PUBLIC PAPERS OF THE PRESIDENTS
OF THE
UNITED STATES

PUBLIC PAPERS OF THE PRESIDENTS
OF THE
UNITED STATES

Ronald Reagan

1988

(IN TWO BOOKS)

BOOK I—JANUARY 1 TO JULY 1, 1988

UNITED STATES GOVERNMENT PRINTING OFFICE
WASHINGTON : 1990

Published by the
Office of the Federal Register
National Archives and Records Administration

For sale by the
Superintendent of Documents
U.S. Government Printing Office
Washington, DC 20402

Foreword

On a warm May day in the year 1988, I had an opportunity no other President of the United States has ever had before; I stood in the Lenin Hills at a podium at Moscow State University and spoke to Soviet students about the glory and wonder of human freedom. That moment crystalized the year.

In the Communist world, glasnost—openness—was frequently invoked but those who lived under the yoke of communism would not accept mere sloganeering. In Afghanistan, a people suffering invasion and occupation began to see the light at the end of a ghastly ordeal. In the Persian Gulf, Southern Africa, and Cambodia, as well, there was progress toward negotiated settlements. All in all, the suffering peoples of the world made it clear they would not stand for the status quo, and for once they were heard.

In the United States, the Senate consented to the ratification of the first treaty ever to ban an entire class of U.S. and Soviet nuclear missiles—a significant accomplishment, indeed.

Ronald Reagan

Preface

This book contains the papers and speeches of the 40th President of the United States that were issued by the Office of the Press Secretary during the period January 1–July 1, 1988. The material has been compiled and published by the Office of the Federal Register, National Archives and Records Administration.

The material is presented in chronological order, and the dates shown in the headings are the dates of the documents or events. In instances when the release date differs from the date of the document itself or when the document was not issued by the Office of the Press Secretary, that fact is shown in the textnote. Every effort has been made to ensure accuracy: Remarks are checked against a tape recording, and signed documents are checked against the original. Textnotes and cross references have been provided by the editors for purposes of identification or clarity. Speeches were delivered in Washington, DC, unless indicated. The times noted are local times. All materials that are printed full-text in the book have been indexed in the subject and name indexes, and listed in the document categories list.

The Public Papers series was begun in 1957 in response to a recommendation of the National Historical Publications Commission. An extensive compilation of messages and papers of the Presidents covering the period 1789 to 1897 was assembled by James D. Richardson and published under congressional authority between 1896 and 1899. Since then, various private compilations have been issued, but there was no uniform publication comparable to the Congressional Record or the United States Supreme Court Reports. Many Presidential papers could be found only in the form of mimeographed White House releases or as reported in the press. The Commission therefore recommended the establishment of an official series in which Presidential writings, addresses, and remarks of a public nature could be made available.

The Commission's recommendation was incorporated in regulations of the Administrative Committee of the Federal Register, issued under section 6 of the Federal Register Act (44 U.S.C. 1506), which may be found in title 1, part 10, of the Code of Federal Regulations.

A companion publication to the Public Papers series, the Weekly Compilation of Presidential Documents, was begun in 1965 to provide a broader range of Presidential materials on a more timely basis to meet the needs of the contemporary reader. Beginning with the administration of Jimmy Carter, the Public Papers series expanded its coverage to include all material as printed in the Weekly Compilation. That coverage provides a listing of the President's daily schedule and meetings, when announced, and other items of general interest issued by the Office of the Press Secretary. Also included are lists of the President's nominations submitted to the Senate, materials released by the Office of the Press Secretary that are not printed full-text in the book, and acts approved by the President. This information appears in the appendixes at the end of the book.

Volumes covering the administrations of Presidents Hoover, Truman, Eisenhower, Kennedy, Johnson, Nixon, Ford, and Carter are also available.

The Chief Editor of this book was William King Banks, assisted by E.B. Swidal.

White House liaison was provided by Marlin Fitzwater, Assistant to the President for Press Relations. The frontispiece and photographs used in the portfolio were supplied by the White House Photo Office.

Martha L. Girard
Director of the Federal Register

Don W. Wilson
Archivist of the United States

Contents

Administration of Ronald Reagan

1988

New Year's Messages of President Reagan and Soviet General Secretary Gorbachev
January 1, 1988

President Reagan's Message

Good evening. This is Ronald Reagan, President of the United States. I'm speaking to you, the peoples of the Soviet Union, on the occasion of the New Year.

I know that in the Soviet Union, as it is all around the world, this is a season of hope and expectation, a time for family to gather, a time for prayer, a time to think about peace. That's true in America, too. At this time of year, Americans travel across the country—in their cars, by train, or by airplane—to be together with their families. Many Americans, of course, came to the United States from other countries, and at this time of year, they look forward to hosting friends and family from their homelands.

Most of us celebrate Christmas or Hanukkah, and as part of those celebrations, we go to church or synagogue, then gather around the family dinner table. After giving thanks for our blessings, we share a traditional holiday meal of goose, turkey, or roast beef and exchange gifts. On New Year's Eve we gather again, and like you, we raise our glasses in a toast to the year to come, to our hopes for ourselves, for our families, and yes, for our nation and the world.

This year, the future of the Nation and the world is particularly on our minds. We're thinking of our nation, because in the year ahead, we Americans will choose our next President. Every adult citizen has a role to play in the making of this decision. We will listen to what the candidates say. We will debate their views and our own. And in November we will vote. I'll still be President next January, but soon after that, the man or woman leading our country will be the one the American people pick this coming November.

As I said, we Americans will also be thinking about the future of the world this year—for the same reasons that you'll be thinking of it, too. In a few months, General Secretary Gorbachev and I hope to meet once again, this time in Moscow. Last month in Washington, we signed the intermediate nuclear forces treaty, in which we agreed to eliminate an entire class of U.S. and Soviet nuclear weapons. It was a historymaking step toward reducing the nuclear arms of both sides, but it was just a beginning.

Now in Geneva, Soviet and American representatives are discussing a 50-percent reduction in strategic nuclear weapons. Perhaps we can have a treaty ready to sign by our meeting in spring. The world prays that we will. We on the American side are determined to try. You see, we have a vision of a world safe from the threat of nuclear war, and, indeed, all war. Such a world will have far fewer missiles and other weapons. Today both America and the Soviet Union have an opportunity to develop a defensive shield against ballistic missiles—a defensive shield that will threaten no one. For the sake of a safer peace, I am committed to pursuing the possibility that technology offers.

The General Secretary and I also anticipate continuing our talks about other issues of deep concern to our peoples—for example, the expansion of contact between our peoples and more information flowing across our borders. Expanding contacts and information will require decisions about life at home that will have an impact on relations abroad.

This is also true in the area of human rights. As you know, we Americans are concerned about human rights, including freedoms of speech, press, worship, and travel. We will never forget that a wise man has said that: "Violence does not live alone and is not capable of living alone. It is necessarily interwoven with falsehood." Silence is a form of falsehood. We will always speak out on behalf of human dignity.

We Americans are also concerned, as I know you are, about senseless conflicts in a number of regions. In some instances, regimes backed by foreign military power are oppressing their own peoples, giving rise to popular resistance and the spread of fighting beyond their borders. Too many mothers, including Soviet mothers, have wept over the graves of their fallen sons. True peace means not only preventing a big war but ending smaller ones, as well. This is why we support efforts to find just, negotiated solutions acceptable to the peoples who are suffering in regional wars.

There is no such thing as inevitability in history. We can choose to make the world safer and freer if we have courage—but then courage is something neither of our peoples have ever lacked. We have been allies in a terrible war, a war in which the Soviet peoples gave the ages an enduring testament to courage. Let us consecrate this year to showing not courage for war but courage for peace. We owe this to mankind. We owe it to our children and their children and generations to come.

Happy New Year! Thank you, and God bless you.

General Secretary Gorbachev's Message

Ladies and gentleman, friends, as we celebrate the New Year, I am glad to address the citizens of the United States of America and to convey to you season's greetings and best wishes from all Soviet people.

The first of January is a day when we take stock of the past year and try to look ahead into the coming year. The past year, 1987, ended with an event which can be regarded as a good omen. In Washington, President Reagan and I signed a treaty on the elimination of intermediate and shorter range missiles. That treaty marks the first step along the path of reducing nuclear arms, and that is its enduring value. But the treaty also has another merit: It has brought our two peoples closer together. We are entering the New Year with a hope for continued progress, progress towards a safer world.

We are ready to continue, fruitfully, the negotiations on reducing strategic arms with a view to signing a treaty to that effect even in the first half of this year. We would like, without delay, to address the problem of cutting back drastically conventional forces and arms in Europe. We are ready for interaction in resolving other problems, including regional ones.

I think it can be said that one of the features of the past year was the growing mutual interest our two peoples took in each other. Contacts between Soviet and American young people, war veterans, scientists, teachers, astronauts, businessmen, and cultural leaders have expanded greatly. Like thousands of strands, those contacts are beginning to weave into what I would call a tangible fabric of trust and growing mutual understanding. It is the duty of Soviet and American political leaders to keep in mind the sentiment of the people in their countries and to reflect their will in political decisions.

The Soviet people are getting down to work in the New Year with an awareness of their great responsibility for the present and for the future. There will be profound changes in our country along the lines of continued *perestroika,* democratization, and radical economic reform. In the final analysis, all this will let us move on to a broad avenue of accelerated development.

We know that you Americans have quite a few problems, too. In grappling with those problems, however, I feel that both you and we must remember what is truly crucial: Human life is equally priceless, whether in the Soviet Union, the United States, or in any other country. So, let us spare no effort to affirm peace on Earth.

Ladies and gentlemen, during the official departure ceremony in Washington, I said with regret that on that visit I had had little chance to see America. I feel, however, that I did understand what is most important about the American people, and that is their enormous stock of good will. Let me assure you that Soviet people, too, have an equally great stock of good will. Putting it to full use is the most noble and responsible task of government and political leaders in our two countries. If they could only do that, what is but a dream today would come true: a lasting peace; an end to the arms race; wider ranging trade; cooperation in combating hunger, disease, and environmental problems; and progress in ensuring human rights and resolving other humanitarian issues. May the coming year of 1988 become an important milestone as we move down that road.

In concluding this New Year address to the people of the United States of America, I wish peace, happiness, and joy to every American family. A happy New Year to all of you.

Note: The President's message was recorded at 11:50 a.m. on December 23, 1987, in the Roosevelt Room at the White House. The General Secretary's message follows the White House press release. They were televised in the United States and the Soviet Union on January 1.

Radio Address to the Nation on Administration Goals
January 2, 1988

My fellow Americans:

This is the first time I will have spoken to you in 1988, so let me begin by saying very simply what your friends and neighbors will have said to you already: Happy New Year! And as Americans, we do indeed have much to be happy about as this New Year commences. Our nation is at peace. Our economy is growing with new jobs being created at the rate of more than 200,000 a month. But of course, there is still much to be done. Join me then in considering some of the issues that we'll be facing as 1988 gets under way.

The first matter I want to mention is one already before the Congress: the confirmation of Judge Anthony Kennedy to a seat on the Supreme Court. The Senate hearings on Judge Kennedy have already taken place. You may have seen portions of the hearings on television. He made clear his belief that it's a judge's job to interpret the law, not make it. And on an issue that affects every American—crime—Judge Kennedy's testimony and record are clear. Judges must respect the rights of the accused, but they must also keep firmly in mind the rights of crime victims and of society itself. The Supreme Court has been one Justice short for many months now. So, I urge the Senate to confirm Judge Kennedy with all due speed.

The next item I want to discuss with you is one that touches on my recent summit meeting with General Secretary Gorbachev of the Soviet Union. You will remember that Mr. Gorbachev and I signed a treaty on the first day of that summit, and now our administration will forward that treaty to the Senate for its advice and consent. You will hear me speak more about this treaty, the intermediate-range nuclear forces treaty, in the days ahead.

For now, let me just say this: Under this treaty, for the first time in history, an entire class of U.S. and Soviet nuclear missiles will be eliminated. The Soviets will be forced to destroy four times as many deployed warheads as will we. And the verification procedures in the treaty are the most stringent in the history of arms control negotiations. What does this add up to? A good deal for the United States and our allies and a step toward a more secure peace for all the world. I welcome the hearings the Senate will hold on this treaty. Yet here again, I urge the Senate to move forward on ratification.

Next, the economy—I don't want to delve into ancient history as this New Year begins, but it's important to keep in mind what the economy our administration inherited some 7 years ago was like: double-digit inflation, the highest interest rates since the Civil War, rising unemployment. Our economic program changed all that and changed it so dramatically that today America has completed its 61st month of economic growth with low inflation. And just what was our economic program? We cut the number of government regulations and slowed the rate of growth of government itself. But most important, we reformed the tax code and cut individual income tax rates, restoring incentives for hard work, risktaking, and innovation.

In an hour, I will be signing the U.S.-Canada free trade agreement, a truly historic pact that will create more jobs and lower prices for consumers on both sides of the border. It is a win-win situation for both countries. Even more importantly, the agreement is an example of the market-opening steps the entire world should be pursuing and which the United States will push in the new Uruguay round of the GATT [General Agreement on Tariffs and Trade negotiations]. Protectionist measures, some of which are in the trade bills passed by the House and Senate, are backward looking, not forward looking.

Finally, of course, 1988 is an election year, a year in which we will choose new officials at all levels and, yes, a new President. To tell you the truth, I've always loved election years—the rallies, the excitement, all of it so American. But more than the excitement, something of immense importance will be taking place, for this year we will be taking stock of ourselves as a nation and deciding in a free and peaceful democratic election—that is still the marvel of much of the world—where our highest hopes and dreams will lead us. Yes, in 1988, the 212th year of our independence and the 201st of our Constitution, ours remains a free nation truly ruled by we the people.

Until next week, thanks for listening, and God bless you.

Note: The President's address was recorded at 12:05 p.m. on December 23, 1987, in the Roosevelt Room at the White House for broadcast at 12:06 p.m. on January 2.

Statement on the United States-Canada Free Trade Agreement
January 2, 1988

I am pleased to announce that Prime Minister Mulroney and I have today entered into an agreement to establish a free trade arrangement between the United States and Canada. In the truest sense, this is an historic agreement for both sides. We will strengthen what is already a deep friendship between our people by enhancing economic opportunities and creating jobs in both countries. Moreover, the agreement firmly establishes that the trade environment between the two countries will in the future be founded on the principle of free and open trade.

This comprehensive agreement will benefit many sectors of the U.S. economy. Canadian and American tariffs will be phased out completely, saving consumers hundreds of millions of dollars while also improving our export opportunities. It will secure access to Canada's market for American manufacturing, agriculture, financial services, and high technology; improve national security through energy sharing; and provide important investment opportunities. Canada will benefit from the agreement in many of these same ways; the pact is truly reciprocal. As the agreement goes into effect, Canada's access to our large domestic market will grow, and Canadian industrial centers will gain opportunities to develop even more important roles in the economy of North America.

The agreement to establish a free trade area has important international implications, as well. It will encourage supporters of free trade throughout the world by demonstrating that governments can remove trade barriers even in the face of protectionist pressures. We hope that the U.S.-Canada example will help set the tone for the Uruguay round multilateral trade negotiations.

Our negotiations with the Canadian Government leading to this agreement incorporated advice from Congress, industry, agriculture, and labor. Our Congress, as well as the Canadian Parliament, will review the agreement fully over the next several months. As this process begins, both sides should be mindful that the decisions they make will help shape the relationship between our countries in the years to come and will send a signal to the rest of the world.

The creation of the world's largest free trade area will be a mark of leadership and presents an historic opportunity to the United States and Canada. We must not let this opportunity slip from our grasp.

Remarks at the Opening of the Bob Hope Cultural Center in Palm Springs, California
January 2, 1988

Thank you very much. I just, in the last few minutes, have made a decision to tell you a little incident in the world of the theater and entertainment. I have told it on a couple of occasions, but I don't know that anything could be more appropriate for that story than this occasion and this beautiful place.

It was some years ago, and someone in the entertainment world had violated the social codes to such an extent that there was quite a hue and cry about it. But it spread to where it was being leveled against all the people in the world of entertainment, and they charged show people with being childish in their thinking, childish in their attitudes—complete children in their ways.

And it remained for a columnist named Irvin S. Cobb to respond. And Irvin said: "If this be true, and if it also be true that when the curtain goes up on eternity all men must approach the gates bearing in their arms that which they have given in life, the people of show business will march in the procession carrying in their arms the pure pearl of tears, the gold of laughter, and the diamonds of stardust they spread upon what might otherwise would have been a rather dreary world. And when at last they reach the final stage door, the keeper will say, 'Open. Let my children in.' "

Tonight marks the inauguration of a bright new home for the preservation and development of culture in America, a special place to house the lively arts. It also marks the inauguration of an award presented by the American people to honor a lifetime of service and achievement. It's appropriate that the first award should go to a gentleman who has practiced the liveliest of arts—comedy—for over six happy decades. Bob Hope has given generously of his valuable time and voluble talent in support of worthy causes, perhaps more than any human being alive today.

Part of the responsibility of my current job is being Commander in Chief of our Armed Forces. As such, I have a special place in my heart, as do all Americans, for all that Bob Hope has done to entertain our servicemen and women overseas, especially in times of conflict and crisis. Bob recently returned from the Persian Gulf, where he let some of our finest young people know how much we love them and how proud we are of the job they are doing. So, you see, this award is not only in recognition of accomplishments past but is also an incentive to future generations to be inspired to carry on the tradition established by Bob Hope.

America has always been a land of optimism and opportunity—a grand combination that has seen us through trying times. Bob Hope has chronicled those times on radio and television and in motion pictures and, through his perceptions and sense of humor, has given us the most precious gift of all: the gift of laughter.

It is my pleasure now to present this award to the man whose name is a description of his life, and where there is life, there is Hope.

Note: The President spoke at 8:50 p.m. in

the McCallum Theatre for the Performing Arts at the center. Following his remarks, he presented Bob Hope with the first America's Hope Award.

Nomination of Jack Katzen To Be an Assistant Secretary of Defense
January 5, 1988

The President today announced his intention to nominate Jack Katzen to be an Assistant Secretary of Defense (Acquisitions and Logistics) at the Department of Defense. He would succeed Robert B. Costello.

Mr. Katzen is currently Deputy Assistant Secretary of Defense for Acquisitions at the Pentagon in Washington, DC. Prior to this, Mr. Katzen was corporate vice president for Avco Corp. in Greenwich, CT, 1978–1986. He was with the General Electric Co. in various capacities from 1956 to 1978: manager, Far East programs, 1972–1978; manager, strategic planning and review, 1971–1972; general manager, advanced programs, 1969–1971; and special systems, 1968–1969.

Mr. Katzen graduated from Carnegie Institute of Technology (B.S., 1942). He was born August 12, 1921, in New York, NY. Mr. Katzen has two children and resides in Greenwich, CT.

Nomination of Roger J. Marzulla To Be an Assistant Attorney General
January 5, 1988

The President today announced his intention to nominate Roger J. Marzulla to be an Assistant Attorney General (Land and Natural Resources Division) at the Department of Justice. He would succeed Frank Henry Habicht II.

Since July 1987 Mr. Marzulla has been Acting Assistant Attorney General for Land and Natural Resources at the Department of Justice in Washington, DC. Prior to this he was Deputy Assistant Attorney General for Land and Natural Resources, 1984–1987; and special litigator for the Land and Natural Resources Division, 1983–1984. He was president and chief legal officer of the Mountain States Legal Foundation, 1981–1982.

Mr. Marzulla graduated from the University of Santa Clara (B.A., 1968) and the University of Santa Clara Law School (J.D., 1971). He was born August 12, 1947, in Glendale, CA. He is married and resides in Washington, DC.

Nomination of L. Francis Bouchey To Be a Member of the Board of Directors of the Inter-American Foundation
January 5, 1988

The President today announced his intention to nominate L. Francis Bouchey to be a member of the Board of Directors of the Inter-American Foundation for a term of 6 years. This is a new position.

Since 1983 Mr. Bouchey has been president of the Council for Inter-American Security in Washington, DC. Prior to this he was public affairs consultant for various civic, educational, and international organizations, 1973–present. Mr. Bouchey was Assistant Director in the Office of Staff Placement for the ACTION agency, 1972–1973; and program analyst for the National Transportation Safety Board at the Department of Transportation, 1971–1972.

Mr. Bouchey graduated from the University of Dallas (B.A., 1966) and Georgetown University (M.A., 1972). He was born October 3, 1942, in Yakima, WA. Mr. Bouchey is married, has two children, and resides in Falls Church, VA.

Remarks at the Presentation Ceremony for the Presidential Rank Awards for the Senior Executive Service
January 5, 1988

I appreciate this opportunity every year to honor and reward a special group of individuals who provide the creativity and energy that ensure the people of the United States the Government they deserve and the Government they pay for. Well, each of you is a tribute to the fact that throughout our government we've got top quality professionals getting the job done.

Thomas Jefferson once said that one of the toughest tasks of any President was finding the right person for the right job. Well, I'm grateful that those of you we honor today are people who worked your way into positions of responsibility and have taken that responsibility seriously.

Now, there's a story I'd like to tell. You knew I'd have one of those. [*Laughter*] There's only one thing: I'm standing here very uncertain right now, because I'm hoping that I haven't told you this one before. [*Laughter*] It's about a young fellow. He had a great feeling for animals and wanted to work with animals. And then one day in the help wanted ads he saw an ad from the zoo. They were advertising for someone to come and work in the zoo. Well, he went down, and he found out that his first job was going to be—if he took the job—to get into a gorilla suit and enter the cage to replace their gorilla who'd died until the one they'd ordered could arrive. But then there would be a regular job for him after he had done that and the real gorilla arrived. Well, he took them on. And he got in the cage, and there he was in the suit and—couldn't just sit around. And when the kids, particularly, were in front of the cage, he started doing tricks and everything he could think of for them. And one day he was swinging on a rope, and he got so enthused he swung over into the lion's cage. And the lion came roaring at him, and he started screaming for help. And the lion jumped on him and said, "Shut up, or you'll get us both fired." [*Laughter*]

I guess whoever was running that zoo was certainly employing innovative problemsolving. [*Laughter*] Seriously though, I know that many of you've saved the Government—and that really means the taxpayers—considerable money. You've done it by your diligence and your intelligence. But you've also done more than that: You've provided leadership. And more often than not, that's worth more than money. Today's awards are designed as a way of saying thank you and letting you know that you are appreciated.

This is my seventh year of being part of this ceremony, and I believe your service warrants my personal congratulations, and I want each of you to know that. This year there are 58 distinguished and 267 meritorious winners, almost double the number that was approved in prior years. Large and small agencies are represented, from civilian executives in the military service to executives in the National Science Foundation.

Thirteen award winners this year come from outside the Washington area. I want to welcome all of you to the Capital, which in so many ways is a company town. But none of us should ever forget the real business of the company takes place in the far reaches of our country and even the world. In fact, 88 percent of the Federal work force is located outside the Washington area.

If I were the CEO of a giant corporation, I couldn't find a better group of executives to run my operation than the nearly 7,000 members of the Senior Executive Service whom you represent here today. America's lucky to have men and women such as yourselves, and I'm proud to have worked with you over these last 7 years. I look forward to a productive year ahead.

So, thank you from the bottom of my heart, and God bless you. And now, Connie Horner, who worked with me at the Office of Management and Budget and has been doing a fine job as Director of the Office of Personnel Management, and Kirke Harper, our Director of Executive Personnel, will help me present the awards.

Note: The President spoke at 1:32 p.m. in Room 450 of the Old Executive Office Building.

Remarks on Signing the Agricultural Credit Act of 1987
January 6, 1988

The President. Thank you all very much. Before saying anything else, I want to thank Senator Lugar. As ranking minority member on the Agriculture Committee, he was instrumental in helping to give this legislation its final shape. Senators Boschwitz, Leahy, and Boren, and Congressmen Madigan and Dingell, as well as other Representatives you see here today, also deserve special mention. And we should thank the members from the House Banking and Energy and Commerce Committees for their hard work.

Now, I hope you'll forgive me if I start off with one of my favorite stories. Whenever farming is the business at hand, I'm reminded of when I was in Las Vegas some years back. I was out on the mashed-potato circuit, and I was there to address the annual Farm Bureau meeting. And on my way into the hall, a fellow, one of the regular visitors in Las Vegas, asked me what was a bunch of farmers doing in a place like Las Vegas. And I couldn't resist. I said, "Buster, they're in a business that makes a Las Vegas crap table look like a guaranteed annual income." [*Laughter*]

But unfortunately, in the past our nation's farmers have had to contend not only with the usual, God-given variables, such as the weather, but with other uncertainties and hardships that were manmade right here in Washington. Many of America's farmers are still suffering from the aftershocks of the runaway inflation of the seventies. As inflation pushed up the price of land, farmers were too often encouraged to overextend themselves in debt. At the same time, in the 3 years prior to 1980, farm costs shot right through the roof—nearly a 50-percent increase, or it amounted to about $44 billion.

Well, since then we've been doing our best to get the situation straightened out, and there's good news for farming. The volume of agriculture exports was up nearly 18 percent in 1987, and we're expecting another 9-percent jump this year, more than doubling our trade surplus of 2 years ago. The U.S. share of world grain trade is rising: from 31 percent in '85–'86 to 36 percent in '86–'87 to an expected 43 percent in '87–'88. Surplus stocks are being reduced. Farm production expenses are down, prices are up, and farm income is at a record high. Meanwhile, land prices are stabilizing, and by the end of 1988, farm debt is expected to have dropped 35 percent from its peak.

Now, that doesn't paint a completely rosy picture for agriculture, however. There are still pockets of financial stress, and high debt and low-income growth in many foreign importing countries combined with global agricultural protectionism still adding to farmers' woes.

Well, today's signing of the farm credit act should help alleviate some of those woes. The act ensures that the Farm Credit System will continue as a principal source of private credit to America's farmers, while at the same time implements many needed reforms to the System to ensure its long-term viability.

Unfortunately, the Congress declined to require the System to provide as much self-help as we believed was appropriate and created new and potentially expensive Federal support mechanisms for secondary markets for private sector agricultural loans. The Congress also added other costly provisions that were not necessary to the health of the Farm Credit System. Of principal concern is the additional forbearance provided to producers that have been substantially delinquent on loans issued directly by the Farmers Home Administration of the United States Department of Agriculture. It makes little sense to add on new and unnecessary spending in this time of deficits, and I urge Congress to reconsider and to take its responsibility for the deficit seriously and to work with us to amend or remove these provisions as soon as possible.

Apart from this bill, there are two encouraging developments for agriculture on the horizon. First, trade negotiations are underway to reform the General Agreement on Tariffs and Trade, to break through the protectionist stranglehold on agriculture and to make the world market in agriculture a free market. American farmers will prosper under these reforms not only because of new access to markets now closed to them but also because trade reform will boost worldwide growth, especially in the less developed countries, where the agricultural trade growth prospects are greatest. As demand increases, American farmers are in a solid position to compete in a more open and expanding world market.

Second, as you know, over New Year's weekend, Prime Minister Mulroney and I hooked up by telephone as we signed a free trade agreement between the United States and Canada. Now, that agreement must be ratified by both nations. This agreement will be vital as we fight back against global protectionism. By persuasion and example, we will show the world what free trade really means: job creation, opportunity, improved international relations, and an upward cycle of prosperity for all nations and their people.

Well, I thank you all. And now it's time to sign the bill. You know, I only had half an hour to read it. [*Laughter*] The bill is signed. All right. Well, thank you all.

Reporter. Mr. President, are you ordering ships out of the Gulf?

The President. I don't answer questions, but that one's easy—no. [*Laughter*]

Note: The President spoke at 11:36 a.m. in the Roosevelt Room at the White House. In his closing remarks, he joked about the lengthy nature of the bill. H.R. 3030, approved January 6, was assigned Public Law No. 100–233.

Executive Order 12623—Delegating Authority To Implement Assistance to the Nicaraguan Democratic Resistance

January 6, 1988

By the authority vested in me as President by the Constitution and laws of the United States of America, including Section 111 of the Joint Resolution Making Continuing Appropriations for the Fiscal Year 1988 (Public Law 100–202) ("the Act"), the Foreign Assistance Act of 1961, as amended (22 U.S.C. 2151 *et seq.*), and section 301 of title 3 of the United States Code, and in order to delegate certain functions concerning the designation of funds to be transferred, the transfer of funds and operation of accounts, it is hereby ordered as follows:

Section 1. The Secretary of State is authorized to perform the functions vested in the President by Section 111 of the Act, except the determination and certification pursuant to Section 111(b)(2), except any request for additional assistance pursuant to Section 111(j)(1), and except as provided in Sections 2 and 3 of this Order.

Sec. 2. The Secretary of Defense is authorized to perform the function, vested in the President by Section 111(a) of the Act, of designating the accounts from which unobligated funds, made available by the Department of Defense appropriations acts for the Fiscal Year 1987 or prior fiscal years, are transferred.

Sec. 3. The Secretary of Defense is authorized to perform the functions, vested in the President by Section 111(b)(1) and (d)(1) of the Act, of designating and transferring unobligated funds made available by the Department of Defense appropriations acts for the Fiscal Year 1987 or prior fiscal years.

Sec. 4. The funds described in Sections 2 and 3 of this Order will be transferred to the account for Assistance for the Nicaraguan Democratic Resistance.

RONALD REAGAN

The White House,
January 6, 1988.

[*Filed with the Office of the Federal Register, 4:47 p.m., January 6, 1988*]

Executive Order 12624—Increasing the Number of Members on the President's Foreign Intelligence Advisory Board
January 6, 1988

By the authority vested in me as President by the Constitution and laws of the United States of America, it is hereby ordered that Executive Order No. 12537 of October 28, 1985, is amended by deleting the word "fourteen" from the second sentence of Section 1 and inserting in its place the word "sixteen."

RONALD REAGAN

The White House,
January 6, 1988.

[*Filed with the Office of the Federal Register, 4:48 p.m., January 6, 1988*]

Nomination of William F. Burns To Be Director of the United States Arms Control and Disarmament Agency
January 7, 1988

The President today announced his intention to nominate William F. Burns to be Director of the United States Arms Control and Disarmament Agency. He would succeed Kenneth L. Adelman.

Major General Burns is currently Deputy Assistant Secretary of State for Arms Control, Bureau of Politico-Military Affairs, at the Department of State, in Washington, DC. Prior to this, General Burns was Joint Chiefs of Staff Representative to the Intermediate-range Nuclear Forces negotiations in Geneva, Switzerland, November 1981–June 1984. General Burns was reassigned to Carlisle Barracks as deputy commandant for the United States Army War College, 1984–1985. In February 1985 he returned to the Pentagon as the Joint Chiefs of Staff Representative to the Intermediate-range Nuclear Forces negotiating group in Geneva, Switzerland, until December 1986.

General Burns has served in the United States Army in various capacities from 1954 to the present: director, special task force, Corps Support Weapons System, Fort Sill, OK, 1981–1982; deputy assistant commandant, U.S. Army Field Artillery School, Fort Sill, 1980–1981; senior liaison officer to Federal Republic of Germany, U.S. Army Training, and Doctrine Command, Bonn, Germany, 1978–1980; commander, 42d Field Artillery Group, U.S. Army Europe, 1976–1978; director of political-economic studies for the department of national and international security studies at the U.S. Army War College, Carlisle Barracks, PA, 1972–1976. Awards and decorations which General Burns has received include the Defense Distinguished Service Medal, Defense Superior Service Medal, the Legion of Merit, the Bronze Star with V Device and three Oak Leaf Clusters, Meritorious Service Medal with two Oak Leaf Clusters, Air Medals, and the Army Commendation Medal with Oak Leaf Cluster.

General Burns graduated from LaSalle College (B.A., 1954) and Princeton University (M.A., 1969). He was born June 23, 1932, in Scranton, PA. He is married, has four children, and resides in Fort Myer, VA.

Designation of James M. Stephens as Chairman of the National Labor Relations Board

January 7, 1988

The President today announced his intention to designate James M. Stephens to be Chairman of the National Labor Relations Board. He has served as a member of the Board since October 1985. He would succeed Donald L. Dotson.

Since 1985 Mr. Stephens has been a member of the National Labor Relations Board in Washington, DC. Prior to this, he was labor counsel for the Committee on Labor and Human Resources for the U.S. Senate, 1981–1985; assistant minority labor counsel for the Committee on Education and Labor for U.S. House of Representatives, 1977–1981; and was an associate with the law firm of Roetzel and Andress in Akron, OH, 1973–1977.

Mr. Stephens graduated from Wittenberg University (A.B., 1968) and Case Western Reserve University (J.D., 1971). He was born September 16, 1946, in Rochester, NY. Mr. Stephens is married, has two children, and resides in Vienna, VA.

Statement on Signing the Computer Security Act of 1987

January 8, 1988

I am pleased today to sign H.R. 145, the Computer Security Act of 1987. This Act will provide the foundation for a comprehensive and consistent approach to computer security throughout the Federal Government. I sign this Act with the understanding that it will neither expand nor restrict the Federal Government's present or future disclosure obligations under the Freedom of Information Act ("FOIA"), 5 U.S.C. § 552, as amended, with respect to information pertaining to Federal computer systems or information stored in those systems. The Act will enhance the ability of the Federal Government to manage and protect its computer resources and represents a significant step forward in the effective use of these new technologies.

RONALD REAGAN

The White House,
January 8, 1988.

Note: H.R. 145, approved January 8, was assigned Public Law No. 100–235.

Statement on Signing the Federal Employees' Retirement System Technical Corrections Bill
January 8, 1988

I have today approved H.R. 3395, an Act making technical corrections to the Federal Employees' Retirement System. The Act contains a number of significant technical and clarifying changes and improvements in the Federal Employees' Retirement System, as well as in the Civil Service Retirement and Foreign Service Retirement systems. While not perfect, these changes will improve the operation of the Government's retirement system for its employees.

Although I have signed H.R. 3395, I want to note my serious objection to a non-germane provision that was added in the Senate immediately before final congressional passage without hearings or the opportunity for the Executive branch or other concerned parties to evaluate and comment on it.

This provision will effectively erect barriers to air carriers that want to provide mail transportation service to rural areas in Alaska, and, in some cases, may well discriminate against existing air carriers. Such restrictions on transporting mail are costly and inefficient and could cause service delays. These restrictions, which undermine market forces and economic efficiency, are contrary to long-standing Federal aviation policy.

Had this provision been presented to me in separate legislation, I would have disapproved it. I therefore strongly urge the Congress to reconsider and repeal this amendment at the earliest opportunity.

RONALD REAGAN

The White House,
January 8, 1988.

Note: H.R. 3395, approved January 8, was assigned Public Law No. 100–238.

Appointment of Juanita Donaghey Duggan as Special Assistant to the President for Public Liaison
January 8, 1988

The President today announced the appointment of Juanita Donaghey Duggan to be Special Assistant to the President for Public Liaison. She will serve as domestic policy liaison.

Since June 1985 Mrs. Duggan has served as Assistant Director for Legislative and Intergovernmental Affairs at ACTION. Mrs. Duggan previously served as professional staff member to Senator Jeremiah Denton (R–AL) on the Senate Committee on Labor and Human Resources, Subcommittee on Family and Human Services, and on the Committee on the Judiciary, Subcommittee on Security and Terrorism.

Mrs. Duggan graduated from Georgetown University (B.S., 1982). She is married and has one son. Mrs. Duggan is a native of Mobile, AL, and resides in Washington, DC.

Appointment of Mary McGeein Schnepper as Special Assistant to the President for Public Liaison

January 8, 1988

The President today announced the appointment of Mary McGeein Schnepper to be Special Assistant to the President for Public Liaison. She will serve as liaison with commerce and professional associations.

Ms. Schnepper joined the public liaison staff in 1983, and since 1986, she has worked with the business community as Associate Director of Business Liaison.

Ms. Schnepper graduated from Mercy School of Nursing, Toledo, OH, and Marymount University, Arlington, VA, (B.S.N.). Ms. Schnepper resides in Arlington, VA, and has four children.

Appointment of Patricia Mack Bryan as Associate Counsel to the President

January 8, 1988

The President today announced the appointment of Patricia Mack Bryan to be Associate Counsel to the President.

Since June 1987 Ms. Bryan has served in the Office of the Counsel to the President. Prior to her position in the White House, she was Acting Deputy Assistant Attorney General and Special Assistant to the Assistant Attorney General, Office of Legal Policy, Department of Justice, 1983–1987, and an associate with the firm of Jones, Day, Reavis & Pogue, 1980–1983.

Ms. Bryan graduated from Gettysburg College (B.A., 1977) and Harvard Law School (J.D., 1980). She was born July 7, 1955, in Philadelphia, PA.

Appointment of Benedict Simms Cohen as Associate Counsel to the President

January 8, 1988

The President today announced the appointment of Benedict Simms Cohen to be Associate Counsel to the President.

Since June 1987 Mr. Cohen has served in the Office of the Counsel to the President. Prior to that, he was an attorney-adviser, Office of Legislative Affairs, Department of Justice, 1986–1987; a clerk to the Honorable Laurence H. Silberman, United States Court of Appeals for the District of Columbia Circuit, 1985–1986; and an associate with the firm of Davis Polk & Wardwell in New York, 1983–1985.

Mr. Cohen graduated from Yale University (B.A., 1980) and the University of Chicago Law School (J.D., 1983). He was born January 9, 1959, in Nashville, TN, is married, and resides in Washington, DC.

Statement on Receiving the Report of the Presidential Task Force on Market Mechanisms
January 8, 1988

I received this afternoon the report from my Task Force on Market Mechanisms. This task force, chaired by former Senator Nicholas Brady, was established in the wake of the events of mid-October, when the securities markets experienced extreme volatility, huge trading volumes, and a precipitous decline in value.

The task force and its staff worked diligently from the beginning, attempting to assemble the data and analyze the events that took place during those tumultuous times. In a period of just 60 days, they have performed an important task and produced a very detailed report.

As I told Senator Brady, the task force analysis is a significant contribution to our understanding of the events of mid-October. I intend to carefully review this report along with the New York Stock Exchange and the Chicago Mercantile Exchange studies and the forthcoming studies by the Securities and Exchange Commission and the Commodity Futures Trading Commission. After that I will decide what actions are warranted.

I want to express my profound appreciation to the task force and its staff for performing so ably under such severe time constraints.

Radio Address to the Nation on the United States-Canada Free Trade Agreement
January 9, 1988

My fellow Americans:

If someone were to ask us as a nation who our best friends are, what would be the answer? It's difficult to imagine any better friends than our neighbors, the Canadians. Our two peoples have lived, side by side, in peace and with the spirit of good will for the better part of two centuries.

Winston Churchill once noted: "That long Canadian frontier from the Atlantic to the Pacific Oceans, guarded only by neighborly respect and honorable obligations, is an example to every country and a pattern for the future of the world." Churchill, as usual, was as profound as he was eloquent. It wouldn't surprise him to find out that the citizens of Canada and the United States are moving together toward a truly historic achievement. Last week Prime Minister Mulroney and I entered into a free trade agreement, which once approved by the United States Congress and the Canadian Parliament will establish our two countries as the world's largest free trade area.

The U.S.-Canadian free trade agreement is the culmination of 18 months of strenuous negotiations between our governments. Both Prime Minister Mulroney and I played an active role in the process, keeping the negotiations on track and ensuring that the outcome would be absolutely fair and equitable. Frankly, I think we've come up with a winner, a winner for people on both sides of the border. Canada and the United States are already each other's largest trading partners. Our bilateral trade in goods and services exceeded $150 billion in 1986. The economic health and national security of our countries are linked. This well-honed treaty will build on these ties that already exist and open up tremendous new potential.

The treaty will, over a 10-year period, eliminate the tariffs and bring down most of the trade barriers that now serve only to tax or impede the commerce between our two peoples. What will this accomplish? Numerous studies have shown that the agreement will mean billions of dollars in new economic growth for both countries each year. This means thousands of new jobs, increased investment, and expanding opportunities. And it's not just the export industries which will reap the rewards. The most easily recognized beneficiaries of this pact will be the consumers of both countries. With enhanced competition, lower prices can be expected as well as greater consumer choice. As for industry, eliminating the obstacles to doing business and wiping out tariffs is going to be a great boon to manufacturing on both sides of the border. Markets will open that have been restricted, sources of raw material and parts that are now made more expensive by tariffs will be available at a lower cost. In short, this treaty is going to be overwhelmingly positive for both Canada and the United States.

This, however, does not mean that there will be no opposition. Whenever there is change, even for the better, there are segments of society that resist—small groups that have a special interest in keeping things the way they are—even at the expense of keeping everybody else from moving forward. Benjamin Franklin, our much venerated Founding Father, saw this, even in his day. Talking about trade he noted: "The more free and unrestrained it is, the more it flourishes; and the happier are all the nations concerned in it. Most of the restraints put upon it," he pointed out, "seem to have been the projects of particulars for their private interest, under pretense of public good."

Well, in approaching the U.S.-Canadian free trade agreement, I would hope that the national interest will overcome the pressure of the private interest, on both sides of the border. I would hope that our peoples, of Canada and the United States and their elected representatives, are able to keep their eyes on the long-term growth and opportunity that will be forthcoming with this agreement rather than short-run dislocation that comes with any change.

In Canada there are those who fear that their national identity might be damaged by a closer association with such a large country as the United States. Well, experience says otherwise. European countries have for decades cooperated closely on trade, yet the national character of each member nation still remains vital and distinctive. Canada, too, has a national character that will not only survive but flourish in an environment of free trade and expanding opportunity.

I have no doubt that history will prove this agreement a boon to both our peoples. And through it, we will be an example to all the world of what free people can accomplish and demonstrate that the path to economic growth, job creation, and security is through negotiation and cooperation, not protectionism.

Until next week, thanks for listening, and God bless you.

Note: The President spoke at 12:06 p.m. from Camp David, MD.

Remarks and a Question-and-Answer Session With Members of the City Club of Cleveland, Ohio

January 11, 1988

Thank you very much. And thank you, Vice President Akers, officers and members of the City Club, Mayor Voinovich. I thank you all very much. And a special hello to Clevelanders Herb and Jody Weinberg, who are the parents of my Assistant Press Secretary, Mark Weinberg. It's great to be in Cleveland today, home of the Browns. And congratulations on your big victory. When I was at Camp David on Saturday, I heard a lot of barking—[*laughter*]—and it wasn't coming from Nancy's dog. [*Laughter*]

But it's also a great pleasure to have this opportunity to address the City Club of Cleveland as you celebrate, as you know, the 75th year in which you've championed the cause of free speech. Seventy-five years—it was just a little bit longer ago that I first exercised my freedom of expression—[*laughter*]—to my mother and her midwife in Tampico, Illinois. So, you could say that we approach the subject from a position of comparable experience. [*Laughter*]

Looking over the distinguished speakers who've preceded me, I couldn't help but think that it is a measure of the high esteem in which your organization is held that you've been able to convince so many politicians to come before you to talk and answer questions. But I'm looking forward to the question-and-answer period later on. After all, I've been assured that Sam Donaldson [ABC News] is not a member of your club. [*Laughter*]

But before then, however, I want to talk to you about an area in which freedom is just as vital as speech and, as the years go by, will become more and more important. I'm talking about the developing economy of the future, an economy of great challenges and even greater opportunities, if only we have the courage to embrace them, to jettison the prejudices and small-mindedness of the past and open our arms to economic freedom on a world scale.

Now, I know a lot of people, when they hear talk about the economy, reach for their wallets to see if they've suddenly become lighter. It's said that if you ask three economists a question, you'll get seven different answers. And that's why with economists, I always have one motto: Trust, but verify. [*Laughter*]

I spoke of the economy of the future, but it's forming right now in the minds and imaginations of entrepreneurs around the globe. It's taking shape in businesses, large and small; in factories and universities; in research and development centers. Powered by an explosion of technological invention and linked by a global network of investment and communications, it is transforming our lives so fast that the so-called conventional wisdom can barely keep up. But the dramatic changes we've already witnessed are only the foreshadowing of things to come.

I will speak of the practical and immediate effects on our economy in a moment, but first it's important to understand that this technological revolution is in a fundamental sense a moral revolution. At its heart is a rejection of the counsels of despair we heard so often in the seventies. Remember the seventies? Rampant inflation, hypertaxation, sky-high interest rates, productivity growth falling through the floor, and the steady erosion of investment incentives.

But worse than the statistics was a kind of collapse of faith. The West, in those years, experienced what can only be described as a crisis of confidence in its most fundamental values. We increasingly heard talk about the so-called convergence of the free world and the Communist bloc. Some said our freedoms were a luxury we could no longer afford. Expert opinion talked of limited resources in a shrinking world. In this future of scarcity, we were told, the free nations would have to sacrifice more and more of their economic and political freedoms and accept increasing government control.

But, as I said, the American people rejected this counsel of despair. They saw that the crisis was not in their values, but in the leadership that no longer believed in them. And they demanded a return to our basic principles—those principles of freedom and enterprise that had always made this country great.

Well, the road back is well-mapped now. We cut taxes, we quashed inflation and deregulated the economy, unleashing the creative energies of the American people. The result never would have been imagined by "expert opinion" 8 years ago—some 14½ million new jobs—more jobs than Europe and Japan created combined. Last year alone, 3 million new jobs were created. Employment—the percentage of all working Americans over 16 years of age, male and female—is at record highs.

Right here in Cleveland, unemployment has dropped from 15 percent in 1979 to certainly less than 10 percent under Mayor Voinovich. Nationwide, black employment has risen 26 percent since November 1982. That's more than twice the rate of job gain for whites. Economics columnist Warren Brookes looked at this record and concluded, and I'll quote: "On every front—jobs, income, even household wealth—this, 1981 through 1986, has been the best 5 economic years in black history."

New business creations are going strong. Manufacturing productivity, one measure of the health of an economy, has reversed its decline of the seventies and is now racking up historic gains averaging an annual growth rate of nearly 5 percent since 1982—more than 1½ times the average of the postwar period. But these numbers, impressive as they are, do more to disguise than to reveal the real nature of our progress. The change is qualitative, not quantitative. We're not merely accelerating the processes of the Industrial Revolution; we're fundamentally transforming them.

Let me give you just one example—the semiconductor, or computer chip. One scientist makes this comparison. If automotive technology had progressed as fast as semiconductor technology in the past 20 years, he says, a Rolls Royce would now cost less than $3, get 3 million miles to the gallon, deliver enough power to drive an ocean liner, and 6 of them would fit on the head of a pin. [*Laughter*] Now, this is more than a mere productivity explosion. Operating in the mysterious world of quantum physics, today's quantum leap in the world's economy—well, the computers signal that. We're rapidly moving from the economy of the Industrial Revolution—an economy feeding on and tied to the Earth's physical resources—to, as one economist titled his book, "The Economy in Mind," in which human imagination and the freedom to create are the most precious natural resources.

Think again of that little computer chip. Those chips, the driving force of the modern economy, are made from the silicon in sand, one of the most common substances on Earth. Their value doesn't come from the physical material that makes them up, but from the microscopic architecture designed into them by ingenious human minds. More and more in this new economy, mind replaces matter, human invention makes physical resources obsolete. Take a typical telecast via satellite like Saturday's Browns' game. That satellite—the product of human invention—replaces thousands of tons of copper dug from the Earth and molded into wire. Rather than being imprisoned in a world of shrinking natural resources, we're transcending them, moving to a new era of seemingly limitless horizons.

Now, this is good news for humanity, but it's bad news for statism. The centrally planned state can dig metal out of the ground or pump oil. Though less efficiently than a free economy, it can operate huge factories and run assembly lines. But it cannot fabricate the spirit of enterprise. It cannot imitate the trial and error of free markets, the riot of experiment that produces knowledge and progress. No government can manufacture the entrepreneur or light that spark of invention. All they can do is let their people go—give them freedom of mind and spirit. A recent issue of Fortune Magazine summed it up in an article called "The Death of Socialism." Even Socialist governments in Western Europe are now cutting tax rates, while the Soviet Union struggles with economic reforms in an attempt to keep from falling farther and farther behind.

Over a century ago, the English economist and philosopher, John Stuart Mill, predicted that the competition between Socialist and free market economies would in the end be decided by which system was "consistent with the greatest amount of human liberty and spontaneity." One hundred years later, the results are in: Socialist and Communist systems have given up their freedoms, and all they've bought with their sacrifice is stagnation and suffering. I'm reminded of the story Adlai Stevenson used to tell of Mrs. Karl Marx at the end of a long and bleak life, and how she would remark how good it would have been if Karl had made some capital instead of writing so much about it. [*Laughter*]

So, instead of convergence, we see an increasing divergence between the free and the unfree. Statist economies stagnate, while the free-market, low-tax countries vault ahead into a new era of growth—into a new world economy. Even more than in the past, this new world economy is a one-world economy. With Americans in the lead, entrepreneurs have created a global electronic network, on line 24 hours a day, sending capital, ideas, goods, and services around the world at near the speed of light.

Research, development, manufacturing, marketing, and investment now all take place on a global level.

Take the example of Boeing. Headquartered in Seattle, it builds its new 767 with airframe parts from Japan and Italy, its engines assembled by American workers in Ohio with parts from Sweden, France, West Germany, and Italy. Or take the example of Honda. They're now building cars in Marysville, Ohio, for sale in Taiwan, and they're now studying the possibility of selling their American-made cars in Japan. In this new world economy, national boundaries are increasingly becoming obsolete. In this new global information age, entrepreneurs follow their investments, and they all flow where there is the greatest stability, the greatest opportunity. Overwhelmingly, they all flow to the United States.

We hear talk about the trade deficit, but we must beware of single-entry bookkeeping. The other side of the ledger shows that the growing, dynamic United States economy has attracted $159 billion in foreign capital into the United States. Trade deficits and inflows of foreign capital are not necessarily a sign of an economy's weakness. During the first 100 years of our nation's history, while we were developing from an agricultural colony to the industrial leader of the world, the United States ran a trade deficit. And now, as we're leading a global movement from the industrial age to the information age, we continue to attract investment from around the world.

Now, some people call this debt. By that way of thinking, every time a company sold stock it would be a sign of weakness, and it would be much better to be a company nobody wanted to invest in rather than one everybody wanted to invest in. Take the case of high-tech, high-growth California. Milton Friedman argues that California's external debt—to other States and other countries—almost certainly dwarfs the external debt of the United States. Does this augur bad days ahead for California? On the contrary, one might argue it's a sign of strength.

Historically, fast-growing economies often run deficits in the trade of goods and services, experiencing net capital investment from abroad. This predictable and, up to a point, desirable process has been accentuated by slow growth in parts of Europe and the need for debt-ridden Third World nations to generate trade surpluses to service their debt. Germany, which has actually lost half-a-million jobs in the last 10 years, has a trade surplus in goods. Mexico has a trade surplus in goods. The United States, which has been the engine keeping the world economy moving forward, has a trade deficit because our growing economy enables us to buy their goods.

Over time, however, these imbalances should be reduced, and there are two ways to do it: We can become more like them, or they can become more like us. We can raise taxes, reregulate our economy, and adopt protectionist legislation of the kind now being considered in Congress. That will effectively slow growth in this nation and stifle international trade. We won't be able to buy their goods and, certainly, no one will want to invest in the United States. The world can all shrink together, and we can all look forward to hearing the experts once again pontificating about convergence and the limits to growth.

The other solution is for them to become more like us: to adopt low-tax, progrowth policies; to encourage trade, not discourage it—to make it freer and fairer and more plentiful; to join with the other nations in a cooperative, upward cycle of growth in which all participate; to embrace the possibilities of the new world economy. In fact, we're beginning to see this happen. Several major industrialized countries have followed the U.S. lead in cutting high marginal tax rates to spur growth. These changes and other market forces are already causing the volume of U.S. exports to boom, with continued growth expected.

May I just interject right here that where some people, complaining about the deficit—and no one complains about it louder than I do—when they complain about it, they cite our reducing taxes in these last several years. Well, I think someone should pay attention to the fact that every time we have reduced the rates, we have increased the total revenue paid in taxes by the people to the Government because there is an incentive for people to earn more and to go out and to experiment, and so forth. And so, no, the deficit has not been caused by the cut in taxes. The deficit would increase if we yielded to those who want us to increase taxes.

I'm not saying there aren't problems. The one that sticks out like a sore thumb is that United States budget deficit. It's an embarrassment and a shame—most dangerous, perhaps, because it signals the complete breakdown of one of the most basic functions of the United States Government. Now, we've made some progress. For the first time in 14 years, the Federal Government spent less, in real terms, last year than the year before. We took $75 billion off of last year's deficit, and the bipartisan congressional leadership joined with me in signing on a 2-year deficit reduction plan. Now, those are steps in the right direction, putting us on the path toward a balanced budget and doing it without the severity of the across-the-board cuts in the Gramm-Rudman-Hollings act.

But there's more to be done. If we're not careful, we'll slip once more into the errors of the past—broken promises and unchecked spending. It's time to get at the root of the problem. It's time to fix the busted budget process. Just before Congress—or Christmas, I should say—Congress delivered a large package to my door. It was the 1,000-page continuing resolution that contained all of the spending authority for the United States Government. It should have been called a continuing irresolution. For the second year in a row, the Congress failed to pass even 1 of the 13 appropriation bills on time; they just bundled them together in a trillion-dollar bonanza.

How about a New Year pledge: a budget that is credible and reliable, a spending plan that is timely and enforceable and does not leave the Government on the brink of default? Thirteen manageable bills and not one gigantic catchall—I will take the pledge, and I hope 535 people who represent you in the Congress of the United States will take the same pledge.

There are some other changes that will reform this process. The Constitution gives the President the authority to veto legislation and the Congress the authority to override that veto. When our forefathers framed that historic document, I'm sure they did not envision the dilemma a President faces today: Either veto the legislation needed to run the Government or sign into law a bill that does little to promote the national welfare. Let me describe a few of its choicer items: Even in this time of Gramm-Rudman, when the national defense is being pared to the bone, Congress has decided that we have a pressing national need for asparagus research. Stone fruit was also provided for generously, but the really big money went to the usual pork-barrel spending projects—roads, highways, and dams—which puts me in mind of another story.

It's about a Congressman, present company excepted—[*laughter*]—who was sitting in his office one day when a constituent comes by to tell him why he must vote for a certain bill coming up. The Congressman sat back and listened. And when he was done, he said, "You know, you're right. You're right, you're absolutely right." And the fellow left happy. And a few minutes later, another constituent came by, but this one wanted him to vote against the bill. The Congressman listened to his reasons, sat back, and said, "You know, you're right. You're right, you're absolutely right." And the second constituent left happily.

Well, the Congressman's wife had dropped by and had been waiting outside the office where she heard these two conversations. And when the second man left, she went in and said, "That first man wanted you to vote for the bill, and you said he was right. And the second one wanted you to vote against it, and you said he was right, too. You can't run your affairs that way." And the Congressman leaned back and said, "You know, you're right. You're right, you're absolutely right." [*Laughter*]

No President should be faced with the all-or-nothing proposition. The time is here for giving the President the same thing that 43 Governors have—a line-item veto. Until that occurs, it's time for the Congress to take the responsibility for seeing that unwarranted appendages are not part of necessary legislation that comes to my desk.

In these years, our country has come together to celebrate the signing and ratification of our Constitution. The more I reflect on that noble document, the more I'm drawn to the same conclusion as George Washington, that it is more than the product of human invention—that divine providence, as Washington believed, must have also lent a hand.

Two hundred years later, this document will serve as a guide not just for this nation but for the world as we enter the 21st century. We sometimes forget that the original purpose of the Constitutional Convention was to find some solution to the trade disputes that were then tearing the States apart. The Connecticut Gazette in 1787 warned that trade disputes between Georgia and Virginia may "impoverish or fatally crush" the commerce of Virginia. Fighting had actually broken out between some States. Blood had been shed. Perhaps as great as the new political unity they achieved in Philadelphia was the economic breakthrough—the principles that would enable America to become the world's largest free trade zone, a continental economy.

When the Constitution was written, it took longer to travel from Washington to Richmond, Virginia, than it does today to travel from Washington to Tokyo. The needs of the new world economy are transcending political boundaries. As many of you know, over New Year's weekend, Prime Minister Mulroney and I signed an historic free trade agreement between the United States and Canada—an agreement, it is my profound hope, that will help pave the way into that new world economy in which national boundaries become like the border between the U.S. and Canada: meeting places rather than dividing lines.

The changing economic realities—in which products are increasingly information and can be transmitted around the world at the speed of light—these new economic realities dictate a world economy. Because of our experience with a continental economy, we are uniquely situated to lead the world into a new era of economic cooperation, to make this "city on a hill" that is America, a global city. The watchword of this new era will be freedom—free enterprise, free trade, freedom to travel, freedom of emigration. Freedom—the emancipation of peoples' creative energies around the world. That's the challenge that has opened up to us in the 1980's. All we need is the courage to meet it.

Thank you all very much. God bless all of you.

Mr. Akers. Mr. President, one of the great traditions of the City Club is the spontaneous, unrehearsed question-and-answer period following each speaker's formal remarks. We are extremely gratified that you have graciously agreed to continue that tradition. Therefore, prior to your entering the room, we held a random lottery and selected eight members of the City Club who'll have the opportunity to pose questions to you at this time. We'll start with the first question at the microphone to the right.

Iran Arms and Contra Aid Controversy

Q. Mr. President, my name may be Sam Donaldson, I'm not sure. [*Laughter*] Roughly quoting a famous Washington secretary: "Sometimes we must act outside the law." Is there ever a time when an administration, or individuals within an administration, can or should act outside the law? And because Sam asks followup questions, I think I will. Are you planning to pardon anyone mired in the Iran-*contra* scandal?

The President. I would have to tell you that first of all, with the special investigators still going forward with their investigation, it would be too early for me to comment on anything of that kind or to make a decision in advance. I would have to wait to see what takes place, whether someone is deemed breaking the law or not. And so, I can't answer your question that directly.

I would have to say that in all of the investigation that went on I did not see any—what I considered lawbreaking that was taking place on the part of anyone in the administration. There were some individuals that had not informed me completely of what was going on in the meetings that were being held with some representatives from Iran. They weren't representatives of the Government, may I add. These were people that contacted us through Israel and wanted to talk to us about better relations with the United States in the event of a new government in Iran, because of the health of the Khomeini. If you'll remember, at that time the Khomeini—almost every other day they were proposing that he wouldn't live out the week.

And so, yes, we accepted that and met with them, but that was not against the law. I checked that out beforehand—that the law did give me the permission to do that and to withhold information from the Congress if I thought it was necessary, particularly for the protection of human lives. And we felt that the people who had asked to meet with us—their lives would be endangered if it became known what they were doing.

Aid to the Contras

Q. Welcome to Cleveland, Mr. President. My question is: Do you think democracy will prevail in Nicaragua if aid is cut off, as Congress threatens to do?

The President. If aid is cut off to the *contras,* I have to believe that the actions of the Sandinistas, right down to the present, are such that they are proving that they have no intention of completely accepting the proposed peace agreement. We have, and we think that that could be a solution. But we believe that the only thing that can bring the *contras*—or bring the Sandinista government, which is a totalitarian Communist government—that can bring it to the negotiating table, is the threat of the *contras*—who are the people of Nicaragua.

And I was interested to note this morning that 10,000 Nicaraguan citizens in the capital, in Managua, yesterday demonstrated against the Sandinista government. And maybe the peace process is the reason why they weren't attacked or arrested and thrown into prison, as anyone else doing that has been in the past. But I believe that right now we're asking for nonlethal help to the *contras.* But I do believe that just as we're helping the people of Afghanistan try to restore freedom to their country, that we—or the Sandinista government is establishing what would be a Soviet satellite state on the soil of the Americas. And I don't think we should tolerate that for one minute.

Sino-Soviet Relations

Q. Mr. President, Mayor George Voinovich, members of the City Club, my name is Arthur Push. Thank you for allowing me to participate in this citadel of free speech.

My question pertains to the Soviets reinviting China to participate in a summit with them. In your opinion, is this an attempt by the Soviets to align themselves with another world power in order to have greater bargaining leverage with the West, or is it Gorbachev's genuine concern to further your and his interest in world peace and begin dealing with the silent giant of the East? And as a typical press tactic, I have a followup. What is your plan in dealing with China? Will you encourage greater trading with them so that the American businesses can tap the tremendous markets in China not only to help them modernize but also help our economy flourish, as well as promoting a free market? Thank you. Sorry for the length.

The President. All right, I'll try to handle both of these in a single answer. I don't know; I couldn't read Mr. Gorbachev's mind as to what his motives might be. But I do know this: that historically, the Soviets—it's almost been an obsession with them, of the great size on their border of China and what a great threat that could be. And right now they have some 53 divisions on the Chinese border, and before the INF agreement, they were trying to maintain some of those weapons that they could continue to have aimed at China. But maybe it is defensive with him; maybe it is simply trying to restore what once was an alliance. But if so, the Chinese have put down some pretty valid considerations that they have got: the Soviets must stop supporting the Vietnamese in their domination and takeover of Cambodia. And there are some other things: again, the removal of the 53 divisions and so forth. The world would be a better place if all those things came about.

On the other hand, I was visiting China at a time when they first began the change in their own system. It was quite thrilling to be there at a time when a Chinese family became the first family to buy an automobile. All the automobiles were government-owned; they didn't belong to the private people. And you waited to see what might happen. And the Government of China put them on television to tell the people what they had done and said to the people, see, work, earn more money. You, too, can buy an automobile.

They're making moderations of the same—at least it seems the same kind that is being proposed in *glasnost* by Gorbachev. But there's no question that if the intent is peace and not what looked for a time like an arms unit, back before the Chinese broke out of the arrangement with them, why, this could well be something that we should not question, but go along with.

But, again, I would recommend to the Chinese in their dealings that—even though he's an affable person and we got along just fine—a Russian proverb: *Dovorey no provorey*—trust but verify.

Q. Thank you very much, Mr. President. Welcome to Cleveland.

The Nation's Economy

Q. Good afternoon, Mr. President. My question is in keeping with your speech's theme: the economy. In recent months, we have seen the U.S. dollar decline in value against foreign currency and the stock market fall drastically. Many economists predict that we are heading into a recession. I would like for you to comment, please, on what you see to be the immediate fate of the economy and what immediate actions you would recommend to avoid a recession.

The President. Well, for one thing, with regard to the dollar, we have an agreement with the most potent trading partners of ours, a number of other nations, about together working to maintain the stability in the ratio of all our currencies. And we are working at that. And what we want is stability in the value of the dollar.

Now, to go on with the other parts of your question and whether there's to be a—you see, I can make jokes about economists, because my degree was in economics. First of all, I don't believe that the dollar or anything outside of Wall Street and the markets had anything to do with the great debacle in October. And that is borne out in the report that has been presented to me by the commission that I appointed, the Brady commission: that what took place was a panic as a result of—well, there were no more than, he says, about 15 firms that were involved in the great change that was taking place in the market; but that it was induced within the marketplace and not from some factor outside.

As to recession, I have to say we have just completed 62 months of expansion. That is the longest period, I think, in the history of our country, certainly the longest period since World War II. Every indices is that we're going to continue to expand; there's going to continue to be an increase in productivity and all. When I spoke about the jobs—just think of this—with 3 million new jobs this last year, as I said, and 14½ million in these 62 months. The potential employment pool of America for statistics is considered to be everyone, male or female, from 16 years of age up. That includes all the people getting an education; that includes all the people retired, not looking for a job. And today the highest percentage in our history, 62.3 percent of all that population's segment, are employed. And I don't think the signs of recession are there.

I'll tell you what does frighten me: When I see sometimes in the media all this great emphasis in quoting people about pessimism and that—well, this looks like there's a recession coming. That could bring on bad times and a recession. If enough people get frightened and say, well, let's not buy a new car this year; let's put it off until next year; or let's not put that new carpet down or buy a refrigerator, let's make the old one do for a while. If enough people do that, you have a recession. They just go on strike and quit buying.

So, I think that we should, more and more, look at the economic facts. And all of the facts about our economy are up and higher than they have been in years and years. And we're continuing to create about a quarter-of-a-million new jobs every month. So, I don't anticipate a recession unless some of those doomcriers scare the people into one—just talk it up.

Public Lands and Recreational Facilities

Q. Good afternoon, Mr. President. Your Commission on American Outdoors provided wide-ranging opportunities for the American public to speak to recreation resource needs and issues, and as you know, their report was finalized and published in 1987. My question to you is: Now that this report has become a reality, expressing that today's recreational needs are more of a necessity than a frill in today's world, what are your thoughts as to the Federal funding responsibility in seeing that these needs are met?

The President. I think you're talking about government landowning and so forth, for recreational purposes and so forth. There has been an increase in that. And I have a map—I wish everyone could see it. It's a map of the United States. And the land owned by the Government is in red, and the rest of the map is white. West of the Mississippi River—your first glance at that map, you think the whole thing is red, the Government owns so much property.

We have been supportive of recreational facilities and so forth, doing that. But there has been, also, a great private sector move, and don't overlook that. That is so American, and we should be so proud of it. This last year, we were asked to send some people to Paris, France, to an international meeting to tell those countries in Europe and others how we supported things of this kind—charities, good causes—privately, because in all those other countries, they thought that was the Government's task—the Government should do it. Well, the Government isn't as good at doing it as the private sector is. Wetlands in this country that are supported by the very people who hunt ducks—and doing it to keep their own sport intact—all kinds of things.

Where there is a specific need, I don't think you can generalize. But I know that we have vastly upgraded our national parks in the last few years, and we're continuing to do that. If there is a particular need in a particular place, fine, but at the same time, I think we should think twice about government ownership and how far it can go in dominating this land of ours. It's something like—what is it now—it's hundreds and hundreds of millions of—well, I'm not going to risk this, because I have the figures, and I can't spin them off the top of my head right now. But I don't know anyplace other than the Soviet Union where the Government owns more than ours does. But it is also land that is deemed to be used for the sport and recreation and outdoor life of the people, and we'll continue to be cooperative with that private sector.

Budget Deficit

Q. Mr. President, you may not have had time to read this morning's Wall Street Journal, but I'd like you to react to the lead sentence, which is: "Calling budget deficits the unwanted and unpleasant stepchild of Reaganomics. The President's task force on the October 19th stock market crash pointed to government red ink as the major cause."

The President. I have no quarrel with the fact that government overspending—deficit spending—is a drag on our economy, and it must be eliminated. The first man who ever proposed no deficit spending was Jefferson, who said it was the great omission of our Constitution that it did not place a limit on the Government's ability to borrow money.

Now we're trying, and it's been a goal of mine. But when I hear them call it a stepchild of mine, I would like to point out something: The President of the United States can't spend a dime; only the Congress can do that. I have submitted, as I'm required by law, every January 4th a budget to the Congress. We have not had a budget since I've been here. We've had continuing resolutions. They call my budget dead on arrival.

And then the only place they're willing to cut is defense spending. But when I came into office, on any given day, 50 percent of our warplanes couldn't fly for lack of spare parts. And almost as many ships in the Navy could not leave harbor for the same reasons. Well, we have rebuilt our military, and one result of that is the INF treaty. The Soviet Union didn't come to the table to bargain with us on arms because they had changed their ways. They know they can't win an arms race if we keep on building and furbishing our defense. But the Congress every year has reduced what we have sought for defense spending.

Now, the reason I went into this is to tell you this: In 5 years, the Congress has cut $125 billion from defense spending, but not to reduce the deficit—because they've added $250 billion to domestic spending that is not defense. So, each time they have been adding on to the spending. The thing is, the great War on Poverty that started under Lyndon Johnson in the middle sixties—from 1965 to 1980, the budget of the United States grew to five times what it had been in '65. The deficit grew to 38 times what it had been in 1965.

I was out on the mashed-potato circuit for years as a private citizen making speeches about deficit spending, because back in—well, for more than 50 years before 1980, there's only been 4 years in which there was a Republican Congress. And the other 46 years in that half-century has been a Democratic Congress. But there have also been only 8 years in which the budget was balanced out of those. And every time people like myself out on the mashed-potato circuit complained and said we should start balancing the budget, their defense was—and maybe some of you can remember this—they would say deficit spending is necessary to our prosperity, and it's no problem, because we owe it to ourselves. And that was their argument for going on with what they were doing.

So, I'm as determined as ever, and that's what Gramm-Rudman-Hollings is all about. You can't do it in 1 year, but we can set ourselves on a course that will reach at year-certain. And then if the Lord is smiling on us—and I hope He'll smile on us—the American people will force the Government to have a balanced budget amendment—that the Government henceforth cannot deficit spend.

Ohio Senate Race

Q. Mr. President, it's certainly an honor to have you here in Cleveland, speaking to the City Club and the people of Cleveland, but it's also, I think, wonderful that you're going to do a little politicking for Mayor Voinovich, who many of us are hoping will be our next Senator. And my question revolves—we all know our current Senator [Howard M. Metzenbaum] is effective in getting publicity and getting his name in the paper, but I wonder how effective he is as far as representing the people of the country and the best interest of the country. And I'd really, sir, like your unbiased opinion. [*Laughter*] Who do you think would make the best Senator and try to help out the people of Ohio?

The President. My unbiased opinion is—[*laughter*]—that the things we've been trying to do, such as balancing a budget and ending deficit spending and keeping this economy going and so forth, has got a 1,000 times better chance of taking place if the next Senator from Ohio is your former mayor, George Voinovich.

Q. Thank you, Mr. President.

The President. Thank you all, and I'm sorry I talked so long here. I've got all kinds of stories about speakers who should not take too long as after dinner or after lunch speakers, and I've violated all of it with my answers here, but you tempted me beyond my strength. I don't often face such wonderful, informative questions as you were asking.

Note: The President spoke at 12:40 p.m. in the Grand Ballroom at the Stouffer Tower City Plaza Hotel. In his opening remarks, he referred to Bruce H. Akers, vice president of the City Club of Cleveland, and Mayor George Voinovich. He also referred to the Cleveland Browns' victory in the National Football League playoffs. Following the question-and-answer session, the President returned to Washington, DC.

Statement by Assistant to the President for Press Relations Fitzwater on the Canada-United States Agreement on the Arctic
January 11, 1988

The Canadian Secretary of State for External Affairs, the Right Honourable Joe Clark, and the Secretary of State, George Shultz, today concluded an agreement on cooperation between Canada and the United States in the Arctic. The agreement affirms the political will of the two countries to cooperate in advancing their shared interests in Arctic navigation, development, and security. It signals the importance which the two countries attach to protection of the unique and fragile environment of the region and the well-being of the inhabitants of the north.

The agreement signed today marks the culmination of 24 months of discussions between the two governments. "This is an important step forward for Canada in the north," Prime Minister Mulroney said today. "While we and the United States have not changed our legal positions, we have come to a practical agreement that is fully consistent with the requirements of Canadian sovereignty in the Arctic. It is an improvement over the situation which prevailed previously. What we have now significantly advances Canadian interests." President Reagan stated: "This is a pragmatic solution based on our special bilateral relationship, our common interest in cooperating on Arctic matters, and the nature of the area. It is without prejudice to our respective legal positions, and it sets no precedents for other areas."

Remarks at the Dedication Ceremony for the Army and Navy Club
January 12, 1988

Well, reverend clergy, General Hittle, General Dawson, Charles Graham, and ladies and gentlemen: In the old days, I'm told, the Army and Navy Club often invited their neighbor, the President, to all their parties. I've also heard that Benjamin Harrison and Grover Cleveland walked over for a toddy or two. Oh, for the good old days. [*Laughter*] If I'd known that the club was this beautiful, Nancy and I would have stopped by long ago, and we would even walk, if the Secret Service would let us.

Well, the word for today is: Congratulations! You've put together a beautiful building and an historic treasure. I'm amazed at your outstanding collection of art, particularly the De Welden sculptures. I've always wondered where old generals and admirals went when they "just faded away." And now I know.

But nothing is more important than keeping alive the gallant tradition of our armed services—a tradition that adds up to a word not just for today but for all time: patriotism. As you know, I've visited our men and women in the armed services and their families all around the world—from Camp Liberty Bell on the demilitarized zone in Korea to Tempelhof Air Force Base in West Berlin—and the one thing that's always struck me the most about them is their dedication to country. They take a little bit of America with them every place they go, no matter how far, to make it more like home. And these men and women are willing to be away from this home that they love so that other countries may remain free. That's one of the great sacrifices they make for our country.

So, I've got a report to bring you from the front. I've talked to admirals and generals alike, on bases from Iceland to Guam, and they've told me stories about how their troops, U.S. troops, are the best trained, best equipped, and best educated troops around. To sum it up, what we have right now is the best darn group of young men and women in uniform that this nation has ever seen, and we're proud of them.

I was honored when you invited me to dedicate your new clubhouse, as the Army and Navy Club begins its second century. General Hittle assures me that I'm among friends. Then, I knew that already. No group of men and women has given more steadfast support to the Commander in Chief, no matter what his name was, no matter what party he represented. And I know I'll never forget the support that you've given me during some of my toughest hours as President. And so, I salute you not only for the help you've given me over the past 7 years but for the help your club has given my predecessors and will give my successors for generations to come.

Upstairs I couldn't help noticing the busts of President Eisenhower and President Truman, but when I saw that picture of General "Hap" Arnold standing in front of a B–17, I had to resist the urge to snap to attention. You know, General Arnold was my boss some 40 years ago, and he ran a tough Air Force. Just ask the fellows on the other side.

General Hittle told me, too, that Gary Cooper filmed many of the scenes of "The Billy Mitchell Court Martial" right here at the club. But he says that the members wouldn't let the cameras in until after midnight, after the members had gone to bed. Well, I'm grateful that you didn't impose that kind of schedule on me. [*Laughter*] And I think Nancy would feel the same way.

In December of 1885, according to your records, after the founders signed the papers of incorporation, they retired to a warm room to drink a toast: "To the club." I'd like to repeat that salute with you today. For a century, the Army and Navy Club has played an important role in the life of the Republic. May the second century eclipse the first. And so, ladies and gentlemen, a salute: "To the club." Thank you.

Note: The President spoke at 11:10 a.m. in the dining room of the club. In his opening remarks, he referred to Brig. Gen. James D. Hittle, USMC, Ret.; Maj. Gen. Donald S. Dawson, USAF, Ret.; and Charles J. Graham; president, vice president, and general manager, respectively, of the club.

Remarks on Signing the Martin Luther King, Jr., Day Proclamation
January 12, 1988

We're here today to honor a man who dedicated his life to the pursuit of a dream. In honoring one man's commitment, we're also rededicating ourselves to the fundamental principle behind that dream. That principle, which goes to the very essence of America, is simply this: that it is self-evident that all men are created equal and that they are endowed by their Creator with certain unalienable rights.

Today we still cherish these rights and values upon which our country was built and for which our forefathers gave their lives, for which Dr. Martin Luther King, Jr., gave his life. The fight for genuine equality of opportunity goes on. It still continues for many Americans today, yet let us not ignore the strides that have been made and the great strides that are being made toward ending discrimination and bigotry in our towns and communities, in our government, and most important, in our own hearts.

And there are many reasons for hope. Advancements in employment and education should not escape our attention. Black employment has risen 26 percent during our expansion. That's more than twice the rate of the job gain of whites. The unemployment rate for black youths has declined dramatically.

Great strides are being made in education, as well. The publication we released last spring, "Schools That Work," describes many schools that are doing a good job educating disadvantaged children. One shining example is the Garrison Elementary School in the South Bronx in New York City. The student population is half black and half Hispanic. The school lies in one of the poorest sections of New York. Yet for the past 5 years, Garrison has ranked in the top 12 percent of New York City schools in reading achievement. By the time they reach the sixth grade, nearly every student performs at or above grade level in both reading and math.

You know, James Madison once said: "A well-instructed people alone can be permanently a free people." Together we strive to ensure that every American receives a sound education and that, in so doing, we secure our freedom, as well. Secretary of Education William Bennett has been leading the charge for higher standards and more discipline. We can give no better gift to our young people than giving them the basic skills needed to reach their potential and fulfill their dreams.

The value of a good education was not lost on Dr. King. He entered Morehouse College at the age of 15 and earned a Ph.D. 11 years later from Boston University. Martin Luther King, Jr.'s own life was one of dreams. It's fitting that we honor the man who went from being a minister in the Ebenezer Baptist Church in Atlanta to being the recipient of the Nobel Peace Prize.

Dr. King said the evening before his assassination: "I just want to do God's will. And he's allowed me to go to the mountain. And I've looked over, and I've seen the promised land . . . so I'm happy tonight. I'm not worried about anything. I'm not fearing any man." These are the words of a man at peace with God and himself, content in the knowledge that what is right will inevitably triumph. He gave his life, as so many of our forefathers did, for his principles. And it is thanks to his strength of character and his God-given talents that the dream he spoke about so eloquently will live on forever.

And now we'll sign the proclamation honoring the 59th anniversary of Dr. Martin Luther King, Jr.'s birth.

Note: The President spoke at 1:17 p.m. in the Roosevelt Room at the White House.

Proclamation 5760—Martin Luther King, Jr., Day, 1988
January 12, 1988

By the President of the United States of America

A Proclamation

Twenty years ago this coming April, Dr. Martin Luther King, Jr., was slain by an assassin in Memphis, Tennessee. Violence and hatred, the enemies against which he offered an uncompromising message of brotherhood and hope, had claimed another victim in a decade of tumult that plumbed the very spirit of this Nation. Martin Luther King was martyred not only for his beliefs, but for the passionate conviction and consistency with which he espoused them. That those convictions prevailed, that his dream of the death of bigotry did not die with his life's ebbing, offered immutable confirmation of his fervent belief that "unarmed truth and unconditional love will have the final word in reality."

Martin Luther King's leadership was of the same character as his dream. It was larger than personality and broader than history. It bore the stamp of the religious tradition that formed his early life and led him to an assistant pastorship at Ebenezer Baptist Church in Atlanta at age 18. It took anchor in what he called the "magnificent words" of the Declaration of Independence and in the Constitution, words he echoed and to which he so often appealed in his speeches and writings against the cruelty and irrationality of segregation and prejudice. His was leadership that spoke to the best in every person's nature and that never failed, even in the face of curses and threats, iron bars and police lines, to turn men's eyes toward "the bright and glittering daybreak of freedom and justice."

Arrested in a march for desegregation on Good Friday, 1963, Martin Luther King wrote from the Birmingham City Jail of his faith in this ultimate dawning of equality: "We will reach the goal of freedom in Birmingham and all over the nation, because the goal of America is freedom. Abused and scorned though we may be, our destiny is tied up with the destiny of America. . . . If the inexpressible cruelties of slavery could not stop us, the opposition we now face will surely fail. We will win our freedom because the sacred heritage of our nation and the eternal will of God are embodied in our echoing demands." Those demands, he saw, were claims to the original promise of the truths our Founders proclaimed "self-evident"—that "all men are endowed by their Creator with certain unalienable rights," among them the "rights to Life, Liberty and the pursuit of Happiness." He called these words a "promissory note to which every American was to fall heir," and he insisted that what was centuries overdue could no longer be delayed.

Martin Luther King's words were eloquent because they were borne not by his tongue alone but by his very being; not by his being alone but by the beings of every one of his fellow black Americans who felt the lash and the sting of bigotry; and not by the living alone but by every generation that had gone before him in the chains of slavery or separation. He brought light to the victims of segregation, but he brought light as well—in a way, illumined by faith, more sorely needed—to its perpetrators. He saw how evil could crush the spirit of both the oppressor and the oppressed, but whereas "unearned suffering" was redemptive, those who were motivated by hatred and inflicted pain had no recourse but to abandon the instruments of prejudice and to change heart.

Through his evocation, by his words and his presence, of transcendent ideals, Martin Luther King pierced to the heart of American society and changed it, irrevocably, for the better. He, and all those who marched with him, overcame. As they did so, so too did the America that Lincoln had said could not stand divided—transmuted now through the toil and blood of its fallen heroes into a land more wholly free. The work of justice and freedom continues, but its goal is less distant, its hardships more tolerable, and its triumph more sure. For these gifts to our Nation, during his lifetime and in the decades past and to come, all Americans join in fitting celebration of the birth of Martin Luther King, Jr.

By Public Law 98–144, the third Monday in January of each year has been designated as a public holiday in honor of the "Birthday of Martin Luther King, Jr."

Now, Therefore, I, Ronald Reagan, President of the United States of America, by virtue of the authority vested in me by the Constitution and laws of the United States, do hereby proclaim Monday, January 18, 1988, as Martin Luther King, Jr., Day.

In Witness Whereof, I have hereunto set my hand this 12th day of January, in the year of our Lord nineteen hundred and eighty-eight, and of the Independence of the United States of America the two hundred and twelfth.

RONALD REAGAN

[*Filed with the Office of the Federal Register, 4:44 p.m., January 12, 1988*]

Letter to the Speaker of the House of Representatives and the President of the Senate Reporting on the National Emergency With Respect to Libya
January 12, 1988

Dear Mr. Speaker: (Dear Mr. President:)

1. I hereby report on developments since my last report of July 10, 1987, concerning the national emergency with respect to Libya that was declared in Executive Order No. 12543 of January 7, 1986. This report is submitted pursuant to section 401(c) of the National Emergencies Act, 50 U.S.C. 1641(c); section 204(c) of the International Emergency Economic Powers Act, 50 U.S.C. 1703(c); and section 505(c) of the International Security and Development Cooperation Act of 1985, 22 U.S.C. 2349aa–9(c).

2. Since my last report on July 10, 1987, there have been two amendments to the Libyan Sanctions Regulations, 31 C.F.R. Part 550 (the "Regulations"), administered by the Office of Foreign Assets Control of the Department of the Treasury. These amendments, comprising sections 550.630 and 550.635 of the Regulations and published in the *Federal Register* at 52 FR 35548 (September 22, 1987), provide for a census of blocked assets held by U.S. persons and a census of claims of U.S. nationals against the Government of Libya and any Libyan entity. Reporting under these sections is mandatory. The submission of a report on a claim against Libya, however, does not constitute the filing with the United States Government of a formal claim for compensation, since no formal claims adjudication program currently exists. There have been no amendments or changes since July 10, 1987, to orders of the Department of Commerce or the Department of Transportation implementing aspects of Executive Order No. 12543 that relate to exports of U.S.-origin commodities and technical data and air transportation, respectively.

3. The major licensing action occurring during the past 6 months under the Regulations involved blocked assets of the Libyan Arab Foreign Bank, held by the London branch of Bankers Trust Company. The Libyan bank had sued in London for release of the funds, and the Commercial Court issued a ruling in *Libyan Arab Foreign Bank* v. *Bankers Trust,* finding no basis under British law for withholding payment of funds held in London and New York under the British deposit contract. In October, after completion of interagency consultation, the Treasury Department licensed Bankers Trust to comply with the London judgment by authorizing the release of approximately $292 million to the Libyan bank, in addition to interest for pre-sanctions breach of contract damages. This licensing action affected only the funds involved in this particular lawsuit.

Other licensing actions included extending one license authorizing a service contractor that had been operating in Libya to sell certain of its equipment in Libya to a Libyan purchaser. Three immediate family members of Libyan nationals registered their eligibility to enter into transactions related to travel to, and residence within, Libya. Two licenses were issued authorizing U.S. persons to obtain services in connection with Libyan patent, trademark, copyright, and other intellectual property protection.

4. Various enforcement actions mentioned in my last report are being pursued, and one case has been brought to trial involving prosecution of persons who allegedly exported petroleum equipment from the United States to Libya through a European conduit.

5. The expenses incurred by the Federal Government in the 6-month period from July 10, 1987, through the present time that are directly attributable to the exercise of powers and authorities conferred by the declaration of the Libyan national emergency are estimated at $623,554. Personnel costs were largely centered in the Department of the Treasury (particularly in the Office of Foreign Assets Control, the Cus-

toms Service, the Office of the Assistant Secretary for Enforcement, the Office of the Assistant Secretary for International Affairs, and the Office of the General Counsel), the Department of State, the Department of Commerce, the Department of Justice, the Federal Reserve Board, and the National Security Council.

6. The policies and actions of the Government of Libya continue to pose an unusual and extraordinary threat to the national security and foreign policy of the United States. I shall continue to exercise the powers at my disposal to apply economic sanctions against Libya as long as these measures are appropriate and will continue to report periodically to the Congress on significant developments, pursuant to 50 U.S.C. 1703(c).

Sincerely,

RONALD REAGAN

Note: Identical letters were sent to Jim Wright, Speaker of the House of Representatives, and George Bush, President of the Senate.

Appointment of George A. Wade as a United States Commissioner on the International Pacific Halibut Commission
January 12, 1988

The President today announced his intention to appoint George A. Wade to be a U.S. Commissioner on the International Pacific Halibut Commission for a term expiring December 12, 1989. This is a reappointment.

Since 1975 Mr. Wade has been chairman and chief executive officer of VWH Co., Ltd., in Seattle, WA. Prior to this he was chairman and president of Pacific Capital Corp., 1968–1975. Since 1968 Mr. Wade has been the majority stockholder and chief executive officer of several controlled entities.

Mr. Wade graduated from Yale University (B.S., 1950) and the University of Washington (M.B.A., 1960; Ph.D., 1975). He was born May 14, 1929, in Seattle, WA. He is married, has five children, and resides in Seattle, WA.

Appointment of Ralph P. Davidson as a Member of the Board of Trustees of the John F. Kennedy Center for the Performing Arts
January 12, 1988

The President today announced his intention to appoint Ralph P. Davidson to be a member of the Board of Trustees of the John F. Kennedy Center for the Performing Arts, Smithsonian Institution, for the remainder of the term expiring September 1, 1994. He would succeed Trammell Crow.

Since 1986 Mr. Davidson has been chairman of the executive committee of the Time, Inc., board of directors in New York, NY. Prior to this he served as chairman of the board of Time, Inc., 1980–1986. Mr. Davidson has been with Time, Inc., since 1954 in various capacities: retail representative for Life magazine, European regional manager of Time International, advertising sales executive, European advertising director in London, managing director of Time International and associate publisher, and vice president and publisher. In 1982 Mr. Davidson was appointed to the President's Commission on Executive Exchange. He is also a member of the Statue of Liberty-Ellis Island Centennial Commission, chairman of the executive committee of the Business Committee for the Arts, and a director of the

New York City Ballet.

Mr. Davidson graduated from Stanford University (B.A., 1950). He served in the United States Navy during World War II. He was born August 17, 1927, in Santa Fe, NM. He is married, has six children, and resides in New York, NY.

Presidential Finding Concerning Alaska Natural Gas
January 12, 1988

This Administration has been dedicated to encouraging free trade and to removing regulatory impediments that inhibit the development of our Nation's natural resources. Proven natural gas reserves in the Prudhoe Bay area of Alaska's North Slope represent approximately 15 percent of total U.S. gas reserves. In addition, undiscovered, recoverable supplies of natural gas from Alaska's North Slope may exceed 100 trillion cubic feet. There can be no doubt the development of Alaskan oil has played an important role in ensuring adequate energy supplies at reasonable prices for American consumers. I believe efficient development of Alaska natural gas will provide similar benefits. Leaving this resource undeveloped benefits no one.

Efficient development of Alaska natural gas on the basis of market financing could encompass the export of some of this gas to other countries. Because world energy markets are interrelated, our Nation will benefit from an enlarged international gas supply. Production of Alaska reserves will increase the amount of secure energy sources available at market prices and, thus, displace less secure or more expensive energy sources, including oil from the Persian Gulf.

Before Alaska natural gas can be exported to nations other than Canada or Mexico, Section 12 of the Alaska Natural Gas Transportation Act (15 U.S.C. 719j) requires me to find exportation "will not diminish the total quantity or quality nor increase the total price of energy available to the United States." In order to make this finding, it has been necessary to assess the relationship of Alaska natural gas to the U.S. energy market.

There exist adequate, secure, reasonably priced supplies of natural gas to meet the demand of American consumers for the foreseeable future. This demand can be met by lower-48 production and already-approved Canadian imports. If necessary, this demand also can be met at lower delivered energy cost by coal, oil, imported liquified natural gas (LNG), natural gas from Mexico, and other energy sources.

Given these facts, exports of Alaska natural gas would represent a judgment by the market that the energy demands of American consumers can be met adequately from other sources at comparable or lower prices. Exports of Alaska natural gas would not diminish the total quantity or quality of energy available to U.S. consumers because world energy resources would be increased and other more efficient supplies would thus be available. Finally, exports would not increase the price of energy available to consumers since increased availability of secure energy sources tends to stabilize or lower energy prices.

Accordingly, I find that exports of Alaska natural gas in quantities in excess of 1,000 Mcf per day will not diminish the total quantity or quality nor increase the total price of energy available to the United States.

This finding removes the Section 12 regulatory impediment to Alaskan natural gas exports in a manner that allows any private party to develop this resource and sets up competition for this purpose. It is my belief that removal of this impediment to private sector development of Alaska's vast natural gas resources, using private sector resources with no government subsidy, will benefit our entire Nation.

This finding represents a determination that the effects of exports of Alaska natural gas on American consumers would comply with the market criteria of Section 12 in the context of current and projected future energy markets and that such exports would be consistent with our comprehensive energy policy. It does not assess the merits or feasibility of a particular project, but rather lets the marketplace undertake a realistic consideration of various options concerning Alaska natural gas. The operation of market forces is the best guarantee that Alaska natural gas will be developed efficiently and that there is an incentive to find additional reserves.

I do not believe this finding should hinder completion of the Alaska Natural Gas Transportation System (ANGTS). This Administration supports the timely, economic development of Alaskan natural resources. To this end the Administration has removed all regulatory barriers to the private sector's expeditious completion of this project. In particular, I want to reaffirm our support for the special regulatory treatment of the "prebuild" portion of ANGTS, including the minimum revenue stream guarantees.

This finding shall be published in the *Federal Register.*

RONALD REAGAN

[Filed with the Office of the Federal Register, 2:39 p.m., January 13, 1988]

Note: The finding, which was released by the Office of the Press Secretary on January 13, was printed in the "Federal Register" of January 15.

Remarks Following Discussions With Prime Minister Noboru Takeshita of Japan

January 13, 1988

The President. It has been a great pleasure to welcome Prime Minister Takeshita on his first visit to Washington since taking office in November. He is the leader of one of the world's great nations and one of America's most valued friends.

Our meetings were constructive and amiable. We discussed the vital issues of the day and established an excellent personal rapport. Good personal relationships between the leaders of Japan and the United States are essential as our two nations strive to confront the challenges of this century and the next.

During our discussions today, Prime Minister Takeshita and I found that our views on international questions coincide to a remarkable degree. We share an abiding commitment to democratic institutions and to free markets to protect freedom and human rights. We are dedicated to improving the economic well-being not just of our own people but of all mankind.

In this regard, I was especially pleased with the Prime Minister's global economic perspective. He outlined significant plans for expanding Japanese domestic demand and stimulating growth. He reviewed Japan's plans to increase its foreign assistance budget next year to an amount second only to that of the United States. And he expressed Japan's determination to continue the process of economic adjustment. The Prime Minister and I discussed and affirmed our support for the economic policy coordination process adopted at the Tokyo and Venice economic summits. A joint statement concerning our bilateral undertakings in that regard will be released shortly.

The U.S.-Japan treaty of mutual cooperation and security is the foundation upon which our relationship is built. I was satisfied to note that U.S.-Japan cooperation in the national security area is strong and growing and that Japan's recently announced budget provides for continued significant increases in the area of national defense. Japan's growing contribution to the maintenance of U.S. forces in Japan is of immense value to the United States. I might add that Japan's national defense program is entirely consistent with the concept of self-defense and in no way poses any threat to others.

During our meetings, I briefed the Prime Minister on the details of last month's summit. We agreed on the benefits of the INF treaty, and he was encouraged by the possibility of even further arms cuts with the Soviet Union. I was gratified that the Prime Minister expressed Japan's fullest support of our actions, and I assured him that we would consult fully with all of our allies as we continue our discussions with the Soviet Union.

The Prime Minister and I recognized the danger posed to our mutual security in the export of certain kinds of high technology. The Prime Minister assured me that Japan has taken the necessary legislative and administrative measures to prevent technology leakage. I told the Prime Minister that I appreciated his actions and his commitment to the vigorous implementation of controls over exports of sensitive technology. The Prime Minister and I concur on the importance of the new nuclear cooperation agreement. We believe it to be a good agreement, and we will exert our best efforts to have it come into force expeditiously.

The Prime Minister noted that Japan's global trade surplus is declining and underlined his determination to address bilateral issues. I was pleased with his assurance that he intends to resolve a particularly difficult trade issue—the problem of access for the U.S. construction industry—in a satisfactory manner. We agree the Uruguay round [of the General Agreement on Tariffs and Trade] must succeed and that revision of the world trading system should include a comprehensive reform of trade in agriculture and services. I expressed appreciation for the Prime Minister's efforts on trade, stressing the urgency of expanding opportunities for U.S. farmers and other exporters at a time of increasing pressure for protectionism here in the United States. We concurred on the importance of keeping trade flowing and barriers down. For our part, I intend to continue my efforts to reduce our budget deficit, improve American competitiveness, and combat protectionism.

We reaffirmed our determination to conclude a new science and technology agreement, with equitable and expanding research benefits for scientists of both countries. I expressed appreciation for Japan's initiatives to provide more than $4 million in science fellowships to American researchers. We also reaffirmed the spirit of the 1983 U.S.-Japan joint policy statement on energy cooperation.

The Prime Minister and I noted with satisfaction political developments in the Republic of Korea and our intention to help make the 1988 Olympic games a success. We also pledged to do our utmost to help the Philippine Government and its people in this period of economic adjustment.

In sum, our talks were positive and forthright, and it's been a great pleasure to have the Prime Minister here with us in Washington. I look forward to being with him again in Toronto this spring.

The Prime Minister. Thank you, Mr. President. I'm extremely pleased with the results of the cordial and candid exchange of views I had with you today. Thanks to your efforts over the past years, Mr. President, the historic INF treaty was signed last month. I look forward to its expeditious entry into force. And as one representing a member of the West, I am determined to firmly support the President in his pursuit of substantive progress in East-West relations, where much remains to be done across a broad spectrum of areas.

The President and I confirm that the cooperative relationship between Japan and the United States, with the unshakable security arrangements as its cornerstone, is essential for the peace and stability of the Asia-Pacific region. I will continue my efforts, with the cooperation of the President, for further strengthening the credibility of the Japan-U.S. security arrangements.

I explained to the President that the Government of Japan has continued to provide the funds necessary for achieving its current defense program. Japan has also continued to increase its host nation support for U.S. forces in Japan, whose stationing is an indispensable part of the Japan-U.S. security system. Moreover, in view of the recent economic conditions adversely affecting the financial situation of U.S. forces, I noted to the President that the Government of Japan has decided on its own initiative to increase further Japan's share of such expenditures.

The President and I agreed that today, more than any other time in history, policy coordination among major countries is required to ensure sustained growth of the world economy and to correct external imbalances. In this respect, we agreed that the roles to be fulfilled by Japan and the United States are of vital importance. We shared the recognition that, together with the measures taken by individual countries, stability of exchange rates is indispensable to the achievement of these goals as described in our joint statement.

Fully aware of the heavy responsibility commensurate with Japan's status in the international economy, I am determined to carry out a vigorous economic management policy with emphasis on domestic demand expansion to promote structural adjustment to the improved market access and to strive for a further steady reduction of the current account surplus.

In this connection, I explained to the President that despite an expected drop in net exports, Japan's growth for fiscal year 1988 is now projected at 3.8 percent, a rate higher than the previous fiscal year, through the formation of the fiscal '88 budget geared toward domestic demand expansion with a substantial increase in public works spending. I also explained the prospect for a $10 billion reduction in Japan's current account surplus for fiscal '88 through these measures. The President highly appreciated my explanation. The President, on the other hand, explained that the measures for budget deficit reduction have been enacted based upon the recognition that deficit reduction is essential to the stability of today's world economy. I paid tribute to the President for his endeavors.

With regard to various economic and trade issues which arise as a matter of course between two increasingly interdependent economies of Japan and the United States, the President and I confirmed the basic posture that their solutions should be sought in the spirit of cooperation and joint endeavors and with the aim of expanding, and not contracting, economic exchanges. I expressed my hope that a mutually satisfactory solution will be reached on the pending issue of access to major Japanese public works on the basis of the proposal that Japan has recently made. I also stated to the President the need for early resolutions of the pending issue of Japan-U.S. semiconductor trade.

The President and I exchanged views on the trade bill currently under deliberation in the U.S. Congress, and I expressed my firm support to the President's determination to contain protectionism. The President and I shared the recognition that this year is especially important for the success of the Uruguay round and agreed that our two countries should take the lead in its promotion.

I explained Japan's intensive efforts to prevent the recurrence of illegal diversion of high technologies. The President highly appreciated the measures which Japan has taken for this purpose. In this connection, I expressed Japan's deep concern about moves in the U.S. Congress toward sanctions against foreign companies, including Toshiba Corporation. The President and I agreed on the importance of enhancing the cooperation in the field of science and technology. I explained about my government's initiatives to increase the number of American scientists who will be invited to Japan for research. The President welcomed these initiatives.

I expressed my views concerning the recycling of funds to the developing countries, including the quantitative and qualitative improvement of our official development assistance, in particular, and stated that in the draft budget for fiscal '88, an increase of 6.5 percent over the previous year was secured for ODA [official development assistance]. In this connection, I was encouraged that the President appreciated highly my recent participation in the ASEAN [Association of South East Asian Nations] summit and my subsequent visit to the Philippines. The President and I affirmed, in particular, to continue our support to the Aquino government and to welcome the Republic of Korea's firm stride along the road of democracy, as evident in the recent Presidential election, as well as to cooperate closely towards the success of the Seoul Olympics this fall.

The President and I agreed on the importance of the new Japan-U.S. nuclear cooperation agreement and its prompt entry into force. The President and I, looking forward to a successful Toronto summit, agreed to meet again in Toronto.

In completing my meeting with you, Mr. President, I feel confident that we have strengthened further the foundation of the relations between our two countries. It is my determination to build upon this basis to make Japan a nation that contributes to the world.

I wish to express my heartfelt appreciation to President and Mrs. Reagan for the warm welcome extended to me and my wife as well as our gratitude to the American people for their kindness and consideration during our stay.

Thank you very much.

Note: The President spoke at 1:39 p.m. in the East Room at the White House. The Prime Minister spoke in Japanese, and his remarks were translated by an interpreter. Earlier, the President and the Prime Minister met in the Oval Office and then attended a luncheon in the Residence.

Joint Statement by the President and Prime Minister Noboru Takeshita of Japan on Economic Issues

January 13, 1988

President Reagan and Prime Minister Takeshita reaffirmed their support for the economic policy coordination process adopted at the Tokyo and Venice Summits. The President and Prime Minister endorsed the economic goals and policies set forth in the December 22 statement of the G–7. They agreed that the achievement of sustained non-inflationary growth and reduced trade imbalances remains a top priority of their economic policies. They welcomed the recent actions of other industrial countries in support of these objectives, and called on the newly industrialized economies to play a more constructive role in fostering a strong world economy with reduced external imbalances.

The President stressed his determination to continue the progress that has been made in reducing the U.S. budget deficit. He indicated that the fiscal 1989 budget to be transmitted to the Congress will continue the effort to reduce the budget deficit and will meet the deficit reduction objectives established in the Gramm-Rudman-Hollings budget legislation. The President also reiterated his pledge to veto protectionist trade legislation while seeking authority for the Uruguay Round of trade negotiations.

Prime Minister Takeshita indicated that Japan will pursue economic policies to continue its strong growth in domestic demand and to reduce its trade surplus. The Prime Minister reaffirmed his commitment to carrying forward structural reform of the Japanese economy through implementation of the recommendations of the Maekawa Report and by accelerating liberalization of domestic financial markets, including deregulation of domestic interest rates. To achieve sustained growth as well as to foster exchange rate stability, the Bank of Japan agrees, under the present stable price conditions, to continue to pursue the current policy stance and to make efforts to accommodate declining short-term interest rates.

The President and the Prime Minister believe that the close coordination of their policies within the framework of the arrangements adopted by the Venice Summit is establishing the fundamental economic conditions for greater stability of exchange rates and that a further decline of the dollar could be counterproductive. In addition, they noted that their authorities are cooperating closely on exchange markets and have developed arrangements to assure the adequacy of resources for their cooperative efforts.

Remarks on Presenting the Presidential Medal of Freedom to Roger L. Stevens
January 13, 1988

Thank you all, and good evening to you all. Special regards, of course, to Roger, Christine, and their family. Roger, you were thrilled almost 40 years ago when the New York Times gave you a good review to your first Broadway production, and by the way, I can understand that. Since taking this job, I've found out just how hard it is to get a good review from the New York Times. [*Laughter*]

Well, tonight, Roger, we're giving your entire life a review, and it's a rave. Born in Detroit, educated at Choate, Roger's schooling ended with the advent of the Depression. He spent 5 years at odd jobs. He pumped gas. He worked on the assembly line in a Ford factory. He spent 6 months in real estate and earned not a penny. And some say he kept himself in pocket money mainly by playing blackjack and poker. [*Laughter*] Then in 1934 Roger sensed that certain old apartment buildings were undervalued. He put money into them and launched his first brilliant career in real estate. Soon he had holdings across the country—Detroit, New York, Seattle. And during the war, he spent 2 years at a naval air station in Florida and took the opportunity to look into Florida real estate. When the war ended, he and his colleagues bought three hotels in Florida and one in South Carolina.

By the mid-1950's, Roger's holdings qualified him as a tycoon, a magnate, a hard-driving real estate giant, but not his manner. No, there was a sense of humility and gentleness about him and always a sense of fun. In the words of a banker who worked with Roger in those days—I'll quote: "Business is a game to him. He makes it fun for you, too, because in dealing with him, you never have to concern yourself about what you'll get out of it. As a matter of fact, you sometimes wonder if he's keeping track of how he'll come out himself." [*Laughter*] Well, it's significant that when Roger engineered the purchase of the Empire State Building the room he selected for his office—there in what was then the tallest, most glamorous building on Earth—the room that Roger selected for his office was a cubbyhole that used to belong to a window washer. [*Laughter*]

Roger kept his files in cardboard boxes scattered around the floor. But as I said, real estate was only the first of Roger's brilliant careers. His second, as a New York theatrical producer, got started in 1949, when Roger staged Shakespeare's "Twelfth Night." The show ran for 48 performances, and Roger lost just a little less than $1,000 on each. But it was up from there—up and up and up. In the fifties and early sixties, Roger had as many as eight shows on Broadway a year. He produced playwrights from around the world: the Frenchman Giraudoux; the Swiss playwright Dürrenmatt; the Welsh poet Dylan Thomas; and the Englishmen, Shaffer, Bolt, and Pinter.

Yet it's for his contributions to American theater that Roger should perhaps be most honored. This is the man who produced "Bus Stop," by William Inge; "Tea and Sympathy," by Robert Anderson; and "Cat on a Hot Tin Roof," by Tennessee Williams. And ladies and gentlemen, Roger Stevens is the man who backed a crazy idea to update "Romeo and Juliet" and place it in New York—backed the idea even after another producer pulled out. And after three decades, the mere mention of that show still has the power to thrill. It was called "West Side Story."

By the way, through much of this period, Roger remained an active player in the real estate market. There's a story about a theatrical producer who needed to speak to Roger about a leading lady. When he was told that Roger was in a banker's meeting about a multimillion-dollar loan for a construction project, the director explained: "How can anybody bother with a hole in the ground when we're casting?" [*Laughter*]

But there's still a third brilliant career to speak of. For it was, as has been said here already tonight, in 1961 that President Kennedy asked Roger to see what he could do about founding a national center for the arts here in Washington. And I might add that we Republicans were especially happy to see Roger take on the assignment. You see, it cut into the time he'd been using to raise money for the Democrats. [*Laughter*]

In Roger's own words: "I thought it was a shame that the world's richest nation did not have a decent place for the performing arts. I thought I'd put it together in 3 or 4 years and go back to New York. But it took 10 years to get the darn thing built, and then somebody had to run it. So, there I was." Well, today the Kennedy Center represents one of our nation's premiere cultural institutions, and more than 20 years later, Roger, there you still are. Now, Roger, if I may, I'd like to ask you to join me here at the podium. Roger?

Roger Stevens, on behalf of a grateful nation, I present to you this nation's highest civilian honor, the Medal of Freedom. And now permit me to read the citation:

"A quarter of the time, I have big hits; a quarter of the time, artistic successes; a quarter of the time, the critics were crazy; and a quarter of the time, I'm crazy." [*Laughter*] It figures out pretty well that way.

That humble assessment is by Roger L. Stevens, Chairman of the John F. Kennedy Center for the Performing Arts, real estate giant, chairman of the first National Council on the Arts, and producer or coproducer of more than 200 plays, including such American classics as "Cat on a Hot Tin Roof" and "West Side Story." Roger Stevens may be humble, but his achievements have enriched our nation's culture beyond measure. Congratulations, Roger. And God bless you. Thank you.

Note: The President spoke at 10:25 p.m. following a dinner in the Corcoran Ballroom at the Four Seasons Hotel. Mr. Stevens had served as Chairman of the Board of Trustees of the John F. Kennedy Center for the Performing Arts.

Statement on the Soviet-United States Nuclear and Space Arms Negotiations

January 14, 1988

Today marks the opening in Geneva of round nine of the nuclear and space talks between the United States and the Soviet Union. Our objective in these talks remains unchanged—achievement of equitable and effectively verifiable arms reduction agreements with the Soviet Union, which lessen the risk of war and make the world safer.

Last month here in Washington, General Secretary Gorbachev and I signed the treaty on intermediate-range nuclear forces (INF). This treaty is truly historic. For the first time, an entire class of U.S. and Soviet nuclear missiles will be eliminated. Through this treaty, we and our NATO allies achieve the goal we set forth in 1979: elimination of the threat posed to our security by Soviet INF missiles.

Under this agreement, the Soviets are required to eliminate deployed INF missile systems capable of carrying almost four times as many nuclear warheads as the deployed systems we will eliminate. Furthermore, the INF treaty provides for the most stringent verification in the history of arms control. The asymmetrical reductions to achieve an equal U.S.-Soviet level and the comprehensive verification provisions of the INF treaty provide important precedents for future arms reduction agreements. The

INF treaty is in the security interests of the United States and our allies.

The treaty now goes to the Senate for its advice and consent as to ratification. I welcome the debate the Senate will hold, and I hope the Senate will move expeditiously in carrying out its important constitutional role. The INF treaty is not, however, an end in itself. It is part of our overall strategy for strengthening peace and ensuring strategic stability. Our focus now will be on achieving 50-percent reductions in U.S. and Soviet strategic offensive nuclear arsenals. We particularly seek to reduce the most destabilizing nuclear arms: fast-flying ballistic missiles, especially heavy intercontinental ballistic missiles with multiple warheads.

Our negotiators returned to Geneva with my instructions to expedite work on a joint draft treaty which meets these objectives. This draft START treaty reflects progress already achieved in Geneva and the areas of agreement that General Secretary Gorbachev and I reached during our meetings in 1985 and 1986. This includes a ceiling of 6,000 warheads on 1,600 delivery vehicles for each side, a ceiling for heavy intercontinental ballistic missiles and their warheads, and counting rules for heavy bombers and their armament. During our meetings in Washington last month, the General Secretary and I made further progress. We reached agreement on a sublimit of 4,900 for the total number of ballistic missile warheads, a counting rule for existing ballistic missiles, and guidelines for effective verification of the treaty.

Despite the progress we have made, important differences remain, including such issues as mobile intercontinental ballistic missiles, sea-launched cruise missiles, and the details of effective verification. A START agreement can be reached this year if the Soviets return to Geneva ready to apply themselves with the same seriousness as the United States. The United States seeks a sound agreement, and we will not negotiate against arbitrary deadlines. It remains my operating principle that we would rather have no agreement than accept a bad one.

Our negotiators will also continue work at Geneva on strategic defense issues. In accordance with my agreement with General Secretary Gorbachev last month, I have instructed our negotiators to work out with the Soviets a separate new treaty calling for observing for a specified period of time the ABM treaty, as signed in 1972, while both countries conduct research, development, and testing as required, which are permitted by the ABM treaty. After this period, and unless otherwise agreed, both countries will be free to choose their own course of action.

During our meetings last month, I made clear to General Secretary Gorbachev my firm commitment to move forward with our Strategic Defense Initiative. I believe that he understands our insistence on investigating fully the feasibility of strategic defenses, especially since, as he acknowledged, the Soviet Union itself has long been conducting its own program in this vital area. SDI offers the best hope of a safer world, one in which Western security would rely less on the threat of retaliation and increasingly on defenses, which threaten no one. SDI is the cornerstone of our security strategy for the 1990's and beyond. SDI is not a bargaining chip but our path to a more secure future.

Our negotiating team—led by Ambassadors Kampelman, Cooper, and Hanmer—returns to Geneva fully prepared to make progress on the difficult issues remaining in both offensive reductions and strategic defense.

Designation of Nancy Schulze as a Member of the Board of Visitors to the United States Air Force Academy
January 14, 1988

The President today announced his intention to designate Nancy Schulze to be a member of the Board of Visitors to the United States Air Force Academy for a term expiring December 30, 1990. She would succeed Henry B. Sayler.

Mrs. Schulze is currently chairman-elect (for 1988) of the Republican Women's Federal Forum, and has been vice chairman of that organization since 1987. She has also been president of the Republican Congressional Wives, 1986–1987. Prior to this, she was a member of the Board of Visitors for the Air University, at Maxwell Air Force Base, in Montgomery, AL, 1985–1986; chairman of the Defense Advisory Committee on Women in the Services (DACOWITS), 1984; and member of the executive committee of DACOWITS, 1983. She was also chairman of a Washington area fundraiser for the American Diabetes Association, 1984–1986.

Mrs. Schulze attended Penn State University. She was born May 27, 1934, in Bryn Mawr, PA. She is married, has four children, and resides in McLean, VA.

Appointment of Robert H. Mendelsohn as a Member of the United States Holocaust Memorial Council
January 14, 1988

The President today announced his intention to appoint Robert H. Mendelsohn to be a member of the United States Holocaust Memorial Council for a term expiring January 15, 1992. He would succeed Willard Fletcher.

Since 1980 Mr. Mendelsohn has been president of Mendelsohn Associates, in Washington, DC. Prior to this he served as an Assistant to the Secretary at the Department of the Interior, July 1980. He has also served as a consultant at the Pennsylvania Avenue Development Corporation; consultant at the Department of the Interior; and project administrator for Terranomics, Inc., 1975–1976.

Mr. Mendelsohn graduated from the University of California at Berkeley, (A.B., 1959). He was born January 11, 1938, in Harlan, IA. Mr. Mendelsohn served in the United States Marine Corps Reserve, 1956–1962. He is married, has one child, and resides in Chevy Chase, MD.

Letter Accepting the Resignation of Robert H. Bork as United States Circuit Judge
January 14, 1988

Dear Bob:

It is with deep sadness that I accept your decision to resign as United States Circuit Judge for the District of Columbia Circuit, effective February 5, 1988. In my many appointments to the Federal bench, I have attempted to select men and women of uncommon intellect, unimpeachable integrity, and a strong, steady temperament—men and women with special gifts for communication and reasoning and with an abiding courage of conviction. You, Bob, epitomize these virtues at their very finest—which is why I turned to you to fill Justice Lewis Powell's seat on the Supreme Court.

The unprecedented political attack upon you which resulted in the regrettable Senate action was a tragedy for our country. All Americans are the poorer today for not having your extraordinary talents and legal skills on the High Court.

And yet, as I read your letter of resignation, I cannot help but feel a warm admiration for the difficult decision you have made. There is, as you state, a lively public debate brewing in this country, fueled in no small part by your confirmation hearings—a debate over the proper role of the judiciary in our system of representative self-government. That debate has advocates who view the courts and the Constitution as mere instruments for political advantage. Effective advocacy of a more traditional approach to the judicial function occurs too infrequently. Your recent experience, against a background of unswerving commitment to the doctrine of judicial restraint, makes you uniquely well suited to carry that debate forward.

For your many years of dedicated public service, especially the last six on the Court of Appeals, your country and I thank you. For your courageous adherence to conviction and refusal to forsake your ideals, your country and I salute you. For daring to embark on this new course in selfless service of the cause of truth and justice in the public arena, your country and I remain in your debt.

While your public service on the Court of Appeals will be sorely missed, I am confident that your writings and other contributions as a private citizen are destined to have a most profound and lasting impact on the Nation.

Best wishes for success in your future endeavors.

Sincerely,

RONALD REAGAN

January 7, 1988

Dear Mr. President:

Six years ago you appointed me to the United States Court of Appeals for the District of Columbia Circuit. That was a great honor and I continue to be grateful to you for it. The task of serving the law and the ends of justice has made the last six years absorbing and fulfilling.

It is, therefore, with great reluctance, and only after much thought and discussion with my family, that I have now decided to step down from the bench. This decision is the more difficult because of what I owe to you, to the many Americans who have written to me in the last six months to express their support, and, indeed, to all Americans our system of justice serves. Because I recognize these debts and obligations, I want to explain the course I have chosen.

The crux of the matter is that I wish to speak, write, and teach about law and other issues of public policy more extensively and more freely than is possible in my present position. As a sitting judge on a very busy court, I cannot devote the time and energy I wish to public discourse. Moreover, constraints of propriety and seemliness limit the topics a federal judge may address and the public positions he may advocate. My experience as your nominee for Associate Justice of the Supreme Court of the United States made me acutely aware of the restrictions on my ability to address issues. For several months various highly vocal groups and individuals systematically misrepresented not only my record and philosophy of judging but, more importantly, the proper function of judges in our constitutional democracy. This was a public campaign of miseducation to which, as a sitting federal judge, I felt I could not publicly respond. What should have been a reasoned national debate about the role of the courts under the Constitution became an essentially unanswered campaign of misinformation and political slogans. If, as a judge, I cannot speak out against this attempt to alter the traditional nature of our courts, I think it important to place myself where I can.

You nominated me to my present court and to the Supreme Court precisely because I do speak for the traditional view of the judge's role under the Constitution. It is a view that goes back to the founding of our nation and was ably articulated by, among others, James Madison, Thomas Jefferson, Alexander Hamilton, and Joseph Story. It has been espoused by the greatest judges in our history. That view, simply put, is that a judge must apply to modern circumstances the principles laid down by those who adopted our Constitution but must not invent new principles of his own.

A few years ago I said:

> In a constitutional democracy the moral content of law must be given by the morality of the framer or the legislator, never by the morality of the judge. The sole task of the latter—and it is a task quite large enough for anyone's wisdom, skill, and virtue—is to translate the framer's or the legislator's morality into a rule to govern unforeseen circumstances. That abstinence from giving his own desires free play, that continuing and self-conscious renunciation of power, that is the morality of the jurist.

That was my view then. It is my view now. Though there are many who vehemently oppose it, that philosophy is essential if courts are to govern according to the rule of law rather than whims of politics and personal preference. That view is essential if courts are not to set the social agenda for the nation, and if representative democracy is to maintain its legitimate spheres of authority. Those who want political judges should reflect that the political and social preferences of judges have changed greatly over our history and will no doubt do so again. We have known judicial activism of the right and of the left; neither is legitimate.

My desire to participate in the public debate on these matters is what prompts my decision to leave the bench at this time. I had considered this course in the past but had not decided until the recent confirmation experience brought home to me just how misfocused the public discourse has become. A great many supporters have written to urge that I continue in public service. The decision I have made will, I believe, allow me to do just that. My views on these matters are of long standing. Because of my experience as your nominee, I am now in a better position to address the issues than ever before.

Though I am sure this decision is the correct one, I find, as the time of my departure draws near, that the prospect of leaving the federal judiciary fills me not merely with reluctance but with sadness. Any lawyer should be deeply honored to be a federal judge and to serve with a nationwide corps of the most dedicated men and women one is likely ever to meet. The work of an appellate judge may be the aspect of the legal profession for which I am best suited. I have actively enjoyed the day-to-day work of judging—the exchanges with lawyers at oral argument, the discussions with colleagues and clerks in arriving at a correct decision, and the effort to craft the best opinion one can. Trying with all one's capacities to do justice according to law is a deeply satisfying experience, both intellectually and emotionally. I will miss it more than I can say. I find some consolation in leaving behind a record of which I believe I may be proud, and one by which I am content to be judged.

In choosing a date for my departure, I have considered, among other factors, the desirability of leaving time for the nomination and confirmation of my successor as well as the importance of beginning my new work without undue delay. It will, however, take a few weeks to complete work on hand. I ask, therefore, that you accept my resignation as Circuit Judge, United States Court of Appeals for the District of Columbia Circuit, effective at the close of business, Friday, February 5, 1988.

With deep gratitude for your confidence in me, for appointing me to this court and nominating me to the Supreme Court, I will always remain

Yours truly,

ROBERT H. BORK

Proclamation 5761—National Sanctity of Human Life Day, 1988
January 14, 1988

By the President of the United States of America

A Proclamation

America has given a great gift to the world, a gift that drew upon the accumulated wisdom derived from centuries of experiments in self-government, a gift that has irrevocably changed humanity's future. Our gift is twofold: the declaration, as a cardinal principle of all just law, of the God-given, unalienable rights possessed by every human being; and the example of our determination to secure those rights and to defend them against every challenge through the generations. Our declaration and defense of our rights have made us and kept us free and have sent a tide of hope and inspiration around the globe.

One of those unalienable rights, as the Declaration of Independence affirms so eloquently, is the right to life. In the 15 years since the Supreme Court's decision in *Roe* v. *Wade*, however, America's unborn have been denied their right to life. Among the tragic and unspeakable results in the past decade and a half have been the loss of life of 22 million infants before birth; the pressure and anguish of countless women and girls who are driven to abortion; and a cheapening of our respect for the human person and the sanctity of human life.

We are told that we may not interfere with abortion. We are told that we may not "impose our morality" on those who wish to allow or participate in the taking of the life of infants before birth; yet no one calls it "imposing morality" to prohibit the taking of life after people are born. We are told as well that there exists a "right" to end the lives of unborn children; yet no one can explain how such a right can exist in stark contradiction of each person's fundamental right to life.

That right to life belongs equally to babies in the womb, babies born handicapped, and the elderly or infirm. That we have killed the unborn for 15 years does not nullify this right, nor could any number of killings ever do so. The unalienable right to life is found not only in the Declaration of Independence but also in the Constitution that every President is sworn to preserve, protect, and defend. Both the Fifth and Fourteenth Amendments guarantee that no person shall be deprived of life without due process of law.

All medical and scientific evidence increasingly affirms that children before birth share all the basic attributes of human personality—that they in fact are persons. Modern medicine treats unborn children as patients. Yet, as the Supreme Court itself has noted, the decision in *Roe* v. *Wade* rested upon an earlier state of medical technology. The law of the land in 1988 should recognize all of the medical evidence.

Our Nation cannot continue down the path of abortion, so radically at odds with our history, our heritage, and our concepts of justice. This sacred legacy, and the well-being and the future of our country, demand that protection of the innocents must be guaranteed and that the personhood of the unborn be declared and defended throughout our land. In legislation introduced at my request in the First Session of the 100th Congress, I have asked the Legislative branch to declare the "humanity of the unborn child and the compelling interest of the several states to protect the life of each person before birth." This duty to declare on so fundamental a matter falls to the Executive as well. By this Proclamation I hereby do so.

Now, Therefore, I, Ronald Reagan, President of the United States of America, by virtue of the authority vested in me by the Constitution and laws of the United States, do hereby proclaim and declare the unalienable personhood of every American, from the moment of conception until natural death, and I do proclaim, ordain, and declare that I will take care that the Constitution and laws of the United States are faithfully executed for the protection of America's unborn children. Upon this act, sincerely believed to be an act of justice, warranted by the Constitution, I invoke the considerate judgment of mankind and the gracious favor of Almighty God. I also proclaim Sunday, January 17, 1988, as National Sanctity of Human Life Day. I call upon the citizens of this blessed land to gather on that day in their homes and places of worship to give thanks for the gift of life they enjoy and to reaffirm their commitment to the dignity of every human being and the sanctity of every human life.

In Witness Whereof, I have hereunto set my hand this 14th day of January, in the year of our Lord nineteen hundred and eighty-eight, and of the Independence of the United States of America the two hundred and twelfth.

RONALD REAGAN

[Filed with the Office of the Federal Register, 10:50 a.m., January 15, 1988]

Note: The proclamation was released by the Office of the Press Secretary on January 15.

Address to the Nation's Students on the Observance of Martin Luther King, Jr., Day
January 15, 1988

Today we honor a man who dedicated his life to the pursuit of a dream—a dream not just for himself but for you, for all of us, for America. And in honoring his commitment, his dedication, his life, we rededicate ourselves to the fundamental principle behind that dream and to the challenge that history has given every American from the founding of our country to the present: the challenge of making that principle and that dream, the American dream, an enduring reality.

Our nation's founders first stated the principle to which Reverend Martin Luther King, Jr., dedicated his life when they wrote: "We hold these truths to be self-evident, that all men are created equal, that they are endowed by their Creator with certain unalienable Rights, and that among these are Life, Liberty and the pursuit of Happiness." Today we continue to cherish those truths and the rights and values upon which our country was founded and for which Americans have, for 200 years, worked and fought and, yes, for which many have given their lives—for which Reverend King gave his life.

Many years ago, from the steps of the Lincoln Memorial, Reverend King reminded us of what America stands for. He reminded us that America has issued a promissory note of full rights for all its citizens. Yes, he reminded us that the destinies of all Americans were tied to one another, that the freedom of all Americans was inextricably bound together. He said that the day must come when all Americans are judged not by the color of their skins but by the content of their character.

The fight—Reverend King's fight—for genuine equality of opportunity goes on, even today. We're all part of it, but we should never forget the strides that have been made and the many reasons for hope. Too often in the past, for example, blacks lagged behind in economic well-being while others advanced. We would hear story after story about how America's promise of opportunity had failed blacks. But since our recovery began more than 5 years ago, black employment has shot forward twice as fast as white employment. Since 1982 the real income of black families has increased almost 40 percent faster than white family income, and the share of black families in the highest income brackets is up by over 70 percent. Last year one leading economic observer looked at this record of opportunity, hope, and achievement and concluded that "on every front—jobs, income, even household wealth—1981 through 1986 were the best 5 economic years in black history."

Great strides are being made in education, as well. The publication we released last spring, "Schools That Work," describes many schools that are doing a good job educating disadvantaged children. One shining example is the Garrison Elementary School in the South Bronx in New York City. The student population is half black, half Hispanic. The school lies in one of the poorest sections of New York. Yet for the past 5 years, Garrison has ranked in the top 12 percent of New York City schools in reading achievement. By the time they reach the sixth grade, nearly every student performs at or above grade level in both reading and math.

You know, one of our Founding Fathers, James Madison, once said: "A well instructed people alone can be permanently a free people." That's why it's so important that every American receives a sound education. That's why it's important that you stick to your studies, work hard, and get your diploma. You'll be doing it for yourself, yes, but also for your family, your friends, your community, and your nation. Make it your first contribution to preserving the American dream for the generations to come.

You know, Nancy and I have asked all of you to just say no to drugs. That way—and by finishing school—you'll just say yes to your future and your dreams. Reverend King and many others through our history have lived and died so you could make those dreams into realities. By doing your best, you can say thank you to them.

In that speech I mentioned at the Lincoln Memorial, Reverend King said that with our faith in America's promise of freedom and opportunity we could "transform the jangling discords of our nation into a beautiful symphony of brotherhood." To move the world towards enduring love and brotherhood is the continuing vocation of the human soul. But we in America are vastly closer today to realizing our national ideals because of Reverend King's life and work.

Let us each, on this day, dedicate ourselves to preserving and expanding the American dream. Let us resolve that future generations will know a new birth of freedom and that this land that Reverend King loved so well and gave so much to will continue to shine with the brilliant hope of all mankind.

Note: The President's address was videotaped at 5:04 p.m. on January 14 in the Roosevelt Room at the White House. It was broadcast on January 15 and 18 on Public Broadcasting Service and Southern Educational Communications Association television stations.

Remarks by Telephone to the Students and Faculty of Martin Luther King, Jr., Elementary School
January 15, 1988

The President. Hello. Mr. Dalton?

Mr. Dalton. Good morning, Mr. President.

The President. Well, it's good to speak to you, and I'm looking forward to saying a few words to your student body there.

Mr. Dalton. We'd like to have you say as much as you would like.

The President. Well, thank you, and welcome to all of you. You know, today is the birthday of a great American hero, Dr. Martin Luther King, Jr., after whom your school was named. So, I thought that if there was any occasion which would justify my interrupting the fine work that you, the students and the faculty, are doing at King Elementary, to have a brief chat, this would be it.

Dr. King was a man who dedicated his life to the pursuit of the dream that one day all Americans would be judged not by the color of their skin but by the content of their character. He was committed to seeing that our nation lived up to its promise of liberty and justice for all. Now, much remains to be done, but ours is a better country today, and each of you has more opportunities because of the hard work and courage of this remarkable man.

We should also be reminded that Dr.

King understood the value of education as a means of helping to accomplish his vision for America. Dr. King once said: "I have the audacity to believe that people everywhere can have an education." Well, he was right. And today minority schools located in the poorest of big city neighborhoods are meeting high academic standards in reading, mathematics, and other vital subjects.

As you young people, the students at King Elementary—you can help fulfill Dr. King's dream by making certain that you try your hardest to take advantage of the great opportunities available to you. Most certainly, that includes being diligent in your studies, and it also means saying no to drugs and those of you who are in any way involved in drugs.

And, Mr. Dalton, I want you to know that this partnership that we have had—the White House and your school—has been very rewarding to all of us, and we're very proud of this relationship that we have with you and your fine students there at the school. And I appreciate very much this chance to speak to you again and wish you all the very best.

Mr. Dalton. We thank you, Mr. President, and we would also like to extend to you and your wife the happiest in 1988 and hope that everything would turn out all right today in your checkup.

Thank you.

The President. Well, thank you very much. And thank you all, and God bless you all.

Mr. Dalton. Goodbye, sir.

The President. Goodbye.

Note: The President spoke at 10:02 a.m. from the Oval Office at the White House to the students and faculty assembled in the school's auditorium. William Dalton was the principal of the school.

Remarks to Reporters on the Nation's Economy
January 15, 1988

I have a brief statement here to read. And I want to warn you now; I cannot take any questions, because already we're pressing our appointment at the hospital, there, for the checkup. So, I will have to go. And besides, you all ought to get in out of the cold.

Well, we've had some more good news on the economic front today. As I've been saying all along, the fundamentals in the United States economy remain sound. Industrial production is up, inflation is down, and this country continues on a long trend of sustained growth with low inflation. The trade deficit for November fell 25 percent from the October level, and exports increased to an all-time record.

Much of the improvement came from our manufacturing sector, again indicating that our competitive position in the world is steadily improving. This news has had a positive impact in the financial markets around the world, but we should not pay undue attention to any one month's trade numbers. The real significance is that over the past 61 months a trend for the American economy has been sustained growth with low inflation, and today's signs indicate that it will continue well into the future.

And thank you all, and we're on our way.

Note: The President spoke at 1 p.m. at the South Portico of the White House prior to his departure for Bethesda Naval Hospital for a physical examination.

White House Statement on the Continuation of Military Aid to Pakistan
January 15, 1988

The President today signed and sent to Congress waivers to the law that would require a cutoff in aid to Pakistan under the Symington and the Solarz amendments because of activities in the nuclear weapons development area. This waiver action was based on the recognition that disrupting one of the pillars of the U.S. relationship with Pakistan would be counterproductive for the strategic interests of the United States, destabilizing for South Asia, and unlikely to achieve the nonproliferation objectives sought by the sponsors.

The Government of Pakistan is aware of our continuing concern over certain aspects of its nuclear program. Despite these problem areas, there are crucial nonproliferation criteria which Pakistan continues to honor. The United States will insist on the maintenance of these restraints even as we work with Pakistan on progress in the areas of concern.

The President's action is preceded by months of extensive consultations with Congress. We have achieved an understanding on the general approach which is reflected in approval by Congress of a 30-month waiver of the Symington amendment and near-full funding for Pakistan for FY '88. The administration pledged to continue pressing Pakistan away from a nuclear weapons option and is obliged to certify annually that Pakistan does not possess nuclear weapons.

The reasons which convinced the administration to waive the Symington amendment also apply to the Solarz amendment, where the waiver applies only retroactively. The Government of Pakistan has pledged that procedures will be tightened to ensure an end to procurement activities in the United States. We will continue to monitor procurement activities in this country to ensure compliance with Pakistan's new procedures.

There is no diminution in the President's commitment to restraining the spread of nuclear weapons in the Indian subcontinent or elsewhere. We will continue to urge Pakistan and India to discuss measures which might be taken to reduce the threat of a nuclear arms race in South Asia. As arms control negotiations between the United States and the Soviet Union begin to bear fruit and set an example, the administration will be seeking still further ways to make this commitment effective.

Radio Address to the Nation on Teenage Drug Abuse
January 16, 1988

My fellow Americans:

This week something happened here in Washington that makes me proud, and I expect you'll feel the same way. It had to do with a report that our Secretary of Health and Human Services, Dr. Otis Bowen, released on Wednesday. Now, most of the time government reports, with all their statistics and dry language, are not particularly interesting. But this one is different, because it has to do with something of deep concern to every American family: attitudes about drug use among America's young people.

For each of the last 13 years, the Government has surveyed America's graduating high school seniors. Every year thousands of seniors in hundreds of schools across America have been asked about the drugs they've used and about what they think of drug use. For many years, what we found out proved pretty discouraging. In the seventies students told of ever more frequent drug use. Many of them said that some drug use, even drugs like cocaine, was okay, nothing to be afraid about. We had a drug epidemic, and too often our national leaders, in government and the media, didn't seem to care.

Drug use, some said, was a victimless crime. No one got hurt. No one suffered. So, what was the big deal? Well, I've often thought that this message that drugs weren't all that bad was part of a larger message. The same people who winked at us about drugs also told us that America's future was bleak. Too often they said that the traditional values of family and community were old fashioned and out of date. It was as if they'd lost faith in the future and wanted the rest of us to lose it, too.

But in communities around America, families, teachers, and young people themselves were finding out that those who said drug use was no big deal, whether they knew it or not, were telling a big lie—and a dangerous one. Just how dangerous we all saw 2 years ago when a promising athlete, a young man whose future could have been written in headlines and in gold, died of a cocaine overdose. Len Bias never got to play professional basketball. But today his mother says that his death may have been a message from God to America's young people: Stay away from drugs—all drugs—all the time.

Well, as you know, others have carried that message, too. For 6 years now, Nancy has been traveling around the country spreading the word. On one trip out West, a student asked her how to turn away from drugs when they were offered. She replied: "Just say no." Since then, thousands of Just Say No clubs have been started in schools around the Nation. Students got the message, in many cases, long before adults.

That brings me back to the report I was telling you about. Maybe you've heard the best news in it already. Last year for the first time since the surveying began, a substantially smaller proportion of high school seniors—one-third smaller—acknowledged current use of cocaine than acknowledged it the year before. But that's not all.

Students are no longer buying the old line that experimenting with cocaine and other illegal drugs is safe. For many years, only about a third of them said that using cocaine once or twice was dangerous. Last year almost half did, and nearly 90 percent said regular use was dangerous. And cocaine use is no longer the "in" thing. In fact, almost all the seniors surveyed—97 percent—disapproved of regular cocaine use. And whether they thought one or two experiments dangerous or not, 87 percent disapproved of even trying cocaine. Use of marijuana and amphetamines is also dropping. More than 10 percent of the members of the class of 1978 said they used marijuana daily. In the class of 1987, it was only about 3 percent, still too many, but much better than it was. And more than 70 percent—more than ever have before—say that regular marijuana use is harmful.

So, the message is out, and America's young people have heard it: Drugs hurt, drugs kill, drug use is nothing to brag about, stay away from drugs. A few minutes ago, I said all this makes me proud. Well, the one thing I've found you can always count on is that when we Americans get a message and decide to do something—watch out—there's nothing that can stop us! I'm proud, as I know you are, of Nancy and of the many adults who've worked against this plague. But most of all, and I know also you join me in this, I'm proud of millions of young Americans who—one by one, or together with their friends—just say no to drugs.

Until next week, thanks for listening, and God bless you.

Note: The President spoke at 12:06 p.m. from Camp David, MD.

Remarks at the 1988 Reagan Administration Executive Forum
January 19, 1988

Thank you very much. My goodness, if they'd have done this for "Bedtime for Bonzo," I never would have left Hollywood. [*Laughter*] Well, thank you all very much, and a special thanks to the members of the Army Band and the Herald Trumpeters—thank them for the spirit and energy they contribute to this event and other events throughout the year.

Well, it is 1988, and before saying anything else, I'd like all of you who've been part of the administration since 1981 to stand. [*Applause*] Well, I think we owe these battle veterans a special round of applause, and you already did that. Thank you.

Words can't express my appreciation to each and every one of you, whether you've been on the team for 7 months or 7 years, for the contribution that you're making. Everything we've accomplished can be traced to your hard work and professionalism, your willingness to work the extra hours and to make the extra phone calls. You're the unsung heroes, the people who've made it happen, and I salute you!

When we came here 7 years ago, we pledged to the American people that we were not here to conduct business as usual, that we intended to bring about a fundamental change of direction for our beloved country. First, we turned around an economy racked by inflation and uncertainty, an economy that was headed into an abyss. We put America back on the high road to growth and expanding opportunity, to hope and improving living standards.

And now, over the years, there's been a lot said about the so-called Reagan luck. Well, being of Irish extraction, sometimes I'm inclined to believe such things. However, I can assure all of you that the great economic expansion our country has enjoyed has had more to do with low tax rates, deregulation, and responsible Federal policies than with leprechauns. In fact, the only people who still seem to believe in tooth fairies and leprechauns are those who've tried to tell us that if we only raise taxes the budget deficit will disappear.

Well, luck, as it is said, is where preparation meets opportunity. And for the first 2 years of our administration, we prepared America for better times. We cut the tax rates. We streamlined government and cut useless regulations. Through our block grant program, we returned power and authority for a number of programs back to the States. But most significant, we turned to the people themselves. We left resources in their hands that others would have taken away. We took the yolk of overregulation off their shoulders. We looked to the entrepreneur instead of the Federal planner, the free enterprise system instead of the bureaucracy. And they proved something I've always believed in, and that is, more often than not, the best thing government can do for a free people is get its hands out of their pockets and get out of their way.

I think we can be proud that our policies, based on an abiding faith in the people, have worked. America is still enjoying the fruits of the longest peacetime expansion in history. The real gross national product, which is the value of all the goods and services produced in the United States, has risen more than 21 percent during this expansion. Inflation, running at double-digit, killer rates in 1979 and '80, has averaged some 3.3 percent since the recovery began. The prime interest rate, which was 21 percent just before we got to Washington, is down to—last month—8.75.

What does all this mean to the American people? It means that more of them are working and a higher percentage of the population is employed than ever before. It means the median after-inflation income of the American family, which was dropping when we got to Washington, increased 4.2 percent in 1986. Homes are again affordable to the average citizen. In March of last year, America built its 100 millionth home.

You know, I wonder sometimes where certain candidates for an office of the other party—why they haven't found out all these figures. [*Laughter*] Don't let anyone tell you that this expansion has excluded the poor and the minorities, as some of them are saying. The poverty rate, which was rising precipitously when we got here, is now declining. That tragic trend we inherited has been reversed. Among minorities, the news is also good. Teenage black unemployment, for example, though still far too high, has been cut dramatically in recent years; and the percentage of blacks in the group of Americans who make over $50,000 has almost doubled since 1982.

Something that seems to be popular of late is suggesting that greed has characterized the 1980's in America. Well, I don't happen to believe that pejorative word is appropriate. We should applaud people who are trying to better their lot, not put them down. One cover story which seemed to be saying the 1980's has been a period of selfishness instead of self-improvement contained a poll which reported that between 1982 and 1987 there had been a 66-percent increase in the number of people who answer yes to this question: Are you involved in any charity or social service activities, such as helping the poor, the sick, or the elderly? And furthermore, we know that between 1980 and 1986 charitable giving shot up 77 percent. So much for the so-called era of greed.

This has been a time of people getting involved and helping one another without waiting for government. It's been a time of increasing hope, of rising standards of living, of economic expansion. And don't let anyone tell you it's all over. We were told it couldn't be done even before we started. The doomsayers then claimed it could never last, yet it has been one of the longest, as I said, peacetime expansions in history.

On the network news we saw story after story that would lead one to conclude that poverty was increasing, and when the statistics finally came out, we found there'd been a significant decline in the poverty rate. We heard the professional pessimists telling us America was being deindustrialized, and then we found out that our industry was making record gains in productivity and that our manufacturing industries were making a big comeback. And now we even hear highly touted analysts telling economic movers and shakers that a report heralding the good news that unemployment is going down is actually bad news.

I don't think the American people believe in this kind of "Alice in Wonderland" economics. I don't think the American people believe good news is really bad news. We can be proud of what's been accomplished. The doomsayers, who can't make the front page or network news unless they've got something bad to say, have been wrong for the last 7 years. And in 1988 we and the American people are going to prove them wrong again.

In the year ahead, we're not going to be on the defensive, shoring up problems and answering our critics. We are moving forward, and I have no doubt that when we look back 1988 will be a year of great accomplishment toward our goals. This is the year when Judge Anthony Kennedy will be confirmed and the Supreme Court will again be brought up to full strength. The Federal judiciary is too important to be made a political football. I would hope, and the American people should expect, not only for Judge Kennedy's confirmation but for the Senate to get to work and act on 27 other judicial nominations that have been left in limbo for quite awhile now.

This is also the year that the United States will strongly affirm that democracy, not communism, is the future of Central America. In a few weeks, Congress will determine if we're to provide the democratic resistance in Nicaragua what they need to survive. The Guatemala peace plan can succeed only if the Sandinistas have reason to compromise and institute democratic reforms. We must have the courage to stand behind those who continue to put their lives on the line for democracy in Nicaragua.

We've learned on another front that standing firm—that strength, not weakness—is the best way to achieve results with our adversaries. Nearly 7 years ago, I proposed the zero option, suggesting the elimination of an entire class of U.S. and Soviet intermediate-range nuclear armed missiles. Many of our opponents called for the so-called nuclear freeze, which would have left Soviet intermediate-range missiles threatening both Europe and Asia. Against great outcries, we and our allies installed our cruise and Pershing II missiles. It was this determination which finally convinced the Kremlin to bargain realistically. I believe we can all be proud that at last month's summit we signed the first agreement between the Soviet Union and the United States that actually reduced our respective nuclear arsenals.

The Senate will begin its review of the INF treaty next week, and while there will be a thorough examination, there should be no reason to delay ratification. Let us note that one stand we took in this arms reduction process concerned our commitment to the Strategic Defense Initiative. SDI will give us the possibility to base deterrence increasingly on defenses which threaten no one rather than on the threat of nuclear retaliation. I would hope that Congress does not, in the months ahead, take away in the committee room what the Soviets were unable to get at the bargaining table. We must push forward in the SDI research and testing.

Progress continues to be made, as well, toward strategic nuclear reductions, and another summit may occur in the near future. But let me note: Arms reductions cannot and will not be pursued in isolation from other areas of deep concern to the American people and the other free people of the world. If relations with the Soviet Union are to improve, if we're to enter into a new period of rapprochement with our adversary, we must see greater respect for human rights. We need to see more freedom and a further opening of the emigration door. We also need to see a peaceful resolution to regional conflicts which Soviet weapons, personnel, and policies now help to prolong.

In particular, the Soviet Government needs to realize that relations with the United States cannot be expected to flourish while Soviet troops remain in Afghanistan. And I can promise all those who love freedom and whose hearts must be with those freedom fighters who struggle for their national survival that the Soviet troops must leave Afghanistan and the United States will never agree to any steps that would put the freedom fighters and Afghan hopes for self-determination at risk.

I am optimistic about the chances for better relations between East and West. Clearly, the people of the world are bounding rapidly into a new era of technology and enterprise. Tremendous advances are being made that are opening up vast new potential. Communist societies, in contrast, stagnate under the heavy hand of repression and the failure of socialism. They must change; relations with the West must improve, or Communist governments will simply be left behind. It's that simple.

And here in this continent, we are about to undertake one of the most truly visionary steps of the 20th century. Early this month, Prime Minister Mulroney and I signed, and I fully expect the Congress to approve, an agreement that will eliminate the tariffs and tear down the barriers that have frustrated and taxed trade and commerce between the United States and Canada. What we are putting in place is the largest free trade area in the world. This historic step will be a source of growth and prosperity on both sides of the border for years to come and be a lasting legacy of which we all can be immensely proud.

The only thing that can keep America back is an unwillingness to do what needs to be done, to do what is within our ability to do. Congress, for example, needs to act to make good on the second year of its agreement to bring down Federal deficit spending. Nothing could give greater confidence to the investing community than responsible action by Washington to bring down the level of deficit spending.

And finally, I'd like to discuss with you personally something that's been of utmost concern to Nancy and me during our stay at the White House. Of all we've been able to do, I'm perhaps the proudest of what we've done to change attitudes in America about the use of drugs. It's no longer fashionable to use drugs. And by the end of this administration, I'd also like to be able to say that it's no longer tolerated.

We've spent much time and money on interdicting drugs, on arresting the traffickers and stopping the flow of drugs from their source. Yet we cannot ignore that as long as there are users the problem will persist. Progress has already been made. The number of daily marijuana users among high school seniors, according to some reports, has dropped from 1 in 9 in 1978 to 1 in 30 in 1987.

In the time left in our administration, I would hope that you'll do everything possible to eliminate drug abuse from the Federal workplace. The Federal Government is the Nation's largest employer, and it should be an example to the rest of the Nation. We've got to make it an example. Can I count on you? [*Applause*] I don't know why I ask. You've never disappointed me.

You've changed and are changing the direction not only of American history but of world history. We have been revolutionaries, and for 7 years the so-called sophisticates have at every turn said our revolution had failed. But again and again they've been wrong, because they've forgotten our secret weapon—the human spirit.

Yes, ours is a revolution for the most powerful yearnings of the spirit: yearning for opportunity, for a better life for your children, for freedom, for true and lasting peace. The yearning of the spirit—in all the history and humanity, no force is stronger or more blessed. So, when you leave here today, remember: One more year, not for the Gipper but for Americans and for all mankind. As they say in showbiz: Let's bring them to their feet with our closing act.

I thank you, and God bless you for all you've done and will do this year. And you've already applauded, so I won't wait for that, because I had something else to follow my speech. And that is I would like to introduce to you some of my small friends from the Young Americans for [Citizens of] America who have a big message for you.

Note: The President spoke at 11:30 a.m. at DAR Constitution Hall at the seventh annual Executive Forum for political appointees of the administration. Following his remarks, a group of children representing Young Citizens of America sang a short medley of patriotic songs.

Statement by Assistant to the President for Press Relations Fitzwater on the Central American Peace Process

January 19, 1988

President Reagan believes that the outcome of the January 15 summit meeting of the Central American Presidents presents important opportunities to further peace and democracy in this troubled region. At the San José summit, there was a clear consensus among the four Central American democratic Presidents that the Sandinistas had not complied with the peace accord. By making his last-minute promises, President Ortega implicitly acknowledged the accuracy of that judgment.

The Guatemala City plan aims at peace and democracy for all of Central America. Its objectives, in combination with the pressures from the Central American democracies and the Nicaraguan democratic resistance, have prompted the Sandinistas to reluctantly promise to diminish their tight control over the Nicaraguan political system and to provide a glimmer of hope to the Nicaraguan people that democracy and freedom may eventually be established.

The key issue is whether Daniel Ortega is really committed to genuine democracy or just seeks the elimination of the Nicaraguan democratic resistance. The Sandinistas' track record is clear and must be considered in evaluating the latest Sandinista offer. There is a need for openmindedness and hope, along with skepticism. We welcome the new promises but note that while Daniel Ortega was in Costa Rica making them his government was arresting prominent democratic leaders inside Nicaragua.

The focus is where it belongs: on the Sandinistas—their promises and their actions. The President believes that continued support for the Nicaraguan democratic resistance will keep the pressure on the Sandinistas to move forward with genuine and enduring democratic reforms. The Nicaraguan democratic resistance is the best insurance policy for keeping the peace process on track and producing a democratic outcome in Nicaragua. This is not the time to falter in our support for the freedom fighters.

Nomination of Carol Pendas Whitten To Be a Member of the National Advisory Council on Educational Research and Improvement
January 19, 1988

The President today announced his intention to nominate Carol Pendas Whitten to be a member of the National Advisory Council on Educational Research and Improvement for a term expiring September 30, 1990. She would succeed Penny Pullen.

From 1985 to 1987, Mrs. Whitten was the Director of Bilingual Education and Minority Languages Affairs at the Department of Education in Washington, DC. Prior to this she was a congressional liaison officer for the Office of Legislative Affairs at the Department of Labor, 1984–1985. She served in various capacities at the Department of Education: special assistant to the Deputy Under Secretary for Management of the Office of Management, 1983–1984; executive assistant to the Acting Director of the National Institute of Education, 1982–1983; and education program specialist for the Women's Educational Equity Act program, 1980–1981.

Mrs. Whitten graduated from Barry College (B.S., 1967; M.S., 1971). She was born December 4, 1945, in New York, NY. She is married, has one child, and resides in Chevy Chase, MD.

Remarks on Presenting the Presidential Citizen's Medal to Brooke Astor
January 19, 1988

The President. Well, Brooke and ladies and gentlemen, good afternoon, and welcome to the White House. We've gathered here today to bestow an honor upon a woman we all know and admire: Brooke Astor. I'll read a citation in just a moment, but that citation is awfully official sounding, and I'd like to add a personal note. You see, Brooke is a friend of ours. Nancy has known Brooke since Nancy was 14. I've known Brooke for a good many years.

There's no way a document can capture her wit, her warmth, no way express her energy and her extraordinary vitality. And, Brooke, there's just no way that Nancy and I can ever thank you enough for all the wonderful moments that you've given us.

And now you're here with me at the podium, and your country wishes to honor you. And therefore, I shall read a citation for the Citizen's Medal:

"Her philanthropies have extended from Carnegie Hall to the Bronx Zoo. She has made the New York Public Library her special project, overseeing the renaissance of that venerable and magnificent institution. She has written two volumes of autobiography and a number of splendid, witty novels. And to all who knew her, she's a joy. And if Brooke Astor feels that she has become a public monument, it is a credit to the public for making her one."

Ms. Astor. That's it?

The President. And now, yes, the presentation of the Citizen's Medal.

Ms. Astor. Oh, thank you, Mr. President. I'm overcome.

The President. Well, congratulations, and God bless you.

Ms. Astor. Mr. President, when can I wear this?

Mrs. Reagan. Anytime.

Ms. Astor. Do I wear it at a big party and pin it on?

The President. Yes, you can. It's yours.

Ms. Astor. That isn't showing off?

The President. No, it's yours. You've earned and deserve it. [*Laughter*]

Ms. Astor. Thank you so much.

The President. And there's a little button that shows, if you choose, that you are the possessor of that.

Ms. Astor. There's the button, yes.

Mrs. Reagan. Wear it anytime.

The President. All right.

Ms. Astor. Thank you so much for this.

The President. And now we shall all adjourn to the Red Room, which is right next door. Gorbachev was very happy with it. [*Laughter*]

Note: The President spoke at 4:30 p.m. in the Blue Room at the White House.

Letter to the Speaker of the House of Representatives and the President of the Senate Transmitting a Presidential Determination on Assistance to the Nicaraguan Democratic Resistance
January 19, 1988

Dear Mr. Speaker: (Dear Mr. President:)

I herewith transmit my determination and certification under Section 111(b)(2)(A) of the Joint Resolution making further continuing appropriations for the fiscal year 1988, and for other purposes (P.L. 100–202), relating to efforts to achieve a cease-fire agreed to by the Government of Nicaragua and the Nicaraguan democratic resistance. I am also transmitting herewith copies of reports to me by the Secretary of State which discuss the negotiation process and describe the failure of the Government of Nicaragua to progress toward the establishment of genuine democracy.

The United States has supported the process for achieving democracy and security set in motion by the accord signed by the Central American Presidents in Guatemala on August 7, 1987. In that accord, the Sandinistas again promised, as they had promised to the Organization of American States in 1979, to move toward genuine democracy with free elections by a truly free people. After the meeting of the Central American Presidents in San Jose, Costa Rica, on January 15 and 16, 1988, the Nicaraguan President issued yet more promises about Nicaraguan actions under the Accord. Deeds, not words, are needed.

The time for Sandinista compliance with the accord has come and gone and the Nicaraguan people and the Central American democracies have waited in vain for the Sandinistas to carry out their promises. It has become increasingly clear that, without the pressure created by a strong Nicaraguan democratic resistance, the Sandinistas will not change their conduct to comply with the promises they have repeatedly made and broken since 1979.

To succeed in bringing democracy to Nicaragua and security to all of Central America, the United States must maintain a steady course in its Central America policy, including its support for the Nicaraguan democratic resistance.

Sincerely,

RONALD REAGAN

Note: Identical letters were sent to Jim Wright, Speaker of the House of Representatives, and George Bush, President of the Senate. The determination was printed in the "Federal Register" of January 21.

White House Statement on the Presidential Determination on Assistance to the Nicaraguan Democratic Resistance
January 19, 1988

The President today made the determination and certification under section 111(b)(2)(A) of the fiscal year 1988 continuing resolution (P.L. 100–202) that permits resumption of transportation of military assistance to the Nicaraguan democratic resistance authorized by the Congress.

Section 111 of the continuing resolution provided for suspension of transportation of military assistance to the resistance on January 12, 1988, and for resumption of such assistance after January 18, 1988, if the President determined and certified to the Congress that:

—no cease-fire is in place that was agreed to by the Government of Nicaragua and the Nicaraguan democratic resistance;

—the failure to achieve such a cease-fire results from the lack of good faith efforts by the Government of Nicaragua to achieve such a cease-fire; and

—the Nicaraguan democratic resistance has engaged in good faith efforts to achieve such a cease-fire.

The President's determination was based on the Secretary of State's findings, set forth in his January 18, 1988, report, that the conditions for resuming assistance to the resistance have been met.

The Sandinistas have a record, beginning with promises to the Organization of American States in 1979 and continuing through the Guatemala accord of August 7, 1987, of making promises of democracy and freedom that they do not keep. After the Central American Presidents summit meeting this past weekend in San José, Costa Rica, the Nicaraguan President issued yet more promises. That very weekend, the Sandinistas' internal security forces executed a wave of arrests and interrogations of leading members of the surviving democratic political elements in Nicaragua. Moreover, while the Nicaraguan President demands unilateral termination of support for the forces of freedom in Nicaragua, the massive flow to the Sandinistas of Soviet-bloc arms continues unabated.

The United States remains fully committed to the achievement of democracy in Nicaragua and security in all of Central America as the essential conditions for a just and lasting peace in the region. The events which have unfolded since the signing of the Guatemala accord on August 7, 1987, have demonstrated once again that a strong Nicaraguan democratic resistance remains essential to the achievement of those conditions.

Recess Appointment of Edward Morgan Rowell as United States Ambassador to Portugal
January 19, 1988

The President today recess-appointed Edward Morgan Rowell, of California, a career member of the Senior Foreign Service, Class of Minister-Counselor, as Ambassador to the Republic of Portugal. He would succeed Frank Shakespeare.

Since August 1985 Mr. Rowell has been Ambassador to the Republic of Bolivia. Mr. Rowell began his career in the Foreign Service in 1956 in training assignments, first as a management analyst and then as a budget examiner. He served as vice consul and economic-commercial officer in Recife, Brazil, in 1958. He then went to Curitiba, Brazil, as consul and principal officer, 1958–1961. In 1961 he returned to the Department as special assistant to the Deputy Assistant Secretary for Inter-American Affairs.

From 1962 to 1964, he was officer in charge of Honduran affairs for the Department and the Agency for International Development. From 1964 to 1965, he was detailed to Stanford University for Latin American studies. In 1965 he served as political officer and deputy chief of section at the U.S. Embassy in Buenos Aires, Argentina. He then became chief of the political section of the U.S. Embassy in Tegucigalpa, Honduras, where he served until 1970. In 1970 he returned to Stanford University Graduate School of Business for senior training. Mr. Rowell then served as a Foreign Service inspector in the Department from 1971 to 1974. From 1974 to 1975, he was deputy director-economic officer in the Office of Iberian Affairs. In 1975 he became deputy director, Office of West European Affairs and then director. In 1978 he went to Lisbon, Portugal, as deputy chief of mission, and from 1983 to 1985 he was a Deputy Assistant Secretary for Consular Affairs.

Mr. Rowell graduated from Yale University (B.A., 1953) and attended Stanford University (1964–1965) and the Graduate School of Business at Stanford (1970–1971). He was born October 13, 1931, in Oakland, CA. He served in the United States Army, 1953 to 1955. Mr. Rowell is married and has three children.

Nomination of Don E. Newquist To Be a Member of the United States International Trade Commission
January 19, 1988

The President today announced his intention to nominate Don E. Newquist to be a member of the United States International Trade Commission for a term expiring December 16, 1988. He would succeed Susan W. Liebeler.

Since 1982 Mr. Newquist has been a senior vice president of corporate relations at the Valero Energy Corp. in San Antonio, TX. Previously, he was vice president for administration at Valero Energy Corp., 1978–1982; vice president for public affairs and employee relations; and assistant vice president for public affairs.

Mr. Newquist graduated from McMurray College (B.B.A., 1966). He was born August 24, 1943, in Stamford, TX, and resides in San Antonio, TX. He served in the United States Navy, 1967–1969.

Letter to the Speaker of the House of Representatives and the President of the Senate Transmitting the Annual Report on National Security Strategy
January 20, 1988

Dear Mr. Speaker: (Dear Mr. President:)

In accordance with section 603 of the Goldwater-Nichols Department of Defense Reorganization Act of 1986 (P.L. 99–433; 50 U.S.C. 404a), I hereby transmit the second annual report on the National Security Strategy of the United States, 1988.

Sincerely,

RONALD REAGAN

Note: Identical letters were sent to Jim Wright, Speaker of the House of Representatives, and George Bush, President of the Senate.

Remarks and a Question-and-Answer Session With Students at Suitland High School in Suitland, Maryland

January 20, 1988

I think I'm the reason why the program was delayed a little this morning. I was late, and the principal has told me I've got to stay after school. [*Laughter*] But it's an honor to be here with you to celebrate all that you've done to make this school so outstanding.

It so happens that visiting a school reminds me of something I heard just the other day. It seems that a certain little boy had reached school age, and his mother worked very hard to make him enthusiastic about the idea—bought him new clothes, told him about the other children he would meet, got him so excited about the project that he eagerly went off on the first day, came home with excellent reports of what school was like. Well, the next morning, his mother went into the bedroom and said he had to get up, and he said, "What for?" She said, "You've got to go to school." He said, "What, again?" [*Laughter*]

Well, it is a pleasure to be at this wonderful school, this school that makes people want to come back. It wasn't so long ago, of course, that Suitland High School had its problems—bad problems: low academic performance, vandalism, poor attendance by both students and teachers alike. Yet today you've turned Suitland around to make it a school noted for its strong sense of purpose and pride, harmony and, yes, academic achievement. I wonder: Would you take a moment to join me in applauding your own remarkable accomplishment? [*Applause*]

Well, now we've heard Principal Hairston and others tell us how this transformation has taken place. And before taking your questions, I'd like to discuss with you how we might work this same transformation in schools all across America. The first point to make is that money alone isn't the answer. From 1963 to 1980, for example, the amount our nation spent on education in real terms more than doubled. Yet during precisely that same period, college board scores fell by almost 90 points. Consider, too, the State of New Hampshire. New Hampshire spends less on education per student than almost every State in the Union. Yet for a number of years now, New Hampshire students have had the Nation's highest SAT scores.

Now, please don't misunderstand me, funding is important, very important. In fact, the amount our country will devote to education this year at all levels of government—local, State, and Federal—will total over $300 billion. But money is only money. Unless it represents genuine commitment—a willingness to work hard at improving American education, to become involved—then money by itself is all but meaningless. You know, I've thought more than once that—back when we were throwing money at education—well, we were sort of like the parent who will buy his child expensive toys and clothes, who will give his child just about anything, except his own time and commitment.

But perhaps the greatest difficulty facing our educators today is this: In too many school systems, if you're a teacher, principal, or superintendent and you do something very good for your students, nothing good happens to you. In a word: There are too few rewards. We need to change that. We need to reward excellence in education as we reward excellence in other fields. We need, in other words, to introduce education to some free-market principles, things like incentives and accountability. An example of incentives is programs now under consideration in some areas, programs that reward teachers and administrations for improved student performance. As for an example of accountability, well, you needn't look any further than Superintendent Murphy's "Applied Anxiety Room." Posted in his office are the test scores showing the performance of all the schools in Prince George's County. And John Murphy holds principals accountable for results. This is the kind of tough, sound management we need in our schools.

Educational excellence also means getting parents involved. It means taking innovative steps to attract and reward good teachers based on their performance. And it means alternate certification: opening up the teaching profession to allow more qualified men and women to enter the field. Excellence means community involvement, and your Advisory Council for Business and Industry, as we've heard, is a fine example of this.

And of course, educational excellence depends on choice. I've long argued that parents should have more choice in determining the schools that their children will attend. I've long argued that more choice would lead to better education. And so, I've advocated tuition tax credits and education vouchers. One form of choice, magnet schools, is one of the things Prince George's County is most noted for and is one of the great success stories of the education reform movement. The success of Suitland's own magnet programs—the Visual and Performing Arts Center and University High School—is a testament to their worth.

In helping to foster magnet schools, we help foster improved education. In 1987 a $4 million Department of Education grant was made to Prince George's County for magnet school programs, such as the kind that you have here at Suitland High School. It's been a good investment. Come to think of it, I wish all Federal dollars got that kind of return. And since I'd like to see magnet schools programs expanded, I'm going to ask the Congress to increase the size of the current program next year by over 50 percent, from $72 million to $115 million. With these additional funds, we can help more schools do what you've done so well in Prince George's County.

Now, I've talked for a while about how we can make our schools better, but I haven't yet told you why I believe this is so important. What it comes down to is this: It is here, in Suitland High and schools like it around the country, that our future is being shaped. Recently the headlines have been full of a term called "superconductivity," as papers struggle to keep up with the seemingly daily breakthroughs in the lab. Only a year ago superconductivity was considered a scientific backwater, a phenomenon with little practical purpose. Now scientists are saying it may change our lives. "It shows all the dreams we have had can come true. The sky is the limit," said one theorist. We're moving from an age of things to an age of thoughts, of mind over matter. It is the mind of man—free to invent, free to experiment, free to dream—that will shape the economy and the world of the future.

Permit me to offer in closing one final message, and it's a message from my heart. If you heard my radio talk last Saturday, then you'll know about a new report on drug use by America's students, including high school students like you. We've had so much bad news about drugs lately, but if you want some good news, just listen. According to the report released by our Secretary of Health and Human Services, Dr. Otis Bowen, last year, for the first time since these surveys began, a substantially smaller number of high school students—one third smaller—acknowledged current use of cocaine than acknowledged it the year before. And cocaine is no longer fashionable—far from it. Ninety-seven percent of the students surveyed disapproved of regular cocaine use, while 87 percent disapproved of even trying it. The use of marijuana and amphetamines is also down.

What it all means is this: America's young people are getting the message. Drugs are ugly. Drugs are nothing to brag about. Drugs kill. And this is so important as you look to the future. You see, in the 21st century, staying employed will mean more than just knowing something. It will mean being able to keep on learning. It will mean having character and discipline and being proud of yourselves. There won't be opportunities in years to come for those who handicap themselves with drug use now.

My young friends, you've done so much already, turning this school around, learning to learn, and learning to look to the future with confidence. I can't tell you how proud I am of you. Keep it up. Keep on saying yes to life. And when it comes to drugs, take a tip from a friend of mine who just happens to be named Nancy Reagan: Just say no.

Thank you. God bless you all.

Mr. Hairston. Mr. President, I understand you have a few minutes remaining. We have some students out in the audience that would like to ask you a few questions.

The President. Alright.

Career Planning

Q. Good morning, Mr. President. My name is Felicia Funderburk. I'm the president of Suitland's Student Government Association. One of the most important questions facing high school seniors today is what college they plan to attend and what career goals they plan to pursue. When you were a high school senior, what career goals did you want to pursue? And how did you plan for it? And what advice can you give young people today as they embark on their careers?

The President. You've asked a question, and I know you're expecting an answer saying something about having decided to do something or other. No, I'm delighted to answer this and encourage you—don't be concerned because you haven't made up your mind. I graduated from college with a degree in economics and sociology and still had not been able to pin down exactly what I wanted to do. Now, at that time, I must say, the demand was just maybe to get a job of any kind, because I graduated at the very depth of the Great Depression—1932. And so, you thought anything might be—but it wasn't until I went back to my summer job to get a little money to go job hunting after I graduated.

My summer job was lifeguarding at a river beach in my hometown. And there were people who came out from the city and corporate heads and so forth with their families every summer. And I taught their children to swim and so forth. And there weren't as many by 1932 with the result of what had happened in the Crash. But one was there, and he told me that if I could tell him what I wanted to do he had contacts with a number of businesses and areas. He would do what he could to get me a job. But he said, "You've got to come back and tell me." And I went home, and I thought, and I finally realized that in spite of my degree in economics and sociology I wanted the theatrical world.

Now, there in the middle of Illinois, I didn't have the nerve to say I wanted to be an actor. [*Laughter*] But radio was pretty new, and I said I wanted to be a sports announcer in radio. Well, he told me then, he said, "Well, I don't have any contacts. There's nothing I can do to help you there." But he said, "Maybe that's better. Let me give you some advice." He gave me the best advice I've ever had. He said, "Now that you've determined that, what you want to do," he said, "you start out knocking on doors, telling people at those doors what you want to do—businesses. And someplace along the line, even in this Depression, you'll find someone in a radio station who knows that his business is going to depend on bringing younger people into the business to carry on. And then you'll get a job." And he says, "Don't get discouraged if you knock on a lot of doors. Remember a salesman sometimes has to make 250 calls before he makes a sale."

It turned out to be the greatest advice I was ever given. And sure enough, one day in a station in Davenport, Iowa, turned down because they had just hired an announcer the day before—and where was I? Why didn't I know they were looking for one? On the way out, after a number of turndowns, I said to myself aloud, "How do you get to be a radio announcer if you can't even get a job in the station?" Well, I've left out one thing. He had told me, "Don't ask to be a sports announcer." He said, "Just ask for anything, because you believe in the future of radio—anything inside the station—and then take your chances on there from getting to what you want."

Well, I got to the elevator, and fortunately, the program director that I'd been interviewed by was arthritic, because I heard the thump of his canes coming down the floor before the elevator arrived. And he was yelling to me to stop and wait. And I did, and he asked me, "What was that you said about sports?" And I told him that that's what my ambition was. And he said, "What do you know about football?" I said, "I played it 8 years." And he said, "Could you tell me about a game and make me see it?" I said, "I think so."

He stood me in front of a microphone in a studio. He said, "When the red light goes on, you start broadcasting an imaginary football game." He said, "I'll be in another room listening." And I remembered a game we played the year before, my senior year. We won in the last 20 seconds of the game with a long touchdown run and so forth. And I could remember enough of the names so that I wouldn't have to fish for names in broadcasting it. So, I started us out in the fourth quarter, with the long, blue shadow settling over the field, and back in our own 35 yard line. Here's the play—has the ball going wide out to the right, cuts back in over—so forth and so on. [*Laughter*] He walked back into the studio, and he said, "Be here Saturday. You're broadcasting the Iowa-Minnesota football game." And that's how I started my career as a sports announcer.

I know I've taken a long time here, but I know that this is a problem at your age—that you're thinking so hard, so many of you, what do I want to do? And don't let it bother you that you haven't made that decision yet. You'll change your mind many times before it comes—the right moment. But then when it comes, just knock on the door, whatever you've chosen to do, and ask until you find somebody that will let you in.

Q. Thank you very much.

The President. I didn't mean to make a second speech, but you touched a nerve. [*Laughter*]

Political Participation

Q. Good morning, Mr. President. My name is Victoria Bell, and I'm a member of the graduating class of 1988. Those of us who are of age have registered to vote. Could you please give us some advice on what a young person's role should be in politics today?

The President. Your role should be in—what is it? I didn't——

Q. On what a young person's role should be in politics today.

The President. In politics? Well, it was the last thing I thought I would ever end up in. [*Laughter*] I had completely different thoughts for most of my life. But I think what you should recognize is this—there is a little figure that says something. The 18- to 24-year-old group of young people happens to be the lowest bracket with regard to voting, the smallest percentage of that bracket votes. We have a society that is unique in the world. It is based on the fact that "we the people" are the Government. Our Constitution differs from all but one other constitution in the world. Our Constitution isn't the Government telling the people what their privileges are: Our Constitution is we the people telling the Government what it can do.

Now, government of that kind can only work if people participate. So, whether you're interested in ever becoming involved in politics yourself, participate by that most fundamental thing of voting. But also when you make up your mind, the thing that you believe in, and whether it's party or what philosophy, then participate. Volunteer in campaigns to be of help, to really participate in what the Government—or who is going to be in the Government. And then, if from that experience you find that you want to actually engage in the issues of the day and having a say about them, then you look around and pick where is the nearest and most available way or level of government and office that you can begin by seeking public office.

And then, when you get that public office, make up your mind—I have told a Cabinet as a Governor of California and a Cabinet as the President of the United States, in discussing all the issues and what we're going to do about something, don't anyone tell me what the best political way is. I don't want to hear what is right or wrong politically. I want to hear what is right or wrong morally about the issue and what we should do, and make that your goal as a participant in government.

Q. Thank you, Mr. President.

Federal Role in Education

Q. Good morning, Mr. President. My name is Larry Bradford. I'm a student with the visual and performing arts program. My question to you today is: Based on what you learned of our school today, what educational programs and policies will your administration be advocating?

The President. What educational programs?

Q. What educational programs and policies will your administration be advocating?

The President. Well, I probably should turn that question over to the Secretary of Education, who is experienced in it, but I would just take a chance myself—if he wants to add anything to this. I think that the first thing we at the Federal level must recognize is that our great system of education is managed by and run by the people at the local and State level. And the Federal Government should be of help where it can, but it should not involve itself in trying to dictate to the schools of America.

Do you want to add to that, Bill?

Secretary Bennett. Couldn't say it better myself. That's for sure. [*Laughter*]

Q. Thank you, Mr. President.

Secretary Bennett. Maybe I would just underline what you said in your remarks, Mr. President. I think you will see emphasis from us on the point that we heard from this table: accountability, choice, high expectations to help the kind of local effort we see here be duplicated all around the country.

The President. We have a great diversity in our education across this great land—in more than education, in the land itself—and that is valuable to us.

Arms Control

Q. Good morning, Mr. President. My name is Audrell Cabiness, and I'm an eleventh-grader here at Suitland. What could future leaders do to ensure the prevention of nuclear war?

The President. Well, wait a minute. I have a little trouble with——

Q. What could future leaders do to ensure the prevention of nuclear war?

The President. What can we all do with regard to preventing a war? Is that what you're talking about?

Q. Yes.

The President. Well, having seen four of them in my lifetime, I'm hoping and praying that we can avoid one. But I do know this: We have to be practical. We have to be realistic. We have to be totally in favor of peace ourselves and doing all that we can to maintain peace.

My first words in my meeting with Gorbachev in Geneva, Switzerland—when he and I met in a room, just the two of us and—well, with interpreters—I said to him that we were in a unique situation, the two of us from these two great powers, that we could perhaps bring on a war or we could bring on peace for the world. And I said I think what we have to recognize is we mistrust each other, and we are both heavily armed. And I said we don't mistrust each other because we're armed. We're armed because we mistrust each other. And so, our goal—even though we're going to talk about trying to reduce weapons and lower the military threat—that our main goal must be to eliminate the mistrust that has caused us to build those armaments. And I think that this country—we have an order now to maintain peace.

The Great Seal of the United States, with the eagle and its head turned—in one claw has arrows and in the other claw has the olive branch, designating peace. The older seal, the one on my desk in the Oval Office—because it's an old, old desk—the eagle is looking at the claw with the arrows. On the ceiling—because the building is newer—on that seal, the eagle is looking at the claw with the olive branch.

Harry Truman, after World War II, decided that our seal should be changed and that our eagle, our bird, should be looking at peace, not war. But at the same time, right now I'm trying to convince the Congress—we have made great strides in this first treaty that has ever been signed of the actual elimination of arms—has come about because we revealed to the world that we were going to deal from strength, that they could have their choice: engage in an arms race with us or join us in eliminating the causes of armament. And so, we're pursuing that. And it's been successful so far, because after several years of turndown, we have signed the first treaty that ever eliminated a total system of nuclear weapons. And that's——

Q. Thank you.

U.S. Trade Deficit

Q. Good morning, Mr. President. My name is Keith Emory, and I'm a senior in the comprehensive school program. My question for you deals with a major issue in the United States: the issue of the balance of trading. What steps do you think the U.S.

Government can take to correct the many trade imbalances that we have with foreign countries?

The President. We're taking those steps as much as we can. But let me point something out. I happen to be one who believes that the imbalance in trade is not the terrible thing that it has been portrayed. Granted that we would like to export more, but for 100 years—while this country of ours was becoming the great economic power that it is—for all those 100 years, we had an imbalance of trade, as we have now. We're the greatest exporter in the world. Now, I could caution you, too. Sometimes our statisticians don't use all the figures they should. For example, by the number of dollars of exports that we have does not include services, just things that are made to sell. I think there might be a little difference if we realized how much money comes in from abroad to insurance companies that sell insurance abroad, the services of that kind. And it would balance up a little better.

But if we're going to be the greatest exporter, we must recognize the right of other countries to export, too, and therefore we're an importer. And I've always—this comes, I guess, from that degree in economics I got—I've always believed that people in America who feel free to buy foreign products, import foreign goods of some kind or another—that's their right to do that. And those people, at the same time that they're sending money abroad, they're replacing that money with a product that has an actual money worth. And it's not that the Government is involved in that. Where the Government is involved is—we have people in our Congress today who want protectionism, high tariffs that will keep people from being able to sell goods in our country without realizing that they can retaliate and then have high tariffs against us selling abroad.

Back in that Great Depression that I mentioned earlier, in 1932, two great mistakes were made in this country and by this country. One, we introduced a thing called the Smoot-Hawley tariff, which made it virtually impossible for anyone to sell anything in America, and that simply spread the Great Depression around the world. And the only thing that ended the Great Depression was World War II. And that was one lesson. The second lesson was the Congress of the United States also then increased the income taxes tremendously from one bracket of 1½ percent to 9 percent, from something like around 20 percent to 63 percent. And immediately, the total amount of revenue that the Government was getting was reduced, even though the rates were higher.

And so, what we're fighting for is free and fair trade around the world, and we've made great progress with some of our trading partners who did have restraints and restrictions. But that open, free trade and, as I continue to insist, low tax rates here on ourselves in our own country, to increase the incentive of people to earn more—we have reduced the taxes in our administration, and the total amount of revenue the Government is getting from that tax has increased mightily. About 1,000 years ago, a man named Ibn-Khaldun said in the beginning of the empire, the rates were low and the revenue was high. At the end of the empire, the rates were high and the revenue was low. So, we're going to stick with what we're trying to do, and we can use all the help that you'll give us.

Q. Thank you, Mr. President.

Administration Accomplishments

Q. Good morning, Mr. President. I am Len Walder, a freshman in the University High School. My question to you is this: What do you feel was your major accomplishment as President, and what would you most like to be remembered for as President of the United States?

The President. Well, I'd just like to be remembered. [*Laughter*] But, well, I'd be satisfied if they just would say I did my best. But now, wait a minute here. You got me so off base here on the first part of that question—what—oh, what accomplishment? It's rather difficult to pick things out of all the things that we tried to turn around and change. The economy was in a shambles when we came here. We were in a great recession. Interest rates were sky high, and inflation was in double digits. We turned all that around. And for 61 months we have had an economic expansion which is the longest period in the history of our nation for an economic expansion. But with all of that, I think I'd rather be remembered for the fact that not too many years ago there was a great pessimism in our country, and people were very critical, and people didn't seem to be very proud of the flag anymore. And today what I get in the mail and what I hear from people when I get out of Washington is that once again they're proud to be Americans. And if I had anything to do with that, that's what I would be most proud of, that once again——

Q. Thank you, Mr. President.

The President. Well, just one line to finish now, and I appreciate very much and apologize for the length of my answers. But this thing about America—I got a letter from a man the other day, and I'll share it with you. This man said you can go to live in Turkey, but you can't become a Turk. You can go to live in Japan, but you cannot become Japanese—or Germany or France—and named all the others. But he said anyone from any corner of the world can come to America and become an American.

Note: The President spoke at 11:50 a.m. in the school auditorium. In his remarks, he referred to Joseph Hairston, principal of the school.

Remarks to Civic Leaders at a White House Briefing on Aid to the Nicaraguan Democratic Resistance
January 20, 1988

Thank you all very much, and welcome to the White House. I often like to start this sort of an event with a joke or an anecdote, but somehow I don't think that's appropriate today. The issue we're here to discuss is perhaps one of the most serious we'll have to face and make a decision on. As you know, Congress will be voting soon on continued aid to the democratic resistance forces in Nicaragua, the *contras*, as they call them, or freedom fighters, as I call them. And if aid doesn't pass, those in Congress who oppose aid to the freedom fighters have made it very plain that they will not allow another vote on this issue to come to the floor. We're at a critical juncture: If Congress votes down aid this time, the decision may well be irrevocable. And if that happens, it's my great fear that we will have abandoned all hope for democracy in Nicaragua and peace in Central America.

Last weekend the leaders of the five Central American nations met to examine compliance with the Guatemala accord. There's no doubt as to their conclusion: The Sandinistas are the biggest obstacle to fulfillment of the plan and to peace and democracy in that region. While the four Central American democracies are in substantial compliance, the Sandinistas are nowhere near. Even the Sandinistas had to admit as much, issuing a separate declaration that outlined additional steps they felt compelled to announce so as to put their behavior in a better light.

I want to talk to you today about why we must keep the pressure on the Sandinistas so that they can't reverse course, so they keep walking down that road to democracy. Because each step they have taken, each reluctant reform, is still easily undone. Daniel Ortega has said that his revolution is irreversible. Our goal in Nicaragua must be to make democracy irreversible.

We welcome the Sandinistas' new promises to abide by the peace plan, and we must hold them to their word. We must make sure that each time the Sandinistas walk through a new door toward democracy we close it behind them—and keep it closed. Only the freedom fighters can do that, only they can be our insurance policy for democracy in Central America. Some say that the freedom fighters are not necessary to keep the pressure on, that the spotlight of world opinion and the Sandinistas' sworn commitment to the Guatemala accord are enough. Well, perhaps it's worth reviewing the historical record to see just how much faith we can put in Sandinista promises.

As I pointed out in my recent address to the Organization of American States, we already have a negotiated settlement with the Sandinistas—the settlement of 1979—in which the United States, together with the other members of the OAS, took the unprecedented action of withdrawing recognition from a sitting government—the Somoza government—and helped bring the Sandinistas to power. As part of that settlement, the Sandinistas promised—and I'm citing from documents signed by the Sandinistas—"free elections, a broad-based democratic government, full guarantee of human rights, fundamental liberties, freedom of religion, union rights, a mixed economy, an independent foreign policy of nonalignment, and a minimum permanent military corps."

It's simply stating the obvious to point out that the Sandinistas have not honored a single one of those promises to the other nations of the Organization of American States. What isn't as widely understood, however, is that we now have documented proof that they never intended to. Barely 2 months after assuming power, the Sandinista leadership met secretly to draft a report known as the 72-hour document, outlining their plans to establish a Communist dictatorship in Nicaragua and spread subversion throughout Central America.

The Sandinistas and their supporters say it was the belligerence of the United States that forced them to go back on their promises, just as they now put all of the blame for their shortcomings on the freedom fighters. But again, let's examine the historical record. Only a day after the Sandinistas finished meeting secretly to draft the 72-hour document, President Carter received Daniel Ortega in the White House and offered his new government our friendship and help. But while we sent the Sandinistas over $100 million in aid—more than any other country—and arranged for hundreds of millions of dollars of loans, the Sandinistas were busy carrying out their plans to eliminate human rights and impose a Marxist totalitarian regime in Nicaragua.

Six months after the meeting in the White House, while the United States aid was still flowing, several Sandinista comandantes took their first official trip to Moscow, the first of many, and signed a communique with the Soviet Communist Party, expressing support for the foreign policy goals of the Soviet Union. But that, one might say, was merely the paperwork; already Soviet military planners were in Nicaragua. Over 30 new military bases were either built or in the process of construction by the time I came into office in 1981. The Sandinista army was becoming the largest, best supplied in all Central America, and the Sandinistas were already assisting the Communist guerrillas in El Salvador—all while American aid flowed to Nicaragua, while our hand was extended in friendship.

I could go on to detail the systematic crushing of all human rights, the torture of dissidents, and the swelling population of political prisoners, the tragedy of hundreds of thousands of Nicaraguan refugees flooding into Costa Rica and Honduras—nearly 1 out of every 10 Nicaraguans is now a refugee. But the record of Sandinista totalitarianism is well known by now. The human destruction of communism on the American mainland is well documented and acknowledged by all sides in this debate. My purpose here is to ask a simple question: How can we expect a regime that has compiled such a history of broken promises, of outright deceit, to abide by the terms of the Guatemala accord unless we keep up the pressure by continuing to aid the freedom fighters?

Recently, Daniel Ortega was up here in Washington talking with Members of Congress, giving them assurances of his commitment to the Guatemala accord. But we know now, from the testimony of a high-level Sandinista defector, Major Roger Miranda, that even while Daniel Ortega was making those promises, the Sandinistas were planning with the Cubans and Soviets to increase their armed forces to 600,000—that's one out of every five men, women, and children in the country.

Shortly after Major Miranda made his revelations public, Defense Minister Humberto Ortega confirmed them, including

Sandinista plans to acquire advanced MiG fighter planes, missiles, and artillery. "Several thousand Nicaraguans," he said, "are now taking courses in the Soviet Union and other Socialist countries to learn to operate the new weapons systems." And the Sandinistas are now developing military facilities that could serve as a launching stage for the Soviet Tu–95 BEAR bomber, a bomber whose range reaches well inside the continental United States. All this, it now turns out, while Daniel Ortega was in the halls of our Congress talking peace. There's a saying I remember from my childhood—and I'm sure you all do, too—that goes "Fool me once, shame on you. Fool me twice, shame on me." But what of the third, fourth, and the fifth times? How does one explain such willful gullibility?

Now the Sandinistas have made more promises. We welcome their promises to lift the state of siege, meet face-to-face with freedom fighters, hold local elections, and release some political prisoners; and we must hold them to those promises. But these limited steps, which still do not bring them into compliance with the Guatemala accord, were taken with extreme reluctance and only after the Sandinistas had been told by certain U.S. Congressmen that failure to do so would result in renewed aid for the freedom fighters.

Was there ever a better argument for aid? It's only the freedom fighters, and the pressure they've brought to bear on the Sandinistas, that has brought us this far. It's only the freedom fighters that can push the Sandinistas so far down the road to democracy that they never go back. The fact is that even if they carry out the steps they've announced, the Sandinistas are still a long way from compliance with the Guatemala accord.

Nearly 6 months after signing, nearly 3 months after the agreed-upon deadline for compliance, thousands of political prisoners are in Sandinista prisons and will remain there even under the newly announced partial amnesty. Opposition groups and human rights activists are harassed and beaten by government mobs. Perhaps the best indication of the Sandinistas' true inclinations was the arrest and intimidation last week of seven leaders of the democratic opposition, released only after a storm of international protest. Some in this country talk as if the Sandinistas would reform if we'd just let them alone. But that's not what the Sandinistas themselves say. Just 5 weeks ago, Daniel Ortega made his true intentions clear. Even if there were elections in Nicaragua and the Sandinistas lost, he said, they would never give up power.

Those who want to cut off funding for the freedom fighters are going to have to explain how Daniel Ortega doesn't really mean what he says. They're going to have to explain that the Sandinistas don't really mean what they say when they talk of turning all of Central America into one "revolutionary fire" and boasting of carrying their fight into Latin America and Mexico. Because right now, what stands between the Sandinistas and their stated intentions, what stands in the way of a Soviet base camp in Central America, are the Nicaraguan freedom fighters. It's clear that it's the freedom fighters, and only the freedom fighters, that have brought the Sandinistas to the negotiating table and have wrung from them the limited reforms they've made. Without the freedom fighters, the hope of democracy in Nicaragua would be lost. The consolidation of totalitarian power would be complete, and the Soviets would have already succeeded in establishing another Cuba—this time on the American mainland.

The Soviets have made their choice. They and their allies have poured billions of dollars of military aid into Nicaragua, at least 20 times more than the United States Congress has given to the forces of the democratic resistance. Next month the American Congress and the American people will have to make their choice, too. As I said, this is the moment of truth, the make-or-break vote on the freedom fighters. If we abandon them now, if Congress votes down aid, we will be abandoning the only real cause for peace and freedom in Nicaragua. We will be consigning the peace process to an obscure footnote in history and handing the Soviet Union one of its greatest strategic victories since World War II.

Throughout history, one of our greatest fortunes and greatest strengths as a nation has been that we're protected on either side by two vast oceans. For almost two centuries, we have not experienced the tragedy of foreign aggression on our mainland. And today we can boast that the thousands of miles of borders that separate us and our neighbors lie unarmed and unfortified. Yes, we've been blessed by history, but that should not make us complacent now that a real—and if we don't act to stop it—irreversible danger is developing to our south.

Imagine the effect on U.S. national security if the Sandinista vision of a Communist Central America is realized and Mexico is threatened. Imagine if, for the first time in this century, we had to concern ourselves with a security threat on our southern border. Imagine our vital sealanes through the Gulf put in jeopardy. The kind of turmoil that exists in the Persian Gulf cannot be allowed to exist in the Gulf of Mexico.

It is willfully naive to think the Soviet Union, beset by a crisis in its own economy, would be pouring billions of dollars into a country on the other side of the world if they didn't see great opportunities there. It's time to realize that the Sandinista Communists and their Soviet mentors are serious people with serious objectives. It's time we got serious, too.

This vote will be remembered by the American people either as the time we acted to support freedom and kept our mainland secure or as the beginning of one of America's most tragic mistakes. Of course, the consequences for Latin America would be even worse. An emboldened Communist left would once again step up the offensive in El Salvador, Costa Rica, Guatemala, and Honduras. The tide of democracy would be reversed as the region descended into a cycle of leftwing violence and military repression. Democracy, caught in the crossfire, would not survive long.

But all this is unnecessary. If we support those fighting for freedom and democracy in Nicaragua, we can keep the peace process on track. We can keep pressure on the Sandinistas to honor the peace plan. We can keep the forward movement of democracy in Latin America safe. And we can prevent the crisis in U.S. national security I described from taking place.

You know, we've heard a lot about how the freedom fighters will never be an effective fighting force. Well, the latest operation against the Las Miñas area disproved that once and for all. Over 7,000 freedom fighters took part in a surprise attack on major military targets and Sandinista gold and silver mines—a source of hard currency for the bankrupt Sandinista economy. In the process, they demolished enemy barracks and overran enemy headquarters. They blew up ammunition dumps and petroleum tanks, destroyed hydroelectric plants, and decommissioned permanently a radar installation the Sandinistas had used to coordinate air strikes against the freedom fighters.

If the Communist guerrillas in El Salvador mounted such a successful attack, you can imagine the headlines, all the people calling for us to cut our losses and get out, to accept the "will of the people." That the freedom fighters can count [mount] such a major operation, moving thousands of troops in secret throughout the length of the country, demonstrates their support among the Nicaraguan people. With our support, the cause of freedom and democracy can prevail.

Probably the most important revelation of Major Miranda was the extent of corruption in the Sandinista regime. While the people go ragged and hungry, denied even basic foodstuffs, the Sandinistas milk their country for huge profits. Humberto Ortega alone has skimmed $1½ million and put it into a secret bank account in Switzerland.

No, it's the corrupt dictators of the Sandinista regime that have no popular support. That's why they must be sustained by billions of dollars of Soviet-bloc aid. The true sentiments of the Nicaraguan people were seen recently when 10,000 people thronged the streets of Managua to demonstrate against the Sandinistas. And believe me, it took real courage for those brave souls to openly defy such a brutal regime.

The freedom tide that has swept Latin America is pushing up against the borders of Nicaragua. It can go either way, and this vote coming up in 2 weeks will be decisive. We have seen with the recent treaty we signed on INF missiles what we can accomplish if we negotiate from a position of strength. We have seen in Afghanistan how the brave resistance of the Mujahidin is forcing the Soviet Union to look for a political solution. We must keep the pressure on in Nicaragua. We must not let up until democracy has taken such firm root that no one can ever pull it out.

The majority of the aid that I will be requesting from Congress is for nonlethal assistance to keep the freedom fighters a viable force until democracy is irreversible in Nicaragua. As I said, the Communist Sandinistas have made their choice. Now we must make ours: a future of freedom and democracy for Nicaragua and its neighbors and peace throughout the region, or turmoil, revolution, and unrest, and a steady advance of Soviet military might toward our southern border. That's the choice. There's no middle way.

Let's make certain that those who come after us say we made the right choice, that when it came time to decide we stood up for freedom and peace—we acted before it was too late, while the costs were still small, to do what was necessary to support democracy and protect the national security of the United States. Thank you all very much, and God bless you.

Note: The President spoke at 2:04 p.m. in the East Room at the White House.

Written Responses to Questions Submitted by the Japanese Newspaper Mainichi Shimbun
January 19, 1988

Death of Daisuke Yamauchi

Before we turn to matters of policy, let me express to you my condolences on the untimely loss of the president of the Mainichi Newspapers, Mr. Daisuke Yamauchi. Mr. Yamauchi knew the United States well, and as Mainichi's bureau chief in Washington, and before that as one of the first Japanese participants in the Fulbright fellowship program, he fostered the close ties that have come to mark our countries' mutual relations over the years. He was also one of the founders of the Fulbright Alumni Association in Japan and its first president. Mr. Yamauchi was an outstanding journalist and a great friend of the United States. He will be missed.

Soviet-U.S. Relations

Q. First of all, please allow me, Mr. President, to congratulate you on your signing of the INF treaty at the U.S.–U.S.S.R. summit. We, the Japanese people, are especially grateful that the principle of global zero has prevailed.

Now, how would you assess the present status of the START negotiations? Will the treaty be ready for signature when you visit Moscow? On the other hand, some of us in Japan feel that the advent of the new superpower relationship might mean the United States and the U.S.S.R. are starting to talk over our heads, so to speak. Would you tell me how you look at the superpower relationship from now on as well as its implications to the U.S. allies?

The President. My recent meeting with General Secretary Gorbachev in Washington resulted in considerable progress toward implementing our goal of 50-percent reductions in U.S. and Soviet strategic offensive arms. We agreed that we would instruct our negotiators in Geneva to work toward the completion of a treaty and related documents at the earliest possible date—if possible, in time for signature during our meeting in Moscow in the first half of 1988.

I don't wish to underestimate the difficulties of this task. In particular, a START agreement presents difficult verification challenges that go well beyond those we faced in INF. However, a START agreement has always been a high priority of mine and would constitute an historic achievement. If the Soviets show a similar commitment to reductions in strategic offensive arms and don't attempt to hold such reductions hostage to restrictions that would cripple SDI, we can conclude an effectively verifiable START agreement.

I firmly believe the achievements to date in U.S.-Soviet relations would not have been possible without the close consultations and unity of purpose between the United States and our allies, both in Europe and in Asia. Through this cooperation we have been able to send a clear message to Moscow that the Western alliance—and when I use that term I have very much in mind our allies in Asia as well as NATO—remains solid and committed to a realistic security policy vis-a-vis the Soviet Union. We have always valued highly the advice and support of your government as we have pursued our dialog with Moscow and will continue to do so in the future. Prime Minister Takeshita and I had a full exchange of views on the appropriate strategy for dealing with Mr. Gorbachev when we met in Washington.

U.S. Economic Policy

Q. In the field of world economy, the dollar exchange rate is coming down again, and stock markets have not quite stabilized yet. What would be your outlook for the world economy in 1988? What would you want Japan, West Germany, and other partners to do?

The President. In the coming year, as our trading sectors more fully adjust to the strong exchange rate signals of the last 2 years, we expect to see continued adjustments in real external imbalances, greater stability in exchange rates, a reduction in uncertainties facing traders, and an improved outlook for investment in our respective economies.

In the United States, we are reducing the budget deficit and the private sector is expanding exports. United States fiscal and monetary policies are encouraging real economic growth, a decline in the trade deficit, and a more stable dollar.

We would ask other countries to pursue the best interests of their consumers by breaking down the structural and policy barriers to imports that prevent them from enjoying a higher standard of living. Other nations also need to build up their domestic infrastructure and generally invest more in their own economies.

Japan-U.S. Relations

Q. What did you achieve through your talks with Prime Minister Takeshita of Japan during his first visit here as our Premier? What sort of personal relationship did you establish with him? May I take this opportunity to ask you your assessment of the U.S.-Japan relationship at present? How would you like to see it develop during 1988?

The President. Prime Minister Takeshita and I achieved a reaffirmation of the importance of U.S.-Japan relations not only to our two countries but to the world. We continued to demonstrate to the world the value of U.S.-Japan cooperation as allies and partners to global peace and prosperity.

I met with Prime Minister Takeshita when he was Minister of Finance, and since he became Prime Minister we have communicated on several occasions and exchanged personal messages. So, it is fair to say we had already established a personal relationship before our recent meeting. If I were to characterize that relationship, I would describe it as the sort of personal relationship one would expect between the leaders of two of the world's largest democracies and the two largest free economies, a relationship based on shared values and interests and mutual trust and respect.

United States-Japan relations are solid. There is hardly an important issue, multilateral or bilateral, on which we do not consult closely and cooperate. We have certain trade differences, but we are addressing them cooperatively, as friends and allies. We will continue to do so.

I expect that the United States and Japan will continue to consult and cooperate closely on a wide range of bilateral and global issues. Not only do we share values and interests, our economies are inextricably entwined, and neither country wants to see relations unravel. I can assure you we are working hard to make sure the bonds between us remain strong.

Japan-U.S. Trade

Q. Retaliatory measures hammered out by the Congress against Kansai Airport issue, as well as Toshiba and semiconductor sanctions, and demands for liberalization of import of rice and other agricultural products are proving to be highly sensitive in Japan, imbued with emotional undertones, making it difficult for Prime Minister Takeshita to implement necessary policy changes. Would there, after all, not be any possibility of compromise conceivable, such as a linkage of sorts between Japan's adoption of a decidedly domestic expansionist policy and lessening of these U.S. demands?

The President. Trade issues in both our countries are often highly sensitive. In dealing with these issues, we should seek solutions that are in the overall best interest of each nation and the international economy and not allow protectionist pressures to hold sway. Japan's expansionary economic policy is part of a coordinated effort to reduce external economic imbalances. This effort has been endorsed by the Group of Seven industrial nations. Increased domestic consumption and infrastructure investment are not an onerous burden for Japan and can help sustain world economic growth.

Q. What would you expect the outcome of the congressional discussions of the trade bill to be? Would you expect it to be less protectionist, in view of the recent economic developments?

The President. I would welcome a trade bill that is not protectionist. However, the current trade bill in Congress still contains a number of protectionist proposals. I will veto any bill that restricts trade, favors special interests to the detriment of the broader national interest, or includes procedural changes that are protectionist. I have urged Congress to jettison the protectionist features of the trade bill. They made little sense when originally proposed, and they make even less sense today. In my view, trade policy should not be confrontational but should help open markets, increase market incentives and efficiency, and make a positive contribution to world economic stability.

The impact of recent economic developments is difficult to predict. It is encouraging that monthly U.S. trade data have begun to show significant progress toward reducing the deficit. Of course, eliminating the deficit will take time. Because of that, protectionist sentiment will not go away quickly. There is also a deeply held view that U.S. markets are far more open to the exports of our trading partners than are their markets to United States exports. Our trading partners should understand and support the need of the United States to significantly increase exports if protectionism is to be contained.

How the U.S. Congress will react to economic developments is even more difficult to predict. I would hope that Congress will reconsider certain protectionist proposals that have passed one or both Houses. My opposition to such protectionist measures is as strong as ever.

East Asia

Q. How would you evaluate the outcome of the recent Korean Presidential election? Are you optimistic about the Seoul Olympic games now? What would be your outlook for another emerging democracy in the Philippines? How would you feel about Prime Minister Takeshita visiting the Philippines before any other country? May I also ask you your outlook for East Asia in 1988?

The President. We were pleased that the Republic of Korea conducted its Presidential election and arrived at a democratic outcome. We look forward to working with Mr. Roh Tae Woo, the President-elect, and will keep open our channels to the opposition. Preparations for the Olympics are on track. I am pleased to see that East-bloc nations and the Soviet Union have accepted invitations. I know that the Republic of Korea remains open to compromise on the Olympics and hope that North Korea will join in this great celebration.

In the Philippines, President Aquino's government offers the best chance for establishing a stable democracy and a prosperous economy. President Aquino enjoys broad popular support, and Filipinos perceive her government as honest and committed to justice. There have been many accomplishments in the Philippines, including adoption of a new constitution, successful conduct of congressional elections, and restoration of economic growth. Prime Minister Takeshita's decision to attend the December ASEAN [Association of South East Asian Nations] ministerial conference in

Manila, thereby visiting the Philippines before any other country, was an admirable demonstration of his government's support for the Aquino government and the ASEAN nations.

I am optimistic regarding prospects for the East Asian nations in 1988. I expect peaceful and stable relations within the region, though Vietnam's continuing occupation of Cambodia is unacceptable and should be ended without delay. We all hope for a relaxation of tensions on the Korean Peninsula and a successful Olympic games, developments that could contribute to better East-West relations. We must support the Aquino government's efforts to promote democracy, stability, and economic reform in the Philippines. We must remain resolute in maintaining our military preparedness against the steady Soviet buildup of forces deployed in East Asia. I foresee continuing economic growth and dynamism for the nations of East Asia in 1988. Given our mutual interest and desire to cooperate in trade and other matters, I see no reason why the East Asian nations cannot join with other nations, especially the United States and Japan, to achieve unprecedented prosperity for the betterment of all mankind.

Japan-U.S. Relations

Q. What would be your long-range outlook, well into the 21st century, of the U.S.-Japan relationship, in terms of the development of the Pacific rim area, as well as for the well-being of the world as a whole? At the same time, how would you see changes in the roles of China and the U.S.S.R. in the Pacific area as well as in the whole world of the 21st century?

The President. I am very optimistic—and with good reason—about the future of U.S.-Japan relations in the coming century. Already we are close allies. We maintain the largest overseas trading relationship in the history of the world, and our global interests coincide in most areas. The reason this remarkable relationship exists is no accident; rather, it stems from the fact that our two nations share a common set of democratic goals and principles and because we both believe in the virtues of an open economic system. I am confident that these shared principles and goals will continue to guide our two nations, and therefore I am equally confident that the excellent relations which now exist between the United States and Japan will continue to flourish in the coming century. In fact, the future of the Pacific rim area as a whole appears very bright in the next century. The principles of free trade and democracy are spreading throughout the world, even into once-dark corners of the Socialist world. America and Japan can work together to advance this trend.

Japan's International Role

Q. Are you satisfied with Japan's effort to build up her self-defense capabilities? And in view of the present level of our defense spending, are you satisfied with Japan's efforts to increase official development assistance and other aids to the Third World? What sort of contribution would you like to see from Japan to the protection of the shipping in the Persian Gulf?

The President. We consider it very important that Japan increase its capability to defend its homeland, territorial seas and skies, and sealanes out to 1,000 nautical miles—goals incorporated in Japan's defense planning. We welcome, therefore, the increase in Japan's defense budget for the coming year, which will enable Japan to fund fully the third year of its current 5-year defense plan. We are also pleased that the budget provides additional funding to increase Japan's support for United States forces stationed in Japan.

We welcome efforts of the Government of Japan to increase aid flows and other financing for Third World countries. In particular, we applaud the plan to double official development assistance by 1990 and the commitment to recycle $20 billion over 3 years to developing countries.

We are pleased with measures undertaken by the Government of Japan to enhance navigational safety and promote peace in the Persian Gulf region. Provision of a navigational aid system, increased aid to Jordan and Oman, and funding for United Nations peace efforts are concrete signs of Japan's political commitment to Western solidarity in our common efforts to assure safe navigation and bring peace to the Gulf.

Note: The questions and answers were released by the Office of the Press Secretary on January 21.

Nomination of Chester E. Norris, Jr., To Be United States Ambassador to Equatorial Guinea
January 21, 1988

The President today announced his intention to nominate Chester E. Norris, Jr., a career member of the Senior Foreign Service, Class of Minister-Counselor, to be Ambassador to the Republic of Equatorial Guinea. He would succeed Francis Stephen Ruddy.

Since 1986 Mr. Norris has been Deputy Representative of the United States on the Economic and Social Council of the United Nations. Prior to this, he was Deputy Executive Director, Secretary of State's Advisory Committee on South Africa at the Department of State in 1986; economic counselor and acting deputy chief of mission and Chargé at the U.S. Embassy in Lagos, Nigeria, 1982–1985; Iranian claims affairs, special commission at the Department of State, 1981–1982; minister-counselor for Economic and Commercial Affairs and acting deputy chief of mission, Jidda, Saudi Arabia, 1979–1981; and Office Director and Acting Deputy Assistant Secretary in the Bureau of International Organization Affairs at the Department of State, 1976–1979. Mr. Norris attended the National War College, 1975–1976. He was director of the United States Trade Centers in London, England, 1972–1975, and in Sydney, Australia, 1970–1972. Mr. Norris was commercial attaché at the U.S. Embassy in Tel Aviv, Israel, 1966–1970. Mr. Norris joined the Foreign Service in 1965.

Mr. Norris graduated from the University of Maine (B.A., 1951) and attended the U.S. Maritime Academy (1946–1947). Mr. Norris was born December 1, 1927, in Bangor, ME. He is married and resides in New York, NY.

Designation of Lawrence M. Hecker as a Member of the Board of Visitors to the United States Air Force Academy
January 21, 1988

The President today announced his intention to designate Lawrence M. Hecker as a member of the Board of Visitors to the United States Air Force Academy, Department of the Air Force, for a term expiring December 30, 1990. He will succeed Terrence O'Donnell.

Mr. Hecker is currently corporate vice president for aviation affairs at Wicat in Stamford, CT. Prior to this he was vice president of flight operations for Western Airlines. From 1984 to 1985, he was senior director of flight operations for Air Atlanta, Inc. In 1983 he formed Consultants for Aviation Training and Operations, an independent consulting group. From 1981 to 1983, he was vice president of operations at Simuflight Training, Inc.

Mr. Hecker served in the U.S. Navy from 1942 to 1953. He attended Georgia Tech (1940–1941) and the U.S. Coast Guard Academy (1941–1943). Mr. Hecker was born on May 7, 1923, in New York City. He is married, has six children, and resides in New Canaan, CT.

Appointment of Roxani M. Gillespie as a Member of the Supplemental Health Insurance Panel

January 21, 1988

The President today announced his intention to appoint Roxani M. Gillespie to be a member of the Supplemental Health Insurance Panel. She would succeed Joseph F. Murphy.

Since 1986 Mrs. Gillespie has been insurance commissioner for the California Department of Insurance in San Francisco, CA, and chief deputy insurance commissioner, 1983–1986. Prior to this she was corporate counsel and vice president of the Industrial Indemnity Co., in San Francisco.

Mrs. Gillespie attended the University of Athens and Boston College of Law (J.D., 1967). She was born April 19, 1941, in Athens, Greece. Mrs. Gillespie is married, has two children, and resides in San Francisco, CA.

Nomination of Eugene J. McAllister To Be an Assistant Secretary of State

January 21, 1988

The President today announced his intention to nominate Eugene J. McAllister to be an Assistant Secretary of State (Economic and Business Affairs) at the Department of State. He would succeed Douglas W. McMinn.

Since 1985 Mr. McAllister has been Special Assistant to the President and Executive Secretary of the Economic Policy Council at the White House in Washington, DC. Prior to this he was Deputy Assistant Director of the Office of Policy Development at the White House, 1983–1985. Mr. McAllister was senior policy analyst in the Office of Economics and Planning at the Office of Management and Budget, 1982–1983, and policy analyst for the Director's Office, 1981. He was a Walker fellow in economics at the Heritage Foundation, 1978–1981.

Mr. McAllister graduated from Loyola University of Los Angeles (B.S., 1974) and the University of California, Davis (M.A., 1976). He was born May 20, 1952, in the Bronx, NY. He is married and resides in Fairfax, VA.

Proclamation 5762—American Heart Month, 1988

January 21, 1988

By the President of the United States of America

A Proclamation

For more than half of this century, diseases of the heart and blood vessels, collectively called cardiovascular diseases, have been our Nation's most serious health problem. Last year, these diseases claimed 973,000 lives, and they caused serious and sometimes permanent illness or disability in still more Americans. Within this family of diseases, the leading killers remained coronary heart disease, which accounted for 524,000 deaths, and strokes, which accounted for 148,000 deaths.

Grim though these statistics may be, other statistics indicate that a corner may have been turned in 1965. Since then, mortality rates for all cardiovascular diseases, and especially for the two leading killers—

coronary heart disease and stroke—have been moving steadily downward. For example, since 1972, mortality rates for all cardiovascular diseases combined have fallen by 34 percent, and those for coronary heart disease and stroke have declined by 35 percent and 50 percent respectively.

One major reason for the decline in cardiovascular mortality rates is that more and more Americans are modifying their habits in the direction of better cardiovascular health. Research has identified factors that increase vulnerability to premature coronary heart disease or stroke, and millions of Americans are acting on that knowledge to eliminate or ameliorate the risk factors that can be modified. These include high blood pressure, diabetes, obesity, and sedentary living. The National Heart, Lung, and Blood Institute, encouraged by the success of its National High Blood Pressure Education Program, has now launched similar programs against two other major risk factors: cigarette smoking and elevated blood cholesterol.

Today, the person stricken with a heart attack has a much better chance of surviving the acute episode, thanks to continued improvement in diagnosis and treatment. More and more of the stricken are reaching the hospital alive, thanks to better recognition of ominous symptoms, widespread teaching of cardiopulmonary resuscitation by the American Red Cross and the American Heart Association, and better-equipped emergency vehicles with better-trained crews.

Many individuals and organizations have contributed to the past four decades of progress against cardiovascular diseases. However, two organizations—the federally funded National Heart, Lung, and Blood Institute and the privately supported American Heart Association—have been in the forefront of this national effort. Since 1948, the two have worked in close cooperation to foster and support increased basic and clinical research in the cardiovascular field, to train new research scientists and clinicians, and to participate in a wide variety of community service and public and professional information activities. Through their efforts, Americans have become more aware of what they can do to live healthier lives.

Much has already been accomplished, but much more remains to be done. Recognizing the need for all Americans to take part in the continuing battle against heart disease, the Congress, by Joint Resolution approved December 30, 1963 (77 Stat. 843; 36 U.S.C. 169b), has requested the President to issue annually a proclamation designating February as "American Heart Month."

Now, Therefore, I, Ronald Reagan, President of the United States of America, do hereby proclaim the month of February 1988 as American Heart Month. I invite all appropriate government officials and the American people to join with me in reaffirming our commitment to finding new or improved ways to prevent, detect, and control cardiovascular diseases.

In Witness Whereof, I have hereunto set my hand this twenty-first day of January, in the year of our Lord nineteen hundred and eighty-eight, and of the Independence of the United States of America the two hundred and twelfth.

RONALD REAGAN

[*Filed with the Office of the Federal Register, 10:16 a.m., January 22, 1988*]

Note: The proclamation was released by the Office of the Press Secretary on January 22.

Letter to the Speaker of the House of Representatives and the Chairman of the Senate Foreign Relations Committee Reporting on the Cyprus Conflict
January 22, 1988

Dear Mr. Speaker: (Dear Mr. Chairman:)

In accordance with Public Law 95–384, I am submitting to you a bimonthly report on progress toward a negotiated settlement of the Cyprus question.

The United Nations Secretary General delivered his latest biannual report to the Security Council on Cyprus on November 30, 1987, a copy of which is attached. The Secretary General highlighted a number of continuing concerns. These included the deadlock in the negotiating process, his persisting unease over the military buildup by both sides on the island, a Greek Cypriot women's march that violated the integrity of the buffer zone, and the continuing presence of students in Varosha. The Secretary General also mentioned that the Committee on Missing Persons (CMP) met frequently during the past 6 months. The CMP is to be commended for efforts to accelerate its investigation and its declaration of a "firm intention to reach a conclusive stage as soon as possible."

The Secretary General underscored the need for the parties to foster an atmosphere that would reduce tensions and to cooperate fully with his new Special Representative. We share the Secretary General's concerns and fully agree with his urgings on cooperation and reducing tensions.

The Secretary General's new Special Representative for Cyprus, Mr. Oscar Camilion, traveled to Cyprus, Greece, and Turkey in early December. Mr. Camilion met with Cypriot Foreign Minister Iacovou, Turkish Cypriot leader Denktash, and high-level officials in Greece and Turkey. We understand that the new Special Representative was well received and is preparing to return to Cyprus in the near future to begin his efforts to help the parties toward the goal of a lasting, mutually acceptable settlement.

The United Nations Security Council unanimously adopted Security Council Resolution 604 on December 14, extending the mandate of the United Nations Force in Cyprus (UNFICYP) for another 6 months. The resolution also requests the Secretary General to continue his mission of good offices in Cyprus.

Unfortunately, the financial condition of UNFICYP, which is totally supported by voluntary contributions, continues to worsen. Seven of the eight troop-contributing countries recently sent joint letters to the Secretary General and to the Security Council President for December (the Soviet Union) pointing out that UNFICYP's accumulated deficit, which they bear, has now passed $160 million. The November 30 Secretary General's report to the Security Council remarks that UNFICYP is fulfilling its mission in an exemplary manner under difficult conditions and that its presence remains indispensable. We concur emphatically with the Secretary General's assessment and continue to urge other countries to increase or initiate contributions to UNFICYP.

We continued active consultations with parties and individuals interested in the Cyprus dispute during the past 2 months. Special Cyprus Coordinator M. James Wilkinson responded to requests for meetings from Cypriot Presidential candidate George Vassiliou and from a delegation of the Cypriot Committee of Relatives of Missing Persons on November 18 and 20, respectively. Special Cyprus Coordinator Wilkinson and Department of State Deputy Assistant Secretary Robert W. Farrand also held separate meetings on December 3 and 4 with a delegation from the Committee for the Restoration of Human Rights throughout Cyprus.

Sincerely,

RONALD REAGAN

Note: Identical letters were sent to Jim Wright, Speaker of the House of Representatives, and Claiborne Pell, chairman of the Senate Foreign Relations Committee.

Statement by Assistant to the President for Press Relations Fitzwater on the Nuclear and Space Arms Negotiations
January 22, 1988

Today the President directed our negotiators at the nuclear and space talks in Geneva to table a draft treaty in the defense and space forum of the negotiations. This step is in fulfillment of the agreement which the President and General Secretary Gorbachev reached at their recent summit in Washington.

In the joint statement following the summit, the United States and Soviet delegations in Geneva were instructed to work out an agreement that would commit the two sides to observe the ABM treaty as signed in 1972 while conducting their research, development, and testing as required, which are permitted by the ABM treaty, and not to withdraw from the ABM treaty for a specified period of time. It was also agreed that such an agreement must have the same legal status as the treaty on strategic offensive arms, the ABM treaty, and other similar legally binding agreements.

The U.S. draft treaty we tabled today would accomplish and advance these goals. It calls for a separate and new treaty that faithfully embodies the elements of agreement reached at the summit. It would help to provide a jointly managed, predictable, precise, and stable basis for developing, testing, and—when proven feasible—deploying advanced defenses against strategic ballistic missiles. Such defenses would decrease the risk of war.

We hope that the Soviet delegation will join us in serious discussions to conclude a defense and space treaty that achieves the important goals which the two leaders identified at the Washington summit. At the same time, we will press ahead with our negotiations to conclude a treaty providing for 50-percent reductions in U.S. and Soviet strategic offensive arms. We hope, with today's tabling of a draft defense and space treaty, to hasten progress toward a safer and more stable world, one with reduced levels of nuclear arms and an enhanced ability to deter war based on the increasing contribution of effective strategic defenses against ballistic missile attack.

Remarks to Participants in the March for Life Rally
January 22, 1988

The President. Hello to you, Nellie Gray——

Miss Gray. Hello, President Reagan.

The President. ——and to all of you in the 15th annual March for Life rally.

Miss Gray. Mr. President, I wanted to welcome you to this 15th March for Life. The prolife Americans are coming here from every State of the Union. We appreciate so much your prolife words, but we do want to mention that we are somewhat disappointed that once again in December you unfortunately were assigning some public monies for abortions here in the District of Columbia. And we do want to ask today, as we join—that even though we have spent a lot of time lobbying with the White House, unfortunately, those monies were appropriated to kill the preborn children in the District of Columbia. We would love to hear from you today, Mr. President, that we will not have any more appropriations for abortions in the District or anywhere else.

The President. Well, Nellie, sometimes these things happen, because, as you know, there are people that are in great disagreement with us. But we are continuing to work and to do our best to end any Federal funding.

Miss Gray. Wonderful. We welcome you, Mr. President, and we await your message now.

The President. Well, all right. The first of your noble marches came just one year after the Supreme Court issued its decision in *Roe* v. *Wade.* And for a decade and a half, you've worked to end the tragedy that—since that day when the Court, in the stroke of a pen, legalized abortion across our nation—has claimed the lives of more than 20 million infants.

Twenty million—that's more than twice the population of New York City and close to the population of all of California. And yet our opponents tell us not to interfere with abortion. They tell us not to impose our morality on those who wish to allow or participate in the taking of the life of infants before birth. Yet no one calls it imposing morality to prohibit the taking of life after a child is born. We're told about a woman's right to control her own body. But doesn't the unborn child have a higher right, and that is to life, liberty, and the pursuit of happiness? Or would our critics say that to defend life, liberty, and the pursuit of happiness is to impose morality? Are we to forget the entire moral mission of our nation through its history?

Well, my answer, and I know it's yours, is no. America was founded on a moral proposition that human life—all human life—is sacred. And this proposition is the bedrock of our national life, the foundation of our laws. It's the wellspring of our Constitution. Courts may ignore it, and they have. They cannot—and I should add—have not denied it. When reverence for life can have no boundaries, when we begin to take some life casually, we threaten all life.

A few years ago, I spoke about the pain that we now know an unborn fetus experiences in the course of an abortion. At the time there was an outcry—enraged criticism and angry denials. But criticism wasn't the only response. It so happened that I received a letter signed by 24 medical doctors, including eminent physicians like the former chief of pediatrics at the St. Louis City Hospital and the president of the New York State Medical Society. They discussed recent advances in medical technology and concluded: "Mr. President, in drawing attention to the capability of the human fetus to feel pain, you stand on firmly established ground."

Well, you know, I couldn't help noticing, that letter received far less coverage than the many derisive attacks that preceded it. Modern medicine treats unborn children as patients. Mothers are advised to calm the fetus with music. Some say that Mozart is particularly soothing. Isn't there enough evidence for even skeptics to admit that those who assert the personhood of the fetus may be right? And if we are to err, shouldn't it be on the side of life? I believe it's time the law caught up with science.

Now, I'm going to ask your support on a few things. We have sent up to Congress the prolife bill. It states that abortion is the taking of a human life and stops all Federal funding of abortion by making the Hyde amendment permanent. It needs your support, and it deserves your support.

We will soon publish regulations that will cut off Federal family planning funds from abortion-related activities. The law prohibits using title X money to encourage or promote abortion in any way. Yet under the current guidelines, title X programs must offer abortion counseling and referrals. It has been argued that this is evenhanded, a way of ensuring that young women are presented with all options. But that's not how it's worked out. Too often, the same title X funded programs that give referrals have financial ties to programs that perform abortions. In practice, young women using their services have sometimes been led to believe that abortion is their best, if not their only option. As one young woman reported recently in a comment on our new regulations: "I was not given a complete picture [by the family planning clinic]. . . . The decision I made for abortion was no decision at all. It was a coercion."

Well, our new regulations will put an end to this conflict of interest in cases where title X funds are involved. They will prohibit using title X money for any program that performs abortions, or counsels or refers for abortions, or promotes abortion through the media, the courts, or anyplace else. They will require family planning programs to be both financially and physically separate from facilities that use abortion as a method of family planning—no mingling of silver. We are getting title X back to Congress' original intent: reducing the number of abortions. But as you know, original intent is controversial these days. We'll need your help in defending these regulations.

Now, before I hang up, let me suggest that we all take a moment for a silent prayer—prayer for wisdom and, since ours is a merciful cause, that we ourselves will know mercy for the suffering of women who have had abortions and for the troubled mind with which so many Americans meditate on this issue. Shall we pray?

[*At this point, the participants prayed silently.*]

Amen.

Good luck, and God bless you all.

Miss Gray. We thank you, Mr. President. And we want to join with you, and we will work to perfect those bills. We also want to include in our prayers and our silent prayers the prisoners of conscience who are in the jails because they have tried to stop the abortions, and we are sorry that Joan Andrews is not with us today. Thank you, Mr. President.

The President. Thank you all. God bless you.

Note: The President spoke at 12:02 p.m. from the Oval Office via a loudspeaker hookup with the rally site. Participants had gathered on the Ellipse for a march to the Supreme Court on the 15th anniversary of the Court's decision in "Roe v. Wade," which legalized abortion. Nellie Gray was president of March for Life. In her closing remarks, she referred to Joan Andrews, who was convicted in Florida of illegal antiabortion activities.

Remarks to Civic Leaders at a White House Briefing on Aid to the Nicaraguan Democratic Resistance
January 22, 1988

Well, good afternoon, and welcome to the White House. I know that you're going to be briefed today on the situation in Central America, so I thought I'd use our time together not in giving you a great deal of background but, very simply, to tell you why I asked the Congress to provide aid to the Nicaraguan democratic resistance, the freedom fighters. Providing aid to the freedom fighters will do much to decide whether the people of Nicaragua ever possess the liberty that we Americans cherish so much. What I'd like to do is tell you four stories—and they're four true stories. Among them, I believe, they express everything that needs to be said.

The setting for the first is Managua itself. The date was just 12 days ago, Sunday, January 10th. The event was a march by 10,000 people through the streets of the Nicaraguan capital to mark the 10th anniversary of the death of newspaper publisher Pedro Joaquin Chamorro. Chamorro was killed by gunmen—gunmen believed to have been supporters of the former dictator, Anastasio Somoza. Yet instead of celebrating the Sandinista regime that overthrew Somoza, the marchers demonstrated against the Communist regime. There were chants of "Communists, get out!" One speaker told the crowd, "The people aren't afraid anymore." Another said, "This is the beginning of democracy, and it can't end today."

By a week ago Sunday, when this march took place, it had been a full 8½ years since the Marxist Sandinistas had overthrown Somoza and established their own regime. We in the United States rightly ask whether the Sandinistas have the support of the Nicaraguan people, and 8½ years is certainly long enough for a people to get to know the true nature of their rulers. Those 10,000 marchers answered our question. Rejection of the Communist regime is not, as some would have it, limited to a few reactionary holdovers from the Somoza years. It runs deep—very deep—among the people themselves. When you hear the second story I'd like to share with you, I think you'll begin to understand why.

In 1984 Prudencio Baltodano was captured by Sandinista soldiers. His crime? He was an evangelical minister, a man of God. The soldiers bound him to a tree, beat him, then used a bayonet to cut off his ears and slit his throat. The soldiers' commander told them Baltodano wasn't "worth wasting a bullet." "Let him die suffering," the commander said. As they left him bleeding, the soldiers taunted him, "Pray and see if God will save you."

Well, God did save Prudencio Baltodano, and just last week he was reunited in Washington, here, with his wife and six children. You see, a church in Gaithersburg, Maryland, has sponsored Reverend Baltodano and his family. The church and some other American friends worked to get his wife and children here to the United States from a refugee camp in Costa Rica, to provide them with clothing, and to help them find housing. To me, the help Mr. Baltodano and his family are being given here in the United States is just as important a part of the story as the suffering they endured in Central America. It reminds us that when we see someone in trouble, when we see someone suffering, we Americans reach out to help. And I'm delighted to see Reverend Baltodano here with us. Welcome!

Well, the people in Nicaragua need our help. That's the meaning of this coming congressional vote. For there can be no doubt that under the Sandinistas the people of Nicaragua are suffering—suffering from the suppression of civil liberties, suffering materially from a national economy that has collapsed under Communist interference and control. It's my firm belief that these are grounds enough for helping the freedom fighters: that when our nation sees neighbors who need help and when it's within our power to extend that help, then it is our duty to do so. Yet as I tell you the third story, you'll see that there is still another reason for us to assist the freedom fighters of Nicaragua. Simply put, the security of Central America and our own nation is at stake.

On October 25th of last year, a high-level member of the Sandinista staff entered the American Embassy in Mexico City and requested political asylum. Major Roger Miranda had been a top aide to Humberto Ortega. Humberto Ortega is in charge of the Sandinista military and the brother of the President, Daniel Ortega, the leader of the Communist regime in Nicaragua. American officials spent weeks debriefing Major Miranda. And then, last December, he was interviewed by a number of news organizations. When the Sandinistas learned that Major Miranda's revelations would be made public, they apparently decided that they had nothing to lose by admitting to them. At a gathering in Managua, Humberto Ortega confirmed some of Major Miranda's most damaging disclosures.

Item: In Ortega's own words, Nicaragua has "a few thousand officers in Cuba and the Soviet Union studying the use of sophisticated weapons."

Item: The Sandinista Communists are training Salvadoran rebels in Managua to use surface-to-air missiles, missiles that could sharply escalate the violence in that country.

Item: The Communists in Nicaragua have made secret agreements with the Soviet Union, Cuba, and East-bloc nations. Major Miranda stated, and Humberto Ortega publicly confirmed, that these pacts call for the Soviet Union and its satellites to help the Sandinistas arm and train 600,000 army troops and civilian militia by the mid-1990's.

Permit me to put that figure into perspective. Six hundred thousand troops will represent one-fifth of the entire population of Nicaragua. It will be as if the United States had Armed Forces of nearly 49 million. But the comparisons with other nations in Central America are more significant. Nicaragua's neighbor to the north, El Salvador, has a population of 5 million, but a military of only some 43,000. Honduras has a population of over 4½ million, a military of only 14,600. Costa Rica, Nicaragua's neighbor to the south, has a population of 2.6 million and no armed forces. Even Mexico, with a population of over 80 million—by far the largest nation in the region—even Mexico has a military of only some 140,000, less than one-fourth the force of 600,000 that the Communists of Nicaragua plan to have in a matter of only a few years.

The meaning of what Major Miranda and Humberto Ortega have stated is clear. The Communist regime in Nicaragua represents a threat to the entire region of Central America. And if it represents a threat to the region that adjoins our southern borders, it represents a threat to us. Already, hundreds of thousands of Nicaraguan refugees have left their country. It is by no means difficult to visualize a situation in which hundreds of thousands of Central Americans seek to escape violence and instability by streaming toward the American Southwest.

My fourth story occurred just last weekend, when the leaders of the five Central American nations met to examine compliance with the Guatemala accord. There's no doubt as to their conclusion: The Sandinistas are the biggest obstacle to fulfillment of the plan and to peace and democracy in the region. While the four Central American democracies are in substantial compliance, the Sandinistas are nowhere near. Even the Sandinistas had to admit as much, issuing a separate declaration that outlined additional steps they felt compelled to announce so as to put their behavior in a better light.

It is clear, as you can see, why we must keep the pressure on the Sandinistas so that they can't reverse course, so that they keep walking down that road to democracy, because each step they've taken, each reluctant reform, is still easily undone. The Sandinistas have said their revolution will spread. Our goal in Nicaragua must be to make sure it's democracy and freedom that spreads.

We welcome the Sandinistas' new promises to abide by the peace plan, but we must hold them to their word. We must make sure that each time the Sandinistas walk through a new door toward democracy we close it behind them—and keep it closed. Only the freedom fighters can do that; only they can be our insurance policy for democracy in Central America.

And let me add something else: Once a cease-fire is in place in Nicaragua and significant progress is being made toward a real and lasting political settlement, the United States is prepared to join in regional security discussions. Our goal is the same as those democracies we've seen emerge in the other Central American countries, the same as those who've been fighting for the freedom they were promised 8½ years ago: an opportunity for all people in that region to have the right to peace, freedom, and democracy.

Some say that the freedom fighters are not necessary to keep the pressure on, that the spotlight of world opinion and the Sandinistas' sworn commitment to the Guatemala accord are enough. Well, perhaps it's worth reviewing the historical record to see just how much faith we can put in Sandinista promises. As I pointed out in my recent address to the Organization of American States, we already have a negotiated settlement with the Sandinistas—the settlement of 1979—in which the United States, together with the other members of the OAS, took the unprecedented action of withdrawing recognition from a sitting government—the Somoza government—and helped bring the Sandinistas to power. As part of that settlement, the Sandinistas promised—and I'm citing from documents issued by the Sandinistas—"free elections, a broad-based democratic government, full guarantee of human rights, fundamental liberties, freedom of religion, union rights, a mixed economy, an independent foreign policy of nonalignment, and a minimum permanent military corps."

Well, it's simply stating the obvious to point out that the Sandinistas have not honored a single one of those promises that they made to all the other states of North and South America. What isn't as widely understood, however, is that we now have documented proof that they never intended to. Barely 2 months after assuming power, the Sandinista leadership met secretly to draft a report known as the 72-hour document, outlining their plans to establish a Communist dictatorship in Nicaragua and spread subversion throughout Central America.

The Sandinistas and their supporters say it was the belligerence of the United States that forced them to go back on their promises, just as they now put all the blame for their shortcomings on the freedom fighters. Well, again, let's examine the historical record—our belligerence.

Only a day after the Sandinistas finished meeting secretly to draft the 72-hour document, President Carter received Daniel Ortega in the White House and offered his new government our friendship and help. But while we sent the Sandinistas over $100 million in aid—more than they received from any other country at that time—the Sandinistas were busy carrying out their plans to eliminate human rights and impose a Marxist totalitarian regime in Nicaragua.

Six months after the meeting in the White House, while U.S. aid was still flowing, several Sandinista comandantes took their first official trip to Moscow—the first of many—and signed a communique with the Soviet Communist Party expressing support for the foreign policy goals of the Soviet Union. But that, one might say, was merely the paperwork. Already, Soviet military planners were in Nicaragua. Over 30 new military bases were either built or in the process of construction by the time I came into office in 1981. The Sandinista army was becoming the largest, best supplied in all Central America, and the Sandinistas were already assisting the Communist guerrillas in El Salvador—all while American aid flowed to Nicaragua, while our hand was extended in friendship.

Well, I could go on to detail the systematic crushing of all human rights, but my purpose here is to ask a simple question: How can we expect a regime that has compiled such a history of broken promises and corruption to abide by the terms of the Guatemala accord unless we keep up the pressure by continuing the aid to the freedom fighters?

Some in this country talk as if the Sandinistas would reform if we would just let them alone, but that's not what the Sandinistas themselves say. Just 5 weeks ago, Daniel Ortega made his true intentions clear: Even if there were elections in Nicaragua and the Sandinistas lost, he said, they would never give up power. The Soviets have made their choice. They and the allies have poured billions of dollars of military aid into Nicaragua—at least 20 times more than the U.S. Congress has given to the forces of the democratic resistance.

In less than 2 weeks, the American Congress and the American people will have to make their choice, too. As I said, this is the moment of truth, the make-or-break vote on the freedom fighters. If we abandon them now, if Congress votes down aid, we will be abandoning the only real cause for peace and freedom and democracy in Nicaragua.

We have the testimony of brave men and women who are speaking to us of things they've seen and heard, the testimony of the 10,000 who marched in Nicaragua, of Prudencio Baltodano and Major Miranda. The freedom fighters are fighting for all of these and, yes, for us, for our own security.

Now let us move to help them. Thank you, and God bless you all.

Note: The President spoke at 2:03 p.m. in the East Room at the White House.

Radio Address to the Nation on Administration Goals
January 23, 1988

My fellow Americans:

This week was the start of the eighth year of my Presidency. And so, as we all do at the beginning of a new year, I'd like to take a few minutes to look ahead at some of the challenges before our nation this year.

By the way, I'll be doing a lot more looking ahead on Monday night, when I'll go up to Capitol Hill to deliver the annual State of the Union Address. The State of the Union is the only statement that the Constitution itself requires the President to give. Almost all Presidents since Woodrow Wilson have delivered States of the Union in person, not just sent up written messages. This will be my seventh time. And let me tell you, the thrill of standing in that place where so many great Presidents have stood and of continuing a tradition that stretches back to George Washington and signifies our determination that, as Lincoln said, a government of, by, and for the people shall not perish from the Earth—well, that thrill never goes away. I'm looking forward to Monday night. I hope you'll tune in.

As I'll tell Congress then, we in Washington have a lot of work ahead of us—for starters, preserving the economic growth of the past 5 years. Last week we had good news on this front. Our trade deficit dropped by 25 percent, but more importantly our exports, which have been climbing for more than a year, shot forward nearly 10 percent in 1 month and reached the highest levels in American history. Yes, American industry is in an export boom, and our economy is strong—in fact, it's the envy of the world.

But we all know that there are still unanswered questions in our economic future—the biggest: Are we going to keep working to reduce our budget deficit? The administration and Congress have made progress, in the Gramm-Rudman-Hollings legislation and in this year's budget compromise, but we need to do more. On Monday I'll remind Congress of some good ideas that are past due for action, like the line-item veto and a balanced budget amendment. And I may have a surprise, too, a way, right now, for Congress to show it's serious about putting the Government's house in order.

No issue that we will take up in the year ahead is more significant than the issue of peace with freedom, whether in this hemisphere or around the world. On Monday I will formally submit to the Senate for advice and consent to ratify the Intermediate Nuclear Forces treaty that General Secretary Gorbachev and I signed in December. It's a good treaty, a solid one with the most extensive verification provisions in history. It will make America and its allies more secure. Monday evening I will remind the Congress that this step toward enduring peace with freedom would never have come if the forces of democracy hadn't been strong, and I'll ask for expeditious Senate action.

In Central America, the key to peace with freedom is also in the strength of the democratic forces. Some say if you're for aid to the freedom fighters in Nicaragua you're against the peace process. Phooey! Even the Sandinistas admit they're talking peace and democracy because of the freedom fighters. Yet to date, the Sandinistas haven't gone through with one concession to democratize that they can't easily reverse once the pressure of the freedom fighters is off. At stake here is whether Nicaragua becomes a Soviet base camp on the mainland of this hemisphere. Imagine if the Sandinista vision of a Communist Central America is realized and Mexico is threatened. The next vote on aid to the freedom fighters may be the most important this Congress casts. On Monday I'll ask Congress to vote yes.

There are great challenges and opportunities in the year ahead. On Monday I will also talk about continuing to bring greater excellence to education. I'll mention ways to raise the quality of our schools. But I'll remind Congress that the most important thing is not to throw quantities of money at education but to tie funding to results and to have a commitment to quality and to State and local control of schools.

So, that's a glimpse of the year ahead. And as I said, you'll hear more Monday night. That's the Nation's future, but let me turn for a minute to something more personal. You may have read about Tabatha Foster. She's 3 years old, was born with a severe birth defect, and recently, in an operating room in Pittsburgh, received five new organs. It will take time and money, as much as $1 million, to return Tabatha to full health. Her parents have exhausted their medical insurance, so a Tabatha Foster Fund has been set up to help them. I know you join me in praying that Tabatha will someday be able to lead a normal life.

Until next week, thanks for listening, and God bless you. And God bless Tabatha Foster.

Note: The President spoke at 12:06 p.m. from Camp David, MD.

Statement by Assistant to the President for Press Relations Fitzwater on the Innovative Emissions Control Technologies Program

January 23, 1988

The President has instructed his advisers to continue discussions with their Canadian counterparts toward completion of a bilateral air quality accord. He reiterated his commitment to implement the recommendations of the 1986 Special Envoys' report, committing fully to proceeding with the Innovative Control Technologies Program.

The Innovative Control Technologies Program is a 5-year, joint Federal and industry $5 billion effort to encourage the development and deployment of innovative technologies designed to reduce powerplant emissions that are thought to cause acid rain. The President will request the full amount of the Federal Government's share in this program.

Additionally, the President has accepted the recommendations of his Task Force on Regulatory Relief, chaired by the Vice President. These recommendations are designed to eliminate regulatory barriers to the deployment of innovative emissions control technologies and to other cost-effective emissions reductions measures. The specific recommendations of the Task Force are:

• Preferential treatment, under the Innovative Control Technologies Program, for projects in States that, for ratemaking purposes, treat innovative technologies the same as pollution control projects. This treatment would recognize the additional risk inherent in demonstration of innovative technologies.

• A Federal Energy Regulatory Commission (FERC) 5-year demonstration program allowing rate incentives for innovative technologies. This would also recognize the risk inherent in demonstration of innovative technologies. FERC already provides this type of incentive in certain circumstances.

• The Environmental Protection Agency (1) encourages the States to consider achieving greater ozone reduction through interpollutant trading and other measures that substitute less expensive nitrogen oxide emissions reductions for more expensive volatile organic compound emissions reductions, (2) encourage the use of "bubbles" between recently built emissions sources, (3) expand commercial demonstration permits for innovative control technologies, and (4) encourage complementary use of emissions "bubbles" and waivers for innovative technology applications.

Message to the Senate Transmitting the Soviet-United States Intermediate-Range Nuclear Forces Treaty

January 25, 1988

To the Senate of the United States:

I am transmitting herewith, for the advice and consent of the Senate to ratification, the Treaty between the United States of America and the Union of Soviet Socialist Republics on the Elimination of Their Intermediate-Range and Shorter-Range Missiles (the Treaty). The Treaty includes the following documents, which are integral parts thereof: the Memorandum of Understanding (the MOU) regarding the establishment of a data base, the Protocol on Elimination governing the elimination of missile systems, and the Protocol on Inspection regarding the conduct of inspections, with an Annex to that Protocol on the privileges and immunities to be accorded inspectors and aircrew members. The Treaty, together with the MOU and the two Protocols, was signed at Washington on December 8,

1987. The Report of the Department of State on the Treaty is provided for the information of the Senate.

In addition, I am transmitting herewith, for the information of the Senate, the Agreement Among the United States of America and the Kingdom of Belgium, the Federal Republic of Germany, the Republic of Italy, the Kingdom of the Netherlands, and the United Kingdom of Great Britain and Northern Ireland Regarding Inspections Relating to the Treaty Between the United States of America and the Union of Soviet Socialist Republics on the Elimination of Their Intermediate-Range and Shorter-Range Missiles (the Basing Country Agreement), which was signed at Brussels on December 11, 1987. The Basing Country Agreement confirms that the inspections called for in the Treaty will be permitted by the five Allied Basing Countries. The Report of the Department of State discusses in detail the terms of the Basing Country Agreement. Also attached for the information of the Senate are the notes exchanged between both the German Democratic Republic and Czechoslovakia and the United States. The notes acknowledge that these countries agree to the United States' conducting inspections, under the Treaty, on their territory. Identical notes also are being exchanged between the Soviet Union and the five Allied Basing Countries.

The Treaty is an unprecedented arms control agreement in several respects. It marks the first time that the United States and the Soviet Union have agreed to eliminate, throughout the world, an entire class of their missile systems. Significantly, the eliminations will be achieved from markedly asymmetrical starting points that favored the Soviet Union. The Treaty includes provisions for comprehensive on-site inspections, including the continuous monitoring of certain facilities, to aid in verifying compliance. To a much greater extent than in earlier arms control agreements between the United States and the Soviet Union, detailed information has been, and will continue to be, exchanged by the Parties in order to facilitate verification of compliance. Finally, the United States and the Soviet Union have agreed on cooperative measures to enhance verification by national technical means.

The missile systems to be eliminated consist of all U.S. and Soviet ground-launched ballistic missiles and ground-launched cruise missiles having a range capability between 500 and 5500 kilometers. The launchers for such missiles and unique elements of their related support structures and support equipment also will be eliminated. The shorter-range missiles to be eliminated under this Treaty are those with a range capability between 500 and 1000 kilometers. They must be eliminated within 18 months after the entry into force of the Treaty. Intermediate-range missiles, having a range capability between 1000 and 5500 kilometers, are to be eliminated in two phases within three years after entry into force of the Treaty. Elimination will take place at designated locations and will be subject to on-site inspection as an aid to verifying compliance.

In the MOU, the United States and the Soviet Union have provided detailed information on the location of all missiles, launchers, and related support structures and support equipment subject to the Treaty. Each Party is required to provide updated data on a routine basis after the Treaty enters into force.

The Treaty provides that on-site inspections are permitted at specified locations in the United States and the Soviet Union as well as in the Basing Countries in Western and Eastern Europe where U.S. or Soviet missiles, launchers, and related support structures and support equipment subject to the Treaty are or have been located. The different types of "short-notice" on-site inspections for which the Treaty provides are designed to contribute to our ability to verify Soviet compliance, while protecting all U.S. and Allied nuclear and conventional forces not subject to the Treaty as well as other sensitive intelligence and defense facilities.

In addition to "short-notice" on-site inspections, the Treaty provides for other types of on-site inspections, including the continuous presence of U.S. inspectors at the Soviet facility at Votkinsk, at which SS–25 and SS–20 missiles have been assembled, and a continuous Soviet presence at the identified facility at Hercules Plant #1, located at Magna, Utah, at which stages of Pershing II missiles formerly were produced.

The Treaty is the culmination of six years of negotiations with the Soviet Union. To a large extent, the Treaty is the result of Allied solidarity in support of the fundamental objectives established by NATO's "dual-track" decision in 1979. Our Atlantic and our Asian and Pacific Allies have been closely involved throughout the period of negotiation, and they fully support the Treaty. The Treaty enhances our collective security by eliminating an entire class of Soviet missile systems that has been a major concern for over a decade. Our European Allies will continue to be well protected by the significant U.S. nuclear forces remaining in Europe, by the independent British and French nuclear deterrents, and by conventional forces, which include over 300,000 U.S. troops.

I believe that the Treaty is in the best interests of the United States and represents an important step in achieving arms reductions that strengthen U.S. and Allied security. Therefore, I urge the Senate's advice and consent to its ratification.

RONALD REAGAN

The White House,
January 25, 1988.

Statement by Assistant to the President for Press Relations Fitzwater on the Soviet-United States Intermediate-Range Nuclear Forces Treaty

January 25, 1988

The President today transmitted the INF treaty to the Senate for its advice and consent to ratification. The treaty, together with its Memorandum of Understanding on Data and Protocols on Elimination and Inspection, was signed on December 8, 1987, by the President and General Secretary Gorbachev.

The INF treaty, when fully implemented, will substantially increase the security of the United States and our European and Asian friends and allies. By eliminating all Soviet ground-launched INF missile systems, a substantial element of the Soviet military threat and an instrument for political pressure and intimidation will have been removed.

The INF treaty, with its asymmetric reductions favoring the United States, provides the first necessary step toward a more secure and stable balance of military forces between the United States and the Soviet Union, which will benefit all mankind. The treaty demonstrates the rewards of negotiating from a position of strength and with the firm support of our allies.

Designation of George R. Salem as a Member of the Board of Directors of the Overseas Private Investment Corporation

January 25, 1988

The President today designated George R. Salem to serve as a member of the Board of Directors of the Overseas Private Investment Corporation, U.S. International Development Cooperation Agency. He would succeed Robert W. Searby.

Since 1986 Mr. Salem has been Solicitor for the Department of Labor in Washington, DC, and Deputy Solicitor, 1985–1986. Previously he was a partner with the law firm of Thompson, Mann and Hutson.

Mr. Salem graduated from Emory College (B.A., 1975), Emory University School of Law (J.D., 1977), and Georgetown University Law Center (L.L.M., 1984). He was born December 24, 1953, in Jacksonville, FL. He is married, has two children, and resides in Springfield, VA.

Address Before a Joint Session of Congress on the State of the Union
January 25, 1988

Mr. Speaker, Mr. President, and distinguished Members of the House and Senate:

When we first met here 7 years ago—many of us for the first time—it was with the hope of beginning something new for America. We meet here tonight in this historic Chamber to continue that work. If anyone expects just a proud recitation of the accomplishments of my administration, I say let's leave that to history; we're not finished yet. So, my message to you tonight is put on your workshoes; we're still on the job.

History records the power of the ideas that brought us here those 7 years ago—ideas like the individual's right to reach as far and as high as his or her talents will permit; the free market as an engine of economic progress. And as an ancient Chinese philosopher, Lao-tzu, said: "Govern a great nation as you would cook a small fish; do not overdo it." [*Laughter*] Well, these ideas were part of a larger notion, a vision, if you will, of America herself—an America not only rich in opportunity for the individual but an America, too, of strong families and vibrant neighborhoods; an America whose divergent but harmonizing communities were a reflection of a deeper community of values: the value of work, of family, of religion, and of the love of freedom that God places in each of us and whose defense He has entrusted in a special way to this nation.

All of this was made possible by an idea I spoke of when Mr. Gorbachev was here—the belief that the most exciting revolution ever known to humankind began with three simple words: "We the People," the revolutionary notion that the people grant government its rights, and not the other way around. And there's one lesson that has come home powerfully to me, which I would offer to you now. Just as those who created this Republic pledged to each other their lives, their fortunes, and their sacred honor, so, too, America's leaders today must pledge to each other that we will keep foremost in our hearts and minds not what is best for ourselves or for our party but what is best for America.

In the spirit of Jefferson, let us affirm that in this Chamber tonight there are no Republicans, no Democrats—just Americans. Yes, we will have our differences, but let us always remember what unites us far outweighs whatever divides us. Those who sent us here to serve them—the millions of Americans watching and listening tonight—expect this of us. Let's prove to them and to ourselves that democracy works even in an election year. We've done this before. And as we have worked together to bring down spending, tax rates, and inflation, employment has climbed to record heights; America has created more jobs and better, higher paying jobs; family income has risen for 4 straight years, and America's poor climbed out of poverty at the fastest rate in more than 10 years.

Our record is not just the longest peacetime expansion in history but an economic and social revolution of hope based on work, incentives, growth, and opportunity; a revolution of compassion that led to private sector initiatives and a 77-percent increase in charitable giving; a revolution that at a critical moment in world history reclaimed and restored the American dream.

In international relations, too, there's only one description for what, together, we have achieved: a complete turnabout, a revolution. Seven years ago, America was weak, and freedom everywhere was under siege.

Today America is strong, and democracy is everywhere on the move. From Central America to East Asia, ideas like free markets and democratic reforms and human rights are taking hold. We've replaced "Blame America" with "Look up to America." We've rebuilt our defenses. And of all our accomplishments, none can give us more satisfaction than knowing that our young people are again proud to wear our country's uniform.

And in a few moments, I'm going to talk about three developments—arms reduction, the Strategic Defense Initiative, and the global democratic revolution—that, when taken together, offer a chance none of us would have dared imagine 7 years ago, a chance to rid the world of the two great nightmares of the postwar era. I speak of the startling hope of giving our children a future free of both totalitarianism and nuclear terror.

Tonight, then, we're strong, prosperous, at peace, and we are free. This is the state of our Union. And if we will work together this year, I believe we can give a future President and a future Congress the chance to make that prosperity, that peace, that freedom not just the state of our Union but the state of our world.

Toward this end, we have four basic objectives tonight. First, steps we can take this year to keep our economy strong and growing, to give our children a future of low inflation and full employment. Second, let's check our progress in attacking social problems, where important gains have been made, but which still need critical attention. I mean schools that work, economic independence for the poor, restoring respect for family life and family values. Our third objective tonight is global: continuing the exciting economic and democratic revolutions we've seen around the world. Fourth and finally, our nation has remained at peace for nearly a decade and a half, as we move toward our goals of world prosperity and world freedom. We must protect that peace and deter war by making sure the next President inherits what you and I have a moral obligation to give that President: a national security that is unassailable and a national defense that takes full advantage of new technology and is fully funded.

This is a full agenda. It's meant to be. You see, my thinking on the next year is quite simple: Let's make this the best of 8. And that means it's all out—right to the finish line. I don't buy the idea that this is the last year of anything, because we're not talking here tonight about registering temporary gains but ways of making permanent our successes. And that's why our focus is the values, the principles, and ideas that made America great. Let's be clear on this point. We're for limited government, because we understand, as the Founding Fathers did, that it is the best way of ensuring personal liberty and empowering the individual so that every American of every race and region shares fully in the flowering of American prosperity and freedom.

One other thing we Americans like—the future—like the sound of it, the idea of it, the hope of it. Where others fear trade and economic growth, we see opportunities for creating new wealth and undreamed-of opportunities for millions in our own land and beyond. Where others seek to throw up barriers, we seek to bring them down. Where others take counsel of their fears, we follow our hopes. Yes, we Americans like the future and like making the most of it. Let's do that now.

And let's begin by discussing how to maintain economic growth by controlling and eventually eliminating the problem of Federal deficits. We have had a balanced budget only eight times in the last 57 years. For the first time in 14 years, the Federal Government spent less in real terms last year than the year before. We took $73 billion off last year's deficit compared to the year before. The deficit itself has moved from 6.3 percent of the gross national product to only 3.4 percent. And perhaps the most important sign of progress has been the change in our view of deficits. You know, a few of us can remember when, not too many years ago, those who created the deficits said they would make us prosperous and not to worry about the debt, because we owe it to ourselves. Well, at last there is agreement that we can't spend ourselves rich.

Our recent budget agreement, designed to reduce Federal deficits by $76 billion over the next 2 years, builds on this consensus. But this agreement must be adhered to without slipping into the errors of the past: more broken promises and more unchecked spending. As I indicated in my first State of the Union, what ails us can be simply put: The Federal Government is too big, and it spends too much money. I can assure you, the bipartisan leadership of Congress, of my help in fighting off any attempt to bust our budget agreement. And this includes the swift and certain use of the veto power.

Now, it's also time for some plain talk about the most immediate obstacle to controlling Federal deficits. The simple but frustrating problem of making expenses match revenues—something American families do and the Federal Government can't—has caused crisis after crisis in this city. Mr. Speaker, Mr. President, I will say to you tonight what I have said before and will continue to say: The budget process has broken down; it needs a drastic overhaul. With each ensuing year, the spectacle before the American people is the same as it was this Christmas: budget deadlines delayed or missed completely, monstrous continuing resolutions that pack hundreds of billions of dollars worth of spending into one bill, and a Federal Government on the brink of default.

I know I'm echoing what you here in the Congress have said, because you suffered so directly. But let's recall that in 7 years, of 91 appropriations bills scheduled to arrive on my desk by a certain date, only 10 made it on time. Last year, of the 13 appropriations bills due by October 1st, none of them made it. Instead, we had four continuing resolutions lasting 41 days, then 36 days, and 2 days, and 3 days, respectively.

And then, along came these behemoths. This is the conference report—1,053 pages, report weighing 14 pounds. Then this—a reconciliation bill 6 months late that was 1,186 pages long, weighing 15 pounds. And the long-term continuing resolution—this one was 2 months late, and it's 1,057 pages long, weighing 14 pounds. That was a total of 43 pounds of paper and ink. You had 3 hours—yes, 3 hours—to consider each, and it took 300 people at my Office of Management and Budget just to read the bill so the Government wouldn't shut down. Congress shouldn't send another one of these. No, and if you do, I will not sign it.

Let's change all this. Instead of a Presidential budget that gets discarded and a congressional budget resolution that is not enforced, why not a simple partnership, a joint agreement that sets out the spending priorities within the available revenues? And let's remember our deadline is October 1st, not Christmas. Let's get the people's work done in time to avoid a footrace with Santa Claus. [*Laughter*] And, yes, this year—to coin a phrase—a new beginning: 13 individual bills, on time and fully reviewed by Congress.

I'm also certain you join me in saying: Let's help ensure our future of prosperity by giving the President a tool that, though I will not get to use it, is one I know future Presidents of either party must have. Give the President the same authority that 43 Governors use in their States: the right to reach into massive appropriation bills, pare away the waste, and enforce budget discipline. Let's approve the line-item veto.

And let's take a partial step in this direction. Most of you in this Chamber didn't know what was in this catchall bill and report. Over the past few weeks, we've all learned what was tucked away behind a little comma here and there. For example, there's millions for items such as cranberry research, blueberry research, the study of crawfish, and the commercialization of wildflowers. And that's not to mention the five or so million [$.5 million] that—so that people from developing nations could come here to watch Congress at work. [*Laughter*] I won't even touch that. [*Laughter*] So, tonight I offer you this challenge. In 30 days I will send back to you those items as rescissions, which if I had the authority to line them out I would do so.

Now, review this multibillion-dollar package that will not undercut our bipartisan budget agreement. As a matter of fact, if adopted, it will improve our deficit reduction goals. And what an example we can set, that we're serious about getting our financial accounts in order. By acting and approving this plan, you have the opportunity to override a congressional process that is out of control.

There is another vital reform. Yes, Gramm-Rudman-Hollings has been profoundly helpful, but let us take its goal of a balanced budget and make it permanent. Let us do now what so many States do to hold down spending and what 32 State legislatures have asked us to do. Let us heed the wishes of an overwhelming plurality of Americans and pass a constitutional amendment that mandates a balanced budget and forces the Federal Government to live within its means. Reform of the budget process—including the line-item veto and balanced budget amendment—will, together with real restraint on government spending, prevent the Federal budget from ever again ravaging the family budget.

Let's ensure that the Federal Government never again legislates against the family and the home. Last September I signed an Executive order on the family requiring that every department and agency review its activities in light of seven standards designed to promote and not harm the family. But let us make certain that the family is always at the center of the public policy process not just in this administration but in all future administrations. It's time for Congress to consider, at the beginning, a statement of the impact that legislation will have on the basic unit of American society, the family.

And speaking of the family, let's turn to a matter on the mind of every American parent tonight: education. We all know the sorry story of the sixties and seventies—soaring spending, plummeting test scores—and that hopeful trend of the eighties, when we replaced an obsession with dollars with a commitment to quality, and test scores started back up. There's a lesson here that we all should write on the blackboard a hundred times: In a child's education, money can never take the place of basics like discipline, hard work, and, yes, homework.

As a nation we do, of course, spend heavily on education—more than we spend on defense. Yet across our country, Governors like New Jersey's Tom Kean are giving classroom demonstrations that how we spend is as important as how much we spend. Opening up the teaching profession to all qualified candidates, merit pay—so that good teachers get A's as well as apples—and stronger curriculum, as Secretary Bennett has proposed for high schools—these imaginative reforms are making common sense the most popular new kid in America's schools. How can we help? Well, we can talk about and push for these reforms. But the most important thing we can do is to reaffirm that control of our schools belongs to the States, local communities and, most of all, to the parents and teachers.

My friends, some years ago, the Federal Government declared war on poverty, and poverty won. [*Laughter*] Today the Federal Government has 59 major welfare programs and spends more than $100 billion a year on them. What has all this money done? Well, too often it has only made poverty harder to escape. Federal welfare programs have created a massive social problem. With the best of intentions, government created a poverty trap that wreaks havoc on the very support system the poor need most to lift themselves out of poverty: the family. Dependency has become the one enduring heirloom, passed from one generation to the next, of too many fragmented families.

It is time—this may be the most radical thing I've said in 7 years in this office—it's time for Washington to show a little humility. There are a thousand sparks of genius in 50 States and a thousand communities around the Nation. It is time to nurture them and see which ones can catch fire and become guiding lights. States have begun to show us the way. They've demonstrated that successful welfare programs can be built around more effective child support enforcement practices and innovative programs requiring welfare recipients to work or prepare for work. Let us give the States more flexibility and encourage more reforms. Let's start making our welfare system the first rung on America's ladder of opportunity, a boost up from dependency, not a graveyard but a birthplace of hope.

And now let me turn to three other matters vital to family values and the quality of family life. The first is an untold American success story. Recently, we released our annual survey of what graduating high school seniors have to say about drugs. Cocaine use is declining, and marijuana use was the lowest since surveying began. We can be proud that our students are just saying no to drugs. But let us remember what this menace requires: commitment from every part of America and every single American, a commitment to a drug-free America. The war against drugs is a war of individual battles, a crusade with many heroes, including America's young people and also someone very special to me. She has helped so many of our young people to say no to drugs. Nancy, much credit belongs to you, and I want to express to you your husband's pride and your country's thanks. Surprised you, didn't I? [*Laughter*]

Well, now we come to a family issue that we must have the courage to confront. Tonight, I call America—a good nation, a moral people—to charitable but realistic consideration of the terrible cost of abortion on demand. To those who say this violates a woman's right to control of her own body: Can they deny that now medical evidence confirms the unborn child is a living human being entitled to life, liberty, and the pursuit of happiness? Let us unite as a nation and protect the unborn with legislation that would stop all Federal funding for abortion and with a human life amendment making, of course, an exception where the unborn child threatens the life of the mother. Our Judeo-Christian tradition recognizes the right of taking a life in self-defense. But with that one exception, let us look to those others in our land who cry out for children to adopt. I pledge to you tonight I will work to remove barriers to adoption and extend full sharing in family life to millions of Americans so that children who need homes can be welcomed to families who want them and love them.

And let me add here: So many of our greatest statesmen have reminded us that spiritual values alone are essential to our nation's health and vigor. The Congress opens its proceedings each day, as does the Supreme Court, with an acknowledgment of the Supreme Being. Yet we are denied the right to set aside in our schools a moment each day for those who wish to pray. I believe Congress should pass our school prayer amendment.

Now, to make sure there is a full nine-member Supreme Court to interpret the law, to protect the rights of all Americans, I urge the Senate to move quickly and decisively in confirming Judge Anthony Kennedy to the highest Court in the land and to also confirm 27 nominees now waiting to fill vacancies in the Federal judiciary.

Here then are our domestic priorities. Yet if the Congress and the administration work together, even greater opportunities lie ahead to expand a growing world economy, to continue to reduce the threat of nuclear arms, and to extend the frontiers of freedom and the growth of democratic institutions.

Our policies consistently received the strongest support of the late Congressman Dan Daniel of Virginia. I'm sure all of you join me in expressing heartfelt condolences on his passing.

One of the greatest contributions the United States can make to the world is to promote freedom as the key to economic growth. A creative, competitive America is the answer to a changing world, not trade wars that would close doors, create greater barriers, and destroy millions of jobs. We should always remember: Protectionism is destructionism. America's jobs, America's growth, America's future depend on trade—trade that is free, open, and fair.

This year, we have it within our power to take a major step toward a growing global economy and an expanding cycle of prosperity that reaches to all the free nations of this Earth. I'm speaking of the historic free trade agreement negotiated between our country and Canada. And I can also tell you that we're determined to expand this concept, south as well as north. Next month I will be traveling to Mexico, where trade matters will be of foremost concern. And over the next several months, our Congress and the Canadian Parliament can make the start of such a North American accord a reality. Our goal must be a day when the free flow of trade, from the tip of Tierra del Fuego to the Arctic Circle, unites the people of the Western Hemisphere in a bond of mutually beneficial exchange, when all borders become what the U.S.-Canadian border so long has been: a meeting place rather than a dividing line.

This movement we see in so many places toward economic freedom is indivisible from the worldwide movement toward political freedom and against totalitarian rule. This global democratic revolution has removed the specter, so frightening a decade ago, of democracy doomed to permanent minority status in the world. In South and Central America, only a third of the people enjoyed democratic rule in 1976. Today over 90 percent of Latin Americans live in nations committed to democratic principles. And the resurgence of democracy is owed to these courageous people on almost every continent who have struggled to take control of their own destiny.

In Nicaragua the struggle has extra meaning, because that nation is so near our own borders. The recent revelations of a former high-level Sandinista major, Roger Miranda, show us that, even as they talk peace, the Communist Sandinista government of Nicaragua has established plans for a large 600,000-man army. Yet even as these plans are made, the Sandinista regime knows the tide is turning, and the cause of Nicaraguan freedom is riding at its crest. Because of the freedom fighters, who are resisting Communist rule, the Sandinistas have been forced to extend some democratic rights, negotiate with church authorities, and release a few political prisoners.

The focus is on the Sandinistas, their promises and their actions. There is a consensus among the four Central American democratic Presidents that the Sandinistas have not complied with the plan to bring peace and democracy to all of Central America. The Sandinistas again have promised reforms. Their challenge is to take irreversible steps toward democracy. On Wednesday my request to sustain the freedom fighters will be submitted, which reflects our mutual desire for peace, freedom, and democracy in Nicaragua. I ask Congress to pass this request. Let us be for the people of Nicaragua what Lafayette, Pulaski, and Von Steuben were for our forefathers and the cause of American independence.

So, too, in Afghanistan, the freedom fighters are the key to peace. We support the Mujahidin. There can be no settlement unless all Soviet troops are removed and the Afghan people are allowed genuine self-determination. I have made my views on this matter known to Mr. Gorbachev. But not just Nicaragua or Afghanistan—yes, everywhere we see a swelling freedom tide across the world: freedom fighters rising up in Cambodia and Angola, fighting and dying for the same democratic liberties we hold sacred. Their cause is our cause: freedom.

Yet even as we work to expand world freedom, we must build a safer peace and reduce the danger of nuclear war. But let's have no illusions. Three years of steady decline in the value of our annual defense investment have increased the risk of our most basic security interests, jeopardizing earlier hard-won goals. We must face squarely the implications of this negative trend and make adequate, stable defense spending a top goal both this year and in the future.

This same concern applies to economic and security assistance programs as well. But the resolve of America and its NATO allies has opened the way for unprecedented achievement in arms reduction. Our recently signed INF treaty is historic, because it reduces nuclear arms and establishes the most stringent verification regime in arms control history, including several forms of short-notice, on-site inspection. I submitted the treaty today, and I urge the Senate to give its advice and consent to ratification of this landmark agreement. [*Applause*] Thank you very much.

In addition to the INF treaty, we're within reach of an even more significant START agreement that will reduce U.S. and Soviet long-range missile—or strategic arsenals by half. But let me be clear. Our approach is not to seek agreement for agreement's sake but to settle only for agreements that truly enhance our national security and that of our allies. We will never put our security at risk—or that of our allies—just to reach an agreement with the Soviets. No agreement is better than a bad agreement.

As I mentioned earlier, our efforts are to give future generations what we never had—a future free of nuclear terror. Reduction of strategic offensive arms is one step, SDI another. Our funding request for our Strategic Defense Initiative is less than 2 percent of the total defense budget. SDI funding is money wisely appropriated and money well spent. SDI has the same purpose and supports the same goals of arms reduction. It reduces the risk of war and the threat of nuclear weapons to all mankind. Strategic defenses that threaten no one could offer the world a safer, more stable basis for deterrence. We must also remember that SDI is our insurance policy against a nuclear accident, a Chernobyl of the sky, or an accidental launch or some madman who might come along.

We've seen such changes in the world in 7 years. As totalitarianism struggles to avoid being overwhelmed by the forces of economic advance and the aspiration for human freedom, it is the free nations that are resilient and resurgent. As the global democratic revolution has put totalitarianism on the defensive, we have left behind the days of retreat. America is again a vigorous leader of the free world, a nation that acts decisively and firmly in the furtherance of her principles and vital interests. No legacy would make me more proud than leaving in place a bipartisan consensus for the cause of world freedom, a consensus that prevents a paralysis of American power from ever occurring again.

But my thoughts tonight go beyond this, and I hope you'll let me end this evening with a personal reflection. You know, the world could never be quite the same again after Jacob Shallus, a trustworthy and dependable clerk of the Pennsylvania General Assembly, took his pen and engrossed those words about representative government in the preamble of our Constitution. And in a quiet but final way, the course of human events was forever altered when, on a ridge overlooking the Emmitsburg Pike in an obscure Pennsylvania town called Gettysburg, Lincoln spoke of our duty to government of and by the people and never letting it perish from the Earth.

At the start of this decade, I suggested that we live in equally momentous times, that it is up to us now to decide whether our form of government would endure and whether history still had a place of greatness for a quiet, pleasant, greening land called America. Not everything has been made perfect in 7 years, nor will it be made perfect in seven times 70 years, but before us, this year and beyond, are great prospects for the cause of peace and world freedom.

It means, too, that the young Americans I spoke of 7 years ago, as well as those who might be coming along the Virginia or Maryland shores this night and seeing for the first time the lights of this Capital City—the lights that cast their glow on our great halls of government and the monuments to the memory of our great men—it means those young Americans will find a city of hope in a land that is free.

We can be proud that for them and for us, as those lights along the Potomac are still seen this night signaling as they have for nearly two centuries and as we pray God they always will, that another generation of Americans has protected and passed on lovingly this place called America, this shining city on a hill, this government of, by, and for the people.

Thank you, and God bless you.

Note: The President spoke at 9:07 p.m. in the House Chamber of the Capitol. He was introduced by Jim Wright, Speaker of the House of Representatives. The address was broadcast live on nationwide radio and television.

1988 Legislative and Administrative Message: A Union of Individuals

January 25, 1988

To the Congress of the United States:

Introduction

In one sentence of 52 words, the Framers of our Constitution announced the proper ends of government in a free society:

"We the People of the United States, in Order to form a more perfect Union, establish Justice, insure domestic Tranquility, provide for the common defence, promote the general Welfare, and secure the Blessings of Liberty to ourselves and our Posterity, do ordain and establish this Constitution for the United States of America."

The six purposes listed in the Preamble for establishing the Constitution serve as a lasting measure of the legitimate role of government. An American President has no more sacred duty than to ensure that the government stays within the constitutional limits that protect individual liberty. In assessing this Administration's policies and proposals now and for the future, the fundamental blueprint remains the Preamble of the Constitution.

In the past 7 years, our Administration has worked to restore a vision of government that was the Founders' own—a vision of a free and self-reliant people, taking responsibility for its own welfare and progress through such time-tested means as individual initiative, neighborhood and community cooperation, and local and State self-government. The return of responsibility and authority to the individual American is now leading to a virtual renaissance in America of liberty, productivity, prosperity, and self-esteem.

Our foreign and defense policies are geared to protect American freedom against external threats, to guarantee that our liberties are secure from the aggressions of those whose values are not founded in human freedom. Protection of liberty today means not just a strong America, but also a common defense with our allies of the free world. It gives me pride to report that our mutual efforts are being rewarded with a new growth of democracy and a renewed respect around the world for this country and what it stands for. At home our challenge remains to achieve full participation in the longest peacetime economic expansion on record—in the almost unlimited prosperity which flows from genuine human freedom.

This statement of Administration policy is organized according to the six basic tenets for which the American people first ordained and established the Constitution:

I. To Form a More Perfect Union

In setting aside the Articles of Confederation for a new Constitution, the Framers acknowledged that the governmental deficiencies of the new Nation were of their own making. They understood that if the American republic were to endure and prosper, its organizing principles would have to be revised. The constitutional system the Framers produced has been the wonder of the free world, but after 200 years some aspects of that system are in need of repair and reform. Accordingly, I propose the following measures to "form a more perfect Union."

A. Balanced Budget Amendment

Before the Great Depression, the idea that the Federal government should balance its budget on a yearly basis was treated as though it were part of the Constitution. The economic crisis, and later World War II, forced the abandonment of this policy. But what may have been necessary in those national emergencies is now a permanent feature of the Federal government.

There is no question that continued Federal budget deficits, fueled by higher spending, are bad for the economy. Unfortunately, our political system makes it extremely difficult to reduce the deficit. The public interest in spending restraint is a generalized one, diffused among the entire citizenry. The special interests favoring spending on any particular program are smaller, but they fight much harder to maintain or increase spending.

Certainly, there are constructive proposals that would help control spending. Since 1981, our budgets have sought billions of dollars in reductions of outdated and outmoded programs. Members of the Congress and private think tanks have also identified wasteful spending. But the political process's inability to overcome inertia, along with the persistence of special interests, has led many Americans to despair of achieving budgetary balance without constitutional reform. That is why 32 States have applied to the Congress to call a constitutional convention for the purpose of proposing a constitutional amendment to require a balanced budget—only two States short of the number required by Article V of the Constitution.

In previous years, the Senate has approved such a balanced budget amendment that would obviate such a convention, but the House has failed to support it. This is clearly the option I prefer to achieve the consitutionally mandated balanced budget desired by the overwhelming majority of the American people.

It is imperative that the Congress consider such an amendment as a major priority for 1988, and I will be a willing partner in that enterprise.

B. Budget Process Reform

It is widely acknowledged, by the Congress, the press, and the American people, that the current budget process is not working. The Budget Act of 1974 was purported to streamline and rationalize the budget considerations by the Congress. The new process was to "force" the various committees to consider their recommendations in the context of the entire budget and ensure that proper attention was paid to the bottom line—the deficit.

In both substance and form, the process has failed. Deadlines are routinely missed or ignored. Enforcement mechanisms are rarely employed. Debates over the same issue occur three and four times a year. And from the size of the deficit, the process has obviously failed to provide fiscal discipline.

Over the last 7 years, total revenues paid to the Federal government have increased by over $250 billion. But total expenditures have increased by some $325 billion. Part of the increased spending, $125 billion, or half of the increase in revenues, was devoted to rebuilding our national defenses. But last year, the government spent $140 billion more on domestic programs than in 1981 and $70 billion more on interest payments due to the deficit. And for every dollar the Congress has cut from my defense request, they have added $2 to domestic spending.

Nowhere is the failure of the budget process more evident than in the annual process of developing the appropriations bills that establish discretionary spending levels making up just under one-half the total budget. The regular process requires that 13 separate appropriations bills be sent to the President well in advance of the October 1 beginning of a new fiscal year. But the norm has been anything but normal—during the last 7 years, the Congress sent only 10 of the 91 required bills on time. In the last 2 years, not one bill has been on time and all 13 have been collapsed into one massive piece of legislation.

These increasingly large spending bills, passed at the last moment before existing funding expires, deny the Congress and the Executive the ability to adequately examine their contents. The Congress cannot truly vote on their merits and the President has little ability to employ a veto.

While Gramm-Rudman-Hollings has helped restore some fiscal discipline, it simply adds another layer to an already broken process. The threat of across-the-board cuts is only partially effective as major portions of the budget are exempt. And G–R–H does not produce what a truly effective budget process should; namely, a thorough consideration of spending priorities within the constraints of available revenues. To assist the next administration in attaining the deficit targets contained in the Gramm-Rudman-Hollings law and achieve a balanced budget within the next few years, the following changes in the budget process are proposed:

• *Joint Budget Resolution.* The budget process has so degenerated in recent years that the Presidential budget is routinely discarded and the congressional one regularly goes unenforced. The product of this breakdown is a concurrent resolution, requiring neither consultation with the Administration nor the signature of the President. As a remedy, I propose that henceforth the Congress and the Executive collaborate on a joint resolution that sets out spending priorities within the revenues available. The requirement of a Presidential signature would force both branches of government to resolve most policy issues before formulating appropriations measures. The budget process could be further improved by including in the budget law allocations by committee as well as by budget function.

• *Individual Transmittal of Appropriations Bills.* The current practice of transmitting full-year omnibus continuing resolutions oversteps appropriation committee/subcommittee jurisdictions. More important, it does not permit the Legislative and Executive branches to exercise proper scrutiny of Federal spending. Therefore, I propose a requirement that appropriations bills be transmitted individually to the President.

• *Strict Observance of Allocations.* During the 1980s, an unacceptable budget practice evolved of disregarding congressionally approved function allocations. Funds regularly were shifted from defense or international affairs to domestic spending. I strongly urge that each fiscal year separate defense and non-defense allocations be made and enforced through a point-of-order provision in the budget act.

• *Enhanced Rescission Authority.* Under current law, the President may propose rescissions of budget authority, but both houses of Congress must act "favorably" for the rescission to take effect. The Supreme Court in the *Chadha* decision (1983) effectively moots even this limited authority. I propose a change of law that would cure the legislative veto defect and require the Congress to vote "up or down" on any Presidentially proposed rescission, thereby preventing the Congress from simply ignoring the rescission or avoiding a recorded vote.

• *Adopt Biennial Budgeting.* The current budget process consumes too much time and energy. A 2-year budget cycle offers several advantages—among them, a reduction in repetitive annual budget tasks, more time for congressional oversight and consideration of key spending decisions in reconciliation, and fewer gimmicks, such as shifting spending from one year to the next. I am calling on the Congress to adopt biennial budgeting, beginning with a trial 2-year Defense budget.

• *Truth in Federal Spending Legislation.* As part of my Economic Bill of Rights proposal, I outlined legislation that provides for "Truth in Federal Spending." Soon I will transmit legislation that will require any future legislation creating new Federal programs to be deficit-neutral; this will be done by requiring the concurrent enactment of equal amounts of program reductions or revenue increases. Additionally, my proposed legislation would require that all future legislation and implementing regulations be accompanied by financial impact statements detailing the measure's likely economic impact, including the effect on State and local governments. Enactment of this proposal would be an important step toward reassuring the American people that the Congress is serious about controlling government spending.

C. Line Item Veto

A President should have the same tools to control spending that 43 governors have. I will forward my proposal for a line item veto. It would allow future Presidents to remove from spending bills those items that are extraneous—without threatening the continuation of vital government programs. The Congress could override each veto by a two-thirds vote in each House. The budget crisis, however, also demands immediate action. For example, last month the Congress presented me with a catchall spending bill with many extraneous and costly provisions, some of which had been considered for the first time in conference. I am asking the Congress immediately to accept the responsibility for making its own processes work, rather than giving up and resorting to a continuing resolution.

D. Super-Majority Tax Amendment

Our Founding Fathers knew that without economic freedom there can be no political freedom. Even before our Nation was full-born, nine colonies assembled in a "Stamp Act Congress" and worked their will to oppose taxation without representation. Today, we must once again resolve to put an end to irresponsible taxation and spending. We have fallen into a costly and dangerous habit, which could threaten our future prosperity, burden future generations, and reduce the incentive of individuals and businesses to create more goods and services.

It is clear that we need a mechanism to control expenditures of Americans' hard-earned money. To this end, I will send to the Congress a proposed constitutional amendment to require a super-majority vote in the Congress in order to increase the tax burden on our citizens. I urge the Congress to act expeditiously in approving this amendment and to send it to the States for ratification.

E. Federalism—Returning Power to the People

At the time of my first State of the Union address, it was apparent that the limited national government envisioned by the Framers had been replaced by a national government whose involvement in domestic affairs was limited only by its own will. The Founders understood that unchecked central authority threatens individual liberties. Accordingly, they constituted a Federal system of government, with all powers not specifically granted by the Constitution to the national government reserved to the States and to the people.

We have sought to revitalize the principle of federalism by reforming the institutional processes of the national government. This past October, I signed Executive Order 12612, which requires Executive officials to ensure that all proposed policies and legislation comply with federalism principles and to conduct a formal federalism assessment as appropriate, and which restricts Federal preemption of State laws. The Congress should review its legislative procedures to determine whether reforms similar to those in Executive Order 12612 are warranted.

The National Governors Association and the Advisory Commission on Intergovernmental Relations, as well as State and local officials, have been examining possible amendments to the Constitution that would restore the structural balance of power between the national government and the States. If we in Washington are unsuccessful in reviving the constitutionally crucial principle of federalism, it may become necessary to consider such proposals.

II. To Establish Justice

For 200 years our Republic has enjoyed a constitutional system that is the envy of the world. By its own terms and by the will of the American people, the Constitution is the supreme law of the land. Yet in recent years, some have advocated and at times have succeeded in promoting a laxity in the observance of the terms of its text. Fortunately, I can count as one of the most satisfying legacies of my presidency the work my Administration has done to restore the foundations of American government through an insistence on the faithful interpretation and observance of the Constitution.

A. Judicial Appointments

In the elections of 1980 and 1984, I promised the American people that I would nominate judges and justices to the Supreme Court who would be faithful to the Constitution. I have kept that promise.

Our written Constitution, adopted and ratified by the people 200 years ago and amended several times since, is our fundamental law. Every government official takes an oath to abide by its provisions. For members of the Congress, this should mean enacting laws only in pursuance of the powers set forth in the Constitution. As President, this means taking care that the laws are faithfully executed. To the courts falls the task of adjudicating cases or controversies according to the Constitution and the laws made under it. In so doing, judges must faithfully interpret the text of the Constitution, as well as laws passed by the Congress, as written, in accordance with their original meaning. To do otherwise would constitute a usurpation of legislative power never intended by the American people. With this in mind, I have been careful to nominate only judges faithful to this principle. I urge the Senate to be guided by the same standards in exercising its constitutional duty in the confirmation process.

Part of faithfully interpreting the law is seeing to it that those convicted of crimes are dealt with fairly but firmly. In this respect, I am particularly proud of my judicial appointments. Federal court records indicate that between 1981, when I first took office, and 1984, the average sentence handed down by a Federal court per conviction increased dramatically—by over 100 percent for rape, over 100 percent for burglary, and over 60 percent for murder. I will continue to nominate judges who are tough on crime. When the Senate adjourned last year, 27 judicial nominations were left pending—an unprecedented number—and other vacancies are yet to be filled as well. The Chief Justice of the United States has stated that the high number of vacancies is contributing to an enormous backlog for the Federal courts. The Senate must act expeditiously to confirm these judges.

B. Civil Rights

Among the greatest imperatives in establishing justice is the elimination of discrimination based on race, sex, and other immutable characteristics. Discrimination based on religion is equally invidious. This Administration has held high the banner of equal opportunity for all Americans, and we will not retreat from the fight against discrimination wherever it exists.

Our achievements have been significant. We have successfully prosecuted racial hate groups and have achieved more convictions for criminal civil rights violations than any previous administration. We have moved aggressively to enforce our Nation's voting rights laws, thereby securing for thousands of citizens the most fundamental of all rights—the right to help shape their future with a ballot.

In desegregating our Nation's public schools, we have placed the emphasis where it should be—on enhancing educational quality for all children.

I am particularly proud of our successes in moving America closer to the constitutional ideal of a color-blind society open to all without regard to race. In the workplace, we have rejected the use of quotas and have insisted on fair treatment in hiring and promotion decisions. And after 3 years of effort by this Administration, the Fair Housing Initiatives Program has finally been authorized. The Federal government will now be able to provide direct assistance to State and local governments, as well as public and private organizations, investigating complaints of housing discrimination. The 20th anniversary of the Fair Housing Act of 1968 is an appropriate time to strengthen the statute by increasing the penalties for those convicted of housing discrimination and by extending the protections of the Act to handicapped persons. This Administration will submit appropriate legislation to achieve this purpose. Every American is entitled to freedom from discrimination—to be judged on the basis of qualification and performance, not on stereotypes and unfair assumptions.

Currently pending in the Senate, however, is a bill whose vague and sweeping language threatens to subject nearly every facet of American life—from the corner grocery to the local church or synagogue to local and State government—to intrusive regulation by Federal agencies and courts. Ironically it does so in the name of civil rights. This Administration opposes this overreaching legislation known as the Civil Rights Restoration Act of 1987 (S. 557). In its stead, I have proposed a bill that provides institution-wide coverage under the appropriate civil rights statutes of educational institutions receiving Federal aid while avoiding an unwarranted expansion of Federal jurisdiction. My proposal, the Civil Rights Act Amendments of 1987 (H.R. 1881), also ensures adequate protection of religious tenets under Title IX and makes clear that no institution must provide insurance coverage for abortions or perform abortions as a condition of the receipt of Federal aid.

C. Protection of Victims of Obscenity and Child Pornography

In establishing justice we must be ever mindful that our cherished constitutional freedoms cannot be distorted to protect activities that exploit the innocent and defenseless. The production and distribution of obscene materials, as well as child pornography, are such activities. Our Administration has made the elimination of these materials a top domestic priority.

The Attorney General's Commission on Pornography report has resulted in several new law enforcement efforts, foremost among these being the establishment of a special enforcement unit within the Department of Justice. In a single operation in 1987 more purveyors of child pornography were federally indicted than at any time in history, and the first Federal obscenity racketeering convictions were recently returned in Virginia. However, much more can be done to protect our children and families if the Congress enacts my proposed Child Protection and Obscenity Enforcement Act of 1987. It would criminalize buying and selling children for use in pornography, and it would also prohibit dial-a-porn and cable obscenity. It would strengthen our laws against organized crime traffic in hard-core obscenity.

D. Legal Services for the Needy

Provision of needed legal services for those who cannot afford them is an important goal of our society. Unfortunately, the current system administered by the Legal Services Corporation (LSC) is not working. Each year the Congress has mandated that a large portion of these funds be allotted to a group of "National and State Support Centers." Since 1975 these law reform think tanks have been criticized for political involvement and have not provided any day-to-day service to the poor—the original intent of the LSC. Instead, they have concentrated on social "law reform," without regard to a particular client's needs. I call on the Congress to disallow LSC funds for political think tanks or "support centers" and through strong and specific legal language to limit any political lobbying by LSC grantees. All LSC funds should be used to assist *directly* the poor in need of legal help.

There is another way in which the needy are being badly served by LSC. A congressionally mandated policy of "Annual Presumptive Funding" precludes the possibility of awarding LSC grants on a competitive basis. LSC must be able to demand results from grantees or give other prospective grantees opportunity better to serve the poor. While stability is desirable, we must be able to weed out inefficient or incapable grantees.

III. TO ENSURE DOMESTIC TRANQUILLITY

The leading threat to domestic tranquillity comes in the form of criminal offenses of citizen against citizen. When I took office crime rates were soaring. The public, with good reason, felt unsafe in our streets and often even in homes and places of work. Determined to give America back to its law-abiding citizens, our country is in the midst of the most vigorous crime-fighting effort in its history. Passage of the Comprehensive Crime Control Act of 1984, appointment to the bench of Federal judges who are tough on crime, and an unprecedented attack on organized crime are efforts that have paid off. In spite of our successes, however, much remains to be done.

A. Restoration of the Federal Death Penalty

Federal statutes currently provide for capital punishment for the offenses of espionage, treason, murder, and certain other felonies such as air piracy. Except in the case of the air piracy statute, enacted in 1973, these death penalty provisions are not accompanied by appropriate procedures required since the Supreme Court's 1972 decision in *Furman* v. *Georgia* to prevent disparate application. In this respect, the Congress has lagged well behind the State legislatures, more than 40 of which have acted to adopt appropriate death penalty procedures since the *Furman* decision.

Fortunately a solution is at hand. The Comprehensive Crime Control Act of 1984 created the United States Sentencing Commission to promulgate sentencing guidelines to insure consistent, tough, and equitable sentencing. The Commission should go forward now to set in place procedures to permit the constitutional imposition of capital sentences for the most serious Federal offenses.

B. Criminal Justice Reform Act

To protect further society from criminals, the Congress should act promptly on the Criminal Justice Reform Act, which I transmitted last year. By statute it would establish uniform procedures that would allow death penalty provisions in current Federal statutes to be enforced according to recent Supreme Court decisions. It also contains important reforms to curb the abuse of *habeas corpus* by convicted criminals and to promote truth in the courtroom by ensuring that evidence obtained by the police through reasonable searches and seizures can be used at trial. These important protections for the public will complete the anti-crime effort we began with the Comprehensive Crime Control Act of 1984. They were approved by the Senate in 1984 and in part by the House of Representatives in 1986. The time has come—this year—to enact them into law.

C. Victims of Crime

In 1982 my Task Force on Victims of Crime pointed out that all too often crime victims suffer doubly—they are first victimized by criminals and then by an inadequate justice system. My Administration has put into effect a number of the Task Force recommendations. The most important of these has been the development of model legislation mandating the protection and fair treatment of crime victims, which by 1986 had become the basis for legislative action in nearly two-thirds of the States. I am directing the Attorney General to press forward on the remaining Task Force recommendations.

D. The Fight Against Terrorism

Innocent Americans and freedom-loving people across the world have become the victims of terrorists. But this Nation will not be held captive to the will and whim of terrorists.

This Administration is considering a series of legislative proposals designed to strengthen our hand against terrorists. These include proposals for the expeditious removal of aliens from the United States who are engaged in terrorist activity and proposals providing for criminal and civil forfeiture of terrorists' assets.

State-sponsored terrorism, fomented by governments whose conduct and support for such acts put them outside the community of nations, remains a scourge on the international scene and a particular threat to our citizens and interests. We must further develop the rule of law against these criminals by denying terrorists the legitimacy of international instruments condoning their activities. The Senate should give its advice and consent to ratification, with certain reservations, of Additional Protocol II to the 1949 Geneva Conventions, which would serve to promote basic human rights. The Administration has rejected Additional Protocol I, which would give combatant status to terrorist organizations, and I welcome congressional support of this decision.

E. Organized Crime

For over a half-century this Nation has been plagued by organized crime. Due to vigorous efforts by Federal investigators and prosecutors, some of the most infamous leaders of organized crime are now facing long jail terms. This progress has come through a new strategy aimed at penetrating crime syndicates and targeting their leadership for prosecution. Strike forces have focused on several major cities such as Cleveland, Kansas City, and Boston. One of our most recent successes was in March of 1987 when a jury in New York returned 18 guilty verdicts in the "Pizza Connection" case involving $50 million in laundered proceeds from heroin sales by an organized crime group. In addition, our Administration's Comprehensive Crime Control Act of 1984 has enabled police to detain pending trial certain organized crime figures who previously could have made bail and has dramatically expanded our ability to seize and forfeit the assets of mob members.

Yet, mob-run crime is still a grave problem. Obscenity, extortion, drug importation and sales, loan sharking, illegal gambling, and murder are all crimes that we intend to hit hard during the remainder of this Administration. Our goal is to put "the mob" out of business through vigorous use of both criminal and civil statutes, by purging organized crime elements from labor organizations, and by targeting the newer, "emerging" organized crime groups to ensure that they never wield the mob's power and influence.

F. Prison Capacity Expansion

One result of our increased efforts to fight crime is that the number of criminals serving time in Federal prisons has increased dramatically—nearly 80 percent since 1981. We anticipate that the Federal inmate population will continue to increase in the future, particularly in light of the enhanced criminal penalties contained in the Anti-Drug Abuse Act of 1986 and the new sentencing guidelines. One of my top priorities for the next year will be to increase substantially the construction of new prison space to accommodate the increased number of criminals being removed from our streets.

G. Drug Free America

In the past 7 years, the Nation has made tremendous gains towards a drug free America. Today, public attitudes are clearly against the use of illegal drugs, and drug awareness is increasing. The national prevention effort has taken off with its own strong momentum. Individuals and communities, businesses and schools are taking a firm stand against the use of illegal drugs. Most important, the number of drug users is down; and our children are showing us that they are willing and able to say "no" to drugs.

We are on our way to a drug free future. Still, illegal drugs continue to destroy the lives and the hopes of hundreds of thousands of Americans each year, especially young people whose future lies before them. Since the beginning of my Administration, I have committed the Federal government to provide national leadership and support to the national crusade, encouraging and assisting private sector efforts and aggressively pursuing Federal responsibilities to stop the supply and use of illegal drugs. The National Drug Policy Board, which I established by Executive order on March 26, 1987, has ensured that our Federal agencies work together effectively and efficiently. The Board has named lead agencies for all facets of the anti-drug program to improve coordination throughout the government and enable us to achieve maximum impact with our resources. To this end, the Board has developed a series of nine interrelated strategies.

Five strategies are aimed at reducing the supply of illegal drugs: enhanced *international* cooperation; stepped-up *interdiction* of drugs coming into the country; improved *intelligence* on drug activities; stepped-up *investigations* to eliminate drug trafficking organizations; and targeting *prosecution* of top drug organizations. Simply put, we are working with our allies throughout the world to reduce the amount of illegal drugs produced or processed; making sure that as little as possible of those illicit drugs enter this Nation; and Federal, State, and local officials are working together to investigate and prosecute to the fullest these merchants of destruction.

And we are working to reduce the demand for drugs. Nancy and I join the millions of parents across the country who know too well that real progress toward the goal of a drug free America will best be measured by preventing individuals who do not use drugs from beginning to use them and by convincing those who do use to stop.

Our four strategies to reduce demand are: *prevention education* to keep young people from becoming drug users; reduction of drug use by *high-risk youths*; improved community-based *treatment* for addicts whose drug habits have removed them from the American mainstream; and fostering attitudes of intolerance toward drug use on the part of *mainstream adults*.

Every American should be able to enjoy a drug free workplace. Schoolchildren should have drug free schools. Every citizen should be able to rely on a Federal work force free from drugs. And every American should be able to enjoy a drug free transportation system. This Administration is working in partnership with private employers and State and local governments to ensure all four.

We are proceeding with a cooperative national effort to reduce and eventually eliminate drugs from government housing projects. The Department of Education issued *Schools Without Drugs* and has mobilized school, parent, and community efforts to take drugs away from young people and give them back their lives.

These efforts have already begun to produce results. In 1987, for the first time since the National Institute on Drug Abuse began its annual survey of high school seniors in the early 1970s, a significant drop—one-third—in current cocaine use was revealed. Ninety-seven percent of the seniors polled disapproved of regular cocaine use, and 87 percent disapproved of even trying it—strong evidence that cocaine use is no longer "in" among young Americans.

Finally, as the Nation's largest employer, the Federal government is committed to establishing a model for a drug free workplace that deals constructively with illegal drug use. We are establishing a broad drug education training program for all employees. The program includes testing of employees holding safety-sensitive positions. For example, the Department of Transportation has already implemented drug-testing programs for employees in such positions, including air-traffic controllers and airline safety inspectors. Indeed, fair and accurate drug testing is one of the few effective ways to ensure that illegal drug users begin the process of rehabilitation. Agency programs that include random testing to identify these drug users will be ready for implementation in 1988. We are putting our money where our heart is. In the past 7 years, there has been a three-fold increase in Federal spending to fight drugs, bringing the total close to $3.5 billion this year.

I worked closely with the Congress to enact the Anti-Drug Abuse Act of 1986, which embodies a national commitment to fight drug abuse through: increased criminal penalties, improved criminal investigation and prosecution, demand reduction, better international cooperation, and more effective interdiction. The Act also established the White House Conference for a Drug Free America. Already it has hosted six regional forums to facilitate information gathering and interchange on various aspects of the drug issue. The Conference will hold a national assembly in Washington next month that will expand upon the findings of the regional conferences, showcase the best of the Nation's efforts, and highlight new proposals for combatting drug use in this country. I look forward to the group's final report this spring in order to work with the Congress to implement its recommendations and promote our vision of a drug free America.

IV. To Provide for the Common Defense

Our government has no higher duty than defense of the freedom of the American people. On this point, Alexander Hamilton and James Madison, two of the most eminent Framers of our Constitution, were in complete agreement. Wrote Alexander Hamilton in *The Federalist,* "The circumstances which endanger the safety of nations are infinite, and for this reason no constitutional shackles can wisely be imposed on the power to which the care of it is committed." James Madison concurred, "The means of security can only be regulated by the means and the danger of attack."

In our constitutional framework, the President and the Congress share the vital responsibility for ensuring our national security. Within this same constitutional framework, however, the President has important independent powers. Both of these constitutional principles apply to the agenda of national security issues we will face in 1988 and beyond.

Our two branches of government clearly share powers in such areas as planning and budgeting for the maintenance of our defense capability; the ratification of treaties, as in the case of the INF Treaty; and foreign economic and security assistance, that vital instrument of our foreign policy. At the same time, the Congress must respect the constitutional wisdom that only the President can act as the effective Executive agent in the conduct of foreign relations. This truth is long established in our constitutional law and practice. And the President, in order to act effectively in the Nation's behalf, needs the flexibility to respond, within the framework of law, to often unpredictable and fast-moving challenges.

In 1980, I promised as my first priority to rebuild our national defenses to meet the Soviet military challenge and to restore America's standing as leader of the Free World. Immediately this Administration went to work to rebuild our military, to restore morale in the services and national pride among our people, and to make America once again the leader of free nations. As a result, we are now able to deal from strength with our adversaries and to promote and sustain the efforts of valiant men and women around the globe who are struggling to win or preserve their freedom. Peace is our goal, but we must guard the power and responsibility to meet every challenge.

A. East-West Relations

On the basis of our renewed strength, and a policy of realism in the pursuit of peace, we have in the past 7 years taken great strides toward a world in which freedom can flourish. In the coming year, we face new challenges and new opportunities, and I hope that the Congress will be my partner in addressing both.

Today I have submitted to the Senate for its advice and consent to ratification the Treaty Between the United States of America and the Union of Soviet Socialist Republics on the Elimination of Their Intermediate-Range and Shorter-Range Missiles. This INF Treaty is the first agreement ever to *reduce* and not simply *limit* the buildup of nuclear weaponry, and it provides for the elimination of an entire class of U.S. and Soviet nuclear missiles. It contains the most stringent verification regime in the history of arms control. This treaty represents the culmination of 6 years of hard negotiation. After the West showed strength and solidarity, the Soviets joined us in an agreement to ban such weapons on both sides.

On the basis of similar strength and fortitude, and support from the American people and the Congress, we are engaged in serious negotiations with the Soviet Union on an agreement that could reduce strategic nuclear offensive forces by 50 percent. The United States and Soviet Union are negotiating for effective verification measures that would make it possible to ratify the U.S.-U.S.S.R. Threshold Test Ban Treaty of 1974 and Peaceful Nuclear Explosions Treaty of 1976.

These accomplishments depend on maintaining our strength. It should now be unmistakably clear that our determined program to rebuild our military strength and my Strategic Defense Initiative have spurred major advances in arms reduction, as well as strengthening our own and allied security. These efforts must not be undercut.

In addition, I must reiterate what I said last year—that legislating Soviet arms control positions into American law is not the way to get good agreements. I will veto legislation that undermines national security and undercuts our negotiating position.

The issue between East and West, of course, is not simply arms control. Efforts by the Soviet Union and its surrogates to suppress freedom are major sources of international tensions. Experience shows these efforts to be significant obstacles to improvements in U.S.-Soviet relations.

Human rights and regional conflicts are key issues on my agenda with the Soviet Union. Unfortunately, I can report to you only very limited improvement in both of these areas. For instance, while a few Soviet political prisoners have been released, and there has been some increase this past year in the emigration of Soviet Jews, many more prisoners remain, and many thousands of Soviet Jews are still denied the basic right to emigrate. Furthermore there has been no significant change in Soviet involvement in or provocation of regional conflicts, despite the repeated Soviet lip service to the need for peaceful solutions.

B. Defense Budget

Our defense budget proposals represent an essential program for maintaining our defensive strength. The defense budget has already been reduced to levels that will require us to delay the achievement of important defense objectives. Anything less will jeopardize not only our national security and that of our allies but also the prospects for fair agreements negotiated with our adversaries.

With this in mind we must continue with the Strategic Modernization Program as an essential guarantor of Free World security at the same time as we seek clear-cut and effectively verifiable strategic arms reductions. We must also continue the modernization of nuclear, conventional, and chemical deterrence forces supporting our commitments to our allies. Additionally, we must ensure that the conventional force disparities between NATO and the Warsaw Pact are redressed through a combination of negotiated reductions and the strengthening of NATO capabilities.

My Strategic Defense Initiative (SDI) is not simply a program of research and development of new technology. It offers hope of a reorientation of strategy—hope for a world in which strategic defenses, which threaten no one and can block a ballistic-missile attack, play a greater role in maintaining deterrence. This is a vital program. It is an investment in a safer world for our children, and it is insurance against violations of arms reduction agreements. It reinforces our negotiating efforts. I will ask the Congress to provide increases in funding necessary for essential SDI research, development, and testing. It is a cornerstone of our security strategy for the 1990s and beyond. And when it is ready, we will deploy it.

Despite reductions in defense funding, we must attempt to maintain the strength of our technology base, pursuing new developments in conventional weapons technology. We must also continue our Armaments Cooperation initiatives with our allies to realize improvement in acquisition management and the advantages of shared technological advances among our allies.

We will maintain, where necessary, the deployment of U.S. military forces throughout the Free World as a deterrent to those who might act to threaten peace and freedom and as evidence of solidarity with our allies and other friendly nations.

We must continue to develop and to exercise our capabilities to respond to low-intensity conflict. These simmering confrontations below the threshold of large-scale conventional war undermine the political, economic, and security interests of the United States and its allies and friends.

We must complete the revitalization of our special operations capability begun early in this Administration and preserve that capability in the ensuing years.

Similarly, we need a vital and effective intelligence capability. We must ensure that this capability is effectively managed and that the President has the ability to employ it flexibly. I will not accept legislation governing the conduct of intelligence activities that does not preserve the flexibility that is required if our intelligence community is to do its job. To improve the military intelligence support to U.S. military commanders, especially in the vital area of human intelligence collection, I am seeking legislation to authorize the Secretary of Defense to establish commercial entities to provide cover for certain Department of Defense foreign intelligence collection activities.

As we address the resource requirements for our defense efforts, we must also streamline the process of resource allocation. For this reason, I urge the Congress to shift fully to a 2-year defense authorization and appropriation cycle. This Administration continues to press initiatives that streamline and strengthen the Federal procurement process to dramatically increase competition in the award of Federal contracts. We are placing particular emphasis on the findings of the Blue Ribbon Commission on Defense Management (The Packard Commission) and especially those recommendations having government-wide effect.

C. Democracy and Freedom

America's goal is both peace and freedom. Americans have always believed that liberty was not the birthright of a fortunate few but of all mankind. And we are inspired in this period by the stirring sight of democracy flourishing anew in many regions of the world—from Latin America to the Philippines to the Republic of Korea.

Most remarkable is the struggle of those directly resisting aggression sponsored by the Soviet Union and its surrogates—in Afghanistan, in Cambodia, in Nicaragua, and in Angola.

I strongly support the cause of the brave Freedom Fighters of Nicaragua. On this issue there have been differences between the Executive branch and the Congress, but there are also shared principles: that there must not be a Cuban or a Soviet-bloc military base in Nicaragua, because such a base would threaten the United States and the other nations in the Hemisphere; that Nicaragua must not pose a military threat to its neighbors or provide a staging ground for subversion or destabilization; and that Nicaragua must respect the basic freedoms and human rights of its own people, including the original pledges the Sandinista regime made to the Organization of American States in 1979.

It is now widely accepted that democracy *within* Nicaragua is the core issue in the conflict in Central America. It is the attempt of the Communist Sandinista regime to consolidate its monopoly of power that has led to armed rebellion. The Guatemala Peace Accord, reached last August, recognizes the importance of democracy within Nicaragua—of total amnesty for political prisoners, of negotiations with the armed resistance for a cease-fire. The outcome of the January 15 San Jose meeting to evaluate compliance with the Guatemala Peace Accord presents important opportunities to further peace and democracy in the troubled Central American region.

At the San Jose Summit there was a clear consensus among the four Central American democratic presidents that the Sandinistas had not complied with the Peace Accord. By making his last-minute promises President Ortega acknowledged the accuracy of that judgment.

The key issue is whether the Sandinistas are now committed to genuine and enduring democracy or do they just seek the elimination of the Nicaraguan Democratic Resistance.

The Nicaraguan Democratic Resistance is the best insurance policy for keeping the peace process on track and producing a democratic outcome in Nicaragua. This is not the time to falter in our support for the Freedom Fighters. The United States must not abandon those fighting for democracy in Nicaragua until true democracy is attained.

In Afghanistan, we maintain our firm and unwavering support for the heroic struggle of the Afghan Resistance against the Soviet occupation. We will never agree to any steps that put the Afghan Resistance, or Afghan hopes for self-determination, at risk.

We support a peaceful solution, but such a solution can be achieved only if the Soviet Union withdraws its forces promptly and completely and allows Afghans themselves to determine their political future. As I reminded Secretary General Gorbachev during the December Summit, a prompt and permanent Soviet withdrawal would open the way to further improvements in U.S.-Soviet relations. Let 1988 be the year that sees an end to the Soviet occupation of Afghanistan.

We shall continue our policy in the Persian Gulf to promote stability in the region, maintain freedom of navigation, and promote peace between Iran and Iraq. This bloody conflict has been prolonged because of Iran's intransigence and its attempts to intimidate and threaten the countries of the area and disrupt freedom of navigation. As a result of our policy, we have broadened and strengthened our relationship with the countries of the Gulf Cooperation Council, and our vital interest in the free flow of oil in and out of the Gulf has been protected. We are actively pursuing an arms embargo resolution against Iran, which has refused to comply with the cease-fire demand of the United Nations Security Council.

At the same time, we will work actively to promote peace between Israel and its Arab neighbors. The violence in the West Bank and Gaza is a vivid reminder of the dangers of the status quo. We, along with those in the area, must work together to give the Palestinians a reason for hope, not despair. Stability in the Middle East requires a just and lasting settlement of the Arab-Israeli conflict—a settlement that both assures Israeli security and recognizes the legitimate rights of the Palestinians. We are committed to achieving such a settlement.

The cause of democracy and freedom worldwide is promoted by our program of economic and security assistance to our allies and friends. Central to our security and to the preservation of peace are our ties with allies and friends, including NATO and our East Asian allies—Japan, Korea, the Philippines, and Thailand. Enormous progress has been made in this decade in restoring America's influence in the world and in expanding the horizons of democracy. To further reduce our foreign assistance programs would be a tragic mistake. Economic assistance, especially when coupled with wise internal policies, helps friendly countries prosper; security assistance helps them carry the burden of their self-defense, often in regions of strategic importance for the Free World. In many cases, our aid programs help countries on whose territory there are facilities that support the mutual defense or whose democratic aspirations we wish strongly to support—such as the Philippines. Our assistance programs have also been vehicles for encouraging structural economic policy reforms that promote prosperity, in part through greater reliance on free markets. This crucial support for basic American goals must be restored.

Since the enactment of comprehensive reform of our Nation's immigration laws in the fall of 1986, the flow of illegal aliens across our southern border has been reduced significantly. Our Nation continues to provide open avenues of legal immigration that each year allow 600,000 people to join our ranks as permanent residents. As in the past, a significant portion of these new arrivals are individuals seeking refuge from oppression in their home countries. I am pleased to report the Department of Justice has taken two important steps toward fairer, more expeditious consideration of the asylum applications of persons suffering persecution because of their religious and political beliefs. An Asylum Policy and Review Unit, charged with reviewing asylum cases, has been created directly within the Department. In addition, a change has been proposed in the Immigration and Naturalization Service that would give specially trained Asylum Officers jurisdiction to interview applicants and render decisions, while preserving for each applicant an opportunity for a new hearing before an independent immigration judge. Our Administration is also studying a further restructuring of the asylum process to ensure that asylum and refugee cases are considered from a humanitarian perspective.

As General Vessey's visit last summer to Vietnam indicated, we remain committed to obtaining the fullest possible accounting of our men missing in action in Southeast Asia.

D. The Economic Dimension of Freedom

We remain active in promoting free economic institutions in the developing world. In this connection, the Administration strongly supports the intent of the Caribbean Basin Economic Recovery Expansion Act, which would extend the Caribbean Basin Initiative (CBI) for an additional 12-year period and enhance the program's duty preferences. While not supporting every specific provision in the bill, such as the one concerning sugar, the Administration shares the goal of strengthening the CBI and is proposing modifications and alternatives to reach that goal. In addition, the Senate should give its advice and consent to the ratification of the Bermuda Tax Treaty, and the Congress should enact the complementary tax law changes. These actions would help regularize our economic ties with this strategically important island.

The United States has been in the forefront of Western nations helping Africa to alleviate food shortages due to drought, war, and destructive economic policies as in Ethiopia. For example, in June 1987 I set a common goal for all U.S. economic policies and programs for Sub-Saharan Africa—to end hunger there through economic growth and private sector development, and I am now implementing that decision. At the same time, we have had some success in promoting economic policy reform in Africa, which is now bringing the benefits of investment incentives and free markets to a number of countries that began their independence burdened by stultifying centralized structures. Senegal, Ghana, Cameroon, Botswana, and Malawi are some of the countries adopting market-oriented reforms.

To meet future oil supply disruptions that might develop, it is important that additional oil reserves be placed in the Strategic Petroleum Reserve to meet our 750-million-barrel target. In the section "Strengthening America's Energy Security," which follows, I outline several steps that will strengthen America's overall energy security.

I am proud that our Administration has instituted an effective and prudent system of safeguarding our strategic interests in East-West trade. We cannot let our adversaries acquire through trade vital technology that would strengthen their military capability against us. At the same time we are determined to harmonize trade control practices with friends and allies both to enhance their effectiveness and to avoid undermining the competitive position of U.S. exports.

V. To Promote the General Welfare

As James Madison observed in *The Federalist*, No. 41, the meaning of the "general welfare" is restricted to that public happiness which the government may promote by its clearly enumerated powers. Permitting general and unlimited powers to government, even though these might be used with the best motives, would render the Constitution useless as a safeguard for individual freedom.

This Administration is deeply committed to decreasing the power of the Federal government to its intended scope and to increasing the power of individuals. These policies establish conditions most conducive to individual initiative and enterprise and, consequently, to the creation of wealth and public well-being. The preservation of freedom, the highest value in our Republic, requires placing the rights of individuals above the power of government. The great challenge of our national government is to use only its carefully enumerated powers in promoting the general welfare by empowering individuals to help themselves.

A. Empowering Individuals To Control Their Own Resources

If individuals are to possess genuine autonomy then they must be free to control their own resources, to enjoy the fruits of their labor, and to keep what they earn, free from excessive government taxation and spending. To further this ideal, I propose the following six specifics:

1. *Tax Policy.* Experience has shown that higher taxes ultimately fuel higher spending and do not improve the deficit. During the past 7 years, tax revenues generally have increased, but spending has still increased 27 percent more than tax revenues. This is the true source of the deficit.

Those who favor higher taxes ignore the impact of such taxes on the economy. By reducing and reforming taxes we have seen unprecedented economic growth, high rates of job creation, and increasing productivity for over 60 months. During this period of time, the Administration has lowered income tax rates and removed the automatic tax increases caused by inflation. Future tax policy must preserve these and other gains made on behalf of the American taxpayer. Tax increases should also be opposed on the basis of their burden on economic growth. These include, but are not limited to, returning to higher marginal rates for individuals or corporations; repealing indexing; creating a value-added tax or increasing excise taxes; increasing taxes on capital or energy sources; and levying new taxes on securities transfers or corporate takeovers.

2. *Reduction of Capital Gains Tax Rate.* The tax reforms accomplished in 1986 did much to remove provisions that inhibit economic prosperity. The most important piece of unfinished business is to reduce the capital gains tax rate to the level that will generate the savings and investment necessary for future economic growth.

Past experience demonstrates that lowering the capital gains tax rate will mean increased realizations of capital gains upon which taxes are paid. When capital gains tax rates increase, investors tend to hold rather than sell their assets. If investors hold their assets until death, they can pass their untaxed gains on to their children, resulting in no income taxes paid on those gains. When the capital gains tax rate was increased in 1969, for example, it led to an immediate reduction in the amount of capital gains realized. By contrast, a reduction in the capital gains tax rate in 1978 and again in 1981 led to significant increases in capital gains realizations.

Reducing the capital gains tax rate to an agreed-upon optimum should be a cornerstone of tax reform for the 1990s. I will consult with the Congress about achieving this rate reduction as soon as possible.

3. *Raise Revenues with User Fees.* The burden of reducing the deficit must not be allowed to hamper the productive element of society—the private sector. Raising new revenues must be confined to areas where they will not burden productivity. I believe that user fees for services are a sensible alternative to a policy where revenues are unrelated to expenditures, where some citizens are singled out for gain while others are excluded. Additionally, user fees promote efficiency by encouraging individuals to use the proper level of government services.

4. *Spending Restraint.* We all recognize that reducing the size of the Federal deficit is a top priority. The 2-year budget agreement that the Congress and I worked out last fall is a first step. But we must go further and reduce the size and the cost of the Federal government. I will apply the following principles in considering new appropriations and authorization legislation, which I urge the Congress also to follow: eliminate pork-barrel spending that uses national funds to benefit local interests; work toward subsidy-free business and agriculture marketing; avoid creation of new entitlement programs and additional cost-of-living increase provisions; direct public assistance to the needy; and provide for necessary discretion to promote efficient administration of Federal programs. Moreover, the Congress should avoid attaching appendages to spending bills that authorize unnecessary programs and go beyond the enumerated powers of the national government.

5. *Government Management Improvements—Government of the Future.* When I became President, one of my earliest priorities was to try to reestablish the proper relationship between the Federal government (which had grown much too large and too powerful) and the State and local governments; and between government and the private sector. In 1981, through our federalism and deregulation initiatives, we placed greater responsibility at the State and local level and in the private sector. We are continuing those efforts.

But as we look forward to the beginning of the 21st century, we need to update our perspective on the proper role of the Federal government and examine what needs to be done to prepare for the changes that will take place. For example, we expect the population to grow to over 268 million people. Changes in technology and communication will link the world's economies, trade, capital flows, and travel as never before. I have asked the Office of Domestic Affairs to work with the President's Council on Management Improvement to conduct an in-depth review and recommend to me by August what further adjustments have to be made in the Federal role to prepare for these anticipated changes. This summer I look forward to receiving their report, "Government of the Future," which will also incorporate plans of my "Reform '88" program.

Meanwhile, those responsibilities that legitimately fall within the enumerated powers of the Executive branch should be managed to deliver quality service to all of our citizens. Our government has a major effect upon the daily lives of all of us through the direct delivery of services, the payment of financial assistance through various entitlement programs, the collection of taxes and fees, and through regulating commercial enterprises. My 1988 management priorities will be to complete the "Reform '88" management improvement program I started 6 years ago; to overhaul the administrative, financial, and credit systems in our Federal government; to implement productivity and quality plans in each agency; and to direct the Office of Personnel Management to examine the needs of the Federal work force of the future.

My goal, therefore, is to ensure that my Administration leaves a "legacy" of good management of today's problems—with plans in place to handle tomorrow's challenges.

6. *Social Security Reports to Participants.* Virtually all workers are required to participate in the social security system. But the

average worker does not know the level of benefits that would be paid his family should he die, become disabled, or retire. As a result he cannot make plans for any supplemental benefits and insurance he may need.

I am pleased to announce that before the year is over the Social Security Administration will begin providing upon request reports similar to those frequently provided to employees who receive private sector benefits. The social security report will contain a clear and detailed statement that outlines a participant's credited earnings and social security taxes for each year; indicates his current eligibility status; and sets forth an estimate in current dollars of the current and future benefits available to him.

B. Freeing the Individual From Government Dependency

It is a fact of American life that many Federal programs, while attempting to help the poor, have made them more dependent on the government. Much is within our reach to help dependent citizens lift themselves to self-sufficiency:

1. *Reducing Welfare Dependency Through Opportunity.* The current welfare system has trapped too many Americans in a dependency on welfare that is hard to break and easy to pass on to succeeding generations. In recent years, a consensus has emerged that it is through work and the acceptance of responsibility that people develop the self-esteem to pull themselves up from dependency.

Last year I launched a major effort to encourage the States, working with established community self-help groups, to undertake a wide range of "workfare" and other responsibility-building reform experiments. Experience has clearly shown that it is in the States that real welfare reform will occur. This was true back in the 1970s in California when we started this movement; it is increasingly the case today. The States' and my objective is to make work and self-sufficiency more attractive than welfare. However, because the current welfare system is so complex and restrictive in its endless rules and restrictions, we need legislation to give the States added flexibility and encouragement to undertake truly innovative and individualized reform experiments.

Last August I endorsed H.R. 3200/S. 1655, legislation that represents a constructive and fiscally responsible approach to reducing welfare dependency. This legislation would help more people become self-sufficient through mandatory participation requirements and a flexible work and training program. It would strengthen our ability to require absent parents to support their children. It also contains the broad waiver authority States need to implement their own ideas and make the welfare system more responsible to the needs of each particular State. I call on the Congress to enact this legislation and not use the present consensus on the need to reform our welfare system as an opportunity simply to expand the benefit levels, which would lead to increased dependency.

Even under the limited authority of current law, many States have undertaken or are planning such experiments. To assist them I have established the Interagency Low Income Opportunity Advisory Board to facilitate "one-stop shopping" for the States as they deal with the Federal government and to advise my Cabinet on the impact of the State proposals on the Federal welfare system.

Recently this Board facilitated multi-program waivers of Federal programs to the States of Wisconsin and New Jersey, enabling them to launch broad-based welfare reform initiatives. Wisconsin's program restructures benefits to make participation in work and training programs more attractive than simply collecting welfare. New Jersey's Reaching Economic Achievement ("REACH") program employs widespread mandatory work requirements, together with the services intended to make long-term employment a reality, and promises savings through reduced case loads. We need more such experiments, emphasizing the close tie we know exists between achievement through work and the feelings of self-worth essential to personal economic independence.

2. *Removing Barriers to Home Ownership.* Historically our freedom has been symbolized by the opportunity for every

American family to own and occupy housing. The success of our economic recovery program has caused inflation and mortgage interest rates to decline, making it easier for more Americans to buy homes. To make housing even more affordable, this Administration is working with home builders and local officials to overcome government delays and cost-adding regulations. I am also pleased that the recently passed housing bill granted permanent authority for the FHA mortgage insurance program that increases the availability of credit to American home buyers. The bill also accepts my recommendations for extending the availability of rental housing vouchers to rural as well as urban areas. These vouchers will give meaningful choice to the individuals intended to be beneficiaries of housing programs. Moreover, the bill endorses the concept of tenant ownership of public housing. In order fully to empower occupants of public housing to own their own homes, I will be acting on the recommendations of the President's Commission on Privatization to develop a proposal to sell at a discount existing public housing to the current occupants, thus mirroring the success this approach has enjoyed in Britain.

3. *Strengthening the Family.* It is one of our country's most basic principles—where there are strong families, the freedom of the individual expands. The strength and stability of the American family provide essential armor for individuals in the fight against poverty. Only a few years ago, the American household of persons related by blood, marriage, or adoption—the traditional definition of the family—seemed in peril.

I have sought to further policies that recognize the importance of a stable family life. For example, the tax reforms of 1986 contributed to family stability by increasing personal exemptions. Last fall I issued an Executive order on the Family requiring that every department and agency review its proposed activities in light of seven standards designed to promote and not harm the family. The Offices of Management and Budget and Policy Development are charged with the responsibility of reviewing future Executive branch activity to ensure that it meets these standards. In addition, the Congress should require a statement that determines the impact legislation will have on the American family.

In March, I will receive a report from the Office of Policy Development on the impact of existing policies and regulations on the family. At that time I will take administrative action and propose legislation necessary to correct policies that do not conform to the family criteria.

4. *Strengthening Communities Through Enterprise Zones.* Despite the economic prosperity enjoyed by most of the Nation, some regions remain economically depressed. The key to revitalizing these areas is not new or expanded government programs, but free enterprise. In 1981, I proposed the creation of enterprise zones in which economically depressed areas could receive tax and regulatory relief in order to expand private economic activity and opportunity within the zones and create jobs in the process.

More than half the States have set up their own enterprise zones, even without Federal incentives. These zones have created new jobs and spurred billions of dollars in capital investment. Their success is testimony to the power of this concept and is just a small indication of how much could be accomplished if Federal incentives were added to those of States and localities. Adding Federal incentives would make existing zones far more economically attractive and successful and would also encourage more State and local zones. Accordingly, I am renewing my call to the Congress to take up effective Federal enterprise zone legislation that will complement the State programs.

5. *Independence Through Excellence in Education.* Individuals well instructed in basic skills, important knowledge, sound values, and independent reasoning are better equipped to participate in America's continued freedom and prosperity. In 1981, however, our educational system was suffering from a 20-year decline in academic achievement. Yet spending per pupil had nearly doubled since 1970, and Federal spending for education had increased over 3,000 percent since 1960. It has now risen to more than $20 billion. But while funding is very important, money without genuine

commitment does not lead to educational excellence.

In 1983, the National Commission on Excellence in Education launched a national renaissance in education by identifying problem areas and suggesting solutions for State and local programs. In its groundbreaking report, *A Nation At Risk,* the Commission recommended that the States and localities return to the basics in curriculum and strengthen high school graduation requirements. Additionally, my Administration urged the States and localities to consider merit pay and competency testing to improve the abilities of educators. As a result of the Commission's and our efforts, some school systems began to turn away from a smorgasbord curriculum and toward a more structured, traditional program designed to educate good citizens and to enable all students to participate in the opportunities our society offers in abundance. But despite this progress, we still have a long way to go. For example, only 5 percent of American 17-year-olds have advanced reading skills; an average high school student takes only 1.4 years of history. In April the Department of Education will complete its review of progress made since the issuance of *A Nation at Risk.*

Last month the Secretary of Education unveiled a model curriculum in a report entitled *James Madison High School.* This report outlined a year-by-year slate of courses in English, social studies, math, science, foreign language, fine arts, physical education, and health, and proposed that they be made graduation requirements for all students. Four years of English would include American, British, and world literature. Three years of social studies would include western civilization, American history, and Principles of American Democracy, with a hefty dose of geography throughout. This is the kind of curriculum that will help America's young people meet the challenges of the next century. Although a public high school curriculum must be set at the State or local level, I hope school officials will examine the model curriculum proposed in *James Madison High School.*

In addition to "back to basics" reforms, American education would benefit from greater parental involvement. In July 1987, as part of my Economic Bill of Rights, I stated that we must recognize the right of parents to have their children educated, publicly or privately, without unreasonable regulation or interference from State or Federal governments. To that end, I am establishing a working group in the Domestic Policy Council that will examine the parental role in education and make recommendations for strengthening parents' rights.

Improving choice in education continues to be an important goal of this Administration. Study after study has found that when parents have a say and are involved in their children's education, the children do better in school. For example, the Congress should authorize a program of giving parents a choice of schools when providing Federal funds to benefit students.

I will continue to encourage efforts to advance parental choice through expansion of the magnet schools program, as well as in the compensatory education programs financed through Chapter 1 of the Education Consolidation and Improvement Act. Compensatory education programs provide additional services to children most in need of extra help in mastering basic skills. Enhancing parental choice is particularly critical in the education of disadvantaged children, who are the focus of the Chapter 1 program.

But I do not intend to stop there. Polls show that millions of Americans would like, but do not have, the ability of choosing the education program and institution that is best for their children. A voucher system at the State level would empower parents. I will ask the Department of Education to develop model voucher legislation and make it available to the 50 States, so that they can implement programs that promote choice in education.

A college education is part of training for tomorrow's challenges. However, since 1980 the cost of a college education has risen more than twice as fast as the Consumer Price Index, and many Americans are wondering whether their children will ever be able to go to college. Colleges set tuition, not the Federal government. It is my hope that our Nation's universities will act to reduce the cost of higher education without sacrificing quality in core fields. To help college students from families of limited means, I propose an increase in the maximum Pell Grant to $2300.

I will also ask the Congress to approve creation of College Savings Bonds. These bonds will offer an incentive for lower- and middle-income families to save now for the future education of their children. Interest on bonds used for this purpose will be free from taxation.

While we do our part to help finance college education, students must do their part and act responsibly. Most do, many do not. The taxpayers will spend over $1.6 billion this year to pay off student defaults. To ensure that tomorrow's students do not lose out because Federal guarantees are abused, the Department of Education will propose a rule holding schools and colleges accountable for excessive rates of default on Guaranteed Student Loans. Schools in which there is a disproportionately high number of student defaults will face the loss of eligibility for student aid.

Other policies addressing this problem include: providing better information to students on their duties when they borrow and when their debts are due; use of the IRS to take money owed out of tax refunds; use of collection agencies and litigation to go after the worst offenders; and increasing the incentives for lenders and guarantee agencies to do a better job of collecting loans.

6. *Protecting the Health of Citizens.* Government promotion of public health has enabled many individuals to participate fully in society. The Federal government now has the opportunity to assist elderly persons who fall victim to catastrophic illnesses and to lead the fight against diseases such as AIDS.

I am asking the Congress to enact my proposal for Federal coverage of catastrophic health care costs incurred by Medicare beneficiaries. This legislation, which I negotiated with the Senate, would provide affordable catastrophic coverage.

Additionally, the Office of Personnel Management has a new proposal before the Congress to help Federal workers deal with long-term health care needs—both nursing home and home health care. This proposal will serve as an example for *privately funded* long-term health care. No new government funds will be needed to provide this additional insurance. It will be made available through the already-existing life insurance program for Federal employees, with a small additional premium from employees enrolled in the program.

We must continue to take preventive measures against AIDS while at the same time treating AIDS victims with compassion and care. Although increased Federal funding is not the only solution, I am proposing $1.5 billion in fiscal 1989 for research, treatment, testing, counseling, and education, up ten-fold since 1985. Administration scientists were centrally involved in the discovery of the Human Immuno-deficiency Virus (HIV), developing the HIV blood antibody test and the anti-AIDS drug AZT. And testing has been initiated in human volunteers for two experimental AIDS vaccines.

However, the primary responsibility for avoiding AIDS lies with the individual. As the Surgeon General, the Secretary of Health and Human Services, and the Secretary of Education have been reminding us all, the best way to prevent AIDS is to abstain from sex until marriage and then to maintain a faithful relationship, as well as to avoid illicit drugs altogether. If the American people follow this wise and timeless counsel, if our schools and families and media communicate it effectively, the spread of AIDS can be greatly diminished.

For our young people, education is crucial for AIDS prevention, and parents have the primary responsibility for this. The Department of Education released *AIDS and the Education of Our Children* last October to assist parents and educators in this effort. This publication reflects my conviction that educational efforts in the schools should be determined locally with deference to parental values.

In 1987 I announced a policy of expanded routine testing, which is essential for early diagnosis and treatment of infected individuals, for protection of the public, and for assisting Federal, State, and local policymakers in dealing with this epidemic. I also established the Presidential Commission on the HIV Epidemic and will receive their final recommendations this summer.

I have directed the Public Health Service to undertake a comprehensive program to determine the extent of HIV infection and full-blown AIDS. We need to know more about the dynamics of this disease, its prevalence, and its rate of spread. Beginning in March 1988, the Centers for Disease Control will produce quarterly reports on the progress in implementing this program.

I am directing the Food and Drug Administration to accelerate its review of new therapeutics, vaccines, blood-screening tests, and other products to fight this disease.

C. Freeing Individuals To Pursue Productive Endeavors

I believe all individuals should have the right to pursue their livelihood in their own way, free from excessive government regulation and government-subsidized competition. Greater personal autonomy, not a paternalistic "industrial policy," is the path to greater American competitiveness. As the 1987 Nobel Laureate in Economics, James Buchanan, recently pointed out:

"We now have in place the scientific and technical tools that enable us to make meaningful comparisons between the workings of an industry in an unregulated, privatized setting and the workings of the same industry in a regulated or controlled setting."

Our experience with deregulation over the past 7 years has demonstrated the superiority of industry inspired by private initiative rather than controlled by Federal regulations. Accordingly, I am instructing my Administration to take all possible measures to provide individual Americans with the greatest possible range of economic opportunities, and I invite the Congress to join me in further deregulating our economy and in promoting free trade among free nations. Here are nine areas on which the Administration will focus:

1. *Deregulation of Key Industries.* Back in 1980, I promised to get the government off the backs of all individual Americans—working men and women, consumers, and businessmen and women. More than 7000 new regulations were issued in my predecessor's last year in office. This had to stop. At my direction, various departments have acted to reduce the scope and cost of Federal regulation. We have accomplished a great deal. For example, we have expedited Federal approval of experimental drugs, making them available to treat serious or life-threatening diseases when other treatments do not work.

Individual Americans have access to more goods and are able to travel more easily and at less cost because of deregulation. Today, for the first time in 30 years, the railroad industry is financially stable because of economic deregulation. Shippers and consumers across the Nation benefit from real cost reductions brought on by more competition. And, despite some problems inevitable in a large, dynamic industry, airline consumers now enjoy about $11 billion per year in lower fares, a great number of flight options, and a safe, efficient air transportation system unequaled by any nation. Our free market policies have worked. Although we must continue our vigilance to assure safety, we must not, in any form, re-regulate these industries.

The current relaxation of Federal regulation of the trucking industry has demonstrated the tremendous potential of individual Americans. Now is the time to complete the deregulation process. I ask that the Congress pass the Administration's Trucking Productivity Improvement Act of 1987 to remove the last vestige of Federal regulation of the interstate trucking industry and ensure that the States do not re-regulate the interstate and intrastate operations of interstate trucking firms. Already the progress of rail and trucking deregulation has made the Interstate Commerce Commission an anachronism. It should be abolished as proposed in legislation sent to the Congress last year.

This Administration has sought to promote the free flow of information among individuals by freeing the telecommunications industry from intrusive government control. In this "Age of Information" America risks losing its position as the world's leader in information and telecommunications technology—not because we lack the talent, the resources, or the will, but because we have needlessly regulated our telecommunications industry.

Another area in which deregulation has promoted individual freedom is the broadcasting and cable industries. I have strongly supported the elimination of the so-called "Fairness Doctrine" as an unconstitutional infringement upon the freedom of the press, and I will continue to resist any legislation that attempts to reverse this Federal Communications Commission (FCC) action. This Administration has also insisted in the courts that the cable industry receive the same First Amendment protection as the print media. This is particularly imperative in light of recent technological changes in the industry. One area where First Amendment rights have been dealt a severe blow is the recent codification of the "cross-ownership" rule. This last minute appendage to the Continuing Resolution prevents owners of newspapers and broadcast stations from even seeking a waiver of the rule and thus violates their First Amendment rights. This change could force the closing of newspapers. I strongly support measures to repeal legislative cross-ownership restrictions that inhibit rather than enhance the free market of ideas.

Where the government does regulate economic activity, this Administration has sought to use market-oriented approaches. For example, in the case of airline landing rights, it is important that individuals be able to freely transfer rights to operate within the regulatory regime. Despite the progress we have made on deregulation, more needs to be done. The Office of Management and Budget therefore will continue to assure that agencies, as they develop proposed regulations, evaluate and make public their findings concerning the effect of proposed Federal regulations on private sector employment and commerce.

2. *Reducing Government Reporting Burdens.* Since 1982, my Executive Office has actively sought to reduce the burden of Federal reporting requirements on every individual and business. Each year we have made sizable reductions in paperwork burdens, totalling 560 million man-hours from Fiscal Year 1981 through Fiscal Year 1986. To improve our efforts, the Office of Management and Budget will issue regulations that will provide a more timely and complete description of proposed reporting burdens. Citizens will be encouraged to report back to OMB when, in their experience, the reporting requirement is unduly onerous. The Office of Management and Budget is systematically simplifying Federal procurement regulations and reducing the paperwork burden imposed upon those who want to compete for contracts with the Federal government.

Similarly, the Census Bureau has substantially improved the questionnaires to be used in the 1990 decennial census. These improvements will reduce the paperwork burden on all American households by using a significantly abbreviated "short" form and by making sure that no more households than absolutely necessary are asked to complete the "long" form. These changes will also improve the quality of the information collected.

3. *Strengthening America's Energy Security.* The economic well-being and future security of this Nation depend upon maintaining and building long-term energy security and strengthening the domestic energy industry. We have made considerable progress. While our economy has greatly expanded, we are using no more energy and less oil than we did 10 years ago, and our strategic oil stocks are five times higher. But more needs to be done.

In May 1987, I offered several proposals to enhance our Nation's energy security. The windfall profit tax has raised little or no revenue since the collapse of oil prices in 1985, yet it discourages long-term investment in new domestic oil production. Moreover, it causes oil producers to engage in purposeless record-keeping. It should be repealed.

Last May I signed legislation eliminating restrictions on natural gas use. The Congress should now act to decontrol the wellhead price of natural gas and provide for open access pipeline transportation. Both measures would lead to less demand for imported oil. I also urge action on the Administration's proposal to deregulate many oil pipelines.

This year the Congress will consider our recommendation concerning oil and gas activities on the coastal plain of the Arctic National Wildlife Refuge—the most outstanding onshore oil and gas frontier in this Nation. The Department of the Interior would manage exploration, development, and production of these potentially vast resources while assuring that environmental safeguards are carefully maintained. The Congress should move expeditiously to enact legislation implementing our recommendation.

Development of our offshore energy resources continues to be vital to our economic and energy security. Last year we developed and implemented a 5-year Outer Continental Shelf (OCS) leasing program. Unparalleled in its responsiveness to State and local concerns, this program meets America's need for domestic energy supplies while it continues to provide protection for our important coastal resources.

Lastly, to ensure the future viability of nuclear power in the United States, the nuclear licensing process should be reformed and the Price-Anderson Act should be reauthorized. I urge responsible congressional action in these areas.

4. *Protecting the Environment Without Unnecessary Government Intrusion.* I have always believed that this Nation does not have to choose between a clean, safe environment and a productive economy. Of course, sometimes trade-offs exist and choices have to be made.

America's program for environmental protection is the most comprehensive in the world. And our environmental accomplishments are impressive. We have dramatically reduced air pollution in our cities and restored thousands of miles of waterways without hampering economic growth. We have cut levels of lead in urban air by nearly 90 percent and cleaned up more than 1000 hazardous dumps and spill sites. And we have made impressive strides in the Superfund hazardous waste cleanup program. Work has been completed at almost 200 sites this year, including many that posed immediate threats to human health and the environment. This brings the total since this program began to over 1000. In addition, work is underway at more than 700 National Priority List sites.

We have recognized the global nature of some environmental challenges and played a leadership role in the world community to meet them. In December, I submitted to the Senate for advice and consent to ratification an international protocol to reduce chemical emissions that may be depleting the stratospheric ozone layer, and I urge early congressional action on this initiative. This protocol is the first time nations of the world have agreed to specific action in order to address a global environmental problem.

Consistent with the report of the National Acid Precipitation Assessment Program, I will again request congressional approval of a 5-year, $2.5 billion program for development of innovative clean coal technologies to reduce further acidic deposition (acid rain) emissions. The Secretary of Energy has begun implementation of the first 2 years' funding provided in the continuing resolution and, at my direction, has formed a panel to advise on innovative technology projects for funding. Additionally, I have reviewed and accepted significant new recommendations from my Task Force on Regulatory Relief that will introduce such new technologies into the marketplace more quickly and efficiently:

- The Department of Energy will permit preferential treatment for innovative clean coal technology projects, recognizing the risk inherent in such demonstrations.
- The Federal Energy Regulatory Commission will support a 5-year demonstration program on rate incentives for innovative technologies.
- The Environmental Protection Agency will support and encourage a variety of means to include "bubbles" and interpollutant trading, to achieve emissions reductions.

5. *Strengthening Financial Markets.* With a view to empowering people to engage in productive activity for mutual gain, I am taking steps to reduce arbitrary second-guessing of markets by government regulators who can scarcely hope to administer financial services more efficiently or fairly.

I reassert my support for the pro-competitive Financial Modernization Act of 1987, which would repeal Sections 20 and

32 of the Glass-Steagall Act prohibiting affiliations between commercial banks and securities firms. It would permit bank holding companies, with Federal Reserve Board approval, to own affiliates that underwrite or deal in securities. I welcome the bipartisan initiatives of the Senate and House Banking Committees in this area, and I encourage the Congress to consider additional reforms that keep financial services open and competitive and allow the development of innovative services to benefit individuals, businesses, and government. In today's global economy, America's financial institutions must be released from this outdated legal framework so that they will be able to remain on the leading edge in the world marketplace.

The market for corporate control is a vital component of our free enterprise economy. This Administration opposes legislation that would have the effect of making takeover activity more costly and difficult. Such efforts prevent the free flow of capital and make American firms less responsive to competitive forces, often at the expense of shareholders.

6. *Protecting Individual's Property Rights.* It was an axiom of our Founding Fathers and free Englishmen before them that the right to own and control property was the foundation of all other individual liberties. To protect these rights, the Administration has urged the courts to restore the constitutional right of a citizen to receive just compensation when government at any level takes private property through regulation or other means. Last spring, the Supreme Court adopted this view in *Nollan* v. *California Coastal Commission.* In a second case, the Court held that the Fifth Amendment requires government to compensate citizens for temporary losses that occur while they are challenging such a government regulatory "taking" in court.

In the wake of these decisions, this Administration is now implementing new procedures to ensure that Federal regulations do not violate the Fifth Amendment prohibition on taking private property; or if they do take a citizen's property for public use, to ensure that he receives constitutionally required just compensation.

7. *Trade and Competitiveness.* To enable individuals to enjoy the benefits of trade with other countries and to engage in productive activity without the burdens of retaliatory trade barriers, I will continue to encourage a free and fair trade policy. U.S. trade policy must reflect the fact that we live and work in a global economy and that our future prosperity lies in establishing stable, open relationships with our trading partners abroad and competitive, unrestrained markets at home. An effective trade policy, therefore, must pursue two interrelated goals: to extend, by example and by negotiation, the benefits of free trade to the world economy and to enhance, through deregulation and privatization, the free operation of the domestic economy. Only in such a competitive environment will American business reach its productive potential and American workers enjoy the just rewards for their labors.

Last February, I submitted to the Congress a program for making the United States more competitive, much of which was contained in the Trade, Employment, and Productivity Act of 1987. There were six elements to that program, each critical to ensuring America's future economic preeminence: increasing investment in human capital; promoting the development of science and technology; better protecting intellectual property rights; enacting essential legal and regulatory reforms; shaping the international economic environment; and continuing to eliminate the Federal budget deficit by reducing domestic spending. Taken as a whole, this program recognized that government must not interfere with the marketplace but should ensure that the underpinnings of American economic success, such as a well-educated work force and a technological edge, remain strong.

Unfortunately, the Congress has failed to recognize the broad nature of the competitiveness problem and instead has placed too much emphasis on protectionist measures that may defer short-lived adjustment pains but harm the future health of the economy. Protectionism serves as a hidden tax on the American economy, crippling once prosperous industries, throwing Americans out of work, and raising costs for consumers. American business comes to rely more heavily on government and less on the marketplace, while Americans watch their standard of living slip away. Despite the soothing words of its advocates, protectionism represents the triumph of special interest over the general interest. This Administration remains committed to working with the Congress to draft responsible trade legislation, but if that legislation is not free of harmful protectionist measures, I will veto it.

The Department of Commerce is taking two important steps to boost U.S. exports. First, it will launch Export Now, an intensive new effort, supported by the private sector, to inform small, medium, and large businesses of the current opportunities to expand exports. This effort will encourage American business to take advantage of favorable exchange rates, of the market-opening actions of this Administration, and of the support our government agencies can give them in entering new overseas markets. Second, the Department will begin the Malcolm Baldrige Quality Awards program to help restore "Made in the U.S.A." as the symbol of the very best products throughout the world.

No sector of our economy would benefit more from international trade reforms than agriculture. One of my proposals to the General Agreement on Tariffs and Trade (GATT) for negotiations under the Uruguay Round is to eliminate worldwide all subsidies that distort agricultural trade and all agricultural import barriers. I propose that these subsidies and restrictions be phased out over 10 years. We are striving for an agreement on agriculture by the end of this year, in order to hasten access of U.S. farmers to export markets now closed to them. I also propose an international harmonization of health and sanitary measures affecting agricultural trade with the aim of eliminating foreign countries' use of them as disguised trade barriers.

The Nation benefits from the excellence of our scientists, engineers, and researchers. Because it is important that business have adequate incentives to fund research here in the United States, we are seeking enactment of a permanent tax credit for firms engaging in research and experimentation to replace the tax credit that expires at the end of this year. In addition, we are seeking legislation that would permit the allocation of at least 67 percent of a U.S. company's research expenses to its domestic income for purposes of the foreign tax credit.

During this Administration, we have also shifted the focus of Federal investment in R&D to basic research, allowing the private sector to transform this fundamental knowledge into technologies and processes necessary to develop products and services that meet the demands of the marketplace. Federal investment in basic research has grown in real terms by 40 percent since 1981. Last year, I issued an Executive order to facilitate citizens' access to such federally funded basic research. In addition, I am asking the Congress to fund incentives to spur American innovation. I am requesting that we now provide monetary awards to accompany our National Medals of Science and Technology. In addition, I am proposing a new Thomas A. Edison Prize that will challenge Americans from all walks of life to use technology to improve the quality of life in the United States and the world.

This Administration has also proposed construction of a Superconducting Super Collider, which is essential to continued U.S. leadership in high-energy physics and America's scientific and technological competitiveness. Presently, the Department of Energy is studying locations in seven States, and late this summer the Secretary of Energy will select the preferred site for the project. We hope that our allies will share the cost of construction and operation of this facility, as well as the benefits it will afford for new discoveries in basic physics.

The freedom to compete in the marketplace is essential to our concept of liberty. Our antitrust statutes were intended to protect this freedom. Sadly they have been transformed into weapons that competitors use against each other and tools for inappropriate government interference in the marketplace. Additionally, American firms find themselves at a competitive disadvantage with foreign competitors because of the burden and uncertainty fostered by some outdated aspects of our Nation's antitrust statutes. Therefore, I again urge the Congress to adopt my proposed antitrust reforms, particularly those that remove disincentives to pro-competitive mergers. In addition, I am asking the Congress to amend the National Cooperative Research Act to permit some types of joint production ventures. While retaining the protection of the antitrust statutes, this change will help U.S. manufacturing firms develop innovative ways to produce goods and services at competitive prices both here and overseas.

For example, the domestic automobile manufacturing industry has made major strides in improving its competitive position, producing higher quality and more fuel-efficient vehicles. Despite these gains in fuel efficiency, the industry remains restricted by current law, which requires automobile manufacturers to "balance" their line of automobiles to include cars and light trucks that meet corporate average miles-per-gallon fuel economy (CAFE) standards. These standards make it more difficult for U.S. firms to produce automobiles that consumers want to buy. This Administration has proposed the Motor Vehicle Information and Cost Savings Act of 1987 to eliminate this requirement for future model years. This legislation would remove a competitive disadvantage for American firms at a time when the purpose of the CAFE standard has been largely realized and would remove the incentive for domestic auto manufacturers to export U.S. jobs.

Another factor affecting U.S. competitiveness is our civil justice system. During the past 2 years, 47 of the 50 States have enacted tort reform legislation. We strongly supported many of these State initiatives, and we will work closely with the States to achieve further reforms wherever possible. In addition, the Administration is encouraged by the progress of the legislation to reduce the costly product liability insurance spiral and will work with the Congress towards the enactment of effective and meaningful reform of product liability law.

Key to promoting investment in ideas, innovation, and research is ensuring that those investments will be protected. Accordingly, I have proposed as part of my superconductivity legislation to raise legal protection for products resulting from patented processes and to prohibit foreign nations from using the Freedom of Information Act to acquire intellectual property developed by the U.S. Government. Additional measures planned include joining the Berne Convention, which provides international protection for intellectual property, demanding adequate protection of intellectual property rights when negotiating treaties, and pushing hard in the GATT Round for high standards for intellectual property protection worldwide.

8. *Free Trade with Canada.* On January 2 Prime Minister Mulroney and I signed a Free Trade Agreement that, when enacted, will mark the beginning of a remarkable new era. It eliminates all tariffs between the United States and Canada over the next 10 years, promotes free trade in energy, and greatly reduces restrictions on investments. The agreement goes beyond most trade agreements and covers services and investment. It is a "win-win" agreement for both the United States and Canada. Moreover, it sends a signal to the rest of the world: protectionism is not inevitable. Rather, with the political will and commitment, all nations can promote freer trade to the benefit of each and every citizen. I will soon transmit a bill to implement this agreement and I urge prompt enactment to ensure that the agreement takes effect on January 1, 1989.

In November, the United States Trade Representative, on my behalf, signed a framework agreement with Mexico for discussions on trade and investment. This framework agreement is an important step forward in our bilateral trade relationship that will enable us to work together to address problems, reduce barriers and, thus, increase trade and investment between our two countries.

9. *Freeing the Individual to Work.* Few laws that a government may impose are more injurious to liberty than restrictions on the right to work, as outlined in my Economic Bill of Rights. Today, we are in the 6th year of an economic recovery that has created 14.5 million jobs. In order to continue and to build on that record of growth, we need policies that recognize the changing nature and changing needs of the work force.

These policies include enhanced training for dislocated workers, so that they are able to adjust to a world requiring new and different skills. Our proposed Worker Adjustment Program will address this need in a comprehensive way while increasing the role of States and localities in determining how these funds are best spent. In addition, we are preparing to give States and localities the flexibility to provide remedial training to disadvantaged youth. For thousands of low-skilled young people, this initiative holds the potential to provide a way out of poverty and into a job.

Indeed, the changes in our work force present other challenges as well. More people are working than ever before in our history. There is fuller work force participation across all sectors, and more women are working than ever before. While this has helped power our tremendous growth, it has also created tension between demands of work and demands of child-rearing. We need to work with State and local governments and the private sector to identify and develop effective solutions, consistent with our efforts to strengthen the family, to foster practical, voluntary ways to ease this tension.

Several threats to our continued job growth can be found in a range of initiatives pending in the Congress, such as employer-provided health care and health insurance; parental leave; advance notification of plant closings; risk notification; an increase in the minimum wage; labor protective provisions; and a ban on employers using polygraphs to prevent theft. Many of these initiatives have been called "mandated benefits," but a more accurate description would be "mandated costs" or "mandated unemployment." Such mandated costs are particularly harmful to our Nation's small businesses, which are leading the way in job creation in our economic recovery. While many of the objectives sought by such legislation are laudable, they are not the proper subject for Federal mandates.

While well intentioned, the added employment costs would reduce job opportunities, lower wages generally, weaken economic growth, and hinder our competitiveness in world markets. In short, they are efforts to make individuals and companies pay for new government programs, mandated by the government but implemented by the private sector. Rather than forcing employers to provide such coverage, with possible serious adverse side effects for some workers, these decisions should be left to voluntary negotiation between employers and employees.

The adoption of "comparable worth" pay standards, another intrusive form of government intervention into the labor market, has also been proposed. The objective is not to provide equal pay for equal work, a concept I fully support and which I enforce as the law of the land. Rather, "comparable worth" proposals seek to determine the worth of completely different jobs and then empower government panels to assign "fair" and "comparable" wages. Proposals that would establish panels of "experts" to determine how much workers can earn would create the kind of planned economy that has stifled economic growth in other parts of the world. Such wage fixing completely ignores the fact that in a free enterprise economy market forces should determine wages.

We should seek to eliminate existing barriers to employment. For example, when I took office I inherited a rule that, for over 40 years, prohibited individuals from working in their homes to produce knitted garments such as sweaters, caps, and scarves. In 1984, we dropped that rule and permitted employers to hire home workers after obtaining a certificate from the Department of Labor authorizing such employment, thus ensuring that the home workers receive the protection of the Fair Labor Standards Act. The restrictions still apply to six other categories of products, and the Department of Labor will be working to extend the certification procedures for five of the six remaining home work industries.

Another proposal in the Congress would raise the minimum wage, thereby creating additional barriers to employment. Today most people who work at the minimum wage are teenagers and others with limited experience who need these jobs to begin their climb up the economic ladder. Few are heads of households. Higher minimum wages will surely force young and inexperienced workers into unemployment. We should permit a special minimum wage differential for teenagers that would increase employment, on-the-job-training, and future wage growth for the least-skilled workers. Reform of other Federal wage statutes, such as Davis-Bacon, is also needed.

We should avoid so-called anti-"double breasting" laws that would bar firms with union labor from having independent affiliates without union contracts. Anti-double breasting laws reduce job opportunities by raising labor costs and should be left to negotiation between employer and employee.

D. Empowering Individuals by Opening Up New Areas for Human Endeavor

One enduring legacy of American frontier society has been a love of bold challenges and wide open vistas. Some 30 years ago we crossed a "new frontier" with a shot into space. Today we continue to face new opportunities and new challenges in opening a limitless universe beyond our tiny globe to exploration and commercial enterprise. But here on Earth as well, whole new sectors of discovery and productivity lie waiting for development through individual creativity and initiative.

1. *Privatization of Government Activities.* Over time, government has accumulated numerous commercial operations, many of which could be performed more efficiently by the private sector. Where such opportunities exist to provide better services at lower cost, we will seek to transfer such services and operations to the most efficient enterprises. This does not imply the abrogation of government responsibility for these services. Rather, it merely recognizes that what matters the most is the cost and quality of the service provided, not who provides it. In addition, there is an important moral consideration—individual liberty would be enhanced and the debilitating effect of public sector growth on human freedom would be reduced.

Even now, government relies extensively on the private sector to provide basic government services in many key programs: the G.I. Bill, Medicare, Medicaid, student loans, food stamps, and many other programs. Further, the government benefits from private sector assistance in disbursing funds electronically, assessing credit worthiness of loan applicants, servicing and collecting payments due the government, and relying on finance accounting systems from the private sector to bring about an extensive upgrading of Executive branch financial management throughout the government. Thus privatization can make government operations more efficient and at the same time provide more convenient service to our citizens.

The Administration sold over $5 billion in government loans to private investors last year, with plans to sell an additional $4 billion in government loans this year. Additionally, we sold the government-owned freight railroad, CONRAIL, to private investors at a price tag of almost $2 billion.

As part of my Economic Bill of Rights, I established the President's Commission on Privatization to accelerate our program of placing greater reliance on the private sector. In its interim report covering government housing programs the Commission recommended expanded use of housing vouchers, tenant management of public housing projects, and sales of public housing units to tenants. The Congress has already enacted a major housing bill that endorses housing vouchers and facilitates the Administration's efforts to encourage tenant management and public housing ownership. Similarly, the Commission has endorsed the sale of government loan assets. The Commission's final report is expected in March and will cover many more opportunities, including prison construction, military commissaries, AMTRAK, Naval Petroleum Reserves, and urban mass transportation. After a careful review of these proposals, legislation will be developed to implement the most promising proposals.

To pursue administrative measures within the Executive branch and implement the findings of the Commission on Privatization, I have created an Office of Privatization within the Executive Office of the President. I have given it the responsibility to investigate and propose privatization opportunities that can be included in my recommendations for the Fiscal Year 1989 Budget.

I will recommend that a comprehensive study be conducted to measure the likely benefits that would occur if we permit the private sector to perform some functions now performed by the United States Postal Service and other government entities.

I will also recommend a series of pilot projects to determine if privatization is the best way to go in other government programs, including operation of minimum security Federal prisons, Federal prison industries, regulatory audits by the U.S. Customs Service, management of Federal multiple-use lands by public and private groups, and waste water treatment facilities funded by Federal grants.

I am further recommending the direct privatization of all or some of several existing government programs where the benefits of privatization are believed to be significant or where studies have already been completed. Included in this category are the Naval Petroleum Reserves, AMTRAK, Federal Crop Insurance, arbitration of tax disputes, government employee housing, the Railroad Retirement Board, the National Finance Center, the National Technical Information Service, the Alaska Power Administration, and the collection of overdue loans to the Federal government. I will also ask for substantially expanded authority to allow individuals to use their private sector credit cards to pay money owed to the government.

In addition, I have recently promulgated an Executive order to foster greater contracting out of services currently provided by the government to private providers, many in America's vital small business community. Study after study, many conducted by the General Accounting Office, demonstrate that savings of between 30 to 40 percent can be achieved by contracting out government work to private business. If all agencies took advantage of contracting-out opportunities, the total savings would amount to $7 billion per year.

2. *New Opportunities in Space.* Nearly 2 decades ago, with courage and bold technological innovation, America pushed back the frontier of space by landing a man on the moon and safely bringing him back. This breakthrough created untold opportunities for scientific discovery and commerce and advanced mankind's age-old dream of exploring space beyond its planetary home.

If America is to continue its leadership in space, we must now forge ahead, exploring space's vast frontier and expanding our free enterprise system to Earth's orbits and beyond. And we must build our long-term space future on a sound foundation that will ensure reliable and economical access to and use of outer space.

I recently adopted an enhanced comprehensive national space policy. This policy reaffirms America's commitment to space leadership as a fundamental national objective and recognizes the importance of both private sector and governmental space activities in achieving critical national goals. And while acknowledging the importance of returning the Space Shuttle to safe, reliable operations, it also stresses that access to space, so vital to America's security and prosperity, must never be limited to any single system.

As a matter of special note, my policy also specifically recognizes the importance of extending the reach of American private commerce to space and establishes goals to guide both civil and national security space efforts in achieving cost-effective, resilient, and reliable means of access to space.

And I am no less deeply committed to the long-range goal of expanding human presence and activity beyond earth orbit and into the solar system, and I invite the Congress to join with me in endorsing and supporting this new long-term goal.

As the first step, I have directed the National Aeronautics and Space Administration to begin a systematic development of space technologies called Project Pathfinder, which will aid us in deciding where this new adventure should take us, and when. The funding proposed for Fiscal year 1989 is $100 million.

Second, I am asking the Congress to maintain our strong national commitment to a permanently manned space station. The Fiscal Year 1989 Budget request includes $1.0 billion to achieve this goal, along with a request for a 3-year appropriations commitment from the Congress totalling $6.1 billion.

Third, I will soon announce a major Commercial Space Initiative that includes administrative and legislative action to nurture entrepreneurship in space. By taking advantage of the private sector's innovative excellence, we can maintain and extend America's leadership in space.

My initiative will have three goals: (1) promoting a strong commercial presence in space—we need the private sector to begin to lay the infrastructure necessary for research and manufacturing in space; (2) assuring a highway to space by building on my previous efforts to promote a strong private expendable launch vehicle industry; and (3) building a solid technology and talent base. The engineers and scientists who will be working in space are in school now. We must give them the tools and the enthusiasm to do the job well.

E. Empowering the People to Participate in the Political Process

Political enfranchisement in America has evolved in the direction of a more participatory republic. Today any legislation in this area should open up more participation in the political process.

1. *Removing Government Interference with the Political Process.* The right to free speech and the right to participate in the democratic process are two of our most fundamental freedoms. In *Buckley* v. *Valeo*, the Supreme Court held that limits on how individuals spend their own resources in the political process can violate the First Amendment. This is a sound principle. We should make sure "campaign reform" will not have the effect of reducing popular participation in the political process or impairing constitutional rights. Today, there are proposals to restrict certain parts of our electoral process. A more beneficial reform would be the requirement of full disclosure of all campaign contributions, including in-kind contributions, and expenditures on behalf of any electoral activities, including those in the context of membership communication.

2. *Protecting Civil Servants from Political Pressure.* The Hatch Act was passed in 1939 in response to scandals involving the administration of funds in New Deal programs. It prohibits Federal civil servants from taking part in certain partisan political activities, such as campaigning for public office, participating in party management, or raising political funds. The Clay Amendments in the Congress would severely erode these prohibitions. Although advanced in lofty terms—"the right of government workers to participate more fully in the political process"—their effect would be to politicize the civil service and reduce public faith in government. Federal workers already enjoy their democratic right to vote and to express their political views in a wide variety of other ways.

We do not want to risk a situation in which Federal employees come to believe that their advancement depends on espousing particular views, perhaps the political views of their superiors. Neither should electoral campaigning be allowed to mar cooperation between the political appointees of the President and the civil service establishment, a cooperation crucial to good government. As I have said in the past, the Hatch Act should not be changed or repealed.

3. *Improving the Civil Service.* The past 7 years have witnessed an increasing commitment by the Nation's Federal civil service to quality in their work and pride in their performance. The abilities of this work force, from the most recently hired clerical worker to the most senior member of the managerial corps, are ready not only to continue the effort to serve the American people, but to take that service to new levels of excellence.

At present, however, the Federal civil service is overregulated by a system that discourages employee initiative and hamstrings government managers with thousands of pages of restrictive rules and regulations. With the major reforms encompassed in my proposed Civil Service Simplification Act, we can provide substantial incentives for top performance, introducing into our Federal government the classic productive values of the American workplace: entrepreneurial freedom and reward for hard work.

VI. To Secure the Blessings of Liberty

It was the need to secure inalienable, God-given rights from oppression that moved our forefathers to institute a new government in America. Among these individual rights, Jefferson wrote, were "Life, Liberty and the pursuit of Happiness." But, as the Founders of our Republic made clear in drafting a new Constitution 11 years later, their intention was not only to secure liberty but the blessings of liberty as well. To attain these blessings would mean cultivating the values that sustain a free people. George Washington advised our Nation in his Farewell Address,

"Of all the dispositions and habits which lead to political prosperity, religion and morality are indispensable supports. In vain would that man claim the tribute of patriotism who should labor to subvert these great pillars of human happiness, these firmest props of the duties of men and citizens. The mere politician, equally with the pious man, ought to respect and to cherish them. A volume could not trace all their connections with private and public felicity."

Following our first President's good counsel, I am leading my Administration in efforts to shore up the moral foundations of our individual freedom:

A. Protection of the Unborn

None are more powerless than the unborn. Since the legalization of abortion-on-demand in 1973, there have been an estimated 21 million abortions in this country. I am committed to reducing the number of abortions in this country and reaffirming life's sacred position in our Nation.

The Congress should pass expeditiously my Human Life Bill. The first section of the bill contains a finding that abortion takes the life of a human being and that *Roe* v. *Wade* was wrong not to recognize the humanity of the unborn child. The second section would enact, on a permanent and government-wide basis, the Hyde Amendment restriction prohibiting Federal dollars from going for abortion unless a mother's life is endangered. In addition, the Congress should pass the Human Life Amendment.

At my direction, the Department of Health and Human Services is about to issue regulations prohibiting the use of Title X funds (approximately $140 million) for any program that performs abortion, counsels for abortion, or promotes abortion through lawsuits, lobbying, or other such activities. The regulations also require that Title X programs separate themselves from programs that engage in abortion activities. It is clear from the legislative record surrounding the passage of Title X that its purpose, far from promoting abortion, was one of offering an alternative to abortion and indeed reducing the number of abortions. For some time the program as enforced was standing its essential purpose on its head, effectively promoting abortion instead of reducing the incidence of abortion as intended by the Congress.

Another loophole often used to circumvent prohibitions on using Federal funds for abortions is the use of psychiatric recommendations. Currently the law allows for Federal funding only when an abortion is necessary to save the life of the mother. This law reflects the consensus that abortion may be considered when there is a physical threat to the mother. I am directing the Secretary of Health and Human Services to issue regulations that reflect this consensus and make it clear that only when there is physical danger to the life of the mother can Federal funds be used for abortion.

In August 1987 I formed an Interagency Task Force on Adoption that delivered its final report to me on November 13. I will act to implement the Task Force recommendations and propose legislation where necessary. Each year over 140,000 children are adopted, yet thousands of childless families still wait for children to adopt. There are 36,000 children awaiting adoption, of which about 60 percent are "special needs" children. Many have physical or emotional handicaps, belong to sibling groups, or are older children; they are generally more difficult to place.

This Administration will also work with the States to encourage model legislation that promotes adoption. California's Pregnancy Freedom of Choice Act, for instance, allows the State to reimburse licensed nonprofit maternity homes for the costs of maternity care and other pregnancy services. Michigan contracts out special needs adoption to private agencies, reimbursing them for the full cost of adoption services up to $10,000. These are exemplary efforts to provide families for children in need of parental love and care.

B. Religious Liberties

The First Amendment protects the right of Americans to freely exercise their religious beliefs in an atmosphere of toleration and accommodation. As I have noted in the past, certain court decisions have in my view interpreted the First Amendment so as to restrict, rather than protect, individual rights of conscience. I have repeatedly affirmed my belief that school prayer on a voluntary basis is permissible, indeed desirable, in the public school. In my State of the Union addresses in 1986 and 1987, I expressed my support for a constitutional amendment that would make it clear that the Constitution does not prohibit voluntary prayer in public schools.

One disturbing development in this area of the law has been the exclusion of religiously affiliated organizations from federally funded programs. A recent lower court decision held unconstitutional my Adolescent Family Life Program because the program included religious organizations among those carrying out its implementation. That decision, if upheld, would effectively require the government to discriminate against religious charitable organizations, even when their participation in a program only serves to further its legitimate secular purpose. The Department of Justice is appealing this ruling that I believe to be inconsistent with the First Amendment. Our forefathers came to this land in large part to secure the rights to freedom of religion and individual conscience that they would later establish as bedrock provisions of our Constitution. We must avoid such perversion of the First Amendment. Rather, as we prepare for the 21st century, we must continue to foster the free exercise of religion that our forefathers understood would provide the moral foundations for American society.

CONCLUSION

These then are the legislative and administrative policies that the Administration will pursue in furtherance of the six purposes for which the American people first ordained and established our Constitution. They have been carefully chosen. For obviously not every policy that a President or a Congress may put forward is compatible with our Constitution, even though that policy might be popular. In order to secure the liberty of individuals and political minorities, the Constitution places a number of carefully considered restrictions on the Federal government. The Congress does not, for example, possess a general legislative power, nor the President the power of decree. The Framers proscribed both as inconsistent with limited, constitutional government. Thanks in large measure to their wisdom, America has enjoyed the blessings of liberty for 2 centuries. It is my belief that the policies presented in this message will contribute to the continuing restoration of the Federal government to a sound constitutional footing and thus preserve these same blessings for our posterity in the 21st century.

RONALD REAGAN

The White House,
January 25, 1988.

Informal Exchange With Reporters
January 26, 1988

Aid to the Contras

Q. Mr. President, are you ready to give a figure on *contra* aid yet?

The President. That's what we're going to discuss this morning, and you'll be hearing about it very soon.

Vice President Bush

Q. What do you think about last night's encounter between Vice President Bush and Dan Rather?

The President. I am only going to talk about the other encounter—*contra* aid. [*Laughter*]

Q. Do you think he upstaged your State of the Union last night? [*Laughter*]

The President. No comment.

Q. Do you think Rather was too tough on the Vice President?

The President. That's, again, no comment.

Q. Well, could you tell us what the Vice President said to you in confidence and help clear up some—[*laughter*]. You could get him off the hook, Mr. President, by telling us what the Vice President urged you about the Iranian arms sales.

The President. No, I think he has been exactly right, that that would set a precedent with regard to private conversations between Presidents and Vice Presidents, and I don't think we have a right to do that.

Q. Was he present when Shultz and Weinberger expressed their objections to this arms sale? There's some confusion about that.

The President. No, he wasn't.

Q. He was not present?

The President. No.

Israeli Response to Palestinian Protesters

Q. Do you think it's civilized to break the arms and legs of protesters?

Senator McCain. Are the Sandinistas still doing that? [*Laughter*]

Q. He answered the question. The Sandinistas and the Israelis are doing it.

The President. That's one of those questions that if I try to ignore it or something I look hard-hearted. And I'm opposed to violence wherever it's possible to avoid violence.

Note: The exchange began at 11:23 a.m., prior to a meeting with congressional leaders in the Cabinet Room at the White House. Dan Rather interviewed the Vice President on the CBS Evening News on January 25. John McCain was a Senator from Arizona.

Message to the Senate Transmitting Amendments to the International Convention on Load Lines, 1966
January 26, 1988

To the Senate of the United States:

I transmit herewith, for the advice and consent of the Senate with a view to acceptance by the United States, amendments to regulations 47 and 48 of Annex II of the International Convention on Load Lines, 1966. The report of the Department of State is also transmitted for the information of the Senate in connection with its consideration of these amendments.

The International Convention on Load Lines establishes uniform principles governing the safe loading of ships on international voyages. The annexes, which form an integral part of the Convention, embody the regulations for determining the location of ships' load lines. The annexes also divide the world's oceans into regions in which particular load lines must be observed depending on the season of the year in which the vessels operate. The amendments to regulations 47 and 48 of the Convention, proposed by the Government of Chile, would redefine the boundaries of the seasonal zones intersecting the coast of Chile. The effect would be to extend the tropical and summer zones toward the south to the advantage of both the Chilean coastal trade and visiting foreign trade.

I believe that the proposed amendments will not be detrimental to United States shipping and should be accepted. I recommend that the Senate give early and favorable consideration to these amendments, and give advice and consent to their acceptance by the United States.

RONALD REAGAN

The White House,
January 26, 1988.

Message to the Congress Transmitting a Report on Federal Greenhouse Effect Research

January 26, 1988

To the Congress of the United States:

In accordance with Section 9 of Public Law 99–383 (100 Stat. 816), I transmit herewith a report on current government activities in the area of research on the so-called "Greenhouse Effect."

While you will note that extensive investigations of the phenomenon are in progress, we do not plan to establish an International Year of the Greenhouse Effect as suggested in the language of Public Law 99–383.

RONALD REAGAN

The White House,
January 26, 1988.

Accordance of the Personal Rank of Ambassador to Alan H. Flanigan While Serving as United States Special Negotiator for Defense Negotiations With Greece

January 26, 1988

The President today accorded the personal rank of Ambassador to Alan H. Flanigan in his capacity as United States Special Negotiator for United States-Greek Defense Negotiations.

Mr. Flanigan is currently United States Special Negotiator for United States-Greek Defense Negotiations at the Department of State in Washington, DC. He entered the Foreign Service in 1966 after serving 6 years as a lieutenant in the United States Navy. His first assignment as a junior officer was to the U.S. Embassy in Lima, Peru. In 1969 he returned to the Department as desk officer for Peru where he served until 1971 when he became special assistant to the Counselor of the Department. Mr. Flanigan was political officer at the U.S. Consulate General in Izmir, Turkey, 1973–1975, and at the U.S. Embassy in Ankara, Turkey, 1975–1978. He was then assigned as officer in charge of Turkish Affairs in the Department, 1979–1981; and Director of the Office of Western European Affairs, 1981–1983. From 1983 to 1987, he served as deputy chief of mission at the U.S. Embassy in Lisbon, Portugal.

Mr. Flanigan graduated from Tufts University (B.A., 1960). He was born July 8, 1938, in Columbus, IN. He is married, has two children, and resides in Alexandria, VA.

Appointment of Maurice Raymond Greenberg as a Member of the Advisory Committee for Trade Negotiations

January 26, 1988

The President today announced his intention to appoint Maurice Raymond Greenberg to be a member of the Advisory Committee for Trade Negotiations for a term of 2 years. This is a reappointment.

Since 1967 Mr. Greenberg has been president and chief executive officer of American International Group, Inc., in New York, NY. Prior to this he was president of American Homes in New York.

Mr. Greenberg graduated from the University of Miami in 1948 and New York

School of Law (LL.B., 1950). He served in the U.S. Army, 1942–1945 and 1951–1953. He was born May 4, 1925, in New York, NY. Mr. Greenberg is married, has four children, and resides in New York City.

Appointment of J. Michael Farrell as Deputy United States Commissioner on the Commission for the Study of Alternatives to the Panama Canal

January 26, 1988

The President today announced his intention to appoint J. Michael Farrell to be Deputy Commissioner of the United States of America on the Commission for the Study of Alternatives to the Panama Canal. This is a new position.

Since 1987 Mr. Farrell has been a partner with the law firm Manatt, Phelps, Rothenberg & Evans in Washington, DC. Prior to this he was General Counsel at the Department of Energy, 1985–1987. From 1981 to 1982, he held several Federal Government appointments including: Private Sector Coordinator of the Caribbean Basin Initiative at the Department of State, Deputy Director, Office of Presidential Personnel at the White House, and Assistant Counsel in the office of the Counsel to the President.

Mr. Farrell graduated from Georgetown University (B.S., 1963; J.D., 1966). He was born March 30, 1941, in Washington, DC. He is married, has three children, and resides in Washington, DC.

Appointment of John E. Washburn as a Member of the Supplemental Health Insurance Panel

January 26, 1988

The President today announced his intention to appoint John E. Washburn to be a member of the Supplemental Health Insurance Panel. He would succeed Bruce A. Bunner.

Since 1983 Mr. Washburn has been director of insurance for the State of Illinois in Springfield, IL. Prior to this he was director of the legislative office in the office of the Governor in Springfield, IL, 1980–1983. Mr. Washburn began his career in State government in 1970.

Mr. Washburn graduated from Northern Illinois University (B.S., 1968). He was born June 10, 1943, in Madison, WI. He is married, has two children, and resides in Chatham, IL.

Nomination of Ronald F. Lehman II To Be an Assistant Secretary of Defense

January 27, 1988

The President today announced his intention to nominate Ronald F. Lehman II to be an Assistant Secretary of Defense (International Security Policy) at the Department of Defense. He would succeed Richard N. Perle.

Since 1986 Mr. Lehman has been United States Negotiator for Strategic Nuclear Arms at the United States Mission to International Organizations, Geneva, for the Department of State in Washington, DC. Previously he was Deputy United States Negotiator for Strategic Nuclear Arms, 1985–1986. Mr. Lehman was Deputy Assistant to the President for National Security Affairs at the White House, 1986, and Special Assistant to the President for National Security Affairs and Senior Director for Defense Programs and Arms Control for the National Security Council at the White House, 1983–1986. He was a U.S. delegation member for the U.S.-Soviet direct communications links talks, 1983–1984, and for the U.S.-Soviet talks on nuclear proliferation, 1982. He was senior adviser to the U.S. delegation for the U.N. Special Session on Disarmament, 1982, and Deputy Assistant Secretary of Defense for the Department of Defense, 1982–1983. He was a member of the professional staff of the Armed Services Committee for the United States Senate, 1978–1982.

Mr. Lehman graduated from Claremont Men's College (B.A., 1968) and Claremont Graduate School (M.A., 1969; Ph.D., 1975). He was born March 25, 1946, in Sanitarium, CA. He served in the United States Army from 1969 to 1971. Mr. Lehman is married and resides in Arlington, VA.

Remarks to Members of the Reserve Officers Association
January 27, 1988

Well, thank you. And General Sandler, General Hultman, distinguished guests and Reserve officers, I'm grateful for this opportunity to be with you and to thank personally all of you in the Reserve Officers Association. The United States of America would not stand as secure and free today if it were not for you. You have the deep appreciation of this President and the rest of our citizenry for your dedication. General Sandler, General Hultman, as a grateful Commander in Chief, I salute you all and those who serve with you.

You know, looking around this room, I can't help but believe that in this gathering I may well hold the longevity record as a Reserve officer. [*Laughter*] I was, in fact, sworn into the Army Reserve as a lieutenant in 1935 at Fort Des Moines, Iowa. And that was back when the cavalry really was the cavalry. [*Laughter*] Now, I understand that both Generals Sandler and Hultman have served at Fort Des Moines. Back in my day, having a general come to visit was a big event.

You know, there used to be a thing called the citizen's military training camps. And then every summer, why, they would have a war game someplace, and they would come in for 2 weeks in an encampment. And then the Reserve officers would be called up, and they'd don uniforms and serve the officers in this thing that was undertaken. And I can't help but remember that one time it was at Fort Omaha. And usually they would invite some top brass from Washington to come out and add a little luster to the scene, in viewing these war games.

And it seems that one young cavalry lieutenant was sent with a message over to the commanding officer of Fort Omaha who was standing with the visiting general. You know, in the cavalry you didn't always know what horse you were on or what they'd given you. His must have had a sore mouth or something, because he came galloping up and then tightened up on the reins for a halt. And that horse just planted all four feet, and he somersaulted right over the horse's head. [*Laughter*] And believe me, he landed on his feet holding the reins in his left hand, and—[*laughter*]—realized he was facing two generals. [*Laughter*] And he snapped to salute. [*Laughter*] And the visiting general, being the ranking one there, very slowly started to respond, but as he did so, he turned to the other one and said, "Does he always dismount like that?" [*Laughter*]

I will always remember my time as a Reserve officer. And let me add that I will always be grateful to you for the support that you've been to our administration over these last 7 years. When it counted, you were there. Your support for a strong national defense, for American leadership and solid alliances, for an activist, profreedom foreign policy has made all the difference.

It has not been easy, but together we've rebuilt America's defenses, which in the last decade had been sorrowfully neglected. Military spending in real terms was permitted to decline by 20 percent during the 1970's. And if there's any lesson from that decade, it is that there's a measurable relationship between the military might of the United States and the state of freedom in the world. By the latter half of the 1970's, the pay level of our active duty personnel had eroded, their weapons were wearing out, spare parts were in short supply, morale hit rockbottom, and reenlistment rates plummeted.

Not by mere coincidence, this was also a time of defeat and despair for the free people of the world. Those who suggest that the Soviet Union's disproportional military spending is a reaction to our own military expenditures need to explain why in the 1970's, when our real spending was going down, the Soviets raced ahead with a massive peacetime buildup. At the same time, Communist forces, supplied and trained by the Soviet Union, pushed forward in Southeast Asia, in Africa, and in Central America. Terrorists wreaked havoc and, much to our European allies' alarm, Soviet intermediate-range missiles, SS-20's, were deployed. Communist expansion and Western retreat were the order of the day.

Victor Hugo once said that "People do not lack strength; they lack will." Well, in 1980, the American people looked deep into their souls and proved to the world that they still had the will to be free and the courage to carry the torch of liberty, just as our forefathers did before us. We rolled up our sleeves and went to work. Since then we've brought up the pay level of our military personnel. We've replenished the stockpiles of spare parts and ammunition. We've put in the hands of those defending us top quality weapons, like the F-16 and the Abrams battle tank. And perhaps most important to these brave young men and women, to whom we owe so much, we restored the pride this country has in those who wear the military uniform of the United States of America.

Today America's military is strong, confident, and standing tall. I can't help but think that if there's one man who deserves credit for the rejuvenation of our forces and the resurgence of American military might, it is the man you honor with this year's Minuteman of the Year award, former Secretary of Defense Cap Weinberger.

Cap inherited what seemed like an overwhelming challenge. When he was appointed, I felt like I'd just handed him a bayonet and given him 2 hours to clear a minefield. [*Laughter*] Cap, for example, was faced with the dilemma of sweeping the waste, fraud, and abuse out of the Pentagon, realizing that every victory would be used against him. And sure enough, when contracts for $400 hammers or $9,000 wrenches were found and corrected, more often than not, it was portrayed in the media as a horror story and used to cast doubt rather than praise on our defense effort.

It's a tribute to their common sense and patriotism that the American people have stuck with us. The national security of the United States is not an inexpensive proposition. It is not a job that can be done with bargain-basement equipment and second-rate weapons. And as a free people, we owe this pledge to our defenders: If they're willing to put their lives on the line for us, we at least must be willing to pay the cost of providing them with the best equipment and weapons available so they can accomplish their mission and come home safely.

I think the American people agree with that as well. They want our country to be secure and America to be a strong force for freedom in the world. Our nation's defense should be a sacred trust, above the political fray and the pressures of partisan consideration. That is the ideal, but let's have no illusions. Three years of steady decline in the value of our annual defense investment have increased the risk of our most basic security interests, jeopardizing earlier hard-won goals. We must face squarely the implications of this negative trend and make adequate, stable defense spending a top goal both this year and in the future. This is what the American people want, and you'd think those with acute political instincts would understand it.

It all reminds me of the story of the gunners mate on the American fighting frigate back in the days of our Revolution, the *Bonhomme Richard*. There he was in the midst of that battle, wounded and lying among the other wounded on the deck—the smoke filling the air and the shot and shell flying—when from the quarterdeck he heard that line, "I have not yet begun to fight." The gunners mate leaned over to another member of the crew and simply said, "There's always somebody who didn't get the word." [*Laughter*]

Thomas Jefferson once noted, "If a nation expects to be ignorant and free, it expects what never was and never will be." It is up to us then to get the word to our fellow citizens. First and foremost, we've got to inform them about the serious consequences—I would even say catastrophic consequences—of cutting off aid and, thus, pulling the rug out from under the democratic resistance in Nicaragua.

Today I'm submitting to the Congress my request for $36 million in additional aid for the freedom fighters in Nicaragua. This request ensures that the democratic resistance can keep the pressure on the Sandinistas to comply with the terms of the Guatemala accord for peace and democracy. Ninety percent of the funds is for nonlethal aid, such as food, clothing, medicine, and the means to deliver it. Ten percent is for ammunition. And this part of the request will be suspended until March 31st to determine if the steps taken by the Sandinistas are irreversible steps to democracy in Nicaragua. In reaching this judgment, I will personally consult the Presidents of the four Central American democracies.

Our approach to the Communist threat in Nicaragua has long been based on a simple principle: diplomacy and pressure in support of freedom and democracy must go hand-in-hand. President Teddy Roosevelt once said, "Diplomacy is utterly useless where there is no force behind it." We've seen the success of this two-track approach elsewhere in the world—in Afghanistan, freedom fighters have forced the Soviet Union to think seriously about a diplomatic solution to that brutal occupation; and in the INF talks, where our decision to deploy intermediate-range missiles a few years ago made possible the agreement I signed this past December.

This same approach may be working today in Nicaragua, although it's too early to tell if Daniel Ortega's promises will be matched by true efforts to allow democracy to flourish or if these promises are just a repetition of things said for nearly 10 years. It is clear, however, that the pressure of the Nicaraguan freedom fighters has forced the Sandinistas to pull back from aggression against their neighbors and to think twice about their continued domestic repression.

Although past efforts to restore peace and establish democracy in Nicaragua have invariably failed, I believe we owe it to ourselves and the people of Central America to explore fully diplomatic avenues toward solving the conflict. But only if we have the tools can diplomacy work. Last November, I pledged at the Organization of American States that if serious negotiations between the Nicaraguan resistance and the Sandinista government were underway, I would ask Secretary Shultz to enter regional talks in Central America with the Presidents of all five countries.

I reiterate that pledge today, and I hope that we may be close to fulfillment of the necessary conditions. The objectives laid out last August in the Guatemala accord and most recently affirmed in San José by the five Presidents are consistent with our goals. I will ask Secretary Shultz to pursue them, just as he pursues the security interests of our country and the democracies of Central America.

We must ask ourselves, however, what will create the conditions for serious negotiations? Recent months have shown clearly that only continued and to the Nicaraguan freedom fighters—aid, I should say—to the Nicaraguan freedom fighters has provided sufficient incentive for the Sandinistas to make concessions, as minimal as those concessions have been. If we remove that incentive—if Congress cuts off aid to the freedom fighters next week—there is little chance that the Sandinistas will bargain seriously.

I intend to make an all-out diplomatic effort to achieve a negotiated settlement leading to democracy in Central America. But success at the negotiating table depends on continued support for the Nicaraguan freedom fighters. We cannot expect diplomacy to work if we ourselves lack the will to negotiate from a position of strength. We cannot go to the bargaining table empty-handed. And that, in the end, would assure a Marxist-Leninist regime on the American mainland. And I didn't come to Washington to preside over the communization of Central America.

We must have the will to do what is right and the courage to stand by other free peoples, whether they're Western Europeans in the NATO alliance, Mujahidin insurgents struggling for their national independence, or Nicaraguan freedom fighters who want nothing more than the democratic government they were promised. Such support makes war less likely; it deters aggression. In the case of NATO, it has provided over 40 years of peace for the European Community. In the Third World, our support affirms to all that aggression comes with a heavy price, and that Americans will not sit back idly and watch brave people—like those in Afghanistan and Nicaragua—beaten into submission.

There is reason for cautious optimism about relations between the East and West. There's evidence of some change in the Soviet Union. We welcome it, but let me reiterate a point I've made before. If there is truly to be a new era, we must see significant changes—a far greater respect for human rights, including the right to emigrate, and an end to Soviet policies that prolong regional conflicts.

On those regional conflicts, we've heard the rhetoric. Now it's time to see the action. If the Soviet leadership wants to improve substantially relations with the West, they must realize that it will not happen while Soviet troops still occupy Afghanistan. We want to see those Soviet troops go home permanently and leave the Afghan people in peace and free to determine their own future.

The people of Afghanistan know, as do so many others around the world, that if peace is to have a chance, if the hope for freedom is to be kept alive, the United States must play a powerful and active role in world affairs. It is an awesome responsibility. President Teddy Roosevelt said it well, "The world has set its face hopefully toward our democracy, and, oh, my fellow citizens, each one of you carries on your shoulders not only the burden of doing well for the sake of your own country but the burden of doing well and seeing that this nation does well for the sake of mankind."

That has never been more true than today as our naval forces patrol the waters of the Persian Gulf, a commitment that already cost the lives of 37 brave men aboard the U.S.S. *Stark*. Yet because of the bravery and professionalism of our military personnel, our friends in that volatile region understand that the United States can be counted on, and our adversaries know that we will not be driven out of the Middle East or anywhere else. We're telling the world in unmistakable terms that the United States is a global power, and we intend to keep her that way.

And let me just add, we went into the Gulf alone. Yet today the naval forces of our allies can also be found patrolling those dangerous waters. They came because they believed it was the right thing to do. It underscores the common interest we share. I can't help but be proud of this kind of cooperation. And I can't help but also be proud that America still has what it takes to lead the way.

Peace through strength. We've heard it a thousand times. The validity of that truism was never more real to me than during my recent summit with General Secretary Gorbachev. In 1981 we faced the challenge of Soviet deployment of a large number of new nuclear-armed intermediate-range missiles threatening our friends and allies in Western Europe and Asia. The Soviets rejected our offer for a zero option, which I proposed in November 1981. Following that, street demonstrators and our political adversaries turned up the heat on us—not the Soviets. Our opponents insisted on acceptance of a so-called nuclear freeze, which would have frozen-in the Soviet advantage. Well, to our credit and that of our allies, we stood firm and moved forward with our deployment of Pershing II's and ground-launched cruise missiles. It was this strength of commitment that brought the Soviets back to the bargaining table in early 1985, following their late 1983 walkout. And it was this strength that ultimately convinced them then to come to an agreement similar to the one I first proposed in 1981, a zero option.

Now I understand the justifiable apprehension about dealing with the Soviet Union. Will Rogers used to say we never lost a war, and we never won a conference. [*Laughter*] Well, let me just note: The cornerstones of any bargaining with the Soviets are strength and realism. I believe, however, there are potential areas, even with a government that is so fundamentally contrary to our own ideals, where it will be mutually beneficial for us to come to an agreement of some kind. It requires the utmost care, and that's what we took in reaching the INF agreement.

We withstood the massive propaganda campaign against deployment of the cruise and Pershing missiles. We understood [withstood] the Soviet pressure to abandon our Strategic Defense Initiative. And I can assure you, SDI will not be given up—under any circumstances—in exchange for an arms control agreement. And let me add now that the world must by now be noting a bit of cynicism in the Soviet campaign against SDI. Mr. Gorbachev himself, in a presummit interview, finally acknowledged his own country's extensive SDI-like program. They have—in effect and in fact—spent roughly $200 billion, many times more than the United States, on strategic defense over the last 10 years.

The Strategic Defense Initiative represents the new potential that technology is opening for mankind, especially the free people of the world. Computerization and miniaturization are changing our way of life. By the end of the next decade, we will have developed an aerospace plane that will take off from airport runways and speed to its destination at up to 25 times the speed of sound. It will be traveling in space—Washington to Tokyo in 3 hours.

But technology alone will not keep us free. Our country will never be able, simply, to put its faith in machines. The true bulwark of our freedom and national independence is to be found in the souls of our people. Our greatest defense lies in their love of liberty and strength of character. It is this that makes us a mighty force for good on this planet. It is this on which our security and our free system of government rely. It is the willingness to accept the heavy burden of responsibility that comes with liberty. Freedom, you see, is not meant for the faint of heart.

Nowhere is the sense of patriotism and responsibility to which I am referring more evident than in the Reserve forces of the United States. Today nearly 1.7 million men and women so serve. We as a country could never hope to match a less than free adversary, a militarized state—and maintain our own freedom at the same time—without a strong Reserve force. Today the Reserves play an increasingly vital role in military planning and in actual operations. In Grenada, Reserve pilots were part of the action. Off the coast of Lebanon, the Reserves relieved our weary sailors on the battleship *New Jersey.* And in everyday assignments, in arduous missions that need to be done, the Reserves are doing their part. You are doing it because you love this blessed land of ours and all she stands for. She cannot stand without you.

There's a story I'd like to close with. It's about a young American marine who fought in the Pacific four decades ago, Private First Class Maurice Roach. In March of 1945, after 3 weeks of heavy fighting, Roach was mortally wounded during the battle for Iwo Jima. A friend, Frank Campbell, now a Catholic priest in Oregon, remembers that before Roach died there on that blood-soaked little island, the young marine turned and whispered, "Tell 'em I did my duty." That same spirit is alive in this room today. It is what keeps our country the last best hope for all mankind. Thank you for all you are doing. God bless you.

Note: The President spoke at 2:20 p.m. in the International Ballroom at the Washington Hilton Hotel. In his opening remarks, he referred to Maj. Gen. Roger W. Sandler and Maj. Gen. Evan L. Hultman, president and executive director of the Reserve Officers Association, respectively.

Statement on the Senate Judiciary Committee Approval of the Supreme Court Nomination of Anthony M. Kennedy

January 27, 1988

The Senate Judiciary Committee's 14–0 vote to approve the nomination of Judge Anthony Kennedy gives us considerable confidence that the Nation will soon have a full Court. The committee has acted responsibly and expeditiously to review his qualifications and favorably report Judge Kennedy to the full Senate. I look forward to a positive vote soon by the Senate that will bring this distinguished and scholarly legal mind to the Court. I am very pleased by the committee action.

Message to the Congress Transmitting a Request for Aid for the Nicaraguan Democratic Resistance

January 27, 1988

To the Congress of the United States:

I herewith transmit a request in accordance with Section 111 of the joint resolution making further continuing appropriations for the fiscal year 1988 (P.L. 100–202) for budget and other authority to provide additional assistance for the Nicaraguan Democratic Resistance. Such assistance is essential to enhance the national security of the United States by advancing the prospects for democracy in Nicaragua and security for all of Central America.

Despite the combined diplomatic efforts of the four Central American democracies and the United States to persuade the Sandinista regime in Nicaragua to move toward democracy and to cease its actions that threaten the security of the region, progress towards these goals is far from complete.

The Sandinistas have repeatedly promised democracy to the people of Nicaragua, first before the Organization of American States in 1979 and, most recently, two weeks ago in the Final Communique of the Central American Presidents at the close of the San Jose Summit. In contrast to these assurances, the Sandinistas' years in power have brought repression and poverty to the Nicaraguan people, not democracy.

It has become clear beyond doubt that, without the steady pressure created by an effective Nicaraguan Democratic Resistance supported by a determined United States, the Sandinistas will neither move toward democracy nor desist from aggression against their neighbors. The United States, in consultation with the governments of the four Central American democracies, is prepared to redouble its diplomatic efforts in support of peace and democracy on the Central American isthmus. However, the success of such efforts depends on the continuation of the pressure that the Resistance provides.

I urge approval of the additional aid I am requesting for the Nicaraguan Democratic Resistance. Congressional approval of this request is essential to assure a democratic future for Central America and to protect the national security interests of the United States.

RONALD REAGAN

The White House,
January 27, 1988.

January 27, 1988

Request for Assistance for the Nicaraguan Democratic Resistance

In accordance with the Constitution and laws of the United States of America, as President of the United States of America, and pursuant to section 111(j)(1) of the joint resolution making further continuing appropriations for the fiscal year 1988 (Public Law 100–202), I hereby request budget and other authority to provide additional assistance for the Nicaraguan democratic resistance, as follows:

Sec. 101. Policy.

(a) *General Policy.*—It is the policy of the United States in implementing this request to advance democracy and security in Central America, and thereby to assist in bringing a just and lasting peace to that region, in a manner compatible with the Guatemala Peace Accord of August 7, 1987 and the Declaration of the Presidents of the Central American Nations at San Jose, Costa Rica on January 16, 1988, and consistent with the national security interests of the United States.

(b) *Specific Policy Objective.*—In pursuing the policy set forth in subsection (a), it is the objective of the United States to enhance its security as well as that of the democratic countries of Central America by assisting in the achievement of—

(1) genuine democracy in Nicaragua;

(2) an end to Soviet, Cuban, and other Communist bloc military or security assistance to, advisers in, and establishment or use of bases in, Nicaragua;

(3) an end to Nicaraguan aggression and subversion against other countries in Central America; and

(4) reduction of the military and security forces of Nicaragua to a level consistent with the security of other countries in the region.

Sec. 102. Transfer of Prior Defense Appropriations for Assistance.

(a) *Transfer and Use.*—Upon enactment of a joint resolution approving this request, there are hereby transferred to the President $36,250,000 of unobligated funds, from the appropriations accounts specified in section 106, to provide assistance for the Nicaraguan democratic resistance, to remain available until expended.

(b) *Earmark for Non-Lethal Assistance Including Human Rights.*—Of the funds transferred by subsection (a), $32,650,000 shall be available only for non-lethal assistance, of which $450,000 shall be available only for strengthening programs and activities of the Nicaraguan democratic resistance for the observance and advancement of human rights.

(c) *Prohibition on Purchase of Aircraft.*—Funds transferred by subsection (a) may not be obligated or expended to purchase aircraft.

(d) *Indemnification of Leased Aircraft.*—(1) The President is authorized to transfer unobligated funds, from the appropriations accounts specified in section 106, solely for the indemnification of aircraft leased to transport assistance for which this request provides and assistance previously, specifically authorized by law for the Nicaraguan democratic resistance.

(2) Not more than $20,000,000 may be transferred under the authority granted by paragraph (1).

(3) The President shall transfer the balance, if any, remaining of funds transferred under paragraph (1) to the appropriations accounts from which such funds were transferred under that paragraph when the funds transferred by subsection (a) have been expended.

(e) *Passive Air Defense Equipment.*—(1) The Department of Defense shall make available to the department or agency administering this request passive air defense equipment (including ground-based radio detection and ranging equipment) to ensure the safety of transportation provided pursuant to this request.

(2) The Department of Defense shall not charge the department or agency receiving equipment under paragraph (1) for such equipment, and shall bear the risk of loss, damage, or deterioration of such equipment during the period of its use under the au-

thority of paragraph (1).

(f) *Initiation of Delivery of Additional Assistance.*—No assistance for which this request provides shall be delivered to the Nicaraguan democratic resistance prior to March 1, 1988.

Sec. 103. Restrictions on Lethal Assistance.

(a) *Prohibition.*—After February 29, 1988, no lethal assistance may be delivered to the Nicaraguan democratic resistance, except as provided in subsection (b).

(b) *Resumption of Lethal Assistance.*—Lethal assistance may be delivered to the Nicaraguan democratic resistance if, after March 31, 1988, the President determines and certifies to the Speaker of the House of Representatives and the President of the Senate that—

(1) at the time of such certification no ceasefire is in place that was agreed to by the Government of Nicaragua and the Nicaraguan democratic resistance;

(2) the failure to achieve the ceasefire described in paragraph (1) results from the lack of good faith efforts by the Government of Nicaragua to comply with the requirements of the Declaration of the Presidents of the Central American Nations at San Jose, Costa Rica on January 16, 1988; and

(3) the Nicaraguan democratic resistance has engaged in good faith efforts to achieve the ceasefire described in paragraph (1).

(c) *Scope.*—The lethal assistance to which subsections (a) and (b) refer is lethal assistance for which this request provides and lethal assistance previously authorized by law.

(d) *Suspension During Ceasefire.*—Delivery of lethal assistance to the Nicaraguan democratic resistance for which this request provides, or which was previously authorized by law, shall be suspended during any period in which there is in place a ceasefire agreed to by the Government of Nicaragua and the Nicaraguan democratic resistance, except to the extent, if any, permitted by the agreement governing such ceasefire.

Sec. 104. General Authorities and Limitations.

(a) *Related Statutes.*—The requirements, terms and conditions of section 104 of the Intelligence Authorization Act, Fiscal Year 1988 (Public Law 100–178), section 8144 of the Department of Defense Appropriations Act, 1988 (as contained in section 101(b) of Public Law 100–202), section 10 of Public Law 91–672, section 502 of the National Security Act of 1947, section 15(a) of the State Department Basic Authorities Act of 1956, and any other provision of law shall be deemed to have been met for the transfer and use consistent with this request of the funds made available by section 102(a) and (d), and the transfer and use of equipment as provided in section 102(e).

(b) *Continuation of Authority to Support, Monitor, and Manage.*—The authority to support, monitor and manage activities for which funds are provided under this request or a law which previously, specifically authorized assistance to the Nicaraguan democratic resistance shall continue until the funds transferred by section 102(a) have been expended.

(c) *Continuation of Limitations.*—Sections 203(e), 204(b), 207, 209(b), 209(c) and 216, and the first sentence of section 203(d), in "TITLE II—CENTRAL AMERICA" in section 101(k) of the continuing appropriations resolution for the fiscal year 1987 (Public Laws 99–500 and 99–591), shall apply with respect to funds made available under this request.

Sec. 105. Required Detailed Statements and Report.

(a) *Incorporation of Detailed Statements and Report by Reference.*—The report of the Secretary of State dated January 27, 1988 and transmitted with this request is hereby incorporated in this section by reference.

(b) *Status of Statements and Report.*—(1) The detailed statements and report, included in the report of the Secretary of State and incorporated in this section by reference, are those required by section 111(j)(4) of the joint resolution making further continuing appropriations for the fiscal year 1988 (Public Law 100–202).

(2) Enactment of the joint resolution approving this request shall not be deemed to constitute agreement or disagreement by

the Congress or any Member thereof with the statements and report incorporated by reference in this section.

Sec. 106. Defense Appropriations Accounts.

The appropriations accounts to which sections 102(a) and 102(d) refer are—

(1) Missile Procurement, Army, Department of Defense Appropriations Act, 1986, as contained in section 101(b) of the further continuing appropriations resolution for the fiscal year 1986 (Public Law 99–190);

(2) Aircraft Procurement, Army, Department of Defense Appropriations Act, 1986, as contained in section 101(b) of the further continuing appropriations resolution for the fiscal year 1986 (Public Law 99–190);

(3) Shipbuilding and Conversion, Navy, Department of Defense Appropriations Act, 1984 (Public Law 98–212); and

(4) Missile Procurement, Air Force, Department of Defense Appropriations Act, 1986, as contained in section 101(b) of the further continuing appropriations resolution for the fiscal year 1986 (Public Law 99–190).

Sec. 107. Definitions.

As used in this request—

(1) the term "lethal assistance" means weapons, weapon systems, and ammunition; and

(2) the term "non-lethal assistance" means assistance other than lethal assistance.

RONALD REAGAN

White House Statement on Aid to the Nicaraguan Democratic Resistance

January 27, 1988

The President today submitted a request to the Congress pursuant to section 111 of the fiscal year 1988 continuing resolution (P.L. 100–202) for $36.25 million of additional aid for the Nicaraguan democratic resistance (NDR) to sustain the resistance. The request ensures that the resistance can continue the pressure on the Sandinista regime to comply with its obligations under the Guatemala accord of August 7, 1987, to bring democracy to Nicaragua.

All funds under the request are derived by transfer from existing defense appropriations. Ninety percent of the funds requested provides nonlethal aid, such as food, clothing, medicines, and the means to deliver it. Ten percent provides for REDEYE air defense missiles, for use against the Sandinistas' Soviet-made Hind helicopter gunships, and ammunition.

The request prohibits the purchase of aircraft to transport aid to the resistance, but permits leasing aircraft. To ensure the availability of leased aircraft, the request authorizes the President to transfer not more than $20 million from defense appropriations to indemnify the owners of leased aircraft in the event of loss, but which will otherwise not be spent. The request also provides for electronic equipment, radar, and other passive air defense equipment to protect the safety of transportation.

The request supports the Central American peace process by providing a clear opportunity for the Sandinista regime to comply with its obligation to establish democracy and to negotiate a cease-fire directly with the resistance. The request prohibits delivery of all lethal aid after February 29, 1988, which is the date on which current authority to deliver lethal aid expires. Thereafter, delivery of lethal aid may begin only if, after March 31, 1988, the President certifies to the Congress that (A) there is no ceasefire in place between the Government of Nicaragua and the resistance, (B) that Nicaragua has not met its obligations to comply with the requirements of the declaration of the Presidents of the Central American nations at San José,

Costa Rica, on January 16, 1988, and (C) that the resistance has negotiated in good faith.

The Congress will consider a joint resolution to approve the President's request under expedited procedures that provide for a vote in the House of Representatives on February 3 and a vote in the Senate on February 4.

Written Responses to Questions Submitted by the Egyptian Newspaper Al Ahram
January 26, 1988

Egypt-U.S. Relations

Q. How would you describe Egyptian-American relations at the moment, with particular reference to the Egyptian economic situation and the problem of the Egyptian FMS [foreign military sales] debt to the United States? How do you see the future of the relationship?

The President. Our relationship with Egypt today is particularly strong. It is a special partnership, deriving its strength from our similar views and interests on so many issues, most notably our mutual commitment to peace and stability in the Middle East. We share the determination to advance the Arab-Israeli peace process, to reduce tensions in the Gulf, to contain the threat of terrorism from which we have both suffered so much, and to promote development and better lives for the people of the region. The bonds between the Egyptian and American peoples are strong, built on many years of cooperation in military, economic, educational, and cultural fields.

We are doing a great deal to help alleviate Egypt's difficult economic situation and its heavy debt burden. We are encouraged by Egypt's efforts to develop a stronger and more vibrant economy. In recognition of these efforts and Egypt's requirements, I recommended to Congress that our assistance levels to Egypt be maintained, despite severe cuts in both overall foreign assistance and U.S. domestic programs. As a result, in fiscal year 1988, Egypt will receive one-fourth of our total worldwide economic support fund assistance and nearly one-third of all foreign military sales assistance, all on a grant basis.

I am proud of the results we have achieved together in our partnership in the economic field, with the cooperation of both the public and private sectors. For instance, U.S. private investors in the oil industry have helped develop Egypt's leading export sector, while providing employment and training for many talented Egyptians. Our official assistance programs have financed power stations, water facilities, and telecommunications equipment, health services, and over 500 schools—all of which have helped raise living standards for many Egyptians and build the base for future economic growth. Looking ahead, I hope we can rely more on our private sectors to generate growth. Experience around the world has shown that this is the best approach to increasing employment and production.

I believe the future of Egyptian-American relations is bright and that our common vision of peace will enable us to continue to work together to meet the many challenges on the horizon in the Middle East and around the world. President Mubarak is a strong and determined leader, and I look forward to discussing a wide range of issues with him when we meet this week.

Egypt's Role in the Middle East

Q. What is your perception of Egypt's role in the Arab world?

The President. Egypt has always occupied a leadership position in the Arab world. This position has recently been reaffirmed publicly by the Arab summit in Amman and the prompt reestablishment of relations with Egypt by the majority of the members of the Arab League. President Mubarak's recent tour of the Gulf States is a further demonstration of the central role Egypt plays in the pursuit of stability and security in the Middle East. I value the counsel of President Mubarak as an Arab leader committed to peace.

Middle East Peace Efforts

Q. In September 1982, you presented the "Reagan plan" for peace in the Middle East. The current situation is clearly explosive, but some elements in Israel favor peace negotiations. Are you considering any new initiatives? Would you support an international peace conference, and do you foresee such a conference taking place before the end of your administration?

The President. Recent events in the West Bank and in Gaza make it clear that the status quo is unacceptable. We must work together with those in the area to give the Palestinians a reason for hope, not despair. Conditions must be improved in the territories, and real movement toward a political settlement of the Arab-Israeli conflict is essential. However, without a new sense of realism on the part of all the parties, this will be difficult. Flexibility must be demonstrated by practical suggestions, and not just by rhetorical posturing.

With my full encouragement and support, Secretary of State Shultz has been working actively to find a way to bridge the gaps on substance and process that have prevented the advent of negotiations. He made some headway during his October 1987 trip to the region but found that important differences remain on both the format and the agenda for bilateral negotiations.

We have not ruled out any means of reaching bilateral negotiations. For nearly 3 years, we have devoted much time and effort to seeing how an international conference could be structured that would result in such negotiations—the only kind that are likely to be productive and meaningful. A conference must facilitate such negotiations, not be a vehicle for avoiding them. We are committed to trying to find a basis that meets the needs of all the parties and gives us a reason to believe that the negotiations can be successful. Our aim, after all, is a comprehensive peace, not just a negotiating process.

The fact that 1988 is an election year in the United States will not reduce our commitment to continuing our efforts on behalf of Middle East peace. The enemies of peace will not rest in 1988; therefore, the proponents of peace must not, either.

Palestinian Human Rights

Q. The United States is a signatory to the 1949 Geneva convention, which includes an article against deportation of people from their homeland. How far are you willing to go to ensure the protection of human rights for Palestinians and to prevent their deportation? Is your concern for their rights equal to your well-established concern for the right to emigrate by other peoples?

The President. The human rights situation in the West Bank and Gaza remains extremely complex. The United States recognizes that Israel, as the occupying power, has legitimate security concerns and responsibilities as well as an obligation to protect the human rights of Palestinians. The United States has a regular dialog with the Government of Israel on human rights, as with other governments. We are, indeed, just as concerned with the human rights of Palestinians as of other peoples and have made it very clear that we oppose deportations and any denial of the due process of law.

Soviet-U.S. Relations

Q. What regional issues will you discuss at the upcoming summit with Secretary Gorbachev?

The President. Let me begin by explaining the current status of our dialog with the Soviet Union on regional issues. Over the past few years, the United States has actively sought to engage the Soviets in a frank exchange of views in the search for constructive and peaceful solutions to conflicts and problems in various regions around the world. Through patience and persistence, we have succeeded in establishing a regular cycle of meetings between U.S. and Soviet experts and policymakers. These discussions have helped each side to understand the other's positions and perspectives. Unfortunately, in many cases we continue to differ on the best means to achieve peaceful solutions.

We Americans are particularly troubled by the use of Soviet forces abroad, as in

Afghanistan, and by wars waged by regimes supported by the Soviet Union against their own peoples or their neighbors. In the course of our dialog, the Soviets have expressed a political commitment to withdraw their forces from Afghanistan and have said this could be completed in 1988. We hope this happens.

When General Secretary Gorbachev and I met in Washington this last December, we agreed that the aim of our regional dialog now should be "to help the parties to regional conflicts find peaceful solutions that advance their independence, freedom, and security."

Afghanistan

Q. Please explain your Afghanistan policy; particularly, is there any connection between the proposed U.S. reduction of forces in the Arabian Gulf and the Soviet withdrawal from Afghanistan? Are you planning to reduce arms shipments to the Mujahidin to encourage a rapid Soviet withdrawal? Are you close to agreement with the Soviets on an interim government in Kabul, and how would you feel about a future alliance between Kabul and Tehran?

The President. We, and the 122 other governments who voted for the Afghan resolution in the last U.N. General Assembly, seek a fair and comprehensive settlement based on the rapid and complete withdrawal of Soviet troops. It must provide for self-determination for the Afghan people, return of the refugees in safety and honor, and a restoration of Afghanistan's independence and sovereignty. It is entirely up to the Afghan people to decide what form of government they have and how they run their country. We sincerely hope that 1988 will be the year in which all Soviet troops leave Afghanistan. Until then, however, we and other governments will continue to provide full support for the Afghan cause.

The Afghan conflict is Moscow's problem. The Soviets must make the necessary decision to get out. Once this has clearly occurred, we would of course use our influence to be helpful. We would favor a neutral, nonaligned Afghanistan, free from foreign interference.

Persian Gulf Conflict

Q. What is happening on U.N. Security Council Resolution 598? Are you getting cooperation from other Security Council members on an arms embargo? Do you plan to reduce the U.S. naval presence in the Gulf? And how do you feel about the creation of a U.N. force?

The President. The United States has pushed hard for the full implementation of U.N. Security Council Resolution 598 since its unanimous adoption on July 20, 1987. Six months after the adoption of Resolution 598, it is clear that, while Iraq has accepted Resolution 598 in all its parts and without imposing conditions, Iran has no intention of negotiating its implementation in good faith. Iran has used the time since the adoption of 598 to build up forces for another offensive against Iraq and to increase attacks upon nonbelligerent shipping in international waters in the Gulf.

Our view is, therefore, that the Security Council should act to adopt an enforcement resolution imposing an embargo on the provision of arms to Iran by any member state. Together with other permanent and nonpermanent members of the Security Council, we are discussing an arms embargo resolution which we hope will receive the unanimous support of the Security Council as soon as possible. We note that the Soviet Union has so far resisted the adoption of an arms embargo, preferring instead to call for further delay and discussion of separate U.N. action related only to the Gulf, ignoring Iran's continuation of the land war.

We have no plans to change the mission of our forces in the Gulf. Our Navy, which is charged with carrying out that mission, continually reviews the composition of our forces there to perform in the best and most efficient way. Our basic commitment remains unchanged.

With regard to proposals for a United Nations naval force in the Gulf, we believe it is essential that the concept for such a force be spelled out clearly. If the proposal is for a U.N. force to help monitor or enforce compliance with an arms embargo, we would be prepared to consider the possibilities seriously once an arms embargo is adopted by the Security Council. We want an arms embargo to be as effective as possible. The Soviet Union, however, has been inconsistent about its concept for a U.N. naval force. The Soviets appear to favor a U.N. naval force that would replace the U.S. and other navies in the area and impose an end to attacks on shipping, while allowing Iran to continue the land war. This represents a deliberate diversion from the full implementation of Resolution 598, which calls for a comprehensive cease-fire.

Note: The questions and answers were released by the Office of the Press Secretary on January 28.

Executive Order 12625—Integrity and Efficiency in Federal Programs

January 27, 1988

By the authority vested in me as President by the Constitution and laws of the United States of America, and in order to coordinate and enhance governmental efforts to promote integrity and efficiency and to detect and prevent fraud and abuse in Federal programs, it is hereby ordered as follows:

Section 1. Establishment of the President's Council on Integrity and Efficiency. (a) There is established as an interagency committee the President's Council on Integrity and Efficiency.

(b) The Council shall be composed of the following members:

(1) The Deputy Director of the Office of Management and Budget, who shall be Chairperson of the Council;

(2) The Associate Attorney General;

(3) The Deputy Director of the Office of Personnel Management;

(4) The Executive Assistant Director-Investigations of the Federal Bureau of Investigation;

(5) The Director of the Office of Government Ethics;

(6) The Special Counsel of the Merit Systems Protection Board;

(7) A designee of the Secretary of the Treasury; and

(8) All civilian Inspectors General, now or hereafter created by statute.

(c) The Chairperson may, from time to time, invite other officials to participate in meetings of the Council.

Sec. 2. Functions of the Council. (a) The Council shall continually identify, review, and discuss areas of government-wide weakness and vulnerability to fraud, waste, and abuse and develop plans for coordinated government-wide activities that attack fraud and waste and promote economy and efficiency in government programs and operations. These will include interagency audit and investigation programs and projects to deal efficiently and effectively with those problems concerning fraud and waste that exceed the capability or jurisdiction of an individual agency. The Council will recognize the preeminent role of the Department of Justice in matters involving law enforcement and litigation.

(b) The Council shall develop policies that will aid in establishment of a corps of well-trained and highly skilled Office of Inspector General staff members.

(c) The Council members should, to the extent of their ability and authority, pay careful attention to professional standards developed by the Council and participate in Council plans, programs, and projects.

(d) The creation and operation of the Council shall neither interfere with existing authority and responsibilities in the departments and agencies, nor augment or diminish the statutory authority or responsibilities of its members.

Sec. 3. Responsibilities of the Chairperson. (a) The Chairperson may appoint a Vice Chairperson from the Council members to assist in carrying out the functions of the Council.

(b) The Chairperson shall, in consultation with the members of the Council, establish the agenda for Council activities.

(c) The Chairperson shall, on behalf of the Council, report to the President on the activities of the Council. The Chairperson shall advise the Council with respect to the reaction of the President on the Council's activities.

(d) The Chairperson shall provide agency heads with summary reports of the activities of the Council.

(e) The Chairperson shall establish, in consultation with the members of the Council, such committees of the Council as deemed necessary or appropriate for the efficient conduct of Council functions. Committees of the Council may act for the Council in their areas of designated responsibility.

(f) The Chairperson shall be supported by the Associate Director for Management and Chief Financial Officer of the Office of Management and Budget who shall advise and assist the Chairperson in the execution of the entire range of responsibilities set forth above.

Sec. 4. Coordinating Conference. (a) There is established as an interagency committee the Coordinating Conference of the President's Council on Integrity and Efficiency.

(b) The Conference shall be composed of the Chairperson of the Council and one representative of each Executive agency, not represented on the Council, determined by the Office of Management and Budget to possess audit and investigative resources. The head of each such agency shall designate as the agency's representative the official who is responsible for coordinating the agency's efforts to eliminate fraud and waste in the agency's programs and operations.

(c) The Chairperson shall convene meetings of the Conference at least quarterly. The Chairperson shall provide for the dissemination to the Conference of appropriate information on the activities of the Council, in order to enable the Conference members, to the extent of their own ability and authority to do so, to implement the coordinated plans, standards, policies, programs, and projects developed by the Council.

Sec. 5. Administrative Provisions. (a) The Director of the Office of Management and Budget shall provide the Council and the Conference with such administrative support as may be necessary for the performance of the functions of the Council and the Conference.

(b) the head of each agency represented on the Council or the Conference shall provide its representative with such administrative support as may be necessary, in accordance with law, to enable the agency representative to carry out his responsibilities.

Sec. 6. Revocation. Executive Order 12301 of March 26, 1981, entitled "Integrity and Efficiency in Federal Programs," is revoked.

RONALD REAGAN

The White House,
January 27, 1988.

[*Filed with the Office of the Federal Register, 10:44 a.m., January 29, 1988*]

Note: The Executive order was released by the Office of the Press Secretary on January 28.

Remarks at the Welcoming Ceremony for President Mohammed Hosni Mubarak of Egypt
January 28, 1988

President Reagan. Mr. President and Mrs. Mubarak, welcoming good friends to Washington and to the White House is one of my more pleasant responsibilities as President. I'm especially pleased today to greet, once again, President Mubarak, a personal friend and a friend of the United States. President Mubarak is the proud leader of a proud land: Egypt, a country with a special fascination for Americans; Egypt, a venerable society rich in culture, a country not unaccustomed to making history.

Americans learn from their earliest school days about Egypt's extraordinary place in the history of civilization. And recent history records that our two countries were partners in one of the monumental events of our era: the securing of peace between Egypt and Israel. The first step toward ending the cycle of violence in the Middle East was as arduous, painstaking, and fraught with danger as any that a country ever made. It was a tremendous accomplishment and a tribute to the vision, courage, and sincere desire for peace on both sides. And, President Mubarak, we're heartened by the progress that continues under your dynamic and responsible leadership.

In the past few months, Arab countries that broke relations with Egypt years ago have resumed diplomatic relations with your country. It's a victory for the cause of peace and a tribute to your steadfastness as well as a recognition that Egypt is again exerting the leadership role it has traditionally played in Arab councils. We applaud you at this moment, when time and events have proven you right.

The United States and Egypt continue to work together to broaden the peace that started with that first step 10 years ago. The recent explosion of violence in the West Bank and Gaza and the sad toll it has taken in lives and injuries, vividly remind us that much remains to be done. The danger of allowing the Palestinian problem to fester is evident and reinforces the urgency of moving toward negotiations: Hard work, creativity, and a willingness to take practical, not merely rhetorical, steps are needed.

Mr. President, if peace is to be achieved, if another giant step is to be made, much depends on Egypt and the United States. We are partners in this endeavor, and Egypt's own experience provides it with special insights. I'm looking forward to discussing with you your ideas as well as our own thoughts on how to ensure that hope displaces despair and real progress is made toward peace.

Both of our countries also look with distress on the seemingly endless conflict between Iraq and Iran. The latter's aggressive measures to intimidate and destabilize other countries in the Gulf and elsewhere in the Middle East are reprehensible and reason for alarm. Both the United States and Egypt strongly support U.N. Security Council efforts to end the war, and we share a firm commitment to freedom of navigation in the region and the security of friendly Gulf Arab States. President Mubarak, as your recent trip to the Gulf clearly demonstrates, Egypt has a vital role to play in the pursuit of these goals; and I'm pleased to have this opportunity to discuss how we can work together to achieve them.

The scope of our cooperation, of course, goes far beyond the formulation of foreign and diplomatic policy. Egypt and the United States have also made common cause in advancing Egypt's economy and bettering the living standard of her people. America's contributions to agriculture, industry, power generation, and private sector development stand as visible symbols of our broader partnership for progress, a partnership that we expect to benefit both our peoples for many years to come.

Mr. President, all Americans are especially delighted that your visit will take you beyond Washington. I hope that in the limited time you have you'll capture a glimpse of America's heart and soul. You'll find it in cities and towns across the country, in businesses, in universities, and in our churches. And there you'll find a love of freedom and a genuine good will to you and the people of Egypt. Your visit, I know, will strengthen the bonds and expand the potential of American and Egyptian friendship.

In closing, I'd like to share with you a bit of history. Some may not realize that the U.S.-Egyptian collaboration on security issues goes back over 100 years. Shortly after the American Civil War, General Charles Pomeroy Stone and General William Wing Loring, together with some 50 other officers from the Union and Confederate Armies, went to Egypt to work with the Egyptian Armed Forces. They worked on military training, helped strengthen coastal defenses, and shared their ideas and their experience.

General Stone left Egypt in 1878, and his

last job after his return to the United States provides a fitting symbol of our enduring relationship. Stone was asked to design and construct the base for a huge statue, designed and constructed by a Frenchman, presented to the United States by the schoolchildren of France. Stone went to work with his usual energy. He gave lectures on Egypt to help finance the project, and enlisted two of his former colleagues from his days in Egypt to help with drafting the plans and erecting the structure. So, Mr. President, when you look at the Statue of Liberty, you can be proud that those who built its solid base spent nearly a decade in the service of Egypt, building a base as well for our relationship.

Today we offer you our warm welcome and celebrate the solid friendship between our countries. President Mubarak, welcome.

President Mubarak. President Reagan, Mrs. Reagan, dear friends, once again we meet in your glorious Capital in order to strengthen the bonds of friendship and understanding between our peoples. The Egyptian people are sending you and each and every American warm greetings and heartiest wishes for success and fulfillment.

They value the United States as a friend and a partner in the search for peace and progress. This friendship is a lasting one, for it is based on mutual respect and a profound conviction that all nations, regardless of origin and decree, share a common interest in the preservation of peace and maintenance of security. Over the years, our American friendship has served as a force of stability and progress; today it remains a source of hope and promise. We are determined to deepen this friendship and intensify our cooperation for our common good.

President Reagan has made a great contribution to the process of strengthening these ties and deepening their roots. He's a man of wisdom and conviction. During the past few years, he has taken many steps for the purpose of enhancing world peace and security. We commend him on his recent achievement and congratulate the American people on the courageous steps that are certain to reduce tension and pave the way for a better future for mankind.

People of good will should build upon it in the years ahead to maintain insecurity—to eliminate insecurity and stop violence and suffering throughout the world. Sincere and concrete and concerted efforts are urgently needed for solving regional conflicts. In this respect, the Middle East is a region that requires special attention and top priority. It is confronted with great challenge and rising dangers. The United States can do much to help all nations of the Middle East to cope with these problems.

A few days ago I met with most of the area's leaders, and it was their consensus that certain steps must be taken urgently and effectively in order to check the continuous deterioration of the situation in different parts of the Middle East. This is needed not only to safeguard the interests of the region's people and save the lives of millions of innocent individuals but also to protect vital American interests.

The futile war which is raging in the Gulf threatens the safety and the security of all parties. It endangers the freedom of navigation and blocks the flow of strategic materials that are essential in international trade as well as the prosperity of many nations. It's an illusion to speak of restricting the theater of operations. Even if it happens, the fallout from the war would certainly spread throughout the region. Therefore the only real solution is to end the war immediately and to bring the dispute to the negotiating table.

The tragic situation in the West Bank and the Gaza is another source of alarm and concern. It is evident that the continuation of occupation and oppression would bring loss to and inflict damage on all the parts without exception. It would badly hurt American interests in the Middle East. It deals a devastating blow to our peace efforts at a time when we are looking for a breakthrough.

In the course of our discussion today, we shall focus on these issues in full awareness of their importance and ramifications. We shall exchange views candidly and sincerely and examine certain ideas designed to generate a new momentum and initiate movement. We realize that many governments are preoccupied this year with domestic matters and international events. But history does not stop, and it is an absolute must that we continue to move forward to attain our objectives. This is the crux of public responsibility.

In the past few weeks we noticed with satisfaction that the United States, under the leadership of President Reagan, has taken courageous steps in the right direction. This active role must continue for our mutual benefit. The risks involved here cannot be compared with the damage that is certain to result from inaction and stagnation.

African problems need greater attention, too. The debt problem is crippling growth and development in most parts of our continent. An equitable solution must be reached if we want to save the lives of millions who face the danger of starvation and fatal disease. On the other hand we cannot accept the continuation of the worsening situation that exists in southern Africa today. The fundamental rights of our fellow Africans are being violated, and their security is being endangered every day. The fight for human rights and the dignity of man—indivisible, and we must maintain our firm commitment to work for a better future for coming generations.

I am looking forward to a stimulating and fruitful discussion with President Reagan and his able associates, and we shall continue to an objective exchange of views during the months ahead. We shall always be guided by the spirit of genuine friendship and sincerity, which has dominated our relations consistently. Together we shall endeavor to serve the cause of peace and derive hope in the midst of despair and frustration. Together we shall overcome. Thank you, Mr. President.

Note: President Reagan spoke at 10:05 a.m. in the East Room at the White House, where President Mubarak was accorded a formal welcome. Following the ceremony, the two Presidents met in the Oval Office.

Appointment of Richard W. Kazmaier, Jr., as a Member of the President's Council on Physical Fitness and Sports, and Designation as Chairman

January 28, 1988

The President today announced his intention to appoint Richard W. Kazmaier, Jr., to be a member of the President's Council on Physical Fitness and Sports. He would succeed George Allen. Upon appointment, he will be designated Chairman.

Since 1975 Mr. Kazmaier has been president of Kazmaier Associates, Inc., in Concord, MA. Prior to this he was general manager of the sports division of Kendall Co., in Boston, 1971–1975. He was president of L&R Industries, Inc., 1969–1970. Mr. Kazmaier has received numerous honors and awards in the field of football: All American, 1950–1951; Heisman trophy, 1951; Maxwell trophy, 1951; Football Hall of Fame, 1966.

Mr. Kazmaier graduated from Princeton University (A.B., 1952) and Harvard University (M.B.A., 1954). He served in the United States Navy, 1954–1963. He was born November 23, 1930, in Toledo, OH. He is married, has six children, and resides in Key Largo, FL.

Nomination of Nanette Fabray MacDougall To Be a Member of the National Council on the Handicapped
January 28, 1988

The President today announced his intention to nominate Nanette Fabray MacDougall to be a member of the National Council on the Handicapped for a term expiring September 17, 1990. This is a reappointment.

Mrs. MacDougall is an actress. She is also active in organizations benefiting the hearing handicapped and other disabled persons. She serves on the boards of the National Captioning Institute, the Better Hearing Institute in Washington, DC, the Ear Research Institute, and the Museum of Science and Industry in Los Angeles. She is past chairman of the National Easter Seal Society for Crippled Children, the National Mental Health Association, and the National Advisory Committee for Education of the Deaf. She has received many awards for her service, including the President's Distinguished Service Award in 1971 and the Eleanor Roosevelt Humanitarian Award in 1964.

Mrs. MacDougall has one child and resides in Pacific Palisades, CA. She was born October 27, 1920, in San Diego, CA.

Proclamation 5763—National Challenger Center Day, 1988
January 28, 1988

By the President of the United States of America

A Proclamation

Two years ago, on January 28, 1986, America lost the seven-member crew of the Challenger. Now as then, we join the families of those gallant Space Shuttle explorers in mourning them and in saluting their courage, vision, and determination.

The families of Challenger's crew members, sharing the bold spirit of the loved and lost, resolved to join in the task of preparing America's coming generations of astronauts and scientists—of inspiring young people and of giving them the opportunity to develop all of the knowledge and capabilities they would need in space and science research.

To that end, the families established a living memorial, the Challenger Center for Space Science Education. The Center will be a tribute to the Challenger crew and to their achievements, their bravery, and their dedication to America's leadership in space. The Center will stimulate and enhance students' search for knowledge and involvement in science, especially the space sciences. The Center, which will rely on private donations, has already established headquarters in our Nation's Capital and is planning regional sites.

The goals of the Center are those of all Americans, as National Challenger Center Day reminds us so well. Let our Nation's continued mission in the exploration of space pay tribute to the Center and to the families, and let it forever salute Challenger's crew and its quest.

To commemorate the members of the Challenger crew, the Congress, by Senate Joint Resolution 201, has designated January 28, 1988, as "National Challenger Center Day" and authorized and requested the President to issue a proclamation in observance of this event.

Now, Therefore, I, Ronald Reagan, President of the United States of America, do hereby proclaim January 28, 1988, as National Challenger Center Day, and I call on the people of the United States to observe this day by remembering the Challenger astronauts who died while serving their country and by reflecting upon the important role of the Center in honoring them and in furthering their goal of strengthening space and science education.

In Witness Whereof, I have hereunto set my hand this twenty-eighth day of January, in the year of our Lord nineteen hundred and eighty-eight, and of the Independence of the United States of America the two hundred and twelfth.

RONALD REAGAN

[*Filed with the Office of the Federal Register, 3:11 p.m., January 28, 1988*]

Toasts at the State Dinner for President Mohammed Hosni Mubarak of Egypt
January 28, 1988

President Reagan. Wendell Phillips once said that "you can always get the truth from an American statesman after he has turned 70 or given up all hope of the Presidency." [*Laughter*] Well, today I welcome you, President Mubarak, as a friend. Coming from a 76-year-old constitutionally prohibited from seeking another term, you can rest assured those sentiments are genuine and come from the heart. [*Laughter*]

This visit is a particularly happy occasion as it provides the opportunity to congratulate you personally on your reelection to a second term as President of Egypt. As a second term veteran myself, however, let me suggest, Mr. President, it doesn't get any easier. [*Laughter*] The referendum that approved your second term reflects the strong confidence that the Egyptian people have in your leadership. We share that same confidence. Nevertheless, Mr. President, we both know that governing a country in which there are divergent political views and a lively opposition is a tough job. We respect your work to broaden participation in the political process and are confident it will help create the stable political environment needed for Egypt to move forward.

Egypt today, under your guidance, is resuming its rightful place in the forefront of world leadership. This is particularly important at a time when the forces of fanaticism and blind hatred threaten the security and stability of the Middle East. Egypt, by again exerting its wise and calming influence, provides the world hope that the serious challenges facing the Middle East can and will be overcome and that the region will be restored to a happier and more tranquil course.

Likewise, President Mubarak, you have wisely and effectively led Egypt onto a course of economic reform and development. The difficult obstacles you and the Egyptian people face are well understood here, too. We, too, learned in our own efforts to strip away years of government intervention in our marketplace how monumental this task can be, how ingrained is the dependence on intervention, and how powerful are the interest groups that resist change. But we're convinced that such vigorous reform is the surest path to economic progress. And, Mr. President, Americans will stand and work with Egyptians in the cause of growing prosperity, just as we do in the cause of peace.

Mr. President, our meetings today were enjoyable and enlightening. And so, you are most welcome. And in saying that, I propose a toast to you, Mr. President, Mrs. Mubarak, the people of Egypt, and to the close and amicable ties that will continue between our peoples and our governments.

President Mubarak. President Reagan, Mrs. Reagan, dear friends, thank you for your kind words and the gracious hospitality. The elegant and warm reception you have accorded us reflects the best tradition of American friendship and genuine openness. It is a tradition that has deep roots in our culture, too. We value friendship and loyalty to friends. As usual, President Reagan and his graceful spouse have made us feel welcome and quite at home the minute we arrived at the White House this morning. They symbolize the American spirit at its best.

My meeting with the President today was another confirmation of my belief that he is a man of wisdom and vision. He is an American in the true sense of the word. I expressed to him my admiration of the relentless efforts he exerted for years to make the world more safe and secure for future generations. His recent achievement in this area will certainly have a lasting effect on world peace and stability. I have no doubt that other steps will follow in the same direction during the months ahead.

I am certain that regional conflicts will figure high on the agenda throughout the year. Of these conflicts, the Middle East problems deserve special attention and priority. Strenuous efforts are needed to stop the war, which is still raging in the Gulf, and set the peace process in motion again. We have to demonstrate to all the parts concerned that peace is the only meaningful and effective way to settle disputes and solve problems. No other formula would work. No other alternative is acceptable. There is no justification at all for the continuation of bloodshed and destruction. As Benjamin Franklin once said: "There never was a good war or a bad peace."

With this in mind, Egypt has not hesitated at any point to take pioneering steps in order to make peace. It is for this reason, too, that I have proposed a few days ago a moratorium on all forms of violence and repression. I am quite convinced that this proposal, which is conceived as a preparatory step towards comprehensive peace, reflects the real sentiment of people of good will and human principles everywhere. No one who looks ahead and thinks of the future can accept the continuation of occupation and oppression. No one can, in good conscience, condone a policy of shooting and beating in a land that is holy to all of us.

What I am proposing here is a policy of hope and positivity to replace despair and fear. I am sure that I am not alone in that, for I am backed by millions of men and women of courage and conviction everywhere. Let me seize this opportunity to thank all those Americans, Israelis, and others who raise their voices in support of peace and in defense of liberty. Their stand will never go unnoticed or unrewarded.

Dear friends, American leaders have worked with Egyptian leaders over the years in order to construct a model for friendship and cooperation among nations. In particular, President Reagan has made a great contribution to the development of friendly relations between Egypt and the United States. We are proud of this friendship, which has been mature enough to overcome all obstacles we have encountered and deep enough to look to the future with hope and promise. The talks we had in the morning added to the reservoir of good will and mutual understanding that exists today between our peoples. As ever, the President was both receptive and responsive. I highly value his opinions and ideas. We shall continue to work together, as we did in the past, in order to serve our common goal of reinforcing peace and promoting progress and stability.

In conclusion, permit me to ask you, ladies and gentlemen, to rise in a tribute to President and Mrs. Reagan, to all our friends who are present this evening, and each and every American. Thank you.

Note: President Reagan spoke at 10:07 p.m. in the State Dining Room at the White House.

Proclamation 5764—American Red Cross Month, 1988
January 28, 1988

By the President of the United States of America

A Proclamation

The remarkable story of the International Red Cross began at Solferino, in northern Italy, exactly 125 years ago, when battling Austrian and French soldiers brought death and destruction to the countryside—and when Swiss traveler Henri Dunant realized that wounded soldiers should receive assistance no matter what their allegiance.

From that compassion at Solferino grew a great tradition and a humanitarian organization that relieves the sufferings of all those wounded not only by war but also by poor health, old age, personal adversity, natural calamity, and so on.

As Americans join people around the globe in observing this anniversary, we reflect that the story could have turned out much differently if Henri Dunant—one man, after all—had ignored Solferino and its victims. Clara Barton, for instance, might never have founded the American Red Cross, and her counterparts in other countries might never have founded sister societies. Life would truly have been different in our land for people who needed blood, or evacuees left homeless by floods, or accident victims, or countless others.

A century and a quarter after Solferino, we have real reason to celebrate the victory for humanity and for international cooperation that sprang from that battlefield. Today, 145 national societies of the International Red Cross offer help without regard to race, creed, cause, or nationality. Like many of these societies, the American Red Cross provides assistance on several fronts, including health and safety, disaster relief, blood, and social services.

Every day, the American Red Cross battles the devastation left by natural disasters. Last year, the Red Cross clothed, fed, or sheltered 450,000 disaster victims, and through the generosity of the American people it provided individuals with $122 million in disaster relief.

The Red Cross also assists military personnel, last year alone helping members of the Armed Forces and their families 2.5 million times. Daily it relays 4,000 messages of birth, death, and illness to military posts worldwide.

The American Red Cross battles potential threats to the blood supply by collecting, and testing for disease, more than half of our Nation's blood supply. Last year, four million volunteers donated blood to the Red Cross, restoring life and health to millions of blood recipients.

The Red Cross also fights hazards to health and safety by training in cardiopulmonary resuscitation, first aid, swimming, water and boating safety, and preparation for parenthood and babysitting. Last year, seven million Americans successfully completed Red Cross courses. Last year, Red Cross chapters also distributed 67 million AIDS brochures and urged the public "to get the facts."

The Red Cross also combats social and economic problems; it helps young mothers, assists the aged, the homeless, and the destitute, and helps immigrants learn English.

These are some of the reasons we all rejoice in the vision and the mission of the American Red Cross, especially in this 125th anniversary year of the International Red Cross.

Now, Therefore, I, Ronald Reagan, President of the United States of America and Honorary Chairman of the American National Red Cross, by virtue of the authority vested in me by the Constitution and laws of the United States, do hereby proclaim the month of March 1988 as American Red Cross Month. I urge all Americans to continue their generous support and ready assistance to the work of the American Red Cross and its more than 2,800 chapters, 1.4 million adult members, and three million youth volunteers.

In Witness Whereof, I have hereunto set my hand this twenty-eighth day of January, in the year of our Lord nineteen hundred and eighty-eight, and of the Independence of the United States of America the two hundred and twelfth.

RONALD REAGAN

[*Filed with the Office of the Federal Register, 10:45 a.m., January 29, 1988*]

Note: The proclamation was released by the Office of the Press Secretary on January 29.

Remarks to the National Conference of State Legislators
January 29, 1988

I'm delighted to welcome President Ted Strickland and all the officers and leadership of the National Conference to the Old Executive Office Building. You know, one of the things I like best about getting together with people from the States is the sense of diversity that it brings out—the different regions, the different accents. And, well, would you be surprised if that reminded me of a story? [*Laughter*]

A Bostonian visited San Antonio, asked a native what was that dilapidated-looking ruin over there. And he said, "That, sir, is the Alamo." Well, he said, "In that building, sir, 136 immortal Texans held off an army of 15,000 of Santa Anna's regulars for 4 days." "Hmm," said the Bostonian, "and who's that man on horseback on that hill over there?" And he said, "Well, that, sir, is a statue of a Texas Ranger. He killed 46 Apaches in single-handed combat and broke up 27 riots in his lifetime. Where you from, stranger?" And he said, "Well, I'm from Boston. We have our heroes there, too. Paul Revere, for instance." And the Texan snorted, "Paul Revere! You mean that man who had to ride for help?" [*Laughter*]

But it's an honor to have this opportunity to speak to you who work at levels of government so close to the people themselves. In a moment, I'd like to discuss the domestic agenda for this, the remaining year of our administration. But if you'll permit me, first I'd like to stress something that we've been working on from the very first: federalism, a topic Secretary [of Transportation] Burnley has just touched on as well.

After all, it was with the intention of keeping government close to the people that the Founding Fathers entrusted the State governments with duties like the protection of property rights and the enforcement of criminal justice—duties that affected the people in their everyday lives. And when Alexis de Tocqueville toured America during the last century, he found that it was the State governments with which the people were the most involved. "Men," he wrote, "are affected by the sovereignty of the Union only in connection with a few great interests, but State sovereignty enfolds every citizen and in one way or another affects every detail of daily life."

Well, when our administration came to office, we took it as one of our chief aims to reawaken the federalist impulse and approach the Constitution with a new fidelity—in short, to restore power to the States. By now you should know how, since 1981, we've worked to widen the scope for independent State decisionmaking. I'm proud to say that our federalism focus is continuing. This past October, I issued an Executive order requiring all Departments and Agencies to do a federalism assessment of all their policies, to make sure they aren't doing things better left to the States.

But despite all we've been doing to promote federalism here in Washington, our efforts take second place to the remarkable new initiatives that you're overseeing in the States. State governments are attracting venture capital. You're fostering international trade. Many States have cut taxes. And more than half the States have set up their own enterprise zones, even without Federal incentives. These zones have created new jobs and spurred billions of dollars in capital investment. In the words of columnist James J. Kilpatrick: "It becomes increasingly evident that the State governments, as a group, are governing more responsibly than the National Government. The most interesting political activity these days is often not in the National Capital but in the State capitals." Well, now, I happen to think that's just what the Founding Fathers had in mind. So, congratulations to you all.

And as I now turn to our domestic agenda, I believe you'll see that, here, too, the States have their role to play. The first item I'd like to mention is one that seems to have made quite an impression during my State of the Union Address this past Monday: the urgent need for budget reform. You may remember that I placed on a table, for everyone in the Nation to see, all 43 pounds of the continuing resolution, the accompanying conference reports, and the reconciliation bill. As if anybody needed any more evidence that the budget process here has completely broken down.

And when I say that producing that huge pile of documents made an impression, I mean literally. You see, when I banged down one of those stacks of paper—if I remember correctly, it was the one weighing 15 pounds—when I banged that document down, I got my finger stuck underneath. [*Laughter*] And here it is 4 days later, and I'm still sore, but not as sore as I am when I consider the budget process we've had to go through, year after year here. This coming year, I intend to use all my powers as President to enforce some simple discipline upon the Federal budget.

In a word, discipline—that's what is missing from the Federal budget process. In 30 days I will return to Congress certain items that should be rescinded. Sure, it will improve our deficit targets, but also it will be a first sign of discipline in a process that's out of control.

But we need other measures to reform the budget process permanently, and here I take a page from the States. The great majority of your State constitutions require balanced budgets. I'd submit that it's about time we passed a balanced budget amendment for the Federal Government. And in your statehouses, no fewer than 43 Governors have the line-item veto. I had it back in Sacramento, myself. The line-item veto is a proper and prudent tool of government, an instrument that gives the Executive the ability to reach into the massive appropriations bills and pare away the waste. It's time we gave that power to all future Presidents. As we push for these measures this coming year, I urge you to join us.

Next, a subject that really belongs to the States: education. You know the story how from 1960 to 1980 overall spending on education more than doubled, while college board scores during the same period fell drastically. We've worked hard to put education at the top of the Nation's agenda and to make certain that we concern ourselves not only with what we spend but with how we spend it. This response has been dramatic. Many States formed task forces on education. In some States, promising new programs, like merit pay for teachers, are being put in place. Still other States have opened the teaching profession to a wider pool of qualified candidates. And in recent years we've seen college board scores actually go up for the first time in nearly 20 years.

This year at the Federal level, we're doing still more to promote imaginative reforms. We're adding money to the budget for the magnet schools program, an idea that has already done much to foster greater achievement among our public schools. We're building greater accountability into our Federal programming by tying funding to results. Secretary [of Education] Bennett has proposed, among other reforms, a much stronger curriculum for our high schools. As Bill puts it, his aim is to promote a "national conversation" on what works in education.

But I don't intend to stop here. Polls show that millions of Americans would like, but do not have, the ability of choosing the education program and institution that is best for their children. A voucher system at the State level would empower parents. I'll ask the Department of Education to develop model voucher legislation and make it available to the 50 States so that they can implement programs that promote choice in education. As we do all this here in Washington, I encourage you in the States to do even more. For as I said in my State of the Union Address, the most important thing we in Washington can do is reaffirm that control of our schools belongs to the States, to local communities and, most of all, to parents and teachers.

Permit me to turn now to an area of shared Federal and State responsibility: welfare. The sad truth is that our welfare programs, State and Federal alike, too often have only made poverty harder to escape. In the fight against poverty, we now know, it's essential to have strong families—families that teach children the skills and values they'll need to succeed in the wider world, families that provide mothers and fathers with comfort, inspiration, and a focus for their labors. Yet when we ask ourselves whether our welfare programs have encouraged family life and values, we must answer: Far from it. Instead, they've subjected poor families to a subtle but constant undermining force, pulling them apart.

Many of you already preside over important welfare innovations. Some of you have shown us how child support enforcement can be improved. Others have launched innovative new programs which require welfare recipients to work or prepare for work. You in the States are attempting to meet what I believe must become the central criterion for all forms of public assistance: not how much money we spend on welfare but how many Americans our programs make independent of welfare. This is what we should be doing at the end of each year, not boasting about how many more people are on welfare that we're taking care of but how many people have we been able to remove from welfare and make independent and self-sufficient. The 50 States present us with the opportunity to apply this criterion in endless ways, experimenting and testing in a manner from which all can profit. Our administration will give the States even more flexibility and encourage still greater reform. Our aim is simple: to replace today's poverty trap with a welfare system that fosters genuine economic opportunity.

I'd like to turn now to a subject that's especially close to Nancy and me: a drug free America. Nancy and so many others have worked tirelessly to change the Nation's attitude toward drugs—to replace what was too often an easy complacency with a hard and clear understanding of just how damaging drug abuse truly is. And one of my proudest moments in office came just a few weeks ago, when I read that our most recent survey of the attitudes of high school students toward drug abuse—you see, cocaine use is on the way down, while marijuana use is at the lowest point since the surveying began. We're making progress, real progress.

The States, of course, have a critical role in amplifying the antidrug measure. Efforts to reduce demand must occur at the State and local level, and they are. The recently enacted legislation in New Jersey and Missouri, for example, to provide swift and certain consequences for illegal drug use reinforce my deep belief that there is no need for a Federal law to do what States can do better. So, I ask you to join Nancy and me in carrying this one simple message to our young people: Say yes to life, and when it comes to drugs, just say no.

Now, it was my intention to focus today on our domestic agenda, but one foreign policy issue has become so important in recent days that I want to share with you my thoughts. That issue, of course, is Central America. Our approach to the Communist threat in Nicaragua has long been based on a simple principle: diplomacy and pressure in support of freedom and democracy must go hand-in-hand. We've seen the success of this two-track approach elsewhere in the world. In Afghanistan, for example, freedom fighters have forced the Soviet Union to think seriously about a diplomatic solution to that brutal occupation.

This same approach may be working today in Nicaragua, although it's too early to tell if Daniel Ortega's promises will be matched by true efforts to permit genuine democracy. What is unmistakable is this: Democracy has a chance in Nicaragua because of one factor alone—the pressure placed on the Communist Sandinistas by the freedom fighters.

I believe we owe it to ourselves and the people of Central America to explore fully diplomatic avenues toward solving the Nicaraguan conflict. We must ask ourselves, however, what will create the conditions for serious negotiations? If Congress cuts off aid to the freedom fighters next week, there is little chance that the Sandinistas will bargain seriously. We cannot expect diplomacy to work abroad if here at home we lack the will to negotiate from a position of strength. So, much depends upon this coming vote—the progress of democracy in Latin America and our own security as a nation. I just have to believe that we owe it to the future to stand by the freedom fighters.

Well, having said that, I thank you all once again for being here today. And by the way, I know that as fellow politicians your hearts start to quicken just a little bit, the way mine does, when we start to head into a campaign season. No two ways about it, last year was not one of my favorites. But that was then, and this is now—an election year, when the people will be heard from. And to tell you the truth, I'm starting to have some fun again. [*Laughter*] Well, again, I thank all of you for being here and for what you're doing, and God bless you all.

Note: The President spoke at 1:17 p.m. in Room 450 of the Old Executive Office Building.

Message to the Congress on Amendments to the Generalized System of Preferences
January 29, 1988

To the Congress of the United States:

I am writing concerning the Generalized System of Preferences (GSP) and Hong Kong, the Republic of Korea, Singapore, and Taiwan. The GSP program is authorized by the Trade Act of 1974, as amended ("the Act").

I am hereby providing notice of my intent to remove Hong Kong, the Republic of Korea, Singapore, and Taiwan from their status as beneficiaries of the GSP program as of January 2, 1989, under Section 504(a)(1) of the Act (19 U.S.C. 2464(a)(1)). All four have achieved an impressive level of economic development and competitiveness, which can be sustained without the preferences provided by the program. Graduating these economies may also enable other less developed countries to benefit more fully from the GSP program.

RONALD REAGAN

The White House,
January 29, 1988.

Statement by Assistant to the President for Press Relations Fitzwater on Amendments to the Generalized System of Preferences
January 29, 1988

Because of their remarkable advancements in economic development and their recent improvements in trade competitiveness, President Reagan today has decided to remove four participants from the trade preference program that permits certain imports from developing economies to enter the United States duty free. Effective January 2, 1989, Hong Kong, the Republic of Korea, Singapore, and Taiwan will be graduated from the Generalized System of Preferences (GSP), a move that will affect nearly $10 billion in imports.

Since its inception in 1976, the Generalized System of Preferences has been a program of temporary incentives rather than permanent tariff advantages. Through the years we have regularly reviewed the 3,000 products from 141 beneficiaries that are eligible for GSP treatment and removed benefits from those products that no longer needed preferential treatment to compete in the U.S. market. Today's action is in keeping with the original intent of the program and with its operation during the past 12 years.

Over the past decade, Hong Kong, the Republic of Korea, Singapore, and Taiwan have made such tremendous strides in their economic development that they can now compete effectively in the United States without preferential treatment. Indeed, they have successfully fulfilled the objectives of the program. Last year nearly 60 percent of GSP benefits went to these four beneficiaries, a disproportionate amount for such advanced economies. Their graduation will open additional opportunities for the remaining beneficiaries—those most in need of the program.

This move should not be interpreted as penalizing any of the beneficiaries being graduated from the program. On the contrary, it reflects the great economic successes they have had. All four are good friends and valued trading partners. But the Generalized System of Preferences is a development program, and when GSP beneficiaries no longer need the program benefits, they should be graduated. America's relationship with these four advanced developing economies has entered a new phase, one that is characterized by greater equality. The United States admires their economic achievements and their advancement toward full partnership in the international trading system. We look forward to continued friendship and even closer economic ties in the years ahead.

Remarks to the University of Miami Hurricanes, the National Collegiate Athletic Association Football Champions
January 29, 1988

The President. Well, thank you all, and please be seated. Not you. [*Laughter*] I don't think there's room for that. Well, thank you all very much. And you know, there was a bit of confusion around here earlier this week. It seems that when I told somebody to expect the Hurricanes on Friday some of the White House staffers battened down the storm doors and ordered up emergency reserves of jellybeans. [*Laughter*] And I had to explain that I wasn't talking about tropical storms, that I'd invited the best college football team in America to come by. And so, welcome, to the 1987 NCAA football champions, the University of Miami Hurricanes, and their coach, Jimmy Johnson.

Jimmy, I just couldn't wait to have you champs come to the White House here to offer you much-deserved praise for the skill, determination, and winning spirit that you've demonstrated this season. And from the looks of a few of your other fans gathered here in the East Room, I'm not the only one impressed, not by a long shot. The whole country honors you today, and I'm pleased to have this opportunity to add my congratulations.

Of course, it's never easy. Yet with Steve Walsh, a sophomore quarterback who completed 18 of 30 passes for 209 yards and 2 touchdowns, and did it against a defense which only gave 7½ points per game all season, you had the odds on your side. Steve, of course you know better than anyone how important the help of running back Melvin Bratton and flanker Michael Irvin was. [*Laughter*] Each of them caught a touchdown pass in the big game. And the Orange Bowl might have come out a little differently without Greg Cox, who kicked a 56- and a 48-yard fieldgoal. And congratulations, Greg, on setting the Orange Bowl record with that 56-yard kick. You know, I kind of feel that if I could just kick some of the spending bills coming across my desk—[*laughter*]—I'd set a few fieldgoal records myself.

Actually, I might just ask Bernard Clark, the Hurricanes' most valuable player, to stand outside the Oval Office and tackle those spending bills. Those 14 tackles that you made in this Orange Bowl are truly impressive and something to be proud of. I ought to know, because I don't know if you're aware of this, but I played football when I was in college. And I had about 14 tackles in my whole 4 years. [*Laughter*] I'm kidding. I'm sure it was at least 16. [*Laughter*]

Seriously, I'd like to take a moment to recognize some other sportsmen: Coach Barry Switzer and the Oklahoma Sooners. They may have lost the game, but they had a winning season and accomplished it with a lot of class. The mark of a great sportsman is grace in defeat, and Coach Switzer exemplifies this. As he said after the game: "The best team won." Well, of course, let me congratulate all of you for having grace in victory, which is also important and not as easy as some people think. As a matter of fact, Knute Rockne once told his team that it really is this thing about being a good loser—it's easier to be a good loser and smile and take it than it is to be a good winner and do it with dignity and grace.

So, the best team did win. So, congratulations, champs. And the Miami Hurricanes are number one! Good luck, and God bless you.

Mr. Foote. Mr. President, my name is Tad Foote, and I'm the president of this university, and I express our deep appreciation and our honor at this invitation. May I present just a few of my colleagues, please, sir.

First of all, the chairman of our board of trustees, Jim McLamore, whom you know, sir—he is also the founder of Burger King, you have met before, and one of the leading Republicans in our part of the United States, as you know—[*laughter*]—our outstanding director of athletics, Mr. Sam Jankovich, standing right next to you, who is presenting you with a ball that has been signed by the Hurricanes; our outstanding coach, Jimmy Johnson, to my right, Mr. President; and his staff. This is the best coaching staff in the United States, President Reagan. And finally, the national champions. They're the big ones. [*Laughter*]

The President. That would be typical—when I was playing, I was usually outsized. [*Laughter*]

Mr. Foote. This has been a great football team, Mr. President. We are extremely proud of the Hurricanes. They've won with class on and off the field. We are deeply appreciative.

May I take this opportunity, please, sir, to wish you the very best during your last year in office; and on behalf of our university, these young men, and all of us, to thank you for your service to the United States. And I present this to you on behalf of the University of Miami as a small token of our appreciation.

Our coach, Jimmy Johnson, Mr. President.

Mr. Johnson. This has to be University of Miami's finest hour. Obviously, we're very proud of these young men winning the national championship, going undefeated; but we're also very proud that they are outstanding young men off the field, on the field, and in the classroom. Mr. President—and we have received all kinds of recognition and awards, having won the national championship, but without question, this is the finest honor that we could ever receive. Thank you.

The President. I am honored.

Mr. Johnson. From the number one national champions, we give this jersey to our number one, President Reagan.

The President. Well, thank you all very much. I don't know whether I'm going to be able to get everybody—a handshake with everybody here or not, but—

Michael Irvin. Please shake my hand. [*Laughter*]

Note: The President spoke at 3:05 p.m. in the East Room at the White House. Tad Foote, president of the University of Miami, gave the President a glass trophy, and Coach Johnson gave the President a football that had been autographed by the members of the team.

Radio Address to the Nation on Aid to the Nicaraguan Democratic Resistance
January 30, 1988

My fellow Americans:

One of the great stories of this decade, a story that goes too often unremarked, involves the movement toward democracy in this, our own Western Hemisphere. Less than 50 percent of the people of Latin America lived in democracies when our administration took office. Today that percentage is more than 90. In the words of President Sarney of Brazil: "Latin America's extraordinary effort to create a democratic order is the most stunning and moving political fact of recent years."

Yet in the face of this broad and sweeping movement toward human freedom, one country has gone in the opposite direction, away from freedom and toward oppression. That country is Nicaragua. Since the Communist Sandinista regime of Nicaragua took power in 1979, its political opposition has been subjected to constant harassment. Freedom of the press was replaced by state censorship. Communist control of the economy has produced hyperinflation and a standard of living that is now nothing short of desperate. Perhaps the most telling fact of all is this: Some 250,000 Nicaraguans, over 10 percent of the entire population, have fled the country.

It would be one thing if Nicaragua, bad as it is, were self-contained. Yet the actual case is much worse. For the Communist regime has placed Nicaragua within the Soviet orbit, embarked upon a massive military buildup, and already begun to send arms and guerrillas into neighboring countries. First, El Salvador, then Guatemala, Honduras, Costa Rica—the Communist Sandinistas have sought to extend violence throughout all of Central America. It could be only a matter of time before serious unrest and instability reached Mexico. Were that to happen, the decade of the nineties could open with hundreds of thousands of refugees streaming toward our own southern borders.

Yet people in Central America have themselves moved to prevent this threat from becoming a reality. First among these are the Nicaraguan freedom fighters. These brave men and women have given up ordinary life to endure the hardship of living in the countryside—virtually always on the move—to fight for freedom in their own country. There was a time when the freedom fighters, with few supplies, little medical support, and dwindling ammunition, were forced to retreat. But in recent months, in large measure because we in the United States have stood with them, the freedom fighters have begun to win major victories, placing intense pressure upon the Communist Sandinista regime to reform.

Outside Communist Nicaragua, the democratic leaders of neighboring Central American countries have worked together to develop a peace plan for the region. Among its provisions, the peace plan calls for all the countries of Central America, including Nicaragua, to respect civil liberties, including freedom of the press and freedom to hold elections.

The Communist regime in Nicaragua—which, as I've said, is under intense pressure from the freedom fighters—has agreed to participate in the regional peace process. So far, the measures the Communists have taken have been extremely limited—the release of a small number of political prisoners, for example, and the lifting of censorship in a very few cases. Yet there is hope that, with the freedom fighters keeping up the pressure, the Communists will observe still further provisions of the peace plan, permitting Nicaragua at least to inch toward the conditions of genuine democracy.

The United States has made every effort to promote a negotiated solution. Since 1981 we have met with the Sandinistas ourselves—bilaterally, multilaterally, and in other diplomatic settings. Four special United States envoys have traveled to the region on at least 40 occasions. Yet it remains vital for us to help the freedom fighters keep the Communist Sandinistas under pressure.

Next week Congress will vote on my request for additional aid for the Nicaraguan resistance. Ninety percent of the $36 million package is for nonlethal support, such as food, clothing, medicine, and the means to deliver those items. Only $3.6 million is for ammunition, and its delivery would be suspended for at least a month to determine whether progress is being made toward a cease-fire. I'm hopeful that will occur, and the ammunition will not be required.

However, if the Sandinistas fail to move forward on the path of peace and democracy, then I will certify to Congress that these supplies must be released. I will make that decision only after the most careful and thorough consultation with Congress and the four Central American democratic Presidents. Those brave freedom fighters cannot be left unarmed against Communist tyranny.

Until next week, thanks for listening, and God bless you.

Note: The President spoke at 12:06 p.m. from the Oval Office at the White House.

Statement on the 44th Session of the United Nations Commission on Human Rights

January 30, 1988

This 44th session of the United Nations Commission on Human Rights takes place at a critical time, when conditions for freedom have seldom been more favorable. The spread of democracy and free elections in Latin America and Asia and the desire for free markets and human rights hold out a beacon for oppressed peoples throughout the world. A witness to mankind's desire for liberty and to the strength of soul possessed by prisoners of conscience is our chief of delegation, Armando Valladares, who suffered for more than two decades in Cuban prisons as a political prisoner. His character and sense of purpose will serve us well in our diplomacy in the Commission.

Many issues face this session. The United Nations has repeatedly affirmed the right of self-determination for the Afghan and Cambodian peoples and deplored overwhelming human rights violations committed by their respective Soviet and Vietnamese invaders. The U.N. also has concerned itself with the serious human rights situation in Iran, whose government continues to suppress fundamental freedoms and persecute members of the minority Baha'i faith. The Commission has furthermore concerned itself with the human rights problems of Chile. We intend to work closely with cooperative delegations to reach constructive and helpful resolutions on such issues as the practice of apartheid by the South African Government.

Yet much remains to be done. One of the principal human rights violators in the Western Hemisphere, Cuba, has escaped attention for many years, but no more. The United States sponsored a resolution last year asking that violations in Cuba be placed on the UNHRC agenda, and we will do so again this year. Religious intolerance, particularly in the Soviet Union, continues to deprive millions of the freedom to worship as they choose. The freedom to emigrate, proclaimed by the Universal Declaration of Human Rights, continues to be denied to large numbers of people, including Soviet Jews, by Communist regimes. In spite of our best efforts, the practice of torture by other governments continues. The abuse of psychiatry to repress political dissidents in the U.S.S.R. is especially repugnant. We will look for deeds, not words, to satisfy world opinion that the U.S.S.R. has ended this practice.

We must not forget other victims of longstanding human rights abuses: Among them are the Baltic nations of Estonia, Latvia, and Lithuania; the Turkish minority in Bulgaria; the Paraguayans; and the peoples of Ethiopia, North Korea, Vietnam, and Nicaragua, where governmental repression is a way of life.

As the trend toward democracy throughout the world continues to gain momentum, we welcome the efforts of the United Nations to accelerate that trend. We pledge our full participation in the struggle for respect for all human rights.

Message on the Observance of National Afro-American (Black) History Month, February 1988
February 1, 1988

February traditionally has been our National Black History Month. In our celebration of this period, all Americans should reflect on the theme, "The Constitutional Status of Afro-Americans into the Twenty-first Century."

Black Americans' mighty contributions to the greatness of this land we call America have been tinged with poignant irony. Though they endured the chains of slavery and segregation, Afro-Americans have fought and died to keep our Nation's flame of liberty burning brightly. Theirs is a chronicle that can best be described as a litany of hope and faith in our Constitution's principles and in the ultimate fulfillment of its promise of equality under God for all.

Our Founding Fathers were the architects of the greatest political document ever written. In its preamble, they recorded their dream of securing "the Blessings of Liberty to ourselves and our Posterity. . . ." The dream of liberty for black Americans found many courageous champions before and during the bloody years of the Civil War, in the Jim Crow era, and in the modern civil rights movement. They saw that the bell of liberty rings hollow unless applied equally to Americans of every race, creed, and color.

The issues of freedom and equality are at the very core of National Afro-American (Black) History Month. This month offers all Americans the chance to learn more about a vital part of our history. But as we learn, we must remember that the battle against the disease known as prejudice cannot be waged and won in one era and forgotten in another. Every generation must renew the fight against injustice.

RONALD REAGAN

Appointment of Nancy P. Dorn as Special Assistant to the President for Legislative Affairs
February 1, 1988

The President today announced the appointment of Nancy P. Dorn as Special Assistant to the President for Legislative Affairs at the White House. She would succeed Lynn Withey.

Ms. Dorn has served as Deputy Assistant Secretary of State for Legislative Affairs since 1986. Prior to her service at the Department of State, she was chief of staff and floor assistant to former Congressman Tom Loeffler of Texas. She served previously on the staff of the Committee on Appropriations of the House of Representatives.

Ms. Dorn is a graduate of Baylor University (B.A., 1981). She was born in Lubbock, TX, on September 18, 1958, and currently resides in Arlington, VA.

Appointment of Harvey Ruvin as a Member of the Advisory Commission on Intergovernmental Relations
February 1, 1988

The President today announced his intention to appoint Harvey Ruvin to be a member of the Advisory Commission on Intergovernmental Relations for a term of 2 years. He would succeed Gilbert M. Barrett.

Since 1972 Mr. Ruvin has been commissioner of Dade County in Miami, FL, and is currently president of the National Association of Counties. Prior to this he was mayor of North Bay Village, FL, 1968–1972.

Mr. Ruvin graduated from the University of Florida in 1959 and the University of Miami (J.D., 1962). He was born June 6, 1937, in New York, NY. He is married, has one child, and resides in Miami, FL.

Appointment of John C. Stone as Special Assistant to the President for Legislative Affairs
February 1, 1988

The President today announced the appointment of John C. Stone as Special Assistant to the President for Legislative Affairs at the White House. He would succeed Richard Prendergast.

Mr. Stone comes to the White House from the Washington consulting firm of Jay Stone and Associates, Inc., where he served as president since its inception in 1982. From 1975 to 1982, he was the chief of staff to Congressman W. Henson Moore (R–LA).

Mr. Stone graduated from Tulane University (B.A., 1964). He served until 1968 as a lieutenant in the United States Navy as an air intelligence officer and participated in two Vietnam combat cruises aboard the U.S.S. *Coral Sea.* He was born December 31, 1942, in Springhill, LA. He is married, has two children, and resides in McLean, VA.

Nomination of Thomas J. Simon To Be a Member of the Railroad Retirement Board, and Designation as Chairman
February 1, 1988

The President today announced his intention to nominate Thomas J. Simon to be a member of the Railroad Retirement Board for the term of 5 years from August 29, 1987. He would succeed Robert A. Gielow. He will be the member at large and as such will serve as Chairman.

Since 1985 Mr. Simon has been Associate Director for Administration for the Office of Personnel Management in Washington, DC. Prior to this he was Director of the Office of Program Initiatives for the General Services Administration, 1982–1985. He was an expert consultant for the Social Security Administration in Washington, DC, 1981–1982; an associate with David M. Griffith and Associates in Northbrook, IL, 1980–1981; principal with Warren King and Associates in Chicago, IL, 1973–1980; and corporate cash manager with Reserve Insurance Co., 1970–1973.

Mr. Simon graduated from St. Louis University (B.S., 1966) and the University of Chicago (M.B.A., 1968). He was born July 13, 1944, in Chicago, IL. He is married, has three children, and resides in Alexandria, VA.

Remarks at the Annual Convention of the National Religious Broadcasters Association
February 1, 1988

Thank you all very much, and thank you for recognizing the greatest blessing that God has bestowed on me. Thank you, Dr. Robert Cook, Dr. Ben Armstrong, Dr. Thomas Zimmerman, Dr. Sam Hart. And by the way, Dr. Hart, I wish I could have delivered my greetings in person at the Grand Old Gospel Fellowship celebration at the Constitution's bicentennial. I understand it was a great event.

It was in 1921 that the healing words of the Gospel first flew like angels over America's airwaves. Since then, religious broadcasting has been a pillar of radio and television in our nation. This programming has helped God's message of salvation enter into millions of lives not just in the United States but in virtually every country of the globe.

Of course, it hasn't always been easy. In the past year your critics—and I can't help noticing how often they're my critics, too—[*laughter*]—your critics have delighted in taking the actions of an isolated few and portraying all broadcast preachers in that light. It won't work.

Long before the revelations about one ministry, you were busy assembling a board of ethics and a code of conduct for your entire field. And you have shown that integrity is a cornerstone of your ministries and are preparing so that in the year 2033 your successors, and maybe many of you, will meet to mark another 45 years of service with accountability to God and man. And I'll tell you what. You make that celebration, and I'll try to make it, too. [*Laughter*] I've already lived some 23 years beyond my life expectancy when I was born—that's a source of annoyance to a great many people in this town. [*Laughter*]

Today America is in the midst of a spiritual revival. From the growth of your radio and television stations to the polls of George Gallup, we see the signs of Americans returning to God. On our campuses the political activism of the sixties has been replaced with the religious commitment of the eighties. Organizations like Campus Crusade for Christ, the Fellowship of Christian Athletes, and Youth for Christ have grown in popularity. And why not, your message is rooted in one sure guide for life, the guide for our Founding Fathers and every generation of Americans as much as for ourselves, the infallible wellspring of our national goodness: the Bible, the inspired word of God.

How ironic that even as America returns to its spiritual roots, our courts lag behind. They talk of our constitutional guarantee of religious liberty as if it meant freedom from religion, freedom from—actually a prohibition on—all values rooted in religion. Well, yes, the Constitution does say that "Congress shall make no law respecting an establishment of religion." But then it adds: "or prohibiting the free exercise thereof."

The first amendment protects the rights of Americans to freely exercise their religious beliefs in an atmosphere of toleration and accommodation. As I have noted in the past, certain court decisions have, in my view, wrongly interpreted the first amendment so as to restrict, rather than protect, individual rights of conscience. What greater legacy could we leave our children than a new birth of religious freedom in this one nation under God? Now, I hear the smart money in this town say we haven't got a prayer, but somehow I believe the man upstairs is listening and that He'll show us how to return to America's schoolchildren the right that every member of Congress has: to begin each day with a simple, voluntary prayer.

At the heart of our Judeo-Christian ethic is a reverence for life. From the Ten Commandments to the Sermon on the Mount, the mission of faith is to cherish and magnify life—and through it God's holy name. Yet since the Supreme Court's decision in *Roe* v. *Wade,* there have been 20 million abortions in America. And as the Bloomington baby case showed, this callousness for life can spill over into other areas, leading to decisions on who is good enough to live and who is not.

All we know about the human spirit contradicts this mechanistic, materialistic view of man. Perhaps you saw in the papers recently the story of a young Irish author, Christy Nolan, who has received one of Britain's most coveted literary awards, the Whitbread Book of the Year award. Some say he's the new James Joyce. Little, except talent, is extraordinary here—talent and the terrible fact that complications at birth left Christy Nolan totally paralyzed. He cannot walk, talk, or control his limbs. He writes using what he calls a unicorn stick attached to his forehead, pecking out the words on a typewriter, a page a day. In his message accepting the award, Christy Nolan wrote: "Imagine what I would have missed if the doctors had not revived me on that September day long ago."

Imagine what so many deemed unworthy of life have missed. Imagine what the rest of us have missed for their absence. Life and the human spirit are absolutes, indivisible. Isn't it time we returned the right to life to the core of our national values, our national customs, and our national laws? [*Applause*]

Our administration is issuing regulations to deny title X family planning money for the support of abortion counseling, abortion promotion, and abortion services. Now, there's going to be a big fight on this, so let me ask you: Can I count on your help to make the regulations stick? [*Applause*] Well, that's what I thought you'd say. [*Laughter*]

There's something else I need your help on, and that's getting Congress to stand by its commitment to the cause of freedom and against the consolidation of a Communist regime in Nicaragua. In approving $100 million in aid to the freedom fighters in 1986, Congress laid down certain preconditions for renewing aid this year, including remindments [requirements] that the freedom fighters demonstrate that they are a proficient fighting force and that they show they have popular backing. Well, in truth, many who voted for those conditions believed there was no way the freedom fighters could meet them, not in the short time they had. They thought they'd found an easy way to get out of further support without taking blame. But the freedom fighters met those conditions.

Now we hear that further aid will jeopardize the peace process. By that reasoning, deploying the Pershing II and ground-launched cruise missiles in Europe should have led to the end of the intermediate nuclear force talks, and in fact, many who now oppose aid to the freedom fighters said it would. But the Senate is now debating ratification of that first agreement ever to eliminate an entire class of U.S. and Soviet nuclear weapons. The principle is the same. Peace doesn't come through the weakness of America and its democratic allies: Peace and freedom come through strength.

We're told that the Sandinistas have at last made hopeful confessions—concessions, I should say—[*laughter*]—they could well make some confessions—[*laughter*]—so more aid would be counterproductive. The problem here is what we've seen over and over again: that the Sandinistas stick to their word only if it's convenient or they're threatened. In 1979, when the Sandinistas came to power with American help, they pledged to President Carter that they would install a pluralistic, democratic government. But even as they were making that promise, they were drafting a blueprint for rule—what is now called the 72-hour document because it came out of a secret 3-day meeting. In it they said that the broad coalition government was only a front to, in their words, "neutralize Yankee intervention."

In other words, the coalition and the promises about democracy the Sandinistas made to the Organization of American States and to us were falsehoods, lies. And we swallowed them. We gave the Sandinistas $118 million over the next 18 months, even as they brought in Soviet and Cuban advisers, began supplying Communist guerrillas in El Salvador and elsewhere, and started to install Communist tyranny in Nicaragua.

The falsehoods have continued. Just over a week ago, I received a letter from Sandinista leader Daniel Ortega in which he said that Nicaragua allows "the full and unrestricted exercise of freedom of speech, debate, and association." Well, just about the time that letter arrived at the White House, in Nicaragua, Sandinista thugs attacked a meeting of mothers of political prisoners.

In October I raised this issue of promises broken when I addressed the Organization of American States. I was particularly concerned about the promises made in 1979 to bring democracy to Nicaragua. A month later, from the same platform, Daniel Ortega replied to me. He said that the pledges of democracy, of individual liberty, of a mixed economy, of freedom of press and religion were—here's his word: "inexistent." Why? Because a political pledge did not have—again from his speech to the OAS—"the force of a legal commitment." Well, he should have been a Hollywood producer. No, so one question must be answered: Sandinista promises of the past have been broken; can we believe them now?

The Sandinista steps toward peace and democratization can be reversed once the pressure from the freedom fighters is removed. The five democratic Presidents of Central America affirmed just weeks ago that the Sandinistas have failed to comply with the regional peace plan. Indeed, the Sandinistas haven't made one concession on their own without a threat hanging over them. And again and again the Sandinistas have shown themselves students of what Lenin said: that "telling the truth is a bourgeois prejudice." It's just this simple: The way to democracy and peace in Nicaragua is to keep the pressure on the Sandinistas taking irreversible steps to comply with the regional peace plan, and giving aid to the freedom fighters now.

You know, the more objections I hear from our critics about aid to the freedom fighters, the more I think of the story of that fellow who went into the Army. I bet you were wondering when I would get to a story. [*Laughter*] The fellow spent hours in boot camp on the firing range learning to shoot. And when he was done with boot camp, they gave him one of those medals that says Marksman on it. He went home—very proud—on leave, and near the edge of town he saw somebody's homemade firing range—a wall, and on the wall lots of chalked bull's-eyes, and in the middle of every bull's-eye a bullet hole. Well, he wanted to see who could shoot like that, and finally he tracked him down—a 7-year-old boy. And he asked the boy, "How did you do that?" The boy answered, "I take my gun; I line up my sights; and I pull the trigger. Then I take my chalk, and I draw a circle around the hole." [*Laughter*]

Well, that's how on target the criticisms of aid to the freedom fighters are. It's time for us to face why, even as the five Central American countries search for peace, the Soviet-bloc continues to pour billions in tanks, bullets, and other assistance into Nicaragua. To quote one of our leading national strategists, Zbigniew Brzezinski: "Potentially at stake in Central America is America's capacity to defend Western interests throughout the world." And he adds: "If the Soviet-Cuban presence in Nicaragua destabilizes the entire region, the United States will inevitably pull back" from Europe and the Pacific to defend our border. Our choice is whether to remove U.S. assistance to the freedom fighters, but is there any discussion about removing Soviet assistance to the Sandinista regime?

But there's something more than security at stake: freedom. Religious persecution under the Communist Sandinistas has been persistent and often brutal—Jews, Catholics, evangelical Christians, and others—all have suffered. Perhaps you know the story of Prudencio Baltodano, a father, a farmer, and an evangelical man of God. Sandinista soldiers tied him to a tree, struck him in the forehead with a rifle butt, stabbed him in the neck with a bayonet, and then cut off his ears. "See if your God will save you," they jeered as they left him for dead. Well, God did save Prudencio Baltodano. He found his way to Costa Rica and then to the United States. Recently his wife and children were located in a refugee camp in

Costa Rica, and through the efforts of the church located here in the Washington area, the family was reunited here in the United States. And Prudencio Baltodano is with us today. Señor Baltodano.

Let me tell you one other story of Sandinista religious repression. I mentioned Campus Crusade for Christ earlier. In late 1985 the Crusade's national director for Nicaragua, Jimmy Hassan, was arrested. For hours, he was harassed, questioned, and put in a tiny cell, questioned again, placed in a cold room, questioned yet again, and had a gun put to his head and the trigger pulled. Thank goodness the gun was empty. The reason for all this: He had been preaching the Gospel to young people. But that's not why I'm telling you his story. No, I thought you'd want to hear his account of what he said to one of his captors when, after hours of interrogation and humiliation, he was released: "I said to him I wanted to leave it clear that as a Christian I loved him, and I wanted him to know Christ."

Is there any force on Earth more powerful than that love? Is there any truth that gives more strength than knowing that God has a special plan for each one of us? Yes, man is sinful, separated from God. But there is God's promise of salvation, even for the least likely of us.

A few weeks ago I received a letter from a family in Wisconsin. The woman who wrote the letter is a widow, her husband was killed in World War II. They enclosed with the letter this prayer:

> Hear me, Oh God; never in the whole of my lifetime have I spoken to You, but just now I feel like sending You my greetings.
>
> You know, from childhood on, they've always told me You are not. I, like a fool, believed them.
>
> I've never contemplated your creation, and yet tonight, gazing up out of my shell hole, I marveled at the shimmering stars above me and suddenly knew the cruelty of the lie.
>
> Will You, my God, reach your hand out to me, I wonder? But I will tell You, and You will understand. Is it not strange that light should come upon me and I see You amid this night of hell?
>
> And there is nothing else I have to say. This, though: I'm glad that I've learned to know You.
>
> At midnight we are scheduled to attack. But You are looking on, and I am not afraid.
>
> The signal. Well, I guess I must be going. I've been happy with You.
>
> This more I want to say: As You well know, the fighting will be cruel, and even tonight I may come knocking at your door. Although I have not been a friend to You before, still, will You let me enter now, when I do come?
>
> Why, I am crying, O God, my Lord. You see what happens to me: Tonight my eyes were opened.
>
> Farewell, my God. I'm going and not likely to come back. Strange, is it not, but death I fear no longer.

That young man did die in that attack, and that prayer was found on the body of a young Soviet soldier who was killed in that combat in 1944.

Thank you all so very much. Usually speaking to an audience I add a God bless you, but I know God already has blessed all of you. Thank you very much.

Note: The President spoke at 2:20 p.m. in the main ballroom at the Sheraton Washington Hotel. In his opening remarks, he referred to Robert A. Cook and Ben Armstrong, president and executive director of the National Religious Broadcasters, respectively; Thomas A. Zimmerman, president of the Lausanne Committee for World Evangelization; and B. Sam Hart, president of the Grand Old Gospel Fellowship. Prior to the President's remarks, Mrs. Reagan was given the Foster Grandparents Award.

Nomination of Howard W. Cannon To Be a Member of the Board of Trustees of the Barry Goldwater Scholarship and Excellence in Education Foundation
February 2, 1988

The President today announced his intention to nominate Howard W. Cannon to be a member of the Board of Trustees of the Barry Goldwater Scholarship and Excellence in Education Foundation for a term of 4 years. This is a new position.

Mr. Cannon is currently president of Howard W. Cannon & Associates in Washington, DC. Prior to this he was a United States Senator from Nevada, 1958–1984. He served in the United States Air Force from 1941 to 1946 and received several awards: Distinguished Flying Cross Air Medal with two Oak Leaf Clusters, Purple Heart, European Theatre Ribbon with eight Battle Stars, and the French Croix de Guerre with Silver Star.

Mr. Cannon graduated from Arizona State College (B.E., 1933) and the University of Arizona (LL.B., 1937). He was born January 26, 1912, in St. George, UT. Mr. Cannon is married, has two children, and resides in McLean, VA.

Designation of Michael W. Grebe as a Member of the Board of Visitors to the United States Military Academy
February 2, 1988

The President today announced his intention to designate Michael W. Grebe to be a member of the Board of Visitors to the United States Military Academy, Department of the Army, for a term expiring December 30, 1990. This is a reappointment.

Since 1970 Mr. Grebe has been a partner with Foley & Lardner in Milwaukee, WI. Prior to this Mr. Grebe was a captain in the U.S. Army, 1962–1967.

Mr. Grebe graduated from the United States Military Academy (B.S., 1962) and the University of Michigan (J.D., 1970). He was born on October 25, 1945, in Peoria, IL. He is married, has two children, and resides in Mequon, WI.

Proclamation 5765—National Consumers Week, 1988
February 2, 1988

By the President of the United States of America

A Proclamation

Across our Nation and around the world, consumers are sending business an important message: there is no substitute for good service, the kind on which companies make their reputations. Under free enterprise, we consumers express our views through our everyday marketplace decisions and require businesses to adapt to our changing consumer choices.

The flexibility of American economic freedom opens the door to many opportunities for consumers and businesses. Both profit from today's increased emphasis on service. Customer-oriented companies that listen to their customers and make the commitment to act on their customers' wishes outperform their self-centered competitors time and again in profitability and customer loyalty. As a result, consumers are finding increasing responsiveness in some corners of the marketplace and are creating a demand for service in others. Indeed, customer service is emerging as a key competitive advantage today, not only in the domestic marketplace, but also in the expanding international arena.

In many industries, service is the product. The service sector accounts for 60 percent of our gross national product and provides some 70 percent of American jobs. Communications, transportation, utilities, banking, accounting, health care, and home maintenance are but a few examples of service industries indispensable to our way of life. Whether the transaction involves goods, services, or both, quality of customer service is a crucial ingredient in the interaction between customer and business, before, during, and after the sale. Service quality is often the factor that distinguishes businesses from one another.

This is the 7th year I have proclaimed National Consumers Week. I initiated National Consumers Week in 1982 to acknowledge and emphasize the significant stake consumers have in our economy. Our economy has three bases, the triad of capital, labor, and consumers; without any one of them the whole economy would lose its balance. Over the past 7 years, I have watched National Consumers Week grow into an established, national event involving millions of Americans in all sectors of our economy. I am proud of the success National Consumers Week enjoys. In recognition of the importance of consumers to our economy, and of service to consumers and business, "Consumers Buy Service" is the theme I have selected for National Consumers Week, 1988.

Now, Therefore, I, Ronald Reagan, President of the United States of America, by virtue of the authority vested in me by the Constitution and laws of the United States, do hereby proclaim the week beginning April 24, 1988, as National Consumers Week. I urge consumers, businesses, educators, community organizations, labor unions, the media, and government officials to identify, emphasize, and promote activities during National Consumers Week that draw attention to the importance of service in consumers' purchasing decisions.

In Witness Whereof, I have hereunto set my hand this second day of February, in the year of our Lord nineteen hundred and eighty-eight, and of the Independence of the United States of America the two hundred and twelfth.

RONALD REAGAN

[*Filed with the Office of the Federal Register, 4:50 p.m., February 2, 1988*]

Proclamation 5766—Small Business Week, 1988
February 2, 1988

By the President of the United States of America

A Proclamation

More than 17 million Americans own a small business; and the rest of us benefit from their ingenuity, enterprise, and hard work. These entrepreneurs employ half of all Americans in the work force. These achievements and the American heritage of economic liberty that helps make them possible are truly fitting reasons for each of us to join in observance of Small Business Week.

Today, small businesses provide well over two-thirds of all new American jobs, as well as 40 percent of our aggregate national output; the bulk of new American products and technologies; and more than two-thirds of all first jobs. The majority of jobs held by younger, older, minority, and female employees are in small business. In the next quarter-century, fully three-fourths of all new jobs created in America will have their genesis in small business.

The development of new enterprises depends on many factors, including the hopes, dreams, and hard work that have always characterized America's entrepreneurs. But it also depends on a climate hospitable to small business—a climate marked by a lack of government interference in the marketplace; low taxes; low interest rates; and the basic freedom to strive for and create progress, prosperity, and opportunity for ourselves and our fellow Americans. Government, the servant of the people, must make sure that it does not harm that climate, which is so necessary to our Nation's well-being and future.

The small business men and women of our land truly follow a great heritage and foster good for America.

Now, Therefore, I, Ronald Reagan, President of the United States of America, by virtue of the authority vested in me by the Constitution and laws of the United States, do hereby proclaim the week of May 8 through May 14, 1988, as Small Business Week, and I urge all Americans to join with me in saluting our small business men and women by observing that week with appropriate ceremonies and activities.

In Witness Whereof, I have hereunto set my hand this second day of February, in the year of our Lord nineteen hundred and eighty-eight, and of the Independence of the United States of America the two hundred and twelfth.

RONALD REAGAN

[*Filed with the Office of the Federal Register, 4:51 p.m., February 2, 1988*]

Nomination of Frances Mathews To Be a Member of the National Advisory Council on Educational Research and Improvement
February 2, 1988

The President today announced his intention to nominate Frances Mathews to be a member of the National Advisory Council on Educational Research and Improvement for a term expiring September 30, 1990. She would succeed Elaine Y. Schadler.

Mrs. Mathews was a talk show host for KCSJ Radio in Pueblo, CO, 1983–1984. Prior to this she was communications clerk for the Wyoming House of Representatives for one session. She was a reporter and then editor for the Guernsey Gazette in Guernsey, WY.

Mrs. Mathews graduated from Montana State University (B.S., 1954). She was born December 24, 1932, in Deer Lodge, MT. She is married, has three children, and resides in Pueblo.

Address to the Nation on Aid to the Nicaraguan Democratic Resistance
February 2, 1988

My fellow Americans:

I want to begin tonight by telling a story, a true story of courage and hope. It concerns a small nation to our south, El Salvador, and the struggle of its people to throw off years of violence and oppression and live in freedom.

Nearly 4 years ago, I addressed you as I do tonight and asked for your help in our efforts to support those brave people against a Communist insurgency. That was one of the hardest fought political battles of this administration. The people of El Salvador, we heard, weren't ready for democracy. The only choice was between the left-wing guerrillas and the violent right, and many insisted that it was the guerrillas that truly had the backing of the people. But with your support, we were able to send help in time. Our package of military aid for El Salvador passed Congress by only four votes, but it passed.

Some of you may remember those stirring scenes as the people of El Salvador braved Communist gunfire to turn out in record numbers at the polls and vote emphatically for democracy. Observers told of one woman, wounded in a Communist attack, who refused to leave the line at the polls to have her wounds treated until after she had voted. They told of another woman who defiantly answered Communist death threats saying, "You can kill me. You can kill my family. You can kill my neighbors. But you can't kill us all." Well, that's the voice of the people determined to be free. That is the voice of the people of Central America.

In these last several years, there have been many such times when your support for assistance saved the day for democracy. The story of what has happened in that region is one of the most inspiring in the history of freedom. Today El Salvador, Honduras, Guatemala, as well as Costa Rica choose their governments in free and open democratic elections. Independent courts protect their human rights, and their people can hope for a better life for themselves and their children. It is a record of success that should make us proud, but the record is as yet incomplete.

Now, this is a map of Central America. As I said, Guatemala, Honduras, El Salvador, and Costa Rica are all friendly and democratic. In their midst, however, lies a threat that could reverse the democratic tide and plunge the region into a cycle of chaos and subversion. That is the Communist regime in Nicaragua called the Sandinistas, a regime whose allies range from Communist dictator Fidel Castro of Cuba to terrorist-supporter Qadhafi of Libya. But their most important ally is the Soviet Union.

With Cuban and Soviet-bloc aid, Nicaragua is being transformed into a beachhead for aggression against the United States. It is the first step in a strategy to dominate the entire region of Central America and threaten Mexico and the Panama Canal. That's why the cause of freedom in Central America is united with our national security. That is why the safety of democracy to our south so directly affects the safety of our own nation.

But the people of Nicaragua love freedom just as much as those in El Salvador. You see, when it became clear the direction the Sandinistas were taking, many who had fought against the old dictatorship literally took to the hills; and like the French resistance that fought the Nazis in World War II, they have been fighting the Communist Sandinistas ever since.

These are the forces of the democratic resistance. The Communist government named them *contras,* but the truth is they're freedom fighters. Their tenacious struggle has helped buy the surrounding democracies precious time, and with their heroic efforts, they are helping give freedom a chance in Nicaragua. A year-and-a-half ago, Congress first approved significant military aid for the freedom fighters. Since then they've been winning major victories in the field and doing what many at first thought impossible: bringing the Communist Sandinistas to the negotiating table and forcing them to negotiate seriously.

From the beginning, the United States has made every effort to negotiate a peace settlement—bilaterally, multilaterally, in other diplomatic settings. My envoys have traveled to the region on at least 40 different occasions. But until this last year, these negotiations dragged on fruitlessly, because the Sandinistas had no incentive to change. Last August, however, with mounting pressure from the freedom fighters, the Sandinistas signed the Guatemala peace plan.

This time, the leaders of the four Central American democracies refused to let the peace negotiations become an empty exercise. When Nicaragua missed the second deadline for compliance, the democratic leaders courageously stood as one to insist that the Sandinistas live up to their signed commitments to democratic reform. Their failure to do so, said the democratic leaders, was the biggest obstacle to peace in the region. The Sandinistas are clearly feeling the pressure and are beginning to take limited steps. Yet at this crucial moment, there are those who want to cut off assistance to the freedom fighters and take the pressure off.

Tomorrow the House of Representatives will be voting on a $36 million bill, a support package to the freedom fighters. Ninety percent is for nonlethal support, such as food, clothing, and medicine, and the means to deliver it. Ten percent is for ammunition. That amount will be suspended until March 31st to determine whether the Sandinistas are taking irreversible steps toward democracy. I'm hopeful this will occur. However, if there is no progress toward a negotiated cease-fire, I'll make a decision to release these additional supplies, but only after weighing carefully and thoroughly the advice from Congress and the democratic Presidents of Central America.

Now, over the past several days, I've met with many Members of Congress, Republicans and Democrats, concerning my proposal. In the spirit of bipartisanship, I will, tomorrow, send a letter to the congressional leadership taking a further step. At the appropriate time, I will invite Congress to act by what is called a sense of Congress resolution on the question of whether the Government of Nicaragua is in compliance with the San José declaration. If Congress adopts such a resolution within 10 days containing this finding, then I will honor this action and withhold deliveries of ammunition in this package.

One thing is clear: Those brave freedom fighters cannot be left unarmed against Communist tyranny. Now, some say that military supplies aren't necessary, that humanitarian aid is enough. But there's nothing humanitarian about asking people to go up against Soviet helicopter gunships with nothing more than boots and bandages. There's no vote scheduled tomorrow in the Soviet Union on continued assistance to the Sandinistas. That assistance will continue, and it won't be just humanitarian.

Our policy of negotiations backed by the freedom fighters is working. Like the brave freedom fighters in Afghanistan who have faced down the Soviet Army and convinced the Soviet Union that it must negotiate its withdrawal from their country, the freedom fighters in Nicaragua can win the day for democracy in Central America. But our support is needed now; tomorrow will be too late. If we cut them off, the freedom fighters will soon begin to wither as an effective force. Then with the pressure lifted, the Sandinistas will be free to continue the consolidation of their totalitarian regime—the military buildup—inside Nicaragua, and Communist subversion of their neighbors.

Even today, with the spotlight of world opinion focused on the peace process, the Sandinistas openly boast that they are arming and training Salvadoran guerrillas. We know that the Sandinistas, who talk of a revolution without borders reaching to Mexico, have already infiltrated guerrillas into neighboring countries. Imagine what they'll do if the pressure is lifted. What will be our response as the ranks of the guerrillas in El Salvador, Guatemala, even Honduras and unarmed Costa Rica, begin to swell and those fragile democracies are ripped apart by the strain? By then the freedom fighters will be disbanded, refugees, or worse. They won't be able to come back.

Let me explain why this should be and would be such a tragedy, such a danger to our national security. If we return to the map for a moment, we can see the strategic location of Nicaragua—close to our southern border, within striking distance of the Panama Canal. Domination of Central America would be an unprecedented strategic victory for the Soviet Union and its allies, and they're willing to pay for it. Cubans are now in Nicaragua constructing military facilities, flying combat missions, and helping run the secret police. The Soviet Union and Soviet-bloc countries have sent over $4 billion in arms and military aid and economic aid—20 times the amount that the United States has provided the democratic freedom fighters. If Congress votes tomorrow against aid, our assistance will very quickly come to an end, but Soviet deliveries won't.

We must ask ourselves why the Soviet Union, beset by an economic crisis at home, is spending billions of dollars to subsidize the military buildup in Nicaragua. Backed by some 2,000 Cuban and Soviet-bloc advisers, the Sandinista military is the largest Central America has ever seen. Warsaw Pact engineers are completing a deep-water port on the Caribbean coast similar to the naval base in Cuba for Soviet submarines. And the recently expanded airfields outside Managua can handle any aircraft in the Soviet arsenal, including the Bear bomber, whose 5,200-mile range covers most of the continental United States.

But this is only the beginning. Last October a high-ranking Sandinista officer, Roger Miranda, defected to this country, bringing with him a series of 5-year plans—drawn up among the Sandinistas, Soviets, and Cubans—for a massive military buildup in Nicaragua extending through 1995. These plans, which Major Miranda makes clear are to be put into effect whether the freedom fighters receive aid or not, call for quadrupling the Sandinista armed forces to 600,000 or one out of every five men, women, and children in the country.

As I speak to you tonight, several thousand Nicaraguans are taking courses in the Soviet Union and Cuba to learn to operate new high-tech missiles, artillery, and other advanced weapons systems. Of grave concern is the fact that the Soviets have scheduled delivery of Soviet MiG aircraft to Nicaragua. Now, if these were just the claims of one defector, no matter how highly placed and credible, some might still find reason to doubt. But even before Major Miranda's revolutions [revelations] were made public, his old boss, Defense Minister Humberto Ortega, confirmed them in a public speech, adding that if Nicaragua chose to acquire MiG's it was none of our business. The introduction of MiG's into Nicaragua would be so serious an escalation that members of both parties in the Congress have said the United States simply cannot tolerate it.

The Miranda revelations can't help but make us skeptical of the recent Sandinista promises to abide by the Guatemala peace accord. The argument is made that the freedom fighters are unnecessary, that we can trust the Sandinistas to keep their word. Can we? It's important to remember that we already have a negotiated settlement with the Sandinistas: the settlement of 1979 that helped bring them to power, in which they promised, in writing, democracy, human rights, and a nonaligned foreign policy.

Of course, they haven't kept a single one of those promises, and we now know that they never intended to. Barely 2 months after assuming power, the Sandinista leadership drafted a secret report called the 72-hour document, outlining their plans to establish a Communist dictatorship in Nicaragua and spread subversion throughout Central America. This is the document in which they detailed their deception. It is now part of the public record, available for all to see.

One day after that 72-hour meeting, President Carter, unaware of their secret plans, received Daniel Ortega here in the White House and offered his new government our friendship and help, sending over $100 million in aid—more than any other country at the time—and arranging for millions more in loans. The Sandinistas say it was U.S. belligerence that drove them into the hands of the Soviets—some belligerence. A short while later, the Sandinista comandantes made their first official trip to Moscow and signed a communique expressing support for the foreign policy goals of the Soviet Union. But that, one might say, was only the paperwork. Already, Soviet military planners were in Nicaragua, and the Sandinista subversion of El Salvador had begun—all while our hand was extended in friendship.

This is not a record that gives one much faith in Sandinista promises. Recently, Daniel Ortega was up in Washington again, this time talking to Members of Congress, giving them assurances of his commitment to the Guatemala peace process. But we now know that at the same time, back in Managua, the Sandinistas were drawing up plans for a massive military escalation in Nicaragua and aggression against their neighbors. Now, as the Sandinistas see the vote on aid to the freedom fighters nearing, they are making more promises. Well, forgive my skepticism, but I kind of feel that every time they start making promises—like that fellow in the Isuzu commercial—there should be subtitles under them telling the real story.

One may hope they're sincere this time, but it hardly seems wise to stake the future of Central America and the national security of the United States on it. The freedom fighters are our insurance policy in case the Sandinistas once again go back on their word. The Sandinistas themselves admit that the limited steps they have taken to comply with the peace accords were promised in order to influence the vote in Congress. Was there ever a better argument for aid?

Even now, with the entire world watching, the Sandinistas have harassed and beaten human rights activists and arrested several leaders of the peaceful democratic opposition, including the editor of La Prensa. Before being interrogated, some were sealed for over an hour in metal lockers, 3 feet square on the floor and 7 feet high. Said one comandante of the opposition: "They are scorpions. They should return to their holes, or we will crush them."

Just a short while ago, the Sandinistas made their true intentions clear. Even if they were forced to hold elections and lost, they said they would never give up power. Responding to the estimate that the Sandinistas have no more than 15-percent popular support, another comandante responded by saying: "That's all right. We can hold on to power with only 5 percent." Now, these are not the words, these are not the actions, of democratic reformers.

Those who want to cut off the freedom fighters must explain why we should believe the promises the Sandinista Communists make trying to influence Congress, but not the threats they make at home. They must explain why we should listen to them when they promise peace and not when they talk of turning all Central America into one "revolutionary fire" and boast of carrying their fight to Latin America and Mexico.

If we cut off aid to the freedom fighters, then the Sandinistas can go back to their old ways. Then the negotiations can become, once again, what they were before: high-blown words and promises and convenient cover, while the Sandinista Communists continue the consolidation of their dictatorial regime and the subversion of Central America. During the last vote in Congress, many who voted for aid to the freedom fighters set conditions on further assistance. They said the freedom fighters must broaden their leadership; they have. They said the freedom fighters must show that they are a viable fighting force and win support from the people. Well, the latest victory in the Las Miñas area proved that.

For several weeks, nearly 7,000 freedom fighters maneuvered in secret throughout the country—something they could only have done with support of the population. In one of the largest military operations in Nicaraguan history, they overran enemy headquarters, routed army barracks, blew up ammunition dumps, petroleum tanks, and other military targets. At one point, they captured a warehouse where grain was being hoarded for the army. The freedom fighters opened the doors and invited the hungry people of the area to take what they needed.

The freedom fighters are inside Nicaragua today because we made a commitment to them. They have done what Congress asked: They have proven their effectiveness. Can we, as a moral people, a moral nation, withdraw that commitment now and leave them at the mercy of the Sandinista regime or turn them forever into refugees—refugees from the country for which they are making such a heroic sacrifice?

What message will that send to the world, to our allies and friends in freedom? What message will it send to our adversaries—that America is a fair-weather friend, an unreliable ally? Don't count on us, because we may not be there to back you up when the going gets a little rough.

By fighting to win back their country, the freedom fighters are preventing the permanent consolidation of a Soviet military presence on the American mainland. By fighting for their freedom, they're helping to protect our national security. We owe them our thanks, not abandonment.

Some talk of containment, but we must not repeat the mistake we made in Cuba. If containment didn't work for that island nation, how much less effective will it be for an expansionist Soviet ally on the American mainland. I will tell you truthfully tonight: There will be no second chances tomorrow. If Congress votes down aid, the freedom fighters may soon be gone, and with them all effective pressure on the Sandinistas.

Our goal in Nicaragua is simple: peace

and democracy. Our policy has consistently supported the efforts of those who seek democracy throughout Central America and who recognize that the freedom fighters are essential to that process. So, my fellow Americans, there can be no mistake about this vote: It is up or down for Central America. It is win or lose for peace and freedom. It is yes or no to America's national security.

My friends, I've often expressed my belief that the Almighty had a reason for placing this great and good land, the New World, here between two vast oceans. Protected by the seas, we have enjoyed the blessings of peace—free for almost two centuries now from the tragedy of foreign aggression on our mainland. Help us to keep that precious gift secure. Help us to win support for those who struggle for the same freedoms we hold dear. In doing so, we will not just be helping them, we will be helping ourselves, our children, and all the peoples of the world. We'll be demonstrating that America is still a beacon of hope, still a light unto the nations.

Yes, a great opportunity awaits us, an opportunity to show that hope still burns bright in this land and over our continent, casting a glow across the centuries, still guiding millions to a future of peace and freedom. Thank you, and God bless you.

Note: The President spoke at 8 p.m. from the Oval Office at the White House. The address was broadcast live by Cable Network News and CONUS Communications. The three major television networks, ABC, CBS, and NBC, declined to broadcast the address.

Statement to the Conference on Disarmament
February 2, 1988

The Conference on Disarmament plays an important role in international endeavors to create a more stable and peaceful world. You resume your work in a year that holds promise for realizing concrete steps toward this universal objective. I am pleased to be able to report to you that we are making discernible progress on all aspects of my administration's comprehensive agenda: reductions in nuclear arms, peaceful settlement of regional conflicts, development of confidence-building measures, and advancement of human rights and fundamental freedoms.

The signing of the INF treaty was an historic event. For the first time, the United States and the Soviet Union will begin reducing nuclear arms. We hope that this beginning will be followed by reaching agreement on our proposal for a 50-percent reduction in U.S. and Soviet strategic nuclear arsenals. In the field of nuclear testing, the United States and U.S.S.R. have begun full-scale, step-by-step negotiations with agreement on the needed verification improvements to existing treaties as the first step. Both sides have also agreed that progress toward banning nuclear tests must be part of an effective disarmament process. In Vienna, we are working out the terms of reference for negotiations on conventional stability in Europe. In addition, we are continuing the process, which was successfully initiated in Stockholm, in the area of confidence-building measures.

The Conference on Disarmament has an impressive agenda. Of special importance is your effort on a convention banning chemical weapons. Progress has been made in narrowing differences of principle; you now face the arduous task of working out the details and finding solutions on issues which affect vital security interests of all our countries. General Secretary Gorbachev and I have reaffirmed our commitment to negotiations in the Conference on Disarmament, which would result in a truly effective, verifiable, and global ban on these terrible weapons. Under the capable leadership of Ambassador Max Friedersdorf, the United States delegation will continue to work with you in resolving this and other difficult issues which engage this forum. I wish you Godspeed.

Note: Ambassador Max L. Friedersdorf read the President's statement at the opening session of the conference.

Remarks Congratulating the Washington Redskins on Winning Super Bowl XXII
February 3, 1988

The President. I'd like to welcome the winners of the 22d Super Bowl, the Washington Redskins; and your coach, Joe Gibbs. Welcome to the White House! Fellas, what else is there to say but Hail to the Redskins!

You know, I noticed that some of your fans painted their faces half-red and half-yellow; some of them wore hog noses; some even climbed lampposts. My staff told me that that wouldn't be very Presidential; but make no mistake about it, I'm just as enthusiastic as your fans!

The Redskins didn't simply enter the history books Sunday night, they rewrote them. In so doing, you gave new meaning to the term "Capital offense"—[*laughter*]—setting 14 Super Bowl records. And if you will allow me a minute, I'd like to list a few of the more impressive individual records: Timmy Smith, 204 yards rushing and two touchdowns; Ricky Sanders, 193 yards receiving, the most combined yards—235, and two touchdowns; and Doug Williams, the Super Bowl most valuable player, with one of the most inspiring performances displayed by any quarterback in football history—340 yards passing, the longest completion in Super Bowl history, 80 yards. That breaks one record and—and four touchdown passes in one quarter—and that breaks one record and ties two others. Way to go, Doug. [*Applause*] You recently showed the world how to overcome adversity and did it with style and grace.

It's noisy, isn't it? [*Laughter*] He's probably on his way to Denver. [*Laughter*] [*The President referred to the sound of a plane flying nearby.*] But, as Dexter Manley might point out—and a happy belated birthday, Dexter—this wasn't a victory accomplished solely on individual feats. No, it was the teamwork of a well-coached organization. This is exemplified by the five team Super Bowl records set Sunday night. So, congratulations go to Joe Gibbs and his excellent coaching staff.

And, Joe, if I could just add one personal criticism. Having spent a share of my life in show business, couldn't you have saved some of those thrilling moments in the second quarter for the last 10 minutes of the fourth quarter, so we could have a big curtain?

But seriously, I'm sure all the Redskins join me in congratulating the Denver Broncos on a fine season. Being number two in the NFL is also something to be proud of. There probably isn't a classier organization to win that runner-up position. Coach Reeves, John Elway, and the rest of the Broncos are true sportsmen.

But today, tomorrow, and the entire year belong to the victorious Redskins and your loyal fans who, thanks to you, are in hog heaven. Once again, congratulations, Redskins, and God bless you.

Joe Gibbs. On behalf of the Redskins, I want to thank the President. And we really feel like that this was a total team and family effort for the Redskins. And by that I mean there was no one individual, as Doug and Ricky and Timmy and everybody else will tell you. It was all of us pulling together. It was special teams; it was our defense—played absolutely superb; our offense; it was our owner, Jack Kent Cooke; Bobby [general manager Bobby Beathard], getting the talent; and our coaching staff, which I'm very thankful for; and most assuredly, all the fans. Everybody out there that belongs to the Redskin family pulled together and helped us get this. And we really did it as America—the same thing as a team effort by every single person in the family. And we thank you very much, and thank you, President.

Bobby Beathard. As a small token of appreciation from the Washington Redskins, we would like to present a small present to President Reagan, making him an official member of the Redskin family. And thanks to everybody out there. We're going to give President Reagan a Washington Redskin jersey.

The President. Thank you very much. I play right guard.

Doug Williams. First of all, on behalf of the Washington Redskins and the President, I'd like to tell him one thing—this is a long ways from Zachary. [*Laughter*] But I have a token of appreciation also. It's a Super Bowl XXII football with both teams engraved on it—Washington Redskins and Denver Broncos. I'm going to give it to the President upon one circumstance—that he run the right play. And the play is trip right, fake zoom, Larry crisscross. [*Laughter*] And he's got to throw it. [*Laughter*]

The President. Where's Ricky Sanders?

Doug Williams. Here he comes.

[*At this point, the President threw a pass to Ricky Sanders.*]

The President. I'm going to go down and shake their hands.

Dexter Manley. I came up with a solution, that we're going to renegotiate the President's contract for 4 more years.

Note: The President spoke at 2:35 p.m. at the South Portico of the White House.

Designation of Roland R. Vautour as a Member of the Board of Directors of the Rural Telephone Bank
February 3, 1988

The President today designated Roland R. Vautour, Under Secretary of Agriculture for Small Community and Rural Development, to be a member of the Board of Directors of the Rural Telephone Bank, Department of Agriculture. He would succeed Richard W. Goldberg.

Since 1987 Mr. Vautour has been Under Secretary for Small Community and Rural Development at the Department of Agriculture in Washington, DC. Prior to this, he was State Director (Vermont, New Hampshire, and U.S. Virgin Islands) for the Farmers Home Administration, 1981–1987. He was founder and owner of Sterling Realty from 1969 to 1981.

Mr. Vautour graduated from the University of New Hampshire (B.A., 1952). He was born January 20, 1929, in Berlin, NH. He is married, has four children, and currently resides in Alexandria, VA.

Statement on the Senate Confirmation of Supreme Court Nominee Anthony M. Kennedy
February 3, 1988

I am extremely pleased that today the Senate has voted, 97 to 0, to confirm my nomination of Judge Anthony M. Kennedy as Associate Justice of the Supreme Court. Judge Kennedy has served with great distinction as a Federal appellate judge in this nation's largest circuit for 12 years. He will make an outstanding addition to the Supreme Court.

By confirming Judge Kennedy as an Associate Justice, the Senate has not only restored to the Nation a full nine-member Supreme Court, it has reaffirmed this country's commitment to the philosophy of judicial restraint. Judge Kennedy believes, as I do, that the role of the judge in our democratic society is faithfully to interpret the law, not to make it; and that it is just as important to protect the victims of crime as it is to protect criminal offenders.

Judge Kennedy represents the best traditions of America's judiciary. I am confident that he will serve the Court and this country well.

Proclamation 5767—National Day of Prayer, 1988

February 3, 1988

By the President of the United States of America

A Proclamation

Americans in every generation have turned to their Maker in prayer. In adoration and in thanksgiving, in contrition and in supplication, we have acknowledged both our dependence on Almighty God and the help He offers us as individuals and as a Nation. In every circumstance, whether peril or plenty, whether war or peace, whether gladness or mourning, we have searched for and sought God's presence and His power, His blessings and His protection, His freedom and His peace, for ourselves, for our children, and for our beloved land.

That was surely so at the very beginning of our Nation, in the earliest days of our quest for independence and liberty. It could only be thus, for a people who recognized God as the Author of freedom; who cherished the ancient but ever new words of Leviticus, "Proclaim liberty throughout all the land unto all the inhabitants thereof" and who cast those words where they would ring out forever, on the Liberty Bell; who affirmed along with Thomas Jefferson that the God Who gave us life gave us liberty as well.

So did they believe, those who gathered in Carpenters' Hall in Philadelphia in 1774, the members of the First Continental Congress. They had come together, in times that tried men's souls, to deliberate in the united interests of America and for our "civil and religious liberties." John Adams later wrote his wife Abigail about what followed: "When Congress first met, Mr. Cushing made a motion that it should be opened with prayer." Some delegates opposed the motion, citing differences in belief among the members; but Sam Adams, that bold lover of liberty and our country, arose to utter words of healing and unity.

"I can hear the prayer," he said, of anyone "of piety and virtue who is . . . a friend to his country." He went on to suggest that a clergyman of a persuasion other than his own open the First Continental Congress with prayer.

And so it happened. Because Sam Adams gave voice to all the goodness, the genius, and the generosity that make up the American spirit, the First Continental Congress made its first act a prayer—the beginning of a great tradition.

We have, then, a lesson from the Founders of our land, those giants of soul and intellect whose courageous pledge of life and fortune and sacred honor, and whose "firm reliance on the protection of Divine Providence," have ever guided and inspired Americans and all who would fan freedom's mighty flames and live in "freedom's holy light." That lesson is clear—that in the winning of freedom and in the living of life, the first step is prayer.

Let us join together, Americans all, throughout our land. Let us join together, in factories and farms, in homes and offices, in places of governance and places of worship, and in outposts everywhere that service men and women defend us. Let us, young and old, join together, as did the First Continental Congress, in the first step—humble, heartfelt prayer. Let us do so for the love of God and His great goodness, in search of His guidance and the grace of repentance, in seeking His blessings, His peace, and the resting of His kind and holy hands on ourselves, our Nation, our friends in the defense of freedom, and all mankind, now and always.

By joint resolution of the Congress approved April 17, 1952, the recognition of a particular day set aside each year as a National Day of Prayer has become a beloved national tradition.

Now, Therefore, I, Ronald Reagan, President of the United States of America, do hereby proclaim May 5, 1988, as a National Day of Prayer. I call upon the citizens of our great Nation to gather together on that day in homes and places of worship to pray, each after his or her own manner, for unity in the hearts of all mankind.

In Witness Whereof, I have hereunto set my hand this third day of February, in the year of our Lord nineteen hundred and eighty-eight, and of the Independence of the United States of America the two hundred and twelfth.

RONALD REAGAN

[*Filed with the Office of the Federal Register, 11:21 a.m., February 4, 1988*]

Letter to the Congressional Leadership on Aid to the Nicaraguan Democratic Resistance
February 3, 1988

Dear ________:

On January 27, I transmitted to the Congress a request for $36.25 million in further assistance for the Nicaraguan democratic resistance. Our goal in Nicaragua is simple—peace and democracy. Our policy has consistently supported the efforts of those who seek democracy throughout Central America and who recognize that the freedom fighters are essential to that process.

Ninety percent of my request is for nonlethal aid, including food, clothing, medicine and transportation. The other ten percent is for ammunition and air defense missiles that would not be available for delivery until after March 31, 1988 pending my certification that:

—at the time of certification, no ceasefire is in place that was agreed to by the Government of Nicaragua and the Nicaraguan democratic resistance;

—the failure to achieve such a ceasefire results from the lack of good faith efforts by the Government of Nicaragua to comply with the requirements of the Declaration of the Presidents of the Central American Nations at San Jose, Costa Rica on January 16, 1988; and

—the Nicaraguan democratic resistance has engaged in good faith efforts to achieve such a ceasefire.

As I have already stated, I would make that certification only after consulting personally with the Congress and the Presidents of the four Central American democracies, and I would give considerable weight to their views on the question of whether Nicaragua has complied with the San Jose Declaration.

Furthermore, in the event that I find it necessary to make such a certification, I will notify the Speaker of the House of Representatives and the President of the Senate of my intention to do so ten days in advance. If the Congress adopts during that ten-day period a concurrent resolution stating that the Government of Nicaragua is in compliance with the San Jose Declaration, then I will refrain voluntarily from making the certification, and the suspension of lethal aid deliveries will continue.

I believe that this arrangement will afford Congress and the Executive branch the opportunity to address jointly the central question of Sandinista compliance with the commitments made at the San Jose Summit. Accordingly, I strongly urge that the Congress give its approval to my request of January 27, which in my judgment will serve to enhance the national security interests of the United States by strengthening the prospects for democracy in Central America.

Sincerely,

RONALD REAGAN

Note: Identical letters were sent to Senate Majority Leader Robert C. Byrd, Senate Minority Leader Robert Dole, House Majority Leader Thomas S. Foley, House Minority Leader Robert H. Michel, and other Members of Congress.

Announcement of the Establishment of the Council of Health Promotion and Disease Prevention
February 3, 1988

The President announced today that he has asked the Secretary of Health and Human Services to establish a Council of Health Promotion and Disease Prevention. This Council will bring experts together to assess current health promotion and disease prevention activities. The Council also will make recommendations for better use of resources and for innovative methods to encourage healthy lifestyles.

Prevention of disease and pursuit of good health is a relatively untapped field of study. The Council's work on health promotion and disease prevention should prove particularly valuable in controlling the increasing costs of health care. The administration appreciates the leadership of Congressman Don Ritter of Pennsylvania, who initiated the proposal to establish the Council.

Statement by Assistant to the President for Press Relations Fitzwater on the House of Representatives Failure to Approve Aid for the Nicaraguan Democratic Resistance
February 3, 1988

We are disappointed that the House of Representatives did not vote to keep pressure on the Sandinistas during the peace process. We thank our many supporters in Congress who worked so hard on behalf of this issue. We will continue consultations with these congressional supporters and others concerning the future of the resistance and the peace process.

Remarks at the Annual National Prayer Breakfast
February 4, 1988

You know, hearing these wonderful young men from Wheaton College here took me down memory lane a little bit, because some years ago, before they were born, and possibly before some of their fathers were born—[*laughter*]—I played football against Wheaton College. And it's kind of nice that I can say here—if one of them asked me—it ended in a tie game. [*Laughter*]

At the risk of sounding facetious, I just want to say here in this room—and as has been so eloquently stated by the people who've spoken already—about the uniqueness of how all of us, from so many different heritages, have come together here in the name of that one man. I have long been unable to understand the atheist in this world of so much beauty. And I've had an unholy desire to invite some atheists to a dinner and then serve the most fabulous gourmet dinner that has ever been concocted and, after dinner, ask them if they believe there was a cook. [*Laughter*]

But I want to thank each of you for being here today and for sharing with us the spiritual message that God has placed in your hearts. God's love shines through every word. His truth is the ultimate power source, and it's always there. It's available to ministers of the Gospel, Presidents, and the local grocery clerk. His comforting hand—well, I could never carry the responsibilities of this high office without it.

Our forefathers drew on the wisdom and strength of God when they turned a vast wilderness into a blessed land of plenty called the United States of America. God has truly blessed this country, but we never should fall into the trap that would detract from the universality of God's gift. It is for all mankind. God's love is the hope and the light of the world.

Recently a letter found its way to my desk, I'm pleased to say, and in that letter was a copy of a prayer. It was sent to me by a woman who had lost her husband in World War II. This prayer had been written and delivered in a shellhole during World War II. It read:

> Hear me, oh God; never in the whole of my lifetime have I spoken to You, but just now I feel like sending You my greetings.
>
> You know, from childhood on, they've always told me You are not. I, like a fool, believed them.
>
> I've never contemplated your creation, and yet tonight, gazing up out of my shell hole, I marveled at the shimmering stars above me and suddenly knew the cruelty of the lie.
>
> Will You, my God, reach your hand out to me, I wonder? But I will tell You, and You will understand. Is it not strange that light should come upon me and I see You amid this night of hell?
>
> There's nothing else I have to say. This, though: I'm glad that I've learned to know You.
>
> At midnight we're scheduled to attack. But You are looking on, and I am not afraid.
>
> The signal. Well, I guess I must be going. I have been happy with You.
>
> This more I want to say. As You well know, the fighting will be cruel, and even tonight I may come knocking at Your door. Although I have not been a friend to You before, still, will You let me enter now, when I do come?
>
> Why, I'm crying, oh God, my Lord. You see what happens to me: Tonight my eyes were opened.
>
> Farewell my God, I'm going, and I'm not likely to come back. Strange, is it not, but death I fear no longer.

And he did not come back. This prayer was found on the body of a young Russian soldier killed in action in 1944. I also received some letters—five letters, in fact—from Russian soldiers in Afghanistan who had deserted their government and their army. Each one of them wrote a letter to me and in that letter revealed their belief in God and that they had deserted not out of fear of battle but because they could not carry out the unholy orders that had been given them.

And just last week, one of those five—we did get them out. Their plea was for sanctuary. One of those five was in my office, a handsome young man in his early twenties. And it was evident—and not only from his letter but from his words—when he was thanking me for what we had done, that he believed in God. And I asked him how much religion did he believe there was in his own country. And he said, well, among young people like myself, it is spreading fast.

So, I know with all of us here, brought together, as we've been told so often this morning, in His name—I just thank you, and God bless you all.

Note: The President spoke at 9:30 a.m. in the International Ballroom at the Washington Hilton Hotel. Prior to his remarks, the Wheaton College Men's Glee Club of Wheaton, IL, sang two hymns.

Statement on the House of Representatives Failure to Approve Aid for the Nicaraguan Democratic Resistance
February 4, 1988

I am deeply disappointed by the House of Representatives' vote against the administration's request for additional assistance to those fighting for freedom and democracy in Nicaragua. I believe this action undercuts the efforts of those brave men and women at a critical juncture in the Central American peace process.

Yesterday's vote was won by those who advance the proposition that the prospects for peace and democracy in Nicaragua are best served by removing military pressure from the Sandinista regime. We have a fundamental difference of opinion. Whatever the case, the Communist regime in Managua should not interpret the House's action as a signal permitting a reversal in steps taken toward fulfillment of the commitments made under the Guatemala accords. I look forward to consulting closely with the Congress to determine whether the Sandinistas are making measurable and timely progress towards attainment of democratic reforms.

Meanwhile, my commitment to peace and democracy in Central America is undiminished. I wish to assure those struggling inside Nicaragua for those values we hold so dear of my personal support. And in the days ahead, I expect to consult with congressional leaders and our friends in Central America as to how best to build on the impressive record of progress our Central America policy has achieved during the past 6 years.

Proclamation 5768—National Tourism Week, 1988
February 4, 1988

By the President of the United States of America

A Proclamation

Every year, millions of Americans and visitors from abroad travel throughout our country to see for themselves the beauty of our land, the hospitality of our people, and the record of our history. They discover the glory and story of America, the evidence and the experience of all the hard-won freedom, justice, and opportunity we and our ancestors have cherished and preserved. National Tourism Week fittingly celebrates tourists, travelers, and those who earn their livelihood by serving them.

Travel and tourism offer countless benefits for Americans and for our guests from other lands, including domestic friendship and international goodwill, enhanced communication and cooperation, and the chance to view and visit natural wonders of limitless variety, city and countryside, and outstanding cultural events. Our comprehensive services and accommodations make U.S. travel and tourism the first choice of world travelers and the world's best buy for the travel dollar.

The travel and tourism industry, once small, is now our third-largest retail trade and second-largest employer. The travel industry directly or indirectly supports nearly seven million jobs and generates some $292 billion in receipts, or 6.4 percent of our gross national product. Internationally, tourism now is the largest business export among America's service industries; it contributes more than $19 billion annually to our balance of trade.

National Tourism Week reminds us not only of the economic, educational, and recreational benefits of travel and tourism but also of the warm and wide welcome that Americans traditionally and gladly offer to neighbors from near and far.

The Congress, by Public Law 100–214,

has designated the week beginning the third Sunday in May 1988 as "National Tourism Week" and has authorized and requested the President to issue a proclamation in observance of this week.

Now, Therefore, I, Ronald Reagan, President of the United States of America, do hereby proclaim the week beginning May 15, 1988, as National Tourism Week. I call upon the people of the United States to observe this week with appropriate ceremonies and activities.

In Witness Whereof, I have hereunto set my hand this fourth day of February, in the year of our Lord nineteen hundred and eighty-eight, and of the Independence of the United States of America the two hundred and twelfth.

RONALD REAGAN

[*Filed with the Office of the Federal Register, 4:08 p.m., February 4, 1988*]

Proclamation 5769—National Women in Sports Day, 1988
February 4, 1988

By the President of the United States of America

A Proclamation

The many achievements of American women in sports at home and abroad are sources of pride and inspiration for all of us. Whether on high school playing fields across our land or in Olympic arenas, female athletes time and again display qualities Americans cherish—not only great ability but also greatness in spirit, courage, and skill.

Reflection on this record of accomplishment reminds us of the many benefits of women's and girls' sports and of the importance of physical fitness for people of all ages and abilities. True physical fitness helps us do our best in life, as well as in sports and physical activities at any level. Women's sports and fitness activities also help develop leadership skills that can carry over into many other areas. Opportunities for female athletes of every background can truly touch the lives of many people for the better and enrich our country. The same is true for greater attention in schools and communities to physical fitness for girls; fitness research; and private, volunteer, and public sports programs.

In recognition of the contributions of women's sports to our country, and of the need for continuing advances in these sports, the Congress, by Senate Joint Resolution 196, has designated February 4, 1988, as "National Women in Sports Day" and authorized and requested the President to issue a proclamation in observance of this event.

Now, Therefore, I, Ronald Reagan, President of the United States of America, do hereby proclaim February 4, 1988, as National Women in Sports Day. I call upon the people of the United States to observe this day with appropriate ceremonies and activities.

In Witness Whereof, I have hereunto set my hand this fourth day of February, in the year of our Lord nineteen hundred and eighty-eight, and of the Independence of the United States of America the two hundred and twelfth.

RONALD REAGAN

[*Filed with the Office of the Federal Register, 10:52 a.m., February 5, 1988*]

Statement by Assistant to the President for Press Relations Fitzwater on Senate Approval of Aid for the Nicaraguan Democratic Resistance

February 4, 1988

We are gratified that the Senate has affirmed its belief in the freedom fighters in Nicaragua. This vote sends an important signal to the Sandinista government that American leaders remain concerned about the peace process and will be watching its progress very carefully.

Nomination of Ernest C. Baynard III To Be an Assistant Secretary of Energy

February 5, 1988

The President today announced his intention to nominate Ernest C. Baynard III to be an Assistant Secretary of Energy (Environment, Safety, and Health) at the Department of Energy. He would succeed Mary L. Walker.

Since 1986 Mr. Baynard has been of counsel at the law firm of Newman & Holtzinger, P.C., in Washington, DC. Prior to this, he was Deputy General Counsel for the Federal Energy Regulatory Commission, 1984–1986, and Associate Solicitor for the Division of Surface Mining at the Department of the Interior, 1983–1984. He was with the law firm of Connole & O'Connell as partner, 1980–1983, and as an associate, 1972–1980.

Mr. Baynard graduated from Trinity College (B.A., 1966) and Georgetown University Law Center (J.D., 1971). He was born August 8, 1944, in Washington, DC. He served in the United States Navy, 1966–1968. Mr. Baynard is married, has four children, and resides in Alexandria, VA.

Remarks on Signing the Housing and Community Development Act of 1987

February 5, 1988

Well, see how many it takes to bring about a happening like this. Well, welcome. You know, when I was a kid, my family used to live over the store. Sometimes I feel like I haven't come all that way—only now, got elevators. [*Laughter*]

Well, again, welcome. And I am pleased today to sign this bill, S. 825, the Housing and Community Development Act of 1987. This comprehensive legislation represents both compromise and cooperation between the administration, the Senate, and the House. Through a concerned effort, the legislation was transformed from a budget buster that would have reversed hard-won housing policy reforms into a rational, cost-effective bill that is fiscally responsible.

Thanks are due to many people for producing this compromise. In particular, Senators like Jake Garn, Pete Domenici, Bill Armstrong, Phil Gramm—the Republican Four Horsemen—deserve our gratitude for holding the line when an unacceptable version of the legislation came before the Senate. Senators Alan Cranston, and Al D'Amato, Dick Lugar, Pete Wilson, Dave Karnes, plus Chairman St Germain, and Representatives Chalmers Wylie, Marge

Roukema, John Hiler, and Steve Bartlett's efforts were instrumental in fashioning out the final compromise with our administration.

S. 825 contains several noteworthy provisions. It makes permanent the Federal Housing Administration's insuring authority. That means we will no longer see temporary suspensions of FHA mortgage programs that benefit young families and other first-time buyers.

A key feature of this housing bill is the permanent authorization of the housing voucher program that we first proposed in 1982. The housing voucher program exemplifies our commitment to community development through public-private partnerships. Vouchers gave families the dignity of choice—the opportunity to choose the type and location of their housing and the ability to be near family and friends and schools and churches or jobs. This legislation puts the private market to work in supplying rental housing by enabling the government to help needy families with vouchers so they can afford to rent housing of their own choosing. This legislation is a big step toward our housing goal of a home for every American family.

In just the last year, our voucher program has helped 100,000 low-income families find housing of their own choosing. We know flexible housing vouchers serve needy families better at substantially less taxpayer cost. And I'm also pleased that this bill authorizes the availability of vouchers to rural areas, but it's very disappointing that the Congress refused to appropriate the funding for a rural housing voucher program this year.

S. 825 provides new opportunities for public housing residents to take control of their own lives by managing or buying their own housing. Joining me are three of our national heroes of the tenant management movement: Kimi Gray, of the Kenilworth-Parkside Resident Management Corporation here in Washington, DC; Bertha Gilkey, of the Cochran Tenant Management Corporation in St. Louis; and Mildred Hailey, the founder of the tenant management movement at the Bromley-Heath Tenant Management Corporation in Boston. And they remind us that ownership or control of one's own residence should be an opportunity for every citizen.

S. 825 provides training and technical support for the establishment of new resident management groups and allows them to reinvest savings from resident management to establish small business enterprises. The resident management enterprises of low-income residents have effectively combated crime and poverty and created new pride through self-management in cities around the country.

This bill also adopts our proposal for modernization of public housing and gives us new tools to combat fraud and abuse in housing and FHA insurance programs. It also includes authority for the designation of enterprise zones—part of an initiative that we proposed in 1981. I'm also gratified by another provision of this bill which authorizes HUD to fund local, private organizations that are working to end housing discrimination. Too often—one case is too many—families and individuals seeking to buy or rent homes still confront bigotry and discrimination. Well, the fair housing initiative program section of this bill will help ensure that such racism will not be tolerated.

Special thanks to Sam Pierce for leading the 3-year fight for this program. Secretary [of Housing and Urban Development] Pierce has been one of the unsung heroes of our administration. His loyalty and hard work, his good sense and commitment can be seen in this bill. Few others could have brought such divergent forces together as Secretary Pierce, and he deserves our appreciation and applause. Thank you, Sam. [*Applause*]

Well now, this housing bill also makes some progress in eliminating ineffective programs, such as the Solar Energy Bank, the Rental Housing Development Grant, and the section 235 subsidy programs. As we work together to reduce the Federal deficit, we need to assure the American people that their tax dollars are being used to meet critical housing and community development needs in a cost-effective way.

There are, of course, a number of provisions in this bill that the administration did not support. Previously enacted cost-saving reforms were eroded, and provisions mandating unnecessary cost increases were included. The rights of landlords and owners and the Government's ability to wisely manage subsidized projects are excessively restricted. In the spirit of cooperation, the administration will work with Congress to see if we can correct these features of the bill.

But on balance, this is a sound compromise. This bill helps keep a lid on new spending while preserving our key housing reforms. It also includes features that will help ensure that our country can efficiently and effectively meet the challenge of America's changing housing needs. In an earlier day, American pioneers would gather together and help newcomers build their homes. That same spirit of good will and cooperation is what made the passage of this bill possible. And now I'll sign it, which is the easiest part of the process. [*Laughter*]

Note: The President spoke at 11:57 a.m. in the Roosevelt Room at the White House. S. 825, approved February 5, was assigned Public Law No. 100–242.

Nomination of Paul Freedenberg To Be an Under Secretary of Commerce
February 5, 1988

The President today announced his intention to nominate Paul Freedenberg to be Under Secretary of Commerce for Export Administration at the Department of Commerce. This is a new position.

Since 1987 he has been Acting Under Secretary for Export Administration. Prior to this Mr. Freedenberg was Assistant Secretary of Commerce for Trade Administration, 1985–1987. He was the staff director for the Subcommittee on International Finance and Monetary Policy for the United States Senate Banking Committee, 1981–1985; the minority counsel to the International Finance Subcommittee, 1979–1981; and served as a member of the minority professional staff for the U.S. Senate Banking Committee, 1977–1979.

Mr. Freedenberg graduated from the University of Illinois (B.A., 1965) and the University of Chicago (Ph.D., 1972). He was born February 17, 1943, in Chicago, IL. He is married, has two children, and resides in Potomac, MD.

Nomination of Mark E. Buchman To Be President of the Government National Mortgage Association
February 5, 1988

The President today announced his intention to nominate Mark E. Buchman to be president of the Government National Mortgage Association at the Department of Housing and Urban Development. He would succeed Glenn R. Wilson, Jr.

Since 1982 Mr. Buchman has been executive vice president and corporate banking division manager of Union Bank in Los Angeles, CA. Prior to this he was with Manufacturers Hanover Trust Co. in various capacities from 1962 to 1982: senior vice president and deputy general manager of the international division, 1980–1982; senior vice president, 1977–1980; various international positions, 1971–1977; Far Eastern representative in Tokyo, Japan, 1966–1971; and junior officer, 1962–1966.

Mr. Buchman graduated from University of Pennsylvania (B.S., 1959). He served in the United States Navy, 1959–1962. He was born June 19, 1937, in Caldwell, NJ. He is married, has two children, and resides in Los Angeles, CA.

Nomination of Richard C. Crawford To Be a Member of the Board of Trustees of the Harry S. Truman Scholarship Foundation
February 5, 1988

The President today announced his intention to nominate Richard C. Crawford to be a member of the Board of Trustees of the Harry S. Truman Scholarship Foundation for a term expiring December 10, 1993. He would succeed Robert Michael Isaac.

Since 1986 Mr. Crawford has been mayor of the city of Tulsa in Oklahoma. Prior to this, he was portfolio manager for Fourth Investment Advisors in Tulsa and Director of Personnel at the National Labor Relations Board.

Mr. Crawford graduated from Ohio State University (B.S., 1959) and served in the United States Army. He was born December 9, 1933, in Columbus, OH. He is married, has two children, and resides in Tulsa.

Remarks During the President's 77th Birthday Celebration
February 5, 1988

The President. And I used to think I wanted an Oscar. [*Laughter*] Oh, believe it or not, I am speechless. [*Laughter*] Oh, I knew that she got away with making the deal with the Soviets for the arms thing and so forth—[*laughter*]—but I never believed that she could accomplish anything like this. [*Laughter*] Incidentally, when was it that you were doing all that stuff with the Russians that I read about? [*Laughter*]

Well, all of you here—and to think that I kept trying to get Howard [Baker] to drop the packages and let me bring them over here. I didn't know why he was going to all that trouble. [*Laughter*] But, yes, it was a surprise, but I don't know of a happier surprise—all of you here, so many of you so dear to both of us. And I couldn't have imagined this in my wildest times. A matter of fact, I had it figured that we'd be just about getting into the helicopter now to go to Camp David, and I'm glad we're not.

But I don't know how to thank you, and Marvin—a song of my very own. [*Laughter*]

Mr. Hamlisch. That's yours.

The President. I've got to take singing lessons. [*Laughter*] But thank you all very much for all that you've done.

Mr. Hamlisch. We're all going to now sing one song that I didn't write, but I think it's the appropriate song.

Note: The President spoke at 1:54 p.m. in the East Room at the White House. Prior to the President's remarks, Marvin Hamlisch, accompanied by members of the Army Band and singer Donna Marie Elio, performed a song he had written entitled "He's Our Man (The Ronald Reagan March)" and presented a framed copy of the score to the President. Following Mr. Hamlisch's remarks, the guests sang "Happy Birthday."

Remarks During the White House Staff's Celebration of the President's 77th Birthday
February 5, 1988

Mr. Baker. Mr. President and ladies and gentlemen: Mr. President, if you are truly surprised—[*laughter*]—after 77 of these happy occasions, your acting skills have lost none of their luster. [*Laughter*] But surprise or not, on behalf of everyone here, your administration, your staff, your political party, and your friends from all over the country, we wish you happy birthday, Mr. President!

And, Mr. President and Mrs. Reagan, as you know, there are two people who've worked especially hard to recognize your birthday in this unique way. One of them, the First Lady, is on my left, and the other is Marvin Hamlisch. And Marvin, Mr. President, has composed a march in honor of your birthday, and it's entitled "The Ronald Reagan March." And the United States Marine Corps Band is ready to let us all hear how it sounds now.

Now, Mr. President, I thought you'd like to know that, now that you've got a march of your very own, we've taken steps to have a circuit installed to Capitol Hill, and any time you think you need to expand your presence in that place, all you have to do is touch a switch in the Oval Office and the Capitol Building will be regaled with the "Ronald Reagan March." [*Laughter*]

And now, Mr. President, to go along with the march, we have here something else for you. We have a gift certificate, which has been prepared by your staff and which I'd like to read. It says, "Gift certificate presented to President Ronald Reagan, redeemable for 1988, the best of 8, from every member of your administration, and expires on January 20th, 1989." Happy birthday!

The President. Well, believe it or not, I am speechless. For the last few hours, I have been surprised as I've never been surprised before. I came over here to have a hasty lunch and get into my Camp David clothes with Nancy and found myself at a luncheon party inside the State Dining Room with a great many friends there. And I think you ought to know—when I think of how long it took the whole Government here to come up with a budget this year—Marvin Hamlisch wrote that march in a week. [*Laughter*]

But to all of you, I can't tell you how—yes, I am surprised, and anyone is a cynic who doesn't think that I am—[*laughter*]—because I just thought that, well, yes, everybody was being very nice. And Howard helped me over here with a few presents that had been delivered in the office, and I thought he was going out of his way to be nice. Didn't know he'd been invited to the lunch, because I didn't know there was a lunch. [*Laughter*]

But to all of you, also, can you imagine what this means. There are more of you here than there lived in the town where I was born. [*Laughter*] There isn't any way to express it. And you know something: It ain't bad having another birthday, even at this stage. [*Laughter*] Here I am, 39 years old. [*Laughter*] I've been that old 39 times now. [*Laughter*] And I wouldn't mind going another 39.

But to all of you all I can say is just thank you all. God bless you all.

Note: The celebration began at 3:05 p.m. at the South Portico of the White House, prior to the President's departure for a weekend stay at Camp David, MD.

Radio Address to the Nation on Drug Abuse and Aid to the Nicaraguan Democratic Resistance
February 6, 1988

My fellow Americans:

On Monday I'll be journeying to North Carolina to participate in a symposium examining one of our country's most serious challenges: the use of illicit drugs. In North Carolina we'll be talking about drug use in the workplace, a problem that, it is estimated, costs our society nearly $100 billion in lost productivity each year and poses a grave threat to our public health and safety.

And public safety is an issue. There was a train wreck in Maryland a little over a year ago, when the crew went through signals that told them to stop. Sixteen people were killed, including two young sisters. Those young victims will never know the joys of life, of marriage, of having their own families. Why did that tragedy occur? Well, the National Transportation Safety Board determined that the engineer ran the stop signals because he was impaired by marijuana.

The time to act has long since passed. The tragedy and heartbreak brought to families throughout our country have already gone too far. Each of us can help by making a personal commitment to be absolutely intolerant of the use of illegal drugs. As Nancy says: "Either you take an active hostile position or you're giving tacit approval."

The next step is to identify the users—not to put them in jail but to do what we can to get them off drugs and to help them to live a drug free life. Drug testing not only permits us to identify users but it has been shown to be a deterrent, as well. In fact, a no-drug policy in the military, which includes screening and testing, has resulted in a two-thirds decline in the number of drug users in uniform. This same commitment could well save money and lives in the private sector. And we're determined that the Federal Government, the Nation's number one employer, lead the way in eliminating the use of illegal drugs in the workplace.

But this challenge isn't the Government's alone: It belongs to all of us. Those using drugs are affecting our lives, hurting others, whether they want to admit it or not. When policemen, judges, mayors, and military officers are gunned down by drug traffickers in countries like Colombia, anyone using drugs in the United States is helping pull the trigger of a murderer's gun. And the death toll also includes those shop owners and police killed during drug-related incidents in our own country. No decent person could want to contribute to such vicious crime, yet everyone who uses illegal drugs, even occasionally, shares the blame.

But it's never too late to quit, and it's never too late to take a stand. I've always believed that, once we've made up our minds, there's nothing we Americans can't accomplish. Making up our minds is the hard part.

Just this week we saw Congress divided on my request for continued assistance to those fighting for freedom in Nicaragua. Both sides claim their goal to be peace and democracy in Central America; the argument is over how to achieve it. To my disappointment, the House of Representatives voted to remove military pressure from the Sandinista regime in Nicaragua. The Senate agreed with me, that we cannot leave the democratic resistance in that country to the mercy of that Communist regime and expect the Sandinistas to democratize out of the goodness of their hearts.

All of this has serious implications for our country's national security and, no less important, has grave implications for those brave souls who are fighting for democracy in Nicaragua—people who trusted us. Their fate, the fate of democracy, and our own security interests depend on the next steps we take.

I understand that some in Congress have already begun to develop an alternative assistance package. I await the details. I will work with the members of both parties to see to it that the fact that we disagree does not mean that America cannot act. What I will not accept, however, is an assistance package that is little more than a disguise for surrender and abandonment.

The Sandinistas made commitments to democracy and pluralism as long ago as 1979. They were not kept. Americans are united in our determination that these latest promises be kept in a timely way. We must act to ensure that freedom is not smothered in that country.

We live in perilous times, my fellow Americans, but also times of great hope and opportunity. The future is up to us.

Until next week, thanks for listening, and God bless you.

Note: The President spoke at 12:06 p.m. from Camp David, MD.

Remarks on Arrival at Duke University in Durham, North Carolina
February 8, 1988

The President. Well, don't stop the music on account of me. Thank you all very much. This is a very warm welcome, and you make me very proud. I appreciate your coming out here on this day, and I'm looking forward to meeting the Duke basketball team. I know they had a pretty fine week. And yesterday it seems that somebody didn't win one for the Gipper. [*Laughter*]

But I know that we're expected for a meeting over on the campus here.

Audience members. Just say no! Just say no! Just say no!

The President. What are they saying?

Did I hear somebody saying just say no? [*Applause*] Well, that's what Nancy let me come down here to talk about, just say no. I don't know whether you'd be interested in knowing where that came from. But Nancy was appearing before a group of students like yourselves, and a girl in the audience spoke up and said, "What do we do when someone offers us drugs?" And Nancy said, "Just say no." And today there are over 10,000 Just Say No clubs in schools and campuses across the country.

Audience members. Just say no! Just say no! Just say no!

The President. So, I can't hear. I can't hear what they're saying.

Well, I know that I've got to move on and get over to the forum and the meeting on this subject that I just mentioned. But again, I just want to tell you this is very heartwarming. You make me very proud, indeed, and I'll try to be deserving of this warm welcome. Thank you very much.

Note: The President spoke at 1:27 p.m. at the university.

Remarks at a Seminar on Substance Abuse in the Workplace in Durham, North Carolina
February 8, 1988

Thank you, Governor Jim Martin, and thanks, too, for that great music by the Duke University Pep Band. I understand I'm the backup speaker today. You had a real star this morning: Secretary of Labor Ann McLaughlin. Governor, Dr. Brodie [president of Duke University], distinguished guests, Duke students—[*applause*]. I figured that was the best way to find out if you were here. [*Laughter*]

Well, this has been a week of champions for me. Last Wednesday the Redskins came to the White House, and today I am visiting the home of Coach K's [Michael Krzyzewski] Duke Blue Devils. I met them out at the airport when we arrived. You've got a champion Governor in Jim Martin and a champion Senator in Jesse Helms. And North Carolina has given our administration champion leaders: Jack Matlock, our Ambassador to the Soviet Union; Jim Burnley, our Secretary of Transportation; and Bill Bennett, our Secretary of Education.

But today we're here to talk about drugs in the workplace, as you've been doing. As I mentioned, earlier today I had the opportunity to hear from some people who know firsthand about what drugs in the workplace can mean. And I've been very impressed, as well, with what our panel here has told me. As you know, Nancy and I have both taken a personal interest in the crusade for a drug free America. Like so many Americans, we watched with greater and greater apprehension during the years when too much of our media and too many of our cultural and political leaders sent out the message that using illegal drugs was okay.

Well, thank God those days are over. Those days of scenes in a movie where you would get laughs out of someone who was high on marijuana, those scenes where everybody—the first thing they did was open a bottle before the scene began on the screen—well, this conference proves that we no longer shrug off illegal drug use. Yes, Americans in all walks of life have seen the truth about drugs. Workers, employers, students, teachers are all saying no to drugs and alcohol.

A few weeks ago we learned that America's students are saying no as never before. For 13 years we have conducted annual surveys of thousands of graduating seniors in high schools across our country: What drugs have they used? How often? What do they think about drug abuse? Well, just last month the survey of the class of 1987 came out, and the news was the best ever. For the first time since the surveying began, a substantially smaller proportion of high school seniors—one-third smaller—acknowledged current use of cocaine than did the year before. Use of marijuana and amphetamines is also dropping. And almost all students said it was wrong even to try a drug like cocaine. So, America's students are getting the message: Drugs hurt; drugs kill.

And let me add, I can't help being proud of the role someone close to me has played in teaching our young people to stay away from drugs. Nancy's doing a great job. And by the way, I'm the only one in the family the Government's paying, but I think she's working more than I am. [*Laughter*] And by the way, she's asked me, as she always does when I speak to an audience that includes young people—please, for your families, for your friends, for yourselves, do what so many others are doing and just say no to drugs and alcohol.

But if we're to achieve our goal of a drug free America, we must reach outside the schools and into the workplace. Now, the professional basketball court may seem like a long way from the average office or factory. But as I heard those personal stories before I came out here, I couldn't help thinking how similar they were to a story about drugs in the workplace that I was planning to tell you.

A few years ago, here in North Carolina, North Carolina State had one of the Nation's most promising young basketball stars. David Thompson led North Carolina State to an NCAA championship before signing a pro contract for over $2 million. After three seasons of brilliant play, he was the highest paid player in the National Basketball Association, and then he got into drugs. Over the next two seasons, his game deteriorated. He became injury- and accident-prone. He started showing up late for practice and got into fights on the court. So, he was traded and eventually cut. Two years ago he filed for bankruptcy—millions and a brilliant career squandered on drugs.

Today David Thompson is pulling his life together. We all pray for his success. And he has this warning: "You never feel like you're going to be the one to get hooked," he says. And he added: "I knew that it was harmful both for me and for my career, but I couldn't stop." And he offers this advice about drugs: "Never try it. It's easy to get involved with, and it's very hard to get out of."

David Thompson was an extraordinary athlete but an all too typical on-the-job drug user. Game deteriorating? Studies show that drug users are two-thirds as productive as nonusers. Lost productivity because of drugs costs America nearly $100 billion a year, and that's like having a pulled hamstring in the race of international commerce.

Injury and accident-prone? Drug users are three or four times as likely to be involved in accidents. For example, a study of airline pilots using flight simulators showed that they had trouble performing standard landing maneuvers as long as 24 hours after smoking a marijuana cigarette. I have heard that the amount of time that marijuana stays in the fat in the body—unlike alcohol leaving so quickly—that it can be up to 4 days that the body is still being affected.

Missing work? In one national study, drug users reported skipping work two or three times as often as nonusers.

Difficult to get along with? Ninety-two percent of all Americans say they don't want to work around someone who gets high during the day, perhaps because drug users act the way they tell researchers they feel: They don't want to be at work—period.

One other thing: As I heard firsthand today, when it's all over and drug users look back on the wreckage of their careers and their lives—like David Thompson—their advice is: "Never, never try it." They wish they never had. They wish someone had discovered their habit earlier and given them help.

Well, that's why we're here. Now, I've heard critics say employers have no business looking for drug abuse in the workplace. But when you pin the critics down, too often they seem to be among that handful who still believe that drug abuse is a victimless crime.

When I hear those critics, with their new version of an old, discredited theory, I remember the story about the man who took the train ride. This is my way of getting to tell you a story. [*Laughter*] The man noticed that the fellow across the aisle was making strange and elaborate gestures and grimaces and then laughing. And finally the man leaned over to ask if anything was wrong. "No, no," the fellow said. "It's just that when I travel I pass the time telling stories to myself." And the man said, "Well, then why do you make faces and gestures as if you were in pain?" And the fellow answered, "Well, every time I start a story, I have to tell myself that I've heard it before." [*Laughter*]

But we've heard the story of victimless crime before, and it's a bad one. The drug user is a victim. His employer is a victim. His fellow employees are victims. The family that depends on his wages are victims. And America—which is only as strong and as competitive as all of us together—America is the victim. It would be hard to find any crime with more victims than drug abuse.

Almost a year-and-a-half ago, we announced a Federal campaign for a drug free workplace. To accomplish this, we proposed to put the Federal Government in the lead, moving toward a drug free workplace for Federal employees. We're encouraging State and local government to follow our example, as well as Federal contractors and all of the private sector. That means you. And I know that the companies represented here have already moved ahead.

I'm proud of the progress we've made, particularly in the military and other areas where an alert mind can mean the difference between life and death. We got a headstart with the military. And since the drug program started there, illegal drug use has gone down by two-thirds. But I know we have a long way to go. The companies here today are leaders, but I know hundreds of others are making progress, too. We in Washington have a lot to learn from you. You're showing how compassion and campaigns for a drug free workplace go hand in hand.

The crusade for a drug free America is being waged on many fronts. In the last 6 years, for the first time ever, we've set up a nationally coordinated attack on drug smuggling. Drug seizures are at an all-time high. Federal drug arrests have increased 66 percent. Arrests of major traffickers have tripled. But in the end, the crusade against drugs will be won not on the shores but in the heart of America. If students, workers, executives, professionals—if all of us decide that there's no place for the enslavement of illegal drugs in this land of the free, then we will win and drugs will lose. And that's our challenge. That's the crusade that you're helping to lead.

You know, there's a great deal of emphasis and people talking about—when I heard a phrase about throwing money at drugs, the idea that it can all be done if we have enough people out there on the borders intercepting. Well, we have intercepted, tons and tons. We have fleets of airplanes and boats and trucks that have been confiscated. And I told some people earlier today, I saw for the first time in my life what $20 million looked like. It was piled up on a table down in Florida, confiscated from drug dealers. And yet as long as there is a profit in it, that isn't enough. The real answer must come from taking the customer away from the drugs, not the other way around.

Then, to those of you—and like some who've spoken here today—who've resolved their problem and cured, they are the greatest exponents. I found that out back, Jim, in my Governor days, when I would try to talk to young people about this when it was first beginning—the emphasis then was on marijuana. And I found out that I might stand there and talk all day, and I wasn't as effective as one individual who could stand up in front of them and say to them, "I've been there. I used to do that." And he can solve more problems in 10 minutes than, as I say, as I could all day. And those are the people, so many of them, who are so unselfishly now joining the crusade. And God bless them and—for all of that you're doing to help—you, to your fellow Americans. I thank you, and God bless you.

Note: The President spoke at 2:15 p.m. at Cameron Indoor Stadium at Duke University. He was introduced by Governor James Martin. Prior to his remarks, the President met with members of the business community. Following the seminar, he returned to Washington, DC.

Nomination of Marc G. Stanley To Be an Assistant Secretary of Commerce

February 8, 1988

The President today announced his intention to nominate Marc G. Stanley to be an Assistant Secretary of Commerce (Congressional and Intergovernmental Affairs). He would succeed Gerald J. McKiernan.

Since 1979 Mr. Stanley has been administrative assistant to Pennsylvania Congressman William Clinger, Jr., in Washington, DC, and serves as adjunct professor to the Washington Semester program of the American University, 1981–present. Prior to this he was administrative assistant to Connecticut Congressman Ronald A. Sarasin, 1973–1978. He was legislative assistant to Pennsylvania Congressman Lawrence Coughlin, 1969–1972, and legislative assistant to New York Congressman Seymour Halpern, 1962–1964.

Mr. Stanley graduated from George Washington University (B.A., 1964) and University of Baltimore (LL.B., 1967). He served in the United States Coast Guard Reserves, 1967–1973. He was born February 18, 1943, in Washington, DC. Mr. Stanley is married, has two children, and resides in Rockville, MD.

Appointment of Charles V. Greener as Special Assistant to the President for Legislative Affairs
February 9, 1988

The President today announced the appointment of Charles V. Greener as Special Assistant to the President for Legislative Affairs at the White House.

Mr. Greener has served since January 1981 as chief of staff to Congressman Bob McEwen (R–OH). Prior to joining Congressman McEwen's staff, Mr. Greener served as executive assistant to Larry Robinson, president and chief executive officer of J.B. Robinson, Inc., in Cleveland, OH. From 1977 to 1978, he was district representative for Congressman Willis D. Gradison (R–OH).

Mr. Greener graduated with honors from Valparaiso University with a bachelor of arts degree in history and political science. He was born July 27, 1954. He resides in Arlington, VA, and has one daughter.

Nomination of Mrs. Lamar Alexander To Be a Member of the Board of Directors of the Corporation for Public Broadcasting
February 9, 1988

The President today announced his intention to nominate Mrs. Lamar (Honey) Alexander to be a member of the Board of Directors of the Corporation for Public Broadcasting for a term expiring March 26, 1991. She would succeed Harry O'Connor.

Mrs. Alexander has been involved in numerous public and community programs. She has served as honorary chairman of the International Year of the Child, 1979–1980; delegate to the White House Conference on Families, 1980; honorary chairman of the Association of Retarded Citizens in Tennessee, 1980–1981; and chairman of the Governor's task force on the prevention of mental retardation, since 1980. Mrs. Alexander currently serves as a member of the Board of Directors for the Public Broadcasting System and Nashville's Council of Community Services.

Mrs. Alexander graduated from Smith College (B.A., 1967). She was born October 12, 1945, in Victoria, TX. She is married to Tennessee Governor Lamar Alexander, has four children, and resides in Nashville.

Appointment of Charles Wohlstetter as a Member of the President's National Security Telecommunications Advisory Committee
February 9, 1988

The President today announced his intention to appoint Charles Wohlstetter to be a member of the President's National Security Telecommunications Advisory Committee. He would succeed John N. Lemasters.

Since 1967 Mr. Wohlstetter has been chairman of the board of Contel Corp. in New York City. Prior to this Mr. Wohlstetter was president of Contel Corp., 1961–1967.

Mr. Wohlstetter graduated from the College of the City of New York (B.A., 1929). He was born April 5, 1910, in Manhattan, NY. Mr. Wohlstetter is married, has three children, and resides in New York City.

Nomination of John E. Higgins, Jr., To Be a Member of the National Labor Relations Board

February 9, 1988

The President today announced his intention to nominate John E. Higgins, Jr., to be a member of the National Labor Relations Board for a term of 5 years expiring December 16, 1992. He would succeed Donald L. Dotson.

Since 1976 Mr. Higgins has been Deputy General Counsel of the National Labor Relations Board in Washington, DC. Previously, he was Deputy Associate General Counsel for the National Labor Relations Board, 1972–1975, and Deputy Assistant General Counsel, 1969–1972. Mr. Higgins also serves as adjunct professor for Catholic University of America Law School.

Mr. Higgins graduated from Boston College (A.B., 1961), Boston University Law School (J.D., 1964), and Cornell University (M.S., 1970). He was born on December 27, 1939, in Medford, MA. Mr. Higgins is married, has three children, and resides in Chevy Chase, MD.

Nomination of Tirso del Junco To Be a Governor of the United States Postal Service

February 9, 1988

The President today announced his intention to nominate Tirso del Junco, M.D., to be a Governor of the United States Postal Service for the remainder of the term expiring December 8, 1991. He would succeed John R. McKean.

Since 1975 Dr. del Junco has been chairman of the department of surgery at Santa Marta Hospital in Los Angeles, CA. Dr. del Junco is currently a member of the board of regents at the University of California and a member of the air resources board for the State of California. Prior to this he was chief of medical staff at Queen of Angels Hospital, 1979, and chairman of the department of surgery, 1972 and 1977. Dr. del Junco has also served as president of the board of medical examiners for the State of California, 1971–1972.

Dr. del Junco graduated from the University of Havana (M.D., 1949). He served in the United States Army as chief of surgery for Camp Hanford Army Hospital in Washington, 1955–1957. He was born April 20, 1925, in Havana, Cuba. He is married, has four children, and resides in Pasadena, CA.

Proclamation 5770—National Child Passenger Safety Awareness Week, 1988

February 10, 1988

By the President of the United States of America

A Proclamation

Motor vehicle crashes are a major cause of death and disabling injury for America's children. The best way to protect children in automobiles is to use child safety seats and other safety restraints on every trip. We must alert parents and concerned citizens of the critical need to make child passenger safety a priority in every community, and we should recognize the thousands of people throughout our Nation who do so as they take part in programs and activities in support of National Child Passenger Safety Awareness Week. Fittingly, this special week falls just before Valentine's Day, when we express love and appreciation to family and friends.

Many people may be unaware that child passenger protection laws requiring the use of child safety seats and belt systems are in place in all 50 States and the District of Columbia. Correctly used, child safety seats are highly effective, reducing the risk of fatality among children under four by about 70 percent and of serious injury by about 67 percent. For older children, studies of the effectiveness of belt systems indicate that they can reduce the risk of fatalities and serious injuries by 40 to 55 percent.

Effective child passenger protection requires awareness that the efficacy of child safety seats and belt systems depends on their correct installation and use. A nationwide effort is underway to boost correct child seat use to 70 percent or higher by 1990 through increasing public awareness and enforcement of child passenger protection laws and alerting parents about the importance of installing the restraints correctly and securing their children in them properly on every trip. With added concern for the proper installation and consistent use of these safety devices, we can prevent tragedies and save the lives of hundreds of children every year.

To encourage the people of the United States to protect their children properly in child safety seats and belt systems; to encourage safety and law enforcement agencies and others to promote greater use of these essential safety devices; and to inform the public about the serious dangers children can face as automobile passengers and the importance of child safety protection devices and their correct use, the Congress, by House Joint Resolution 402, has designated the week of February 7–13, 1988, as "National Child Passenger Safety Awareness Week" and authorized and requested the President to issue a proclamation in observance of this week.

Now, Therefore, I, Ronald Reagan, President of the United States of America, do hereby proclaim the week of February 7–13, 1988, as National Child Passenger Safety Awareness Week. I ask all Americans to make sure that their children are fully protected by the correct use of child passenger protection devices. I call upon concerned citizens and government officials to observe this week with appropriate ceremonies and activities in reaffirmation of our commitment to universal and correct use of child passenger protection devices.

In Witness Whereof, I have hereunto set my hand this tenth day of February, in the year of our Lord nineteen hundred and eighty-eight, and of the Independence of the United States of America the two hundred and twelfth.

RONALD REAGAN

[*Filed with the Office of the Federal Register, 10:52 a.m., February 11, 1988*]

Proclamation 5771—Save Your Vision Week, 1988
February 10, 1988

By the President of the United States of America

A Proclamation

To have healthier eyes, one needs the healthy attitude of caring for those eyes—and of recognizing how much they contribute to life, learning, independence, work, recreation, and the enjoyment of visual beauty. Thanks to recent advances in the treatment and prevention of eye disease, the possibility of keeping good vision for life is now excellent.

Regular eye checkups are a must. With improved diagnostic techniques and new treatments, we can now stop many potentially blinding diseases even before they begin to affect vision. But many treatments can save vision only if problems are detected early, often before a person notices any symptoms.

Ensuring a lifetime of healthy eyes begins at infancy. Even an infant with healthy-looking eyes may have an unsuspected vision problem that only an eye specialist can detect. We now know that parts of the brain involved in vision cannot develop without early stimulation. If children are to see normally, congenital cataracts, lazy eye, or misaligned eyes must be treated early.

Other eye diseases usually begin in middle age. For example, if glaucoma is detected before any vision is lost, an eye doctor can prescribe one of the new drugs that can check the disease's impact.

The many eye diseases associated with aging need not be disabling. For instance, in cataracts, the cloudy lens can be surgically removed and an artificial lens implanted. In another age-related disease, leaky blood vessels develop in the back of the eye, often doing irreparable damage in only weeks or months. Laser treatment can usually stop the destruction and save the remaining vision.

Laser treatment can also save the sight of some people who risk visual loss due to diabetes. The earlier the intervention, the less the potential vision loss.

To encourage our citizens to cherish and protect their sight, the Congress, by joint resolution approved December 30, 1963 (77 Stat. 629, 36 U.S.C. 169a), has authorized and requested the President to proclaim the first week in March of each year as "Save Your Vision Week."

Now, Therefore, I, Ronald Reagan, President of the United States of America, do hereby designate the week beginning March 6, 1988, as Save Your Vision Week. I urge all Americans to participate in this observance by making eye care and eye safety an important part of their lives. I also invite eye care professionals, the communications media, and all public and private organizations committed to the goal of sight conservation to join in activities that will make Americans more aware of the steps they can take to protect their vision.

In Witness Whereof, I have hereunto set my hand this tenth day of February, in the year of our Lord nineteen hundred and eighty-eight, and of the Independence of the United States of America the two hundred and twelfth.

RONALD REAGAN

[*Filed with the Office of the Federal Register, 2:46 p.m., February 11, 1988*]

Note: The proclamation was released by the Office of the Press Secretary on February 11.

Nomination of William Evans To Be an Under Secretary of Commerce

February 11, 1988

The President today announced his intention to nominate William Evans to be Under Secretary of Commerce for Oceans and Atmosphere. This is a new position.

Since 1986 Dr. Evans has been Assistant Administrator of the National Oceanic and Atmospheric Administration (NOAA) for Fisheries in Washington, DC, and is currently Chairman of the Marine Mammal Commission, 1984–present. Prior to this he was executive director and senior scientist for Hubbs-Sea World Research Institute, 1977–1986. He was head of the bioanalysis group of the biosystems division at the Naval Undersea Center, 1974–1976, and advance study fellow and visiting scientist for the National Marine Fisheries Service at the Southwest Fisheries Center, 1972–1974.

Dr. Evans graduated from Bowling Green State University (B.S., 1953), Ohio State University (M.A., 1954), and the University of California at Los Angeles (Ph.D., 1975). He was born October 11, 1930, in Elkhart, IN. He is married, has two sons, and currently resides in Silver Spring, MD.

Nomination of Daniel G. Amstutz for the Rank of Ambassador While Serving as Chief United States Agricultural Negotiator for the Multilateral Trade Negotiations
February 11, 1988

The President today announced his intention to nominate Daniel G. Amstutz for the rank of Ambassador during his tenure of service as chief agricultural negotiator in the Uruguay round of multilateral trade negotiations.

Since 1983 Mr. Amstutz has been Under Secretary of Agriculture for International Affairs and Commodity Programs, in Washington, DC. Prior to this he was a general partner with Goldman, Sachs and Company, 1978–1982. From 1972 to 1978, he was president of Cargill Investor Services, Inc. Mr. Amstutz has also served on the trade expansion subcommittee of the President's Export Council, the administration's trade policy review group, and the Advisory Committee for the Commodity Futures Trading Commission. He is also a member of the National Commission on Agricultural Trade and Export Policy.

Mr. Amstutz graduated from Ohio State University (B.S., 1954). He was born November 8, 1932, in Cleveland, OH, and resides in Arlington, VA.

Message to the Senate Transmitting the Mexico-United States Legal Assistance Treaty
February 11, 1988

To the Senate of the United States:

With a view to receiving the advice and consent of the Senate to ratification, I transmit herewith the Treaty on Cooperation between the United States of America and the United Mexican States for Mutual Legal Assistance, signed at Mexico City on December 9, 1987.

I transmit also, for the information of the Senate, the report of the Department of State with respect to the Treaty.

The Treaty is one of a series of modern mutual legal assistance treaties being negotiated by the United States in order to counter more effectively trans-border criminal activities. The Treaty should be an effective tool to combat a wide variety of modern criminals including members of drug cartels, "white-collar criminals," and terrorists. The Treaty is self-executing and utilizes existing statutory authority.

The Treaty provides for a broad range of cooperation in criminal matters. Mutual assistance available under the Treaty includes: (1) the taking of testimony or statements of witnesses; (2) the provision of documents, records, and evidence; (3) the execution of requests for searches and seizures; (4) the serving of documents; and (5) the provision of assistance in procedures regarding the immobilizing, securing, and forfeiture of the proceeds, fruits, and instrumentalities of crime.

I recommend that the Senate give early and favorable consideration to the Treaty and give its advice and consent to ratification.

RONALD REAGAN

The White House,
February 11, 1988.

Appointment of Julian E. Kulas as a Member of the United States Holocaust Memorial Council
February 11, 1988

The President today announced his intention to appoint Julian E. Kulas, of Illinois, to be a member of the United States Holocaust Memorial Council for a term expiring January 15, 1993. This is a reappointment.

Since 1957 Mr. Kulas has been a self-employed attorney with the law office of Julian E. Kulas, and since 1977 he has been president of First Security Federal Savings Bank in Chicago, IL. Mr. Kulas is also vice president (and former president) of the Ukrainian Congress Committee of America, president of the Ukrainian-American Democratic Organization of Illinois, and chairman of the Helsinki Monitoring Committee of Chicago.

Mr. Kulas graduated from De Paul University (B.A., 1957; J.D., 1958). He was born June 5, 1933, in Boratyn, Poland. Mr. Kulas is married, has three children, and resides in River Forest, IL.

Appointment of Stanley C. Pace as United States National Chairman for United Nations Day, 1988
February 11, 1988

The President today announced his intention to appoint Stanley C. Pace to be the United States National Chairman for the 1988 United Nations Day. He will succeed J. Willard Marriott, Jr.

Since 1986 Mr. Pace has been chairman and chief executive officer of General Dynamics Corp. in St. Louis, MO, and vice chairman, 1985. Prior to this, he served the Tapco Group in various capacities: assistant manager, 1954–1958; general manager, 1958–1965; executive vice president, 1965–1977; and president, 1977–1985. Mr. Pace served in the U.S. Air Force from 1943–1954.

Mr. Pace graduated from the United States Military Academy (B.S., 1943) and California Institute of Technology (M.S., 1949). Mr. Pace was born on September 14, 1921, in Waterview, KY. He is married, has three children, and currently resides in St. Louis, MO.

Proclamation 5772—Lithuanian Independence Day, 1988
February 11, 1988

By the President of the United States of America

A Proclamation

Seventy years ago, on February 16, 1918, the Lithuanian National Council declared the independence of Lithuania and established the Republic of Lithuania. This restoration of Lithuania's sovereignty was recognized around the world—even by the Soviet Union, in 1920. Lithuania joined the League of Nations in 1921, and for the next two decades Lithuanians enjoyed liberty and self-determination under a government that fostered political and religious freedom for all citizens.

Then, in June 1940, the year after the signing of the Molotov-Ribbentrop Pact, the Soviet Union invaded and illegally occupied Lithuania and the other Baltic States. The United States unequivocally condemned this violation of national sovereignty and national integrity, and ever since then our policy has remained consistent. We have never recognized the forcible incorporation of Lithuania into the Soviet Union, and we never will.

Observance of the anniversary of Lithuania's Declaration of Independence is natural for Americans, who faithfully celebrate our own Independence Day each year. America has long been a beacon of hope to Lithuania, because Americans cherish their self-determination, individual liberty, and independence—the God-given rights the Lithuanian people seek to reclaim in the face of religious and political persecution, forced Russification, and ethnic dilution. It is therefore fitting to show our solidarity with the people of Lithuania.

We join in Lithuania's proud and solemn remembrance of the 70th anniversary of its independence, and together with people the world over we share the spirit and the hope of the Lithuanian people as they commemorate that day. Among the Lithuanian people the spirit of liberty remains unbroken—the spirit of a true leader of her people, Nijole Sadunaite, whose sacrifices for country and conscience continue so courageously to the present day, and who wrote from the Gulag, "Our brief days on earth are not meant for rest, but to participate in the struggle for the happiness of numerous hearts"; the spirit of the freedom marchers of Vilnius, Lithuania's capital, and of Kaunas; the spirit of every time and place where bold sons and daughters remember their heritage and their highest ideals.

To demonstrate our common commitment to the cause of freedom, the Congress, by Senate Joint Resolution 39, has designated February 16, 1988, as "Lithuanian Independence Day" and has authorized and requested the President to issue a proclamation in observance of this day.

Now, Therefore, I, Ronald Reagan, President of the United States of America, do hereby proclaim February 16, 1988, as Lithuanian Independence Day. I call upon the people of the United States to observe this day with appropriate ceremonies and activities in reaffirmation of their devotion to the just aspirations of all peoples for self-determination and liberty.

In Witness Whereof, I have hereunto set my hand this 11th day of February, in the year of our Lord nineteen hundred and eighty-eight, and of the Independence of the United States of America the two hundred and twelfth.

RONALD REAGAN

[*Filed with the Office of the Federal Register, 10:18 a.m., February 12, 1988*]

Appointment of Craig P. Coy as a Member of the President's Commission on White House Fellowships
February 11, 1988

The President today announced his intention to appoint Craig P. Coy to be a member of the President's Commission on White House Fellowships.

Since 1987 Mr. Coy has been assistant to the Chairman of the National Drug Policy Board for the Office of the Attorney General at the Department of Justice in Washington, DC.

Mr. Coy graduated from the United States Coast Guard Academy (B.S., 1972) and Harvard University (M.B.A., 1983). He served in the United States Coast Guard, 1972–present. He was born February 21, 1950, in Willows, CA. Mr. Coy is married, has two children, and resides in Arlington, VA.

Remarks at the Annual Conservative Political Action Conference Dinner
February 11, 1988

It's great to be here, and I thank you. [*Applause*] No, please. It's great to be here tonight, and I'm delighted to see so many old friends. And now let's get right to it.

First, there's the INF treaty. How do you think I felt when Gorbachev called a week and a half ago and asked me if our first group of on-site inspectors could be the Denver Broncos' pass defense? [*Laughter*] And then along came the House vote on *contra* aid. I felt so terrible I nearly called Dan Reeves and John Elway to tell them what a rough week I'd had.

But seriously, while the Denver Broncos are all terrific athletes and people, each one of us has to congratulate the Washington Redskins. [*Applause*] Believe me, the House action on the *contra* vote was a missed chance at a victory for peace in Central America. It's great to know there're some people in Washington who play to win. And believe me, I'll be getting back to that topic in a few minutes.

By the way, something odd happened just before I got here tonight that I think you should know about. I got a message from Dave Keene reminding me that this was the eve of Lincoln's birthday and suggesting I go upstairs and check on the ghost in Lincoln's bedroom. I did. And what do you know, there was Stan Evans dressed as Abe Lincoln. [*Laughter*] And he kept saying, "Listen to Jesse Helms." [*Laughter*]

Actually, I do want to thank you for that warm welcome, but I hope tonight isn't going to be like what happened to that fellow I knew back in Hollywood in those movie days—and, oh, how I hope I haven't told you this one before. [*Laughter*]

We had an actor that was in Hollywood, and he was only there long enough to get enough money to go to Italy, because he aspired to an operatic career. And then after some time there, in Milan, Italy, where he was studying, he was invited to sing at La Scala, the very spiritual fountainhead of opera. They were doing "Pagliacci," and he sang the beautiful aria, "Vesti la giubba." And he received such thunderous and sustained applause from the balconies and the orchestra seats that he had to repeat the aria as an encore. And again, the same sustained, thunderous applause, and again he sang "Vesti la giubba." And this went on until finally he motioned for quiet, and he tried to tell them how full his heart was at that reception—his first time out. But he said, "I have sung 'Vesti la giubba' nine times now. My voice is gone. I cannot do it again." And a voice from the balcony said, "You'll do it till you get it right." [*Laughter*] Well, let's get it right tonight. And let's start where we should start.

A couple of weeks ago, I talked about the state of our Union, and tonight I'd like to talk about something that I think in many ways is synonymous: the state of our movement. During the past year, plenty of questions have been asked about the conservative movement by some people who were surprised to find out back in 1980 that there was such a thing. I mean a powerful new political movement capable of running a victorious national campaign based on an unabashed appeal to the American people for conservative ideas and principles.

Well, we conservatives have been in Washington now for awhile, and we occasionally need to remind ourselves what brought us here in the first place: our unshakable, root-deep, all-encompassing skepticism about the Capital City's answer to the UFO, that bizarre, ever-tottering but ever-flickering saucer in the sky called the prevailing Washington wisdom.

And right now some of the Potomac seers are saying we conservatives are tired; or they're saying we don't have a candidate, that we don't know what to do with ourselves this year. I even hear some of those candidates in the other party saying how easy it's going to be to win the Presidency for their liberal agenda, because they can run on—of all things—this administration's economic record. [*Laughter*] Boy, have I got news for them. They're seeing flying saucers again. [*Laughter*] I've even got a quote for them. It's from Napoleon, the morning of Waterloo, at breakfast with his generals. This is true. He said: "I tell you what; Wellington is a bad general. The English are bad trips [troops]. We'll settle the matter by lunchtime."

Well, my fellow conservatives, I think that's exactly what this year is about—settling the matter by lunchtime, letting the liberals in Washington discover, once again, the lesson they refuse to learn, letting them know just how big our election year will be—because of booming economic growth and individual opportunity—and how big an election year ball and chain they've given themselves with a 7-year record of opposition to the real record, but most of all, letting them know that the real friends of the conservative movement aren't those entrenched in the Capital City for 50 years.

The real friends of the conservative movement are an entity that gets heard from in a big way every 4 years and who, I promise you, are going to be heard from this year. I'm talking about those who, if the case is aggressively put before them, will vote for limited government, family values, and a tough, strong foreign policy every single time. I'm talking about those believers in common sense and sound values, your friends and mine, the American people.

You see, those who underestimate the conservative movement are the same people who always underestimate the American people. Take the latest instance. As I mentioned, in recent months some people—and I'm not mentioning any names, because I don't want to build up any candidacies before New Hampshire, but you know who they are—have actually taken on themselves of proving to the American people that they've been worse off under this administration than they were back in the Carter years of the seventies.

Now, I agree with you; this takes some doing. [*Laughter*] How do they manage it? Well, you see, any statistical comparison of the two recent administrations would start with 1977 to 1981 as the budget years of the last administration and 1981 to 1987 as the pertinent years for this one. Now, that sounds reasonable enough. But our opponents have a new approach, one that would have embarrassed even the emperor's tailors.

They take the year 1977, go up to 1983, and then they stop. So, you see, not only do 1984 and 1985 not get counted in their data base, but they include in this administration's economic record 4 years of the last Democratic administration. As columnist Warren Brookes pointed out in an article published in the Washington Times this week: "All of the foreshortened Reagan gains are nullified by the Carter losses; so they look like no gains at all or, worse, losses." Our successes, in short, are statistically buried under the last administration's failures.

But the truth is otherwise, because under the last administration real per capita disposable income rose at only 1-percent annual rate, only half the 2-percent rate of increase under this administration—a gain that has totaled 12.4 percent in 6 years. Under the last administration, median family income declined 6.8 percent, while under this administration, it went up 9.1 percent. Or take real after-tax labor income per hour. If you use the approach adopted by our liberal critics, you see a 4½-percent decline. But the truth is that that figure fell 8½ percent under the last administration, and we turned this around and accounted for an 8.9-percent increase.

Under the last administration, the average weekly wage went down an incredible 10 percent in real terms, which accounted for the worst drop in postwar history. Here again, we've stopped the decline, and that's not to mention what all this has meant in terms of opportunity for women, for blacks, and minorities—the very groups our opponents say they most want to help. Well, since the recovery began, 70 percent of the new jobs have been translated into opportunities for women; and black and other minority employment has risen twice as fast as all other groups. Minority family income has also increased at a rate over 40 percent faster than other groups. In addition, since 1983, 2.9 million people have climbed out of poverty, and the poverty rate has declined at the fastest rate in more than 10 years.

So, think for a moment on what these statistics mean and the kind of political nerve and desperation it takes to try to sell the American people on the idea that in the 1980's they never had it so bad. The truth is we're in the 63d month of this nonstop expansion. Real gross national product growth for 1987 was 3.8 percent, defying the pessimists and even exceeding our own forecast—which was criticized as being too rosy at the time—by more than one-half percent. Inflation is down from 13½ percent in 1980 to only around 4 percent or less this year. And there's over 15 million new jobs.

So, believe me, I welcome this approach by the opposition. And I promise you every time they use it I'll just tell the story of a friend of mine who was asked to a costume ball a short time ago. He slapped some egg on his face and went as a liberal economist. [*Laughter*]

Now, the reason I spell out these statistics and stress this economic issue should be very clear. You know some cynics like to say that the people vote their pocketbook. But that's not quite the point. Economic issues are important to the people not simply for reasons of self-interest. They know the whole body politic depends on economic stability. The great crises have come for democracies when taxes and inflation ran out of control and undermined social relations and basic institutions.

The American people know what limited government, tax cuts, deregulation, and the move towards privatization have meant: It's meant the largest peacetime expansion in our history. And I can guarantee you they won't want to throw that away for a return to budgets beholden to the liberal special interests.

No, I think the economic record of conservatives in power is going to speak for itself. But now let's turn to another area. For two decades we've been talking about getting Justices on the Supreme Court who cared less about criminals and more about the victims of crime, Justices who knew that the words "original intent" referred to something more than New Year's resolutions and fad diets. [*Laughter*] And then, 7 months ago a seat opened on the Supreme Court. And even before our first nominee was announced, a campaign was planned unlike any that has ever been waged for or against a judicial nominee in the history of our country. And let me acknowledge once again my admiration for one of the courageous defenders—not only in our time but in all time—of the principles of our Constitution, yes, of its original intent: Judge Robert Bork.

One of America's most cherished principles, the independence and integrity of our judiciary, was under siege. And the American people, who have always been the ultimate guarantors of the Constitution, began to say, with clarity and finality, it must never happen again. So, when I nominated a judge who could as easily have been my first nominee, there was hardly a peep of protest. And Judge Kennedy is now going to be Justice Kennedy. And since our opponents won't, I'll let you in on a secret: Judge Kennedy will be just the kind of Justice that you and I've been determined to put on the Court. Anyway, any man who teaches law school in a tricorner hat and a powdered wig is okay by me on original intent. [*Laughter*]

Let's look at how far and how successfully we've carried the battle into the lower courts. Just look at the statistics on criminal sentencing. In few places can you see more clearly the collapse of the liberal stranglehold on our courts. The most recent statistics show Federal judges imposed prison sentences that averaged 32 percent longer than those handed down during 1979. Robbery sentences were 10 percent longer; drug offenses, 38 percent longer; and weapons offenses, 41 percent longer.

The great legal debates of the past two decades over criminal justice have, at their root, been debates over a strict versus expansive construction of the Constitution. The Constitution, as originally intended by the framers, is itself tough on crime and protective of the victims of crime. For so long, the liberal message to our national culture was tune in, turn on, let it all hang out. And now they see conservatives taking the lead as our nation says no to drugs and yes to family and absolutely to schools that teach basic skills, basic values, and basic discipline. And it's no wonder that our nation admires a man who believes in teaching values in education and talks turkey to teachers, parents, and educators, such as our Secretary of Education, Bill Bennett.

And so, I say to you tonight that the vision and record that we will take aggressively to the American people this November is a vision that all Americans—except a few on the left—share; a vision of a nation that believes in the heroism of ordinary people living ordinary lives; of tough courts and safe streets; of a drug free America where schools teach honesty, respect, love of learning and, yes, love of country; a vision of a land where families can grow in love and safety and where dreams are made with opportunity. This is the vision. This is the record. This is the agenda for victory this year.

Well, that's the record then on the economy and the social issues. Now let's turn to foreign policy. I want to be clear tonight about the vote on *contra* aid. It was a setback to the national security interests of the United States and a sad moment for the cause of peace and freedom in Central America. Until now the carrot-and-stick approach has worked in forcing a Communist regime to relax some of its repression. But now the action by the House of Representatives removes one part of that formula and goes only with the carrot. The effect of this vote then was to trust the promises of democracy of the Sandinista Communists—the kind of promises that no Communist regime in history has ever carried out and that this regime was likely to carry out only under continued pressure. The effect of this vote was to rest the hopes for peace and democracy in Central America purely and simply on the word of the Communist regime in Managua. This course is—and I repeat—a risk to America's national security.

But you know I read something the other day, and it's worth a note here. One of those opposing aid to the freedom fighters said it was important to get a 20-vote margin. Well, as you know, it was nothing like that. If we could have turned around four or five votes, we would have won. Last week's vote was not the final word, only a pause. Last week the bad news was the lost vote in the House, but the good news was our support in the Senate and the overwhelming number of House Republicans who voted with us and those 47 Democrats who braved the threats of reprisals to vote for *contra* aid.

So, let me make this pledge to you tonight: We're not giving up on those who're fighting for their freedom, and they aren't giving up either. I'll have more to say on this in a few weeks. For now, I'll leave it at this: Get ready. The curtain hasn't fallen. The drama continues.

While we're on foreign policy, let me turn for just a moment to what I said in that December interview while Mr. Gorbachev was here. You know, Ben Wattenberg was one of the journalists there, and he brought up a speech that I made back in 1982 to the British Parliament. And he asked me if what I really was saying was what I said in England: that if the West remained resolute, the Soviets would have to, at some point, deal with its own internal problems and crises; that the tides of history are shifting in favor of the cause of freedom.

Well, I believed then, and I believe now, that we must consider what we're seeing—or the steps in that direction. This hardly means accepting the Soviets at face value. Few of us can forget what that has led to in the past. F.D.R. was quoted as saying during his dealings with the Soviets in '44: "Stalin doesn't want anything but security for his country. And I think that if I give him everything I possibly can and ask nothing from him in return, noblesse oblige, he won't try to annex anything and will work with me for a world democracy and peace."

Well, no, there is no room for illusion. Our guard is up. Our watch is careful. We shall not be led by—or misled by atmospherics. We came to Washington with a commonsense message that the world is a dangerous place, where the only sure route to peace and the protection of freedom is through American strength. In no place has this thesis of peace through strength been tested more than on the matter of intermediate-range nuclear forces, INF.

In deploying over 400 SS–20's, with over 1,200 warheads, against our friends and allies in Europe and Asia over the past decade, the Soviets were playing a high-stakes game of geopolitical blackjack. The prize was Europe; the strategy, discredit America's deterrence and undermine the NATO alliance. But we and our allies turned over a winning hand, deploying in Europe Pershing II and ground-launched cruise missiles that provided an effective counter to the new Soviet missiles; and Moscow finally stopped upping the stakes.

What I would like to see is for some of those who've been praising our INF treaty to show they've learned its true lesson and vote to maintain an adequate defense budget, our work on a strategic defense against ballistic missiles, and yes, aid to the freedom fighters in Nicaragua.

And while we're on the subject of our nation's defense, you know, there's a man I want to talk about tonight who said once that "the definition of happiness was service to a noble cause." No one has done that better, and tonight I salute Cap Weinberger for all he's done for America.

But at the same time we must not look at any single step alone. We must see not just the INF treaty but also the advance of SDI and, most important, the growing democratic revolution around the globe against totalitarian regimes. We should engage the Soviets in negotiations to deter war and keep the peace. But at the same time, we must make clear our own position, as I have throughout these negotiations.

In sitting down to these negotiations, we accept no moral equivalency between the cause of freedom and the rule of totalitarianism. And we understand that the most important change of all is this: that containment is no longer enough; that we no longer can be satisfied with an endless stalemate between liberty and repression; that arms reduction negotiations, development and testing of SDI, and our help for freedom fighters around the globe must express the clear goal of American foreign policy—to deter war, yes; to further world peace, yes; but most of all, to advance and protect the cause of world freedom so that someday every man, woman, and child on this Earth has as a birthright the full blessings of liberty.

We've seen dramatic change in these 7 years. Who would have guessed 7 years ago that we would see tax rates drop from 70 percent to 28 percent, the longest peacetime economic boom in our history, or a massive shift in world opinion toward the ideas of free enterprise and political freedom.

I know some of you are impatient with the pace of this change. But if I might repeat a story I told when I addressed you for the first time as President. I had the pleasure in appearing before a Senate committee once while I was still Governor. And I was challenged there, because there was a Republican President in the White House at the time, who'd been there for some time—and hadn't we corrected everything that had gone wrong? And the only way I could think to answer him is I told him about a ranch many years ago that Nancy and I acquired. It had a barn with eight stalls in it, in which they kept cattle—cows. We wanted to keep horses. Well, the accumulation within the stalls had built up the floor to the place that it wasn't even tall enough for horses in there. [*Laughter*] And so, there I was, day after day, with a pick and shovel, lowering the level of those stalls, which had accumulated over the years. And I told this Senator who'd asked that question that I discovered that you didn't undo in a relatively short time what it had taken some 15 years to accumulate. [*Laughter*]

We've been not only undoing the damage of the past, we've put this nation on the upward road again. And in the process, the differences between the liberals and conservatives have become clear to the American people. We want to keep taxes low; they want to raise them. We send in budgets with spending cuts, and they want to ignore them. We want the balanced budget amendment and the line-item veto, and they oppose them. We want tough judges and tough anticrime legislation; they hold them both up in the Congress—you'd be surprised how many judges are waiting out there before they—so that they have to pass on them before they can take their office, and they've been waiting for months. We want a prayer amendment; they won't let it come to a vote in the House. We stress firmness with the Soviets; they try to pass legislation that would tie our hands in arms negotiations and endanger our defenses.

But I say we have a program and a plan for the American people, a program to protect American jobs by fighting the menace of protectionism, to move forward at flank speed with SDI, to call America to conscience on the issue of abortion on demand, to mention, as I did in my State of the Union Address, the overwhelming importance of family life and family values.

That's a case to take to the American people. That's a fighting agenda. I intend to campaign vigorously for whoever our nominee is, and tonight I ask each of you to join me in this important crusade. Let's ask the American people to replenish our mandate. Let's tell them if they want 4 more years of economic progress and the march of world freedom they must help us this year—help us settle the matter before lunchtime, help make 1988 the year of the Waterloo liberal. I just have to add here, when you look at the figures overall, that they have the nerve even to still be out there and campaigning. [*Laughter*]

We mustn't just think that electing the President is enough. We've been doing that for more than half a century. In the 50 years between 1931 and 1980, only 4 years in that period was there a Republican majority in both Houses of the Congress—2 years in Eisenhower's regime, 2 years in Truman's. But for 46 of those 50 years, they controlled the Congress. Every Democrat President, except for those 2 years, had a Democratic Congress. Every Republican President had a Democratic Congress, except for those 2 years in Eisenhower's regime. And now, in the last 7 years added to that—yes, for 6 of those years we had one House. But except for the 4 years, for 58 years it will be our opponents holding the House of Representatives, where so much legislation and authorization for spending and so forth comes in. And in all those 58 years, there have only been 8 single years in which there was a balanced budget. So, who's at fault for the deficit today?

Back when the War on Poverty began, which poverty won—[*laughter*]—from 1965 to 1980—in those 15 years, the Federal budget increased to five times what it had been in '65. And the deficit increased to 38 times what it had been just 15 years before. It's built-in; it's structural. And you and I need to get representatives not only in the executive branch but out there in the Legislature so that we can change that structure that is so built-in and that threatens us with so much harm.

Well, I've gone on too long for all of you here, but I couldn't resist, because you're the troops. You're out there on the frontier of freedom. One young soldier over there in Korea, one of our men, saluted me when I visited there and very proudly said, "Mr. President, we're on the frontier of freedom." Well, so are you. Thank you. God bless you all.

Note: The President spoke at 9:32 p.m. in the Regency Ballroom at the Omni Shoreham Hotel. In his remarks, the President referred to David A. Keene, chairman of the American Conservative Union, and newspaper columnist M. Stanton Evans.

Written Responses to Questions Submitted by the Mexican Newspaper Notimex
February 10, 1988

Mexico-U.S. Relations

Q. At the beginning of your administration, some of your officials considered Mexico as the next Iran. Six years later Mexico is still there, and after some rocky times, the relations are considered very good on both sides of the border. One year before the end of your term, what is your actual assessment of the bilateral relations, and what is still to be done?

The President. "Mexico as the next Iran" was a phrase used briefly by one former official. It was never the judgment of my administration. I think it's true to say that relations between the United States and Mexico today are strong and productive. In the past 5 years, working pragmatically on the many problems we jointly face, we've reached mutually beneficial agreements on trade and investment; cooperated closely to help Mexico manage its foreign debt burden; and addressed unique issues of immigration, energy, and the environment along our common border.

The past few months, in particular, have seen an unprecedented number of new agreements reached between our two countries. In November we signed a bilateral framework understanding on trade and investment, which in conjunction with the GATT process will help us to reduce barriers to trade and investment between our countries. In early December we signed a mutual legal assistance treaty, which will assist both countries in combating a wide variety of criminal activity ranging from drug cartels to white collar criminals. Also, in December the United States was pleased to play a role in the Government of Mexico's plan to exchange debt for new bonds. In addition, we have recently signed agreements on steel, beer, wine, and distilled spirits, and we are close to concluding a major new civil aviation agreement. And at the end of the February 13 meeting in Mazatlán, we will sign a new 4-year textile accord and a telecommunication agreement.

President De la Madrid and I have worked to place U.S.-Mexican relations on a new path. Much work remains to be done. In the time we have left in office, we must build on the progress we've made so that we can turn over to our successors a better relationship. It must be equipped to manage the growing ties between our two peoples and deal with the problems we both face. We must continue to work closely to combat narcotics trafficking and the other common maladies that hinder our ability to cooperate even more closely.

Q. In your last State of the Union Address, you said that trade will be the foremost concern of your February meeting with President Miguel De la Madrid. For years you've sponsored a proposal for a North American common market, but given the economic disparities between the two countries, how could Mexico be an equal partner with the United States? From your position, which would be the Mexican role and/or advantage in such an economic alliance? Could you be more explicit on the idea of a North American agreement of economic freedom?

The President. We are seeing the beginnings of an historic restructuring of the Mexican economy, of Mexico's trade relationships with the United States, specifically, and the world, in general. In recent years, under the leadership of President De la Madrid, Mexico has undertaken a number of important steps. As I mentioned already, Mexico has acceded to the General Agreement on Tariffs and Trade (GATT) and signed with the United States last November a bilateral framework understanding on trade and investment.

The recently signed framework understanding is a symbol of the special relationship which exists between our two nations as well as a recognition that both countries will gain from the continued liberalization of bilateral trade and investment flows. My February 13 meeting with President De la Madrid will serve to affirm and build upon this progress. Through the framework process, as through the multilateral trade negotiations taking place in the GATT, both of our governments are committed to working toward the progressive reduction of barriers to trade and investment. We see these steps as providing a solid foundation on which to build towards freer flows of trade and investment of benefit to both our nations.

Mexican Economic Reforms

Q. Two years ago, Secretary [of the Treasury] James Baker proposed a plan to help heavily indebted countries to resume growth to avoid defaults. Yet 2 years later, growth has not resumed, and the debt problem is one of the main weaknesses of the international economy. There are, however, some signs of progress, like the U.S. backed Mexican bond-for-debt swap. Is the United States prepared or willing to go further in these or other kinds of measures?

The President. The program for sustained growth proposed by Secretary Baker in October 1985 is a dynamic program for encouraging the adoption of policies which experience in many countries has shown lead to sustained growth. The program recognizes the need for new loans from development banks and commercial banks in support of these reforms. Recently the program has been expanded through the menu approach to include a variety of financial instruments, such as debt-equity swaps, bonds, and trade credits, in addition to general balance-of-payment loans as options in commercial bank financing packages.

We welcome the innovative proposal developed by the Government of Mexico to allow foreign creditors to exchange their loans at a discount for long-term bonds issued by Mexico. The voluntary debt-bond swap program designed by Mexico is consistent with our efforts to encourage market-oriented solutions to the problems of developing countries. Our policy recognizes that each country is unique and must work with its creditors to devise the solutions most appropriate to its economic and financial position.

The economic policy reforms begun by President De la Madrid have helped put Mexico in a position to work out mutually beneficial agreements with its creditors. His farsighted efforts to open up the Mexican economy and revitalize domestic industries are helping place Mexico on the path of sustained economic growth. We remain ready to assist Mexico's continuing and creative efforts to manage its external debt.

Soviet-U.S. Nuclear Test Ban

Q. The United States and the Soviet Union are on the beginning of the long path to nuclear disarmament. The Group of Six has offered to help monitor the nuclear test ban. Would you accept such help, since the real conflict between the United States and the Soviet Union seems to be in terms of the so-called low-intensity conflict?

The President. The United States shares the desire of the Group of Six for concrete arms control measures. We and the Soviets have agreed that a comprehensive ban on nuclear testing must be linked to an effective disarmament process which must include the elimination of nuclear weapons. Our immediate priority in the area of nuclear testing limitations is reaching an agreement on essential verification improvements to the Threshold Test Ban Treaty (TTBT) and the Peaceful Nuclear Explosions Treaty (PNET).

These treaties are bilateral, and our verification concerns with them are of a bilateral nature. We believe that bilateral discussions will best serve progress in this area. If the Soviet Union agrees to essential verification procedures, I will request Senate advice and consent to ratification of these treaties. Once the treaties are ratified, the United States will immediately propose negotiations on ways to implement a step-by-step parallel program—in association with a proposal to reduce and ultimately eliminate all nuclear weapons—of limiting and ultimately ending nuclear tests.

Central American Peace Process

Q. Your administration seems to have identified the Central American peace plan as directed only to Nicaragua and the demise of the Sandinista regime. But it is not so, and the democratization of Nicaragua means not only national dialog and a cease-fire but elections that the Sandinistas could win. In any case, it is likely that they will remain as an important political force in Nicaragua. Is the United States disposed to accept this outcome? Could you explain the U.S. plans in Central America beyond the Nicaragua solution, whatever it is?

The President. Nicaragua under the Sandinista regime is out of step with the rest of Central America, which has moved decisively toward democracy in the last decade. Simply put, attention has focused on Nicaraguan compliance, because Nicaragua has the farthest to go in meeting its commitments under the peace plan.

Salvadorans, Guatemalans, and Hondurans are moving toward the sort of stable, popular system that has served their Costa Rican neighbors so well. In 1979 Nicaraguans overthrew Somoza with similar hopes for their country, but the Sandinistas hijacked the revolution for their own purposes and dashed the hopes of the many democratic forces that helped bring down Somoza. In doing so, they imposed on the people of Nicaragua an alien ideology and the totalitarian controls associated with Soviet-style regimes, which also threaten their neighbors. This is what led to the creation of a national resistance and, ultimately, civil war.

Through the Central American peace plan, Nicaragua's neighbors have given the Sandinistas a clear message: Democratize, because until a democratic Nicaragua takes control of its own future, its problems will continue to be the problems of the entire region. Nicaragua's key problem is not just a matter of words or particular elections, it is a matter of unilateral monopoly of power in a closed society. One day Daniel Ortega says he won't give up power in an election; the next day he says he will. Incidentally, in the last few weeks other Sandinista comandantes have tried to explain why they don't have to abide by free elections. What all this means is that Central Americans can't settle for promises. They did that once and are paying the price today. Nicaragua's democratic neighbors agree with us that Sandinista compliance with the regional peace accord will make or break the plan.

You asked whether the United States could live with the Sandinistas being a political force in Nicaragua. That's not up to us; that's a decision the Nicaraguan people must be allowed to make for themselves. Democracy and development are at the heart of our policy there. The monopoly ambitions of the Sandinista front are only a temporary obstacle standing between Central Americans and the freedom and prosperity they so desperately want and deserve.

Note: The questions and answers were released by the Office of the Press Secretary on February 12. One of the questions referred to the Group of Six, which consisted of India, Sweden, Argentina, Mexico, Tanzania, and Greece. Its principal aims were peace and nuclear disarmament.

Statement by Assistant to the President for Press Relations Fitzwater on the Soviet-United States Nuclear and Space Arms Negotiations
February 12, 1988

On Monday, February 15, the United States and the Soviet Union will resume step-by-step negotiations on nuclear testing with the opening of round two of these talks in Geneva. The nuclear testing talks represent a practical approach—as the President has long advocated—to nuclear testing limitations which are in our national security interest.

In undertaking these talks, the United States and the Soviet Union agreed, as a first step, to negotiate effective verification measures for two existing, but unratified nuclear testing treaties: the Threshold Test Ban Treaty (TTBT) and the Peaceful Nuclear Explosions Treaty (PNET). Once our verification concerns have been satisfied and the treaties ratified, we will propose that the United States and the Soviet Union immediately enter into negotiations on ways to implement a step-by-step program—in association with a program to reduce ar ultimately eliminate nuclear weapons—limiting and ultimately ending nuclear te: ing.

We are making progress toward our goal of effective verification of the TTBT and the PNET. During General Secretary Gorbachev's visit to Washington in December, the United States and the Soviet Union agreed to design and conduct joint verification experiments intended to facilitate agreement on effective verification of these two treaties. These joint experiments, which will take place at each other's nuclear test site, will provide opportunities to measure the yield of nuclear explosions using techniques proposed by each side. Through these experiments, we hope to provide the Soviet Union with all the information they should need to accept U.S. use of CORR-

TEX—the most accurate technique we have identified for verification of the TTBT and the PNET.

We and the Soviets also agreed to visit each other's nuclear test sites for the purpose of familiarizing ourselves with the conditions and operations at those test sites. These unprecedented visits, which build on an idea the President first proposed in September 1984, took place last month in a constructive and cooperative atmosphere.

With a better understanding of the practical problems associated with conducting these experiments, we now have the information needed to design the experiments. The two sides have agreed to begin this work immediately upon resumption of negotiations on Monday. We hope that the sides will continue to make expeditious progress in these talks.

Radio Address to the Nation on the President's Trip to Mexico
February 13, 1988

My fellow Americans:

Today I am meeting with Mexican President De la Madrid in Mazatlán, Mexico, so I've prerecorded this radio talk. Over these last 7 years, maintaining a constructive and friendly relationship with our neighbors to the south has been one of the highest priorities of our administration. As we review what has transpired, there is every reason to be pleased.

The leaders of our two nations are aware that good relations and cooperation between us are invaluable to both our peoples. And that's why the meetings between our top leadership have been frequent and our talks at those meetings comprehensive. My meeting today with President De la Madrid will cover a number of issues—from economic concerns, to our mutual commitment to fight drug traffickers, to the security challenges facing the hemisphere.

Mexico is our fourth largest trading partner and we, correspondingly, are Mexico's largest trading partner. Our commercial ties are strong and of great benefit to people on both sides of the border. We've worked hard to make it that way. Last November we signed a new framework understanding that underscored our special trade and investment relationship. During our meetings in Mazatlán, President De la Madrid and I will reaffirm our commitment to take advantage of every opportunity to strengthen the commercial ties between our peoples.

One thing that cannot be overemphasized is that a healthy and expanding Mexican economy is in the interest of the United States. We want Mexico to grow and prosper. And that's why we've done our best and will continue to do our best to help find solutions to the vexing problems of Mexico's international debt. Innovative, market-based methods of managing this burden are being explored, such as Mexico's offer to exchange debt for long-term bonds.

At the same time, we've been working with our Mexican counterparts on such things as a new textile accord, a telecommunications agreement—which will be signed in Mazatlán today—and a new civil aviation agreement, which is in the final stages of negotiations. I hope that one day all of this will be seen as the initial steps leading toward an historic freeing of commerce and trade throughout the continent.

We're just now beginning to tap the unmeasurable potential between Mexico and the United States. This can certainly be seen in the Immigration Reform and Control Act, passed by Congress in 1986. This law offers protections for more than a million undocumented immigrants living in the United States, many of whom are from Mexico. It provides a means for them to find legal employment in our country and to participate openly and freely in our society. Population movement and employment are subjects being examined closely by joint U.S. and Mexican commissions. A study of the issues and frank dialog between us is essential, and I am gratified by the responsible long-term approach the Mexican Government is taking in this sensitive area.

We have found that there are honest and concerned officials on both sides of the border who are dedicated to the same ideals. Nowhere is that more clear than in the battle against drug traffickers. American and Mexican policemen and law enforcement officials have lost their lives in this fight. We've been allies with brave individuals, men and women of integrity who are putting their lives on the line against this evil and the corruption and bloodshed that follows in its trail.

I might add that each and every one of us can make a contribution to winning this war against drugs. First, by refusing to use illegal drugs ourselves and, second, by helping others to get off drugs—and the traffickers would go out of business if people quit buying illegal drugs. That's the real solution, and it's up to each and every one of us to be a part of the solution.

Finally, my talks with President De la Madrid will also cover the security threat to this hemisphere. Since 1980 we've witnessed an impressive expansion of democracy throughout the Americas. However, this progress cannot be taken for granted. The establishment of totalitarian regimes, supported by Cuba and the Soviet Union, is a threat to stability and freedom. Nowhere is that threat more acute than in Central America. I would hope that the United States and Mexico will find common interest in opposing any such totalitarian threat.

The peoples and Governments of United States and Mexico are and ought to be friends. Our national interests dictate it; our peoples demand it. It is in this spirit that I meet today with President De la Madrid. I will pass on to the people of Mexico your very best wishes.

Until next week, thanks for listening and God bless you.

Note: The President's address was recorded at 11:45 a.m. on February 11 in the Oval Office at the White House. It was broadcast at 12:06 p.m. on February 13.

Remarks at the Welcoming Ceremony for President Reagan in Mazatlán, Mexico
February 13, 1988

President De la Madrid. Your Excellency Ronald Reagan, President of the United States of America, members of his party, ladies and gentlemen: On behalf of the people and the Government of Mexico, I am very pleased to extend a most cordial welcome to the President of the United States of America and to the distinguished members of his party.

This is the sixth time that we two Presidents have met and, on balance, this type of top-level communication between the governments of our countries has shown itself to be both effective and useful. On the basis of personal friendship and direct, frank communication, we two Presidents have periodically had the opportunity to review issues of interest to us and to improve the manner in which our relations are conducted.

I must gratefully acknowledge President Reagan's interest in maintaining our relations within an atmosphere of mutual cordiality, dignity, and respect. We have dealt successfully with delicate issues and broadened the basis for cooperation, which, as neighbors, our two countries require. Today we can affirm that our relations are conducted on a very positive level. There is fluid and wide-ranging communication between the two governments, and we have institutional mechanisms, not only to solve but also to prevent problems.

I am certain, Mr. President, that on this occasion, perhaps the last time we meet as Presidents, we will strengthen the basis for good and productive relations and discuss as frankly as we always have the problems on our agenda. President Reagan, I cordially welcome you and also the members of your party.

President Reagan. President De la Madrid, distinguished guests, people of Mexico: This is a momentous occasion for me. Over 5 years ago, President De la Madrid and I first met near the border in Tijuana. We dedicated ourselves to building on the strength, friendship, and cooperation that are traditional bonds between our two countries. We resolved to address the daily concerns of our citizens with mutual respect and understanding. We set out to make progress on difficult issues and to discuss areas of disagreement with the candor of good friends. The personal rapport we developed has served the interests of both our peoples.

Today Mexico and the United States stand together as we strive to meet the perplexing challenges that face our nations. We can be proud of what has been accomplished in so short a period. We have created dynamic commercial ties that lay the foundation for a stronger and expanding trade relationship and more competitive economies. We have worked together to find positive and creative solutions to a threatening international debt problem. We have established strong new mechanisms to deal with border matters. We have strengthened law enforcement cooperation, reducing the ability of criminals to take advantage of different jurisdictions.

Today we will meet again in the spirit of good will and cooperation that has been the hallmark of our relations. Today we help pave the way for a new generation of political leaders in both our countries who will soon follow us and build on the foundation we've laid. That foundation is cemented by our shared values and common goals: a better quality of life for our peoples, opportunities for our children, and the dignity of living peacefully in free and democratic societies. Much still needs to be done to achieve these goals, but we can be proud of the legacy we leave.

Mr. President, next year we will commemorate the 100th anniversary of the founding of the U.S.-Mexico International Boundary and Water Commission. The Commission has been a success, a model for others throughout the world. It is concrete and living proof that two nations can live as neighbors, deal with the reality of a 3,000-kilometer border, and respect each other's sovereign independence and identity.

There will be no greater monument to this upcoming anniversary, which marks a century of Mexican-American cooperation, than the current high plane of relations between the leaders of our countries and the bonds of family, commerce, and friendship between our peoples. This is the spirit in which I come today. Thank you, and God bless you.

Note: The President spoke at 12:17 p.m. at the Camino Real Hotel, where he was accorded a formal welcome with full military honors. The Presidents' remarks were translated by interpreters. Following the ceremony, they met with U.S. and Mexican officials at the hotel.

Informal Exchange With Reporters on Drug Trafficking
February 13, 1988

Q. Mr. President, are you surprised at the relationship that the DEA [Drug Enforcement Administration] had—the close relationship with Noriega [Commander of Panamanian Defense Forces] and the fact that so much of this drug dealing was going on, and he didn't report it, or they didn't?

The President. Helen [Helen Thomas, United Press International], you know I'm not taking questions here. But on that—I'm not going to comment on something that is presently before the court, as it is now.

Q. Well, did you——

Q. Mr. President, will you certify to Congress this month that Mexico has fully cooperated in drug enforcement?

The President. Well, we're going to be discussing a whole number of things here in our meetings, and——

Q. President De la Madrid says that demand is the big problem with this drug thing.

The President. Always has been.

Note: The exchange began at 12:50 p.m. at the Camino Real Hotel in Mazatlán, Mexico. Following the exchange, President Reagan met with President Miguel De la Madrid Hurtado.

White House Statement on the Meeting Between President Reagan and President Miguel De la Madrid Hurtado in Mazatlán, Mexico

February 13, 1988

President Reagan and President De la Madrid met privately for approximately 45 minutes with only notetakers present. President Reagan congratulated President De la Madrid on his 5 years of leadership and for the modernization that he had brought to Mexico. The President stressed that during the tenure of the two Presidents significant successes had been achieved in trade, investment relations, drug enforcement, commercial ventures, and general economic improvements.

The President stressed the importance of the drug problem for our two countries. He raised the issue of certification to Congress by March 1 and urged the Mexican President to work even harder on drug eradication. President De la Madrid emphasized his deep concern and intensive efforts to deal with the drug problem. He said he condemns narcotics and would have more to say on the matter publicly later. President De la Madrid quoted a number of statistics concerning their drug enforcement activities. President Reagan recognized that Mexico has been very cooperative in fighting drugs, but also pointed out that "this is the year we have to show results."

The two leaders also discussed Central American policy. The President repeated his commitment to the peace process and to his support for the resistance. President De la Madrid said his country has been supportive of the Esquipulas plan [Guatemala accords]. They also discussed East-West relations, and the President commented on his recent summit meeting with General Secretary Gorbachev.

Toast at a Luncheon Hosted by President Miguel De la Madrid Hurtado in Mazatlán, Mexico

February 13, 1988

President De la Madrid, members of the Mexican and U.S. delegations, friends, this is the sixth time President De la Madrid and I have met, as he told us, since 1982. I am extremely pleased with our discussions and with the remarkable record of accomplishment since we last met in Washington.

Our commercial relations are perhaps the most dramatic example of this progress. The signing of our new framework understanding last November marked the beginning of a special trade and investment relationship between our countries. Today we have rededicated ourselves to work together through the framework process and in the GATT [General Agreement on Tariffs and Trade] to seize every opportunity to expand commerce between us. One day I hope these steps will be seen as part of the historic evolution toward the free and unimpeded trade and investment on this continent and in the Western Hemisphere.

There are, of course, obstacles to overcome, not the least of which is a persistent debt problem. There is, however, reason for optimism on this account. Innovative, market-based ideas on how to manage the international debt problem are emerging. Mexico's plan to exchange debt for long-term bonds is but one example.

And cooperation on the debt is but one of the many areas where progress is being made. Agreements that have been reached or are near in several areas—such as textiles, telecommunications, and civil aviation—are positive steps forward. We can also point to the successful management of difficult environmental problems along our common border. Under the agreement we signed in 1983, we're meeting our responsibilities. This is exemplified by the recently signed contingency plan on hazardous substances.

Population movement and employment needs will continue to be crucial factors in our relationship. And I'm gratified by the new dialog we've undertaken on these subjects and by the establishment of U.S. and Mexican commissions to study these questions jointly. In 1986 the United States Congress passed, and I signed into law, the Immigration Reform and Control Act, intended to reestablish control of our borders. It offers protections for well over a million undocumented immigrants living in the United States, many of whom are from Mexico, by providing a means for them to find legal employment and to participate openly and freely in our society.

The mutual legal assistance treaty signed in December has already been ratified by the Mexican legislature. A few days ago I transmitted this treaty to the United States Senate for prompt ratification so that cooperation against criminals can be intensified. And as for the fight against criminals, Mr. President, perhaps our most serious undertaking has been the battle against the scourge of international drug trafficking and the use of these drugs in our societies. The people of the United States are now turning away from drugs. Drug use is no longer fashionable, and in most circles it's no longer tolerated. My wife, as you're aware, has taken the lead in an energetic program to combat drug abuse. Our success, measured by the number of people rejecting drugs, should curb the demand that fuels the trafficking.

This menace threatens the fabric of both our societies. The heartache and corruption brought on by these traffickers are pervasive. President De la Madrid, if the decent people of our two societies are to win, it requires cooperation and a mutually reinforcing effort. And, Mr. President, I'm certain we are both committed to victory in this war against drugs and the evil it has wrought on our peoples.

Our first responsibility to our citizens is to assure them an environment where they can raise their families in peace and freedom and prosperity. And that is why our commitment to democracy in our hemisphere must be unshakable. Totalitarian societies—such as those in the Soviet Union, Cuba, and now Nicaragua—have demonstrated for all to see that tyranny doesn't work. Mexico and the United States have a common interest in stable, free, and democratic governments in this hemisphere. I would hope this common interest will manifest itself in a common stand against the expansion of totalitarianism.

A year from now, new Presidents will be in office in both our countries. They will be challenged, as have you and I, Mr. President, to achieve real, measurable progress on matters that concern us both because they affect the daily lives of our people. In the past 5 years, we have demonstrated that we can cooperate to achieve creative, mutually beneficial solutions, and this is a valuable legacy that we leave to our successors.

Mr. President, I want to say publicly before we part that I truly believe history will honor you for the wise and politically courageous way you're guiding Mexico on the difficult but ultimately rewarding path to economic recovery and national development. This is an effort worthy of our admiration, our respect, and our support. And I know that with continued perseverance it will be crowned with success. I also believe, Mr. President, that you and I together have turned the relationship between the United States and Mexico in a new, more constructive direction that our successors can build upon.

When I arrived today, I spoke of the

foundation for Mexican-American relations that we've laid these last 5 years. Well, you know, one of my first jobs as a young man was digging foundations at a construction site. I worked there with strong, decent men whose hard work was a necessary part of the building process. President De la Madrid, it's been an honor for me to work with you and your colleagues, to labor beside you, and to have your friendship. Our peoples will live better lives for what we've done together. I can think of no goal better than that.

So, I propose a toast to you and to relations between the United States and Mexico. And may they always be as sunny as the skies here today over Mazatlán.

Note: President Reagan spoke at 3:31 p.m. in the Salon Mazatlán at the Camino Real Hotel in response to a toast by President De la Madrid. Following the luncheon, President Reagan traveled to his ranch in Santa Barbara County, CA.

Statement by Assistant to the President for Press Relations Fitzwater on the Deployment of Strategic Nuclear Missiles in Cuba

February 15, 1988

The SS–4 and SS–5 missile sites established in Cuba between late August and mid-October 1962 were confirmed as having been destroyed in that year. We also are confident that the missiles were removed from Cuba at that time. We have had extensive intelligence collection directed at Cuba since 1962 and have no evidence that SS–4, SS–5, or other strategic missiles have been deployed there.

Proclamation 5773—National Visiting Nurse Associations Week, 1988

February 17, 1988

By the President of the United States of America

A Proclamation

For the last century, visiting nurse associations have sent skilled and dedicated nurses to care for homebound patients throughout our country. Today, approximately 20,000 nurses in nearly 500 associations care each year for nearly a million Americans, adults and children alike. This tradition of caring service has provided indispensable help to countless people and has truly earned visiting nurses the gratitude and the esteem of their countrymen.

Visiting nurse associations have won great professional respect as well for their adherence to the highest standards in offering personalized home health care. Visiting nurses often work under adverse conditions and at personal sacrifice, working long hours and traveling great distances to minister to the sick at home and to teach people sound health practices.

The contributions of visiting nurses also help community health services meet today's demand for nursing. Patients released from acute care institutions, the chronically ill, and the physically and mentally handicapped all receive the many benefits of visiting nurses' care and services.

Many volunteers assist the work of visiting nurse associations, serving on boards of directors and offering every kind of support, from visiting patients to staffing offices to delivering meals on wheels.

The activities of visiting nurses and those who support their fine work deserve our praise, thanks, and encouragement, now and always.

The Congress, by Public Law 100–246, has designated the period of February 21 through February 27, 1988, as "National Visiting Nurse Associations Week" and has authorized and requested the President to issue a proclamation in observance of this week.

Now, Therefore, I, Ronald Reagan, President of the United States of America, do hereby proclaim the period of February 21 through February 27, 1988, as National Visiting Nurse Associations Week. I call upon the people of the United States to observe this week with appropriate ceremonies and activities in support of America's visiting nurses and their reverence and respect for the worth and the dignity of the patients for whom they care.

In Witness Whereof, I have hereunto set my hand this seventeenth day of February, in the year of our Lord nineteen hundred and eighty-eight, and of the Independence of the United States of America the two hundred and twelfth.

RONALD REAGAN

[*Filed with the Office of the Federal Register, 11:22 a.m., February 18, 1988*]

Note: The proclamation was released by the Office of the Press Secretary on February 18.

Remarks on Presenting the Fiscal Year 1989 Budget to Congressional Leaders

February 18, 1988

The President. Thank you all for coming down here this morning. Seven years ago today, I submitted our economic recovery program which has resulted in 63 months of economic growth. And today I'm sending our fiscal year 1989 budget to the Congress. This budget fits within the second year of the bipartisan budget agreement that we reached last November, and it also meets the deficit reduction targets of Gramm-Rudman-Hollings, and it contains no increases in taxes. And in this budget, we have increased funding for drug interdiction and treatment, funding for our air traffic safety, education, science, and space; and we've increased by 38 percent the level of funding for the fight against AIDS.

And while meeting these domestic priorities and our national security needs, this budget does not increase taxes—again, consistent with our budget agreement. And these recommendations to the Congress, along with budget reform proposals, improve government management; and continued efforts toward privatization will continue the economic growth that we've all witnessed these past 5 years. And now I'm hoping we can work together through the budget process this year, sticking to our agreement and completing the appropriations process before the end of this fiscal year.

Republican Presidential Campaign

Reporter. Mr. President, are you going to call in Senator Dole and Vice President Bush and give them a little lesson on the 11th Commandment? [*Laughter*]

The President. I'm not going to talk about anything but the budget. [*Laughter*]

Q. Are you pleased about the way the campaign's going on the Republican side at this point?

The President. I'm—no comments.

Abduction in Lebanon

Q. Sir, is there anything you can do for Colonel Higgins?

The President. There, I have to tell you we're doing everything we can. We're trying to find out as much as we can, and we'll try to get him located. And certainly we want to rescue him.

Congressman Conte. You have a sizable increase in here for education, Mr. President——

The President. Pardon?

Congressman Conte. You have a sizable increase in this budget for education, and we want to thank you—some of us who have been fighting for it for many years now.

Note: The President spoke at 10:40 a.m. in the Cabinet Room at the White House. Lt. Col. William R. Higgins, USMC, was abducted in Tyre, Lebanon, on Febuary 17. He was a member of the United Nations Truce Supervision Organization.

Message to the Congress Transmitting the Fiscal Year 1989 Budget
February 18, 1988

To the Congress of the United States:

As we consider the state of our Nation today, we have much cause for satisfaction. Thanks to sound policies, steadfastly pursued during the past 7 years, America is at peace, and our people are enjoying the longest peacetime economic expansion in our Nation's history.

By reordering priorities so that we spend more on national security and less on wasteful or unnecessary Federal programs, we have made freedom more secure around the world and have been able to negotiate with our adversaries from a position of strength. By pursuing market-oriented economic policies, we have uncorked the genie of American enterprise and created new businesses, more jobs, improved production, and widespread prosperity. And we have done all this without neglecting the poor, the elderly, the infirm, and the unfortunate among us.

Seven Years of Accomplishment

Let me note a few of the highlights from our Administration's record of accomplishment:

- The current expansion, now in its sixty-third month, has outlasted all previous peacetime expansions in U.S. history. Business investment and exports are rising in real terms, foreshadowing continued economic growth this year and next.
- Since this expansion began, 15 million new jobs have been created, while the unemployment rate has fallen by 5 percentage points—to 5.7 percent, the lowest level in nearly a decade. By comparison, employment in other developed countries has not grown significantly, and their unemployment rates have remained high.
- Inflation, which averaged 10.4 percent annually during the 4 years before I came to office, has averaged less than a third of that during the past 5 years.
- The prime interest rate was 21.5 percent just before I came into office; it is now 8.5 percent; the mortgage rate, which was 14.9 percent, is now down to 10.2 percent.
- Since 1981, the amount of time spent by the public filling out forms required by the Federal Government has been cut by hundreds of millions of hours annually, and the number of pages of regulations published annually in the *Federal Register* has been reduced by over 45 percent.
- Between 1981 and 1987, changes in the Federal tax code, including a complete overhaul in 1986, have made the tax laws more equitable, significantly lowered earned income tax rates for many individuals and corporations, and eliminated the need for 4.3 million low-income individuals or families to file tax forms.
- At the same time, real after-tax personal income has risen 15 percent during the past 5 years, increasing our overall standard of living.
- The outburst of spending for means-tested entitlement programs that occurred in the 1970's has been curbed. Eligibility rules have been tightened to retarget benefits to the truly needy, and significant progress has been made in improving the efficiency and effectiveness of these programs.
- We have begun the process of putting other entitlement programs on a more ra-

tional basis. This includes medicare, which was converted from cost-plus financing to a system that encourages competition and holds down costs.

• Federal spending for domestic programs other than entitlements has been held essentially flat over the past 5 years, while basic benefits for the poor, the elderly, and others in need of Federal assistance have been maintained. This is a dramatic improvement over the unsustainably rapid annual growth of these programs that prevailed before 1981.

• The social security system has been rescued from the threat of insolvency.

• Our defense capabilities have been strengthened. Weapons systems have been modernized and upgraded. We are recruiting and retaining higher caliber personnel. The readiness, training, and morale of our troops have been improved significantly. Because we are stronger, enormous progress has been achieved in arms reduction negotiations with the Soviet Union.

• Federal agencies have undertaken a major management improvement program called "Reform '88." This program has two main objectives: to operate Federal agencies in a more business-like manner, and to reduce waste, fraud, and abuse in government programs.

• Some functions of the Federal Government—such as financing waste treatment plants—are being transferred back to State and local governments. In other instances—such as water projects—State and local governments are bearing a larger share of costs, leading to more rational decision-making in these areas.

• Finally, we have made real progress in privatizing Federal activities that are more appropriate for the private sector than government. Notable examples include the sale of Conrail, the long-term lease of National and Dulles Airports, and the auction of billions of dollars in loan portfolios.

• Related to this shift away from the Federal budget are our achievements on cost sharing and user fees, shifting the cost of projects and programs where appropriate to non-Federal sources.

While we have reason to be proud of this record of achievement, we must be vigilant in addressing threats to continued prosperity. One major threat is the Federal deficit.

Deficit Reduction, the Agreement, and G-R-H

If the deficit is not curbed by limiting the appetite of government, we put in jeopardy what we have worked so hard to achieve. Larger deficits brought on by excessive spending could precipitate rising inflation, interest rates, and unemployment. We cannot permit this to happen, and we will not.

BUDGET SUMMARY

[In billions of dollars]

	1987	1988	1989	1990	1991	1992	1993
Receipts	854.1	909.2	964.7	1,044.1	1,124.4	1,189.9	1,258.1
Outlays	1,004.6	1,055.9	1,094.2	1,148.3	1,203.7	1,241.0	1,281.3
Surplus or deficit (−)	−150.4	−146.7	−129.5	−104.2	−79.3	−51.1	−23.3
Gramm-Rudman-Hollings deficit targets	−144.0	−144.0	−136.0	−100.0	−64.0	−28.0	0.0
Difference	6.4	2.7	−6.5	4.2	15.3	23.1	23.3

Note.—Totals include social security, which is off-budget.

The Congress acknowledged the pressing need to reduce the deficit when, in December 1985, it enacted the Balanced Budget and Emergency Deficit Control Act, commonly known for its principal sponsors as the Gramm-Rudman-Hollings (G-R-H) Act. This Act committed both the President and the Congress to a fixed schedule of progress toward balancing the budget.

In 1987, the budget deficit was $150 billion—down $71 billion from the record level of $221 billion reached in 1986. This was also a record decline in the deficit. To some extent, however, this improvement represented one-time factors, such as a high level of receipts in the transitional year of tax reform. Economic forecasters predicted that without action the 1988 and 1989 deficits would be higher than the 1987 level. In order to prevent this, and to preserve and build upon the 1987 deficit-reduction progress in a realistic fashion, last fall the Congress modified the G-R-H Act. Specifically, it required that the 1988 deficit target be $144 billion and the target for 1989 be $136 billion.

Last year, members of my Administration worked with the Leaders of Congress to develop a 2-year plan of deficit reduction—the Bipartisan Budget Agreement. One of the major objectives of the budget I am submitting today is to comply with that agreement—in order to help assure a steady reduction in the deficit until budget balance is achieved.

The Bipartisan Budget Agreement reflects give and take on all sides. I agreed to some $29 billion in additional revenues and $13 billion less than I had requested in defense funding over 2 years. However, because of a willingness of all sides to compromise, an agreement was reached that pared $30 billion from the deficit projected for 1988 and $46 billion from that projected for 1989.

In submitting this budget, I am adhering to the Bipartisan Budget Agreement and keeping my part of the bargain. I ask the Congress to do the same. This budget does not fully reflect my priorities, nor, presumably, those of any particular Member of Congress. But the goal of deficit reduction through spending reduction must be paramount. Abandoning the deficit reduction compromise would threaten our economic progress and burden future generations.

This budget shows that a gradual elimination of the deficit is possible without abandoning tax reform, without cutting into legitimate social programs, without devastating defense, and without neglecting other national priorities.

Under the Bipartisan Budget Agreement, progress toward a steadily smaller deficit and eventual budget balance will continue, but this projected decline rests on two assumptions: continued economic growth, and implementation of the Agreement. If the economy performs as expected, and if the Bipartisan Budget Agreement reflected in this budget is adhered to, the deficit should decline to less than 3 percent of GNP in 1989. For the first time in several years, the national debt as a proportion of GNP will actually fall. Reducing the deficit and the debt in this manner would bring our goal of a balanced budget and a reduced burden on future generations much closer to realization.

Moreover, adherence to the Agreement, as reflected in this budget, will ensure the achievement of additional deficit reductions in future years, because in many cases the savings from a given action this year will generate deficit savings in subsequent years. Given the good start made in 1987, we have an opportunity this year to put the worst of the deficit problem behind us.

Meeting National Priorities

In formulating this budget, I have endeavored to meet national priorities while keeping to the terms of the Bipartisan Budget Agreement and the G-R-H Act. In essence, the Agreement limits the 1988-to-1989 increase in domestic discretionary program budget authority to 2 percent. To address urgent national priorities insofar as possible within this overall 2 percent limit, my budget proposes that some programs—such as those for education, drug enforcement, and technology development—receive larger funding increases, while others are reduced, reformed, or, in some cases, terminated.

High-priority programs must be funded adequately. One of our highest priorities is to foster individual success through greater educational and training opportunities. For example:

- I propose an increase of $656 million

over the $16.2 billion appropriated for 1988 for discretionary programs of the Department of Education. Although State and local governments fund most education activity, Federal programs provide crucial aid for the poor, the handicapped, and the educationally disadvantaged.

• I have proposed reform of our overcentralized welfare system through State experimentation with innovative alternatives. In addition, my initiative would overhaul current employment and training programs for welfare recipients, and strengthen our national child support enforcement system.

• By emphasizing housing vouchers, I would provide housing assistance to 135,500 additional low-income households in 1989—8 percent more than the 125,000 additional households receiving housing subsidies in 1988.

• Ineffective programs to assist dislocated workers would be replaced by an expanded $1 billion worker readjustment program (WRAP) carefully designed to help those displaced from their jobs move quickly into new careers.

In addition, I am proposing funds to strengthen U.S. technology and make America more competitive. For example:

• I propose a continued increase in federally supported basic research aimed at longer-term improvements in the Nation's productivity and global competitiveness. This budget would double National Science Foundation support for academic basic research, increase support for training future scientists and engineers, and expedite technology transfer of Government-funded research to industry.

• I would provide $11.5 billion for space programs, including: essential funding for continued development of America's first permanently manned Space Station; increased support for improving the performance and reliability of the space shuttle; a major new initiative, the Advanced X-ray Astrophysics Facility, for space science; further support to encourage the commercial development of space; and a new technology effort, Project Pathfinder, designed to develop technologies to support future decisions on the expansion of human presence and activity beyond Earth's orbit, into the solar system.

• I also recommend $363 million in 1989 to initiate construction of the Superconducting Super Collider (SSC), including $283 million for construction and $60 million for supporting research and development. The SSC as currently envisaged will be the largest pure science project ever undertaken. It will help keep this country on the cutting edge of high energy physics research until well into the next century.

This budget also reflects my belief that the health of all our citizens must remain one of our top priorities:

• I continue to urge enactment of an affordable self-financing insurance program through medicare to protect families from economic devastation caused by catastrophic illness.

• To attack the scourge of AIDS, I propose $2 billion for additional research, education, and treatment in 1989—a 38 percent increase over the 1988 level and more than double the Federal Government's effort in 1987. This includes $1.3 billion in funding for the Public Health Service.

• Building upon the Nation's preeminence in basic biomedical research, I seek a 5.1 percent increase for non-AIDS research at the National Institutes of Health;

Our fight against drug abuse must continue, as well as our efforts to protect the individual against crime:

• For expanded law enforcement, including efforts targeted at white collar crime, organized crime, terrorism and public corruption, I propose $4.5 billion—an increase of 6 percent over 1988.

• For drug law enforcement, prevention, and treatment programs, I propose $3.9 billion in 1989, a 13 percent increase over the 1988 level.

• To relieve prison overcrowding and adequately house a growing inmate population, I would provide $437 million—more than double the $202 million devoted to Federal prison construction in 1988.

Other areas of Federal responsibility receive priority funding in this budget:

• For the Federal Aviation Administration to continue its multi-year program to modernize the Nation's air traffic control systems, I would provide $1.6 billion—a 44 percent increase over the level of 1988.

• To improve coordination of Federal rural development programs and to redirect funding toward needy rural areas and program recipients, I propose a rural development initiative to be coordinated by the Secretary of Agriculture.

• To carry out the joint recommendations of the U.S. and Canadian Special Envoys on Acid Rain, I recommend total funding of $2.5 billion for innovative clean coal technology demonstration projects over the period 1988 through 1992.

• I also recommend an expansion of hazardous waste cleanup efforts, with an increase in Superfund outlays of some $430 million in 1989.

• To continue filling the Strategic Petroleum Reserve (SPR) at the current rate of 50,000 barrels per day, I would provide $334 million in 1989. Contingent upon the enactment of legislation authorizing the sale of the Naval Petroleum Reserves (NPR), I would provide an additional $477 million to bring the fill rate up to 100,000 barrels per day, and an additional $208 million to establish a separate 10 million barrel defense petroleum inventory to offset the disposition of the NPR.

• To improve the speed and accuracy of tax processing and expand information services provided to taxpayers, I would provide a $241 million increase for the Internal Revenue Service. These funds are designed to assure smooth implementation of the 1986 tax reforms.

Maintaining peace in a troubled world is the most important responsibility of government. Fortunately, during the past 7 years, our defense capabilities have been restored toward levels more consistent with meeting our responsibility to provide an environment safe and secure from aggression. Specifically, combat readiness has been improved, and our forces have been modernized.

The proposals for national security contained in this budget represent an essential minimum program for keeping America safe and honoring our commitments to our friends and allies. Anything less would jeopardize not only our security—and that of our friends and allies—but also would dim the prospects for further negotiated agreements with our adversaries.

As called for in the Bipartisan Budget Agreement, my budget requests defense funding of $299.5 billion in budget authority and $294.0 billion in outlays for 1989. It also provides for about 2 percent real growth in these programs in future years. Also, as called for in the Agreement, my budget requests $18.1 billion in budget authority for discretionary spending for international affairs. This includes $8.3 billion in security assistance to allied and friendly countries where the United States has special security concerns.

Needed Programmatic Reforms

Incentives.—It is essential to continue to change the incentive structure for many domestic Federal programs to promote greater efficiency and cost-effectiveness. This budget proposes to create such needed incentives.

Many Federal programs offer payments without sufficient regard for how well taxpayers' money is being spent. For example, farm price support programs, under the Food Security Act of 1985, are much too costly. I plan to continue pushing for the elimination of artificially high price supports, thereby reducing the need for export subsidies. In particular, I plan to propose amendments to the Act to modify the counterproductive sugar price support program that currently poses significant problems in the areas of trade policy, foreign policy, and agricultural policy. The importance of agricultural trade to the economic health of the farm sector and the Nation as a whole mandates increased reliance on free markets, not government largess.

The budget proposes certain reforms in the medicare program in order to achieve the savings agreed to in the Bipartisan Budget Agreement. First, as justified by the results of several independent studies, I propose to reduce the add-on payment for teaching hospitals under the prospective payment system (PPS) for indirect medical education from 7.70 percent to 4.05 percent, the best estimate of the added costs incurred historically by teaching hospitals. Second, I propose to limit medicare overhead payments for graduate medical education and make consistent varying secondary payor enforcement mechanisms. To reduce escalating supplementary medical insurance costs and help slow future increases in beneficiary premiums, I propose to limit payments for certain overpriced physician procedures, limit payments for durable medical equipment and supplies, and eliminate a loophole in the payment process for kidney dialysis. In total, these reforms would reduce spending for medicare by $1.2 billion from the level that would occur if current law were continued. Spending for the medicare program would still increase by 7 percent from 1988 to 1989.

Although the provision of needed legal services for those who cannot afford them is an important goal in our society, the current system earmarks a large portion of the funding to "National and State Support Centers" that have been criticized for political involvement. I urge Congress to disallow use of Federal funds for such "think tanks" and limit the use of funds to the *direct* assistance of the poor in need of legal aid.

The Government often continues programs at the Federal level that are no longer needed. This is the case with rural housing programs, the Economic Development Administration, urban mass transit discretionary grants, urban development action grants, sewage treatment, Small Business Administration direct loans, housing development action grants, the housing rehabilitation loan program, and economic development programs of the Tennessee Valley Authority. Efforts to reverse this situation have been undertaken by prior administrations as well as my own, but the limited results to date indicate the difficulty of curbing excessive government involvement in these areas.

Regulatory Relief.—For 7 years I have worked to reduce the excess burdens of government regulation for all Americans—working men and women, consumers, businesses, and State and local governments. As a result, various departments and agencies have reduced the scope and costs of Federal regulation. Federal approval of experimental drugs has been expedited, making them available to treat serious or life-threatening diseases when other treatments do not work. Excessive burdens on State and local governments are being lifted. Access to goods and services has been made easier, and at less cost. Federal reporting requirements on individuals and businesses have been eased, as well as the paperwork burden on those who wish to compete for contracts with the Federal Government. Under the leadership of the Presidential Task Force on Regulatory Relief, headed by the Vice President, the Administration will continue these and other efforts to lessen the burden of excessive government regulation.

As a case in point, my budget proposes termination of the Interstate Commerce Commission, contingent upon enactment of legislation that completes deregulation of the motor carrier industry. There is no justification for continued economic (as opposed to safety) regulation of surface transportation, and there is a substantial argument against it. As a result of economic deregulation of trucking and railroads, consumers save tens of billions of dollars each year, and the industry is healthier, more innovative, and better able to adapt to changing economic circumstances. This is no time to turn back the clock.

Privatization.—The government and the private sector should do what each does best. The Federal Government should not be involved in providing goods and services where private enterprise can do the jobs cheaper and/or better. In some cases, the fact that no private provider exists is a reflection of government policy to prohibit competition—as with first class mail service. In other cases, an absence of private providers reflects a government policy of providing large subsidies—as with uranium enrichment. Invariably, the taxpayer ends up paying more for less.

Accordingly, my budget proposes that a number of Federal enterprises be transferred back to the private sector, through public offerings or outright sales. Following our successful sale of Conrail and auctioning of $5 billion in selected loan portfolios, I am proposing the sale not only of the Naval Petroleum Reserves, but also of the Alaska Power Administration, the Federal Government's helium program, excess real property, and a further $12 billion in loan portfolios. In addition, I have proposed legislation to authorize a study of possible divestiture of the Southeastern Power Administration, and plan to study possible privatization of our uranium enrichment facilities, as well as ways of making the U.S. Postal Service more efficient through greater reliance on the private sector. Such "privatization" efforts continue to be a high priority of this Administration, and I look forward to acting on the final recommendations of the Privatization Commission, which I established last September.

Privatization does not necessarily imply abrogation of government responsibility for these services. Rather, it recognizes that what matters is the service provided, not who provides it. Government has an inherent tendency to become too big, unwieldy, and inefficient; and to enter into unfair competition with the private sector.

The Federal Government should also depend more on the private sector to provide ancillary and support services for activities that remain in Federal hands. Therefore, I am proposing the development of a private mediating institution to reduce the backlog of cases before the U.S. Tax Court. I propose that the private sector be relied upon for booking functions for concessional food programs. I also encourage the complete privatization of wastewater treatment plants, certain mass transit projects, the Department of Agriculture's National Finance Center, and the Rural Telephone Bank.

In addition, our Administration plans to initiate privatization and commercialization efforts involving Federal prison industries, relying on a private space facility for microgravity research opportunities in the early 1990's, commercial cargo inspection, military commissaries, Coast Guard buoy maintenance, and the management of undeveloped Federal land. Moreover, my budget proposes that the work associated with certain Federal employment positions be reviewed for the feasibility of contracting their responsibilities out to the private sector as yet another way to increase productivity, reduce costs, and improve services.

One of the best ways to test the worth of a governmental program or a particular project is to shift some of the cost of that program or project to the direct beneficiaries. We have done that, for example, with water resources development projects. As a result, local sponsors and users choose to proceed only on the projects that are most important and most cost effective.

Management Improvements.—As we all know, the Federal Government has a major effect upon our daily lives through the direct delivery of services, the payment of financial assistance through various entitlement programs, the collection of taxes and fees, and the regulation of commercial enterprises. As the 21st century approaches, the Federal Government must adapt its role in our society to meet changing demands arising from changing needs and requirements. At the turn of the century, the U.S. population will exceed 268 million, with a greater proportion of elderly requiring more specialized services. The Nation will operate at a much faster pace as changes in technology and communication link the world's economies, trade, capital flows, and travel as never before.

I have asked the Office of Domestic Affairs and the Office of Management and Budget to work with the President's Council on Management Improvement to conduct an in-depth review and recommend to me by this August what further adjustments in the Federal role should be made to prepare for the challenge of government in the 21st century. This summer I will receive their report, "Government of the Future." I also intend to complete the "Reform '88" management improvement program I started 6 years ago to overhaul the administrative, financial, and credit systems in our Federal Government; to implement productivity and quality plans in each agency; and to examine the needs of the Federal work force of the future. I want to leave a legacy of good management of today's programs, with plans in place to handle tomorrow's challenges.

Efforts to improve the management of the Federal Government must be continued. We have all heard stories of the horrible waste that occurs in the Federal Government. Some of it is obvious—like the billions of dollars in unneeded projects that were included in the thousand-page 1988 spending bill that was dropped on my desk last December. Some are not obvious—like the billion dollars in unnecessary interest expense the government paid, year after year, because it lacked a cash management system, or the billions of dollars lost annually for lack of a credit management process to ensure collection of the trillion dollars in loans owed the Federal Government.

In July 1980, I promised the American people: "I will not accept the excuse that the Federal Government has grown . . . beyond the control of any President, Administration or Congress . . . we are going to put an end to the notion that the American taxpayer exists to fund the Federal Government. The Federal Government exists to serve the American people . . . I pledge my Administration will do that." I have delivered on that promise.

The first step was taken within months after my inauguration when I formed the President's Council on Integrity and Efficiency, composed of the agency Inspectors General. By the time I leave office, they will have delivered savings of over $110 billion in reduced waste, fraud, and abuse to the American people.

Then, in March 1982, I initiated the world's largest management improvement program with these words: "With Reform '88 we're going to streamline and reorganize the processes that control the money, information, personnel and property of the Federal bureaucracy." I told my Cabinet at that time that "we have six years to change what it took twenty or thirty to create—and we came to Washington to make changes!" I have followed up on that commitment. The President's Council on Management Improvement has overseen this effort, and is generating significant results.

These efforts are described in greater detail in my *Management Report,* which is being submitted concurrently. They can succeed only if all Federal managers and employees work together. Therefore, I propose in this budget a new approach to paying Federal employees who increase their productivity. I ask the Congress to modify the current system of virtually automatic "within-grade" pay increases for the roughly 40 percent of employees eligible each year to one that is based on employee performance. This will give Federal employees stronger incentives to improve service delivery and reduce costs to the taxpayer.

The Budget Process

As I have stressed on numerous occasions, the current budget process is clearly unworkable and desperately needs a drastic overhaul. Last year, as in the year before, the Congress did not complete action on a budget until well past the beginning of the fiscal year. The Congress missed every deadline it had set for itself just 9 months earlier. In the end, the Congress passed a year-long, 1,057-page omnibus $605 billion appropriations bill with an accompanying conference report of 1,053 pages and a reconciliation bill 1,186 pages long. Members of Congress had only 3 hours to consider all three items. Congress should not pass another massive continuing resolution—and as I said in the State of the Union address, if they do I will not sign it.

I am asking for a constitutional amendment that mandates a balanced budget and forces the Federal Government to live within its means. A constitutional amendment to balance the Federal budget—and a provision requiring a super-majority vote in the Congress to increase taxes—would impose some much-needed discipline on the congressional budget process. Ninety-nine percent of Americans live in States that require a balanced State budget, and a total of 32 States already have passed resolutions calling for a convention for the purpose of proposing a balanced budget amendment to the U.S. Constitution.

Also, I am asking the Congress for a line-item veto, so that my successors could reach into massive appropriation bills such as the last one, cut out the waste, and enforce budget discipline. Forty-three State Governors have a line-item veto; the President should have this power as well. As Governor of the State of California (1967–1975), I used the line-item veto 943 times. The California State legislature upheld each of these vetos, even though both Houses were controlled by the opposition party.

In addition, I propose the following further reforms to the budget process:

(1) *Joint budget resolution.* The budget process has so degenerated in recent years that the presidential budget is routinely discarded and the congressional budget resolution is regularly disregarded. As a remedy, I propose that henceforth the Congress and the Executive collaborate on a joint resolution that sets out spending priorities within the receipts available. The requirement of a Presidential signature would force both branches of government to resolve policy differences before appropriations measures must be formulated. The budget process could be further improved by including in the budget law allocations by committee as well as by budget function.

(2) *Individual transmittal of appropriation bills.* The current practice of transmitting full-year continuing resolutions skirts appropriations committee-subcommittee jurisdictions. More importantly, it does not permit the Legislative and Executive branches to exercise proper scrutiny of Federal spending. Therefore, I propose a requirement that appropriations bills be transmitted individually to the President.

(3) *Strict observance of allocations.* During the 1980s, an unacceptable budget practice evolved within the Congress of disregarding congressionally approved function allocations. Funds regularly were shifted from defense or international affairs to domestic spending. I strongly urge that each fiscal year separate national security and domestic allocations be made and enforced through a point of order provision in the Budget Act.

(4) *Enhanced rescission authority.* Under current law, the President may propose rescissions of budget authority, but both Houses of Congress must act "favorably" for the rescission to take effect. In 1987, not a single rescission was enacted, or even voted on, before expiration of the 45-day deadline. I propose a change of law that would require the Congress to vote "up or down" on any presidentially proposed rescission, thereby preventing the Congress from ducking the issue by simply ignoring the proposed rescission and avoiding a recorded vote.

(5) *Biennial budgeting.* The current budget process consumes too much time and energy. A 2-year budget cycle offers several advantages—among them, a reduction in repetitive annual budget tasks, more time for consideration of key spending decisions in reconciliation, and less scope for gimmicks such as shifting spending from one year to the next. I call on the Congress to adopt biennial budgeting.

(6) *Truth in Federal spending.*—As part of my Economic Bill of Rights, I will shortly transmit legislation that will require any future legislation creating new Federal programs to be deficit-neutral. In addition to requiring the concurrent enactment of equal amounts of program reductions or revenue increases, my proposal would require that all future legislation and regulations be accompanied by financial impact statements, including the effect on State and local governments.

Adoption of these reforms should enable the Federal Government to make informed decisions in a deliberate fashion that fosters rational priorities. The American people deserve no less from their elected representatives.

Conclusion

Looking back over the past 7 years we can feel a sense of pride in our accomplishments. Important tasks remain, however. The large and stubbornly persistent budget deficit has been a major source of frustration. It threatens our prosperity and our hopes for lessening the burden on future generations.

Two years ago, the Legislative and Executive branches of government responded to this threat by enacting the G-R-H Act, which mandated gradual, orderly progress toward a balanced budget over the next several years. My budget achieves the 1989 target of the amended Act while preserving legitimate programs for the aged and needy, providing for adequate national security, devoting more resources to other high-priority activities, and doing so without raising taxes.

My budget also embodies the Bipartisan Budget Agreement reached last November. In presenting this budget, I am keeping my end of the bargain. I call upon the Congress to uphold its end—by ensuring that appropriations and other legislation are in full accord with the Agreement. By exercising this measure of restraint and self-discipline, we can secure great benefits for the Nation: a lower budget deficit, reduced demand on credit markets, more stable financial markets, a steadily declining trade deficit, and continued prosperity with non-inflationary growth. And, by reforming the budget process, the Congress can improve its decisionmaking and garner the thanks of a grateful public. Surely, these are small prices for what is at stake.

RONALD REAGAN

February 18, 1988.

Note: The message was not issued as a White House press release.

Nomination of David L. Chatfield To Be a Member of the National Credit Union Administration Board

February 18, 1988

The President today announced his intention to nominate David L. Chatfield to be a member of the National Credit Union Administration Board for the remainder of the term expiring August 2, 1989. He would succeed P.A. Mack, Jr.

Since 1980 Mr. Chatfield has been senior vice president of corporate development for Alaska U.S.A. Federal Credit Union in Anchorage, AK. Prior to this he was president of the Alaska Credit Union League and Alaska League Services, Inc., 1978–1979. From 1976 to 1978, he was director of political action development for the Credit Union National Association, Inc., in Washington, DC.

Mr. Chatfield attended Ohio State University and Arapahoe Community College. He was born September 30, 1940, in Columbus, OH. He is married, has four children, and resides in Anchorage, AK.

Nomination of Alan Marshall Elkins To Be a Member of the Board of Regents of the Uniformed Services University of the Health Sciences

February 18, 1988

The President today announced his intention to nominate Alan Marshall Elkins to be a member of the Board of Regents of the Uniformed Services University of the Health Sciences, Department of Defense, for a term expiring May 1, 1993. He would succeed David I. Olch.

Since 1969 Dr. Elkins has been chief of psychiatry of Maine Medical Center in Portland, and president of the medical staff, 1980. Prior to this, Dr. Elkins was director of community psychiatry for St. Luke's Hospital Center in New York City, 1965–1969, and associate attending psychiatrist, 1961–

1969. He was senior examiner of the American Board of Psychiatry and Neurology, 1969–present.

Dr. Elkins graduated from Dartmouth College (A.B., 1952) and Boston University School of Medicine (M.D., 1957). He served in the United States Army Medical Corps Reserve, 1956–1965. He was born December 20, 1930, in Boston, MA. He is married and resides in Cape Elizabeth, ME.

Nomination of Robert Earl Farris To Be Administrator of the Federal Highway Administration
February 18, 1988

The President today announced his intention to nominate Robert Earl Farris to be Administrator of the Federal Highway Administration at the Department of Transportation. He would succeed Ray A. Barnhart.

Since 1986 Mr. Farris has been Deputy Administrator of the Federal Highway Administration at the Department of Transportation in Washington, DC, and is currently a member of the board of consultants of the Eno Foundation for Transportation. Prior to this, he was commissioner of the Department of Transportation for the State of Tennessee, and chairman of the National Council of Public Works Improvement, 1985–1986.

Mr. Farris attended the United States Marine Corps Radar-Radio Technical School; Harvard University, John F. Kennedy School of Government; and the University of Virginia Transportation Executive Institute. He served in the United States Marine Corps, 1946–1952. He was born March 7, 1928, in Etowah, TN. Mr. Farris is married, has two children, and resides in Washington, DC.

Remarks at the Swearing-In Ceremony for Anthony M. Kennedy as an Associate Justice of the Supreme Court of the United States
February 18, 1988

The President. Mr. Chief Justice, members of the Court, and ladies and gentlemen, welcome to the White House, and thank you for coming to witness this historic occasion. This ceremony is the culmination of our constitutional process, which involves each of the three branches of government. I've had the honor of nominating Judge Kennedy to be an Associate Justice of the United States Supreme Court. The Senate has confirmed my nomination, and I now ask that Chief Justice William Rehnquist administer the constitutional oath of office to Judge Kennedy.

Chief Justice Rehnquist. Thank you, Mr. President. Before I administer the oath, let me say on behalf of my colleagues and all of us how grateful we are to you for having this very fine ceremony in the White House. We appreciate it.

[*At this point, Justice Kennedy was sworn in.*]

Justice Kennedy. Mr. President and Mrs. Reagan, Chief Justice and Mrs. Rehnquist, distinguished and esteemed guests and friends: My family joins me, Mr. President, in again expressing our deep appreciation for the confidence and the trust that you've reposed in us. And we thank you, Mr. President, and we thank you, Mr. Chief Justice, for this gracious reception and for the warm welcome you've given us to the Court and to this city. We feel very much at home here. It is a singular privilege to succeed to the place left by Justice Powell, who served the Court and the country with such wisdom and distinction.

In this year, the bicentennial, it is appropriate to recognize an essential truth, and that is that the Constitution of the United States is the single fact, the single reality, the single idea, the single moral principle that sets the United States apart from other nations, now and throughout history. I shall honor the Constitution. And at this gracious assembly and ceremony, it is appropriate to note also that the Presidency, the Congress, and the courts are committed to the Constitution and to the rule of law and to the heritage of freedom.

Thank you very much.

The President. Mr. Chief Justice and members of the Court, ladies and gentlemen, almost 200 years ago, President Washington sent a letter inviting five men to become the first Associate Justices of the United States Supreme Court. In that letter, Washington wrote: "Considering the judicial system as the chief pillar upon which our National Government must rest, I have thought it my duty to nominate such men as I conceived would give dignity and luster to our national character."

Well, we gather here today to welcome as the newest Associate Justice of the Supreme Court a man I've known and respected for more than a decade and who, like those Washington nominated, will give dignity and luster to our national character: Anthony M. Kennedy.

Judge and now Justice Kennedy—sounds good, doesn't it—[*laughter*]—takes a distinguished seat on the High Bench. It was first held by one of those initial Washington appointees: John Rutledge. A century and a half later, Hugo Black filled it. And for more than a decade, it has been graced with the service of one of the great gentlemen of the American judiciary, a Justice widely acclaimed for his decency and fairness: Justice Lewis Powell.

Like his distinguished predecessor, Justice Kennedy's career has been marked by his devotion to a simple, straightforward, and enduring principle: that we are a government of laws, not of men. Our Constitution, our form of government, is built on a bedrock value: self-government, yes, but self-government with a purpose—which is individual liberty.

We often say that to preserve liberty the Bill of Rights was added after ratification, but we should not forget that the framers in Philadelphia didn't put a Bill of Rights in their original document, because they believed that the system they'd constructed—with all its checks and balances and its restrictions on the Federal Government's powers—was a sufficient safeguard of freedom. This system was their answer to what they saw as, and what was, an almost impossible dilemma.

The framers had gone to Philadelphia with a clear mandate to, as the Annapolis convention had instructed, "render the Constitution of the Federal Government adequate to the exigencies of the Union"—which was to say, to give it the power to tax, to regulate interstate commerce, and to raise an army and navy to defend the Nation. The absence of these powers under the Articles of the Confederation had led to trade wars among the States, local rebellions, international humiliation, the exhaustion of the Government's finances, and the ruin of the economy.

The question the framers asked was: How can the central government receive the power to govern without also receiving the power to oppress? Their answer, as we know: Define and divide power. The National Government got only so much, the States and the people kept the rest. And what the Federal authorities received, the framers distributed, some to the legislature—and in fact, some to one House and some to the other and some to the entire legislature—then some to the executive and some to the judiciary.

As Hamilton noted, the judiciary—I had trouble with that, didn't I?—[*laughter*]—the judiciary they created was the "least dangerous" branch because it had "neither force nor will, but merely judgment." And, yes, the Convention did discuss giving judges more expansive powers. There was a move to establish a so-called council of revision, a panel drawn from the courts that could veto legislation because it was dumb or distasteful, whether or not it was constitutional—I'm the only one that can do it because it's dumb and distasteful—[*laugh-*

ter]. But Madison spoke for the proposal, and so did others. But in the end, the Convention listened to a different voice, one not in the room on those hot summer days, yet heard clearly nonetheless: that of the French constitutional philosopher Montesquieu, who had warned that "there is no liberty if the power of judging be not separated from the legislative powers."

And so, the role assigned to judges in our system was to interpret the Constitution and lesser laws, not to make them. It was to protect the integrity of the Constitution, not to add to it or subtract from it—certainly not to rewrite it. For as the framers knew, unless judges are bound by the text of the Constitution, we will, in fact, no longer have a government of laws, but of men and women who are judges. And if that happens, the words of the documents that we think govern us will be just masks for the personal and capricious rule of a small elite.

Well, Justice Kennedy has shown a consistence and courageous dedication to preserving ours as a government of laws, and that's why I nominated him. In more than 12 years on the bench of the 9th Circuit, he won the respect of his colleagues and of the entire legal community. Lawyers and judges of all persuasions characterize him as fair, openminded, and scholarly. And considering the unusual division and intensity of views in the legal community of his circuit, that says a lot. And besides, anyone who teaches law in a powdered wig and a tricornered hat is all right by me on original intent. [*Laughter*]

So, to Justice and Mrs. Kennedy and the entire family, congratulations, good luck, and God bless you. And now I know that Justice Kennedy looks forward to greeting each of you in a few moments.

Note: The President spoke at 4:03 p.m. in the East Room at the White House.

Appointment of Herbert D. Katz as a Member of the United States Holocaust Memorial Council
February 18, 1988

The President today announced his intention to appoint Herbert D. Katz to be a member of the United States Holocaust Memorial Council for a term expiring January 15, 1993. This is a reappointment.

Since 1965 Mr. Katz has been president of Sajik Corp. in Hollywood, FL. Prior to this he was a partner with the law firm of Koneig & Katz, 1959–1973.

Mr. Katz graduated from Wharton School of Finance, University of Pennsylvania (B.S., 1951) and Harvard Law School (J.D., 1954). He served in the United States Coast Guard, 1954–1957. He was born June 13, 1929, in Uniontown, PA. Mr. Katz is married, has five children, and resides in Hollywood, FL.

Message on the Management of the United States Government
February 18, 1988

I am proud to report on the continued success of my Administration's efforts to better manage the Federal Government. Keeping the machinery of government well oiled and up-to-date is a difficult and often frustrating task, but it is absolutely essential if the American people are to have the quality of Federal services they deserve.

Historians and scholars often speak of "the American experiment." They are dead right: that is exactly what we are. We are an experiment to prove that men and women are not only capable of governing themselves, but that free, democratic institutions are superior to any other. Our people have every right to expect that their National Government perform its appointed tasks in a timely, efficient, and courteous fashion.

When I assumed office, I realized there were many tasks the Federal Government was not performing as well as it might. I saw too many examples of government inefficiency that tended to produce excessive costs, inadequate service, or both. To correct these defects, I initiated a governmentwide management improvement strategy that I called "Reform '88."

Our first step was to ask one of the classic questions of good management: Should we be performing a particular task at all? One of the root causes of waste and inefficiency at the Federal level is that the Federal Government has taken on responsibilities that lie outside its proper sphere of action. Accordingly, wherever appropriate, we eliminated Federal regulatory programs and tried to terminate other programs that are unnecessary or duplicative of private sector activities. In other cases we returned Federal programs to the States or to the private sector to operate. Administrative overhead was reduced and cost-effectiveness enhanced by consolidating many Federal programs into block grants and turning them over to the States. Similar gains were realized by selling Government-owned enterprises like Conrail to private bidders. Further gains can be made by increased use of private sector ancillary and support services for activities where government plays a continuing role. In other areas, the Federal Government can scale back operations and reduce barriers to competition, in order to encourage private alternatives.

Second, we launched an all-out campaign against fraud, waste, and abuse at the Federal level. We expanded the role of our agency Inspectors General and made greater use of oversight mechanisms such as internal controls. Over the past 7 years, we have gone after the unscrupulous contractors who bilk the Pentagon, the doctors who overcharge the Medicaid program, the welfare chiselers who collect benefits to which they have no right, the embezzlers who line their pockets with the taxpayers' money, and the deadbeats who evade taxes or will not repay Federal loans. Individuals and corporations have been prosecuted to the fullest extent of the law for cheating the government, and the number of abuses has been substantially curtailed. As a result, billions of dollars have either been saved or put to better use by Federal agencies.

Third, we have worked to improve individual agency operations by managing the agencies better and making their resources go further. Through intensive management review of agency programs, implementation of the recommendations made by the President's Private Sector Survey on Cost Control, and the budget review, we homed in on unique agency problems and assisted their managers in solving them. No major agency was exempt from this effort.

Fourth, for the first time in history, we developed and are implementing governmentwide management systems to collect and analyze information concerning finances, personnel, and other administrative responsibilities. The Federal Government now has uniform accounting systems that will soon be used by every Executive branch agency. The government's credit policies and loan programs are likewise being carried out in a uniform manner—with the result that these credit programs are now being operated in a manner comparable with practices in the private sector. In the same way, our practices for handling cash receipts and disbursements have been improved, and new technology has been applied to improve the timeliness of transactions and reduce the potential for abuse. Information on the work performed by government employees is now standardized and collected uniformly, as are details on government property and procurement.

Lastly, and most importantly, we are making Federal agencies more productive. I realize that productivity, efficiency, and quality control are terms more often associated with private, profit-making enterprises than with government. Yet, I have long believed that they should apply to government as well. We owe our "customers"—the American people—the highest standards of service. Major strides have been made in improving the timeliness and efficiency of Federal Government operations. For example, a new automated passport system has enabled the State Department to issue passports in about half the time it used to take—and the Department has done this at a time when passport applications have increased by 20 percent. The Commerce Department is using a similar system to speed the issuance of export licenses. The Food and Drug Administration has reduced the time it takes to test and approve new medical devices by about one-third—without cutting corners on safety. The Federal Aviation Administration is implementing new ways to speed passenger planes in and out of airports. The Internal Revenue Service is accelerating the processing of tax returns. And these are just a few of our many accomplishments.

Although we have achieved much already, not every initiative we have begun will be completed before the end of this Administration. Some additional implementing work will remain, especially in completing systems for managing government operations and in planning for the 21st century. Nevertheless, our work to date will leave a firm foundation on which future Administrations can build. This is the "management legacy" that my Administration will leave behind for our successors.

The record recounted here in this report to the Congress is one of solid accomplishment—a record that speaks for itself. This report is organized in six parts:

- *First,* this message to you on what the management agenda for this Administration has been, and how far we have gone toward implementing that agenda over the past 7 years.
- *Second,* an overview of government in the year 2000 and our plans to be prepared for the changes it will require.
- *Third,* a summary of accomplishments and our goals for the coming year in our priority areas of credit, financial management, productivity, improved services through technology, procurement, and privatization.
- *Fourth,* a description of the roles played by key agencies such as the General Services Administration, the Office of Personnel Management, and the Department of the Treasury, as well as special organizations such as the President's Council on Management Improvement, and the President's Council on Integrity and Efficiency—both of which have been invaluable in their support and assistance. This section also includes detailed plans, agency by agency, for the implementation of our goals in each of our priority areas, and our legislative agenda.
- *Fifth,* official reports to the Congress, required each year, recording and analyzing our progress to date.
- And *Sixth,* a collection of additional data on selected aspects of the management program.

I have been deeply gratified by the professionalism and spirit of cooperation with which Federal executives and employees have assisted in realizing the management goals of this Administration. We can be very proud of our joint effort to date, but on no account can we be content with what has been done so far. Genuine reform will require continuing dedication and a devotion to stated management goals that endures long after my time in office has expired.

If we know anything about the future, we know that the pace of change—already swift—will be even faster. It is no idle question to ask how democratic institutions will manage to keep up. Americans in the 21st century will have additional, and perhaps different, needs and expectations of their government. To meet those needs and expectations, we must prepare now by overhauling, modernizing, and streamlining the machinery of our Federal system.

Accordingly, I have asked the President's Council on Management Improvement, working with my Office of Domestic Affairs and the Office of Management and Budget, to review these issues, and report to me in August of this year with recommendations for actions to be taken.

The result of their effort should be a blueprint for government in the 21st century: better governance over those things that are truly Federal in nature, increased responsiveness to the needs and demands of the American people, and less taxpayer dollars spent on the administration of government.

A more productive, better managed government, with a workforce that delivers excellence—this is an important part of the legacy I plan to leave to future Presidents and the America they serve.

RONALD REAGAN

February 18, 1988.

Note: The message was not issued as a White House press release.

Message to the Congress Transmitting the Annual Economic Report of the President
February 19, 1988

To the Congress of the United States:

My first *Economic Report,* issued in 1982 after a year in office, could look only to the future for encouraging economic news. The task of rebuilding the economy was just beginning, and hard choices were being made. Inflation had begun to come down from double-digit rates, but America was mired in recession, its second in as many years. Today, however, we can point to real, solid economic progress. The policies of this Administration have spurred and sustained a record economic expansion—the longest in U.S. peacetime. Fifteen million new jobs have been created during this expansion, with strong gains widespread across industries and demographic groups. Real gross national product (GNP) has risen nearly 23 percent during these 5 years of growth.

And the accomplishments are not all in the past. Our policies will continue to contribute to rising standards of living in the years ahead. By enhancing private incentives and opportunities for work, investment, and entrepreneurship, we have laid the groundwork for growth far into the future. To ensure that the renewed energy of the private sector remains a force for growth, we must continue our efforts to bring down the Federal deficit through restraint on spending, to resist the siren song of protectionism, to support policies that foster noninflationary economic growth, and to rein in government when it threatens to make our markets less open, our industries less responsive, or our economy less flexible.

The Economic Expansion

Since November 1982, the U.S. economy has grown without interruption and without a resurgence of inflation. Only twice before in our Nation's history—but never during peacetime—has recorded economic growth continued for so long. During the current expansion a strong increase in employment, combined with low rates of inflation and higher productivity growth, have meant rising standards of living for the American people.

Employment has increased dramatically, and all demographic groups have benefited. While overall employment has risen about 15 percent since November 1982, employment of blacks has increased by more than 25 percent and employment of Hispanics by more than 40 percent. Correspondingly, unemployment rates—especially among minorities—have fallen rapidly, although those rates are still unacceptably high. I believe that all who want jobs should be able to obtain employment commensurate with their skills and abilities.

As the unemployment rate has declined by almost one-half, some have claimed that the new jobs are low-quality, dead-end positions, while others have argued that booming employment has put us on the verge of another round of inflation. Neither view is accurate. The facts show that the strongest job growth has been in the higher paid, high-skill occupations. The bulk of the new jobs created have been full-time positions in occupations that pay well. While it is true that the number of jobs in manufacturing has risen more slowly than in the service-producing sector of the economy, this is a reflection of the innovation of American business and the skill of American workers, not a sign that the United States is "deindustrializing." The share of manufacturing output in total output actually has risen over the course of the expansion, and it is now above its postwar average. However, rapid increases in manufacturing productivity have meant slower growth in employment in this sector. This strong productivity growth, in combination with the downward adjustment of the dollar's exchange rate, has lifted the competitiveness of our products on world markets. Around the globe, products "Made in the U.S.A." are becoming more common and more sought after.

Moreover, I do not believe that our economy has yet reached its full potential, or that our economic growth threatens price stability. Growth can and should continue. With sound and stable economic policies, saving and investment will be encouraged, and the Nation's productive capacity will continue to expand. I remain committed to the goal of price level stability, and I view the decline in inflation during my Administration as a major accomplishment. I would not take lightly the prospect of a resurgence of inflation. But economic growth itself will not lead to a spiral of worsening inflation; only irresponsible economic policies would do that.

Our economic projections show inflation slowing during the coming years, even as output grows at a robust average annual rate of 3.2 percent. But continued economic progress requires that policymakers adhere to forward-looking principles, pursuing the long-term best interests of the Nation through a sustained commitment to growth and stability. The prospects for growth in the immediate future have been diminished somewhat by last year's plunge in the stock market, as well as by the increase in interest rates and tightening of monetary policy during 1987. Nevertheless, I anticipate that the U.S. economy will continue to post gains in 1988, as the expansion moves through its 6th year.

The past 5 years have marked an outstanding period of economic growth in the United States. It has been unusual in its longevity, unusual for the fact that inflation has remained subdued, and unusual relative to the performance of other industrial economies. Between 1982 and 1986, American businesses, large and small, created two and one-half times as many new jobs as Japan and the major industrial countries of Europe combined. In 1987 this trend appears to have continued, as the U.S. economy again generated new jobs at a remarkable rate. The U.S. unemployment rate has fallen 5 percentage points, and now stands well below those in most other major industrialized countries, where unemployment rates have yet to recover fully from the last recession. Overall, we have not lost jobs because of foreign trade. Instead, growth-oriented policies of lower and fairer taxes, reduced interference by government, and free and open international trade have been a source of strength for the economy. Indeed, the U.S. economy has flourished, and the outlook is full of promise.

The Role of Government in the Economy

It is hard to believe that at the beginning of the 1980s the prevailing attitude toward the economy could best be described as despair. Inflation and interest rates had ratcheted higher with each successive business cycle, and, as the economy suffered through its second recession in 2 years, the goal of sustainable growth appeared increasingly elusive. Amid double-digit inflation and unemployment rates, there were calls for the Federal Government to do more and more, thereby compounding the failed policies of the past. Instead, I took government policy back to the basics, and the last 5 years of economic growth testify to the vitality of free markets and the productivity of the American people. Government intrusions in the Nation's economic life have been reduced, and the private sector has responded with an explosion of activity, creating new products and new jobs at a very rapid rate.

The Federal Government has an important role to play in the Nation's economy, but it is a limited role. As a general proposition, economic decisions should be left to the private sector, which has been our economy's strength throughout its history, or to State and local governments when the issues cannot be handled satisfactorily by the private sector. Only in issues truly national in scope is there a role for the Federal Government.

We have made efforts to restrain Federal spending, to limit it to only the government's vital functions, and those efforts have borne fruit. Last fiscal year, for the first time in 14 years, Federal outlays, after adjustment for inflation, declined. Government spending on goods and services absorbs resources that might be used better by the private sector, and any Federal outlay must be financed eventually by inflation or taxes. Because there is no free lunch, we must make the hard choices, funding only those programs that are in the best interest of the Nation, not those that happen to have the most influential lobbyists. For example, while a strong national defense is rightly the responsibility of the Federal Government, a continued proliferation of pork-barrel projects is not. America's sense of fair play is violated when hard-earned tax dollars are needlessly turned over to powerful special interests.

In the conduct of macroeconomic policies, we have turned away from the stop-and-go policies of the past. My Administration has adopted a long-term view that fiscal policy determines the division of economic activity between the public and private sectors and is not meant to respond to every rise and fall in the economic data. Similarly, monetary policy should provide adequate liquidity for sustained noninflationary growth. Together, these policies create a stable environment in which individuals and businesses can plan for the future and make the most of their economic opportunities.

For too long the Federal Government has interfered unnecessarily in private economic decisions. There is a legitimate, although limited, role for the Federal Government in certain industries—for example, in ensuring the safety and soundness of the Nation's banking and payments systems. But many government regulations impede the operation of markets, inhibit competition, or impose costs on firms and raise the prices faced by consumers, without providing commensurate benefits. Regulations that interfere with the efficient use of labor, investment, and raw materials ultimately reduce our productive potential, making this country worse off.

While my Administration has been successful in reducing many regulations and intrusions into markets, much remains to be done. We must lessen remaining disincentives to work, diminish the burden of Federal regulations, and dismantle government programs that needlessly subsidize inefficient producers. In particular, we must release financial institutions from outdated legal restraints, eliminate the remaining controls on interstate trucking, deregulate natural gas, and repeal mileage standards for new automobiles. We must resist appeals for even more government intervention that would introduce additional inefficiencies, such as requiring advance notification of layoffs and plant closings. With few exceptions, the private sector is best able to allocate resources to their most highly valued uses, and it should be allowed to do so without excessive paperwork and restrictions. That is why privatization, deregulation, and private sector initiatives have been important elements of my economic program. I believe in the inherent dynamism of the private sector, and I believe that the most constructive thing government usually can do is simply get out of the way.

The International Environment

This Administration has been a force for economic change in the United States and, by our example, in the world at large. Our proven market-oriented policies are being adopted in more and more countries around the globe, as they recognize the high costs of big government and the harmful effects of stifling the entrepreneurial spirit.

In order to enhance growth and economic opportunity, many nations have followed our lead, undertaking reductions in sky-high tax rates that diminish incentives to work, save, and produce. In addition, tax reform is becoming a worldwide movement. Just as in the United States, tax reform abroad promises to end many distortions and inefficiencies, allowing businesses and individuals to make decisions about production and investment in order to increase their economic well-being, rather than simply to reduce their tax bills.

From continent to continent, the benefits of privatization and deregulation are becoming appreciated. Even China, and perhaps now even the Soviet Union, appear to be edging toward freer economic systems. Instead of viewing private enterprise as the adversary, many governments now see it as their best hope for progress and prosperity. Developing as well as industrialized nations are reducing market rigidities and interferences, thereby expanding economic freedom and opportunity for their citizens.

In those developing countries that encourage investment and private enterprise, the ensuing economic growth should contribute to lessening their debt problems. The debt burden carried by developing countries is not just their problem; we all have a vital interest in finding solutions that promote growth and protect open international financial markets. And we will continue to work with all who display a real determination to deal with this difficult issue.

The United States has been a constructive force in the world economy, not only by demonstrating the benefits of private enterprise, but also by our commitment to free trade and international economic cooperation. In addition, this Nation's strong demands for imports helped support output growth abroad during much of this decade. The world economy has become increasingly interdependent, as trade has multiplied and financial markets have become essentially global.

To continue to reap the benefits of an open international trading system, we are committed to reducing further the barriers that interfere with the free flow of goods, services, and capital. To this end, the United States has entered into, and will continue to seek out, bilateral and multilateral agreements to lower impediments to international commerce. The Free-Trade Agreement recently negotiated with Canada is an historic accomplishment. Once the necessary implementing legislation is passed, it will establish the largest international free-trade area in the world. At the same time, in the Uruguay Round of the multilateral negotiations under the General Agreement on Tariffs and Trade, we have been working to lower trade barriers worldwide. In that forum, we have placed special emphasis on eliminating spiraling subsidies to agricultural production and harmful barriers to agricultural imports, on establishing and enforcing adequate protections for intellectual property, on liberalizing trade in services, and on ensuring evenhanded treatment of foreign investment. Through these avenues and others, we will continue to pursue the goal of free and fair trade, which can only expand opportunity and prosperity both at home and abroad.

The Challenges Ahead

The American people elected me to this office with a vision of a reinvigorated economy, and I have watched that vision become reality. The resurgence of America has confirmed my optimism. The accomplishments of the last 7 years should inspire us, but not blind us to the important challenges that remain.

Foremost among our challenges is the continued high level of Federal spending and the budget deficit. Federal receipts last year were $255 billion above their level in 1981; nevertheless, the deficit has nearly doubled since then, bloated by a $326 billion increase in outlays. Although we have succeeded recently in slowing the growth of spending, and the deficit declined by $71 billion in the last fiscal year, the deficit is still too large.

Recent progress in controlling Federal outlays notwithstanding, as a percent of GNP, outlays remain well above the postwar average. The government continues to spend too much, absorbing resources that could be put to better use by the private sector. There are several essential functions of the Federal Government, such as providing a strong national defense and ensuring an appropriate safety net for those in need, but in many areas the government's presence is oppressive and unnecessary.

Tax increases are not the key to eliminating the deficit. Some taxes are unavoidable—the necessary functions of the Federal Government must be paid for. But tax reform and the cuts that have been instituted in income tax rates represent successful efforts to find less distorting, less burdensome, and more equitable means of financing government. Undoing tax reform through tax increases would affect economic activity adversely by raising uncertainty about government policy and reducing incentives to work and produce. Rather, in coming years we should look to ways to enhance incentives for investment in future productive capacity, including reducing the tax rate on capital gains.

The Gramm-Rudman-Hollings law and our recent agreement with the Congress on a 2-year budget-trimming package have charted the course for additional deficit reduction. Those are steps in the right direction. But the budget process itself remains a major obstacle to eliminating the deficit. And I am not the only one to have noticed that the budget process is a disaster; a recent survey of Members of Congress identified it as a major source of frustration. The process is not working and it must be reformed; discipline and responsibility must be restored.

Current budget practice is to deliver a pair of mammoth bills that must be passed and signed in a matter of hours—or the government has to shut down. This is not responsible government, and I will not sign another of these behemoths. This budget process does not serve the best interests of the Nation, it does not allow sufficient review of spending priorities, and it undermines the checks and balances established by the Constitution.

So that such massive appropriations bills do not have to be an all-or-nothing proposition, I have asked for the line-item veto, a power that 43 State Governors already have. With a line-item veto, future Presidents could pare away waste and enforce budget discipline. In addition, expanded rescission powers would allow the Executive to cut unnecessary spending on programs that, in many cases, have outlived their usefulness. Finally, to ensure that balanced budgets become a permanent feature of our fiscal landscape, the legislatures of 32 States have asked for—and I endorse—a constitutional amendment to force the Federal Government to live within its means. These steps must be taken, because the current budget process is impending budget progress. By its very nature, the democratic process is often messy and unfocused. But we know that democracy works and that tough decisions can be made. We must rise to the challenge again and prove that we can craft sound budgets through a sensible process.

We also must resist efforts to push the Nation into protectionism. Our foreign trade deficit is very large, but it has turned the corner in real terms. Last year foreign trade contributed significantly to our economic growth. Moreover, further improvements are on the way. At this point especially, it would be a tragic mistake to attempt to close the trade gap by closing our markets. Isolating U.S. markets could only lead to global downward spiral in trade and economic activity.

My administration is committed to working diligently with the Congress to draft responsible trade legislation, but if that legislation is not free of harmful protectionist measures, I will veto it. Our goal is to see the trade deficit reduced in an environment of sustained economic growth and low inflation. To this end, we are working with the other major industrial countries to coordinate economic policies that sustain noninflationary economic growth, encourage an orderly reduction of international imbalances, and thereby foster stability of exchange rates.

We must maintain the confidence of foreigners and our citizens alike in the ability of the United States to generate profitable investment opportunities and to follow responsible economic policies. The vitality of free and open markets, full of opportunity and promise, is the best foundation for investment. We must see to it that our tax structures and regulations do not discourage saving and investing. We must encourage investment not only in plant and equipment, but also in the American people themselves. Education, skills, research and development—these are some of the most fruitful areas for investment; expanded knowledge enhances the productive potential of our most valuable resource, our people.

Conclusion

America is blessed with great gifts—abundant land and natural resources, a diverse and hard-working people, an unshakable tradition of democratic values. My confidence in America has been shown to be well-founded over these past few years. The economy has been revitalized, and the record peacetime economic expansion has brought with it renewed opportunities and enhanced well-being. We set ourselves a formidable task: to reduce and to rationalize the role of government in the economy. That effort has been richly rewarded. During our watch, the U.S. economy again has shown its strength.

But our job is not finished. The Federal budget must be controlled in order to build a solid foundation for future economic growth. And I will not be satisfied until all Americans share in this prosperity; there are still too many enmeshed in poverty and without jobs. We must rise to our remaining challenges, heartened by our triumphs and inspired by the resilience of a resurgent America.

RONALD REAGAN

The White House,
February 19, 1988.

Note: The message was not issued as a White House press release.

Message to the Congress Reporting Budget Deferrals
February 19, 1988

To the Congress of the United States:

In accordance with the Impoundment Control Act of 1974, I herewith report three new deferrals of budget authority totaling $3,570,665,449 and ten revised deferrals of budget authority now totaling $4,973,643,337.

The deferrals affect programs in the Departments of Agriculture, Defense-Military, Defense-Civil, Energy, Health and Human Services, and Transportation.

The details of these deferrals are contained in the attached report.

RONALD REAGAN

The White House,
February 19, 1988.

Note: The attachment detailing the deferrals was printed in the "Federal Register" of March 2.

Statement on the Designation of Caspar W. Weinberger and Andrew L. Lewis Jr., as Members of the National Economic Commission
February 19, 1988

I am today designating Caspar Weinberger and Drew Lewis to the National Economic Commission. These appointments, along with those announced today by the Republican leaders of the House and Senate, complete the current membership of the Commission.

This Commission, which was created in last year's reconciliation bill, is charged with making recommendations on reducing the Federal deficit and is to issue its report on March 1 of next year. The Commission should also examine the current budget process as part of their deliberations.

I am very pleased that these two men have agreed to lend their considerable expertise to the Commission. While Cap most recently served as my Secretary of Defense, he has had extensive government experience at OMB and HEW as well as in State government in California. He knows the budget inside and out and is familiar with a broad range of Federal programs. Drew has exhibited his many abilities in both the public and private sector; he served as my Secretary of Transportation and is currently at Union Pacific.

As I have said before, I believe when all aspects of the budget are reviewed the primary policy problem will be viewed not as a lack of revenues but an inexorable growth in spending. Over the last 7 years, revenues have increased by $250 billion, but spending has increased by $325 billion. And while defense has necessarily grown, it accounted for only $125 billion, or less than 40 percent, of the increase.

Remarks Following Discussions With Chancellor Helmut Kohl of the Federal Republic of Germany

February 19, 1988

The President. It's been a very great pleasure to meet with Chancellor Kohl again for a friendly and highly useful discussion. This year marks the 40th anniversary of a series of events that have shaped the destiny of our two countries. In 1948 the United States stepped forward and helped spark the postwar recovery of West Germany and Europe and assisted in starting the constitutional process that created a West German state. In response to Soviet challenges, we launched the Berlin airlift and aided in laying the foundation for collective security and the economic integration of Western Europe.

It was in this crucible of events that the modern relationship between the Federal Republic of Germany and the United States was forged, a relationship that has prospered and many times proven its value to both our countries. As befits good friends, the Chancellor and I have met regularly since we assumed office. Our discussions reflect the richness of our relationship and the many interests we share. I especially benefit from hearing the Chancellor's views on world problems.

Among the many subjects we discussed today was the state of the NATO alliance, including our common defense efforts and arms control strategy. I thanked the Chancellor for his support throughout the long INF negotiations and now for the treaty itself. This treaty represents a major political victory for NATO, a success far beyond what many thought possible. It carries important lessons on how successfully to negotiate arms reductions with the Soviet Union. We also reviewed progress on the NATO alliance's next arms control priorities. These include negotiations toward a 50-percent reduction in strategic arms, a verifiable global ban on chemical weapons, and redressing the serious imbalances in conventional forces in Europe.

We agreed that we must deal with the Soviet Union from a position of realism, strength, and alliance unity. And we agreed that the alliance must maintain both military strength and readiness. These are the underpinnings and preconditions of any successful dialog with the Soviet Union. Only a strong West can have a positive influence on the way in which the Soviet Union deals with other countries and with its own people; we know that a weak Western alliance cannot. The NATO summit meeting early next month will provide an opportunity to continue discussion of these important matters within the alliance as a whole.

The Chancellor and I also discussed economic and trade issues. In particular, I told the Chancellor that I supported the efforts he's made to stimulate the West German economy, and I expressed the hope that he would do more. The Chancellor, in turn, welcomed our efforts to reduce the United States Federal deficit. We both agreed on the need to avoid trade protectionism. Protectionism would be an economic disaster for both our countries.

In the course of our discussions, we also touched on a subject close to both our hearts: the city of Berlin and its brave people. We both agreed that they must be included in whatever benefits improved East-West relations may bring. We look forward to a positive response to the invitation the Western powers extended last December to the Soviet Union to join with us in taking steps to improve the lives of Berliners.

The Chancellor's visits to Washington are always welcome. We'll be seeing each other again soon at the NATO summit in Brussels. And until then, we do not say goodbye but *aufwiedersehen* [until we meet again].

Chancellor Kohl. Mr. President, ladies and gentlemen, my visit to Washington—and this is my ninth bilateral meeting with President Reagan—is a return visit to the memorable visit the President paid to Berlin and Bonn last June.

The Berlin initiative announced by you, Mr. President, was one of the points on which we focused in our conversation. I once again expressed my appreciation and gratitude to President Reagan for this initiative, and I assured him that the Federal Republic and the Federal Government will do all it can in order to make its contribution towards the success of this initiative. In the meantime, the three Western protective powers have entered into talks with the Soviet Union on this issue, and the President assured me that Secretary of State Shultz, on the occasion of his forthcoming visit to Moscow, will make it plain to his Soviet interlocutors that Berlin must be included from the very beginning in positive developments of West-East relations.

Mr. President, I might take this opportunity to express my appreciation for having issued a proclamation declaring the 6th of October, 1987, German-American Day. And I may request you to make this a permanent feature.

We had intensive exchanges on the present state of West-East relations. Never in the postwar history has the United States of America and the Soviet Union been engaged in such an intensive dialog at the highest level as in the last few years. And with the INF agreement, the third summit meeting between you, Mr. President, and General Secretary Gorbachev has for the first time in history opened the way towards genuine disarmament. And I have seized this opportunity, once again, to express my congratulations to the President on this success—the success which will be your success and which will always be linked with your Presidency.

The INF agreement is in the interest of the United States of America; it's in the interest of the Atlantic alliance; and it is, not least, also in the interest of our own country. Nobody who has objections as far as this agreement is concerned, be it here in Washington or somewhere else in the United States, can point to the Federal Republic of Germany. And that is the reason why yesterday, when I had talks and meetings with the leadership of the Senate, I pleaded in no uncertain terms in favor of the ratification of this agreement without any restricting amendments.

Mr. President, you referred to the present negotiations concerning START. The Government of the Federal Republic of Germany vigorously supports a 50-percent cut of the strategic offensive potential of either power, because this step is not only in the interest of the United States of America but it would also be in the very real interest of the Federal Republic of Germany and of Western Europe. Mr. President, we staunchly support a worldwide ban on chemical weapons, and we support the early adoption of a mandate for negotiations on conventional stability in the whole of Europe, from the Atlantic to the Urals.

In accordance with the decisions taken by the alliance in Reykjavik and in Brussels, I have supported the position that, in conjunction with the establishment of a conventional balance and the global elimination of chemical weapons, tangible and verifiable reductions of nuclear systems of shorter range should also be reached. The objective being equal ceilings, no zero resolution, no denuclearized zone—and least of all, in Europe. We were in agreement that all these disarmament questions and issues as well as the necessary measures to preserve our common security should be combined and form an overall concept for our alliance. And we think that the forthcoming NATO summit meeting must be an incentive for that and give new impulses to that effort.

We have agreed that we will remain in bilateral contact as far as all these issues are concerned. And along this line—and the President and I myself were in complete agreement on that—trust and confidence between West and East must be further developed and intensified, and this would also include the solution of regional conflicts as well as ensuring respect for human rights, particularly so in the countries of the Warsaw Pact.

Mr. President, you have just made the same point, and we are all in agreement that we will be able to face up to the tasks ahead of us. And this new phase can be mastered only when we show unity, coherence, and the closest measure of coordination and consultation. Now, Mr. President, I would like to take this opportunity here to express, as Chancellor of the Federal Republic of Germany, before the American public, that we are fully aware of the fact that the Federal Republic of Germany knows that only together, with their allies, and only together with the support of all the free nations of Western Europe and the United States of America, will it be possible to attain its legitimate aim of easing, in the interest of the people, the consequences of the division of our country and to make the frontier between East and West more permeable. We are belonging to the West, and that is the way it will be also in the future.

Mr. President, I came here not only in my capacity as Chancellor of the Federal Republic of Germany but also as the Chairman and the President of the European Community. I was able to report to you about the successful conclusion of this summit meeting—the European Community—we had a week ago in Brussels and the measures we agreed upon there, particularly the restriction in the limitation of agricultural production and our commitment to the maintenance and to the support of the common policy favoring continued free trade all over the world—were some of the main positions we have taken there. And I also assured you that we will certainly not adopt a tax on oils and fats.

Mr. President, it has been a reassuring experience in all the visits I paid to you here in the White House, that as far as our commercial relations, trans-Atlantic commercial and economic relations are concerned, we have always renewed our commitment to the concept of a free trade and to rejection of protectionism. That this is part of the spirit in which we are facing these tasks and in which we will be able to live up to the tasks of the future.

Mr. President, once again, I thank you very much for the extremely friendly atmosphere for our exchanges and for the support I've been receiving from you, from the members of your Cabinet, and the members of your staff. These have been 2 short days I spent here in Washington, but I think these were 2 good days. And I think it is this spirit in which we will go on working also in the future together. Thank you.

The President. Mr. Chancellor, your suggestion during your last visit for a U.S.-German Youth Exchange Council has resulted in the recent establishment of a body of prominent Americans and Germans who have accepted the challenge to expand youth exchanges between our two countries. I fully support the work of this youth exchange council and share your strong personal commitment to advancing mutual understanding, particularly between the younger generations in our two countries. I am, therefore, especially pleased to be able today to exchange with you, in the presence of Director Wick and Professor Weidenfeld, the two coordinators of U.S.-German cooperation, copies of the documents establishing the U.S.-German Youth Exchange Council.

Chancellor Kohl. Mr. President, I think what we have just done is more important than anything else we could have possibly done. We discussed the issues, the great international issues, but what we have done here concerns the future. It relates to the next generations, and I think they will form their opinion and their judgment about what we have done by measuring us against this background. And I think they will enable us to live up and to stand up to that measurement if we will be able to go on along this line. Thank you very much.

Note: The President spoke at 1:31 p.m. in the East Room at the White House. In his closing remarks, he referred to Charles Z. Wick, Director of the U.S. Information Agency, and Werner Weidenfeld, Coordinator of German-American Cooperation. The Chancellor spoke in German, and his remarks were translated by an interpreter. Earlier, the President and the Chancellor met in the Oval Office and then attended a luncheon in the Residence.

Designation of Michael R. Farley as Chairperson of the National Council on Vocational Education
February 19, 1988

The President today designated Michael R. Farley as Chairperson of the National Council on Vocational Education. He would succeed J. Fernando Niebla.

Since 1965 Mr. Farley has been president of Farley and Associates, a company dealing with family and business insurance and estate and income tax planning for small businesses.

Mr. Farley graduated from the University of Arizona (B.S., 1967) and the American College of Life Underwriters (C.L.U., 1972). He served in the U.S. Army Signal Corps, 1967–1969. Mr. Farley was born March 6, 1944, in Los Angeles, CA. He is married, has three children, and resides in Tucson, AZ.

Radio Address to the Nation on the Federal Budget
February 20, 1988

My fellow Americans:

This week I transmitted to Congress our proposed budget for 1989. This budget fulfills the second-year obligations of a bipartisan agreement I hammered out last November with the leaders of Congress. We then, after arduous negotiations, agreed on a plan to reduce Federal deficit spending by over $75 billion in 2 years. If Congress upholds its commitments and stands firm against pressures for increased spending—pressures that reached a peak during election years—solid results will be forthcoming.

And progress already has been made. If our proposed budget is enacted, deficit spending will have dropped from $221 billion in fiscal year 1986 to $130 billion in fiscal year 1989. As a proportion of gross national product, it will have been cut by more than half since 1983. The legislative and executive branches, by living up to our commitments of last November, are demonstrating the kind of responsible leadership expected by the electorate.

The budget we've transmitted is true to that spirit. It reduces the level of deficit spending while at the same time holds the line against any general tax increase. It remains firm in our commitments to essential domestic programs. It also includes funding for the minimum defense program needed to keep our country safe and necessary to honor our commitments to our friends and allies. Anything less would not only jeopardize our national security but also dim prospects for further negotiated agreements with our adversaries.

We've proposed a trim budget that keeps the lid on spending and yet still recognizes that some increases are justified. For example, we're actually calling for Congress to spend substantially more on education, combating AIDS, the war against drugs, and improving air safety, while keeping discretionary domestic spending within predetermined limits.

The long-term solution to the plague of deficit spending, however, is not prudence this year or next. What's needed is reform that will bring discipline and accountability to the budget process. Exemplifying the shortcomings, last year the Federal budget was slapped together into a single behemoth bill and delivered to me hours before the Federal Government was due to run out of money. I was faced with the decision to either sign, without time for careful consideration, or see the Federal Government shut down. I pledged during the State of the Union, after plopping down 43 pounds of paper sent to me by Congress, that I would never sign another catchall continuing resolution. I'm pleased that at least 34 Senators and a good number of Congressmen, including many in the leadership, have indicated that they, too, do not want a repeat of last year's budget mayhem.

Make no mistake, we have the opportunity to put our fiscal house in order and to reform the budget process. We've proven time and again that, by working together, partisanship can be put aside and progress can be made when the national interest is at stake. It took cooperation from both sides of the aisle, for example, to put in place an economic recovery program that has given this country the longest peacetime expansion in history. Inflation and interest rates have been kept down. Family income is up. And we've created over 15 million new jobs since the recovery began.

Being mindful of the suffering that comes with unemployment, that last figure is a matter of particular pride for me. And as our economy has grown, unemployment has dropped to its lowest level since 1979. But that statement doesn't come near to describing the success we've enjoyed. Today more people have jobs and a higher percentage of our work force is employed than ever before. Since the recovery began, we've created more new jobs than in all of Western Europe and Japan combined. And even the meaning of unemployment figures is sometimes not fully understood. Our 7 million unemployed citizens are often thought of as people who have lost their jobs, as they're sometimes described in the media. In fact, less than half of the unemployed are job-losers. Fifty-five percent are new entrants, mainly young people looking for their first jobs; reentrants, individuals who left the work force, perhaps to raise a family, and are now seeking to get back in; or job-leavers, who voluntarily left their jobs to change locations or occupations.

We, of course, need to remain concerned about each and every citizen who is seeking work and should not be satisfied until everyone who wants a job—a good job—has one. One person enduring the pressures and frustrations of unemployment is too many. That is why responsible Federal spending and taxing policies—policies that foster growth and expand opportunity for all our citizens—are so important. That is what the budget that I have just sent to Congress is all about.

Until next week, thanks for listening, and God bless you.

Note: The President spoke at 12:06 p.m. from Camp David, MD.

Toast at a White House Dinner Honoring the Nation's Governors
February 21, 1988

I think there are at least two of us in this room who have a great feeling of nostalgia right about now, because it isn't the last time for you, but it is for us under these same circumstances. And we're going to miss this very much. We're delighted, Nancy and I, to welcome you once again to the White House. Seven years ago some of you were our first guests for a state dinner, and since then I've thought that was the right way to begin. I'm wondering now if we might have started something. I don't want to tie my successor's hands. So, let me say that as a Governor I always thought that before a new President began entertaining heads of state from around the world he should show that first things come first and spend an evening with the heads of our 50 sovereign States and our territories.

We've just finished a year-long celebration: the bicentennial of the drafting of the Constitution. You know, the framers had a way of referring to the States as opposed to the Federal Government. They said "the people." For example, James Madison once noted that "the people" called the Constitutional Convention, meaning the States did, and Congress just sort of tagged along trying to catch up and take credit. But there's a wisdom in saying "the people" to mean the States, a wisdom that until a few years ago was too often forgotten. The founders gave us a Federal system in the first place, because the best government of, by, and for the people is not the National Government but State government.

In the past 7 years, we've tried to return that seminal wisdom to Washington. We've taken federalism seriously. We've lived and breathed it, not just paid lip service to it. Federalism has been an integral part of our policies. For example, we've done our best to make certain that the Federal Government doesn't increase taxes and drain away the revenue base on which State and local governments depend. We've loosened Federal grant guidelines and regulations in general and given States more room to experiment in areas like welfare reform that were once tightly controlled. And we've worked in partnership with you to improve the quality of education.

We've also remembered that part of federalism is recognizing that the States are laboratories of democracy. And so, we've tried to get Congress to follow the lead of the States in one of the most important matters before the Government: the Federal budget. You know, I remember it used to be thought of as sophisticated to say that the Federal Government was so much wiser than State government, and that was why it should be kind of a big brother to the States, telling them what to do and how to do it. Well, the Federal budget process should put an end to that myth once and for all. Not one of you would put up with the mess that we have here in Washington at budget time.

Federal debt, after taking out for inflation, held steady or declined from the late forties until 1974, when it started to soar. Our budget system of checks and balances has become unchecked and unbalanced. That's why I want the Federal Government to follow the lead of so many of the States and give the American people a balanced budget amendment and the next President a line-item veto.

Now, before I take my seat, I ask all of you to join me in raising a glass to one of America's outstanding Governors and your chairman—he's feeling lonely right now; his State just lost half its population—[*laughter*]—and to another distinguished Governor and your vice chairman: to John Sununu and Jerry Baliles.

Note: The President spoke at 9:07 p.m. in the State Dining Room. Governors John H. Sununu of New Hampshire and Gerald L. Baliles of Virginia were chairman and vice chairman, respectively, of the association. In his closing remarks, the President referred to the departure of journalists from New Hampshire following the Presidential primary.

Remarks to Members of the National Governors' Association
February 22, 1988

Thank you all very much, and welcome to the White House again. It was wonderful to see you all at our dinner here last night. As you know, I recently visited Mexico to meet with President De la Madrid. And I was reminded in that visit of when I was

Governor of California and had been asked by the then-President to go down and represent him there. And like many of you, I've traveled to other countries, also, than the United States. But on this first visit to Mexico, I gave a speech to a rather large audience and then sat down to rather unenthusiastic and scattered applause. And I was embarrassed and tried to cover all of that, because what made it worse was that the next speaker up was speaking in Spanish, which I didn't understand, but he was getting interrupted virtually every line with most enthusiastic applause. So, I started clapping before anyone else and longer than anyone else until our Ambassador leaned over and said to me, "I wouldn't do that if I were you. He's interpreting your speech." [*Laughter*] Well, as I said last night, it's nice to be talking to not one but almost half a hundred heads of state, and with no interpretation required—at least not usually.

I'd like to pick up today on a subject from last night: giving government back to the people, giving many of the responsibilities not specifically stated in the Constitution as Federal functions back to the States and localities where they belong. I remember when we first came to this town over 7 years ago. When you started to talk about federalism, you sometimes felt like a lone voice crying in the wilderness.

It's like the time Abraham Lincoln found his entire Cabinet, with the exception of one member, ranged against him on an issue. Lincoln had a way at times like that of stopping action for the moment and telling a story—I think that habit sort of goes with this job. So, Lincoln told the story of a man at an Illinois revival meeting who fell asleep halfway through the preacher's sermon. And the preacher was getting really inspired, and he challenged the congregation, "All of you who are on the Lord's side, stand up." And of course, everyone stood up, except for one man who was still sound asleep. And then the preacher in a bellowing voice called out, "And all of you who are on the side of the devil, stand up." At that point, the man woke up, arose, and was standing there all alone. And he said, "I didn't exactly understand the question, but I'll stand by you, parson, till the last," he said. "But it seems to me we're in a hopeless minority." [*Laughter*]

Well, we're no longer a hopeless minority. Together, you and I, over the past 7 years, have begun to return balance to the relationship between the Federal Government and the States. This past October, I signed an Executive order that restricts the Federal Government from preempting State laws and requires that all proposed policies and legislation comply with the principles of federalism. And I commend Governor Sununu and the National Governors' Association in your efforts to examine ways—including constitutional amendments—to restore the balance of power between the National Government and the States. Federalism, as arcane and maybe even antiquated as it may sound to some, is gaining momentum, with success following success. As States and localities take on more of their rightful responsibilities, they're showing that they can teach the all-wise Federal Government a thing or two.

Not one of our efforts of the past will be more crucial than working to ensure the protection of our children, families, and neighborhoods. As I said in the State of the Union, one of our most important responsibilities is to provide the very best opportunities for the generation that will follow us. Isn't that the dream of every parent, that their children's future will be even better than theirs? Our job is to make sure that government policies are geared to protecting and nurturing our most precious natural resource: our children.

Education, of course, is an essential element. One can't read the writings of our Founding Fathers today without being impressed by the faith that they put in education—the faith they had that an educated populace would guarantee the success of this great experiment in democracy that they were undertaking. Such a strong faith in education must have been based not just on wishful thinking but on sound observation, observation that the American style of education—not just for the few, not just for the elite, but for all—was working. And so, one can't help but believe they knew what they were doing when they quite consciously left the responsibility to educate the

American people up to the States.

I suppose it's the destiny of every second generation or so to think for awhile that maybe they're wiser than our Founding Fathers. And it's the destiny of the generation that follows to realize that this almost certainly is not true and to try to bring the Nation back to its first principles. The mystique of Washington, of big government, held sway for 40 years; and even as the dollars spent on education increased by over 3,000 percent, the quality of education in this country precipitously declined. It seems odd to us now that people would actually believe that a collection of bureaucrats sitting in a building in Washington, DC, could actually do a better job designing and running our children's education than the thousands of communities and millions of parents who know intimately their children's needs.

In the last few years, we've arrested the decline in American education by returning to the fundamental common sense of our Founding Fathers and the fundamental common sense of parents across this nation. The States have begun to reassert their authority in education, and many of you Governors have been leading the charge. And with this new renaissance of federalism has come a wealth of new ideas, innovation, and experiment, but more needs to be done.

Secretary [of Education] Bennett makes, I think, an interesting analogy. He says that if you serve a child a rotten hamburger in America, Federal, State, and local agencies will investigate you, summon you, close you down, whatever. But if you provide a child with a rotten education, nothing happens, except that you're liable to be given more money to do it with. Well, we've discovered that money alone isn't the answer. I'd like to mention a few steps that could be taken now—in 1988—to drastically improve the education our children are getting. These are, of course, primarily matters for local and State authorities to resolve, but I'd like to use my bully pulpit to urge a few changes.

Now, nothing is more important to good education than good teachers, yet in most States unnecessary regulations and requirements block talented people from entering the field. Governor Kean of New Jersey recognized the problem and instituted a new alternative certification program that has been an unqualified success in opening up the teaching profession to all those who have something to offer, increasing the number of applicants to teaching jobs, and improving the quality of teachers. We also need more accountability in our educational system. That means merit pay at all levels of the system so that those who are doing a good job are encouraged and rewarded. It also means giving parents a greater choice of the school their child will attend. I've long supported various mechanisms to increase parental choice, including tuition tax credits, vouchers, and magnet schools. It's now clear from the experience of many cities and school districts that increased choice leads to increased competition and better schools—so, better teachers, more accountability, but also better content.

"A Nation at Risk" said our high school students should have 4 years of English and 3 years of math, science, and social studies. Many States have moved in the direction of these requirements, but only 3 States have adopted them. In any case, requiring that students take the key subjects is only the first step; we need to make sure that our students study the basics, but also raise the standards in those courses. Now, it's not for the Federal Government to specify content of curricula, but I urge educators and citizens to take a look at Bill Bennett's recent proposed model high school curriculum and to make sure that our schools are giving students as rich and challenging a curriculum as they deserve and as equality of opportunity demands.

Perhaps the greatest test of federalism is how we meet the urgent need for welfare reform—how successful we are in fashioning local and community solutions to problems that would destroy families, or worse, keep families from forming in the first place. With a variety of innovative programs, the States are moving forward to meet this challenge, and I think we have reason to be optimistic that in the diversity of these approaches we may find new answers. And that's why I strongly support the Brown-Michel bill on welfare reform. This cost-effective proposal allows for States to demonstrate their ideas for reform of a system that is just not working for poor people. And I know that many of you have already developed demonstration programs, and we hope that more of you will do so.

Another problem for which the States are looking for solutions is child care. Once again, the Brown-Michel bill will permit you to develop your own ideas on child care, ideas that will treat child care in the way that is best for you and the families in your communities, instead of having the Federal Government jump in.

And now, if I might, I'd just like to sound a note of caution. It's natural in politics—when there's a perceived need in the country, when people are calling out for solutions, they look to government first. Often government has a role, a crucial and a necessary one. Still, maybe it's my conservative bent, but I can't help but feel uneasy sometimes. Some describe a conservative as he who would rather sit and think, and others describe him as someone who would rather just sit.

A program on PBS some time ago described in devastating detail how our current welfare program, originally designed to raise people out of poverty, has become a crippling poverty trap, destroying families and condemning generations to a dependency. Economist Walter Williams, in "The State Against Blacks," details how many laws and regulations—also originally designed with a progressive social purpose—have just the opposite effect. They keep the poor poor. Now, much of the push for child care is designed to rectify the ills of earlier programs, and many of these efforts are timely and good. But in this area, more than any other, government should tread carefully, humbly, because we're dealing with the most fundamental element of human society: the family.

Of course, one of the best things we could do for families is obliterate drug use in America. Our society's come a long way in 8 years, from do your own thing to just say no. Again, States are taking the lead in helping to make our society intolerant to drug use with stiff penalties and sure and swift punishment for offenders.

And one final word if I may. Over the last year, many of you've been traveling abroad as sort of special trade emissaries, and you've done a tremendous job working to improve trade and open foreign markets to American goods. Well, at this moment, we have before us an unprecedented opportunity to demonstrate to the world just what we mean by free and fair trade. I'm talking about the Canada free trade agreement—the first ever of its kind and scope.

At this moment in history, we have a choice. We can go the way that some are proposing—threats, tariffs and retaliation, and a shrinking world trade system, or openness, expansion, and freer and fairer trade, bringing an upward cycle of prosperity to all who participate. The first leads inevitably and inexorably to Smoot-Hawley. And the second—well, I mentioned our Founding Fathers earlier.

Their primary purpose in calling for a Constitutional Convention in 1787 was to solve the trade disputes between the States that were tearing our young nation apart. Fighting had actually broken out between some States. Blood had been shed. Perhaps as great as the political unity they achieved in Philadelphia in 1787 was the economic breakthrough—the principles that would enable America to become the world's largest free trade zone, a continental economy.

We now have the chance to expand that free trade zone to include our largest trading partner: Canada. And I hope I can count on your support for this historic agreement. As with our Founding Fathers, it will, in many cases, mean transcending the special interests of the moment—no matter how valid they may be in themselves—and looking to the broader interest not just of one State or not just of the United States, but of an entire world whose freedom and prosperity depend on an open and expanding cycle of free trade.

Well, I've gone on long enough. You know, there's a story about Henry Clay, the Senator from Kentucky known for his biting wit. One time in the Senate, one Senator in the middle of a seemingly interminable speech turned to Clay and said, "You, sir, speak for the present generation, but I speak for posterity." And Clay interrupted him and said, "Yes, and you seem resolved to speak until the arrival of your audience." [*Laughter*]

Well, I'll cut it shorter than that. Thank you very much, and God bless you all.

Note: The President spoke at 10:03 a.m. in the East Room at the White House. In his remarks, he referred to Gov. John H. Sununu of New Hampshire, chairman of the association.

Message to the Senate Transmitting the Canada-United States Legal Assistance Treaty

February 22, 1988

To the Senate of the United States:

With a view to receiving the advice and consent of the Senate to ratification, I transmit herewith the Treaty between the Government of the United States of America and the Government of Canada on Mutual Legal Assistance in Criminal Matters, with Annex, signed at Quebec City on March 18, 1985. I transmit also, for the information of the Senate, the report of the Department of State with respect to the Treaty.

The Treaty is one of a series of modern mutual legal assistance treaties being negotiated by the United States in order to counter more effectively criminal activities. The Treaty should be an effective tool to prosecute a wide variety of modern criminals including members of drug cartels, "white-collar criminals," and terrorists. The Treaty is self-executing and utilizes existing statutory authority.

The Treaty provides for a broad range of cooperation in criminal matters. Mutual assistance available under the treaty includes: (1) the taking of testimony or statements of witnesses; (2) the provision of documents, records and evidence; (3) the execution of requests for searches and seizures; (4) the serving of documents; and (5) the provision of assistance in proceedings relating to the forefeiture of the proceeds of crime, restitution to the victims of crime, and the collection of fines imposed as a sentence in a criminal prosecution.

I recommend that the Senate give early and favorable consideration to the Treaty and give its advice and consent to ratification.

RONALD REAGAN

The White House,
February 22, 1988.

Address to the Citizens of Western Europe

February 23, 1988

This is Ronald Reagan, speaking to you, the citizens of the North Atlantic alliance, over the satellite channels of WORLDNET and the Voice of America. In just a few days, I'll be flying to Europe to meet with the heads of the governments of our North Atlantic allies, and this will be our first meeting since General Secretary Gorbachev and I signed the Intermediate Nuclear Forces agreement in Washington in December. That agreement represented a step toward world peace and world freedom, and it was a major victory for the Atlantic alliance. So, at next week's meeting we'll celebrate the success of a policy we launched over 8 years ago, and we'll ask ourselves, What next? Today I'd like to share with you some thoughts we in America have about the alliance, the INF agreement, and the road ahead.

The Atlantic alliance is the core of America's foreign policy and of America's own security. Preservation of a peaceful, free, and democratic Europe is essential to the preservation of a peaceful, free, and democratic United States. If our fellow democracies are not secure, we cannot be secure. If you are threatened, we're threatened. If you're not at peace, we cannot be at peace. An attack on you is an attack on us. This is not simply a matter of treaty language, important as treaty language is. It is an enduring reality—as enduring as the reality that a threat to the security of the State of Maine or New York or California is a threat to the security of all 50 American States. Simply put: An attack on Munich is the same as an attack on Chicago.

We Americans did not come easily or willingly to the lesson of how closely America's peace and freedom are tied to Europe's. We had a tradition dating back to President Washington of avoiding permanent alliances. And yet twice in this century when peace and freedom were under siege in Europe, one way or another, we found ourselves part of the struggle. At the end of the Second World War, we hoped that peace, freedom, and democracy were at last secure in Europe forever. Even though the United States had a monopoly for a number of years on nuclear weapons, we did not seek to exploit the advantage for territorial or any other kind of gain. We went home, took off our uniforms, put on our civilian clothes, and got back to the normal life with our families and our communities. Europeans often say that we Americans are naive. Well, four decades ago, perhaps we were.

Soon we learned that the postwar world was not to be as we, through all those years of fighting, had prayed it would be. We watched with growing apprehension and dismay as the Soviet Union turned its back on the commitment made at Yalta to conduct free and open elections in Eastern Europe. Throughout Eastern Europe, the Red Army remained a fully mobilized army of occupation. And there were attempts to subvert the democracies of Western Europe and then the Soviet adventure in Greece, not unlike what the Soviets are doing today in Central America.

As Western Europe, with help from our Marshall plan, rebuilt, all our nations began to face the nature of the Soviet threat to the democracies. And so, beginning with the Brussels treaty in 1948, which established the Western European Union, and then the North Atlantic treaty 1 year later, which included Canada and the United States as well as other European nations, we drew together for our common safety and peace. As President Harry Truman said when he signed the North Atlantic treaty: Through this partnership "we seek to establish freedom from aggression and from the use of force in the North Atlantic community." And he added: "This is the area which has been at the heart of the last two world conflicts. To protect this area against war will be a long step toward permanent peace in the whole world."

Well, peace has been the alliance's goal, the purpose of its forces and its strategies. And for almost 40 years, peace has been its achievement—an unprecedented period of European peace in which we in the democracies have lived in freedom and prospered. NATO's strategy for peace has always been simple: Prevent aggression before it starts. Be strong enough, be determined enough so that no adversary would think even for a moment that war might pay.

At first, NATO's atomic monopoly gave peace a nuclear umbrella of protection. Later, a more flexible response became necessary so that we could answer any attack in kind. Yes, strategic nuclear weapons as well as other nuclear weapons were and are still necessary. As President Mitterrand said in December: "Between East and West, world peace has been guaranteed by nuclear balance." But we recognized in the mid-sixties that the strategic nuclear balance alone is not sufficient to keep the peace. The alliance's adversaries must not believe that our only possible response to a limited attack is to begin an intercontinental nuclear exchange. If they do, they may doubt that we would risk such a response and be tempted to test us.

That, of course, is why the Soviet deployment of SS–20 intermediate-range nuclear missiles starting in the late seventies was such a threatening challenge. The SS–20 wasn't just a new weapon but an entirely new level of threat to which NATO had nothing comparable. Without provocation or warning, the Soviet Union was shaking the fundamental structure of European peace.

How did the West respond? In 1977 Chancellor Schmidt brought the Soviet SS–20 threat to the forefront of our attention. In December 1979 NATO made the dual-track decision. First, the United States would negotiate with the Soviets, attempting to persuade them to withdraw the SS–20's or to agree to the lowest possible equal U.S. and Soviet levels. Second, as long as the Soviets kept these missiles, NATO would go ahead and deploy a limited number of its own INF missiles—the U.S. Pershing II's and ground-launched cruise missiles. The aim of this decision was not to fill Europe with more missiles; just the opposite. As Valery Giscard d'Estaing has said: Its "preferred goal was to compel the Soviet Union to eliminate the SS–20's."

And now we have succeeded. It wasn't easy. Europeans know that only too well. You saw the many demonstrations, many of them violent, protesting deployment. You heard the angry voices accusing the United States and NATO of warlike intentions. You went through election campaigns fought over deployment. You watched as the Soviets, playing to pacifist sentiments, rejected my 1981 proposal for the total elimination of longer range INF missiles as unrealistic and not serious; later, walked out of negotiations and—both before and after they returned—issued one ultimatum after another. You witnessed the courage of your leaders as they stood by the alliance decision, above all, the leaders of the five basing countries: Britain, Belgium, Italy, the Netherlands, and the Federal Republic of Germany.

Now many of the same people who fought NATO's policy every step of the way claim credit for its success. The antideployment forces have won, they say. Well, Prime Minister Thatcher had it right when she said recently that, in her words, "but for the firmness of NATO," to go forward with deployment, "the INF agreement would never have been signed." And as she noted: "The SS–20's would still have been up, and we should have had no means of persuading the Soviets of taking them down." And it is not just SS–20's that will come down but SS–4's and the Soviet shorter range INF missiles, the SS–12's and SS–23's, which themselves were a growing threat to NATO's security, capable of carrying conventional or chemical as well as nuclear warheads. Yes, the INF agreement is a victory for NATO. It should be a lesson to NATO's critics.

I recognize that not everyone is completely at ease with the agreement. Some worry about the Soviet conventional and chemical advantage and that removing the Pershing II's and ground-launched cruise missiles would leave Western Europe more vulnerable to these Soviet forces. Some are concerned about the link between the United States and European pillars of NATO. With these weapons gone, they ask: Is peace still secure?

Well, I'm happy to say that the answer is yes! The approximately 4,000 nuclear weapons that will remain in Europe are a strong link between the pillars of NATO, as are the more than 300,000 American servicemen and women and their families who live and work in Europe. And those nuclear weapons that will remain are dispersed throughout NATO, not concentrated in one country, and do not, by the way, put any one country at special risk. Ensuring the peace requires that these nuclear weapons stay where they are until we can achieve a better balance of conventional forces on the continent. Because of them and the Soviet knowledge that we have them, we can maintain the balance that maintains the peace.

You see, the United States remains steadfastly committed to the NATO strategy of flexible response, and we in the United States will do our part to ensure that NATO maintains all the modern forces, both conventional and nuclear, needed to uphold that strategy. After all, our goal is not a nuclear-free or a tank-free or an army-free Europe but a war-free Europe. A war-free Europe is what we have today; a war-free Europe is what we want to preserve.

As we look to NATO's next decade, we must make sure that all of our forces for peace, including our nuclear forces, remain modern and effective. This will require constant work, because military machinery wears out or becomes obsolete. And it will require being smart about the weapons and equipment we develop and buy, so we get the best value for our money. I'm pretty tightfisted myself, so I've been glad to see that NATO is taking efficiency seriously.

Better coordination among West European nations will also help in defense planning or in other areas, as we've seen in the Persian Gulf. And let me add that we in America welcome multilateral and bilateral defense cooperation among our European partners of the sort that the Western European Union and the Germans and the French and other governments have demonstrated within the overall framework of the alliance. Such cooperation and coordination are essential to strengthening the European pillar of the alliance and, thereby, the alliance as a whole.

We Americans will do our part in keeping the alliance strong. Our troops will stay in Europe, a guarantee that our destiny is coupled with yours. We will keep our forces, including the strategic nuclear umbrella, strong and up to date.

And we will press forward with our Strategic Defense Initiative. I can't help noting that initially there was great confusion about our SDI program. Some called it Star Wars. They said it would dangerously expand the reach of American arms into space. But now the recognition has grown that this technology will not expand the threat of arms but limit it. It will protect and defend people. SDI holds the promise of lifting from mankind the burden of nuclear terror and making this a safer world.

The United States is not alone in pursuing a strategic defense. In the last decade the Soviets have spent $200 billion on strategic defense. It would be a fatal mistake not to pursue this program. Even before it becomes leakproof, strategic defense will strengthen deterrence. It can make anyone who might think about disabling the West with a first strike think again, because it will undermine Soviet confidence in the military success of an attack.

But keeping our forces ready and able is hardly the only item on the alliance agenda. We want a safer world, one with smaller forces and fewer weapons while maintaining the essential balance that keeps the peace. That's the goal of the strategic arms reduction talks underway now in Geneva—a 50-percent reduction in the strategic arsenals of both the United States and the Soviet Union.

We in the alliance have also long sought to redress the imbalances in conventional forces in Europe. We also want greater openness, more confidence, and increased security, which benefit all nations. The first priority of any new negotiations must be to eliminate conventional capabilities for surprise attack and large-scale offensives. The United States hopes that the Warsaw Pact countries will join with the Atlantic allies in focusing on correcting the imbalances, above all, in tanks and artillery, which are the most threatening ground forces. A safer peace requires that neither side be able to mount a massive conventional attack without warning.

More balance between East-West conventional forces will require substantial reductions by the Warsaw Pact countries—bigger reductions than any we might make, because their forces are so much bigger and more threatening. And we must be able to verify that they are keeping their forces at the negotiated levels. This may sound ambitious, but we've learned from the alliance's success with the INF treaty that solidarity, determination, and perseverance can turn ambitious dreams into realities.

Finally, we're seeking in arms control talks in Geneva an effective, verifiable, and truly global ban on all chemical weapons. Strategic arms reductions, conventional arms balance, an effective ban on chemical weapons—these are our post-INF negotiating priorities. And yet as we approach these negotiations, we again hear the voices that call on us to turn back from our strategy of combining strength with negotiations. They say the Soviets under a new leader have changed—in the era of *glasnost* we can trust the Soviets more.

But can we afford to forget that the policy called *glasnost* is separated from the era of the gulag by fewer years than NATO has existed? In fact, the policy called *glasnost* coexists today with the reality of political repression in the Soviet Union. We cannot afford to forget that we are dealing with a political system, a political culture, and a political history going back many decades, even centuries. Swings between *glasnost* and the gulag are not new or even peculiar to the Soviet regime. In history they recurred again and again as the throne passed from czar to czar, and even within the reign of a single czar. We cannot afford to mortgage our security to the assessed motives of particular individuals or to the novel approaches of a new leadership, even if we wish them well. We must stick with the strategy of strength and dialog that has kept the peace and brought us a remarkable achievement in the INF treaty.

Let's remember the issue for NATO is not today or tomorrow; it's what will Europe look like in 15 years? The Soviets talk about openness in international affairs. Last year at the Berlin Wall, I noted that there are simple ways for them to demonstrate that they are serious about openness. They can begin on the border of East and West. They can allow expanded commercial air service to Berlin so it can become one of the chief aviation hubs of central Europe. They can join Britain, France, and the United States in bringing more international meetings to Berlin. They can allow young people from East Berlin to visit the Western sectors and take part in cultural events there. They can join the Western sector powers in allowing and encouraging international sports events to take place throughout the city.

And they can tear down the Berlin Wall. To the Soviets today I say: I made my Berlin proposals almost 9 months ago. The people of Berlin and all of Europe deserve an answer. Make a start. Set a date, a specific date, when you will tear down the Wall. And on that date, bring it down. This would be an impressive demonstration of a true commitment to openness.

Throughout Eastern Europe and within the Soviet Union itself, we look for the Soviet leadership to demonstrate its seriousness about its Helsinki commitments to human rights. We look for an end to Soviet sponsorship of regional conflicts and for the Soviets to allow more and more people-to-people exchanges between East and West. These are pillars on which an enduring improvement in relations must be built.

For you see, the basic differences between East and West have nothing to do with the level of arms. We do not distrust each other because we're armed; we're armed because we distrust each other. It's a question of values, of beliefs, of moral principles. You can see it in a thousand ways. How did the Soviets treat Germany and the German people after the war? How did the democracies? How do the Soviets treat Third World nations like Afghanistan or Ethiopia today? How does the West? What is the condition of Eastern Europe today? What is that of Western Europe? Or take a simpler thing: What do the Soviets mean by words like democracy, freedom, and peace? Not, I'm sorry to say, what we mean.

Negotiations between East and West do not imply moral equivalency of our two systems or ways of life. We must never forget to say this publicly and say it repeatedly: So long as the difference between East and West is the difference between oppression and freedom; so long as Europeans in the East cannot worship and speak freely; so long as gigantic armies are poised in Eastern Europe, facing west, training to attack first—just as NATO's troops are trained only to defend when attacked; so long as this is the state of our world, NATO's strategy and reason for being must remain to stop aggression before it happens.

I mentioned earlier what President Truman said when he signed the North Atlantic treaty. On that occasion he also noted, speaking of the alliance, that "we are like a group of householders, living in the same locality, who decide to express their community of interests by entering into a formal association for their mutual protection." During the past four decades we in the alliance have, if anything, grown even closer together.

Today, in a sense, we live not simply in the same locality but in a single house, a house that may someday include all of mankind among its residents: the house of democracy. "In my Father's house are many mansions." In the house of democracy are many languages and many national heritages, but one ideal: the dignity of man, or as Abraham Lincoln said, the belief that "no man is good enough to govern another without that other's consent." All of us honor this truth. All of us are united in defending it. We have raised high the roof beam of this great structure of an alliance to shelter that truth from all the winds that blow and all the bears and wolves that prowl.

Yes, the Atlantic community is the house of democracy. The Atlantic alliance is the guardian of Europe's greatest legacy to the ages—human freedom and democratic rule. This is the challenge before the alliance now: to remain strong so that generations to come will know peace and freedom just as we do. Thank you, and God bless you.

Note: The President spoke at 9 a.m. from the Map Room at the White House. The address was broadcast live by the U.S. Information Agency's Voice of America and WORLDNET television.

Letter Accepting the Resignation of James H. Webb, Jr., as Secretary of the Navy
February 23, 1988

Dear Jim:

It is with regret that I accept your resignation as Secretary of the Navy, effective February 22, 1988.

During the past four years, you have served our country with honor and courage, just as you have throughout your distinguished career. As my first Assistant Secretary of Defense for Reserve Affairs, you played a major role in revitalizing the reserve components of our Armed Forces. You were instrumental in restoring confidence and pride in one of our most noble national traditions—the concept of the American citizen-soldier.

Since taking the helm a year ago as Secretary of the Navy, you continued to press forward the highest standards of excellence throughout the Navy and Marine Corps. From the most remote outposts to the lecture halls of Annapolis, your commitment to the quality of our military capability and the well-being of our men and women in uniform has been undivided.

As your service to this Administration comes to a close, I want to thank you for the selflessness and loyalty that you have always personified. In the end, it is these qualities that will ensure that freedom endures in this generation and in every generation to come.

Godspeed in all your endeavors.

Sincerely,

RONALD REAGAN

February 22, 1988

Dear Mr. President:

Over the past three months the Department of Defense has been struggling to implement a mandated 33 billion dollar reduction of the FY 89 budget approved by you last year. The Navy Department was directed to absorb a significant share of this reduction, which eventually became approximately 12 billion dollars.

Like many others, I have serious concerns regarding the entire budget reduction process. First, the Department of Defense has been required to absorb cuts at a ratio almost twice as great as non-defense programs. Second, many Defense reductions themselves have been made in the wrong areas, and without clear strategic thought. I am particularly upset with the nature of the cuts as they affect the Department under my authority.

On three separate occasions, the uniformed and civilian leadership of the Navy Department provided the Secretary of Defense with proposed cuts totaling the amount required to meet the budget reduction, but which also would preserve the cherished goal of your administration to rebuild our Navy to a minimum level of 600 ships. In each case the advice of this senior leadership, concurred in by the Joint Chiefs of Staff, was ignored. I can only conclude that the decision to reduce the level of our fleet to a point that it may never reach the 600 ship goal was motivated by other than military and strategic reasoning.

During the four years I have served in your Administration, I have repeatedly expressed my gratitude at your decision to rebuild the greatest Navy in the world. Since I became Secretary of the Navy last year, I have stated just as frequently my belief that the force levels of our sea services remain minimal and must not be reduced. Even in the current budget environment such force levels could have been maintained. Since recommendations to that effect were rejected by your Secretary of Defense, I am unable to support him personally, or to defend this amended budget during budget deliberations. Consequently, I find it necessary to resign from my position as Secretary of the Navy.

Thank you for the opportunity to have served our country during four of our nation's most critical and productive years.

Respectfully yours,

JAMES H. WEBB, JR.

Nomination of William L. Ball III To Be Secretary of the Navy
February 23, 1988

The President today announced his intention to nominate William L. Ball III to be Secretary of the Navy. He would succeed James H. Webb, Jr.

Since February 1986 Mr. Ball has served as Assistant to the President for Legislative Affairs at the White House. Prior to that time, he was Assistant Secretary of State for Legislative and Intergovernmental Affairs, 1985–1986. From 1981 to 1985, he was administrative assistant to Senator John Tower of Texas. In 1981 he also served as chief clerk of the Senate Armed Services Committee. In 1978 he served as administrative assistant to Senator Herman Talmadge of Georgia. He served as a regular officer in the United States Navy from 1969 to 1975.

Mr. Ball graduated from the Georgia Institute of Technology (B.S., 1969). He was born June 19, 1948, in Belton, SC. He is married, has two children, and resides in the District of Columbia.

Message to the Congress Transmitting Proposed Legislation on Superconductivity Competitiveness
February 23, 1988

To the Congress of the United States:

I am pleased to transmit today for your immediate consideration and passage the "Superconductivity Competitiveness Act of 1988." This legislation is needed to help translate U.S. leadership in science into leadership in international commerce.

Scientific advances in superconductivity have taken place at a remarkable pace recently. In the estimation of one noted physicist, in the past year we have made 200 years worth of progress. As additional breakthroughs occur, the effect on our standard of living—indeed, our way of life—could be dramatic and unprecedented, in areas as diverse as transportation, energy, health care, computers, and communication.

By funding basic research, the Federal government has played a key role in these scientific breakthroughs. In Fiscal Year 1987, the Federal government spent about $55 million in superconductivity research. In Fiscal Year 1988, the Federal government will spend significantly more—increasing the annual spending to more than $100 million. Ultimately, however, our success in superconductivity will depend on the private sector, which will make the critical decisions on how much capital, time, and effort to invest in commercializing superconductivity.

On July 28, 1987, I announced an 11-point superconductivity initiative designed to help the private sector in its efforts to commercialize superconductivity. This initiative has these three objectives:

- To promote greater cooperation among the Federal government, academia, and American industry in the basic and enabling research that is necessary to continue to achieve superconductivity breakthroughs;
- To enable the U.S. private sector to convert scientific advances into new and improved products and processes more rapidly; and
- To better protect the intellectual property rights of scientists, engineers, and other professionals working in superconductivity.

The Superconductivity Competitiveness Act of 1988 ("the Act") is a key part of this initiative. It will help ensure our readiness in commercializing recent and anticipated scientific breakthroughs.

Title I of the Act states the title of the legislation.

Title II amends the National Cooperative Research Act (NCRA) to cover joint production ventures. This is a particularly important step toward allowing U.S. firms to become more competitive with firms overseas in moving important research involving superconductivity and other fast-moving high technology areas from the laboratory to the marketplace.

Title II recognizes that unless U.S. firms are encouraged to organize their research and development activities in the most efficient manner possible, they cannot compete effectively with overseas firms. I should stress that the purpose of the NCRA is not to provide firms with immunity for anticompetitive behavior. Our antitrust statutes will continue to protect American consumers and businesses from harmful practices where they occur. This extension of the NCRA should promote innovation and productivity and will permit this country to maintain—or in some instances to regain—its position of world technological leadership.

Title III of the Act increases the protection of the U.S. patent laws for holders of U.S. process patents. Currently, there is no court-ordered remedy for patent infringement when a product made overseas, using a process that is patented in the United States, is imported into the United States. Title III would establish such a remedy and would permit U.S. manufacturing patent process holders to sue for injunctive relief and damages. (Relief of this nature is already available to process patent holders for products made in the United States using processes patented in the United States.) Title III would not extend the territorial application of American law. It would not prevent a foreign manufacturer from using a process overseas that is patented in the United States, as long as items manufactured under that process are not exported to the United States.

Title IV of the Act would provide protection for certain commercially valuable scientific and technical information generated in Federal government-owned and -operated laboratories. In particular, Title IV recognizes that commercially valuable scientific and technological information generated in Federal facilities loses potential commercial value when it is released wholesale under the Freedom of Information Act (FOIA). In addition, mandatory disclosure of such information under FOIA could encourage U.S. competitors to exploit the U.S. science and technology base rather than making investments in their own research and development infrastructure. Under Title IV, Federal agencies will be required to withhold information of this nature requested under the Freedom of Information Act where disclosure could reasonably be expected to harm the economic competitiveness of the United States. This Title is *not* intended to end the U.S. tradition of sharing the benefits of our excellence in science and technology; it merely provides that the Freedom of Information Act may not always be the appropriate or best avenue for doing so.

I should note that my Administration is currently developing a uniform policy to permit Federal contractors to own the rights to technical information that they develop for the government. This is intended to provide these contractors with proprietary rights equal to those of other firms that submit technical information to the government that was developed at private expense. Because our policy in this area is still under development, Title IV has been drafted to apply only to Federal government-generated, government-owned scientific and technical information.

Title V specifies the effective date of the Act.

There is a growing realization that, although the United States has long been a leader in breakthroughs in the laboratory, it has occasionally failed to convert these breakthroughs into commercial applications. This Act, in conjunction with the other components of our superconductivity initiative, can and will speed the process of commercialization. There is no time to waste in this effort. I urge the Congress to act promptly and favorably upon this legislative proposal.

RONALD REAGAN

The White House,
February 23, 1988.

Appointment of Alan Michael Kranowitz as Assistant to the President for Legislative Affairs
February 23, 1988

The President today announced the appointment of Alan Michael Kranowitz as Assistant to the President for Legislative Affairs at the White House. He is presently Deputy Assistant to the President with primary responsibility for liaison with the House of Representatives. He will replace William L. Ball III, who the President will nominate to be Secretary of the Navy.

Mr. Kranowitz served previously as chief of staff to Congressman Tom Loeffler (R–TX), as a professional staff member on the Senate Republican Policy Committee, and as Assistant Director for Legislative Affairs at the Office of Management and Budget. In 1971–1975, Mr. Kranowitz served as a Director of Legislative Affairs at the Department of Housing and Urban Development under Secretaries George Romney, James Lynn, and Carla Hills.

Mr. Kranowitz graduated from Yale University (B.A., 1963). He was born March 19, 1941, in New Britain, CT. He is married, has two children, and resides in Bethesda, MD.

Message to the Congress Transmitting Proposed Legislation To Promote Truth in Federal Spending
February 24, 1988

To the Congress of the United States:

I am forwarding today for your immediate consideration and prompt passage a legislative proposal entitled the "Truth in Federal Spending Act of 1988."

On November 20 of last year, I agreed with congressional leaders on a package designed to reduce the Federal deficit. That Bipartisan Budget Agreement between the President and the joint leadership of the Congress reflects a strong consensus that Federal spending must be brought under control.

Continued spending growth, particularly

where wasteful or unnecessary, adds to the Federal deficit and absorbs resources that would otherwise be employed more fruitfully in the private sector of the economy. The Bipartisan Budget Agreement represents an important step in reducing spending growth. But protecting the Federal budget from special interest, budget-busting legislation requires a continued, ongoing commitment. Despite recent encouraging efforts to bring the Federal budget deficit under control, major problems persist.

On July 3 of last year, when I outlined our Economic Bill of Rights, I described a proposal for the legislation that I am forwarding to the Congress today. It is designed to discourage wasteful Federal spending by requiring both the Legislative and Executive branches of government to be fully accountable for their respective actions. Key provisions of this draft bill would:

—Insure that all legislation that would result in increased Federal spending is deficit-neutral by requiring the concurrent enactment of equal amounts of program reductions or revenue increases;

—Require that all legislation include a "financial impact statement" detailing the measure's likely economic effects upon the private sector and State and local governments;

—Require that regulations and proposed regulations promulgated by Executive branch agencies also be accompanied by financial impact statements; and

—Permit waiver of the requirements of the Act during time of war or during a national security emergency.

In making this important proposal, one point deserves special emphasis. In complying with the deficit neutrality requirements of the Truth in Federal Spending Act of 1988, some may be tempted simply to shift spending requirements, either expressly or implicitly, from the Federal government to State and local governments. This is not, however, and should not be interpreted as being, the intent of this initiative. Instead, through enactment of this landmark legislation, we seek to achieve an historic breakthrough: to make the *Federal Government*—both the Legislative and Executive branches—more fully accountable for its actions and the effects of those actions on all the citizens of our Nation and, in so doing, get its fiscal house in order.

Enactment of the Truth in Federal Spending Act of 1988 will help us to carry out the important goals reflected in the Bipartisan Budget Agreement of November 20, 1987. It will also continue the important work we have accomplished in reducing or eliminating needless Federal expenditures. It is worthy of broad, bipartisan support. Accordingly, I urge its prompt and favorable consideration.

RONALD REAGAN

The White House,
February 24, 1988.

Message to the Senate Transmitting the Annual Report of the United States Arms Control and Disarmament Agency
February 24, 1988

To the Congress of the United States:

I am pleased to transmit the 1987 Report of the United States Arms Control and Disarmament Agency. It reviews the negotiation process used in achieving the INF Treaty and contains a copy of the Treaty itself. That Treaty, signed by General Secretary Gorbachev and me on December 8, 1987, is the first treaty of the nuclear era requiring the elimination of an entire category of U.S. and Soviet nuclear weapons.

The report provides information about the ongoing negotiations for a 50-percent reduction to equal levels in U.S. and Soviet strategic nuclear offensive arms, an effective and verifiable ban on chemical weapons, and the correction of disparities in conventional forces. Also described are the ancillary activities of the Arms Control and Disarmament Agency in support of our arms control policies and, concomitantly, the security of the United States.

The INF Treaty constitutes a breakthrough in verification, the most far-reaching in the history of arms control, and should serve as a guide for other treaties to come. The political and economic advantages of carefully negotiated and effectively verifiable arms reductions hold great promise for peace, security, and continued prosperity for our country. The 1987 record of progress toward those goals is contained in this 27th ACDA Report.

RONALD REAGAN

The White House,
February 24, 1988.

Remarks Following Discussions With Prime Minister Anibal Cavaco Silva of Portugal

February 24, 1988

The President. It has been a pleasure and an honor for me to meet today with Prime Minister Cavaco Silva on his first official visit to Washington. Portugal is a founding member of the North Atlantic Treaty Organization, a valuable friend and an ally. We salute Portugal's impressive transition to democracy and its continuing commitment to the collective defense of the West. Beyond the shared values and common interests that link our two countries, the Portuguese-American community has made a lasting contribution to American society that we can all appreciate.

Mr. Prime Minister, you and I have just concluded a most useful discussion covering a broad range of international as well as bilateral issues of importance. Southern Africa, the Middle East, and Afghanistan were among the topics we covered today, and I'm grateful for your advice and counsel, Mr. Prime Minister. High also on our list of topics was the agenda for the NATO summit, where we will meet again next week. I listened intently to the Prime Minister's views on East-West issues. I brought him up to date on recent developments in U.S.-Soviet relations and our plans for the Moscow summit. Secretary Shultz discussed his meeting with Soviet Foreign Minister Shevardnadze. Prime Minister Cavaco Silva briefed us on Portugal's assessment of the recent European Community summit in Brussels and the current political and economic situation in Portugal.

As our meeting today underscored—while trying to improve relations with adversaries—America still remains strong and unflinching in its commitments to our friends. The core of our foreign policy is our permanent partnership with our fellow democracies in the Atlantic alliance, on which the global balance of power and the cause of freedom so crucially depend. Be assured, we will never sacrifice the interests of our allies and friends in any agreement with the Soviet Union. The people of the United States and the people of Portugal are united with all other free peoples in the cause of freedom and the responsibility of maintaining the peace. The United States, Mr. Prime Minister, and Portugal are doing their part in this historic adventure. We're honored to have such friends.

These are challenging times. From our cordial and candid conversation, I know that we share similar goals and many of the same concerns. Portugal's role as a key and trusted ally is much appreciated here. We applaud Portugal's desire to modernize its armed forces and to play a more active role in NATO's collective defense efforts. Our commitment to assist Portugal in these efforts remains firm, ever within the context of the harsh budget realities that we all face. The task of leadership is to rise to challenge. I believe from our meeting today our two governments will accelerate the pace of our extensive cooperation and develop even further the close and mutually beneficial relationship which has traditionally existed between our two countries.

The Prime Minister. Mr. President, this morning we had the opportunity to have a useful exchange of ideas on the strengthening of the Atlantic alliance in a perspective of peace and security for the Western World, on the relations between our two countries, and finally, on the international situation. Portugal's and the United States positions converge toward the need for firmness and cohesion in the Western world.

I reiterated to President Reagan the Portuguese Government's support of the INF agreement and the continuation of the dialog with the Soviet Union. I expressed my firm belief that Western Europe's defense is not feasible without the United States commitment in the framework of NATO. I am sure that, at the next NATO summit meeting which will be held in a few days, we will have the opportunity to restate our common determination to strengthen the Atlantic alliance as a requisite for the preservation of peace and our common values. I informed President Reagan of the conclusions of the last European Council and the prospects for building a united Europe and for Portugal's development and modernization.

In the context of Portugal-U.S.A. relations, I reasserted our desire to maintain a preferential relationship since Portugal, being the United States maritime frontier with Europe, is a strategically important ally and wishes to remain a close and reliable ally.

A few differences have emerged regarding the agreement signed between our two countries in 1983, in the context of the defense agreement, which has bound us since 1951; namely, the legitimate Portuguese expectations regarding assistance levels granted to Portugal by the United States. We approach this subject in the spirit of openness that should guide relations between friends and allies. I stressed the difficulties that will result for Portugal if that assistance were curtailed, particularly at a time when we are committed to the reequipment of our armed forces and trying to modernize the country in an effort that cannot be deferred. I stated to President Reagan, that the Portuguese Government intended to request that consultations be held in the terms of the agreement.

In holding these consultations, we do not have the intention of ceasing or reducing the facilities enjoyed by the United States in Portuguese territory but rather to identify and overcome existing difficulties. As friends and allies, we want to look for solutions that will meet our common interests, so as to ensure a framework of cooperation to strengthen the preferential relations that exist between our two countries.

When we analyzed the international situation, we gave special relevance to the situation in Southern Africa, a region where Portugal has important responsibilities to fulfill. I am gratified by the ongoing talks between the United States and the Angolan Governments—which are a positive step in the peace process—and by the support provided to Mozambique.

Mr. President, I wish to express my appreciation for the opportunity to meet with you on this occasion which, I am sure, has contributed to strengthen the relations between our two countries as well as the Atlantic alliance's cohesion.

Note: The President spoke at 1:30 p.m. at the South Portico of the White House. The Prime Minister spoke in Portuguese, and his remarks were translated by an interpreter. Earlier, the President and the Prime Minister met in the Oval Office and then attended a luncheon in the Residence.

Remarks Announcing the "Export Now" Campaign
February 24, 1988

Thank you, Secretary Verity, Van Smith, and Jack Murphy. I'm especially pleased also that Governor Baliles is here today. He and several other Governors realize the importance of healthy, robust trade and have been champions of such international commerce. I couldn't be more pleased to join you today to launch the "Export Now" campaign. America loves a winner, and I think this campaign exemplifies the winning spirit of American enterprise and competition.

Although the doomsayers haven't grasped the magnitude of what is happening in international commerce, our manufacturers, farmers, and world traders are already in the process of regaining America's share of world markets. Just a single figure tells the story. In the last quarter of 1987, our exports in real terms—that's the volume of goods after adjusting for any change in prices—were up 20 percent from the same period a year earlier. That's over five times the growth in our domestic economy. Who says we've lost the spirit of the Yankee trader?

We're in the midst of a great trade turnabout. Why? Well, there are several parts to the answer, as you all know. Obviously, the fact that the dollar's exchange rate is now at a far more realistic level is of great significance. One of the primary goals of "Export Now" is to drive home the point to middle-sized and smaller businesses that new opportunities are emerging because of the adjustment in the value of the dollar.

In short, exporting, for American businesses—large and small—is now a profitable option. At the current exchange rates, many American companies can now quote a lower price to their customers in Hamburg or Antwerp or Osaka than their competitors and still make a higher profit than on sales in our own domestic market. Of course, quoting a good price is only half the battle.

Quality products and good service are also part of the trade equation. And in the last few years, American industry has been going through an unprecedented period of renovation, computerization, and modernization. The commitment behind the dramatic changes I'm talking about resulted from the rude shock American business experienced when hit by the wave of imports some years ago. But our corporate leaders and working men and women did not give up, not in the least. They slimmed down. They became more efficient. They shut down obsolete plants. They worked to develop a new spirit of cooperation between management and labor, and placed much greater emphasis on quality and getting the job done right.

And now, as the exchange rate adjustments have opened new opportunities, our business community is ready to meet the competition. You know, there's a saying in sports, "No pain, no gain." Well, American business has taken the pains, and now it's ready for the gains. What we don't need now, however, is protectionism that undermines all the progress we've made. I strongly urge Congress to send me a trade bill that does not imperil our ability to export by causing other countries to close their markets. U.S. businesses are in the process of recapturing old markets—we shouldn't shoot ourselves in the foot after we've worked so hard and are in a position to win the race.

There are provisions in the legislation currently in conference that encourage exports, and we don't want to lose those, but there are also some totally objectionable provisions—including measures that are GATT-illegal [General Agreement on Tariffs and Trade] and reduce U.S. competitiveness. We ask for your support to ensure that we don't end up with an economy-killing protectionist bill.

I visited a number of plants last year in various parts of the United States, and I must say I was deeply impressed by what I saw—whether it was at Harley-Davidson in Pennsylvania, Dictaphone in Florida, Broan in Wisconsin, or Somerset Technologies in New Jersey. The working people of this country are ready and willing to compete head on. And I happen to believe that on a level playing field they can outproduce and outdo anyone, anywhere. Again, America's greatest asset is the character of our own people. I challenge anyone who says the United States is in some kind of decline to just look at the current export figures. We're beginning to beat our major competitors, both in third markets as well as in exporting to them directly. Let me give you just a couple of real world examples.

Back in 1973, when American auto manufacturers needed help in complying with the Clean Air Act, Corning Glass Works developed the catalytic converter. For 3 years, Corning dominated that market, but by 1977 Japanese makers of catalytic converters had come up with a superior and less expensive product. Detroit automakers gave Corning a choice: meet the competition head-on within 12 months or lose their business. Through union cooperation and worker participation from the factory floor to the boardroom, Corning did just that—it came up with a better and more competitively priced converter. Corning not only kept Detroit's business but is now making inroads in the Japanese market.

Argus Fire Control, Incorporated, doused all the fires it could find in America. Dick Thomas, president of the firm, said, "I figured I either had to come up with another product or find another market." Well, today, Argus sells in 15 foreign countries.

Change is the order of the day for a dynamic and expanding economy. Today new opportunities are opening as the people of the free world are brought closer together by technology and the elimination of political barriers to commerce. A great milestone in this evolutionary process will be the adoption of the U.S.-Canada free trade agreement. Our own businesses—big and small—need to be ready for the expanding horizons that will result from this historic agreement.

Bill, your "Export Now" program has come along at exactly the right time, and I'm delighted to support this initiative. I also want to commend Jim Abdnor, the Administrator of the Small Business Administration, who has been working to stimulate small businesses' interest in exporting. The conditions are right. We're already off to a great beginning in export growth. And now let's show the world what we can do.

Thank you all very much.

Note: The President spoke at 2:04 p.m. in Room 450 of the Old Executive Office Building to business leaders. In his opening remarks, he referred to Secretary of Commerce C. William Verity, Jr.; Van P. Smith, chairman of the board and president of the Ontario Manufacturing Corp.; John J. Murphy, chairman and chief executive officer of Dresser Industries; and Gov. Gerald L. Baliles of Virginia. "Export Now" was a public-private partnership designed to encourage U.S. exports.

The President's News Conference
February 24, 1988

International Issues

The President. On the networks at last! [*Laughter*] Good evening. Before I take your questions, I have a brief opening statement.

Secretary of State George Shultz today reported to me on his recent trip to Moscow, and it was encouraging. Progress continues to be made on our four-part agenda, and the commitment remains to do all that we can to advance the cause of peace and to settle regional conflicts.

In the Middle East, it's time for all parties to rid themselves of old ideas and stances that cannot work and to begin a serious process of negotiation and reconciliation. Any process that is undertaken must meet Israel's security needs and satisfy the legitimate rights of the Palestinians. Secretary Shultz leaves tonight for the Middle East to see if practical and real progress can be made that provides a pathway to a comprehensive settlement, and he carries with him my full support.

There's another regional conflict that has serious implications for our country's security interests: Nicaragua. Our policy consistently has been to bring peace and freedom to all of Central America. Today four of the five Central American countries choose their governments in free and open democratic elections. Independent courts protect their human rights, and their people can hope for a better life for themselves and their children. One country, Nicaragua, with its Communist regime, remains a threat to this democratic tide in the region.

So, our message to the people of Nicaragua tonight is the same as it has been for the past 7 years: freedom based on true democratic principles. In the past several months, there have been some limited steps taken by the Communist regime in Nicaragua toward reform. Now is not the time to reverse that process.

So, there's no argument that all of us seek peace and democracy in Nicaragua, and the difference is how to achieve that goal. On February 3d, Congress voted on continued support for the democratic resistance in Nicaragua, and to my disappointment, the majority in the House of Representatives voted to remove the pressure of the democratic resistance on the Sandinista regime. However, the Senate agreed with me that we cannot leave those fighting for freedom in Nicaragua at the mercy of the Communist regime and expect the process toward democracy to move ahead.

We've already seen what happens when pressure is removed. In just 2 short weeks, the Sandinistas threatened the only free press in that country and rejected a cease-fire proposal made by the mediator, Cardinal Obando, which incorporated the essential elements laid out and agreed to last August. And in the first 2 months of 1988, Soviet military assistance to Nicaragua has almost doubled, compared to the same period in 1987. These do not represent signs of peace; these remain troubling indications of a regime determined to crush its opposition and threaten its neighbors.

There is a choice. We must act to ensure that freedom is not smothered in Nicaragua and to guarantee that these latest promises will be kept in a timely way.

End of statement, and Helen [Helen Thomas, United Press International]?

Israeli-Occupied Territories

Q. Mr. President, through the years you've been very eloquent on the subject of human rights in the Soviet Union and Nicaragua. The question really is: Why have you never condemned the treatment of the Palestinians in the occupied areas—shooting unarmed protesters, beating people to death, children, trying to bury some alive? And I'd like to follow up.

The President. Helen, we have spoken to the Government there, and we've also spoken to the Palestinian leadership, because there is every evidence that these riots are not just spontaneous and homegrown. But we have spoken, and that's part of the reason why the Secretary of State is going back over there. We don't support that sort of thing, and we are trying to persuade all the participants to try to arrive at a solution representing justice for all.

Q. Well, if you want that and you say you believe in security for Israel and legitimate rights of the Palestinians, why don't you go on the public record now and say that there should be an exchange of removal of the occupation and of peace?

The President. Well, I don't think it's up to us to dictate the settlement in the Middle East.

Q. Well, we certainly are great supporters of Israel, so we certainly have some influence.

The President. Yes, and we have used that a number of times and are using it now. But we think that—and the thing that is taking the Secretary of State there—we think that the necessity is for all who are represented in that situation, on both sides, should come together, when you stop to think that legally a state of war still exists there in the Middle East, between the Arab nations and Israel, and that it's time for us to arrive at a true peace and recognize the rights of all.

American Hostages in Lebanon

Q. Mr. President, Shi'ite militiamen are scouring southern Lebanon for Colonel Higgins, the American kidnaped last week, and you've expressed a determination to get him out. Can you say that the same intense efforts, the same kind of dragnet, will be used to find the other American hostages, one of whom, Terry Anderson, is about to mark the end of his third year in captivity?

The President. We have never given up on that. As you can realize, it's very frustrating to try and establish a location, knowing of course that you are governed by the fact that unwise action on our part could bring about harm to the hostages. But we've never let up, and we never will, in trying to obtain the freedom of all the hostages.

Q. Sir, Pat Robertson said today that his Christian Broadcasting Network once knew the location of American hostages in the Middle East, and that the United States, in effect, missed an opportunity to rescue them. I understand he's clarified that remark, but I wonder if you have any thoughts about the tone that he's setting in this campaign.

The President. Well, all I can say—I don't want to comment on the campaign, but I can only say this: that it would be very strange if he actually did have information as to the location of those hostages. Isn't it strange that no one in our administration was ever apprised of that? We have tried our best, and through every kind of channel, to establish their whereabouts, because that's the beginning of efforts to try and get them free. But if he thought that he knew, he kept it to himself.

Trude [Trude Feldman, Transfeatures]?

Middle East Peace Efforts

Q. Mr. President, as of now, is there any change in our policy of not talking with the PLO [Palestine Liberation Organization], in light of the fact that there are reports out of Geneva that Mr. Arafat is now ready to accept U.N. Resolution 338 and 242?

The President. Well, I know that this is one other thing we're pursuing. If he really is, and if he is willing to acknowledge the right of Israel to exist as a nation—this has been one of the blocking points, that how do you sit down and try to get into a talk about peace when someone says they have no right to even exist? And I'm sure that the Secretary of State is apprised of that fact and will see what we can do there.

Q. And given—may I follow up?

The President. Yes?

Q. And given the 40-year hostility in the area which has been built up, how can you as the "Great Communicator" try to alleviate some of the antagonism between the Israelis and the Palestinians before you leave office?

The President. Well, we are trying to and will continue to try to. That's a goal that I would think would be one of the greatest achievements of this administration—if before I leave, we could bring about a peace in the Middle East.

Israeli-Occupied Territories

Q. Mr. President, whom precisely are you criticizing when you say that the riots are not homegrown and not spontaneous?

The President. Well, we have had—it's a little difficult for me, because there's some things that I shouldn't be saying. But we have had intimations that there have been certain people suspected of being terrorists, outsiders coming in, not only with weapons but stirring up and encouraging the trouble in those areas. Now, that isn't something you can go out and say we absolutely know, but certainly the violence is both ways.

Q. But it would seem, sir, that that's still a generalization if you say some people from the outside. Can't you not be specific and say just who it is?

The President. No, because I get into areas there that would be violating security rules, and I don't think I should.

Q. The PLO? Russians?

The President. What?

Q. PLO? Russians?

The President. No, no.

Iraqi Pipeline Plan

Q. Mr. President, it's my understanding that in 1985 your national security adviser, Robert McFarlane, briefed you on the Iraqi pipeline project and got and gained your approval for it. In light of the difficulties that your Attorney General, Mr. Meese, is encountering now, could you explain your position on the pipeline and tell me if you think it was a good idea at that time?

The President. I have no recall of knowing anything about this pipeline plan until fairly recently, and then found out with regard to the transmittal of the letters that have now been turned over to the special investigator. And this was about the first information that I recall having. Now, I can't say to you that I was given information earlier, because I just have to tell you if I was I have totally forgotten—that I have no knowledge of anything of that kind.

Q. Well, Mr. President, does it trouble you at all that your dear friend Mr. Meese has become entangled in this project, and it has yet been another case which has brought him, some would say, embarrassment?

The President. Let me just say one thing. I have every confidence in his integrity. I've known him for more than 20 years, but I cannot comment in any way on this case that is now before a special investigator.

Sam [Sam Donaldson, ABC News]?

South Africa

Q. Mr. President, the white minority government of South Africa has now effectively banned activities by dissenting organizations, even when those activities are peaceful. What is your view on that, and what can you do, if anything, to reverse it?

The President. Well, the State Department has already contacted them about that, and we are making our own feelings clear that they should be working toward a multiracial democracy and not oppressing political organizations there. And we've made our feelings clear about that.

Q. Well, sir, may I follow up? Have you considered sending aid to the freedom fighters—the ANC [African National Congress] or any other organization—against this oppression just as you send aid to other freedom fighters around the world?

The President. No, we have not involved ourselves in that, other than things such as the sanctions and so forth. We have tried our best to be persuasive in this very difficult problem and to find—or to encourage a better solution.

Q. Well, what's the difference?

The President. Well, the difference is that we don't have an armed insurrection going as we have in some other countries, and we have a great division even among the people who are being oppressed. It is a tribal policy more than it is a racial policy, and that is one of the most difficult parts here.

Bill [Bill Plante, CBS News]?

Government Ethics

Q. Mr. President, throughout your administration, when members of your Cabinet or members of the administration have been accused of any kind of wrongdoing or simply of bad judgment, it's been your policy generally to say nothing. Is your loyalty more important to you than the perception that the members of the Government must be above reproach?

The President. No, Bill, and I have to say that I do not favor violations of ethics or laws at all in or out of government, but I do want to call your attention to one thing. I think—and this has gone on pretty much throughout the time that I've been here—that there is a kind of lynch mob atmosphere that takes place, and people are—the memories are there of this person, that person, and so forth. But no attention is paid to the fact of how many of them, when it actually came to trial, was found to be totally innocent, but in the meantime, they have been smeared nationwide. And it's very difficult for people to remember what the outcome was. They only remember the other of the—in other words, guilt was by accusation and not by actual trial and conviction. And I could call to your attention too, Ray Donovan, Jim Beggs of the space program—both of them totally cleared of any wrongdoing whatsoever. And this has been true of a great many others. But those that were doing something wrong and were apprehended and it was proven on them, they're no longer with us.

Q. Well, sir, people have asked if—as in the case of the Iran-*contra* affair, when the committee which investigated it noted that you never condemned the actions of those members of your staff who were involved—the question was raised whether your silence meant that you did not find their actions objectionable?

The President. No, when they came under the judgment of the law and the judgment was made and—great regret if someone was guilty of wrongdoing—but they were punished accordingly.

Soviet-U.S. Trade

Q. Mr. President, what are you doing to make things easier for corporations to trade with the Soviet Union in nonstrategic items, such as food processing, pharmaceuticals, automotive, and hotels, for instance? And do you believe the Soviet Union should join GATT, the General Agreement on Trade and Tariffs? And will you discuss these and other trade items with Mr. Gorbachev in your forthcoming summit?

The President. Well, I can't relate to you discussions about those particular things with him. But I do know that there has been consideration of them involving themselves in the GATT procedure; and that, of course, is being reviewed among those of us who are participants now. But I don't know whether that answers your question or not, but our trade with the Soviet Union is restricted mainly on the basis of where we might be giving them technology and information that could be used one day against us.

Iran Arms and Contra Aid Controversy

Q. Mr. President, I know you have to remain neutral in the Republican race, but you could clear up a major issue right now by telling us whether George Bush, in fact, did have reservations about the sale of arms to Iran; whether he had reservations about Israel's role in that policy; and whether, in fact, he's telling the truth when he tells us that he did have those reservations?

The President. Yes, in the general discussion, and that's not unusual here. I've ordered our people on Cabinet matters or anything else, and I want to hear what they really feel. I don't want to be surrounded by yes-men. And, yes, there were reservations, but I'm not going to go into—just as he wouldn't go into the private discussions that we may have had.

But I think it's time for me to point out what the opposition was based on of anyone who did oppose. Particularly, it's been revealed that Secretary Weinberger and George Shultz both objected. They did not object, the idea that we were trading arms for hostages. Their objection—they knew what we were trying to do. This had been a request that came to us from some people not in the Government of Iran but who wanted to privately meet with us on how there could be a better relationship if and when the day came that there was a new government in Iran. And if you'll remember, back in those days, almost every other day there was speculation that the health of the Khomeini was failing to where there might be this contest of a new government.

Their objection was—what we had done, we'd gotten this request; and in dealing with it, in this conversation with these private individuals, we pointed out our feelings about terrorism and so forth. They agreed with us. And the thing was that they, the Hizballah, as we know, is philosophically attuned to Iran. The idea was that they could perhaps influence the Hizballah to give up some of our hostages. And indeed, as the talks went on, they did. We got two of them free.

But their objection was that if and when this became known, as it would be, it would be made to appear that we were trading hostages for—or arms for hostages. Now, we were giving these arms to these individuals, because we felt that maybe they could influence the Hizballah. We weren't dealing with the kidnapers at all. And this was what the whole situation was. But it turned out that George and Cap and those who had doubts were right in that when it did become known, by way of a henchman of the Ayatollah, then everyone just automatically said that—and to this day are saying—it was arms for hostages.

Republican Presidential Campaign

Q. On the issue of George Bush and his role though, this has become one of the major issues between the Vice President and Senator Dole. Now, although you have to remain neutral, as the author of the 11th Commandment, thou shall not criticize one's fellow Republican, do you have any advice for these two men, and aren't you getting a little concerned that they might be hurting the Republican chances by their very bitter political feud?

The President. Well, whether I am concerned or not, I am not going to comment on things like that. I am going to say that they know my feelings, all of them, about the 11th Commandment.

Q. No advice at all to them?

The President. Jerry [Jeremiah O'Leary, Washington Times]?

Defense Spending

Q. Mr. President, the resignation of Secretary of the Navy Webb has ignited a controversy about your buildup of the United States Navy. And the question is: Are you satisfied—[*inaudible*]—the budget cuts in the military have not damaged our national security, and are you still committed to a 600-ship Navy at a time when the Soviets are not cutting their navy?

The President. I am committed at the 600-ship Navy. And I want you to know, Jerry, that from the very beginning, since I've been here, the Congress has cut my request for defense every time. And sometimes, they have tried to pretend that that is in an effort to reduce the deficit spending and so forth. But in a 5-year period, the Congress cut my defense budgets a total of $125 billion at the same time that they increased my request for domestic programs by $250 billion. And this budget which is now being attributed to me—no, this isn't as low as they originally wanted to cut it, but it was as high as we could get it in the negotiations for the present budget. And it has been harmful.

But let me tell you that in 1980, when we came here, the Navy had 479 vessels, and by 1987, we had 568. And by next year, it will be 580. And so, what has happened is that there will be a little delay in the achieving of the 600-ship Navy. But I can't help but remind—or tell all of you, when I was campaigning in 1980 and knew the state of our defenses, I was faced with the question. And some of you will recall I did a lot of campaigning on, question-and-answer basis. At almost every gathering, there would be a question: Well, if I came to a choice between deficit spending and buildup of our defense structure, which would I choose? And every time, I said, in responsibility, I would have to choose the buildup of our defenses. And every time, in every audience in America that I said that to, gave me an applause that was almost an ovation for saying that.

Q. The second part of the question was: Is it a threat to the national security that the Navy is not going to have 600 ships on the schedule that you had in mind?

The President. I don't think right at the moment—and with the way we're progressing in various treaties and so forth—I don't believe that the threat is that immediate, and because very shortly we will achieve our 600. We want 15 carriers and their squadrons, and we've just launched the 15th carrier, 100 nuclear-powered attack submarines, and 4 battleships, and we're achieving that.

Panamanian Drug Trafficking

Q. Mr. President, you must certify by March 1st whether Panama has been cracking down on drug trafficking through that country or whether aid to Panama should continue to be suspended. What are you going to do?

The President. Well, I can't give you the answer yet, because we're still working on that and still collecting the facts as to what their effort has been at trying to intercept the drugs and join us in that campaign. But as you said, March 1st we will be giving the answer.

Q. Sir, if I could follow up: Some officials in your administration have suggested that if Noriega [Commander of the Panamanian Defense Forces] would step down and go into exile, that you would stop the prosecution of him on drug charges. Would you consider that kind of deal?

The President. No, and I'm not going to comment on something of this kind. This man has been indicted by a Federal grand jury, and so I'm not going to make any comment of that kind, nor have we made any advances or suggestions of that kind to the Government of Panama. What we would like to see is a return to democracy and a civilian government in Panama, and not this domination by—literally—a military dictator.

Federal Reserve Board Chairman

Q. Mr. President, Federal Reserve Chairman Alan Greenspan today objected to pressure from the administration regarding the formulation of monetary policy, such as was contained in the budget and the Economic Report and a Treasury letter to Federal Reserve Board members. Don't you have confidence in your appointee to the Fed, Alan Greenspan, as the Chairman?

The President. Yes, I do. And I'm going to have to find out what this is all about that you're talking about, because nothing of that kind had been directed to me.

Aid to the Contras

Q. Mr. President, back to the *contra* aid question. In your opening statement, you seemed to suggest that the Sandinistas are taking advantage of Congress not coming through with *contra* aid to withdraw some of the concessions they had made. With Congress about to consider new humanitarian aid—both a Democratic and a Republican plan—is it worth it to pass humanitarian aid without military aid?

The President. Well, I think the only comment that I can make there is that anything that will keep the freedom fighters as a pressure on the Sandinistas is worth doing. Just as when we tried to pass our own bill and narrowly failed, you could see that the military aid was down the road aways—it was not necessary right now. The other aid—humanitarian aid—is more imminent. And so, if we can get that, that's fine, and then we'll take our chances on the other in trying to get it. But they do still have some military stores for a limited period of time.

Q. If I may follow up on that point, sir: In the two plans that are being considered, the Democrats want the Defense Department to deliver whatever stores and supplies are authorized. The Republican plan would give that responsibility to the CIA. Do you favor either course?

The President. I certainly would favor the CIA. I think that involving our military when there is no need to is very rash and foolish, because you would be putting our military into a combat situation, and this is what we've been trying to avoid in Central America all the way.

Abduction of Lt. Col. William Higgins

Q. In that regard, Mr. President, I'd like to ask you about the latest hostage situation. Do you think it was responsible for your administration to allow a marine lieutenant colonel, William Higgins, to operate in southern Lebanon at a time when eight Americans were already being held in that country and when your own State Department was recommending against travel there and considering the ramifications of the abduction of William Buckley, earlier?

The President. I don't think that you can use that as a measure of where officers can be assigned to duty. They're in a dangerous business to begin with. And we are a part of the United Nations, and we have obligations to the U.N. with regard to the UNIFIL force [United Nations Interim Force in Lebanon] that has been there for a number of years now. And this particular officer happened to volunteer when there was a vacancy at that spot—volunteered for that. And I think that we have to have the confidence—and I do have the confidence in men like him—that someone would have a hard time getting secrets that could harm this country from a person of that kind.

Q. Mr. President?

The President. No, I was——

Presidential Campaign

Q. Mr. President, to follow up on Bill's question earlier, Democratic National Chairman Paul Kirk this morning called your administration the sleaziest and most corrupt in recent American history. Even if you have full confidence in people like Ed Meese, that they will be cleared, do you have any concern that all these charges and all these investigations are going to be used effectively by the Democrats against all the Republican candidates in 1988?

The President. I don't know whether they're going to be used effectively or not. I know they're going to be used—they have been for quite some considerable time now. As a matter of fact, if anyone listened for more than 15 minutes to their candidates, he would decide that we're in an economic slump, we're burdened by inflation, high interest rates, and unemployment, when at the moment none of those things are true. And we have a higher percentage of our potential employee pool employed than ever in our history and are continuing the longest expansion—economic expansion—in our history. And tomorrow morning, I think you'll find a little good news, along about 8:30 a.m. tomorrow morning, is going to be released with regard to the economy. So, I just think that, you know, the kids will play—[*laughter*]—and as long as they want to do that, but I hope it'll easily be forgotten.

Federal Budget

Q. Mr. President, the budget that you have proposed to Congress would eliminate three housing programs for the homeless. It would make deep cuts in an emergency food program, and it would end a job training program for the homeless. Do you believe that the problem of the homeless is less pressing now than just a year ago, when you signed legislation from Congress to create these programs?

The President. No, but I do know that we're doing a great many things, and we also are keeping track of the extent to which the private sector is joining in and helping on this. And this budget is the result of long, long weeks of negotiation with the Democrats and ourselves, and I think that we're meeting the problems.

Again, I also have to say this: that sometimes our budget in programs can reflect another program we've had going, which is a management program. And we have had a team for a considerable period of time now that has been actually investigating the management practices of government programs as compared to the way they're done in the private sector. And there are millions and millions of dollars that are being saved. So that something that maybe looks smaller does not mean that the people in need are going to get less; it means that we're able to provide that with less administrative overhead. When I came here from a governorship, as a Governor, I had seen Federal programs administered in our State in which it was costing the Federal Government $2 for every dollar that reached a needy person. This is something we've been trying to change, and we've made some progress in it.

Q. Mr. President, just to follow up on the budget; the Chairman of your Council of Economic Advisers told us last week that the deficit might have a good side if it forces your successor and Congress to make choices in social programs. Do you see a good side to the deficit?

The President. I have said that I think that there is a great reform that is needed throughout many of those programs. And it is a reform to where we can get these programs to where their goal will be to remove people from dependency and make them independent of government help instead of doing what we've been doing for too many years now—and that is, actually involving them in dependency to the place where they never can get out. We've made them permanently dependent on government, and we're trying to change that, correct that.

Q. Thank you.

The President. Thank you, Helen. I'm going to run for it now.

Note: The President's 43d news conference began at 8 p.m. in the East Room at the White House. It was broadcast live on nationwide radio and television.

Appointment of Robert B. Barker as an Assistant to the Secretary of Defense

February 25, 1988

The President today announced his intention to appoint Robert B. Barker to be Assistant to the Secretary of Defense for Atomic Energy. This is a new position.

Since 1985 Dr. Barker has been Assistant to the Secretary of Defense for Atomic Energy at the Department of Defense in Washington, DC. Prior to this he was Deputy Assistant Director of the Bureau of Verification and Intelligence at the Arms

Control and Disarmament Agency, 1983–1985. Dr. Barker also worked at the Lawrence Livermore National Laboratory as assistant associate director for arms control, 1982–1983; special projects division leader, 1978–1982; and evaluation and planning division leader, 1973–1978.

Dr. Barker graduated from Dartmouth College (A.B., 1960) and Syracuse University (Ph.D., 1966). He was born March 9, 1939, in New York, NY. He is married, has three children, and resides in Arlington, VA.

Nomination of Kenneth J. Beirne To Be an Assistant Secretary of Housing and Urban Development

February 25, 1988

The President today announced his intention to nominate Kenneth J. Beirne to be an Assistant Secretary of Housing and Urban Development (Policy Development and Research). He would succeed June Q. Koch.

Since 1987 Mr. Beirne has been a freelance writer. Prior to this he was General Deputy Assistant Secretary for Policy Development and Research at the Department of Housing and Urban Development, 1984–1987; senior adviser to the Deputy Under Secretary for Intergovernmental Relations, HUD, 1981–1984; and served as a management and political consultant, 1979–1981. Mr. Beirne was executive director of the Republican Party of Kentucky, 1981. He was the recipient of the Secretary's Award for Excellence at the Department of Housing and Urban Development in 1987.

Mr. Beirne graduated from the University of Notre Dame (A.B., 1968) and Claremont Graduate School (Ph.D., 1973). He was born November 3, 1946, in the Bronx, NY. Mr. Beirne is married, has five children, and resides in Burke, VA.

Nomination of Barbara McConnell Barrett To Be Deputy Administrator of the Federal Aviation Administration

February 25, 1988

The President today announced his intention to nominate Barbara McConnell Barrett to be Deputy Administrator of the Federal Aviation Administration, Department of Transportation. She would succeed Richard H. Jones.

Since 1985 Mrs. Barrett has been a partner with Evans, Kitchel and Jenckes, P.C. in Phoenix, AZ. Prior to this, she was Vice Chairman of the Civil Aeronautics Board, 1983–1984, and executive assistant to chairman, 1982–1983. She was associate general counsel and assistant secretary for Southwest Forest Industries, Inc., 1980–1982, and a corporate attorney for the Greyhound Corp., 1976–1980.

Mrs. Barrett graduated from Arizona State University (B.S., 1972; M.B.A., 1975; J.D., 1978). She was born December 26, 1950, in Indiana County, PA. She is married and currently resides in Paradise Valley, AZ.

Nomination of Hugh Hewitt To Be Deputy Director of the Office of Personnel Management
February 25, 1988

The President today announced his intention to nominate Hugh Hewitt to be Deputy Director of the Office of Personnel Management. He would succeed James E. Colvard.

Since 1986 Mr. Hewitt has been General Counsel at the Office of Personnel Management in Washington, DC. Prior to this he was General Counsel for the National Endowment for the Humanities, 1986. Mr. Hewitt was Assistant Counsel at the White House, 1985–1986, and Special Assistant to Attorneys General Smith and Meese, 1984–1985.

Mr. Hewitt graduated from Harvard College (A.B., 1978) and University of Michigan (J.D., 1983). He was born February 22, 1956, in Warren, OH. He is married, has one child, and resides in Oakton, VA.

Executive Order 12626—National Defense Stockpile Manager
February 25, 1988

By the authority vested in me as President by the Constitution and laws of the United States of America, including the Strategic and Critical Materials Stock Piling Act (50 U.S.C. 98 *et seq.*), as amended, section 3203 of the National Defense Authorization Act for Fiscal Year 1988 (Public Law 100–180), and section 301 of Title 3 of the United States Code, it is hereby ordered as follows:

Section 1. The Secretary of Defense is designated National Defense Stockpile Manager. The functions vested in the President by the Strategic and Critical Materials Stock Piling Act, except the functions vested in the President by sections 7, 8, and 13 of the Act, are delegated to the Secretary of Defense. The functions vested in the President by section 8(a) of the Act are delegated to the Secretary of the Interior. The functions vested in the President by section 8(b) of the Act are delegated to the Secretary of Agriculture.

Sec. 2. The functions vested in the President by section 4(h) of the Commodity Credit Corporation Charter Act, as amended (15 U.S.C. 714b(h)), are delegated to the Secretary of Defense.

Sec. 3. The functions vested in the President by section 204(f) of the Federal Property and Administrative Services Act of 1949, as amended (40 U.S.C. 485(f)), are delegated to the Secretary of Defense.

Sec. 4. In executing the functions delegated to him by this Order, the Secretary of Defense may delegate such functions as he may deem appropriate, subject to his direction. The Secretary shall consult with the heads of affected agencies in performing the functions delegated to him by this Order.

RONALD REAGAN

The White House,
February 25, 1988.

[*Filed with the Office of the Federal Register, 10:58 a.m., February 26, 1988*]

Statement by Assistant to the President for Press Relations Fitzwater on General Manuel Noriega of Panama
February 25, 1988

We understand that President Delvalle today dismissed General Noriega from his position as Commander of the Panama Defense Forces. At this time we want to reiterate our unqualified support for civilian constitutional rule in Panama. There is but one legitimate sovereign authority in Panama, and that is the Panamanian people exercising their democratic right to vote and elect their leadership in a free society.

Nomination of Jill E. Kent To Be an Assistant Secretary of the Treasury
February 26, 1988

The President today announced his intention to nominate Jill E. Kent to be an Assistant Secretary of the Treasury (Management). She would succeed John F.W. Rogers.

Since 1985 Ms. Kent has been Principal Deputy Assistant Secretary for Finance and Management at the Department of the Treasury in Washington, DC. Prior to this she was Chief of the Treasury and General Services Branch at the Office of Management and Budget, 1984–1985. From 1981 to 1984, Ms. Kent was a senior budget examiner at OMB, responsible for the Internal Revenue Service account. She was Acting Chief of Legislative Reference at the Department of Health and Human Services, 1978–1980.

Ms. Kent graduated from the University of Michigan (B.A., 1970) and George Washington University (J.D., 1975; LL.M., 1979). She was born June 1, 1948, in Detroit, MI. Ms. Kent is married and resides in Washington, DC.

Nomination of Frank DeGeorge To Be Inspector General of the Department of Commerce
February 26, 1988

The President today announced his intention to nominate Frank DeGeorge to be Inspector General of the Department of Commerce. He would succeed Sherman Maxwell Funk.

Since 1982 Mr. DeGeorge has been Deputy Inspector General at the Department of Commerce in Washington, DC. Prior to this he was Associate Deputy Administrator for Administration at the Veterans Administration, 1981–1982. He was Principal Deputy Assistant Secretary for Conservation and Renewable Energy at the Department of Energy, 1980–1981, and Deputy Chief Financial Officer, 1979–1980.

Mr. DeGeorge graduated from La Salle College (B.S., 1951) and completed graduate studies at the University of Delaware (1954–1955). He was born September 18, 1929, in Philadelphia, PA. He served in the United States Marine Corps, 1951–1953. He is married, has four children, and resides in College Park, MD.

Nomination of Robert H. Brumley II To Be General Counsel of the Department of Commerce
February 26, 1988

The President today announced his intention to nominate Robert H. Brumley II to be General Counsel of the Department of Commerce. He would succeed Douglas A. Riggs.

Since 1985 Mr. Brumley has been Deputy General Counsel at the Department of Commerce in Washington, DC, and Special Assistant to the General Counsel, 1983–1985. Prior to this Mr. Brumley was a partner in the firm of Chenault, Brumley and Chenault, 1979–1983.

Mr. Brumley graduated from East Tennessee State University (B.S., 1974) and the University of Tennessee College of Law (J.D., 1977). He was born July 19, 1948, in Cherry Point, NC. He served in the United States Marine Corps, 1970–1972, and the USMC Reserves, 1972-present. He is married, has two children, and resides in Aylett, VA.

Nomination of Robert L. Pettit To Be Associate Deputy Secretary of Transportation
February 26, 1988

The President today announced his intention to nominate Robert L. Pettit to be Associate Deputy Secretary of Transportation. He would succeed Jennifer Lynn Dorn.

Since 1986 Mr. Pettit has been a partner with the law firm of Wiley, Rein & Fielding in Washington, DC. Prior to this, he was senior legal adviser to Commissioner Mary Dawson at the Federal Communications Commission, 1982–1986; an associate with the law firm of Fletcher, Heald & Holdreth, 1978–1982; and an attorney with the Renewal and Transfer Division of the Federal Communications Commission, 1977–1978.

Mr. Pettit graduated from the University of Missouri (B.A., 1974) and Duke University School of Law (J.D., 1977). He was born August 14, 1952, in Springfield, MO. Mr. Pettit is married, has two children, and resides in Washington, DC.

Nomination of Karen Borlaug Phillips To Be a Member of the Interstate Commerce Commission
February 26, 1988

The President today announced his intention to nominate Karen Borlaug Phillips to be a member of the Interstate Commerce Commission for a term expiring December 31, 1991. She would succeed Malcolm M.B. Sterrett.

Since 1987 Mrs. Phillips has been minority chief economist at the United States Senate Committee on Finance in Washington, DC. Prior to this she was tax economist for the United States Senate Committee on Finance, 1985–1987. Mrs. Phillips also worked as a professional staff member at the United States Senate, Committee on Commerce, 1982–1985.

Mrs. Phillips graduated from the University of North Dakota (B.A., 1977; B.S., 1977). She was born October 1, 1956, in Long Beach, CA. She is married and resides in Alexandria, VA.

Appointment of Julius Belso as a Member of the National Council on Vocational Education
February 26, 1988

The President today announced his intention to appoint Julius Belso to be a member of the National Council on Vocational Education for a term expiring January 17, 1991. He would succeed J. Fernando Niebla.

Since 1981 Mr. Belso has been a partner with Biro-Belso Real Estate in New Brunswick, NJ. Prior to this he was chairman of the board for Magyar Savings and Loan Association, 1984–1987.

Mr. Belso graduated from the Agricultural Institute of Hungary in 1938. He was born August 12, 1918, in Kerkakutas, Zala Megye, Hungary. He is married and resides in New Brunswick, NJ.

Nomination of Jesse D. Winzenried To Be Director of the Securities Investor Protection Corporation, and Designation as Vice Chairman
February 26, 1988

The President today announced his intention to nominate Jesse D. Winzenried to be Director of the Securities Investor Protection Corporation for a term expiring December 31, 1990. He would succeed Roger A. Yurchuck. Upon confirmation, he will be designated Vice Chairman superseding the announcement of December 11, 1987, naming Frank G. Zarb as the intended Vice Chairman.

Mr. Winzenried has served with Crown Central Petroleum Corp. as group vice president, director, and member of the executive committee of the board of directors, 1974–1981. Prior to this, he was vice president of the Coastal States Gas Corp., 1969–1974.

Mr. Winzenried graduated from the University of Wyoming (B.S., 1945), the University of Denver (M.S., 1946), and New York University (Ph.D., 1955). He was born June 13, 1922, in Byron, WY. He served in the United States Air Corps, 1942–1943. Mr. Winzenried has three children and resides in Cody, WY.

Statement by Assistant to the President for Press Relations Fitzwater on the Situation in Panama
February 26, 1988

We condemn all efforts to perpetuate military rule in Panama, including efforts to remove President Delvalle from office. We want to reiterate our unqualified support for civilian constitutional rule in Panama. There is but one legitimate sovereign authority in Panama, and that is the Panamanian people exercising their democratic right to vote and elect their leadership in a free society. We have also initiated a series of consultations to learn the views of other countries in the hemisphere with regard to this situation.

Radio Address to the Nation on Drug Abuse and Aid to the Nicaraguan Democratic Resistance
February 27, 1988

My fellow Americans:

This Monday Nancy and I will be attending a very special meeting in Washington. It's a gathering of concerned citizens from every walk of life who are working with us to develop a national strategy to fight drug abuse in America. This is part of the White House Conference for a Drug Free America, which was established last year by Executive Order 12595.

A decade ago, drug abuse was ignored and, in some circles, was even glamorized. It was fashionable. Comedians joked about drugs, trivializing the problem. Well, there was legitimate reason for concern. Fathers and mothers saw their children wasting their lives. Husbands and wives felt helpless as a loved one destroyed a marriage. And as is so often the case, the children suffered most.

I can't help but be proud that my wife, Nancy, took on the challenge of mobilizing our people against this evil. She came up with the formula that will make all the difference: Just say no. It's as simple as that. It's going to require all of us working together, however, to help those we love and care for to just say no and live right.

We've already made progress. First and foremost, that complacent attitude has been replaced with vigorous and active involvement. Not only is the use of illegal drugs no longer accepted but is, in many circles, no longer tolerated. The old line about drug use being a victimless crime is being replaced with an understanding that the money spent on drugs, even by casual users, ends up financing murderers in South America as well as on our own streets.

On Monday, the members of the White House Conference will be joined by some 2,000 other activists who are dedicated to a drug free America. Whatever recommendations they ultimately make, it is clear there are no easy answers. We must continue to seek every opportunity to stop the sale and use of illegal drugs. Nancy, I know, has dedicated her life to this not just as First Lady but as parent and good citizen. Our commitment will not end when we leave Washington at the end of my term. Nancy and I are dedicated to working with you in the years ahead to secure the gains we've made and to keep our country moving toward the goal of a drug free America.

This is truly a national crusade. Government will do its part. Drug interdiction and well-equipped law enforcers are necessary. Each one of us has a role to play. The strategy that is emerging will depend on the widest range of citizen involvement. And I know I can count on you, because you feel as strongly about this as Nancy and I do.

We want everyone to have the opportunity for a productive, meaningful life. That also requires our country to be secure, which is why we've been so concerned about events in Central America. Democracy has been progressing in that region, but one area where totalitarianism has a foothold could well undo all that's been accomplished. Nicaragua, with its Communist regime, represses its own people and threatens its neighbors. Well, if there's any lesson we've learned, it is that freedom and peace go hand in hand, so it is imperative we see democratic progress in Nicaragua. And in the past several months, under pressure from the democratic resistance, there have been some limited reforms there.

On February 3d, to my disappointment, however, the majority in the House of Representatives voted to remove pressure for further democratic reform. The Senate, on the other hand, agreed with me that we cannot leave those fighting for freedom in Nicaragua at the mercy of the Communist regime and expect the process toward democracy to move ahead.

And already we can see warning signs. In just 2 short weeks, the Sandinistas threatened the only free press in the country and rejected a cease-fire proposal which incorporated the essential elements laid out and agreed to last August. And in the first 2 months of 1988, Soviet military assistance to

Nicaragua has almost doubled, compared to the same period in 1987. These are serious matters, and it's not time for wishful thinking. We must face reality in Central America, or we will face the consequences. We must have a policy, everywhere in the world, based on realism and strength.

Next week, I'll be in Brussels meeting with our NATO allies to assure them America is ready and willing to stand with them to keep the peace with freedom that we have gained together through the alliance these past 40 years.

Until next week, thanks for listening, and God bless you.

Note: The President spoke at 12:06 p.m. from the Oval Office at the White House.

Written Responses to Questions Submitted by the South Korean Newspaper Dong-A Ilbo
February 24, 1988

Democracy in South Korea

Q. With the inauguration of Mr. Roh Tae Woo, Korea will celebrate its first peaceful transfer of power. Since Korea has only experienced authoritarian rule, and not true democracy under a good or enlightened President, could you tell us the secret of being such a leader, and what can be done in Korea to bring expanded democracy?

The President. Over the past few decades, Korea has impressed the world with its economic miracle of rapid growth. In the past year, Korea has matched that economic progress with a kind of political miracle, setting a new course toward an open and democratic political system. The 1987 Presidential election marked an important milestone in that process. It is, however, important to remember that democracy is a process, not an end point. Americans value democracy, because it is a dynamic system that changes as a nation changes.

As you know, I met President-elect Roh in Washington last year. He impressed me as a man committed to the democratization of your country, because he knew that was what Koreans, including himself, wanted. I understand that President-elect Roh likes to refer to his having big ears. That is really the key to leadership in a democratic society. You have to listen carefully before you make decisions. Sometimes—especially when you have a wide-open election year as we have now—some may not like the results, but accept them and understand the different ways in which others see problems.

South Korea-U.S. Trade

Q. In a political sense we expect closer cooperation between the United States and the new Korean government, but economically (trade) we expect increased tensions in the short term. What can be done to keep these tensions under control so that this area tracks the political area?

The President. Korea and the United States are longtime allies and friends. The relationship has become closer, stronger, and more complex over the years. You are now our seventh largest trading partner. Korean and American businessmen routinely visit one [an]other. We have a growing Korean-American community living in our country. All of these trends are very positive, yet sometimes overlooked.

Change has also brought some new stresses—notably in the trade and exchange rate areas. There are real problems. Working together, as we have done for so many years in other areas, I am sure that we can solve these issues. The key is remembering that it is in our mutual interest to find good solutions. Participation in the international open-market system that has enabled Koreans to prosper has both benefits and responsibilities. Korea must be willing to accept responsibilities commensurate with its new, increased role in the international economic system.

Tensions on the Korean Peninsula

Q. Could you characterize how the recent improvement in U.S. relations with the Soviets can contribute to reduction of tensions on the Korean Peninsula? In the coming U.S.-Soviet summit would you encourage the Soviet leader to play a more active role in restraining or completely stopping North Korea's terrorist actions, including jeopardizing the 1988 Seoul Olympics?

The President. The United States and Soviet Union and everyone else in the region should be cooperating to reduce tensions on the Peninsula, as well as in the world as a whole. We hope that improved U.S.-Soviet relations will help move things in that direction and, of course, improve the situation in other areas of the world, too.

The key problem in Korea is North Korea's proclivity to use violence. The world was shocked again by the recent murder of 115 innocent people aboard KAL 858 by North Korea. A successful incident-free Olympics in Seoul this September is in everyone's interest. The prospect of North Korean—or anyone else's—attempts to disrupt the games through violence is a danger that we and the Soviets can agree to work against.

We hope that Moscow will use its close relations with Pyongyang to urge moderation and to encourage the resumption of direct North-South contacts on practical ways to reduce tension. It is time for the North to eschew violence and get down to the serious business of resuming dialog with Seoul. If it does, it may be able to join in the peace, progress, and prosperity other nations in the region have begun to share.

South Korea-Eastern Bloc Relations

Q. How do you assess possible diplomatic initiatives of the new Korean Government toward the East bloc, including the Soviet Union? Is there a role for the United States to play in helping improve Korean-East bloc relations?

The President. In recent years the Republic of Korea has made some progress in expanding contacts with the Eastern bloc. The Olympics will emphasize how this has happened. Continued progress in this direction is inevitable since Korea has so much to offer—products and expertise in the economics of free-enterprise industrialization. We support further movement and further opening in whatever appropriate ways that Korea may ask.

South Korea-U.S. Relations

Q. What are the chances for a U.S.-Korean summit with Mr. Roh Tae Woo, either in Washington or Seoul, and when could that take place?

The President. We have a close alliance with Korea and always welcome the opportunity for such discussions. Our people meet and share views all the time. Talk now of the details of summits and such seems a bit premature, since President-elect Roh is only now being sworn in and is busy setting up his new administration.

Note: The questions and answers were released by the Office of the Press Secretary on February 29.

Remarks at a Meeting of the White House Conference for a Drug Free America
February 29, 1988

The President. Thank you very much, Lois. And let me just say here how much Nancy and I admire the job Lois has been doing. On my desk in the Oval Office, I have a little sign that says: There is no limit to what a man can do or where he can go if he doesn't mind who gets the credit. And I can't think of anyone who is a better example of that truth about quietly getting things done than Lois Herrington. Lois, I speak for everyone here in saying thanks for the great job that you do.

All of us are here today to talk about the campaign for a drug free America. Now, I've said this once or twice in public and many times at home, but I can't say it too often. There are few things that I'm more proud of than the work Nancy has done in the fight against drugs. And in a moment I'll talk about money and law enforcement and so forth. They're important, no doubt, but Nancy has addressed something more fundamental. She's touched the conscience and consciousness of the Nation. She's helped teach hundreds of thousands of our young people to just say no to drugs and alcohol. Nancy, I'm so proud. And I'll confess that I've been nursing a little guilt, too. I'm the only one in the family the Government's paying. [*Laughter*]

We're fighting the crusade for a drug free America on many fronts. In the past 7 years, we've, for the first time ever, set up a coordinated Federal, State, and local campaign against drug smugglers. Among other things we've enlisted the military in the battle, including Navy ships and AWAC planes. We've also set up 13 Federal, State, and local strike forces to investigate and prosecute major drug rings. We've substantially increased the number of Federal prosecutors and agents. And we've strengthened the laws so that, for example, we can now dispose of property that was bought with drug money. We don't have to give it back.

The results? Last year, Federal drug agents confiscated over half a billion dollars' worth of drug-related assets. They closed down 682 clandestine laboratories. And they seized 92,000 pounds of cocaine. These are all records. We've taken fleets of airplanes, boats, and trucks from smugglers and dealers. I visited Florida some time back and saw for the first time what $20 million looks like. It was piled up on a table, confiscated from drug dealers. I've heard stories of our planes tracking drug planes and landing right behind them on the runways, agents jumping out and making the arrest.

To get around us, smugglers have had to find new ways of hiding their product. We've discovered drugs in hollowed out lumber and in bathrooms and luggage compartments in airplanes. One morning in Tennessee a man woke up and found a body in his driveway. It was wearing an unopened parachute and carried a large package of cocaine. An air smuggler had tried to elude pursuers by bailing out of his plane. Drug seizures are at an all-time high. Federal drug arrests have increased 66 percent. Arrests of major traffickers have tripled. And in the past 8 years, prison sentences for those convicted of drug law violations have increased by 44 percent, to an average of more than 6 years per sentence.

And that's how we're fighting on what you might call the supply side of the crusade against drugs. But as significant as stopping smugglers and pushers is, ending the demand for drugs is how, in the end, we'll win. That's why the best news I've heard in a long time was the recently released annual survey of high school seniors. For 13 years we have asked thousands of graduating seniors what drugs they use, how often, and what they think about drug abuse. For the first time a substantially smaller proportion of the seniors—one third smaller—acknowledged current cocaine use than did the year before. Use of marijuana and amphetamines is also dropping. Better still, almost all students said it was wrong even to try a drug like cocaine.

With all the headlines about how we're losing the drug war, let's keep in mind the progress we've made. Many drug-related problems now are not because more people are turning to drugs—in fact, the number of users has leveled off and may be falling—but because so many got hooked when the message went out that illegal drugs were acceptable.

This conference couldn't have happened 8 years ago—not enough people cared. Now almost everyone cares. Your communities are looking to you for leadership. So, let me ask you to take back home the message that illegal drugs are one thing no community in America can, should, or needs to tolerate—in schools, in workplaces, in the streets, anywhere. America is already starting to take that message to heart. That's why I believe the tide of battle has turned, and we're beginning to win the crusade for a drug free America.

Now, rather than go any further, I'll stop

here. President Eisenhower once said that the great thing about this job was no one could tell you to sit down. [*Laughter*] Well, almost no one. [*Laughter*] Nancy, you're on.

Mrs. Reagan. Thank you, Mr. President. I know who's boss in the family. [*Laughter*] I can't tell you how good it feels to be here at this conference with so many people united in a common purpose. Although the drug problem is still destructive, the Nation has come a long way in its battle against drugs, and your presence here today proves it.

At least we realize there is a drug problem today. In Saturday's Washington Post, there was one page in which every article was a local drug story. And there was another local drug story on the front page. We must face the fact that drugs are tearing our communities apart.

Although I've been deeply concerned about this problem since my days in Sacramento, over the past nearly 8 years, I've focused mainly on education, on prevention, and on the need to change attitudes. Although we're making progress, still many ignorant ideas persist. And one of the worst is the casual user's justification that drug use is a victimless crime, that drugs don't hurt anyone except the person who's using them. Yet there are consequences to drug use beyond an individual's personal and selfish high. And that's what I'd like to talk to you about this morning.

A few weeks ago the drug cartel murdered Colombia's Attorney General, Carlos Mauro Hoyos, who was active in trying to halt cocaine traffic to the United States. Half a dozen men in 3 jeeps ran his car into a curb, sprayed it with machine gun fire, and killed his two bodyguards. Mr. Hoyos was later found, blindfolded and handcuffed, his skull shattered with bullets. And, ladies and gentlemen, the people who casually use cocaine are responsible, because their money bought those bullets. They provided the high stakes that murdered those men plus hundreds of others in Colombia, including supreme court justices, 21 judges handling drug cases, and scores of policemen and soldiers.

The notion that the mellow marijuana user doesn't hurt anyone is just as phony. As a result of an intensive effort by the Drug Enforcement Administration in Guadalajara, Mexico, and particularly Special Agent Enrique Camarena, over 10,000 acres of marijuana that were ready for harvest and eventual sale in the United States were destroyed. And this caused a major financial loss for a notorious trafficking group. On February 7, 1985, less than 3 months after the destruction of the 10,000-acre plantation, Special Agent Camarena was kidnaped by the traffickers. He was tortured and beaten to death. And this country's casual marijuana users cannot escape responsibility for their fellow American's death, because they, in effect, bought the tools for his torture.

As you know, many others have had their lives taken to protect our society from the corruption of drugs. Two DEA agents in California were killed just this month. Last week, while guarding the home of a witness in a drug crime, a rookie policeman in New York was assassinated in a patrol car. The traffickers and dealers will murder anyone who stands in their way. Recently an innocent young girl in Los Angeles was shot to death in the crossfire between two rival drug gangs. And who will tell the grief-stricken families that drug use is a victimless crime?

The casual user may think when he takes a line of cocaine or smokes a joint in the privacy of his nice condo, listening to his expensive stereo, that he's somehow not bothering anyone. But there is a trail of death and destruction that leads directly to his door. The casual user cannot morally escape responsibility for the action of drug traffickers and dealings. I'm saying that if you're a casual drug user you're an accomplice to murder. The casual user also cannot morally escape association with those who use drugs and then endanger the public safety. The message from casual use is that drugs are acceptable, that they can be handled, that somehow it's simply a matter of dosage. Casual use sets the tone for tolerance and that tolerance has killed.

Anne and Arthur Johnson are from Potomac, Maryland. They're with us today, and I'll introduce you to them later. On January 4, 1987, the Johnson's daughter, 20-year-old Christy, was taking the train to New York to visit her sister before heading back to classes at Stanford University. The Sunday afternoon Amtrak train was crowded with students returning to school and families returning home from Christmas and the New Year's holidays. Unknown to the passengers, a Conrail locomotive passed several warning signals and crossed into the path of the Amtrak train. The crash killed 16 innocent people and injured 175 others. Christy never made it to her sister's; she was killed in the crash.

The investigation determined that the engineer and brakeman on the Conrail train were smoking marijuana prior to the crash—16 people killed because of an engineer's personal indulgence in a joint of marijuana. Now, don't tell the Johnsons that casual drug use is a victimless crime. And don't try to tell the Johnsons that drugs hurt no one but the user. Several of the families of the victims who were killed in the wreck testified before the Senate last week in favor of mandatory drug testing for railroad personnel. The engineer and the brakeman also called for such testing, saying that alcohol and drug use was widespread within the industry. Senator Danforth told the families: "You won't win this quickly; you have to fan the flame of rage." And that's exactly what we must do—we must fan the flame of rage.

Ladies and gentlemen, I want to make it impossible for casual users to escape responsibility for any innocent death due to drugs. I want to make them fully face the brutality of drug use. I don't mind admitting that I have reservations about telling the following two stories, because they're real stories of anguish and inhuman brutality. Yet Betty Jean Spencer and Vince and Roberta Roper can't ignore the brutality of drugs. They live with it every day. They're with us today, and if they can't forget, neither should we.

First, let me tell you about Betty Jean Spencer. Mrs. Spencer was at home in her rural farmhouse in Indiana with her four sons. They were 14, 16, 18, and 22 years old. Four men barged into the house, men out on bail on drug trafficking. The men didn't know her. They didn't know her sons. Mrs. Spencer says they were obviously high on something. They were laughing about the other people they were going to kill when they finished there. They ordered Mrs. Spencer and her four sons to line up face down on the floor, and then the men began shooting them at point-blank range with a shotgun. Mrs. Spencer miraculously survived two shotgun blasts to the back of her head, but her sons were murdered. And the men are in prison.

That's a brutal, brutal story. And it makes me angry. And no one—absolutely no one—should be allowed to say that drug use is a victimless crime. No one should be able to get away with the argument that drugs are a harmless, private indulgence.

Finally let me tell you about the nightmare that Vince and Roberta Roper must endure. Their daughter, Stephanie, a 22-year-old student, was returning to school in Maryland when her car broke down. Two men offered assistance. They drove her a short distance in their car, pulled a gun on her, and each raped her. They drove to another location and raped her again. They then decided to kill her. I don't want to repeat what they did to her, but we can't ignore the brutality of drugs. One of the men whipped Stephanie on the head with a chain, and as she tried to run away, he shot her. He then poured gasoline on her and set fire to her. Both men were users of PCP, LSD, amphetamines, barbiturates—virtually any drug they could obtain.

Now, who would dare stand before the Ropers and tell them that drug use is a victimless crime? What apologist for casual drug use will look the Ropers in the eye and say it's all a matter of moderation? Who could be so brazen? Yet the attitude prevails.

Applause isn't appropriate, but a hug or a squeeze of the hand when you leave might mean a lot. But I'd like to introduce you to Betty Jean Spencer, and Anne and Arthur Johnson—[*applause*]—Vince and Roberta Roper. Thank you. [*Applause*] Let's each of us help here: Promise them that we won't let anyone forget the brutality of drugs.

You know, in the field of drug and alcohol abuse there's something called the enabling concept: If I don't do something about your behavior, then I enable it to happen. Society's attitude has enabled the casual drug user to avoid facing his role in the murder and brutality behind drugs. We can no longer let the casual user continue without paying the moral penalty.

We must be absolutely unyielding and inflexible in our opposition to drug use. There's no middle ground. We must be as adamant about the casual user as we are about the addict. And whereas the addict deserves our help, the casual user deserves our condemnations, because he could easily stop, and yet he chooses not to do so. He must be made to feel the burden of brutality and corruption for which he's ultimately responsible. We must get the message out: We will not stand for illicit drug use of any kind—period.

And there's another message I'd like to get out to all of you here today, and that's a message of gratitude for your involvement in the fight against drugs. You're the people who will eventually turn the tide. You're the ones who will make the difference. Many of you have been with me from the very beginning in one capacity or another. And I want you to know that when my husband and I return to California I'm not giving up my interest and concern about this. You can't get rid of me. In fact, I'll be actively involved in the Nancy Reagan Center in Los Angeles to be run by Phoenix House. The center will include a residential high school for young people in treatment, a training unit, and a research unit. I hope that the center will become a place where we can develop new methods, test new approaches, and discover new answers.

Anne Morrow Lindbergh once wrote: "One can never pay in gratitude, one can only pay 'in kind' somewhere else in life." And I'm hoping that this center will be one way I may repay all of you for the support and love and encouragement you've given me over the past 8 years. Thank you for your support, and thank you for what you're doing for our nation.

Note: The President spoke at 10:10 a.m. in the Regency Ballroom at the Omni Shoreham Hotel. In his opening remarks, the President referred to Lois H. Herrington, chairman and executive director of the Conference.

Remarks at the Annual Leadership Conference of the American Legion
February 29, 1988

Thank you Commander Comer, and thank you all very much. Congressman Conte, President Behrend, General Turnage, and members of the American Legion and American Legion Auxiliary, it's wonderful to have you here in Washington. As you may have noticed, this isn't like other cities. I've heard that one of the networks is considering a midseason replacement with a new dramatic series set in Washington; it's called Capitol Hill Street Blues. [*Laughter*]

But it's great to be with the Legion once again. You're always so kind in your reception. But I want you to know that the trappings of office haven't gone to my head—I still wear the same size American Legion hat you gave me in 1980. In fact, I made the same point to Interior Secretary Don Hodel the other day. I said, "Don, you can't let high office go to your head. And speaking of heads, how much room is there left on Mount Rushmore?" [*Laughter*]

But as you may know, I'll be traveling to Brussels tomorrow to attend a summit with the leaders of the North Atlantic alliance. But I wanted to stop by here first to talk about our hopes and plans for the alliance, because it is, after all, many of you and the servicemen the Legion represents who made that alliance possible, who with their courage and sacrifice brought 40 years of peace to Europe and security to the United States.

Coming here, I was reminded of something Ernie Pyle wrote in France during the final days of World War II. I suppose there are more than a few of us here who remember Ernie Pyle and his simple, honest words that meant so much. Sitting under an apple tree in a lovely green orchard, he thought of the end of the war. Peace would come, he knew, but there would be no return to innocence.

"Last night," he said, "we had a violent electrical storm around our countryside. The storm was half over before we realized that the flashes and the crashings around us were not artillery but plain old-fashioned thunder and lightning. It will be odd to hear only thunder again. You must remember that such little things as that are in our souls and will take time. And all of us together will have to learn how to reassemble our broken world into a pattern so firm and so fair that another great war cannot soon be possible."

A pattern so firm and so fair—before Ernie Pyle, friend of the GI, was laid to rest on Okinawa, the United States and the war-ravaged democracies of Europe set about that great enterprise. We embraced our old enemies and made them friends. We set about reconstructing a continent, replacing hurt and harm with a helping hand. Soon would follow the Marshall plan, an example of national charity and generosity unparalleled in history.

I've often said that there is something unique about the American form of patriotism, the kind so gloriously on display here at the Legion. It is not an exclusive attachment; it is not jealous or chauvinistic: It's the affirmation of man's deepest desires for the rights and liberties given him by his Creator. American patriotism is, quite simply, the call to freedom, everywhere, for all peoples. And that's why the American flag is more than a national flag. It has been, throughout our history, the hope and encouragement of freedom-loving peoples everywhere.

There's an account of two of America's greatest postwar statesmen traveling to Hungary soon after the war. Budapest lay devastated by weeks of street fighting, but there was rejoicing in the city. The Soviet occupiers had allowed a free election, and the anti-Communists had won a clear majority. Cheering Hungarians thronged the streets, blocking the way to the American mission. Recalled one of the diplomats: "There was an enormous crowd celebrating the victory under the American flag." He said, "It made me very humble to see how much these people looked to the United States as the protector of their freedom." And recalled the other: "Here was the hope of the world—the American flag."

The jubilation, of course, didn't last. The Hungarians did not have long to celebrate their freedom before it was snatched away from them. Soon, to use Winston Churchill's famous phrase, an iron curtain was to descend across Europe. While we had defeated one form of totalitarianism, another—just as implacable, just as greedy—threatened our hopes for a new world living in peace and freedom, a new pattern so firm and so fair that it would forever be secure.

As Churchill wrote: "In war, one must show resolution; in victory, magnanimity; in peace, good will." In this new cold war, as it was called, in this uneasy peace, we would be called upon to match our good will with resolution not just for today or tomorrow but for the long haul. We would be called upon to match the magnanimity of the Marshall plan with the tough realism and determination of NATO.

Today NATO has kept the peace in Europe and helped keep America secure for 40 years. Eight Presidents from both parties, with strong bipartisan support from Congress and the American people, have shown a clear resolution to our adversaries: A free and democratic Europe is essential to a free and democratic America. We have let there be no doubt in the Soviets' minds: An attack on free Europe would be the same as an assault on the United States. The core of our foreign policy and of our national security is our permanent partnership with our fellow democracies in the Atlantic alliance, on which the cause of freedom so critically depends. We will never sacrifice the interests of our allies and friends in any agreement with the Soviet Union.

Our commitment to the Atlantic alliance has not been inexpensive, but the tragic lessons of two world wars teach us that it has been cheap at the price. Today a rebuilt, prosperous, free Europe is taking on more of the burdens of defense. In the event of a short-warning attack, 90 percent of the defending troops would be European. And despite sluggish economies on the continent, two-thirds of our allies will be increasing their defense contributions this year.

Military aggression is not the only threat from the East. The Soviets' time-honored tactic of political intimidation designed to split the alliance was never better seen than at the time of NATO's INF deployments in response to the Soviets' SS–20's. Threatening to boycott negotiations, the Soviets mounted the most intensive campaign of political pressure any of us can remember. For a while it appeared they might be successful. The papers were full of predictions that our allies would cave. So-called peace movements sprang up trumpeting a line very close to that of the Soviets. If they had had their way, of course, the Soviet SS–20's would remain permanently in place, pointed at every major city in Europe.

But the Soviet effort to split the alliance failed. The allies refused to be intimidated and went ahead with the deployments as planned. The result—the historic treaty signed last December that, for the first time, eliminates an entire class of U.S. and Soviet nuclear missiles. Let me say one thing about the treaty: It is not based on trust. We can't forget that the very reason for NATO was the Soviets' aggressive expansionism in Eastern Europe and abrogation of their sworn commitments under the Yalta agreement.

Being, as I am, an old member of the cavalry—back in a time when the cavalry still rode horses—[*laughter*]—I know that even animals learn from experience. I was in a picture once in Hollywood, and one of the character actors there was the well-known Big Boy Williams—230 pounds of him. And there was a scene where Big was up there on one of those high, boarded wagons, and he was to drop down onto the horse and take off. And in the rehearsal, he did, and took off. And then they said, "Okay, roll the cameras." They called for action, and Big dropped down right on his back on the ground. [*Laughter*] The horse had felt him fall on him once; he wasn't going to stay there for the second time around. [*Laughter*] That was in a picture called "Santa Fe Trail." [*Laughter*]

So, we've learned from experience, too. And as I said to General Secretary Gorbachev—and I think the point struck home—when it comes to treaties with the Soviet Union, our policy is *dovorey no provorey*, which, as everyone knows by now, I think, means trust, but verify.

During the years of these negotiations, new realities have come into play—new realities that present new opportunities. In particular, in recent years we've seen the emergence among some of our European allies of a willingness, even an eagerness, to seek a larger, more closely coordinated role for Western Europe in providing for its own defense within the overall framework of the alliance. And we Americans welcome this.

For these four decades, NATO has, in effect, represented an alliance between a number of partners and one very senior partner. Yet today our European allies have risen from the ruins of war to vitality, prosperity, and growing unity as a continent. And so, I would submit that now the alliance should become more and more one among equals, an alliance between continents. In the words of former Secretary of State Henry Kissinger: The time has come for our country "to welcome a European identity in defense, which in the end is bound to spur Atlantic cooperation."

We will continue to push for verifiable 50-percent reductions in the strategic arsenals of the U.S. and U.S.S.R. and for a verifiable and truly global ban on chemical weapons. But at the same time, the serious imbalance of conventional forces in Europe must be addressed as an equally high priority. This imbalance represents an unacceptable threat to the West. Warsaw Pact tanks and artillery far outnumber our own. Ours are positioned for defense, theirs for an offensive attack.

There is a role for arms control negotiations here, but as a supplement to a policy of strength, not as a substitute. We have learned from experience: The only effective way to negotiate with the Soviets is from a position of strength. The Warsaw Pact's numerical superiority and the Soviet strategy, which emphasizes surprise attacks, means that our remaining nuclear forces are fully capable of supporting NATO's flexible response strategy. At the same time, we must modernize our chemical weapons to deter Soviet first-use, and we must provide for conventional forces that are capable of protecting free Europe.

And when talking about our efforts to secure a peaceful future, nothing could be more important than our Strategic Defense Initiative, SDI—a strategic defense that threatens no one, that could someday make nuclear weapons obsolete. The technology for SDI is developing more rapidly than many would have thought possible. No, technology isn't holding SDI back, but year after year Congress cuts our budget requests for SDI. General Secretary Gorbachev has stated publicly, before the American people, that the Soviets have their own SDI program, that they're doing everything we're doing. Now is not the time to cut back on SDI.

General Secretary Gorbachev talks about *perestroika,* or restructuring at home. Well, it's time for some *perestroika* in the Warsaw Pact. It's time for the removal of Soviet troops from Eastern Europe and the abandonment of Soviet offensive strategy on the continent. On my last trip to Europe, I went to Berlin and visited that infamous wall that cuts such an ugly scar through the heart of Europe. The wall that encircles the free sectors of that city is part of a vast system of barriers—of barbed wire, guard towers, dog runs, and machine guns—that divides the continent, divides nations, peoples, families.

For years, especially in the seventies, the cognoscenti spoke of the so-called superpower conflict in value-neutral terms, as if there was no essential difference between Western democracies and Soviet communism. Any suggestion that a system that denies its people their God-given liberties was fundamentally evil was met with ridicule. Well, I challenge those people to go to Berlin and look upon that wall, look upon the works of tyranny.

The question can be asked: How can we ever achieve a lasting peace with a regime that is so scared of its own people that it must imprison them behind barbed wire? And that's why I said to Mr. Gorbachev: If you really want *glasnost,* if you really want openness, tear down that wall.

The unnatural division of Europe remains one of the major sources of tension between the West and the Soviet Union. We accept no spheres of influence. We accept no legal division of Europe. Our policy can be based on only one principle: the right of people everywhere to self-determination, to freedom, and to the basic rights granted them by their Creator. So, the meeting of the Atlantic democracies in Brussels this week will come at a time when, in many ways, our alliance has never been stronger or more unified—also at a time when the challenges before us have never been greater.

Let me just say a few words here about Congress and defense spending. It seems ironic to me that so many of those who welcome, as they should, our historic agreement to eliminate an entire class of U.S. and Soviet INF missiles in Europe and Asia continue to undercut our ability to negotiate from strength by voting year after year to cut necessary defense spending. In the seventies we tried dealing with the Soviets and their clients from a position of weakness. The result: Angola, Cambodia, Afghanistan, Nicaragua, and at the negotiating table an arms control treaty so flawed that a Senate controlled by the President's own party spiked it. If Congress continues to unilaterally make major defense cuts that amount to strategic concessions to the Soviets, we could find ourselves back in the position we were in during the late seventies: dangerously weak and ill-prepared.

We don't have to stretch our memories back too far to remember that the American people twice, by overwhelming majorities, voted clearly and emphatically for something that all of us here believe in: They voted for peace in the only way it can ever be secured; they voted for peace through strength.

Today the people of Afghanistan are setting an example for all of us—of courage, heroism, and strength. I can assure you: We will not let them down. We will not agree to any steps that put the Afghan freedom fighters or Afghan hopes for self-determination at risk. And the fact there's progress now in the Afghan diplomacy—because we stood by our friends—should teach a lesson in another similar situation closer to home.

As you know, Congress will be voting

again on continued aid to the freedom fighters in Nicaragua. I hope Members of Congress will remember one thing: Those freedom fighters are inside Nicaragua today, because we made a commitment to them. Are we going to cut them off now and leave them defenseless against the Sandinistas? If we do, who will ever trust in the United States of America again? How long can we remain a world power if we gain a reputation for pulling the plug on the people who have placed their trust in us, people fighting for their own freedom and for our national security?

Before the last vote, I warned Congress: You may cut off aid to the freedom fighters, but Soviet deliveries to the Sandinistas won't stop. And in fact, Soviet military assistance to the Sandinistas was nearly doubled in the first 2 months of this year compared to the same period in 1987. Congressional opponents of aid argued that the peace process would flourish and the Sandinistas would democratize if we cut off our assistance to the freedom fighters. Well, it's been 3 weeks, and exactly the opposite has happened.

Cardinal Obando y Bravo was forced to suspend the most recent round of peace talks because of Sandinista obstructionism. And Sandinista rhetoric has become ever more warlike, full of promises to crush the resistance. And the Sandinistas continue to tighten their grip on the suffering country—threatening La Prensa; sending out the government directed *turbas,* or mobs, to harass dissidents; and expanding their system of political prisons. That's the Sandinistas for you. At the same time they promise a general amnesty, they're building more political prisons. They've gone from 2 to 16 prisons.

Recently a document was found on a Communist terrorist killed in battle in El Salvador. And let me quote a few lines: "The defeat of the *contras* would be a grave strategic defeat for the United States," it says, and goes on, "The failure of the *contras* and the acceptance of the Nicaraguan revolution for the United States can be a total global strategic change." I could not have said it better myself, except to add, of course, that this total global change will not be in our favor. Unless the freedom fighters remain a viable force, the peace process will quickly become what it was before: an empty charade, dragging endlessly and fruitlessly on, while the Soviets continue their military buildup on the American mainland.

The American people are watching, and Congress knows it. And some say they're willing to support some type of humanitarian aid but are doing everything they can do to disband the freedom fighters. But there's nothing humanitarian about asking people to go up against Soviet attack helicopters armed only with boots and bandages. Whatever package emerges from the Congress must include a provision for expedited procedures that would allow us to request additional military aid to the freedom fighters should the peace process break down.

We will not leave the freedom fighters to be picked off one by one—picked off by Sandinistas heavily equipped by the Soviet Union. With our help, the freedom fighters have been winning major victories in the field. With our help, they can keep the pressure on the Sandinistas to force them to democratize.

Preventing the consolidation of a pro-Soviet regime on the American mainland is a crucial test of national security. If Central America goes Communist, it would be a setback for America of incalculable proportions. I won't stake the future of the Western Hemisphere on Sandinista promises. There is no alternative: United States security demands a free and democratic Nicaragua. Nothing less will do. And let me just add that I'm aware of the Legion's tremendous support for our Central America policy, and I just want you to know I thank you from the bottom of my heart.

And finally, I'd like to turn to another side of the world: Asia. I understand you'll be hearing today about our efforts to account for our missing servicemen in Southeast Asia and Korea. Many of you here today were their comrades-in-arms. You fought the same battles, flew the same missions. Those men were fighting a noble cause. They were fighting for America and for freedom. We will never forget them. And that's one reason why I'm renewing today the personal commitment I made to the families of our POW's and MIA's: We will not give up. We will not relent until we bring our American heroes home.

Now, I can't resist just one last thing here before I go. I have become a collector of jokes that I can absolutely establish are told among the Soviet citizens. They tell them to each other, and reveals they've got a great sense of humor. But also they've got a pretty good sense of realism about their government.

This one happens to do—I was mentioning about the Berlin Wall and why it must come down. This is a story that is told in East Germany about that wall. It seems that their leader, Mr. Honecker, was attracted to a very lovely young lady, and he was making all sorts of promises. And then she said, "Well, all I want is—I want the Wall to be torn down." And he said, "The Wall to—oh," he said, "I know. You want to be alone with me." [*Laughter*] I haven't told that one to Secretary General Gorbachev yet, but I will. I'll get around to it. [*Laughter*]

I want to thank you all very much. God bless all of you.

Note: The President spoke at 1:26 p.m. in the main ballroom at the Sheraton Washington Hotel. In his opening remarks, the President referred to John (Jake) P. Comer, national commander of the American Legion; Representative Silvio O. Conte of Massachusetts; Pearl Behrend, president of the American Legion Auxiliary; and Thomas K. Turnage, Administrator of Veterans Affairs.

Executive Order 12627—Amending the President's Commission on Privatization
February 29, 1988

By virtue of the authority vested in me as President by the Constitution and laws of the United States of America, and in accordance with the Federal Advisory Committee Act, as amended (5 U.S.C. App. I), it is hereby ordered that section 2(d) of Executive Order No. 12607 of September 2, 1987, entitled "President's Commission on Privatization" is amended by deleting "March 1, 1988" and inserting in lieu thereof "March 31, 1988."

RONALD REAGAN

The White House,
February 29, 1988.

[*Filed with the Office of the Federal Register, 10:21 a.m., March 1, 1988*]

Message to the Senate Transmitting a Protocol to the Belgium-United States Convention on Taxation
February 29, 1988

To the Senate of the United States:

I transmit herewith, for Senate advice and consent to ratification, the Supplementary Protocol Modifying and Supplementing the Convention between the United States of America and the Kingdom of Belgium for the Avoidance of Double Taxation and the Prevention of Fiscal Evasion with Respect to Taxes on Income, together with a related exchange of notes. The Supplementary Protocol and the exchange of notes were signed at Washington on December 31, 1987. I also transmit for the information of the Senate the report of the Department of State with respect to the Protocol.

Pending the successful conclusion of a comprehensive new income tax convention, the Supplementary Protocol will make certain improvements in the existing convention intended to promote the development of economic relations between the United States and Belgium.

It is most desirable that this Protocol be considered by the Senate as soon as possible and that the Senate give advice and consent to ratification.

RONALD REAGAN

The White House,
February 29, 1988.

Message to the Congress Transmitting the Report on the Reduction of Federal Travel Expenses
February 29, 1988

To the Congress of the United States:

In accordance with section 512 of the Labor, Health and Human Services, and Education, and Related Agencies Appropriations Act, 1988, included in Public Law 100–202, I herewith transmit a report specifying my determination of the uniform percentage necessary to reduce outlays for travel, transportation, and subsistence by $23.6 million in accounts within this appropriations act in Fiscal Year 1988. Federal agencies have been instructed to make the required reductions.

RONALD REAGAN

The White House,
February 29, 1988.

Message on the Observance of St. Patrick's Day, 1988
February 29, 1988

Nancy and I are proud and pleased to wish everyone a Happy St. Patrick's Day, especially Irish Americans and all of Ireland's own, at home and around the globe.

On St. Patrick's Day I seek to remind America and the world of the debt we owe to the Irish people, who through the ages have created and perpetuated a unique heritage of faith and freedom, of humor and hope, of scholarship and sanctity and sacrifice.

With faith and fearlessness St. Patrick brought Christianity to Ireland a millennium and a half ago. The annals reveal the Irish people's eagerness to embrace the faith and to keep it; that trait remains to this day, a tribute to the Apostle of Ireland and to his flock in every generation.

St. Patrick's Day is a time to recall as well the many links between Ireland and America—perhaps, as some say, from the days of pre-Columbian Irish seafaring monks, but surely ever since the Irish people have known America as a land of liberty, justice, and opportunity.

As the ballad says, "And now to conclude and finish, as I have no more to say"—May America and Ireland always cherish each other and the kinship in which we hold St. Patrick's Day. And may God ever be our shield and our guide.

RONALD REAGAN

Appointment of Kay Wheless Woodward as Special Assistant to the President and Director of the Office of Cabinet Affairs

February 29, 1988

The President today announced the appointment of Kay Wheless Woodward to be Special Assistant to the President and Director of the Office of Cabinet Affairs at the White House.

Mrs. Woodward recently served as Deputy Assistant Secretary for Congressional Affairs at the Department of Labor. She was named Legislative Director in the Office of Congressional Affairs at the Department of Labor in 1985. Previously she served as legislative affairs officer in the Office of the U.S. Trade Representative, (November 1982–May 1985); legislative writer, office of congressional relations, U.S. Chamber of Commerce, 1981–1982; director of operations, Coalitions for America, 1979–1981; and staff assistant for the Senate Republican Steering Committee, 1977–1978.

Mrs. Woodward graduated from Hollins College (B.A., 1977). She was born on January 25, 1955, in Raleigh, NC. She is married and resides in Alexandria, VA.

Remarks on Departure for the North Atlantic Treaty Organization Summit Meeting in Brussels, Belgium

March 1, 1988

The President. Thank you all very much, and good morning.

Audience members. Good morning.

The President. I'm going to Europe to meet with a group of friends and colleagues: the leaders of the North Atlantic alliance. We and our foreign affairs and defense ministers see a good deal of each other, just as friends should. But the meeting that begins in Brussels tomorrow will be special. It'll be the first time in almost 6 years that leaders of all the NATO countries have met together for a summit.

Much has happened in those 6 years that we can be very proud of, including the INF treaty with the Soviet Union that removes an entire class of U.S. and Soviet nuclear weapons—weapons that, on the Soviet side, have held the European continent at risk. That historic agreement was possible because the alliance's steadfast political and military resolve backed up our negotiations with the Soviets. But the purpose of this summit is not self-congratulations. Our responsibility is to the future, and it will be to the future that we turn our attention tomorrow.

Our first priority is to maintain a strong and healthy partnership between North America and Europe, for this is the foundation on which the cause of freedom so crucially depends. We will never sacrifice the interests of this partnership in any agreement with the Soviet Union. NATO's agenda for peace and freedom has always been ambitious, and it must remain so.

In the arms control area, we will continue to press for Soviet agreement to 50-percent reductions in the strategic nuclear forces on both sides and for a truly global and verifiable ban on chemical weapons. My colleagues and I will be working to give negotiations on conventional forces a new start as well. We will also discuss Soviet behavior toward its own citizens and toward other countries, since problems of human rights and external aggression remain key obstacles to long-term improvement of East-West relations.

If our common approach to the East over the years has given coherence to our message of peace and world freedom, it has been our unwavering commitment to defend ourselves that has given it credibility. Arms reduction can only succeed if it is backed up by a strong defense. My Atlantic colleagues and I will rededicate ourselves to maintaining the deterrent that has protected our freedom and prosperity for almost 40 years. I will repeat to my colleagues my strong conviction that American troops will remain in Europe, under any administration, so long as Europeans want them to stay.

We can be rightfully proud of these 40 years of peace that our common commitment has brought, but the job is not finished. We in the alliance will not be satisfied merely with a record period without war. We seek nothing less than permanent peace with freedom in Europe and the North Atlantic. This bold objective can be attained, but we must have the courage to follow the course that we've set for ourselves. For four decades the combination of a strong common defense and pursuit of dialog with the East has been a winning formula for NATO. It is a combination that can lead us to a future of peace, freedom, and prosperity for generations to come.

Thank you, God bless you, and thank you all for coming out here to see us off. Thank you.

Reporter. Mr. President, what are you going to do about Noriega in Panama?

The President. It's under discussion right now.

Q. Is there anything that the U.S. can do?

The President. That's what we're trying to find out.

Note: The President spoke to supporters and members of the White House staff at 8:28 a.m. at the South Portico of the White House.

Designation of Manfred Eimer as Acting Director of the United States Arms Control and Disarmament Agency

March 1, 1988

The President today designated Manfred Eimer as the Acting Director of the United States Arms Control and Disarmament Agency.

Since 1983 Mr. Eimer has been Assistant Director (Verification and Intelligence) at the United States Arms Control and Disarmament Agency. Prior to this he was Executive Director at ACDA, 1973–1983. From 1970 to 1973, he was Assistant Director (Intelligence) and Assistant Director (Electronic Warfare and Reconnaissance), Defense Research and Engineering, at the Department of Defense. He was vice president (engineering) at the Space General Corp./Aerojet General Corp., 1963–1970.

Mr. Eimer graduated from California Institute of Technology (B.S., 1947; M.S., 1948; and Ph.D., 1953). He was born August 11, 1925, in Vienna, Austria. Mr. Eimer is married, has three children, and resides in Potomac, MD.

Letter to Congressional Leaders on the Proposed Civil Rights Restoration Act of 1987

March 1, 1988

*Dear*__________:

I am writing to advise you of my deep concern with the "Civil Rights Restoration Act" (S. 557), also called the "Grove City" bill, which the House is scheduled to consider shortly. I will veto the bill if it is presented to me in its current form.

Preservation of the civil rights of Americans is an important function of government. In the area directly affected by the

Grove City decision of the Supreme Court—education—my Administration has supported the effort to end discrimination against women, such as in collegiate athletics. In this and other areas, we remain committed to the effort to eradicate invidious discrimination in American society.

Unfortunately, the Grove City bill dramatically expands the scope of Federal jurisdiction over State and local governments and the private sector, from churches and synagogues to farmers, grocery stores, and businesses of all sizes. It diminishes the freedom of the private citizen to order his or her life and unnecessarily imposes the heavy burden of compliance with extensive Federal regulations and paperwork on many elements of American society.

The bill poses a particular threat to religious liberty. It interferes with the free exercise of religion by failing to protect the religious tenets of schools closely identified with religious organizations. Further, the bill establishes unprecedented and pervasive Federal regulation of entire churches and synagogues whenever any one of their many activities, such as a program to provide hot meals for the elderly, receives any Federal assistance. Moreover, and in further contrast to pre-*Grove City* coverage, entire private elementary and secondary school systems, including religious systems, will be covered if just one school in such a private system receives Federal aid.

I regret that the Members of the House of Representatives were not given the opportunity to consider and solve these and the many other problems with the bill through the normal process of committee consideration. I urge the House to correct these deficiencies.

Sincerely,

RONALD REAGAN

Note: Identical letters were sent to Jim Wright, Speaker of the House of Representatives; Robert H. Michel, Minority Leader of the House of Representatives; and Representative F. James Sensenbrenner, Jr., of Wisconsin. The letter was released by the Office of the Press Secretary on March 2.

Remarks Following the North Atlantic Treaty Organization Summit Meeting in Brussels, Belgium
March 2, 1988

The President. I promised a statement. I have a statement. Today's meetings have been extremely productive. There is a strong sense of unity in the alliance, as reflected in the statement on conventional imbalance in Europe. This document is a major step forward for the alliance. The most direct threat to our security and to stability in Europe lies in the Soviet Union's massive military presence at a level far exceeding its defense needs.

First, effective defenses are vital. We're determined to ensure that the alliance's defenses remain strong. We'll continue to cooperate on better and more efficient ways to maintain our defenses. Second, we also seek to strengthen stability through effective and verifiable conventional arms reduction. Large asymmetrical reductions in the Warsaw Pact tanks and artillery, which pose the greatest threat to peace, are essential in meeting this goal; but arms reduction is not enough. Arms are only the symptom, not the cause of the political division of Europe between free and unfree societies. In addition to arms reductions, we also look for greater respect for the human rights and fundamental freedoms on which lasting security and stability in Europe ultimately depend.

During my meetings in Brussels, I have kept close watch on the situation in the Middle East. Secretary Shultz briefed me fully on his negotiating efforts, and it's clear all countries in the region believe it is useful for the United States to remain engaged in this process. We'll spare no effort in our search for a comprehensive peace settlement. I have directed Secretary Shultz to return to the Middle East tomorrow to continue his discussions.

Thank you.

NATO

Reporter. Mr. President, if I could try a question I asked you earlier: Some critics are saying that at this summit you're papering over some of the real differences within NATO about burden-sharing and what to do about modernizing with short-range nuclear weapons.

The President. I have to say first that that is the only question. I'm going to get back where it's warm now. But that's the only question—that actually there's no foundation for the question. There are no great fundamental differences there. I have never seen such harmony and togetherness as we have. And all of the statements that were made today—and every head of state had an opportunity to speak in there—all of them were supportive of what's going on and what we're doing.

Q. Disagree about anything, sir?

The President. What?

Q. Disagree about anything in all those hours?

Secretary Shultz. Here's the conventional arms——

Q. Mr. Secretary, I never got it hand-delivered. [*Laughter*] Did the President disagree about anything, though, sir?

The President. No.

Q. Nothing?

The President. No.

Middle East Peace Process

Q. Mr. President, what do you think that the Secretary can accomplish by going back to the Middle East when, in fact, he returned last night with no concrete signs of progress there?

The President. Well, he came back here temporarily to participate in what was going on here today, and now he's going back.

Note: The President spoke at 5:30 p.m. outside of Chateau Stuyvenberg. A tape was not available for verification of the contents of the remarks.

Letter to Congressional Leaders on Aid to the Nicaraguan Democratic Resistance

March 3, 1988

*Dear*________:

Today the House of Representatives will once again address the issue of continued assistance to Nicaragua's Freedom Fighters, a matter of great national security concern.

The case for such support is compelling. If we do not sustain the Nicaraguan Resistance, we face the prospect of a consolidated Marxist-Leninist regime on the American mainland and prolonged troubles for Nicaragua's democratic neighbors. If, on the other hand, meaningful assistance is provided, we can enhance the prospects for democracy inside Nicaragua and advance the cause of regional peace in accordance with the Guatemala Accords of August 1987.

It is, of course, not only the mere fact of continued assistance to the Freedom Fighters which is important. The quantity, nature and means of delivery of such help are also vital factors. I have said in the past and continue to maintain that our aid must be sufficient to sustain the Resistance in the field, provide equipment indispensable to those purposes and include effective means for transporting approved materials into Nicaragua under extraordinarily hazardous conditions.

This brings me to the question of the alternative assistance packages which the House will consider today. It is my considered judgment that the aid package offered by the Democratic Leadership does not meet the essential criteria I have outlined above. Their proposal will not enable us to sustain the Freedom Fighters inside Nicaragua at anywhere approximating their present numbers. The proposal would alter the delivery arrangements to DOD responsibility, a notion which I am not prepared to accept. And, finally, the Democratic Leadership's proposal would not assure a future vote on further assistance should the peace process fail to produce the results we all hope for. Without such provision it is quite obvious that all the Sandinistas have to do is play a waiting game instead of bargaining seriously with their internal opponents and democratic neighbors.

In contrast, the alternative put forward by the House Republican Leadership meets the minimum criteria I have outlined. Program responsibility would remain in the tried and tested hands of experienced professionals who have amply satisfied their oversight committees with their competence and thorough accountability. And, of course, the Republican alternative provides for expedited procedures in case of eventual need, an element which I consider indispensable to any package which ultimately emerges from the Congress.

Today could represent a watershed in our policies toward Central America. One avenue will lead to rapid debilitation of the Resistance and further encouragement of Sandinista intransigence. The other could keep alive prospects for democracy and meaningful talks toward peace. For the reasons set forth, I strongly urge you and your colleagues to vote against the proposal of the Democratic Leadership and in favor of the Republican package.

Sincerely,

RONALD REAGAN

Note: Identical letters were sent to Robert H. Michel, Minority Leader of the House of Representatives, and Representative Charles W. Stenholm of Texas.

Statement by Assistant to the President for Press Relations Fitzwater on the North Atlantic Treaty Organization Summit Meeting in Brussels, Belgium
March 3, 1988

The meeting of the NATO alliance concluded with extemporaneous remarks by President Reagan concerning the values of the alliance in the free world. The President spoke eloquently and with great feeling concerning the unique role of the alliance in preserving freedom. The President praised the solidarity of NATO and the strengths that emanate from each country's commitment to one another.

The President cautioned that, while General Secretary Gorbachev speaks of reforms and restructuring, many of the Soviet policies are unchanged. The President referred to the words of Demosthenes when he said: "Surely, no man would judge another by his words and not his deeds. That certainly is true when considering the Soviet Union. I am not a linguist, but I recall the Russian proverb: *Dovorey no provorey.* That means trust but verify." The President said that East-West relations continue as a source of world tension, but that the alliance was poised as never before to negotiate with the East.

"The media seems to thrive on fights more than friendship," the President said. "They continue to ask: Are you papering over great differences here? Well, I haven't found them. Our alliance is strong and united. The United States believes our destiny rests with the maintenance of this alliance. We often say that if the bomb is dropped in Amsterdam it is the equivalent of dropping a bomb on Chicago. As long as we maintain that attitude, I don't believe a bomb is going to drop on anyone."

Speaking of the Soviet Union, the President said: "We don't have to go to war. We have to see to it that the Soviets won't go to war. If they realize that war with one of us is really war with all of us, they won't start one. So, we must just stay strong, united, and dedicated to one another."

The President told the moving story of soldiers who had deserted the Soviet Army in Afghanistan, because they had been ordered to kill women and children. These Soviet military members instead made the difficult decision to defy those orders and desert to the West. "Their hope for freedom was placed in us," the President said. "And indeed the hopes of freedom for people all around the world are placed in us."

"Our people admire and respect NATO. There is no thought in our country of the United States shortchanging this alliance. We are with you, and we intend to stay with you until lasting peace is achieved."

Remarks to Reporters Following the North Atlantic Treaty Organization Summit Meeting in Brussels, Belgium

March 3, 1988

The President. Good afternoon. My alliance colleagues and I have just concluded our latest round of consultations on the full range of issues facing us. First, let me say that the state of the alliance is excellent. We're strong, we're united, we're prosperous, and we're free.

This is the second full-fledged alliance summit that I've attended. Some of my colleagues and I also met here following my first meeting with Mr. Gorbachev. So, while this is a special occasion, it is also only one element of the much larger pattern of close and continuous consultations that is a fundamental reason for the success of this alliance.

NATO will soon begin its fifth decade. The North Atlantic alliance is the most successful in history. While other alliances have been formed to win wars, our fundamental purpose is to prevent war while preserving and extending the frontiers of freedom.

The INF treaty is the most recent NATO success. My colleagues and I are all justifiably proud of that achievement. It was the direct result of our steadfastness and persistence in carrying out the two-track decision that we made as an alliance over 8 years ago. It goes without saying that our allies support this treaty, and every leader solidly reaffirmed its value to the security concerns of the alliance. So, now our focus turns on meeting the challenges of the future.

During the past 2 days we went over the full range of issues that affect our collective security. I reiterated the strong bipartisan support that exists for the alliance in the United States and the commitment that American troops will remain in Europe, under any administration, so long as the need for a forward defense of our common values remains. We cannot and will not put our peace and freedom, and that of our children and their children, at risk. All of us understand the absolute necessity of maintaining the credibility of our deterrent. We will never trade that credibility away at the negotiating table, and we won't give it away through neglect.

The most direct threat to our security and to stability in Europe lies in the Soviet Union's massive military presence. The alliance has given its needs a lot of thought, knows what it wants to do, and has programs that it has committed to carry out. And there's no doubt the alliance stands on strength and unity.

The alliance is the most dynamic force for improvement of East-West relations. From our meetings here, our commitment is to move forward to meet our defense requirements while continuing discussions on our four-part agenda with the new Soviet leadership. The alliance has agreed on its arms control priorities and is ready to get down to business. NATO fully supports my effort to negotiate deep reductions in strategic weapons.

So, while arms reduction is a part—but only a part—of our discussions, progress in this area must always be based on enhancing our security, not substituting for it. Our alliance has guaranteed peace in Europe and the North Atlantic for almost 40 years. I am more confident than ever, after these 2 days of meetings, that the alliance remains on the right path and that, as always, we have the courage and the will to follow it.

Let me conclude by noting that this will be one of the last alliance meetings for Secretary General Peter Carrington. Lord Carrington has been at the helm of the alliance and NATO for 4 crucial years. He has steered this ship of 16 states with a steadiness that has earned our unbounded admiration. I'm sure that I speak for all my colleagues in expressing our heartfelt thanks to Lord Carrington and our best wishes to Dr. Manfred Wörner, whose strong hand will soon be at the helm. The West has no better champions than these two distinguished statesmen.

And Secretary Shultz will now take your questions.

Reporter. Why did the alliance skirt the tough issues—the modernization and burden-sharing? Why did you skirt those issues?

Secretary Shultz. Do you want me to handle that?

The President. Here's the man that's going to answer the questions.

Nicaragua

Q. Mr. President, Ortega has dismissed Cardinal Obando y Bravo. Does that concern you, sir?

The President. He concerns me by just being there.

Note: The President spoke at 12:12 p.m. in the Luns Press Theatre at North Atlantic Treaty Organization Headquarters.

Declaration of the Heads of State and Government Participating in the Meeting of the North Atlantic Council in Brussels, Belgium
March 3, 1988

A Time for Reaffirmation

We, the representatives of the sixteen members of the North Atlantic Alliance, have come together to re-emphasize our unity, to assess the current state of East-West relations, to review the opportunities and challenges which lie ahead, and in so doing:

—to reaffirm the common ideals and purposes which are the foundation of our partnership;

—to rededicate ourselves to the principles and provisions of the Washington Treaty of 1949;

—to reassert the vital importance of the Alliance for our security, and the validity of our strategy for peace.

The Purposes and Principles of Our Alliance

2. Our Alliance is a voluntary association of free and democratic equals, united by common interests and values. It is unprecedented in its scope and success. Our security is indivisible. Our Alliance is dedicated to preserving peace in freedom and to collective self-defence, as recognised by the United Nations Charter. None of our weapons will ever be used except in response to attack.

3. Our concept of a balanced security policy as set out in the Harmel Report has successfully stood the test of time. It remains valid in its two complementary and mutually reinforcing approaches: political solidarity and adequate military strength, and, on that basis, the search for constructive dialogue and co-operation, including arms control. The ultimate political purpose of our Alliance is to achieve a just and lasting peaceful order in Europe.

4. The security in freedom and the prosperity of the European and North American Allies are inextricably linked. The long-standing commitment of the North American democracies to the preservation of peace and security in Europe is vital. The presence in Europe of the conventional and

nuclear forces of the United States provides the essential linkage with the United States strategic deterrent, and, together with the forces of Canada, is a tangible expression of that commitment. This presence must and will be maintained.

Likewise, a free, independent and increasingly united Europe is vital to North America's security. The credibility of Allied defence cannot be maintained without a major European contribution. We therefore welcome recent efforts to reinforce the European pillar of the Alliance, intended to strengthen the transatlantic partnership and Alliance security as a whole.

The Atlantic Alliance cannot be strong if Europe is weak.

5. Our aim will continue to be to prevent any kind of war or intimidation. By maintaining credible deterrence the Alliance has secured peace in Europe for nearly forty years. Conventional defences alone cannot ensure this; therefore, for the foreseeable future there is no alternative to the Alliance strategy for the prevention of war. This is a strategy of deterrence based upon an appropriate mix of adequate and effective nuclear and conventional forces which will continue to be kept up to date where necessary.

6. While seeking security and stability at lower levels of armaments, we are determined to sustain the requisite efforts to ensure the continued viability, credibility and effectiveness of our conventional and nuclear forces, including the nuclear forces in Europe, which together provide the guarantee of our common security. Taking into account the structure of the Alliance, each of us undertakes to play his part in this joint endeavour in a spirit of solidarity, reaffirming our willingness to share fairly the risks, burdens and responsibilities as well as the benefits of our common efforts.

7. We seek a just and stable condition of peace in which the sovereignty and territorial integrity of all states are respected and the rights of all individuals, including their right of political choice, are protected.

We want gradually to overcome the unnatural division of the European continent, which affects most directly the German people. We will continue to uphold the freedom and viability of Berlin and to support efforts to improve the situation there.

The search for improved and more stable relations with the Soviet Union and the other countries of Eastern Europe is among our principal concerns. We call upon these countries to work with us for a further relaxation of tensions, greater security at lower levels of arms, more extensive human contacts and increased access to information. We will continue the effort to expand co-operation with the East wherever and whenever this is of mutual benefit.

East-West Relations: The Way Ahead

8. We have noted encouraging signs of change in the policies of the Soviet Union and some of its allies. This creates the prospect for greater openness in their relations with their own people and with other nations. We welcome such progress as has been already achieved in certain areas. But we look beyond pronouncements for tangible and lasting policy changes addressing directly the issue dividing East and West.

9. However, we have to date witnessed no relaxation of the military effort pursued for years by the Soviet Union. The Soviet Union persists in deploying far greater military forces than are required for its defence. This massive force, which the Soviet Union has not refrained from using outside its borders, as is still the case in Afghanistan, constitutes a fundamental source of tension between East and West. The steady growth of Soviet military capabilities, as it affects every region of the Alliance, requires our constant attention.

10. We will continue to be steadfast in the pursuit of our security policies, maintaining the effective defences and credible deterrence that form the necessary basis for constructive dialogue with the East including on arms control and disarmament matters.

To meet our security needs in the years to come will require ever greater efficiencies in the application of our scarce resources. We are therefore determined to expand our practical co-operation in the field of armaments procurement and elsewhere. In this context we recognise the challenges to our industrially less advanced Allies and the need to address them through mutual assistance and co-operation.

11. Arms control is an integral part of our security policy. We seek negotiations not for their own sake but to reach agreements which can significantly reduce the risk of conflict and make a genuine contribution to stability and peace. We shall work together vigorously and on the basis of the closest consultation to this end.

12. Our representatives to the North Atlantic Council continue actively the further development of a comprehensive concept of arms control and disarmament as directed in the Statement of our Ministers at Reykjavik in June 1987.

13. The recently concluded INF agreement between the US and the Soviet Union is a milestone in our efforts to achieve a more secure peace and lower levels of arms. It is the impressive result of the political courage, the realism and the unity of the members of the Alliance. The treaty's provisions on stringent verification and asymmetrical reductions provide useful precedents for future agreements. We look forward to its early entry into force.

14. Consistent with their security requirements, the fifteen Allies concerned will make use of all possibilities for effectively verifiable arms control agreements which lead to a stable and secure balance of forces at a lower level. For them, the comprehensive concept of arms control and disarmament includes:

—a 50% reduction in the strategic offensive nuclear weapons of the US and the Soviet Union to be achieved during current Geneva negotiations;

—the global elimination of chemical weapons;

—the establishment of a stable and secure level of conventional forces, by the elimination of disparities, in the whole of Europe;

—in conjunction with the establishment of a conventional balance and the global elimination of chemical weapons, tangible and verifiable reductions of American and Soviet land-based nuclear missile systems of shorter range, leading to equal ceilings.

15. Recognizing the urgency and central importance of addressing the conventional force imbalances in Europe, we have adopted a separate statement on conventional arms control.

16. The resolution of East-West differences will require progress in many fields. Genuine peace in Europe cannot be established solely by arms control. It must be firmly based on full respect for fundamental human rights. As we continue our efforts to reduce armaments, we shall press for implementation on the part of the governments of the Soviet Union and of other Eastern countries of all of the principles and provisions of the Helsinki Final Act and of the Madrid Concluding Document. We support the continuation and strengthening of the CSCE process. It represents an important means of promoting stable and constructive relations on a long term basis between countries of East and West, and, moreover, enhances closer and more fruitful contacts between peoples and individuals throughout Europe. We call upon all participating states to make every effort for an early conclusion to the CSCE follow-up meeting in Vienna with a substantial and balanced final document.

17. We agree that the speedy and complete withdrawal of Soviet troops from Afghanistan and the effective restoration of that country's sovereignty would be of major significance. It is against these criteria that we shall assess General Secretary Gorbachev's recent statements.

18. We hope that at their forthcoming summit in Moscow President Reagan and the General Secretary Gorbachev will be able to build upon the progress achieved at their Washington meeting last December. We strongly support the efforts of the United States. These fully accord with our consistent policy to seek, through high-level dialogue, early and substantial progress with the Soviet Union on a full range of issues, including greater respect for human rights, arms control, a lessening of regional tensions, and improved opportunities for bilateral contacts and co-operation.

19. Reflecting upon almost four decades of common endeavour and sacrifice and upon the results achieved, we are confident that the principles and purposes of our Alliance remain valid today and for the future. We are united in our efforts to ensure a

world of more secure peace and greater freedom. We will meet the opportunities and challenges ahead with imagination and hope, as well as with firmness and vigilance. We owe no less to our peoples.

Note: The following sentence appeared at the bottom of the last page of the declaration: "Greece recalled its position on nuclear matters." The declaration was not issued as White House press release.

Remarks to United States Armed Forces at a Departure Ceremony in Brussels, Belgium
March 3, 1988

Thank you all for coming out here on what is not exactly a sunshiny day. Could I just tell you, you've made me very proud by coming out this way to see me off. But you've made me even more proud by the fact of what you represent. You are the largest American delegation in Europe. And you're here serving our country, some of you with regard to the European Community, some with regard to the alliance, and then, many of you are here also just representing our government and certainly the military. I am so proud of the detachment that is here assigned to the NATO alliance and that is defending America as well as the peace of the world.

Well, God bless you all. And you know what? I'm going to issue an Executive order: I'm going to get in the airplane, and you get out of here and get out of this nasty weather before you catch cold. All right. Thank you all. God bless you all.

Note: The President spoke at 3:49 p.m. at Zaventem Airport in Brussels, Belgium. Following his remarks, he returned to Washington, DC.

Statement on the House of Representatives Disapproval of Aid to the Nicaraguan Democratic Resistance
March 3, 1988

The House has once again failed to approve an aid package for the Nicaraguan democratic resistance. I call on the House and Senate to act urgently to develop an aid package which is effectively deliverable and of sufficient quantity to sustain the Nicaraguan freedom fighters. If not, the prospects for peace and democracy inside Nicaragua will diminish quickly.

Proclamation 5774—Department of Commerce Day, 1988
March 4, 1988

By the President of the United States of America

A Proclamation

This year marks the 75th year of service to our Nation by the United States Department of Commerce; three-quarters of a century ago, on March 4, 1913, the Department was established in its current form. Its mission of fostering, promoting, and developing the domestic and foreign commerce of the United States has ever since remained both vital and truly worthy of public recognition.

Throughout this century the Department of Commerce has helped Presidents and the Congress develop policies to support our economic growth, our scientific and technological advancement and security, and our international trade. The Department provides business and government planners with critical data they need for intelligent decision-making, urges inventors and entrepreneurs to bring products to the marketplace, encourages firms to seek legitimate export opportunities, and makes sure that fair trade laws are enforced vigorously. The Department of Commerce also supplies oceanic information and formulates telecommunications and information policy.

The employees of the Department of Commerce have always reflected the finest traditions of public service. That was surely true of the Department's late Secretary, Malcolm Baldrige, and our present Secretary, C. William Verity, Jr.

In recognition of the contributions of the Department of Commerce and the dedication of its officers and employees, the Congress, by Senate Joint Resolution 251, has designated March 4, 1988, as "Department of Commerce Day" and has authorized and requested the President to issue a proclamation in observance of that day.

Now, Therefore, I, Ronald Reagan, President of the United States of America, do hereby proclaim March 4, 1988, as Department of Commerce Day, and I urge the people of the United States to observe this day with appropriate ceremonies and activities.

In Witness Whereof, I have hereunto set my hand this fourth day of March, in the year of our Lord nineteen hundred and eighty-eight, and of the Independence of the United States of America the two hundred and twelfth.

RONALD REAGAN

[*Filed with the Office of the Federal Register, 10:18 a.m., March 4, 1988*]

Nomination of Gordon A. Smith To Be an Assistant Secretary of Defense
March 4, 1988

The President today announced his intention to nominate Gordon A. Smith to be Assistant Secretary of Defense (Command, Control, Communications and Intelligence) at the Department of Defense. He would succeed Donald C. Latham.

Since 1986 Mr. Smith has been Deputy Director of the Strategic Defense Initiative Organization at the Pentagon. Prior to this he was president and chief operating officer of Fairchild Space Operations Co. and corporate vice president for operations at Fairchild Industries.

Mr. Smith graduated from Swindon Technical College in the United Kingdom (1957) and George Washington University (M.S., 1978; Ph.D., 1982). He was born April 1, 1934, in Swindon, United Kingdom. Mr. Smith is married and resides in Derwood, MD.

Nomination of W. Allen Moore To Be an Under Secretary of Commerce

March 4, 1988

The President today announced his intention to nominate W. Allen Moore to be Under Secretary of Commerce (International Trade Administration) at the Department of Commerce. He would succeed S. Bruce Smart.

Since 1985 Mr. Moore has been chief of staff for the United States Senate Committee on Commerce, Science, and Transportation in Washington, DC. Prior to this he was director of legislation for United States Senator Jack Danforth, 1977–1985. He was a consultant to the Board of Directors of CETEC Corp. in California, 1982–1986; Associate Director for Policy and Planning for the White House Domestic Council, 1975–1977; and vice president and general manager of the Seneca Corp., 1973–1975.

Mr. Moore graduated from Pomona College (B.A., 1966) and Stanford University (M.B.A., 1971). He was born January 25, 1945, in Glendale, CA. He is married and resides in Arlington, VA.

Nomination of Jan W. Mares To Be an Assistant Secretary of Commerce

March 4, 1988

The President today announced his intention to nominate Jan W. Mares to be an Assistant Secretary of Commerce (Import Administration) at the Department of Commerce. He would succeed Paul Freedenberg.

Since 1985 Mr. Mares has been Senior Policy Analyst for the Office of Policy Development at the White House. Prior to this he was Assistant Secretary of Energy for International Affairs, 1985, and Assistant Secretary for Policy, Safety and Environment, 1984.

Mr. Mares graduated from Harvard University (B.A., 1958; LL.B., 1963) and Massachusetts Institute of Technology (M.S., 1960). He was born December 12, 1936, in St. Louis, MO. He is married, has two children, and resides in Washington, DC.

Nomination of Donna F. Tuttle To Be Deputy Secretary of Commerce

March 4, 1988

The President today announced his intention to nominate Donna F. Tuttle to be Deputy Secretary of Commerce. She would succeed Clarence J. Brown.

Since 1983 Mrs. Tuttle has been Under Secretary of Commerce for Travel and Tourism in Washington, DC. Prior to this, she was state finance chairman for the Carol Hallet campaign for Lieutenant Governor of California, 1982; state finance director for the Mike Curb Committee, 1981–1982; and speaker's bureau chairman for the State of California for the Reagan-Bush campaign and national chairman for Youth for Reagan, 1980.

Mrs. Tuttle graduated from the University of Southern California (B.A., 1969). She was born April 21, 1947. She is married, has two children, and resides in Washington, DC.

Nomination of Edward R. Hamberger To Be an Assistant Secretary of Transportation
March 4, 1988

The President today announced his intention to nominate Edward R. Hamberger to be an Assistant Secretary of Transportation (Governmental Affairs). He would succeed Rebecca Gernhardt Range.

Since 1981 Mr. Hamberger has been with the law firm of Lipsen, Hamberger, Whitten and Hamberger, serving as managing partner since 1982. Prior to this he was General Counsel and Special Counsel to the Chairman as well as Director for Public Participation for the National Transportation Policy Study Commission, 1977–1979. He served as staff director and legal counsel of the House Republican Policy Committee, 1979–1980.

Mr. Hamberger graduated from Georgetown University (B.A., 1973; M.S., 1975; and J.D., 1977). He was born May 28, 1950, in Pottsville, PA. Mr. Hamberger is married, has two children, and resides in Bethesda, MD.

Appointment of Two Members of the Advisory Committee to the Pension Benefit Guaranty Corporation
March 4, 1988

The President today announced his intention to appoint the following individuals to be members of the Advisory Committee to the Pension Benefit Guaranty Corporation:

For a term expiring February 19, 1990:

Richard M. Prosten, of the District of Columbia. He would succeed Roger F. Martin. Since 1970 he has been director of research, industrial union department at the AFL–CIO in Washington, DC. Prior to this he was collective bargaining coordinator, industrial union department, AFL–CIO, 1964–1970. He was born July 2, 1941, in Boston, MA. He is married, has two children, and resides in Washington, DC.

For a term expiring February 19, 1991:

Eugene B. Burroughs, of California. This is a reappointment. Since 1987 Mr. Burroughs has served as a senior adviser for the Prudential Asset Management Co., Inc., in San Diego, CA. Prior to this he was executive vice president of M.D. Sass Association, Inc., 1985–1987. Mr. Burroughs graduated from Benjamin Franklin University (B.A., 1955). He was born August 22, 1931, in Washington, DC. Mr. Burroughs served with the United States Marine Corps, 1952–1955. He is married, has two children, and resides in Rancho Santa Fe, CA.

Nomination of Richard V. Backley To Be a Member of the Federal Mine Safety and Health Review Commission
March 4, 1988

The President today announced his intention to nominate Richard V. Backley to be a member of the Federal Mine Safety and Health Review Commission for a term of 6 years, expiring August 30, 1994. This is a reappointment.

Since 1982 Mr. Backley has been a Commissioner for the Federal Mine Safety and Health Review Commission in Washington, DC. Prior to this, he was an administrative law judge for the Civil Aeronautics Board, 1975–1978, and an administrative law judge for the Bureau of Hearings and Appeals for the Social Security Administration, 1975.

Mr. Backley graduated from De Paul University (B.A., 1951; LL.B., 1955). He was born on July 21, 1927, in Chicago, IL. He served in the U.S. Navy, 1945–1948 and 1951–1952. Mr. Backley is married, has three children, and resides in Fairfax, VA.

Appointment of William A. Schambra as a Member of the National Historical Publications and Records Commission
March 4, 1988

The President today announced his intention to appoint William A. Schambra to be a member of the National Historical Publications and Records Commission for a term expiring December 26, 1991. This is a reappointment.

Since 1983 Mr. Schambra has been a resident fellow at the American Enterprise Institute, serving as assistant director for the Project to Study the Constitution at AEI, 1979–1983. Prior to this he was associate editor of Public Opinion magazine, 1977–1979.

Mr. Schambra graduated from James Madison College (B.A., 1971), Northern Illinois University (M.A., 1974; Ph.D., 1983). He was born March 27, 1949, in Freeport, TX. Mr. Schambra is married, has one child, and resides in Alexandria, VA.

Appointment of Albert D. Wheelon as a Member of the President's National Security Telecommunications Advisory Committee
March 4, 1988

The President today announced his intention to appoint Albert D. Wheelon to be a member of the President's National Security Telecommunications Advisory Committee. He would succeed Allen E. Puckett.

Since 1987, Dr. Wheelon has been chairman and chief executive officer of Hughes Aircraft Co. in Los Angeles, CA. Dr. Wheelon joined Hughes Aircraft Co. in 1966 as vice president for engineering and was executive vice president of the company, 1986–1987. He has been a member of the President's Foreign Intelligence Advisory Board and the President's commission investigating the space shuttle *Challenger*.

Dr. Wheelon graduated from Stanford University (B.S., 1949) and Massachusetts Institute of Technology (Ph.D., 1952). He was born January 18, 1929, in Moline, IL. He is married, has two children, and resides in Los Angeles, CA.

Nomination of Stanley J. Glod To Be Chairman of the Foreign Claims Settlement Commission of the United States
March 4, 1988

The President today announced his intention to nominate Stanley J. Glod to be Chairman of the Foreign Claims Settlement Commission of the United States at the Department of Justice for the remainder of the term expiring September 30, 1988. He would succeed Bohdan A. Futey.

Since 1969 Mr. Glod has been practicing law in Washington, DC. From 1968 to 1969, he was an associate professor of international and comparative law at the University of Virginia School of Law.

Mr. Glod graduated from John Carroll University (A.B., 1958), Georgetown University Law Center (J.D., 1961), and the University of Munich (S.J.D., 1967). He was born June 28, 1936, in Altoona, PA. He serves in the United States Army, 1958–present. Mr. Glod has four children and resides in Alexandria, VA.

Nomination of Two Members of the Board of Trustees of the Harry S. Truman Scholarship Foundation
March 4, 1988

The President today announced his intention to nominate the following individuals to be members of the Board of Trustees of the Harry S. Truman Scholarship Foundation for terms expiring December 10, 1993:

Margaret Truman Daniel, of New York. This is a reappointment. Since 1954 Mrs. Daniel has been working as an author. Mrs. Daniel graduated from George Washington University (A.B., 1946; Litt. D., 1975), Wake Forest University (L.H.D., 1972), and Rockhurst College (H.H.D., 1976). She was born February 17, 1924, in Independence, MO. She is married, has two children, and resides in New York.

Gary Eugene Wood, of Texas. He would succeed Gloria Ann Hay. Since 1985 Mr. Wood has been director of governmental relations at Baylor University. Prior to this he worked as a finance professor at Baylor University from 1979 to 1985. Mr. Wood graduated from Baylor University (B.B.A., 1966), University of Florida (M.A., 1967), and the University of Texas (Ph.D., 1977). He was born December 9, 1943, in Houston, TX. He is married, has one child, and resides in Waco, TX.

Appointment of Maiselle D. Shortley as a Member of the National Advisory Council on Adult Education
March 4, 1988

The President today announced his intention to appoint Maiselle D. Shortley to be a member of the National Advisory Council on Adult Education for the remainder of the term expiring July 10, 1989. She would succeed George F. Meyer, Jr.

Since 1987 Mrs. Shortley has been chairman of the National Conservative Political Action Committee in Alexandria, VA. Prior to this, she was Deputy Associate Director for Volunteer Liaison of ACTION, 1985–1987; Deputy Assistant Secretary for Communications and Community Relations at the Department of Defense, 1984–1985; and Confidential Assistant in the Office of Public Liaison at the White House, 1981–1984.

Mrs. Shortley graduated from Dumbarton

College (B.A., 1964). She was born August 1, 1942, in North Adams, MA. She is married, has one child, and resides in McLean, VA.

Nomination of Walter C. Wallace To Be a Member of the National Mediation Board
March 4, 1988

The President today announced his intention to nominate Walter C. Wallace to be a member of the National Mediation Board for the term expiring July 1, 1990. This is a reappointment.

Since 1982 Mr. Wallace has been a member of the National Mediation Board in Washington, DC. Prior to joining the Board in October 1982, he was in the private practice of law and labor arbitration. From 1973 to 1975, he was president of the Bituminous Coal Operators Association.

Mr. Wallace graduated from St. John's College, St. John's University (B.A., 1948), and Cornell Law School (LL.B., 1951). He was born March 25, 1924, in New York City. He served in the United States Army, from 1943 to 1945. Mr. Wallace is married, has one child, and currently resides in Washington, DC.

Designation of James L. Kolstad as Vice Chairman of the National Transportation Safety Board
March 4, 1988

The President today designated James L. Kolstad as Vice Chairman of the National Transportation Safety Board for a term of 2 years. He would succeed Patricia A. Goldman.

Since 1987 Mr. Kolstad has been a member of the National Transportation Safety Board. Prior to this he was vice president of the Pat Thompson Co., a communications brokerage firm in Denver, CO. He was the senior director of communications and public affairs for Frontier Airlines from 1978 to 1985. From 1973 to 1978 Mr. Kolstad was the Director of the Office of Community and Congressional Relations for the Civil Aeronautics Board. Prior to this he was a Presidential advance man at the White House, 1972–1973.

Mr. Kolstad graduated from the University of Montana (B.A., 1960). Mr. Kolstad was born on March 3, 1939, in Washington, DC. Mr. Kolstad has one child and resides in Alexandria, VA.

Accordance of the Personal Rank of Ambassador to Armando Valladares While Serving as Head of the Delegation to the United Nations Commission on Human Rights
March 4, 1988

The President today accorded Armando Valladares the personal rank of Ambassador in his capacity as Head of the United States Delegation to the 44th Session of the United Nations Commission on Human Rights meeting February 2-March 12, 1988, in Geneva, Switzerland.

Mr. Valladares was appointed by the President as Representative of the United States on the Human Rights Commission of the Economic and Social Council of the United Nations on November 30, 1987. Since 1984 he has been president of the European Coalition for Human Rights in Cuba. He spent 20 years as a political prisoner in Cuba. Mr. Valladares is an author and poet, and among several books he has written are "From My Wheelchair" and "Against All Hope." He was adopted by Amnesty International as a prisoner of conscience.

Mr. Valladares graduated from the Instituto de Segunda Ensenanza de Marianano in Havana, Cuba (B.A., 1954). He was born May 30, 1937, in Pinar Del Rio, Cuba. He is married, has two children, and resides in Alexandria, VA. Mr. Valladares became a naturalized United States citizen in January 1987.

Statement on the House of Representatives Disapproval of Aid to the Nicaraguan Democratic Resistance

March 4, 1988

By its action last night, the House of Representatives again failed to approve further assistance for the Nicaraguan freedom fighters. Without renewal of aid soon, the resistance will cease to provide the pressure necessary to ensure that the Sandinista regime honors its promises under the Guatemala accord of August 1987 and the San José Declaration of January 1988 to bring about democracy in Nicaragua.

I ask the House of Representatives and the Senate to act swiftly to renew assistance to the freedom fighters. Key elements of such a package should include:

—sufficient nonlethal assistance to sustain the resistance in the field;

—a safe and effective means for delivering; and

—procedures for expedited consideration by the Congress of a future Presidential request for additional aid if efforts to negotiate a cease-fire are unsuccessful.

In the days ahead, I will be consulting with bipartisan supporters in both Chambers to put together an effective package for aid to the resistance. Prompt renewal of assistance to the resistance remains essential to advance the national security interests of the United States.

Radio Address to the Nation Following the North Atlantic Treaty Organization Summit Meeting in Brussels, Belgium

March 5, 1988

My fellow Americans:

As many of you know, I recently returned from Brussels, Belgium, where I met with the leaders of the North Atlantic alliance. I'm glad to say that the Western alliance remains a strong and unified guardian of the free world, ready to meet the many challenges before us.

In all of my meetings with allied leaders there was a unity of purpose and resolve that I found heartening and uplifting. That strength and unity have never been more sorely tested or better proven than in the events leading up to, and making possible, the recent signing of our historic treaty with the Soviet Union to eliminate an entire class of U.S. and Soviet nuclear weapons. Let me, if I may, review those events, because they provide a lesson that was much on my mind this week in Brussels, a valuable lesson about the only effective way to deal with the Soviet Union: from a position of strength.

INF refers to intermediate-range nuclear forces. They only became an issue in the seventies and early eighties when the Soviets began targeting their new SS–20 missiles against every major city in Western Europe and our friends in Asia, as well. The free nations had no comparable weapon to counter this new threat. So, NATO agreed on what we called a dual-track policy. We would negotiate with the Soviets to get them to remove their missiles or to reduce them to the lowest possible equal level, and we would also deploy our own forces to counter their new threat.

Well, the Soviets tried every play in the book to keep NATO from deploying these weapons. They stalled; they threatened. Finally, they walked out of the negotiations in Geneva when we did begin deploying. The political pressure brought to bear on Western Europe was immense. Many said our allies couldn't take it and they'd cave in. Demonstrations erupted in many of the capital cities in Europe, and the demonstrators' line was very similar to the Soviets'—No NATO deployments. In the United States, the so-called nuclear freeze movement gained strength. Well, if those demonstrators had gotten their way, there would be no INF treaty. There would be no agreement with the Soviet Union to reduce, for the first time in history, nuclear armaments. The Soviet SS–20's would still be in place, threatening the populations of Western Europe and Asia. The lesson learned: One must always negotiate with the Soviets from a position of strength.

At this NATO meeting, we talked with our allies about ways to apply this lesson. After the removal of the Soviet intermediate-range missile threat, our highest priorities are: first, to negotiate a 50-percent reduction in strategic arms; second, to address the fact that the Warsaw Pact conventional forces, arrayed offensively along the Iron Curtain, far outnumber NATO's; and third, to address the problems created by the continued Soviet maintenance of the world's largest chemical weapons arsenal.

That's why continued modernization of NATO forces, nuclear and conventional, is essential. Most of you have heard of SDI—our Strategic Defense Initiative that may one day make ballistic missiles obsolete. At the same time, we must continue to pursue NATO's conventional defense initiative to develop high-tech conventional weapons that may be an important part of the answer to the Soviets' aggressive strategy on the European continent.

These issues were on our agenda in Brussels. We resolved there to press for large, asymmetrical reductions to Warsaw Pact conventional forces, for example, tanks and artillery. General Secretary Gorbachev talks at home about *perestroika*—that's Russian for restructuring. Well, it's time for some restructuring in the Warsaw Pact. It's time for the abandonment of the Soviet offensive strategy on the continent.

We must never forget that arms reduction is not enough. Armaments are only the symptom, not the cause, of a much deeper division between free societies and the unfree. That division is at its heart a moral division. Perhaps it is best symbolized by the Berlin Wall and the horrible barrier that cuts down the center of Europe, dividing nations, peoples, families. The question must be asked: When can we ever hope to achieve a real and lasting peace with a regime that is so fearful of its own people that it must imprison them behind barbed wire? That's why, when I visited the Berlin Wall last year, I issued a challenge to Mr. Gorbachev: If you really want *glasnost,* if you really want openness, tear down that wall!

So, let me conclude by saying, I found this week in Brussels what the Atlantic alliance has demonstrated now for 40 years: that a peace built on strength can and will endure. And I am convinced, after our meeting, that the alliance of free nations has never been stronger.

Until next week, thanks for listening, and God bless you.

Note: The President spoke at 12:06 p.m. from the Oval Office at the White House.

Remarks at the Annual Conference of the Veterans of Foreign Wars
March 7, 1988

Thank you, Commander Earl Stock, and it's good to see here Ladies Auxiliary President Joan Katkus. I've always said it's a pleasure and an honor to speak before a meeting of the Veterans of Foreign Wars. You are the men who, from the Marne to the Bulge, from Okinawa to Omaha Beach, from the Chosin Reservoir to Hamburger Hill, have defended America's heritage and fought for the freedom not only of our nation but peoples all over the world.

Today as veterans you're still defending freedom. Whether it's supporting adequate defense budgets or aid to the freedom fighters in Nicaragua or teaching America's young people the meaning of our precious rights through your Voice of Democracy program, the members of the VFW are still on the front lines, still leading the charge, and still showing what true patriotism really means. That's why when you sound the bugle this is one old rider in the horse cavalry who snaps to attention.

As you may know, I returned last Thursday from a 2-day visit to Europe, where I met with the leaders of the other Western allies, and I'll talk about that meeting in a moment. At another time, I might have liked to take a few more days over there, see some sights, and maybe buy Nancy a few presents. But I had a meeting here in Washington I couldn't miss. I've told you this before, and it's true as ever. I'd travel halfway around the world to meet with the VFW.

Let me say here something that I regard as an obvious truth, but one that seems to need repeating. America owes a great debt to its fighting men. And it's a debt that our nation will carry as long as it lives, for without our fighting men, our nation would not live. That's why I don't understand those who would so easily forget. I'm speaking about those who would turn their backs on the men missing in action in Southeast Asia. We have a moral bond as sacred as any a free people can make with one of their own to close no books, write no last chapters, reach no final conclusions until we have the fullest possible accounting of every soldier, airman, aviator, marine, and civilian lost in Laos, Cambodia, or Vietnam.

To you who came home, the Emergency Veterans' Job Training Act I signed at your convention in New Orleans 5 years ago and the new GI bill I signed last June are the least we can do to show America's gratitude. And as you know, I believe we also should create a Cabinet-level Department of Veterans Affairs.

I've always found that Americans are deeply grateful to our veterans—even those Americans who aren't too good at showing it. This is my way of sliding into a story. While it doesn't concern an American veteran, it's about a great allied fighting man. It was during World War II, and British Field Marshal Montgomery had come to America to help spur the war effort. A dinner was held in his honor in Hollywood. Sam Goldwyn, one of the founders of MGM, was to toast Field Marshal Montgomery. And when the time came, Sam, who has a reputation for misspeaking, got up, waited for silence, then after a few words said, "I propose a toast to Marshall Field Montgomery." [*Laughter*] Well, Jack Warner was sitting next to Sam and tried to help. And he said, "Montgomery Ward, you mean." [*Laughter*]

Well, as I said a moment ago, I've just returned from meeting with the leaders of our North Atlantic allies. And next year, the alliance marks its 40th anniversary. Its achievement has been simple and historic: 40 years of freedom and democracy in Western Europe—and without armies clashing anywhere on the continent. Since the fall of Rome more than 1,500 years ago, Europe has known few longer periods of total peace. Americans, including some of you, have helped keep that peace and preserve that freedom. As President Kennedy told our troops in Germany 25 years ago: "Millions sleep peacefully at night, because you stand in this field." You know when I hear about peace marchers in Europe or here I think of our young men and women in uniform. They're the real peace marchers.

At the meeting last week, the Atlantic alliance celebrated one of the great achievements of its history. More than a decade ago, without warning, without provocation, the Soviet Union challenged the strategic balance in Europe and stationed an entirely new level of weapon, one for which NATO had no fully effective deterrent: the intermediate-range SS–20 nuclear missile. To keep the balance that keeps the peace, NATO had to meet this challenge, and meet it NATO did. In 1979 it voted to deploy U.S. intermediate-range nuclear forces. It also voted to press for a U.S. negotiation with the Soviets on this issue.

Shortly after I came into office, I proposed that our negotiators should work for what we called the zero option—remove all U.S. and Soviet longer range INF missiles. You may recall that some of our critics said I couldn't be serious, that this was just a ploy to ambush arms control and put it out of commission for the duration. The Soviets said they would walk out of negotiations if we went ahead with deployment. Well, we did, and they did.

But NATO stuck to its guns. In the face of heavy political fire, the leaders of NATO moved forward. Many faced demonstrations at home, and some of those demonstrations turned to violence. But eventually, after the missiles went in place, the Soviets returned to the bargaining table, and today we have the agreement our critics said was impossible: the zero option. Now, I can't think of any better demonstration of what you and I've been saying for years: that the road to peace is through American and free world strength.

And no one should ever forget that you helped America stand its ground against the political assault here at home and finally to take the hill in arms talks. Yes, once again you defended our nation's security, peace, and freedom. And now your support is needed on another front. I hope that you, the members of the VFW, will vigorously support ratification of the INF treaty.

And by the way, let me just tell you, I wouldn't have signed that or any other agreement with the Soviets if I didn't believe we could effectively verify it. The networks have been having fun in the last few months playing clips of my statement just after I came to office that the Soviets reserved to themselves the right to lie and cheat for their own ends. They say I've changed. I've got news for them. [*Laughter*] If I trusted the Soviets, I wouldn't have insisted on the strict verification provisions that we have in this treaty—the toughest that have ever been adopted. Now, maybe they call that trust. Well, if so, it must be the kind of trust a sage meant when he said, "Trust everybody, but cut the cards." [*Laughter*]

But something amazing has happened since Mr. Gorbachev and I signed the INF agreement in Washington in December. In Europe and here at home, some of the very same people who told us not to deploy the Pershing II and ground-launched cruise missiles, who said we were being provocative and that our defense buildup in general was a step back in the safety of the world—these same people are now taking credit for the INF agreement. They say that the agreement is a victory for what they've been calling for: cuts in defense, eliminating or scaling back vital weapons systems. Well, as a great general said once at the Battle of the Bulge, "Nuts!" [*Laughter*]

The truth is just the opposite. This is not the time to drop our guard. It's time to look forward and ask what we must do to keep the peace not only in Europe but around the world. And the answer is the same as it's always been: Keep America and its allies strong. In Europe this means continuing to modernize our remaining nuclear forces and modernizing our conventional forces as well, giving them what is called smart weapons that help even the odds against the much larger armies of the Warsaw Pact. It's just this simple: If we're going to put young Americans in harm's way, we owe them the best weapons money can buy.

Keeping America strategically strong means going forward, as well, with our research, development, and testing on a strategic defense against ballistic missiles. SDI is America's best guarantee that the Soviets will stick to their agreements in arms reductions. It's also protection against an accidental missile launch and against some madman who might take over a country that can get ballistic missiles. In short, as I've said before, it's an insurance policy, and we're not the first ones the agent has visited.

The Soviets have been spending far more money developing strategic defenses than we have and have been doing it longer. In the last decade, they've poured roughly $200 billion into their programs. In 2 weeks, we mark the fifth anniversary of our Strategic Defense Initiative, and in that time, we've spent only $13 billion—less than 7 percent what the Soviets spent in the decade. To give you an idea of the magnitude of the Soviet efforts, they've assigned 10,000 of their top scientists and engineers to their military laser program alone. It would be foolhardy not to pursue SDI, and that's why America must research, develop, and test SDI. And when it's ready, we must deploy it.

Now that we have the INF treaty, our negotiating priorities are a 50-percent reduction in strategic arms; a conventional arms balance in Europe; and an effective, verifiable, and truly global ban on all chemical weapons. We'll need to keep up our strength if we're to succeed, and that's why the Congress must not further reduce the defense budget.

Not long ago I saw a letter from your commander to Members of Congress. He sent it following his recent visit to Central America, and I think he summed things up as well as anyone ever has when he said that, in his words: "The real issue before the Congress and the country is not the *contras*, it is communism in Central America."

You know, recently the Government of El Salvador found documents on the body of a Communist courier. The papers included a review of the situation in Central America, and in those papers it said: "The defeat of the *contras* would be a grave strategic defeat for the United States, especially if we take into account the geopolitical position of Central America." Well, the VFW understands this. The Communists in Central America understand this. The Soviets understand this. It's time that Congress understood it, too. A Soviet base on the American mainland is a pistol pointed at the heart of the Americas.

During the first round of debate on aid to the freedom fighters a few weeks ago, one of the congressional leaders opposing aid said that we shouldn't keep money flowing to the *contras*, because for every dollar we gave them, the Soviets would give the Sandinistas five. Well, he ought to remember something Pericles, the great leader of ancient Athens, said: "The secret of liberty is courage." Too many of the opponents of aid to the freedom fighters claim to be the heirs of Franklin Roosevelt, who told us when the odds are stacked against us that America had a rendezvous with destiny and then led us to the fight, and of Harry Truman, who helped Greece and Turkey stand up to communism and led us into NATO.

You know, when I listen to the critics and their claims to be what F.D.R. and Truman would be today, it reminds me of a time I was on the set of a movie that happened to involve Irving Berlin. As a matter of fact, it was called "This is the Army." I was already in the Army, but some of us on active duty were sent back temporarily to be in that film, which as you all know, all the proceeds went to Army emergency relief. Well, Irving Berlin, who had written that and who had written the first one in World War I, "Yip Yip Yaphank," was on the set. And Irving asked if he couldn't play one part there, because there was a flashback to World War I, and Irving wanted to sing his song "Oh, How I Hate to Get Up in the Morning." [*Laughter*] Now, he's a great writer of songs, not particularly a great singer of songs. [*Laughter*] And as we were filming that scene and he, in his World War I uniform, was singing, one of the crew leaned over to me and whispered, "If the fellow that wrote that song could hear this guy sing it, he'd roll over in his grave." [*Laughter*]

Courage hasn't exactly been the watchword of some opponents of *contra* aid. Harry Truman said: "The buck stops here." But last week, aid opponents tried to pass the buck of responsibility for abandoning in the field the young men and women of the democratic resistance. And that ploy failed, as it should have. Now it's time for Congress to show that it knows you can't have real peace negotiations when one side has helicopter gunships and the other has bandages. Recently, Daniel Ortega has said he's going to crush the freedom fighters, and he has thrown out the peace mediator, Cardinal Obando y Bravo. You know where Ortega stands. Isn't it time for Congress to have the courage to show where it stands?

You better than anyone know that Americans have never lacked for courage. On the eve of the Second World War, an observer from another country said: "Most people think Americans love luxury and that their culture is shallow and meaningless. It's a mistake. I can tell you that Americans are full of the spirit of justice, fight, and adventure." Those were the words of Japan's senior admiral in the war, Admiral Yamamoto, who added: "Japan cannot beat America."

In thousands of foxholes and trenches, cockpits and decks, around the world, the American spirit of justice and the just fight, our love of freedom and devotion to the dignity of man have been the hope of millions for liberty and a better life. You more than anyone else know what courage it has taken. It was courage like that of Sergeant Howard Collette, whose bomber was hit over the Celebes, and as it plunged toward the Pacific, he was heard over the radio reading aloud from his pocket Bible to his wounded comrades, calming them, comforting them, as he and they fell to their final rest.

On every continent and ocean in this century, Americans have left such stories. Courage is our mark, freedom and democracy our gift to mankind. And you, who know this so well, help us keep it that way forever. Thank you, and God bless you.

Note: The President spoke at 10:34 a.m. in the Sheraton Ballroom at the Sheraton Washington Hotel.

Remarks to Media Executives at a White House Briefing on Drug Abuse

March 7, 1988

I'm delighted all of you could come by today. The question before us is a simple one: What value do we place on human dignity and on human worth? I realize that's rather bluntly put. But you know, one of the things I've been intrigued by while I've held this job is an attitude in government that says every approach to public policy issues must be complicated and indirect. Now, come to think of it—and I know this will come as a surprise—it kind of reminds me of an anecdote from back in the days when I was also in the media business, in radio.

And most of you will remember for those radio dramas the sound-effects man and all of the things that he devised, from coconut shells that he would pound on his chest to be a horse galloping and so forth. This one particular time at WHO-Des Moines, rehearsing for a play there, and there was a sound effect that called for water falling on a board. And the sound-effect man went to work. He tried sand on a drum, and he tried rice on cardboard and peas on something else. And he was going on, and he couldn't get anything that sounded, through the microphone, like water on a board. And it was getting near show time, and somebody suggested trying water on a board. [*Laughter*] And you know, it sounded just like water on a board.

Well, that may seem a long way from the drug problem, but it isn't. Trying water on the board is really what we've tried to do with America's problem. You see, so much has changed during the past few years that I'm not sure many of us remember the skepticism that greeted early antidrug efforts. There were even those who questioned whether drugs were that much of a threat to society. Well, we're wiser now, and sadly so. We know that the price our society and our children have paid for laxity about what is quite simply a public health menace of the first order. Which is what brings us here today.

I know most of you in the media are cautious about being part of joint efforts with any government agency, and as a general rule, I think this caution is well-advised. But on certain matters of life and death, on questions of national survival, I think there's room for common purpose between us. The fact that those of us here today and people from almost every walk of life are now allied on this issue indicates a new public consensus, a consensus that has developed around what we just talked about, a very simple, very direct set of propositions: that drugs hurt, that drugs kill, that each of us must in our daily lives just say no to drug use and drug users. And saying no doesn't just mean a private refusal to use drugs: It also means taking active steps against drugs or drug use whenever it occurs and whenever we see it.

Now, this set of very direct propositions has had impact. For the first time, we're seeing progress—progress measured in statistics, but also in something much more profound: a change in awareness across America, a change that puts the goal of a drug free generation within our grasp. The most recent survey of the Nation's high school seniors is indicative of the change. Even more revealing than the fact that one-third fewer seniors acknowledged current use of cocaine in 1987 than the year before, almost all the students said it was wrong even to try a drug like cocaine. So, America, and especially young people, are realizing that we have a drug abuse problem and that illegal drugs are deadly and wrong.

It's gratifying to see that in homes, schools, businesses, and communities across the United States the wall of denial is crashing down. We're also recognizing that individual freedom does not include the right to self or social destruction. Drug use is not a victimless crime; it is not a private matter. While we must be concerned with the personal consequences for the individual, we must demonstrate our great concern for the millions of innocent citizens who pay the high price for the illegal drug use of some. These costs are measured by crime and terrorism. One recent study suggests as much as 50 to 75 percent of crime is drug-related. There is also lost productivity, increased health care costs, continuing threats to worker and public safety, the transmission of AIDS, and an overall degradation of our society.

If I could interject right here: In a community in California several years ago, before we began to get as serious as we are about this problem, the Santa Barbara Police Department—they were pretty much aware of the users and so forth, and on a weekend they rounded all they could gather, rounded them up, and put them in the hoosegow for the weekend. And they did it as an experiment. The burglary rate in Santa Barbara dropped to virtually zero while those users were off the street.

So, we're also overcoming an erroneous perception of the illicit drug user as powerless to act against drug availability, peer pressure, or his or her general lot in life. In fact, our nation's law enforcement officers, while hitting the pushers and suppliers with a force greater than ever before, acknowledge that the drug abuse problem will ultimately be solved by preventing nonusers from ever starting to use illegal drugs and getting current users to quit.

Finally, we're having to face squarely those things which we've built into our culture that enable illegal drugs to exist in our society. As citizens and individuals, we're realizing that, although government must do everything possible to help, a solution to the drug problem will only come when each of us directly confronts and rejects the cultural acceptance of illegal drug use in our daily lives.

In 1981 there were a lot of people who believed drug abuse was so rampant that we were defenseless to do anything about it. But as I said, we're taking down the surrender flag that has flown over so many drug efforts; we're running up a battle flag. We can fight the drug problem, and we can win. This call was answered by concerned citizens from around the country who were committed not only to fighting drug use but to achieving that drug free generation of young Americans that is now our goal.

Last week Nancy and I spoke to over 2,000 such individuals at the White House

Conference for a Drug Free America. Believe me, not so long ago, this conference would not have been possible. And there are still those who continue to say that, because we have not quickly solved a problem which took decades to develop, we should throw in the towel. Let's remember that our actions today are an investment in the future.

We know there are a large number of individuals, primarily those who acquired their drug-use habits in the sixties and seventies, who persist in using illegal drugs. And this persistent demand for illegal drugs is met by sometimes seemingly limitless supply. But a surge in drug-related crimes, deaths by overdose, births of drug-addicted and drug-impaired babies, and even the destabilization of national governments by traffickers should not be viewed as harbingers of defeat in our war on drugs. These events should instead strengthen our resolve to stop this insidious evil once and for all.

No, America's awakening to its drug problem has not come easily. We remember a nation stunned after the death of Len Bias. The same rude awakening has occurred only recently in the Washington, DC, area and nationally as to the stranglehold of drug criminals on foreign governments. But believe me, with each jolt into reality, we strengthen our offenses and move closer to a drug free America. Remember, the shock of recognition is not a sign of defeat; it's the beginning of victory.

Many important campaigns are now underway. Businesses are taking strong action against drug use in the workplace. Several States, such as New Jersey and Missouri, have enacted stricter laws against illegal drug use and trafficking. A number of important initiatives are underway to achieve drug free schools, drug free public housing, and drug free transportation. Our law enforcement officials have aggressive offenses underway. We're working to improve treatment and to increase the drug users' incentives for seeking help. And we're working internationally with the individual countries and organizations, like the United Nations, to stem growth, production, and transit of narcotics.

And here your own work has been particularly important. Long gone are the days when drug coverage focused on what the Government was—or too often, was not—doing to solve the drug problem. Today drug abuse is the subject of major industry initiatives and in-depth specials on the nightly news, daily newspapers, and weekly magazines. Also gone are the days when drug use was frequently glamorized in movies and television, on radio, and in print. Today the media is revealing the deadly truth about drugs and why each of us must take a stand.

So, in addition to your individual efforts, I hope you will keep up your tough reporting on this story. This means holding government officials accountable, of course, but it also means keeping a close eye on trends in drug use in America and reporting to your readers fully and fairly about those efforts. Let me assure you that when Nancy and I see stories about how far we have to go in this battle, we welcome them.

I also want to mention at least some of your individual programs. The Academy of Television Arts and Sciences is actively promoting an ongoing awareness of the drug abuse problem to be reflected in everything which is broadcast. The National Association of Broadcasters is now in its fifth year of the NAB on-air initiatives, which include a variety of major programs against drug and alcohol abuse. The Media-Advertising Partnership for a Drug Free America, the largest antidrug use advertising campaign ever attempted, is working toward a $1½ billion in volunteered media time and space to"unsell" illegal drugs. The 3 major TV networks, 13 cable networks, 13 radio networks, and the Nation's newspapers and magazines are donating space and time for the media-advertising partnership antidrug use advertisements. The Miami Herald has published more than 175 anti-drug use public service ads, many of them full-page, since joining the campaign just last year. Capital Cities/ABC broke with its tradition of local autonomy for its many print and broadcasting properties in 1984 after the death of an employee due to a drug overdose. They implemented a companywide substance abuse policy.

In addition, ABC contributed 482 commercials, half in prime time, to media-advertising partnership spots in the past 9 months. The Boston Herald launched "Say No To Drugs," a major community-based drug education campaign designed to help combat drug abuse among young people in the greater Boston area. The Chicago Sun-Times has teamed up with WLS-TV Chicago in "Say No To Drugs." The Motion Picture Association has produced a series of antidrug messages, which are shown before their feature films in movie theaters across the country.

I don't want to brag, but one of these PSA's features my own leading lady. All of these initiatives liberally [literally] represent billions of dollars in expertise and coverage, which has been invaluable in moving toward a drug free America. And this is just to mention a few examples of the excellent work that all of you are doing.

So, on behalf of the next generation of Americans—the many lives that will be saved and whose futures will be bettered—I want to extend a heartfelt thank you to each one of you. Thank you, and God bless you.

Note: The President spoke at 1:30 p.m. in the Indian Treaty Room of the Old Executive Office Building. In his remarks, he referred to Len Bias, a University of Maryland basketball player who died of a drug overdose in 1986.

Proclamation 5775—Women's History Month, 1988
March 7, 1988

By the President of the United States of America

A Proclamation

Women's History Month is a time for us to recognize and salute women's contributions to the American family and to society. Women have been making these contributions since this continent was explored and settled and America won its independence.

Women continue to strengthen the family and enrich our lives with intellectual gifts, creative talents, and an indomitable spirit—in business, government, volunteer activities, religious life, education, health, the military, sports, the arts, and many other areas. Historians will record the accomplishments of women at home as well, chronicling the tremendous contributions countless women have made by helping to raise children who adhere to the moral, ethical, civic, and patriotic principles that have made us, and kept us, a great country. We should be proud and grateful as we celebrate Women's History Month.

The Congress, by Senate Joint Resolution 262, has designated the month of March 1988 as "Women's History Month" and authorized and requested the President to issue a proclamation in observance of this event.

Now, Therefore, I, Ronald Reagan, President of the United States of America, do hereby proclaim March 1988 as Women's History Month. I call upon all Americans to observe this month with appropriate ceremonies and activities.

In Witness Whereof, I have hereunto set my hand this seventh day of March, in the year of our Lord nineteen hundred and eighty-eight, and of the Independence of the United States of America the two hundred and twelfth.

RONALD REAGAN

[*Filed with the Office of the Federal Register, 4:17 p.m., March 8, 1988*]

Note: The proclamation was released by the Office of the Press Secretary on March 8.

Remarks to Members of the United States Winter Olympic Team
March 8, 1988

The President. Thank you all very much, and welcome to the White House. Somebody once stopped Louis Armstrong on a street in New York City and asked him how to get to Carnegie Hall. "Practice," he said, "practice, practice, practice." Well, that's how each of you got to the Olympics. And I must tell you, we have hundreds of groups here each year, but I can't think of any that I'm prouder of than you. Years of practice and years of dedication, years of dreaming and working for your dreams have made each one of you—medal or no medal—an American champion and an American success story.

America cheered when Bonnie Blair won her gold and bronze medals, setting a world record in the 500 meters. And when she was asked how she did it, Bonnie said, "I think I just got it on guts." Well, one thing I noticed on TV when Bonnie won: that "Blair Bunch," Bonnie's family as well as her friends from the Champaign, Illinois, Police Department, cheering her on. I have a hunch that love and support of both family and community helped Bonnie find those guts.

And while we're on gold, Brian Boitano, is there anyone who's soared the way you did in your gold medal-winning long program? Eric Flaim flew as he captured 1 silver in the 1500 meters and just missed 3 bronzes. And Jill Watson and Peter Oppegard, you were a thrill to watch as you captured your bronze medal. And like Bonnie, each of you has had that backing of family and community over the years, and that backing has given you the strength to compete with grace and sportsmanship. And Debi Thomas, sometimes when I look at everything you've done and are doing—Olympic skater, pre-med student—I wonder if your name should be Debi or Superwoman. I know that you draw a lot of your strength from the strength and love and example of your mother. Yes, you were disappointed with your bronze, but the grace with which you accepted your disappointment won you a gold medal in the heart of every American.

Talking about gold medals from America's heart, there's one that goes to Dan Jansen for his courage, and one that goes to his family, too. Their devotion to each other captured the heart and earned the admiration of our entire land. Dan, you received the United States Olympic Committee's Olympic Spirit Award, and everyone here and around the country applauds the committee's choice. You dedicated that honor to your sister, her memory, and your entire family. And now you're back in competition and number one in World Cup points. Yes, your family is very precious in your life, and if recently a cause of great sadness, it is also a source of great strength. And that strength is an inspiration to the entire world.

Now, I won't forget the demonstration events: freestyle skiing—gold in the aerials. Melanie Palanik, in my book anyone who even tries freestyle aerial skiing deserves a medal. [*Laughter*] And silvers in men's and women's ballet—Lane Spina and Jan Bucher. Finally, in disabled skiing, we had a sweep in the women's modified giant slalom: Diana Golden, Cathy Gentile, silver—that was gold for Diana Golden. I left out one of the golds, didn't I? [*Laughter*] Cathy Gentile, silver, Martha Hill, bronze, while Greg Mannino won a silver in the men's. Your performances inspired us all.

Now, there's been a lot of talk—too much talk in my opinion—about the number of medals that weren't won. The heart of the Olympics is the sport and the competition. It's the exuberance of the hockey team. It's Bonny Warner breaking new ground in American women's luge. It's the pride of Marion, Indiana, at the performance of Wayne and Natalie Seybold in pairs skating. And, yes, it's the spirit of Pam Fletcher, who returned to the slopes 2 hours after breaking her leg in a practice run to cheer for her teammates. It's striving with the support and love of family and community to be the best you possibly can be, because you love your sport and—win, lose, or draw—you love the competition. And for that, all of you get gold medals. There's one thing you can remember above all. Just being here in those uniforms and being where you were puts you a world apart from just literally millions of other people, and every one of you has a right to be proud.

Thank you all for being here, and God bless you.

Mr. Boitano. I think winning medals is one thing, but I think the thing that I'll, and we'll, most remember about Calgary is the outstanding support that not only all of our teammates gave us but that we got from our own country. It filled me personally with so much patriotism. And I think, speaking on behalf of all of the athletes, that we're very appreciative to be a part of this country, and we really respect it a lot. Bonnie Blair would like to make a presentation to make President Reagan a part of our team.

[*At this point, the President was given a Winter Olympic uniform.*]

The President. Thank you. Well, thank you all very much.

Ms. Blair. Thank you for everything.

Mr. Helmick. Mr. President, as president of the United States Olympic Committee, I'd like to thank you. And I want to tell you, the President of the United States, that I think that we had 165 heroes representing the United States up in Calgary. Men and women who won their regionals, their nationals, their trials, and since then have gone on to win world championships and world cups. And each one of them—there's 165 stories of personal struggles, personal sacrifices, not only sacrifice of their time but economic sacrifice. And the Congress of the United States and you, Mr. President, have done something to really help the economic sacrifice, and that is the passage of the Coin Act, which is going to bring new resources to help support these athletes in their Olympic challenges. And on behalf of the United States Olympic Committee and this team and the summer team going to Seoul, I want to thank the Congress and the President for the Coin Act. Thank you very much.

The President. Thank you all very much.

Note: The President spoke at 2:01 p.m. in the Rose Garden at the White House.

Statement by Assistant to the President for Press Relations Fitzwater on the Situation in Panama

March 8, 1988

The United States welcomes the statements issued by President Delvalle, Vice President Esquivel, and the political parties and Civilian Crusade of Panama favoring a government of national reconciliation. This is a blueprint for progress toward democracy in Panama. We support their goal of restoring democratic government and civilian constitutional order. Once this goal has been achieved, we will work cooperatively with the Government of Panama toward the recovery of Panama's financial and economic health. The United States remains committed to fulfilling its Panama Canal treaty obligations, and we are prepared to resume working with the Panamanian Defense Forces under the treaty once civilian rule and constitutional democracy are established.

Executive Order 12628—United Nations Industrial Development Organization
March 8, 1988

By virtue of the authority vested in me as President by the Constitution and laws of the United States of America, including Section 1 of the International Organizations Immunities Act (22 U.S.C. 288), and in order to facilitate United States participation in the United Nations Industrial Development Organization, it is hereby ordered as follows:

Section 1. The United Nations Industrial Development Organization, whose Constitution was ratified by the United States on August 2, 1983, and entered into force on June 21, 1985, is hereby designated as a public international organization entitled to enjoy the privileges, exemptions, and immunities conferred by the International Organizations Immunities Act. This designation is not intended to abridge in any respect the privileges, exemptions, or immunities that such organization has acquired or may acquire by international agreements or by Act of Congress.

Sec. 2. This Order shall be effective immediately.

RONALD REAGAN

The White House,
March 8, 1988.

[*Filed with the Office of the Federal Register, 10:27 a.m., March 9, 1988*]

Remarks at the Unveiling of the Knute Rockne Commemorative Stamp at the University of Notre Dame in Indiana
March 9, 1988

Thank you. And, Moose, when I was young and reading about George Gipp, I never thought I'd come back as the Gipper. [*Laughter*] Well, thank you, Reverend Malloy and Governor, Lieutenant Governor, distinguished guests. And a special hello to the Rockne family. I brought with me Dick Lyng, our Secretary of Agriculture and Notre Dame's representative in the Cabinet, and the five—not the four—horsemen from Congress—South Bend's own Jack Hiler, our quarterback in this effort. You'll recognize one of America's truly great sports legends and four other distinguished alumni: Joe McDade, Dan Lungren, Dave Martin, and Ben Blaz.

It's a pleasure to visit once again the home of the Fighting Irish. With St. Patrick's Day coming up and after seeing those film clips, it brings to mind another deathbed scene. You know, apparently the town rogue of one small Irish hamlet lay on his deathbed as the priest prepared for the atonement. "Do you renounce the devil?" "Do you renounce him and all his works?" the priest asked. And the rogue opened one eye and said, "Father, this is no time for making enemies." [*Laughter*]

But, it's great to be back here. I've said this before, but I want you to know the first time I ever saw Notre Dame was when I came here as a sports announcer, 2 years out of college, to broadcast a football game. You won, or I wouldn't have mentioned it. [*Laughter*] And then, of course, I was here with Pat O'Brien and a whole host of Hollywood stars for the world premier of "Ḱnute Rockne." Now, let me explain, I may be saying the name differently, but when we made the picture we were told, and Bonnie [Mrs. Knute Rockne] upheld it to us, that it was Ḱnute—not Knute. So, you'll have to get used to me saying it that way.

"Knute Rockne: All American"—how I had wanted to make that movie and play the part of George Gipp. Of course, the goal was—or the role was a young actor's dream: It had a great entrance, an action middle, and a death scene right out of the opera. [*Laughter*] But it was more than that. I know that to many of you today Rockne is a revered name, a symbol of greatness and, yes, a face now on a postage stamp. But my generation, well, we actually knew the legend as it happened. We saw it unfold, and we felt it was saying something important about us as a people and a nation. And there was little room for skepticism or cynicism; we knew the legend was based on fact.

I would like to interject here, if I could, that it's difficult to stand before you and make you understand how great that legend was at that time. It isn't just a memory here and of those who knew him, but throughout this nation he was a living legend. Millions of Americans just automatically rooted for him on Saturday afternoon and rooted, therefore, for Notre Dame. Now, of course, the Rockne legend stood for fairplay and honor, but you know, it was thoroughly American in another way. It was practical. It placed a value on devastating quickness and agility and on confounding the opposition with good old American cleverness. But most of all, the Rockne legend meant this—when you think about it, it's what's been taught here at Notre Dame since her founding: that on or off the field, it is faith that makes the difference, it is faith that makes great things happen.

And believe me, it took faith—and a lot of it—for an unknown actor to think that he could get the part of George Gipp. I was under contract to Warner Brothers, but I had been all over the studio talking about my idea for a story. Having come from sports announcing to the movies, I said I thought that the movies ought to make the life story of Knute Rockne. And then one day I picked up the Daily Variety and read where Warner Brothers was announcing that they were making the life story of Knute Rockne and were starting to cast the film. Well, all I'd ever wanted was to play the Gipper if they some day made the film. And I approached Pat O'Brien, who was going to play Rockne—he'd been my choice—and he told me bluntly that I talked too much and that's where Warner's got the idea. [*Laughter*] And I told him what my ambition was, and he said, "Well, they're looking for a name actor." But Pat did intervene with the head of the studio, the top producer, Hal Wallis. Hal was, to put it mildly, unimpressed with my credentials. [*Laughter*] He started by telling me I didn't look big enough for the part.

Well, I wasn't very polite, because I told him, "You're producing the picture, and you don't know that George Gipp weighed 5 pounds less than I weigh right now. He walked with a kind of a slouch and almost a limp. He looked like a football player only when he was on the field." And then I went home, because some cameramen had told me that the fellas in the front office, they only knew what they saw on film. And I dug down in the trunk and came up with my own pictures of myself playing football in college and brought them back and showed them to Hal Wallis.

Well, he finally let me do a test for the part, and Pat O'Brien, knowing of my nervousness and desire, graciously agreed to be a part of it and play in the scene with me. Well, of course, I had an advantage. I had known George Gipp's story for years, and the lines were straight from Knute Rockne's diary. And the test scene was one that said something about what Rockne liked to see in his players. It was George Gipp's first practice. You saw that scene where he was told to get into uniform. And Rockne told him to carry the ball, and Gipp just looked back at Rockne and cocked an eyebrow and said, "How far?"

Well, I mentioned all this because, as I say, Knute liked spirit in his ball players. Grantland Rice tells us that once when he was working with the four backfield stars who became known as the "Four Horsemen" the fellow named Jimmy Crowley just couldn't get it right. Now, you know, I never tell ethnic jokes anymore unless they're about the Irish. [*Laughter*] But in view of the spirit of this occasion, maybe I can be permitted some leeway. Rockne, who, by the way, was Norwegian, was commonly called the "Swede." He finally got exasperated after Crowley muffed a play and hollered, "What's dumber than a dumb

Irishman?" And without missing a beat, Crowley shot right back, "A smart Swede." [*Laughter*]

Well, that was Rockne. And you know, not too long ago I was questioned about the George Gipp story. And this interviewer had really done his research. In fact, he'd even gone back and talked to my old football coach, Ralph McKenzie, at Eureka College, who was 91 years old, and asked him about my football career. Well, now, I've been through a lot of interviews, but believe me, I tensed up at hearing that. And apparently Mac described me as "eager, aggressive, better on defense, overall an average football player—but an outstanding talker." [*Laughter*]

Well, anyway, I was asked whether I knew that George Gipp was no angel, that he played in some pool games and card games in his time. And of course, that was true, and I said so. But it was also true of George Gipp—and it is legitimately part of the legend—that he used his winnings from those games to buy food for destitute families and to help other students pay their way through Notre Dame. And the reason he got so sick and later died from pneumonia was because he had promised a former teammate who had become a high school coach that he would give his students some pointers. Author James Cox tells us it was during that training session in Chicago that an icy wind blew in across Lake Michigan and the Gipper first felt the ache and sore throat that would lead to the illness that would take his life. You see, there were no miracle drugs in those days. And a promising young life was ended, but the point is, George Gipp couldn't forget a friend.

And I've always thought that it was no mere coincidence that the legend of George Gipp and Knute Rockne emerged from this great institution of higher learning not simply because of its academic excellence but because it stands among the winds of subjectivity for lasting values and principles that are the heart of our civilization and on which all human progress is built—Notre Dame not only educates its students in the development of honesty, courage, and all the other things we call character. Rockne once wrote: "Sportsmanship means fairplay. It means having a little respect for the other fellow's point of view. It means a real application of the Golden Rule."

And I know a fine example of this is the charitable care 80 of you students give the handicapped children at the Logan Center. This and other acts of good will say much about your generation. There are those who suggest the 1980's have been characterized by greed. Well, charitable giving is up. I think our detractors are looking in the wrong places. If they want to see the goodness and love of life of this generation, the commitment to decency and a better future, let them come here to Notre Dame. It's a place where the Golden Rule, the legend of Rockne, and the idea of religious faith still live.

Rockne stressed character. He knew, instinctively, the relationship between the physical and moral. That is as true of nations as it is of people. Charles Lindbergh, also a hero of that time, once said: "Short-term survival may depend on the knowledge of nuclear physicists and the performance of supersonic aircraft, but long-term survival depends alone on the character of man." Rockne believed in competition, yet he did not rely on brute force for winning the victory. Instead, he's remembered as the man who brought ingenuity, speed, and agility into this most American of sports.

May I interrupt myself here for a second and tell you something else about him? As a sports announcer, I was told by many of the great coaches in this land whose teams had played against Notre Dame teams under Rockne that one of their hardest problems when playing Notre Dame was that their team worshiped Rockne—[*laughter*]—that they were fans of his, and that when they came out in the field the first thing they looked for was where was this great, great coach. Rockne, you see, was a man of vision. And that's how he came by his reputation as someone larger than life and a miracle man. Because of his tremendous success in sports, it's easy to forget that he was something else as well, something not too many people knew about him. He was also a man of science, having taught chemistry here at Notre Dame for 4 years. I must believe that he would not be at all surprised at the enormous advances that have taken place over the five decades since his death.

Much has been said about the technological revolution in which we are living. Every time we turn around, it seems to be staring us in the face. Typewriters are being replaced in corporate offices throughout the country by highly efficient word processors. With the almost universal proliferation of copy machines, carbon paper has almost gone the way of the buggy whip. Not only deregulation, but design and technology have made our airlines more efficient.

The American workplace, in recent years, has undergone a dramatic transformation. Just in the last 5 years, manufacturing productivity of our working people has increased 4.7 percent annually. And from the plant floor to the corporate boardroom, there is more cooperation, a sense of common purpose, more of a winning spirit, and state-of-the-art equipment and machinery available to do the job. I've seen it in the many companies that I've visited all across this nation, and I've heard it from the working people themselves. And don't let all the gloom and doomers tell you any different. There's a will to succeed evident in our land. I happen to have always believed in the American people. Don't ever sell them short. Given the proper tools and a level playing ground, our workers can outproduce and outcompete anyone, anywhere.

It's a far different picture than the agonizing sight of a decade ago, when many were counting out American workers and American industry. We were told that Americans would no longer go the extra mile, no longer had the drive to excel; that our country was in decline and that we, as a people, should lower our expectations. Well, today we see an America ready to compete, anxious to compete. In fact, our workers are so productive that foreign companies are opening plants in the United States, sometimes to manufacture products for export to other countries. Our industrial base, contrary to a totally false yet widespread impression, is strong and, in fact, is growing. We've added almost 300,000 manufacturing jobs in the last 6 months, and that trend is continuing. There are over 19 million manufacturing jobs today, about the same as the last 20 years, while manufacturing output is up almost 40 percent over the last 5 years. And unemployment continues to decline. In short, American industry is lean and mean and ready to meet the competition head on. I predict that as this year progresses we will see American manufacturing reemerge as the leading force in the world marketplace. Exports will, in fact, race ahead and lead our domestic economy.

What is propelling our country forward?—that fundamental element of the American character that no tyranny and few of our competitors can ever hope to match. Knute Rockne knew and appreciated it—the creative genius and omnipresent optimism of our people. We had faith in them these last 7 years, and they did the rest. That's why, instead of giving up, we set our sights high. We didn't raise taxes, drain the investment pool, and tell our working people and business leaders to hunker down and prepare for the worst, to lower their expectations. We asked them to dream great dreams, to reach for the stars. We left resources in the private sector that others would have drained into the bureaucracy.

The heavy investment made in our economy during the early part of this decade is paying off now, in a big way. President Franklin Roosevelt once said: "The only limit on our realization of tomorrow will be our doubts of today." Well, together, we, the American people, have proven the doubters wrong, time and again. We've done it by keeping our eyes on the future, by setting our sights on what can be done rather than on complaining about how much there is to do. We've done it by viewing every problem as an opportunity. I happen to believe in something former astronaut John Swigert once said: "Technology and commitment can overcome any challenge."

The individual investment made in companies, large and small; the retraining of our work force to handle the jobs in this technological age; the search for new ideas and innovative approaches; the modernization of older industries and investment in the new; energy, creativity, and, yes, hard work on a massive scale throughout our country, from the bottom up—this is the foundation of our prosperity and the impetus for national progress. Our program has been to foster innovation and to keep our country in the forefront of change.

And that's why last year we committed ourselves to building the world's largest particle accelerator, superconducting supercollider to maintain our leadership in high-energy physics research and America's scientific and technological competitiveness. That's why we're developing a space plane that by the end of the century will take off from a runway, but once at high altitude will rocket into near space and zip to its destination at 10 and even 20 times the speed of sound. And that's why I'm proposing to Congress in my fiscal year '89 budget a new Thomas A. Edison prize program, offering monetary awards to any American who can develop workable, groundbreaking technologies that could improve our quality of life. And that's why scientists right here at Notre Dame are blazing trails in superconductivity research, finding ways so that this breakthrough technology can be put to use for the betterment of all mankind. Because someday, because of research being done here, transcontinental railroads will slide heavy cargoes on a magnetic cushion, cheaply and quickly across the country. Perhaps our energy costs will drop below anything we could have imagined a decade ago.

Rockne exemplified the American spirit of never giving up. That spirit is the reason why you and your generation are going to succeed. That's why we're not just going to compete, we're going to win. And that's also why this year we'll see the return of the American space shuttle, symbolic of America's tenacity. We never give up. And I cannot help but believe that the heroes of the *Challenger* will be cheering along with the rest of us when the United States reclaims its rightful leadership role in leading the conquest of this, the last frontier.

Technology in these last decades has reshaped our lives. It's opened vast opportunity for the common man and has brought all of mankind into one community. Today worldwide communications and transportation have linked productive citizens of every free land. Through advances in medicine, our people are living longer, and the quality of their later years has been vastly improved. I like to remind people that I've already lived some 23 years longer than the average life expectancy when I was born. That's a source of frustration to a number of people. [*Laughter*]

And you know there are always those who say the problem's too big, it can't be helped, let's prepare for the worst. But a few years ago, we heard that about the drug problem here in America. But a few people, including my roommate, Nancy—[*laughter*]—said it was time for action, not gloom and doom. And the statistics are starting to show what her commitment and the commitment of millions of others has accomplished. Not only did a recent survey of high school seniors show that one-third fewer seniors acknowledged current use of cocaine in 1987 than the year before, but almost all the students said it was wrong to even try a drug like cocaine.

We still have a long way to go, and when Nancy and I see stories saying just that in the newspaper, we welcome them. But let's also remember that the shock of recognition is not a sign of defeat: It's the beginning of victory. And victory will be ours. And I hope that each of you will join us in saying that drugs hurt, drugs kill, that each of us must just say no to drugs and drug users, and most of all in giving America what America deserves: your very best. And that means a drug free generation. And may I challenge you? Why not? Why not make your generation the one that said, once and for all, no more drugs in the United States of America or the world?

Excellence too is returning to our schools. We've learned what's always been known here at Notre Dame: that values are an essential part of educational excellence. Throughout the Nation, parents and teachers are gaining greater control over local curriculums, emphasizing basics and making their children's education a priority in all of our lives. And they're right to do so, because all of the wonderful gains I've talked about so far, especially those gains built on the growth of technology, depend on young Americans who know how to think, calculate, write, and communicate.

Now, there are those who see a dark side to our technological progress. Yes, they admit our well-being has been enhanced in so many ways. Technological advances now are making it more likely, for example, that our natural resources will be spared as long-haul telephone lines and electrical cable give way to the satellite transmissions and computer chips. I spoke to the young people of Europe not long ago via our WORLDNET system and reminded them that only a short time ago such a transmission would have required thousands of tons of copper wire and other resources. Instead, our talk was transmitted quickly, cheaply, efficiently, almost miraculously from our continent to theirs, via satellite.

Yet it is pointed out that, regretfully, as man has advanced into this new age, so has his capability to kill and destroy; and it's no longer just those in uniform who are victimized. In World War I, more than 8 million military personnel lost their lives and over 12 million civilians died. During the Second World War, almost 20 million in uniform lost their lives; however, there were about 14 million civilians killed. And if there's ever another such conflagration, a Third World War, hundreds of millions will lose their lives. And it's estimated that 90 percent of the casualties will be civilian.

When I was in college, I remember a debate in one of my classes. This was back in the days when the bomber was just being recognized as the potent weapon that it later became in the post-World War I days. Our class debated whether or not Americans—people who, to our way of thinking, stood for high moral standards—would ever drop bombs from an airplane on a city. And the class was about evenly divided. Half felt it might be necessary. The others felt bombing civilians would always be beyond the pale of decency, totally unacceptable human conduct, no matter how heinous the enemy. Well, a decade later, few, if any, who had been in that room objected to our country's wholesale bombing of cities. Civilization's standards of morality had changed. The thought of killing more and more people, noncombatants, became more and more acceptable.

Well, today, technology is pointing toward a way out of this dilemma. It's given us the promise of basing our security in the future on protection rather than the threat of retaliation. SDI offers a chance to reverse not only the nuclear arms buildup but also to reverse the trend that in effect has put a lower and lower value on human life. Technology offers you young people who debate in today's classroom an option that threatens no one and offers a shield rather than ever sharper, more deadly swords. It offers you young people a chance to raise the moral standards of mankind.

When I came here in 1981 for one of the first major addresses of my Presidency, I acknowledged the difficulties we faced in the world, not only the threat of nuclear war but also totalitarian expansion around the world, especially in places like Afghanistan. But I also said that in avoiding these two unacceptable choices of nuclear confrontation or totalitarian rule the West had a secret resource of strength: the spiritual values of our civilization and the essential decency and optimism of our peoples.

And something that got a warm response from you undergraduates, but was treated very skeptically in Washington, was my suggestion that these values were so strong and this inner strength was so great that, in the long run, the West would not contain communism: We would transcend communism, that the era of the nuclear threat and totalitarian darkness would someday be put behind us, that we would look again with all the people of the Earth to the bright, sunlit uplands of world peace, world prosperity, and yes, world freedom. How much has changed since those days. And as we look back at 7 years of peace as well as progress in arms reductions and the hope of a Soviet exit from Afghanistan, we can be pleased that the inner strength of our nation and our civilization is increasingly apparent with every day that passes.

And that inner strength is what Notre Dame and the legend of Rockne are all about. You know, so much is said about Rockne's influence on his ballplayers, but actually he liked to talk about their influence on him. In his autobiography, he described his inability to sleep one night before a big game. So, he was up early in the lobby and saw 2 of his boys come down the stairs and go out, and then others came and followed them. And though he had a pretty good idea of what was going on, he decided to follow along. "They didn't realize it," he said in his diary, "but these youngsters were making a powerful impression on me." And he said, "When I saw them walking up to the Communion rail to receive and realized the hours of sleep they had sacrificed, I understood what a powerful ally their religion was to them in their work on the football field."

And after Rockne found—here at Notre Dame—his own religious faith, a friend of his at the University of Maryland asked him if he minded telling him about it. "Why should I mind telling you?" he said. "You know all this hurry and battling we're going through is just an expression of our inner selves striving for something else. The way I look at it is that we're all here to try and find, each in his own way, the best road to our ultimate goal. I believe I've found my way, and I shall travel it to the end." And travel it to the end he did. And when they found him in the Kansas cornfield where the plane had gone down, they also found next to him a prayer book and at his fingertips the rosary of Notre Dame, the rosary of Our Lady. Someone put it so well at the time: Knute Rockne did more spiritual good than a thousand preachers. His career was a sermon in right living.

Yes, we've seen more change in the last 50 years, since Knute Rockne was with us, than in all the other epics of history combined. You are the beneficiaries of this, and it is you who'll continue the struggle and carry mankind to greater and greater heights. As Americans, as free people, you must stand firm, even when it's uncomfortable for you to do so. It won't always be easy. There will be moments of joy, of triumph. There will also be times of despair, times when all those around you are ready to give up.

It's then I want you to remember our meeting today. And "some time when the team is up against it and the breaks are beating the boys, tell them to go out there with all they've got and win just one for the Gipper. I don't know where I'll be then, but I'll know about it, and I'll be happy." Good luck in the years ahead, and God bless you all. Thank you.

Note: The President spoke to the students and faculty at 1 p.m. at the Joyce Athletic and Convocation Center. In his remarks, he referred to Moose Krause, a former player on a Rockne team; Father Edward Malloy, president of the University of Notre Dame; Gov. Robert Orr; Lt. Gov. John Mutz; and Representatives John Hiler of Indiana, Joseph McDade of Pennsylvania, Dan Lungren of California, David Martin of New York, and Ben Blaz of Guam. Following his remarks, the President participated in the unveiling of the stamp. He then attended receptions for university officials and guests and for Indiana State Republican Party members. Following the receptions, the President returned to Washington, DC.

Letter to the Speaker of the House of Representatives and the President of the Senate on Nuclear Cooperation With EURATOM
March 9, 1988

Dear Mr. Speaker: (Dear Mr. President:)

The United States has been engaged in nuclear cooperation with the European community for many years. This cooperation was initiated under agreements concluded over 2 decades ago between the United States and the European Atomic Energy Community (EURATOM), which extend until December 31, 1995. Since the inception of this cooperation, the Community has adhered to all its obligations under those agreements.

The Nuclear Non-Proliferation Act of 1978 amended the Atomic Energy Act of 1954 to establish new nuclear export criteria, including a requirement that the United States has a right to consent to the reprocessing of fuel exported from the

United States. Our present agreements for cooperation with EURATOM do not contain such a right. To avoid disrupting cooperation with EURATOM, a proviso was included in the law to enable continued cooperation until March 10, 1980, if EURATOM agreed to negotiations concerning our cooperation agreements, which it did.

The law also provides that nuclear cooperation with EURATOM can be extended on an annual basis after March 10, 1980, upon determination by the President that failure to cooperate would be seriously prejudicial to the achievement of U.S. non-proliferation objectives or otherwise jeopardize the common defense and security and after notification to the Congress. President Carter made such a determination 8 years ago and signed Executive Order No. 12193, permitting continued nuclear cooperation with EURATOM until March 10, 1981. I made such determinations in 1981, 1982, 1983, 1984, 1985, 1986, and 1987 and signed Executive Orders Nos. 12295, 12351, 12409, 12463, 12506, 12554, and 12587 permitting continued nuclear cooperation through March 10, 1988.

In addition to numerous informal contacts, the United States has engaged in 12 rounds of talks with EURATOM regarding the renegotiation of the U.S.-EURATOM agreements for cooperation. These were conducted in November 1978, September 1979, April 1980, January 1982, November 1983, March 1984, May, September, and November 1985, April and July 1986, and September 1987. Further progress in the talks is anticipated this year.

I believe that it is essential that cooperation between the United States and the Community continue, and likewise, that we work closely with our allies to counter the threat of nuclear explosives proliferation. A disruption of nuclear cooperation would not only eliminate any chance of progress in our talks with EURATOM related to our agreements, it would also cause serious problems in our overall relationships. Accordingly, I have determined that failure to continue peaceful nuclear cooperation with EURATOM would be seriously prejudicial to the achievement of U.S. non-proliferation objectives and would jeopardize the common defense and security of the United States. I intend to sign an Executive order to extend the waiver of the application of the relevant export criterion of the Nuclear Non-Proliferation Act for an additional 12 months from March 10, 1988.

Sincerely,

RONALD REAGAN

Note: Identical letters were sent to Jim Wright, Speaker of the House of Representatives, and George Bush, President of the Senate.

Executive Order 12629—Nuclear Cooperation With EURATOM
March 9, 1988

By the authority vested in me as President by the Constitution and statutes of the United States of America, including Section 126a(2) of the Atomic Energy Act of 1954, as amended (42 U.S.C. 2155(a)(2)), and having determined that, upon the expiration of the period specified in the first proviso to Section 126a(2) of such Act and extended for 12-month periods by Executive Orders Nos. 12193, 12295, 12351, 12409, 12463, 12506, 12554, and 12587, failure to continue peaceful nuclear cooperation with the European Atomic Energy Community would be seriously prejudicial to the achievement of U.S. non-proliferation objectives and would otherwise jeopardize the common defense and security of the United States, and having notified the Congress of this determination, I hereby extend the duration of that period to March 10, 1989. Executive Order No. 12587 shall be superseded on the effective date of this Executive Order.

RONALD REAGAN

The White House,
March 9, 1988.

[Filed with the Office of the Federal Register, 10:40 a.m., March 10, 1988]

Nomination of George Arthur Trail III To Be United States Ambassador to Malawi
March 10, 1988

The President today announced his intention to nominate George Arthur Trail III, a career member of the Senior Foreign Service, Class of Minister-Counselor, as Ambassador to the Republic of Malawi. He would succeed Weston Adams.

Before joining the Foreign Service in 1965, Mr. Trail was an assistant professor of naval science at Rice University in Houston, TX, 1963–1965, and a financial analyst for the Ford Motor Co. in 1965. He took language training at the Foreign Service Institute, 1965–1966, and his first overseas assignment was consular officer in Munich, Germany, 1966–1967. Thereafter he became trade and investment officer at the U.S. Embassy in Bonn, and in 1968 was assigned as the political officer in Freetown, Sierra Leone. In 1970 he returned to Washington and served first as the Liberian desk officer, 1970–1972, and as a congressional fellow for a year at the offices of Congressman Lee Hamilton and Senator Lee Metcalf. Mr. Trail served as principal officer at the American consulate in Kaduna, Nigeria, 1973–1975, and political-military officer in Bangkok, Thailand, 1975–1978. He was Deputy Director of the Office of West African Affairs in the Department of State, 1978–1980; consul general in Johannesburg, 1980–1984; and deputy chief of mission in Nairobi, Kenya, where he served until August 1987, when he was assigned to the Bureau of African Affairs in the Department of State.

Mr. Trail graduated from Franklin and Marshall College (A.B., 1958) and the University of Houston (B.S., 1965). He served in the United States Navy, 1959–1963. He was born October 16, 1936, in Chambersburg, PA. He is married, has four children, and resides in Chambersburg, PA.

Nomination of Barry M. Goldwater, Jr., To Be a Member of the Board of Trustees of the Barry Goldwater Scholarship and Excellence in Education Foundation
March 10, 1988

The President today announced his intention to nominate Barry M. Goldwater, Jr., to be a member of the Board of Trustees of the Barry Goldwater Scholarship and Excellence in Education Foundation. This is a new position.

Since 1983 Mr. Goldwater has been in private practice as an investment banker, and since 1984, as a general partner in Hambrose Leasing in New York. Previously Mr. Goldwater represented the 20th Congressional District of California as a Member of the U.S. House of Representatives, 1969–1982. From 1962 to 1969, he was a stockbroker with Noble-Cook, Inc.

Mr. Goldwater graduated from Arizona State University (B.S., 1962). He was born July 15, 1938, in Los Angeles, CA. He has one child and resides in Studio City, CA.

Nomination of M. Alan Woods To Be a Member of the Board of Directors of the Inter-American Foundation
March 10, 1988

The President today announced his intention to nominate M. Alan Woods to be a member of the Board of Directors of the Inter-American Foundation for a term expiring September 20, 1992. He would succeed M. Peter McPherson.

Since 1987 Ambassador Woods has been Administrator of the Agency for International Development (AID). Prior to this, he was Deputy United States Trade Representative with the rank of Ambassador, 1985–1987; vice president-technology for Sears World Trade, 1983; and vice president of DGA International, 1977–1983. He was Assistant Secretary of Defense (Public Affairs), 1976–1977; Special Assistant to the Secretary and Deputy Secretaries of Defense, 1975–1976; and Principal Deputy Assistant Secretary of Defense (Public Affairs) in 1975. Ambassador Woods was Deputy Director of the Presidential Personnel Office at the White House, 1974–1975.

Ambassador Woods graduated from American University (B.A., 1967). He was born October 13, 1945, in St. Louis, MO. He is married and resides in Washington, DC.

Interview With Christine Ockrent of TF–1 Television of France
March 10, 1988

Israeli-Occupied Territories

Q. Mr. President, your administration has been putting a lot of pressure on Israel to come to a solution in the occupied territories. Are you disappointed at the lack of results so far?

The President. Well, no, because I believe that peace is inevitable. I don't think that anyone—we may have some differences there as to how to achieve it, but I don't think anyone believes that we can go on just with a constant state of warfare and unrest. And I believe that we have presented for discussion a pretty good solution that would remove some of the problems besetting the people in the occupied territories.

Q. Prime Minister Shamir has already expressed his opposition to Secretary Shultz's plan. He will be coming here next week.

The President. Yes.

Q. What kind of additional pressure do you intend to put on him?

The President. Well, I don't think it's so much pressure as it is just an attempt at persuasion. But also, I'd like to point out that his Cabinet is pretty evenly split on the solution. So, it isn't a case of outside pressure there. He has a great element in his own government that sees merit in the proposals that we've made.

Israeli Elections

Q. Would early Israeli elections be considered an American success in your view?

The President. Frankly, I haven't given much thought to that and to their election process there as to whether it would or not. I know that he has now broached that subject. And yet if they were held, maybe it is that he would believe that he might have more support for his position, because the other faction, then, in the election is the one that is already differing from the Prime Minister and supportive of what we've proposed.

Israeli Censorship

Q. Do you share the view that Israel should ban all television coverage from the troubled areas?

The President. Well, I'm a great believer in a free press and the right of the people to know, and so I would have to be opposed to it, thinking that they want to conduct operations in which they would rather not have public knowledge of them.

Middle East Peace Settlement

Q. What would be the ultimate goal if Secretary Shultz was to succeed? Would it be to have an international conference on the Middle East with a seat for your friend, Mr. Gorbachev?

The President. Well, this is a problem, because you have a situation there where the Soviet Union has not recognized Israel as a nation. That's very difficult to have someone participating in a conference of that kind who doesn't even believe in the right of statehood of the other country. What we've also thought is not the kind of international conference that would seek to impose a settlement. I don't think that really is the province of the other countries, but to be helpful and see if we could not join in helping arrive at a solution that would once and for all end the hostilities. I think most of the world tends to forget that war between Israel and the Arab States still is a fact. It has never been settled. There has never been any peace agreement arrived at, and it would be a great achievement if once and for all that state of war came to an end.

Global Economy

Q. Mr. President, after more than 7 years here at the White House, in a capsule view, how would you qualify the global shift of economic power in the world? Would you say that this country is a fading empire, that Europe is in economic decline, and that Japan is the emerging world power today?

The President. Well, I would say quite the contrary—not as to whether Japan is an emerging power. I think that having been Governor of a State on the Pacific Basin, in the western part of our country, I believe that the old adage "Go west young man" still holds true, that the Pacific rim is something very great economically for the future. It is coming into being as a great economic force.

Q. Is Europe in economic decline, in your view?

The President. No, I don't believe so. But I'm speaking of the developing nations when I speak about the other. But I would think the reverse is true. I believe that with our economic summit, that our turning away from protectionism to the extent that we are, and our efforts to even do more of that with the GATT [General Agreement on Tariffs and Trade] treaty and all, that we've made great improvement in world economy. And we have to face the fact that it is a world economy, that none of us anymore can believe that we can stand off and just achieve prosperity by ourselves.

Deficit Reduction

Q. The U.S. budget deficit has reached unprecedented proportions. Don't you feel that in a way it means the failure of liberal economic policy that you pursued?

The President. You're speaking of our Federal budget deficit——

Q. Indeed.

The President. ——not in the trade deficit? Yes, for over 50 years this country has been running deficits. As a matter of fact, it's almost 60 years now in which there have only been 8 individual years in which there was not a budget deficit. It was a false economic theory that was adopted by one of our two political parties and that party happened to control the Legislature for most of these 60 years. And it has been proven false. So, what we've been doing for these 7 years is trying to get on a path leading toward a balancing of the budget, the elimination of deficit spending. It has reached a point that you couldn't do it in one year. You couldn't suddenly pull the string and say——

Q. Not even in two terms—two Presidential terms?

The President. Well, you see I was still up against that Legislature with that other philosophy. But I do believe that that's one of the things that's happened in these 7 years—is that instead of the argument as it had been for more than half a century, in which those who believed in deficit spending defended it, and they said, oh, this brings prosperity, this is necessary to do this. Now that argument, which was a fallacious argument, is gone, and the only debate between us now is how best to achieve the balanced budget. There is no longer anyone defending deficits.

French Elections

Q. You don't want to take sides in this Presidential election in this country, but whom would you support in France?

The President. I think I should remain neutral there, also, that that would be best for all of us. And I wouldn't want to seem to be trying to involve myself in what the course of the French people should be.

Q. You would have no personal preference? Because you know all our candidates, or most of them.

The President. Well, I think my philosophy there would have to be the same as it is here in our own election process: that until decisions are made as to who the nominees are going to be, I will remain neutral.

Q. Has President Mitterrand given you any tip in Brussels, a few days ago, as to what his own personal behavior would be?

The President. No, no, he hasn't.

Note: The interview began at 10:35 a.m. in the Map Room at the White House.

Interview With Alastair Burnet of ITN Television of the United Kingdom
March 10, 1988

Soviet-U.S. Relations

Q. Mr. President, do you trust Mr. Gorbachev?

The President. Well, let me say, I used a Russian proverb. I'm not a linguist, but I did learn this and have used it several times in his presence. If I'm pronouncing it correctly, it is *dovorey no provorey.* It means trust but verify. And I think that's the policy that has to be followed. I have cited Demosthenes, who a thousand years or two back in the Athenian marketplace said: "What sane man would let another man's words rather than his deeds tell him who is at peace and who is at war with him?"

Q. Then are you not in a great hurry to get a strategic arms agreement with him that you can sign in Moscow?

The President. Well, this is one of the problems. It's a pretty complex negotiation that is going on. Apparently, both sides would like to get this 50-percent reduction in weapons, but it's a little more complex than the INF treaty that we did agree to because of the verification features and all. So, I am acting on a supposition that he also wants the treaty. And it's a case of not setting a deadline whereby you have to hurry and maybe accept something less than is possible simply to meet a deadline. So, we've set no date, but we're working just as hard as we can to arrive at an agreement.

Q. Will you go to Moscow if you can't get an agreement in advance?

The President. Oh, yes, because I think there are other things. Our negotiations at the summit meetings and our discussions have been on a number of things—not only the arms control but the regional problems, Afghanistan, Nicaragua, things of that kind, and also human rights. We believe that that is of great importance if the relations between our countries is to improve, that there must be some solution to these things that we think are such violations of human rights. And we've made progress in all of our meetings on all of these subjects. And so, I'm looking forward to the summit. It will be nice if we have reached a point at which, as we did here, we could sign that treaty. But if not, I think we would continue to discuss it, make progress, and eventually come to a signing.

Q. Why do you suppose Mr. Gorbachev would want to make progress with you rather than wait, say, for your successor?

The President. Well, you know, there might be some merit in the fact that we now know each other. We've laid a groundwork of relationship. And someone coming in new—and he remembers his own experience coming in—there would be probably a wait while someone else established themselves in the position and you discovered what their ideas were and so forth. So, I think that probably he would like to get some things wound up because of all the groundwork that's been laid.

Nuclear Weapons in Europe

Q. Do you agree with Mrs. Thatcher that it would be foolish for anyone to expect a nuclear-free Europe for many, many years?

The President. I do agree. And I think that probably what she is saying is something that I've also said, but that hasn't been recognized as much. And that is that this idea that came into being of a nuclear-free Europe at the same time that we're all aware that in conventional weapons the Soviet Union is far in advance of NATO—and it is only the presence of some of the nuclear, particularly tactical weapons, that have redressed that imbalance. So that before you could ever look to a nuclear-free Europe or world you would have to have an establishment of parity between the forces in conventional weapons.

On the other hand, I believe that as we continue with our Strategic Defense Initiative, the seeking of a defensive weapon—there never has been an offensive weapon yet in the world that has not led to a defense, even the sword and the shield. And I believe that it is possible to come up with a defensive system that can render the nuclear weapons obsolete. Because I have said—as a matter of fact, to your Parliament, when they graciously allowed me to address them—I have said a nuclear war cannot be won and must never be fought. There can't be a victor in a nuclear war. Where do we live after we have poisoned the Earth?

Q. Are you reinforcing America's nuclear capacity in Britain?

The President. I try to refrain from speaking in such details, as matters that are strategy, that I don't think should be discussed. So, I can't go beyond that. I don't want to talk about systems that—that, I think, is information that should be held.

Q. But many people do think that the INF treaty, for example, made it necessary for you to reinforce American nuclear capability.

The President. Well, the truth is that there are still a great many nuclear weapons in NATO, in the tactical and battlefield-type weapons. We still have our Trident submarines and so forth and are going forward with those programs. And I think the enemy's well aware of that. So, I don't think that first fear that was expressed by some people that INF was in some way lowering our defensive strength.

Let me point out that it was the Soviet Union that came along with a nuclear weapon that was targeted on all the leading targets and cities and so forth of Europe. NATO had nothing to match it. NATO appealed to us—this was before I was in office here—for weapon systems to provide a defense—or not a defense, a deterrent, I should say. And when I came in office, I inherited this situation.

Well, first we asked the Soviet Union to withdraw those weapons. And they refused. And then we went forward with the deployment of our own match to their weapons. And if you'll remember, there was great objection on the part of many people to that. At the same time, however, that we went forward, and the Soviets were quite upset and left the table. I proposed to the Soviets that we would join them in a zero-zero option. And again, there was some scorn about that—as if I had done something that could not possibly happen. And the Soviets left the bargaining table. But they returned.

Soviet-U.S. Relations

Q. Would that be the special advice that you would give to your successor——

The President. Yes.

Q. ——after 7 years in the White House?

The President. Yes. The special advice—and was proven very simply with this particular thing we're talking about—and that is: Deal from strength. Twice the Soviet Union walked away and said they wouldn't discuss things with us. We persisted in implementing and putting the weapons in, deploying them, and they came back. And now we have a treaty. That zero-zero has eliminated an entire weapon system for both sides. So, peace through strength is very common sense.

Presidential Election

Q. And who is your successor going to be?

The President. That, I can't say. In this position, in our country, I'm the titular head of the party, and with all of the primaries going on—until a nominee is selected, I must remain neutral.

Note: The interview began at 10:47 a.m. in the Map Room at the White House.

Interview With Dieter Kronzucker of ZDF Television of the Federal Republic of Germany
March 10, 1988

Berlin Wall

Q. Mr. President when you have been last year in Germany, you said that the wall should be torn down. Is this a topic you might take up with Mr. Gorbachev again when you go to Moscow?

The President. That could very well enter the conversation. I've made no secret about my feeling about that, and, yes, I'd be very happy to speak to him about it.

East-West Relations

Q. Do you think German reunification could be taking place somewhere along the line in the East-West dialog?

The President. Well, couldn't that grow from such things as I also suggested? In addition to tearing down the wall, and without going so far as to offer an opinion about reunification, I said that couldn't Berlin then become a city in which maybe some things—for example, Olympics games, meetings, international meetings and so forth—could take place, and also a change in the whole aerial position, aircraft position so that Berlin could once again become a hub for international air traffic. And then maybe, from all of those things, reunification could grow.

Q. Is the summit in Moscow just a continuation process of the East-West dialog, or could there come out some concrete results?

The President. Well, we have achieved some results with them, because mainly we have talked about regionalism, things like Afghanistan and Nicaragua and so forth. We've talked about human rights and the violation there and what an effect that has on our trying to improve relations with each other. And we have made gains. There has been a softening in their position on human rights, and they have freed political prisoners and so forth. We think they have a long way to go to meet our standard of human rights. And also, we see now his determination to leave Afghanistan. So, no, we talk about all those differences that are between us as well as the arms matters. And obviously we've made progress now in that with the treaty that has already been signed and the one that is being negotiated now.

Administration Goals

Q. Mr. President, you have another 9 months—your Presidency. What is the problem number one in U.S.A. you would like to tackle during these remaining 9 months?

The President. Well, there are a number of things in which we've made progress that I would like to see us speed up the progress. Economically, for example, we're on the path now toward returning to the balanced budget idea. For almost 60 years, the opposition party has been, in the main, in control and has practiced a policy of budget deficits. We at least now—the argument about whether you should or should not deficit spend has changed to where, for these last 7 years, it is only a case of, well, how fast do you restore the balance, and how do you—what methods do you use to restore a balanced budget? So, we've made a gain there. I would like to see us act faster with that—some modernization of our budgeting process that I think is very lacking right now.

Then, we have one spending area in which there is controversy. And that is when I took office, on any given day, half of our military aircraft couldn't fly for lack of spare parts. Half of our naval vessels couldn't leave port for the same reason or for lack of crew. And I said that, even with my intent to try and eliminate the deficit, if it was a choice between eliminating the deficit or rebuilding and refurbishing our national security I would have to choose the national security. And we did. We made great progress. Only in this last year or so, that now that—again, the opposition party has a majority in both houses of our legislature. They have forced reductions in defense spending on us that I think are very detrimental and are going to remove some of the advantage that we have gained, and I would hope that we could change and continue to restore and reach our defense targets. I think that peace comes through strength.

There are some other things of that kind, some changes—we as you know, a unique thing about our country, we are a federation of sovereign States. And a great deal of authority has been left in the hands of local government and the State governments. Clear back when Franklin Delano Roosevelt ran for election, his promise was to restore the authority and autonomy to those local levels of government that had been unjustly seized, as he put it, by the Federal Government. Well, things didn't get better over the years, but we have embarked on a program of restoring that Federal balance, restoring the sovereignty of the States. And we've made progress in it, just as we've made great progress in improving the business management of government. We estimate that in these few years, we have reduced the amount of paperwork imposed on our citizens, on our businesses, and on our local levels of government by 600 million man-hours of work a year. And I would like to see this continue. There are some social reforms I would like to see also.

Views on the Presidency

Q. And do you still enjoy to be President—looking forward to?

The President. Well, maybe people are surprised to hear this, but yes, I do enjoy it. I was out there as a citizen making speeches and arguing about things and campaigning for individuals for government posts and so forth, and then to—I never expected this—but to find myself in a position where I can actually deal with the problems is very exciting, indeed.

Q. If you look back at the last 7 years, that it's mainly the accomplishments you like to remember, or is there some failure you would say, I wouldn't repeat it again—remembering, for example, your visit in Bitburg, '85, in the war cemetery in Germany? Do you regret that?

The President. Not at all. Not at all. I thought that it was very worthwhile, and I came home with a message also for our own people: that I think the courage of your country in maintaining those evidences of the horror of the Holocaust and bringing your own young people in to see them so that this can never happen again—I think is something that you have every reason to be proud of.

The First Lady

Q. Mr. President, a last question. A President of the United States, especially in such a large country, and considering the complicated governing system, is very heavily reliant on his advisers.

The President. Yes.

Q. Is it that your wife is your main adviser?

The President. [*Laughter*] No, and she's very embarrassed about the press stories that for some reason continue to say that. No, she has been a good and faithful wife, and I share secrets with her and my problems and all of that. But, no, I'm surrounded by people that I have appointed to the Cabinet positions and all. And I have made it very plain from the first that I want to hear from them their views on these problems. Even if they differ with what my own might be, I want to hear that from them. And one thing I do not want to hear. I do not want to hear the political ramifications on any problem, whether it is good politically to do something. All I want from them is their opinion as to whether is it good or bad for the people of this country. And then I will make the decision, having heard them out.

Note: The interview began at 10:59 a.m. in the Map Room at the White House.

Message to the Congress on Revisions to the 1988 Fiscal Year Appropriations
March 10, 1988

To the Congress of the United States:

I ask the Congress to consider the rescission or repeal of the wasteful, unnecessary, or low priority spending projects that were included in the full-year fiscal 1988 Continuing Resolution (P.L. 100–202). These are the projects that, if I were able to exercise line item veto authority, I would delete. They consist of Congressional directives and amendments concerning activities which are unnecessary and for which my administration has not requested funds. It is my hope that the funds appropriated for these projects will not be spent as directed and can instead be spent on worthwhile projects or retained by the Treasury to lower the deficit. Accordingly, I am informally asking that the Congress review these projects, appropriations, and other provisions line by line and either rescind or repeal them as soon as possible. I reserve the option of transmitting at a later date either formal rescission proposals or language that would make the funds available for more worthwhile purposes, for any or all of these items.

Since I assumed this office, the Congress has appropriated billions of dollars for questionable purposes, much of it in the context of massive spending bills passed in great haste that not even Congress had an adequate chance to evaluate. Because current law so severely restricts my ability to impound or not spend appropriated funds, I again appeal to the Congress to provide the Chief Executive with permanent line item veto authority. In the meantime, I urge your prompt attention to this request for legislative action in order to avoid these unnecessary expenditures of taxpayer dollars.

The details of these projects are set forth in the attached letter from the Director of the Office of Management and Budget.

RONALD REAGAN

The White House,
March 10, 1988.

Statement Requesting Revisions to the 1988 Fiscal Year Budget Appropriations
March 10, 1988

In my State of the Union Address, I said I would send back to Congress examples of spending items that are wasteful, unnecessary, and low priority, and that if I had a line-item veto I would have struck from the legislation. That list is being formally transmitted to the Congress today. I urge the Congress to review these items and rescind, repeal, or amend them as soon as possible.

The items I have chosen represent only the more excessive examples from the continuing resolution itself. I have not included fundamental policy differences, such as major program terminations, that I have with the Congress. Nor have I included the many earmarks that appear in the report language accompanying the appropriations. The report itself is never sent to me and, as the Supreme Court has said, has no force of law. In fact, I am directing all executive agencies to provide a full justification before they expend any funds to comply with these earmarks. And I am not including even more items tucked away inside the other piece of legislation I received in December, the reconciliation bill, that actually increase the deficit without benefit to the taxpayers.

I believe the American people can see by this exercise why I have consistently appealed for a line-item veto. We need to restore some discipline to our budget process. Does the Congress have the discipline to vote on these projects and take this next step?

As I have said, I have limited this initial list, and as a result—while it will have an immediate beneficial effect—it will not, by itself, solve our budget problems. I urge the Congress to take the necessary action on this limited list in order to avoid these unnecessary expenditures of taxpayers' dollars. It is another step on the road to a balanced budget, a demonstration in discipline. Perhaps, having taken this step, we can move even further.

Statement on Economic Sanctions Against Panama
March 11, 1988

The United States has had a long and mutually productive relationship with Panama. The people of the United States consider the people of Panama to be near neighbors and friends. The historic Panama Canal treaties exemplify the close cooperation that has traditionally characterized the friendship between the two countries, which created one of the great engineering works of the human race.

Out of concern for our friendship, we have been saddened and increasingly worried in recent years as Panama's political crisis deepened. Our policy with respect to the situation in Panama is clear: We strongly favor a rapid restoration of democracy and the resumption by the Panamanian Defense Forces of a role consistent with constitutional democracy. In the present circumstances, I believe that General Noriega would best serve his country by complying with the instruction of President Delvalle to relinquish his post. In so doing, General Noriega would contribute very substantially to reducing political tensions and set the stage for a prompt transition to democracy in Panama. Until such a time as democratic government is restored in Panama, the United States cannot proceed on a business-as-usual basis.

Today, therefore, I have taken a number of steps against the illegitimate Noriega regime that will contribute significantly to the goal of a democratic, stable, and prosperous Panama. I have directed that actions be taken to suspend trade preferences available to Panama under the Generalized System of Preferences (GSP) and the Caribbean Basin Initiative.

Further, in keeping with the spirit of our war against drugs, I have ordered that Panama be subject to intensified scrutiny by our Immigration and Customs Services in order to apprehend drug traffickers and money launderers. Moreover, because we recognize President Delvalle as the lawful head of government in Panama, I have directed that all departments and agencies inventory all sources of funds due or payable to the Republic of Panama from the U.S. Government, for purposes of determining those that should be placed in escrow for the Delvalle government on behalf of the Panamanian people.

In that light, I have directed that certain payments due to Panama from the Panama Canal Commission be placed in escrow immediately. This step is in complete compliance with our obligations under the terms of the Panama Canal treaties. I am prepared to take additional steps, if necessary, to deny the transfer of funds to the Noriega regime from other sources in the United States.

We have welcomed the recent statements issued by President Delvalle, the political parties, and the Civilian Crusade of Panama calling for a government of national reconciliation. We support their goal of restoring democratic government and constitutional order. Once Panamanians achieve this goal, the United States is fully prepared to work with the Government of Panama to help quickly restore Panama's economic health. The United States has been, and remains, committed to fulfilling faithfully its obligations under the Panama Canal treaties. We are also prepared to resume our close working relationships with the Panamanian Defense Forces once civilian government and constitutional democracy are reestablished.

Remarks to Business Leaders at a White House Briefing on International Trade
March 11, 1988

Thank you all very much, and welcome to the White House complex. White House complex—that's what they call these buildings. That's because nothing in Washington is ever simple. [*Laughter*]

Well, we're here to talk about America's strength in international trade. And seeing each of you—manufacturers large and small, people who know about trade not just in theory but in practice, people who don't hide from a challenge but compete with the best of American ingenuity and energy—yes, knowing you and knowing America's working men and women, as well, I know why today American exports are the highest they've been in the entire history of the United States of America.

Now, to see the charges that some of our critics throw around, you'd never guess that we export so much as a paper clip. You've heard their charges: the deindustrialization of America, the decline of the middle class, the loss of American jobs. We keep knocking them down with facts. We hit them with the more than 15 million jobs created since our recovery began. We keep pounding away at the fact that these are better, higher paying jobs, as well as that after years on a falling roller coaster the real income of the average American has risen steadily now for 5 years. We throw at them a three-punch combination of surging manufacturing exports, the longest peacetime expansion on history, and the reality that more Americans are at work today than ever before. And after all this, you'd think they'd stay on the mat and wait for the bell, slip back into the locker room in shame. But, no, they just keep coming up with new charges and new demands for a return to old and discredited policies. You know, this Washington sparring match—in one form or another, it's been going on since the day I took office.

And it reminds me of a story back in my Hollywood days, happened to be a fight that took place outside a party that was going on at some Hollywood personality's home. And the fight was between the late John Huston, the director, and Errol Flynn, the actor. Now, if any of you remember the shape that Errol was in and John Huston and his belly, you can guess how the fight went. Two punches and John was flat on the ground. So, Errol splashed some water on him and helped him up, and John started hitting him again. Errol decked him again and threw water on him again, helped him up. And John took a swing again, dropped to the floor. Finally, Errol doused him with one last bucket of water and, when Huston came around, leaned over and whispered very kindly, "John, you have no chance. I was a professional fighter. Please don't be a fool." And you know, as Huston told it later, he said, "When Errol said that to me, I knew I had him." [*Laughter*]

Well, today we're here to knock down again some of those fellows that are taking the wild swings. And the wildest is that American manufacturing and American workers are losing out in international trade. As Al Smith used to say: "Let's look at the record." Over the past 15 months, the volume of exports has been growing four times as fast as the volume of imports. And much of this export surge is in manufacturing exports. Today industry after industry is finding itself in an export boom. As Business Week magazine reported recently: "Basic manufacturers, once considered a dying breed, are selling products many thought wouldn't even be made in the United States any longer—escalators to Taiwan, machine tools to West Germany, lumber to Japan, shoes to Italy."

The dollar has helped, of course, but what's happening here goes beyond the dollar. On one hand, since 1980 the United States manufacturing economy has increased its productivity more than three times as much as in the previous 7 years. The result is that, as one German manufacturing expert put it recently, the United States is, in his words, "the best country in the world in terms of manufacturing costs." The other reason for our manufacturing export boom is, in a single word, entrepreneurship—smaller businesses that are growing rapidly and seeking new markets. Since our recovery began, businesses with 100 or fewer people and businesses that are 5 years old or less have created most of the new jobs in America. They are also responsible for many of our exports, like one small furniture manufacturer from St. Louis who visited Europe late last year. It was kind of a busman's holiday. He started looking at European furniture. And he said, "I discovered that my products were a lot better and cheaper." Now he's selling tables and chairs to Scandinavia.

All of this adds up to one thing. As economics writer Warren Brookes reported recently: "One of the best kept secrets in economic circles these days is that the Reagan administration could end with a bang, not a whimper, as the Nation makes an apparently successful shift to an export-led economy." Well, I'm very grateful to Mr. Brookes for saying that. Those were his words, not mine. You'd think this would all be cause for rejoicing here in Washington—not among our critics. They've been predicting economic disaster for 5 years. They've waited; they've been patient. Now they're tired of waiting. Some of the provisions they've put in the trade bill now before the House-Senate conference would hurt American jobs, American competitiveness, and the entire American economy.

For example, when David Birch, MIT's expert on job creation, asked why the United States has so much more entrepreneurship and, therefore, so much more job creation than Europe, he found some straightforward answers. Among these were, as he's written: "Regulations are much more onerous in Europe than in the United States, eliminating much of the flexibility that is the bread and meat for entrepreneurs." And to point out the principal villain, he added: "Europeans face a host of rules governing their right to close down facilities, fire workers, and relocate operations . . ." So, what does our trade bill include? Well, America's first national rules restricting a company's right to close down facilities and relocate operations.

Another example, this week Honda began exporting its first cars from America to Japan. Foreign investment has helped create new American jobs and American exports. It has contributed to the rising productivity of American manufacturing that I mentioned earlier. So, what does the trade bill include? New disclosure requirements that would dampen and discourage foreign investment from coming into this country.

One final example, potentially the most serious: Today over 10 million American jobs depend on imports, exports, or both. We're continuing a pattern that began in our first days as a nation. In periods when our total international trade has expanded, the number of jobs has risen. When trade has fallen, so have jobs. Since the end of World War II, the expansion of international trade has been in the framework of the General Agreement on Tariffs and Trade, the GATT. Not 5 people in 100 can tell you what GATT is, but without it the world would long ago have fallen back into the cycle of protection and retaliation, every country for itself—a cycle that helped to bring on the worldwide Great Depression of the 1930's.

Mandatory retaliation provisions could require me and future Presidents to take actions in direct violation of the GATT. If enacted, they could weaken the international trading system and could require the President to start trade wars. It's a bad proposal under any circumstance, but it's particularly bad now that American exports are soaring and American manufacturers are exporting as never before and so are vulnerable to retaliation as never before. Yes, too many backers of the trade bill talk about making America more competitive but support provisions that would bench some of the best competitors on our team. They talk about saving jobs, but they want provisions that have the potential to destroy thousands if not millions of American jobs. They talk about learning from the Japanese, but why did they have to take their lesson from Kamikaze pilots? [*Laughter*]

I've mentioned three problems we have with the trade bill. There are many, many more—more than there's time to touch on here. But we've listed them in detail for the conference members and said how strongly we feel. My veto pen remains ready and available if the final work product of the conference remains antitrade, anticonsumer, antijobs, and antigrowth. But my hope, which I believe you share, is that I won't have to use that pen. The administration is working diligently with the Congress to avoid that, to get a trade bill that will complement our efforts to promote trade, exports, jobs, and productivity, not stymie them.

Now, you all know that the House-Senate conference on the trade bill is working away and plans to finish its job by Easter. While there's much left to do in this process, it got off to a good, constructive start earlier this month by throwing overboard many objectionable provisions. We just hope that the rest of the other 16 subconferences will follow the example of flagship subconference number one and that the flagship subconference will continue on this constructive course. As they continue their work, I would note that on Tuesday those who had predicted that protectionism would be embraced in the South were proven wrong. The American people know that putting up walls around our country is a prescription for ruin, not renewal.

What the world and the United States need now is more trade and more open trade. And that's why we've pushed for a new GATT round that includes the most ambitious multilateral trade negotiation agenda in history. That's why we've negotiated an historic trade agreement with Canada that will expand jobs, growth, and opportunity on both sides of the border.

As Congress considers the Omnibus Trade bill, it can either help or hinder a free and open trading system. Let me suggest that provisions on the trade bill stick to five rules. One, that they're GATT legal. Two, that they not provoke retaliation against our bombing export business—wait a minute—our booming export business—[*laughter*]—or U.S. firms abroad. Three, that they not restrict the flexibility of U.S. business to adjust to foreign competition. And four, that they not tie the hands of U.S. negotiators who are working to open markets abroad. And five, sort of summing it all up, a kind of golden rule, don't pass any trade law that we wouldn't want another nation to pass in just the same form, regulating Americans who do business there. The golden rule—it's not a bad way to do business, in the home or in the marketplace, around the world. I hope we can count on the support of each of you in the next few weeks. Now is not the time to turn out the lights on America's export boom.

Now, before I stop, I thought I'd tell you one final story. In hearing all the incredible doomsday talk from the critics about our economy and their equally incredible talk about how they're going to fix things, I couldn't help remembering an old Hollywood story about Sam Goldwyn and his studio's advertising office. The advertising director took a poster to Sam promoting "We Live Again," which starred Anna Sten. The poster read, "The directorial genius of Mamoulian, the beauty of Sten, and the producing genius of Goldwyn combined to make the world's greatest entertainment." Goldwyn looked it over solemnly and said, "That's the kind of ad I like." He said, "Facts, no exaggeration." [*Laughter*] And now I can use that word I used before. By the way, the movie bombed. [*Laughter*]

Well, that's all I have to say except to thank you all for being here and for what you're doing, and God bless all of you.

Note: The President spoke at 1:18 p.m. in Room 450 of the Old Executive Office Building.

Radio Address to the Nation on International Trade
March 12, 1988

My fellow Americans:

I'd like to talk to you today about our nation's trade policy. I can't think of a recent economic issue that has generated more heat and less light, yet has more importance to our long-term national interest, than trade.

Throughout the 7 years I've been in office, professional doomsayers have latched onto one issue after another as evidence of an American decline. They can't seem to acknowledge the obvious good news that surrounds us—the low inflation, the over 15 million new jobs since November 1982, and the longest peacetime economic expansion of the century. Trade is only the most recent subject of lamentation by our critics. For them, our trade deficit is an excuse for getting the Government more involved in private business decisions. They say that Americans can't compete with foreign workers, so we should slow imports by erecting protectionist trade barriers. As usual, the doom merchants are wrong. The United States economy remains the most dynamic and exciting one on the globe. Our entrepreneurs, our can-do spirit, and our economic freedom are the envy of the world. The pessimism used to justify protectionism is totally unfounded.

Let's clear up a few myths. First, the trade situation is improving far more quickly than people realize. Economists may disagree on the impact of the trade imbalance, but there is no disagreement that there has been a remarkable turnaround in the real trade deficit. Since the third quarter of 1986, the merchandise trade deficit in real terms has declined 18 percent. And over the past 15 months, the volume of exports has grown over 4 times as fast as the volume of imports. Clearly, we are in an export boom. American industries, particularly manufacturers, are setting records. Unfortunately, there's a threat to all this good news. I'm talking about the trade bill pending in Congress. Adopting protectionist measures and starting trade wars now would be like closing the barn door just as the horse is trying to get back in. The best way to keep our exports growing is to keep international trade expanding. And that brings me to another myth: that Congress can pass a law that will reduce the trade deficit without destroying our prosperity. Legislation can reduce a trade deficit only if it reduces economic activity. If people are not working, they're not trading. We had a trade surplus and 25-percent unemployment in the Great Depression.

A protectionist trade bill is a serious threat to our export boom. It's a serious threat to the millions of American jobs that depend upon international trade. It is filled with scores of provisions that are protectionist and defeatist. My veto pen is ready if the final bill remains antitrade, anticonsumer, antijobs, and antigrowth. However, the administration is willing to work diligently with Congress to produce a bill that would increase our international competitiveness and complement our efforts to promote trade, exports, jobs, and productivity, not stymie them.

All those working on the bill should take a deep breath, take another look at the trade outlook, and work together in a constructive spirit. It is still possible to write a bill that I can sign. Indeed, I'm encouraged by reports on the status of the trade bill negotiations. The conference committee working on the final draft of the bill has already eliminated a number of troublesome provisions, including illegal quotas, budget-busting giveaways, and protectionist measures. Many objectionable provisions remain, including proposed procedural changes in the law, but I'm hopeful that in the next phase these will be jettisoned. Only wholesale elimination of many of the existing items will produce a bill I can sign.

Regardless of whether I sign trade legislation this year, we will continue our free and fair approach to trade policy. We will challenge unfair trade practices of other countries in order to achieve a level playing field for American industries. We will negotiate to knock down trade barriers on a bilateral or multilateral basis. In that regard, we will seek early enactment of the U.S.-Canada free trade agreement and push for concrete progress in the upcoming Uruguay round of trade negotiations. Finally, we will continue to coordinate economic policies with our major trading partners, thereby helping to maintain a favorable international climate for trade expansion.

America's open market is its great strength, not its weakness. International trade has helped bring unparalleled prosperity to the American people. It would be a tragic mistake to surrender to doubt and defeatism just when our prospects are looking so bright. I have confidence in America, and I'm sure you do too.

Until next week, thanks for listening, and God bless you.

Note: The President spoke at 12:06 p.m. from Camp David, MD.

Interview With Arrigo Levi of Canale 5 Television of Italy
March 10, 1988

Administration Goals

Q. Mr. President, you have less than 1 year's work left as a President. And do you still expect to achieve something important in the final 10—11 months left?

The President. Well, there are some things pending that I think are of importance and that I believe we can achieve, and I'm going to keep working right down to the last minute.

Q. Which things, for instance, a strategic arms agreement?

The President. Yes, oh, yes. We're going to pursue that and hope that well before my time is up we will have that resolved. But there are other things here in our own domestic problems. I think that our budgeting process that has led to the deficit spending over the last almost 60 years must be corrected. And I am going to be fighting for legislation to achieve that. And for my successor—that he could have some things I haven't had, such as what's called a line-item veto—the power to pick things out of a legislation and veto them. And we still have further to go in the building up of our national security. And that is important to me, as is our relationship with our allies in Europe and NATO.

Soviet-U.S. Relations

Q. You have made that important agreement, and there may be others to come with the Soviet Union. Now, people remember that you had once called the Soviet Union the evil empire. And they also wonder has the Soviet Union changed, or have your views changed? Or both?

The President. My views haven't changed. But you must remember that the Soviet leaders, when I first came into office, kept dying. And finally there was little chance to work with any of them on some of the things that I thought should be straightened out. Now there is a new leader, and he does seem to want to make some changes in their system. I have read his book "Perestroika," and I know of his theories on *glasnost.* And so, we have been able to reach agreement on some of the things that we've discussed in our summit meetings. I always take up the matter of human rights, and there has been an improvement in that. Regional conflicts—and we see them now—this leader wanting to get out of Afghanistan. So, I think progress can be made, but as I have frequently said to him—I'm not a linguist, but I have learned a Russian proverb that I use on him every once in awhile: *Dovorey no provorey*—trust but verify.

Q. Does he approve of your proverb? He once complained that you tell him that too often.

The President. I know. I know. He told me that.

Q. But you do like each other? It's an important question for people of the whole world.

The President. I have found that, yes, that we can discuss things and in an affable manner, and he is totally unlike the other leaders before him that I had dealt with.

Strategic Defense Initiative

Q. Mr. President, you sometimes have been described as the first passivist of the White House, meaning that your aim is to make nuclear weapons obsolete through SDI. Is that a foregone and lost hope?

The President. No, not at all. As a matter of fact, we're still going forward, and we've made progress. And there have been breakthroughs. I believe that the Strategic Defense Initiative that we're working on can be such an effective defense, that it makes so much more sense than thinking that a deterrent in which we're trying to keep the peace by threatening to blow each other up, that if we can come up with a defensive weapon—and I have expressed to General Secretary Gorbachev my belief that we'd be willing to share it—that if we could have a defense that did render those weapons obsolete—because I have stated many times that I do not believe that a nuclear war can be won nor should it be fought. Where would a victor live after we'd poisoned the Earth with an exchange of these multiple weapons that we have?

Arms Control

Q. Do you feel that you have made some progress in convincing Gorbachev, and the Russians in general, of the importance of defensive systems?

The President. Well, we have the one treaty signed already now—the intermediate-range weapons. That was targeted on every principal city in Europe, and now it no longer exists. And we're now trying to negotiate a treaty that would reduce by half the strategic ballistic missiles. But to those people who talk denuclearization and think that somehow I am suggesting something that might be dangerous to Europe—not at all. I recognize that the tactical nuclear weapons that we have and the airborne weapons and so forth are necessary to balance the great superiority that the Soviet Union has achieved in conventional weapons. And until those weapons can be reduced and we achieve a defensive parity there, until then, you cannot go on with further denuclearization.

President's Legacy

Q. What would you like future historians to remember as your main achievement, and what would you like them to forget as your main failure?

The President. Oh, my.

Q. Let's take one at a time. Maybe if we had time——

The President. I don't know. That's so hard to pick out.

Q. The achievement or the failure?

The President. On the economic side, I think we've made great progress in changing a philosophy that was here in our land in which the political debate was between how much more deficit spending the Government should do. Now that whole argument has been changed, and it's down to, well, what is the best way to eliminate or reduce the deficit spending. And the argument is how to reduce the spending, not between one side that wants to spend more as against the other. I'm proud of that, and I hope that before I leave we can have some improvements in our budgeting process that will be adopted by our government. I am proud of that. I'm also proud of the fact that when I came into office our national defense was quite a shambles. On any given day, half our military aircraft couldn't fly for lack of spare parts. Today we have achieved a great improvement in our military. And I think the fact that we have signed this INF treaty with the Soviet Union is evidence of the fact that peace comes through strength.

Q. We didn't say anything about what failure was, but the girl says you have no time to remind us of your failures. Maybe there were none, that's too much.

The President. No, I am sure there were things I would have—I think there were some things that, whether they were failures or whether they were just terrible disasters—one, namely, the terrorist murder of some 240 of our young marines is a tragedy I will never forget. And I will never forget the families that I met with of those young men.

Q. Do you feel good looking back at your 8 years at the White House and beyond that, your career as an actor, and union organizer? How does that make you feel?

The President. Well, I think the Lord has blessed me very much, and I am truly grateful to Him. I hope I can be deserving of the good things that He's bestowed on me.

Note: The interview began at 11:10 a.m. in the Map Room at the White House and was released by the Office of the Press Secretary on March 14.

Letter to the Speaker of the House of Representatives and the President of the Senate Transmitting the Report on Activities of United Nations Member Countries
March 14, 1988

Dear Mr. Speaker: (Dear Mr. President:)

Pursuant to Title V, Section 528 of the Foreign Assistance and Related Programs Appropriations Act, 1987, as contained in Public Law 99–500, I am transmitting herewith the report on the activities of countries within the United Nations and its specialized agencies.

This report assesses the degree of support of United States foreign policy in the United Nations context by the governments of countries that are members of the United Nations.

In addition, this report includes the report required of the Secretary of State under Section 117 of Public Law 98–164 on the performance of U.N. member countries in international organizations.

Sincerely,

RONALD REAGAN

Note: Identical letters were sent to Jim Wright, Speaker of the House of Representatives, and George Bush, President of the Senate.

Appointment of Roman Popadiuk as Special Assistant to the President and Deputy Press Secretary for Foreign Affairs
March 14, 1988

The President today announced the appointment of Roman Popadiuk to be Special Assistant to the President and Deputy Press Secretary for Foreign Affairs. He will succeed J. Daniel Howard. Mr. Popadiuk has been an Assistant Press Secretary for Foreign Affairs at the White House since July 1986.

Mr. Popadiuk has been a career Foreign Service officer since 1981. He served in Mexico City from 1982 to 1984, where he did consular and political work and was special assistant to the Ambassador. From 1984 to 1986, he had a tour with the Department of State and the National Security Council. Prior to joining the Foreign Service he was an adjunct lecturer in political science at Brooklyn College in New York City.

Mr. Popadiuk was born on May 30, 1950. He received a B.A. from Hunter College in 1973 and a Ph.D. from the City University of New York in 1981. He is married to the former Judith Ann Fedkiw. They have four children and reside in Bethesda, MD.

Message to the Congress Transmitting the Annual Report on International Activities in Science and Technology
March 14, 1988

To the Congress of the United States:

In accordance with Title V of the Foreign Relations Authorizations Act for Fiscal Year 1979 (Public Law 95–426), I am transmitting the Administration's annual report on international activities in science and technology (S&T) for Fiscal Year 1987. The report reflects a U.S. commitment to international scientific and technological cooperation of impressive range and depth.

New breakthroughs in 1987 demonstrated the increasing importance of international cooperation in science and technology. The discovery of superconductivity at high temperatures has the potential to revolutionize the way we work and live; international agreement on a protocol concerning protection of the ozone layer was a major accomplishment which will benefit future generations.

Official, government-to-government science and technology cooperation, such as our highly successful cooperative programs with India and China, supports our foreign policy objectives, as well as the mission objectives of the domestic agencies involved. Through the space sciences and environmental agreements we engaged in practical cooperation with the Soviet Union, while the signing of an S&T agreement during the Vice President's September 1987 visit to Warsaw provided a visible signal of our desire to improve relations with Poland. Such international cooperation should provide positive science and technology benefits to involved domestic U.S. agencies commensurate with their cost.

United States preeminence in science and technology has been a major force in our leadership of the free world since World War II. Today we are putting new emphasis on assuring continued U.S. strength in science and technology in the years ahead. Employing science and technology to improve American industry's competitiveness is a major objective of this Administration. On April 10, 1987, I issued an Executive order to facilitate industry access to federally funded research and development and to assure more effective access by American researchers to developments in science and technology abroad. In negotiating new S&T agreements, we are seeking equitable access by American researchers to foreign research facilities, balance in the contributions and benefits for countries participating in the agreements, and assurance of protection for intellectual property rights.

We are working with our economic partners and allies to ensure that all industrialized countries make equitable contributions to the world scientific enterprise. We are negotiating with Japan to restructure our Head of State-level S&T agreement to reflect new realities, including Japan's prowess in science and technology.

In numerous developing countries, science and technology are instrumental in furthering U.S. foreign policy objectives. Agency for International Development-funded programs continue to produce major advances in the health sciences and increased global stability through improved agricultural output, while facilitating the entry of American vendors into overseas markets.

To implement the U.S.-Brazil Presidential S&T initiative announced in September 1986, a distinguished binational panel of scientific experts met twice during 1987 and identified priority areas of research for cooperative projects. The recommendations of that eminent panel will be considered by the U.S.-Brazil Joint Commission for an expanded program of cooperation, as envisioned in the 1986 initiative.

Impressive gains were made in Fiscal Year 1987 in utilizing our S&T relations to enhance America's defensive capabilities through increased foreign participation in the Strategic Defense Initiative and through other cooperative S&T activities, such as those carried out under NATO auspices. At the same time we have negotiated several agreements that significantly strengthen free-world efforts to control illicit transfer of advanced technology to potential adversaries.

Participation in international science and technology activities is vital to U.S. national security in the broadest sense. Science and technology can be a powerful force to enrich cooperative relations with friends and adversaries, as well as to strengthen our Nation's competitive posture in the economic arena. International cooperation can accelerate the rate of scientific discovery and the development of new technologies to meet the needs and challenges of the future. In many cases, the benefits of such cooperation accrue first to the partners in the joint effort, and such returns make it feasible to sustain a long-term commitment to cooperation. Ultimately, however, all the world's people are beneficiaries. I remain committed to the belief that international cooperation in S&T is vital to the future prosperity and security of our Nation and of the earth.

RONALD REAGAN

The White House,
March 14, 1988.

Remarks to the Institute for Foreign Policy Analysis at a Conference on the Strategic Defense Initiative
March 14, 1988

Well, Dr. Pfaltzgraff, thank you, and thank you all very much. Let me say it's a great honor to be addressing so many distinguished scientists, business leaders, and academics, so many who live the life of the mind and use their talents for the benefit of mankind.

I want to thank the Institute for Foreign Policy Analysis, a staunch ally when it comes to strategic defenses, for bringing this first-class group together on SDI's fifth anniversary. And it's good to see so many other friends here as well: Dr. Teller, who is proof that life begins at 80—[*laughter*]—and 3 of SDI's best friends in the Congress, Senators Wallop and Quayle, Congressman Chappell; and the frontline offense of our strategic defense team, Ambassador Rowny, General Abrahamson, and Bill Graham. And we're all hoping this even will be chronicled in his indubitable fashion by Tom Clancy. [*Laughter*]

It hardly seems like 5 years since we first embarked together on this noble enterprise to find an alternative to nuclear terror. When I addressed the American people on that March 1983 day, I said it was time to turn the great technological might of our nation not to inventing ever more deadly weapons of destruction but instead to creating new instruments of peace—defensive technologies that harm no one. I said it would take years, probably decades, of effort. There would be setbacks and failures as well as successes. But we could not ignore this great challenge: to develop the means of rendering ballistic missiles impotent and obsolete. If anything, we overestimated the technological challenge back then. The technologies of our Strategic Defense Initiative have progressed more rapidly than many of us ever dreamed possible. The creative genius and ingenuity of U.S. and allied scientists and engineers and the steadfast support of so many in this room have helped make that rapid progress possible.

But if we've learned anything in 5 years, it's that it's sometimes easier to bring into being new technologies than it is to bring about new thinking on some subjects. Breakthroughs in physics are sometimes easier than breakthroughs in psyches. Perhaps the most astounding reaction to the announcement of our Strategic Defense Initiative was the sudden conversion of many on a certain side of the political spectrum to the strategy of mutual assured destruction, whose very appropriate acronym is MAD. I remember that only a few months before the announcement of SDI I received a letter from 41 academic leaders, presidents, and board chairmen of many of our most distinguished colleges and universities. And in that letter they called upon me to, and I quote, "to make a major investment in planning, negotiating, and cooperating to establish civilized, effective, and morally acceptable alternatives to nuclear war." We could no longer rely on the notion, they said, that, "no nation with nuclear weapons will pull the trigger." Well, I couldn't agree more. In fact, I've been waiting for another letter from that same group supporting SDI. [*Laughter*] I guess the mails are just a bit slow. [*Laughter*] I do promise to write back right away.

The philosopher John Stuart Mill said, I think aptly, that "no great improvements in the lot of mankind are possible until a great change takes place in the fundamental constitution of their modes of thought." Sometimes, however, it's not so much mankind in general as it is the experts who have trouble changing the fundamental constitution of their modes of thought. The fact is, it would probably stop any inventor dead in his tracks if he listened for too long to the advice of experts in his field.

Throughout history, it seems, they have agreed on one basic principle: Progress must stop at the limits of their expertise. [*Laughter*] I'm fond of quoting Charles Duell, the Commissioner of the United States Office of Patents, who advised President McKinley in 1899 to abolish the Patent Office because, he said, "Everything that can be invented has been invented." [*Laughter*] Of course, Presidents aren't immune from such blunders either. There's the story of Rutherford B. Hayes, who said after witnessing a scientific demonstration, "That's an amazing invention, but who would ever want to use one of them?" He was talking about the telephone.

Well, we've had our share of naysayers when it comes to SDI as well. But some of the difficulties they said were insurmountable have already been surmounted much more rapidly and effectively than anticipated. For example, our Delta 180 and, most recently, 181 tests, demonstrating among other things our ability to track fast-moving targets in space and distinguish between dummy warheads from the real thing, showed a technical ability that some scientists, concerned and otherwise, had said could not be achieved so quickly. But, you know, I don't give up hope for our opponents. It has been estimated that the sum total of human knowledge doubles every 8 years. Maybe they just need a little bit more time.

Now, for the impressive technological feats that we've recently seen, immense credit goes to the brilliant and hard-working scientists and engineers who made them possible. And I want them to know they are not working late into the night to construct a bargaining chip. They are building a better future, free from the nuclear terror, and generations to come will thank them. We'll continue to research SDI, to develop and test it, and as it becomes ready, we will deploy it.

There's one serious problem that the SDI program has had a great deal of difficulty with, however. It would probably be listed in the physics textbooks under the heading, "Inertial Resistance of Large Bodies"—[*laughter*]—in this case, some in the United States Congress. In every one of the last 4 years, Congress has cut back on our requests for SDI funding. And those cuts have already set the program back 1 to 2 years. In what can only be described as a self-fulfilling prophecy, they have voted down funding because they say SDI won't work.

Well, it won't if we don't develop it and test it. Congress should realize that it's no longer a question of whether there will be an SDI program or not. The only question will be whether the Soviets are the only ones who have strategic defenses, while the United States remains entirely defenseless. It seems to me that it was a watershed event when General Secretary Gorbachev, after years of concerted Soviet efforts to kill our SDI program and deny their own efforts in this area, stated publicly on TV to Tom Brokaw [NBC News] and the American people that when it comes to SDI "the Soviet Union is doing all that the United States is doing."

Well, everything, one might add, and more. The Soviet defense effort, which some call Red Shield, is now over 15 years old, and they have spent over $200 billion on it. That's 15 times the amount that we have spent on SDI. The Soviets already have the world's only deployed ABM defenses. Congress, in effect, killed our ASAT program. The Soviets already have an operational antisatellite system. While the United States Congress cuts back on our SDI, 10,000 top Soviet scientists and engineers work on their military laser program, alone.

Even now that the Soviets have acknowledged their own SDI-like program, some in Congress would bind us to an artificially restrictive interpretation of the ABM treaty that would effectively block development of our SDI program and perpetuate the Soviets' advantages in advanced strategic defenses. This effort makes even less sense when the Soviets aren't even abiding by the ABM treaty, while we are. Virtually all experts, even some of our biggest critics, agree that the Soviet construction of the large, phased-array radar at Krasnoyarsk is an out-and-out violation of the ABM treaty.

A few months ago, I raised a serious specter. I pointed out that it is not only in the development of strategic defenses that the United States could be left behind. A recent report released by the Department of Defense called "The Soviet Space Challenge" warns that the Soviet space program points in one disturbing direction, and I quote: "the methodical pursuit of a war-fighting capability in space." Soviet launch capacity far outstrips our own. We should be concerned that, together with the longstanding program and the construction of the Krasnoyarsk radar as part of an updated early warning system, the Soviets may be preparing a nationwide ABM defense of their territory. In other words, they may be preparing to break out of the ABM treaty. In that eventuality, without SDI, we would be dangerously unprepared.

There has been a tendency by some in Congress to discuss SDI as if its funding could be determined purely by domestic considerations, unconnected to what the Soviets are doing. Well, that is, to put it plainly, irresponsible in the extreme. The fact is that many Americans are unaware that at this moment the United States has absolutely zero defenses against a ballistic missile attack. If even one missile were to be accidentally fired at the United States, the President would have no way of preventing the wholesale destruction of American lives. All he could do is retaliate—wipe out millions of lives on the other side. This is the position we find ourselves in; to perpetuate it forever is simply morally untenable. Vengeance is not the American way. It certainly cannot form any plausible longstanding basis for Western strategy if a better form of deterrence can be established. Flexible response has worked. And we, of course, remain committed to our present strategy, but we remain equally committed to our search for a safer way to deter aggression.

It can be said that the old discredited policy of MAD is like two adversaries holding loaded guns to each other's head. It may work for awhile, but you sure better hope you don't make a slip. People who put their trust in MAD must trust it to work 100 percent—forever, no slip-ups, no madmen, no unmanageable crises, no mistakes—forever.

For those who are not reassured by such a prospect, and I count myself among their number, we must ask: Isn't it time we invented a cure for madness? Isn't it time to begin curing the world of this nuclear threat? If we have the medicine, can we in good conscience hold out on the patients? I believe that, given the gravity of the nuclear threat to humanity, any unnecessary delay in the development and deployment of SDI is unconscionable. And that's why we'll move forward, when ready, with phased deployments of SDI.

As of last August, the Department of Defense has begun focusing on six specific defensive technologies, and they are now moving ahead with them to the demonstration and validation phase. The development and deployment of an initial phase, when it is ready, will be undertaken in such a way that it provides a solid foundation for a continued evolution toward a fully comprehensive defense system, which is SDI's ultimate goal. Among the objectives of this first phase will be to strengthen deterrence by denying the Soviet Union confidence in their ability to achieve any objectives through the use of ballistic missiles. It will also protect the population of the United

States and its allies against an accidental launch of ballistic missiles. Every extra minute that we leave the population of the West defenseless against ballistic missiles is one minute too long.

Equally important, SDI will continue to prove an irresistible force behind offensive arms reductions. Our SDI program, in fact, already has helped to make this world safer because, along with NATO's INF deployments, it was one of the major factors that led to the treaty signed by General Secretary Gorbachev and myself that will for the first time reduce the nuclear arsenals threatening mankind. It was an historic reversal of the trend of more and more nuclear weapons, and SDI helped make it happen.

At the same time, we must work to strengthen our conventional deterrence. SDI will likely prove instrumental here, too, by providing high-tech spinoffs for NATO's Conventional Defenses Initiative, CDI, that could help to address the imbalance of forces in Europe. And SDI helps to solve what is perhaps the greatest paradox of arms reduction: that reductions, if not carefully managed, could mean greater instability and risk. As arms are reduced to lower and lower levels, each violation could become more and more threatening. SDI can play a key role in solving this paradox of nuclear arms reductions. We may build an edifice of peace and arms reductions, but just like your homes, it needs an insurance policy against fire and theft. SDI is it: vital insurance against Soviet cheating.

A few days ago, when I went to Notre Dame, nostalgia was much the order of the day, but I did bring up an issue, a very serious issue. I spoke about when I was in college and a debate that I remember having in one of my classes in those post-World War I days, when the bomber was just being recognized as the potent weapon that it later became. Our class debated whether or not Americans—people who, to our way of thinking, stood for high moral standards—would ever drop bombs from a plane on a city. And the class was about evenly divided. Half felt it might be necessary. The other felt that bombing civilians would always be beyond the pale of decency, totally unacceptable human conduct, no matter how heinous the enemy. We believed that young men in America would refuse such an order. But a decade later, during World War II, few, if any, who had been in that room objected to our country's wholesale bombing of cities under the hard pressures of total war. Civilization's standards of acceptable conduct had changed.

It's hard to say they changed for the better. We have the opportunity to reverse this trend, to base the peace of this world on security rather than threats, on defense rather than on retaliation. Those who say it can't be done, who stand in the way of progress and insist that technology stops here—I plead with them to consider what they're saying. For no matter how effective arms reduction negotiations ever are, we can never "uninvent" the nuclear weapon. We can never erase the knowledge of how to build a ballistic missile. If they were able to succeed in stopping SDI, then we would be left forever with that loaded pistol to our heads, with an insecure and morally tenuous peace based forever on the threat of retaliation.

But the world is rapidly changing, and technology won't stop here. All we can do is make sure that technology becomes the ally and protector of peace, that we build better shields rather than sharper and more deadly swords. In so doing, maybe we can help to bring an end to the brutal legacy of modern warfare. We can stop the madness from continuing into the next century. We can create a better, more secure, more moral world, where peace goes hand in hand with freedom from fear—forever.

Thank you all very much. God bless you all.

Note: The President spoke at 10:56 a.m. in the Regency Ballroom at the Omni Shoreham Hotel. In his opening remarks, he referred to Dr. Robert L. Pfaltzgraff, Jr., president of the Institute for Foreign Policy Analysis; Dr. Edward Teller, Associate Director Emeritus of the Lawrence Livermore National Laboratory; Senators Malcolm Wallop of Wyoming and Dan Quayle of Indiana; Representative Bill Chappell, Jr., of Florida; Edward L. Rowny, Special Advisor to the President and Secretary of State on Arms Control Matters; Lt. Gen. James A. Abrahamson, USAF, Director of Strategic Defense Initiative Organization; William R. Graham, Jr., Science Advisor to the President and Director of the Office of Science and Technology Policy; and novelist Tom Clancy.

Remarks to Supporters of Israel at a White House Briefing on United States Foreign Policy
March 15, 1988

I was thinking on the way over here what a great idea this event is and wondering why we don't get together more often. You know, it kind of reminds me of the fella who asked his friend what the problem really was: ignorance or apathy. And the friend responded, "I don't know, and I don't care." [*Laughter*]

Well, I doubt there's a person in this room who can be accused of suffering from either of those defects. Each one of you is alive to the issues of the day. Each one of you has made your family proud and your country grateful for the active role that you've taken in community and world events and especially for your loyalty to the United States and Israel and to the wonderful work of the United Jewish Appeal. I believe you also know where I stand. As I look back on these last 7 years, I remember many emotional, many poignant moments, but few, believe me, will ever match those times I have spent with you, especially on those occasions when we commemorated the victims of the Holocaust and pledged to each other and the world: Never again.

Those of us in this room are as one on this point: We know what Israel is. We know what Israel means. And as I will tell the Prime Minister tomorrow, when it comes to Israel, the United States is not a bargainer or a broker: The United States is a friend and an ally. And that's why one of the things I'm proudest of is the steps we've been able to take during this administration to build a stronger foundation of enduring friendship and cooperation. For example, strategic cooperation—something other administrations shied away from—is now a commitment our two governments have made to each other. It responds to our mutual needs and is a reminder to all that no wedge will be driven between the United States and Israel.

Our commitment to close relations and to Israel's security has been reflected in our foreign aid levels, our commercial cooperation of research and defense, and the vital and historic free trade agreement that we have signed. Our commitment to Israel's security is also reflected in our latest peace initiative. Making progress toward peace in the Middle East not only serves mutual interests, it is urgent. It's in America's and Israel's interest to develop a credible basis on which to make progress, one that promises to overcome stalemate and make genuine reconciliation possible. That's why I'm delighted that Prime Minister Shamir is here.

And let me underscore one point that I hope needs no underscoring: Our policy has as its basis—and this is a first principle in any negotiation—the assuring of Israel's freedom and security. We will not leave Israel to stand alone, nor will we acquiesce in any effort to gang up on Israel. Peace will not be imposed by us or by anyone else. It will and must come from the genuine give-and-take of negotiations. That's what we're working to set in motion now.

And while our work on behalf of Israel is a vital part of why we're there today, I would be remiss if I didn't speak to you about other efforts to make U.S. foreign policy consistent and strong. Only a few years ago, some Americans were beginning to question what we stood for in the world. Our nation has now regained its confidence and sense of purpose. We've returned to proclaiming enthusiastically the democratic ideals that inspired our Founding Fathers and the Founding Fathers of Israel. And I think this vigorous foreign policy is good, of course, for Israel because the United States is thought of today as a strong nation and a reliable ally. This has helped move the process of peace forward throughout the world, and it has enhanced the security with all our friends and allies.

And what I hope you've noticed during the past few years is that we have moved American foreign policy away from the notion that mere containment is enough, that we have willingly and openly proclaimed to the world that our goal is not just peace but freedom as well, that we seek not separate spheres of influence or a simple balance of power or a deadening stalemate with totalitarianism, that we seek instead a day when every person in every land will share fully in the blessings of freedom. And that's the core of our foreign policy: protecting the security of the United States while advancing the cause of world freedom and democratic rights. It's in this context that I think you can understand why we've moved forward boldly on a broad range of foreign policy issues like SDI, the Persian Gulf, and aid to those fighting against Communist tyranny.

That last subject is particularly appropriate. I want to take a moment of your time to talk about it, and I hope you'll give some thought to this after we part today. You know, so frequently, I have found that the measure of any regime or government can be taken by its official attitude toward anti-Semitism.

And as most of you know, few regimes today so blatantly sanction and practice official anti-Semitism as the Sandinista Communists in Nicaragua. The Jewish community has been forced out almost entirely. Managua's one synagogue has been defaced and firebombed. And Nicaragua has officially aligned itself with Mu'ammar Qadhafi of Libya and of course the PLO, an organization that has again revealed its true colors, opposing our efforts of peace and trumpeting its responsibility for a sickening terrorist attack on a bus carrying Israeli men, women, and children. It's no accident that Sandinista leaders were trained in the seventies by the PLO, and the PLO has established a presence in Nicaragua. So, too, one of the hijackers some years ago of an El Al airliner was a Sandinista. He died in the attempt and is now a national hero. They have named a geothermal plant after him. And of course, the Sandinistas have led the way in sponsoring recent anti-Israel resolutions in the U.N.

So, I think it's time that some in Congress who want to turn away from the reality of leftwing anti-Semitism face the facts about the anti-Semitism of the Sandinistas as well as their ties to the PLO and other terrorist groups. It is the Nicaraguan freedom fighters who are resisting this kind of moral corruption. It is the freedom fighters who are fighting for the political, civil, and human rights of Jews and Christians in Nicaragua. It is the freedom fighters who must be sustained and supported in this struggle.

You know, I just don't understand the inability of some people to realize what the Sandinistas are all about. Only the other day we saw newspaper accounts of the Castro connection in international drug dealing. So, too, the evidence has been compelling for a long time that the Sandinistas have been involved in such drug trafficking. In one of my TV addresses on the subject of *contra* aid, I showed a picture of a drug smuggler's aircraft landing in Nicaragua at a military airfield and being met by Nicaraguan officials and soldiers. And the Commission on Organized Crime, chaired by Judge Irving Kaufman, concluded that top-level members of the Sandinista leadership were involved in the international drug trade. Well, anyway, the point that I'm making here is that all of us have a stake in what happens in Nicaragua as we do in the fate of Central America in general.

You know, many people early on said that we could not save El Salvador, and our aid package passed by only a few votes. And now democracy is prospering in El Salvador, Honduras, Costa Rica, and Guatemala. Nicaragua is the odd man out and a menace to the cause of regional democracy. But the struggle in Nicaragua goes on, and with Congress' help, we'll see to it that democracy wins there too.

So, I hope you can see how these issues are interrelated and how our foreign policy is not just strong for the sake of being strong, that we seek to do more than just project national pride and firmness. Our real motivation, our root motivation is the cause of human freedom, and this has no small bearing on the mutual concerns that bring us here today.

As all of you know, I expect to be in Moscow one of these days for a summit meeting with Mr. Gorbachev. As it was at the Washington summit and the summits before that, the issue of Soviet Jewry will, I assure you, be high on our agenda. The General Secretary knows of my profound concern on this point and of your concern as well. And I'll be making this very plain again in Moscow.

So, let me conclude then by thanking you for all you've done on behalf of the issues of Soviet Jewry and Israel's security. The safety and security of the United States and the safety and security of Israel are all part of a larger cause, the cause of human rights for every man, woman, and child on this Earth. And today, as we meet here, let's rededicate ourselves to that cause. Thank you very much.

Note: The President spoke at 11:53 a.m. in Room 450 of the Old Executive Office Building to members of the Prime Ministers Council, major contributors to the United Jewish Appeal.

Nomination of Michael E. Zacharia To Be an Assistant Secretary of Commerce
March 15, 1988

The President today announced his intention to nominate Michael E. Zacharia to be an Assistant Secretary of Commerce (Export Administration) at the Department of Commerce. This is a new position.

Since 1987 Mr. Zacharia has been Deputy Assistant Secretary for International Trade Controls at the Department of State in Washington, DC. Prior to this, he was a partner with the firm of Weintraub, Genshlea, Hardy, Erich & Brown, 1983–1987; Special Counsel to the Under Secretary for International Trade at the U.S. Department of Commerce, 1982–1983; and a White House fellow, serving as special assistant to the Deputy Secretary of State, 1981–1982. He was a participating associate for the firm of Fulbright & Jaworski, 1978–1981.

Mr. Zacharia graduated Phi Beta Kappa from the University of California, Berkeley (A.B., 1973) and the University of California, San Francisco (J.D., 1976). He was born April 14, 1952, in Chicago, IL. He is married, has three children, and resides in Annandale, VA.

Nomination of Susan S. Suter To Be Commissioner of the Rehabilitation Services Administration at the Department of Education
March 15, 1988

The President today announced his intention to nominate Susan S. Suter to be Commissioner of the Rehabilitation Services Administration at the Department of Education. She would succeed Justin W. Dart, Jr.

Since 1984 Mrs. Suter has been director for the Illinois Department of Rehabilitation Services in Springfield, IL; and executive associate director of the Illinois Department of Rehabilitation Services, 1982–1984. Prior to this, she was State coordinator for the International Year of Disabled Persons for the State of Illinois, Office of the Governor, 1981–1982; director of community services for the Illinois Developmental Disabilities Advocacy Authority (IDDAA), 1980–1981; and developmental disabilities planning specialist for the Governor's planning council on developmental disabilities, 1979–1980.

Mrs. Suter graduated from the University of Illinois (B.S., 1972) and Eastern Illinois University (M.S., 1984). She was born April 16, 1950, in Evanston, IL. She is married, has one child, and resides in Springfield, IL.

Appointment of John F.W. Rogers as Chairman of the Advisory Council on Historic Preservation

March 15, 1988

The President today announced his intention to appoint John F.W. Rogers to be Chairman of the Advisory Council on Historic Preservation for the remainder of the term expiring June 10, 1989. He would succeed Cynthia Jeanne Grassby Baker.

Mr. Rogers is currently group vice president of operations for Oliver Carr Co. in Washington, DC. Prior to this he was Assistant Secretary for Management at the Department of the Treasury, 1985–1987. From 1981 to 1985, he was Assistant to the President for Management and Administration and Director of the Office of Administration at the White House. He also served as director and general manager of the Committee for the 50th American Presidential Inaugural. Prior to joining the White House staff, he was executive assistant to the director of the White House transition team, and assistant to the president for administration at the American Enterprise Institute for Public Policy Research.

Mr. Rogers graduated from George Washington University (B.A., 1978). He was born April 15, 1956, in Seneca Falls, NY, and currently resides in Washington, DC.

Appointment of Harlan Hockenberg as a Member of the President's Commission on White House Fellowships

March 15, 1988

The President today announced his intention to appoint Harlan (Bud) Hockenberg to be a member of the President's Commission on White House Fellowships. This is an initial appointment.

Since 1964 Mr. Hockenberg has been senior partner with Davis, Hockenberg, Wine, Brown, Koehn and Shors in Des Moines, IA. Prior to this he was a partner with Abramson, Myers and Hockenberg, 1958–1964.

Mr. Hockenberg graduated from the University of Iowa (B.A., 1949; J.D., 1952). He was born July 1, 1927, in Des Moines, IA. He served in the United States Navy from 1945 to 1946. He is married, has three children, and resides in Des Moines.

Statement by Assistant to the President for Press Relations Fitzwater Urging Clemency for South Africa's Sharpeville Six
March 15, 1988

The President has directed that a demarche be delivered immediately to the South African Government urging clemency for the Sharpeville Six on compassionate and humanitarian grounds. We have been in consultation with other governments on this matter and understand that similar appeals will be made to the Government of South Africa by Britain and West Germany, among others. We trust the South African Government will respond favorably to these requests for clemency. An act of compassion such as this by the South African Government would be welcomed by all Americans.

Note: The Sharpeville Six were a group of blacks convicted in connection with the death of township councillor Jacob Dlamini on September 3, 1984.

Executive Order 12630—Governmental Actions and Interference With Constitutionally Protected Property Rights
March 16, 1988

By the authority vested in me as President by the Constitution and laws of the United States of America, and in order to ensure that government actions are undertaken on a well-reasoned basis with due regard for fiscal accountability, for the financial impact of the obligations imposed on the Federal government by the Just Compensation Clause of the Fifth Amendment, and for the Constitution, it is hereby ordered as follows:

Section 1. Purpose. (a) The Fifth Amendment of the United States Constitution provides that private property shall not be taken for public use without just compensation. Government historically has used the formal exercise of the power of eminent domain, which provides orderly processes for paying just compensation, to acquire private property for public use. Recent Supreme Court decisions, however, in reaffirming the fundamental protection of private property rights provided by the Fifth Amendment and in assessing the nature of governmental actions that have an impact on constitutionally protected property rights, have also reaffirmed that governmental actions that do not formally invoke the condemnation power, including regulations, may result in a taking for which just compensation is required.

(b) Responsible fiscal management and fundamental principles of good government require that government decision-makers evaluate carefully the effect of their administrative, regulatory, and legislative actions on constitutionally protected property rights. Executive departments and agencies should review their actions carefully to prevent unnecessary takings and should account in decision-making for those takings that are necessitated by statutory mandate.

(c) The purpose of this Order is to assist Federal departments and agencies in undertaking such reviews and in proposing, planning, and implementing actions with due regard for the constitutional protections provided by the Fifth Amendment and to reduce the risk of undue or inadvertent burdens on the public fisc resulting from lawful governmental action. In furtherance of the purpose of this Order, the Attorney General shall, consistent with the principles stated herein and in consultation with the Executive departments and agencies, promulgate Guidelines for the Evaluation of Risk and Avoidance of Unanticipated Takings to which each Executive department or agency shall refer in making the evaluations required by this Order or in otherwise taking any action that is the subject of this Order. The Guidelines shall be promulgated no later than May 1, 1988, and shall be disseminated to all units of each Executive department and agency no later than July 1, 1988. The Attorney General shall, as necessary, update these guidelines to reflect fundamental changes in takings law occurring as a result of Supreme Court decisions.

Sec. 2. Definitions. For the purpose of this Order: (a) "Policies that have takings implications" refers to Federal regulations, proposed Federal regulations, proposed Federal legislation, comments on proposed Federal legislation, or other Federal policy statements that, if implemented or enacted, could effect a taking, such as rules and regulations that propose or implement licensing, permitting, or other condition requirements or limitations on private property use, or that require dedications or exactions from owners of private property. "Policies that have takings implications" does not include:

(1) Actions abolishing regulations, discontinuing governmental programs, or modifying regulations in a manner that lessens interference with the use of private property;

(2) Actions taken with respect to properties held in trust by the United States or in preparation for or during treaty negotiations with foreign nations;

(3) Law enforcement actions involving seizure, for violations of law, of property for forfeiture or as evidence in criminal proceedings;

(4) Studies or similar efforts or planning activities;

(5) Communications between Federal agencies or departments and State or local land-use planning agencies regarding planned or proposed State or local actions regulating private property regardless of whether such communications are initiated by a Federal agency or department or are undertaken in response to an invitation by the State or local authority.

(6) The placement of military facilities or military activities involving the use of Federal property alone; or

(7) Any military or foreign affairs functions (including procurement functions thereunder) but not including the U.S. Army Corps of Engineers civil works program.

(b) Private property refers to all property protected by the Just Compensation Clause of the Fifth Amendment.

(c) "Actions" refers to proposed Federal regulations, proposed Federal legislation, comments on proposed Federal legislation, applications of Federal regulations to specific property, or Federal governmental actions physically invading or occupying private property, or other policy statements or actions related to Federal regulation or direct physical invasion or occupancy, but does not include:

(1) Actions in which the power of eminent domain is formally exercised;

(2) Actions taken with respect to properties held in trust by the United States or in preparation for or during treaty negotiations with foreign nations;

(3) Law enforcement actions involving seizure, for violations of law, of property for forfeiture or as evidence in criminal proceedings;

(4) Studies or similar efforts or planning activities;

(5) Communications between Federal agencies or departments and State or local land-use planning agencies regarding planned or proposed State or local actions regulating private property regardless of whether such communications are initiated by a Federal agency or department or are undertaken in response to an invitation by the State or local authority;

(6) The placement of military facilities or military activities involving the use of Federal property alone; or

(7) Any military or foreign affairs functions (including procurement functions thereunder), but not including the U.S. Army Corps of Engineers civil works program.

Sec. 3. General Principles. In formulating or implementing policies that have takings implications, each Executive department and agency shall be guided by the following general principles:

(a) Governmental officials should be sensitive to, anticipate, and account for, the obligations imposed by the Just Compensation

Clause of the Fifth Amendment in planning and carrying out governmental actions so that they do not result in the imposition of unanticipated or undue additional burdens on the public fisc.

(b) Actions undertaken by governmental officials that result in a physical invasion or occupancy of private property, and regulations imposed on private property that substantially affect its value or use, may constitute a taking of property. Further, governmental action may amount to a taking even though the action results in less than a complete deprivation of all use or value, or of all separate and distinct interests in the same private property and even if the action constituting a taking is temporary in nature.

(c) Government officials whose actions are taken specifically for purposes of protecting public health and safety are ordinarily given broader latitude by courts before their actions are considered to be takings. However, the mere assertion of a public health and safety purpose is insufficient to avoid a taking. Actions to which this Order applies asserted to be for the protection of public health and safety, therefore, should be undertaken only in response to real and substantial threats to public health and safety, be designed to advance significantly the health and safety purpose, and be no greater than is necessary to achieve the health and safety purpose.

(d) While normal governmental processes do not ordinarily effect takings, undue delays in decision-making during which private property use is interfered with carry a risk of being held to be takings. Additionally, a delay in processing may increase significantly the size of compensation due if a taking is later found to have occurred.

(e) The Just Compensation Clause is self-actuating, requiring that compensation be paid whenever governmental action results in a taking of private property regardless of whether the underlying authority for the action contemplated a taking or authorized the payment of compensation. Accordingly, governmental actions that may have a significant impact on the use or value of private property should be scrutinized to avoid undue or unplanned burdens on the public fisc.

Sec. 4. Department and Agency Action. In addition to the fundamental principles set forth in Section 3, Executive departments and agencies shall adhere, to the extent permitted by law, to the following criteria when implementing policies that have takings implications:

(a) When an Executive department or agency requires a private party to obtain a permit in order to undertake a specific use of, or action with respect to, private property, any conditions imposed on the granting of a permit shall:

(1) Serve the same purpose that would have been served by a prohibition of the use or action; and

(2) Substantially advance that purpose.

(b) When a proposed action would place a restriction on a use of private property, the restriction imposed on the use shall not be disproportionate to the extent to which the use contributes to the overall problem that the restriction is imposed to redress.

(c) When a proposed action involves a permitting process or any other decision-making process that will interfere with, or otherwise prohibit, the use of private property pending the completion of the process, the duration of the process shall be kept to the minimum necessary.

(d) Before undertaking any proposed action regulating private property use for the protection of public health or safety, the Executive department or agency involved shall, in internal deliberative documents and any submissions to the Director of the Office of Management and Budget that are required:

(1) Identify clearly, with as much specificity as possible, the public health or safety risk created by the private property use that is the subject of the proposed action;

(2) Establish that such proposed action substantially advances the purpose of protecting public health and safety against the specifically identified risk;

(3) Establish to the extent possible that the restrictions imposed on the private property are not disproportionate to the extent to which the use contributes to the overall risk; and

(4) Estimate, to the extent possible, the potential cost to the government in the

event that a court later determines that the action constituted a taking.

In instances in which there is an immediate threat to health and safety that constitutes an emergency requiring immediate response, this analysis may be done upon completion of the emergency action.

Sec. 5. Executive Department and Agency Implementation. (a) The head of each executive department and agency shall designate an official to be responsible for ensuring compliance with this Order with respect to the actions of that department or agency.

(b) Executive departments and agencies shall, to the extent permitted by law, identify the takings implications of proposed regulatory actions and address the merits of those actions in light of the identified takings implications, if any, in all required submissions made to the Office of Management and Budget. Significant takings implications should also be identified and discussed in notices of proposed rule-making and messages transmitting legislative proposals to the Congress, stating the departments' and agencies' conclusions on the takings issues.

(c) Executive departments and agencies shall identify each existing Federal rule and regulation against which a takings award has been made or against which a takings claim is pending including the amount of each claim or award. A "takings" award has been made or a "takings" claim pending if the award was made, or the pending claim brought, pursuant to the Just Compensation Clause of the Fifth Amendment. An itemized compilation of all such awards made in Fiscal Years 1985, 1986, and 1987 and all such pending claims shall be submitted to the Director, Office of Management and Budget, on or before May 16, 1988.

(d) Each Executive department and agency shall submit annually to the Director, Office of Management and Budget, and to the Attorney General an itemized compilation of all awards of just compensation entered against the United States for takings, including awards of interest as well as monies paid pursuant to the provisions of the Uniform Relocation Assistance and Real Property Acquisition Policies Act of 1970, 42 U.S.C. 4601.

(e)(1) The Director, Office of Management and Budget, and the Attorney General shall each, to the extent permitted by law, take action to ensure that the policies of the Executive departments and agencies are consistent with the principles, criteria, and requirements stated in Sections 1 through 5 of this Order, and the Office of Management and Budget shall take action to ensure that all takings awards levied against agencies are properly accounted for in agency budget submissions.

(2) In addition to the guidelines required by Section 1 of this Order, the Attorney General shall, in consultation with each Executive department and agency to which this Order applies, promulgate such supplemental guidelines as may be appropriate to the specific obligations of that department or agency.

Sec. 6. Judicial Review. This Order is intended only to improve the Internal management of the Executive branch and is not intended to create any right or benefit, substantive or procedural, enforceable at law by a party against the United States, its agencies, its officers, or any person.

RONALD REAGAN

The White House,
March 15, 1988.

[*Filed with the Office of the Federal Register, 4:53 p.m., March 16, 1988*]

Note: The Executive order was released by the Office of the Press Secretary on March 16.

Appointment of Craig O. McCaw as a Member of the President's National Security Telecommunications Advisory Committee
March 16, 1988

The President today announced his intention to appoint Craig O. McCaw to be a member of the President's National Security Telecommunications Advisory Committee. He would succeed M. Kenneth Oshman.

Since 1985 Mr. McCaw has been chairman and chief executive officer for McCaw Communications Co. in Kirkland, WA, and president and chief executive officer, 1970–1985. Mr. McCaw has been District I director for the National Cable Television Association (NCTA) Board of Directors, a member of NCTA's State-local government committee, and a member of State Cable Associations in Washington.

Mr. McCaw graduated from Stanford University (B.A., 1973). He was born August 11, 1949, in Centralia, WA. He is married and currently resides in Bellevue, WA.

Remarks Following Discussions With Prime Minister Yitzhak Shamir of Israel
March 16, 1988

The President. It's been a pleasure to meet with Prime Minister Shamir again and to have this opportunity to review with him the important issue of peace in the Middle East. We have a unique relationship with Israel, a relationship of trust, friendship, and shared ideals. I think we can be proud of the achievements that we've made over the last 7 years in giving more substance and dimension to the strong ties between Israel and the United States. In the remainder of my term, we'll continue to work to strengthen those ties.

The main topic of our discussion today was the search for peace in the Middle East. We've seen a new sense of urgency on the part of many in the region and a wide recognition of the reality that the status quo is unacceptable. Our efforts have been geared toward trying to find a reasonable and practical way to make real progress—progress that will assure the security of Israel and its neighbors and achieve the legitimate rights of the Palestinians.

The present situation is a challenge and an opportunity to move decisively to break the deadlock that has lasted far too long. I hope we will not lose this opportunity. Today Prime Minister Shamir and I discussed the proposal for moving forward rapidly to peace negotiations, which Secretary Shultz left with Israel, Jordan, and Syria during his recent visit. We believe this proposal offers a realistic and achievable way to change the relationship between Israel and the Arabs. It's a concrete demonstration of my commitment to finding a solution to the Arab-Israeli conflict through a negotiating process that would begin soon. As I told Prime Minister Shamir, the United States is prepared to be an active partner in this process, and we hope that all the parties involved will seize this opportunity.

So, let's be clear about several things. The United States will not slice this initiative apart and will not abandon it. And those who will say no to the United States plan—and the Prime Minister has not used this word—need not answer to us; they'll need to answer to themselves and their people as to why they turned down a realistic and sensible plan to achieve negotiations. This is a time for all the parties to the conflict to make decisions for peace.

Prime Minister Shamir and I also reviewed our countries' robust and vital bilateral relationship. As you know, Israel has been designated one of our major non-NATO allies and friends, and we have developed a solid basis of strategic cooperation between our two countries. Strategic cooperation is a symbol of our converging needs and our mutual commitment to ensuring that no wedge will ever be driven between us. I want to add that Prime Minister Shamir and I both remain very concerned about the many thousands of Jews that remain in the Soviet Union and yearn to emigrate or fully express their Jewish identity. The plight of Soviet Jewry shall remain at the top of my agenda in my discussions with Secretary Gorbachev.

As I bid farewell to Prime Minister Shamir, I wish him and the people of Israel a happy 40th anniversary. Our prayer is that this anniversary will mark the beginning of the era of peace and accommodation in the Middle East.

The Prime Minister. Thank you, Mr. President. This visit to Washington has given me an opportunity to meet again with President Reagan, Secretary of State Shultz, Secretary of Defense Carlucci, and Secretary of the Treasury Baker. My colleagues and I have also met with congressional leaders and other friends in the Congress, in the administration, and in the general public.

I am indebted to the President for this kind invitation. It affords me the opportunity to discuss matters of common concern and to deepen the friendship and understanding between our two countries. In the talks with the President and with Secretary Shultz, we reviewed the state of U.S.-Israel relations and the efforts to advance peace in the Middle East. Mr. President, we have always been in complete agreement with the principle of negotiating from a position of strength for which you have always stood. We have stepped up efforts to seek a framework for conducting direct peace negotiations between Israel and those of its Arab neighbors that we hope will join us in the quest for peace.

Israel has welcomed the American involvement and the Secretary's efforts in this search. We have confidence in the American role because we share the same goal of peace with security for all the countries in the Middle East. I have strong reservations concerning the proposed international conference which, in my view, is not conducive to peace. Some months ago I accepted a proposal by Secretary Shultz to launch direct negotiations with the blessing of the U.S.-Soviet summit in order to grant international legitimacy for the negotiations for those states desiring it. Unfortunately, it was rejected. Nevertheless, I shall be ready to consider a similar proposal. Israel firmly believes that those who are prepared to live with each other in peace must learn to negotiate directly with each other. We remain committed to the Camp David accords, which have provided a workable agreed framework for peace between Israel and each of its Arab neighbors.

Mr. President, these are difficult times for Israel. We shall overcome them in the best possible way consonant with our tradition and our eagerness to prevent the loss of lives. Mr. President, on the eve of Israel's 40th anniversary, the people and Government of Israel are united in hailing the deep friendship and the close cooperation between our two countries. This friendship has reached unprecedented levels under your leadership. We have established a strategic cooperation agreement between Israel and the United States, a free trade area agreement between our two countries, and the designation of Israel as a major non-NATO ally of the United States. We are confident that a solid foundation of friendship between Israel and the United States will remain unshaken in spite of occasional differences of opinion that may arise.

I am sure I speak for all the people of Israel and for peace-loving persons everywhere when I express our gratitude for your untiring efforts to reduce tensions in the world and to bring peace to our wartorn region. We will continue to do our utmost to cooperate in the search for peace. I return to Jerusalem confident that with the friendship and understanding of the United States Government and its people we shall succeed. Thank you.

Note: The President spoke at 1:25 p.m. in the East Room at the White House. Earlier, the President and the Prime Minister met in the Oval Office and then attended a luncheon in the Residence.

Proclamation 5776—Freedom of Information Day, 1988
March 16, 1988

By the President of the United States of America

A Proclamation

Freedom of Information Day reminds us of some of our most important principles. "We the People," as the framers of the Constitution called us in the Preamble, govern ourselves through representative government. All of us, of course, have the right to do so. We are best able to do so when every citizen is informed on matters of public importance and can therefore take full part in civic affairs and in the exercise of fundamental rights. We can all be grateful indeed to the Founders who through the Constitution—including the Bill of Rights—provided for freedoms for all Americans that make a well-informed electorate possible.

No one understood these principles more thoroughly than James Madison, our fourth President, whose birthday, March 16, is the occasion for Freedom of Information Day. Long before he became President, he served as chief recorder of the Constitutional Convention; he was perhaps the most influential architect of our charter of liberty and limited government. Throughout life he championed conditions that could foster responsive government, such as a free press and a vigorous flow of information among the public, tempered with the recognition that for legitimate government to function, some matters must remain outside the public domain. He maintained this balance eloquently when he helped draft the Bill of Rights, and especially the First Amendment, while restricting access to most of the documents that form the Constitutional record.

Two centuries later, Madison's ideals continue to strengthen our Nation. We Americans cherish our freedoms and use them; we thrive on the benefits of free exchanges with those who represent us in government and discharge the public trust. This interaction requires forthrightness in government and public access to most government information. Indeed, the responsible flow of such information to the public is entirely compatible with the necessary and proper protection of vital public interests such as national security, privacy, and effective law enforcement.

On the anniversary of President Madison's birth, let us celebrate our history and heritage of freedom of information by remembering and revering the life and example of this wise and generous patriot and lover of liberty.

The Congress, by Senate Joint Resolution 126, has designated March 16, 1988, as "Freedom of Information Day" and authorized and requested the President to issue a proclamation in observance of this event.

Now, Therefore, I, Ronald Reagan, President of the United States of America, do hereby proclaim March 16, 1988, as Freedom of Information Day, and I call upon the people of the United States to observe this day with appropriate ceremonies and activities.

In Witness Whereof, I have hereunto set my hand this sixteenth day of March, in the year of our Lord nineteen hundred and eighty-eight, and of the Independence of the United States of America the two hundred and twelfth.

RONALD REAGAN

[*Filed with the Office of the Federal Register, 4:52 p.m., March 16, 1988*]

Message to the Senate Returning Without Approval the Civil Rights Restoration Act of 1987 and Transmitting Alternative Legislation
March 16, 1988

To the Senate of the United States:

I am returning unsigned with my objections S. 557 and transmitting for your prompt consideration the Civil Rights Protection Act of 1988. The Congress should enact legislation designed to eliminate invidious discrimination and to ensure equality of opportunity for all Americans while preserving their basic freedoms from governmental interference and control. Regrettably, the bill presented to me fails to achieve that objective.

There is no matter of greater concern to me than ensuring that our Nation is free of discrimination. Our country has paid a heavy price in the past for prejudices, whether based upon race, gender, ethnic background, religion or handicap. Such attitudes have no place in our society.

It was with this commitment in mind that in the wake of the Supreme Court's 1984 *Grove City College* decision, I voiced my support for legislation that would strengthen the civil rights coverage of educational institutions that existed prior to that decision. I have repeatedly endorsed legislation to do just that. Today I am sending to Congress a bill that goes further than the legislation previously endorsed. This proposed bill is intended to accommodate other concerns raised during Congressional consideration of the *Grove City* issue.

Our bill advances the protection of civil rights. It would:

—prohibit discrimination against women, minorities, persons with disabilities, and the elderly *across the board* in public school districts, public systems of higher education, systems of vocational education, and private educational institutions which receive *any* Federal aid.

—extend the application of the civil rights statutes to *entire* businesses which receive Federal aid as a whole and to the *entire* plant or facility receiving Federal aid in *every* other instance.

—prohibit discrimination in *all* of the federally funded programs of departments and agencies of State and local governments.

Our bill complements well our body of existing Federal civil rights laws. But even more remains to be done. For example, I have urged the Congress to enact responsible legislation to deal with some obvious failures of the Fair Housing Act of 1968, including the need to protect persons with disabilities.

Congress, on the other hand, has sent me a bill that would vastly and unjustifiably expand the power of the Federal government over the decisions and affairs of private organizations, such as churches and synagogues, farms, businesses, and State and local governments. In the process, it would place at risk such cherished values as religious liberty.

The bill presented to me would diminish substantially the freedom and independence of religious institutions in our society. The bill would seriously impinge upon religious liberty because of its unprecedented and pervasive coverage of churches and synagogues based on receipt of even a small amount of Federal aid for just one activity; its unprecedented coverage of entire religious elementary and secondary school systems when only a single school in such a system receives Federal aid; and its failure to protect, under Title IX of the Education Amendments of 1972, the religious freedom of private schools that are closely identified with the religious tenets of, but not controlled by, a religious organization.

Businesses participating in Federal programs, such as job training programs, would be subject to comprehensive Federal regulation. While some proponents of S. 557 have claimed that it would not apply to farmers who receive Federal crop subsidies or food suppliers who accept food stamps, the ambiguity in the statute and its legislative history indicates that these exemptions should be made explicit.

A significant portion of the private

sector—entities principally engaged in the business of providing education, health care, housing, social services, or parks and recreation—would for the first time be covered nationwide in all of their activities, including those wholly unrelated activities of their subsidiaries or other divisions, even if those subsidiaries or divisions receive no Federal aid. Again, there was no demonstrated need for such sweeping coverage.

Further, this bill would be beyond pre-Grove City law and expand the scope of coverage of State and local government agencies. Under S. 557, any agency of such a government that receives or distributes such assistance would be subject in all of its operations to a wide-ranging regime of Federal regulation, contrary to the sound principles of federalism.

The cost and burdens of compliance with S. 557 would be substantial. The bill would bring to those it covers—which is most of America—an intrusive Federal regulatory regime; random on-site compliance checks by Federal officials; and increased exposure to lawsuits, which are costly to defend even when you win.

Moreover, such legislation would likely have the unintended consequences of harming many of the same people it is supposed to protect. For example, persons with disabilities seeking to enhance their job skills are not helped if businesses withdraw from Federal job-training programs because of their unwillingness to accept vastly expanded bureaucratic intrusions under S. 557. Business groups have indicated many of their members may do just that.

The Civil Rights Protection Act that I am proposing today addresses the many shortcomings of S. 557. The Civil Rights Protection Act would protect civil rights and at the same time preserve the independence of State and local governments, the freedom of religion, and the right of America's citizens to order their lives and businesses without extensive Federal intrusion.

The Civil Rights Protection Act contains important changes from S. 557 designed to avoid unnecessary Federal intrusion into the lives and businesses of Americans, while ensuring that Federal aid is properly monitored under the civil rights statutes it amends. The bill would:

—Protect religious liberty by limiting coverage to that part of a church or synagogue which participates in a Federal program; by protecting under Title IX, the religious tenets of private institutions closely identified with religious organizations on the same basis as institutions directly controlled by religious organizations; and by providing that when a religious secondary or elementary school receives Federal assistance, only that school, and not the entire religious school system, becomes subject to the Federal regulation.

—Ensure that the reach of Federal regulation into private businesses extends only to the facility that participates in Federally funded programs, unless the business, as a whole, receives Federal aid, in which case it is covered in its entirety. The bill also states explicitly that farmers will not become subject to Federal regulation by virtue of their acceptance of Federal price support payments, and that grocers and supermarkets will not become subject to such regulations by virtue of accepting food stamps from customers.

—Preserve the independence of State and local government from Federal control by limiting Federal regulation to the part of a State or local entity that receives or distributes Federal assistance.

In all other respects, my proposal is identical to S. 557, including the provisions to ensure that this legislation does not impair protection for the lives of unborn children.

I urge that upon reconsidering S. 557 in light of my objections, you reject the bill and enact promptly in its place the Civil Rights Protection Act of 1988.

RONALD REAGAN

The White House,
March 16, 1988.

Note: S. 557, which passed over the President's veto on March 22, was assigned Public Law No. 100–259.

Message to the Congress Transmitting Alternative Civil Rights Legislation
March 16, 1988

To the Congress of the United States:

In returning to the Senate without my approval S. 557, the "Grove City" bill, I urged the Congress to enact promptly, in lieu of S. 557, my alternative proposal, the "Civil Rights Protection Act of 1988."

My proposal, which is enclosed, would address the many serious shortcomings of S. 557, as explained in the attached copy of the veto message on the bill.

I pledge my wholehearted support in working with the Congress to enact promptly this carefully crafted and effective alternative to S. 557.

RONALD REAGAN

The White House,
March 16, 1988.

Statement by Assistant to the President for Press Relations Fitzwater on the Deployment of United States Armed Forces to Honduras
March 16, 1988

In light of the significant cross-border incursion by Sandinista armed forces into Honduras from Nicaragua, and at the request of the Government of Honduras, the President has ordered the immediate deployment of an infantry brigade task force consisting of two battalions of the 82d Airborne Division from Fort Bragg, North Carolina, two battalions from the 7th Infantry Division at Fort Ord, California, plus supporting units to Palmerola Air Force Base in Honduras for an emergency deployment readiness exercise.

In addition to its value as a test of the proficiency of our military units, this exercise is a measured response designed to show our staunch support to the democratic Government of Honduras at a time when its territorial integrity is being violated by the Cuban- and Soviet-supported Sandinista army. This exercise is also intended as a signal to the governments and peoples of Central America of the seriousness with which the United States Government views the current situation in the region. The duration of this exercise has not been decided. The brigade task force will not be deployed to any area of ongoing hostilities.

Note: Marlin Fitzwater read the statement to reporters at 10:16 p.m. in the Briefing Room at the White House.

Statement on the Situation in Ireland
March 17, 1988

St. Patrick's Day is a joyous occasion on which we celebrate the Irish heritage in America and the ties of kinship, culture, and values which the American and Irish people share. The friendship between our two nations, treasured for generations, will continue to be strengthened by our shared commitment to democracy, justice, and peace.

It is appropriate to pause in our celebrations today to consider the still unresolved problems in Ireland. Northern Ireland continues to suffer from senseless violence, which tragically we have seen repeated in recent days, and high unemployment. We can best address these problems by supporting those who seek peaceful settlements to disputes and rejecting those who seek solutions through terror. Concerned Americans can help by refusing financial or moral support to any Irish terrorists.

We support the Governments and people of the United Kingdom and of Ireland in their work for justice, progress, and reconciliation in Northern Ireland. Our government welcomed the landmark Anglo-Irish agreement when it was signed in 1985. It has already yielded important results. As an expression of our continuing support, the United States is contributing $120 million to the International Fund for Ireland to promote economic progress and reconciliation—the goals of the agreement. Reconciliation and an end to discrimination in the workplace can best be accomplished in an environment of economic growth. We therefore support economic development, the creation of new jobs, and equal employment opportunity in Northern Ireland.

Let all Americans and people of good will resolve on this St. Patrick's Day to work toward a future of peace and prosperity for Ireland.

White House Statement on the President's Request To Transfer Funds for Critical Federal Programs

March 17, 1988

The President today requested the Congress to transfer funds to critical programs, make other offsetting reductions, and provide additional support for some entitlement programs, such as veterans. This request is fully in accord with our 2-year bipartisan budget agreement.

These transfers are few, but of critical importance. First, the Coast Guard is currently hampered in its drug interdiction efforts because the Congress failed to appropriate sufficient funds. This change would restore $60 million to allow the Coast Guard to maintain its efforts to stop drugs from entering this country. Second, within the Department of Justice, program revisions are necessary to cover ongoing expenses as a result of the Mariel Cuban prison riots. A budget amendment for FY 1989 is also included to provide for the reconstruction of these prisons. Third, NASA's request is necessary to support additional personnel for shuttle recovery operations—personnel previously approved by the Congress. And fourth, the Small Business Administration is experiencing an unforeseen demand for disaster loans.

In addition to these transfers, other changes are needed to make additional funds available. For example, unanticipated currency fluctuations have severely depleted accounts for the Board for International Broadcasting. The Department of Defense requires additional authority to reprogram funds later in the year for INF verification. This request also includes several entitlement programs that are not under the control of the appropriations committees nor subject to the strictures of the budget agreement. There are several veterans' programs, including replenishment of the revolving fund for housing loans, that require immediate action. Finally, the judiciary is requesting $57 million in additional funding to cover FY 1988 pay raises. The executive branch is required by law to simply transmit this request without review or alteration.

As with the President's FY 1989 budget submission, this package complies fully with the budget agreement. The President urges the Congress to act expeditiously on this request while maintaining the integrity of our 2-year budget plan.

Nomination of E. Allan Wendt for the Rank of Ambassador While Serving as Senior Representative for Strategic Technology Policy at the State Department

March 17, 1988

The President today announced his intention to nominate E. Allan Wendt, a career member of the Senior Foreign Service, Class of Minister-Counselor, for the rank of Ambassador during his tenure of service as Senior Representative for Strategic Technology Policy in the Office of the Under Secretary of State for Coordinating Security Assistance Programs.

Mr. Wendt has been serving in this position since May 1987. He entered the Foreign Service in 1959, first as a personnel officer and then as staff aide. From 1961 to 1963, he served as vice consul at the American Consulate General in Dusseldorf, Federal Republic of Germany. He then returned to the Department of State, serving as watch officer in the operations center, 1963–1964, and in the Personnel Office in the Bureau of East Asian and Pacific Affairs, 1964–1966. Mr. Wendt was economic/commercial officer and commercial attaché at the U.S. Embassy in Saigon, Vietnam, 1967–1971; and economic/financial officer at the U.S. Mission to the European Communities, 1971–1974. He then became a senior fellow with the Council on Foreign Relations in New York, 1974–1975; and Director of the Office of International Commodities in the Bureau of Economic and Business Affairs, 1975–1979. From 1979 to 1981, Mr. Wendt was Counselor for Economic and Commercial Affairs at the U.S. Embassy in Cairo, Egypt. In 1981 he served as Deputy Assistant Secretary of State for International Energy Resources Policy in the Bureau of Economic and Business Affairs until October of 1986, when he studied Arabic at the Foreign Service Institute until May of 1987.

Mr. Wendt graduated from Yale University (B.A., 1957). He received a degree from Institut d'Etudes Politiques in 1959 and Harvard University (M.P.A., 1967). He was born November 8, 1935, in Chicago, IL, and currently resides in Washington, DC.

Remarks at a St. Patrick's Day Luncheon in Alexandria, Virginia

March 17, 1988

The President. Well, thank you very much. I know that they've got me scheduled. So, I just have a minute or two to say something here, and first of all, a very great thank you to Pat Troy, the owner of this particular place. Jack Kilpatrick and I—this has been a very happy surprise. We just thought we were coming over here for a St. Patrick's Day lunch. [*Laughter*] It was quite a surprise, but a very pleasant surprise.

You know, my father told me when I was that high that the Irish built the jails in this country and then filled them. [*Laughter*] And then I—no, I'll tell you, you're thinking what I did, and for a long time I was very chary about saying anything. I didn't know why he was so proud of that—[*laughter*]—until I got a ticket once from a Chicago cop. [*Laughter*] And when I heard that brogue I found out what he meant. [*Laughter*] The police forces of America are largely Irish. So, by now, I can tell you, I've got a pub named after me in Ballyporeen. [*Laughter*] But I just want you to know—you know, I'm very leery about ethnic jokes now in my position. [*Laughter*] So, the only ones I can tell are Irish. [*Laughter*]

Well, no, I really set out to tell you that on that same trip to Ballyporeen, where I found that pub, I went up on Cashel Rock later, where St. Patrick erected the first cross in Ireland. And the young Irish guide who was showing me around took me through the cemetery, and he stopped beside one very ancient, large tombstone there. And the inscription on the tombstone read: "Remember me as you pass by. For as you are, so once was I. And as I am, you too will be. So, be content to follow me." And that was too much for some Irishmen of more recent vintage—[*laughter*]—who had scratched underneath, "To follow you I am content. I wish I knew which way you went." [*Laughter*]

Well, I thank you all for this, and a happy St. Patrick's Day to all of you. And why didn't I find this place 7 years ago? [*Laughter*]

Mr. Troy. That's because you were in the Eire Pub in Boston, that's why. [*Laughter*] Can't keep out of the damn places, can you? [*Laughter*]

The President. No, it's those people over there that tell me where I'm going everyday.

Audience member. We love you!

The President. Well, again, thank you very much, and thank all of you.

Mr. Troy. Let's hear it for our President—President Reagan! [*Applause*]

Note: The President spoke at 1:12 p.m. at Ireland's Own restaurant.

Remarks at a St. Patrick's Day Luncheon Hosted by Speaker of the House of Representatives Jim Wright
March 17, 1988

Well, Seamus Wright—[*laughter*]—I'll keep this brief. On St. Patrick's Day, you should spend time with saints and scholars, so of course, you know, I have two more stops I have to make. [*Laughter*] I turned back to the ancient days of Ireland to find a suitable toast, and I think I have found it. St. Patrick was a gentleman who through strategy and stealth drove all the snakes from Ireland. Here's toasting to his health—but not too many toastings lest you lose yourself and then forget the good St. Patrick and see all those snakes again. [*Laughter*] I believe that, you know, let those who love us, love us, and those who don't love us, let God turn their hearts. And if He won't turn their hearts, let Him turn their ankles so we'll know them by their limp. [*Laughter*]

May you have warm words on a cold evening and a full moon on a dark night and a smooth road all the way to your door.

Note: The President spoke at 1:52 p.m. in the Speaker of the House of Representatives' Dining Room at the Capitol.

Statement by Assistant to the President for Press Relations Fitzwater on the Report of the President's Commission on Privatization
March 18, 1988

Today the President received the report of the President's Commission on Privatization. Chairman Linowes and members of the Commission worked hard to prepare this final report, and they are to be congratulated on an excellent achievement. The Commission's spirit of bipartisanship, as well as the diverse backgrounds of its members, make the Commission's forward-looking recommendations especially useful as we consider what steps are needed to attain an appropriate division of responsibilities between the Federal Government and the private sector.

The work of the Commission on Privatization is close to the President's philosophy of government. He campaigned for the Presidency on a platform of limited government, and one of the earliest priorities of this administration was to reestablish the proper relationship between the Federal Government, which had grown too big and powerful, and the private sector. We are continuing those efforts, and the Commission's report today is an important contribution to them. The Commission's recommendations on privatization will prove greatly helpful to this and future administrations and to the Congress in achieving a proper balance between the public and private sectors. The President commends the members of the Commission for an excellent achievement.

Letter to the Speaker of the House of Representatives and Chairman of the Senate Foreign Relations Committee Reporting on the Cyprus Conflict

March 18, 1988

Dear Mr. Speaker: (Dear Mr. Chairman:)

In accordance with Public Law 95–384, I am submitting to you a bimonthly report on progress toward a negotiated settlement of the Cyprus question.

The Republic of Cyprus held presidential elections in mid-February 1988 and elected George Vassiliou, an independent candidate, as President of the Republic for a five-year term. I sent a message of congratulations to President Vassiliou noting the friendly, warm relations that exist between our two countries. I expressed the hope that his election would be the signal for progress in the search for a lasting, mutually acceptable settlement of the Cyprus problem.

There have been recent developments that reinforce my belief that there is an opportunity at this time to make real progress toward a settlement of the dispute. The new Special Representative of the United Nations Secretary General, Mr. Oscar Camilion, arrived in Cyprus shortly after the election of President Vassiliou and expressed his hope that there will be progress in the near future. Prior to his departure for Cyprus, Mr. Camilion met with U.S. Ambassador to the United Nations Vernon Walters and with the U.S. Special Cyprus Coordinator M. James Wilkinson. Our representatives voiced full support for Mr. Camilion's efforts and for the good offices mission of the U.N. Secretary General.

We also have seen the development of a new climate between Greece and Turkey as a result of the recent meetings between Prime Ministers Papandreou and Ozal. The two leaders have resolved to increase their cooperation and to work toward lasting solutions of the issues dividing Greece and Turkey. We welcome this development and the resultant building of confidence and lessening of tensions in the area. This new dialogue in the Greek-Turkish relationship can serve as an example and positive force in the region.

While there are thus hopeful signs, it remains for the parties directly involved to work diligently toward the common goals of peace and justice. Leaders of both sides face a challenge requiring patience and the exercise of farsighted statesmanship. I want to reemphasize that the Government and people of the United States of America remain committed to helping them work toward a lasting, mutually acceptable settlement.

Sincerely,

RONALD REAGAN

Note: Identical letters were sent to Jim Wright, Speaker of the House of Representatives, and Claiborne Pell, chairman of the Senate Foreign Relations Committee.

Announcement of the United States Delegation of Observers for Elections in El Salvador
March 18, 1988

The President today announced the members of the United States delegation of election observers to the March 20, 1988, legislative/municipal elections in El Salvador. The President believes that this round of elections represents yet another example of the development and consolidation of democracy in Central America.

The delegation of U.S. observers will be cochaired by Senator Richard Lugar and Congressman Jack Murtha. The other members of the delegation are:

Senator Christopher S. Bond
Congressman Mickey Edwards
Congressman John Kasich
Congressman John Rowland
Congresswoman Beverly Byron
Congressman Alan Mollohan
Howard Penniman, elections expert, American Enterprise Institute
Mario Paredes, executive director, Northwest Regional Center for Hispanics (New York)
Merom Brachman, retired chairman, Ohio Ethics Commission
Eugenia Kemble, executive director, Free Trade Union Institute
Susan Kaufman-Purcell, Council on Foreign Relations (New York)
John White, former chairman, Democratic National Committee
Devier Pierson, Pierson Semmes and Finley
James Dyer, Deputy Assistant to the President
Ambassador Edwin G. Corr, U.S. Ambassador to El Salvador
Fritz Korth, advisory member, International Foundation for Electoral Systems
Betsy Warren, Principal Deputy Assistant Secretary of State for Legislation

In contrast to recent developments in Panama and Nicaragua, El Salvador's democratic elections demonstrate the commitment of the Government and citizens of El Salvador to democratic processes and rule. The Communist guerrillas of El Salvador, the Farabundo Marti National Liberation Front (FMLN), who have been supported by Nicaragua's Communist regime since 1979, have chosen not to participate in the elections and have instead engaged in the acts of violence and terrorism to intimidate citizens and disrupt the elections. But as has been demonstrated in the past, the determined and courageous people of El Salvador have never succumbed to the violence and threats from the FMLN. They have voted in record numbers in a progression of elections from 1982 on, repudiating the Communist FMLN and affirming their commitment to democracy. The President strongly supports the people of El Salvador and their democratic aspirations and is demonstrating this support by sending this delegation.

Executive Order 12631—Working Group on Financial Markets
March 18, 1988

By virtue of the authority vested in me as President by the Constitution and laws of the United States of America, and in order to establish a Working Group on Financial Markets, it is hereby ordered as follows:

Section 1. Establishment. (a) There is hereby established a Working Group on Financial Markets (Working Group). The Working Group shall be composed of:

(1) the Secretary of the Treasury, or his designee;

(2) the Chairman of the Board of Governors of the Federal Reserve System, or his designee;

(3) the Chairman of the Securities and Exchange Commission, or his designee; and

(4) the Chairman of the Commodity Futures Trading Commission, or her designee.

(b) The Secretary of the Treasury, or his designee, shall be the Chairman of the Working Group.

Sec. 2. Purposes and Functions. (a) Recognizing the goals of enhancing the integrity, efficiency, orderliness, and competitiveness of our Nation's financial markets and maintaining investor confidence, the Working Group shall identify and consider:

(1) the major issues raised by the numerous studies on the events in the financial markets surrounding October 19, 1987, and any of those recommendations that have the potential to achieve the goals noted above; and

(2) the actions, including governmental actions under existing laws and regulations (such as policy coordination and contingency planning), that are appropriate to carry out these recommendations.

(b) The Working Group shall consult, as appropriate, with representatives of the various exchanges, clearinghouses, self-regulatory bodies, and with major market participants to determine private sector solutions wherever possible.

(c) The Working Group shall report to the President initially within 60 days (and periodically thereafter) on its progress and, if appropriate, its views on any recommended legislative changes.

Sec. 3. Administration. (a) The heads of Executive departments, agencies, and independent instrumentalities shall, to the extent permitted by law, provide the Working Group such information as it may require for the purpose of carrying out this Order.

(b) Members of the Working Group shall serve without additional compensation for their work on the Working Group.

(c) To the extent permitted by law and subject to the availability of funds therefor, the Department of the Treasury shall provide the Working Group with such administrative and support services as may be necessary for the performance of its functions.

RONALD REAGAN

The White House,
March 18, 1988.

[*Filed with the Office of the Federal Register, 11:23 a.m., March 21, 1988*]

Statement by Assistant to the President for Press Relations Fitzwater on the Formation of the Working Group on Financial Markets

March 18, 1988

In view of the extraordinary events in the financial markets in 1987 and the findings of the numerous market studies, including studies by Federal agencies, self-regulatory organizations, and the President's Task Force on Market Mechanisms, it is clear that further, closely coordinated work needs to be done. Despite our financial system's notable success in withstanding the shock of those events, we need to ensure that the public is protected by assuring financial integrity of the markets during periods of significant price changes.

We also must be concerned about the quality and fairness of our markets for all participants and the willingness of individuals and institutions to participate in these markets. In addressing these issues, we must keep clearly in mind the vital national interest in preserving the efficiency and international competitiveness of our financial markets and institutions.

To these ends, the President is asking the Secretary of the Treasury to chair a select Working Group on Financial Markets to coordinate the Government's efforts to evaluate recommendations and to seek the resolution of the complex issues involved. The other Working Group members will be the Chairmen of the Board of Governors of the Federal Reserve System, the Securities and

Exchange Commission, and the Commodities Futures Trading Commission.

The President expects that they will consult with the various exchanges, clearinghouses, self-regulatory bodies, and major market participants as they proceed. He has asked the Working Group to consult also with the Congress as this work progresses. The goals of the Working Group are twofold: first, to ensure the continued integrity, competitiveness, and efficiency of our nation's financial markets, and second, to maintain the public's confidence in those markets. Much can be done within the existing legal framework by both regulators and market participants, but the President has asked the Working Group to consider also whether any legislature changes are necessary.

In the President's judgment and that of his senior advisers, the major items the Working Group should address are investor confidence, credit and settlement system risks, and maintenance of orderly, efficient, and internationally competitive markets. The issues raised by the several studies that in our view merit the greatest attention are listed below. None of them is simple, and while deserving high priority, may not be resolved quickly or without considerable reflection. A significant number of issues have been suggested by most of the reports and commentators, while others have had more limited support. The list, which was developed in consultation with all members of the Working Group, is not intended to include all of the suggestions made nor all of the items that may be addressed by the Working Group; nor is it intended to imply an endorsement of all items listed. The major issues the President has asked the Working Group to address are attached.

Issues for Consideration

A. Investor Confidence

1. Adequacy of mechanisms to address intermarket front-running and price manipulation.
2. Expansion of information dissemination and trade processing capacities of exchanges, member firms, service bureaus, and clearing systems.
3. Better evaluation and enforcement of affirmative market-maker obligations.
4. Adequacy of customer protection rules and their enforcement in all markets.
5. Adequacy of regulatory agency and self-regulatory organization resources and staffing levels.
6. Assessment of a variety of approaches to assuring better access and order execution for individuals' orders.

B. Credit System Issues

1. Coordination of clearing system operations and information exchange.
2. Adequacy of private sector capital for futures floor traders, market-makers, broker-dealers, and futures commission merchants, including any appropriate revisions of capital rules.
3. Adequacy and clarity of private sector credit arrangements for exchange settlement systems and market participants.
4. Progress toward on-line clearing and same-day trade comparisons for all equity and derivative products.
5. Changes in margin requirements and additional security deposits for financial protection against price-spike volatility, settlement capability for variation margin, and positions with concentrated risk.
6. Establishment of harmonized leverage requirements for uncovered customer positions in cash and derivative markets.

C. Market Mechanisms

1. The desirability of simultaneous, brief trading halts in all markets based on clear authority and carefully established and known standards.
2. Coordination of openings and continuing trading of index futures and options with the trading of the underlying stocks.
3. Establishment of separate trading of index "baskets" of stock.
4. Providing for or requiring physical delivery for settlement of index futures and options.
5. Development of block trading procedures for index futures and options on futures.
6. Revision of the equity market short-sale rules.
7. Use of "open outcry," "one price auc-

tion," and specialist book disclosure approaches in large, intraday order imbalance situations in specialist markets to facilitate price discovery and market clearing and minimize intermarket disruptions and discontinuities.

8. Emergency measures to restrict large, rapid liquidations of positions.

9. Preestablished standards for shortened trading hours for all markets in periods of sustained heavy volume.

10. Investigation of the usefulness of enhanced reporting requirements for broker-dealer recordkeeping, large trader tracking systems, and program trades, with due consideration to financial privacy concerns and international capital flows.

11. Imposition of price limits for index futures and options.

12. Full day closings in response to specified price moves.

13. Restrictions on access to the DOT system for program trades based on either volume or price move limits.

14. Price limits on individual stocks.

15. Aggregate cash and derivative market position limits.

D. Regulatory Structure

1. Careful consideration of the desirability of more formal intermarket coordination and cooperation mechanisms, different regulatory regimes, a "tie-breaking referee" for intermarket issues, or emergency powers.

2. Development of mechanisms for international coordination on multimarket issues.

Proclamation 5777—National Agriculture Day, 1988
March 18, 1988

By the President of the United States of America

A Proclamation

As a Nation we are blessed deeply and in many ways. The agriculture that sustains us is truly one of those blessings. We do well to give thanks for our bountiful crops. They are the yield of our fertile fields; of the skills and cooperation of countless Americans, including farmers, ranchers, scientists, farm organizations, commerce, and government; and, surely, of the liberty in which the American people are free to work, create, and produce for their mutual benefit.

Some of the world's best farmland is here in our country; roughly half of the land in the contiguous United States has a capacity for crop production. Our bounty supplies needs both at home and abroad; today, one American farmer produces enough food and fiber for 114 people. Our agricultural production, processing, and marketing provide jobs, generate wealth, and strengthen our economy, our standard of living, and our position in world trade markets. Thanks to our agricultural efficiency, American consumers, on average, spend less of their income on food than do citizens of any other nation.

As we give thanks for our rich harvests, let us be sure to express gratitude to all those in agriculture and its related endeavors who through the years have contributed so much to our Nation and the world and who continue to shape and to share the spirit and the heritage of the American people.

The Congress, by Senate Joint Resolution 265, has designated March 20, 1988, as "National Agriculture Day" and authorized and requested the President to issue a proclamation in observance of this event.

Now, Therefore, I, Ronald Reagan, President of the United States of America, do hereby proclaim March 20, 1988, as National Agriculture Day. I call upon the people of the United States to observe this day with appropriate ceremonies and activities.

In Witness Whereof, I have hereunto set my hand this eighteenth day of March, in the year of our Lord nineteen hundred and eighty-eight, and of the Independence of the United States of America the two hundred and twelfth.

RONALD REAGAN

[Filed with the Office of the Federal Register, 11:22 a.m., March 21, 1988]

Note: The proclamation was released by the Office of the Press Secretary on March 19.

Radio Address to the Nation on the Deployment of United States Forces to Honduras and the Strategic Defense Initiative

March 19, 1988

My fellow Americans:

There was a nice celebration of St. Patrick's Day up on Capitol Hill this week, but believe me, that wasn't the only reason Congress knew I had my Irish up. On two issues vital to our national security, I had some stern words for some of our lawmakers.

The first has to do with the safety of our hemisphere. Back in the early 1980's, there were those who argued that the prospects for democracy in Central America were bleak and we would do little to prevent Marxist dictatorships there. But after the administration built a consensus, Congress finally passed our economic and military aid program, and today the countries of Costa Rica, El Salvador, Honduras, and Guatemala are democratic. Indeed, tomorrow, El Salvador—the nation some in Congress were gloomiest about—will host congressional and municipal elections, just one more sign of a successful democratic reform in that nation and region.

However, in one Central American nation, Nicaragua, the cause of freedom is in grave peril. Up until the end of last month, the United States had been aiding the freedom fighters who've been trying to restore democracy by resisting the regime of Soviet-backed Sandinista Communists. However, just as the heroic efforts of the democratic resistance have forced the Communists to cut back on their aggression abroad and to make peace concessions, the Congress, in a close vote, decided to cut off aid to the freedom fighters.

Since the Congress rejected our package of assistance for those fighting for freedom in Nicaragua, the Communist dictators have done exactly as we predicted. Instead of giving peace a chance, the aid cutoff is giving the Communist dictators a chance—a chance they long hoped for, a chance to smash their opponents. They have hardened their negotiating position. They have fired the mediator, Cardinal Obando y Bravo. They have sent mobs of thugs against peaceful opposition groups. And now, instead of negotiating for a cease-fire, they have launched a major military assault on the weakened *contras,* invading democratic Honduras in the process.

Now, from the beginning, our Central American policy has been designed to prevent another Cuba and to let the people of Nicaragua win back their freedom and their independence from the Soviet Union on their own, to do this without having to commit American military personnel. But now, because of Congress' aid cutoff last month, the Sandinistas have mounted their major cross-border incursion into Honduras. In response, and at the request of President Azcona, we have sent American military units to Honduras to conduct an emergency readiness exercise. Our purpose is to send a signal to the Governments and peoples of Central America about the seriousness with which we view the situation.

The freedom fighters are in desperate need of support. If they are to remain a viable and effective force, they must have assistance now. There is not a moment to spare. If urgently needed help does not reach them soon, we face the prospect of a collapse of the democratic resistance, the attendant consolidation of a Marxist-Leninist regime in Nicaragua, and an increased threat to Nicaragua's democratic neighbors. Ultimately, we will face a national security crisis of the first order and an enormous human tragedy.

Now, another vital security matter where the Congress has not been doing its job has involved our work on a strategic defense against ballistic missiles. This coming week marks the 5th anniversary of my call for just such a Strategic Defense Initiative, or SDI. I am taking this occasion to note that the Soviets have been making extensive progress on their own SDI-like program in the last few years. Indeed, the Soviets may be preparing a nationwide defense, which would mean a breakout from the restrictions of the ABM treaty, which prohibits a massive deployment of such a system. However, at the very moment when the Soviets are so far along in their efforts, Congress has been cutting back ours. Every year Congress has cut the SDI budget. We are now 1 to 2 years behind schedule, and this despite the fact that the actual SDI program is progressing faster than we expected. But our scientists and engineers must have Congress' support, and they must have it soon.

So, I can't think of two more vital national security issues than these: preventing the establishment of a Soviet beachhead in Central America and erecting a defense shield that will reduce the nuclear threat that has so overshadowed the postwar era. That's why we cannot permit some in Congress to take dangerous risks with America's national security.

Until next week, thanks for listening, and God bless you.

Note: The President spoke at 12:06 p.m. from the Oval Office at the White House.

Nomination of G. Philip Hughes To Be an Assistant Secretary of Commerce
March 21, 1988

The President today announced his intention to nominate G. Philip Hughes to be an Assistant Secretary of Commerce (Export Enforcement). This is a new position.

Since 1986, Mr. Hughes has been Deputy Assistant Secretary for Technology Transfer and Control at the Department of State in Washington, DC. Prior to this he was Director for Latin American Affairs for the National Security Council, 1985–1986. Mr. Hughes was Deputy Assistant to the Vice President for National Security Affairs for the Office of the Vice President, 1981–1985; Assistant Director for Intelligence Policy for the Office of the Secretary of Defense, 1979–1981; research fellow for the Brookings Institution, 1978–1979; and assistant analyst for national security and the international affairs division for the Congressional Budget Office, 1975–1978.

Mr. Hughes graduated from the University of Dayton (B.A., 1972), Tufts University (M.A., 1974; M.A., 1975), and Harvard University (M.P.A., 1978). Mr. Hughes received the Secretary of Defense Medal for Distinguished Public Service, 1985. He was born September 7, 1953, in Dayton, OH. He is married and currently resides in Falls Church, VA.

Nomination of Frederick M. Bernthal To Be an Assistant Secretary of State
March 21, 1988

The President today announced his intention to nominate Frederick M. Bernthal to be Assistant Secretary of State for Oceans and International Environmental and Scientific Affairs. He would succeed John Dimitri Negroponte.

Since 1983 Dr. Bernthal has been Commissioner for the United States Nuclear

Regulatory Commission in Washington, DC. Prior to this, he was chief legislative assistant for U.S. Senator Howard Baker, 1980–1983, and legislative assistant, 1978–1979. He was associate professor of chemistry and physics at Michigan State University, 1975–1978, and assistant professor, 1970–1975. Dr. Bernthal was visiting scientist for Niels Bohr Institute at the University of Copenhagen, 1976–1977, and staff postdoctoral scientist at Yale University, 1969–1970.

Dr. Bernthal graduated from Valparaiso University (B.S., 1964) and the University of California at Berkeley (Ph.D., 1969). He was born January 10, 1943, in Sheridan, WY. He is married, has one child, and resides in Washington, DC.

Remarks on Signing the Afghanistan Day Proclamation
March 21, 1988

Well, we're gathered here today to mark the beginning of a new year for the valiant, freedom-loving people of Afghanistan. We may be approaching an historic moment. We all hope that what we hear from Moscow means there will be a complete and irreversible withdrawal of all the Soviet forces from Afghanistan, that the Afghan people will be able to freely determine their own future, and that the millions of refugees can return to their homes with dignity. The struggle for freedom waged by the people of Afghanistan is inspiration to free people all over the world. We have supported them in their effort to liberate their country from foreign domination, and we'll continue that support as long as it's needed. As a free people we can do no less, for their struggle is our struggle.

And with that said, I shall sign the proclamation.

Note: The President spoke at 1:35 p.m. in the Roosevelt Room at the White House.

Proclamation 5778—Afghanistan Day, 1988
March 21, 1988

By the President of the United States of America

A Proclamation

March 21 marks the beginning of a new year in a bitter decade for the people of Afghanistan. This may well be a climactic year, and we hope with the Afghan people that it will see the complete withdrawal of Soviet troops and self-determination for the people of Afghanistan. For more than 8 years, the courageous Afghans have suffered and died under the boot of the Soviet Army, which invaded to prop up an illegitimate, unrepresentative, and discredited regime. Let us take this occasion, therefore, to remember the sorrow and to salute the heroism of the Afghan people. They have fought valiantly and against heavy odds to free themselves from the yoke of oppression—from assaults on their liberty, their sovereignty, their dignity, their lives, and their very way of life.

It now appears possible that the tenacity and tremendous sacrifices of the Afghan people will bear fruit in the coming period. The Soviet leadership seems to have finally recognized that the will of the Afghan people to be free cannot be broken. Indications of Soviet willingness to withdraw are an important step forward, though their seriousness can be proven only by the actual, and total, removal of Soviet troops from Afghan soil. To be acceptable, Soviet withdrawal must be complete, irreversible, and verifiable.

Our objectives have been and remain: prompt and complete withdrawal of Soviet forces; restoration of Afghanistan to an independent, nonaligned status; self-determination for the Afghans; and return of refugees in safety and honor. I reiterated this commitment and our support for the brave Afghan Mujahidin in my meeting last November with Afghan Alliance leader Yunis Khalis. I said the same to General Secretary Gorbachev last December.

The United States Government has also repeatedly told the Soviet leadership that any guarantees of noninterference that they and we would undertake must be symmetrical. An agreement at Geneva must not serve as a pretext for continued Soviet military support to the discredited minority Kabul regime. Some 120 members of the United Nations have voted year after year for self-determination in Afghanistan, recognizing that the present government in Kabul does not represent the Afghan people but is a direct result of outside interference. The Mujahidin and the refugees are the true voice of the Afghan people.

I am proud of the strong support provided the Afghan cause over the past 7 years by my Administration, by the United States Congress, and by the American people. Our commitment to the freedom of the Afghan people will not end should the Soviets withdraw. We will join other nations and international organizations to help the Afghans rebuild their country and their institutions; millions of men, women, and children will be returning to a country devastated by Soviet aggression.

The United States has consistently supported the Afghans in their long ordeal. That support will continue. We will rejoice with them when true peace is achieved and Afghanistan once again takes its rightful place in the community of nations. Let us pray and strive to make sure that this moment of liberation will come soon.

Now, Therefore, I, Ronald Reagan, President of the United States of America, by virtue of the authority vested in me by the Constitution and laws of the United States, do hereby proclaim March 21, 1988, as Afghanistan Day. I call upon the people of the United States to observe this day with appropriate ceremonies and activities.

In Witness Whereof, I have hereunto set my hand this 21st day of March, in the year of our Lord nineteen hundred and eighty-eight, and of the Independence of the United States of America the two hundred and twelfth.

RONALD REAGAN

[*Filed with the Office of the Federal Register, 4:50 p.m., March 21, 1988*]

Nomination of George F. Murphy, Jr., To Be Deputy Director of the United States Arms Control and Disarmament Agency
March 21, 1988

The President today announced his intention to nominate George F. Murphy, Jr., to be Deputy Director of the United States Arms Control and Disarmament Agency. He would succeed David F. Emery.

Since 1986 Mr. Murphy has been a consultant with the American Nuclear Energy Council in Washington, DC. Prior to this, he was director of the Senate National Security Office, 1977–1986; executive director of the Joint Committee on Atomic Energy, 1975–1977; deputy director of the Joint Committee on Atomic Energy, 1968. He served in the Central Intelligence Agency, 1950–1958.

Mr. Murphy graduated from Harvard University (A.B., 1949). He was born May 1, 1924, in Boston, MA. He served in the United States Army Air Corps, 1942–1946. Mr. Murphy is married, has two children, and resides in Bethesda, MD.

Remarks to the House of Representatives Republican Conference
March 22, 1988

Our job in the next few months is to keep the leadership on the other side of the aisle from ramming through legislation that would send the longest peacetime economic expansion on record into a tailspin. You know the legislation I mean—plant closing regulations, protectionist trade legislation, a huge hike in the minimum wage which will guarantee unemployment for millions of poor urban teenagers, costly new entitlement programs, and hidden tax increases. Yes, working together, we've kept the rascals in the majority in line. The stakes in our continued success are high. When economist Jude Wanninski was asked not long ago why the stock market crashed on October, he replied—here are his words—"the perception that the Congress, controlled by the Democratic Party, which is a party of pessimists, believes we must have protectionist trade legislation, we must have tax increases, we must even have a recession" and the fear that Congress might have seized control of economic policy from the administration. Well, thanks to you, in the last several months we've proven to the world that the party of faith, hope, and opportunity is still in the driver's seat.

In a vote you may cast today, you can reassure the world once again. I'm talking about the so-called Civil Rights Restoration Act of 1987, commonly known as the Grove City bill. Equality before the law is the American standard. We can never allow ourselves to fall short. Discrimination is an evil, pure and simple, and cannot ever be tolerated. Ending discrimination and protecting civil rights are not, however, the issues at stake here. The real issue is that accepting one dollar in Federal aid, direct or indirect, would bring entire organizations under Federal control, from the charitable social service organizations to grocery stores to churches and synagogues.

Over the weekend a spokesman for the National Federation of Independent Businesses said that, "There is a lot of confusion out there." The group is telling all small businessmen that it would like to sustain the President's veto so that an alternative can be passed which clarifies who is covered and who isn't. "Confusion" is exactly the right word. As Bob Michel and Trent Lott said so aptly—the House was given almost no opportunity to amend the bill to make its intent clear. Jim Sensenbrenner was given a one-shot amendment which would have been very helpful if it had passed, but the Rules Committee gave the rest of you no opportunity to strengthen the bill on the floor so that the American public could know for sure what the legislation accomplished.

I ask you, therefore, to sustain my veto so that we Republicans can demonstrate our commitment to civil rights and our resolve to overturn the Grove City decision in a responsible manner. With my veto message on the Grove City bill, I transmitted to Congress the Civil Rights Protection Act of 1988, which is designed to ensure equality of opportunity and eliminate discrimination, while preserving our basic freedoms. It would strengthen the civil rights coverage of education institutions and accommodate other concerns raised during congressional consideration of the Grove City issue. It would extend the Federal civil rights laws to an entire plant or facility receiving Federal aid, but it would not single out certain sectors of our economy for nationwide coverage, as S. 557 would. If my veto is sustained, this is the bill that Republicans can all help move through the Congress to strengthen the protections afforded the civil rights of our citizens.

Now, let me turn to another area: our national security. If anyone still doubted what you and I've been saying for years—that the road to peace is through the strength of America and its friends—you'd think the INF treaty would have set their doubts to rest. But apparently it hasn't. The same issue is at stake in Central America today, and the same people are making the same old mistakes. Those who led the fight against our package of assistance to the democratic resistance cannot escape responsibility for what happened. Immediately after the House vote against our package of aid to the freedom fighters, Daniel Ortega called for the "complete and total defeat" of the *contras*. Our critics—the ones who told us that taking pressure off of the Sandinistas would move them in a more democratic direction—these critics dismissed Ortega's words as "idle rhetoric." We know now that physical preparations for the incursion began immediately.

This incursion is no mere political mistake by the Sandinistas. It is part of a broad offensive that is both military and political. It is meant to deliver a knockout blow to the democratic resistance. And rather than pointing the way to more democracy, the cutoff of aid has also been followed by more harassment and oppression in Nicaragua—including attacks with rocks, chains, and pipes by Sandinista-sponsored mobs on political demonstrations; the harassment of opposition journalists; and not-so-veiled threats to the opposition parties. Rarely has a political proposition been tested so fully and conclusively. Opponents of our package of aid to the freedom fighters said that little or no assistance would mean more democracy and less war, but just the opposite has occurred.

The truth about Nicaragua is getting out. Early last week, for example, I spoke to major contributors to the United Jewish Appeal and got a warm response when I talked about Sandinista anti-Semitism and Sandinista ties to drugs, Castro, and terrorism. I mentioned that Sandinista leaders had been trained by the PLO, and the one hijacker who died in a PLO hijacking of an El Al airline was a Sandinista who now has a powerplant named after him in Nicaragua. I mentioned the attacks on Managua's only synagogue. And I mentioned, too, the line from the Commission on Organized Crime report tying members of the Sandinista leadership to international drug trafficking.

This issue is not going away and will be coming back to the Hill again. We're determined to get continued assistance for the resistance. And if we stick together, this time we'll make it. It's issues like these I've mentioned today, issues that will chart the course of America into the next century, that make me determined to leave the next Republican President a more Republican House of Representatives. We've got a lot of work left before this old cowboy climbs up on his horse and rides off into the sunset. But I have a feeling that when the credits roll up on the screen for the hit show "GOP Administration—1981 to 1989 and Beyond," the last credit will read: "Don't miss the exciting sequel: 'A GOP House of Representatives in the nineties.'"

Thank you, and God bless you.

Note: The President spoke at 9:16 a.m. in the Caucus Room at the Cannon House Office Building.

Statement by Assistant to the President for Press Relations Fitzwater on the Establishment of the United States Nuclear Risk Reduction Center

March 22, 1988

The President has directed the establishment of the United States Nuclear Risk Reduction Center in the Department of State and has approved the designation of Assistant Secretary of State for Politico-Military Affairs H. Allen Holmes as the first Director, United States Nuclear Risk Reduction Center. These steps provide for the implementation of the agreement between the United States of America and the Union of Soviet Socialist Republics on the establishment of Nuclear Risk Reduction Centers, which was signed at the White House on September 15, 1987.

Under this agreement, which is of unlimited duration, each party is committed to establish a Nuclear Risk Reduction Center in its capital, staffing its center as it deems appropriate. The U.S. and Soviet centers will communicate by direct satellite communication links, which are capable of rapidly transmitting full texts and graphics. To help ensure the smooth operation of the centers, the U.S. and Soviet representatives will hold regular meetings at least once each year. The Nuclear Risk Reduction Centers will pass notifications required under a number of existing and, possibly, future arms control agreements, as well as "good will" notifications, which may be provided at the discretion of either party. In particular, the centers will be used to transmit the notifications required under the INF treaty once that treaty enters into force. The centers are expected to begin operation in April.

Ambassador Holmes will retain his responsibilities as Assistant Secretary of State for Politico-Military Affairs. He will be assisted in the day-to-day management of the center by a staff director appointed by the Department of State and a deputy staff director appointed by the Department of Defense. The centers will operate 24 hours a day.

The President is pleased to announce this step, which advances his efforts to increase strategic stability and to reduce the risk of war through accident or miscalculation. The ribbon cutting ceremony for the U.S. center will take place at the Department of State at 11:35 this morning. Secretary Shultz and Foreign Minister Shevardnadze will participate.

Nomination of Robert S. Gelbard To Be United States Ambassador to Bolivia
March 22, 1988

The President today announced his intention to nominate Robert S. Gelbard, a career member of the Senior Foreign Service, Class of Minister-Counselor, as Ambassador to the Republic of Bolivia. He would succeed Edward Morgan Rowell.

Since 1985 Mr. Gelbard has been Deputy Assistant Secretary for the Bureau of Inter-American Affairs at the Department of State. Previously, he was Director of the Office of Southern African Affairs, 1984–1985, and Deputy Director of the Office of Western European Affairs of the Bureau of European and Canadian Affairs, 1982–1984. From 1978 to 1982, he was first secretary in Paris, France; financial economist for the Office of European Regional Political and Economic Affairs for the Bureau of European and Canadian Affairs, 1976–1978; and an international economist for the Office of Development Finance at the Bureau of Economic and Business Affairs, 1973–1975. He served as a principal officer, 1971–1972, and consul, 1970–1971, in Porto Alegre, Brazil. Mr. Gelbard joined the Foreign Service in 1967, and served in the Peace Corps in Bolivia, 1964–1966, and in the Philippines, 1968–1970.

Mr. Gelbard graduated from Colby College (A.B., 1964) and Harvard University (M.P.A., 1979). He was born March 6, 1944, in Brooklyn, NY. He is married, has one child, and resides in Washington, DC.

Remarks to State and Local Republican Officials on Federalism and Aid to the Nicaraguan Democratic Resistance
March 22, 1988

Well, ladies and gentlemen, President Owens, thank you all very much. It's good to have you all here in Washington. As you may have noticed, Washington, DC, isn't like other cities. Harry Truman, a man famous for saying exactly what he meant in a very few words well chosen, once said of Washington, it's the kind of city that if you want a friend you should find a dog. [*Laughter*] Well, that isn't true today, at least. I've counted on your friendship and support going on 8 years now. Eight years we've hung tough and hung together, often against seemingly overwhelming odds. Anybody who has come up through elected politics as a Republican knows how important that solidarity is.

It's like a story our first Republican President, Abraham Lincoln, once told when he found out all but one of his Cabinet officers ranged against him on an important issue. His story was about a man who fell sound asleep during a revival meeting and didn't hear when the minister said, "All of you who are on the side of the Lord, stand up." Of course, everyone stood up immediately, except for this one man, who was still asleep. But the preacher was only getting started and bellowed out, "All of you who are on the side of the devil, stand up." Well, at that the man woke up and standing as straight as he could said, "I didn't exactly understand the question, parson, but I'll stand by you to the end. It does seem we're in a hopeless minority." [*Laughter*] Well, as Republicans, you may be in a minority in terms of numbers at this year's meeting of the National League of Cities, but always remember, the ideals and beliefs that you stand for are the majority beliefs in this United States of America. On everything from education to crime, federalism to welfare reform, to keeping the American economy a growth and opportunity economy, the people of this country agree with you.

Now, I know you've heard from Beryl Sprinkel [Chairman of the Council of Economic Advisers] here, and from Senator Baker [Chief of Staff to the President] and Frank Donatelli [Assistant to the President for Political and Intergovernmental Affairs], so I'll try to keep this brief. As Henry the Eighth said to each of his 6 wives, "I won't keep you long." [*Laughter*] But there are so many issues before us that I want to cover.

The first is federalism. I remember how the pundits snickered at that idea at first. But those of us who have actually served at the State and local level know it's not in Washington but in the States, the cities, and communities of this country where the real work gets done. And we know from experience that the 10 most frightening words in the English language are, "I'm from the Federal Government, and I'm here to help." [*Laughter*] Well, federalism has become the wave of the future. Just last October, I signed Executive Order 12612. Everything in this town has a number attached to it—usually a large one. But this order is a breakthrough. We took a lesson from the environmental movement, and now when any agency in the executive branch takes an action that significantly affects State or local governments, it has to prepare a federalism impact statement, which only seems proper to me. The Federalist system given us by our Founding Fathers is a precious natural resource, and every bit as much as our environment, it should be cherished and protected.

Now it's time for Congress to join us and pass a truth-in-spending initiative that requires that all legislation include a financial impact statement, detailing the measure's likely economic effects upon the private sector and State and local governments. Last month I sent to the Congress the Truth in Federal Spending Act of 1988. I hope you'll join with me and urge the Congress to promptly enact this legislation. We see the momentum of federalism in the move in States across our country to reform welfare. In my State of the Union Address, I said that some years ago the Federal Government declared a War on Poverty and poverty won. Instead of providing a ladder out of poverty, welfare became a net of dependency that held millions back. Instead of hope, we've too often bred despair and futility.

It's time, as I said to Congress, for the Federal Government to show a little humility, to let a thousand sparks of genius in the States and communities around this country catch fire and become guiding lights. You know, on the subject of federalism, I remember back when I was Governor; we had something that was a bit more common back then—campus protests. And one thing the protesters would often chant was that we should give power back to the people. I guess they didn't realize how closely I was listening. [*Laughter*]

Yes, we've made tremendous progress with federalism, but all that progress and more could be destroyed by one bill that I vetoed last week, but some hope to pass over my veto. I'm talking about the so-called Civil Rights Restoration Act of 1987. Equality before the law is the American standard. We can never allow ourselves to fall short. Discrimination is an evil, pure and simple, and cannot ever be tolerated. And there are already laws, many laws, on the books to protect our civil rights. We can ensure equality of opportunity without increasing Federal intrusion into State and local governments and the private sector.

The truth is, this legislation isn't a civil rights bill. It's a power grab by Washington, designed to take control away from States, localities, communities, parents, and the private sector and give it to Federal bureaucrats and judges. One dollar in Federal aid, direct or indirect, would bring entire organizations under Federal control—from charitable social organizations to churches and synagogues. To give just one example, if a church or a group of churches operates a nearby summer camp open to all faiths, and that camp uses surplus Federal property, not only the camp but the entire church or group of churches would come under Federal control—even if the church itself received no aid.

What does that mean? It means masses of new paperwork, random on-site compliance reviews by Federal bureaucrats, and a field day for lawyers—we'd see lawsuits multiply faster than flies in springtime. The Grove City bill would force court-ordered social engineers into every corner of American society. And that's why I won't play politics with such a vital issue. I won't cave to the demagoguery of those who cloak a big government power grab in the mantle of civil rights. I have vetoed the Grove City bill, and I ask every Senator and Representative to rise above the pressures of an election year, to make a stand for religious liberty by sustaining my veto of this dangerous bill.

Now, as a reasonable alternative, I've transmitted to Congress the Civil Rights Protection Act of 1988, which is designed to ensure equal opportunity while preserving our basic freedoms. This bill properly addresses the Supreme Court's decision in the Grove City case. It would strengthen the civil rights coverage of educational institutions and accommodates other concerns raised during congressional consideration of the Grove City issue. It also would preserve the independence of State and local governments by limiting Federal regulation to that part of a State or local entity that receives or distributes Federal assistance. It's hard to believe that anyone who thinks seriously about the current Grove City bill would ever support it.

It's like the story about a Congressman sitting in his office one day when a constituent comes by to tell him why he must vote for a certain piece of legislation. The Congressman sat back, listened, and when he was done he said, "You're right. You know, you're absolutely right." The fellow left happy. A few minutes later, another constituent came by, and this one wanted him to vote against the bill. The Congressman listened to his reasons, sat back, and said, "You know, you're right. You're right. You're absolutely right." Well, the second constituent left happy. The Congressman's wife had dropped by and was waiting outside the office when she heard these two conversations. When the second man left, she went in and said, "That first man wanted you to vote for the bill, and you said he was right. And the second one wanted you to vote against it, and you said he was right, too. You can't run your affairs that way." And the Congressman said, "You know, you're right. You're right. You're absolutely right." [*Laughter*]

The inability of some in Congress to say no to special interests is right now the biggest threat to our prosperity and our democratic way of life. And that's why few election years will be more important than 1988. As you know, reapportionment comes up just 3 years later, in 1991. Having Republicans in State and local offices is the only hope we have of getting a fair deal, and that's all we're asking for: an end to the antidemocratic and un-American practice of gerrymandering congressional districts.

In 1984 there were 367 congressional races contested by both parties. In the races, Republicans won half a million more votes than the Democrats, but the Democratic Party won 31 more seats. In California, one of the worst cases of gerrymandering in the country, Republicans received a majority of votes in the '84 congressional races, but the Democrats won 60 percent more of the seats. The fact is gerrymandering has become a national scandal. The Democratic-controlled State legislatures have so rigged the electoral process that the will of the people cannot be heard. They vote Republican but elect Democrats. A look at the district lines shows how corrupt the whole process has become. The congressional map is a horror show of grotesque, contorted shapes. Districts jump back and forth over mountain ranges, cross large bodies of water, send out little tentacles to absorb special communities and ensure safe seats. One democratic Congressman who helped engineer the gerrymandering of California once described the district lines there as his contribution to modern art. [*Laughter*] But it isn't just the district lines the Democrats have bent out of shape: It's the American values of fair play and decency. And it's time we stopped them.

Frank Fahrenkopf and the Republican Party have challenged the Democrats' gerrymandering in court, but ultimately it's in the State legislatures that the battle for fairness must be won. And that's why Republicans are going to have to campaign with all our heart and soul for Republican State legislative candidates. I promise you this: As far as the President of the United States is concerned, he's not going to be sitting around his garden sniffing roses in 1988. I'm going to be out on the campaign trail, telling the American people the truth about how the electoral process has been twisted and distorted and that it's time to give the vote back to the people. And I'm going to be telling them, in the name of the American system and in the name of fairplay: Vote Republican in 1988.

One final note, if I may. It's on a subject that concerns State and local officials and every American—every citizen who cherishes our freedom and shares a concern for our national security. I'm talking about the crisis developing in Nicaragua. No, crisis is not too strong a term. Those who voted to cut off aid to the freedom fighters claimed it would bring peace to Nicaragua. We pleaded with them that abandoning our friends in the region was no way to bring peace. We warned that even though we cut off the freedom fighters the Soviets would continue their massive aid to the Communists. And as I pointed out in my press conference, Soviet military aid to the Communist Sandinista regime doubled in the first 2 months of this year compared to last year. Well, our worst fears have come to pass. Only 7 weeks after the first vote in Congress, the Sandinista Communists have launched an offensive against the freedom fighters, hoping to deliver a killer blow before anyone can come to their rescue. The freedom fighters, with all aid cut off, sit trapped inside Nicaragua, prey for the Sandinistas and their Soviet-supplied weapons. Who can't but question whether the only plan that Daniel Ortega ever intended for the democratic resistance was their elimination?

The House leadership, who played hardball to win the vote to cut off aid, now says it won't accept responsibility for the destruction of the freedom fighters. Well, if the freedom fighters are extinguished and Communist rule is consolidated in Nicaragua, the American people will be the ones to decide who is responsible. Congress must immediately redress the grave mistake they've made and send aid urgently to the freedom fighters before it's too late. In every forum available to you, with your constituents and with your Representatives in the Congress, make your feelings on this issue known, and do it now because soon it may well be too late.

Well, I've spoken for long enough. I'm reminded of the quip that Henry Clay once made when one of his antagonists in the Senate, in the middle of a dull and lengthy speech, turned to him and said, "You, sir, speak for the present generation. I speak for posterity." Clay interrupted him and said, "Yes, and you seem resolved to keep on speaking till the arrival of your audience." [*Laughter*] Well, I won't do that today. I've said enough. Thank you all very much. God bless you all.

Note: The President spoke at 11:47 a.m. in Room 450 of the Old Executive Office Building. In his opening remarks, he referred to Donna Owens, president of the National Conference of Republican Mayors and Municipal Elected Officials.

Remarks at a Fundraising Reception for Senator Chic Hecht of Nevada
March 22, 1988

It's good to be here and to see one of my oldest and truest friends, a former Senator and a former Governor, but always a current statesman, Paul Laxalt. For both Paul and me, one of the highest priorities of this election year is to make sure that another old and true friend stays where he belongs: in the United States Senate. And, of course, I'm talking about Senator Chic Hecht.

Now, we're all together on that. That's why we're here. And don't think I'm not aware of and don't appreciate what each of you is doing to help Chic. And I just heard, as evidence, of what you've done. Well, I am, and I do. Chic is going to have a tough race. We all know that. But he's a scrapper. Time and again his opponents, as well as the press, have underestimated him, given him up for goners, only to see him out ahead of the pack on election day. This year they've been writing him off again, as you were told. You didn't know you were using a couple of my lines. [*Laughter*] He was 31 points down in the polls just a while back, and that didn't phase Chic. He got to work, and now it's the opposition that's sweating. And he's narrowed that gap, as you've been told, to just 7 points, and he's closing fast.

That's the kind of spirit I like. It reminds me of reading a poll about another candidate in January 1980. [*Laughter*] It was taken at a National Press Club luncheon here in Washington on the eve of the primary season. Those in attendance were asked who would be the next President of the United States. Jimmy Carter got a large number of votes and so did Teddy Kennedy. But there was one candidate on the Republican side who got so few votes from the wise men of Washington that it wasn't even reported in the lineup.

Like Chic, I've had a career of being underestimated. [*Laughter*] It started a number of years back. I was under contract to Warner Brothers Studio, and when I announced that I was running for Governor and somebody told Jack Warner that, Jack thought a moment, and he said, "No, uh, uh. Jimmy Stewart for Governor—Reagan for best friend." [*Laughter*] So, I have a hunch that being underestimated will turn out to be Chic's secret weapon. Chic's going to be reelected because he stands for the kind of principles Nevada wants and America needs represented, the principles that brought so many of us here to Washington 7 years ago and brought Chic to join us 2 years later.

Through 3 Congresses, Chic and I've worked together for lower tax rates and tax reform, for strong measures like a Gramm-Rudman to put a collar on congressional spending, for a strategic defense against ballistic missiles, for judges and justices who would return the tradition of judicial restraint to the American judiciary, for a strong defense, and to support those brave souls fighting for freedom in our hemisphere and around the world. But we began working side by side long before Chic came here to Washington. Chic joined with me in 3 Presidential campaigns spanning two decades to bring our principles here to Washington. And once he made it here himself, he's stood with me more often than all but a handful of Senators, as Paul has told you.

Yes, we believe in the same things, for which I'm grateful. I sure wouldn't want to fight against Chic Hecht too often. He's got a stubborn, independent streak. He's the kind of Senator who doesn't make a lot of noise; he just gets things done for Nevada and the Nation, and more often than not he comes out on top. Nevada may be the Silver State, but Chic Hecht has gone for the gold medal among Senators, and so far as I'm concerned, he's won it.

Now I'd like to turn to a matter that shows just how critical it is to put Chic and men and women like him in the next Congress. I'm talking about Central America and the situation in Nicaragua. Last week's Sandinista attack on Honduras was greeted by too many in Congress not as the proof that funding the freedom fighters is the one way—the only way—to get the Sandinistas to the peace table and keep them there. No, one Senator spoke for too many when he shook his head about the political mistake of those in Managua—as if they'd stumbled in some primary or caucus.

Well, maybe if these critics thought for a moment, they'd just see what the nature of this so-called mistake really was. Troop movements, small-team reconnaissance missions, the positioning of fuel and supplies—in short, the logistical preparations for the incursion—began just after Congress voted to reject our package of aid to the democratic resistance. We saw it happening. This was a precise and carefully prepared operation that showed the influence of outside advisers and must have required several weeks to plan. It was not some spontaneous Sunday afternoon outing.

In other words, counting back to when we first saw logistical preparations commence and before that to when planning would have had to start, this invasion was beginning or underway even as, in late February, a group of liberal House Democrats sent a letter to anti-aid lobbyists saying that, in their words: "Nothing will bring peace faster than destroying *contra* hopes for more military aid." This was the same period in which we were warning that an end to congressional aid would set back, not advance, the cause of peace and democracy in Nicaragua.

Preparations for the incursion were continuing when Sandinista mobs were breaking up peaceful demonstrations in Managua—something they'd eased off on as the congressional vote on aid to the freedom fighters approached—but this time their attacks showed a savagery that had rarely been displayed before, as thugs pounded demonstrators with clubs and metal bars. And believe me, they did not just do this to their fellow men. They did it to groups of women and ladies who were simply walking in the streets and protesting various things the Sandinistas were doing. The stage for the attack was set even before Daniel Ortega fired the peace mediator, Cardinal Obando y Bravo, and boasted he was going to crush the *contras.*

Well, now we know he had reason to believe he could. The attack he knew was approaching involved multiple combat battalions, thousands of troops, and the close support of MI–17 and MI–25 attack helicopters—Soviet craft. Were the signs of danger ever clearer? Yet throughout this time our critics were saying over and over that only by stopping aid would we give the peace process a chance. I'm not questioning the sincerity of our critics, only their judgment.

And I'm saying that we need—America needs—more men and women on both sides of Capitol Hill with the good judgment of Chic Hecht. He's understood what's been going on in Central America from the first, and as on so many matters, I've always found him to have a cool, clear head. And I know that others have recognized these qualities in Chic as well. He's been endorsed by the Chamber of Commerce, and I understand that he just received the coveted Watch Dog of the Treasury Award. You know, he told you he was a businessman, and he is. And you know, principles of the kind that are just commonplace out in the private sector and in the business world are still in great need in our Nation's Capital.

I like to tell a little story about a community that decided they were going to raise their signal sign—or traffic signs and street signs and so forth from only being 5 feet high to 7 feet high so they would be more visible to drivers in automobiles. And the Federal Government came in and said, oh, we have a plan. We'll do that for you. We'll lower the streets 2 feet. [*Laughter*]

America needs Chic Hecht. And sincerely, I hope the next President will be a Republican and that he'll need him, too. So, I know what you're going to do, and thank you, and God bless you. A young man from the University of Nevada, Las Vegas, just before we came in, presented me with this. My name on it. And it's for those Runnin' Rebels. And I'm going to take it home with me. All right. Thank you all very much.

Note: The President spoke at 6:04 p.m. in the Grand Ballroom at the Sheraton Grand Hotel. In his closing remarks, he referred to a red windbreaker that was given to him by a University of Nevada student.

Remarks at a White House Briefing for Members of the American Business Conference

March 23, 1988

Thank you. And I was listening, and I almost didn't come out here. [*Laughter*] Well, thank you, and thank you all, and welcome once again to the White House complex.

You know as well as I do that Washington isn't always the easiest city in which to achieve a sense of shared purpose or common vision. Indeed, I'm often reminded of Harry Truman's famous comment on our Nation's Capital. He said, "If you want a friend in Washington, get a dog." [*Laughter*] But between this administration and the American Business Conference, there has been true friendship from the very first. It's been a friendship based not upon politics but upon convictions: the conviction, above all, that it's in economic freedom that men and women can give the fullest expression of their inborn creativity; that it's an economic freedom that leads most directly to economic productivity and growth.

In 1981 ABC was a cofounding member of the Tax Action Group, a group that proved crucial in convincing Congress to pass our historic tax cut. This means that you not only participated in the shaping not only of American history but of world history. For, I don't know whether you're aware of it, but the tax cut revolution has spread to nations as diverse as India, Indonesia, and Canada. And it was just last week that the British unveiled in the House of Commons tax reform for Great Britain—a reform that I'm convinced will contribute to the already growing British economy. England may be the mother of parliaments, but from the Boston Tea Party to this administration, it's the United States that has been the mother of tax revolts. You know, that's a pretty good line. I can hardly wait to try it out on Margaret Thatcher. [*Laughter*]

In 1983 I made a trip to Boston to demonstrate our commitment to high-tech entrepreneurship. I stopped at the Millipore Corporation and spent most of a full and happy day listening to America's winning companies and their formulas for economic growth. In 1984 you of ABC issued your historic study on the cost of capital, a study that gave us vital clues on how to keep our economic recovery gaining strength. In 1985 it was while addressing you that I warned the would-be tax hikers in Congress that I had my veto pen at the ready and dared them to make my day. In 1986 ABC played a key role in passing Gramm-Rudman-Hollings and our historic tax reform. In 1987 you of ABC took a lead role in forming COMET [Coalition for Open Markets and Expanded Trade], the free trade coalition, a coalition that, from its inception, has helped me to stave off protectionist legislation. And now in 1988 you of ABC represent one of the leading advocates of the trade accord between the United States and Canada, one of the most important trade agreements ever concluded.

And in a moment, I'd like to discuss world trade with you in some detail. But before I do so, it's clear from all I've just said that we have indeed been through a great deal together, you and I. And I just want to pause for a moment and let you know how much your friendship and support have meant to me, and to say: From my heart, I thank you.

Yet there's a great deal still to do in these remaining 10 months, and so to get on with business, let's consider for a moment America's role in international trade. Now, you'd think the United States never exported so much as a paper clip. The truth is that today America can claim surging manufacturing exports, the longest peacetime expansion on record, and the reality that more Americans are at work today than ever before. And in today's climate, I can just see some of those people out there saying, "Oh, yes, but that's because of the increase in population." Well, there's an answer to that. We have the highest percentage of the potential work pool employed than ever in the history of our nation. So, that takes care of the increase in population charge.

But the critics never learn. Since the third quarter of 1986 the volume of American exports has been growing some 4 times as fast as the volume of imports. And much of this export surge is in manufacturing exports. Industry after industry is finding itself in an export boom. As Business Week magazine reported recently: "Basic manufacturers, once considered a dying breed, are selling products many thought wouldn't even be made in the United States any longer—escalators to Taiwan, machine tools to West Germany, lumber to Japan, and shoes to Italy." Well, the dollar's helped, of course. But what's happening here goes beyond the dollar.

Since 1980 the United States manufacturing economy has increased its productivity more than 3 times as much as in the previous 7 years. The result is that, as one German manufacturing expert put it recently, the United States is "the best country in the world in terms of manufacturing costs." Well, all of this adds up to one thing, as another economics writer reported recently: "One of the best kept secrets in economic circles these days is that the Reagan administration"—thank you—"could end with a bang, not a whimper, as the Nation makes an apparently successful shift to an export-led economy." And I rehearsed some of those remarks before I came in, and it's absolutely true. I have not quacked once. [*Laughter*]

Too many backers of the trade bill currently under consideration in Congress talk about making America more competitive, but support provisions that would do just the opposite. They talk about saving jobs, but they want provisions that have the potential to destroy thousands, if not millions, of American jobs. We've listed our objections to this bill in detail for the House-Senate conference members. My veto pen remains ready and available if the final work product of the conference remains antitrade, anticonsumer, antijobs, and antigrowth. But my hope, which I believe you share, is that I won't have to use that pen.

Now, you all know that the House-Senate conference on the trade bill is working away and plans to finish its job soon. The conference process got off to a good, constructive start earlier this month; however, many objectionable provisions remain, including proposed procedural changes in the law. But I'm hopeful that in the next phase these will be jettisoned. Only wholesale elimination of many of the existing items will produce a bill that I can sign.

But there's another vital trade matter before the Congress, one that gives the Congress the opportunity to take positive and, indeed, historical action. I refer, of course, to our free trade agreement with Canada. Already, our two nations generate the world's largest volume of trade. Canada is by far our largest trading partner. And consider this one fact alone: The United States exports more to the province of Ontario than to the entire country of Japan. With this agreement, Canada and the

United States will be the largest free trade area on Earth. As Prime Minister Mulroney has said: "It will bring us to a new decade and a new century, on the leading edge of the world's trade and commerce."

Well, we're tearing down the walls, the tariffs, that block the flow of trade and eliminating the tangle of restrictions and regulations that bind our commerce and inhibit economic cooperation. As this agreement takes effect, Americans and Canadians will conduct business, invest, and trade where they like, rejecting beggar-thy-neighbor policies, and putting aside special interests in favor of the common interest. We've broken new territory by covering areas, such as investment and services, traditionally beyond the scope of trade agreements. What better example could there be for the GATT [General Agreement on Tariffs and Trade] Uruguay round, which is currently underway in Geneva. But success will depend in large part on people like you who are willing to operate in a truly free environment for trade and investment. And I'll be looking for your support in obtaining congressional approval for this historic, pathbreaking agreement.

Now, I know it's bad manners to quote oneself, so please forgive me if I read you a few lines from a speech I delivered all the way back in November of 1979: "A developing closeness between the United States, Canada, and Mexico could serve notice on friend and foe alike that we're prepared for a long haul, looking outward again and confident of our future; that together we're going to create jobs, to generate new fortunes of wealth for many, and provide a legacy for the children of each of our countries. Two hundred years ago, we taught the world that a new form of government, created out of the genius of man to cope with his circumstances, could succeed in bringing a measure of quality to human life previously thought impossible." Well, let us dare to dream, I said, of some future date, when the map of the world shows a North American continent united in commerce, committed to freedom where borders become what the U.S.-Canadian border is today: a meeting place rather than a dividing line.

My friends, I look forward to working with you once again in behalf of the economic freedom in which we both so deeply believe. Yes, let us dare to dream, and let us work on to make our dreams come true.

I'm going to finish with just one thing. I know I should have quit long ago, but it's just a little item that, during the war when I was flying a desk for the Air Corps, in uniform—[*laughter*]—I came across something that has been kind of a symbol of government to me and its mistakes. There was a warehouse full of filing cabinets. Someone had inspected them and found that they didn't even have historical interest, and there was no absolute use to them whatsoever. So, in that military type of correspondence, we started up through the channels a letter requesting permission to destroy those files so that we could use those file cases for things current. And all the way it went up, being endorsed, till finally the top level. And then it came back down being endorsed all the way, permission granted for the destruction of those files providing copies are made of each one. [*Laughter*]

Oh, thank you. God bless you all.

Note: The President spoke at 11:01 a.m. in Room 450 of the Old Executive Office Building.

Statement on the Fifth Anniversary of the Strategic Defense Initiative

March 23, 1988

Today marks the fifth anniversary of a program vital to our future security. On March 23, 1983, in announcing our Strategic Defense Initiative—SDI—I put forward the vision of a safer and more secure future for our children and our grandchildren, a future free from the threat of the most dangerous weapon mankind has invented: fast-flying ballistic missiles. It was on that date that I challenged our best and brightest scientific minds to undertake a rigorous program of research, development, and testing to find a way to keep the peace through defensive systems, which threaten no one. If we can accomplish this, and I am more and more convinced that we can, we will no longer have to face a future that relies on the threat of nuclear retaliation to ensure our security.

The Soviets not only are ahead of us in ballistic missiles but also are deeply engaged in their own SDI-like program. If they are allowed to keep their near monopoly in defenses, we will be left without an effective means to protect our cherished freedoms in the future. But with our own investigation of defenses well underway, we have been able to propose to the Soviets at our arms negotiations in Geneva that both of us protect our nations through increasingly effective defenses, even as we cut back deeply our strategic offensive arms. SDI, in fact, provided a valuable incentive for the Soviets to return to the bargaining table and to negotiate seriously over strategic arms reductions. And as we move toward lower levels of offense, it will be all the more important to have an effective defense.

The SDI program is progressing technologically even faster than we expected. We have demonstrated the feasibility of intercepting an attacker's ballistic missiles. We have made rapid progress on sensors, the eyes and ears of a future defensive system. And our research has produced useful spinoffs for conventional defenses and for medicine, air traffic control, and high-speed computing. The problems we face now are largely political. Every year, Congress has cut back the SDI budget. We are now 1 to 2 years behind schedule. Some of our critics question SDI because they believe we are going too fast and doing too much, while others say we should move now to deploy limited defenses—perhaps to protect our own missiles. While such a defense may initially strengthen today's uneasy balance, SDI's goal is to create a stronger, safer, and morally preferable basis for deterrence by making ballistic missiles obsolete. Thus, we seek to establish truly comprehensive defenses, defenses which will protect the American people and our allies.

The American people can never be satisfied with a strategic situation where, to keep the peace, we rely on a threat of vengeance. And we must recognize that we live in an imperfect, often violent world, one in which ballistic missile technology is proliferating despite our efforts to prevent this. We would be doing a grave and dangerous disservice to future generations if we assumed that national leaders everywhere, for all time, will be both peaceful and rational. The challenge before us is of course difficult, but with SDI, we are showing already that we have the technological knowhow, the courage, and the patience to change the course of human history.

Remarks Announcing the Soviet-United States Summit Meeting in Moscow

March 23, 1988

The President. A very brief announcement—we've begun our meetings, and of course, as you know, they're going to resume. We've only had a short time together, the Foreign Minister and myself, but can announce that it has been agreed: The Moscow summit will be from May 29th through June 3d—I'm sorry—June 2d, May 29, June 2d. Mr. Minister, do you have any——

Reporter. Mr. President, do you think you'll have an arms control treaty by then, sir?

Q. Do you think you'll have an arms control treaty to sign at that summit when you go to Moscow, sir?

The President. I have no way to answer that now. We're——

Q. Can you make enough progress to at least have agreement in principle, Mr. President?

The President. Well, I think we had an agreement in principle that even led to this before we even started. Both sides had said we want to look toward a certain proportionate decrease in arms.

Q. Then why aren't you going to sign one?

Q. What will you accomplish then, sir, at the——

The President. What?

Q. What will you accomplish with a summit if you cannot sign an agreement?

The President. Well, there are a number of other subjects that we continue to discuss with each other.

Q. Will you only go to Moscow?

The President. Look, I can't——

Q. Have you made progress on verification, Mr. President? What are the obstacles? The Intelligence Committee is warning that the Soviets might cheat.

The President. I can't report on anything else. Andrea [Andrea Mitchell, NBC News], I can't take any further questions.

Q. Mr. Foreign Minister, can we ask you a question, sir?

The Foreign Minister. We have set the date, and now we shall take care of good substance, good content, for the summit.

Soviet Withdrawal From Afghanistan

Q. Mr. Foreign Minister, can you tell us whether you've made progress with an agreement for withdrawal from Afghanistan?

The Foreign Minister. There is progress, yes.

Q. Have you agreed to withdraw?

Q. ——for withdrawal before the Geneva accords?

Note: The President spoke at 11:54 a.m. in the Rose Garden at the White House. Soviet Foreign Minister Eduard Shevardnadze spoke in Russian and his remarks were translated by an interpreter. The President and the Foreign Minister then attended a luncheon in the Residence.

Nomination of Joy Cherian To Be a Member of the Equal Employment Opportunity Commission

March 23, 1988

The President today announced his intention to nominate Joy Cherian to be a member of the Equal Employment Opportunity Commission for a term expiring July 1, 1993. This is a reappointment.

Since 1987 Dr. Cherian has been a member of the Equal Employment Opportunity Commission in Washington, DC. Prior to this he was director of international insurance law for the American Council of Life Insurance, 1983–1987. He has worked for the American Council of Life Insurance since 1973.

Dr. Cherian graduated from University of Kerala, India (B.S., 1963; B.L., 1965), Catholic University (M.A., 1974; Ph.D., 1974), and George Washington University (M.C.L., 1978). Dr. Cherian was born May 18, 1942, in Kerala State, India. He is married, has two children, and resides in Wheaton, MD.

Proclamation 5779—Modifying the Implementation of the Generalized System of Preference and the Caribbean Basin Economic Recovery Act

March 23, 1988

By the President of the United States of America

A Proclamation

1. I have determined that, under section 802(b) of the Trade Act of 1974 (the Act) (19 U.S.C. 2492(b)), as amended by the Anti-Drug Abuse Act of 1986 (Pub. L. 99–570, 100 Stat. 3207), during the previous year Panama has not cooperated fully with the United States, and has not taken adequate steps on its own, in preventing narcotic and psychotropic drugs and other controlled substances produced or processed, in whole or in part, in Panama or transported through Panama, from being sold illegally within the jurisdiction of Panama to United States Government personnel or their dependents or from being transported, directly or indirectly, into the United States, and in preventing and punishing the laundering in that country of drug-related profits or drug-related monies.

2. Pursuant to section 802(a) of the Act (19 U.S.C. 2492(a)), I have decided to deny until further notice the preferential tariff treatment under the Generalized System of Preferences (GSP) and the Caribbean Basin Economic Recovery Act (CBERA) now being afforded to articles that are currently eligible for such treatment and that are imported from Panama.

3. Section 604 of the Act (19 U.S.C. 2483) confers authority upon the President to embody in the Tariff Schedules of the United States (TSUS) (19 U.S.C. 1202) the relevant provisions of that Act, of other acts affecting import treatment, and of actions taken thereunder.

Now, Therefore, I, Ronald Reagan, President of the United States of America, acting under the authority vested in me by the Constitution and the statutes of the United States of America, including but not limited to sections 604 and 802 of the Act, do proclaim that:

(1) General headnote 3(e)(v)(A) to the TSUS is modified by striking out "Panama" from the enumeration of independent countries whose products are eligible for benefits under the GSP.

(2) General headnote 3(e)(vii)(A) to the TSUS is modified by striking out "Panama" from the enumeration of designated beneficiary countries whose products are eligible for preferential treatment under the CBERA.

(3) No article the product of Panama and entered, or withdrawn from warehouse for consumption, into the United States on or after the effective date of this Proclamation shall be eligible for preferential tariff treatment under the GSP or under the CBERA.

(4) This Proclamation shall be effective with respect to articles entered, or withdrawn from warehouse for consumption, on or after the fifteenth day following the date of the publication of this Proclamation in the *Federal Register.*

In Witness Whereof, I have hereunto set my hand this twenty-third day of March, in the year of our Lord nineteen hundred and eighty-eight, and of the Independence of the United States of America the two hundred and twelfth.

RONALD REAGAN

[*Filed with the Office of the Federal Register, 10:25 a.m., March 24, 1988*]

Nomination of L. Clair Nelson To Be a Member of the Federal Mine Safety and Health Review Commission
March 23, 1988

The President today announced his intention to nominate L. Clair Nelson to be a member of the Federal Mine Safety and Health Review Commission for a term of 6 years expiring August 30, 1994. This is a reappointment.

Since 1982 Mr. Nelson has been a Commissioner for the Federal Mine Safety and Health Review Commission in Washington, DC. Prior to this Mr. Nelson was senior vice president for the Champion International Corp., 1955–1982.

Mr. Nelson graduated from Utah State University (B.S., 1939) and George Washington University (J.D., 1947). He was born June 2, 1918, in Logan, UT. He served in the United States Army from 1941 to 1946. Mr. Nelson is married, has four children, and resides in McLean, VA.

Executive Order 12632—Exclusions From the Federal Labor-Management Relations Program
March 23, 1988

By virtue of the authority vested in me as President by the Constitution and laws of the United States of America, including Section 7103(b) of Title 5 of the United States Code, and in order to exempt certain agencies or subdivisions thereof from coverage of the Federal Labor-Management Relations Program, it is hereby ordered as follows:

Section 1. Determinations. The agencies or subdivisions thereof set forth in Section 3 of this Order are hereby determined to have as a primary function intelligence, counterintelligence, investigative, or national security work. It is also hereby determined that Chapter 71 of Title 5 of the United States Code cannot be applied to these agencies or subdivisions in a manner consistent with national security requirements and considerations. These agencies or subdivisions thereof are hereby excluded from coverage under Chapter 71 of Title 5 of the United States Code.

Sec. 2. Relationship to Executive Order No. 12559. The determinations set forth in Section 1 of this Order are the same determinations that I made at the time of and as a predicate to my issuance on May 20, 1986, of Executive Order No. 12559, which was issued for the same purpose as this Order. On July 10, 1987, Executive Order No. 12559 was held by a United States District Court to be incomplete as a matter of form, and therefore invalid, because it did not expressly set forth these determinations. *AFGE* v. *Reagan*, Civil No. 86–1587 (D.D.C.). These determinations were not expressly set forth in the text of Executive Order No. 12559 because all that Order did was amend Executive Order No. 12171 by adding the agencies or subdivisions referred to in Section 1 of this Order to the list in Executive Order No. 12171 of entities excluded from coverage of the Federal Labor-Management Relations Program, and these determinations were already expressly set forth in the text of Executive Order No. 12171, which remains in effect (as amended). This Order is not intended to reflect any belief that the form of Executive Order No. 12559 was invalid, but is intended solely to accomplish the purpose of that Order.

Sec. 3. Amendment of Executive Order No. 12171. Executive Order No. 12171 is amended by deleting Section 1–209 and inserting in its place:

Sec. 1–209. Agencies or subdivisions of the Department of Justice. (a) The Office of

Enforcement and the Office of Intelligence, including all domestic field offices and intelligence units, of the Drug Enforcement Administration.

(b) The Office of Special Operations, the Threat Analysis Group, the Enforcement Operations Division, the Witness Security Division and the Court Security Division in the Office of the Director and the Enforcement Division in Offices of the United States Marshals in the United States Marshals Service.

RONALD REAGAN

The White House,
March 23, 1988.

[Filed with the Office of the Federal Register, 10:28 a.m., March 24, 1988]

Nomination of Susan E. Alvarado To Be a Governor of the United States Postal Service

March 24, 1988

The President today announced his intention to nominate Susan E. Alvarado to be a Governor of the United States Postal Service for the term expiring December 8, 1996. She will succeed Ruth O. Peters.

Since 1987 Ms. Alvarado has been vice president of governmental relations for E. Bruce Harrison Co., Inc., in Washington, DC. Prior to this she was vice president of congressional liaison for the National Association of Broadcasters, 1983–1986. From 1981 to 1982 Ms. Alvarado was a legislative assistant to the Vice President of the United States. She served as legislative assistant to Senator Ted Stevens from 1976 to 1980.

Ms. Alvarado graduated from Ohio State University (B.A., 1975). She was born May 11, 1954, in Alexandria, VA, and currently resides in Alexandria.

Appointment of William P. Longmire, Jr., as a Member of the President's Cancer Panel

March 24, 1988

The President today announced his intention to appoint William P. Longmire, Jr., to be a member of the President's Cancer Panel for a term expiring February 20, 1991. This is a reappointment.

Since 1984 Dr. Longmire has been professor of surgery emeritus at UCLA Medical Center's department of surgery in Los Angeles, CA. Prior to this he was a professor of surgery at the UCLA Medical Center, 1948–1984.

Dr. Longmire graduated from Johns Hopkins (M.D., 1938). He was born September 14, 1913, in Sapulpa, OK. He served in the United States Air Force, 1952–1954. Dr. Longmire is married, has two children, and resides in Los Angeles, CA.

Remarks and a Question-and-Answer Session With Students and Faculty at Oakton High School in Vienna, Virginia
March 24, 1988

The President. I know that two of your Congressmen, Frank Wolf and Stan Parris, are with us here today. I hope they haven't been talked into leaving their present occupation and—[*laughter*]. Should we move the class outdoors? [*Applause*]

Well, you know, being here in school today sort of reminds me—well, would you mind if I told you one of my favorite stories about schools? It seems a little boy had to take home a bad report card. And the next day back in his classroom he walked up to his teacher and said, "Teacher, last night my daddy told me that if my grades didn't improve, somebody was going to be in big trouble. So, I'd be careful if I were you." [*Laughter*]

But it's not so very long ago that all of American education needed to improve, or we were all going to be in big trouble. Back in 1983 a report entitled "A Nation at Risk"—that report itself said that the educational foundations of our society were being eroded by "a rising tide of mediocrity that threatens our very future as a nation and a people." Well, it was time to stem that tide, to get our educational house in order, or to suffer the consequences.

I'm particularly pleased to have the opportunity to learn about what Fairfax County has done to improve the quality of your teachers. You have become leaders in promoting excellence in the teaching profession, and I'm here to find out more about what works. Next month Secretary Bennett will turn in to me a homework assignment—yes, even Cabinet members have homework assignments—one that I gave him last March, asking for a status report on American education. Come to think of it, Bill, that's an awfully long time to complete an assignment. [*Laughter*] But don't worry; your work so far has been "A-plus." But the Secretary's report will tell us what kind of progress we've made over the last 5 years, and it will tell us what things we still must do. Secretary Bennett, I'm looking forward to reading your report and to continuing to work closely with you on specific ways that we can improve education. There are few areas of American life as important to our society, to our people, and to our families as our schools.

By the way, if I could just interject something here, if there's anybody who proves that learning doesn't have to be dull, that education and fun can go together, it's our nation's Secretary of Education, Bill Bennett. Secretary Bennett has a law degree and a Ph.D. in philosophy—that's pretty serious-sounding stuff. But he also happens to be an expert on something many of you probably know quite a lot about: rock 'n' roll. [*Laughter*] And I'll prove it.

Bill, who sang "Rock Around the Clock"?

Secretary Bennett. Bill Haley and the Comets.

The President. Name the two lead singers of the Drifters.

Secretary Bennett. Clyde McPhatter and Ben E. King.

The President. And what's at the top of this week's Top Forty?

Secretary Bennett. I don't have the foggiest idea, Mr. President.

The President. You mean, you don't know the answer?

Secretary Bennett. No, sir.

The President. But, Bill, everybody knows that this week's number one song is Michael Jackson's "Man in the Mirror." [*Laughter*] But, don't feel bad, Bill; two out of three isn't bad. But there's a serious point here, one I hope you'll always remember. Learning and fun can go together. And in many ways, the more you know, the more fun you can have.

Now, some of you may have heard that I've taken to visiting schools lately to find out firsthand what's going on. I must say these trips have strengthened my confidence in our country's future. The reason? When you visit schools like Oakton, you realize that they just don't come any better or any brighter than America's students and teachers.

Two months ago I visited Suitland High School in Prince George's County, Maryland. A few years ago Suitland had problems, bad problems—low academic performance, poor attendance by both students and teachers. But Suitland High School turned itself around, and it did so in large part by supporting some of the key articles of the education reform movement: parental choice in the form of magnet schools and increased accountability on the part of students, teachers, and administrators alike.

Now I've come to Oakton. I've done so to pay tribute to your school and to your superintendent, Robert Spillane, for his outstanding efforts on behalf of excellence in education in Fairfax County. And I'm especially impressed by all you've done in attracting and retaining good teachers. And it's teaching that I'd like to speak about for a moment or two today. It seems to me that given the job that teachers do, given the number of young lives they affect, teachers deserve at least as much praise and thanks and honor as those in any other profession in our society. So, I wonder: Would you students join me for a moment in applauding your own teachers here at Oakton? [*Applause*] You don't know what you've just done. I come from a business where getting a hand was the most important thing in life.

You know, I have to tell you a little story, if I could, about a teacher that had an impact on my life. And this happens, and will happen to all of you, as the years go on. Yes, I remember a teacher. I was in his office one day—and not by invitation—by order. [*Laughter*] He was the principal as well as the English teacher in our school at that time. And in the course of his words to me he said, "Reagan, it doesn't matter much to me what you think of me now. What I'm concerned about is what you'll think of me 15 years from now." Well, I guess I just took that in stride. But, well, after 15 years I had the pleasure of telling that man how much an impact he had made on my life and then, those many years later, how important he was to me in all the things that I was doing. And to increase the pleasure I get from that memory was that it was only a short time later that I heard he had departed, he had left us, died. But I was able to tell him, and he had been right about when I would remember about him.

I was very pleased the other day to read of a poll that shows a sharp increase among college students who intend to enter the teaching profession. And I'm curious—having heard some remarks about this very subject just a moment ago—could the students in this audience who are just thinking that maybe they might become teachers please raise their hands? I see from up here a scattering of more hands than you down there probably. So, well, good for you.

I'd like to tell you something about an American hero, Sam Houston. He once wrote—in his lifetime, Sam Houston was a frontiersman, a soldier, a general, a U.S. Senator, a Governor, and yes, even a President—President of the Republic of Texas. And for a while in Maryville, Tennessee, he was a teacher. Years later, as Sam Houston looked back over a lifetime of accomplishments, he wrote that being a teacher gave him a higher feeling of dignity and self-satisfaction than any other office or honor he had ever held. Well, that speaks volumes.

Now, just why have we seen this increase in teaching lately—this increased interest, I should say. Well, in part, it's because we've begun to reward excellence in the teaching profession—as you've been told already—just as we reward excellence in any other profession. We've begun to introduce free-market principles like incentives and accountability in education. Listen, for a moment, to the recommendations of the "Nation at Risk" report: "Salaries for the teaching profession should be increased and should be professionally competitive, market-sensitive, and performance-based. Salary, promotion, tenure, and retention decisions should be tied to an effective evaluation system that includes peer review so that superior teachers can be rewarded, average ones encouraged, and poor ones either improved or terminated."

The report also recommended that "qualified individuals, including recent graduates with mathematics and science degrees, graduate students, and industrial and retired scientists could, with appropriate preparation, immediately begin teaching in these fields." And you heard that that's taking place here and is approved in your county. And it said that "incentives should be made available to attract outstanding students to the teaching profession." Well, today we can see that Fairfax County has taken these recommendations to heart. Your blue ribbon commission pointed to the necessity of recruiting and maintaining excellent teachers, and said that the people of Fairfax County are willing to pay more for good teachers if there is assurance of quality control and accountability. The school board approved the plan, and Dr. Spillane met with the teachers to get their advice and support.

Fairfax County has shown the Nation how to upgrade the teaching profession by demonstrating how to attract and retain good teachers. Career ladders, performance-based pay, and other initiatives help to keep good teachers in the profession. Everybody benefits—students, parents, and teachers. To improve the quality of the teaching force, Virginia is moving toward requiring a prospective teacher to have a bachelor of arts degree in a subject area rather than an education degree. Virginia also allows teachers to enter the profession through the alternate certification route. Your alternate certification allows school systems to draw from an expanded pool of qualified teachers and enables qualified ex-military personnel, scientists, engineers, and others to become teachers. I wonder, Superintendent Spillane, do ex-Presidents qualify for this program? [*Laughter*] Well, there you have it. It's no mystery. It's a miracle. We know what works in education, and we understand, in particular, the vital importance of good teaching.

There's one topic in this regard that's of special importance to Nancy and me: putting an end to drug abuse. When it comes to drugs and education, let me just say this: If a school has a drug problem, then we might as well stop and forget about improving education through qualified teachers, a solid curriculum, high expectations, performance-based pay, or any other reform measure. If students are using drugs, then no education can work. If kids are using drugs, they won't learn. It's that simple. It's that awful. And so, we need to get tough on drugs, on drug pushers, but also on drug users. We need to get drugs out of our schools and our neighborhoods. We need to get drugs out of our children's lives. So, I commend Fairfax County for your efforts—commend you from my heart—and urge you to continue the good fight.

You know, let me just say something to you here and issue a challenge. You stop to think: not only the drugs and the effect they have on people and the destruction that they can create but that there are some soulless people who are living in the veritable lap of luxury, with literally billions of dollars, at the highest standard of living, and paying no taxes or supporting no worthwhile operation. They are supported by those who are their customers. Why shouldn't your generation—now with the changes that we've tried to make in your behalf—why don't you make up your minds that your generation is going to be the one that decides there will be no more drug customers in this country of ours, that you are going to eliminate drugs by taking away their customers? Your generation will be the one that makes that change overall in the United States.

I've talked quite a lot about teaching this afternoon, and there's one story that just about says it all when it comes to the importance of teachers. The story comes from Robert Bolt's play, a drama called "A Man For All Seasons." It's about Thomas More, a great man who lived in England some 400 years ago. The story goes like this. A young man, Richard Rich, approached Sir Thomas for advice on prospective careers. Rich is a bright and ambitious young man and is considering law or politics. But instead Sir Thomas More makes this suggestion: "Why not be a teacher? You'd be a fine teacher—perhaps even a great one." "And if I was," asked Rich, "well, who would know about it?" And Sir Thomas in the play replies, "You, your pupils, your friends, God—not a bad public, that."

Well, that isn't a bad public. It's our teachers' public. And I've come here today to pay tribute to you for your efforts. And to you here at Oakton High who have done so much to foster good teaching and an understanding of teaching's importance, on behalf of a great many people in this country, I thank you.

Now, it so happens that in order to give Secretary Bennett that pop quiz I did a little homework myself. And to tell you the truth, I was really struck by Michael Jackson's song, "Man in the Mirror." It's a wonderful song. It's full of energy and drive and, of course, that helps to make the point that I was talking about earlier: learning and fun go together. After all, Michael Jackson and the others involved have spent years training as musicians, learning to read and write music, mastering vocal techniques, becoming highly skilled at playing various musical instruments. The result of all this training and education? Well, as I said, the result is a wonderful, powerful song. But the song has a powerful moral as well: "I'm starting with the man in the mirror. I'm asking him to change his ways."

Well, it's true—whether the problem is improving education or eliminating drug abuse or helping the homeless—whatever the challenge, individual initiative and responsibility is always part of the answer. And so, as I thought about the message I'd like to leave with you, as I considered what word I could give to you, in your youth, and for many years, well, I decided that this week's top song would do just fine.

My young friends, you've given me such a gift today—the gift of your energy, your exuberance, and your love of learning. And, always to remember: "No message could be any clearer. If you want to make the world a better place, just start with the man in the mirror." Thank you, and God bless you all.

Ms. Thomas. Thank you very much, Mr. President. The students have a few questions that they would like to ask you if you would be willing to answer them.

The President. I'd love to.

Academic Standards

Q. Mr. President, do you feel that the pressure to achieve and the competition between students in the United States is as great today as it was in your high school days?

The President. Is it as great today?

Q. Yes, sir.

The President. Yes, it is because the period that I was referring to—back then, we had not entered into that decline that seemed to come upon us in later years. I don't know what caused it, but it did happen. But, no, we had curriculums that were stiff and required courses that you had to take. And you find out later that they were very beneficial—in taking them. And also, we had a great feeling about our land. Maybe part of it was because I'm old enough that that was in the immediate postwar era, post-World War I. [*Laughter*]

Liberal Arts

Q. Mr. President, the Secretary of Education's decision to place emphasis on math and science programs took away the strength of the arts program. How can we achieve a balance between the subjects?

The President. Well, again, I could refer to the past. I think you can have that balance—depends a lot on you. But that principal that I spoke about that had such an imprint on my life—because not only the principal and the English teacher but by virtue of that particular class—he also directed all the school plays and the drama club plays. And many years later in Hollywood I once said to myself, I haven't come across a director yet that was better than B.J. Frazier. So, it's there, and it's possible. And I don't think they detract at all. Even though I spoke and asked some of you if you were thinking about being teachers, let me say another word of encouragement. If you're still pondering and you haven't thought of what you want to be in life, don't get discouraged. I graduated from college unable to say exactly what I wanted to do with my life. So, the broadest exposure you get to all of these subjects—the compulsory ones, math and science and all the rest—all of them are going to help you one day answer that question for yourself.

Homelessness

Q. Mr. President, do you feel the problem of the homeless is one the Federal Government should tackle? And if not, how can it be resolved?

The President. Frankly, I think the problem of the homeless, like so many other problems, actually belongs at the local community and State level, with the Federal Government ready to help in any way that it might be able to in which something would come properly under the Federal Government's province. But you see, that's one of the great secrets of this country that we tended to forget for about 40 or 50 years. As we started going into more and more Federal domination and Federal interference in local programs, including education, we played a hand in the decline of education by thinking that in addition to doing some added funding we could use that as an excuse for the Federal Government trying to run the public schools. The schools for a long time have been run in this country best when they're closer to the people in the communities where the parents and the students are. And so, I have to say that in this particular thing that you've raised, the problem of the homeless, is best known by the people in the community where it's taking place—why they're homeless, can see them as individuals instead of a mass of faceless people that the Federal Government just thinks of in numbers. So, as I say, if there is a way in which the Federal Government's help can be used, whether it is in financing or what else, actually the administering of this belongs right back where the people are.

Q. Thank you, Mr. President.

U.S. Involvement in Panama

Q. Mr. President, because of the recent uprising in Panama, will it be necessary to resume U.S. military control in Panama for the safety of the Canal Zone?

The President. No, we're going to abide by the Canal treaty, and we're not going to be the big Colossus of the North once again coming into our smaller neighbors' places of living and business and trying to guide and direct them. They have a very difficult problem there. We think that they're moving toward solving it with the reaction of the people to the man that has caused so much of this problem. We want to be of help in any way we can, and so we've helped them in that regard in the economic restraints that we've put down there so that there can be pressure focused on this particular individual. But, no, there's no danger of us coming in with our power and muscle and saying this is the way it has to be.

President's Future Plans

Q. Mr. President, what are you going to do when you step down from the Presidential spotlight?

The President. Hmmm. [*Laughter*] I'm a little old to be a teacher, in spite of what I said earlier. [*Laughter*] Well, I tell you, I do have some ambitions for when that time comes. There are some things that I would like to crusade for that I could not crusade for while I'm President—some I could but some others that I couldn't—because it would seem as if I was selfishly doing it in my own interest.

For example, I would like to start calling to the attention of the people of this country the flaw in the 22d amendment to the Constitution, passed a few years ago, which says a President can only serve two terms. Now let me explain something here. The reason I have to wait is because, as I say, I couldn't dare open my mouth and do this in my own behalf while I'm here, and I don't want to. But what I want to call to the people's attention is: The President is the only one in government who is elected by all the people, and it seems to me that that constitutional amendment, which was born out of vengeance against Franklin Delano Roosevelt—I think that that amendment is an infringement on the democratic rights of the American people, who should be allowed to vote for who they want as long as they want and—[*applause*].

And also, I'm going to crusade for some other things, too, like the line-item veto and the—[*laughter*]—43 Governors had it. I had it when I was Governor of California. I line-item vetoed out of budgets 943 times in 8 years and was never overridden once. Now, in California, the legislature takes a two-thirds majority to pass the budget, and then they send it to the Governor. And it only takes two-thirds of a majority to override a veto. But when I found spending things in that budget and I vetoed them 943 times, you could not get the same two-thirds majority in the legislature when that was exposed all by itself out there—not buried in the whole budget—you couldn't get two-thirds of them to override my veto, not once.

So, those are some things that I'd like to go out and get on what I call the mashed-potato circuit and—speaking and—because when you, the people—[*laughter*]—no, when you arouse yourself and—[*laughter*]—when you decide that there's something you want done, I think your two Congressmen over here—[*laughter*]—will tell you, they hear in Washington.

Invitation to Attend Graduation

Q. Mr. President, will you honor Oakton High School with your presence at graduation?

The President. There was some laughter between you and me before, and I didn't hear your question. [*Laughter*]

Q. Will you honor us with your presence at graduation?

The President. Was I—what? [*Laughter*]

Q. Will you honor us with your presence at graduation in June?

The President. Oh! [*Laughter*] Well, I don't know whether that's possible. You know, you've heard that the President is the most powerful man in the country, if not the world and so forth. I have to tell you something: Every day they hand me a piece of paper that tells me what I'm going to be doing that day—[*laughter*]—for every 15 minutes of that day. And long before graduation time, I'm sure that my schedule—first, I suppose, I should ask you the date of your graduation.

Q. June 15th.

The President. June 15th. It is very possible that I will be in Canada at the economic summit that is held every June, every year. But I won't know that for a while yet.

Audience Members. Awww!

The President. If it were possible, I would be most happy to join you.

Q. Okay, thank you.

Mr. Spillane. Mr. President, on behalf of the entire staff of this school and all of us in Fairfax County, we want you to have this remembrance of your visit here: a schoolhouse that plays "School Days." And we very much appreciate the opportunity to listen to you today, and thank you.

The President. Well, thank you very much.

Note: The President spoke at 2 p.m. in the Oakton High School auditorium. Ms. Laura Thomas, principal of the school, introduced the question-and-answer session.

Nomination of David O'Neal To Be an Assistant Secretary of Labor
March 25, 1988

The President today announced his intention to nominate David O'Neal to be Assistant Secretary of Labor for Mine Safety and Health. He will succeed David A. Zegeer.

Since 1985 Mr. O'Neal has served as Deputy Director of the Bureau of Land Management for the Department of the Interior in Washington, DC. Prior to this he was president of O'Neal Inns, Ltd., 1984–1986, president of O'Neal Printing, 1982–1984, and executive vice president of Aviation Systems International, 1981–1982.

Mr. O'Neal graduated from St. Louis College of Pharmacy (B.S., 1962). He served in the U.S. Marine Corps, 1956–1959. He was born January 24, 1937, in Belleville, IL. Mr. O'Neal has two children and resides in Arlington, VA.

Nomination of Elaine L. Chao To Be a Commissioner of the Federal Maritime Commission, and Designation as Chairman
March 25, 1988

The President today announced his intention to nominate Elaine L. Chao to be a Federal Maritime Commissioner for the remainder of the term expiring June 30, 1991. She would succeed Edward V. Hickey, Jr. Upon confirmation, she will be designated Chairman.

Since 1986 Miss Chao has been Deputy Administrator of the Maritime Administration for the Department of Transportation in Washington, DC. Prior to this she was vice president for syndications of BankAmerica Capital Markets Group, 1984–1986. From 1983 to 1984, she was a White House fellow with the Office of Policy Development, and a senior lending officer in the European Banking Division for Citibank, N.A., 1979–1983.

Miss Chao graduated from Mount Holyoke College (A.B., 1975) and Harvard University Graduate School of Business Administration (M.B.A., 1979). She was born March 26, 1953, in Taipei, Taiwan, and currently resides in Washington, DC.

Informal Exchange With Reporters Prior to a Meeting With President Joaquin Balaguer Ricardo of the Dominican Republic
March 25, 1988

Q. Is everything calm and peaceful in the Dominican Republic?

President Balaguer. Yes, everything is calm and peaceful—as peaceful and tranquil as it can possibly be in today's world.

Q. How about our country, Mr. President? Is our country peaceful and tranquil, too?

President Reagan. I would say the situation is normal.

Nicaraguan Cease-Fire Agreement

Q. How about the cease-fire talks? Are you happy with the outcome?

President Reagan. Well, I only have to say, of course, that we've looked forward to this and hope it continues. But, I still think that—just as in some other meetings that have gone on in which I've been involved—I think that we should keep in mind that both parties must be dedicated to the things that are said and agreed to at those meetings.

Q. Sounds like you are suspicious they won't be.

President Reagan. I think there's reason to have caution. They have a past record that indicates that we should be.

General Noriega of Panama

Q. Are we going to see General Noriega in the Dominican Republic?

President Reagan. No, that's not far enough.

Missile Sites in Saudi Arabia

Q. Mr. President, there have been suggestions that the Israelis might attack the new Saudi missile sites. How would the United States feel about that?

President Reagan. Well, naturally, we would be totally opposed to any such thing and hope that they're not considering any such act.

Gridiron Dinner

Q. Are you all set for the Gridiron?

President Reagan. Is one ever set for that?

Dominican Republic-U.S. Relations

Q. President Reagan, can we ask you some questions about the relations with the Dominican Republic and the United States? Is there a possibility of getting more help from the United States of America Republic in terms of the sugar war, things like this?

President Reagan. As you know, we've had some problems both ways, with the Congress and matters of that kind, but I can assure you that we feel that the relationship we have with the Dominican Republic is of the best, and we treasure it and hope to continue that close relationship.

Note: The exchange began at 11:40 a.m. in the Oval Office at the White House. President Balaguer spoke in Spanish, and his remarks were translated by an interpreter.

Remarks Following Discussions With President Joaquin Balaguer Ricardo of the Dominican Republic
March 25, 1988

President Reagan. It has been my great pleasure to have met with President Balaguer. His remarkable leadership has been an important element in the significant, positive role that the Dominican Republic has played in regional affairs.

President Balaguer has been a driving force throughout his country's democratic development. In 1966 he led democracy's return to the Dominican Republic after years of political uncertainty and turmoil. Indeed, he is, in many ways, the father of Dominican democracy. It's a great honor to have him here. The United States and the Dominican Republic traditionally have enjoyed very close and warm relations. Our meeting today reflected the important historical, cultural, political, and economic ties that bind our two countries. We discussed the economic problems that face us and examined possible solutions.

President Balaguer described the serious impact that low world sugar prices and declining market access are having on the Dominican Republic. I applaud his government's courageous efforts to meet difficult economic and developmental challenges through diversification and private sector investment. The United States Government wants to participate in these processes. Within our budget limitations, we will continue to support development and growth in the Dominican Republic.

Sharing a common hemisphere and democratic beliefs, we examined important political developments elsewhere in the Caribbean and Latin America. We are both concerned by recent events in Central America and Panama. I deeply appreciate President Balaguer's insights into these issues. We both hope for democratic and peaceful solutions to the problems of the region. We want to see an end to the pursuit of military solutions and to the massive Soviet armament that fuels that pursuit. I congratulated the President on his government's role in hosting the first Nicaraguan peace talks mediated by Cardinal Obando y Bravo. We discussed bilateral cooperation in the critical area of narcotics. I want personally to thank President Balaguer for his assistance in combating illegal narcotics in the Caribbean. His government's efforts have been crucial, and we look forward to continued cooperation on this matter of national and hemispheric security.

So, thank you again, Mr. President, for coming to visit me today in Washington. You're a close and good friend of the United States; a leader dedicated to freedom, democracy, and peace; a trusted ally. I wish you well and look forward to working with you as our two countries face the challenges of the future. Thank you, and God bless you.

President Balaguer. Mr. President, this is a beautiful spring day to pay this visit on President Ronald Reagan, which is a great honor to me, but not really to me, but an honor which is really a distinction on my country. I have told President Reagan today of not only my personal admiration but that of the whole people of the Dominican Republic for himself, personally, for his policies as a leader of the world in the defense of human rights, and for the progress of democratic regimes in Latin America and throughout the world.

Together we have reviewed the bilateral problems and issues between our two countries. We have also reviewed the problems affecting other Latin American countries. All these countries have been inspired by President Reagan's policies in the areas of democracy, liberty, and for helping the weak toward economic recovery. The Dominican Republic has received a great deal of help from the Reagan administration, especially in terms of the Caribbean Basin Initiative. This is the most constructive initiative which has ever come to Latin America. It is the most practical initiative and the one from which we have derived the most advantage. And here I include the Good Neighbor Policy of Roosevelt and the Alliance for Progress of President Kennedy, because those were theoretical abstractions, whereas the Caribbean Basin Initiative has been a pragmatic movement which has achieved a great deal of practical good for our countries.

The Dominican Republic specifically has improved its economy, has progressed, has established a large number of free trade zones, opening foreign industries, and thus has reduced its unemployment rate a great deal. Also, the Reagan plan has permitted us to export more to the United States because of the lowering, or total elimination, of tariffs. We have exported more clothes, more apparel, manufactured in the Dominican Republic, as well as other products—which we have now started exporting to the United States, thanks to the lowering of tariff barriers, with once again, the consequence of lowering unemployment.

There are problems which subsist in our relations, especially in connection with the lowering of our sugar quota, but this we have discussed with President Reagan and with his senior advisers in this area of expertise. We also discussed the subject this morning on Capitol Hill with a number of Senators who are friends of the Dominican Republic. We found there a very receptive climate and feel confident that the problem will be solved, taking into account the interests of both of our countries. Our talks today regarding our policies vis-a-vis other countries of the region have been ones in which we have agreed on almost every point. We agreed, for example, on the subject of Haiti and on our discussions of other countries which are our neighbors. And we have almost total and virtual agreement between the two countries.

It is a great pleasure to me now to thank you, President Reagan, very warmly for your hospitality, for your great cordiality and an honor which this visit has done to my country, the Dominican Republic. If when I get home I am asked if I come with my hands full or my hands empty, I will say that my hands are very full—full of friendship, full of affection, and full of admiration for the United States and for its President, Ronald Reagan. My admiration for Ronald Reagan is nothing new. It is something which I have always spoken of, saying that he is not only a leader of his country and of the continent but a world leader—with his revolutionary economic policies, his loyalty to democratic regimes everywhere, and his fight against drug trafficking in the world.

And here I would like just to interject a word of admiration for Mrs. Reagan—for Nancy, the First Lady, whose human struggle against drug trafficking stands as an example to women all over the world, especially in Latin America, which is suffering so much from this scourge, telling us all that we all must make our own efforts to eradicate this plague in order to save the youth of this generation and succeeding generations.

Thank you, President Reagan. Believe me, your economic policies leading to the recovery of the American economy are also leading to the recovery of economies throughout the world. You will continue always to be an inspiration and a guide to me. I am always conscious of your struggle to increase the defense of human rights, to reduce unemployment, to solve the social problems of the world—things that we will do together and we will always remember in the Dominican Republic.

Once again, thank you, Mr. President.

Reporter. Mr. President, sir, the Senate wants you to take stronger action against Panama. They voted today. Will you consider that?

President Reagan. We're considering everything, but I can't take any more questions.

Q. What do you want Secretary Shultz to say to the Palestinians, Mr. President?

President Reagan. I can't now.

Note: President Reagan spoke at 1:31 p.m. in the Rose Garden at the White House. President Balaguer spoke in Spanish, and his remarks were translated by an interpreter. Earlier, the two Presidents attended a luncheon in the Residence.

Proclamation 5780—Greek Independence Day: A National Day of Celebration of Greek and American Democracy, 1988

March 25, 1988

By the President of the United States of America

A Proclamation

The United States and Greece are old allies and friends. Our nations and peoples are bound by interests, kinship, values, and a record of common achievement. Ancient Greek ideals of freedom fueled our own struggle for independence, and American friends supported Greece's effort to forge a modern nation in 1821.

Over the years, millions of Americans of Greek ancestry have enriched and strengthened the United States. In this century, Americans and Greeks fought and died together in three wars. The Truman Doctrine, which helped Greeks preserve their independence and launch Greece toward prosperity, is a proud achievement of American foreign policy. Today, Greece and the United States are partners in the NATO alliance, which has kept the peace and preserved freedom for nearly 40 years.

The democracy we so cherish began in Greece a millennia ago. The grandeur the ancient Greeks left has endowed modern Americans and modern Greeks with democracy's promise of liberty. Today, the world is still inspired by the eternal values and aspirations for which modern Greeks reached when they began their quest for independence on March 25, 1821.

Saluting our common fealty to democracy and its defense, and recognizing the bonds between the United States and Greece, the Congress, by Senate Joint Resolution 218, has designated March 25, 1988, as "Greek Independence Day: A National Day of Celebration of Greek and American Democracy" and has authorized and requested the President to issue a proclamation in observance of this event.

Now, Therefore, I, Ronald Reagan, President of the United States of America, do hereby proclaim March 25, 1988, as Greek Independence Day: A National Day of Celebration of Greek and American Democracy, and I urge all Americans to join in appropriate ceremonies and activities to salute the Greek people and Greek independence.

In Witness Whereof, I have hereunto set my hand this 25th day of March, in the year of our Lord nineteen hundred and eighty-eight, and of the Independence of the United States of America the two hundred and twelfth.

RONALD REAGAN

[*Filed with the Office of the Federal Register, 10:18 a.m., March 28, 1988*]

Remarks and a Question-and-Answer Session With the Members of the Center for the Study of the Presidency
March 25, 1988

The President. Thank you very much, and welcome to the White House. I know you don't think you're in the White House, but somehow—you know Washington. They call it the White House complex. Washington is complex. [*Laughter*]

Well, I can't think of groups that are more welcome here than those sponsored by the Center for the Study of the Presidency. For more than two decades, the center has contributed to our understanding of the high office that for a brief time the American people have entrusted to me. Under the leadership of Gordon Hoxie, the center has helped both the country at large and the men who've held this office to see more clearly the institution and the challenges of the day that the Presidency and its trustee face.

The modern Presidency is, like everything else in our system, the product of both the founders' design and later practice. I remember this every time I give a press conference. Perhaps you know that historians date the Presidential press conference back to our sixth Chief Executive, John Quincy Adams. Before that, Presidents didn't have press conferences. But it seems that every morning before dawn, Adams would stroll down to the Potomac River, take off his clothes and take a swim. [*Laughter*] And one summer day a woman—not a man—of the press followed him to the river. And after he'd plunged in, she popped from the bushes, sat on his clothes, and demanded an interview. [*Laughter*] She told him that if he tried to come ashore before she was finished, she'd scream. So Adams held the first press conference up to his neck in water. [*Laughter*] I know how he felt. [*Laughter*] By the way, the reporter's name was Anne Royall. I don't think it's true that she's the great, great, great grandmother of Sam Donaldson. [*Laughter*]

I'm told that this weekend, at the center's 19th annual student symposium, you will be examining "Congress and the Presidency in Economic and Foreign Policy." One of the most important tools that the President has, both in economic policy and in foreign policy, is the veto. From the very beginning there were repeated attempts to get around the intent of the framers when they gave Presidents this tool. The entire scope of the veto was challenged.

As Edward Corwin's classic study, "The President," points out: "Naturally the veto power did not escape the early talent of Americans for conjuring up constitutional limitations out of thin air. People said the veto was solely the means furnished the President for carrying out his oath to 'preserve, protect, and defend the Constitution' and was not validly usable for any other purpose. They said that it did not extend to revenue bills, having never been so employed by the King of England, and that it was never intended to give effect merely to Presidential desires." But these challenges to the plain and straightforward meaning of the Constitution all failed.

Today we're facing another challenge to the use of the Presidential veto. In recent years, Congress has unjustifiably diminished the veto's utility, particularly when it comes to the budget. You may remember that I had a costar when I delivered the State of the Union Address this year. It was that 1,000-page continuing resolution that Congress sent to me last December and gave me only 10 hours to study and then sign or shut down the Government. I've been reluctant—as I believe any President should be—to allow the Government to stop functioning. So, for the second year running, I signed a single monster bill that funded most of the Government. But as I told Congress in January, never again. Next time I veto, and they can choose whether to shut the Government down or not.

But the question I would ask you is: Doesn't the new practice of creating gigantic continuing resolutions require a new and better response? Can anything but enactment of a line-item veto provide the leverage we need to curb wasteful and unnecessary spending?

In the mid-seventies, Congress shoved the President aside in the budget process. It legislated major shifts in the checks and balances of budgetmaking power. And the results came immediately. Before that, Federal deficit with inflation taken out had been steady or falling for a quarter of a century. Since then, it's been in a steep climb.

In my years in the White House, I've seen one Member of Congress after another call for lower deficits and less spending and then go out and vote for more spending. Some, of course, just want more spending, but many are sincere. They are caught in what scholars call a "prisoner's dilemma." If nearby districts or States get Federal dollars, they feel they have to match it or look bad to the folks back home.

The fact is that there is only one way, once and for all, to stop them before they spend again. And that's to restore the role in the budget process of the only elected official who speaks not for local interests but for the interest of the entire Nation: the President. And the way to do that is with the line-item veto.

You know, we say that the States are the laboratories of democracy and have been since our earliest days. Is there any provision of government that has been more successfully tested on the State level than the line-item veto? Forty-three Governors have it. When I was Governor of California, I used it 943 times and was never overridden once. I found that somehow things got in the budget that just couldn't live in sunlight, and that's all the line-item veto is—a way for the President to let some sunlight into the dark, dank caverns of the budget process.

Well, I've just about used up my time. You know, there's a story about one of my favorite Presidents—Calvin Coolidge—who, as you know, was famous for using a few, a very few, well-chosen words. He'd just made a campaign speech when a woman ran up to him and exclaimed, "Oh, Mr. Coolidge, what a wonderful address. I stood up through it." Coolidge said, "So did I." [*Laughter*]

Well, thank you all, and God bless you. And I'm going to take a few minutes here—I know I don't have much time, and I hope that some of you won't mind if I limit this to the students present—that they must have, as a part of your meeting, a few questions still about the Presidency. The reason I'm shutting out those of you who might be on the faculty is, I had trouble with questions from you back when I was in college. [*Laughter*]

As a matter of fact, two from my alma mater, Eureka College, are here today. Twenty-five years after I graduated, Eureka brought me back and gave me an honorary degree. And all that did was compound the sense of guilt I've nursed for 25 years—[*laughter*]—because I thought the first one they gave me was honorary. [*Laughter*]

Well, does someone have a question that they——

Civil Rights Legislation

Q. Mr. President, I would like to thank you for vetoing the recent so-called civil rights legislation recently sent through Congress. After your veto, why do you think you had problems getting enough Senators or Congressmen to help you sustain your veto? And if you would have had the line-item veto, what specific aspects of that civil rights legislation do you think you could have vetoed?

The President. Well, the things that I would have changed with the line-item veto are what made me veto the bill. I'm not against the whole purpose of that bill. As a matter of fact, I sent up a bill that called for it—virtually what was in this one—except for the provisions that were in there that would now give the Federal Government regulating control over everybody down to a farmer or a mom and pop grocery store or anything else. That's what I had against the bill. I'm not against extending civil rights. But it was so written that if—well, as I said in one of my statements, if a church or a group of churches, for example, put together, as many of them do, a summer camp, and if that summer camp happened to, let's say, be located on Federal land or surplus land or anything of that kind, automatically, all of the churches involved in that would be subject to Federal regulation.

And thus they would be—well, I can tell

you what that excess regulation can do, and maybe there are some here from the—physicians in the colleges and universities—that know. It was not too many years ago in the Federal Government—we've been trying to get the Federal Government out of things where it doesn't belong and get them back to local and State control and so forth. I actually learned of a college like that that many of you go to. The college's average cost for administrative overhead was $50,000 a year. Federal regulations imposed brought that up to $500,000 a year just for the administrative overhead and the paperwork that was required of the Government rules. And I don't think it improved education a bit.

Foreign and Domestic Spending

Q. Mr. President, hello. I'd first like to say thank you for providing a renewed sense of unity and patriotism to American citizens.

The President. Thank you.

Q. But what I'd like to ask you is: Do you anticipate a decrease in foreign aid and perhaps an increase in domestic aid throughout the United States?

The President. Well, actually, there has been a decrease now mandated by Congress on foreign aid. And frankly, it has set us back a great deal. Foreign aid isn't just a charity that—for example, it includes security features, also. And it helps other countries provide for their own defense where, because of our own national interest, if they can't do that, we have to. And ours is more expensive than their own homegrown variety. So, we're trying to reverse that.

I just met with another President of one of our Caribbean nations today, and this hit them very hard. And their economy is virtually strapped because of cutbacks that were made by the Congress. So, I think we've got to look with—it's so easy to say, well, we've got so many problems, what are we doing helping these people over here? Well, we do live in the world with them, and you can't be isolationist anymore, and certainly not a country like ours.

So, I hope that we can reverse this trend and begin to restore some of that. With regard to aid throughout our country, let's get something straight. For example, aid to education, we've always believed, is a local and State responsibility. And it was not too many years ago that under the New Deal—Federal Government decided to get itself involved. But the Federal Government only contributes 7 percent of the total cost of education. But for that 7 percent, the Federal Government gets greedy and wants a lot more privilege and authority over education than they've bought for 7 percent.

But with regard to need—here we're looking at welfare reforms, also. Because again, I once found a program when I was Governor, a Federal program, that the administration overhead was $2 for every $1 they got to a needy person. We believe that some reforms are needed to make it more practical than that. And right now, the most effective aid to the people is coming from what I call the private sector. Last year, private individuals and groups and organizations raised $84 billion for charitable causes for the needy.

Someone—I better—young lady right back there?

The President's Legacy

Q. I just was wondering, now that you're in your last year, what do you think is your greatest accomplishment, or one of your greatest, and what would you like to be remembered for in history books? [*Laughter*]

The President. I try not to think of the history books—[*laughter*]—very much about that, contrary to what a lot of people say. I think it's—I've always looked at this job, as I indicated it in my remarks—you don't become President, you are given temporary custody of an institution called the Presidency. And you don't have any right to go around changing its traditions or rules or anything else, as some have tried to do. But when we came into office, we were in quite an economic bind. Inflation was in double digits, unemployment was up—well, we really were in something of a recession. Interest rates—the prime rate was 20.5 percent. And we set out to make some economic changes.

Maybe one thing that I'll remember with joy—I don't know whether anyone else will—having gotten my degree in economics, that makes me able to tell ethnic stories about economists—[*laughter*]—I had always believed, and put it into practice over great opposition—and that was the most important part of our economic reform—was the reduction of the marginal tax rates. A man named ibn-Khaldun, a few centuries ago said that at the beginning of the empire the rates were low and the revenue was high. He said at the end of the empire the rates were high and the revenue was low.

Well, over all the objections, we cut the marginal tax rates, and that has been the most important part of our economic recovery. We have the highest percentage of the potential labor pool in America employed that we've ever had in our history. We have had the longest economic expansion that we've ever had in the history of our country. And, I can tell you that when you look at the revenues for the tax rates, they have vastly increased all the way across as we reduced the rates. At the lower rates, more money is coming into the Government. Well, I'd always believed that back from my days in school during the Great Depression, and so I think I'll remember that with great pleasure.

But I think what you mentioned a little while ago, also—after all of the rioting and the cynicism that came out of the Vietnam experience, and the campus riots and all, I found that a great many of our military wouldn't dare leave the base without getting into civilian clothes. And I decided that maybe we needed a change of attitude in this country. And today, we have it. I think our country has once again discovered a pride in being an American. And I can tell you there's nothing I'm more proud of than the young men and women—your age—who are in our military today, and they're volunteers. And they wear the uniform; they don't take it off to go out among us civilians anymore. And I'm very proud of what has been accomplished there.

But you continue, and then I think I'm getting to the place where I have to quit.

Tactical Nuclear Weapons

Q. Hello, Mr. President. My question is that in a TV documentary I saw that we have nuclear weapons in Europe that a single person can carry and which are effective over a 1-square-mile area. If such weapons fall into the hands of terrorists, how could we prevent them from smuggling them into the country when we cannot do enough to stop the drug trafficking and the entry of illegal aliens to our southern borders?

The President. Well, all I can tell you is that we have a very elaborate program of security for anything nuclear, including even the plants where things like that are constructed. And I think it is as effective a program as we possibly can have. I think, also, you're probably talking about a type of nuclear weapon that is not included in the INF agreement where we've gotten rid of a whole system for the first time of nuclear weapons.

I'm speaking of the tactical battlefield weapons, which would be what you were referring to there. Those weapons we cannot start trying to reduce until we engage the Soviet Union in reduction of conventional weapons. They have such a great superiority that the only thing that evens us out in the NATO line are those tactical nuclear weapons. If we got rid of them, we would automatically put the Soviets in a tremendous superiority with the conventional. And I've already notified the General Secretary, and he's expressed a willingness to sit down and talk about them. So, once we can get this START treaty on top of the INF, then we'll go after the conventional weapons, and when those are equal, then we can go after the short-range tactical nuclear weapons.

Now——

Civil Rights Legislation

Q. Hello, Mr. President. My question is in regards to your veto on the civil rights legislation—excuse me—[*laughter*]—legislation. I, in fact, was not in favor of your veto; however, you did express that you had an alternate plan. I'd like to know some of what that involved or detailed.

The President. Well, it was the thing we've been trying ever since to reverse the Grove City ruling, and so it was basically what was the most apparent thing in the program that I vetoed, or the bill that I vetoed, except that they added, as I've said, all those other things of controls in there.

Well, virtually, there was a Senate bill on the floor about the same time that the one that I vetoed had been on the floor, and that one was defeated in favor of this other one. And my bill was very similar to that Senate bill. So, in trying to persuade some legislators to vote to sustain my veto, I reminded them that their record showed that they had voted for that other bill and then voted when they didn't get that, voted for this one. And I said, I'm giving you a chance to vote again on the same kind of bill you wanted to pass before as that Senate bill.

And I think there was a concern about some of them that they would appear to the folks back home as if they were against civil rights. Well, I want to tell you, I have—long before the term was ever coined—I have been a devotee of civil rights. I grew up in a family—one brother, my mother and father, and we grew up with the belief that the ugliest sin in the world was discrimination and prejudice. And so, all my life has been over on that side. I had to be, or I'd have been laced. [*Laughter*]

But I've tried to explain there; it was only those other factors that they gave the open door for excessive government regulation. For example, when I said, all the other people—well, this grocery store—if people came into that grocery store with food stamps, that automatically made them subject to Federal regulation and things of that kind that were never intended. And that's all I wanted cleaned up.

So, I've just talked to our people. Now, since our veto wasn't sustained, I've talked to them. But why don't we pick out one-by-one those things now that are in that legislation that's been passed and introduce legislation one at a time to get those other things canceled.

Q. So your bill has approximately the same elements, however, you didn't want——

The President. That's right—the main feel of the bill that I vetoed, yes.

Q. Thank you.

The President. Well, could I take just one more? [*Laughter*] You ought to know I'm late. I've got somebody waiting to—[*laughter*]. I can't take any more after this one.

Iran Arms and Contra Aid Controversy

Q. Mr. President, you once referred to Oliver North as a national hero. Now that he has been indicted, are you going to pardon him and Poindexter?

The President. Now, wait a minute, I'm having a little trouble hearing.

Q. You once referred to Oliver North as a national hero. Now that he has been indicted, are you going to pardon him and Poindexter?

The President. I still think Ollie North is a hero. And at the other hand—and any talk about what I might do or pardons and so forth—I think with the case before the courts, that's something I can't discuss now. But from my—I just have to believe that they're going to be found innocent because I don't think they were guilty of any lawbreaking or any crime.

I've got to take a second and tell you something that—[*laughter*]—you know. The whole so-called Iran scandal—I find it hard to think of scandal in connection with it. We were contacted by some individuals, not the Government of Iran. And these individuals—there was great talk at that time that Khomeini was maybe not going to live out the week. They knew that there would be factions striving for leadership. These individuals wanted to discuss with people from our side how to establish better relations with the United States.

Well, we, behind the scenes, have been trying for years to get an end to the Iran-Iraq war, for example. So I said, yes, we'll meet with them. Incidentally, they came through a third country in the Middle East and that country recommended them to us as being dependable people. Our people met with them. It had to be secret because, obviously, they were risking their lives for doing such a thing. They'd be—I don't know that they haven't been executed. I've never heard of them since this whole thing blew up in the press. But our people met with them. And then the word came back that those people asked if we could make a kind of token sale of arms to them, which they would turn over to the military. And this, they said, would first of all confirm that our people really were representing the top in government, but also that it would give them a prestige they might need when the day came that they were going to try to redirect the Government of Iran.

Well, I had told our people when the word came to me to go back that we had a rule that we didn't do business with countries that practice terrorism, and Iran practices terrorism. Well, they came back with the statement that they wouldn't and they didn't, and they gave some individual incidents to show their opposition to terrorism.

Well, I thought about it, and there was a lot of objection among some of our people and all—and debated. And I knew that the Hizballah [radical Shi'ite terrorist group operating in Lebanon] has a kind of philosophical relationship with Iran. So, I said, all right, to prove their credentials—the Hizballah are holding our people hostage—tell them, yes, we'll do this if they will use their influence to see if they can't convince the Hizballah to release our hostages. And it was a token shipment of arms, and they were sent. I didn't put it on there that they don't get the arms unless—we delivered the arms. And they were delivered then by somebody to the—from the other side of the ocean into Iran. They were given to the military, and we got our money back—exactly what we had asked for. At the same time, we had two hostages released, and we were supposed to have in 48 hours another two. And that was when that leak in a newspaper in Lebanon revealed this secret operation of ours, so we never did get the other two hostages back.

And it wasn't until then that our Attorney General discovered a memo that seemed to indicate that there was more money than we had received, although we had received the price we asked. And I immediately took him and went before the joint leadership of the Congress and told them what we'd discovered—we had no explanation for it, but were going to try to find out; that I'd asked for a special investigator and also that I had appointed a commission to look into this and see what was going on because this money was supposed to be in a Swiss bank account.

Now, that's the whole extent of the so-called scandal—what our intent was and what happened. And you know something? After all the investigation, today I still don't know who got that extra money or where it came from. I'm hoping to find out.

But I didn't mean to get into that long an answer. But I wanted you to know that I have some definite reason for still thinking that Ollie North is a hero.

All right. Thank you all.

Note: The President spoke at 2:25 p.m. in Room 450 of the Old Executive Office Building.

Message to the Congress Transmitting the Annual Report on Nuclear Nonproliferation

March 25, 1988

To the Congress of the United States:

I have reviewed the activities of the United States Government departments and agencies during the calendar year 1987 related to preventing nuclear proliferation, and I am pleased to submit my annual report pursuant to section 601(a) of the Nuclear Non-Proliferation Act of 1978 (Public Law 95–242).

The report concludes that the United States during 1987 continued to make significant progress in its efforts to achieve its non-proliferation goals.

As I have indicated in previous statements to the Congress, my central arms control objective has been to reduce substantially, and ultimately to eliminate, nuclear weapons and rid the world of the nuclear threat. The prevention of the spread of nuclear explosives to additional countries is an indispensable part of our efforts to meet this objective. I intend to continue my pursuit of this goal with untiring determination and a profound sense of personal commitment.

RONALD REAGAN

The White House,
March 25, 1988.

Radio Address to the Nation on Soviet-United States Relations and Trade Legislation
March 26, 1988

My fellow Americans:

This week, as our thoughts begin to turn toward Easter, the cause of peace among nations is foremost in our minds, a cause that was also at the top of our work agenda here in Washington as I received Soviet Foreign Minister Shevardnadze at the White House. My talks with him were cordial but, as you might expect, to the point.

During Mr. Shevardnadze's stay, I announced May 29th through June 2d as the dates for my summit meeting in Moscow with the leader of the Soviet Union, General Secretary Gorbachev. And of course, this was good news. The last U.S.-Soviet summit in the U.S.S.R. was 14 years ago, so this meeting will give me and, in a sense, you, the American people, an opportunity to convey the message of peace and freedom to the Soviet people. But let me also say that while lengthy talks held between Secretary Shultz and Mr. Shevardnadze at the State Department were useful, they also made clear how difficult the issues are between the United States and the Soviet Union.

Now, some progress was made here and there in various areas, but there's much more that needs to be done, given the importance of the topics discussed. Our agenda with the Soviet Union deals not only with arms reduction but also regional matters, human rights, and people-to-people exchanges. And as our discussions continue in each of these areas, I can assure you that the United States will sign only those agreements that are in our best interest. Let me also assure you, as negotiations continue on efforts to further reduce United States and Soviet strategic nuclear arms, that my administration will carefully review such proposals. Still, we've come a long way in our attempts to deal with the Soviets and to further the cause of peace and freedom around the world. The next summit will help. How much, we'll have to see.

An important accomplishment of the first few summits, however, will be before the United States Senate Foreign Relations Committee next week for approval; this is the INF treaty on intermediate-range nuclear forces that Mr. Gorbachev and I signed when he was here for the Washington summit last December. It's an important vote, and I'm hopeful the Senate will, as it exercises its constitutional duty, speedily approve what amounts to the first real nuclear arms reductions ever achieved.

Now, some of you've heard me say before that our progress with the Soviets is based on their awareness that we have no illusions about them and on our determination to deal from a position of strength. Now, that strength means, of course, keeping our defenses ready and second to none; but it also means a strong and vigorous economy and a place for America as the world leader in trade. That's why the other matter that is being considered in the Congress is of critical importance; that is the legislative conference on trade legislation.

Last year, there was trade legislation coming through the Congress that would have meant serious risks to America's prosperity and indeed the world's. Fortunately, working with our administration, Congress has made some progress in producing a sounder bit of legislation. However, the legislation now before a conference committee still contains provisions that would restrict trade, deter investment in the United States, require mandatory retaliation that invites trade wars, and unnecessarily hamper my prerogatives as President. For example, one proposal still very much alive would create an obligation for the Government to help each and every company that can't keep up with legal, totally fair imports—in effect an entitlement program for businesses that can't compete.

So, my hope is that the Congress will stay on course and that we will settle on a bill that avoids the great danger of choking off international trade and slowing down economic growth. I will not sign a bill that imperils our economy and threatens growth. And by the way, that economic growth keeps coming right along. Only this week we heard that the gross national product growth for last year was 4 percent. Now, this was higher than our own expectations—expectations that, by the way, were criticized as too rosy a scenario when we first made them. Well, the rosy scenario was even rosier than the one the critics were down on. It just shows what can happen when spending and taxes are held down and trade is encouraged. In fact, right now much of our economy is being driven by the growth in exports that bad trade legislation would discourage.

So, you can see there's much on our minds this week in Washington. And before anyone looks prematurely forward to the arrival of the Easter Bunny, I hope Congress will stay focused on the important matters this week: the INF treaty and trade legislation.

Until next week, thanks for listening, and God bless you.

Note: The President spoke at 12:06 p.m. from the Oval Office at the White House.

Remarks to Reynolds Metals Company Employees in Richmond, Virginia
March 28, 1988

Thank you all very much, and thank you Bill Bourke, for that kind introduction. And thanks to Chairman Reynolds for hosting this event, and thank you all very much. And I'd like to say hello, too, to your Senator John Warner, who is down there, and your Congressman Bliley. I've already said hello to them because I brought one of them with me. [*Laughter*] But this has all been fascinating, and there's much that I want to say because I think I've seen a magic show already today. [*Laughter*] But I realize I'm only one of several speakers in this forum, so as Henry the Eighth said to each of his six wives, "I won't keep you long." [*Laughter*]

Today, in my tour of your plant, I saw an example of why American exports are the highest they've been in the entire history of the United States of America. It's called American free enterprise. Today it's increasingly becoming a high technology operation. And I just wish that all of the negativists who talk about the decline of America or say that we can't compete overseas—I wish they'd come to this plant and take a look. It might open their eyes.

America is now in the 64th straight month of economic expansion. That's the longest peacetime expansion in our nation's history, beating out the previous record by 6 months already. And we're still going strong. Gross national product rose nearly 5 percent this quarter and a strong 4 percent for the whole of 1987. Such growth in the fifth year of an expansion probably also belongs in the record books. But I don't think one of those 64 months has gone by without some expert or some politician predicting imminent disaster. Sometimes we'll be lucky and escape only with a recession; sometimes it's another Great Depression, according to the so-called experts. I'm sorry, but it seems to me that these people are out of touch. During the Great Depression the prediction that "prosperity is just around the corner" became a point of ridicule. The reverse is true today. We've heard during the longest, strongest expansion in our history that "calamity is just around the corner."

It's a little like that old story of the traveling salesman who was having kind of a rough day of it and finally gave up and dropped into a local diner and wearily ordered a cup of coffee and a couple of eggs and a few kind words. And the waitress brought the order, put down the eggs, and put down the coffee, and said, "Will there be anything else?" Well, he said, "What about the kind words?" She said, "Don't eat them eggs." [*Laughter*]

Our administration has no higher priority than the protection of America's economic security. For nearly 8 years, we've fought for policies that have enhanced that security. I'll match our program of low taxes, free and fair trade, reduced increases in government spending, and reductions of Federal regulations against our opponents' calls for more protectionism, higher taxes, and big government spending programs any day of the week. I suspect you'll be hearing more about these two approaches in the months ahead. But the fact is you have to give our critics credit. They're running perhaps the greatest myth-making operation in history. The myths keep evolving as they encounter contrary evidence, but the myth makers don't give up. The three big ones today are the deindustrialization of America, the decline of the middle class, and the loss of American jobs.

The reality, of course, is over 15½ million new jobs created since the recovery began, and reversing the trend of the late seventies, these new jobs are bigger and better and higher paying jobs. The reality is that after years of high inflation in which the American people saw their buying power shrink beyond recognition the real income of the average American has been rising steadily for 5 years. The reality is that manufacturing exports are surging, and manufacturing productivity is at an all-time high and rising rapidly. Since 1980 the United States manufacturing economy has increased its productivity almost three times as much as in the previous 7 years. One German manufacturing expert put it succinctly: The U.S., he said, is simply "the best country in the world in terms of manufacturing costs." And the economist Warren Brookes predicted that we will make the shift to an export-led economy, said that '88 "could end with a bang."

Now, you'd think this would all be cause for rejoicing in Washington—not among our critics. They've been predicting economic disaster for 5 years. They've waited. They've been patient. And now they've seized their opportunity. They've got a trade bill before Congress that could squelch productivity, destroy American competitiveness, and make all their doomsday myths a reality. In an apparent attempt to import "Euro-malaise," they've written in European-style regulations that would create America's first national rules restricting a company's right to close down facilities and relocate operations. Another example: Honda recently began exporting its first cars from America to Japan. Foreign investment has helped create new American jobs and American exports. It has contributed to the rising productivity of American manufacturing that I mentioned earlier.

So, what do some in Congress propose including in the trade bill? New disclosure requirements that would dampen and discourage foreign investment from coming into this country. But potentially the most serious are mandatory retaliation or automatic protection provisions that could require me and future Presidents to take actions that would be in direct violation of the GATT and seriously harmful to the national interest. If enacted, they could weaken the international trading system and could require the President to start trade wars. It's a bad proposal under any circumstance, but it's particularly bad now that American exports are soaring and American manufacturers are exporting as never before and so are vulnerable to retaliation as never before.

And, yes, too many talk about making America more competitive, but support provisions in the trade bill that would bench some of the best competitors on our team. They talk about saving jobs, but they want provisions that have the potential to destroy thousands, if not millions, of American jobs. They talk about learning from the Japanese, but why did they have to take their lesson from Kamikaze pilots? [*Laughter*]

You may have been reading lately that the trade bill is making good progress, that a lot of protectionist provisions have been jettisoned. Well, there is some truth to that, but there's a long way to go before the legislation does more good than harm to the U.S. economy. Now, I'll veto if I must. Only wholesale elimination of the objectionable provisions will produce a bill that I can sign. I won't let them destroy the American growth economy. But I'd rather work with Members of Congress to bring about not just an acceptable bill but one that genuinely improves upon our current law.

There are any number of positive things that can be accomplished: renewed negotiating authority so that we can continue to produce compacts like the historic Canada free trade agreement that is so important and that Bill Bourke mentioned. We've advocated a new program that would provide training to workers who are displaced as our economy becomes more competitive. And there are many reforms to existing U.S. laws, such as protection of patents and copyrights and streamlining export controls that would enhance our ability to export. As they continue their work in Congress on this bill, I would note that on Super Tuesday those who had predicted that protectionism would be embraced in the South were proven wrong.

I've often talked about Senator Reed Smoot and Representative Willis Hawley and the bill they coauthored that brought about the collapse of the world trading system and helped send America into the decline of the Great Depression—the Smoot-Hawley tariff. Well, both of them felt that a bit of demagoging about trade was good politics. It certainly did get them in the history books. And what many people don't realize is that they were both thrown out of office 2 years later when the voters had time to see the effects of their bill. Protectionism isn't just bad economics, it's bad politics. I think the American people have decided that one Great Depression is enough, and they aren't going to give the trade demagogues a second chance.

History points in the opposite direction: more trade, not less; increasing cooperation, not isolationism and retaliation; expanding global networks of investment, production, and communication, not mercantilist national economics shrinking behind tariff barriers. And that's why we've pushed for a new GATT round, which has now been launched to negotiate the most ambitious multinational trade agenda in history. This took some doing at the economic summits that we hold each year with several of our trading partners, and why, as was mentioned earlier, we've negotiated an historic trade agreement with Canada that will expand jobs, growth, and opportunity, as you've been told, on both sides of the border.

The transformation of Reynolds Aluminum that we saw here today is part of a larger picture. The world economy is in the midst of a profound transformation. It's been called the information age, the computer age, the technological revolution. America can either accept the challenge, as you here at Reynolds have done, or we can opt out of competition and, therefore, miss out on the new horizons opening before us.

Let me just end by giving one example that shows just how profound that transformation is. The driving force of the technological revolution is the almost daily revolution in semiconductor technology. Now, to give an idea of the change our generation has wrought, one scientist has made this comparison: If automotive technology had progressed as fast and as far as semiconductor technology has in the last 20 years, he says, a Rolls Royce today would cost less than $3; it would get 3 million miles to the gallon; it would deliver enough horsepower to drive an ocean liner; and six of them would fit on the head of a pin. [*Laughter*] This is more than simply a productivity explosion. Operating in the mysterious realm of quantum physics, today's computers signal a quantum leap into a new world economy.

Reynolds has put that quantum power to work for it, and to work for U.S. competitiveness. America is still the leader in innovation and entrepreneurial drive. And if we're willing to compete, I have no doubt we'll be the ones leading the way into the new century and the new world economy. And, Bill, when I was listening to you a moment ago, I want to tell you, this is what we're up to with our trading allies in the world, and we want to bring about that very thing you mentioned with regard to our ability to compete on a fair and level playing field, and that's what we're going to keep driving for until we get it—all the way.

You know, lately, I've got a new hobby, and it's kind of made me stick around longer than I should when I'm speaking. [*Laughter*] I've been collecting stories that are told in the Soviet Union by their people, among themselves, which reveal they've got a great sense of humor, but they've also got a pretty cynical attitude toward their system. And I told this one—Bill, you'll have to hear it again—I told it in the car. I didn't tell this one to Gorbachev. [*Laughter*] You know, there's a 10-year delay in the Soviet Union of delivery of an automobile. And only 1 out of 7 families in the Soviet Union own automobiles. It's a 10-year wait. And you go through quite a process when you're ready to buy, and then you put up the money in advance. And this happened to a fellow—and this is their story that they tell, this joke—that this man, he laid down his money, and then the fellow that was in charge said to him, "Okay, come back in 10 years and get your car." And he said, "Morning or afternoon?" [*Laughter*] And the fellow behind the counter said, "Well, 10 years from now what difference does it make?" And he said, "Well, the plumber's coming in the morning." [*Laughter*]

Well, I really meant it about magic. And I just—here, in the plant I was just through, I saw what I think is miraculous—and total accomplishment of yours from the machinery that performs the miracles to the miracles that they perform. And I just want to thank you all for letting me be a part of this, and I'll go home feeling a little taller than when I left Washington.

So, I thank you all, and God bless you all.

Note: The President spoke at 3:26 p.m. in the main lobby of the headquarters building. In his opening remarks, he referred to Bill Bourke, president and chief executive officer, and David Reynolds, chairman of the board of directors. Prior to his remarks, the President attended a Virginia State Republican Party fundraising reception at the Hyatt Richmond Hotel. He also toured the foil plant.

Remarks Following a Visit to the Reynolds Metals Company in Richmond, Virginia

March 28, 1988

The President. Bill, thank you very much. Your good Senator John Warner is here with me. I'm going to take him back to Washington and put him back to work. [*Laughter*] You know, I've been told that you all heard what I was saying in there to the others. Is that right?

Audience members. Yes!

The President. Well, then, you know that I finished by telling a story that I said I haven't told to Gorbachev. I think I'll tell you a story that I have told to him. [*Laughter*] It seems that they were having some trouble with speeders in the Soviet Union, even though they don't have many automobiles. So, an order was issued that everybody, no matter who it was, caught speeding get a ticket. And one day General Secretary Gorbachev was coming out of his country home. He's late getting to the Kremlin. So, he told his driver to get in the backseat and he'd drive. And down the road he went, past two motorcycle policemen. One of them took out after him. In just a few minutes, he was back with his buddy. And the buddy said, "Well, did you give him a ticket?" And he said, "No." He said, "You didn't? Why not? We're supposed to give everyone a ticket." He said, "No, he was too important." But he said, "Who was it?" "Well," he said, "I couldn't recognize him. But his driver was Gorbachev." [*Laughter*]

Well, I've got to tell one more, and then I've got to go back to Washington and get to work, too. Another story that's a favorite of the people over there is they like to tell stories about us and their people in arguments about the two countries. And this was an argument in which the American, trying to prove how great this country is, said, "Look, I can walk into the President's Oval Office. I can pound the desk and say, 'Mr. President, I don't like the way you're running our country.'" And the Russian said, "I can do that." He said, "You can?" He said, "Yes. I can walk into the Kremlin to the General Secretary's office. I can pound on his desk and say, 'Mr. General Secretary, I don't like the way President Reagan's running his country.'" [*Laughter*]

Well, that's enough, here. You've stood here long enough. And I just want to thank you all for not only a great welcome, but, as I told you in those remarks in there, you're performing miracles, and you make me so proud of what you're all doing and what America means and why we can hold our own with anyone in the world and better them.

Thank you very much. God bless you all.

Note: The President spoke at 3:55 p.m. outside of the headquarters building. In his opening remarks, he referred to Bill Bourke, president and chief executive officer of the company. Following his remarks, the President returned to Washington, DC.

Executive Order 12633—Amending the Code of Conduct for Members of the Armed Forces of the United States
March 28, 1988

By virtue of the authority vested in me as President by the Constitution and laws of the United States of America, and as Commander in Chief of the Armed Forces of the United States, in order to remove gender specific terms, Executive Order No. 10631, of August 17, 1955, as amended, is further amended as follows:

Section 1. The second paragraph is amended to read as follows: "All members of the Armed Forces of the United States are expected to measure up to the standards embodied in this Code of Conduct while in combat or in captivity. To ensure achievement of these standards, members of the armed forces liable to capture shall be provided with specific training and instruction designed to better equip them to counter and withstand all enemy efforts against them, and shall be fully instructed as to the behavior and obligations expected of them during combat or captivity.".

Sec. 2. Articles I, II, and VI of the Code of Conduct for Members of the United States Armed Forces, attached to and made a part of Executive Order No. 10631, are amended to read as follows:

"I

"I am an American, fighting in the forces which guard my country and our way of life. I am prepared to give my life in their defense.

"II

"I will never surrender of my own free will. If in command, I will never surrender the members of my command while they still have the means to resist.

"VI

"I will never forget that I am an American, fighting for freedom, responsible for my actions, and dedicated to the principles which made my country free. I will trust in my God and in the United States of America.".

RONALD REAGAN

The White House,
March 28, 1988.

[*Filed with the Office of the Federal Register, 11:27 a.m., March 29, 1988*]

Nomination of Dennis M. Devaney To Be General Counsel of the Federal Labor Relations Authority
March 28, 1988

The President today announced his intention to nominate Dennis M. Devaney to be General Counsel of the Federal Labor Relations Authority for a term of 5 years. He would succeed John Carl Miller. Mr. Devaney has been serving as Acting General Counsel since March 17, 1988.

Since 1982 Mr. Devaney has been a Board Member of the U.S. Merit Systems Protection Board in Washington, DC. Prior to this he was an Attorney with Tighe, Curhan, Piliero & Case, 1979–1982. Mr. Devaney was a legislative representative with Philip Morris Inc., 1979; counsel for the Food Marketing Institute, 1977–1979; and assistant general counsel for the U.S. Brewers Association, 1975–1977. From 1972 to 1975, he was a law clerk with the NASA Goddard Space Flight Center in Greenbelt, MD.

Mr. Devaney graduated from University of Maryland (B.A., 1968; M.A., 1970) and Georgetown University Law Center (J.D., 1975). He was born February 25, 1946, in Cheverly, MD. He served in the United States Navy, 1970–1972. Mr. Devaney is married, has two children, and resides in Columbia, MD.

Message on the Observance of National Volunteer Week, April 17–23, 1988
March 28, 1988

I am pleased and proud to greet and congratulate everyone celebrating this week in tribute to America's volunteers.

Voluntarism is rooted in the world's religions and cultures, and just as those religions and cultures have found haven in America so has the spirit of neighborly compassion that Emerson envisioned when he wrote, "The only gift is a portion of thyself." Throughout our history Americans have reached out in service to others, near and far, and thereby strengthened their communities, our country, and the entire world. From the smallest act of kindness to the dedication of a lifetime, volunteers respond in times of joy and tragedy alike. From the smallest child to the most venerable senior citizen, more than half of all Americans give of their time and energy in private sector initiatives—for each other.

Voluntarism's essence is the willingness to share blessings and the courage to pursue an ideal. Voluntarism's currency is love, and volunteers measure their riches in terms of what they freely give their countrymen and the people of the world. National Volunteer Week is a time to recognize America's volunteers and to challenge ourselves to add powerful new chapters to the story of this cherished national tradition.

My heartfelt thanks, and Nancy's, to America's volunteers. You truly give the world a lift. God bless you, and God bless America.

RONALD REAGAN

Proclamation 5781—Cancer Control Month, 1988
March 28, 1988

By the President of the United States of America

A Proclamation

In the continuing struggle against cancer, Americans have put their trust in research; today we can affirm that the public trust has been rewarded. Just a few years ago, the cancer cell was seen as a deadly, unsolvable mystery. The mystery is still complex, but today it is considered solvable. We now know a good deal about what the cancer cell does and how it does it.

We have begun to see cancer not as a random event, but as an error in the normal process of growth and development. Researchers have found minute but critical differences in the genes of normal and cancer cells. They have identified and isolated oncogenes, which play a role in changing normal, healthy cells to cancer. And, with every passing day, scientists come closer to understanding how and when oncogenes "turn on" and transform cells.

In time, our knowledge of how oncogenes work may help cure many patients, improve the quality of life for others, stave off recurrences for still others, and enable us to prevent cancer before it starts.

New knowledge about cancer prevention and treatment has improved the outlook for cutting the cancer death rate. With regard to prevention, we now know that type of diet, exposure to the sun, and use of tobacco can trigger events in the cell that cause up to 80 percent of all cancers.

We can reduce our risk of cancer if we take a few sensible steps. Adding fiber and reducing fat in our diet can significantly cut cancer incidence and mortality; we should choose more fruits, vegetables, and whole-grain breads and cereals and cut down on fatty meat, eggs, dairy products, and oils in cooking and salads. Researchers have shown that overexposure to the sun's rays causes skin cancer; they advise us all to wear protective clothing and to use sunscreens to reduce the risk of this illness. The biggest culprit—responsible for 30 percent of all cancer deaths—is smoking and other tobacco use. The scientific evidence linking cigarette smoking to cancers of the lung and mouth is undeniable. Smoking also contributes to cancers of the bladder, pancreas, and kidney. The message is clear: stop smoking or, better yet, don't start.

The U.S. Public Health Service has found that when people are warned about health hazards, they tend to change their habits for the better. More and more of our citizens want information to help protect their health. Of course, the ideal solution is not to let cancer happen; by modifying the way we live, we can greatly reduce our chances of developing this disease.

This year, the American Cancer Society celebrates its 75th anniversary. The work of the American Cancer Society, the National Cancer Institute, and other organizations devoted to cancer research and control has made a difference. Only a few years ago, it was hard to imagine the tremendous progress we see today. Survival rates have improved for 7 of the 10 major forms of cancer; more than 5 million Americans diagnosed with cancer are alive in 1988. Early detection continues to improve the chances of successful treatment; some 385,000 Americans diagnosed with cancer in 1988 will be alive 5 years from now. Once deadly forms of cancer are now yielding to combined treatments of surgery, radiation, drugs, and new biological agents, such as interleukin-2. A diagnosis of breast cancer no longer requires an inevitable mastectomy. Children with leukemia are being treated successfully and living to become productive adults.

In 1938, the Congress of the United States passed a joint resolution (52 Stat. 148; 38 U.S.C. 150) requesting the President to issue an annual proclamation declaring April to be "Cancer Control Month."

Now, Therefore, I, Ronald Reagan, President of the United States of America, do hereby proclaim the month of April 1988 as Cancer Control Month. I invite the Governors of the fifty States and the Commonwealth of Puerto Rico, and the appropriate officials of all other areas under the United States flag, to issue similar proclamations. I also ask the health care professionals, communications industry, food industry, community groups, and all other interested organizations and individual citizens to unite during this month to reaffirm publicly our Nation's continuing commitment to control cancer.

In Witness Whereof, I have hereunto set my hand this twenty-eighth day of March, in the year of our Lord nineteen hundred and eighty-eight, and of the Independence of the United States of America the two hundred and twelfth.

RONALD REAGAN

[*Filed with the Office of the Federal Register, 11:50 a.m., March 30, 1988*]

Note: The proclamation was released by the Office of the Press Secretary on March 29.

Remarks and an Interview With Gannett Foundation Fellows
March 29, 1988

The President. I'm going to impose on you here this morning before taking your questions—that there are a number of major issues being discussed on the Hill today, INF ratification and the *contra* aid bill. But I want to take a couple of minutes, if I could, to talk to you about the trade bill.

America's now in its 64th month of economic expansion. That's the longest peacetime expansion in the history of our country, and we're still going strong. Gross national product is up; exports are up. And we continue to create new jobs—15½ million since the expansion began. There's no time for protectionism. I could argue that there is never a time for it, but now is definitely not the time. It's not the time for mandatory retaliation against our trading partners, and it's not the time to violate our GATT [General Agreement on Tariffs and Trade] agreements, and it certainly is not the time to close our borders to foreign investment while we are pressing to open other borders to U.S. investors.

We can pass a trade bill that will improve our current trade laws, protecting patents and copyrights, and streamlining export controls, and renewing negotiating authority that makes historic compacts like the Canada free trade agreement possible. We can have that kind of a trade bill, and I won't sign one unless we do.

But now, that's enough of that, and I'm pleased to see you and have you all here. Frequently throughout these last several years we've gone out and invited people like yourselves who are outside the White House press corps, or even the beltway press, to come in here, and it has always been a pleasure to take your questions.

Federalism

Q. Mr. President, we often hear local officials complain that your budget priorities force them to swallow Federal programs they can't afford, so they reach their taxing limits and cut basic services. Do you take responsibility for what California counties, for instance, called their unrelenting fiscal crisis?

The President. Their unrelenting what?

Q. Fiscal crisis.

The President. Well, the reverse of all of that is really true. There are some programs that we've cut simply because we've been able to make administrative improvements. I came here with a memory fresh in my mind as Governor of California of coming across a government program to help the needy in which the administrative overhead was $2 for every dollar delivered to a needy person, and set out to do something about that. Some programs, we have thought, are not proper for the Federal Government. But at the same time, one of the things that had been imposed on local and State government by the Federal Government was the usurpation of authority and autonomy that belonged at the local and State level.

And the Federal Government actually had acquiescence, in that over a great many years, by simply taking up so much of the taxing potential that not enough was left for local or State government for the things that they might want to do. And this then was the excuse for the Federal Government to step in with things that, as I say, properly belonged at that other level. Well, now, with our very beginning of our recovery program, it was based on tax reductions and the idea of thus reopening sources of taxation that other elements of government or levels of government could call upon.

Q. Are they in trouble then just because they haven't been willing to raise taxes to take advantage of that?

The President. I would have to see the specific case as to what that was about, but I'd like to call to your attention that the Federal—or the State and local governments basically have, while we've been running budget deficits, have basically been achieving surpluses. As a matter of fact, if you take the total national deficit and add in local and State government—the total cost of all government in the United States—you would find that the deficit is not as—well, it isn't—there are other countries that have greater deficits than we do if you figure all of that. It's at the Federal level that we're still excessively spending.

And I could call attention to the fact that way back in 1932 Franklin Delano Roosevelt ran for office, and part of his platform was to restore authority and autonomy to States and local governments that had been unjustly seized by the Federal Government. And we have a program we call federalism in which we're trying to restore fully that concept that the United States is a federation of sovereign States.

Q. Thank you.

Death of U.S. Marines in Lebanon

Q. Mr. President, if you could change one major policy decision that you've made during your administration, what do you think it would be?

The President. My goodness. [*Laughter*] Well, all of them were made in good faith. [*Laughter*] Changed or not—just offhand, I can't think. Well, I can think of one that turned out so disastrously that we had to withdraw from it. And that is that we—in company of 3 other countries—4 countries, in an effort to try and bring peace in the Middle East and to Lebanon—that when we discovered that the Lebanese military forces—well, Lebanon itself was occupied by military groups that belonged to kind of private warlords, you might almost say, and that the military of Lebanon could not go out and restore government control over the country unless there was some protection for the people left behind in Beirut. And we, in company with three of our allies, decided that we would send in, as you know, forces to maintain order. We would not be out there fighting those private armies, but our forces would be there to keep order in the city where there was no order, keep order there while the Lebanese military did what—or the—yes, Lebanese military did what it was supposed to do.

Well, the funny thing is that was working. I got a letter from a woman there who told me that for the first time in 8 years she was able to allow her daughter to go to school, that it was safe once more. But because it was successful, that's when the terrorist attacks began and the sniping of the military—not only of ours but the others, our allies—car bombings and so forth. And finally, that great disaster, that car bomb that brought down the building at the airport in Lebanon and killed 241 Americans.

It can be questioned as to the wisdom of putting them in there. They had not been billeted in that building, but it was steel and concrete construction. And out where they were, encamped around the airport, which was part of our duties, there were victims of sniping, things of that kind. And the commanding officers, having that kind of structure available, moved these men in there as a place for the nights, not thinking about a suicide bombing that simply drove a truck into the building with the explosives that blew them up. And then we had to retreat. And another reason we had to retreat and give up was it began to be more evident, also, that the Lebanese military was divided in its loyalties and were loyal to some of these, what I called warlords, to the extent that it was difficult to get them in many instances to take action against the forces they were supposed to be clearing out.

Oliver North

Q. Mr. President, last week you said you still think Oliver North is a hero, despite his indictment on conspiracy, theft, and fraud charges. If requested, will you testify on his behalf? And can you tell us why you still consider him to be a hero?

The President. Yes, I will tell you that. I don't know what his situation will be with regard to giving testimony or not. But I think I was too short in my remark when I answered the question. It was a specific question: Did I still consider him a hero? I should have augmented that and said why, and that is look at the record and at the honors and the medals that have been awarded him for bravery in combat. And I have to say those were heroic actions and he is a valid hero. And that was what my answer was based on, although, as I said, I should have augmented it as I did here and reminded them of his war record.

Q. Well, do you think the allegations of shredding documents and lying to Congressional and Justice Department investigators tarnished that heroism?

The President. You have said allegations, and now you come down to what is a kind of a sore point with me about a lot of the things that have been going on with regard to people in our administration. And that is that someplace along the line many of us have forgotten that you are innocent until proven guilty beyond reasonable doubt. And what has happened, I think, in the case of this kind is it's just everyone is accepting guilt on the basis of accusation. And I say they've got a right to be presumed innocent until someone proves them guilty of the charges.

Now, I see that I'm getting a signal here. He isn't just restless. [*Laughter*] It means that my time is up, and that I'm supposed to leave here. But I'm going to turn this over to my Chief of Staff, Senator Howard Baker, and he'll continue to take your questions. And I'm sorry that I have to quit. I've been enjoying this. As a matter of fact, I want to tell you just something before I go. I enjoy taking your questions more than I do from the White House press corps. [*Laughter*]

Note: The interview began at 11:23 a.m. in the Roosevelt Room at the White House.

Proclamation 5782—Education Day, U.S.A., 1988
March 29, 1988

By the President of the United States of America

A Proclamation

Education that emphasizes the ethical values and principles upon which America was founded, and upon which all civilization rests, remains as vital to our country today as ever in our past. History, reason, experience, and the desires of the human heart teach us that individuals and nations alike need, in addition to technical knowledge and skills, all the wisdom, guidance, and inspiration that ethical values provide. We ourselves possess these treasures only because our ancestors cherished and preserved them through the ages; we are duty-bound to pass them along to our children, who need them and seek them just as much as we and members of every generation have needed them and sought them.

These truths are known and practiced now by more and more citizens and educators. One group that exemplifies this is Hasidic Judaism's worldwide Lubavitch movement, led by Rabbi Menachem Mendel Schneerson. It is fitting that we salute his lasting achievements in education, as well as those of his late wife, the Rebbetzin Chaya Moussia Schneerson; of their many colleagues; and of everyone who fosters education that incorporates our prized heritage of ethical values.

In recognition of Rabbi Schneerson's dedication to our educational system, and in celebration of his 86th birthday, the Congress, by House Joint Resolution 470, has designated March 29, 1988, as "Education Day, U.S.A." and authorized and requested the President to issue a proclamation in observance of this day.

Now, Therefore, I, Ronald Reagan, President of the United States of America, do hereby proclaim March 29, 1988, as Education Day, U.S.A., and call upon the people of the United States, and in particular our teachers and other educational leaders, to observe that day with appropriate ceremonies and activities.

In Witness Whereof, I have hereunto set my hand this twenty-ninth day of March, in the year of our Lord nineteen hundred and eighty-eight, and of the Independence of the United States of America the two hundred and twelfth.

RONALD REAGAN

[*Filed with the Office of the Federal Register, 11:51 a.m., March 30, 1988*]

Remarks at the Presentation Ceremony for the American Cancer Society Courage Awards

March 29, 1988

The President. In my years at the White House, I've had the privilege of meeting with many extraordinary people—political leaders, both national and international, men and women who've performed heroic deeds, astronauts, sports champions, all kinds of distinguished achievers. These are all people who've made their mark on the world, and meeting them is one of the nicest parts about being President. But I can't imagine a group of individuals that is more representative of the finest in our country than you who have been chosen to receive the American Cancer Society Courage Awards. I've been given information about all of you—where you come from, your ages, occupations, the kind of cancer that you have experienced. You're not only a cross section of the American people, you are living proof that the quality of courage is universal.

There's a terrible fear that comes when you're told that you have cancer, a fear that is the same whether you are 8 or 80. But that fear was not the end for you, but a challenge. And that's where that courage begins. First you accept the challenge to fight cancer in any way you can. And for all of you here today, your battle with cancer has become more than a personal battle. That is because you've all made conscious decisions to help others who have cancer. Many of you are active volunteers for the American Cancer Society. Some are officers in their units or divisions. Some have written books or worked on instructive videotapes. You've all used your experiences with cancer to help others come to terms with cancer in their lives.

Nancy and I faced that same decision ourselves. We made a conscious decision that it was important to "go public" with the fact that—in both her case and mine—good medical supervision, early detection, and prompt treatment were the keys to victory over cancer. People need to know that cancer isn't something to run and hide from. Cancer is a fact that must be faced and dealt with. You have all done that, and with extraordinary courage.

Here are just a few examples. After an operation on her tongue, Marcia Williams Kling took speech therapy and within 4 months was back entertaining preschoolers on her own television program. Connie Haines also beat cancer and continues to entertain the public. After two operations and 3 years of chemotherapy, Connie is back and as melodious as ever.

I was interested in discovering that members of this group not only have shown courage in a difficult time but truly achieved triumphant victories over the physical aftereffects of cancer. Just look at how the members of this group spend their spare time: camping, motorcycling, swimming, and running. In spite of an amputated leg, one Courage Award winner is a silver medalist in three-track snow skiing at the Special Winter Games. Others have enrolled in a wilderness survival program or else used their excess energy in engaging in ballet, gymnastics, soccer, or judo.

Another one of the Courage Award winners is a remarkable young man. And when I say young, I mean young. He was 6 when they found he had cancer in his body. They didn't give him much chance to survive. But Jason Gaes did. Here's what he has to say: "The reason I wanted to write a book about having cancer is because in every book I read about kids with cancer they always die. I want to tell you kids don't always die. If you get cancer, don't be scared, 'cause lots of people get over having cancer and grow up without dying, like Mike Nelson and Doug Cerny and Vince Varpness and President Reagan and me." [*Laughter*] Those are the words I'm reading from his book.

Well, it's an honor being in Jason's book, but every one of the American Cancer Society Courage Award winners is very special. You're here to be recognized for your courage and for your zest for life, and I'm proud to salute you all today.

And I'm proud to present to you, Jill Ireland, the 1988 Cancer Courage Award. Jill and Charlie [Bronson], your courageous battle against cancer is an inspiration to others. In the acknowledgement to your book, "Life Wish," you write that upon being told about the cancer you would have loved to talk to someone who had had the disease. Well, by sharing your story, the fears and the triumphs, you've become a companion for the many others going through the isolation of catastrophic illness. And for that, I thank you. And on behalf of the many whose lives you've touched, it is my honor to present to you this award.

Ms. Ireland. Thank you, Mr. President. From one survivor to another, I accept this prestigious award on behalf of my family, myself, and I share it with cancer patients everywhere. Thank you.

Mr. Eyre. Mrs. Reagan, we owe you a special debt of gratitude for speaking up so frankly about your personal experience with breast cancer. You have reported and renewed confidence in the use of mammography, a lifesaving technique. You are a visible example of strength and courage to women and Americans all across the Nation. We feel proud to honor you as the recipient of the American Cancer Society Courage Award. And to present this award, I would like to ask Chairman Kay Horsch to join me.

Mrs. Horsch. "The American Cancer Society salutes Nancy Reagan for her personal courage in her battle against cancer and for the hope and inspiration she gives all Americans in the fight for life and health, 1988, signed Ronald Reagan."

Mrs. Reagan. Thank you very much. I'm very honored to receive this award from Ronald Reagan. [*Laughter*] I can't say that it's an award that I dreamed of getting when I was growing up, but that's what happens sometimes in life. And if you can help other people to deal with this problem, then that makes you feel good. And I hope that's what's happened. Thank you very much.

Note: The President spoke at 1:47 p.m. in the Rose Garden at the White House. Harmon J. Eyre was president of the American Cancer Society.

Message to the Senate Transmitting the Belgium-United States Legal Assistance Treaty
March 29, 1988

To the Senate of the United States:

With a view to receiving the advice and consent of the Senate to ratification, I transmit herewith the Treaty between the United States of America and the Kingdom of Belgium on Mutual Legal Assistance in Criminal Matters, signed at Washington on January 28, 1988. I transmit also, for the information of the Senate, the report of the Department of State with respect to the Treaty.

The Treaty is one of a series of modern mutual legal assistance treaties being negotiated by the United States in order to counter more effectively criminal activities. The Treaty should be an effective tool to prosecute a wide variety of modern criminals including members of drug cartels, "white-collar criminals," and terrorists. The Treaty is self-executing and utilizes existing statutory authority.

The Treaty provides for a broad range of cooperation in criminal matters. Mutual assistance available under the Treaty includes: (1) the taking of testimony or statements of witnesses; (2) the provision of documents, records, and evidence; (3) the execution of requests for searches and seizures; (4) the serving of documents; and (5) the provision of assistance in locating, tracing, immobilizing, seizing, and forfeiting proceeds of crime, and restitution to the victims of crime.

I recommend that the Senate give early and favorable consideration to the Treaty and give its advice and consent to ratification.

RONALD REAGAN

The White House,
March 29, 1988.

Proclamation 5783—Fair Housing Month, 1988
March 29, 1988

By the President of the United States of America

A Proclamation

This April is a milestone in the history of civil rights. It marks the 20th anniversary of the passage of Title VIII of the Civil Rights Act of 1968, popularly called the "Fair Housing Act," which declared as a national policy that housing throughout our country be made available to all citizens on the basis of equality and fairness. The Act outlaws any discrimination in the sale, rental, or financing of housing because of race, color, religion, sex, or national origin.

The Fair Housing Act reflects Americans' willingness and determination to make sure that housing is available to all without discrimination. In the 2 decades since its passage, judicial and administrative enforcement and public and private efforts to induce voluntary compliance with the law have helped countless people obtain the housing they desire. America truly has succeeded in moving closer to the ideal of a society open to all.

Every American is entitled to freedom from discrimination in housing; the 20th anniversary of the Act is an appropriate time for all of us to reaffirm our dedication as a Nation to the principles of equal opportunity on which the Fair Housing Act is grounded.

The Congress, by Public Law 100–248, has designated April 1988 as "Fair Housing Month" and authorized and requested the President to issue a proclamation in observance of this event.

Now, Therefore, I, Ronald Reagan, President of the United States of America, do hereby proclaim April 1988 as Fair Housing Month.

In Witness Whereof, I have hereunto set my hand this twenty-ninth day of March, in the year of our Lord nineteen hundred and eighty-eight, and of the Independence of the United States of America the two hundred and twelfth.

RONALD REAGAN

[*Filed with the Office of the Federal Register, 11:52 a.m., March 30, 1988*]

Remarks to Science Honors Students on the Supercollider Program
March 30, 1988

Thank you, Dr. Weinberg. And thank you all very much, and welcome to the White House. It's a great pleasure to have so many present and future scientific pioneers in the Rose Garden with us today. Along with Members of Congress and the administration, we have no fewer than four Nobel laureates in the audience as well as many of the top science students from the Department of Energy's Science Honors Program. I'm tempted to paraphrase an earlier President who once said there's never before been so much talent assembled in one place in the White House since—well, since I hosted the Washington Redskins on the South Lawn last month. [*Laughter*]

But the reason we're here, of course, is to talk about the superconducting supercollider, as you've probably guessed already. I have to confess that when I first heard about this place where things go round and round at great speeds and then crash into each other I thought they were talking about a Presidential campaign. [*Laughter*] At first I was a little nervous addressing so many distinguished scientists on a subject of such complexity, but then I realized these are people who spend their days talking about things called quarks, which some claim exist in two places at the same time. And I thought, why worry? [*Laughter*]

The fact is, I envy the students here today because they exist in a world that seems to put no limits on the imagination. Outer space used to be called the final frontier, but today we've begun to tap another frontier—inner space—whose infinitesimal constellations hold out infinite possibilities. It may be a cliche, but it's nevertheless true that the pace of progress is constantly accelerating. I think one of the reasons I've always had so little patience with those who talk about the limits to growth is that in my lifetime I've seen those limits shattered again and again by questing minds. When I was very young, horsepower was still the kind you fed with hay. Powered flight was still a relatively new thing. And before the turn of the century, we plan to have men living and working in stations in space and a new hypersonic plane that can fly from here to Tokyo in less than 3 hours.

I know that some people may question the practical applications of the superconducting supercollider. The strange world of subatomic particles they may think will never be more than an arcane interest to a few highly specialized scientists. But the truth is, the practical applications of this knowledge are already changing the way we live. One of my favorite examples is from the computer industry. One scientist describes the progress in that industry by making this comparison: "If automotive technology had progressed as fast and as far as superconductor technology has in the last 20 years," he says, "a Rolls Royce today would cost less than $3, get 3 million miles to the gallon, and six of them would fit on the head of a pin." [*Laughter*]

Well, the technological revolution he's describing is transforming our world, and it was only made possible by the knowledge scientists have brought back from their explorations of inner space. Every time someone turns on his desk computer, makes a phone call, or plays a video game, he's plugging into that mysterious world of quantum physics. The superconducting supercollider is the doorway to that new world of quantum change, of quantum progress for science and for our economy. In the face of ever-increasing global competition, the United States must maintain the leading edge in science and technology, and building the world's largest particle accelerator is a visible symbol of our nation's determination to stay out front. Benjamin Franklin once said that an investment in knowledge pays the best interest.

I want to commend you all on your cause, your vision, and the message of progress and competitiveness you carry with you today. And it's my hope that Congress will show equal vision by approving funding to initiate construction of the supercollider. I think all they'd need to do is meet with some of these students here today to see that it is our responsibility to the next generation to keep America a place where we can dream big dreams and then make them real.

I have to interject something here before I conclude. In my lifetime—and only the recent part of my lifetime—after about 25 years in movies and so forth, I was representing the General Electric Theatre on television. And I visited one of their plants in Schenectady early on, and they proudly took me in and showed me what turns out to be the first computer. They called it an electric brain. It would have—well, it would have fit in the Rose Garden here, but it was about as long as from the edge of the platform to the bushes over there and almost as thick. And that is what—I just thought of that when I mentioned here someone sitting down to his desk computer—that, in just those years, from there up to here, is what has happened. So, maybe that fellow about the Rolls Royce was right—six of them on the head of a pin.

Well, I just want to thank you all very much for being here and for allowing me to participate, and God bless all of you.

Note: The President spoke at 11:10 a.m. in the Rose Garden at the White House. In his opening remarks, he referred to Steven Weinberg, professor of physics at the University of Texas, who presented him with a letter from six physicists supporting the administration's efforts in the field of superconductivity.

Remarks at the Swearing-In Ceremony for William L. Ball III as Secretary of the Navy

March 30, 1988

The President. Before we begin, I'd like to ask Rear Admiral John McNamara, United States Navy Chief of Chaplains, to say a prayer.

[*At this point, a prayer was offered.*]

The President. Please, be seated. We're all gathered here to welcome into the Office of Secretary of the Navy as my representative on Capitol Hill an outstanding public servant who has won the respect of the leaders of both parties and to whom I've repeatedly turned for help and advice for the past 2 years: Will Ball.

You know, sometimes you find that someone else has put things in a way you just can't improve upon. When Senator Talmadge introduced Will to the Senate Armed Services Committee, he said, "One prerequisite for the Secretary of the Navy is character. Will Ball has character in abundance." And he added, "The second prerequisite is patriotism, which Will Ball also has in abundance." Well, I second that all the way. Will takes over the Navy at a critical time. The defense budget has now been cut for 4 consecutive years. And yet we must maintain the gains this administration has made in rebuilding our naval and military capabilities. The good ship—or the 600-ship Navy remains our goal. Will's job will be to skipper our naval forces through some troubled waters, while keeping our Navy and Marine Corps team second to none.

Every good captain is concerned about the welfare of the men and women under his command. Will served 3 years aboard ship. He's had his sea legs for years, and he knows what matters to those who swab the decks, land on the shores, man the guns, fly the planes, live in the subs, and sail the oceans of the world in the cause of freedom. Keeping reenlistments high and the quality of our recruits the best it's ever been will be Will's other big assignment. That's never been easy, given the demands on our people who must deploy at sea for long periods of time and be separated from their families. This is but one of the challenges unique to the Navy facing our new Secretary, and I'm confident he's the man for the job. It's no secret that Will has a big job ahead of him. But I have a feeling that Will is just the fellow to give up a—or to give a few up on the Hill a dose of that old-time religion. After all, he's the son of a Baptist preacher, and I've seen he's a pretty good preacher himself when he gets going. [*Laughter*]

That puts me in mind of a story that they used to tell about someone who once had his office just down the hall, back when this magnificent room belonged to the Secretary of the Navy. It concerns Teddy Roosevelt, who, as you know, served for a time as Assistant Secretary of the Navy. Well, you remember Teddy—strong-willed, persuasive, and nothing could stop him. There used to be a story about him, that after he died, he got to heaven. And on his first day in heaven, he told Saint Peter, "Your choir is weak, inexcusably weak. You should reorganize it at once." And Saint Peter said, "All right," and gave T.R. the job. "Well," Teddy said, "I'll need 10,000 sopranos, 10,000 altos, and 10,000 tenors." "But what about the basses?" asked Saint Peter. Teddy said, "Don't worry about that. I'll sing bass." [*Laughter*] A one-man bass section—well, that's your job now, Will.

Good luck, and God bless you. And now we'll have the swearing-in.

[*At this point, Secretary Ball was sworn in.*]

Secretary Ball. Thank you, Mr. President. You honor me and my family by your presence here, and I shall be forever grateful to you for the privilege of serving on your staff and for this great opportunity you have given me. I also want to thank my new boss, Secretary [of Defense] Carlucci, for being here; my former boss, Secretary [of State] Shultz, for being here; and the other members of the Cabinet who could join us today. I especially appreciate the many Members of Congress who have come down from the Hill on a very busy day to be with me in this historic room to share this special moment. I want to express special gratitude to Senator Howard Baker for his guidance and leadership and his patience with me as Chief of Staff. And of course, I will forever owe a debt of gratitude to John Tower for the opportunities and the lessons and the inspiration that he gave to me years ago.

And it was just 23 years ago that I received a message from another gentleman in this room, when I was a senior in high school, and my mother called from home and said I'd received a telegram. And she, as an inquisitive mother would want to do, opened it, and it was a message from my senior Senator saying that I had been accepted in the Navy's ROTC program. And it was that message that began my forthcoming association with the Navy. One week ago, that same senior Senator called me and told me that the Senate had just confirmed me as Secretary of the Navy. And I don't know of any duty that a constituent could ask a senior Senator to do more than that which Strom Thurmond has done for me and for my family down through the years.

Mr. President, on Monday I had occasion to visit the *Coral Sea,* the aircraft carrier, and she's just returned from a 6-month deployment with the 6th Fleet in the Mediterranean. On that great ship I was immediately able to see one of the many legacies that you will leave to history. This particular legacy is perhaps the one that matters most to those who serve at sea. It is indeed written on the faces of those *Coral Sea* sailors, in their spirit and dedication. It can be seen in the cleanliness of the fire rooms and engine rooms far below decks. It signifies what you have done, Mr. President, for our seagoing people, who are proud once again, thanks to you. And I might add that as befits a ship that so reflects the accomplishments of this President in office, the nickname given to the *Coral Sea* is the "Ageless Warrior." [*Laughter*]

I am ready to assume my duties, Mr. President, and with the continued support and assistance of the Congress, we on your Navy and Marine Corps team will remain strong and prepared and will plan wisely for our future so that we can stay that way. As you have time and again explained to the American people, it is only by doing so that we can expect to preserve the peace and ultimately extend the special gift that is freedom to people the world over. Thank you.

Note: The President spoke at 11:47 a.m. in the former office of the Secretary of the Navy at the Old Executive Office Building.

Appointment of Phillip D. Brady as Deputy Counsel to the President
March 30, 1988

The President today announced the appointment of Phillip D. Brady to be Deputy Counsel to the President. He replaces Jay Stephens.

Since 1985 Mr. Brady has been Deputy Assistant to the Vice President. Prior to joining the Vice President's staff, he served in the Department of Justice as Acting Assistant Attorney General for the Office of Legislative and Intergovernmental Affairs, 1984–1985, and Associate Deputy Attorney General, 1983–1984; Director, Congressional and Public Affairs, Immigration and Naturalization Service, 1982–1983; Director, Region IX, ACTION Agency, 1981–1982; legislative counsel, Representative Daniel E. Lungren, 1979–1981; deputy attorney general, California Department of Justice, 1978–1979; and an associate in the law firm of Spray, Gould and Bowers, 1976–1978.

Mr. Brady graduated from the University of Notre Dame (B.A., 1973) and the Loyola University School of Law (J.D., 1976). He was born May 20, 1951, in Pasadena, CA. Mr. Brady is married and has three children and resides in Arlington, VA.

Appointment of William J. Landers as Associate Counsel to the President
March 30, 1988

The President today announced the appointment of William J. Landers to be Associate Counsel to the President.

Since 1983 Mr. Landers has served at the Department of Justice, most recently as Deputy Associate Attorney General and previously as Special Counsel to the Assistant Attorney General (Criminal Division). Prior to that, he was an Assistant United States Attorney in Los Angeles, 1979–1983; deputy city attorney in Los Angeles, 1978–1979; and an associate with the law firm of Parker, Milliken, Clark & O'Hara, 1976–1978.

Mr. Landers graduated from Loyola University of Los Angeles (B.A., 1973) and the Loyola University School of Law (J.D., 1976), where he was editor-in-chief of the law review. He was born October 17, 1951, in Kansas City, MO, and resides in the District of Columbia.

Nomination of F. Clifton White To Be a Member of the Advisory Board for Radio Broadcasting to Cuba
March 30, 1988

The President today announced his intention to nominate F. Clifton White to be a member of the Advisory Board for Radio Broadcasting to Cuba for a term of 2 years. This is a new position.

Since 1982 Mr. White has been director of the John M. Ashbrook Center for Public Affairs in Ashland, OH, and president of F. Clifton White & Associates, Inc., in Greenwich, CT, since 1961. Since 1958 Mr. White has been director of the Public Affairs Council in Washington, DC.

Mr. White graduated from Colgate University (A.B., 1940). He was born June 13, 1918, in Leonardsville, NY. He served in the United States Air Force, 1941–1946. He is married, has two children, and resides in Greenwich, CT.

Designation of Harry Amory Cahill as Deputy United States Representative on the United Nations Economic and Social Council
March 30, 1988

The President today designated Harry Amory Cahill, a career member of the Senior Foreign Service, Class of Minister-Counselor, to be Deputy Representative of the United States of America on the Economic and Social Council of the United Nations. He would succeed Chester E. Norris.

Mr. Cahill is currently Acting Deputy Representative on the Economic and Social Council of the United Nations in New York City. Mr. Cahill has served as principal officer and consul general at the U.S. consulate general in Bombay; on detail at the Department of Commerce, 1982–1983; deputy chief of mission at the U.S. Embassy in Colombo, 1979–1981; senior seminar, 1978–1979; counselor for economic affairs at the U.S. Embassy in Lagos; and Chief of the Division of Business Relations at the Department of State, 1974–1975.

Mr. Cahill graduated from Manhattan College (A.B., 1951) and George Washington University (M.S., 1972). He served in the United States Army, 1951–1954. He was born January 10, 1930, in New York City. Mr. Cahill is married, has six children, and resides in McLean, VA.

Proclamation 5784—Actors' Fund of America Appreciation Month, 1988
March 30, 1988

By the President of the United States of America

A Proclamation

For more than a century, the members and friends of the Actors' Fund of America have served the entertainment world by helping show people to aid their own in time of need. This long tradition of concern and compassion for fellow workers truly touches the lives of thousands for the better, exemplifies and perpetuates America's volunteer spirit, and is worthy of every recognition.

The Actors' Fund assists, in addition to actors, true entertainment professionals who work in any capacity in ballet, circus, the legitimate stage, motion pictures, opera, radio, television, and variety. Its many services and benefits are designed to accommodate the unique needs of those in show business. In wartime and in peacetime, the members of the Actors' Fund have sought to foster the well-being of their fellow entertainers and of all their fellow countrymen. Their active and effective service remains a tribute to them and a blessing for countless people.

The Congress, by Public Law 100–195, has designated the month of April 1988 as "Actors Fund of America Appreciation Month" and authorized and requested the President to issue a proclamation in observance of this event.

Now, Therefore, I, Ronald Reagan, President of the United States of America, do hereby proclaim April 1988 as Actors' Fund of America Appreciation Month. I call upon all Americans to observe this month with appropriate ceremonies and activities.

In Witness Whereof, I have hereunto set my hand this thirtieth day of March, in the year of our Lord nineteen hundred and eighty-eight, and of the Independence of the United States of America the two hundred and twelfth.

RONALD REAGAN

[*Filed with the Office of the Federal Register, 11:11 a.m., March 31, 1988*]

Proclamation 5785—National Know Your Cholesterol Month, 1988
March 30, 1988

By the President of the United States of America

A Proclamation

Coronary heart disease is the leading cause of death in the United States—each year responsible for more than 1.5 million heart attacks, 500,000 of them immediately fatal. High blood cholesterol is one of the three controllable risk factors for coronary heart disease, along with high blood pressure and cigarette smoking.

More than a quarter of adult Americans have blood cholesterol levels that put them at a significantly increased risk of coronary heart disease. Most Americans are aware of their blood pressure levels, but less than half have had their cholesterol checked and less than 10 percent know their blood cholesterol level. Extensive studies have shown that elevated levels of blood cholesterol lead to early development of hardening of the arteries and coronary heart disease, and that the higher the cholesterol, the higher the risk. Now there is firm evidence that lowering high blood cholesterol reduces that risk.

The National Cholesterol Education Program, a joint program by the Federal government, medical groups, voluntary health organizations, industry, and State and local health agencies, has undertaken a campaign to educate professional, patient, and public audiences about the importance of lowering a high blood cholesterol level. The program urges all Americans to learn about the relationship among blood cholesterol, diet, and heart disease; to have their cholesterol level checked; and to know what their number means. The program's long-term goal is to reduce the death and disability from coronary heart disease that is attributable to elevated levels of blood cholesterol.

Each American should know his or her cholesterol level and should take measures to reduce too-high levels. The test is simple and quick; a sample of blood is obtained and the total blood cholesterol level is measured. A high level can be reduced, with diet as the primary approach and drug therapy if needed.

To make all Americans aware of the importance of monitoring their cholesterol, the Congress, by Senate Joint Resolution 244, has designated April 1988 as "National Know Your Cholesterol Month" and has authorized and requested the President to issue a proclamation in observance of this occasion.

Now, Therefore, I, Ronald Reagan, President of the United States of America, do hereby proclaim the month of April 1988 as National Know Your Cholesterol Month. I invite the American people to join with me in reaffirming our commitment to the resolution of the problem of high blood cholesterol.

In Witness Whereof, I have hereunto set my hand this thirtieth day of March, in the year of our Lord nineteen hundred and eighty-eight, and of the Independence of the United States of America the two hundred and twelfth.

RONALD REAGAN

[*Filed with the Office of the Federal Register, 11:12 a.m., March 31, 1988*]

Proclamation 5786—Run to Daylight Day, 1988
March 30, 1988

By the President of the United States of America

A Proclamation

Each year, up to 1.8 million Americans, most of them under age 30, suffer head injuries; and more than 50,000 survivors of such injuries will experience long-term physical and mental difficulties and often need extended care and rehabilitation in returning to productive lives. Advances in medical treatment now save the lives of many people with severe head injuries; improvements in long-term rehabilitation need to continue.

Run to Daylight, a nonprofit organization concerned with improving rehabilitation for survivors of head injuries, is sponsoring a 3,600-mile run across the United States this year—the "Run to Daylight." This event will begin in San Francisco on April 1 and end in Boston on June 30.

The "Run to Daylight" will remind Americans about the rehabilitation needs of survivors of head injuries and will help the National Head Injury Foundation, which is dedicated to improving life for survivors of head injuries and their families and to developing and supporting programs to prevent such injuries.

The Congress, by Public Law 100–268, has designated April 1, 1988, as "Run to Daylight Day" and has authorized and requested the President to issue a proclamation in observance of this occasion.

Now, Therefore, I, Ronald Reagan, President of the United States of America, do hereby proclaim April 1, 1988, as Run to Daylight Day. I urge the people of the United States to learn more about head injuries; to foster appropriate efforts to discover more effective ways to prevent and treat head injuries and rehabilitate head-injured persons; and to aid head injury victims and their families who suffer the severe physical, psychological, and financial burdens of such injuries.

In Witness Whereof, I have hereunto set my hand this thirtieth day of March, in the year of our Lord nineteen hundred and eighty-eight, and of the Independence of the United States of America the two hundred and twelfth.

RONALD REAGAN

[*Filed with the Office of the Federal Register, 11:13 a.m., March 31, 1988*]

Note: The proclamation was released by the Office of the Press Secretary on March 31.

Nomination of Michael P.W. Stone To Be Under Secretary of the Army
March 31, 1988

The President today announced his intention to nominate Michael P.W. Stone to be Under Secretary of the Army. He would succeed James R. Ambrose.

Since 1985 Mr. Stone has been Assistant Secretary of the Army (Financial Management) in Washington, DC. Prior to this, he was with the United States Agency for International Development from 1982 to 1985 as Director of Caribbean Basin Initiative Affairs and mission director in Cairo, Egypt. He was with Sterling Vineyards in Napa Valley, CA, as president and director, 1973–1982, and vice president, general manager, and director, 1968–1973.

Mr. Stone graduated from Yale University (B.A., 1945). He was born June 2, 1925, in London, England. He served in the United States Navy, 1943–1946. Mr. Stone is married, has two children, and resides in Washington, DC.

Appointment of Carlyle Gregory, Jr., as Special Assistant to the President and Deputy Director of the Office of Political Affairs
March 31, 1988

The President today announced the appointment of Carlyle Gregory, Jr., to be Special Assistant to the President and Deputy Director of the White House Office of Political Affairs.

Prior to joining the White House staff, Mr. Gregory founded the American Campaign Academy and served as its president. The academy is a political training school for campaign professionals. From 1981 to 1985, Mr. Gregory was with the National Republican Congressional Committee as field director for the southern region and later as the director of the department of training and speakers.

Mr. Gregory is a 1975 graduate of Washington & Lee University. He is married and resides in Virginia.

Statement on Signing the Bill Authorizing Appropriations for the Bureau of the Mint for Fiscal Year 1988
March 31, 1988

I am today approving H.R. 2631, a bill "To authorize appropriations for the Bureau of the Mint for fiscal year 1988, and for other purposes."

In approving this legislation, I note that section 3 of the bill establishes a "Buy America" requirement for the purchase of materials, supplies, and services related to the production of coins by the United States Mint, which is part of the Department of the Treasury. It requires the Secretary of the Treasury to grant preference to U.S. producers and suppliers over producers and suppliers whose principal place of business is in a foreign country that does not accord U.S. companies the same competitive opportunities for its mint's procurements as it accords to domestic companies. This requirement, standing alone, conflicts with certain of our Nation's international obligations.

In particular, the United States is a party

to the Agreement on Government Procurement of the General Agreement on Tariffs and Trade (GATT). The Procurement Agreement requires entities (e.g., government agencies) specified by a party upon its accession to the Agreement to accord national treatment to the products and suppliers of other parties. When we acceded to the Procurement Agreement, the United States designated the Department of the Treasury, including the Mint, as an agency subject to the Agreement. Certain other parties elected not to designate their mints as subject to the Procurement Agreement; however, they may have designated other agencies that the United States excluded from its coverage. Forbidding the Mint from accepting bids from suppliers in countries that are parties to the Procurement Agreement, but that do not accept bids from United States suppliers with respect to their mint procurements, could be viewed by our trading partners as violating our obligations under the GATT Procurement Agreement.

Canada is one of the parties to the Procurement Agreement that has not designated its mint as subject to the Procurement Agreement. Canada and the United States recently signed a Free Trade Agreement. Among other things, the Free Trade Agreement reaffirms, and incorporates by reference, the rights and obligations of the Procurement Agreement. Thus, failure by the United States to grant Canada national treatment with respect to procurements by the Mint could also bring into question our obligations under the Free Trade Agreement, once it enters into force following approval of the implementing legislation which I will submit to the Congress.

Fortunately, section 3 of H.R. 2631 permits the Secretary of the Treasury to waive the Buy America provision in certain circumstances (i.e., when he finds that compliance with the provision would be inconsistent with the public interest or the cost to be unreasonable). The public interest of the United States includes adhering to our international obligations, and these obligations should be taken into account by the Secretary of the Treasury in making procurements affected by section 3 of this bill.

RONALD REAGAN

The White House,
March 31, 1988.

Note: H.R. 2631, approved March 31, was assigned Public Law No. 100–274.

Statement on Signing the Nevada-Florida Land Exchange Authorization Act of 1988
March 31, 1988

I am pleased to sign into law S. 854, the "Nevada-Florida Land Exchange Authorization Act of 1988."

This law authorizes and directs the exchange of approximately 38,840 acres of public land in Nevada for some 4,650 acres of Florida wetlands of equal value owned by the Aerojet-General Corporation. Aerojet would be entitled to lease an additional 14,000 acres in Nevada for 99 years. The Nevada lands will be transferred with a variety of stipulations for the protection of wildlife.

These lands will be used for the construction of rocket manufacturing, assembly, and testing facilities. Placing them in private ownership not only will expand significantly the tax base of the affected counties, but will also provide major employment opportunities in these areas.

The lands acquired by the United States will be sold to the South Florida Water Management District, a State agency, and used to augment the water conservation activities of that agency. These include both the protection of drinking water for the millions of people living in the Miami area and the maintenance of proper water flows into Everglades National Park.

The funds resulting from that sale will be

utilized for purchase of important wildlife habitat at two National Wildlife Refuges in Florida to aid in the effort to preserve the endangered Key Deer and the Manatee.

I particularly congratulate Senator Chic Hecht and Congresswoman Vucanovich, the primary sponsors, for their leadership role in seeing this project through to completion. The other members of the Nevada and Florida delegations also deserve considerable credit for the time and effort they have devoted to securing passage of this legislation. Florida, Nevada, and the Nation benefit from enactment of this bill. Everyone who has been involved should consider this a job "well done."

RONALD REAGAN

The White House,
March 31, 1988.

Note: S. 854, approved March 31, was assigned Public Law No. 100–275.

Statement by Assistant to the President for Press Relations Fitzwater on the Transfer of United States Funds to Panama

March 31, 1988

We commend those persons who are resisting General Noriega's threats and intimidations to provide him with financial resources. We urge all U.S. companies and persons to comply with the lawful requests of President Delvalle concerning payment of financial obligations to the Government of Panama. Meanwhile, the U.S. Government is taking the following steps in support of the legitimate Government of Panama:

1. United States Government payments due the Government of Panama are to be deposited in an account of the Government of Panama at the Federal Reserve Bank of New York. This account will be set up at President Delvalle's request.

2. The Department of Justice will participate in actions by private parties who have debts to the Government of Panama to declare that President Delvalle is the leader of the recognized Government of Panama. Pursuant to court orders, the Secretary of the Treasury will assist in the establishment of an account to be available for the deposit of funds.

3. The Internal Revenue Service will issue guidance to U.S. taxpayers explaining how tax credit may be claimed for Panamanian income taxes paid into an account to be specified at the Federal Reserve Bank of New York.

Through these measures, we are giving U.S. companies and persons an incentive and opportunity not to provide financial support to the Noriega regime. Should these measures prove insufficient, we will review additional legal steps that may be necessary to deny transfer of funds to the Noriega regime from U.S. companies and persons.

These measures are in addition to the following actions that were announced on March 11:

1. Withdrawal of trade preferences available to Panama under the Generalized System of Preferences and the Caribbean Basin Initiative.

2. Increased scrutiny of Panama by the Immigration and Customs Services in order to apprehend drug traffickers and money launderers.

3. Placing in escrow certain payments by the Panama Canal Commission to the Government of Panama.

The United States remains committed to the goal of restoring democratic government and constitutional order in Panama. When that goal is achieved, the United States is fully prepared to work with the Government of Panama to help restore quickly Panama's economic health. In addition, the U.S. Government is providing one-quarter million dollars to support the Caritas emergency feeding program in Panama. We will continue to examine the food needs of the poor in Panama.

Proclamation 5787—Amending the Generalized System of Preferences
March 31, 1988

By the President of the United States of America

A Proclamation

1. Pursuant to Title V of the Trade Act of 1974, as amended (the Trade Act) (19 U.S.C. 2461 *et seq.*), in Proclamation 5365 of August 30, 1985 (50 FR 36220), I designated specified articles provided for in the Tariff Schedules of the United States (TSUS) (19 U.S.C. 1202) as eligible for preferential tariff treatment under the Generalized System of Preferences (GSP) when imported from designated beneficiary developing countries.

2. Pursuant to section 504(c) of the Trade Act, as amended (19 U.S.C. 2464(c)), those beneficiary developing countries not designated as least-developed beneficiary developing countries are subject to limitations on the preferential treatment afforded under the GSP. Pursuant to section 504(c)(5) of the Trade Act, as amended, a country that has not been treated as a beneficiary developing country with respect to an eligible article may be redesignated with respect to such article if imports of such article from such country did not exceed the limitations in section 504(c)(1) (after application of paragraph (c)(2)) during the preceding calendar year. Further, pursuant to section 504(d)(1) of the Trade Act, as amended (19 U.S.C. 2464(d)(1)), the limitation provided in section 504(c)(1)(B) shall not apply with respect to an eligible article if a like or directly competitive article was not produced in the United States on January 3, 1985.

3. Pursuant to sections 503(a) and 504(a) of the Trade Act, as amended (19 U.S.C. 2463(a) and 2464(a)), in order to subdivide and amend the nomenclature of existing items for the purposes of the GSP, I have determined, after taking into account information and advice received under section 503(a), that the TSUS should be modified to adjust the original designation of eligible articles. In addition, pursuant to Title V of the Trade Act, as amended, I have determined that it is appropriate to designate specified articles provided for in the TSUS as eligible for preferential tariff treatment under the GSP when imported from designated beneficiary developing countries, and that such treatment for other articles should be terminated. I have also determined, pursuant to section 504(a) and (c)(1) of the Trade Act, that certain beneficiary countries should no longer receive preferential tariff treatment under the GSP with respect to certain eligible articles. Further, I have determined, pursuant to section 504(c)(5) of the Trade Act, that certain countries should be redesignated as beneficiary developing countries with respect to specified previously designated eligible articles. These countries have been excluded from benefits of the GSP with respect to such eligible articles pursuant to section 504(c)(1) of the Trade Act. Last, I have determined that section 504(c)(1)(B) of the Trade Act should not apply with respect to certain eligible articles because no like or directly competitive article was produced in the United States on January 3, 1985.

4. In Proclamation 5758 of December 24, 1987 (52 FR 49129), I suspended the preferential treatment afforded under the GSP to articles imported from Chile and removed Chile from the enumeration in TSUS general headnote 3(e)(v)(A) of independent countries whose products are eligible for benefits under the GSP. In order to take such suspension into account, I have determined that the TSUS should be modified to remove references to particular articles imported from Chile which had been ineligible for preferential treatment under the GSP.

5. Section 604 of the Trade Act (19 U.S.C. 2483) confers authority upon the President to embody in the TSUS the substance of the relevant provisions of that Act, of other acts affecting import treatment, and of actions taken thereunder.

Now, Therefore, I, Ronald Reagan, President of the United States of America, acting under the authority vested in me by the Constitution and laws of the United States, including but not limited to Title V and section 604 of the Trade Act of 1974, do proclaim that:

(1) In order to provide preferential tariff treatment under the GSP to certain designated eligible articles, and to provide that one or more countries should no longer be treated as beneficiary developing countries with respect to certain eligible articles for purposes of the GSP, the TSUS are modified as provided in Annex I to this Proclamation.

(2)(a) In order to provide preferential tariff treatment under the GSP to certain countries which have been excluded from the benefits of the GSP for certain eligible articles imported from such countries, following my determination that a country not previously receiving such benefits should again be treated as a beneficiary developing country with respect to such article, the Rates of Duty Special column for each of the TSUS items enumerated in Annex II(a) to this Proclamation is modified: (I) by deleting from such column for such TSUS items the symbol "A*" in parentheses, and (II) by inserting in such column the symbol "A" in lieu thereof.

(b) In order to provide that one or more countries should no longer be treated as beneficiary developing countries with respect to an eligible article for purposes of the GSP, the Rates of Duty Special column for each of the TSUS items enumerated in Annex II(b) to this Proclamation is modified: (I) by deleting from such column for such TSUS items the symbol "A" in parentheses, and (II) by inserting in such column the symbol "A*" in lieu thereof.

(3) General headnote 3(e)(v)(D) to the TSUS, listing those articles that are eligible for benefits of the GSP except when imported from the beneficiary countries listed opposite the enumerated TSUS items for those articles, is modified as provided in Annex III to this Proclamation.

(4)(a) In order to provide benefits under the GSP to specified designated eligible articles when imported from any designated beneficiary developing country—

(I) the Rates of Duty Special column for TSUS items 112.01, 131.27, 141.15, 141.83, and 755.15 is modified by inserting in the parentheses the symbol "A," immediately before "E" in each such item; and

(II) the Rates of Duty Special column for TSUS items 309.20 and 309.21 is modified by inserting the rate of "Free (A)" for each such item.

(b) In order to terminate preferential tariff treatment under the GSP for articles imported from all designated beneficiary developing countries, the Rates of Duty Special column for TSUS item 610.74 is modified by deleting the symbol "A*," in parentheses.

(5) The eligible articles imported from designated beneficiary developing countries and provided for in TSUS items 534.96 and 737.22 shall not be subject to the limitations of section 504(c)(1)(B) of the Trade Act, as amended.

(6) Effective with respect to articles the product of Israel that are entered, or withdrawn from warehouse for consumption, on or after the dates specified in Annex IV to this Proclamation, the rate of duty set forth in the Rates of Duty Special column followed by the symbol "I" in parentheses for each of the TSUS items enumerated in such Annex shall be deleted and the rate of duty provided in such Annex inserted in lieu thereof.

(7) The modifications made by this Proclamation shall be effective with respect to articles both: (a) imported on or after January 1, 1976, and (b) entered, or withdrawn from warehouse for consumption, on or after July 1, 1988.

In Witness Whereof, I have hereunto set my hand this 31st day of March, in the year of our Lord nineteen hundred and eighty-eight, and of the Independence of the United States of America the two hundred and twelfth.

RONALD REAGAN

[*Filed with the Office of the Federal Register, 4:48 p.m., April 1, 1988*]

Note: The annexes to the proclamation were printed in the "Federal Register" of April 5. The proclamation was released by the Office of the Press Secretary on April 1.

Executive Order 12634—Delegating Authority to Provide Assistance and Support for Peace, Democracy, and Reconciliation in Central America
April 1, 1988

By virtue of the authority vested in me as President by the Constitution and laws of the United States of America, including H.J. Res. 523, as enacted on April 1, 1988 ("the Act"), the Foreign Assistance Act of 1961, as amended (22 U.S.C. 2151 *et seq.*), and section 301 of title 3 of the United States Code, and in order to delegate certain functions concerning the designation of amounts to be transferred from specified accounts, the transfer of funds, and related personnel matters, it is hereby ordered as follows:

Section 1. The Secretary of Defense, in consultation with the Administrator of the Agency for International Development, is authorized to perform the functions, vested in the President by Sections 3(b) and (e), 4(a)(2), 8, and 9 of the Act, of transferring unobligated funds from the accounts specified in Section 6 of the Act.

Sec. 2. The Director of the Office of Management and Budget is authorized to perform the function, vested in the President by Section 4(d) of the Act, of approving the detailing of personnel to the Agency for International Development.

Sec. 3. The Secretary of Defense is authorized to perform the function of designating the amounts of unobligated funds, made available by the Department of Defense Appropriations Act, 1986, as contained in section 101(b) of the further continuing appropriations resolution for the fiscal year 1986 (Public Law 99–190), which are to be transferred from each of the accounts specified in Section 6.

RONALD REAGAN

The White House,
April 1, 1988.

[*Filed with the Office of the Federal Register, 4:50 p.m., April 1, 1988*]

Radio Address to the Nation on the Federal Role in Scientific Research
April 2, 1988

My fellow Americans:

Passover and Easter are festivals of hope. That's why this weekend is a good time for all of us to reflect on the enduring importance to mankind of hope and faith in the future. And nowhere do our hopes take more visible form than in the quest of science.

Science has grown, and with it, the fascination it holds for all of us. But as the pursuit of science has become ever more nationally and even multinationally funded, it has also become more expensive. The problem here is that science, unlike a bridge or an interstate highway or a courthouse, has no local constituency. Today, when we're witnessing some of the most exciting discoveries in the history of science, things similar to the breakthroughs associated with Einstein, Galileo, and Newton, Federal funding for science is in jeopardy because of budget constraints.

That's why it's my duty as President to draw its importance to your attention and that of Congress. America has long been the world's scientific leader. Over the years, we've secured far more patents than any other country in the world. And since World War II, we have won more Nobel prizes for science than the Europeans and Japanese combined. We also support more of what is called basic research; that is, research meant to teach us rather than to invent or develop new products. And for the past 40 years, the Government has been our leading sponsor of basic research.

The remarkable thing is that although basic research does not begin with a particular practical goal, when you look at the results over the years, it ends up being one of the most practical things government does. For example, government-sponsored basic research produced the first laser. Today, less than three decades later, lasers are used in everything from microsurgery to the transmission of immense volumes of information and may contribute to our Strategic Defense Initiative that promises to make ballistic missiles obsolete. Well, I think that over the past 50 years the Government has helped build a number of particle accelerators so scientists could study high energy physics. Major industries, including television, communications, and computer industries, couldn't be where they are today without developments that began with this basic research.

We cannot know where scientific research will lead. The consequences and spinoffs are unknown and unknowable until they happen. In research, as Albert Einstein once said, imagination is more important than knowledge. We can travel wherever the eye of our imagination can see. But one thing is certain: If we don't explore, others will, and we'll fall behind. This is why I've urged Congress to devote more money to research. After taking out inflation, today's government research expenditures are 58 percent greater than the expenditures of a decade ago. It is an indispensable investment in America's future.

Let me tell you about just a few of the many projects we'll fund this year. This year we'll begin work on the great grandchild of those particle accelerators that have meant so much to our economic growth. It's called the superconducting supercollider. And it will harness the galloping technology of superconductivity, so we can explore subatomic particles in ways we've never been able to before. We'll also continue developing the space station. When it's in orbit, the space station will let us perform once impossible experiments in the weightless and sterile environment of outer space and understand our world and universe. And we're developing new technology to allow man eventually to journey beyond Earth's orbit. Astronaut Senator Jake Garn and others in Congress have given the space program the support it needs to once again reach for the stars.

Meanwhile, back on Earth, we will be pursuing breakthroughs in biotechnology that promise to revolutionize medicine, agriculture, and protection of the environment. We're working on new ways to spread the seeds of Federal research. Working with universities across the country, we have established 14 engineering research centers devoted to basic research on emerging technologies. And we're planning 10 to 15 new science and technology centers to do the same thing in the fields of general science. All of these centers will work with industries so that what they discover can quickly lead to new and better and internationally competitive products. All of this and more is before Congress now.

Some say that we can't afford it, that we're too strapped for cash. Well, leadership means making hard choices, even in an election year. We've put our research budget under a microscope and looked for quality and cost effectiveness. We've put together the best program for the taxpayers' dollars. After all, the American tradition of hope is one we can't afford to forget.

Until next week, happy Easter and Passover. God bless you.

Note: The President spoke at 9:06 a.m. from his ranch in Santa Barbara County, CA.

Proclamation 5788—National Former Prisoners of War Recognition Day, 1988
April 1, 1988

By the President of the United States of America

A Proclamation

It is truly fitting that America observe April 9 in recognition of our former prisoners of war; that date is the 46th anniversary of the day in 1942 when U.S. forces holding out on the Bataan Peninsula in the Philippines were captured. Later, as prisoners of war, these gallant Americans were subjected to the infamous Bataan Death March and to other inhumane treatment that killed thousands of them before they could be liberated. In every conflict, brutality has invariably been meted out to American prisoners of war; on April 9 and every day, we must remember with solemn pride and gratitude that valor and tenacity have ever been our prisoners' response.

That is clear from the words of then-Captain Jeremiah Denton, USN, when he and other U.S. prisoners of war were freed in 1973 after years of captivity in North Vietnam. "We are honored to have had the opportunity to serve our country under these difficult circumstances," Captain Denton said. Implacable and incredible courage, endurance, faith, and patriotism were behind those words—eloquent and immortal testimony to the spirit of America's Armed Forces in the Vietnam War and throughout our history.

The term "difficult circumstances" referred to nothing less than physical and mental torture, starvation, disease, separation from loved ones, and deprivation of medical treatment—an ordeal that for some, in every conflict, did not end until death. To their brave families we offer solace and salute. To our former prisoners of war who endured so much, we say that with your example and with God's help we will seek to meet the standards of devotion you have set; we will never forget your service or your sacrifice.

The Congress, by Public Law 100–269, has designated April 9, 1988, as "National Former Prisoners of War Recognition Day" and authorized and requested the President to issue a proclamation in observance of this event.

Now, Therefore, I, Ronald Reagan, President of the United States of America, do hereby proclaim April 9, 1988, as National Former Prisoners of War Recognition Day, and I urge all Americans to observe this day of remembrance with appropriate ceremonies and activities.

In Witness Whereof, I have hereunto set my hand this first day of April, in the year of our Lord nineteen hundred and eighty-eight, and of the Independence of the United States of America the two hundred and twelfth.

RONALD REAGAN

[*Filed with the Office of the Federal Register, 3:04 p.m., April 5, 1988*]

Note: The proclamation was released by the Office of the Press Secretary on April 5.

Statement on Signing the Montreal Protocol on Ozone-Depleting Substances
April 5, 1988

I am pleased to sign the instrument of ratification for the Montreal protocol on substances that deplete the ozone layer. The protocol marks an important milestone for the future quality of the global environment and for the health and well-being of all peoples of the world. Unanimous approval of the protocol by the Senate on March 14th demonstrated to the world community this country's willingness to act promptly and decisively in carrying out its commitments to protect the stratospheric ozone layer from the damaging effects of chlorofluorocarbons and halons, but our action alone is not enough. The protocol enters into force next January only if at least 11 nations representing two-thirds of worldwide consumption of chlorofluorocarbons and halons ratify the agreement. Our immediate challenge, having come this far, is to promote prompt ratification by every signatory nation.

I believe the Montreal protocol, negotiated under the auspices of the United Nations Environment Programme, is an extremely important environmental agreement. It provides for internationally coordinated control of ozone-depleting substances in order to protect a vital global resource. It requires countries that are parties to reduce production and consumption of major ozone-depleting chemicals by 50 percent by 1999. It creates incentives for new technologies—chemical producers are already working to develop and market safer substitutes—and establishes an ongoing process for review of new scientific data and of technical and economic developments. A mechanism for adjustment of the protocol is established to allow for changes based upon the review process. The wisdom of this unique provision is already being realized.

Data made available only during the last few weeks demonstrate that our knowledge of ozone depletion is rapidly expanding. For our part, the United States will give the highest priority to analyzing and assessing the latest research findings to assure that the review process moves expeditiously.

The Montreal protocol is a model of cooperation. It is a product of the recognition and international consensus that ozone depletion is a global problem, both in terms of its causes and its effects. The protocol is the result of an extraordinary process of scientific study, negotiations among representatives of the business and environmental communities, and international diplomacy. It is a monumental achievement.

Statement by Assistant to the President for Press Relations Fitzwater on Immigration Amnesty

April 6, 1988

Just over a year ago the President signed into law the most sweeping immigration reform in more than three decades. Among the provisions of the new law was a generous legalization or amnesty provision that allows persons who are unlawfully in the United States to become legal residents if they meet certain requirements.

In general, they must have lived here continuously with only brief absences since prior to 1982, and they must have been contributing members of our society and free from serious criminal violations of our laws. More than 1¼ million persons have already come forward to accept this one-time amnesty provision in the immigration laws. They are made up of nearly every nationality. By their actions in this country over the past 6 years, they have demonstrated that they deserve the privilege of remaining here in a fully legal status without having to live in an underground society and fearing discovery of their unlawful existence in this great nation. Like other immigrants who have come through normal, lawful channels, they have shown a great willingness to work and contribute to our nation while sharing in our economic well being.

But the time to apply for citizenship under this amnesty provision will end on May 4, 1988. There may still be those who for one reason or another have not taken advantage of this one-time opportunity. If they do not do so soon, they will be left behind while their brother and sister immigrants enjoy living in the daylight of liberty. The President calls on all Americans to do whatever is in their power to remind their neighbors, friends, coworkers, and others who may be living outside our immigration laws, but are eligible for legal residence, that the time is growing short for them to come forward and join us as recognized members of our nation and our society. And he urges those who may be eligible to attain this privilege and benefit to do so promptly.

Proclamation 5789—National Student-Athlete Day, 1988
April 6, 1988

By the President of the United States of America

A Proclamation

The American people in recent years have recognized the need for a return to solid educational achievement in our schools and colleges. Parents, educators, and students realize the lasting value of an education that imparts thorough skills in reading comprehension, composition, and mathematics and that provides a fundamental understanding of our country's heritage of liberty and of the entire body of wisdom and knowledge to which our civilization is heir. One of the many beneficial results of this focus on sound education is a reemphasis on the role of academic life for our Nation's student athletes.

For decades, we have cheered our high school and college athletes as they have played the sports our country loves. Sometimes lost in "the tumult and the shouting," however, is the realization that, of every 10,000 student athletes, only one ever becomes a professional athlete; that the one who does so can expect a professional career of less than 4 years; and that the other 9,999 must rely for a living not on their athletic skills but on their educational background and a truly worthwhile academic degree.

We rightly support and salute our student athletes for their accomplishments on the diamond, the gridiron, the hardwood, the track, and every sort of playing field; but we must also do the same for athletes and all students for what they accomplish in the classroom as well. Parents, teachers, and coaches fulfill their obligations to student athletes by expecting and by fostering the high academic performance that is everyone's key to a bright, rather than a blighted, future. That is something for all of us to remember and to act upon, on National Student-Athlete Day and always.

The Congress, by House Joint Resolution 513, has designated April 6, 1988, as "National Student-Athlete Day" and authorized and requested the President to issue a proclamation in observance of this event.

Now, Therefore, I, Ronald Reagan, President of the United States of America, do hereby proclaim April 6, 1988, National Student-Athlete Day, and I call upon the people of the United States to observe this day with appropriate programs, ceremonies, and activities.

In Witness Whereof, I have hereunto set my hand this sixth day of April, in the year of our Lord nineteen hundred and eighty-eight, and of the Independence of the United States of America the two hundred and twelfth.

RONALD REAGAN

[*Filed with the Office of the Federal Register, 11:21 a.m., April 7, 1988*]

Proclamation 5790—Dennis Chavez Day, 1988
April 6, 1988

By the President of the United States of America

A Proclamation

April 8, 1988, is the Centennial Anniversary of the birth of New Mexico's Dennis Chavez, the first native-born Hispanic elected to the United States Senate and for many years the highest-ranking Hispanic in the Federal government. All Americans join the people of the Land of Enchantment and Hispanic Americans throughout our country in saluting the memory of this public servant, who left school as a child to help support his family and went on to become a lawyer, State Representative, U.S. Representative, and U.S. Senator.

Without a high school education, Dennis Chavez served as an interpreter of Spanish during Senator A. A. Jones's successful Senatorial campaign and in 1918 became a Senate clerk. He passed a special entrance examination for Georgetown University Law School and returned to New Mexico to practice law after earning his law degree in 1920. He was a New Mexico State Representative in 1923–24. In 1930 he won a seat in the U.S. House of Representatives, and in 1935 he was appointed to fill a vacancy in the United States Senate. He won election in his own right the next year and was reelected four times; he died in office on November 18, 1962.

As a Senator, Dennis Chavez chaired the Committee on Public Works and served on the Defense Appropriations Subcommittee. He sought the well-being of every American and displayed lasting concern for those in need. Dennis Chavez truly exemplified the dedication of the public servant and won distinction in the service of New Mexico and of his Nation; to this day, his life and career symbolize the countless achievements of Hispanic Americans and demonstrate the opportunity America offers.

The Congress, by Senate Joint Resolution 206, has designated April 8, 1988, as "Dennis Chavez Day" and authorized and requested the President to issue a proclamation in observance of this event.

Now, Therefore, I, Ronald Reagan, President of the United States of America, do hereby proclaim April 8, 1988, as Dennis Chavez Day. I urge Government agencies and the people of the United States to observe this day with appropriate programs, ceremonies, and activities.

In Witness Whereof, I have hereunto set my hand this sixth day of April, in the year of our Lord nineteen hundred and eighty-eight, and of the Independence of the United States of America the two hundred and twelfth.

RONALD REAGAN

[*Filed with the Office of the Federal Register, 11:22 a.m., April 7, 1988*]

Proclamation 5791—National Productivity Improvement Week, 1988
April 6, 1988

By the President of the United States of America

A Proclamation

Our Nation has long enjoyed a high standard of living, thanks especially to our high productivity, which has accounted for about half our economic growth over the last century. Productivity affects our total output of goods and services, helps keep inflation low, and is vital to our ability to compete in U.S. and foreign markets.

Until the mid-1960s, overall U.S. labor productivity grew at a commendable average rate of 3.2 percent each year. But it slowed to under 2 percent in the 1970s, and last year increased by just under 1 percent. Fortunately, productivity in manufacturing continued at a robust rate and increased by 3.3 percent in 1987. However, the rate of growth in the service sector, which accounts for more than 70 percent of U.S. employment, was less than 1 percent in 1987.

We must accelerate productivity growth in the service and other sectors. Good performance in productivity is especially necessary now that we are in world markets for most goods and services, and because many of our foreign competitors can target the U.S. market using state-of-the-art technology.

Government's job is to create a healthy climate in which private sector productivity growth can flourish. We have done this. We have adopted sound policies to reform internal laws, to encourage inventors to create better products and processes, to reduce burdensome regulations, to stimulate investment in research and development, and to strengthen private sector access to federally funded science and technology. These achievements provide a solid foundation for the private sector to build upon.

Our businesses and their individual leaders must continue their efforts to increase productivity by adopting new technologies and management innovations and by better strategic planning in the increasingly competitive international context.

Productivity is now intertwined with quality. To encourage U.S. companies to strengthen their quality, I have endorsed a major initiative, the Malcolm Baldrige National Quality Award, that will honor U.S. manufacturing firms, service companies, and small businesses for improving their goods and services. This initiative pays fitting tribute to a great Secretary of Commerce who fostered improvement during every assignment he took on.

To encourage Americans to understand the importance of productivity growth to their economic welfare, the Congress, by Senate Joint Resolution 223, has designated the week of April 10 through April 16, 1988, as National Productivity Improvement Week and authorized and requested the President to issue a proclamation in observance of this event.

Now, Therefore, I, Ronald Reagan, President of the United States of America, do hereby proclaim the week of April 10 through April 16, 1988, as National Productivity Improvement Week. I call upon the people of the United States and especially our business leaders, educators, workers, and public officials to observe this week with appropriate ceremonies and activities in a spirit of rededication to improving our Nation's productivity.

In Witness Whereof, I have hereunto set my hand this sixth day of April, in the year of our Lord nineteen hundred and eighty-eight, and of the Independence of the United States of America the two hundred and twelfth.

RONALD REAGAN

[*Filed with the Office of the Federal Register, 11:23 a.m., April 7, 1988*]

Letter to the Speaker of the House of Representatives and the President of the Senate Reporting on Japanese Whaling Activities
April 6, 1988

Dear Mr. Speaker: (Dear Mr. President:)

On February 9, 1988, Secretary of Commerce C. William Verity certified under Section 201(e) of the Magnuson Fishery Conservation and Management Act of 1976, as amended (Packwood-Magnuson Amendment) (16 U.S.C. 1821(e)) and Section 8 of the Fishermen's Protective Act of 1967, as amended (Pelly Amendment) (22 U.S.C. 1978), that Japan has conducted whaling activities that diminish the effectiveness of the International Whaling Commission (IWC) conservation program. This letter constitutes my report to the Congress pursuant to subsection (b) of the Pelly Amendment.

The certification of the Secretary of Commerce was based on the issuance by the Government of Japan of permits to its nationals, allowing them to kill Southern Hemisphere minke whales for research purposes, despite a 1987 resolution adopted by the IWC. This resolution recommended that Japan not issue permits until uncertainties in their scientific research proposals were resolved. A revised Japanese research proposal had been reviewed by a special meeting of the IWC Scientific Committee and had not succeeded in satisfying the Committee that the defects in the research program had been cured.

Shortly after the Secretary's certification, the IWC adopted a second resolution on February 14, 1988, recommending that Japan not proceed with its revised research program. Japan has continued its whaling activities notwithstanding this second resolution.

Given the lack of any evidence that Japan is bringing its whaling activities into conformance with the recommendations of the IWC, I am directing the Secretary of State under the Packwood-Magnuson Amendment to withhold 100 percent of the fishing privileges that would otherwise be available to Japan in the U.S. Exclusive Economic Zone. Japan has requested the opportunity to fish for 3,000 metric tons of sea snails and 5,000 metric tons of Pacific whiting. These requests will be denied. In addition, Japan will be barred from any future allocations of fishing privileges for any other species, including Pacific cod, until the Secretary of Commerce determines that the situation has been corrected.

The sanctions being imposed are the strongest possible under the Packwood-Magnuson Amendment. The immediate and prospective effects of a 100 percent reduction of fishing allocations, coupled with Presidential review in the near future, is the most effective means of encouraging Japan to embrace the IWC conservation program. Therefore, I will not impose at this time the sanctions available under the Pelly Amendment against Japanese fish products imported into the United States. I am asking Secretary Verity, in cooperation with Secretary Shultz, to monitor Japanese whaling practices during the next few months and to report to me no later than December 1, 1988.

I also am directing the Secretary of Commerce and the Secretary of State to continue consultations with our IWC partners to ensure that we bring to a halt all whaling that diminishes the effectiveness of the IWC's conservation program, specifically including that under Japan's contested research program. Our actions taken today and in the future should encourage all nations to adhere to the conservation programs of the IWC.

Sincerely,

RONALD REAGAN

Note: Identical letters were sent to Jim Wright, Speaker of the House of Representatives, and George Bush, President of the Senate.

Executive Order 12635—Prohibiting Certain Transactions With Respect to Panama

April 8, 1988

By the authority vested in me as President by the Constitution and laws of the United States of America, including the International Emergency Economic Powers Act (50 U.S.C. 1701 et seq.), the National Emergencies Act (50 U.S.C. 1601 et seq.), and section 301 of title 3 of the United States Code,

I, Ronald Reagan, President of the United States of America, find that the policies and actions in Panama of Manuel Antonio Noriega and Manuel Solis Palma constitute an unusual and extraordinary threat to the national security, foreign policy, and economy of the United States and hereby declare a national emergency to deal with that threat.

Section 1. I hereby order blocked all property and interests in property of the Government of Panama that are in the United States, that hereafter come within the United States, or that are or hereafter come within the possession or control of persons located within the United States. For purposes of this Order, the Government of Panama is defined to include its agencies, instrumentalities and controlled entities, including the Banco Nacional de Panama and the Caja de Ahorros.

Sec. 2. Except to the extent provided in regulations which may hereafter be issued pursuant to this Order:

(a) Any direct or indirect payments or transfers from the United States to the Noriega/Solis regime of funds, including currency, cash or coins of any nation, or of other financial or investment assets or credits are prohibited. All transfers, or payments owed, to the Government of Panama shall be made into an account at the Federal Reserve Bank of New York, to be held for the benefit of the Panamanian people. For purposes of this Order, the term "Noriega/Solis regime" shall mean Manuel Antonio Noriega, Manuel Solis Palma, and any agencies, instrumentalities or entities purporting to act on their behalf or under their asserted authority.

(b) Any direct or indirect payments or transfers to the Noriega/Solis regime of funds, including currency, cash or coins of any nation, or of other financial or investment assets or credits, by any United States person located in the territory of Panama, or by any person organized under the laws of Panama and owned or controlled by a United States person, are prohibited. All transfers, or payments owed, to the Government of Panama by such persons shall be made into an account at the Federal Reserve Bank of New York, to the held for the benefit of the Panamanian people. For purposes of Section 2(b), "United States person" is defined to mean any United States citizen, permanent resident alien, juridical person organized under the laws of the United States, or any person in the United States.

Sec. 3. Sections 1 and 2 shall not be deemed to block property or interests in property of the Government of Panama, including, but not limited to, accounts established at the Federal Reserve Bank of New York as described in section 2, with respect to which transactions are authorized by, or on behalf of, the recognized representative of the Government of Panama as certified by the Secretary of State, or are otherwise authorized in regulations which may hereafter be issued pursuant to this Order. Section 2 shall not be deemed to prohibit interbank clearing payments.

Sec. 4. The measures taken pursuant to this Order are intended to extend the effectiveness of actions initiated in cooperation with the Government of Panama and its President, Eric Arturo Delvalle, and are not intended to block private Panamanian assets subject to the jurisdiction of the United States or to prohibit remittances by United States persons to Panamanian persons other than the Noriega/Solis regime.

Sec. 5. This Order shall take effect at 4:00 p.m. Eastern Daylight Time on April 8, 1988, except as otherwise provided in regulations issued pursuant to this Order.

Sec. 6. The Secretary of the Treasury, in consultation with the Secretary of State, is authorized to take such actions, including the promulgation of rules and regulations, and to employ all powers granted to me by the International Emergency Economic Powers Act, as may be necessary to carry out the purposes of this Order. The Secretary of the Treasury may redelegate any of these functions to other officers or agencies of the Federal Government.

Sec. 7. Nothing contained in this Order shall confer any substantive or procedural right or privilege on any person or organization, enforceable against the United States, its agencies or its officers, or the Federal Reserve Bank of New York or its officers.

This Order shall be transmitted to the

Congress and published in the *Federal Register.*

RONALD REAGAN

The White House,
April 8, 1988.

[Filed with the Office of the Federal Register, 12:04 p.m., April 11, 1988]

Note: The Executive order was printed in the "Federal Register" of April 12.

Letter to the Speaker of the House of Representatives and the President of the Senate Reporting on the National Emergency With Respect to Panama
April 8, 1988

Dear Mr. Speaker: (Dear Mr. President:)

Pursuant to section 204(b) of the International Emergency Economic Powers Act, 50 U.S.C. section 1703, and section 201 of the National Emergencies Act, 50 U.S.C. section 1621, I hereby report that I have exercised my statutory authority to declare a national emergency and take the following measures:

(1) Block all property and interests in property of the Government of Panama that are in the United States, that hereafter come within the United States, or that are or hereafter come within the possession or control of persons located within the United States, except for transactions that are authorized by, or on behalf of, the recognized representatives of the Government of Panama as certified by the Secretary of State;

(2) Prohibit all direct or indirect payments or transfers from the United States or from any U.S. persons or subsidiaries in Panama to the Noriega/Solis regime.

The prohibitions are effective immediately and are subject to regulation by the Secretary of the Treasury.

I am enclosing a copy of the Executive Order that I have issued making this declaration and exercising these authorities.

I have authorized these steps in response to the unusual and extraordinary threat posed by the actions of Manuel Antonio Noriega and Manuel Solis Palma, to challenge the duly constituted authorities of the Government of Panama. In taking these measures we have acted in cooperation with the authorized representatives of the Government and in support of the efforts of the Panamanian people to foster constitutional, democratic government in Panama.

The steps taken today follow the previous measures we have taken in coordination with the authorized representatives of the Government of Panama, including the decision to deposit United States Government payments owed Panama in an account established at President Delvalle's request at the Federal Reserve Bank of New York, and removal of trade preferences under the Generalized System of Preferences and the Caribbean Basin Initiative. These further steps reaffirm our commitment to democratic government in Panama and our belief that Noriega would best serve his country by complying with the instruction of President Delvalle to relinquish his post.

The people of the United States and the people of Panama have shared a long and mutually productive relationship, exemplified by the historic Panama Canal Treaties. The United States has been, and remains, committed to fulfilling faithfully its obligations under the Panama Canal Treaties. We are prepared to resume our close working relationships with the Panamanian Defense Forces once civilian government and constitutional democracy are re-established.

Sincerely,

RONALD REAGAN

Note: Identical letters were sent to Jim Wright, Speaker of the House of Representatives, and George Bush, President of the Senate.

Statement by Assistant to the President for Press Relations Fitzwater on the National Emergency With Respect to Panama
April 8, 1988

The President has declared a national emergency under the authority of the International Emergency Economic Powers Act (IEEPA) and ordered that the United States Government take steps in addition to those announced on March 11 and March 31 to increase economic pressure on the Noriega regime. The President, by Executive order, has ordered the following steps, effective immediately:

—blocking assets of the Government of Panama in the United States;

—prohibiting payments by all people and organizations in the United States to the Noriega regime; and

—prohibiting payments to the Noriega regime by all U.S. people and organizations in Panama, including U.S. branches and subsidiaries.

These measures will provide further support to the efforts of the people of Panama and President Eric Delvalle to restore democratic government and constitutional order in Panama. Passed in 1977, the IEEPA is available to the President to deal with an unusual and extraordinary external threat to the national security, foreign policy, or economy of the United States.

Radio Address to the Nation on Economic Growth and the Intermediate-Range Nuclear Forces Treaty
April 9, 1988

My fellow Americans:

You've probably heard that some of our political opponents are very concerned about the state of our economy. And I have to tell you I don't blame them. If I were in their shoes, I'd be worried too.

You see, April marks the 65th straight month of the longest peacetime expansion in U.S. history. In that time, we've created nearly 16 million jobs. They're better and higher paying, too, which is one reason why the real income of the average American has been rising steadily for the last 5 years. The percentage of Americans employed is the highest in history, and the unemployment rate continues to drop down to its lowest level since 1974. Since 1980 U.S. manufacturing has increased its productivity almost 3 times as fast as in the 7 previous years. Inflation remains low, while the gross national product growth this year and last has exceeded even our own optimistic expectations.

Somehow our opponents have convinced themselves that this record growth, vibrant job creation, and more productive economy is bad news. And they say it's all the fault of Reaganomics. Well, I'd love to take the blame, or credit, as the case may be, but that just wouldn't be fair. All we did was get government out of your way. We cut taxes, inflation, and regulations; and we let the American people take back their own economy and run with it. In their effort to prove that this economic boom we're in is really a bust, our opponents have had to weave some pretty tall tales. One of those they tell about America is that we're threatened by foreign investment. Well, to paraphrase what Joe Friday used to say in "Dragnet": "Let's just look at the facts, ma'am." Yes, foreigners now hold about 12 percent of U.S. public debt, but that's down from 16 percent in 1978. Foreign resources also accounted for 10 percent of total credit-market funds last year—exactly the same as in the mid-1970's. But even so, foreign investment isn't something to be scared of. It brings us a host of benefits, including jobs and lower interest rates for all Americans, whether they be homebuyers, small businessmen, consumers, or farmers.

Writer-economist Warren Brookes makes a very good point: "What difference does it make," he asks, "whether a Japanese company owns a factory in Detroit or in Marysville, Ohio? Could someone seriously think they might dismantle it brick by brick, and ship it back to Japan in the middle of the night?" I wonder if the workers in those plants think foreign investment is such a bad thing, or the nearly 3 million other Americans employed by foreign firms in the United States, whose payrolls add up to more than $70 billion and that pay about $8 billion in income taxes to the United States Treasury.

The fact is we live in a global economy. We can be glad people in other countries choose to invest in the vibrant and growing U.S. economy rather than their own nations. I don't blame them. I think America's a pretty good investment, too. Right now, however, there's a trade bill working its way through Congress that could go a long way toward making America a bad investment for Americans and foreigners alike. At this moment, we've not seen the final bill. But from what we already know, we still have very—underline very—serious reservations. We'll continue to work with the full conference and the congressional leadership to clear up these problems. But the bottom line is this: I will veto a bad trade bill before I will let a bad trade bill veto our economic expansion.

Another important matter facing the Nation today is the INF treaty, which I signed with General Secretary Gorbachev at our Washington summit meeting last December. This treaty will, for the first time, eliminate an entire class of U.S. and Soviet missiles. We called this the zero-option when I first proposed it in 1981. The treaty also requires the Soviet Union to make far greater reductions now in its missile systems to reach equality with us. This is an historic precedent, and we will apply it to other arms negotiations as well. Finally, the treaty has the most comprehensive verification regime in arms control history. This too is an important precedent for other negotiations, particularly those on strategic arms, where an even more elaborate verification regime will be required.

In sum, this treaty represents what can be accomplished when we negotiate from a position of strength. Action on it is now up to the United States Senate, which must give its advice and consent to ratification. I hope it will be given expeditious consideration by the full Senate, and I urge all Senators to provide their advice and consent without reservation. It is a solid treaty, and it enhances the security of our country and our allies.

Until next week then, thank you for listening, and God bless you.

Note: The President spoke at 9:06 a.m. from his ranch in Santa Barbara County, CA.

Remarks at the Annual Convention of the National Association of Broadcasters in Las Vegas, Nevada
April 10, 1988

Thank you, Eddie Fritts, and thank all of you. Well, here we are in one of the entertainment meccas of the world. And I know that all of you have just one thing on your mind—foreign policy. [*Laughter*] But it's a special honor for me to be able to speak to the National Association of Broadcasters because, as you've just been told, broadcasting and I go back a long way. I mean a very long way. [*Laughter*] Come to think of it, the first group like this that I ever addressed was called the National Association of Towncriers. [*Laughter*]

For those of you with television stations, I have an announcement. As you know, I've never liked big government. And that was one of the reasons I was opposed to the so-called fairness doctrine, as you've already been told—that particular legislation which I vetoed. And I think you'll agree, there's no reason to substitute the judgment of Washington bureaucrats for that of professional broadcasters.

And now, while I'm on this subject, I wonder whether I could enlist your help. I nominated Bradley Holmes to the FCC [Federal Communications Commission] last December, and last fall, Susan—well, that was in the fall, and Susan Wing this past December. Now, until these nominations are confirmed by the Senate, the FCC can't operate effectively; yet for all these months, the Senate has failed even to hold confirmation hearings, much less bring the nominations to a vote. So, just let me just ask you: Isn't it high time the Senate took action? [*Applause*]

But as I say, I've never liked big government. Yet sometime before I leave office, I do intend to enact a very important new regulation: one limiting the number of commercials during my old movies. [*Laughter*]

It truly is an honor to have this opportunity to address you of the National Association of Broadcasters as you gather here under the theme, "Broadcasting and Democracy: The Winning Ticket." It's an honor, in particular, because these remarks represent an historic moment for both the Presidency and American broadcasting. It was back in 1923 that Warren Harding became the first President to speak over that newfangled piece of equipment, the radio. In 1946 Harry Truman became the first President to speak by way of television, followed by Dwight Eisenhower, who, in 1955, became the first President to be seen on color television. Today, just six short decades after Warren Harding first spoke over the radio, these remarks of mine are being recorded on HDTV, high-definition television. I'm told that HDTV represents an advance as dramatic as that from black and white to color—a new and powerful manifestation of the broadcasting industry.

This technological creativity—from primitive, early radio to HDTV and satellite transmissions during my own lifetime—has, of course, transformed American life. But I would submit that it promises to transform world affairs as well, and this is a subject that I'd like to come back to. The truth is that there is no setting in which the cause of peace and human freedom is ever far from our minds. And so, I'd like to take a moment to address foreign policy not only because of the coming summit but because I believe lessons have emerged during these past 7 years that will endure far beyond this administration.

Now, a few words about an issue that is important to both the Washington summit last year and to the coming Moscow summit next month: arms reductions. I cannot, of course, describe to you the detail of the talks we've engaged in with the Soviets, or are engaged at the moment. Rather, I'd like to discuss with you our fundamental approach to arms reduction.

The first point is that we insisted upon arms reductions. We refused, in other words, to be drawn into an elaborate arms control process that could very well lull us and our allies into a false sense of security. After all, it was in a climate of arms control and so-called détente during the 1970's that the Soviet Union continued their pursuit of the biggest arms buildup in all history—a buildup of nuclear and conventional forces alike—while we in the United States permitted our own deterrent capability to weaken.

At first, many critics viewed the goal of genuine arms reductions as unrealistic, even, according to some, misleading, even put forward in bad faith. They claimed our administration was making proposals that the Soviets would simply never agree to. But by the autumn of 1985, you in the media began reporting a Soviet willingness to consider a 25-percent, then a 40-percent, and finally a 50-percent reduction in strategic arms. We do not know yet whether we can reach an agreement with the Soviets on such a dramatic production—or reduction in strategic arms in time for the Moscow summit. But the negotiations are going forward, earnestly and in good faith, and that in itself is historic.

With regard to our zero-option proposal for intermediate-range nuclear forces, or as we call it, INF, the critics again derided our position as unrealistic when we first advanced it in 1981. Today it's my hope that the Senate will move expeditiously to give its advice and consent to the INF treaty that Mr. Gorbachev and I signed last December in Washington so we can exchange instruments of ratification next month in Moscow.

If you will, contrast these events with the Soviet attitude when the United States ordered [offered] deep cuts in nuclear arms to Moscow at the beginning of 1977. You'll recall that the Soviets rejected that American offer out of hand. Why? And what has changed in the meantime? Here, I believe, we come upon two points of tremendous importance for the Moscow summit and the whole future of American-Soviet relations.

First, the United States in the 1970's slashed our defense budgets and neglected crucial defense investment. We were dealing, in short, from a position of weakness. Well, today we're dealing from a position of strength. Second, the United States, those 11 years ago, had not yet shown what might be called a tough patience—a willingness to stake out a strong position, then stand by it as the Soviets probed and made their counteroffers, testing American determination. Why should the Soviets have agreed to a joint cut in 1977, when they had reason to believe the United States would go on permitting the strength of its deterrent forces to erode, when the Soviets had reason to believe, in other words, that in dealing with the United States they could get something for nothing? Yet today the Soviets understand that we can be tough enough and patient enough to hold out, that to improve their own position the Soviets themselves must bargain.

But I said when I first ran for President that our nation needed to renew its strength. Some called me bellicose, even a warmonger. Some claimed that we should deal with the Soviets not by rebuilding our own defenses but by engaging in a nuclear freeze, a freeze that would permanently ratify Soviet nuclear superiority. Well, I speak today—as I will speak increasingly in these months—of the lessons we've learned. Now we know, without doubt, that strength works, that strength promotes the cause of freedom and, yes, the cause of peace. I do not claim this achievement for my own.

Bipartisan support in the Congress has proven crucial in rebuilding our nation's defenses. It's my fervent hope that this bipartisan coalition can be sustained and enlarged, in particular, to support strategic defenses for America and our allies. My concern—my grave concern—about efforts to cut the defense budget—this is no time to weaken our defenses, not now, when we've been through so much to rebuild them, when our strong defenses have brought us so far in dealing with the Soviets.

Admittedly, defense is expensive. But it's not so expensive when you understand that it represents an investment in our own freedom and in world peace, and it's not so expensive when you consider what would happen if our defenses were permitted to fail. And so, in the coming campaign and for the years ahead, I would say to all involved in American politics—and I'm sure you here today agree: Wherever our parties may differ in our dealings with the Soviets, let them always agree. I didn't say that exactly correctly. No matter how much we may divide and be divided in our relations with the Soviets, let us always agree: We must be patient, and yes, America must be strong.

Important as they are, arms reductions have represented only one aspect of our four-part agenda for dealing with the Soviets—the other three being human rights; regional conflicts; and bilateral, people-to-people exchanges. This in itself represents another achievement, for we've gone from containment—the mere defense of our interests—to a strategy based upon the expansion of freedom.

Nowhere has the world movement toward freedom and democracy been more in evidence than in what might be called the outposts of Soviet expansionism. For in Afghanistan, Cambodia, Africa, and, yes, Nicaragua, we see domestic insurgencies directed against Communist tyrants. And it's been a central part of our new strategy, part of our new commitment to the expansion of freedom, to help them.

With regard to Nicaragua, it's no secret that I believe Congress should have done more, much more, to aid the freedom fighters. But the recent vote to send humanitarian aid will do much good. And I want to restate my commitment—my unshakable commitment—to stand by the freedom fighters and their efforts, in every way, to bring peace and democracy to their country.

Between now and the time I leave for Moscow, I'll be speaking at greater length about human rights and regional conflicts. In the very near future, we anticipate the signing in Geneva of an agreement that will result in the total withdrawal of Soviet forces from Afghanistan. Now, if that accord is complied with and the Soviets withdraw irrevocably from that long-suffering country, this will be a great victory for its heroic people, whom we shall continue to support. It'll also be a major contribution to the improvement of East-West relations.

But today, if I may, I'd like to talk for a moment about the bilateral relations between our two nations. It was at the Geneva summit in 1985 that General Secretary Gorbachev and I endorsed a new expansion in people-to-people exchanges between our two nations. Since then, exchanges of all kinds have begun taking place. Some have rightly received enormous publicity—the performance of pianist Vladimir Horowitz in Moscow, for example, or the Bolshoi Ballet's tour of the United States. Others have been quietly going forward—student exchanges, fine arts exhibitions, exchanges between academics and scientists. All of this has its impact. No Soviet citizen can return to his country from the United States seriously believing that America represents an aggressive power. No American can return from the Soviet Union without having his understanding of that country—and, yes, of what it means to be an American—deeply enriched. And so, in Moscow next month, I'll seek to expand these people-to-people exchanges still further.

But I'd like to consider as well the implications of another kind of exchange, one that I touched on at the very beginning of my remarks: the information exchange, an exchange borne of high technology. To be sure, no revolution in our time is more striking, far-reaching, and profound than the revolution in technology and communications. The semiconductor and countless other breakthroughs have ushered in a new burst of economic creativity. We have products today—the lap-top computer, for example—that were quite literally undreamed of just a decade ago. Instantaneous communications have made possible the growing integration of world markets. And, yes, the new communications technologies have made it harder and harder for totalitarian states to control the information that reaches their peoples. All of this says a great deal about the nature of the two world systems.

In the West, as I've suggested, we see rising standards of living, medical breakthrough after breakthrough, enormous economic and technological creativity. And in the Communist world? Well, Khrushchev may have said, "We will bury you," but today when we look at the Communist world, what we see is a vast economic stagnation. Today the Soviet Union cannot—and remember, this is some seven decades after the revolution—cannot feed its own people. And consider this: Endless shortages and long lines force the average Soviet family to spend 2 hours shopping every day just to obtain the necessities of life. It is not too much to claim that it lies in the very nature of freedom to promote growth and prosperity. Just as the technological revolution says much about the future [nature] of our two systems, so, too, it suggests a great deal about their future.

Maintaining a state monopoly on information is already becoming more and more difficult. States that depend now on the consent of their people, but on—not on the consent of their people, I should say, but on a rigid control of information those people receive—such states will come under increasing pressure. So, too, economic growth has already come to rely less and less upon the labor of the hands and the sweat of the brow, and more and more upon the genius of the human mind. Consider, for example, the cover story of last week's Forbes magazine.

The article, by the author and economist George Gilder, described coming developments in computer technology, focusing on the work and views of the California Institute of Technology's physicist Carver Mead. The article was entitled, "You Ain't Seen Nothing Yet." "Mead," Gilder writes, "believes that new developments in electronics are opening right now opportunities for entrepreneurial creativity and invention unprecedented in the history of technology. The current transition promises yet another 10,000-fold increase in the cost-effectiveness of computing in the next decade. Silicon slices with as many as 10 billion linked transistors will become possible." And listen, if you would, what Mead himself is quoted as saying: "The entire Industrial Revolution enhanced productivity by a factor of about 100. The Microelectronic Revolution has already enhanced productivity in information-based technology by a factor of more than a million, and the end isn't in sight yet." And Mead goes on to say of coming developments: "We're not going to need the Federal Government to come in and bail out all our electronics. We're going to do just fine, thank you." Well, I know what you're thinking, and it's true: That last remark warmed my heart considerably.

But what does this technological revolution mean for the future of the world order? It means that nations will have to grant to their scientists complete freedom of inquiry; to their businessmen and entrepreneurs, freedom to invest, to risk, to create new products and with them new markets; to their entire economies, the freedom to grow and grow, unburdened by heavy taxation and unimpeded by needless regulation. This represents, as I said, the true challenge of openness to the Communist world. For the Soviets and their clients must open their countries to ever-wider freedoms, or they'll see their economies—indeed, their whole way of life—fall further and further behind.

Well, I don't want to go on too long. This is, after all, Las Vegas, and outside, just a moment ago, I saw a fellow trading 10 passes to the Reagan talk for one ticket to Frankie Valli. [*Laughter*] I'm mindful, too, that bringing things to a good conclusion is always a tricky business. You were told that I was a sports announcer—WHO, Des Moines. Well, back in those days, the great evangelist, Aimee Semple McPherson, was making a tour of the country, holding revival meetings, and one of them in Des Moines. Now, the station thought it would be a good idea—an enterprising public relations man—to interview Aimee Semple McPherson. But why they picked a sports announcer to interview that noted evangelist, I'll never know. But there we stood in the studio, and I asked her several, what I thought were appropriate, questions. And then she answered graciously, but then went into a very fervent plea about the success of her meeting. And I sat down, until suddenly, I heard her saying good night to our radio audience. And I looked up at the clock, and there were only 4 minutes to go. Well, I didn't know enough about Aimee Semple McPherson that I could fill 4 minutes.

So, I got up—and in those days of radio and disk jockeys and so forth, I started thanking the noted evangelist, Aimee Semple McPherson, and so forth. But I did like this—[*At this point, the President made a gesture.*]—which means get a record ready. And the fellow out in the control room, through the window, reached out—there was always records around there for such contingencies—and picked one up and put it on the table. I said, "Ladies and gentlemen, we conclude this broadcast by the noted evangelist, Aimee Semple McPherson, with a brief interlude of transcribed music." I expected nothing less than the "Ave Maria." The Mills Brothers started singing, "Minnie the Moocher's Wedding Day." [*Laughter*] She never did say goodbye. She just slammed the studio door as she—[*laughter*]—went out.

But to return to world affairs, you may recall that when I was in Berlin last year, I challenged Mr. Gorbachev to tear down the Wall, that grim reminder of all that divides East from West, the Communist world from the free. But there is another wall that divides us, an invisible wall. It's the wall the Communist world has erected against the free flow of information and ideas. It's the wall that prevents the Communist world from joining the West in this dazzling new age of prosperity and creativity. And as I challenged him in Berlin before the Washington summit, I challenge Mr. Gorbachev here today before the summit in Moscow—challenge him to tear down this other wall, this grim, invisible wall of oppression.

Mr. Gorbachev and I have already addressed each other's people on television, and this was helpful. But I challenge Mr. Gorbachev to open the Soviet Union more fully to Western media. Western newspapers and journals should become freely available to Soviet citizens. Soviet airwaves should be opened to Western broadcasts. And, yes, the Soviets should open their country to books, all books. Here I have a specific first step to suggest. Mr. Gorbachev, open the Soviet Union to the works of a great man and an historic author. Open the Soviet Union to the works of Solzhenitsyn. We have been too long divided, East from West. Tear down this wall, Mr. Gorbachev, that our peoples might come to know one another and together build the world anew.

Well, I made a promise to myself, as Henry the Eighth said to each of his six wives, that I wouldn't keep you long. [*Laughter*] So, thank you all, and God bless you all.

Note: The President spoke at 10:45 a.m. in the Hilton Pavilion at the Las Vegas Hilton Hotel. He was introduced by Edward O. Fritts, president and chief executive officer of the National Association of Broadcasters.

Nomination of Paul D. Taylor To Be United States Ambassador to the Dominican Republic

April 11, 1988

The President today announced his intention to nominate Paul D. Taylor, of New York, a career member of the Senior Foreign Service, Class of Minister-Counselor, as Ambassador to the Dominican Republic. He would succeed Lowell C. Kilday.

Since 1985 Mr. Taylor has been Deputy Assistant Secretary of State for Inter-American Affairs. From 1981 to 1984, he was deputy chief of mission in Guatemala and Chargé d'Affaires in 1984. Mr. Taylor entered the Foreign Service of the United States in 1963. He has been assigned to posts in Quito, Ecuador; Bangkok, Thailand; Saõ Paulo, Brazil; Madrid, Spain; and Guatemala City, Guatemala.

Mr. Taylor graduated from Princeton University (A.B., 1960) and Harvard University (M.P.A., 1967). He was born May 16, 1939, in Lockport, NY. Mr. Taylor is married, has three children, and resides in Chevy Chase, MD.

Nomination of Walter Leon Cutler To Be United States Ambassador to Saudi Arabia

April 11, 1988

The President today announced his intention to nominate Walter Leon Cutler, of Maryland, a career member of the Senior Foreign Service, Class of Career Minister, to be Ambassador to the Kingdom of Saudi Arabia. He would succeed Hume Alexander Horan.

Mr. Cutler joined the Foreign Service of the United States in 1956 and was first assigned as a consular officer in Yaounde, Cameroon, 1957–1959. In 1959 he returned to Washington as a Foreign Affairs officer in the Executive Secretariat of the State Department. In 1961 Mr. Cutler was named staff assistant to the Secretary of State; political officer in Algiers, Algeria, 1962–1965; and principal officer at the U.S. consulate in Tabriz, Iran, 1965–1967. Mr. Cutler was then assigned as political officer at the U.S. Embassy in Saigon, Vietnam, 1969–1971, and returned to Washington to serve as special assistant in the Bureau of East Asian

Affairs, 1971–1973. He became a member of the senior seminar on foreign policy at the Foreign Service Institute for 1 year. From 1975 to 1979, he was Ambassador to the Republic of Zaire; Senior Deputy Assistant Secretary of State for Congressional Affairs, 1979–1981; Ambassador to the Republic of Tunisia, 1982–1984; Ambassador to the Kingdom of Saudi Arabia, 1984–1987; and diplomat-in-residence for the School of Foreign Service at Georgetown University, 1987–1988.

Mr. Cutler graduated from Wesleyan University (B.A., 1953) and Fletcher School of International Law and Diplomacy (M.A., 1954). He was born November 25, 1931, in Boston, MA. Mr. Cutler is married, has three children, and currently resides in Bethesda, MD.

Proclamation 5792—National Child Care Awareness Week, 1988
April 11, 1988

By the President of the United States of America

A Proclamation

Caring for children is the primary responsibility of a parent. It is the task around which family life is organized, a major factor in every decision parents make about their own and their family's future, from choice of jobs and schools and neighborhoods to the selection of books, films, and every other form of instructional material or entertainment that will influence the development of the child's character and personality. Child care is also an organizing principle of society, for it is the primary means of transmitting knowledge, traditions, and moral and religious values from one generation to the next.

Sound public policy must support the family in its mission of child care. To do so effectively, public policy must increase and strengthen, not narrow and dilute, the variety of child care options open to families. It must help ensure that child care serves as an adjunct and buttress to parental guidance and love; that it reflects as far as possible the actual preferences of parents for the personal care of their precious offspring; and that it is inherently flexible, to avoid the establishment of practices or programs that defeat these ends and undermine either the well-being of children or the health of the economy.

Heightened interest in child care is a result of tremendous growth and change in the U.S. work force. Between 1982 and 1986, American business created two and one-half times as many new jobs as Japan and the major industrial countries of Europe combined. Our country is well into its sixth consecutive year of expansion—a peacetime record. Women, particularly, are moving into the salaried labor force in large numbers, and their unemployment rate has dropped nearly a full percentage point in the past year alone. According to the Bureau of Labor Statistics, nearly half of all mothers with a child under one year of age work. Today one family in six is headed by a single, divorced, or widowed woman.

Americans have responded to these changes in a number of ways, reflecting the many options parents desire and need. Family members—a sibling or grandparents—and students provide both full- and part-time day care. Churches have developed effective day care programs that supplement custodial care with the religious atmosphere many parents seek. State-licensed facilities managed by public agencies or private entities have rapidly expanded, as have corporate child care programs. Moreover, the landmark tax reform bill I signed in 1986 included a provision beneficial to all families facing child care decisions: the near doubling—to $2,000 by 1989, with indexing thereafter—of the per-child personal exemption. This measure has restored at least a fraction of the exemption's original worth to families and more realistically reflects the rising cost of caring for children.

To be fair to all families, child care policy analysis must recognize the contributions of women who work, those who would prefer to work part-time rather than full-time jobs, and homemakers who forgo employment income altogether to raise children at home. Surely all of these are "working mothers." As policy options are reviewed and implemented, we must also continue to assess carefully the growing body of research data on the effects of various forms of child care on the emotional, psychological, and intellectual development of children.

I ask all Americans to join with me in honoring the parents, relatives, schools, churches, and institutional child care providers who take on the enormously important task of child care. Theirs is a sacred trust gladly assumed for the future of our Nation. National Child Care Awareness Week affords us a welcome opportunity to offer them recognition and encouragement.

The Congress, by Senate Joint Resolution 260, has designated the week beginning April 10, 1988, as "National Child Care Awareness Week" and authorized and requested the President to issue a proclamation in observance of this week.

Now, Therefore, I, Ronald Reagan, President of the United States of America, do hereby proclaim the week beginning April 10, 1988, as National Child Care Awareness Week.

In Witness Whereof, I have hereunto set my hand this eleventh day of April, in the year of our Lord nineteen hundred and eighty-eight, and of the Independence of the United States of America the two hundred and twelfth.

RONALD REAGAN

[*Filed with the Office of the Federal Register, 10:54 a.m., April 12, 1988*]

Proclamation 5793—Pan American Day and Pan American Week, 1988
April 11, 1988

By the President of the United States of America

A Proclamation

For nearly six decades, observance of the annual Pan American Day has told the world that the nations of the Western Hemisphere share a unique harmony of ideals—the love of liberty, independence, and democracy; the willingness to seek these treasures and to preserve them wherever they are found; and firm and profound opposition to totalitarianism. Each year the United States joins with countries throughout the Americas in pledging fidelity to these ideals so vital to our future.

Almost a century ago, in Washington, D.C., the First International Conference of American States made the idea of hemispheric unity a reality by establishing the International Union of American Republics, the predecessor of the Organization of American States (OAS). The common aspirations of the peoples of the Americas for freedom, independence, democracy, peace, security, and prosperity inspire the OAS, which is charged with upholding and defending these critical objectives within the Inter-American System.

The past decade has witnessed several victories for freedom and democracy in the Americas. Ten years ago, the great majority of Latin Americans lived under oppression; today, more than 90 percent of the people of the Americas live under democratic government. We can all be truly grateful for these transformations to democracy.

On April 30, the OAS will celebrate the 40th Anniversary of the signing of its Charter in Bogota in 1948—a Charter that declares, "the solidarity of the American States and the high aims which are sought through it require the political organization of those States on the basis of the effective exercise of representative democracy." This principle continues to encourage brave men and women in the fight for liberty and democracy.

The OAS Charter establishes the basis for hemispheric cooperation in the peaceful settlement of disputes, economic and social development, education, and the protection of human rights. In recent years, the OAS has added a new dimension to its regional problem-solving by creating the OAS Drug Abuse Control Commission to combat narcotics trafficking and drug abuse. The United States of America accords special priority to the crucial work of the OAS in the fields of human rights and narcotics control.

The foundations of the Inter-American System emerged from the Americas' independence movements, but its consolidation dates from the signing of the OAS Charter; so it is especially fitting that we renew our commitment to the principles of the Organization of American States and its Specialized Agencies on Pan American Day this year as 40th Anniversary celebrations take place.

Now, Therefore, I, Ronald Reagan, President of the United States of America, by virtue of the authority vested in me by the Constitution and laws of the United States, do hereby proclaim Thursday, April 14, 1988, as Pan American Day, and the week of April 10 through April 16, 1988, as Pan American Week. I urge the Governors of the fifty States, the Governor of the Commonwealth of Puerto Rico, and officials of other areas under the flag of the United States of America to honor these observances with appropriate ceremonies and activities.

In Witness Whereof, I have hereunto set my hand this eleventh day of April, in the year of our Lord nineteen hundred and eighty-eight, and of the Independence of the United States of America the two hundred and twelfth.

RONALD REAGAN

[*Filed with the Office of the Federal Register, 10:55 a.m., April 12, 1988*]

Remarks Announcing the Signing of the Afghanistan Accords
April 11, 1988

Before welcoming our visitors, our guests here today, I have a brief announcement. I have to make it here because that's where the press is, and it's for them. I've just received a briefing from my national security advisers on the contents of the proposed Geneva agreements on Afghanistan that would provide for the complete withdrawal of Soviet occupation forces from that country. I believe the U.S. can now join the Soviet Union as a guarantor of the Geneva instruments. I've therefore asked Secretary [of State] Shultz to represent us at a signing ceremony for the historic accords as scheduled to take place in Geneva later this week.

This development would not have been possible had it not been for the valiant struggle of the Afghan people to rid their country of foreign occupation. We take great pride in having assisted the Afghan people in this triumph, and they can count on our continued support. We also pledge our continued friendship and support to the Government and people of Pakistan, who have so generously hosted millions of Afghan refugees during this period of Soviet domination of Afghanistan.

Note: The President spoke at 1:52 p.m. in the Rose Garden at the White House.

Remarks on Greeting the 1988 National Collegiate Athletic Association Men's and Women's Basketball Champions
April 11, 1988

And now let's bring on the NCAA basketball champions of Louisiana Tech and the University of Kansas. [*Applause*] Well, thank you, and thank you all too—and welcome to the White House. I want to join with the Members of Congress from Louisiana and Kansas, your loyal fans, and the whole Nation in congratulating you.

You know, when I was a boy my nickname was "Dutch." Looking at all of you, I sort of wonder why it wasn't "Shorty." [*Laughter*] Come to think of it, being here with you reminds me of one of my experiences in college. It was freshman year and just after the football season ended. And after playing football, I thought I might go out for basketball, too. I went to the gym, and I saw a few people just about your size, and thought to myself, "I think swimming is the sport for me."

But to the women of Louisiana Tech, congratulations! You had a lot of great games this season, but none was greater than the last one. With the Lady Techsters trailing 33 to 19 at halftime, coach Leon Barmore found himself telling his team, "You don't quit in anything. You don't quit in life. No matter what happens, be proud of your efforts when it's over so you can live with yourselves the rest of your life." "Any other game when we'd be behind by that many points," forward Erica Westbrooks said, "we'd be all upset. This time we kept thinking that it had to be in us. We had to keep digging and finding it within ourselves." Well, Coach, Erica, and all of the Lady Techsters—you found it. And I just have a certain feeling that you're going to be able to live with yourselves pretty darned well.

Congratulations go as well to coach Larry Brown and the University of Kansas Jayhawks. Now, it's no secret that at the beginning of the NCAA tournament, you Jayhawks—well, I suppose the way to put it is to say that you weren't exactly favored to win. [*Laughter*] So, what happened is a testament to determination, to hard work—lots and lots of hard work, to pride, to teamwork, and the courage to dream.

And perhaps nothing exemplifies the true meaning of teamwork than the support you've all given to Archie Marshall and the untiring support Archie Marshall has given to you. In my opinion, that's just the way it should be. As the soft-spoken Danny Manning said to a jammed room of reporters after the final game: "I'd like for you guys to put this in your articles. For anyone who's ever been in a national tournament like this, keep your head up and work hard and anything can happen. To those who said it couldn't happen—well, we're number one."

And to coach Larry Brown, the man who did so much to make this a championship season, I know Jayhawk fans everywhere are rejoicing that, next year, I'm the only one moving back to California.

Well, they're both great stories, the stories of these two teams, these two fighters who happened to turn themselves into national champions. And if I could offer a thought to each of you young players, it would be this: Remember the lessons you've learned this season, the lessons about hard work and never quitting, about digging down into yourselves when you seem to be behind. Because what you've learned in basketball will be a strength to you all your lives. Especially here, in this great land of opportunity. Because it's true, if you keep your head up and work hard in America, anything can happen.

So again, congratulations on your exciting victory, and God bless you all. And have you thought about a game between—[*laughter*]—all right, God bless you.

Note: The President spoke at 1:53 p.m. in the Rose Garden at the White House.

Nomination of Rush Walker Taylor, Jr., To Be United States Ambassador to Togo
April 11, 1988

The President today announced his intention to nominate Rush Walker Taylor, Jr., of Texas, a career member of the Senior Foreign Service, Class of Counselor, as Ambassador to the Republic of Togo. He would succeed David A. Korn.

Mr. Taylor joined the Foreign Service in 1962 and was assigned as third secretary and vice consul, Yaounde, Cameroon, 1962–1964; staff assistant to the Ambassador, Rome, Italy, 1965–1966; and vice consul, Florence, Italy, 1966–1967. He returned to Washington in 1967 to serve on the Italian desk, 1967–1969; and then as staff officer for the Executive Secretariat at the Department of State, 1969–1970. Mr. Taylor was named staff assistant, 1970, and Special Assistant to the Secretary of State, 1971. He was then assigned as principal officer at the consulate in Oporto, Portugal, 1972–1975; deputy chief of mission in Nassau, the Bahamas, 1975–1978; staff of the Inspector General, 1979–1981; Director of the Office of Press Relations for the Bureau of Public Affairs at the Department of State, 1981–1983; and Executive Director and Vice Chairman of the U.S. Delegation for the International Telecommunications Union High Frequency World Administrative Radio Conference, 1983–1984. Since 1985 Mr. Taylor has been deputy coordinator and principal deputy director for the Bureau of International Communications and Information Policy. In 1986 he was temporarily detailed as Chargé d'Affaires in Guinea-Bissau.

Mr. Taylor graduated from Harvard University (A.B., 1956) and the University of Virginia Law School (LL.B., 1959). Mr. Taylor was born November 3, 1934, in Little Rock, AR. He served in the United States Army, 1959–1961. He is married, has three children, and resides in Arlington, VA.

Nomination of Henry F. Cooper for the Rank of Ambassador While Serving as United States Negotiator for Defense and Space Arms
April 11, 1988

The President today announced his intention to nominate Henry F. Cooper, of Virginia, for rank of Ambassador during his tenure of service as United States Negotiator for Defense and Space Arms.

Dr. Cooper entered government service in 1980 as Deputy to the Assistant Secretary of the Air Force for Research, Development and Logistics. From 1983 to 1985, he was Assistant Director of the Arms Control and Disarmament Agency, and from 1985 to 1987, he was Deputy Negotiator for Defense and Space Arms. Prior to his government service, he was a member of the senior technical staff, program manager and deputy director of R&D Associates.

Dr. Cooper was born November 8, 1936, in Augusta, GA. He graduated from Clemson University (B.S., 1958; M.S., 1960) and New York University (Ph.D., 1964). He served in the United States Air Force, 1964–1972. He is married, has three children, and resides in McLean, VA.

Nomination of Stephen R. Hanmer, Jr., for the Rank of Ambassador While Serving as United States Negotiator for Strategic Nuclear Arms

April 11, 1988

The President today announced his intention to nominate Stephen R. Hanmer, Jr., of Virginia, for the rank of Ambassador during his tenure of service as United States Negotiator for Strategic Nuclear Arms.

Since 1978 Mr. Hanmer has served at the Department of Defense in various positions: nuclear plans officer in the U.S. mission to NATO, Director of the Office of Theater Nuclear Force Policy in the Office of the Assistant Secretary of Defense for International Security Policy, Acting Principal Deputy Assistant Secretary of Defense for International Security Policy, and personal representative of the Secretary of Defense on the START delegation. From 1986 to 1987, Mr. Hanmer was Deputy Negotiator for Strategic Nuclear Arms.

Mr. Hanmer graduated from the Virginia Military Institute (B.S., 1955) and the University of Southern California (M.S., 1964). He was born August 15, 1933, in Denver, CO. He served in the U.S. Army, 1956–1977. Mr. Hanmer is married, has three children, and resides in Falls Church, VA.

Nomination of Mark T. Cox IV To Be Alternate United States Executive Director of the International Bank for Reconstruction and Development

April 11, 1988

The President today announced his intention to nominate Mark T. Cox IV to be United States Alternate Executive Director of the International Bank for Reconstruction and Development for a term of 2 years. He would succeed Hugh W. Foster.

Since 1972 Mr. Cox has been with the First Chicago Corp. in several capacities: vice president and head of Western Hemisphere Capital Market Group Mexico in Golden Beach, FL, 1985–1987; vice president and regional manager for the State of Florida, 1983–1985; vice president and representative in Saõ Paulo, Brazil, 1978–1983; vice president and treasurer of First Chicago Investments Canada Limited, 1977–1978; and assistant vice president and general manager in Port-au-Prince, Haiti, 1974–1977.

Mr. Cox graduated from Columbia University (B.A., 1966; M.B.A., 1971). He was born July 14, 1942, in Cheyenne, WY. He served in the United States Army Reserve, 1967–1969. He is married and resides in Golden Beach, FL.

Nomination of Joseph Wentling Brown To Be a Member of the Board of Directors of the State Justice Institute

April 11, 1988

The President today announced his intention to nominate Joseph Wentling Brown to be a member of the Board of Directors of the State Justice Institute for a term expiring September 17, 1989. This is a new position.

Since 1971 Mr. Brown has been a partner with Jones, Jones, Bell, Close & Brown in Las Vegas, NV. Prior to this he was an associate attorney with Laxalt, Bell, Berry, Allison & LeBaron, 1969–1971.

Mr. Brown graduated from the University of Virginia (B.A., 1965) and Washington & Lee University (LL.B., 1968). He was born July 31, 1941, in Norfolk, VA. He served in the United States Marine Corps Reserve, 1963–1969. He is married, has four children, and resides in Las Vegas, NV.

Proclamation 5794—John Muir Day, 1988
April 11, 1988

By the President of the United States of America

A Proclamation

April 21 is the 150th Anniversary of the birth of John Muir, naturalist, explorer, conservationist, author, champion of the American wilderness, and proponent of national parks. This Sesquicentennial Celebration reminds us of our debt to this native of Scotland who traversed our country, our continent, and the world to study and describe mountain and forest and glacier and glade, and who left us a vision of utmost respect for the wilderness and all it embodies.

After studying at the University of Wisconsin and revealing an aptitude for mechanical invention, Muir decided to embark on "the study of the inventions of God"—in the "university of the wilderness." Both observant and eloquent, he began journeys and journal-keeping to investigate nature. Success as a horticulturalist near Martinez, California, gave him the wherewithal to travel and study for a lifetime. He walked throughout his beloved Golden State, all America, and many other lands to record his observations and wrote books and articles on natural phenomena and especially on the forests he loved.

John Muir understood, and helped others to see, the significance and beauty of the wilderness—and to realize that it should be protected for future generations. The establishment of our tremendous national park system, and the practice of sound conservation policies by industry, government, and private citizens, owe much to this pioneer, who along with Robert Underwood Johnson led the fight for the creation in 1890 of what is now Yosemite National Park; who in 1903 hosted President Theodore Roosevelt in Yosemite; who wrote, "The forests of America, however slighted by man, must have been a great delight to God; for they were the finest He ever created."

Let all who revere America's natural heritage, and see in it a timeless treasure dependent upon our stewardship, pause on April 21 in grateful remembrance of John Muir, a man who forever expressed his credo in the words, "In God's wildness lies the hope of the world . . ."

The Congress, by Senate Joint Resolution 245, has designated April 21, 1988, as "John Muir Day" and authorized and requested the President to issue a proclamation in observance of this event.

Now, Therefore, I, Ronald Reagan, President of the United States of America, do hereby proclaim April 21, 1988, as John Muir Day, and I call upon the people of the United States to observe this day with appropriate ceremonies and activities.

In Witness Whereof, I have hereunto set my hand this eleventh day of April, in the year of our Lord nineteen hundred and eighty-eight, and of the Independence of the United States of America the two hundred and twelfth.

RONALD REAGAN

[*Filed with the Office of the Federal Register, 10:56 a.m., April 12, 1988*]

Appointment of William J. Maroni as Special Assistant to the President and Executive Secretary of the Economic Policy Council
April 12, 1988

The President today announced the appointment of William J. Maroni to be Special Assistant to the President and Executive Secretary of the Economic Policy Council. He would succeed Eugene J. McAllister.

Since October of 1987 Mr. Maroni has served as an Assistant Secretary of Labor (Congressional Affairs). Prior to this he served as Deputy Under Secretary of Labor for Congressional Affairs. From 1981 to 1985, he headed the Legislative Affairs Office in the Office of the United States Trade Representative, first as director of congressional affairs and then as an Assistant United States Trade Representative. From 1978 to 1981, Mr. Maroni served as legislative assistant to Senator John H. Chafee of Rhode Island.

Mr. Maroni received a bachelor's degree from Harvard College. He was born January 17, 1955, in Providence, RI. He is married, has one child, and resides in Washington, DC.

Nomination of Lemoine V. Dickinson, Jr., To Be a Member of the National Transportation Safety Board
April 12, 1988

The President today announced his intention to nominate Lemoine V. Dickinson, Jr., to be a member of the National Transportation Safety Board for the remainder of the term expiring December 31, 1988. He would succeed Patricia A. Goldman.

Since 1982 Mr. Dickinson has been special assistant to the Vice Chairman of the National Transportation Safety Board in Washington, DC. Prior to this he was special assistant to the Deputy Secretary at the Department of Transportation, 1981–1982. He was a senior policy analyst for the Office of Technology Assessment at the U.S. Congress, 1977–1981. From 1975 to 1977, he was a technical staff/research engineer for Mitre Corp.

Mr. Dickinson graduated from the University of Maryland (B.S.C.E., 1966; M.S.C.E., 1973; Ph.D., 1975). He served in the United States Army Corps of Engineers, 1968–1971. He was born September 23, 1943, in Washington, DC. Mr. Dickinson is married and currently resides in Alexandria, VA.

Statement by Assistant to the President for Press Relations Fitzwater on the Trade Bill
April 12, 1988

The President has said before that he would like to be able to sign a trade bill that will open markets and improve America's international competitiveness. The 17 subconferences have made notable progress in moving toward such a bill, but further improvements must be made. The administration is prepared to continue working with the congressional leadership and the full conference on an acceptable bill. As the full conference moves to complete its work, the President has asked Secretary Baker,

Senator Baker, and Ambassador Yeutter to make themselves available to resolve the remaining problems. But let there be no misunderstanding: The President will not hesitate to veto a trade bill that will hurt America's economic prosperity.

Statement by Assistant to the President for Press Relations Fitzwater on the Afghanistan Accords

April 12, 1988

The Geneva accords call for four instruments as outlined by Secretary Shultz yesterday in the briefing room. In addition, the Secretary noted our insistence that the obligations of the guarantors be symmetrical. We are satisfied that the Soviets understand our view and intent regarding the guarantees, i.e., that they must be symmetrical. Our position on this issue will be made publicly clear to all parties in a statement the United States will issue at the time of the signing.

Nomination of Richard Newton Holwill To Be United States Ambassador to Ecuador

April 12, 1988

The President today announced his intention to nominate Richard Newton Holwill to be Ambassador to the Republic of Ecuador. He would succeed Fernando Enrique Rondon.

Since 1983 Mr. Holwill has been a Deputy Assistant Secretary for Inter-American Affairs at the Department of State. He has also been a member of the Board of Directors of the Panama Canal Commission since 1983. Prior to this, he was vice president of government information for the Heritage Foundation, 1981–1983; vice president of Energy Decisions, Inc., 1980; and consultant and managing editor of Energy Decisions, 1977–1980. From 1974 to 1977, he was a White House correspondent for National Public Radio.

Mr. Holwill graduated from Louisiana State University (B.A., 1968). He was born October 9, 1945, in Shreveport, LA. He served in the United States Marine Corps, 1969–1971. He is married, has two children, and resides in Washington, DC.

Nomination of George Edward Moose To Be United States Ambassador to Senegal

April 12, 1988

The President today announced his intention to nominate George Edward Moose, of Maryland, a career member of the Senior Foreign Service, Class of Minister-Counselor, as Ambassador to the Republic of Senegal. He would succeed Lannon Walker.

Since 1987 Mr. Moose has been Director of the Office of Management Operations at the Department of State and Deputy Director, 1986–1987. Prior to this, Mr. Moose was: Ambassador to the People's Republic of Benin, 1983–1986; Deputy Political Counselor for the United States Mission to the United Nations, 1980–1983; and international affairs fellow of the Council on Foreign Relations, 1979–1980. Mr. Moose was also Deputy Director in the Office of Southern African Affairs, 1978–1979; Special Assistant in the Office of the Under Secretary for Political Affairs, 1977–1978; analyst for the Office of African Affairs in the Bureau of Intelligence and Research, 1974–1976; and political officer at the U.S. Embassy in Bridgetown, Barbados, 1972–1974. Mr. Moose joined the Foreign Service in 1967.

Mr. Moose graduated from Grinnell College (B.A., 1966). He was born June 23, 1944, in New York City. He is married and resides in Washington, DC.

Nomination of Patrick Butler To Be a Member of the National Council on the Humanities

April 12, 1988

The President today announced his intention to nominate Patrick Butler to be a member of the National Council on the Humanities, National Foundation on the Arts and the Humanities, for a term expiring January 26, 1994. He would succeed Walter Berns.

Since 1985 Mr. Butler has been the vice president of Times Mirror in Washington, DC. Prior to this he was the president of Patrick Butler & Co., 1982–1985. From 1980 to 1982, Mr. Butler was the staff vice president of RCA Corp. He served as special assistant to Senate Republican Leader Howard H. Baker, Jr., 1978–1980.

Mr. Butler attended the University of Tennessee. He was born October 25, 1949, in Hartselle, AL. Mr. Butler is married, has three children, and resides in Bethesda, MD.

Remarks at a White House Briefing for Members of the Young Presidents' Organization

April 13, 1988

Thank you all very much, and thank you, Ken, and welcome to the White House. I am delighted to have you here to wrap up what I know has been a whole series of meetings and briefings that you've had with top officials of the administration. The Young Presidents' Organization has an extraordinary membership. I can't help but admire men and women who are already being called president when they're 40. [*Laughter*] It took some of us a little bit longer. Come to think of it, though, I've often wondered, does president of my union of Screen Actors Guild before I was 40 count? [*Laughter*] So, I'm one of you. [*Applause*]

Well, what you've accomplished so early in life means that your biggest success still lies ahead. I know that you're—well, now that you are used to being called president, no one knows where you might wind up. We certainly need risk-taking, bottom-line chief executives like you to serve in government. I've been very fortunate to have in my administration former members of YPO like Jack Courtemanche, who isn't here with us this morning, but three others that are: Carl Covitz, Bob Tuttle, and Joe Wright. And without men and women drawn from the private sector, it is easy for the Federal Government to become unresponsive and out of touch.

Soon after we got here, I commissioned a task force to reduce excessive government regulation, which I asked Vice President Bush to head up. And thanks to that effort, we were able to eliminate some of the needless regulations that had built up and to subject all new proposed rules to the most careful scrutiny. And the result has been pretty practical. The *Federal Register*, which lists all regulations, is just a little more than half the size that it was when we came here, and the estimate is that we have eliminated among people—just citizens, small—or community and State governments and so forth, businesses—600 million man-hours a year of work filling out government forms in answer to the regulations. A lot of you know personally the sort of paperwork the Federal Government can require.

I remember the old story about a businessman who after many years of dutifully keeping the records and documents required by the Federal Government in his particular business, and with the files really piling up, he wrote the Government asking if he still needed to keep all the old documents. And a letter came back saying, "Well, it's okay, you can throw away any papers more than 8 years old provided you make copies of each one of them first." [*Laughter*]

Here in the Old Executive Office Building, you know, they tell me that officially we're in the White House, but I'm still not used to that. You see, back before the Federal Government was a growth industry, this one building housed most of the executive branch of government. But after a couple of world wars that changed, and existing Federal departments grew and new ones sprang up. And when each agency got its own complex, the White House sort of adopted this beautiful old building. After all, it's just across the street.

Well, I'm happy to report that the Federal Government is not growing that way anymore, but many of your businesses are. And that's the best sort of news for America. In fact, I'll bet that it has been your companies that have needed the new office space in the last few years because the economy is in the longest peacetime expansion in U.S. history. April marks the 65th straight month of economic growth. And during this period, we have created nearly 16 million new jobs, and they're better and higher paying too. And in fact, the U.S. has created about 2½ times as many new jobs as the other leading industrialized nations all put together. No government program can do that, but companies like yours did. Today a greater percentage of our citizens is working than any other time in our history.

I have to try something out. Did you ever know—I didn't know before I got here—what is considered the potential employment pool in America and upon which the statistics are based? It is everyone, male and female, 16 years of age and up, regardless of whether they're going to school, regardless at the other end whether they're retired—they're all considered a part of that pool. Well, when you say the highest percentage of that pool is employed, 62.3 percent of all of that group presently are employed in the United States. It's no coincidence that while we've held down the rate of growth in government, the private economy has been booming—real GNP grew by nearly 5 percent in the fourth quarter last year and inflation remains low. And because you are out there in the vanguard of American business, I don't have to tell you that economic growth is more than statistics, it's the cumulative daily efforts of men and women like yourselves.

As Business Week Magazine reported recently, "Basic manufacturers, once considered a dying breed, are selling products many thought wouldn't even be made in the United States any longer—escalators to Taiwan, machine tools to West Germany, lumber to Japan, and shoes to Italy." Well, since the third quarter of 1986 the volume of American exports has been growing some 4 times as fast as the volume of imports. And it's thanks to you, not the Government, that since 1980 the United States' manufacturing has increased its productivity roughly 3½ times as fast as in the previous 8 years. The result is that, as one German manufacturing expert put it recently, the United States is "the best country in the world in terms of manufacturing costs."

It's thanks to the private sector that the real income of the average American has been rising steadily for the last 6 years. The Federal Government did one thing to contribute to this: we got out of your way as much as we could. So, when American business created new wealth for the country, it flowed to the American people and was not diverted to Washington to fund new bureaucracies and spending programs.

What the Federal Government needs to do now is what each of you always does—balance the budget—and not by raising taxes but by controlling spending. If we can continue the progrowth policies of the last 7 years, I believe that the next decade will be known as the "Roaring Nineties." Our country is poised for even greater economic growth in the years ahead because we've opened up the economy, lowered tax rates, and restored the ideal of limited government and free enterprise.

America will face choices this fall that will determine what lies ahead for American business and the economy. And I want to ask you to become active and involved this year because the stakes are too high and the choice too clear for it to be left up to others. If the policies under which your companies have flourished are reversed, how could your companies' bottom line not suffer? We cannot afford to have American businessmen once again treated like a bunch of hired hands laboring on the Federal farm, where the folks in Washington act as if what you produce belongs to them.

I can't help but say—once back when I was Governor of California—interject here about how that attitude can grow in government. We, one year, gave back $850 million of surplus in California to the taxpayers—just told them to reduce what they gave us in their taxes, and we'd make it up with that surplus. And one Senator stormed into my office one day, and he said—I think he said—there is no excuse for giving back that public money to the people. [*Laughter*]

Well, we've cut the top personal income tax rate by more than half—making U.S. tax rates among the lowest in the world—and revenues have increased, not decreased, with those cuts. And right now, all of our trading partners and neighbors are going through the same thing and making the same kind of tax cuts. We've proved that lower rates enhance economic growth and greater growth results in higher tax collections. We've demonstrated that American business and entrepreneurship are second to none. Let's keep America moving forward.

I ask each of you in the coming months to direct some of your talent, energy, and leadership to the choices that lie before us. In doing so, you'll be serving your country as citizens, serving your companies and industries as corporate leaders, and helping to preserve and build the jobs, growth, and opportunity that working Americans depend on. After you leave here, I want you to remember this building and think whether next year and beyond, America will be constructing new plants and offices for expanding businesses like yours, or will we be raising more and more Federal office buildings to tax, regulate, and stifle the energy, imagination, and enterprise of the American people.

The choice we face is a very simple one. Is the Federal Government going to grow, or is your business going to grow? I want to let you know that I'm on your side. Thank you for all that you have done to make America stronger and more prosperous. I thank you all, and God bless you all.

[*At this point, a portrait of the President and Queen Elizabeth II on horseback outside of Windsor Castle was given to the President.*]

Well, I can't tell you how happy I am. And yes, the Queen and I did go riding when we were guests there at Windsor Palace on a visit. She's a good rider. [*Laughter*] I have to take a second and tell you something about that. I knew about her and her riding before she invited me there to join her, and I had known it because earlier, when I was in England way back in 1949, I was invited to visit the Royal Mews. That at Buckingham Palace is the stable and indoor riding hall and all. And she had just become the commander of—as their—I can't remember which regiment it is, but cavalry regiment.

And therefore, she had to ride, leading them in parades and so forth as a princess. And the man that was taking me through, that was in charge of the stables, was telling me about her and how they trained her. They get all the household help down there with towels and tin pans and so forth all around the riding hall. And they would bring her in, and she would ride around that hall while they made all the clatter and noise they could possibly make to distract the horse. And she was ready for the first parade in London. But he spoke very admiringly of her courage and how quickly she developed this ability to ride. And like all of us that expose ourselves to horses, once you've learned how, which she had to do, she found out she loved it. So, she's now—that's one of her sports.

But, oh, I don't know whether to give that to the Presidential Library or not. [*Laughter*] I've already made up my mind. [*Laughter*] Thank you very much. Thank you all.

Note: The President spoke at 11:01 a.m. in Room 450 of the Old Executive Office Building. In his opening remarks, the President referred to Kenneth M. Duberstein, Deputy Chief of Staff.

Message to the Senate Transmitting the Bahamas-United States Legal Assistance Treaty
April 13, 1988

To the Senate of the United States:

With a view to receiving the advice and consent of the Senate to ratification, I transmit herewith the Treaty between the United States of America and the Commonwealth of The Bahamas on Mutual Assistance in Criminal Matters, signed at Nassau on June 12 and August 18, 1987, with related notes. I transmit also, for the information of the Senate, the report of the Department of State with respect to the Treaty.

The Treaty is one of a series of modern mutual legal assistance treaties being negotiated by the United States in order to counter criminal activities more effectively. The Treaty should be an effective tool in prosecuting a wide variety of modern criminals, including members of drug cartels, and "white-collar criminals." The Treaty is self-executing and utilizes existing statutory authority.

The Treaty provides for a broad range of cooperation in criminal matters. Mutual assistance available under the Treaty includes: (1) taking testimony or statements of witnesses; (2) provision of documents, records, and evidence; (3) execution of requests for searches and seizures; (4) transfer of persons in custody for testimonial purposes; (5) serving documents; (6) locating persons; (7) exchanging information; (8) immobilizing forfeitable assets; and (9) any other matter mutually agreed upon.

I recommend that the Senate give early and favorable consideration to the Treaty, with related notes, and give its advice and consent to ratification.

RONALD REAGAN

The White House,
April 13, 1988.

Proclamation 5795—National Stuttering Awareness Week, 1988
April 13, 1988

By the President of the United States of America

A Proclamation

The uniquely human ability to communicate thoughts through speech allows us to share our ideas almost as quickly as they occur, with little conscious effort. But for the more than three million Americans who stutter, speech is associated with struggle. Rapid-fire repetitions of sounds, prolonged vowels, and verbal blocks disrupt the smooth and easy flow of speech and limit the spontaneous exchange of ideas and feelings. Many stutterers suffer frustration and embarrassment that can lead to harmful emotional stress.

Stuttering has a tendency to be inherited, and it affects four times as many males as females. Children usually outgrow stuttering before reaching adulthood. When the disorder continues or begins in adults, it is considered chronic and very difficult to control.

Just what causes stuttering is not yet known, but research is providing clues. In normal speech, the brain and more than 100 muscles of the vocal system work together to produce fluent sounds. Within the larynx, one set of muscles contracts to pull the vocal folds apart and works in close coordination with the set of muscles that allows the folds to close. In stuttered speech, however, these muscle sets do not coordinate properly, preventing normal movement of the vocal folds.

Focusing on this specific malfunction, scientists at the National Institute of Neurological and Communicative Disorders and Stroke (NINCDS) have developed a promising, but as yet experimental, treatment for severe chronic adult stutterers. Injections to the larynx temporarily paralyze one of the muscles, easing the disruptive tug-of-war between opposing muscles and thereby improving speech.

The NINCDS leads the Federal government's research effort on stuttering, funding projects around the country in addition to conducting studies in its own laboratories. Research supported by private voluntary health agencies adds to the growing pool of knowledge. These private organizations also provide invaluable counseling and other services to stutterers and their families. Together, Federal and private groups call attention to simple ways the public can help; for example, many stutterers actually improve their speech when listeners know to be patient and supportive.

To enhance public awareness of stuttering, the Congress, by Public Law 100–263, has designated the period of May 9 through May 15, 1988, as "National Stuttering Awareness Week" and authorized and requested the President to issue a proclamation in observance of that event.

Now, Therefore, I, Ronald Reagan, President of the United States of America, do hereby proclaim the period of May 9 through May 15, 1988, as National Stuttering Awareness Week, and I call upon the people of the United States to observe that week with appropriate ceremonies and activities.

In Witness Whereof, I have hereunto set my hand this thirteenth day of April, in the year of our Lord nineteen hundred and eighty-eight, and of the Independence of the United States of America the two hundred and twelfth.

RONALD REAGAN

[*Filed with the Office of the Federal Register, 12:08 p.m., April 14, 1988*]

Proclamation 5796—Gaucher's Disease Awareness Week, 1988
April 13, 1988

By the President of the United States of America

A Proclamation

Gaucher's disease, the most common of a group of inherited disorders known as lipid storage diseases, afflicts more than 20,000 Americans. It most commonly strikes people of Eastern European Jewish descent, affecting approximately one in every 2,500 people in this group.

Investigators at the Federal government's National Institute of Neurological and Communicative Disorders and Stroke (NINCDS) discovered that Gaucher's disease is caused by the failure of the body to produce an enzyme needed to break down fatty substances called lipids that arise from the normal renewal of the body's cells and tissues. In Gaucher's disease, a specific lipid builds up in body tissues, causing enlargement of the spleen and liver, bone pain, and fractures. In severe cases, serious neurological disorders may occur.

NINCDS scientists and other investigators supported by both public and private funds have narrowed the search for effective management and treatment of this disease. It is now possible to identify carriers of Gaucher's disease. The gene responsible for producing the needed enzyme has been cloned and its structure in normal individuals and Gaucher's disease patients is being studied. Scientists are continuing to refine techniques for replacing the missing enzyme as a useful form of therapy. They are also examining methods that may eventually allow them to replace the defective gene and provide a permanent cure.

Gaucher's patients are further encouraged and sustained by the work of dedicated voluntary health agencies such as the National Gaucher Foundation. These groups provide information and services to patients and their families and work closely with the NINCDS to promote research. When Gaucher's disease is finally conquered, it will be thanks to the cooperative efforts of both private and Federal agencies.

To enhance public awareness of Gaucher's disease, the Congress, by Public Law 100–254, has designated the week beginning October 16, 1988, as "Gaucher's Disease Awareness Week" and authorized and requested the President to issue a proclamation in observance of that week.

Now, Therefore, I, Ronald Reagan, President of the United States of America, do hereby proclaim the week beginning October 16, 1988, as Gaucher's Disease Awareness Week, and I call upon the people of the United States to observe that week with appropriate ceremonies and activities.

In Witness Whereof, I have hereunto set my hand this thirteenth day of April, in the year of our Lord nineteen hundred and eighty-eight, and of the Independence of the United States of America the two hundred and twelfth.

RONALD REAGAN

[*Filed with the Office of the Federal Register, 12:09 p.m., April 14, 1988*]

Remarks at the Annual Convention of the American Society of Newspaper Editors
April 13, 1988

The President. Thank you all, and let me say a special thank you to your chairman, David Lawrence, and your president, the distinguished editor of one of America's great newspapers, Katherine Fanning. For just a minute there, I thought I was still at the Gridiron. [*Laughter*]

When he stood before this group almost 27 years ago, President Kennedy said that, "The President of a great democracy such as ours and the editors of great newspapers such as yours owe a common obligation to the people to present the facts with candor and in perspective." Well, I certainly agree. Whether one is working in the Oval Office or in the newsrooms of America, whether one is putting together the Nation's policies or the next day's edition, the purpose is the same: the continuing purpose of defending America's liberties and passing them on to the next generation. And truth be told, in the greater scheme of things, you are—I hesitate to say this—more essential to that common pursuit than I am. And that's why freedom of the press is, and must always be, above politics—something all jurists and all legislators and all Presidents agree on. As Jefferson said—and he was right: "When the press is free and every man able to read, all is safe."

Now, not all Presidents have been that generous. I've told this story before, and if you've heard it, I hope you'll just bear with me. That's the nice thing about this job; you get to quote yourself shamelessly—and if you don't, Larry Speakes will. [*Laughter*] But as you may know, historians trace the Presidential press conference back to a Chief Executive who was quite reticent with the press, John Quincy Adams. He didn't hold press conferences. But it seems that every morning before dawn Adams would hike down to the Potomac, strip off his clothes, and swim. And one summer day, a woman of the press, under orders from her editor, followed him. And after he'd plunged into the water, she popped from the bushes, sat on his clothes, and demanded an interview. [*Laughter*] And she told him that if he tried to wade ashore, she'd scream. So, Adams held the first press conference up to his neck in water. [*Laughter*] I know how he felt. [*Laughter*]

But I've always believed that the key to good press relations is tact, candor, and seeing most things from the point of view of editors and reporters. Sort of like Lyndon Johnson. [*Laughter*] There's a story about Johnson when he was Vice President. He was coming off the Senate floor when he ran into a reporter for the New York Times. Johnson grabbed him, shouted, "You, I've been looking for you," pulled him into his office, and began a long harangue about something or other. About halfway through, he scribbled a note on a scrap of paper, buzzed his secretary, and gave it to her. She was back in a minute with another note. He glanced at it while he talked and then threw it away. And eventually the reporter got out, but as he left the outer office, he saw the note that Johnson had written lying on the secretary's desk. It said, "Who's this guy I'm talking to anyway?" [*Laughter*]

Well, I know who you are, and I'm not here to harangue. I'm going to keep my copy crisp and clean—who, what, where, when, why, and how, with no extra words. And for my lead—something that's at the top of the page in any election year and certainly this one—the economy. It's time to take a blue pencil to the nonsense that some who are applying for my job are circulating about our economy. We've heard about hundreds of thousands of lost jobs, the decline of the middle class, and the deindustrialization of America—and this is at a time when our nation is in the longest peacetime expansion on record, is creating hundreds of thousands of jobs each month, has a larger proportion of the work force employed than ever before, has been seeing real personal and family income climb ever since our expansion began, and is exporting more than ever in our history.

So, it's time to cross out the false charges and put in a little perspective. Yes, there is something happening in America's economy. It's new. It's powerful. And on the whole, it's good, creating more and better jobs for our nation, making us vastly more productive and more competitive around the world. And there's no better place to see just what it is than in the newsrooms and pressrooms of your papers.

When I got out of the movie business and first tried for public office, most of the newspapers that covered my race for Governor ran on technology just one generation removed from Gutenberg, the technology of the first industrial revolution, linotypes and the rest. Today, less than a quarter century later, you are reporting, editing, and publishing the news about the current Presidential campaign with a technology that is light-years removed from anything that preceded it. Computer stations to write, light pencils to edit, lap-top word processors that let reporters file finished copy in seconds over the phone, satellite hookups to shoot entire issues to remote printing plants—these incredible transformations have opened vast new horizons to you and your staffs. The result is that while, in what you might call the manufacturing end of newspapers—for example, printing and running presses—employment is about the same today as in 1960, in the service end, reporters and editors in particular, employment has boomed. Newspapers now have almost half again as many people on the job as 27 years ago, and pay is better.

Yes, here is the real story about what's happening to our economy. Newspapers were the first on the street with the speed-of-light technology of the computer age. What you did in the sixties and seventies, the rest of American industry has been doing in the seventies and eighties. And that doesn't mean that we're deindustrializing or becoming a hollow service economy or that our paychecks are shrinking. It does mean that we're becoming much more productive, and so we're spending more time, energy, and manpower on the thought that goes into our products. The story behind the story is that's just what we must do to grow and prosper and stay the world's leader.

You know, all those fellows who talk about us becoming a nation that flips each other's hamburgers and takes in each other's laundry—they owe you who represent what we're really becoming a retraction. If the retraction ever comes—and I'm not holding my breath—it'll rank right up there with what must be history's greatest retraction. I'm told it appeared years ago in one of our newspapers—I won't say which one. And talk about getting a story wrong, it read, and I'm quoting now, "Instead of being arrested, as we stated yesterday, for kicking his wife down a flight of stairs and hurling a lighted kerosene lamp after her, the Reverend James P. Wellman died, unmarried, 4 years ago." [*Laughter*]

Now, I've talked a lot about technology and the economy, but there is a greater truth that gives life and strength to technology in your industry and throughout our economy, and that's freedom. Here in Washington, about a half mile from the White House, stands a monument to one of the early fathers of modern medical technology, an 18th century physician. It's a gray stone statue of the man sitting in his chair in a pose of contemplation. Behind his head is a mosaic of brilliant colors, as if these colors depicted the quality of his thought. Technology, like literature, like journalism, flourishes in our land because we have the freedom to bring the brilliant mosaics in our minds to life. I'm talking here about the first amendment, although technology is not, strictly speaking, a first amendment issue. But our freedom of expression, of debate, of the unfettered airing of ideas is the great plain on which our technological harvest grows.

There is a titanic struggle in the world today. I've often characterized it as the struggle between freedom and totalitarianism, but you could as easily call it the struggle between the pen and the sword, between the first amendment of our Constitution and article 6 of the Soviet Constitution—that's the one that places the party over the country. More and more, the tide of battle seems clear, at least on one front. As America and the free industrial nations leap ahead through technological time, the Soviet Union and its clients are falling farther and farther behind. How can a blindfolded society keep its balance on the Earth's ever-shifting industrial base when the only way is to take the blindfold off and allow the people to see the world and its kaleidoscopic wonders?

Soviet leaders talk about *glasnost*. We in the West have taken this to mean a new freedom of expression, a new flow of information and ideas, a response to the pressures of a changing world. And yet, though some sharp criticism appears in the Soviet press, we know other criticism is stifled. Some publicized prisoners of conscience are released, but others remain in camps and wards. Some people are allowed to demonstrate, but peaceful protests by Jewish women in Moscow and Leningrad, by Latvians in Riga, by Estonians in Tallinn, and by the Armenians are suppressed or forcibly put down. The Ukrainian Catholic Church remains underground. Teaching Hebrew to Jewish children remains a crime. This is why Natan Scharanskiy, among others, warns that, in his words, "*Glasnost* is not a form of freedom. It's just a new set of instructions on what is and isn't permitted."

We don't minimize the importance of what's happening in the U.S.S.R., and we hope that the Soviet Union will, indeed, become a freer society. And this is why, as a matter of conscience, we must press the Soviets to do better and not allow them to beguile themselves and us with half measures. And no one is more important in keeping the truth, favorable and unfavorable, before our nation, the world, and the Soviets themselves than you. Millions in the Soviet bloc look to you to tell their stories. They know that if you do their lives will become better, for the Soviet leaders have always had an acute ear for Western media, and that's true of Mr. Gorbachev as well. I guess what I'm saying is not all that different from what the founding editor of the Chicago Times, Wilbur Storey, said more than a century ago: "It is a newspaper's duty to print the news and raise hell." Now, do that half as well with the Soviet leaders as you do with me—[*laughter*]—and you can make *glasnost* mean something. [*Laughter*]

Let me suggest some first steps you might join me in, in encouraging the Soviet leaders to take. Mr. Gorbachev and I addressed each other's people on television. This was helpful. But now we should move even further and see the Soviet Union open more fully to Western media. Western newspapers and journals, for example, should be freely available to Soviet citizens—books, too. And here, let me repeat a challenge I made recently. Mr. Gorbachev, open the Soviet Union to the works of a great man and historic author. Open the Soviet Union to the works of Solzhenitsyn.

The struggle between the pen and the sword is worldwide, and despite the moral force of freedom and the disadvantages of totalitarianism, the final outcome is by no means certain. And wherever the battle is joined, you, willingly or unwillingly, are in the field. During the period leading up to the cease-fire negotiations in Nicaragua, the Sandinistas acknowledged that they were going forward with internal reforms because they wanted the aid vote in Congress to go their way. They were playing to you in the press and through you to the country and Congress.

I don't often quote from Washington Post editorials. [*Laughter*] I won't say the Post is aggressive, but the first thing I hear each morning is the paper hitting the front door of the White House. Ben Bradlee has it delivered by cruise missile. [*Laughter*] Yet after the Nicaraguan cease-fire agreement, the Post observed that "The cease-fire accord has the superficial appearance of an agreement between equals. But with the war, the Sandinistas were hurting badly, while with the aid cutoff, the *contras* were collapsing." And the Post continued, "It has been argued by the anti-*contra* left that the Sandinistas could not reasonably be expected to democratize while facing a mortal threat. It follows that, being no longer under the gun, they can reasonably be expected to honor their pledges to democratize." And the editors concluded, "Those Americans who have repeatedly urged others to 'give peace a chance' now have an obligation to turn their attention and their passion to ensuring democracy a chance."

Well, the Post is not alone in this view. Costa Rican President Arias has said that "There can be no peace without democracy in Central America." Now the question is: Are we taking steps toward democracy in Nicaragua, or are the Sandinistas biding their time, waiting for the attention to wander, whereupon they will crush the disarmed opposition? I support democracy in Nicaragua. If the cease-fire brings democracy, I'm for it. If it does not, we will ask what will. To advance democracy has been my policy for 7 years. It hasn't changed.

Last week the opposition newspaper, La Prensa, had to stop publishing for several days because it was denied newsprint, in direct violation of the Central American peace agreement. La Prensa is no friend of the Sandinistas. This January, its editor and publisher said that "In 8 years we have gone from Somoza to a dictatorship that is even worse, with a Marxist-Leninist ideology." Well, perhaps this denial of newsprint was a one-time thing. Perhaps it won't happen again. We hope it's not a sign that the Sandinistas are starting, as we warned they might, to revert to oppression now that pressure from the democratic resistance is off.

What a contrast between what's happened in Nicaragua and the course of events, and American policy, in Afghanistan. The freedom fighters are on the verge of a great victory over tyranny and aggression. The United States will continue unchanged its support for the freedom fighters and their fierce struggle for what is rightfully theirs: the right to determine their own country's future.

If success comes in Afghanistan—and I am confident it will—it will remind us of an enduring truth: Peace and justice in these kinds of conflicts do not come just by wishing for them, but by helping those willing to fight for them. The brave people of Afghanistan will have succeeded because of their own heroism and also because they had substantial and consistent international support, not the here-today-gone-tomorrow backing Congress has given the *contras.* No one has insisted that we strangle the Mujahidin in order to give peace a chance. Ask yourself: Where would the negotiations over Afghanistan be today if we had taken that line? On the contrary, the Senate in a unanimous vote urged the opposite—that we maintain our support for the Mujahidin. And they were right.

The question of democracy in Central America will not die and will not fade away. We will be judged on how we address it not merely by voters and readers but by our grandchildren and great-grandchildren. Yes, we are engaged in a great struggle to determine if this hemisphere will be free, whether millions will be ruled by the sword or will rule themselves with the pen. And more than in the Halls of Congress, more than in the Oval Office, more than in the jungles or at the bargaining tables of Latin America, this struggle will be won or lost in your newsrooms and editorial offices. If you do not forget the cause of democracy, neither will the American people. So, this is my message and appeal to you today: Remember that not only are you the guardians of the American people's right to know, you are in a larger sense guardian of the hopes of people all over the world. They look to you to tell their story.

Now, before I finish, let me turn to another matter of great concern. In the last few weeks, we've seen cover stories, television specials, and front page articles on the war against drugs. One frequent refrain has been, as the New York Times this Sunday wrote: "No administration has signed—or spent more money to stem the flow of drugs into this country. But we are losing ground." Well, let me offer a slightly different view. Yes, we've done more than ever before, and right now we're holding our own. We've stopped America's free-fall into the drug pit. We're getting our footing to climb out. We're paying now for the indifference of the seventies.

But to just take two of many signs of progress—the number of drug users has leveled off and may be dropping, and almost all high school seniors now say it's wrong even to try cocaine—these are big changes from just a few years ago. We've gone after smugglers and dealers as never before. The big international arrests of the last few weeks are just one result of this. And we've enlisted the military. And let me say, if you want to see effective leadership, take a look at Vice President Bush's role in this. While others talked about leading the military into the fray against drugs, the Vice President has led. And the result: Last year the Navy steamed some 2,600 ship days, while military planes flew more than 16,000 hours in the fight against illicit drugs. But in the end, this effort will be won not on foreign battlefields but on the homefront. When all of us insist that drug abuse is not only not for us but intolerable in family, friends, neighbors, acquaintances—anywhere by anybody—then we'll win. We're not there yet, but we're on our way.

Thank you. God bless you.

Ms. Fanning. President Reagan has agreed to take questions. I want to remind you that questions should be asked only by ASNE members. Would you please come to a microphone, state your name and the name of your paper, and I'll recognize you from here. I think I'll take the prerogative of asking the first question, if I may, Mr. President.

Larry M. Speakes

You spoke eloquently of the free flow of information, and yet, as you referred in jest, your former press spokesman, Larry Speakes, has confessed that he manufactured quotes for you. Would you tell us, please, did you approve of that process, and will you continue to allow that to happen in your White House?

The President. I was not aware of that and just learned it recently, as all the rest of you did, in the words in his book. And I can tell you right now that I have no affection for these kiss-and-tell books that are being written, and I find them entirely fiction.

President's Agenda

Q. Jimmy Denley, Birmingham Post Herald, in Alabama. Mr. President, as you near the end of two terms in the White House, what is the one thing you want the public to remember you most for as President, and do you expect to take any specific action in the next few months to enhance that image?

The President. Oh, my goodness. I never know how to answer that question because, frankly, I'm just going for the day-to-day battle here and haven't thought about how I'm going to be remembered. I'll be pleased if they remember me at all. [*Laughter*] And I'm going to continue pushing as hard as I can for some of the things, in these last months, that are part of the economic reform and the things that we brought about to see if they can't be planted permanently and not something that will just go away when someone else comes in. And among those are things like—well, for example, I'm getting pretty soon—they're sending me the first budget I've ever had since I've been here. The law tells me I have to submit a budget, and it always turned into a continuing resolution. And I think that we do need a constitutional change. We need an amendment that will ban—as Jefferson once asked right after the acceptance of the Constitution—that will ban the Federal borrowing. And the second thing, to bring about an end to the deficits that—when I'm out of here, I'm going to campaign for as hard as I am while I'm in here, and that is the line-item veto. I used it 943 times as a Governor of California with a hostile, other-party legislature and was never overridden once. And in California, two-thirds of the people have to vote—or the legislature have to vote to pass the budget, and only two-thirds to overturn a veto. The same two-thirds that would vote to send those pork items up buried in the whole budget wouldn't vote to overturn my veto when they had to appear and stand up for them, singly, where the people could see them. So, I think I'm just going to continue the battle until the last day and then head for the ranch.

Soviet-U.S. Relations

Q. Mr. President, Robert Morton, New York City Tribune. During the summit, you gave an interview to some columnists in which you said that you no longer believed the Soviet Union was intent upon world domination. If you had heard yourself say that 8 years ago, what would you have thought, and what led you to change your mind?

The President. Well, I didn't exactly say what has been quoted that I said there. I called attention to the fact, in discussing this new leader—you know, I was here several years before one of them lived long enough for me to meet with him. [*Laughter*] And I called attention to the fact that maybe there were some differences with some of the things he was proposing, in that he was the first and only Russian leader to this day who had never, in appearing before the Communist Congress, pledged himself to carry on the Marxist idea of a one-world Communist state. Now, I just called attention to that. As to whether it was an oversight or he didn't think it was necessary or not, I don't know. But I thought it was something that we should keep in the back of our minds when we were negotiating instead of what we have faced over the years in previous Russian leaders. But I did not ask us to accept that. As a matter of fact, I only know one little phrase in Russian, and I've used it to where he's sick of it, and I love it. And that is: *Dovorey no provorey*—trust but verify.

President's Reading Habits

Q. Mr. President, I'm Tim Gallagher, from the Albuquerque Tribune, in Albuquerque, New Mexico. If I can go back to the kiss-and-tell book by Mr. Speakes for just a moment, he said in that book that you rarely read daily newspapers, that you read news summaries that are prepared for you. I wonder if you could tell this very interested audience how much time you spend reading daily newspapers each day.

The President. Well, I begin with the comics—[*laughter*]—a lifetime habit—and then my next turn is to the editorial pages. And I say that in the numbers because there are more than one paper that come to breakfast with me. And I do as much as I can then before I have to run for the office. And then it is true that I rifle through the clippings they get because they bring those in also from papers that I don't get—from out of Washington, or out of the beltway—papers from across the country. And I do look at that. But he's wrong when he implies that I don't read the papers. Yes, I do. So, you're not getting away with anything.

Afghanistan

Q. Lou Urenick, from the Portland, Maine, Press Herald. Mr. President, what's your assessment of the opposition of Afghan rebels to the peace plan that's shaping up in that region? Many of them say they'll continue to fight on.

The President. We expect them to. And I'm just sorry about the fact that evidently they misunderstand, as many of our other people have—our own citizens have misunderstood. The Geneva accords that we've been negotiating on and picking back and forth at each other for a long time—we have finally reached an agreement, and there is nothing in that agreement that is going to prevent us from supplying the Mujahidin as long as they need it and as long as the Soviet Union continues to supply the Afghan forces in their puppet government that they're leaving behind. So, there's no restriction on us; the Mujahidin are going to continue to have our help.

Race Relations

Q. Ben Johnson, Columbia Missourian. Mr. President, during this conference, we've talked a lot about race relations in this country. This is the 20th anniversary of the Kerner commission report. I'm sure many of us would be interested in your assessment, in this year when we have a black man running for President, of the status of race relations in this country.

The President. Well, I hope that race will not be a part of this campaign in any way. And I'm sorry that in the campaign that's going on with one candidate of the black race that it seems that more attention is being paid to the difference in color than is being paid to what he is actually saying. And I have to believe that a great many of us would find ourselves in great disagreement with the policies that he is proposing and that we would perhaps be more vocal about them if it wasn't for concern that that be misinterpreted into some kind of a racial attack.

Contrary to what some people say, the most frustrating thing that I have endured since I have been here in the image making that goes on is that I have been portrayed so often as, in some way, a racist and prejudiced in regard to racial matters. And it's hard for me to take because I grew up in a family in which that was considered the greatest sin—prejudice and discrimination. And all my life—back when I was a sports announcer and broadcasting major league baseball, I was one of the little handful across the country that continued to editorialize for the breaking of the ban and the allowing of blacks into organized baseball. And it's carried on through my life.

And as I say, I regret that this has become a factor. The candidates should all be based on what are their policies and what is it that they would propose to do. And I will be very frank with you: I find a great disagreement with some of the things that are being proposed by Jesse Jackson. But I also find a great deal of disagreement with his fellow candidates in that party, which is why I'd suggest that everybody should vote Republican. [*Laughter*]

Q. Thank you, sir.

Presidential Campaign

Q. Mr. President, a little more on your political, unbiased opinions: I'd like to ask you to assess the 1988 race, and where you see it going, and how will it end?

The President. Oh, you've caught me in a weak spot. When I was a sports announcer, I was superstitious about ever talking about who was going to win the game or whether they would. And I wouldn't even mention that the pitcher was pitching a no-hit ball game because superstition has it that then you'll jinx him if you do. And to ask me to predict what's going to happen here—well, I think in the Republican Party, of course, it has now narrowed down to one candidate. But even so, there's a convention to be held. And on the other side, I don't know whether the candidates now campaigning—whether any one of them is going to wind up at the convention with the nomination or whether there will be a brokered convention or whether the Democratic Party will go afield seeking to draft someone who has not been campaigning in the primaries. And I just refuse to try and make a guess on this.

Nicaragua

Q. Mr. President, one of the senior administration officials was quoted last week as saying that the *contra* war is over and that the resistance forces have been effectively dismantled. Mr. President, do you agree with this? And also, several years ago you said that your intention was to get the Sandinistas to cry uncle. Have they gotten you to cry uncle instead?

The President. No, and if I find that unnamed official, he may not be official. [*Laughter*] No, I don't believe it's over. And I believe that—with all my heart and soul—that the pressure that is being imposed on Nicaraguan citizens that are being called the *contras,* who have taken up arms to try and bring about the continuation of the revolution that had them in conflict with Somoza as a dictator and who was denying democratic rights—and they were succeeded by the Sandinistas, who not only seized the government and took it over for themselves after the armed revolution but violated the agreement of the revolutionaries to the Organization of American States that they would install democracy as we know it, a pluralistic democracy and so forth. But in doing so we forget there were other revolutionaries that fought beside them, but who were not part of a longtime organization. And so, they were ousted, some exiled, some imprisoned. And many of those are now in what we call the *contras.* And I think we have an obligation to support those people until—call it crying uncle—I meant that the Sandinistas would permit the people of Nicaragua to make their decision on the kind of government they wanted.

Q. What are you willing to do if they do not follow through with the democratic reforms?

The President. What's that?

Q. What action are you willing to take if they don't follow through with the democratic reforms?

The President. Well, I think it would be unwise of me to talk about any further things that might be done. Let them go to sleep every night wondering what we'd do.

Banking Industry

Q. Mr. President, I'm Tom Vale, of the Cleveland Plain Dealer. Sir, do you feel that the banking system of the United States is in trouble?

The President. I think it has some troubles, yes, that have grown out of the—well, some of the problems that were left with us by double-digit inflation with loans and so forth. And we know that, through the Government and the institutions that we have in government to help, we're giving as much help as we can there. I don't think that it is a problem that could suddenly bring disaster down upon us and end this expansion and this economic growth that we're having. But we're going to continue to try and help. And as I say, when you think back to the almost sudden change from inflation to what we have now, that meant that there were a lot of loans that were based on collateral that no longer has the value that it did back in the inflationary era, and problems of that kind are bothering us.

Ms. Fanning. Thank you, Mr. President. We really appreciate your coming and spending time with us today.

The President. Well, thank you.

Note: The President spoke at 1:34 p.m. in the Grand Ballroom at the J.W. Marriott Hotel.

Letter to the Speaker of the House of Representatives and the President of the Senate Transmitting the Report on the Export-Import Bank of the United States
April 14, 1988

Dear Mr. Speaker: (Dear Mr. President:)

This report is being transmitted pursuant to Section 7(a)(2) of the Export-Import Bank Act of 1945, as amended (12 U.S.C. 635e(a)(2)). I have determined that the authority available to the Bank for fiscal year 1988 is sufficient for loans but may be more than sufficient to meet the current estimate of the guarantee needs of the Bank. This estimate was based upon the transactions already approved, applications received by the Bank, and projections of the level of business for the remainder of the fiscal year.

It is not possible to estimate precisely the amount of guarantee authority that will be needed. However, given the likelihood of continued economic growth within the United States as well as the general recovery throughout the world, there is a reasonable prospect that demand for Eximbank's guarantees and insurance could accelerate in the remainder of fiscal year 1988, and require the commitment of amounts greater than currently estimated of the existing guarantee authority.

Therefore, I am not seeking any legislation to rescind any authority of the Bank. I have concluded that the statutory fiscal year 1988 limits for Eximbank authority should be retained unchanged.

Sincerely,

RONALD REAGAN

Note: Identical letters were sent to Jim Wright, Speaker of the House of Representatives, and George Bush, President of the Senate.

Letter to the Majority and Minority Leaders of the Senate on Assistance to Mexico and the Bahamas
April 14, 1988

Dear ________:

The Senate has before it resolutions to disapprove my certification of Mexico and The Bahamas under Section 481 (h) of the Foreign Assistance Act. Passage of these resolutions could result in more drugs entering the United States, not less. In the case of Mexico, significant damage to a broad range of major U.S. interests would also result. I strongly urge the Senate to vote both resolutions down.

Mexico

I understand a number of Senators are attracted by the idea that a "national interest" certification would send Mexico a needed message regarding the drug menace, while protecting the extensive bilateral and foreign policy interests we have there. Unfortunately, this would not be the case.

I have already sent that message, both in my February 13 meeting with President de la Madrid in Mazatlán and in the statement accompanying my "full cooperation" certification. It is absolutely clear, from the Mexican President's words and his Government's subsequent actions, that the message was received and understood.

Should the Congress now overturn the Administration's "full cooperation" certification, the political impact in Mexico would be harmful to U.S. interests. We believe, for example, that Mexico—although it would continue to fight the drug traffic on its own—would terminate U.S. ties to its aerial eradication program and reject the $14.5 million in direct anti-drug aid we currently provide. The ability of the DEA to operate efficiently in Mexico might also be impaired. The result would almost certainly be an increase in the flow of drugs to the United States.

The political impact of decertification by the United States would adversely affect every aspect of our relationship with Mexico, including trade, investment, immigration and vital border-area cooperation. The U.S. would become an issue in Mexico's current election campaign, and a more constructive bilateral relationship would become politically difficult for the next Mexican president. The political left and other elements in Mexico opposed to closer ties to the U.S. would get a new lease on life.

Moreover, I believe my certification decision was correct. While we fault Mexican efforts in some areas, we should not overlook the many positive actions they have taken. For instance: Mexico was the first Latin American country to sign and ratify a Mutual Legal Assistance Treaty with us; in 1987, they increased by 26% their eradication of marijuana while slightly improving opium poppy eradication; their seizures of all drugs in 1987 were up (cocaine by 75%; opium derivative 12%, and marijuana 400%); they arrested 9,800 persons for trafficking including nine major (class 1) narcotics violators.

In sum, I believe it would be both unfair and counterproductive for Congress to disapprove my certification of Mexico as a fully cooperating country.

The Bahamas

On March 1, I recommended full certification for The Bahamas. As with Mexico, the April 12 vote by the full Senate Foreign Relations Committee to deny such certification could seriously jeopardize our joint efforts to counter the flow of narcotics through that country.

When this issue comes before the Senate, it is important that this potential damage be avoided. I would like to review my rationale for full certification.

We have received excellent operational level cooperation from the Bahamian government. To date, no U.S. government request has been denied.

The Bahamas is the only country in the world which allows U.S. law enforcement units to enter its territory in hot pursuit of drug targets. These decisions reflect a political will by the Bahamian government to fight narcotics trafficking.

As a result of our bilateral, cooperative efforts, there was a 300% increase in marijuana and cocaine seizures in 1987 compared to 1986. Last year's seizures amounted to over 24,860 pounds of cocaine and 146.5 tons of marijuana.

Likewise, the Bahamian government made progress in 1987 in key areas of enforcement, investigation, and prosecution. A Mutual Legal Assistance Treaty (MLAT) was signed, and the Bahamian parliament now has passed implementing legislation. Negotiations have been proceeding extremely well on a new modern extradition treaty which would greatly broaden the scope of extraditable offenses. Tough new asset forfeiture laws have been enacted. Bahamians are taking steps to prosecute corruption offenders. And a new special drug court, and a proposal for a second, should relieve the over-burdened legal system.

With operational level cooperation excellent and anti-corruption efforts improving, we want to encourage and strengthen those Bahamians, including officials at the highest level, who clearly want to do more. Again, as with Mexico, I feel strongly the congressional action to overturn my recommendation for certification for The Bahamas would be seriously counterproductive and unjust.

Sincerely,

RONALD REAGAN

Note: Identical letters were sent to Robert C. Byrd and Robert Dole, Majority and Minority Leaders of the Senate, respectively.

Nomination of Daniel Anthony O'Donohue To Be United States Ambassador to Thailand
April 14, 1988

The President today announced his intention to nominate Daniel Anthony O'Donohue, of Virginia, a career member of the Senior Foreign Service, Class of Minister-Counselor, as Ambassador to the Kingdom of Thailand. He would succeed William Andreas Brown.

Mr. O'Donohue is currently the Principal Deputy Director of the Department of State Policy Planning Staff. He was the U.S. Ambassador to Burma from 1983 to 1987. Prior to this, he was Principal Deputy Director of Politico-Military Affairs at the Department of State, 1978–1981; deputy chief of mission at the U.S. Embassy in Bangkok, Thailand, 1977–1978; Executive Assistant to the Under Secretary for Political Affairs, 1976–1977; Office Director of Korean Affairs, 1974–1976; and political counselor for the U.S. Embassy in Seoul, Korea, 1972–1974. From 1971 to 1972, he was a student at the Army War College. He has served as a political officer for the U.S. Embassy in Seoul, Korea, 1960–1964; and vice consul of the consulate general in Genoa, Italy, 1958–1959. Mr. O'Donohue joined the Foreign Service in 1957.

Mr. O'Donohue graduated from the University of Detroit (B.S., 1953) and Wayne State University (M.P.A., 1958). He was born October 27, 1931, in Detroit, MI. He is married, has five children, and resides in Alexandria, VA.

Statement by Assistant to the President for Press Relations Fitzwater on the Trade Bill
April 15, 1988

The President has said he would like to be able to sign a trade bill that will open markets and improve America's competitiveness. The Congress made good progress in moving towards such a bill, although further reasonable improvements still need to be made.

The bill does improve our negotiating authority. It strengthens our hand in taking action against unfair trade practices. It helps us protect our intellectual property rights. Unfortunately, it still contains the plant-closing provision and other nontrade provisions that are injurious to a dynamic economy and America's future prosperity. Our negotiators yesterday were encouraged to believe that the plant-closing provision would be eliminated. Later, however, we were told that after certain consultations took place they could not remove that provision. The labor unions apparently would sacrifice the entire trade bill for this provision.

While the administration would be willing to accept a positive trade bill, we cannot accept a bill that includes seriously flawed elements that will hurt America's competitiveness and economic success. If the bill reaches the President in its present form, the President will veto it.

Remarks at a Luncheon for Members of Vote America
April 15, 1988

I'm delighted that all of you could be here today. And as Joe Rogers knows, I'm an enthusiastic admirer of the work that you're doing.

You know, one of the things I've continually talked about during the past few years was how impressive this young generation of Americans really is. And everywhere I've gone in this country, I've been moved to see their interest in our nation and in the issues before us. In fact, I'd like to tell a story about when one of our Ambassadors visited an American armored cavalry regiment stationed on the NATO line in Germany.

He returned to his helicopter, and as he did so, he was followed by a young, 19-year-old soldier. The soldier asked him if he could get a message to the President, and the Ambassador said, well, sometimes getting messages to the President was part of his job. And the soldier then said, "Well, will you tell him we're proud to be here, and we ain't scared of nothin.' "

Well, a while ago, the Ambassador was in Washington, and he told me the sequel to that incident. I'd repeated the story in a talk program, and there on that base in—it was on the Voice of America—and there on that base in Germany, the young soldier heard that broadcast and knew that I'd received the message. His commanding officer said that he ran down the company street yelling, "The system works! The system works!" [*Laughter*]

And that's why all of you are here today and giving so generously of your time. You want all young Americans to know what the young soldier knew: that the system does work. But you also want them to know something else that soldier knew, and that is that democracy takes time and personal effort. And that's why we're dedicated to the goals of Vote America.

This generation is a generation that's bright with hope, filled with energy, and ready to make a difference. They're talented and optimistic. But for all of that, they also have the lowest percentage of voters. So, it's up to us to remind young Americans that the first step in democratic involvement is voting. With Vote America, you're doing tremendous work. The commercials, the partnership programs, the curriculum materials, the votemobiles, and the mobilization of corporate America are all part of your extraordinary effort to get Americans out to vote. This private sector initiative is bearing fruit, and I'm hopeful we'll see abundant evidence of that in the voting percentages for 1988.

So, all I can say is keep up the great work. And believe me, I hope this project is put on the front burner. The future of our young leaders represents the future of America. And again, because this is a priority of mine, I want to express my personal thanks to each of you. However, beyond this personal interest, our country also owes you a debt of gratitude for your dedication to our young citizens.

You know, I have opportunities every once in a while now to go to a school or college and appear on the campus and speak there. And having been Governor for 4 years at a time when if I went to a campus I would have started a riot and been hung in effigy—[*laughter*]—it's quite a change. And believe me, to stand there and say something that normally might be responded to by an ordinary audience with applause, and then the many times I've heard instead them chanting, "U.S.A.! U.S.A.! " it really sends you out of the room about 3 inches taller than when you came in.

Well, speaking of getting out of the room, I'm going to see each of you in the Blue Room down the line here for a handshake, which I wasn't able to do at the beginning of our lunch here. So, I'm going to thank you here, and God bless you. And I'm going around, and I'll meet you there in the Blue Room. Thank you all.

Note: The President spoke at 1 p.m. in the State Dining Room at the White House.

Nomination of James Eugene Burnett, Jr., To Be Chairman of the National Transportation Safety Board
April 15, 1988

The President today announced his intention to nominate James Eugene Burnett, Jr., to be Chairman of the National Transportation Safety Board for a term of 2 years. This is a reappointment.

Since 1981 Mr. Burnett has been a member of the National Transportation Safety Board in Washington, DC. While on this Board, he has been: Chairman, 1982–1984; Vice Chairman for a brief period in 1984; resuming the position of Chairman, 1984 to present. Prior to this, he was a juvenile judge in Van Buren County, AR, since 1973, and a city judge in Damascus, AR, since 1979. He was special associate justice of the Supreme Court of Arkansas, 1981, and has been a practicing attorney since 1973.

Mr. Burnett graduated from the University of Arkansas (B.A., 1970) and the University of Arkansas Law School (J.D., 1973). He was born September 20, 1947, in Little Rock, AR, and currently resides in Arlington, VA.

Message to the Congress Transmitting the Annual Report of the National Science Board
April 15, 1988

To the Congress of the United States:

I am pleased to submit to the Congress a report of the National Science Board entitled *Science and Engineering Indicators—1987.* This report is the eighth in a continuing series in which important aspects of the status of American science and engineering are examined.

The importance of scientific and engineering research to the well-being of our Nation is widely recognized. Science and engineering play a vital role in maintaining our Nation's defense, improving its health, and increasing its economic productivity.

I commend *Science and Engineering Indicators—1987* to the attention of the Congress and those in the scientific endeavor.

RONALD REAGAN

The White House,
April 15, 1988.

Radio Address to the Nation on Drug Abuse and Trafficking
April 16, 1988

My fellow Americans:

The news has been bad lately, and that's good. And here's why. You've probably been hearing reports about Panamanian strong man General Noriega, who's been indicted for drug trafficking, and his struggle to stay in power despite pressure from his own people and our government to step down. You've also been hearing about the drug-related arrests of many street gang members in Los Angeles. And then, too, there's the news about congressional investigations of organized crime's involvement in the drug trade.

Now, these news reports reflect an important change since the start of our administration in 1981. At the time, we faced a crisis of crime stemming from the illegal drug trade, especially in south Florida. At my urging, Vice President Bush headed up a task force that performed invaluable service by coordinating the activities of all law enforcement agencies in the area and for the first time brought to bear against the drug smugglers the full weight of Federal resources. This included high-tech military equipment and the resources of the intelligence community.

Less than a year later, I went over to the Justice Department to announce a sweeping effort to break the back of organized crime in America. And a key part of this approach was the hiring of more than 1,000 new agents and prosecutors as part of 12 regional drug task forces based on the south Florida model. We also set up a President's Commission on Organized Crime that did landmark work in tracing the international connections of the domestic drug trade, pointing out the usefulness of drug testing, and exposing not only the old style Mafia's involvement in the drug trade but also the danger of new, emerging crime gangs. In addition to all this, we got enacted sweeping legislative initiatives like the Comprehensive Crime Control Act of 1984 and the Anti-Drug Abuse Act of 1986.

This early attention to the criminal side of the drug problem, which has translated into a tripling of the overall antidrug budget, is now paying dividends. Cocaine seizures have increased by over 1,800 percent, arrests of major drug traffickers have increased by almost 200 percent, and well over $500 million in drug-related assets were seized in 1987 alone. And this kind of success at the Federal level would not be possible without an unprecedented degree of Federal, State, and local cooperation. Here in Washington this commitment is best evidenced by our Cabinet-level National Drug Policy Board, as well as the Vice President's National Narcotics Border Interdiction System, and the Department of Justice's Organized Crime Drug Enforcement Task Forces.

But emphasizing the criminal side of the drug problem is only part of defeating the drug menace. Thanks to the efforts of Nancy's Just Say No campaign, Americans are understanding that the permanent way to end the drug menace is to deny the drug pusher his market—to stop demand. And that means education and prevention. It means understanding that drug use is not a victimless crime—that drugs kill and maim and finance the criminal underground. It means accepting the concept of user responsibility. It means realizing that those who use drugs are, in Nancy's words, making themselves accomplices to murder.

Now, in addition to prevention and education and drug law enforcement, we have also been emphasizing the international side of the problem. When we came into office there were drug eradication programs underway in only two countries. Today that number is 23. In fact, this administration has signed an unprecedented number of mutual legal assistance treaties, extradition treaties, and eradication agreements. The unprecedented indictment of Panamanian leader Noriega for drug trafficking by a U.S. grand jury is a further indication of our nation's resolve to end the foreign supply of drugs. His nation is in a crisis of his making.

But, as I said at the beginning, the fact that we're seeing more media coverage of the drug problem and the heat put on people like General Noriega and the street gangs in Los Angeles, or organized crime in general, is good news. Public awareness about the destructiveness of illegal drugs is at an all-time high. Americans are increasingly saying no to drugs. A recent survey of high school seniors showed a significant drop in cocaine and marijuana use.

We have a long way to go before we have a drug free America, and I hope the media keeps emphasizing that point. But it's also true America has awakened to this problem. That's quite a change from just a decade ago. So, that's the good news, the very good news, about the bad news of drug abuse.

Until next week, thanks for listening, and God bless you.

Note: The President spoke at 12:06 p.m. from Camp David, MD.

Statement by Assistant to the President for Press Relations Fitzwater on the United States Military Strike in the Persian Gulf
April 18, 1988

Acting under his authority as Commander in Chief, the President has directed United States forces at 1 a.m. eastern daylight time today to strike Iranian military targets in the southern Persian Gulf. Our forces attacked oil platforms at Sirri and Sassan in the southern Gulf. These platforms are used as command and control radar stations for the Iranian military. The attacks are underway at this time. These actions were taken in response to Iran's recent resumption of mine-laying in international waters and its mine attack on the U.S.S. *Samuel B. Roberts*. The Government of Iran has been repeatedly warned about the consequences of such hostile acts.

Our actions were taken following consultations with congressional leadership and after informing friendly governments. They are designed and intended to deter further Iranian mining. They represent a measured response to Iran's unlawful use of force against the United States and to Iran's numerous violations of the rights of other nonbelligerents. And they constitute a lawful exercise of the United States inherent right of self-defense under article 51 of the United Nations Charter. Appropriate notification of such actions is being provided to the President of the United Nations Security Council.

We have repeatedly told Iran that we do not desire military confrontation, but the Government of Iran should understand that we will protect our ships and our interests against unprovoked attacks. We urgently seek an end to tensions in the region and to the Iran-Iraq war. This would benefit the people of both nations who have suffered so much from the brutal conflict. We urge Iran to accept Security Council Resolution 598 and to agree to its rapid and comprehensive implementation. Iran has nothing to gain from continuation of the war. The Department of Defense will brief later this morning as we have more details come in. We're receiving details on a continuing basis at this time.

Note: Marlin Fitzwater read the statement to reporters at 3:33 a.m. in the Briefing Room at the White House.

Nomination of S. Jay Plager To Be Administrator of the Office of Information and Regulatory Affairs
April 18, 1988

The President today announced his intention to nominate S. Jay Plager to be Administrator of the Office of Information and Regulatory Affairs at the Office of Management and Budget. This is a new position.

Since 1987 Mr. Plager has been Associate Director for Human Resources, Veterans and Labor at the Office of Management and Budget in Washington, DC. Prior to this Mr. Plager was counselor to the Under Secretary at the Department of Health and Human Services, 1986–1987. From 1977 to 1984, he was dean of Indiana University School of Law, and professor of law since 1977.

Mr. Plager graduated from the University of North Carolina (A.B., 1952), the University of Florida (J.D., 1958), and Columbia University (LL.M., 1961). He was born May 16, 1931, in Long Branch, NJ. He served in the United States Navy and United States Naval Reserve, 1948–1971. Mr. Plager is married to Commissioner Ilene H. Nagel, of the United States Sentencing Commission, in Washington, DC, and has three children.

Nomination of John K. Stewart To Be a Member of the Board of Directors of the National Consumer Cooperative Bank

April 18, 1988

The President today announced his intention to nominate John K. Stewart to be a member of the Board of Directors of the National Consumer Cooperative Bank for a term of 3 years. This is a new position.

Since 1978 Mr. Stewart has been president of the John Stewart Co. in San Francisco, CA. Prior to this he was vice president-operations for Barcelon-Berger Management Corp., 1975–1978. He was with Henkle-Stewart Partnerships, 1975–1981, and was vice president of Community Technology Corp., 1971–1975.

Mr. Stewart graduated from Stanford University (B.A., 1956). He was born June 2, 1934, in San Francisco, CA. He is married, has three children, and resides in San Francisco.

Appointment of Joyce Newman as a Member of the National Council on Vocational Education

April 18, 1988

The President today announced his intention to appoint Joyce Newman to be a member of the National Council on Vocational Education for a term expiring January 17, 1991. This is a reappointment.

Since 1982 Mrs. Newman has served as a travel consultant in North Woodmere, NY. Prior to this Mrs. Newman worked as an interviewer at the department of occupational resources, 1979–1982.

Mrs. Newman graduated from the University of Kentucky (A.B., 1958). She was born January 29, 1936, in New York City. She is married, has three children, and resides in North Woodmere, NY.

Remarks to Representatives of Volunteer Youth Groups

April 18, 1988

The President. Thank you all very much. It's a pleasure to welcome all of you here to the White House for the kickoff to National Volunteer Week. I know we're across the street from it, but they still consider this part of the White House.

Volunteering to help your neighbor is an old American tradition—and among our most distinctive traditions. From the time of our founding to the present, it's one of the things that foreign visitors most often note when they come to visit this country. You may know of one foreign visitor, a Frenchman—maybe you've heard of him—called Alexis de Tocqueville. He toured the United States in the early 19th century. He wanted to find out how we did and what we were doing. And then he returned home and wrote about what he had seen here. And one thing he said was this: "I have often seen Americans make great and real sacrifices to the public welfare. They hardly ever failed to lend faithful support to one another." And in thinking why this was, he concluded that, in his words, "The free institutions which the inhabitants of the United States possess and the political rights of which they make so much use remind every citizen that it is the duty as well as the interest of people to make themselves useful to their fellow creatures."

Well, yes, as de Tocqueville saw so clearly, voluntarism—and what some of us call private sector initiatives—go hand in hand with freedom. I like to think that helps explain why in the last 8 years Americans have been volunteering more than ever. In these years when we've pulled back the hand of government and increased personal freedom, we have also seen a revolution of compassion sweep our land. Charitable giving has soared by 77 percent, and more Americans than ever before are volunteering their time to help their community and those in need. The figure for just 1 year, last year, as it was given to me, was that $84 billion was raised in the United States just by various groups like your own, for doing worthwhile things in this country.

You can see this revolution of compassion, of course, at work in such longstanding national organizations as the Red Cross and Project Hope and, here in the Government, the Peace Corps. But even more, you can see it where the cameras and microphones too often fail to turn—in hometowns and neighborhoods, churches, and synagogues. You can see it in Huntsville, Alabama, where the United Way brought together young volunteers from all over the city to write and record a rap against drug and alcohol abuse. It's a rhyming, rhythmic production that the group has performed all over town and on television. And it's getting out, as never before, in Huntsville a message that every young person, and every American for that matter, should hear: When it comes to drug and alcohol abuse, just say no!

But the revolution of compassion is, most of all, a person-to-person revolution. It's Kevin Gounaud, 15, of Springfield, Virginia, who heard about the need for a drive to raise food for the needy. Kevin pulled together 40 of his friends, and together they knocked on 3,000 doors and collected 500 bags of food for those who don't have enough. The revolution of compassion is Pamela Dawley, 17, of Hanover Park, Illinois. Several years ago, through her Girl Scout troop, Pamela organized a drive to collect books to send to needy young people in Mexico. After the 1986 earthquake, Pamela organized an event that raised $1,400 to help the people who had lived in a Mexico City housing project that the quake destroyed. The revolution of compassion is Mike Evans, 16, of Kalamazoo, Michigan. Mike gets around in a wheelchair, and that just seems to mean that he gets around faster than the rest of us. This year, on top of his schoolwork, Mike has volunteered more than 200 hours in everything from tutoring elementary school students to doing data entry for a local community organization that helps handicapped adults. And, yes, the revolution is Andrea Adams, 17, of Kokomo, Indiana. Andrea, who has done so much—it's hard to know what to mention. But after helping start a United Way project to help students at her high school, she met, through the project, another girl whose parents had abused her and thrown her out of her home. The girl was sleeping on the streets and attending school during the day. Andrea, with the support of her parents, invited the girl to come and live with Andrea's family. And today, thanks to Andrea, Andrea's family, and her own determination, that young lady has a high school diploma.

You know, when I hear stories like those of Andrea and all of you, I can't help thinking that the people who talk about ours being a decade of greed ought to be ashamed of themselves. They have so misheard the voices of American compassion and the voices of America singing that it reminds me of a story about an old friend of mine who understood what the American spirit is all about, but who occasionally misheard things himself. His name was John Wayne. We called him, in Hollywood, Duke. Well, one day the Duke was on the set, filming a scene, and he'd just delivered a big and important line when the director shouted "cut," and came up to him, and he said, "Duke, you've got to deliver that line with a little more awe." Well, sure enough, on the next take, the Duke looked up, opened his mouth, and began the line saying, "Aw." [*Laughter*]

When I want to hear what our great nation is all about, I listen not to the cynics but to people like you. This year Americans are joining together to expand voluntarism beyond anything we've ever seen before. It's called Give 5, and it means why don't we all take it upon ourselves to give 5 hours a week and/or 5 percent of our income to charitable causes and worthy goals.

Not only is voluntarism national, it's becoming international. In just 2 weeks, in London, American and British business and community leaders will gather to discuss voluntarism and charitable giving at the first British-American Conference on Private Sector Initiatives. One important topic they will take up will be inspiring the spirit of community service in the leaders of tomorrow. I wish that those attending this conference could meet each of you, because you embody that great spirit. Albert Einstein once said, "It's every man's obligation to put back into the world at least the equivalent of what he takes out of it." And that's what the great American tradition of neighbor helping neighbor is all about. And that's what each of you is doing.

You know, I receive so many letters about things that are going on, and I just received this morning a memorandum from within the White House staff there. And I thought I would bring it along, since it came just before I came over here. On Saturday, 29 White House staff members and friends participated in a special preview project for Christmas in April, the annual program to repair the homes of the poor, the elderly, and the handicapped. Now, that started as a local thing in a town in Texas, where in April, all year long, the people go around finding homes of the elderly or the aged—or, I mean, of the poor or the handicapped, that need work—shingling of roof, painting, plumbing repairs, and so forth. And then, in April volunteers from all over the city come forth, and they go to these homes and do all of this work. They're amateurs at it, but they're pretty handy also at it. I didn't know until I came to Washington that that had already spread from people hearing it in other communities and has spread here to Washington. So, we decided the White House should get involved, too. Skilled and unskilled volunteers spent that day, just this last Saturday, plastering, painting, and doing carpentry at the home of an elderly widow in Northwest Washington.

And additionally, Paolo Biscioni, an organizer of the upcoming British-American Conference on Private Sector Initiatives, came from London, England, and participated in that effort, and he's here this morning. I just ran into him a little while ago in the Oval Office. On April 30th—that's the real Christmas in April day—another White House team of volunteers will join 2,500 other workers in the citywide Christmas in April project to repair 83 other homes. I thought that maybe you'd like to hear that little item in connection with all that you are doing.

Well, I thank you for it, and a great many other people thank you for all that you're doing. And God bless all of you. Thank you. I understand I'm just supposed to stand aside here for a moment, as something's going to happen.

Ms. Cobb. Thank you, Mr. President, for recognizing the accomplishments of the youth volunteers. I am Kendalle Cobb, a youth volunteer with the United Way. Greetings from California! [*Laughter*] There are many volunteer youth groups represented here today, and we are all thrilled to be here with you, one of the country's greatest volunteers.

To me, there are many wonderful things about volunteering, but one of the greatest is that volunteering always makes me feel that I can make a difference. Though many of us are still in high school, our effort can improve the quality of life of others and in so doing can better the world. Thank you for inspiring us and again reminding us that our future lies in helping one another. I agree with you, Mr. President, there is a revolution of compassion sweeping this country, and the youth of today will carry this revolution through the 21st century.

Now, on behalf of all youth volunteers across the country, I would like to present to you a Young America Cares T-shirt. We hope that you will treasure it, because when you care, you're among the very young at heart. Thank you.

The President. Thank you very much. Thank you all very much. God bless you. And you know something, I have a feeling that the 21st century, when another generation—yours—replaces all of us, things are going to be just fine not only in America but in the world. Thank you all very much.

Note: The President spoke at 11:06 a.m. in Room 450 of the Old Executive Office Building.

Proclamation 5797—Crime Victims Week, 1988
April 18, 1988

By the President of the United States of America

A Proclamation

The principle of liberty and justice for all is one of our Nation's most fundamental goals and responsibilities. The vicious conduct of criminals against innocent, law-abiding citizens, however, continues to victimize millions of Americans each year. Our heritage of liberty and justice for all is threatened by this toll, so all of us—government officials, the criminal justice system, opinion-makers, and members of the public—must heed and help crime victims. Crime Victims Week is a fitting time for reflection on ways to assist fully those of us whose unalienable rights have been violated by criminals.

Victims of crime carry a burden inconceivable to others, and America is turning its attention to their plight. We must always remember that the responsibility for crimes lies with those who commit them, not with the innocent victims. Seven years ago, my Administration took some first steps toward meeting crime victims' needs. Since then, we have made great progress, with the President's Task Force on Victims of Crime, the Attorney General's Task Force on Family Violence, and the President's Child Safety Partnership. The Victims of Crime Act of 1984 established a Crime Victims Fund in the U.S. Treasury that is financed by penalty assessments on all convicted Federal defendants. The same Act also authorized U.S. Attorneys to recover the proceeds of literary endeavors of certain violent criminals.

Across our Nation, private citizens and groups, criminal justice personnel, service providers, and victims of crime themselves are helping—working for legislative reforms, monitoring court procedures, accompanying law officers to crime scenes, offering emotional support to crime victims and their families, and sparing countless people from the unjust burdens imposed by lack of concern or understanding. Those who so successfully attend to the needs and rights of innocent victims of crime deserve our gratitude and our assistance as they seek "liberty and justice for all."

The Congress, by Senate Joint Resolution 234, has designated the week beginning April 17, 1988, as "Crime Victims Week" and authorized and requested the President to issue a proclamation in observance of this event.

Now, Therefore, I, Ronald Reagan, President of the United States of America, do hereby proclaim the week beginning April 17, 1988, as Crime Victims Week. I urge government officials and all citizens to continue to help crime victims and to treat them with respect, consideration, compassion, and fairness, for the sake of justice and human dignity.

In Witness Whereof, I have hereunto set my hand this eighteenth day of April, in the year of our Lord nineteen hundred and eighty-eight, and of the Independence of the United States of America the two hundred and twelfth.

RONALD REAGAN

[*Filed with the Office of the Federal Register, 10:53 a.m., April 19, 1988*]

Remarks at a White House Meeting With the Associated General Contractors of America
April 18, 1988

The President. Well, thank you all, and it's good to see Jim and Delcie Ann Supica here. And it's a pleasure to welcome all of you here today, especially since we see so many familiar faces. Before I get into my remarks, however, I have something in the nature of a bulletin that I would like to impose on you.

Earlier today our Navy made a measured response to Iran's latest use of military force against U.S. ships in international waters, as well as its continued military and terrorist attacks against a number of nonbelligerents. Following the destruction of the two Iranian military platforms, whose personnel evacuated after our warning, several Iran naval vessels and small boats attempted to engage our ships and aircraft. Three Iranian naval vessels and at least two small boats were sunk or very severely damaged.

We've taken this action to make certain the Iranians have no illusions about the cost of irresponsible behavior. We aim to deter further Iranian aggression, not provoke it. They must know that we will protect our ships, and if they threaten us, they'll pay a price. A more normal relationship with Iran is desirable, and we're prepared for it. But such a relationship is not possible so long as Iran attacks neutral ships, threatens its neighbors, supports terrorism, and refuses to end the bloody war with Iraq.

Now I'll get on with the business of the day. I was looking over my notes from our last meeting, back in 1986, and I noticed that I told you about one of my first jobs as a young man, working for a contractor who was remodeling old homes. I was just 14 years old—by the way, it's not true that the homes that we were remodeling were log cabins. [*Laughter*] As I say, I was just 14 years old; and as I told you, by the time the summer was over, I'd dug out foundations, laid hardwood floors, shingled roofs, and learned a respect for good, honest labor that has stayed with me all my life. But my notes show that I never did tell you just how it was that I left that construction work.

Well, it was on that summer job—this time digging trenches for foundations. And one hot morning I was swinging my pickax, working away, swinging and digging. It so happened that I had the pick up over my head, ready to bring it down in another blow, when the noon whistle blew. And I just stepped out from under the pickax and didn't finish the blow—it was after 12 o'clock—and walked out from under it. And right behind me, I heard some words that my mother had told me never to use. [*Laughter*] I turned around, and there was my boss, standing there, with the point of the pick stuck in the ground right between his feet—I missed him by about a half an inch. And although I can't say for certain, looking back, but I have the feeling that it may have been at that moment, looking into his face, that I first entertained the thoughts of going into show business. [*Laughter*]

But it is indeed a pleasure to have you here, and I wanted to speak to you today in large measure to give you my thanks. You're the ones, after all, who build our roads and put up our buildings, who do so much to help keep America growing. And as President, I extend to you the respect and gratitude of the Nation. But more than that, I owe you, as well, a personal debt of gratitude, for you've done much to make this administration a success.

I referred a moment ago to our meeting in '86. But there was an earlier meeting as well, all the way back in 1981. I asked you then to support our economic recovery program. You did so, even though in the short term many of your firms went through some tough times. But you knew that in the end it was free enterprise, not government regulation, not high taxes or big government spending, but free enterprise, that had led to the building of a great America. And I like to point out that the *Federal Register*, which lists all new regulations, is just a little more than half the size it was when we came here. The estimate is that we eliminated for our citizens and small businesses some 600 million man-hours a year of work just filling out government forms in answer to the regulations. You knew that what America needed as she entered the 1980's was a new birth of economic freedom.

As I said, it was tough at first for some of you, very tough. But today the American economy is in the longest peacetime expansion in U.S. history. Indeed, this month, April, marks the 65th straight month of economic growth. We've created nearly 16 million new jobs—jobs that on balance are better and higher paying. Altogether, the United States has created close to twice as many new jobs as the other leading industrialized nations combined. During this expansion, a greater percentage of our population is employed than at any other time in our history: 62.3 percent of our total potential employment pool is currently at work. Now, maybe you might be like me; I didn't know at first how they figured what was the potential employment pool. And a little over 60 percent of that doesn't sound so well if you're thinking of the entire population. Well, I found out that that potential pool is everyone, male and female, from 16 years of age up, including all the retirees and the people on Social Security, all the kids that are still going to school and not looking for jobs and so forth. And so, that is 62.3 percent—the highest percentage ever in the history of the United States—have jobs.

And the real income of the average American has been rising steadily for the last 6 years. Even areas of our economy that were long thought to be in special trouble have begun to show signs of new creativity and prosperity. As Business Week magazine reported recently: "Basic manufacturers, once considered a dying breed, are selling products many thought wouldn't even be made in the United States any longer—escalators to Taiwan, machine tools to West Germany, lumber to Japan, and shoes to Italy." Since the third quarter of 1986, the volume of American goods exported has been growing some four times as fast as the value [volume] of imported goods. And since 1980 U.S. manufacturing has increased productivity roughly 3½ times as fast as in the previous 7 years. The result is that, as one German manufacturing expert put it recently, the United States is "the best country in the world in terms of manufacturing costs."

And of course your own industry, too, has grown with the new prosperity. Between 1980 and 1987, total new construction grew 24 percent, for an average annual rate of 3.1 percent. The nonresidential sector grew by 4 percent annually, with an overall growth rate of 32 percent. That's not bad, not bad at all.

The American construction industry is not only prospering here in the United States, it also faces new opportunities abroad because the Japanese Government has announced a large-scale public works program. And Japan, in particular, offers vast potential for American construction firms. Just last month we reached an agreement with Japan that will permit American companies to bid, for the first time, on major Japanese construction projects, giving them a much-needed foothold in this important market. Since American construction firms are the most experienced and competitive in the world, I challenge you to take full advantage of this opportunity. Government can create opportunities by knocking down unfair barriers, but businesses themselves must follow through with the proposals, creativity, and workmanship that made America the leader in this field.

And because we've opened up the economy, lowered tax rates, and restored the ideal of limited government and free enterprise—for all these reasons, America today stands poised for even greater economic growth in the year ahead. But even as we celebrate all that we have accomplished, we must acknowledge that hanging over the future are some enormous ifs. If we keep tax rates down, economic incentives will remain strong. If we get government spending under control, the private sector can continue to grow without fear that it will become crowded out by the public sector. If we continue to combat needless regulations, we can keep the economy from suffocating beneath redtape. If—and I know this is an issue that especially concerns you—if we prevent government from mandating additional costs on business. And so, the ifs continue—on and on and on.

Now, I'm not about to launch into a campaign speech; there will be enough for that in the days to come. I could mention, however, that some of the campaign speeches I've been hearing must have been living in another country for the last few years, not this one. [*Laughter*] In any event, my main purpose in speaking to you today has been, as I said, to offer you my thanks. But more than we owe each other thanks, we owe gratitude to this great land of opportunity and freedom, thanks that we must never cease to repay by remaining active in the political life of the nation. For to be sure, America will face choices this fall that will determine perhaps the entire economic course of the coming decade. Will it be economic growth or the growth of big government? Will it be free enterprise or the steady erosion of free enterprise by an ever-expanding Federal bureaucracy?

And so, I ask each of you to direct some of your talent, energy, and leadership in the coming months to the choices that lie before us. And I know somewhere in your minds there's probably a voice saying, but I'm a contractor, not a politician. Well, there was a time—it's getting to be quite a while ago, now—but there was a time when I wondered just how involved I should become in public affairs. I'll never forget the reaction of my old boss at Warner Brothers, Jack Warner, when he first heard that I was running for Governor of California. He said, "Oh, no, no. Jimmy Stewart for Governor, Reagan for best friend." [*Laughter*] And then there was the time back in the early days of the picture business when Jack Warner's brother Harry was first told about the development of motion picture sound—talking pictures. Harry's reaction was one that I was often reminded of during my early days in public life. He said simply, "Who the heck wants to hear actors talk?" [*Laughter*]

But of course I'm not asking you to become professional politicians, merely to remain engaged in the life of the Nation—as engaged as you've been so successfully during these past 7½ years. The choice is simple: Is big government going to grow, or is your economy going to grow? And so, I thank you one last time for all you've done. And I say to you as well, we can't afford to rest. We must keep America strong—strong and growing.

Now I'm going to do something here to finish that I hadn't really planned on doing. But talking about the difference between government and the private sector—the greatest example we have of that, of course, is the Soviet Union. And I have a new hobby. I collect stories, jokes that I can prove are told between the Russian people, that they tell. They reveal that if we ever got to know them we'd find they have a great sense of humor. Also, they have a pretty cynical attitude about their government.

Now, one example is a story they tell—you know, you have to wait 10 years there for delivery after you order an automobile. And so, a fellow had finally gotten the money together and was going to buy an automobile—only about one out of seven families have them in that country—and he went through all the paperwork and everything and finally signed the last paper, laid down his money. And then the man behind the counter said, "Come back in 10 years and get your automobile." And the man said, "Morning or afternoon?" [*Laughter*] And—wait, wait. The fellow behind the counter says, "Well, what difference does it make 10 years from now?" And he said, "Well, the plumber is coming in the morning." [*Laughter*] I've thought about, but haven't gotten around to, telling that to Gorbachev in our next meeting. [*Laughter*]

Well, thank you all, and God bless you all.

Mr. Supica. Mr. President, the construction industry loves you and salutes you because you have restored and expanded the faith, the hope that was so badly needed to keep this nation great. You know America to its deep heart's core. You have stayed closely in touch with the hearts and the minds and the souls of Americans. In 1981 AGC named you our man of the year. You have always been our man of the hour, sir. Today, Mr. President, you honor us again.

Now, Mr. President, in our own special way, we want to honor you. Like the great American eagles that soar over this great nation, well, you have aspired to a better and stronger America and a safer world. And you, sir, have led the way. As a small gesture of the construction industry's regards for you, our nation's number one builder, I have the privilege of presenting you the Associated General Contractors of America's Eagle Award. May God bless you, Mr. President, Mrs. Reagan, and God bless America. Thank you very much.

The President. Thank you very much. I am honored, greatly honored. I thank you all very much. I'm going to impose on you for just a second. I am going to tell you one of those Russian stories that I did tell to Gorbachev. [*Laughter*] In view of your remarks—Russian and American, they have a lot of stories of that kind—arguing about our two countries. The American said, "Look, I can walk into the Oval Office. I can pound the President's desk, and I can say, 'Mr. President, I don't like the way you are running our country.' " And the Russian said, "I can do that." The American said, "You can?" He said, "Yes, I can go into the Kremlin to the General Secretary's office, pound his desk, and say, 'Mr. General Secretary, I don't like the way President Reagan's running his country.' " [*Laughter*]

Note: The President spoke at 1:52 p.m. in Room 450 of the Old Executive Office Building. In his opening remarks, he referred to Mr. and Mrs. James W. Supica. Mr. Supica was president of the Associated General Contractors of America.

Appointment of David Spears Addington as Deputy Assistant to the President for Legislative Affairs

April 18, 1988

The President today announced the appointment of David Spears Addington as Deputy Assistant to the President for Legislative Affairs. Mr. Addington has served as Special Assistant to the President for Legislative Affairs since July 21, 1987.

Prior to joining the White House staff, Mr. Addington served as the minority chief counsel for the Committee on Foreign Affairs of the House of Representatives. He served previously as an Assistant General Counsel at the Central Intelligence Agency and as counsel to the Subcommittee on Legislation for the Permanent Select Committee on Intelligence of the House of Representatives.

Mr. Addington received the degree of bachelor of science in foreign service (summa cum laude) from Georgetown University School of Foreign Service in 1978 and received the degree of juris doctor (with honors) from Duke University in 1981. He was admitted to the practice of law in Virginia and the District of Columbia in 1981. Mr. Addington was born January 22, 1957. He is married to Dr. Linda L. Werling and resides in Rockville, MD.

Appointment of Nelson C. Ledsky as Special Assistant to the President for National Security Affairs

April 18, 1988

The President today announced the appointment of Nelson C. Ledsky as Special Assistant to the President for National Security Affairs and Senior Director, European and Soviet Affairs Directorate. He will succeed Fritz W. Ermarth.

Mr. Ledsky has been a member of the staff of the National Security Council at the White House since April 1987. A career Foreign Service officer, Mr. Ledsky served as Deputy Director of the Policy Planning Staff at the Department of State from mid-1985 to March 1987. Before that, from 1981 to 1985, he was U.S. Minister in Berlin. Other assignments of Mr. Ledsky in the Foreign Service have included positions as Deputy Assistant Secretary of State for Congressional Relations; Office Director for Southern Europe; and Deputy Director of the Office of Central European Affairs. Mr. Ledsky's overseas assignments have included West Germany, Nigeria, and Guyana.

Mr. Ledsky is a graduate of Western Reserve University in Cleveland, OH, and Columbia University in New York City. He is married to the former Cecile Waechter and has three children.

Nomination of Robert South Barrett IV To Be United States Ambassador to Djibouti
April 18, 1988

The President today announced his intention to nominate Robert South Barrett IV, of Virginia, a career member of the Senior Foreign Service, Class of Minister-Counselor, as Ambassador to the Republic of Djibouti. He would succeed John Pierce Ferriter.

Mr. Barrett's last position with the Department of State was as chief of senior assignments in the Bureau of Personnel, 1986–1987. Prior to this position, he served as: Deputy Director for North Africa, 1985; assistant examiner of the Board of Examiners, 1984; and acting Syrian desk officer, 1983. Mr. Barrett also served as Middle East adviser to the United States delegation to the United Nations for the 1983 and 1984 General Assemblies. Previously, he was deputy chief of mission in Beirut, Lebanon, 1980–1982; and Chargé d'Affaires in Antananarivo, Madagascar, 1977–1980. Mr. Barrett has served as Deputy Director for East Africa, 1974–1977, and first secretary/political officer in Saigon, Vietnam, 1971–1974. Mr. Barrett joined the Foreign Service in 1953, serving in Isfahan, Tehran, Phnom Penh, Paris, Fort de France, and Saigon.

Mr. Barrett graduated from Princeton University (A.B., 1950) and the University of Wisconsin (M.S., 1963). He was born July 3, 1927, in Berlin, Germany. He served in the United States Navy, 1945–1946, and the United States Army, 1950–1952. He is married, has two children, and resides in Washington, DC.

Nomination of William Graham Walker To Be United States Ambassador to El Salvador
April 18, 1988

The President today announced his intention to nominate William Graham Walker, a career member of the Senior Foreign Service, Class of Minister-Counselor, as Ambassador to the Republic of El Salvador. He would succeed Edwin G. Corr.

Mr. Walker joined the Foreign Service in 1961 and served as a consular officer from 1962 to 1964 in Lima and Arequipa, Peru, and from 1964 to 1966 in Naha, Okinawa, Japan. In 1967 he returned to Washington to serve as the desk officer for Argentina at the Department of State. In 1968–1969, Mr. Walker received university training in Latin American studies at UCLA, following which he was posted as a political officer in Rio de Janeiro, Brazil, 1962–1972. From 1972 to 1974, Mr. Walker served as an intergovernmental affairs officer at the Environmental Protection Agency in San Francisco, CA.

He was then assigned as chief, political section, at the American Embassy in San Salvador, El Salvador, from 1974 to 1977. In 1977–1978, Mr. Walker returned to Washington and was assigned as a State Department fellow with the Council on Foreign Relations in New York. From 1978 to 1980, Mr. Walker served as a Foreign Service inspector in Washington, following which he served as the deputy chief of mission in Tegucigalpa, Honduras, from 1980 to 1982, and deputy chief of mission in La Paz, Bolivia, from 1982 to 1985. Since 1985 Mr. Walker has been a Deputy Assistant Secretary of State in the Bureau of Inter-American Affairs in Washington.

Mr. Walker graduated from the University of Southern California (B.A., 1960). He was born June 1, 1935, in Kearny, NJ, and served in the United States Army, 1957–1958. He is married, has four children, and resides in Rockville, MD.

Remarks at a White House Ceremony Honoring Law Enforcement Officers Slain in the War on Drugs

April 19, 1988

The President. Well, thank you all for your greeting this morning, and welcome reverend clergy, Nancy, Attorney General Meese, Members of the Congress, diplomats, and members of our Cabinet, and distinguished guests.

Today we're gathered to honor, as you've been told, the brave public servants who have fallen in the war on drugs. These men took a solemn oath to uphold the law. They accepted the dangerous work of defending our communities, our borders, our families from the scourge of narcotics. And in the line of duty, these courageous citizen soldiers paid the ultimate price. Some died close to home in the towns where they were born. Others fell in foreign lands. But they were each lost to us far too soon. And they each made their love for this country and for us, their countrymen, something real that they lived each day.

Today and in days to come, it'll be our turn to show our love for them. We can show our love by teaching our children to just say no to drugs, by teaching them to choose life, by helping them to live in the world God made, not in an artificial, drug-induced world of false hopes and permanent darkness, of imaginary freedom, but absolute slavery. America's liberty was purchased with the blood of heroes. Our release from the bondage of illegal drug use is being won at the same dear price. The battle is ultimately over what America is and what America will be. At our founding, we were promised the pursuit of happiness, not the myth of endless ecstasy from a vial of white poison. We won our personal freedom so that we could serve God and man, so that we could freely produce and create and build a nation of strong families, rich farms, and great cities. We struggled for liberty in order to cherish it and defend it and transmit it undiminished to our children and theirs.

What sort of a nation is America? The kind that produces heroes like Enrique Camarena Salazar, Eddie Byrne, Terry McNett, and many others who gave their lives in the battle against illegal drugs. We're the kind of country that will pull together and sacrifice to rid ourselves of the menace of illegal drug use because we know that drugs are the negation of the type of country we were meant to be.

In New York City, a young rookie cop, Eddie Byrne, was sitting in his patrol car protecting a government witness in a drug case. On February 26th, at 3:30 a.m., Eddie Byrne was shot in the head three times at point-blank range. His father, a retired police lieutenant, said, "If my son, Eddie, sitting in a police car, representing and protecting us, can be wasted by scum, then none of us is safe." Newspaper accounts say he was ordered killed by a drug kingpin in order to send a message to the police.

Enrique Camarena Salazar, special agent

of the Drug Enforcement Administration, was conducting an undercover investigation in Guadalajara, Mexico, to smash a ring of drug traffickers. He was kidnapped, tortured brutally, and killed.

Terry McNett, a detective in the Sedgwick County, Kansas, sheriff's office, was part of a team raiding the house of an alleged crack dealer in Wichita 2 months ago. After entering the house, Detective McNett, 36 years old, a 15-year police veteran, was shot twice in the right eye and killed.

For these men and for all men and women in this country and around the world who've perished in the war on drugs, I would like to ask that we observe a moment of silence on this solemn occasion. Would you join me?

Amen.

We rededicate ourselves to continue their struggle. It's a struggle of which we've all been a part and one in which we've worked together.

The United States is joined by other countries in a common battle against drugs. I've received a report from Attorney General Meese on his recent trip, that he mentioned in his remarks, to the Dominican Republic, Colombia, Ecuador, Peru, and Bolivia. And I'm particularly encouraged by the commitment he received from the leaders of those countries to heighten efforts in the crusade against narcotics trafficking. The drug enforcement and justice officials overseas have our full support.

I want to pay special tribute to the many sacrifices made by our international allies in this fight. In Colombia alone, 12 supreme court justices, an attorney general, justice minister, and scores of other judicial and law enforcement officials have lost their lives. The traffickers in Colombia have also extended their terror beyond its borders. In 1987 former justice minister, and then Ambassador to Hungary, Enrique Parejo was shot and nearly killed in Budapest at the direction of traffickers. Fortunately he survived and last week received PRIDE's Spirit of Freedom Award. We have the honor of his presence today and salute his courage. Recently, Colombia's Chief Prosecutor, Attorney General Carlos Hoyos, while fighting his country's war on drugs, was abducted and murdered. Similarly, officials from Bolivia, Mexico, Peru, Thailand, and other nations have perished in this international struggle. These giants of courage and the brave men and women like them around the world will be remembered in our prayers.

When I spoke to our nation's police chiefs 7 years ago, we pledged a united effort against the menace of illegal drugs. And since then, important progress has been made. Since 1981 the antidrug law enforcement budget has tripled, and another 13 percent increase has been requested. No-nonsense Federal judges are part of the war on crime. Drug convictions have more than doubled since 1979, with prison sentences 40 percent longer. And last year new, tougher sentencing guidelines were issued. The Comprehensive Crime Control Act, passed in 1984 after a long effort—passed with the help of Members of the Congress who are here today—they helped put drug dealers out of business by confiscating their assets. Last year over $500 million in ill-gotten assets were seized. The Anti-Drug Abuse Act, which I signed into law in October, 1986, contributed additional tools to our effort.

Our antidrug effort spans the Federal Government. It is coordinated by the Cabinet-level National Drug Policy Board chaired by Attorney General Meese. The coordination of Federal, State, local, and international drug enforcement is at an all-time high. Under the leadership of the Vice President, our national drug interdiction system has enabled unprecedented levels of narcotics to be seized enroute from source countries and at our border by law enforcement agencies. These efforts were significantly assisted by the U.S. military, which last year provided more than 16,000 hours of air surveillance and over 2,500 ship days of maritime support in the war against drugs.

Drug eradication programs are now underway in 23 countries. That's up from just two in 1981. And to stem demand for illegal drugs, more funds than ever before are being spent on drug education and public awareness, and I've requested a further 12-percent increase in that.

We can list the accomplishments in this war, but by themselves these efforts, impressive as they may seem, are still not enough. It'll never be enough until we have fully honored the memory of those who have perished and until we have won for them, and for ourselves, a drug free America.

I'm especially proud of the antidrug work that Nancy has done, which is an act of love beyond anything money can achieve and which has changed the way we talk and think about drugs. You see, we too often forget how the level of drug abuse reached the proportions that it did. Back in the 1960's and 1970's, America crossed a deadly line. The use of illegal drugs became not just condoned but even celebrated by a permissive cultural establishment whose slogan was "Just Say Yes." It was a time when all the restrictions on personal behavior were under attack. Some liberal politicians decried our prohibitions on drugs as conservative, moralistic, reactionary, and old-fashioned—or simply remained silent that there even was a drug problem. Many universities adopted a hands-off attitude toward so-called recreational drug use, and the entertainment industry produced films and music that promoted and legitimized the drug subculture. When our young people looked for guidance and direction, instead of finding positive role models warning them of the dangers of drugs, they would too often see celebrities portraying drug use as cool, hip, and with it. What greater shame can there be? With the active encouragement of the progressive culture, our young people began to use drugs—not to rebel but to fit in.

And tragically, countless thousands of young lives were needlessly destroyed. The truth was that drugs are killers, but for nearly a generation that vital message was ignored by a whole group of people who should have known better. The leaders of that destructive generation remain the forgotten accomplices in the epidemic of illegal drug use; they cannot escape blame when a law enforcement officer dies in the battle.

The good news is that America is on the attack in the fight against drugs. Our young people are turning away from illegal drug use and learning to say, just say no. Almost all of the high school seniors, in the latest annual survey, said that it was wrong to even try a drug like cocaine. And the number using cocaine and marijuana fell significantly. Whole communities are working as never before toward the goal of a drug free America.

USA Today reports that in Philadelphia the police department has trained 25,000 residents to observe, identify, and report drug dealers under its town watch program. In Boise, Idaho, the police work with a group called Parents and Youths Against Drug Abuse to promote drug education. In Jackson, Mississippi, a group of teenagers is fighting back by forming Teens on Patrol to act as the eyes and ears for the local police force. These efforts serve as fitting tributes to the fallen heroes that we honor here today. Our heroes embody the courage and commitment that built America and which will see us through this battle. Let us, through our efforts, keep faith with these men and their sacrifice.

Six months ago, I sent to the Congress a new and important piece of legislation, the Criminal Justice Reform Act of 1987, that would provide a powerful new deterrent to violent crime and narcotics trafficking. This critical legislation takes on the drug syndicates on their own terms. It says that when narcotics racketeers kill and are convicted they will face execution. In 1986 the House of Representatives twice approved this provision, but this year neither the House nor the Senate Judiciary Committees have yet taken up this bill. It is time to back up the rhetoric on the drug problem with action. And I call upon the House and Senate to vote promptly on my bill providing for capital punishment when a death results from drug dealing and when a DEA or other law enforcement officer is murdered. When drug syndicates commit murder, our sympathy should be with the victims, not the killers. It's time for the Congress to pass this bill and make it law. It's time for us to send our own message to people who kill cops.

Our antidrug efforts are working. The heroic sacrifices made by America's law enforcement officers and by public servants from around the world have not been in vain. They have made a difference, a difference that will save lives and assure our children a better future in the type of America they deserve to grow up in. Our dream is a nation of drug free communities, drug free workplaces, drug free homes, and drug free schools. And that is what these men died for, and that is what we must work for.

In the crusade for a drug free America, these heroes gave all that they had and all that they were. Let us do all that we can to honor their memory. Through our prayers, let us be with them. Through our work, let us commemorate their sacrifice. And through our achievement, let us celebrate their lives. Together we can achieve what they died for—a drug free America. Thank you, and God bless you.

Attorney General Meese. Thank you, Mr. President, for those inspiring remarks, which highlight our being here today. In your remarks you mentioned the heroes we are commemorating. Among those are two agents from the Drug Enforcement Agency, one of the key institutions in our struggle against drug abuse. We're pleased to have representing our drug law enforcement organizations, Jack Lawn, the Administrator of DEA, seated here on the dais. Jack has been honored recently by his election as president of the International Drug Enforcement Conference.

We had a tragedy in the DEA recently, when two special agents, Paul Seema and George Montoya, were killed in the course of a heroin investigation near Los Angeles. In that operation, one of their colleagues, special agent José Martinez, was wounded. We thank God that he survived, and we're pleased to have him with us today. Surely, no one is a more worthy spokesman for those who risked their lives in the course of the battle against drugs than Mr. Martinez. And so, it is my great honor at this time to ask special agent Martinez to step up and say a few words.

Mr. Martinez. First of all, I'd like to take this opportunity to thank all my friends, family, and everyone in the DEA family, and all the other law enforcement officers and community for their support while I was hospitalized, and the general public for their encouragement to me—all the letters I received. And I would also like to thank everyone for the encouragement that was shown to the loved ones of my slain fellow agents, Paul Seema and George Montoya. I am thankful for the greater public concern about drug abuse. And thank you, Mr. President and Mrs. Reagan, for your contributions to this awareness.

Those of us in drug enforcement are committed to the task of removing drugs from our society, knowing and accepting the dangers involved. At the same time, many in society rationalize the drug use as being a victimless crime and not harmful to anyone. Paul Seema and George Montoya were victims of society's demand to satisfy their desire for drugs. Not until people quit using drugs will it become safer for those of us in law enforcement and the rest of society. Thank you.

The President. The Attorney General tells me I can just conclude it. [*Laughter*] I didn't bring a whistle, and I can't think of a good get-off line, except I think that what we have just heard from this young man, his lovely wife—I think all of us know what's at stake here. And I think all of us are going to continue doing this until it's a chapter of our history that we can look back upon, but know that we'll never see that chapter repeated again in our nation's history. God bless you all. Thank you for what you're doing.

Note: The President spoke at 11:47 a.m. in Room 450 of the Old Executive Office Building.

Photographic Portfolio

10

Overleaf: Walking with Soviet General Secretary Mikhail Gorbachev in Red Square in Moscow, May 31. ***Left:*** With British Prime Minister Margaret Thatcher outside 10 Downing Street in London, June 3. ***Above right:*** With President Mohammed Hosni Mubarak of Egypt in the Oval Office, January 28. ***Center right:*** Participating in a forum on education held at Oakton High School in Vienna, VA, May 24. ***Below right:*** At a Republican congressional fundraising dinner at the District of Columbia Convention Center, May 11.

Above left: At a St. Patrick's Day luncheon in the Speaker of the House of Representatives' Dining Room at the Capitol, March 17. ***Below left:*** With Secretary of State George Shultz and Secretary of the Treasury James A. Baker III in Toronto, Canada, June 20. ***Above right:*** Arrival of President Kenan Evran of Turkey, June 27. ***Below right:*** At the state dinner in St. Vladimir's Hall at the Kremlin in Moscow, May 30.

Above left: Greeting 1988 Winter Olympic medal winners in the East Room, March 8. ***Center left:*** At a luncheon with teachers in the Roosevelt Room, April 26. ***Below left:*** Touring the Reynolds Metals Company in Richmond, VA, March 28. ***Right:*** Walking at Camp David, MD, January 1. ***Overleaf:*** Speaking at the Veterans of Foreign Wars Washington Conference, March 7.

283
CALIFORNIA

Nomination of Salvatore R. Martoche To Be a Member of the National Mediation Board
April 19, 1988

The President today announced his intention to nominate Salvatore R. Martoche to be a member of the National Mediation Board for the term expiring July 1, 1991. He would succeed Helen M. Witt.

Since 1986 Mr. Martoche has been Assistant Secretary for Enforcement at the Department of Labor. Prior to this, he was United States Attorney for the Western District of New York, 1982–1986. He has also been a member of the Attorney General's Advisory Committee, 1983–1986; serving as Vice Chairman, 1984, and Chairman, 1985. Mr. Martoche was an attorney in private practice, 1969–1982, and assistant counsel to the majority for the New York State Senate, 1974–1982. From 1972 to 1981, he was the administrator for the Erie County Bar Association of the Pre-Trial Services Agency, Inc.

Mr. Martoche graduated from Canisius College (B.S., 1962) and the University of North Dakota School of Law (J.D., 1967). He was born October 12, 1940, in Buffalo, NY. He is married, has three children, and resides in Alexandria, VA.

Letter to the Speaker of the House of Representatives and the President Pro Tempore of the Senate on the United States Military Strike in the Persian Gulf
April 19, 1988

Dear Mr. Speaker: (Dear Mr. President:)

On April 14, 1988, the USS SAMUEL B. ROBERTS struck a mine in international waters of the Persian Gulf. Lookouts on the ROBERTS had spotted three mines lying perpendicular to the ship's course and about 700 yards away. The ROBERTS struck a mine set deeper than the others and not visible from the ship. Ten servicemen were injured. The detonation caused a nine-foot hole in the ship's hull near the main engine room, below the water line; a split in the ship's bulkhead between the main engine room and an auxiliary machinery room; and a fire. The ROBERTS is now safely in a repair facility.

An examination of the mines remaining in the water established that they were M–08 mines, the same type Iran was caught placing in the water from the IRAN AJR on September 21, 1987. They had been freshly laid in an area transited by U.S. convoys. No barnacles or marine growth were on the mines. Most important, the mines bore markings of the same type and series as on those laid by the IRAN AJR. No doubt exists that Iran laid these mines for the specific purpose of damaging or sinking U.S. or other non-belligerent ships. We have warned Iran repeatedly against such hostile acts.

In response to this attack on the ROBERTS and commencing at approximately 1:00 a.m. (EDT), April 18, 1988, Armed Forces of the United States assigned to the Joint Task Force Middle East, after warning Iranian personnel and providing an opportunity to escape, attacked and effectively neutralized the Sassan and Sirri Platforms, which have been used to support unlawful Iranian attacks on non-belligerent shipping. While these events were taking place, an Iranian helicopter and small boats attacked an oil rig and the U.S.-flag vessel WILLI TIDE in the Mubarak oil field. In response, U.S. A–6 aircraft attacked three Iranian Boghammar small boats, sinking at least one.

Subsequently, U.S. Forces were attacked by the Iranian PTG JOSHAN, FFG

SAHAND, and FFG SABALAN. In response to these attacks, U.S. Forces severely damaged or sank the Iranian vessels. Iranian F–4 fighters also approached the USS SIMPSON and the USS WAINWRIGHT in a threatening manner; the SIMPSON and WAINWRIGHT fired at the aircraft, causing their retreat.

Search and rescue efforts were undertaken to locate a missing AH–1 Cobra helicopter from the WAINWRIGHT. The helicopter had two men on board. As of 7:00 a.m. (EDT) today, the search and rescue efforts were continuing.

These necessary and proportionate actions by U.S. Armed Forces were taken at my specific direction in the exercise of our inherent right of self-defense, recognized in Article 51 of the United Nations Charter, and pursuant to my constitutional authority with respect to the conduct of foreign relations and as Commander in Chief. We have completed these self-defense actions and consider the matter closed.

Since March 1987, I and members of my Administration have provided to Congress letters, reports, briefings, and testimony in connection with developments in the Persian Gulf and the activities of U.S. Armed Forces in the region. In accordance with my desire that Congress be kept fully informed on this matter, I am providing this report consistent with the War Powers Resolution. I look forward to cooperating with Congress in pursuit of our mutual, overriding aim of peace and stability in the Persian Gulf region. In this connection, I regard the continued presence of U.S. Armed Forces to be essential to the achievement of that aim. Our Forces remain prepared to take any additional action necessary to protect themselves, U.S.-flag vessels, and U.S. lives.

Sincerely,

RONALD REAGAN

Note: Identical letters were sent to Jim Wright, Speaker of the House of Representatives, and John C. Stennis, President pro tempore of the Senate.

Remarks at a Senate Campaign Fundraising Reception for Pete Dawkins of New Jersey
April 19, 1988

Senators, distinguished guests, you know, more than half a century ago, there was a halfback at the University of Chicago who was so powerful, so skilled, and so dashing that he became a hero to millions of football-loving Americans, including a certain young fellow named Dutch Reagan. In 1935 this great halfback, Jay Berwanger, received a new award, and the tradition of the Heisman Trophy was born. Jay Berwanger is with us here tonight, and I couldn't begin without telling him and all the Heisman Trophy winners who are gathered here what a great honor it is to be in their presence.

College football has certainly come a long way since the day when President White of Cornell refused to permit his football team to play against the University of Michigan. President White said—this was back in the 1870's—and I quote: "I will not permit men to travel 400 miles merely to agitate a bag of wind." [*Laughter*] You know, I told President White I thought he was overreacting. [*Laughter*]

But, Pete, Judi [Mrs. Dawkins], and everyone, we're here this evening less to celebrate Pete Dawkins' past as an athlete than to show our support for his future as, yes, the next United States Senator from the great State of New Jersey. Athlete, scholar, soldier, businessman—Pete Dawkins is one of the finest candidates to compete in the elections of 1988. But I'll go even further: Pete Dawkins is one of the finest candidates I've ever known. The reason goes beyond Pete's extraordinary competence and skill. It has to do with his deepest values—with his fierce belief in freedom, in the family, in economic opportunity for all.

On the issues, Pete has already staked out forthright positions. He stands with me in wanting to keep your taxes low in order to keep our economy growing. He's staunch in his support of the Strategic Defense Initiative, which Pete has rightly called a step "to reduce the threat of nuclear arms." And he understands the need to keep the pressure on Soviet-backed regimes by supporting those struggling for freedom around the world, especially in Afghanistan and, yes, in Nicaragua.

This election will determine whether we'll continue on the path we began in 1981—a growing, expanding economy at home and a strong and secure America abroad—or whether we'll return to the failed policies of the past—high taxes, increasing inflation and unemployment, a stifling bureaucracy, and weakness abroad. Our opponents are saying that America wants to return to the good old days of the 1970's. Well, I don't know about you, but I don't think that's what the public wants. [*Laughter*] We're prepared to move forward into the next decade and tackle the new challenges that it offers.

Pete Dawkins is running for the Senate because he believes in the new America, not the old; because he believes America should be strong, not weak; because he believes we should discipline the Federal budget, not the family budget; and because he knows that tax hikes in Washington are seldom used to cut the deficit, just to go on spending. If I could just add one personal note: As President, I've seen the Senate in Republican hands. It was during my first 6 years. And I've seen it run by the Democrats, as it is today. Believe me, this country needs Pete to come down here and help return the Senate to GOP control.

But to turn for a moment from the Nation as a whole to the State of New Jersey, the State so many of you serve and cherish. Under the outstanding leadership of Governor Kean, New Jersey has changed in recent years, changed dramatically. There was a time not too long ago when New Jersey was becoming thought of as one huge, unmanageable sprawl, as a State that was being taken over by the most unpleasant aspects of the big cities in neighboring States. Today New Jersey is rightly seen as a State that has made a comeback—a State of economic growth, but of compassion for its less fortunate citizens; a State of reform and good government; a State where, for millions of Americans, life is good, very good. Today there's a new New Jersey. Isn't it time for New Jersey to have a new Senator? [*Applause*] I hope Governor Kean won't mind when he hears about this, but every time I think of Pete, there's a phrase that goes through my mind. "Pete Dawkins and New Jersey—perfect together." [*Laughter*]

Now, with all of these football greats here, if you'll permit me, I'd like to close with a football story. Back when I was in Hollywood, one day I picked up the Daily Variety and read where Warner Brothers was announcing that they were making the life story of Knute Rockne. Well, that's all I'd thought about from the time I—hadn't been in Hollywood too long, and that was on my mind, having been a sports announcer. And all I ever wanted though, if they made the story, was to play the Gipper. And I approached Pat O'Brien, who intervened with the producer who was going to do the Rockne story. Well, he was, to put it mildly, unimpressed with my credentials. [*Laughter*] He started by telling me I didn't look big enough for the part. Well, I wasn't very polite because I told him, "You're producing the picture and you don't know that George Gipp weighed 5 pounds less than I weigh right now. He walked with a kind of a slouch, almost a limp. He looked like a football player only when he was on the field."

And then I went home because some cameramen, in those early days, had told me that the fellas in the front office only knew what they saw on film. And I dug down in the trunk and came up with my own pictures of myself playing football in college and brought them back and showed them to the producer. Well, believe it or not, he let me do the test. And Pat O'Brien, knowing of my nervousness and desire, graciously agreed to be a part of it. Normally, stars of that standing do not help someone out in a screen test. They leave that to someone of lesser importance.

But, of course, I had an advantage. I'd known George Gipp's story for years, and the lines were straight from Knute Rockne's diary. The test scene was one that I'll never forget, one that said something about what Rockne liked to see in his players. It was George Gipp's first practice. Rockne told him to carry the ball for the scrubs. And Gipp just looked back at Rockne, cocked an eyebrow, and said, "How far?" Well, he answered that question himself by carrying the ball 60 yards through the varsity the first time he got his hands on it. Incidentally, as he came back with the ball, having scored the touchdown—came back with the ball, he tossed it to Rockne and said, "I guess the boys are just tired." [*Laughter*]

Well, as I say, Knute liked that spirit in his ballplayers. Grantland Rice tells us that once when he was working with the four backfield stars who became known as the Four Horsemen, the fellow named Jimmy Crowley just couldn't get it right on one play. Now, you know, I never tell ethnic jokes anymore unless they're about the Irish. [*Laughter*] Rockne, who, by the way, was Norwegian, but was commonly called "the Swede"—he finally got irritated after Crowley muffed a play again and hollered, "What's dumber than a dumb Irishman?" And without missing a beat, Crowley said, "A smart Swede." [*Laughter*]

But to be serious, Pete Dawkins reminds me of George Gipp more than a little. Pete's a fine man, a likable man, a man who loves his country. And Pete is a man of determination. You don't go from being a polio victim at age 11 to winning the Heisman Trophy without lots and lots of determination. On the football field, in combat, in scholarship, in business, and yes, in the United States Senate, you can tell Pete Dawkins to carry the ball; and Pete will say, "How far?"

Well, I'm very proud and pleased to be here. Never thought I'd be associating with that many Heisman Trophy winners—[*laughter*]—but also, I know where your hearts are with regard to this coming election. Do everything you can, and buttonhole those neighbors. The one big trouble today with a lot of people who think like us is that they just have forgotten to vote and think they can just go their way and everything will turn out all right.

Well, the thing to remind those that don't go to the polls anymore what Will Rogers once said. He said: "The people you send to public office are no better and no worse than the people who send them there. But they're all better than those who don't vote at all." So, get out there, get out the vote, and I'll be waiting here to greet a new Senator from New Jersey. Thank you very much.

Note: The President spoke at 7:49 p.m. in the Promenade at the Grand Hotel.

Remarks at the Electronic Industries Association's Annual Government-Industry Dinner

April 19, 1988

I thank you for that welcome, and a special thank you to your chairman, John Mitchell, and your president, Peter McCloskey, the reverend clergy. And let me also give my congratulations to your Medal of Honor winner for this year, educator, scientist, executive, and leader, Joseph Boyd. And I know that I am not an after-dinner speaker tonight. [*Laughter*] And I assure you that I will keep that in mind. [*Laughter*]

I will, as Henry VIII said to each of his six wives, "I won't keep you long." [*Laughter*] But it's a pleasure to appear before this, the oldest and largest organization representing the cutting edge of America's technological future, the industries that are leading the way for America and the world into the third industrial revolution. Henry David Thoreau once said that "This world is but a canvas for our imaginations." And if any people in the world prove that, it's you. Time and again over the past 100 years, electronics has bounded beyond the imaginations of even the most sophisticated observers.

Ninety-one years ago, for example, one of the most distinguished scientists not only of his time but of all time, Lord Kelvin, offered this assessment of what was then only a theoretical possibility: radio. He said, and these are his words, "Radio has no future." [*Laughter*] Well, less than 30 years later the father of radio, Lee DeForest, showed that he wasn't infallible either when he said that, "While theoretically and technically television may be feasible, commercially and financially I consider it an impossibility." [*Laughter*] And then there was the president of a major computer company who said only 11 years ago, and I'll quote again: "There is no reason for any individual to have a computer in their home." [*Laughter*]

Yes, when I look at the history of your industries, it reminds me of a story about a producer I once knew in Hollywood. I was under contract to the Warner Brothers, and one of the brothers, Jack Warner—you may remember the classic film "The Story of Louis Pasteur." It concerned, of course, the great French scientist and ignored many doubters in the scientific community of his time and succeeded in developing the pasteurization process for sterilizing milk. It starred Paul Muni and won him an Academy Award, an Oscar. It was an outstanding movie and a hit. But Jack was very skeptical about making it. He finally agreed only under protest. It would be a bust, he predicted, because, after all, it was, just as he said, "the story of a milkman." [*Laughter*]

Well, tonight I'd like to talk with you about our nation's commitment to leadership and imagination, and your role in America's future. I'm talking about our space program. I believe it is time to look ahead and envision breaking the bounds of earthbound imagination and to begin to conceive of a 21st century. The national aerospace plane is an important investment in our future. Its technologies will yield routine access to space. We will be capable of taking off from Dulles Airport in a second generation shuttle, leaping into space, and docking with the space station, almost like taking off from Washington for London. Not only the Moon but the entire solar system beckons, which is why I have issued a new national space policy that reaffirms the goal of U.S. leadership in space and sets a new long-term goal of expanding human exploration into the solar system. In the coming year's budget I've asked for $100 million to initiate Project Pathfinder. I've said "initiate"; the Pathfinder technology will lay the foundation for potential manned and unmanned missions beyond the Earth's orbit. And I look to the time, before the end of the first decade of the next century, when we may have manned visits to other planets.

The space station is vital to our leadership in space and contributes to our preeminence in manned space flight. Some say we can't afford the space station. I ask you: Can America ever afford to stop dreaming great dreams? And can we afford to jettison the next generation of technical spinoffs? Just think about the thousands of discoveries, all the commercial and industrial products and techniques that came because we developed the technology to go to the Moon. We hear a great deal about American competitiveness. Other nations often cite our major scientific programs as among our greatest competitive advantages, and they're right. Tonight I ask Congress and all the American people to join me in making the long-term investment required to advance U.S. leadership in space. We must begin that investment by funding the increases I've proposed for our civil space program. Can we afford to stop our exploration and wait for others to pass us?

And exploration is not all we want. Recently, we announced that it would be the policy of the Government to encourage private sector investment and involvement in outer space. We are now committed to being the anchor tenant in a privately financed, constructed, and operated commercial research and manufacturing facility. We'll help develop a highway to space by using private launch services to the greatest extent feasible, and we're working to win legislation to limit liability for commercial launch providers. We'll make equipment, like the external fuel tanks of the shuttle fleet, available to private commercial and nonprofit ventures in space. And we're looking at ways to avoid precluding or deterring American private enterprise in taking commercial advantage of the unique aspects of the space environment.

To do our part in building on the base of technology and talent we'll need, we're instituting policies to turn federally funded discoveries into commercial products and technologies. We're encouraging Federal scientists, engineers, and technicians to take sabbatical years to teach at any level of American education. We're opening the way for even greater contacts between NASA and schools and universities. And we're emphasizing the importance of the superconducting supercollider to the advancement of science.

It's a future beyond the most distant star in our dreams that beckons us. And to those who say it can't be reached, that it's impossible, I'd just point toward your industries and ask if a few years ago they thought what you are doing today would also be impossible. Carver Mead, professor of computer sciences at the California Institute of Technology, recently noted that "the entire Industrial Revolution enhanced productivity by a factor of about 100. The Microelectronic Revolution has already increased productivity in information-based technology by a factor of more than a million, and the end isn't in sight yet." Is that the accomplishment of people who listened when others used the word impossible?

More than any other group, you embody America's capacity to dream. More than any other group, yes, we've challenged America's scientists to help find a safe and effective means to protect our borders and those of our allies by developing technologies for the Strategic Defense Initiative. Five years ago, I proposed SDI, and much to my satisfaction, we've made tremendous progress in that research. We must not stop dreaming because a few naysayers insist on limiting our options for a safe and secure future.

I ask each of you today to carry out your dreams and to continue to make this nation the greatest innovator in the world. I ask you today to help us all with our feet on the ground to look to the stars and, in doing that, to remain number one in technology here on Earth. And if even some of you still think that maybe I'm being too optimistic, you're hearing all this from a fellow who was a second lieutenant in the horse cavalry. [*Laughter*] With that, I think it's high time that you enjoy dinner. I thank you all. God bless you all.

Note: The President spoke at 8:38 p.m. in the Grand Ballroom at the J.W. Marriott Hotel.

Proclamation 5798—Jewish Heritage Week, 1988
April 20, 1988

By the President of the United States of America

A Proclamation

The heritage of the Jewish people finds expression in America today just as in the days of our Founders. During Jewish Heritage Week, we recall that throughout our history the American people have drawn inspiration from and analogies to Jewish history. That history—which in this century alone includes the horrors of the Holocaust, the establishment of the modern State of Israel, and the current struggle of Soviet Jewry for freedom—symbolizes humanity's long and continuing quest for liberty.

Happily, the United States, the land of the free, has become home to a thriving Jewish community whose members have made inestimable contributions to our national life. Jews have distinguished themselves in virtually every field, to the benefit of us all. Jewish Heritage Week, which this year includes April 21, the 40th anniversary of the founding of Israel, is a fitting occasion for us to study once again the lessons of Jewish history and to rededicate ourselves to the ideals of freedom for all peoples.

The Congress, by House Joint Resolution 527, has designated the period of April 17 through April 24, 1988, as "Jewish Heritage Week" and has authorized and requested the President to issue a proclamation in observance of this event.

Now, Therefore, I, Ronald Reagan, President of the United States of America, do hereby proclaim the period of April 17 through April 24, 1988, as Jewish Heritage Week. I call upon the people of the United States, interested organizations, and Federal, State, and local government officials to observe this week with appropriate ceremonies and activities.

In Witness Whereof, I have hereunto set my hand this twentieth day of April, in the year of our Lord nineteen hundred and eighty-eight, and of the Independence of the United States of America the two hundred and twelfth.

RONALD REAGAN

[*Filed with the Office of the Federal Register, 4:39 p.m., April 20, 1988*]

Proclamation 5799—Law Day, U.S.A., 1988
April 20, 1988

By the President of the United States of America

A Proclamation

For more than three decades our country has observed May 1 as Law Day, U.S.A., in grateful recognition that our free Republic is a government of laws, not men. On Law Day, U.S.A., we join in proud commemoration of America's legacy of liberty, justice, and self-government, and we pause to salute those past and present who have served and sacrificed to win and protect our freedom and to preserve law and tranquility in our communities—including the men and women of law enforcement whose daily courage and dedication make our laws and liberties a living reality.

Because ours is a government by consent of the people, we are our own lawgivers; hence, the virtuousness of our laws depends on our individual and civic virtues. That is truly something to remember on any Law Day, U.S.A., but especially in a national election year, when we recall how important it is that each of us be familiar with our rights and liberties and with the legal and political guarantees of our freedoms. Only through knowledge, awareness, and love of country can we take full part in the self-government that is ours as Americans to perpetuate.

This is why all Americans of legal voting age should make up their minds, this year and each year, to vote in every election for which they are eligible and to observe all election laws faithfully. By voting, we have our say in who our representatives are and thereby in the shaping of laws that affect us, our communities, our States, and our Nation. We should always remember that those who vote not only demonstrate their voice in public affairs but also exercise one of the precious rights for which brave people around the globe today fight and die just as did our ancestors. Let us understand that our voting is a way to keep faith with them, with our fellow citizens, with the brave Americans who defend us at home and abroad, and with all who cherish our American heritage of liberty, justice, and equality before the law.

Now, Therefore, I, Ronald Reagan, President of the United States of America, in accordance with Public Law 87–20 of April 7, 1961, do hereby proclaim Sunday, May 1, 1988, as Law Day, U.S.A. I urge the people of the United States to use this occasion to reflect on our birthright of freedom, to express gratitude to those who protect our country and our communities, to familiarize themselves with the need to vote, and to encourage and assist others to vote. I ask the legal profession, schools, public bodies, libraries, courts, the communications media, businesses, the clergy, civic, service, and fraternal organizations, and all interested individuals and organizations to join in efforts to focus attention on voting. I also call upon all public officials to display the flag of the United States on all government buildings on Law Day, U.S.A.

In Witness Whereof, I have hereunto set my hand this 20th day of April, in the year of our Lord nineteen hundred and eighty-eight, and of the Independence of the United States of America the two hundred and twelfth.

RONALD REAGAN

[*Filed with the Office of the Federal Register, 4:40 p.m., April 20, 1988*]

Executive Order 12636—Establishment of Emergency Board No. 213 To Investigate a Railroad Labor Dispute
April 20, 1988

Establishing an Emergency Board to Investigate a Dispute Between the Chicago and North Western Transportation Company and Certain of its Employees Represented by the United Transportation Union

A dispute exists between the Chicago and North Western Transportation Company and certain of its employees represented by the United Transportation Union.

The dispute has not heretofore been adjusted under the provisions of the Railway Labor Act, as amended ("the Act").

This dispute, in the judgment of the National Mediation Board, threatens substantially to interrupt interstate commerce to a degree such as to deprive a section of the country of essential transportation service.

Now, Therefore, by the authority vested in me by Section 10 of the Act, as amended (45 U.S.C. 160), it is hereby ordered as follows:

Section 1. Establishment of Board. There is established, effective April 22, 1988, a board of three members to be appointed by the President to investigate this dispute. No member shall be pecuniarily or otherwise interested in any organization of railroad employees or any carrier. The board shall perform its functions subject to the availability of funds.

Sec. 2. Report. The board shall report its finding to the President with respect to the dispute within 30 days from the date of its creation.

Sec. 3. Maintaining Conditions. As provided by Section 10 of the Act, as amended, from the date of the creation of the board and for 30 days after the board has made its report to the President, no change, except by agreement of the parties, shall be made by the Carrier or the employees in the conditions out of which the dispute arose.

Sec. 4. Expiration. The board shall terminate upon the submission of the report provided for in Section 2 of this Order.

RONALD REAGAN

The White House,
April 20, 1988.

[*Filed with the Office of the Federal Register, 4:41 p.m., April 20, 1988*]

Announcement of the Establishment of Emergency Board No. 213 To Investigate a Railroad Labor Dispute
April 20, 1988

The President announced today that he has established, effective April 22, 1988, Presidential Emergency Board No. 213 to investigate a current dispute between the

Chicago and North Western Transportation Company (CNW) and certain of its employees represented by the United Transportation Union. The President, by Executive order, established the Emergency Board on the recommendation of the National Mediation Board, which found that the dispute threatens to interrupt interstate commerce to a degree that would deprive a section of the country of essential transportation services.

The CNW employs over 8,000 persons and in terms of revenue generated is the 8th largest railroad in the United States. The railroad is a major link in our interstate rail network, as a number of major U.S. Class I railroads rely on the CNW to receive or forward their traffic. The CNW handled nearly 1.5 million carloads and over 80 million tons of traffic in 1986. This represents 7 percent of total rail carloads nationwide and 15 percent of all traffic moved in the western territory.

The great majority of CNW traffic is handled in connection with other railroads. More than one-third of CNW's traffic originates on its lines and is forwarded to connecting lines; another one-fourth is received from other rail carriers and terminated on the CNW. Bridge traffic (received from one carrier and subsequently passed along to another carrier) accounts for 21 percent. Only 16 percent represents local shipments (those that both originate and terminate on CNW lines). The largest commodity handled by the CNW in terms of revenues is coal, which accounted for 14 percent of its annual revenues in 1986, 28 percent of its total carloads, and 7 percent of all U.S. rail coal loadings. Grain traditionally has been a major commodity for CNW, including wheat in the Northern Plains and corn in the Missouri and Mississippi River Basins. Grain accounts for 13 percent of CNW-originated carloads, representing 12 percent of all western railroads' grain originations and 9 percent of rail loadings of grain nationwide.

In addition to its freight-handling activities, the railroad is the major rail passenger provider for the city of Chicago, handling approximately 40,000 passengers daily. Alternatives to this commuter rail service are limited. As a result, the Chicago area would suffer a substantial disruption of normal business activities in the event of a strike.

Consequently the President has invoked the Emergency Board procedures of the Railway Labor Act, which in part provide that the board will report its findings and recommendations for settlement to the President within 30 days from the date of its creation. The parties must then consider the recommendations of the Emergency Board and endeavor to resolve their differences without engaging in self-help during a subsequent 30-day period.

Message to the Congress Transmitting the Netherlands-United States Social Security Agreement
April 20, 1988

To the Congress of the United States:

Pursuant to Section 233(e)(1) of the Social Security Act, as amended by the Social Security Amendments of 1977 (P.L. 95–216, 42 U.S.C. 433(e)(1)), I transmit herewith the Agreement between the United States of America and the Kingdom of the Netherlands on Social Security that consists of two separate instruments: A principal agreement and an administrative arrangement. The Agreement was signed at The Hague on December 8, 1987.

The U.S.-Netherlands Agreement is similar in objective to the social security agreements already in force with Belgium, Canada, the Federal Republic of Germany, Italy, Norway, Spain, Sweden, Switzerland, and the United Kingdom. Such bilateral agreements provide for limited coordination between the United States and foreign social security systems to overcome the problems of gaps in protection and of dual coverage and taxation for workers who move from one country to the other.

I also transmit for the information of the Congress a comprehensive report prepared by the Department of Health and Human Services, which explains the provisions of the Agreement and provides data on the number of persons affected by the Agreement and the effect on social security financing as required by the same provision of the Social Security Act.

The Department of State and the Department of Health and Human Services join with me in commending the U.S.-Netherlands Social Security Agreement and related documents.

RONALD REAGAN

The White House,
April 20, 1988.

Nomination of Arch Madsen To Be a Member of the Board for International Broadcasting
April 20, 1988

The President today announced his intention to nominate Arch Madsen to be a member of the Board for International Broadcasting for the remainder of the term expiring May 20, 1989. He would succeed Lilla Burt Cummings Tower.

Mr. Madsen is currently president of Bonneville International Corporation Broadcast House in Salt Lake City, UT. Prior to this he was president of several broadcast stations in Salt Lake City. Mr. Madsen has served the broadcast community in both civic and community capacities.

Mr. Madsen was born December 4, 1913, in Provo, UT. He is married, has five children, and resides in Salt Lake City.

Nomination of Fowler C. West To Be a Commissioner of the Commodity Futures Trading Commission
April 20, 1988

The President today announced his intention to nominate Fowler C. West to be a Commissioner of the Commodity Futures Trading Commission for the term expiring April 13, 1992. This is a reappointment.

Since 1982 Mr. West has been a Commissioner of the Commodity Futures Trading Commission in Washington, DC. Prior to this, he was staff director for the House Committee on Agriculture, 1973–1982, and staff consultant, 1971–1973. Mr. West was also administrative assistant to Congressman W.R. Poage, 1969–1971.

Mr. West graduated from Baylor University (B.A., 1963), George Washington University (M.A., 1980), and Georgetown School of Law (J.D., 1988). He was born July 6, 1940, in Waco, TX. He is married, has three children, and currently resides in Alexandria, VA.

Nomination of William H. LeBlanc III To Be a Commissioner of the Postal Rate Commission
April 20, 1988

The President today announced his intention to nominate William H. LeBlanc III to be a Commissioner of the Postal Rate Commission for the term expiring November 22, 1994. This is a reappointment.

Since 1987 Mr. LeBlanc has been Commissioner of the United States Postal Rate Commission in Washington, DC. Prior to this, he was president and general manager of Baton Rouge Supply Company, Inc., 1980–1987, and a general manager working with management teams of six family-owned businesses, 1972–1980.

Mr. LeBlanc graduated from Louisiana State University (B.S., 1972). He was born May 15, 1948, in Baton Rouge, LA. He served in the United States Marine Corps, 1967–1970. He is married, has three children, and resides in Silver Spring, MD.

Statement by Assistant to the President for Press Relations Fitzwater on Israel-United States Relations
April 21, 1988

Today, on the 40th anniversary of Israel's independence, the United States and Israel have signed a memorandum of agreement (MOA). This MOA formalizes and perpetuates the bilateral U.S. and Israeli consultative groups that meet periodically to discuss joint military, security assistance, and economic developmental questions. The MOA reiterates for the public record our longstanding relationship of strategic cooperation with Israel. Strategic cooperation can only succeed when there are shared interests, including the commitment to building peace and stability in the region. It reflects the enduring U.S. commitment to Israel's security. That commitment will never flag. The U.S. commitment to peace will also not flag. The President knows that a strong Israel is necessary if peace is to be possible. He also knows that Israel can never be truly secure without peace.

To that end, the President has asked Secretary of State Shultz to continue his peacemaking efforts, seeking a comprehensive settlement which will assure Israeli security and provide for the legitimate rights of the Palestinian people. The President remains convinced that our peace initiative is balanced and offers the only realistic basis on which to make progress. The President reiterates his appeal to the leaders in the region not to miss this opportunity to move ahead and get to productive peace negotiations. This is an objective that Israel has fervently sought over the last 40 years.

Nomination of Mary A. Ryan To Be United States Ambassador to Swaziland
April 21, 1988

The President today announced his intention to nominate Mary A. Ryan, a career member of the Senior Foreign Service, Class of Minister-Counselor, as Ambassador to the Kingdom of Swaziland. She would succeed Harvey F. Nelson, Jr.

Ms. Ryan entered the Foreign Service of the United States in 1966 and was first assigned as a consular and administrative officer in Naples, Italy, 1966–1969. She was assigned as personnel officer at the American Embassy in Tegucigalpa, Honduras, 1970–1971, and subsequently served as a consular officer at the American consulate general in Monterrey, Mexico. In 1973 she returned to Washington and was assigned as administrative officer in the Bureau of African Affairs from 1973 to 1975, and as a post management officer in the Bureau of African Affairs, 1975–1977. From 1977 to 1980, she was a career development officer in the Bureau of Personnel. In 1980 Ms. Ryan received French language training, followed by assignments as administrative counselor in Abidjan, Cote d'Ivoire, 1980–1981, and Khartoum, Sudan, 1981–1982. From 1982 to 1983, she served as an inspector in the Office of the Inspector General in the Department of State, and Executive Director of the Bureau of European and Canadian Affairs, 1983–1985. Since 1985 Ms. Ryan has been the Executive Assistant to the Under Secretary of State for Management.

Ms. Ryan graduated from St. John's University (B.A., 1963; M.A., 1965). She was born October 1, 1940, in New York, NY, and currently resides in Washington, DC.

Remarks to the World Affairs Council of Western Massachusetts in Springfield
April 21, 1988

Mark Cohen and Sue Root, reverend clergy, Mr. Mayor, members of the Council here—the World Affairs Council—it's great to be here in Springfield, to get out of Washington, and to find out what people are really thinking. Nobody writes me anymore since they raised the postal rates. [*Laughter*] Actually, though, coming here today violates one of Washington's most important rules: Nobody in government likes to appear in public this soon after April 15th. [*Laughter*] But I do know all about Springfield—the fact basketball was invented here and that tremendous Hall of Fame you have. In fact, Tip O'Neill always tried to get me to come to Springfield. [*Laughter*] "Believe me, Mr. President," he used to say, "you'll love Springfield. They have a Hall of Fame there for people who only work a few hours a day." [*Laughter*]

But I'm delighted to be here with you, and especially in the State where America's own struggle for freedom began. "I'm well aware," John Adams wrote in 1776, "of the toil and blood and treasure that it will cost us to support and defend these States. Yet through all the gloom, I can see the rays of ravishing light and glory." Historians have wondered ever since what it was that made men like Adams and that outnumbered band of colonists believe they could overthrow the power of the mightiest empire on Earth. How appropriate it seemed, 5 years later, when the British band played at Yorktown, "The World Turned Upside Down." Truly, the predictions of the wiser heads in Europe had been proven wrong. The boldness, the vision, and yes, the gift for dreaming of a few farmers, merchants, and lawyers here on these shores had started a revolution that today reaches into every corner of the world, a revolution that still fires men's souls with the ravishing light and glory of human freedom.

As members of the World Affairs Council, as active students of global politics, all of you here today can testify to how unlikely the prospects for freedom seemed at the start of this decade. You can recall democracy on the defensive in country after country, an unparalleled buildup of nuclear arms, hostages in Iran, the Soviet invasion of Afghanistan, predictions of economic contraction, and global chaos, ranging from food and fuel shortages to environmental disaster. All of these were the unrelenting themes of so much of what we read and heard in the media.

With the economic recovery of the United States and the democracies, however, much of this talk abated. And this economic recovery, anticipated in Massachusetts in 1981 and '82 with reduced State and local tax rates, was itself rooted in the insight that was at the heart of the revolution begun here two centuries ago. Trust the people, let government get out of the way, and leave unharnessed the energy and dynamism of free men and women.

But I've come here today to suggest that this notion of trusting the power of human freedom and letting the people do the rest was not just a good basis for our economic policy, it proved a solid foundation for our foreign policy as well. That's what we've given to the people, why we have repeated what they instinctively knew, but what the experts had shied away from saying in public. We spoke plainly and bluntly. We rejected what Jeane Kirkpatrick calls moral equivalency. We said freedom was better than totalitarianism. We said communism was bad. We said a future of nuclear terror was unacceptable. We said we stood for peace, but we also stood for freedom. We said we held fast to the dream of our Founding Fathers: the dream that someday every man, woman, and child would live in dignity and in freedom. And because of this, we said containment was no longer enough, that the expansion of human freedom was our goal. We spoke for democracy, and we said that we would work for the day when the people of every nation enjoyed the blessing of liberty.

Well, at first, the experts said this kind of candor was dangerous, that it would lead to a worsening of Soviet-American relations. But far to the contrary, this candor made clear to the Soviets the resilience and strength of the West; it made them understand the lack of illusions on our part about them or their system. By reasserting values and defining once again what we as a people and a nation stood for, we were of course making a moral and spiritual point. And in doing this, we offered hope for the future, for democracy; and we showed we had retained that gift for dreaming that marked this continent and our nation at its birth.

But in all this we were also doing something practical. We had learned long ago that the Soviets get down to serious negotiations only after they are convinced that their counterparts are determined to stand firm. We knew the least indication of weakened resolve on our part would lead the Soviets to stop the serious bargaining, stall diplomatic progress, and attempt to exploit this perceived weakness. So, we were candid. We acknowledged the depth of our disagreements and their fundamental, moral import. In this way, we acknowledged that the differences [that] separated us and the Soviets were deeper and wider than just missile counts and number of warheads. As I've said before, we do not mistrust each other because we are armed; we are armed because we mistrust each other. And I spoke those words to General Secretary Gorbachev at our very first meeting in Geneva.

And that was why we resolved to address the full range of the real causes of that mistrust and raise the crucial moral and political issues directly with the Soviets. Now, in the past, the full weight of the Soviet-American relationship all too often seemed to rest on one issue: arms control, a plank not sturdy enough to bear up the whole platform of Soviet-American relations. So, we adopted not just a one-part agenda of arms control but a broader four-part agenda. We talked about regional conflicts, especially in areas like Afghanistan, Angola, and Central America, where Soviet expansionism was leading to sharp confrontation. We insisted on putting human rights on our bilateral agenda, and the issue of Soviet noncompliance with the Helsinki accords. We also emphasized people-to-people exchanges, and we challenged the Soviets to tear down the artificial barriers that isolate their citizens from the rest of the world. As for the final item on the agenda, arms control, even that we revised. We said we wanted to go beyond merely establishing new limits that would permit even greater buildups in nuclear arms. We insisted on cutting down, reducing, not just controlling, the number of weapons—arms reductions, not just arms control.

And now this approach to the Soviets—public candor about their system and ours, a full agenda that put the real differences between us on the table—has borne fruit. Just as we look at leading indicators to see how the economy is doing, we know the global momentum of freedom is the best leading indicator of how the United States is doing in the world. When we see a freely elected government in the Republic of Korea; battlefield victories for the Angolan freedom fighters; China opening and liberalizing its economy; democracy ascending in Latin America, the Philippines, and on every other continent—where these and other indicators are strong, so too is America and so too are our hopes for the future.

And yet even while freedom is on the march, Soviet-American relations have taken a dramatic turn into a period of realistic engagement. In a month I will meet Mr. Gorbachev in Moscow for our fourth summit since 1985. Negotiations are underway between our two governments on an unparalleled number of issues. The INF treaty is reality, and now the Senate should give its consent to ratification. The START treaty is working along. And I know that on everyone's mind today is this single, startling fact: The Soviets have pledged that next month they will begin withdrawing from Afghanistan. And if anyone had predicted just a few years ago that by the end of this decade a treaty would be signed eliminating a whole class of nuclear weapons, that discussions would be moving along toward a 50-percent reduction in all strategic nuclear arms, and that the Soviets had set a date certain for pulling out of Afghanistan, that individual would have faced more than a little skepticism. But that, on the eve of the fourth summit, is exactly where we are.

So, let me now summarize for you some of the issues that need crucial definition as we approach this summit. Let's begin with Afghanistan. History records few struggles so heroic as that of the Afghan people against the Soviet invasion. In 8 years more than a million Afghans have been killed; more than 5 million have been driven into exile. And yet, despite all this suffering, the Afghan people have fought on—a determined patriotic resistance force against one of the world's most powerful and sophisticated armies. Yes, their land has been occupied, but they have not been conquered. Now the Soviets have said they've had enough. The will for freedom has defeated the will for power, as it always has, and I believe, always will.

But let me say here that the next few months will be no time for complacency, no time to sit back and congratulate ourselves. The Soviets have rarely before, and not at all in more than three decades, left a country once occupied. They have often promised to leave, but rarely in their history, and then only under pressure from the West, have they actually done it. Afghanistan was a critical, strategic prize for the Soviets. The development of air bases near Afghanistan's border with Iran and Pakistan would have dramatically increased the Soviet capability to project their power to the Strait of Hormuz and to threaten our ability to keep open that critical passage. We believe that they still hope to prop up their discredited, doomed puppet regime, and they still seek to pose a threat to neighboring Pakistan, to whom we have a longstanding defense commitment.

So, we ask have the Soviets really given up these ambitions? Well, we don't know. We can't know until the drama is fully played. We must make clear that any spreading of violence on the part of the Soviets or their puppets could undo the good that the Geneva accords promised for East-West relations.

The Soviets are now pledged to withdraw their forces totally from Afghanistan by next February 15th at the latest. In the meantime, they know that as long as they're aiding their friends in Kabul we will continue to supply the Mujahidin by whatever means necessary. Let me repeat: We will continue to support the Mujahidin for as long as the Soviets support the Kabul regime. The Soviets understand that this is our position and that we wouldn't have entered into this agreement without it. And it's more than a position. This is a hard and fast commitment on my part, backed up by a unanimous resolution of the United States Senate.

From the start, our policy in Afghanistan has, of course, been directed at restoring that country to an independent, nonaligned status, in which the Afghan people could decide their own future and to which their refugees could return safely and with honor—the same goals as those stated in successive United Nations General Assembly resolutions over the years. But these aren't the only goals of our policy there. In a broader sense, our policy is intended to nurture what you might call more normal relations between East and West.

You see, just as a Soviet Union that oppresses its own people, that violates the Helsinki accords on human rights to which it is a party, that continues to suppress free expression and religious worship and the right to travel—just as such a Soviet Union can never have truly normal relations with the United States and the rest of the free world, neither can a Soviet Union that is always trying to push its way into other countries ever have a normal relationship with us. And that's what has happened in countries like Angola, Nicaragua, and Ethiopia: The Soviet Union has helped install or maintain client regimes against the will of the people.

None of these regimes has brought peace or a better life to their people. Each has brought misery and hardship. Each is an outrage to the conscience of mankind, and none more so than Ethiopia. Two years ago a pitying world believed that at last the hopes of all compassionate people had been realized and that the famine in Africa had come to an end. Humanity prayed that it would never again see pictures of children with bloated stomachs or hear stories of families dying one by one as they walked dozens of miles to reach feeding stations. But now in one country the famine has returned. Ethiopia suffers from drought, yes, and even more it suffers from inadequate agricultural policies. But now to drought and failed policy has been added a third, even more deadly element: war. The Ethiopian Army has recently suffered major defeats in its long war with the Eritrean secessionist forces. The combination of drought and the dislocations of war is the immediate cause of famine in that part of the country. But the Ethiopian regime recently ordered all foreign famine relief workers to leave the afflicted northern region. That leads us to the horrible conclusion that starvation and scorched earth are being considered as weapons to defeat the rebellion.

The subject of Ethiopia has long been on the U.S.-Soviet agenda, but now it is more urgent because of this tremendous human catastrophe in the making. Is the world to know another holocaust? Is it to see another political famine? The Soviets are the principal arms supplier and primary backer to the regime in Addis Ababa. They're also supplying 250,000 tons of food this year. They can stop this disaster before it happens. And I appeal to them to persuade the Ethiopian regime, as only they can, to change its decision and to allow the famine relief efforts to continue. And let me add, I hope, as well, that the Soviet Union will join us and other concerned governments in working toward a peaceful, negotiated solution to the civil war.

You know, Ethiopia, of course, for that matter in every country in which the Soviets have imposed a regime, the issues of human rights and regional conflicts merge into one greater issue: that of Soviet intentions, designs, and behavior both home and across the Earth. Several years ago the French political thinker and writer, Jean-François Revel, reported on a conversation that a member of the French Cabinet had with a high Soviet official. The Soviet official, in reviewing the history of the 1970's said, as Revel writes: "We took Angola, and you did not protest. We noted the fact and included it in our analyses." The Soviet official continued: "Then we took Mozambique. Forget it; you don't even know where it is. Then we took Ethiopia, a key move. No reply." And he went on, "Then we took Aden and set up a powerful Soviet base there. Aden! On the Arabian Peninsula! In the heart of your supply center! No response." And the Soviet official concluded by saying, "So, we noted, we can take Aden."

The years of Western passivity in the face of Soviet aggression ended, of course, 7 years ago. But the issue here is that the mentality that produced such analyses, as the Soviet official called them, has not ended. Until it does, the world cannot know true peace.

That's a lesson we should apply closer to

home, in Nicaragua. A few months before the Soviets launched their invasion of Afghanistan, the Soviets also helped Sandinista Communists in Nicaragua to steal a democratic revolution. The Communists promised democracy and human rights, but they instead imposed a cruel dictatorship, massively militarized, and began a secret war of subversion against Nicaragua's peaceful neighbors. The people of Nicaragua took up arms against the Communists, and they've fought a valiant struggle. But our Congress, instead of giving the Nicaraguan resistance the same steady support the Afghans have received, has repeatedly turned aid on and off. Even now, while the Soviet bloc pours half a billion dollars of arms a year into Nicaragua, Congress has denied the freedom fighters the support they need to force the Sandinistas to fulfill their democratic promises. I think it's about time that Congress learned the lessons of Afghanistan.

America, by supporting freedom fighters against brutal dictatorships, is helping to advance the values we hold most dear: peace, freedom, human rights, and yes, democracy. At the same time, we're helping to secure our own freedom by raising the cost of Soviet aggression and by extending the battle for freedom to the far frontier. Some say the Soviet Union is reappraising its foreign policy these days to concentrate on internal reform. Well, clearly, there are signs of change. But if there is change, it's because the costs of aggression and the real moral difference between our systems were brought home to it. If we hope to see a more fundamental change, we must remain strong and firm. If we fulfill our responsibility to set the limits, as well as offering constructive cooperation, then this could indeed turn out to be a turning point in the history of East-West relations.

By starting now to show real respect for human rights and abandoning the quest for military solutions to these regional conflicts, the Soviet Union would also be working to build trust and improve relations between our two countries. Regional conflicts and human rights are closely intertwined. They are issues of moral conscience. They're issues of international security. Because when a government abuses the rights of its own people, it is a grim indication of its willingness to commit violence against others.

Two of the most basic rights that we've called on the Soviets to comply with under the Helsinki accords are the right to emigrate and the right to travel. How can we help but doubt a government that mistrusts its own people and holds them against their will? And what better way would there be to improve understanding between the United States and the Soviet Union than to permit free and direct contact between our two peoples? In the new spirit of openness, why doesn't the Soviet Government issue passports to its citizens? I think this would dramatically improve U.S.-Soviet relations.

Of course, the World Affairs Council here is a major sponsor of USIA's International Visitors Program. So, I don't have to tell you the importance of people-to-people exchanges. And I want to personally—to thank all of you who have provided assistance and hospitality to foreign visitors. I just left a meeting in the Oval Office to come up here, and that meeting brought about by Director Wick of USIA was a meeting with an assemblage of media and publishing people from the Soviet Union. That, I think, is a first in our relationship. I have often reflected in public on how if our planet was ever threatened by forces from another world all nations and all people would quickly come together in unity and brotherhood.

You here today at the World Affairs Council understand better than most this lesson about how much all of us have in common as members of the human race. It is governments, after all, not people, who put obstacles up and cause misunderstandings. When I spoke at the United Nations several years ago, I mentioned some words of Gandhi, spoken shortly after he visited Britain in his quest for independence in India. "I am not conscious of a single experience throughout my 3 months in England and Europe," he said, "that made me feel that after all East is East and West is West. On the contrary, I have been convinced more than ever that human nature is much the same, no matter under what clime it flourishes, and that if you approached people with trust and affection, you would have tenfold trust and thousandfold affection returned to you."

Well, you in the World Affairs Council have done much praiseworthy work in this area. And I'm hopeful that American foreign policy, based as it has been on strength and candor, is opening a way to a world where trust and affection among peoples is an everyday reality. This is my hope as I prepare to leave for Moscow. I'm grateful for your prayers and for your support. I thank you, and God bless you.

[*At this point, the President answered questions from the audience.*]

U.S.-Soviet Summit Meeting in Moscow

Q. Mr. President, my question to you, sir, is what will be the central theme of your message that you'll carry to the people of the Soviet Union next month, and how will the Senate's ratification of the INF treaty, or in the alternative, the Senate's failure to ratify the treaty, affect that message?

The President. Now, did you—the last part—are you speaking of the INF treaty and the failure of ratification?

Q. Yes.

The President. Well, let me answer that part first and then get to the other. I think it would be very, well, upsetting, and it would put a strain on the summit if the Senate has not ratified the treaty by the time we go there. And we're hoping and praying they will, and yet their scheduling of it for discussion and debate is such that I'm very concerned that possibly we may have to go without it having been ratified.

Now, as to the message to the Soviet people, I don't know how much contact we'll be able to have with them. We're going to try. We have been providing lists by name of individuals in the Soviet Union to the General Secretary and his people, and so far, I have to say there has been quite a response in their allowing these refuseniks we've named to emigrate—most of them to the United States, but many to Israel and to other countries. We've provided some more lists before this meeting, and we will be talking about that.

But to the people—I have a feeling that the people of the Soviet Union, as well as what Gandhi said about the people everywhere—that if we had a chance and they had a chance for more contact, we would find that they were very much like us. They have a great sense of humor, and I think they tend to be very friendly. I'm not going to burden you with it now, but I have a new hobby. I'm collecting jokes that I can find are told by the Russian people, among themselves, that reveal that sense of humor as well as a little cynicism about their own system. But I'm looking forward to meeting—and meeting with some of the refuseniks.

Q. Well, I've been to the Soviet Union, and they are a very nice people. You will enjoy it.

Foreign Trade Policies

Q. Mr. President, I'd just like to ask you one question about the trade deficit and foreign trade policy here in America. What do you think the United States people should look for in the next election—for a candidate that would have a policy that would help this country tackle the trade deficit and compete at a more stronger rate with, say, Japan and West Germany on a manufacturing base?

The President. Well, if you'll forgive me, you've got an administration now that has been trying to do something about the trade deficit. We have continuously reduced the trade deficit. We have not brought it to where there is no trade deficit as yet. And this last one, even though they said, oh, why the deficit went up a little bit—they didn't say little bit, they made it sound horrendous—something about around $13 billion-plus in this trade deficit. But what they didn't announce was that our exports were at their highest level that they've been so far. And it so happened that also there was—because of a little lowering in the price of the dollar—there was a little increase in imports at the same time, so that there was still a deficit. But we have continued, in the years we've been here, every year, to have an increase in our exports.

I'll tell you, though, something. I don't feel the way about the trade deficit that I do about deficit spending here within our own country. In the 70 years, back when our country was growing from its colonial beginnings into the great industrial power that it is today, every one of those 70 years we had a trade imbalance. There were things that we hadn't learned to produce yet in our own country, and so forth. And yet that was our great period of growth. Now, with all of this trade imbalance, these last 65 months have been the longest period of economic expansion in the history of the United States.

Now, I've said repeatedly, the trade bill that is now before the conference comes to me as it is, I will veto it not because I'm against a trade bill but because they've loaded on so many items—and one item in particular that would be very restrictive on business and industry in America. And I have served notice that if that item is in there I can't sign it. But if I do have to veto it, I will immediately call on the Congress to adopt a trade bill that is similar to this one without those things that have been added on. Because we've been working in the economic summit as hard as we can to bring about changes in the GATT treaty—that's the general tariff and trade agreement of the industrial nations of the West and Japan.

All we've been asking for is not protectionism but asking for a free and fair area so that we're all playing on a level field. If they've got restrictions on our exports coming into their country, then we're going to respond. We've gotten some great changes made. So, I'm very optimistic and not concerned as much about that trade imbalance. It'd be fine to change it, but the imbalance I want to get is a Congress that will join truly in eliminating the reckless spending that has us overspending. And then I would look for all your support in having a change in the Constitution that says hereafter it'll be against the Constitution to have a trade—or not a trade in, but to have a deficit spending situation in our country.

Drug Abuse and Trafficking

Q. Mr. President, good afternoon. I'm a sophomore English major at Springfield College. My question to you this afternoon: Are you considering any military intervention when it comes to stifling drug traffic into the United States? If so, will it be on an—wide, lateral, or bilateral basis and to what scale?

The President. Are you talking about just using the military in helping against the drug menace and——

Q. As far as increasing.

The President. Well, we have been. For the first time, we have been utilizing the military. There are some laws that limit what you could ask the military to do. But last year alone, there were 16,000 flying hours of surveillance by our military aircraft in helping us interdict the drugs coming into America. And there were 2,500 full sailing days of the Navy out there patrolling and helping us interdict this drug entry.

I have to tell you though, we have done a remarkable job. Incidentally, we've increased our spending with regard to drugs and the fighting of the drug abuse. We have increased that—tripled it—since we've been here. But that is not going to do the job, as much as we have to keep on intercepting those drugs. Last year we confiscated $500 million of assets of the drug dealers and still the problem is with us. I think Nancy set out on the course that we must all do more to bring about. You can't totally ever, with the boundaries we have, shut off the influx of drugs. The deal is: Take the customer away from the drugs. Turn the customer away from drugs. I'm sure you've heard about the Just Say No idea in drugs.

Q. Certainly.

The President. Would you be interested in knowing how easily things can get started? Nancy was talking to a group of school children in Oakland, California. And a little girl asked, "What do we do if somebody offers us drugs?" And Nancy said, "Just say no." That's where it started. There are now over 12,000 Just Say No clubs in the schools of the United States. I think you have a followup.

Q. No.

The President. No?

Q. That will suffice. Thank you. Thank you very much.

The President. Well, thank you.

Administration Accomplishments

Q. How do you solve all the questions in

America, Mr. President? [*Laughter*]

The President. Have we solved all the questions in America? I—[*laughter*]—no, I'd be the first to say no. As a matter of fact, we probably haven't heard some of them yet. [*Laughter*] But we're working on it.

When we came here, we found a situation—came to office—found a situation in which our country was in the economic doldrums. We had double-digit inflation. We had great unemployment. And we had some pretty high taxes. And we set out on an economic recovery program that was aimed at changing that. And also, I had always felt before I came here that there was a growing spiritual hunger in the United States to once again believe, and believe not only in the Almighty but in this country of ours.

So, we answered some of those questions. We found out that by cutting the tax rates the Government got more revenue than it did at the higher rates, because when there's an incentive and you can keep more of the money that you're earning, people earn more money. One percent of our highest taxpayers when we came here was actually paying 18 percent of the total tax revenue from the income tax. When we reduced their rates, that 1 percent is now paying 26½ percent of the total revenue. And yet we still have some people saying we must tax the rich, we must go after them. And those taxes, I think, helped start us very much on the road of economic recovery.

In these last 5 or 6 years, we have now created 16 million new jobs. And the family income average is higher than it has ever been before. Inflation is under control; it's no longer double digit. And one of the things I will always be very proud to see is that Americans are proud once again, to be Americans.

Middle East Peace Efforts

Q. Mr. President, you have for years tried to bring peace to the Middle East. Can we rely on your administration to continue to move Israel to settle the Palestinian question on a more evenhanded basis?

The President. We're going to keep on trying as hard as we can. We feel that the coming together in negotiations, sitting down at a table with the other countries—you know, most of us have forgotten that technically the state of war still exists between the Arab nations and Israel. But we're not going to cure it until we come together and find out how we can arrive at a fair settlement of the differences between those peoples.

I can't resist telling you a little joke. It's kind of cynical—very cynical in a matter of fact—about the Middle East. It has to do with a scorpion that came to a creek and wanted to cross and said to the frog there, "Would you carry me across because scorpions can't swim." And the frog said, "Why, you'd sting me, and I'd die." And the scorpion said, "That would be silly, because if I stung you and you died, I'd drown." Well, that made sense to the frog, so he said, get on, started ferrying him across. And in midstream the scorpion stung him. And the frog in his dying said to the scorpion, as they were both dying, said, "Why did you do that? Now we're both going to die!" And the scorpion said, "This is the Middle East." [*Laughter*]

Q. Does that mean, Mr. President, that the United States is going to move closer to address the Palestinians directly?

The President. Yes, there are some among them that we have refused on principle to address, such as Arafat, because Arafat has refused to recognize the right of Israel to exist as a nation. And I don't think that there's any negotiation between someone who just says, you're not even a nation, I won't talk to you. Israel is a nation, recognized as such by almost all of the civilized world. And so, this is what we're seeking—are Palestinian leaders who are agreeable to coming together and with the other Arab States.

We have worked very hard also to make the other Arab States aware that—even in addition to our agreement and the security, we agree, of Israel—that we want to and can be fair and friends with them. And so we have established a relationship that I think is growing very much about—that we have the trust of a great many of the Arab States. And a number of those are willing to join in this kind of negotiation that we want to achieve.

Q. Thank you, Mr. President. It's very refreshing to hear you say you are going to open up negotiations.

The President. Yes.

Stealth Bomber and Arms Control

Q. Hello, Mr. President. I'd just like to tell you what an honor and totally unexpected privilege it is for me to ask you a question here. My question has to do with the article that was in the Wall Street Journal today about the Stealth bomber—the artist's sketch of it, and after all these years of secrecy, why it was unveiled now. Perhaps it has something to do with your foreign trip and how the Stealth program is going to be incorporated with the Star Wars defense system?

The President. Well, this is, of course, a form of conventional weapon, an airplane and a bomber, and I think the timing was probably somewhat accidental about revealing this photo. What has happened is we have just reached the testing point. So, very shortly that plane will be in the air and visible to all. So, there didn't seem to be any more reason to keep it secret. And I don't think it will hurt at the summit. [*Laughter*]

Q. Well, I hope it helps.

The President. Well, I hope so, too. And I know this is the final question, but I would just like to say to you that—because there is some misunderstanding about that and about treaties, like the START treaty that we're trying to get—we don't know—it doesn't look likely that—that treaty is so much more complicated than the INF treaty, that there's a great question as to whether it could be ready for signature at the summit. But we've never set a deadline on when it can be worked out. We don't want a fast treaty; we want a good one. And there are some lack of understanding on the part of some people. I've read some columns that think that our emphasis on reducing nuclear weapons means that we're going to allow the Soviet Union to wind up with that great superiority they have in conventional weapons, and won't that be to our disadvantage? I think you all should know that as we continue any further development of eliminating nuclear weapons we'll now have to follow negotiations in conventional weapons to reduce to parity so that no one is left with an advantage over the other as we go on eliminating nuclear weapons, if we can. So, that is definite. And I have informed the General Secretary that that must take place, and he has expressed a willingness to talk on reducing our conventional weapons.

Well, I know that you were the sixth, and that was all. Can I do something terrible here? The press knows I do this. I mentioned that hobby of mine. So, as long as I can't answer any more questions, can I conclude in just telling you one of those jokes which illustrates the sense of humor—[*applause*]. And this is one that I told to Gorbachev.

It seems that they recently issued an order that anyone that's caught speeding must get a ticket. And you know that most of the driving there is done by the Politburo, by the—or the bureaucracy. They're the ones with cars and drivers and so forth. So, it seems that one morning Gorbachev himself came out of his country home, knew he was late getting to the Kremlin, told his driver to get in the back seat and he'd drive. And down the road he went, past two motorcycle policemen. One of them took out after him. In a few minutes, he's back with his buddy, and the buddy said, "Did you give him a ticket?" He said, "No." "Well," he said, "why not? We were told that anyone caught speeding was to get a ticket." He said, "No, no, this one was too important." "Well," he said, "who was it?" He says, "I don't know. I couldn't recognize him, but his driver was Gorbachev." [*Laughter*]

Note: The President spoke at 1:04 p.m. at the Springfield Civic Center. In his opening remarks, he referred to Mark Cohen and Sue Root, president and executive director of the World Affairs Council, respectively; Rev. Andrew Wissemann; and Mayor Richard Neal, of Springfield. Following his remarks, the President returned to Washington, DC.

Remarks at the Annual White House Correspondents Association Dinner
April 21, 1988

The President. Thank you all, and I'm delighted to be here. My, what a crowd. Looks like the index of Larry Speakes' book. [*Laughter*] It's good to see Norm Sandler, and your incoming president, Jerry O'Leary.

In his book, Larry said that Jerry used to fill his coat pockets with pastry. Jerry denies it. Earlier tonight, just to be safe, I told him, keep his hands off my dinner roll. [*Laughter*] Larry also said that preparing me for a press conference was like reinventing the wheel. It's not true. I was around when the wheel was invented, and it was easier. [*Laughter*] But even Howard Baker's writing a book about me. It's called, "Three By Five, The Measure of A Presidency." [*Laughter*] Mike Deaver, in his book, said that I had a short attention span. Well, I was going to reply to that, but—oh, what the hell, let's move on to something else. [*Laughter*]

Now, I forgot to acknowledge Yakov Smirnoff. I've heard him before, and he's a very funny man. And I just have an idea here. Why don't you and I have a little fun? How would you like to go to the summit as my interpreter? [*Laughter*]

But the media has certainly had a lot to report on lately. I thought it was extraordinary that Richard Nixon went on "Meet The Press" and spent an entire hour with Chris Wallace, Tom Brokaw, and John Chancellor. That should put an end to that talk that he's been punished enough. [*Laughter*] And of course, you've been reporting on the New York primary. I'm afraid that Dukakis' foreign policy views are a little too far left for me. He wants no U.S. military presence in Korea anymore, no U.S. military presence in Central America, and no U.S. military presence at the Pentagon. [*Laughter*] Dukakis got great news today, though, about the Jimmy Carter endorsement—he isn't getting it. [*Laughter*]

George Bush is doing well. George has been a wonderful Vice President, but nobody's perfect. [*Laughter*] I put him in charge of antiterrorism, and the McLaughlin Group is still on the air. [*Laughter*] But with so much focus on the Presidential election, I've been feeling a little lonely these days. I'm so desperate for attention I almost considered holding a news conference. [*Laughter*] I've even had time to watch the Oscars. I was a little disappointed in that movie "The Last Emperor." I thought it was going to be about Don Regan. [*Laughter*] Of course, I still have lots of work here. There is that Panamanian business going on. One thing I can't figure: If the Congress wants to bring the Panamanian economy to its knees, why doesn't it just go down there and run it? [*Laughter*]

Ladies and gentlemen, this is the last White House Correspondents Dinner that I'll be attending. We've had our disagreements over the years, but the time I've spent with you has been very educational. [*Laughter*] I used to think the fourth estate was one of Walter Annenberg's homes. [*Laughter*] As my goodbye, I'm not going to stand up here and deliver one of those worn-out, sentimental homilies about the press and the Presidency. Neither of us would believe it. [*Laughter*]

A President may like members of the press personally, and I do—Jerry and Norm and Johanna and Lou and so many others of you—but a President institutionally seeks to wield power to accomplish his goals for the people. The press complicates the wielding of that power by using its own great power, and that makes for friction. Every President will try to use the press to his best advantage and to avoid those situations that aren't to his advantage. To do otherwise results in a diminution of his leadership powers. The press is not a weak sister that needs bracing. It has more freedom, more influence, than ever in our history. The press can take care of itself quite nicely. And a President should be able to take care of himself as well.

So, what I hope my epitaph will be with the White House correspondents, what every President's epitaph should be with the press is this: He gave as good as he got. [*Laughter*] And that I think will make for a healthy press and a healthy Presidency. And I think all that's left to say is to thank you for inviting me, and thank you for your hospitality.

[*At this point, Yakov Smirnoff entertained the audience.*]

Mr. O'Leary. Before I propose a toast to the President and his lady, I want to thank Mr. Reagan for the great job he gave me at the National Security Council when the old Washington Star folded. Some job that was. I was put in the same office with Ollie North, and I reported directly to Bud McFarlane and Admiral Poindexter. [*Laughter*] If I'd—knew what was going on then, I would have paid more attention. [*Laughter*]

I had some problems, too, with Larry Speakes. I do not carry Danish pastry in my pocket, nor the President's rolls. Larry, I always thought, has done for Press Secretaries what the Boston Strangler did for door-to-door salesmen. [*Laughter*]

In 1982 I resigned to join the Washington Times so that I could see the President more often. Mr. President, this is a sentimental and somewhat emotional occasion. It's the seventh, and I hope it's not the last time, that you and Mrs. Reagan will honor us with your presence—that it means something to us.

So, ladies and gentlemen, if you will please rise and join in a toast to the President and the First Lady. Mr. President, to your health, to your happiness, and to your future success.

Audience members. Hear! Hear!

The President. After some of the things that you've said, and many of the things that Yakov said, it's pretty stupid to get back up here and try to follow all of that. [*Laughter*] That's why I went on first. [*Laughter*] Well, this has been a wonderful evening, as they all have been. And I think maybe—there is one thing that did bother me, though, O'Leary, and that is that, when you asked everyone to stand, Walter Annenberg has always told me that in Philadelphia, you only rose to toast the dead. [*Laughter*] I took my pulse and figured I'm still here. [*Laughter*]

But I think there is a toast—I try to think here a—if I said to Nancy, let us toast all of you, well then, you'd all be standing there, and we'd be the only ones having a drink. [*Laughter*] And what could you say. I think there's a toast that we all can have, and Yakov made that pretty evident also.

I had a letter recently from a man, and he made an observation that had never occurred to me before. He said, "You can go to live in a country like France, but you cannot become a Frenchman. You can go to live in Greece, but you cannot become a Greek." And he named a few other countries and said you could there. And then he added, "but anyone, from any corner of the world can come to America and become an American." And we've just seen an example of how wonderful that is from our most recent American, who was just up here. So, I think something we can all drink to, while we're standing and before we go home, is to this God-blessed land. And let us hope that all of us will feel in our hearts that we've done all we can to keep this great miracle country alive in the world, because the world is a better place because of us. To the United States of America!

Audience members. Hear! Hear!

Mr. O'Leary. Ladies and gentlemen, the President and Mrs. Reagan have to go back to the White House now. And we request that you please remain in your places until they have left. And thank you all for coming. It's been a marvelous evening. Good night.

Note: The President spoke at 10:10 p.m. in the International Ballroom at the Washington Hilton Hotel. He was introduced by Jeremiah O'Leary, White House correspondent for the Washington Times and the new president of the White House Correspondents Association.

Proclamation 5800—National Organ and Tissue Donor Awareness Week, 1988

April 21, 1988

By the President of the United States of America

A Proclamation

The generosity for which the American people have always been known shines clearly today in the willingness of many people to become organ and tissue donors so that others might live or have an opportunity to enjoy a fuller life. Thousands of Americans will receive an extraordinary gift this year—a kidney, heart, liver, pancreas, a combination of heart and lung, skin, a cornea, bone, or bone marrow. The great majority of these gifts will have been possible only because a caring American agreed to donate an organ or tissue for transplantation.

We can all take pride in this generosity; yet the need for additional transplants remains great. Thousands of Americans will wait this year for a well-matched organ or tissue to become available. For some, no donor may be found. The decision to volunteer as an organ donor is a significant act of personal sacrifice. Fortunately, knowledge about organ donorship has spread in recent years. Groups in our communities stand ready to answer questions about organ and tissue donation. The American Council on Transplantation and school, church, and community groups are involved. Many States give people the chance to sign donor authorization cards when they complete their driver's license forms. Others require hospitals to offer people the opportunity to donate under appropriate circumstances.

Encouragement of organ and tissue donation must always be accompanied, of course, by thorough reflection and complete information. Recent medical and technological developments are posing new moral and ethical questions about transplantation in certain circumstances. Individuals, and society as a whole, must carefully consider these questions so that we never undercut our reverence for the sanctity God vests equally in the life of every person, from the moment of conception until natural death.

The Congress, by Public Law 100–273, has designated the week of April 24 through April 30, 1988, as "National Organ and Tissue Donor Awareness Week" and authorized and requested the President to issue a proclamation in observance of this occasion.

Now, Therefore, I, Ronald Reagan, President of the United States of America, do hereby proclaim the week of April 24 through April 30, 1988, as National Organ and Tissue Donor Awareness Week. I ask health care professionals, public and private service organizations, and all Americans to join in supporting this humanitarian cause.

In Witness Whereof, I have hereunto set my hand this twenty-first day of April, in the year of our Lord nineteen hundred and eighty-eight, and of the Independence of the United States of America the two hundred and twelfth.

RONALD REAGAN

[*Filed with the Office of the Federal Register, 4:34 p.m., April 22, 1988*]

Note: The proclamation was released by the Office of the Press Secretary on April 22.

Nomination of Charles Ray Ritcheson To Be a Member of the National Council on the Humanities
April 22, 1988

The President today announced his intention to nominate Charles Ray Ritcheson to be a member of the National Council on the Humanities, National Foundation on the Arts and the Humanities, for the remainder of the term expiring January 26, 1990. He would succeed William Barclay Allen.

Since 1984 Mr. Ritcheson has been the university librarian, dean, and vice provost/ university professor for University of Southern California's Doheny Memorial Library in Los Angeles, CA, and professor of history, 1977–1984. From 1974 to 1977, he was a cultural attaché for the U.S. Embassy in London, England.

Mr. Ritcheson graduated from Oklahoma University (B.A., 1946) and Oxford University (Ph.D., 1951). He served in the United States Navy Reserve, 1945–1946. He was born February 26, 1925, in Maysville, OK. Mr. Ritcheson is married, has six children, and currently resides in Los Angeles, CA.

Message to the Congress Transmitting the Annual Report on Aeronautics and Space Activities
April 22, 1988

To the Congress of the United States:

I am pleased to transmit this report on the Nation's progress in aeronautics and space during calendar year 1986. The report is provided in accordance with Section 206 of the National Aeronautics and Space Act of 1958, as amended (42 U.S.C. 2476).

It is with great sadness that we mourn the passing of the brave men and women aboard the Space Shuttle Challenger, but it is more important to remember them for their bravery and pursuit of challenge. I believe they would be proud of the challenge we have undertaken to move the Nation forward into a new era of space flight, one more stable, more reliable, and safer than before.

Space activities continue to provide vital support to U.S. national security interests. In response to expendable launch vehicle failures as well as the Challenger tragedy, the Department of Defense has embarked on a space launch recovery program that will provide for more assured access to space and reduce the backlog of critical national security payloads that were scheduled for launch on the Space Shuttle. In addition, critical space communications, navigation, meteorology, and surveillance programs continue to make vital contributions that enhance the effectiveness of our military forces and strengthen the overall deterrent posture of the United States. Also, space-related research conducted in support of the Strategic Defense Initiative continues to make impressive progress toward a more safe and secure future.

In 1986, the National Aeronautics and Space Administration and the Department of Defense initiated the joint National Aero-Space Plane research program that could result in an entirely new family of aerospace vehicles. Also, NASA and the Department of Defense examined and continue to study space transportation requirements for the late 1990's and early years of the 21st century. This study could lead to future development and technology efforts associated with advanced manned and unmanned space transportation systems aimed at providing increased responsiveness, flexibility, and reliability, as well as learning the costs of assured access to space while meeting evolving payload requirements.

Advanced planning continued for a permanently manned Space Station. At my request, our friends and allies cooperated with us in the initial planning and design phases of the Space Station. In addition to helping us build an enhanced facility, their investments will help to strengthen free world ties in space science and exploration.

During the year, we continued to unlock the mysteries of the universe. In January 1986, Voyager 2 become the first spacecraft to fly past Uranus, transmitting over 7,000 images of that planet and its rings and moons. The fastest known spinning binary pulsar was discovered.

In studies of the Earth and its environment, scientists continued to observe conditions from Earthbound and spaceborne platforms and to participate in interdisciplinary research activities that will allow better understanding and prediction of environmental problems throughout the world.

As most of you are aware, space is no longer just the domain of the United States and the Soviet Union. It has become a highly competitive international arena where more and more nations are vying for economic, scientific, and military advantages. Continued advances in aeronautics and space technology will strengthen the Nation's scientific capabilities and develop the technological infrastructure needed to maintain U.S. national security interests as well as economic competitiveness.

Because of the Challenger tragedy, the year 1986 was a difficult one for all of us who support U.S. space activities. In the aftermath of Challenger, we established goals to restructure and strengthen our space planning and organizations. I believe we have made considerable progress toward realizing these goals, which will allow the United States to return space transportation capabilities to safe and reliable operation.

RONALD REAGAN

The White House,
April 22, 1988.

Message to the Senate Transmitting the Thailand-United States Legal Assistance Treaty
April 22, 1988

To the Senate of the United States:

With a view to receiving the advice and consent of the Senate to ratification, I transmit herewith the Treaty between the Government of the United States of America and the Government of the Kingdom of Thailand on Mutual Assistance in Criminal Matters, signed at Bangkok on March 19, 1986. I transmit also, for the information of the Senate, the report of the Department of State with respect to the Treaty.

The Treaty is one of a series of modern mutual legal assistance treaties being negotiated by the United States in order to counter more effectively criminal activities. The Treaty should be an effective tool to prosecute a wide variety of modern criminals including members of drug cartels, "white-collar criminals," and terrorists. The Treaty is self-executing and utilizes existing statutory authority.

The Treaty provides for a broad range of cooperation in criminal matters. Mutual assistance available under the Treaty includes: (1) taking testimony or statements of witnesses; (2) providing documents, records, and evidence; (3) serving documents; (4) executing requests for searches and seizures; (5) transferring persons in custody for testimonial purposes; (6) locating persons; (7) initiating proceedings upon request; and (8) assisting forfeiture proceedings.

I recommend that the Senate give early and favorable consideration to the Treaty and give its advice and consent to ratification.

RONALD REAGAN

The White House,
April 22, 1988.

Nomination of Warren J. Baker To Be a Member of the National Science Board
April 22, 1988

The President today announced his intention to nominate Warren J. Baker to be a member of the National Science Board, National Science Foundation, for a term expiring May 10, 1994. This is a reappointment.

Since 1979 Mr. Baker has been president of California Polytechnic State University in San Luis Obispo, CA. Prior to this, he was a professor and vice president of academic affairs at the University of Detroit, 1976–1979; assistant professor of civil engineering, 1966–1967; and associate professor, 1967.

Mr. Baker graduated from the University of Notre Dame (B.S., 1960; M.S., 1962) and the University of New Mexico (Ph.D., 1966). He was born September 5, 1938, in Fitchburg, MA. Mr. Baker is married, has four children, and currently resides in San Luis Obispo.

Remarks at a White House Briefing for the American Legislative Exchange Council
April 22, 1988

The President. Thank you all very much, and a special thank you to your chairman, Senator Owen Johnson, to your executive director, Connie Heckman, and there happens to be a fellow, I think, down here that—a longtime old friend who founded this organization, Don Totten. And, well, welcome to the White House complex. The White House complex—they call it that because nothing in Washington is ever simple. [*Laughter*]

Now, I've been warned recently about starting so many of my talks with a joke or two—sort of along the lines of a story that Lincoln used to tell. It concerned two Quaker ladies who were discussing Lincoln and Jefferson Davis and the progress of the Civil War. And the first lady said, "I think Jefferson will succeed." And the second asked, "Why does thee think so?" She said, "Because," the first one, "Jefferson is a praying man." "And so is Abraham Lincoln a praying man," said the second lady. "Yes," replied the first lady, "but the Lord will think Abe is joking." [*Laughter*]

Well, I'm not joking when I say that every one of the eight times I've met with you these 8 years I've wished more like you were in our Congress. And yet I'm also glad you're where you are: leading our conservative revolution in the State legislatures of America. Yes, when we talk about federalism here in Washington, we're really talking about putting the States more and more in charge. And that means that if what we conservatives believe in, if the principles that we stand for, are to succeed and prevail, we will need more conservatives like you in our State legislatures.

Already you're leading not only the States but the Federal Government as well in an agenda of hope for the future. In areas like tort reform, drug legislation, AIDS testing and research, welfare reform, privatization, and education reform, you've been way out in front of the pack. In fact, when I look at all you've done—and in areas like welfare reform, for example—I can't help wondering about that old argument for federalism. It used to be said that if we gave the States more power they'd show that they had the maturity to handle as well as Congress handles its power. Talk about faint praise. [*Laughter*] Well, we'd be lucky if Congress had your maturity, your foresight, and your wisdom.

Nowhere is this more true than in spending. Most of you have to balance your budgets. It's a requirement of your State constitutions. Everyone knows that's not the case here in Washington. It should be. But Congress usually won't act without a little friendly prodding, and you can do that. Thirty-two States have passed resolutions calling for a constitutional convention to draft a balanced budget amendment. As my good friend Ed Feulner, president of the Heritage Foundation, wrote recently about the prospects of making it 33, in Ed's words: "With 33 States on board, Congress would feel enormous pressure to take control of the situation, lest it be cut out of the process, as a convention would do." Now, I prefer Congress to deal with the issue directly. But if they don't, a good nudge in the right direction will get their attention.

Getting the Federal Government's fiscal house in order is part of the unfinished business of our revolution. And despite the odds, I'm convinced that, one way or another, it'll be done. You see, on this issue, as on so many others, we've changed the terms of national debate. Eight years ago, who would have thought that Democrats would run for President saying they were against deficits. They remind me of a story about Mae West, the movie star. She was on the set one day with another actress who was on edge because she thought Mae West was upstaging her. Finally, this other actress turned to the director and said West's timing was all wrong, and to West she said, "You forget I've been an actress for 40 years." West replied, "Don't worry, dear. I'll keep your secret." [*Laughter*]

But you'd never know it to hear those fellows on the other side who want to pick up the lease here when mine runs out, but we're in the longest peacetime expansion on record. Inflation is under control. A greater proportion of Americans are at work today than ever before in our history. After a falling roller coaster ride of almost a decade, real family income has risen strongly ever since our recovery began. Our expansion is creating hundreds of thousands of new jobs a month, and taken as a whole, these jobs pay better than the jobs already in the economy. Far from deindustrializing, as those other fellows say our nation is doing, many of our manufacturing industries are running near capacity. Far from losing out in world competition, which they also claim is the case, we're exporting now more than ever before in our history.

But the danger in all the false doomsday talk about our national economy is that it will stampede us to do the wrong things, things that really make things bad. And that's the trouble with the trade bill now working its way toward my desk. I'd like to be able to sign trade legislation this year. I've worked in good faith with Congress to produce an acceptable bill. Such a bill would open markets and improve America's competitiveness. And while the legislation working through Congress does enhance our negotiating authority in the ongoing international trade talks and helps us protect intellectual property rights, both good measures, it contains provisions that are unacceptable.

Put simply, on key provisions in the trade bill, the Democratic leadership in Congress has caved in to pressure from organized labor. The plant-closing restriction in the bill would make American industry less competitive—not the way to go if you want to reverse the trade imbalance and save jobs. In fact, the restriction would cost jobs. One example of how—since our recovery began, most net new jobs in the United States have come from companies that were 5 years old or less, entrepreneurial companies, both very large and very small. Europe, on the other hand, has had little entrepreneurship and almost no new—net new jobs.

Recently one of our leading experts on job creation asked why. And he found some straightforward answers including, as he's written, that "regulations are so much more onerous in Europe than in the United States, eliminating much of the flexibility that is bread and meat for entrepreneurs." And what regulations hurt entrepreneurs and their job-creating powers most? In his words, "Europeans face a host of rules governing their right to close down facilities, fire workers, and relocate operations." So, this is how the supporters of the plant-closing restriction would help America's workers—by copying Europe in ways that have led to Europe actually losing jobs between 1980 and today, the same period in which we have created over 15 million new jobs.

One Washington lobbyist recently said of my veto threats: "I think he's crying wolf." Try me! [*Laughter*] If this bill is unloaded on my desk, I'll stamp it reject and ship it back to where it was made. By the way, that same lobbyist added that he was sure that, in his words, "the administration doesn't want to go into the next election without a trade bill." Well, if they want a trade bill, it's time they took out those provisions that have nothing to do with improving American trade.

I hope Congress will produce a good trade bill this year. Indeed, I want Congress to produce a good trade bill, and I'll work to secure it. But that depends on the leadership in both Houses. Are they willing to put national interest above special interest? If so, we can all join together to help keep America strong and growing.

Let me close by saying thank you for all you've done and all you will do, and with an appeal to each of you. This is my last meeting with you as President. You're not only today's leaders of our revolution in the States, you are the next generation on the Federal level. So, never forget how much we've done and how fast. Just a few years ago, most of us would have said that it would take decades to make as much progress as we've made in just 8 years. There's still much left to do. But if you persevere, it can be done. America is depending on you. The hopes of our young people are depending on you. And the cause of freedom is depending on you. In a way that few are ever privileged to know, the whole world is in your hands. So, again, I just want to say a heartfelt thank you to all of you, and God bless you.

Senator Johnson. Mr. President, we're very honored that you've met with us again as you have in the past. We're grateful for your longstanding support which you've rendered to ALEC. We'd like to take this opportunity today to present you with a token of our appreciation, and at this time I'd like to ask Don Totten to step forward—your old friend, and our first chairman. He was going to unveil that picture. He doesn't have to unveil it—[*laughter*]—but I'll go through the motions as we rehearsed it.

Mr. President, for 8 years we've joined with you in striving for limited government, lower taxes, and more effective judicial and educational institutions. We're deeply appreciative of your achievements and your longstanding relationship with ALEC from your days as Governor of California to the present time. It's with great admiration and appreciation that we present you with this portrait, which you will receive for the Ronald Reagan Presidential Library, along with a set of 50 of the State flags in honor of your service to the country and your service to federalism. Thank you, and God bless you.

Mr. Totten. Mr. President, you've been an inspiration to us all, especially ALEC. We look forward to when you, constitutionally, can run again. [*Laughter*]

The President. I thought that picture looked like somebody familiar that I should know when I came in. [*Laughter*] Well, I thank you all very much, and thank you for that.

I have to say one more thing. When I used that figure 33 of States that would go for a constitutional convention, maybe I ought to tell you that 33 was my lucky number. [*Laughter*] It was my number on my jersey when I played football. I was the 33d Governor. And even when we were buying a ranch—and I was on pins and needles as to whether we were going to get it—and friends of ours down in Los Angeles kind of handling the thing called me up on the phone one day, and he said, "I just thought you would like to know that on today, the 3d of December, at 3:33 p.m. this afternoon, escrow closed. The ranch is yours." [*Laughter*] Tony Dorsett, the great star of the Dallas football team, somehow got wind of this and my feeling about it. So, I now have a Dallas football jersey with the number 33 on it—[*laughter*]—after they'd won the Super Bowl.

Okay, well, thank you all very much.

Note: The President spoke at 12:13 p.m. in Room 450 of the Old Executive Office Building.

Appointment of Gloria Ann Duus as a Member of the National Advisory Council on Indian Education

April 22, 1988

The President today announced his intention to appoint Gloria Ann Duus to be a member of the National Advisory Council on Indian Education for a term expiring September 29, 1990. This is a reappointment.

Since 1986 Mrs. Duus has been owner and president of Ya'hteeh Development Services in Yahtahey, NM. Prior to this, she was the program director for the Office of Navajo Women, 1984–1986, and a staff assistant in the Office of the Chairman/Vice Chairman, 1983–1984. She served as the project director for the Navajo division of education, 1981–1982.

Mrs. Duus graduated from the University of Utah (B.S., 1974) and Northern Arizona University (M.S., 1982). She was born March 6, 1951, in Brigham City, UT. She is married, has three children, and resides in Yahtahey, NM.

Nomination of Francis Anthony Keating II To Be an Associate Attorney General

April 22, 1988

The President today nominated Francis Anthony Keating II to be Associate Attorney General at the Department of Justice. He would succeed Stephen S. Trott.

Mr. Keating is currently serving as an Assistant Secretary of the Treasury (Enforcement), a position he has held since 1985. Prior to this Mr. Keating served as the United States Attorney for the Northern District of Oklahoma, 1981–1985. He was a member of the Oklahoma Senate, 1974–1981, and he was elected a member of the Oklahoma House of Representatives in 1972. From 1971 to 1972, Mr. Keating was State prosecutor for Oklahoma. He also served as a Special Agent for the FBI, 1969–1971.

Mr. Keating graduated from Georgetown University (B.A., 1966) and the University of Oklahoma Law School (J.D., 1969). He was born in Tulsa, OK, is married, and has three children.

Statement on Signing the Prescription Drug Marketing Act of 1987

April 22, 1988

I am today signing H.R. 1207, the "Prescription Drug Marketing Act of 1987," with mixed feelings.

On the one hand, I support the expressed goal of this legislation, which is to reduce potential public health risks that may result from the distribution of mislabeled, subpotent, counterfeit, or adulterated prescription drugs in the secondary source market, the so-called "diversion market." The investigations and prosecutions involving counterfeit and diverted drugs that have been conducted by the Department of Justice during the past few years have demonstrated that the principal factor facilitating the illegal activity that this bill is designed to combat is the almost total lack of traceability of drug products in the diversion market. This bill, to some extent, provides a response to this problem.

On the other hand, I have grave reservations about the bill's provision that would require States to adhere to Federal standards when licensing wholesale drug distributors. This provision represents a substantial intrusion into traditional State responsibilities and prerogatives. The States have always had the primary role in the regulation of wholesale drug distributors, and this bill would substitute the Federal Government for the States in that role.

This provision of H.R. 1207 is contrary to fundamental principles of federalism upon which our Constitution is based. Accordingly, I have directed the Department of Justice to submit to the Congress legislation repealing this portion of the bill, and I urge the Congress to enact this legislation promptly.

I am also troubled about the bill's provision that would generally prohibit certain types of beneficial competition in the sale of pharmaceuticals by hospitals and other health care providers. Such competition from innovative health care providers can benefit consumers through increased choices and lower prices, and should be encouraged, rather than discouraged. To be specific, I am very concerned that this legislation could impose on the sick and the elderly increased prices for prescription drugs. Consequently, I have requested the Attorney General to monitor the implementation of this portion of the bill and to make recommendations for remedial actions if warranted.

Finally, although the lack of traceability of drug products in the diversion market is a valid concern that I share, the magnitude of the public health problem created by diverted drugs is still not clear. I am therefore also concerned by provisions of the bill requiring use of substantial amounts of scarce Federal public health resources to police these practices.

Despite these concerns, I am willing to accept the view of the Congress that H.R. 1207 can assist in preventing potential health and safety problems for the American public. For this reason, I am approving this bill.

RONALD REAGAN

The White House,
April 22, 1988.

Note: H.R. 1207, approved April 22, was assigned Public Law No. 100–293.

White House Statement on the 10th Anniversary of the Committee for the Defense of the Unjustly Persecuted

April 22, 1988

In April the Committee for the Defense of the Unjustly Persecuted, known by its Czech initials, VONS, will mark 10 years of monitoring human rights abuse in Czechoslovakia. VONS grew out of the Czechoslovak human rights initiatives, Charter 77, as an effort to document the plight of those individuals and their families who suffer from various forms of oppression within Czechoslovakia.

Despite persecution and past imprisonment of some of its members, VONS provides a vital source of information on the status of human rights in Czechoslovakia. We note the 10th anniversary of VONS with great admiration for the dedication and courage of its members, both inside and outside Czechoslovakia, and deep regret at the conditions which spawned the Committee and continue to compel its work. We encourage the Government of Czechoslovakia to respect its international commitments on human rights and to extend to its citizens basic freedoms, which all people have the right to enjoy.

Radio Address to the Nation on the Trade Bill and the Persian Gulf Conflict

April 23, 1988

My fellow Americans:

There's a memorable bit of dialog between Claude Rains and Humphrey Bogart in the movie "Casablanca." Rains, playing the Vichy French police inspector, asked Bogart why he came to Casablanca; and Bogart says it was for "the waters." "But this is the desert," replies Rains, "there are no waters here." And Bogart, unflappable as ever, responds, "I was misinformed."

Well, when it comes to the issue of trade, the American people have been misinformed. We seem to hear every night on the evening news that the trade deficit is looming over our economy, threatening at any moment to plunge us back into a second Great Depression. Well, I'm sorry to disappoint these doomcriers, but the economy is strong and getting stronger. What you don't hear so often on the news is that the trade deficit has turned around. Exports are at record levels, factories are expanding, and more Americans have jobs than ever before in our history. Whether it's cars, steel, or high technology, the label "Made in the U.S.A." is seen more and more around the world. This good news doesn't get reported too much because the rising price of imports makes it seem like we're importing more. The truth is when you account for price changes the trade deficit has decreased and is now 20 percent smaller than it was during the third quarter of 1986.

The fearmongers had their heyday last October, when the stock market fell 508 points in 1 day of trading. Many blamed the merchandise trade deficit and predicted a dire future for the U.S. economy. Depression, recession, catastrophe, and calamity was all we heard. Well, I said at the time, the U.S. economy was in great shape. And in fact, in the 6 months since Black Monday, we've seen unemployment drop from 5.9 percent to 5.5, the lowest since 1974. We've had 6 more months of real growth in the longest peacetime expansion in U.S. history. And that growth has been impressive, a 4.8 percent during the last quarter of 1987—some catastrophe.

Not simply content with predicting disaster, some in Congress have put together legislation that would damage our ability to compete with our trading partners. Everyone talks about wanting a level playing field, but what Congress would be doing is putting American workers and industries on the field with one hand tied behind their backs. They call this a trade bill, but there's a lot in it that has nothing to do with trade.

Yes, I want a trade bill, and we've been working with Congress in good faith to produce a bill that would open markets and improve America's competitiveness, but we must guard against enacting legislation that would reverse the gains of the past 5 years. The draft legislation does contain a number of important measures: It enhances our negotiating authority in the ongoing international trade talks, repeals the windfall profits tax, and creates a retraining program for workers who've been laid off. We strongly support these measures. But it also contains provisions that are unacceptable. I've made it very clear to Congress: I will veto this bill, and I am confident that my veto will be sustained. Then I'll work vigorously to secure responsible trade legislation and urge the congressional leadership to schedule prompt action on the new bill. As long as I'm President, we're going to keep traveling the road we're on, one of free and fair trade, record sustained growth, job creation, rising incomes, and technological leadership into the 21st century.

Now, I'd like to turn for a moment to events this past week in the Persian Gulf. The actions that our forces took in the Gulf were a measured response to Iran's resumption of minelaying and continued aggression against nonbelligerents. We have completed these self-defense actions and consider this incident closed.

I am extremely proud of the courage and resourcefulness of our military personnel in the Persian Gulf. Their performance under very difficult circumstances has been superb. We're also very pleased with the role that the European allies are playing in a cooperative effort to counter the Iranian mining threat and to help protect freedom of navigation. Such cooperative efforts, supported by our Gulf Arab friends, offer the best means of deterring Iran and enhancing Gulf security. Working together, we can also put new life into the U.N. Security Council's efforts to end the increasingly bloody, inhumane Iran-Iraq war and remove the root cause of tensions in the Gulf. Our role in this war is neutral, and we do not seek to confront Iran. However, its leaders must understand that continued military and terrorist attacks against nonbelligerents and refusal to negotiate an end to the war will be very costly to Iran and its people.

Until next week, thanks for listening, and God bless you.

Note: The President spoke at 12:06 p.m. from Camp David, MD.

Message to the Congress on the Continuation of the National Emergency With Respect to Nicaragua
April 25, 1988

To the Congress of the United States:

Section 202(d) of the National Emergencies Act (50 U.S.C. 1622(d)) provides for the automatic termination of a national emergency unless, prior to the anniversary date of its declaration, the President publishes in the *Federal Register* and transmits to the Congress a notice stating that the emergency is to continue in effect beyond the anniversary date. In accordance with this provision, I have sent the enclosed notice, stating that the Nicaraguan emergency is to continue in effect beyond May 1, 1988, to the *Federal Register* for publication. A similar notice was sent to the Congress and the *Federal Register* on April 21, 1987, extending the emergency beyond May 1, 1987.

The actions and policies of the Government of Nicaragua continue to pose an unusual and extraordinary threat to the national security and foreign policy of the United States. If the Nicaraguan emergency were allowed to lapse, the present Nicaraguan trade controls would also lapse, impairing our government's ability to apply economic pressure on the Sandinista government and reducing the effectiveness of our support for the forces of the democratic opposition in Nicaragua. In these circumstances, I have determined that it is necessary to maintain in force the broad authorities that may be needed in the process of dealing with the situation in Nicaragua.

RONALD REAGAN

The White House,
April 25, 1988.

Notice of the Continuation of the National Emergency With Respect to Nicaragua
April 25, 1988

On May 1, 1985, by Executive Order No. 12513, I declared a national emergency to deal with the threat to the national security and foreign policy of the United States constituted by the situation in Nicaragua. On April 21, 1987, I announced the continuation of that emergency beyond May 1, 1987. Because the actions and policies of the Government of Nicaragua continue to pose an unusual and extraordinary threat to the national security and foreign policy of the United States, the national emergency declared on May 1, 1985, and subsequently extended, must continue in effect beyond May 1, 1988. Therefore, in accordance with Section 202(d) of the National Emergencies Act (50 U.S.C. 1622(d)), I am continuing the national emergency with respect to Nicaragua. This notice shall be published in the *Federal Register* and transmitted to the Congress.

RONALD REAGAN

The White House,
April 25, 1988.

[Filed with the Office of the Federal Register, 3:37 p.m., April 25, 1988]

Note: The notice was printed in the "Federal Register" of April 27.

Remarks on Receiving a Report on American Education
April 26, 1988

Secretary Bennett. Mr. President, ladies and gentlemen, I am pleased to present to you, Mr. President, and to the American people the first copy of a new Department of Education report entitled "American Education: Making it Work." Mr. President, as you'll recall, on March 26th of last year, at an education symposium in Columbia, Missouri, you gave me a homework assignment: the preparation of a report assessing America's educational progress since 1983, when the National Commission on Excellence in Education 5 years ago today declared us a "nation at risk." You asked that this report tell the American people how far we've come and what still needs to be done, what reforms have worked and what principles should guide us as we move ahead. Well, here's the gist of my report, Mr. President.

American education has made some progress in the last few years. The precipitous downward slide of previous decades has been arrested, and we have begun the long climb back to reasonable standards. Our students have made modest gains in achievement. They are taking more classes in basic subjects. And the performance of our schools has slightly improved. All this is encouraging. We are doing better than we were in 1983. But we are not doing well enough, and we are not doing well enough, fast enough. We are still at risk. The absolute level at which our improvements are taking place is unacceptably low. Widespread and fundamental reforms remain necessary. What these reforms are is not mysterious. Indeed, identifying what works, establishing the ideas and practices that make for effective schools, has been a signal accomplishment of the reform movement to date. Extending and applying the lessons of what works to every school in every community and State in the Nation is the task that lies ahead of us.

To do this, we need, we believe, to pursue five basic avenues of reform. First, we need to strengthen the content of our elementary and high school classes and provide our students with a solid core curriculum of basic studies. Second, we need to do a better job of extending equal intellectual opportunity to all our students by dramatically improving the education that is provided to minority and disadvantaged children. Third, we need to revive and restore a healthy ethos of achievement, discipline, and hard work in all our schools. Fourth, we need more effective and sensible methods of recruiting and rewarding good teachers and principals for our schools. And finally, we need to make American education accountable for results. We need to hold our school system responsible for doing its job, and we need to hold our schools responsible for ensuring that our students are learning.

We know how to achieve these goals. Necessary reforms are described and explained in this report. We know there is wide public support for these goals and reforms. The American people endorse by overwhelming margins almost every significant proposal made in this report. And we know that if we fail to act on such proposals, our schools cannot meaningfully improve.

If our schools are to improve, the powerful resistance to reform must be overcome. It can be. The Nation's modest success over the past 5 years is both proof of reform's possibilities and a summons to all of us for renewed effort. All Americans concerned for the quality of our children's education—Governors, legislators, educators, and parents—must become knowledgeable, aggressive, and courageous proponents of education reform.

I offer this report to you, Mr. President, as a guide to our future work together. It is work for our children and our country. I know you agree with me that there are few things more important than this work. So, here it is, Mr. President.

Mr. President, I know the audience is eager to hear from you, and I want to tell you that in this audience are many principals and teachers. And I know since the time you were a young boy, you've been comfortable in the presence of teachers and principals. [*Laughter*]

The President. Well, that was my story. [*Laughter*] Well, I thank you, Secretary Bennett. And I'm pleased to see David Gardner and other members of the National Commission on Excellence in Education back here with us today. Let me begin by welcoming all of you to the White House. When I was a boy in school, now and then I was, as Bill has indicated, shall we say, "invited" to visit the principal's office. Today at least a few of you are letting me return the favor. [*Laughter*] I hope you'll feel more comfortable than I did. [*Laughter*]

But as Bill Bennett said, it was 5 years ago that we first issued our report on the state of education in the United States, "A Nation at Risk." Brenda Lee is with us today. She has my admiration and the Nation's. And another star who is with us today is Jaime Escalante. Jaime Escalante has taught calculus at Garfield High School, a predominantly Hispanic inner-city school in Los Angeles, since 1974. And when he arrived there, Garfield was terrorized by gangs and close to losing its accreditation. And Jaime set out to prove that their kids could learn math as well as any—with incredible success. In 1982 his students did so well on the advanced placement calculus exam that the Educational Testing Service in Princeton couldn't believe their eyes. They thought the Garfield students must have cheated. Escalante advised his students to take the test again, and they served [scored] as well or better. Today, thanks to Mr. Escalante, Garfield has one of the best calculus programs in America. A movie about Mr. Escalante, "Stand and Deliver," has just been released, which is particularly gratifying to me. Too often my old industry glorifies the wrong kind of people. Jaime Escalante and those at Garfield High School are the kinds of people movies ought to glorify, and this time the movies did.

Well, I had lunch today with Mr. Escalante, Miss Lee, and four other extraordinary educators, and over the last few years I've visited a number of schools dedicated to quality—from Jacksonville, Florida, to Chattanooga, Tennessee, to Columbia, Missouri, and, yes, to Suitland, Maryland, and Vienna, Virginia, just outside of Washington. I've heard and seen how far we've come.

Well, I'm going to back a ways here and pick up some other things before I get too far along that line. You know, that report that I mentioned first, it concluded that, in its words: "If an unfriendly foreign power had attempted to impose on America the mediocre educational performance that exists today, we might well have viewed it as an act of war." It helped heighten and accelerate a wave of education reform in States and communities all around the country. Last year Secretary Bennett and I had a chance to hear about some of those reforms when we flew out to Columbia, Missouri, and attended a conference there that was sponsored by the Secretary's department and the National Governors' Association. At that conference I gave Bill a little homework assignment—well, maybe not that little, since I knew he'd need a whole year to complete it. [*Laughter*] I wanted a full progress report.

Yes, some States had installed career ladders, merit pay, and other means of rewarding good teachers. Many schools were placing a new emphasis on quality and discipline, more homework, more attention to basic skills, more attention to what works, that is, to results. This was truly revolutionary after two decades in which money had been the only measure of progress in education, and in which, while Federal spending on education went steadily up, test scores fell steadily down and too many schools accepted the fashions of the day—the fashions of liberal culture—that held traditional standards in scorn.

It appeared in the newspapers and is about a guidance counselor who asked a class what they should do if they found a purse with $1,000 in it. The class decided that returning it would be neither right nor wrong, just dumb. And when they asked what the counselor thought, he said he wouldn't force his values on them. He told the reporter, and I'm quoting now: "If I come from the position of what is right and what is wrong, then I'm not their counselor." Well, it reminds me of what someone once said that if God had been a liberal, we wouldn't have 10 Commandments, just 10 suggestions. [*Laughter*] Plato once said that "the direction in which education starts a man will determine his future life."

When we've looked at schools that work across the country, we've found that the key to what works is not money or being in a prosperous neighborhood but establishing a direction, that is, setting standards. And that's what Edison Primary School in the inner-city area of Dayton, Ohio, does. Almost all of the students at Edison come from low-income families. When they first enter the school, many suffer from intellectual understimulation and other problems associated with poverty.

And Principal Brenda Lee, that I mentioned before, combats that with love and caring and by teaching each child to do his or her best. In her more than 5 years at the school, she has strengthened the academic program. She established a schoolwide homework policy and required that students demonstrate that they are ready to be promoted before they're promoted. With the help of outside volunteers, she set up a tutoring program. She also got to know parents, meeting them first at bus stops or on the playground. Now more than 50 volunteer to help at the school each day, and having their parents care like that is an incentive for the children to do well. Another incentive is the Student of the Month Award that Principal Lee established to recognize and encourage excellence. The result of all of this is that in just 3 years students doing math at or above grade level went from 40 percent to 64 percent, while those reading at or above grade level rose from 65 to almost 80 percent.

Yes, the reverse, to get back where I was earlier, in the decline in test scores is no accident, but I also know that we still have a long way to go, as Bill said. I'm confident that this report will help us find the way. As I'm told the report notes, we've all heard the arguments of those who believe education reform will fail: that it will take much more steadfastness than the American people possess, much more money than we are willing to pay, or a more fundamental transformation of society than we're willing to bring about.

Well, I reject these arguments. American education can be made to work better, and it can be made to work better now. The first step is to identify where we stand and what needs to be done, and that has largely been done. Now, there is a second step: We must overcome the obstacles that block reform. Successful reform won't come about from the top down. Central planning doesn't make economies healthy, and it won't make schools work, either. How can we release the creative energies of our people? By giving parents choice, by allowing them to select the schools that best meet the unique needs of their children, by fostering a healthy rivalry among schools to serve our young people. Already, the power of choice is revitalizing schools that use it across the Nation. We must make education reform a reality. And if we act decisively, American education will soon work much better than it does today, and we'll provide our children with the schools they deserve.

Educators like Jaime Escalante and Brenda Lee give us examples of how good American education can be. But a few good examples aren't enough. Every school in America must be a good example. Every school in America needs to have a solid curriculum of basic studies. Every school in America needs to offer its students equal intellectual opportunity that knows no distinction of race, class, or family background. Every school in America needs to have an ethos of achievement, moral quality, discipline, and hard work. Every school in America needs to be able to recruit and reward good teachers and principals. And all of American education needs to be accountable for the only result that matters: student learning.

I believe we can do it. We know what works. It's already working at schools around the country. It just needs to be done everywhere. Every American child deserves the kind of school that Brenda Lee runs. Every American child deserves the kind of teaching that Jaime Escalante provides. So, let's dedicate ourselves to giving it to them.

I thank you all, and God bless you all. If my old principal could see me now. [*Laughter*]

Note: The President spoke at 2:13 p.m. in the East Room at the White House. In his opening remarks, he referred to David P. Gardner, Chairman of the National Commission on Excellence in Education.

Nomination of Jane A. Kenny To Be Deputy Director of ACTION
April 26, 1988

The President today announced his intention to nominate Jane A. Kenny to be Deputy Director of ACTION. She would succeed Henry M. Ventura.

Since 1986 Miss Kenny has been Director of VISTA and Student Community Service Programs at ACTION in Washington, DC. Prior to this she was Director of the Executive Secretariat at the General Services Administration, 1985–1986. She worked for the Office of the Vice President as a Special Assistant, 1984–1985, and was Executive Director of the Regulatory Secretariat, 1982–1984. She also worked for the 1981 Presidential Inaugural Committee and the 1980 Reagan-Bush campaign.

Miss Kenny graduated from the College of New Rochelle (B.A., 1967) and American University (M.P.A., 1977). She was born October 5, 1945, in Hartford, CT, and currently resides in Arlington, VA.

Nomination of Wendy Monson DeMocker To Be an Assistant Secretary of Transportation
April 26, 1988

The President today announced his intention to nominate Wendy Monson DeMocker to be an Assistant Secretary of Transportation (Public Affairs). She would succeed Dale A. Petroskey.

Since 1987 Mrs. DeMocker has been Press Secretary to the Secretary at the Department of Transportation in Washington, DC, and Director of Public Affairs for the Federal Railroad Administration at the Department of Transportation, 1983–1987. Prior to this she was assistant press secretary to Senator David Durenberger, 1980–1983.

Mrs. DeMocker graduated from the University of Minnesota (B.A., 1979). She was born October 4, 1957, in Virginia, MN. She is married and resides in Oakton, VA.

Appointment of George F. Moody as a Member of the Board of Governors of the American National Red Cross, and Redesignation as Principal Officer

April 26, 1988

The President today announced his intention to appoint George F. Moody to serve as a Governor on the Board of Governors of the American National Red Cross for a term of 3 years. This is a reappointment. He will also be redesignated to act as the principal officer of the corporation.

Since 1980 Mr. Moody has been president and chief executive officer for the Security Pacific Corp. in Los Angeles, CA. Since 1969 Mr. Moody has served Security Pacific National Bank in various capacities: as executive vice president, vice chairman, president and chief executive officer. Mr. Moody has also served as chairman and principal officer of the American National Red Cross, the Board of Governors, and the Executive Committee since 1985 and was vice chairman in 1984.

Mr. Moody attended Riverside City College. He was born July 28, 1930, in Riverside, CA. He is married, has four children, and resides in Whittier, CA.

Appointment of Al Cardenas as a Member of the Board of Directors of the Federal National Mortgage Association

April 26, 1988

The President today announced his intention to appoint Al Cardenas to be a member of the Board of Directors of the Federal National Mortgage Association for a term ending on the date of the annual meeting of the stockholders in 1989. This is a reappointment.

Since 1987 Mr. Cardenas has been senior partner with the law firm of Greenburg, Traurig, Askew, Hoffman, Lipoff, Rosen, and Quentel, P.A. in Miami, FL. Prior to this he was a partner with the law firm of Broad and Cassel.

Mr. Cardenas graduated from Florida Atlantic University (B.A., 1969) and Seton Hall University (J.D., 1974). He was born January 3, 1948, in Havana, Cuba. Mr. Cardenas is married, has four children, and resides in Miami, FL.

Nomination of Marian North Koonce To Be a Member of the National Council on the Handicapped

April 26, 1988

The President today announced his intention to nominate Marian North Koonce to be a member of the National Council on the Handicapped for a term expiring September 23, 1990. This is a reappointment.

From 1945 to 1980, Mrs. Koonce was an independent operator for Real Estate Management in Santa Barbara, CA.

Mrs. Koonce attended the University of Texas. She was born August 11, 1924, in Yoakum, TX. She is married, has six children, and resides in Santa Barbara, CA.

Proclamation 5801—Mother's Day, 1988
April 26, 1988

By the President of the United States of America

A Proclamation

Maternal love is the first tangible bond any human being knows. It is a tie at once physical, emotional, psychological, and mystical. With all of the words that have been written about motherhood, all of the poems of tribute and gratitude that have been penned through the ages, all of the portraits of a mother and child that have been painted down the centuries, none has come close to expressing in full the thankfulness and joy owing to mothers.

The mark of motherhood, as the story of Solomon and the disputed infant in the first Book of Kings shows, is a devotion to the well-being of the child so total that it overlooks itself and its own preferences and needs. It is a love that risks all, bears all, braves all. As it heals and strengthens and inspires in its objects an understanding of self-sacrifice and devotion, it is the parent of many another love as well.

The arms of a mother are the newborn's first cradle and the injured child's first refuge. The hands of a mother are the hands of care for the child who is near and of prayer for the one who is far away. The eyes of a mother are the eyes of fond surprise at baby's first step, the eyes of unspoken worry at the young adult's first voyage from home, the eyes of gladness at every call or visit that says she is honored and remembered. The heart of a mother is a heart that is always full.

Generation after generation has measured love by the work and wonder of motherhood. For these gifts, ever ancient and ever new, we cannot pause too often to give thanks to mothers. As inadequate as our homage may be and as short as a single day is to express it—"What possible comparison was there," a great saint wrote of his mother, "between the honor I showed her and the service she had rendered me?"—Mother's Day affords us an opportunity to meet one of life's happiest duties.

In recognition of the contributions of mothers to their families and to our Nation, the Congress, by a joint resolution approved May 8, 1914 (38 Stat. 770), has designated the second Sunday in May each year as Mother's Day and requested the President to call for its appropriate observance.

Now, Therefore, I, Ronald Reagan, President of the United States of America, do hereby request that Sunday, May 8, 1988, be observed as Mother's Day. I urge all Americans to express their love and respect for their mothers and to reflect on the importance of motherhood to the well-being of our country. I direct government officials to display the flag of the United States on all Federal government buildings, and I urge all citizens to display the flag at their homes and other suitable places on that day.

In Witness Whereof, I have hereunto set my hand this twenty-sixth day of April, in the year of our Lord nineteen hundred and eighty-eight, and of the Independence of the United States of America the two hundred and twelfth.

RONALD REAGAN

[*Filed with the Office of the Federal Register, 2:34 p.m., April 27, 1988*]

Appointment of Roger L. Stevens as a Member of the President's Committee on the Arts and the Humanities
April 26, 1988

The President today announced his intention to appoint Roger L. Stevens to be a member of the President's Committee on the Arts and the Humanities. This is an initial appointment.

Since 1961 Mr. Stevens has been Chairman of the John F. Kennedy Center for the Performing Arts in Washington, DC.

Mr. Stevens attended the University of Michigan. He was born March 12, 1910, in Detroit, MI. He served in the United States Navy during World War II. Mr. Stevens is married, has one child, and currently resides in Washington, DC.

Remarks at the Welcoming Ceremony for Prime Minister Brian Mulroney of Canada

April 27, 1988

The President. Bienvenue, Brian et Mila. [Welcome, Brian and Mila.] Nancy and I welcome you in the name of all Americans. Your visit is more than the last Washington meeting of two fortunate Irishmen who became leaders of their two countries. Together, we're looking ahead to a new era of growth and well-being for our two countries. In 1988 we're witnessing a dream come into being that many on both sides of the border have worked for: an agreement created to drastically reduce trade and tariff barriers between our two great nations. We shall show by deed and dedication, after the legislative process has been completed, that the lowering of tariffs and trade barriers is the way to a more prosperous world. Protectionism is out, and trade expansion is in.

We're embarking on an exciting new beginning. Our free trade agreement is recognized beyond North America as a venture never before attempted on such a scale by two sovereign and independent nations. When accepted by Parliament and Congress, the agreement will become one of the most important achievements of my tenure in Washington. President Eisenhower asked "the free world to recognize that trade barriers, although intended to protect a country's economy, often in fact shackle its prosperity." Ike would be satisfied, I'm certain, with our efforts this past year. We are unshackling our trading relationship in a broad-based effort to make our two countries more prosperous at home while making ourselves more competitive abroad. We're players in a world economy, and our free trade agreement will help make us the world-class competitors we must be.

Our agreement is remarkable in many ways. It has balance and offers mutual gains for two huge trading partners. Permit me, Brian, to salute the very special and dedicated Canadians and Americans who worked to put this agreement together and who made it happen. We both fielded teams of big league negotiators, and the agreement is indeed a product of their combined abilities. Our countries and peoples have been well served.

I am confident that the legislatures in both of our countries will vote favorably on this historic free trade agreement. Important as that step is, there are still other steps to be taken on the global economic stage. You and I will be meeting again, in Toronto this June, at the economic summit, where we will have discussions with our colleagues from Europe and Japan. We hope to move the process of international economic coordination forward. These discussions will also speed the way to what we trust will be a successful GATT [General Agreement on Tariffs and Trade] round of negotiations. We know that Canada shares with us our concerns about those many barriers to agricultural and services trade that are damaging to world trade.

We both attach great importance to GATT. While the tasks of the present round are formidable, it is essential that we give substance to a comprehensive multilateral reform of the international trading system. This will not be easy to accomplish, but it must be undertaken. And our objectives must include meaningful progress on agriculture. Agriculture is fundamental to both our economies, and it is an export area in which we're highly competitive in a free and open world market. The United States actively seeks the elimination of all subsidies in agriculture as a top priority. Together we must be successful in order to restore market forces in world agriculture.

Cooperation is the hallmark of our relationship in other areas. We will be working with Canada on the largest cooperative high-technology project we have ever undertaken: the permanently manned civil space station. Cooperation has also been the basis of our nearly 80-year tradition of shared concern for our environment. Much has already been done, and experts on both sides of the border recognize the results that have been achieved. Both our countries have made substantial progress in improving air quality. We have advanced our efforts to improve the water quality of the Great Lakes. More can be done to protect our environment as science clearly points the way, but make no mistake, we are moving.

Ours is a relationship of people and their ability to hold personal relationships across a national border. They form them easily and quickly, in good times and during times of stress. Today warm and close professional working ties are enjoyed and valued by service men and women of both our armed forces. It has made for an everyday camaraderie that has become both unique among Armed Forces and commonplace in our bilateral security relations. It is of great benefit to the smooth operation of NORAD and NATO and our shared responsibilities for the defense of North America.

In recent years we've been heartened by Canada's renewed efforts to strengthen its military forces—efforts forcefully spelled out in last year's defense white paper. With this strengthening has gone the Canadian Government's commitment to enlarge its contribution to the defense effort of the West and to support this commitment with the necessary budgets. This is but another illustration of a shared sense of purpose that Canada and the United States nurture to make the alliance stronger.

As I prepare for Moscow, I welcome your thoughts on how we can further relieve international tensions. Thus, Brian, we have our work, as always, cut out for us during our visit. Let's go to it.

The Prime Minister. Mr. President and Mrs. Reagan, Vice President Bush, Mrs. Bush, and Secretary Shultz, and friends: I want to thank you, Mr. President, for your kind words and generous welcome. It's a pleasure to be back among good friends.

The friendship between our people stretches back generations and stretches across a continent. Our relationship is a model for civilized conduct. It reflects what is best in the democratic values on which free societies are based. On more than one occasion we have made common cause in the defense of the values we hold dear, and we remain vigilant in the defense of freedoms we cherish. As one of my distinguished predecessors, John Diefenbaker, once put it—he happened to be a conservative as well, Mr. President—"We are the children of our geography, products of the same hopes, faith, and dreams."

Last year, Americans made almost 37 million visits to Canada, the world's largest tourist invasion, save one, which would be the nearly 45 million visits made last year by Canadians to the U.S. And I think that gives you an indication, Mr. President, of what really goes on in February in Canada. [*Laughter*] Don't try and call a meeting. [*Laughter*] You would be quick to note an imbalance in those figures, and I point this out to Secretary Baker—there's an imbalance in those figures, an imbalance in your favor. But I assure you, we have no plans to legislate against it.

Mr. President, I was determined when I took office to approach relations between our countries in a spirit of openness and perseverance in dealing with the problems that faced us. I found in you a leader of warmth and directness. We have met regularly. In fact, our series of annual meetings is unprecedented in the history of Canada-U.S. relations, and I would hope that it is now a permanent feature of our relationship. In the President's second term of office and in what I hope will be known afterwards as my first—[*laughter*]—we have done much to repair and refurbish the relationship between Canada and the United States. I haven't the slightest doubt that the

President could go on and on—to quote Mrs. Thatcher's noted turn of phrase—but I gather you have something in this country called the 22d amendment. But the principles we set out for ourselves at Quebec in 1985, by this President and myself, I believe have served us well.

We have reinforced our links in the largest trading partnership in the history of the world. In January the President and I signed the free trade agreement, under which both countries stand to gain. As Secretary Baker said in Ottawa last week, this achievement will grow in stature and importance over time. Its geopolitical potential is most significant. And I, too, want to pay tribute to Jim Baker and Clayton Yeutter for the very constructive role they played with our top people at a most critical juncture of the negotiations. The implications of the free trade agreement go far beyond our border and far beyond the shores of this continent, for what transpires between the world's largest trading partners holds a certain significance in the multilateral context.

We have renewed our defense relationship with the modernization of air defense arrangements and enhanced contributions to NATO. We have reached a pragmatic solution on the issue of transit through the Northwest passage. The issue of acid rain remains a challenge for us. This, as you said in Quebec City, Mr. President, is a problem that belongs to both of us. We must continue, and we shall, to work together for an equitable solution to this important challenge.

And so, we have a good deal to discuss together and with our officials. I look forward to my lunch today with Secretary Shultz, as well as my meetings with the congressional leadership and, in a special way, my meetings with the Vice President.

I want to thank you again for the warmth and genuineness of your welcome. Mila and I are delighted to be with you and Nancy again. And if I may conclude, Mr. President, I will by concluding with a remark that you made to me in Quebec City when you were leaving, as you observed Nancy and Mila getting out of their car to come and join us. And you took one look at it, and you said to me, "Brian, well, for two Irishmen, we certainly married up." [*Laughter*] Thank you, Mr. President.

Note: The President spoke at 10:10 a.m. at the South Portico of the White House, where Prime Minister Mulroney was accorded a formal welcome with full military honors.

Informal Exchange With Reporters Prior to a Meeting With Prime Minister Brian Mulroney of Canada
April 27, 1988

George Bush

Q. Mr. President, now that Vice President Bush has gone over the top, are you ready to officially end your position of neutrality in the Republican Party race?

The President. Well, I'm going to have to arrive at that since there are no others entering or not. It's so recent. I haven't even congratulated him yet—which I'm going to do in a short while—about his going over the top. But——

Q. But you are ready to do that, are you not, sir?

The President. Well, let us see.

Attorney General Edwin Meese III

Q. There's a story today in the Wall Street Journal, sir, about a secret plan of a number of your top advisers to pressure out Ed Meese. Are you aware of this?

The President. I shouldn't answer, but I have to tell you that, no, I'm not aware. And I thought the story was completely inaccurate.

Q. Would you support that kind of a plan, sir?

The President. No.

Q. Can you envision any circumstances under which you would ask the Attorney

General to leave?

The President. Well, if he had a complete change of character.

Q. Mr. President, was the Gipper let down by the Orioles last night?

Acid Rain

Q. What are you going to say to the President about acid rain, sir?

The Prime Minister. Pardon?

Q. What are you going to say to the President about acid rain? You mentioned it in your speech.

The Prime Minister. Well, we're going to try and move along toward resolution—a very——

Q. Do you expect one?

The Prime Minister. ——complicated transboundary problem. I hope we get a solution. I don't expect anything within moments. But we have been making movement, and we hope to make a lot more.

Q. Do you really feel the U.S. is dumping garbage in your backyard, Prime Minister?

The Prime Minister. Pardon?

Q. Do you really feel the U.S. is dumping garbage in your backyard?

The Prime Minister. Oh, I think that it's very clear that acid rain has that effect on the environment in the Eastern United States and in Canada. Yes. That's a normal fact——

Q. Mr. President, are you going to respond to his concerns? Are you going to do something about acid rain?

The Prime Minister. Well, we've been trying to work on it——

The President. Yes, this will be a subject we'll be discussing.

Q. Mr. Prime Minister, why were your comments on acid rain considerably toned down from your recent statement in New York?

The Prime Minister. Did you think so?

Q. Yes.

Q. Yes, substantially.

The Prime Minister. Oh, maybe I'll be saying a few things later on today. This was a welcoming ceremony. It wasn't the United Nations. I'm going to be making three or four other speeches today, and I think that if you're interested in acid rain you won't be disappointed.

Q. Are you concerned, Prime Minister, that the United States is talking in Geneva about possibly increasing certain emissions?

The Prime Minister. Well, we'll be discussing the whole problem of acid rain momentarily. And I suppose—within minutes. I'll let you know.

Q. ——concerns about that should increase?

The Prime Minister. Yes, sure. The President knows that.

Note: The exchange began at 10:34 a.m. in the Oval Office at the White House.

Executive Order 12637—Productivity Improvement Program for the Federal Government

April 27, 1988

By virtue of the authority vested in me as President by the Constitution and laws of the United States of America, including the Budget and Accounting Act of 1921, as amended, and in order to further improve a comprehensive program for the improvement of productivity throughout all Executive departments and agencies, it is hereby ordered as follows:

Section 1. There is hereby established a government-wide program to improve the quality, timeliness, and efficiency of services provided by the Federal Government. The goal of the program shall be to improve the quality and timeliness of service to the public and to achieve an annual average productivity increase of 3 percent in appropriate functions. Each Executive department and agency will gradually include appropriate functions in the Productivity Improvement Program, so that by 1991 all appropriate functions are covered.

Sec. 2. As used in this Order, the term:

(a) "Productivity" means the efficiency with which resources are used to produce a government service or product at specified levels of quality and timeliness;

(b) "Appropriate functions" means those agency program functions that produce measurable outputs in the form of services to the public;

(c) "Public" means a customer outside the organization, such as citizens, businesses, State and local governments, other countries and/or their citizens, other agencies, the military;

(d) "Outputs" means products or services delivered to the public;

(e) "Measurement system" means both the specific measures used to determine whether standards of quality, timeliness, and efficiency of services are being met, and the procedures for the collection and reporting of data resulting from application of productivity measures;

(f) "Organizational performance standard" means a statement that quantifies and describes the desired level of quality, timeliness, and efficiency of services to be provided by an organization;

(g) "Management review" means the review by the Director of the Office of Management and Budget, as part of the budget process of agency accomplishments and plans for management and productivity improvements.

Sec. 3. The head of each Executive department and agency shall:

(a) Develop a complete inventory of all appropriate functions to be included in the productivity program, use the agency's planning process to review current functions, and develop agency goals and objectives for improvement in services to the public.

(b) Develop and submit annually to the Office of Management and Budget a productivity plan. Each plan shall conform to the policy guidance issued by the Director of the Office of Management and Budget, pursuant to Section 5 of this Order, and shall:

(1) set forth the agency's productivity goals and objectives;

(2) target priorities for the year and expand coverage each subsequent year to additional appropriate functions, with the objective of complete coverage of all appropriate functions by 1991;

(3) describe the proposed actions designed to make the agency's operations and delivery of services more efficient and responsive;

(4) describe the methods, including efficiency reviews and cost comparisons with the private sector, that the agency will use either to improve its own service, or to make use of commercial services available in the private sector when it is economical to do so; and

(5) describe the measurement systems to be used by the agency to gauge quality, timeliness, and efficiency.

(c) Implement the productivity program after the Management review by the Director of the Office of Management and Budget as provided in Section 6.

(d) Assess annually the agency's progress toward achieving objectives and priorities, including documented gains and cost savings. This assessment will form the basis of the agency's report to the President as required by Section 4.

(e) Designate a senior official responsible for guiding the agency's productivity improvement program.

(f) Inform agency managers and employees that they are expected to be responsible for improvements in the quality, timeliness, and efficiency of services.

(g) Include productivity and quality improvement goals in the performance appraisals of managers and supervisors.

(h) Encourage employee participation in the productivity program through employee training, employee involvement in work-related decisions, incentives, recognition, and rewards and by taking actions to minimize negative impacts on employees that may occur as a result of the productivity program.

Sec. 4. The head of each Executive department and agency shall report annually to the President through the Domestic Policy Council on accomplishments achieved under the plan. The annual report will form the basis of the Management Report to the Congress.

Sec. 5. The Director of the Office of Management and Budget is authorized to:

(a) Develop and promulgate goals, policies, principles, standards, and guidelines for the effective administration of this Order by Executive departments and agencies; and

(b) Identify and propose the elimination of statutory and regulatory barriers that inhibit opportunities to make improvements in productivity.

Sec. 6. The Director shall review, through the management review process, each agency's productivity plan based upon the requirements and guidance issued pursuant to Section 5 of this Order. Nothing in this Section shall be construed as displacing agency responsibilities delegated by law.

Sec. 7. The Director of the Office of Management and Budget shall submit to the Congress, in conjunction with the President's budget, a report on productivity plans and accomplishments of the agencies and the government as a whole.

Sec. 8. The Director of the Office of Personnel Management shall:

(a) Review Federal personnel policies and programs and make or recommend such changes as are appropriate to support productivity improvement;

(b) Review incentive policies and programs for Federal employees and make or recommend such changes as are appropriate to increase the productivity of the Federal Government;

(c) Develop and implement training programs for Federal employees in support of productivity improvements;

(d) Review policies and programs for Federal employees who may be displaced by productivity improvements and make or recommend such changes as are appropriate to ensure that such policies and programs will minimize any adverse impact on Federal employees.

Sec. 9. Executive Order No. 12552 of February 25, 1986, is hereby superseded.

RONALD REAGAN

The White House,
April 27, 1988.

[*Filed with the Office of the Federal Register, 11:01 a.m., April 28, 1988*]

Toasts at the State Dinner for Prime Minister Brian Mulroney of Canada
April 27, 1988

The President. Nancy and I are delighted to again host an evening that brings Americans and Canadians together. No gathering could be more enjoyable and nothing is less unusual. Canadians and Americans congregate the world over on the least provocation. An inviting border has made us close and easygoing neighbors.

The essence and the strength of the relations between our two countries are people. Our people naturally get along well together. We share our triumphs and victories as we share our adversities. And when at times we spar, we do so without rancor, and we work out our differences. May this very special and productive spirit of cooperation remain in place. As John Diefenbaker so ably put it, "Our peoples are North Americans; we are the products of the same hope, faith, and dreams."

Well, your visit comes as we're on the threshold of a major event, important and historic to you and me and the nations we lead. I speak of our recently signed free trade agreement. Years ago British Admiral Beatty voiced the sense of our trade agreement when he explained what defends our common border: "nothing but the sound common sense and sound good will of two practical nations." Well, our new agreement makes much common sense and sets the stage for much good will. We shall avoid the perils of protectionism and gain the advantages of each country producing what each is best able to bring to market. Generations of Canadians and Americans will know you as the farsighted leader who proposed the free trade agreement. It will prove to be as big and as important as the magnitude of our bilateral trade. It signals to our trading partners that we are sincere in our belief that lowering tariffs and trade barriers is clearly the only answer to the distortions growing in world trade.

Your visit has allowed us to address issues other than trade. We share common concerns regarding the many aspects of the environment. Progress is being made. There is yet much we can do to make our shared continent a more comfortable and healthy place on which to live.

We've had important discussions of questions of peace and security. Canada's role is critical for the security of the Atlantic community. Canada's contribution to NATO is to be increased, which all your allies welcome. And I have seen at firsthand, Brian, the constructive contribution you've made personally in alliance deliberations like the NATO summit in March.

This is our fourth and my final summit. They started high on the ramparts of Quebec, and we've never lowered our lofty goals and objectives. I regret, however, that I could never reach those same high notes that the Prime Minister's voice so easily reached in song. [*Laughter*] These have been enjoyable meetings, useful meetings, and they've created bonds between us that have been seen as refreshing—as they have been hopeful to the execution of my office. In the process you've won my respect for your wise counsel and admiration for your leadership.

Mr. Prime Minister, you can look back on the years of our summits as a period in which you successfully achieved the goals you set out before you took office. You've achieved an important constitutional breakthrough. You have seen the Canadian economy grow and unemployment fall during your tenure in office. You have achieved a special place in history with our free trade agreement. Above all, you've been a strong and persistent advocate for Canada, liberally applying your adage that "we can disagree without being disagreeable." You have taught all of us about Canada's point of view on issues important to Canada while at the same time being a good neighbor and a firm friend. There can be little doubt that relations between the United States and Canada have prospered these last 4 years, and I thank you for both the effort and the success.

And now, excuse me just one second. To the Queen of Canada, to my good friend and good neighbor, Prime Minister Brian Mulroney, and Mrs. Mulroney, and to the enduring bond between our two North American peoples.

The Prime Minister. Mr. President and Mrs. Reagan, and *chers amis* [dear friends], I rise to propose a toast to the President of the United States and the First Lady. I rise also in a personal sense on behalf of Mila and myself to toast our friendship with Ronald and Nancy Reagan. For just as this is a glittering occasion of state, it is also a special one for us. This visit marks the last time we will be under this roof at a state dinner as guests of the Reagans. This is not to say, Ron, that I have no expectation of being here again—[*laughter*]—subject to the approval of the voters in Canada this year or next. And we'll be seeing the Reagans again at the economic summit in Toronto in June. But this is the last of our home-and-home visits, which began in Quebec City in 1985. I believe these annual meetings begun by our two administrations have now become part of the institutional framework of Canada-U.S. relations.

I suppose that too much can be made of special relationships between countries, and too much can probably be made of personal relationships between leaders. I don't think that's the case between these two countries or these two leaders. But the fact is that Canada and the United States are one another's best friends and largest trading partners. It's also a fact that Ronald Reagan and I happened to hit it off at the beginning and have got along ever since. This is not to say that either one of us has ever lost sight of the national interest of his own country, but it has helped us define the mutual interest of both our countries. And often, as we did on one or two issues today, we will disagree while continuing to search for common ground.

Those of us who hold elective office are called politicians. There's no dishonor in that. But I have seen Ronald Reagan, the statesman. I want briefly to speak to that tonight from the perspective of a friend in the eighth year of his Presidency. We're looking tonight at a period in American and world history that will in large measure, when the day is done, be known as the Reagan era. For the first time in almost 30 years an American President is completing two full terms of office.

The Reagan years have been a time of peace and prosperity. There have been moments of great difficulty and regional crisis, but the peace has been preserved. When Ronald Reagan came to this house as President, he was accused of saber rattling. In the event while strengthening Western security, he paved the way for historic arms reductions in the INF agreement and opened the door to strategic arms reductions. This is the legacy of a man of peace.

The forthcoming Moscow summit is a significant opportunity for the further reduction of East-West tensions. And the President goes with the hopes and prayers of all his allies for another successful meeting with General Secretary Gorbachev; for, as the President himself has said, a nuclear war cannot be won and must never be fought.

When Ronald Reagan came to this house, the world was on the brink of the deepest recession in half a century. As he prepares to leave it next January, the United States and Western economies are in their 6th consecutive year of unprecedented recovery and expansion. When he leaves office, his popularity will be undiminished and his place in history secure.

I want to just say, parenthetically, something that happened to me in August of 1987. It was a Sunday, and I was reading the New York Sunday Times. And I was struck by this headline. And here's, I think, a direct quote, though I'm speaking from memory. The quote is, "Reagan's Popularity Plummets To 59 Percent." [*Laughter*] You see, right there, one sees the fundamental difference between Canada and the United States. [*Laughter*] It's language. [*Laughter*] "Plummet" clearly does not mean the same thing in Canada—[*laughter*]—as the United States. Now, what I did that day after I finished reading the Times was, I called the President up. He was at Camp David, and I said, "Did you read the Times?" He said, "Yes, I did." And he didn't sound so enthusiastic. [*Laughter*] I said, "I don't know how to break this to you, but on a good day, Margaret Thatcher, Helmut Kohl, and I together would be happy with 59 percent." [*Laughter*] Look, I'll settle for 39 percent. [*Laughter*]

Every leader of a democracy knows the turbulence and the challenges that free societies exemplify. Every leader worth his salt knows the joys of high accomplishment and the sadness of hopes unfulfilled. But history is usually generous to those who show leadership, who brought prosperity, who strengthened freedom, and who kept the global peace. Ronald Reagan has done these things, while never losing his engaging manner and his warm, good humor.

When you look around this house, you get a sense not only of history but of serenity and continuity and of how much Nancy Reagan has contributed to that. She has brought her own brand of commitment and elegance to the White House. She has brought as well her own sense of public purpose to addressing the tragedy of drug abuse not only in your country but throughout the Western Hemisphere. As a Prime Minister and a head of government, I know something of the pressures and tensions on relationships and families that come with these jobs. And of all the world capitals, nowhere is the curiosity greater and the pressure higher than here in Washington. In this unique and demanding climate, Nancy Reagan has been more than a model of grace; she has demonstrated exemplary qualities of loyalty and resolve, which I believe are to her great credit.

On an occasion such as this, one speaks briefly of the achievements, the agenda between our countries, and I'll be very brief. The agenda is comprehensive, the issues are complex, and the solutions are, as President Kennedy once said in regard to Canada-U.S. relations, "neither easy nor automatic." As for the achievements, there is still work for you, Mr. President, to get the free trade agreement ratified by Congress. This is a tremendous accomplishment—the largest trade agreement ever negotiated between two sovereign countries—and it opens up a world of new possibilities and prosperity for both our peoples on both sides of the border. And one of the reasons we made that agreement is that President Reagan believed in the initiative from the beginning and stayed with it to the end.

Engraved on the mantlepiece of this room, there is a quotation, I believe, from the first occupant of this house. I quote it because it applies to the present occupant of this house: "May none but honest and wise men," President John Adams wrote, "ever rule under this roof." Ronald Reagan has been both honest and wise, and for us and for Canada he has been a good and a valued friend.

Ladies and gentlemen, I ask you to rise as I propose a toast to the President of the United States and Mrs. Reagan: To the President and Mrs. Reagan.

Note: The President spoke at 9:57 p.m. in the State Dining Room at the White House.

Remarks on Signing the Augustus F. Hawkins-Robert T. Stafford Elementary and Secondary School Improvement Amendments of 1988

April 28, 1988

Thank you all very much, and let me get right to the business at hand. Excellence in education is a key to the health and well-being of society. That's why when I came into office in 1981 I brought a mandate from the American people to turn over a new leaf in education, to rededicate ourselves to the highest standards of achievement and excellence in our nation's schools. Over the last 8 years we've made much progress. And working together with Congress; State and local governments; parents; teachers; charitable, religious, and community organizations; and business, we have begun to turn back what our education commission 5 years ago called "a rising tide of mediocrity that threatens our very future as a nation and a people."

Well, we've taken a firm and uncompromising stand against drugs in our nation's schools. We've encouraged a return to basics and common sense in primary and secondary education. And we have shifted authority away from distant Federal bureaucracies and returned it to parents, principals, and school boards.

As Secretary Bennett's report this week makes clear, much remains to be done. We remain, as that earlier commission said, "a nation at risk." But today, more than ever before, the American people, the Federal Government, and the States are working together, and not at cross-purposes. We all have come to realize what is at stake: our standard of living, the cohesiveness and unity of our society, our moral standards, and in short, our future.

The legislation that I'll sign today is a product of that common purpose. H.R. 5, the Augustus F. Hawkins-Robert T. Stafford Elementary and Secondary School Amendments of 1988, reauthorizes and improves a wide variety of Federal programs at the elementary and secondary school level. At the same time, it recognizes a fundamental truth: that the primary responsibility for educating these children lies with the local communities and the States, and not with the Federal Government.

The school improvement act will further this important but supplementary role of the Federal Government in elementary and secondary education. It will extend programs for the disadvantaged and other students with special needs, stimulate education innovation and reform, enhance local control and flexibility, improve program accountability, and focus program benefits on those with the greatest need. I'm pleased to note that the bill reauthorizes the magnet school program and expands parental choice. I'm also pleased to see that the bill amends the Bilingual Education Act in ways that provide greater flexibility to local school districts in the selection of instructional approaches. This administration has struggled for several years to amend Federal bilingual requirements so that we may more effectively teach students English. I'm also pleased that the bill enhances parental involvement in programs for disadvantaged children. Parents are, after all, our first and most important teachers.

These central features of the bill echo the themes that the Vice President, Secretary Bennett, and I have been sounding, and I'm pleased that they received overwhelming bipartisan support in both the House and the Senate. From the beginning, we worked with the Congress, educators, and interested members of the public to ensure legislation that would improve basic education for America's youth. I want to commend the Members of Congress who are here today for their leadership in guiding this bill through the Congress.

I want to note that this bill renames the Guaranteed Student Loan Program after Bob Stafford. Bob has had a major influence on Federal education policy for many years, and I commend him on his distinguished career.

I urge the Congress to focus in the appropriations process on the existing, successful programs that this bill reauthorizes. It is these current programs that offer the greatest promise of educational opportunity and educational excellence to our nation's children.

H.R. 5 also contains provisions making "Dial-A-Porn" services a criminal misdemeanor. I commend Congress for joining the administration's longstanding efforts to combat hardcore obscenity. I am bound to note, however, as much as it displeases me, that current Supreme Court jurisprudence is unfriendly to parts of this bill. And I hope that the courts and the Congress will work with the administration to do as much as is permitted by the Constitution to enforce the provisions of this statute.

On balance, H.R. 5 is a solid achievement, one that deserves to be signed, which I am about to do right now.

[*At this point, the President signed the bill.*]

Now I'm going to do what the little 11-year-old girl told me to do in a letter that she wrote to me when I first reported here for duty. She told me all the things I was going to have to deal with and then said, "Now get over to the Oval Office and go to work." [*Laughter*]

Note: The President spoke at 1:39 p.m. in Room 450 of the Old Executive Office Building. H.R. 5, approved April 28, was assigned Public Law No. 100–297.

Nomination of Charles A. Gargano To Be United States Ambassador to Trinidad and Tobago
April 28, 1988

The President today announced his intention to nominate Charles A. Gargano to be Ambassador to the Republic of Trinidad and Tobago. He would succeed Sheldon J. Krys.

Since 1984 Mr. Gargano has been the president of G.M. Development, Inc., in Islip, NY. Prior to this he was vice president and general supervisor of construction and engineering for J.D. Posillico, Inc., 1983–1984. Previously, he was Deputy Administrator at the Department of Transportation for the Urban Mass Transportation Administration, 1981–1983; vice president and general supervisor of construction and engineering for J.D. Posillico, Inc., 1963–1981; and a construction engineer for John Oeschlin, Inc., 1961–1963.

Mr. Gargano graduated from Farleigh Dickinson University (B.S., 1976; M.B.A., 1977). He was born October 28, 1934, in Avellino, Italy. Mr. Gargano is married, has two children, and resides in Dix Hills, NY.

Appointment of Allan H. Meltzer as a Member of the President's Economic Policy Advisory Board
April 28, 1988

The President today announced his intention to appoint Allan H. Meltzer to be a member of the President's Economic Policy Advisory Board. This is an initial appointment.

Since 1957 Dr. Meltzer has been a professor at Carnegie-Mellon University in Pittsburgh, PA, and since 1980 he has been a John M. Olin Professor of Political Economy and Public Policy at Carnegie-Mellon. He has been a visiting professor at Harvard University, the University of Chicago, the University of Rochester, the Yugoslav Institute for Economic Research, the Austrian Institute for Advanced Study, the Getulio Vargas Foundation in Rio de Janeiro, and the City University, London. Dr. Meltzer also is an author of several books, and his writings have appeared in numerous journals.

Dr. Meltzer graduated from Duke University (A.B., 1948) and the University of California, Los Angeles (M.A., 1955; Ph.D., 1958). He was born February 6, 1928, in Boston, MA. He is married, has three children, and resides in Pittsburgh.

Appointment of John C. Howard, Jr., as a Member of the National Commission on Agricultural Policy
April 28, 1988

The President today announced his intention to appoint John C. Howard, Jr., to be a member of the National Commission on Agricultural Policy. This is a new position.

Since 1962 Mr. Howard has been the owner-manager of J.C. Howard Farms and J.C. Howard Grain Co. in Deep Run, NC. He is currently serving on the North Carolina Board of Agriculture.

Mr. Howard graduated from North Carolina State University (B.S., 1962). He was born May 29, 1941, in Lenoir, NC. He is married, has four children, and resides in Deep Run, NC.

Nomination of Helmuth J. Naumer To Be a Member of the National Museum Services Board
April 28, 1988

The President today announced his intention to nominate Helmuth J. Naumer to be a member of the National Museum Services Board, National Foundation on the Arts and the Humanities, for a term expiring December 6, 1992. He would succeed Donald Moncrief Muchmore.

Since 1987 Mr. Naumer has been director of the Office of Cultural Affairs for the State of New Mexico and has served as president of the Museum of New Mexico Foundation since 1986. Prior to this, he was president of the San Antonio Museum Association, 1979–1986; executive director of the Pacific Science Center Foundation, 1976–1979; and executive director of the Fort Worth Museum of Science and History, 1962–1976.

Mr. Naumer graduated from the University of New Mexico (B.A., 1957). He was born May 7, 1934, in Santa Fe, NM, and currently resides in Santa Fe.

Executive Order 12638—Delegation of Functions Relating to the Implementation of the Inter-American Convention on Letters Rogatory and Additional Protocol

April 28, 1988

On October 9, 1986, the Senate gave its advice and consent to ratification of the Inter-American Convention on Letters Rogatory and Additional Protocol. The instrument of ratification was signed by the President on November 10, 1986. The Convention and Additional Protocol require that contracting states designate central authorities to give effect to the Convention's provisions.

In order that the Government of the United States of America may give full and complete effect to the Convention and Additional Protocol, it is expedient and necessary that the Department of Justice perform certain functions.

Now, Therefore, by virtue of the authority vested in me by section 301 of Title 3 of the United States Code and as President of the United States of America, it is ordered as follows:

Section 1. Designation of United States Central Authority. The Department of Justice is designated as the Central Authority to transmit and process letters rogatory and to otherwise proceed in conformity with applicable provisions of the Convention and Additional Protocol.

Sec. 2. Additional Designations. The Department of Justice is authorized to make additional designations provided for in the Convention and Additional Protocol.

RONALD REAGAN

The White House,
April 28, 1988.

[*Filed with the Office of the Federal Register, 12:20 p.m., April 29, 1988*]

Proclamation 5802—National Child Abuse Prevention Month, 1988

April 28, 1988

By the President of the United States of America

A Proclamation

All Americans have great reason to regret and to seek to repair the alarming incidence and prevalence of child abuse and neglect that continue throughout our country. Each year many American children suffer child abuse, and every year many perish in these attacks. The incidence of child abuse and neglect cuts across every income level and geographic area in our land.

This tragic situation is unacceptable—and preventable. Dedicated individuals, private and civic groups, and government bodies are doing much to protect children, but, unfortunately, much remains to be achieved. Caring for children is, of course, the responsibility of parents; but neighbors, relatives, and friends must help protect children when parents or others attack or neglect them. We will truly prevent child abuse and protect our youngsters only to the extent that we cherish children as gifts from our Creator; foster deep and abiding reverence for the innocence and the God-given individual dignity and worth of every child; and treasure the sanctity of every human life.

It is in this spirit that we must assure America's children a loving, safe, and healthful environment. The members of professions, such as law enforcement, social work, church, medicine, mental health, and education, must continue to do their part, as must concerned individuals. Let all Americans reflect on our obligation to children and to families, and then let us put our compassion into action.

The Congress, by Senate Joint Resolution 246, has designated April 1988 as "National Child Abuse Prevention Month" and has authorized and requested the President to issue a proclamation in observance of this event.

Now, Therefore, I, Ronald Reagan, President of the United States of America, do hereby proclaim April 1988 as National Child Abuse Prevention Month. As we observe this time, let us all consider our responsibility for the wholesome and secure development of our children.

In Witness Whereof, I have hereunto set my hand this twenty-eighth day of April, in the year of our Lord nineteen hundred and eighty-eight, and of the Independence of the United States of America the two hundred and twelfth.

RONALD REAGAN

[*Filed with the Office of the Federal Register, 12:19 p.m., April 29, 1988*]

Proclamation 5803—Loyalty Day, 1988
April 28, 1988

By the President of the United States of America

A Proclamation

Loyalty Day, May 1, is a day we set aside to promise allegiance to our country; to revere our heritage of individual freedom, limited government, and respect for every man's divinely bestowed dignity; and to reaffirm our sacred trust to preserve, for our children and for all generations to come, this blessed land of liberty we call America.

We Americans have both pledged and practiced loyalty from the moment the first patriots conceived the idea of a new and independent Nation where only freedom would reign—where people would live as free as God made them and where tyranny alone would never find welcome. We have given our loyalty generously, in times of peace and times of peril. That we will always do, God willing.

Loyalty Day says much about the meaning of our country. In other parts of the world, as we know, totalitarian states proclaim May 1 a day of fealty and require a show of loyalty from the people. No such demand is needed here, of course, because in America we are blessed to be able to govern ourselves; "We the People" are in charge, and we need give our loyalty not to self-appointed rulers but to liberty.

The self-government that protects our rights and liberties has been won and defended in each generation by loyal Americans. That remains true, of course, of our gallant service men and women at home and in a hundred foreign climes. It is true as well of every American in home or office, in factory or farm, in hall of government or place of worship, who calls upon the Author of Liberty to guide and bless our land; of every citizen who cherishes brotherhood and patriotism; of every boy and girl who begins the day with the Pledge of Allegiance to the Flag.

The allegiance we Americans owe, and give gladly, on Loyalty Day and throughout our lives, is to a land and an ideal that beckon human hearts today just as always, here and around the globe—the land of the free, where the only command and the only loyalty are freedom's way and freedom's sway.

To foster loyalty and love of country, the Congress, by joint resolution approved July 18, 1958 (72 Stat. 369; 36 U.S.C. 162), has designated May 1 of each year as "Loyalty Day."

Now, Therefore, I, Ronald Reagan, President of the United States of America, do hereby proclaim May 1, 1988, as Loyalty Day, and I call upon all Americans and patriotic, civic, fraternal, and educational organizations to observe that day with appropriate ceremonies. I also call upon all government officials to display the flag of the United States on all government buildings and grounds on that day.

In Witness Whereof, I have hereunto set my hand this twenty-eighth day of April, in the year of our Lord nineteen hundred and eighty-eight, and of the Independence of the United States of America the two hundred and twelfth.

RONALD REAGAN

[*Filed with the Office of the Federal Register, 12:17 p.m., April 29, 1988*]

Remarks on Presenting the Congressional Gold Medal to Lady Bird Johnson

April 28, 1988

The President. Thank you all very much, and welcome to the White House. Or should I say that for all of us—here at the White House and on Capitol Hill—welcome back, Lady Bird, it's good to have you home. [*Laughter*]

Mrs. Johnson. Thank you, sir.

The President. Some of the duties that come with this job of being President are more enjoyable than others, but nothing could give me more pleasure than honoring one of our finest First Ladies with the Congressional Gold Medal.

I would bet that not 1 American in 10 could tell you who Claudia Alta Johnson is—[*laughter*]—but the whole Nation came to love, admire, and respect Lady Bird Johnson, as she was her husband's most important aide, and he served his country for 7 years here in the White House. When she first met L.B.J., then a former schoolteacher and executive secretary to Congressman Kleberg in Austin, Lady Bird said, and I'll quote, "I knew I'd met something remarkable, but I didn't know quite what." [*Laughter*] Well, it didn't take Lyndon long to figure out what we all came to know later—that he'd met someone quite remarkable, too—because he proposed to her on the second date.

Sam Rayburn, L.B.J.'s political mentor, said that marrying Lady Bird was the best thing Lyndon had ever done, and though his career and his Presidency were filled with many momentous achievements, I think we'd all have to agree. As skilled businesswoman, unofficial diplomat and spokesman for America, regent for the University of Texas—Lady Bird has had an impressive career in her own right. Her concern for the poor and underprivileged helped inspire a nation. Her efforts to beautify America, continuing up to today, still blossom in our Nation's Capital and beside our nation's highways.

In 1941, when L.B.J. was in Congress, the Johnsons were invited to a reception at the White House; and Lady Bird wrote in her diary afterwards, "I went to my first—will it be my last and only—dinner at the White House!" [*Laughter*] There were probably times in later years when you were the hostess of your umpteenth state dinner at the White House, when you wished it had been your last. [*Laughter*] But few First Ladies have carried off their unofficial, but, as I can attest, essential roles with more energy and dedication than you. As you once said, the First Lady is elected by a constituency of one, and there's no doubt that the best candidate won. [*Laughter*]

It certainly took a strong-willed First Lady to complement a President few would ever have called a milquetoast. [*Laughter*] "Earthy" is more often the adjective used. I remember one story of the time that L.B.J. was speaking to a group in North Carolina, and after about 50 minutes, the audience became restless. Lady Bird wrote a note on a piece of paper saying "close soon" and slipped it to him. [*Laughter*] L.B.J. took it, held it up, and read it aloud to the audience. [*Laughter*] And then, after the laughter died down, he continued with his speech. [*Laughter*]

Well, before someone hands me a note, I

will close these remarks, simply saying that it gives me the greatest pleasure to present Claudia Alta Johnson with this special gold medal.

Mrs. Johnson. Mr. President, Mrs. Reagan, I know very well how gracious and generous this is of you in your busy, demanding lives to give this time to make this such a great day for me and my family and many of my friends. And I also think what it really means is a salute to all those people all over this great land who are working to preserve and to enhance the natural beauty of America. I thank you.

The President. Now, we're going to slip out the way we came in, all of us, and then when they release you we will have a chance to see and greet each one of you individually right down here in the hall. So, we shall be saying hello in just a few minutes.

Note: The President spoke at 5:05 p.m. in the East Room at the White House. After the ceremony, the President hosted a reception for Mrs. Johnson in the Residence.

Statement on Signing the Big Cypress National Preserve Addition Act

April 29, 1988

I have today approved S. 90, the "Big Cypress National Preserve Addition Act," with the understanding that additional legislation will be forthcoming this year to provide for Federal acquisition of the private land to be added to the Preserve through a land exchange, which would eliminate any direct cost to the Federal government of expanding the Preserve.

S. 90 amends the Act that established the Big Cypress National Preserve in Florida by adding 146,000 acres of private land to the 575,000-acre Preserve. It requires the acquisition of the surface rights to these lands through a joint Federal-State effort in connection with the planned construction of Interstate Highway 75 through the area.

The cost of the Department of the Interior for purchasing the surface rights to these lands under the provisions of S. 90 would require $40 to $65 million in new appropriations. The Administration has consistently advised the Congress that this cost is excessive and will oppose any appropriations for this purpose. To avoid this cost, and in recognition of the important role of the Big Cypress National Preserve in conserving nationally significant fish, wildlife, and other natural resources in southern Florida, the Department of the Interior has entered negotiations to acquire the private land to be added to the Preserve through an exchange with the private landowners.

Such an exchange would require additional legislation, since the lands involved are in different States. I have been assured by the congressional delegation from Florida that legislation approving the Administration's exchange proposal will soon be considered by the Congress. I urge prompt passage of such legislation, which will not only provide the same protection that S. 90 provides, but also will generate Federal receipts of nearly $35 million resulting from the exchange.

RONALD REAGAN

The White House,
April 29, 1988.

Note: S. 90, approved April 29, was assigned Public Law No. 100–301.

Proclamation 5804—National Arbor Day, 1988
April 29, 1988

By the President of the United States of America

A Proclamation

"He who plants a tree / Plants a hope," wrote Lucy Larcom years ago in her poem, "Plant a Tree"; that thought has surely motivated every American who has ever celebrated Arbor Day, given his neighborhood and Nation the lovely and lasting gift of trees, or sought to conserve our natural forest heritage. In this spirit we can all join in observing an Arbor Day in which we resolve to renew and expand our knowledge of and appreciation for trees and our understanding of the importance of trees and forests to our country and to the entire world.

In the last century, Americans began to realize the wisdom and the necessity of replenishing our supply of trees for their many natural benefits and so that our use of wood for fuel, lumber, and other products would not impoverish future generations. The idea of Arbor Day caught the imagination of many people; for example, on the first Arbor Day, in Nebraska in 1872, citizens of that State planted a million trees, and they added about 350 million more in the next 16 years.

This tradition continues, on Arbor Day and every day; we Americans have planted more trees each year for the last 6 years, and last year's total acreage of trees planted was a record. Arbor Day remains a time for planting and caring for trees in our cities, towns, and countryside, and it should also remind us to learn more about trees and forests and how to protect them at home and guard against desertification and destruction abroad.

Our celebration of Arbor Day should always be tinged with the spirit that the 19th-century poet Henry Cuyler Bunner captured so well in "The Heart of the Tree":

What does he plant who plants a tree?
  He plants, in sap and leaf and wood,
  In love of home and loyalty
And far-cast thought of civic good—
His blessings on the neighborhood
  Who in the hollow of His hand
  Holds all the growth of all our land—
A nation's growth from sea to sea
Stirs in his heart who plants a tree.

The Congress, by Senate Joint Resolution 247, has recognized the last Friday of April 1988 as "National Arbor Day" and has authorized and requested the President to issue a proclamation in observance of this day.

Now, Therefore, I, Ronald Reagan, President of the United States of America, do hereby proclaim Friday, April 29, 1988, as National Arbor Day. I call upon the people of the United States to observe this day with appropriate programs, ceremonies, and activities.

In Witness Whereof, I have hereunto set my hand this twenty-ninth day of April, in the year of our Lord nineteen hundred and eighty-eight, and of the Independence of the United States of America the two hundred and twelfth.

RONALD REAGAN

[*Filed with the Office of the Federal Register, 4:44 p.m., April 29, 1988*]

Letter to the Speaker of the House of Representatives and the President of the Senate Reporting on the National Emergency With Respect to Nicaragua

April 29, 1988

Dear Mr. Speaker: (Dear Mr. President:)

I hereby report to the Congress on developments since my last report of October 30, 1987, concerning the national emergency with respect to Nicaragua that was declared in Executive Order No. 12513 of May 1, 1985. In that Order, I prohibited: (1) all imports into the United States of goods and services of Nicaraguan origin; (2) all exports from the United States of goods to or destined for Nicaragua except those destined for the organized democratic resistance; (3) Nicaraguan air carriers from engaging in air transportation to or from points in the United States; and (4) vessels of Nicaraguan registry from entering U.S. ports.

1. The declaring of emergency was made pursuant to the authority vested in me as President by the Constitution and laws of the United States, including the International Emergency Economic Powers Act, 50 U.S.C. 1701 *et seq.,* and the National Emergencies Act, 50 U.S.C. 1641 *et seq.* This report is submitted pursuant to 50 U.S.C. 1641(c) and 1703(c).

2. The Office of Foreign Assets Control (FAC) of the Department of the Treasury issued the Nicaraguan Trade Control Regulations effective May 7, 1985, implementing the prohibitions in Executive Order No. 12513, 50 Fed. Reg. 19890 (May 10, 1985). There have been no changes in those regulations in the past 6 months.

3. Since my report of October 30, 1987, fewer than 70 applications for licenses have been received with respect to Nicaragua, and the majority of these applications have been granted. Of the licenses issued in this period, most either authorized exports for humanitarian purposes, covering medical supplies and animal vaccines, or extended authorizations previously given to acquire intellectual property protection under Nicaraguan law. Certain licenses authorized the exportation of equipment to *La Prensa,* an opposition publication that had been shut down by the Sandinista regime for a period of time. The FAC's director testified at a congressional hearing concerning FAC's licensing policy with respect to humanitarian donations to Nicaragua. Food, medicine, and clothing donated to relieve human suffering are exempt from the embargo, and Treasury and State have established guidelines for the licensing of donations of other goods.

4. Since my last report it has come to my attention that the Department of the Treasury has completed the following enforcement actions: (a) late in 1987, a U.S. aviation company paid $80,000 as the initial installment of $300,000 in civil and criminal penalties imposed pursuant to a negotiated plea agreement for the exportation of cargo aircraft and spare parts to Nicaragua via Panama; (b) a Canadian corporation paid a fine of $3,840 for the attempted importation of 25 cases of Nicaraguan frozen lobster tails into the United States; and (c) on January 26, 1988, a 15-count indictment was returned by a Federal Grand Jury in Miami, Florida, against four codefendants for the operation of Nicaraguan front companies that provided over $1 million in computers and other commodities to the Central Bank of Nicaragua via Panama.

5. The trade sanctions complement the diplomatic and other aspects of our policy toward Nicaragua. The deteriorating economic situation in Nicaragua was one of the principal reasons for the Sandinistas' pledge to meet the democratization and national reconciliation provisions of the Guatemala Accord (also known as the Arias Peace Plan) and to sign a preliminary cease-fire agreement with the Nicaraguan Resistance on March 23. It is essential that pressure be maintained to induce the Sandinistas to undertake serious and productive dialogue concerning a permanent cease-fire with the Nicaraguan Resistance and with all democratic opposition groups concerning democratization in Nicaragua. The trade sanctions

are part of a larger policy seeking a democratic outcome in Nicaragua by peaceful means.

6. The expenses incurred by the Federal Government in the period from November 1, 1987, through April 30, 1988, that are directly attributable to the exercise of powers and authorities conferred by the declaration of the Nicaraguan national emergency are estimated at $190,079, all of which represents wage and salary costs for Federal personnel. Personnel costs were largely centered in the Department of the Treasury (particularly in the Customs Service, as well as in FAC and the Office of the General Counsel), with expenses also incurred by the Department of State and the National Security Council.

7. The policies and actions of the Government of Nicaragua continue to pose an unusual and extraordinary threat to the national security and foreign policy of the United States. I shall continue to exercise the powers at my disposal to apply economic sanctions against Nicaragua as long as these measures are appropriate and will continue to report periodically to the Congress on expenses and significant developments pursuant to 50 U.S.C. 1641(c) and 1703(c).

Sincerely,

RONALD REAGAN

Note: Identical letters were sent to Jim Wright, Speaker of the House of Representatives, and George Bush, President of the Senate.

Proclamation 5805—Amending the Generalized System of Preferences

April 29, 1988

By the President of the United States of America

A Proclamation

1. Pursuant to subsections 501(1) and (4), 502(c)(2), and sections 504 and 604 of the Trade Act of 1974, as amended (the Trade Act) (19 U.S.C. 2461(1) and (4), 2462(c)(2), 2464, and 2483), I have determined that it is appropriate to terminate the preferential tariff treatment under the Generalized System of Preferences (GSP) for articles that are currently eligible for such treatment and that are imported from Hong Kong, the Republic of Korea, Singapore, and Taiwan. I have determined that these countries are sufficiently advanced in economic development and improved in trade competitiveness that continued preferential treatment under the GSP is not warranted.

2. Subsections 501(1) and (4) of the Trade Act provide that, in affording duty-free treatment under the GSP, the President shall have due regard for the effect such action will have on furthering the economic development of developing countries and the extent of the beneficiary developing country's competitiveness with respect to eligible articles. Subsection 502(c)(2) provides that, in determining whether to designate any country a beneficiary developing country under this section, the President shall take into account the level of economic development of such country. Section 504 authorizes the President to withdraw, suspend, or limit the application of duty-free treatment under the GSP with respect to any article or to any country upon consideration of the factors set forth in sections 501 and 502(c) of the Trade Act.

3. Pursuant to subsection 504(f) of the Trade Act (19 U.S.C. 2464(f)), I have determined that it is appropriate to terminate the preferential tariff treatment under the GSP for articles that are currently eligible for such treatment and that are imported from Bahrain, Bermuda, Brunei Darussalam, and Nauru. Such termination is the result of my determination that the per capita gross national product for each such country for calendar year 1985 (calculated on the basis of the best available informa-

tion, including that of the World Bank) exceeds the applicable limit provided in subsection 504(f).

4. Subsection 504(f) provides that if the President determines that the per capita gross national product (calculated on the basis of the best available information, including that of the World Bank) for any beneficiary country for a calendar year subsequent to 1984 exceeds the applicable limit for the determination year in question, such country shall not be treated as a beneficiary developing country under this Act after the close of a 2-year period.

5. Previously, two of these countries, Brunei Darussalam and Singapore, were designated as members of an association of countries treated as one country for purposes of section 503(b)(2) of the Trade Act, as amended (19 U.S.C. 2463(b)(2)). In order to take into account the termination of benefits under the GSP for articles imported from these two countries, I have determined that it is appropriate to terminate the designations of Brunei Darussalam and Singapore as members of ASEAN and to modify general headnote 3(e)(v)(A) to the Tariff Schedules of the United States (TSUS) (19 U.S.C. 1202) to reflect such termination. Further, in order to reflect the termination of benefits under the GSP for articles imported from Hong Kong, the Republic of Korea, Singapore, and Taiwan, I have determined that it is appropriate to delete from general headnote 3(e)(v)(D) to the TSUS and from the pertinent TSUS items all references to particular products of these countries which are currently excluded from preferential tariff treatment under the GSP.

6. Section 604 of the Trade Act authorizes the President to embody in the TSUS the substance of the relevant provisions of that Act, of other acts affecting import treatment, and of actions taken thereunder.

Now, Therefore, I, Ronald Reagan, President of the United States of America, acting under the authority vested in me by the Constitution and laws of the United States of America, including but not limited to Title V and section 604 of the Trade Act, do proclaim that:

(1) General headnote 3(e)(v)(A) to the TSUS, setting forth those countries whose products are eligible for duty-free treatment under the GSP, is modified—

(a) by deleting "Bahrain", "Brunei Darussalam", and "Nauru" from the enumeration of independent countries, by deleting "Bermuda" from the enumeration of non-independent countries and territories, and by deleting "Brunei" from the enumeration of members of the Association of South East Asian Nations (ASEAN) and by inserting "except Brunei Darussalam" after "Association of South East Asian Nations (ASEAN)"; and

(b) by deleting "Korea, Republic of", "Singapore", and "Taiwan" from the enumeration of independent countries and by deleting "Hong Kong" from the enumeration of nonindependent countries and territories, by deleting "Singapore" from the enumeration of members of the Association of South East Asian Nations (ASEAN) except Brunei Darussalam, and by modifying "Association of South East Asian Nations (ASEAN) except Brunei Darussalam" to read "Association of South East Asian Nations (ASEAN) except Brunei Darussalam and Singapore".

(2) No article the product of any such country and imported into the United States after the effective dates of this Proclamation shall be eligible for preferential tariff treatment under the GSP.

(3) General headnote 3(e)(v)(D) to the TSUS, listing those articles that are eligible for benefits of the GSP except when imported from the beneficiary countries listed opposite the enumerated TSUS items for those articles, is modified as provided in Annex I to this Proclamation.

(4) The Rates of Duty Special column for each of the TSUS items enumerated in Annex II to this Proclamation is modified: (a) by deleting from such column for such TSUS items the symbol "A*" in parentheses, and (b) by inserting in such column the symbol "A" in lieu thereof.

(5) (a) Paragraph (1)(a) of this Proclamation shall be effective with respect to articles entered, or withdrawn from warehouse for consumption, on or after July 1, 1988.

(b) Paragraphs (1)(b), (3), and (4) of this Proclamation shall be effective with respect to articles entered, or withdrawn from warehouse for consumption, on or after January 1, 1989.

In Witness Whereof, I have hereunto set my hand this twenty-ninth day of April, in the year of our Lord nineteen hundred and eighty-eight, and of the Independence of the United States of America the two hundred and twelfth.

RONALD REAGAN

[Filed with the Office of the Federal Register, 2:14 p.m., May 2, 1988]

Note: The annexes to the proclamation were printed in the "Federal Register" of May 4.

Letter to the Speaker of the House of Representatives and the President of the Senate on Amendments to the Generalized System of Preferences

April 29, 1988

Dear Mr. Speaker: (Dear Mr. President:)

I am writing to notify you of my intent to remove certain countries from beneficiary status under the Generalized System of Preferences (GSP). I am also modifying my January 29, 1988, notification to the Congress on the GSP program. The GSP program is authorized by the Trade Act of 1974, as amended ("the Act").

On May 19, 1987, I determined that the 1985 per capita gross national product (GNP) of Brunei Darussalam, Bermuda, Bahrain, and Nauru had exceeded the maximum level permissible under section 504(f) of the Act. Therefore, I intend to terminate the beneficiary status of these four countries. My decision will take effect on July 1, 1988.

With regard to my January 29, 1988, notification to the Congress concerning my decision to graduate Taiwan, the Republic of Korea, Hong Kong, and Singapore from the GSP program on January 2, 1989, the effective date of graduation has been changed to January 1, 1989.

Sincerely,

RONALD REAGAN

Note: Identical letters were sent to Jim Wright, Speaker of the House of Representatives, and George Bush, President of the Senate.

Letter to the Speaker of the House of Representatives and the President of the Senate Transmitting the District of Columbia Budget

April 29, 1988

Dear Mr. Speaker: (Dear Mr. President:)

In accordance with the District of Columbia Self-Government and Governmental Reorganization Act, I am transmitting the District of Columbia Government's Fiscal Year 1989 Budget and Fiscal Year 1988 Budget supplemental.

There are two issues that affect both the Fiscal Year 1989 Budget submitted to the Congress on February 18, 1988, and the Fiscal Year 1989 Budget of the District of Columbia Government. First, I want to reaffirm my concern that none of the funds appropriated for the District of Columbia, including locally generated funds, should be used for abortion unless the life of the mother would be physically endangered if the fetus were carried to term. Accordingly, the District of Columbia Budget that I am hereby submitting goes beyond the current Section 117 of the District of Columbia Budget in that it restricts the use of both the District's Federal and locally generated funds for abortion.

Secondly, I request your support for the initiative in the Fiscal Year 1989 Budget that requires the District Government to bill Federal establishments directly for the water and sewer services provided. The District has had the technical capacity to bill individual Federal establishments since Fiscal Year 1985. The Fiscal Year 1989 Budget proposal to have Federal establishments make their water and sewer payments directly to the District Government will only treat the District like other State and local governments, which bill Federal agencies directly for these services. This direct billing will achieve better efficiency and accountability for services rendered. Thus, it is unnecessary for the Fiscal Year 1989 Budget to include a separate lump-sum amount in the Federal payment to the District of Columbia for water and sewer services provided. I urge the Congress to enact this needed reform in order to avoid the experience of the 1988 Continuing Resolution where the Congress increased the deficit unnecessarily by adding $32.6 million to the requested Federal payment when many Federal agencies already had sufficient funds to pay the District directly. To address previous congressional concerns about the District's ability to bill Federal establishments directly, I am submitting legislation that specifically authorizes the District to bill Federal agencies directly.

Sincerely,

RONALD REAGAN

Note: Identical letters were sent to Jim Wright, Speaker of the House of Representatives, and George Bush, President of the Senate.

Proclamation 5806—National Trauma Awareness Month, 1988
April 29, 1988

By the President of the United States of America

A Proclamation

We can do a great deal of good for ourselves and our fellow Americans the more we realize the toll traumatic injury takes each year in our country—and the more we understand that the extent of this toll is unnecessary, unacceptable, and preventable. National Trauma Awareness Month is an excellent chance for all of us to learn and to do more about the prevention and treatment of traumatic injury.

Traumatic injury is a major public health problem that mainly affects young people; it kills more Americans before age 34 than do all diseases combined. Each year, some 140,000 citizens lose their lives to traumatic injury, and 400,000 suffer severe and often permanently disabling brain or spinal cord injury. Some of the many causes include motor vehicle-related injuries, murder, suicide, and falls.

It is up to all of us to learn how to reduce the risk of traumatic injury to ourselves and our children. Citizens can initiate behavior changes and sustain them, and volunteer groups, civic organizations, private businesses, health care providers, researchers, academia, and government can all help discover and implement new and more effective ways of preventing and treating traumatic injury and of assisting victims and their families. Let us always remember that our efforts in this regard will be a blessing to ourselves, our families, and our neighbors.

The Congress, by House Joint Resolution 373, has designated May 1988 as "National Trauma Awareness Month" and authorized and requested the President to issue a proclamation in observance of this occasion.

Now, Therefore, I, Ronald Reagan, President of the United States of America, do hereby proclaim the month of May 1988 as National Trauma Awareness Month. I urge the people of the United States to observe this month with appropriate ceremonies and activities.

In Witness Whereof, I have hereunto set my hand this twenty-ninth day of April, in the year of our Lord nineteen hundred and eighty-eight, and of the Independence of the United States of America the two hundred and twelfth.

RONALD REAGAN

[*Filed with the Office of the Federal Register, 2:15 p.m., May 2, 1988*]

Message on the Observance of National Nurses Week, May 1–7, 1988
April 29, 1988

I am delighted to send warmest greetings to everyone celebrating National Nurses Week, especially to America's dedicated corps of nursing professionals.

One has only to imagine for a moment a world without nurses to realize how vital their services are. In hospitals and ambulatory settings, in the inner city, in rural and metropolitan communities, in homes and on military posts—wherever a need exists—nurses are there working diligently to serve and to protect the health of our people. It's not an easy task. Nurses work all hours and long hours, respond to shortages of nursing personnel, and face many other adverse conditions.

No medical staff person spends more time with individual patients than nurses do. In addition to their technical skills, they must bring to their duty stations a generous dose of compassion in dealing with patients who are severely ill and in need not only of constant care but also of emotional support and encouragement. To perform their tasks in a rapidly changing scientific environment, nurses must continually study to keep abreast of developments in the health care field.

Nurses have responded to these challenges with the highest commitment to excellence, helping make all of us the beneficiaries of the finest health care in the world. For this they deserve our profound gratitude and respect.

Nancy and I gladly salute our Nation's nurses during this special week of recognition. God bless you.

RONALD REAGAN

Radio Address to the Nation on Free and Fair Trade
April 30, 1988

My fellow Americans:

This week in Washington, trade was the talk of the town, and important talk it was. I've often mentioned trade issues in these broadcasts. And with your help during these last few years, we've been able to resist attempts to block free and fair trade. It hasn't been easy, because not a few politicians still think the way to reelection is to portray themselves as the great friend of the American worker by pushing protectionism. It's been up to us to point out that over the long run this approach halts growth and costs jobs, but as I say, with your help this message has gotten through.

Believe me, this ability to resist protectionism—along with our commitment to lower taxes, less spending, and fewer regulations—has made a huge difference in all of our lives. I don't think any of us can easily forget that sense of desperation Americans felt a few years ago as they saw inflation driving the weekly grocery bill up and up, the value of their savings shrinking, jobs growing increasingly scarce, and economic growth going down to virtually nothing. Well, all that's been changed around.

Just this week, Beryl Sprinkel, the head of my Council of Economic Advisers, went down to the White House briefing room to deliver this quarterly report on the state of the economy. Some experts, who had noted we're in the 65th month of our economic expansion, were saying a slowdown was inevitable, and others, noting last October's stock market plunge, made dire predictions about what the economy was going to do in the first quarter of this year. But the results were exactly what we had hoped for and, in fact, what we had predicted: The economy is moving along at a moderate rate of growth, and inflation is well under control.

My fellow Americans, I remember only too well working in 1981 on my first televised speech describing "the worst economic mess since the Great Depression" and wondering even then how long it would take us to repair the damage. Well, thanks to the dynamics of less government and more free markets, the damage has been repaired—and repaired much faster than anyone could have originally hoped. And that's why I'm certain you don't want me or Congress taking any risks with this progress. And that's also why I've made it clear that I'm going to be very severe with any trade legislation coming out of Congress that threatens America's prosperity.

For the last year, we've all been working on a trade bill here, one that initially contained many objectionable provisions. Working with Members of Congress, we managed to remove almost all of these bad provisions. Unfortunately, however, when it comes to safeguarding prosperity, almost can never be good enough. The current legislation, despite all the hard work, still has provisions that threaten economic growth. These provisions are comprised mainly of demands for unnecessary, burdensome, and costly regulation of private industry. Provisions range from rules on plant closing notifications to restrictions on exports. Unfortunately, these provisions serve the special interests and not the Nation's interests. They would reduce the flexibility of our economy and render us less able to respond to the realities of the international marketplace. In short, they would make us less competitive, not more.

This bill did pass the Congress this week, but the good news is the vote showed we have the strength to sustain a Presidential veto. And you can be sure that this bill is going to get a veto, but fast. And then all Congress has to do is drop the ruffles, frills, and flourishes put there for the special interests, and we can have a trade bill, and have it soon. As I have stated repeatedly, I want a trade bill and will work vigorously to secure one. I urge the congressional leadership to schedule prompt action on a bill immediately after my veto is sustained. It is time to set aside the special interests and advance America's interests by passing trade legislation that will assist, not impede, our dynamic economy.

In the meantime, I'm delighted to tell you that there was some good news on trade this week. Prime Minister Mulroney of Canada was in town, and we discussed our two nations' pending agreement on an historic free trade zone between the United States and Canada. This is the kind of trade legislation we need—legislation that promotes growth and prosperity and keeps America away from the protectionism that once cost the world and our country so much.

Until next week, thanks for listening, and God bless you.

Note: The President spoke at 12:06 p.m. from the Oval Office at the White House.

Remarks at the Annual Meeting of the United States Chamber of Commerce
May 2, 1988

Thank you very much, and thank you, Ed Donley. And a special thank you to Vice Chairman and Chairman-to-be Bill Kanaga and to President Dick Lesher. And to Chairman Ollie Delchamps—and I hope he's listening in—let me say, get well soon, Ollie. We all want to see you back in the saddle and riding tall. And a thank you to my favorite rock group. [*Laughter*]

You know, looking around at you who've been both generals and soldiers in the crusade we brought to Washington years ago, it reminds me of an old Hollywood story. I know you're shocked to hear that. [*Laughter*] Anyway, it was on the evening in 1939 when "Gone with the Wind" premiered. And that first showing was in Atlanta, and Margaret Mitchell, the author of the book, sat next to Clark Gable. And it came to the famous scene in which Scarlett O'Hara is nursing what looks like a single wounded soldier, and the camera pulls back and reveals thousands of Confederate troops, many also injured. And as those thousands appeared on the screen, Gable heard a little gasp next to him. And Mitchell leaned over to him and whispered, "My Lord, Mr. Gable, if we'd had as many soldiers as that, we'd have won the war." [*Laughter*]

Well, looking at all of you, I know why we've won so much of our war these last few years. When the history of our time is recorded, I believe that you, the members of the United States Chamber of Commerce, will occupy a place that few can match. I've heard talk over the years about a Reagan revolution, but in many ways I believe it would be better to call what we've done your revolution. You gave us your drive. You gave us your support. And let me say to two personal heroes of mine, Dick Lesher and Richard Rahn [vice president of the chamber]—and I know everyone here will second this—for 8 years here in Washington you have given us energy, wisdom, intellect, and leadership, and that's why we've come so far. The victory ribbons on your regimental colors read like a list of the great legislative battles over economic policy in this decade: Gramm-Latta, Kemp-Roth, Gramm-Rudman-Hollings. And let me interject my thanks to all of you for also standing with us in a battle we lost: the battle to sustain my veto of the Grove City legislation.

But to return to economics, today perhaps we're a little blase about our incredible accomplishments, but who in 1979 would have thought it possible that in less than a decade the top marginal tax rate on personal income would drop from 70 percent to less than half of that, that the era of high inflation be brought to an end, and that without reigniting the inflation we could light the torch of economic growth and see its lustrous beacon shine for longer than has ever been recorded in peacetime.

Eight years ago, in the now-distant epoch of double-digit inflation, 20-percent interest rates, and official handwringing about the limits of growth and the fatigue of our national economic mettle, we said—you and I—that the way to rebuild America was to restore faith in the greatest constructive force of all: the American spirit of enterprise. And to those who called for more government planning, more regulations, and even more taxes, we said that, in a nation, as in a man or a woman, economic success is not a matter of bricks, mortar, balance sheets, or subsidies. No, if a national economy is to soar, first the inventive, enterprising, pioneering, dreaming entrepreneurial spirit of the Nation's people must soar. And that meant not more regulations, but fewer; not more government decoration [direction], but less; and, yes, not higher taxes, but lower taxes.

You know, sometimes I think that government tries to be a little like the politician of the opposite party who was seeking the oratorical heights, and he said, "If they don't stop shearing the sheep that lay the golden egg, they'll pump it dry." [*Laughter*]

Well, I can't help remembering the fear and trembling and utter disbelief that greeted the arrival of our creed here in Washington. Sometimes it reminded me of a scene of a horrified crowd in some old science fiction film—"Attack of the Killer Tomatoes," maybe. [*Laughter*] Well, it occurs to me as I approach the end of my Presidency that the unparalleled resistance that greeted our policies and that we still face, despite our unparalleled success, was born of more than an ordinary political clash. After all, the struggle between those wanting more and less government spending was not due to Washington—new to Washington, I should say. Neither was the struggle between those who wanted higher and lower taxes, or less defense versus a strong defense. No, our arrival in Washington represented not another skirmish among partisans but a collision of constellations. As George Gilder has written, in his words: "The central conflict in the economy pits the forces of statist bureaucracy against entrepreneurs." And he adds that on one side are those who believe the economy, the Nation, and the world require, as he puts it, "control by large corporations and governments." On the other are those who believe our future depends on "small companies, entrepreneurs, inventors, and creators." And that's his list, not mine.

Yet before we came to Washington, the powers that be saw the economy as a kind of a repertory theater: a few well-known actors—business, labor, government—performing a few well-known plays. Well, we said this is not the way the world works; that there's a great surging, yearning, creative energy in this land of questing freedom; and that because of it, America is continually being born anew. New companies, new technologies bloom and have their day. Some grow; some fade. Some businesses become titanic overnight; others remain tiny. But just because this process of conception, birth, and growth is so fertile, so diverse, and so dynamic, government cannot regulate it, subsidize it, or control it. Government had just better get out of the way and let it happen.

You know, I sympathize with the liberals. When we first started talking about the economy in these terms, they predicted disaster. We predicted growth. And this year more people have been at work than ever before in the history of our country. A greater proportion of the work force has been employed than ever before. And after a decade of a falling roller coaster, real family income has been rising steadily ever since our expansion began more than 5 years ago. Exports are high and climbing. And in industry after industry, American manufacturing is the world leader. Unemployment is the lowest in almost 14 years, and month after month brings new word of hundreds of thousands of new American jobs. And over 90 percent of these new jobs are from businesses that are 5 years old or less; that is, entrepreneurial businesses, just the kind we've been talking about and the liberals dismissed.

You've got to hand it to our critics, though. With all that good news mounting, they didn't give up. When the stock market fell last October, they could hardly wait to dance on the grave. And when I said the economy was strong, they said I was "irrelevant." Well, the first quarter economic figures came out last week. You've seen them. Gross national product, up; domestic demand, up; personal consumption, up; durable goods spending, up; spending on services, up; business, fixed investment, up at a 21-percent annual rate; wages and salaries, up; exports, up. My question is: Who's irrelevant now?

It used to be, if you were a liberal and things just weren't going your way here, you could find friends abroad. Well, even that's getting harder. India, France, New Zealand, Australia, and now Great Britain have followed this new path and have adopted the recipe for what some call the American miracle. Yes, they've begun to cut tax rates, privatize state-owned industry, and reduce regulations. France even presented the Legion of Honor to a supply-side alumnus of our administration, saying it was "for the renewal of economic science and policy after a half century of state intervention."

Well, yes, it's hard being a liberal today. It's a little like the story of when Mark Twain, at the time a young and relatively unknown writer, first met Ulysses Grant. General Grant was always a man of few words, and Twain was flustered and couldn't think of a thing to say. And after a long silence between them, Twain stammered, "General, I'm embarrassed. Are you?" Well, the liberals should be embarrassed.

To an economy that is strong and hearty, they're trying to feed a junk-food diet filled with empty calories. Some of the emptiest are in a box marked the "Trade bill." The plant-closing restriction is the bill's worst provision, although not the only bad one. Mandatory plant-closing notification has no place in Federal law. It's a subject for labor-management negotiations, not government regulation. And before they start to argue with me on that, let me remind them, I was elected president in my union 6 times. And by the way, I'm calling it plant-closing notification because that's what it's called in the press. But it covers wholesalers, retailers, services—every sector. And it applies to layoffs as well as closings.

You may have seen articles lately saying, "Well, this restriction is not all that bad." Well, yes it is. It's a shackle on smaller companies that want to take the leap and become large—one more risk, and a big one, if they cross the threshold and fall under the regulation, an important reason to say, let's hold off growing that big for awhile. And it's a ticking bomb in the back seat of any medium-size or larger company that is stripping down and overhauling so it can keep on the track with foreign racers.

The bill's elaborate exemptions that tell who must give notice and who doesn't have to will detonate lawsuits sending managers to the courtroom just when they're most needed in the factory pulling their weight. Whenever the choice is a close call about whether a company is so distressed that it doesn't have to give notice, legalities will swamp the crucial economics of holding customer loyalty and maintaining creditor confidence—and, so, of saving American jobs.

Well, those who are for the provision insist that it won't hurt us because, after all, many European countries have similar restrictions themselves. Yep, and that's among the reasons for Europe's poor job performance over the last 6 years. If we had done as poorly, our unemployment rate would be up like theirs, not down from 10.8 percent to 5½ percent. What would organized labor say then? Anyone who would copy Europe in this way is no friend to American workers. For America, plant-closing restrictions are like playing Russian roulette with a machine gun—a sure loser. I've said it loud and clear again and again: I want to sign the right trade legislation this year. For example, greater protection for intellectual property and greater negotiating authority in the current round of international trade negotiations are good ideas, and they're in the bill, but they don't make up for so much else. In the form it was passed, I will veto the trade bill.

The future or the past, that's what's at stake in the trade bill, and that's what's been at stake in every battle we've fought together these last 8 years. In essence, our opponents want to move the United States toward what Latin American economists like Hernando de Soto have called a mercantilist system. As Peruvian writer Mario Vargas Llosa has described it, this means, in his words, "a bureaucratized, regulating state that puts the principle of redistribution of wealth over creation of wealth." And as Llosa concludes, redistribution has "meant the concessions of privileges and monopolies to small private elites that depend on the state and on which it, in turn, is dependent."

Well, making America's economy more like that may not seem smart. Well, for those who look at the transformation of our industrial base with trepidation, it offers great comfort. Our opponents want to seize the seasons and stop time from flowing by. They look to the future with fear. They fear new technologies, new businesses, new international competition. We look to the future with hope and optimism. And why shouldn't we? We've made a long journey and, despite all the predictions of disaster, a good one. We aren't at the end yet. Of course, in the years ahead, as we work to reduce further the disincentives in the tax code, we should cut the capital gains tax. When you tax something, you get less of it. The capital gains tax is a tax on innovation, and we need more innovation, not less.

We also must get control of Federal spending, once and for all. Congress has had control of the budget process for 14 years and made a mess of it. One thousand page continuing resolutions you can hardly lift—forget about vetoing by the line, I'm ready to veto by the pound. [*Laughter*] But it's time to strengthen the President's hand in the budget process. It's too late for me to have the benefit of this, but it's time to give the Presidency what 43 Governors have, what I had as Governor of California and used 943 times without getting overridden once—a line-item veto. We need a 2-year budget cycle and more privatization. Last year Congress cut the Coast Guard and gave the money to Amtrak. I'd rather stop all subsidies to Amtrak and give those dollars to the Coast Guard to fight drugs. And most important, we need a no-fault insurance policy for taxpayers—insurance against reckless spending—a balanced budget amendment to the Constitution.

Now, this is just a short distance on the path of our unfinished journey. We're like the pioneers who settled this great land, who struggled across the prairie, who braved the mountain passes and deserts, who conquered a vast frontier. It is love and faith that drive us on—love of the liberty and opportunity that America has offered so many for so long; faith that we, with our strength and our wit, can, like the pioneers and the patriots before us, help build, preserve, and perpetuate that heritage. It is a great gift God has given each of us—making us Americans. Who knows why some are so blessed. It's a mystery we cannot fathom but can only adore and be thankful for.

In these last 8 years you've shown your thanks by helping to rekindle America's fire of opportunity and optimism, by helping to ensure that it would burn for the generation to come, by feeding the flame that will guide our journey into the future. Yet the journey is not over, and without you, America could yet turn back. So many hopes rest with you—so many dreams. And this is my appeal to you, my old comrades in arms, on this, our last gathering of my Presidency: Don't let that fire dim! Keep America on the path to the future. Do this not for me but for this land we love and cherish so well. Thank you, and God bless you all.

Note: The President spoke at 11:02 a.m. at DAR Constitution Hall. He was introduced by Edward Donley, former chairman of the U.S. Chamber of Commerce.

Statement by Assistant to the President for Press Relations Fitzwater on the President's Meeting With Prime Minister Harri Holkeri of Finland

May 2, 1988

The President welcomed Prime Minister Harri Holkeri to the White House as part of the celebration of the Year of Friendship with Finland and discussed the President's upcoming trip to Helsinki and the Moscow summit. Prime Minister Holkeri presented the President with a medal commemorating the 350th anniversary of the first Finnish settlement in America in what is now Wilmington, Delaware.

During the 30-minute Oval Office meeting, the President said that progress had been made in U.S. relations with the U.S.S.R. and expressed appreciation for Finland's support for that policy. The President noted that the Helsinki Final Act symbolizes recent efforts to overcome the East-West division of Europe and to build security and cooperation. Prime Minister Holkeri is visiting the United States to open a Finnish exhibit in Philadelphia related to the Year of Friendship with Finland designated by Congress and the President.

Appointment of Andrew H. Card, Jr., as Deputy Assistant to the President and Director of the Office of Intergovernmental Affairs
May 2, 1988

The President today announced the appointment of Andrew H. Card, Jr., to be Deputy Assistant to the President and Director of the Office of Intergovernmental Affairs at the White House. He would succeed Gwendolyn S. King.

Mr. Card is presently serving as a senior consultant on Vice President George Bush's Presidential campaign. He served at the White House previously as Special Assistant to the President for Intergovernmental Affairs, working primarily with the Nation's Governors. Prior to this he was vice president of CMIS Corp., a computer software engineering firm located in Vienna, VA. He served as a representative to the General Court of the Commonwealth of Massachusetts in 1975–1982 and was named one of the Nation's outstanding legislators in 1982 by the National Republican Legislators' Association. In 1982 Mr. Card was a candidate for the Republican nomination for Governor of Massachusetts.

Mr. Card received a bachelor of science degree in engineering from the University of South Carolina and attended the United States Merchant Marine Academy. He was born May 10, 1947. He is married, has three children, and resides in Springfield, VA.

Appointment of Gerald J. McKiernan as Special Assistant to the President for Legislative Affairs
May 2, 1988

The President today announced the appointment of Gerald J. McKiernan to be Special Assistant to the President for Legislative Affairs (House).

Prior to joining the White House staff, Mr. McKiernan served as the Chief of Staff to Secretary of Commerce William Verity and as Assistant Secretary of Commerce for Congressional and Intergovernmental Affairs. He served previously as the Director of Congressional Affairs for the International Trade Administration at the Department of Commerce. Prior to joining the Reagan administration, he served 10 years on Capitol Hill as a principal aide to Congressman Stewart B. McKinney of Connecticut's 4th Congressional District.

A native of New Haven, CT, Mr. McKiernan entered government service after a career in journalism. He has a degree in communications from the University of New Haven. Mr. McKiernan is married to the former Linda Lehrman. They have one child and reside in Chevy Chase, MD.

Nomination of Charles S. Whitehouse To Be an Assistant Secretary of Defense
May 2, 1988

The President today announced his intention to nominate Charles S. Whitehouse to be an Assistant Secretary of Defense (Special Operations and Low Intensity Conflict) at the Department of Defense. He would succeed Chapman B. Cox.

From 1975 to 1978, Mr. Whitehouse was Ambassador of the United States to the

Kingdom of Thailand. Prior to this, he was Ambassador to Laos, 1973–1975, and deputy chief of mission and counselor in South Vietnam, 1972–1973. He was Acting Deputy Assistant Secretary of State for East Asian-Pacific Affairs, 1970–1971, and regional director of AID in South Vietnam, 1969–1970. Mr. Whitehouse was deputy chief of mission and counselor in Guinea, 1966–1969, and attended the National War College, 1965–1966. He was an international relations officer, 1962–1965, and special assistant to the Under Secretary of State for Economic Affairs, 1956–1959. He was a political officer at the U.S. Embassy in Cambodia, 1954–1956, and at the U.S. mission in Istanbul, Turkey, 1952–1954.

Mr. Whitehouse graduated from Yale University (B.A., 1947). He served in the United States Marine Corps, 1943–1946. He was born November 5, 1921, in Paris, France. Mr. Whitehouse is married, has three children, and resides in Marshall, VA.

Nomination of Henry R. Folsom To Be a Commissioner of the Postal Rate Commission

May 2, 1988

The President today announced his intention to nominate Henry R. Folsom to be a Commissioner of the Postal Rate Commission for the term expiring October 14, 1994. This is a reappointment.

Since 1982 Mr. Folsom has been a Commissioner for the Postal Rate Commission in Washington, DC. Prior to this he was a consultant for Water Resources Agency, 1981. He worked for E.I. du Pont de Nemours and Co. for 35 years. Mr. Folsom has also been an adjunct professor in urban affairs and public policy at the University of Delaware.

Mr. Folsom graduated from the University of Delaware (B.S., 1936). He was born July 19, 1913, in Wilmington, DE. He is married and resides in Arlington, VA.

Nomination of William W. Erwin To Be a Member of the Board of Directors of the Farm Credit System Assistance Board

May 2, 1988

The President today announced his intention to nominate William W. Erwin to be a member of the Board of Directors of the Farm Credit System Assistance Board, subject to the provisions prescribed by P.L. 100–233.

Mr. Erwin started farming full-time in 1949 and is now president of the Triple E Farm, Inc., in Etna Green, IN. He is also a partner in Earl & Erwin. He has also served as Deputy Under Secretary of Agriculture for Rural Development, 1972–1973, and Assistant Secretary of Agriculture for Rural Development, 1973–1975.

Mr. Erwin graduated from the University of Illinois (B.A., 1949). He was born September 28, 1925, in Plymouth, IN. He served in the United States Air Corps, 1944–1945. Mr. Erwin is married, has three children, and resides in Bourbon, IN.

Nomination of Edwin J. Delattre To Be a Member of the National Council on the Humanities
May 2, 1988

The President today announced his intention to nominate Edwin J. Delattre to be a member of the National Council on the Humanities, National Foundation on the Arts and the Humanities, for a term expiring January 26, 1994. He would succeed George Carey.

Since 1986 Dr. Delattre has been the Lynde and Harry Bradley Distinguished Fellow in Applied Ethics for the Ethics in Public Policy Center in Washington, DC. Prior to this he was president of St. John's College, 1980–1986. He was also director of the national humanities faculty, 1976–1980, and a faculty member at the University of Toledo, 1968–1976.

Dr. Delattre graduated from the University of Virginia (B.A., 1963) and the University of Texas at Austin (Ph.D., 1970). He was born September 4, 1941, in Detroit, MI. He is married, has one child, and resides in Fairfax, VA.

Nomination of Richard J. Schwartz To Be a Member of the National Museum Services Board
May 2, 1988

The President today announced his intention to nominate Richard J. Schwartz to be a member of the National Museum Services Board, National Foundation on the Arts and the Humanities, for a term expiring December 6, 1992. He would succeed Louis Roman DiSabato.

Since 1985 Mr. Schwartz has been president of Richard J. Schwartz Corp. in New York City and president of David Schwartz Foundation. Prior to this Mr. Schwartz joined Jonathan Logan, Inc., in 1960 and has served as: executive vice president, president and chief operating officer, chief executive officer, and chairman of the board.

Mr. Schwartz graduated with a bachelor of arts degree from Cornell University. He was born December 29, 1938, in New York City. He is married, has two children, and resides in Scarborough, NY.

Message to the Congress Transmitting the German Democratic Republic-United States Fishery Agreement
May 3, 1988

To the Congress of the United States:

In accordance with the Magnuson Fishery Conservation and Management Act of 1976 (Public Law 94–265; 16 U.S.C. 1801 *et seq.*), I transmit herewith an Agreement effected by exchange of notes April 12, 1988, extending for the period of 2 years from July 1, 1988, until July 1, 1990, and amending to conform with current United States law the Governing International Fishery Agreement between the Government of the United States of America and the Government of the German Democratic Republic, signed at Washington on April 13, 1983. The exchange of notes together with the present Agreement constitute a Governing International Fishery Agreement within the requirements of Section 201(c) of the Act.

United States fishing industry interests have urged prompt consideration of this Agreement, and, similarly, I request that the Congress give favorable consideration to this Agreement at an early date to avoid disruption of ongoing cooperative fishing ventures.

Since 60 calendar days of continuous session, as required by the legislation, may not be available before the current Agreement is scheduled to expire, I recommend that the Congress consider passage of a joint resolution to bring into force the Agreement of April 12, 1988.

RONALD REAGAN

The White House,
May 3, 1988.

Remarks on Signing the Asian/Pacific American Heritage Week Proclamation
May 3, 1988

Please be seated, and thank you and welcome, Members of the Congress, honored guests, and ladies and gentlemen. I am delighted to join you today in celebrating the great contributions made to the United States by citizens of Asian and Pacific island heritage. As you all know, next week marks the 10th Asian/Pacific American Heritage Week. And this occasion is being celebrated throughout the country. One of the events is a nationwide poster contest. And the picture is right here, and we're pleased to have the winning artist here with us today. She is a high school senior from Potomac, Maryland, Serena Lin. Congratulations, Serena.

Our country draws special strength from our rich cultural heritage and the shared values that unite America. Asian-Pacific Americans represent the full breadth of the American experience. For some, their family roots reach deep into American history and the building of this nation. Even before the American Revolution, the first sailors from the Philippines were settled here. Other citizens have only recently come to our shores. They're among our newest Americans—who, like immigrants before them, have a unique appreciation for the freedom and opportunity this country offers.

Citizens of Asian and Pacific heritage have enriched America in irreplaceable ways, but at the same time each person's story is distinctly American, each is a reaffirmation of the kind of country we are and the values that make us strong and free. I think of Wendy Gramm, whose grandfather came from Korea as a contract laborer to cut sugarcane in Hawaii. Wendy's father went on to become vice president of the same sugar company that her grandfather had worked for in the fields. And last February, Wendy was confirmed by the Senate as Chairman of the Commodity Futures Trading Commission, and I can't help but note that one of the commodity futures she now oversees is cane sugar. [*Laughter*]

I think of Hoang Nhu Tran, who as a child saw Americans in uniform defending his native country of South Vietnam from Communist aggression. And when North Vietnam violated the Paris peace accords and Saigon fell, Hoang and his family were forced to flee. And they came to America. Last year, Hoang graduated from the United States Air Force Academy, and he was valedictorian of his class.

I think of Sam Hayakawa. Born in Canada to Japanese immigrant parents, he came to the United States as a graduate student and never left. He once wrote: "I was advised in my youth that there were many jobs and careers I could not hope to aspire to because of my race." Well, he became a noted expert on semantics, president of San Francisco State University. And at the age of 70—the same year he took up scuba diving—[*laughter*]—he was elected to the United States Senate from California.

I think of Elaine Chao, whose father came here from Taiwan with just about

$800. He worked hard and saved for 3 years to bring the rest of his family over. Elaine was eight when she boarded a freighter and made the long, slow journey across the Pacific to Los Angeles, then down through the Panama Canal, then up to New York Harbor, where a little girl saw the Statue of Liberty for the first time. She became a banker, did multimillion-dollar ship financing, then was named a White House Fellow. On Friday, Elaine was confirmed as Chairman of the Federal Maritime Commission, the first American of Asian-Pacific heritage ever to hold this position.

Well, for many groups, education has been a key ingredient in realizing the American dream. And one area in which Asian-Pacific Americans have particularly excelled is in education. Their accomplishments are proof that respect for learning, family encouragement—plus a whole lot of hard work and diligent study—pays off with high grades, advanced degrees, and successful careers. I know there's a growing concern that some universities may be discriminating against citizens of Asian and Pacific heritage, accepting a lower percentage of these applicants than get admitted from other groups, despite their academic qualifications. Well, to deny any individual access to higher education when it has been won on the basis of merit is a repudiation of everything America stands for.

Let everyone be clear, especially all recipients of Federal education funds, that the use of informal exclusionary racial quotas, or any practice of racial discrimination against any individual violates the law, is morally wrong and will not be tolerated. The U.S. Commission on Civil Rights has noted the problem of racially-motivated violence and harassment directed at Asian-Pacific Americans. And in this regard, I have something to say about the hostile racial undercurrent that sometimes accompanies the agitation for protectionism. A few years ago, in Detroit, Vincent Chin, a citizen of Chinese-American heritage, was beaten to death by two men enraged over car imports from Japan. The point is this: Political differences over trade policy are one thing, and we can debate them, but racially-tainted appeals cross a very dangerous line. They're an affront to this country, and they threaten the tranquility and safety of all of us here at home.

Americans of Asian and Pacific heritage are one of the most successful groups in this country. What they've achieved is a great reaffirmation of the American values of work, education, family, and community. They've made this country the land of opportunity. They've distinguished themselves in many fields, from science and medicine to agriculture and commerce. They've contributed to our public life through the arts and literature, and also in government. Asian-Pacific Americans are part of the rich tapestry of American life. It's a tribute to the unifying power of America that such a diverse group whose members often have different national heritages, religious faiths, and historical experiences all come together to celebrate this occasion and to reaffirm our common bond as citizens of the United States. Let me give special praise to the Asian Pacific American Heritage Council, whose help brings people together—or, whose work, I should say, helps bring people together, and makes this special week of celebration a reality.

And now it is my Irish-English—[*laughter*]—privilege to sign the proclamation.

Note: The President spoke at 11:40 a.m. in the Roosevelt Room at the White House.

Proclamation 5807—Asian/Pacific American Heritage Week, 1988
May 3, 1988

By the President of the United States of America

A Proclamation

We do well to salute Americans of Asian and Pacific ancestry for their accomplishments and for those of their forebears who through the decades have offered our land their talents, their determination, and a truly immeasurable gift, the treasure of their ancient heritages.

The contributions of Asian and Pacific Americans and their cultural vitality have benefited the United States in countless ways. Not least among them have been deep appreciation of the unalienable rights to life, liberty, and the pursuit of happiness that form the core of the American ethos, and the willingness and ability to defend these treasures always. Asian and Pacific Americans have won distinction in every field, and continue to strengthen our Nation with industry, initiative, and love of country; that is cause for rejoicing among all Americans, during Asian/Pacific American Heritage Week and the entire year.

Now, Therefore, I, Ronald Reagan, President of the United States of America, by virtue of the authority vested in me by the Constitution and laws of the United States, do hereby proclaim the week beginning May 8, 1988, as Asian/Pacific American Heritage Week. I call upon the people of the United States to observe this week with appropriate ceremonies and activities.

In Witness Whereof, I have hereunto set my hand this 3rd day of May, in the year of our Lord nineteen hundred and eighty-eight, and of the Independence of the United States of America the two hundred and twelfth.

RONALD REAGAN

[*Filed with the Office of the Federal Register, 2:51 p.m., May 4, 1988*]

Proclamation 5808—National Digestive Disease Awareness Month, 1988
May 3, 1988

By the President of the United States of America

A Proclamation

Digestive diseases rank second among all of the causes of disability due to illness in the United States, and account for one-tenth of the economic burden of illness in our land. Their social and economic impact is enormous; half of all Americans are affected by them at some time during life. More Americans are hospitalized for digestive diseases than for any other family of illness.

In recent years major advances have taken place in digestive disease research, but efforts to determine their causes and to develop ways to prevent and treat them have only begun. Knowing the impact of these diseases and of the critical need for research in this field, private, scientific, and governmental organizations have committed themselves to increasing public awareness and understanding of gastrointestinal diseases.

In recognition of the fourth anniversary of the National Digestive Disease Education Program and of the importance of all efforts to combat digestive diseases, the Congress, by House Joint Resolution 421, has designated the month of May 1988 as "National Digestive Disease Awareness Month" and has authorized and requested the President to issue a proclamation in observance of this month.

Now, Therefore, I, Ronald Reagan, Presi-

dent of the United States of America, do hereby proclaim May 1988 as National Digestive Disease Awareness Month. I urge the people of the United States and educational, philanthropic, scientific, medical, and health care organizations and professionals to take part in appropriate activities to encourage further research into the causes and cures of all types of digestive disorders.

In Witness Whereof, I have hereunto set my hand this third day of May, in the year of our Lord nineteen hundred and eighty-eight, and of the Independence of the United States of America the two hundred and twelfth.

RONALD REAGAN

[*Filed with the Office of the Federal Register, 2:52 p.m., May 4, 1988*]

Proclamation 5809—National Drinking Water Week, 1988

May 3, 1988

By the President of the United States of America

A Proclamation

Americans are thankful for the amount of water with which our country is blessed—for our more than two million miles of streams, our more than 30 million acres of lakes and reservoirs, our other surface waters, and our subterranean reserves known as aquifers. We also appreciate our public water systems, whose complex processes provide us with some 12 billion gallons of generally inexpensive and high-quality drinking water daily.

We can be grateful too for the Americans who are helping to bring safe drinking water to millions in the developing world through the efforts of charitable, business, and other private groups and the Agency for International Development. From providing technical assistance to water systems in burgeoning cities to helping construct one-pipe water stands in countless villages in Africa, Asia, and Latin America, dedicated Americans are bringing water to a thirsty world. Water supplies in those developing lands mean improved health and well-being and often presage better productivity and economic vitality that benefit us all.

Less than a century ago, epidemics of waterborne disease were a major public health threat in our country. Today, behind every drop of good drinking water are dedicated individuals such as scientists, engineers, elected officials, water plant owners and operators, regulatory officials, and citizen groups, whose unceasing efforts allow us to enjoy the world's best drinking water.

We must be aware, however, that we do face some difficulties regarding drinking water. Lead eroding from the lead pipes and solder used in some water systems is causing health problems, especially for children; natural contaminants such as radon need attention in many water systems; and man-made contaminants are at levels of concern in some water supplies. Controlling these problems will be a challenge, but not one beyond our abilities or our determination.

State and local governments continue their efforts in this regard, and the Safe Drinking Water Act of 1974, as amended in 1986 (Public Law 99–939), enlists the help of the Environmental Protection Agency in preserving and improving our drinking water. Because of this law and growing public concern, dramatic changes in public water systems over the next 5 years are likely to affect every community.

Consumers and the private sector help protect and improve drinking water by checking the quality of local systems and regional supplies and by working with utilities and State and local officials to protect and improve them. They help preserve water supplies by supporting wellhead protection and watershed control measures. And consumers encourage improved operation and maintenance of water facilities, increased monitoring, replacement of aging pipes and equipment, and installation of new treatment technologies where necessary.

We desire drinking water of the highest quality and realize that our large water supply is neither limitless nor without expense. Knowing that good drinking water is a precious resource and one of the world's most important products, we need to continue to understand and identify potential hazards, how such hazards enter our water supply, and the best means to eliminate them.

The Congress, by Senate Joint Resolution 185, has designated May 2 through May 8, 1988, as "National Drinking Water Week" and has authorized and requested the President to issue a proclamation in observance of that occasion.

Now, Therefore, I, Ronald Reagan, President of the United States of America, do hereby proclaim May 2 through May 8, 1988, as National Drinking Water Week. I call upon the people of the United States and government officials to observe that week with appropriate programs, ceremonies, and activities to enhance public awareness about drinking water and recognition of the benefits of drinking water.

In Witness Whereof, I have hereunto set my hand this third day of May, in the year of our Lord nineteen hundred and eighty-eight, and of the Independence of the United States of America the two hundred and twelfth.

RONALD REAGAN

[*Filed with the Office of the Federal Register, 2:53 p.m., May 4, 1988*]

Proclamation 5810—Father's Day, 1988
May 3, 1988

By the President of the United States of America

A Proclamation

Once again we celebrate Father's Day, by tradition the third Sunday in June, a day to honor and salute fathers everywhere for their love and devotion.

As a weary child tumbles into his father's arms, to be lifted up and carried, he feels his father's strength and is content. In that perch he is like a captain, confidently scanning the horizons of his world, secure in the knowledge that his ship will carry him safely through any threatening seas. Children, vulnerable and dependent, desperately need such security, and it has ever been a duty and a joy of fatherhood to offer it.

Being a father requires strength in many ways; above all, it requires character. Raising a family is no easy task, of course, but one of trial, frustration, and disappointment. Great strength and more than a little courage are needed to persevere, to fight discouragement, and to keep working for the family. In that strength, and with God's grace, fathers find the patience to teach, the fortitude to provide, the compassion to comfort, and the mercy to forgive. All of this is to say that they find the strength to love their wives and children selflessly. And it is above all for this wondrous, mysterious love that fathers shower upon their families, and that allows them to ceaselessly put their families' needs first, that we honor fathers with their own special day.

Our gratitude is not limited to Father's Day, but remains constant; indeed, there are not enough days in the year to express it properly. Still, it is fitting that on such a day the American people pause to celebrate all fathers for their loving care for their youngsters. Our Nation can only continue to prosper if our families prosper. Nothing can replace the family's role as prime nurturer and educator of children, and nowhere are our country's shared values more effectively transmitted to future generations.

So let us thank all fathers on this day; but, above all, let us each take this occasion to express our thanks and our affection to our own fathers, whether we can do so in person or in prayer. We are perhaps no longer little children riding on our fathers' shoulders, yet we will forever feel their firm and loving guidance through life's challenges.

Now, Therefore, I, Ronald Reagan, President of the United States of America, in accordance with a joint resolution of the Congress approved April 24, 1972 (36 U.S.C. 142a), do hereby proclaim Sunday, June 19, 1988, as Father's Day. I invite the States and communities and people of the United States to observe that day with appropriate ceremonies as a mark of appreciation and abiding affection for their fathers. I direct government officials to display the flag of the United States on all Federal government buildings, and I urge all Americans to display the flag at their homes and other suitable places on that day.

In Witness Whereof, I have hereunto set my hand this third day of May, in the year of our Lord nineteen hundred and eighty-eight, and of the Independence of the United States of America the two hundred and twelfth.

RONALD REAGAN

[*Filed with the Office of the Federal Register, 2:54 p.m., May 4, 1988*]

Remarks at a White House Briefing on Religious Freedom in the Soviet Union
May 3, 1988

Thank you all very much, and welcome to the East Room of the White House. This room has seen many important people—Presidents, diplomats, world statesmen—and none more important, none of greater faith and moral courage, than these four men that we are honored to have with us: Father Shibayev, Reverend Matveiuk, Mykola Rudenko, and Iosif Begun. I promise that the witness of faith that you have brought here today will not be confined within these four walls, or forgotten when this meeting is ended. I will carry it in my heart when I travel to the Soviet Union at the end of this month. And I will say that the most fitting way to mark the millennium of Christianity in Kiev Rus would be granting the right of all the peoples and all the creeds of the Soviet Union to worship their God, in their own way.

You have, of course, been hearing this afternoon about the first signs of progress. The presence of these four men here today is testimony to the fact that our witness here in the West can have an impact. Some Soviet dissidents have been allowed to emigrate. Some churches are allowed to organize and file for recognition, and recently the Soviets have said they will allow a printing of language Bibles. These are encouraging signs, and we welcome them. What we hope for ultimately is a willingness to see continued change in the spirit of *glasnost,* when it comes to matters of religion. Perhaps the process is beginning. We noted that General Secretary Gorbachev said recently, and I'll quote: "Mistakes made with regard to the church and believers in the 1930's and the years that followed are being rectified." Well, we sincerely hope and pray that this will be the case.

While some new churches are being built and others, mostly Russian Orthodox, have been allowed to reopen, many other congregations are denied recognition and, therefore, legality. The Ukrainian Catholic Church, the Uniate Church, is still closed, outlawed, and persecuted. Religious instruction of children outside the home—Sunday schools, Hebrew schools, or even confirmation classes, and the production of religious study material are all still illegal activities. And about those Bibles, the authorities have promised to print 100,000 copies for a country of 280 million people. Yet now, there are at least signs by Soviet authorities of a new law on the freedom of conscience, reflecting the interests of religious organizations.

So, while every positive step taken by the Soviets is welcomed, we realize that this is just a beginning. Let me also say, in particular, that the rights of Soviet Jews have taken up much of our official time, and this is very close to my heart. Our hope is for the doors to open fully to emigration and to full freedom for all faiths.

So, the earlier predictions by some that once the grandmothers died nobody would remember that there had been a church in Russia are wrong. Instead, the church in Russia is still full of grandmothers, women who were little children in 1917, and they're joined by the younger generation, longing to satisfy the need, the hunger, that no manmade institution in any society can ever fulfill. Today roughly 90 million people in the Soviet Union, or nearly a third of the population, proclaim some form of belief in God.

And it is not surprising that revolutions devoted to reshaping man as if he were so much clay deny one of the most basic teachings of Judeo-Christian belief: that after God shaped Adam from dust, he breathed into him the divine principle of life. There's a wonderful passage in "Doctor Zhivago," in which Pasternak speaks of his bitter disillusionment with the philosophy of materialism and the bloody revolution it has spawned. "When I hear people speak of reshaping life," he says, "I fall into despair. People who can say that have never understood a thing about life—they have never felt its breath, its heartbeat. They look on it as a lump of raw material that needs to be processed by them, to be ennobled by their touch. But life is never a material, a substance to be molded. Life is the principle of self-renewal, it is constantly renewing and remaking and changing and transfiguring itself, it is infinitely beyond your or my obtuse theories about it."

The history of the 20th century has too often been brutal and tragic, but it has taught us one lesson that should fill our hearts with hope and joy, for we have found that the more religion is oppressed, the greater the attempt to extinguish that life principle, that divine spark—the more it glows. History is etched with stories of those who suffered religious persecution, yes, but it also tells of transcendence, devotion, and sanctity, even conversion.

We think of the strengthened conviction Alexander Solzhenitsyn gained in prison, and the case of the Soviet psychiatrist Anatoliy Koryagin, recently released after serving 6 years in prison. He sought baptism as soon as he emigrated. And we think of heroism and courage that can only remind us of the early Christian martyrs. One such is Anna Chertkova, recently released after being held in a Soviet psychiatric hospital since 1973 for no other crime than her faith; or Alfonsas Svarinskas, a 62-year-old Lithuanian priest, who has spent 18 years in prison and is not scheduled to be released until 1990. He is gravely ill and has petitioned for permission to go abroad to receive medical care; or Bishop Julijonas Steponavicius, in internal exile since 1961 for refusing to collaborate with the authorities.

How many men and women have had their faith tested? Now we see some people who have served prison sentences for the unauthorized practice of religion being released. And no one has been imprisoned on that ground for the last 2 years. Our hopes and prayers are for this expression of change by the Soviet authorities to continue.

The faith of the peoples of the Soviet Union is pure and unbreakable. As Moses led his people from bondage in Egypt, as the early Christians not only withstood pagan Rome but converted an empire, we pray that the millennium of Christianity in Kiev Rus will mean freedom for the faithful in Russia, in the Ukraine, the Baltic States, and all the regions of the Soviet Union. And if we pray, we might want to use the words of the 22d Psalm:

> "In Thee our fathers trusted; they trusted, and Thou didst deliver them.
> "To Thee they cried out and were delivered; in Thee they trusted and were not disappointed."

I have to add a little something here. Recently, a woman wrote me a letter and enclosed in the letter was a copy of what can only be called a prayer. But the story of that—it's in that single page—of a young Russian soldier in a shellhole in World War II, knowing that his unit was going to announce—or going to advance the attack, looking up at the stars and revealing for the first time that he had been taught all his life that there was no God. But now he believed there was. And he looked up at the heavens and spoke so sincerely and said, "Maybe before the night is over I'll be coming to You. And I hope You will forgive what I believed for so long, the foolishness, because I know now there is a God." And that letter was found on the body of the young soldier who was killed in the coming engagement. I thought sometimes of taking it to Moscow with me—maybe the General Secretary might like to read it.

Well, thank you all very much. God bless you.

Note: The President spoke at 2:44 p.m. in the East Room at the White House.

Remarks and a Question-and-Answer Session With Members of the National Strategy Forum in Chicago, Illinois
May 4, 1988

The President. Thank you Morris Leibman, Governor Jim Thompson, Attorney General Harding [Hartigan]—that's all right—[*laughter*]—and Michael Galvin, and someplace in the audience here I brought with me one of the Congressmen so you'd know that it isn't true that we're totally separated—your Congressman here, Dennis Hastert. Well, it's just a pleasure to be in Chicago—Chicago has always been my kind of town—and an honor to be able to speak to you, the members of the National Strategy Forum.

I'll keep my remarks brief today so that we'll have ample time for questions. I can't help but reflect here at the opening that it can be pretty tough in this State for a Chief Executive. In fact, let me tell you what the Illinois State Register had to say about the occupant of the White House. They said, and I quote, "the craftiest and most dishonest politician that ever disgraced an office in America." Of course, they weren't talking about me. That was Abraham Lincoln, they said. [*Laughter*] It may have been that kind of treatment in the press that led Lincoln to answer this way when he was asked what it felt like to be President. Well, he said—you've heard Lincoln is supposed to have said—about the man who was tarred and feathered and ridden out of town on a rail. And a man in the crowd asked him how he liked it, and his reply was that if it wasn't for the honor of the occasion, he'd rather walk. [*Laughter*] Come to think of it, I must be doing something right.

As you know, our agenda for the U.S.-Soviet relations has four main parts: regional conflicts, bilateral exchanges, arms reductions, and human rights. I've spoken elsewhere at some length about the first three, and today I'd like to take a moment to discuss with you the subject of human rights.

We Americans, of course, often speak about human rights, individual liberties, fundamental freedoms. We know that the promotion of human rights represents a central tenet of our foreign policy. We even believe that a passionate commitment to human rights is one of the special characteristics that helps to make America, America. It was Lincoln himself who said that the Declaration of Independence granted liberty not to our nation alone but "gave promise that in due time the weights should be lifted from the shoulders of all men." And it's important to note that this American emphasis on human rights represents much more than merely a vague respect for human dignity. No, part of our heritage as Americans is a very specific and definite understanding of human rights, a definition of human rights that we can assert to challenge ourselves and our own institutions and that we can hold up as an example for all the world.

Ultimately, our view of human rights derives from our Judeo-Christian heritage and the view that each individual life is sacred. It takes more detailed form in the works of the French and English writers of the 18th century Enlightenment. It is the notion that government should derive its mandate from the consent of the governed, this consent being expressed in free, contested, regular elections. And there you have a first human right: the right to have a voice in government, the right to vote.

Elected governments would reflect the will of the majority, but the Enlightenment writers and our own Founding Fathers gave the concept of human rights still more definite, specific form. For they held that each individual has certain rights that are so basic, so fundamental to his dignity as a human being, that no government, however large the majority it represents, no government may violate them—freedom of speech, freedom of religion, freedom of assembly, freedom of the press. These and other rights enshrined in our Constitution and Bill of Rights consist in severe limitations upon the power of government. And this is another basic point: They are rights that every citizen can call upon our independent court system to uphold. They proclaim the belief—and represent a specific means of enforcing the belief—that the individual comes first, that the Government is the servant of the people, and not the other way around. That contrasts with those systems of government that provide no limit on the power of the Government over its people.

Within the Soviet Union, decisionmaking is tightly concentrated at the top. The authority of the Communist Party is not determined by a document—a constitution, if you will—but by the leadership who determine what is right for the people. Rights such as free speech, free press, and free assembly are granted if they are "in accordance with the interests of the people and in order to strengthen and develop the Socialist system." And that last line I was quoting.

I have in the past stressed these contrasts between the United States and the Soviet Union: the fundamental and profound differences between our philosophies of government and ways of life. And I've always said that our negotiations must be undertaken with precisely this sort of realism, this sort of candor. And yet while establishing this context is essential, and reminding ourselves of these basic distinctions always useful, today I have something additional in mind. For, in recent months, the Soviet Union has shown a willingness to respect at least some human rights. It is my belief that there is hope for future change, hope that in the days ahead the Soviets will grant further recognition to the fundamental civil and political rights of all. But before discussing our hopes for the future, I'd like to turn for a moment to a subject that the Soviets themselves often raise.

The United States may recognize civil and political rights, but what of economic and social rights? The Soviets point out, for example, that the United States has an unemployment problem. Or they point to the American problem of homelessness or to racial discrimination. Well, it deserves a full response. To begin with, so-called economic and social rights belong to an essentially different category from civil and political rights. The economic and social conditions in any society are constantly changing—new social groupings constantly taking shape, as yours did, new markets forming as old markets disappear. And yet there's nothing shifting about civil and political rights like freedom of speech or worship; they are constant and immutable, forever basic to the dignity of each human being. They are fundamental—fundamental to everything.

Yes, the United States has social and economic shortcomings—unemployment, for one. As a free people, we've created an economic expansion that over the past 5 years has created nearly 16 million new jobs, but we still recognize we need to do more. Homelessness is indeed a problem, an agonizing one. To some extent, we are bound in dealing with it by our very commitment to liberty, for while we seek to help the homeless in every way possible, we must avoid at all costs coercive solutions. It's true that, as a free people, we spend hundreds of millions of dollars a year through our Federal, State, and local governments to care for the homeless. As a free people, our churches, synagogues, and a host of volunteer organizations do much to provide the homeless with food, clothing, and medicines. And yet there is no denying that a problem remains. Racial discrimination—our strides as a free people during just the past three decades have been dramatic. Yet the problem lingers, and we continue to battle bigotry and prejudice. The problems, as I said, are serious. No one would seek to deny them. Yet in freedom we are constantly confronting them, criticizing ourselves, seeking to do better, in full view for all to see.

But consider, if you will, the economic conditions of the Soviet Union. Now, I do not mean to suggest that the Soviet economy has made no progress. But the limited successes of the past arose largely from constant additions to the labor force and the availability of inexpensive resources. Now that these have been to a great extent depleted, there remains a gap between the Soviet Union and the West. Indeed, given the enormous advances in Western technology, that gap is likely to widen. Now, I do not bring this up simply for the sake of sounding critical. I mention it here because in recent months—and this is a development of tremendous significance—in recent months they've begun to mention it themselves, just like Americans do about their problems. Soviet economists have published articles about Soviet shortages. One recent article dealt with the inadequacies of Soviet housing. The Soviet press now carries stories about the need for progress. And, of course, Soviet economic progress is one of Mr. Gorbachev's chief aims.

And this brings us back to the subject of the day: human rights. For I believe that the Soviets may be coming to understand something of the connection, the necessary and inextricable connection, between human rights and economic growth. The connection between economic productivity and certain kinds of freedom is obvious. Private plots of land make up only 3 percent of the arable land in the Soviet Union, but on them is raised a quarter of all of the produce. The free flow of information, to provide another example, will clearly prove vital for Soviet science and technology to have hope of reaching new and higher standards.

And yet there's a still deeper connection. For it's the individual who is always the source of economic creativity, the inquiring mind that produces a technical breakthrough, the imagination that conceives of new products and markets. And in order for the individual to create, he must have a sense of just that—his own individuality, his own self-worth. He must sense that others respect him and, yes, that his nation respects him enough to permit him his own opinions, respects the relationship between the individual and his God enough to permit him to worship as he chooses, even respects him enough to permit him, if he chooses to do so, to leave.

The Soviets should recognize basic human rights because it's the right thing to do. They should recognize human rights because they have accepted international obligations to do so, particularly in the Helsinki Final Act. But if they recognize human rights for reasons of their own—because they seek economic growth or because they want to enter into a more normal relationship with the United States and other nations—well, I want to say here and now, that's fine by me. The indications, as I've said, have been hopeful. Over the past 3 years, some 300 political and religious prisoners have been released from labor camps. More recently, the incarceration of dissidents in mental hospitals and prisons has slowed and in some cases stopped completely. And while the press remains tightly controlled by the party and state, we've seen the publication of stories on topics that used to be forbidden—topics like crime, drug addiction, corruption, even police brutality.

Now, these changes are limited, and the basic standards contained in the Helsinki accords still are not being met. But we applaud the changes that have taken place and encourage the Soviets to go further. We recognize that changes occur slowly, but that's better than no change at all. And if I may, I'd like now to share with you a brief summary of the human rights agenda that I'll be discussing in my meetings in Moscow. It has four aims.

First, freedom of religion—despite the recent relaxation of some controls on the exercise of religion, it is still true that the churches, synagogues, mosques, or other houses of worship may not exist without government permission. Many have been imprisoned in the past for acts of worship. And yet, to quote the Universal Declaration of Human Rights, "Everyone has the right to freedom of thought, conscience, and religion." And General Secretary Gorbachev has indicated a willingness to consider a new law on the freedom of conscience.

Second is freedom of speech. There are still many serving long prison sentences for offenses that involve only the spoken or written word. Yet the clear, internationally recognized standard, as defined, once again, in the Universal Declaration of Human Rights, is that, and I quote, "Everyone has the right to freedom of opinion and expression." And today there's more such freedom in the Soviet Union than 2 years ago. Many persons imprisoned for expressing dissenting views have been released from prison. This issue can be removed by granting full recognition to this basic human right. And I know you join me in urging the freeing of people imprisoned for nothing more than the expression of their views.

Emigration, third, has long represented a matter of great concern to us. The Universal Declaration states that "Everyone has the right to leave any country, including his own, and to return to his country." Well, it's true that during the past 12 months, the rate of people permitted to leave the Soviet Union has been significantly higher than during the preceding 6 years. And it's true as well that the number of those permitted to leave for short trips, often family visits, has gone up. We're heartened by this progress. Our hope is that the Soviets grant all their peoples full and complete freedom of movement. And one point in particular: The Soviets refuse many the right to leave on the grounds that they possess secret information, even though they had ended their secret work many years before and whatever information they had has become public or obsolete. I hope that such cases will be rationally reviewed and the decision will be made to free these people and their families.

And this brings me now to the fourth and final area I want to discuss: making the progress more permanent. As I've said a number of times now, we welcome the human rights progress that the Soviets have made and believe there is good reason to hope for still more. Yet it's only being realistic to point out that we've seen progress in the Soviet Union before. Khrushchev loosened things up a bit. The intellectual and cultural life of the Soviet Union underwent a kind of thaw, a kind of springtime. But it was a springtime followed by winter, for Khrushchev's relaxations were reversed. And for the nearly three decades until our own day, oppression and stagnation once again became the determining characteristics of Soviet life. And that's why those of us in the West, both publicly and in direct conversation with the Soviets, must continue to make candor and realism the basis of our bilateral relationship. My Chief of Staff, Howard Baker, told me recently of an old Tennessee saying: "Plain talk—easy understood." Well, exactly. And just as previous hopeful moments in Soviet history ended all too soon, so, too, *glasnost,* today's new candor, will succeed if the Soviets take steps to make it permanent, to institutionalize it.

Freedom of religion, freedom of speech, freedom to emigrate, and the willingness to make new freedoms permanent—these are our hopes, these are our prayers for the future of human rights in the Soviet Union, in the world, in our own country. In granting greater liberty, I am confident that the Soviets will discover that they've made possible economic growth. But even more important, this recognition of human rights will advance the cause of peace. For in the words of Andrei Sakharov, a man who suffered much under the Soviet system, but who has also experienced the benefits of *glasnost*—he says: "I am convinced that international confidence, mutual understanding, disarmament, and international security are inconceivable without an open society with freedom of information, freedom of conscience, the right to publish, and the right to travel and choose the country in which one wishes to live. Peace, progress, and human rights—these three goals are insolubly linked."

Well, since I've been speaking today about the relationship of human rights and economic progress, let me say a few words about the present situation in Poland, a nation with which millions of Americans share bonds of kinship. We hope and pray that the Polish Government will hear the voice of the Polish people and that economic freedom, reform, and recovery will soon begin. The Polish have long been ready for it.

Now in concluding, I just want to say something that I've said many times to students. I delight in having an opportunity to speak on campuses or in high schools or something. And I like to point out something about our Constitution. And you'd be surprised how new the thought is to all of them because they say all the other nations have constitutions. And I've read an awful lot of them. And many of them, most of them, contain some of the same clauses that ours do. But I said, the difference is so tiny in ours that it is overlooked, and yet it is so great it tells the entire difference. Three words: "We the People"—our Constitution is a document in which we the people tell the Government what it can do, and it can do nothing that isn't contained in that document. All those other constitutions are documents in which the Government is telling the people what it will let them do. And it's wonderful to see the look on their faces and to think that, well, maybe you've established another little shingle on the roof of patriotism where they're concerned. I told this one night at a dinner table in the White House, when the person beside me was the Crown Princess of Japan. They were there on a trip to our country. And very quietly she said something to me. I was only wrong in one respect. Since World War II, the Japanese Constitution now also says, "We the People," and they have copied us. And I was very happy to be corrected.

Well, thank you all, and God bless you. And now I'm very happy to take some questions.

Mr. Friedman. Thank you, Mr. President. Mr. President, we all thank you for your remarks, and now we come to the moment where we have a question-and-answer session. The rules of engagement, Mr. President, are these: The members have had an opportunity to write written questions—hopefully legibly. We've had ushers pass among the tables, and the questions are now safely contained in a fishbowl.

The President. All right.

Mr. Friedman. And the reason for that is that it is very important that these questions be drawn on a random basis, which I shall do now.

Persian Gulf

The first question, Mr. President, is this: What will be the continued policy for a U.S. presence in the Persian Gulf?

The President. What will be the——

Mr. Friedman. What will be the continued policy——

The President. Oh.

Mr. Friedman. ——for a United States presence in the Persian Gulf?

The President. What it has been since as far back as 1949. And that is: Those are international waters, and no nation has a right to interfere or block those international waters to the traffic of the world. And we're going to stay there as long as it takes to see that they're recognized by everyone as international waters.

Mr. Friedman. Thank you, Mr. President.

Nuclear Waste

The second question is this: How will we dispose of nuclear wastes?

The President. Oh. [*Laughter*] Well, as you know, there were a number of target areas in States that were named for that. And then a commission is investigating everyone, and then we'll name what they believe are the correct places and the best places for the safety of the people and the disposition of that nuclear waste. I realize that somebody's going to think it's too close to them when it happens, but you've got to put it someplace. [*Laughter*]

Soviet-U.S. Summit Meeting in Moscow

Mr. Friedman. The third question, Mr. President, is this: In your judgment, what major objectives will Secretary Gorbachev be trying to achieve in the forthcoming Moscow summit?

The President. Well, for one thing, we both do have, and are awaiting ratification in both countries, of the INF treaty—because they also have a ratification process, just as we do with our Senate. And I am hopeful, and I know he is, that a part of that time could be spent with our signing, or recognizing that it has been signed, and it's in action.

The START agreement, which is the desire to reduce strategic nuclear weapons, missiles, by half, 50 percent, but down to parity—that's something that most people—some of those who are complaining about what we might be doing with that treaty—it's not just that each of us are going to come down 50 percent; we're going to come down to an equal number between the two nations, of warheads and missiles—missiles to carry them. But it's far more complicated than the INF treaty was. And it's doubtful if we are going to—we, our people, and theirs, are working in Geneva all the time, and have been steadily, but there are many complex issues there having to do with verification and things of that kind. And so, our desire that we would be able to sign the START treaty at this Moscow summit, as we did the other one at the Washington summit, may not happen. But then, what we have to say is: We must not be bound by a calendar date. We don't want a fast treaty; we want a good one. And if it is not properly worked out before we get there, then I think that that will be one of the things we will discuss while we're there and see if we can advance it a little, but eventually that we will sign that treaty.

I was very pleased when the Soviet Foreign Minister [Eduard Shevardnadze], on a recent visit to the United States—he didn't say he was quoting a line of mine, but he said it—I say that in case Larry Speakes is in the audience—[*laughter*]—but the line that he said was, "A nuclear war can never be won and must never be fought." Well, I said that to the British House of Parliament and to the Japanese Parliament a few years ago.

But we will also be discussing the things that I mentioned in my speech here. I'm willing to give him the benefit of the doubt up to a point—a point in which, as I say, is—the only thing I can say in Russian is, *Dovorey no provorey*. And he's tired of hearing me say it. It means: "Trust but verify." [*Laughter*] But I give him the benefit of the doubt, that faced with the economic problems that he has—*glasnost* with him—he really is attempting to get that, and so I would hope that in our discussions, that maybe we could be helpful to him in suggestions as to how he might better bring that about. And that, I think, is preferable to staging a kind of contest with him so that someone looks like a winner or loser. And we very definitely will be on that subject of human rights because we are both signatories to a Helsinki pact that has us both pledging to observe those human rights. And I think that to go on with a better relationship between the two countries—that is absolutely essential.

Yesterday, in the White House, I met with four individuals who had all been imprisoned in the Soviet Union. And we had a hand, I think, in getting them released, and they came here. You're talking to a clergyman who was in [prison] 18 years, and during the 18 years, his son was beaten to death. And we think there is some hope, and that's what we're going to deal with.

Is that all of them? Let's take one more.

Mr. Friedman. The fourth question of five, Mr. President, is this—well, there is always a good question, and this is the one: Would you autograph my book, "I Was a Democrat for the FBI and Other Selected Short Stories"?

The President. Yes, I'd be very pleased to do that autograph.

Mr. Friedman. And also, Mr. President, I would be very happy to see the person who made that question. [*Laughter*]

The President. You don't see anyone volunteering.

Mr. Friedman. Sam Donaldson.

Arms Control

Mr. Friedman. Mr. President, the fifth and final question of this session is this: What do you consider to be the most important need in international relations?

The President. The important——

Mr. Friedman. What do you consider to be the most important need in international relations?

The President. Oh, my goodness. [*Laughter*] That is quite a question, and how to get at it? I think the need is, well, just actual frankness and a desire for a peaceful solution. I think maybe I'd answer it this way: In my frustration sometimes—you know, actually, if you count some of the things going on in smaller countries and all, there've been about 114 wars since World War II. But I've often wondered, What if all of us in the world discovered that we were threatened by a power from outer space—from another planet. Wouldn't we all of a sudden find that we didn't have any differences between us at all—we were all human beings, citizens of the world—and wouldn't we come together to fight that particular threat. Well, in a way, we have something of that kind today—mentioning nuclear power again. We now have a weapon that can destroy the world, and why don't we recognize that threat more clearly and then come together with one aim in mind: How safely, sanely, and quickly can we rid the world of this threat to our civilization and our existence.

Note: The President spoke at 12:51 p.m. in the Grand Ballroom at the Palmer House Hotel. In his opening remarks, he referred to Morris Leibman and Michael Galvin, chairman and president, respectively, of the forum; Gov. James R. Thompson, Jr.; and State Attorney General Neil F. Hartigan. Richard Friedman, vice chairman of the forum, moderated the question-and-answer session. Prior to his remarks, the President attended an Illinois State Republican fund-raising reception in the Crystal Room at the hotel. Following the luncheon, the President returned to Washington, DC.

Proclamation 5811—National Defense Transportation Day and National Transportation Week, 1988

May 5, 1988

By the President of the United States of America

A Proclamation

Transportation is essential to American life. Our safe, fast, economical, and convenient movement of people and goods is the cornerstone of our country's social and economic welfare and of our national defense. Now, as in the past, our transportation systems—highways, airports, inland waterways, railroads and public transit, our merchant fleet and the Great Lakes and St. Lawrence Seaway—provide a superior emergency response network and are available as a critical component of our national defense. As our citizens travel in record numbers for business or pleasure, our local, State, and Federal governments continue to work with the transportation industry to enhance transportation safety.

The growth of our Nation and the development of transportation have been intertwined throughout our history. Those who first explored this vast country were followed by pioneers who established settlements. Most of the road routes, river systems, and ocean ports used by our earliest settlers are still in use today. Many of our great cities originated as towns that were starting or end points for transportation systems. As trade and commerce grew, transportation provided the necessary link to vital resources that in turn enabled further national growth. On land and water, in the air, and in space, our transportation systems have become an essential element of our Nation's economic health, providing indispensable services and generating employment for millions of people.

This week we acknowledge the contributions of the dedicated people who build, maintain, and safeguard our transportation systems—from the flagman on a highway project to the space engineer. We honor those who led the way in the development and improvement of ships, waterways, motor vehicles, highways, trains, airplanes, and our newest transportation vehicles, spacecraft. The recent announcement of our National Space Policy means that we continue to call for the help of modern-day pioneers on the frontiers of space technology. With public and private cooperation, our Nation is building a highway to space that will serve as an economic bridge to the 21st century.

In recognition of the importance of transportation and of the millions of Americans who serve and supply our transportation needs, the Congress has requested, by joint resolution approved May 16, 1957 (36 U.S.C. 160), that the third Friday in May of each year be designated as "National Defense Transportation Day"; and by joint resolution approved May 14, 1962 (36 U.S.C. 166), that the week in which that Friday falls be proclaimed "National Transportation Week."

Now, Therefore, I, Ronald Reagan, President of the United States of America, do hereby proclaim Friday, May 20, 1988, as National Defense Transportation Day and the week of May 15 through May 21, 1988, as National Transportation Week. I urge the people of the United States to observe these occasions with appropriate ceremonies that will give full recognition to the citizens and groups that operate the transportation systems of our country.

In Witness Whereof, I have hereunto set my hand this fifth day of May, in the year of our Lord nineteen hundred and eighty-eight, and of the Independence of the United States of America the two hundred and twelfth.

RONALD REAGAN

[*Filed with the Office of the Federal Register, 4:32 p.m., May 5, 1988*]

Nomination of James P. Moore, Jr., To Be an Assistant Secretary of Commerce

May 5, 1988

The President today announced his intention to nominate James P. Moore, Jr., to be an Assistant Secretary of Commerce (Trade Development) for the International Trade Administration at the Department of Commerce. He would succeed Charles E. Cobb, Jr.

Since 1986 Mr. Moore has been Principal Deputy Assistant Secretary of Commerce for International Economic Policy. Prior to this he was Deputy Assistant Secretary of Commerce for Trade Information and Analysis, 1983–1985. Since 1984 Mr. Moore has been head of the United States delegation to the Industry Committee of the Organization for Economic Cooperation and Development in Paris, France. He was a member of the Board of Advisers of the National Air and Space Museum at the Smithsonian Institution, 1981–1983. He has also been a legislative assistant and counselor to Congressman Charles Pashayan, Jr., 1979–1980, and legislative assistant to Congressman William M. Ketchum, 1977–1979.

Mr. Moore graduated from Rutgers University (B.A., 1975) and the University of Pittsburgh (M.A., 1976). He was born April 24, 1953, in Joliet, IL, and currently resides in Arlington, VA.

Nomination of Charles E. Cobb, Jr., To Be an Under Secretary of Commerce

May 5, 1988

The President today announced his intention to nominate Charles E. Cobb, Jr., to be Under Secretary of Commerce for Travel and Tourism at the Department of Commerce. He would succeed Donna F. Tuttle.

Since 1987 Mr. Cobb has been Assistant

Secretary of Commerce (Trade Development) for the International Trade Administration at the Department of Commerce. Previously, he was chairman and chief executive officer of Arvida Disney Corp., 1972–1987. He is also a former director and chief operating officer of the Penn Central Corp. and a group president of Penn Central.

Mr. Cobb graduated from Stanford University (B.A., 1958; M.B.A., 1962). He served in the United States Naval Reserve, 1958–1960. He was born May 9, 1936, in Fresno, CA. He is married, has two children, and resides in Washington, DC.

Message on the Observance of Cinco de Mayo, 1988
May 5, 1988

I am delighted to join the people of Mexico and all those of Mexican heritage in the United States in celebrating Cinco de Mayo, the historic anniversary of Mexican independence and freedom.

On May 5, 1862, Mexican troops led by General Ignacio Zaragoza defeated invading French forces at the Battle of Puebla. The Mexicans, though greatly outnumbered, were carried on to victory by their unswerving belief in liberty and independence. Today, Cinco de Mayo stands as a symbol of the love of democracy and freedom which continues to burn in the hearts of men and women throughout the Americas.

Mexico and the United States share a proud tradition of courage and conviction. As neighbors both in spirit and locale, we look to the future with faith in our continued friendship. The United States has indeed been blessed by her citizens of Mexican descent, and I am confident that our two peoples will continue to grow in friendship and mutual enrichment.

On this special day, I am happy to send warm congratulations and good wishes to the people of Mexico, our citizens of Mexican descent, and all who cherish liberty. *Que Dios los bendiga!*

RONALD REAGAN

Nomination of Jeffrey Davidow To Be United States Ambassador to Zambia
May 5, 1988

The President today announced his intention to nominate Jeffrey Davidow, of Virginia, a career member of the Senior Foreign Service, Class of Counselor, as Ambassador to the Republic of Zambia. He would succeed Paul Julian Hare.

Mr. Davidow entered the Foreign Service of the United States in 1969 and was first assigned as a junior officer at the American Embassy in Guatemala City from 1970 to 1972. From 1972 to 1974, he served as political officer in Santiago, Chile, and as political officer in Cape Town/Pretoria, South Africa, 1974–1976. He returned to Washington in 1976 to fill the position of desk officer in the Office of Southern African Affairs and was a congressional fellow from 1978 to 1979. He was head of the liaison office at the U.S. Embassy in Harare, Zimbabwe, 1979–1982, and a fellow at the Center for International Affairs at Harvard University, 1982–1983. From 1983 to 1985, he served as Director of the Office of Regional Affairs, and Director of the Office of Southern African Affairs, 1985–1986. Mr. Davidow currently holds the position of deputy chief of mission at the U.S. Embassy in Caracas, Venezuela.

Mr. Davidow graduated from the University of Massachusetts (B.A., 1965), and the

University of Minnesota (M.A., 1967). He was born January 26, 1944, in Boston, MA. He is married, has two children, and resides in Springfield, VA.

Appointment of Margaret F. Nelson as a Member of the National Advisory Council on Indian Education
May 5, 1988

The President today announced his intention to appoint Margaret F. Nelson to be a member of the National Advisory Council on Indian Education for a term expiring September 29, 1990. She would succeed Michael L. Stepetin.

Since 1984 Dr. Nelson has been an associate professor at Oklahoma State University and an assistant professor, 1980–1984. She has also served in an instructor/adviser capacity for Oklahoma State University, 1970–1979.

Dr. Nelson graduated from Northwestern State University (B.A., 1969) and Oklahoma State University (M.A., 1971; Ph.D., 1979). She was born August 16, 1922, in Claremore, OK. She is widowed, has five children, and resides in Stillwater, OK.

Proclamation 5812—National Older Americans Abuse Prevention Week, 1988
May 5, 1988

By the President of the United States of America

A Proclamation

Each year during May, through the vehicle of Older Americans Month, our Nation honors its senior citizens for their many contributions to our country, its communities, and its families. The vast majority of older Americans are active members of society—working, creating, volunteering, or simply enjoying the fruits of long years of service to others. As parents and grandparents, they extend their contributions through formation of coming generations of our citizens—their children and grandchildren. The commerce of love between generations—fulfillment of a duty and recognition of a debt—is a ballast that steadies our national enterprise on its voyage from past to future.

Not every older American leads an ideal life, however. Regrettably, some suffer from abuse and neglect, wounds all the more grievous for everything these citizens have done to build and strengthen this land of liberty. For these men and women, years that should be full of satisfaction and appreciation become instead manacles of torment and disrespect from which they cannot escape.

Abuse can take many forms—physical, mental, or emotional. It can come from family members, friends, or professionals; it can even be self-inflicted. Neglect is also a form of abuse, a manifestation of carelessness that can be seen even in situations where an elderly person's basic needs for food and shelter are being met. Loneliness, of course, is its most obvious sign, and fortunately the most easily cured by others.

Abuse and neglect reach their ultimate expression, of course, in occasional cases of—and even organized calls for—euthanasia of the elderly infirm. Older Americans have done their duty. In their twilight years, especially, it is our duty to them that matters. No elderly person should live in fear that he or she is a burden to others or that his or her life will be cut short for reasons of utility or convenience. We can never have too many reminders that the gift of life is ours to cherish and preserve from malice and harm until natural death.

Across our country, State and Area Agencies on Aging, social service, and law enforcement agencies are supporting programs to deal effectively with the difficult problems posed by abuse of the elderly. I urge every concerned American to help ensure that local programs are available to educate people about these problems and to assist both the older person and the abuser to get the help they need.

The Congress, by Senate Joint Resolution 222, has designated the week of May 1 through May 7, 1988, as "National Older Americans Abuse Prevention Week" and has authorized and requested the President to issue a proclamation in observance of the week.

Now, Therefore, I, Ronald Reagan, President of the United States of America, do hereby proclaim the week of May 1, 1988, through May 7, 1988, as National Older Americans Abuse Prevention Week. I urge all government agencies, every community, and every American to observe this period with appropriate activities and to strive to assure that every older American can enjoy what the poet called that honor, love, and obedience "that should accompany old age."

In Witness Whereof, I have hereunto set my hand this fifth day of May, in the year of our Lord nineteen hundred and eighty-eight, and of the Independence of the United States of America the two hundred and twelfth.

RONALD REAGAN

[*Filed with the Office of the Federal Register, 12:05 p.m., May 6, 1988*]

Proclamation 5813—Public Service Recognition Week, 1988
May 5, 1988

By the President of the United States of America

A Proclamation

Government employees, with their commitment to excellence and diversity of skills, contribute significantly to the leadership of the United States in the world. These dedicated men and women are a valuable national resource, serving in the Executive, Legislative, and Judicial branches at all levels of government, and dealing with nearly every aspect of national life.

Government employees provide such a broad range of services that few citizens remain unaffected by their work. They defend our Nation, enforce the laws, help protect the environment, maintain vital transportation systems, work to prevent the entry and abuse of illegal drugs, administer the Social Security system, conduct health research, help parents teach their children, and perform countless other vital tasks for society. These public servants have also helped develop innovative technologies to show the way in the critical fields of defense, health care, agriculture, and industry.

In recognition of the indispensable contributions made by government employees, the Congress, by Senate Joint Resolution 242, has designated the period commencing May 2, 1988, and ending May 8, 1988, as "Public Service Recognition Week" and has authorized and requested the President to issue a proclamation calling for observance of this week.

Now, Therefore, I, Ronald Reagan, President of the United States of America, do hereby proclaim the week of May 2, 1988, through May 8, 1988, as Public Service Recognition Week. I urge the people of the United States and all levels of government to participate in appropriate ceremonies to recognize the vital role of government employees.

In Witness Whereof, I have hereunto set my hand this fifth day of May, in the year of our Lord nineteen hundred and eighty-eight, and of the Independence of the

United States of America the two hundred and twelfth.

RONALD REAGAN

[*Filed with the Office of the Federal Register, 12:06 p.m., May 6, 1988*]

Proclamation 5814—World Trade Week, 1988
May 5, 1988

By the President of the United States of America

A Proclamation

Setting aside a week in celebration of international trade is a fitting way to remind ourselves of the countless benefits of world trade for Americans and for people around the globe, and to remember that freedom is, and must be, an essential element in economic life—individual, national, and international.

International trade can link individuals and nations alike by providing opportunities for the interchange of goods and services, the fruit of human talents that transcend boundaries of geography and culture. The key ingredient in every act of trade is freedom. Only freedom respects the inherent rights, dignity, conscience, and worth of individuals; only freedom encourages individuals to develop their creative abilities to the fullest and to command fair return for their labor; and only freedom provides a rational and humane basis for economic decision-making. The freedom of exchange that is at the heart of every genuine economic transaction benefits all parties and builds competition, enterprise, prosperity, justice, cooperation, and social well-being as people achieve economic success by finding their fellowman's unmet needs and filling them well.

Our country's prosperity likewise depends on our ability to identify needs and markets for goods and services and to meet them well. Our free market economy, our belief in free but fair trade on a global basis, and the American people's ingenuity and ability all make our products among the world's most competitive—and we intend to keep it that way.

My Administration has worked to improve the climate for international trade by seeking a renaissance in American competitiveness. Last year, as American goods regained price competitiveness overseas, exports hit a record level; more than 407,000 manufacturing jobs were created; and employment surged, with more Americans in the labor force than ever before. Exports spell opportunity for American business; thousands of U.S. firms have increased their profit margins by exporting, and thousands are beginning to discover their untapped potential to succeed in export markets. This year's World Trade Week theme, "Export Now," champions the message that I have joined the Secretary of Commerce in sending and exemplifies America's winning spirit.

Foreign markets are now more open to American goods than in the past, but we have far to go in the quest to undo unfair restrictions on trade. We seek to encourage removal of foreign barriers to free trade, but we simultaneously work to discourage domestic protectionism—more accurately described as "destructionism," because it stifles progress and prosperity by preventing competition and economic transactions that people everywhere desire and need. We also reiterate the intention of the United States Government to ensure that our trade policies serve to reinforce our national security interests around the world. International trade policies and practices must promote the causes of freedom, human rights, and economic growth everywhere.

World Trade Week is a truly appropriate time to remember the many benefits international trade has conferred on our country and to reflect on the many blessings the spread of economic freedom has brought, and can bring, to people in every nation.

Now, Therefore, I, Ronald Reagan, Presi-

dent of the United States of America, by virtue of the authority vested in me by the Constitution and laws of the United States, do hereby proclaim the week beginning May 22, 1988, as World Trade Week. I invite the people of the United States to join in appropriate observances to reaffirm the great promise of international trade for creating jobs and stimulating economic activity in our country and for generating prosperity everywhere freedom reigns.

In Witness Whereof, I have hereunto set my hand this fifth day of May, in the year of our Lord nineteen hundred and eighty-eight, and of the Independence of the United States of America the two hundred and twelfth.

RONALD REAGAN

[*Filed with the Office of the Federal Register, 12:07 p.m., May 6, 1988*]

Remarks on the Unemployment Rate and an Informal Exchange With Reporters
May 6, 1988

The President. Okay. Well, I have just a brief announcement here to make, then you can all—well, you can all get out of here. [*Laughter*] The good news on the economy continues: Unemployment is the lowest it's been since 1974, and the proportion of our population working is at an all-time high. The figures have been given out this morning that the rate of unemployment is 5.4 percent, but this thing of the proportion of the population—out of what is considered to be the potential employment pool, all of the age groups for jobs—62.2 percent of that pool is now employed. And one of the best barometers of the state of our economy is to see more people working. Today's report, coupled with those of the last 2 weeks, shows that the economy continues to grow at a moderate pace, and inflation is under control.

End of announcement.

Former White House Officials' Memoirs

Q. Mr. President, do you feel betrayed by the books that some of your former aides have written? Mr. Regan's [former Chief of Staff to the President] book is coming out this weekend.

The President. Well, I've tried to avoid commenting on all the kiss-and-tell books, but I doubt that they will be on my reading list either.

Q. What would your book-writing advice be to Cabinet members and advisers who are still around?

The President. Well, I trust all these people. [*Laughter*]

Q. Has Regan sent you his book yet?

The President. What?

Q. Has Regan sent you his book?

The President. No, and I don't think he's going to send one unless I'm prepared to send a check in return. [*Laughter*]

Q. Are you angry at him?

The President. What?

Q. Are you angry at him? Do you think you feel betrayed?

The President. Well, I will say this, that I would have preferred it if he decided to attack me. And apparently from what we hear, he's chosen to attack my wife, and I don't look kindly upon that at all.

Q. Thank you.

Q. You can rebuttal, you know, in your memoirs—[*laughter*]—when and if.

The President. I carry a pen all the time, Helen [Helen Thomas, United Press International].

Note: The President spoke at 11 a.m. in the Cabinet Room at the White House, prior to a Cabinet meeting.

Executive Order 12639—Administration of Foreign Relations and Related Functions
May 6, 1988

By virtue of the authority vested in me as President by the Constitution and laws of the United States of America, including section 621 of the Foreign Assistance Act of 1961, as amended (22 U.S.C. 2381), and section 301 of Title 3 of the United States Code, and in order to delegate certain functions concerning foreign assistance to the Secretary of State, the Secretary of Defense, and the Director of the International Development Cooperation Agency, it is hereby ordered as follows:

Section 1. Section 1–102(a) of Executive Order No. 12163, as amended, is further amended by amending paragraphs (9) and (10) to read as follows:

"(9) section 538 of the Foreign Operations, Export Financing, and Related Programs Appropriations Act, 1988 (as enacted in Public Law 100–202), to be exercised by the Administrator of the Agency for International Development within IDCA; and

"(10) the first proviso under the heading "Population, Development Assistance" contained in Title II of the Foreign Operations, Export Financing, and Related Programs Appropriations Act, 1988 (as enacted in Public Law 100–202), to be exercised by the Administrator of the Agency for International Development within IDCA.".

Sec. 2. Section 1–201(a)(11) of Executive Order No. 12163, as amended, is further amended by inserting "and (e)" after "620C(d)".

Sec. 3. Section 1–201(a) of Executive Order No. 12163, as amended, is further amended by amending paragraph (22) to read as follows:

"(22) Section 402(b)(2) of Title 10 of the United States Code, which shall be exercised in consultation with the Secretary of Defense;".

Sec. 4. Section 1–201(a) of Executive Order No. 12163, as amended, is further amended by deleting "and" at the end of paragraph (25) and by amending paragraph (26) to read as follows:

"(26) sections 513, 527, 528, 542, 561, 570, 571, 586(c), and 590 of the Foreign Operations, Export Financing, and Related Programs Appropriations Act, 1988 (as enacted in Public Law 100–202);".

Sec. 5. Section 1–201(a) of Executive Order No. 12163, as amended, is further amended by inserting the following new paragraphs at the end thereof:

"(27) the fourth proviso under the heading "Southern Africa, Development Assistance" contained in Title II of the Foreign Operations, Export Financing, and Related Programs Appropriations Act, 1988 (as enacted in Public Law 100–202);

"(28) the proviso relating to tied aid credits under the heading "Economic Support Fund" contained in Title II of the Foreign Operations, Export Financing, and Related Programs Appropriations Act, 1988 (as enacted in Public Law 100–202), which shall be exercised in consultation with the Administrator of the Agency for International Development;

"(29) subsection (c)(2) under the heading "Foreign Military Sales Debt Reform" contained in Title III of the Foreign Operations, Export Financing, and Related Programs Appropriations Act, 1988 (as enacted in Public Law 100–202), and section 572 and section 573(c) of that Act, each of which shall be exercised in consultation with the Secretary of Defense. In addition, section 573(c) shall be exercised in consultation with the Director of the United States Arms Control and Disarmament Agency.

Sec. 6. Section 1–301 of Executive Order No. 12163, as amended, is further amended to add the following section:

"(f) The functions conferred upon the President under section 573(d) of the Foreign Operations, Export Financing, and Related Programs Appropriations Act, 1988 (as enacted in Public Law 100–202)."

Sec. 7. Section 1–701 of Executive Order No. 12163, as amended, is further amended:

(1) in subsection (d) by deleting "670(a)(2)" and inserting in lieu thereof "670(a)"; and

(2) by amending subsection (g) to read as follows:

"(g) Those under sections 130, 131, 504 and 505 of the ISDCA of 1985".

RONALD REAGAN

The White House,
May 6, 1988.

[Filed with the Office of the Federal Register, 11:13 a.m., May 9, 1988]

Proclamation 5815—National Safe Boating Week, 1988
May 6, 1988

By the President of the United States of America

A Proclamation

As a people whose land is blessed with a bounty of rivers, lakes, and streams, Americans have always prized the relaxation and pleasure of the open water. "You feel mighty free and easy," Twain's Huck Finn said, "and comfortable on a raft." This quality of the American spirit has made recreational boating one of the most steadily popular and rapidly growing leisure-time activities in the United States.

Each year, however, our Nation's waterways become more crowded with new and faster watercraft as well as an increasing number of traditional vessels. Despite this fact, boating remains one of the least regulated transportation activities. It is essential, therefore, that all operators be familiar with the rules and courtesies of safe boating. National Safe Boating Week reminds all Americans who use the Nation's waterways to educate themselves about and to respect the dangers of the marine environment and to learn how to operate watercraft in a safe and prudent manner.

Boating has its very own "rules of the road." An operator needs to know a great deal before going out on the water. For this reason, the theme of this year's National Safe Boating Week is "Know Before You Go." Those who operate small boats for fishing, hunting, and other sporting activities should have detailed knowledge of the boats they are using, their handling characteristics, how to safely load them, how to prevent them from capsizing, and how to operate and maintain their equipment. In case of an emergency, all boat operators and riders should know how to use their craft's safety devices and be certain they will work as intended; for example, life jackets should be checked, tested, and properly fitted. In addition, boaters need to be watchful for potentially dangerous situations. They must have a thorough knowledge of the waters they are using, the particular hazards they may encounter, and the prospects for environmental conditions such as tides, currents, temperature, and weather that may be dangerous. To avoid collisions and keep traffic moving, all boaters should know the Navigation Rules and the courtesies of safe boating. Most of all, boaters should know their own limitations so that they do not involve themselves and others in situations beyond their skill or physical endurance.

One especially dangerous problem for boaters is the use of alcohol or drugs. Wise boaters will avoid the use of alcohol and drugs while operating a vessel. That wisdom is backed by the law: Operation of a vessel while intoxicated is a major impediment to safety and is now a Federal offense punishable by hefty civil and criminal penalties.

Boating safety is the responsibility of all who use America's waterways. Let National Safe Boating Week be the start of a major campaign to educate boaters to "know before they go."

To promote boating safety, the Congress enacted the Joint Resolution of June 4, 1958 (36 U.S.C. 161), as amended, authorizing and requesting the President to proclaim annually the week commencing on the first Sunday in June as "National Safe Boating Week."

Now, Therefore, I, Ronald Reagan, Presi-

dent of the United States of America, do hereby proclaim the week beginning June 5, 1988, as National Safe Boating Week. I invite the Governors of the States, Puerto Rico, the Northern Mariana Islands, the Virgin Islands, Guam, and American Samoa, and the Mayor of the District of Columbia, to provide for the observance of this week.

In Witness Whereof, I have hereunto set my hand this sixth day of May, in the year of our Lord nineteen hundred and eighty-eight, and of the Independence of the United States of America the two hundred and twelfth.

RONALD REAGAN

[*Filed with the Office of the Federal Register, 11:12 a.m., May 9, 1988*]

Radio Address to the Nation on the Soviet-United States Intermediate-Range Nuclear Forces Treaty
May 7, 1988

My fellow Americans:

Next week the full United States Senate is expected to begin floor debate on the treaty on intermediate-range nuclear forces, known as the INF treaty. You'll recall that Soviet General Secretary Gorbachev and I signed this treaty at our summit meeting in Washington last December. The treaty represents a landmark accomplishment, an historic accomplishment, because, once implemented, it will bring about the elimination of an entire class of American and Soviet nuclear missiles.

Before our nation can commit itself to a treaty, our Constitution provides that the Senate must give its advice and consent. And therefore, last January I formally submitted the INF treaty to the Senate for its consideration. The duty of the Senate in giving its advice and consent to treaties is vital to maintaining our separation of powers, and the role of the Senate is considering the—in considering, I should say, the INF treaty—it's essential.

Senior officials of the administration have been working closely with the Senate. Officials from our State and Defense Departments, our intelligence community, and our arms control agency have provided many hours of testimony before three separate Senate committees, painstakingly responding to the detailed questions posed to them by the Senators on these committees. In addition, Senators have addressed to the administration numerous letters about the treaty and more than 1,200 written questions. We have provided full written responses. So, you'll see that we've worked very hard to meet any Senate concerns over the treaty. And as I've assured the Senate, we'll continue to do so.

Now that the Senate Foreign Relations Committee has approved the INF treaty, the entire Senate will be called on to discharge its constitutional responsibility to provide its advice and consent to the INF treaty. As this debate is about to begin in the historic Senate Chamber, permit me to take a moment to review with you the treaty's background.

The INF treaty is the result of years of hard work by American officials, officials who, in representing you in our negotiations with the Soviet Union, held fast to the key security objectives that had been set out by the United States and our NATO allies. At one point the Soviet Union actually walked away from the table and stayed away from the talks for almost a year and a half. When in early 1985 the Soviets finally returned, we repeated our call for the elimination of this entire class of U.S. and Soviet missiles—my zero option proposal, first put forward all the way back in 1981.

And in 1987 it was the Soviet Union that finally, after 2½ more years of negotiating, came around to the American position. To sum up: In the INF negotiations, we held fast to what we wanted, and we got it. And this is what comes of negotiating from strength. It's the same successful formula—dealing from strength—that we're applying to our other negotiations with the Soviet Union as well. And I assure you: If we don't get what we want in these other areas—in other words, if we do not get good treaties—there will be no treaties.

It's my hope that, in recognition of the important role they play in this process, the 100 Members of the United States Senate will now proceed expeditiously in their debate on the INF treaty. It is, after all, a solid treaty, carefully negotiated; a treaty that stands on its own substantive merits; a treaty that will enhance the security of our country and that of our European and Asian allies now threatened by the various Soviet missiles that will be removed once the treaty is implemented. Senate approval of the treaty will enable us to get on with the job of eliminating these nuclear missiles. It will also allow us to put into action the elaborate verification regime that we achieved in the INF treaty. The most stringent in arms control history, it will enable us to verify effectively that the Soviets are indeed complying with all of the treaty's provisions.

I know that you, the American people, strongly support this INF treaty. And on Capitol Hill, the House of Representatives has already given the treaty its endorsement by an overwhelming vote of 393 to 7. Now that the treaty is moving to floor debate in the Senate, let the debate be vigorous and full, and let it proceed without delay. For I'm confident that the final vote will indeed give advice and consent to this historic treaty, the historic step toward a safer peace.

Until next week, thanks for listening, and God bless you.

Note: The President spoke at 12:06 p.m. from Camp David, MD.

Proclamation 5816—National Maritime Day, 1988
May 9, 1988

By the President of the United States of America

A Proclamation

National Maritime Day reminds us that the American merchant marine has always been essential to our national security and economic growth—and reminds us as well that the men and women of the merchant marine deserve our gratitude every day. The importance of the merchant marine to our national defense was never more clear than in World War II, when, at a cost of more than 6,000 lives and with the loss of 733 ships, the American merchant marine never faltered in delivering cargo for our Armed Forces throughout the world. Earlier this year, these merchant seafarers received veteran status for their valiant service.

Today, the merchant marine continues its roles in trade and defense—and the sailors of our commercial fleets continue to exhibit the patriotism and the many skills that have ever characterized them and their predecessors. It is truly fitting that we pause to salute these seafarers and all other Americans who support them and guard the lifelines of the sea that sustain us all.

In recognition of the importance of the merchant marine, the Congress, by joint resolution approved May 20, 1933, has designated May 22 of each year as "National Maritime Day" and authorized and requested the President to issue annually a proclamation calling for its appropriate observance. This date was chosen to commemorate the day in 1819 when SS SAVANNAH left Savannah, Georgia, on the first transatlantic steamship voyage.

Now, Therefore, I, Ronald Reagan, President of the United States of America, do hereby proclaim May 22, 1988, as National Maritime Day. I urge the people of the United States to observe this day by displaying the flag of the United States at their homes and other suitable places, and I request that all ships sailing under the American flag dress ship on that day.

In Witness Whereof, I have hereunto set my hand this ninth day of May, in the year of our Lord nineteen hundred and eighty-eight, and of the Independence of the United States of America the two hundred and twelfth.

RONALD REAGAN

[*Filed with the Office of the Federal Register, 10:54 a.m., May 10, 1988*]

Proclamation 5817—National Fishing Week, 1988
May 9, 1988

By the President of the United States of America

A Proclamation

This year we again observe a period of special recognition for the place of fishing, both commercial and recreational, in American life. The lore of fishing is, of course, part of American tradition, from Huck Finn to Ernest Hemingway's Nick Adams. Today fishing continues to provide enjoyment for some 60 million American sport fishermen and women and to enhance our economy in many ways.

Our natural resources offer us some of the world's most bountiful fishing. Commercial fishing supplies us with a tremendous amount of food and other products, and recreational fishing contributes some $25 billion to our economy each year and employs some 600,000 people. Fishermen know firsthand the joys of fishing—it is an ideal family activity, for instance—and realize the need for careful stewardship of our sport and commercial fishery resources. The private sector works closely with government at the Federal, State, and local levels to fund fishery conservation restoration projects throughout the States and Territories.

Fishing's countless additions to our economy, our way of life, and our attitude toward our natural resources are all excellent reasons for the American people to celebrate National Fishing Week in a spirit of appreciation for the hardworking members of the commercial and recreational fishing industries and of the place of fishing in our national history and heritage.

The Congress, by Senate Joint Resolution 190, has designated the week of June 6 through June 12, 1988, as "National Fishing Week" and authorized and requested the President to issue a proclamation in its observance.

Now, Therefore, I, Ronald Reagan, President of the United States of America, do hereby proclaim the week of June 6 through June 12, 1988, as National Fishing Week. I call upon the people of the United States and government officials to observe this week with appropriate programs, ceremonies, and activities.

In Witness Whereof, I have hereunto set my hand this ninth day of May, in the year of our Lord nineteen hundred and eighty-eight, and of the Independence of the United States of America the two hundred and twelfth.

RONALD REAGAN

[*Filed with the Office of the Federal Register, 10:55 a.m., May 10, 1988*]

Nomination of Christopher W.S. Ross To Be United States Ambassador to Algeria
May 9, 1988

The President today announced his intention to nominate Christopher W.S. Ross to be Ambassador of the United States to the Democratic and Popular Republic of Algeria. He would succeed L. Craig Johnstone.

Mr. Ross entered the Foreign Service in 1968 as an officer of the U.S. Information Agency. In this capacity, he served as junior officer trainee in Tripoli, Libya, from 1969 to 1970; branch public affairs officer in Fez, Morocco, 1970–1973; information officer in Beirut, Lebanon, 1973–1976; and as public affairs officer in Algiers, Algeria, 1976–1979. In 1979 he was detailed to the Department of State and served as deputy chief of mission and Chargé d'Affaires at the American Embassy in Algiers, 1979–1981; public affairs adviser of the Bureau of Near Eastern and South Asian Affairs, 1981–1982; Special Assistant to the Special Presidential Envoys to the Middle East, 1982–1984; Director of Regional Affairs of the Bureau of Near Eastern and South Asian Affairs, 1984–1985; and Executive Assistant to the Under Secretary of State for Political Affairs from 1985 to the present.

Mr. Ross graduated from Princeton University (A.B., 1965) and the School of Advanced International Studies, Johns Hopkins University (M.A., 1967). He was born March 3, 1943, in Quito, Ecuador. He is married, has one child, and resides in Washington, DC.

Designation of David Korn as Chairman of the National Cancer Advisory Board
May 9, 1988

The President today designated David Korn as Chairman of the National Cancer Advisory Board for the term expiring March 9, 1990. This is a reappointment.

Dr. Korn has served as a member of the Board since 1984. Since 1984 he has served as dean of the Stanford University Medical Center, and vice president since 1986.

Dr. Korn graduated from Harvard University (B.A., 1954; M.D., 1959). He was born March 5, 1933, in Providence, RI. He is married, has three children, and resides in Stanford, CA.

Nomination of Edward Noonan Ney To Be a Member of the Board for International Broadcasting
May 9, 1988

The President today announced his intention to nominate Edward Noonan Ney to be a member of the Board for International Broadcasting for a term expiring April 28, 1991. This is a reappointment.

Since 1986 Mr. Ney has been chairman of Paine Webber/Young & Rubicam Ventures in New York City. Mr. Ney has been with Young & Rubicam since 1951, serving as chairman, chief executive officer and president, vice president, and account supervisor.

Mr. Ney graduated from Amherst College (B.A., 1946). He was born May 26, 1925, in

St. Paul, MN. He served in the United States Navy during World War II. Mr. Ney is married, has three children, and resides in New York.

Nomination of Charles C. Cox To Be a Member of the Securities and Exchange Commission
May 9, 1988

The President today announced his intention to nominate Charles C. Cox to be a member of the Securities and Exchange Commission for the term expiring June 5, 1993. This is a reappointment.

Since 1983 Mr. Cox has been a member of the Securities and Exchange Commission in Washington, DC, and chief economist for the Securities and Exchange Commission, 1982–1983. Prior to this, he was an assistant professor of management at Texas A&M University, 1980–1982, and director of the John M. Olin Fellowship Program, 1981–1982. From 1972 to 1980, he was an assistant professor of economics at Ohio State University.

Mr. Cox graduated from the University of Washington (B.A., 1967) and the University of Chicago (A.M., 1970; Ph.D., 1975). He was born May 8, 1945, in Missoula, MT. He is married and resides in Washington, DC.

Remarks at the Presentation Ceremony for the Small Business Person of the Year Awards
May 9, 1988

Well, I'd like to welcome Senator Abdnor and the State Small Business Persons of the Year, whom we're honoring today. And I think you recognize my bodyguard here—[*laughter*]—the Vice President.

Now, as some of you know, my admiration for President Calvin Coolidge has often been remarked. "Silent Cal" didn't say much, but when he did, his observations were simple and quietly eloquent. And he is perhaps best remembered for his statement that "the business of America is business." I'm reluctant to tamper with President Coolidge's remarks, but a brief and important addition might be this: "The business of America is small business."

All of us can be very proud of the contributions of this nation's 18 million small businesses. The record, quite simply, is incredible. Small business provides well over two-thirds of all new jobs; about 40 percent of our aggregate national output; the bulk of new products and technologies; most of the jobs generated for younger, older, and female workers; and over 66 percent of all first jobs, and, consequently, the initial on-the-job training in basic work skills. And just to take one area, almost every energy-related innovation of this century has come from small business, including the air conditioner, the gasoline engine, and the electric light.

Today about 13 million Americans are engaged in some entrepreneurial activity, either full-time or part-time. The number of part-time entrepreneurs has increased five-fold in recent years. We've seen in the past 5 years the longest unbroken period of peacetime growth on record. The climate necessary to nurture small business development has never been better.

Clearly the economic policies of the 1980's, which have led to an unprecedented turnaround in inflation, from 12 percent to about 4 percent, coupled with commercial interest rates coming down by more than half since we took office, have made it immensely easier to start up a small business and keep it going.

And the 7th annual report on small business, which I am sending to the Congress this week, shows the unparalleled growth of small business not only in the past year but in each year since 1980. Small business has driven this country ahead with over 4.4 million new business starts. And I'm especially pleased that small business has been the first path of economic success for unprecedented numbers of women and minorities, people who started small businesses and became a part of America's economic mainstream. And you can be sure small business had a large role in Friday's economic news. Unemployment was down by two-tenths of 1 percent to 5.4 percent—the lowest rate since August of 1974.

During the next 25 years small business will provide nearly three-fourths of the 43 million new jobs this country will require. Small business will meet this challenge by virtue of its quicker response time, its flexibility, its willingness to take risk, and its willingness to face the very real possibility of failure. In the United States, we have the freedom to fail as well as to win. It is this readiness to risk, this suspension of disbelief as some call it, that sets us apart and drives us to new heights of accomplishment.

Let me leave you with this thought: Small business is about hopes and dreams. It's about making dreams come true—the dreams of men and women who lie awake at night and consider how they can improve their lot in life. Those dreams, those hopes, are a singular and great natural resource.

Today I have the happy duty to announce the Small Business Persons of the Year. This process, culminating in this selection, has been difficult and competitive. There are many fine contestants, and they're to be heartily commended. As in any event—in business, in sports, in politics—someone must be declared the winner. Now, it doesn't mean necessarily that the other contestants have lost, because all of them are winners in their own right and well worthy of being finalists in this event. And that includes many of you who are here today.

And this 1988 Small Business Persons of the Year are Ben Cohen and Jerry Greenfield. Ben Cohen and Jerry Greenfield truly stand out as an example of what American free enterprise is all about. Just 10 years ago, they gave up working for others and founded Ben and Jerry's Homemade, Inc. Beginning with 2 employees in 1978, the company now employs 200, and the $8,000 in startup money now generates annual sales of $30 million, selling in grocery stores in 35 States and in 45 ice cream parlors around the country. And now, I'm going to quit talking and present the awards. Thank you, and God bless you.

Reporter. Mr. President, will you continue to allow astrology to play a part in the makeup of your daily schedule, sir?

The President. You asked for it. I can't, because I never did.

Note: The President spoke at 1:50 p.m. in the Rose Garden at the White House.

Message to the Congress Transmitting the Annual Report on the State of Small Business
May 9, 1988

To the Congress of the United States:

This seventh report to the Congress on the state of small business continues the positive story of earlier messages. Small businesses continue to make significant contributions in expanding industries and in new job growth. Industries dominated by small firms created 1.3 million new jobs in 1987; over 600,000 businesses were incorporated. As the American people enjoyed the longest peacetime expansion in our history, the overall trend for small business remained clear: low interest rates, steady growth, and stable prices have allowed small businesses to thrive.

It is a pleasure to report that the small business news continues to be good news. A wider appreciation of the innovation, the competitive strength, and the quality of life that small firms bring to our economy is an important goal for all who are interested in the long-term economic health of our Nation. We need to understand the small business sector because ignorance of its contributions and inattention to the effect of government activities on it will result in policies that squelch the vitality of small firms.

Over the last 7 years, the policies of this Administration have dramatically improved opportunities for the millions of men and women who are our entrepreneurs. Inflation, which ran at double-digit rates in 1979 and 1980, has averaged 3.3 percent since the recovery began. The prime interest rate, which was 21.5 percent just before I came to Washington, has been below 10 percent for almost 3 years. Lower tax rates, reduced regulation, and streamlined government have made our small business economy the envy of other nations.

The continuation of this strong small business record is a national priority. There is still much to be done. Important changes in Federal policies can further increase the opportunities for businesses to start up and expand. At the same time, we must be wary of proposals that directly attack the flexibility, adaptability, and innovative abilities of small business. If we saddle employers with excessive burdens of economic and personal risk, if we direct the Nation's savings to excessively high levels of government consumption, if we fail to provide opportunities for coming generations of entrepreneurs, then our economic leadership is clearly at risk.

We have made choices in this Administration, choices in favor of innovation, in favor of private enterprise, and in favor of jobs for millions of men and women. In fact, since 1980, the private sector of our economy has produced 13.8 million new jobs. A majority of these jobs have been in small businesses, whose constant testing of new markets, new ideas, and new ways of doing things assures our future strength. Policies to allow this activity to flourish have been the cornerstone of our economic agenda.

Tax rates have been slashed, leaving more resources in the hands of millions of Americans who operate or invest in small businesses. Business tax rates are at their lowest level since 1941; individual rates, which apply to the greatest number of small business owners, are at their lowest since 1931. Changes in tax rules have reduced the impact of tax-induced acrobatics on business decision-making. Estate-tax reform has allowed thousands of family-owned businesses to stay under family ownership.

Continued deregulation in transportation, communications, and financial services has allowed thousands of new firms to flourish and many thousands of new jobs to be established as firms discover new markets and better ways of performing old tasks. Elimination of many hours of Federal paperwork has allowed business managers to devote more of their valuable time to managing the business. With improved economic analysis, pursuant to my Executive Order No. 12291 and the Regulatory Flexibility Act, millions of dollars in regulatory costs have been avoided or eliminated. In hundreds of individual regulatory proceedings, we chose to reduce regulations, to search for alternatives that promote responsible, independent decisions by businesses. We chose not to believe that blind faith in the efficiency of regulation is the only answer to society's problems.

Reforms of our Federal procurement system have opened up new opportunities for small businesses to compete and have ensured that the government is a responsible business partner. Today, we do a better job paying our bills on time, and we draw on small businesses for a greater share of the $380 billion of goods and services purchased in 1987 by the Federal Government. This increased competition in Federal procurement assures us that tax dollars are spent more wisely.

The emergence of the private sector as a major provider of research and development support is one of the most important developments in science and technology in the last two decades. Approximately one-half of U.S. R&D expenditures are funded by private sources, up from about one-third in 1965.

We have sought to draw on the energy of firms large and small. The Small Business Innovation Development Act, the National Cooperative Research Act, and the creation of a tax credit for research and development expenses have refocused efforts to develop new products and ideas. Reductions in patent fees for small firms and steps to automate the patent system are making it simpler for small companies to protect their inventions.

I count as one of the central accomplishments of this Administration the shift in the debate on these issues. The steps we have taken to improve the small business climate reflect a new and broader understanding by policymakers. Affordable credit, stable markets, simpler Federal regulations, and lower tax rates all combine to benefit thousands of people whose days—and sometimes nights—are occupied in pursuing their individual entrepreneurial dreams.

Much remains to be accomplished on the small business agenda. Many of the policy changes recommended by delegates to the 1986 White House Conference on Small Business are still before us. All of us must work hard to ensure that past gains are solidified and expanded.

Small business concern about the size of the Federal deficit is as warranted today as it was during the White House Conference in August 1986. I welcome small business support for a line-item veto, and I hope that the Congress will give future presidents the same authority that 43 governors have to pare the fat out of massive appropriations bills.

Similarly, our budget process needs the discipline of a constitutionally required balanced budget. Small business owners understand this, and I invite the Congress to join me and the plurality of Americans in supporting such a measure. A government that lives within its means will free billions of dollars in private resources for yet greater small business growth.

Progress in reducing Federal spending will allow more firms, large and small, to expand into world markets, a necessity as our economy becomes increasingly interconnected with those of other nations. Negotiations to reduce trade barriers around the world are underway. Small business owners will find considerable opportunity in new markets opened by the historic trade agreement we have signed with our largest trading partner, Canada. Legislative approval of the agreement with Canada and success in other negotiations will reduce tariff and other barriers to American products and expand opportunities for our service and agricultural sectors. Our economy is increasingly integrated into the world economy; we need the resources, talent, and energy of small business to meet the competitive challenges ahead.

In addition to reducing barriers to trade among nations, we need to make sure that our domestic laws and regulations do not themselves act as barriers to increased competitiveness. Small business owners have felt the effects of such constraints quite sharply, and the small business agenda highlights the types of policies we must work toward. For example, product liability reform has been an important goal of both small firm owners and this Administration.

The Congress currently has before it several bills that aim at the heart of independent business decision-making. These are bills that layer rules, mandates, and employer obligations on top of each other in an effort to regulate the relationship between employers and their workers. Federally mandated leave and health care, duplicative notice requirements on workplace safety, advance notice of layoffs and plant closings or across-the-board increases in the minimum wage combine to limit the flexibility that is the strength of small firms and indeed the strength of our economy. Uniform, inflexible Federal requirements are not the best answer to the issues these bills address.

I urge the Congress to listen to the small business owners who have increased overall employment so dramatically, who have produced a disproportionate share of innovations, and who make our economy different from, and more lively than, that of other nations. Government did not create these jobs or produce these innovations. It cannot be presumed that this national resource—small business—can continue to flourish as it has in the past if it is overly burdened with mandates and obligations or with excessive taxation and regulation.

The report that follows, prepared by the Small Business Administration, details the latest information available on the state of the small business economy. It encourages all of us who have a hand in shaping Federal policy to redouble our efforts to ensure that all Americans who wish to can turn ideas and dreams into businesses and jobs.

RONALD REAGAN

The White House,
May 9, 1988.

Designation of Edward E. Hood, Jr., as Vice Chairman of the President's National Security Telecommunications Advisory Committee
May 9, 1988

The President today announced his intention to designate Edward E. Hood, Jr., as Vice Chairman of the President's National Security Telecommunications Advisory Committee for a term of 1 year. He would succeed Paul W. Henson.

Since 1979 Mr. Hood has been vice chairman of the board and executive officer at General Electric Co. in Fairfield, CT, and senior vice president and sector executive of technical systems and material at General Electric Co., 1977–1979. Mr. Hood has been with the General Electric Co. since 1957 serving in various capacities.

Mr. Hood graduated from North Carolina State (B.S., 1952; M.S., 1953). He was born September 15, 1930, in Boonville, NC. He served in the United States Air Force, 1952–1956. Mr. Hood is married, has two children, and resides in New Canaan, CT.

Remarks on Presenting the Presidential Medal of Freedom to Lord Peter Carrington
May 10, 1988

The President. I know that here we have the NATO Ambassadors. We have some Members of our Congress, other guests. And, Peter and Lady Carrington, we're all here today to honor you on the occasion of your final visit to the United States as NATO Secretary General. You've done a magnificent job at NATO. Your efforts on behalf of all of us during the past 4 years have set a new standard. But we're recognizing something more than simply 4 years of a job well done. Your stewardship of the alliance has continued a life's work in support of human decency and the ideal of freedom—the very basis of the compact for peace we call NATO. It is that commitment and that contribution which the American people are honoring today.

Your first taste of working in this alliance came as a highly decorated tank commander of the Grenadier Guards during World War II. I'm sure, Peter, that there have been times as you've presided over the North Atlantic Council, with its 16 sovereign members seemingly going off in as many directions, when you've been reminded of the confusion of the battlefield. You may even have had a moment or two when you preferred the confusion of the battlefield. [*Laughter*] But one of your special gifts has always been an ability to find common ground, and nowhere is that more important than at NATO.

When you took over the reins in 1984, common ground seemed a precious, scarce commodity in the alliance. The decision by NATO to deploy Pershing II and ground-launched cruise missiles in response to the Soviet SS–20 threat had placed a number of allied governments under enormous political pressure. The Soviets were waging an aggressive propaganda campaign aimed squarely at the cohesion and unity of NATO, and those were difficult days. But our adversaries have rarely understood the strength of our democratic societies and political leadership, and they certainly had not taken your measure, Peter. No one did more to hold the alliance consensus of INF together than Peter Carrington. You believed in NATO when it counted, and that spirit has been contagious.

The results of your leadership speak for themselves. Recognizing that we would not back down, the Soviets returned to the bargaining table in Geneva. And last December General Secretary Gorbachev and I signed the INF treaty. What it should have taught us is that political solidarity with our allies and a shared willingness to do what is necessary to defend ourselves are the indispensable keys to better relations across the board with the Soviet Union.

Keeping a firm hand on the NATO tiller has not been your only accomplishment, Peter. You've also shown uncommon vision in charting the way ahead. As frustrating as it must be at times to have to accommodate to so many views in NATO, you have understood perhaps better than any of us that it is in our diversity and independence that we find our strength. Reconciling the occasionally differing views of the European members of the alliance with those of the North Americans—on a special challenge—you have quipped to me that it can be cold and lonely out there in the mid-Atlantic, where you do your work. But just as your leadership fortified the alliance during INF, it has been your gift of statesmanship which has brought our transatlantic partnership to a level of unity and common purpose unparalleled in the history of NATO.

If there was any doubt about where the alliance was heading in the earlier part of this decade, that doubt is surely gone today. Under your able hand, we have recommitted ourselves to the indispensable task of maintaining our capacity to defend ourselves and each other. You have set in motion major new programs within NATO to help all the member states better utilize the defense resources which our publics have entrusted to us. We and our partners have settled on an arms control agenda which can move the world to a new era of international political relations. Perhaps most important, you have personally symbolized the higher values which hold the alliance together: political and economic freedom, the protection of basic human rights, and a fundamental decency in the way in which nations deal with each other.

You will be sorely missed at NATO, Lord Carrington. Believe me, I know a hard act to follow when I see one. But as I said at the outset, your 4 years in Brussels have been only a small part of four decades of commitment to the ideals which unite the West. I am confident that you will continue to channel your singular talents and energy to the service of all that the alliance represents.

And so without further ado, let me, on behalf of the American people, present you with this nation's highest civilian honor, the Presidential Medal of Freedom. And let me read this citation:

"Foreign Secretary, Defense Minister, Parliamentary leader, and tank commander, Peter Alexander Rupert Carrington, the Sixth Baron Carrington, has proved himself the devoted servant of Her Majesty's government, a friend of the American people, and the faithful defender of human freedom.

"As Secretary General of the North Atlantic Treaty Organization, his tireless efforts have at a critical moment in history strengthened the cause of peace and freedom for all humanity. For his selfless service the American people honor him and extend to him their gratitude and warmest affection."

This is our highest civilian award, the American Medal of Freedom.

Lord Carrington. Thank you. Mr. President, you must realize how deeply honored and moved I am by the award which you have just given me, and immensely grateful. I know how rare an honor it is for an

American to be granted the Presidential Medal of Freedom. How much more so for a foreigner—but a foreigner, as you have reminded me, who sits marooned in the middle of the Atlantic, not obviously the world's most hospitable ocean. The NATO General Secretary does indeed have to detach himself from his own national roots if he is fully to serve the interests of the alliance, and particularly if he is going to keep the transatlantic bridge in good repair.

Now, you, Mr. President, have made that task for me an easy, an enjoyable, and a satisfying one. Your door has always been open to me. You have always been ready to listen when I've tried to convey the views of your European allies and my impression of the state of our alliance. And my task was not only made easy by your openness to me personally but also by your leadership of the alliance.

Throughout your Presidency, you've shown us a dynamic America—sure of herself and sure of where she's going. Your European allies have greatly benefited from the results and the vigor of your leadership. And when you met them in the NATO Council, as you last did just 2 months ago in Brussels, yours was a reassuring and a strengthening presence. You've seen to it that America's defenses remain strong, and thus that our collective security was preserved. With clarity and force you've shown how Atlantic security is indivisible, how its tight mesh unites all the 16 member countries of the alliance. We're united in the strategy to defend our peoples, our homelands, and our freedom.

And you have reminded us that to deter any potential aggressor we must maintain together a balance of conventional and nuclear forces. And your own and the American people's commitment to our collective security can, of course, be seen most clearly in the presence of 300,000 American troops you've stationed in Europe. And less visible, but of course equally important, are the U.S. strategic nuclear forces, which are the ultimate guarantor of our security. But security must go hand in hand with political effort to enable all of us to live more sensibly together. And we have in the INF treaty an historic agreement, the first negotiated reduction in nuclear forces since the advent of those terrifying weapons. And that in itself may hold out the promise of even better things to come.

Sir, we would not have managed without you. You and Vice President Bush have been supported by statesmen and public servants of great quality. George Shultz has been a rock of stability. He has taken Herculean pains to consult your European allies over every move in our relations with the Soviet Union. Frank Carlucci and Cap Weinberger have restored to American forces in the alliance a dynamism and an elan which could not have been imagined 8 years ago.

Mr. President, over the years it's so often been said that NATO is in crisis or that the alliance is beset by danger. No one would pretend that we don't have our problems and our challenges. But as I once said, though that we may not always as an alliance sing in unison, we nearly always manage to sing in harmony. And as I leave NATO after 4 rewarding years, I am as optimistic about the future of the alliance as I was when I first became associated with it, now over 30 years ago. And not least because the generous and the farsighted spirit of the American people continues to live today through the leadership which you, Mr. President, have given us in these last 8 years.

Note: The President spoke at 1:18 p.m. in the Roosevelt Room at the White House. Earlier, the President and Lord Carrington had lunch in the Residence.

Executive Order 12640—The President's Committee on Employment of People With Disabilities
May 10, 1988

By virtue of the authority vested in me as President by the Constitution and laws of the United States of America, and in order to provide for the carrying out of the provisions of the Joint Resolution approved July 11, 1949, ch. 302, 63 Stat. 409, as amended, and the provisions of the Rehabilitation Act of 1973, P.L. 93–112, Section 501 (a)–(f), as amended, it is ordered as follows:

Section 1. Establishment and Composition of the President's Committee. (a) There is hereby established the President's Committee on Employment of People with Disabilities (hereinafter referred to as the Committee or as the President's Committee).

(b) The Committee shall be composed of a Chairman and not more than four Vice Chairmen, who shall be appointed by and serve at the pleasure of the President, and of so many other members as may be appointed thereto from time to time by the Chairman of the President's Committee from among persons (including representatives of organizations) who can contribute to the achievement of the objectives of the Committee. Members appointed by the Chairman shall be appointed for a term of 3 years and may be reappointed. The Chairman of the President's Committee may at any time terminate the service of any member of the President's Committee, except any member appointed by the President.

(c) The Chairman of the President's Committee, upon the advice of the Executive Committee (hereinafter provided for), may designate as, or invite to be, associate members of the President's Committee any heads of Federal departments or agencies that have responsibility for training and rehabilitation services or advocate activities touching the field of interest of the Committee or that are leading employers of individuals with disabilities.

(d) Representatives of business, industry, labor, private organizations, public agencies, other concerned organizations, and individuals with disabilities who are not members may be invited to attend meetings of the Committee.

Sec. 2. Functions of the Committee. The President's Committee shall provide advice and information as to the development of maximum employment opportunities for people who are physically disabled, mentally retarded, and mentally ill. To this end the Committee shall advise the President as to information that can be used by employers, labor unions, and national and international organizations, suggest programs for public education, and suggest methods of enlisting cooperation among organizations and agencies, Federal, State, and local officials, Governors' and local Committees on Employment of People with Disabilities, professional organizations, organized labor, and appropriate international organizations. In carrying out these functions vested in it by the Rehabilitation Act, as amended, the Committee shall be guided by the general policies of the National Council on the Handicapped and shall work closely with the Department of Labor, the Department of Education, the Department of Health and Human Services, the Veterans' Administration, State employment security agencies, and State vocational rehabilitation agencies.

Sec. 3. Executive Committee. (a) There is hereby established the Executive Committee of the President's Committee on Employment of People with Disabilities. The Executive Committee shall be composed of the Chairman of the President's Committee, who shall also be the Chairman of the Executive Committee, the Vice Chairman of the President's Committee, and so many additional members as will provide an Executive Committee of not less than 15 and not more than 30 members. The said additional members shall be appointed for a term of 3 years by the Chairman of the President's Committee from among the members of the President's Committee or otherwise. The Chairman of the President's

Committee may at any time terminate the service of any member of the Executive Committee.

(b) The Executive Committee shall advise and assist the Chairman of the President's Committee in the conduct of the business of the President's Committee and, as authorized by the President's Committee or the Chairman thereof (with due regard for the responsibilities of other Federal agencies), shall study the problems of people with disabilities in obtaining and retaining suitable employment, invite authorities in the various professional, technical, and other pertinent fields to advise it in the exploration of those problems, and review plans and projects for advocating the employment of people with disabilities.

Sec. 4. Advisory Council. There is hereby established the Advisory Council on Employment of People with Disabilities, which shall advise the President's Committee with respect to the responsibilities of the Committee. The Council shall be composed of the Chairman of the President's Committee, who shall also be the Chairman of the Council, and of the following-named officers, or their respective alternates: Secretary of State; Secretary of the Treasury; Secretary of Defense; The Attorney General; Secretary of the Interior; Secretary of Agriculture; Secretary of Commerce; Secretary of Labor; Secretary of Health and Human Services; Secretary of Housing and Urban Development; Secretary of Transportation; Secretary of Education; Chairman, Equal Employment Opportunity Commission; Administrator of General Services; Director, Office of Personnel Management; Director, United States Information Agency; Administrator of Veterans' Affairs; and The Postmaster General.

Sec. 5. Administrative and Incidental Matters. (a) The President's Committee, the Executive Committee, and the Advisory Council shall each meet on call of the Chairman of the President's Committee at a time and place designated by the Chairman. In the case of the President's Committee and the Executive Committee, the Chairman shall call at least one meeting and two meetings, respectively, to be held during each calendar year.

(b) In the absence of designation by the President, the Chairman of the President's Committee may from time to time designate a Vice Chairman of the President's Committee to be one or more of the following-named in the absence of the Chairman: Acting Chairman of the President's Committee, Acting Chairman of the Executive Committee, and Acting Chairman of the Advisory Council. The Chairman of the President's Committee shall from time to time assign other duties to the Vice Chairmen thereof.

(c) The Chairman of the President's Committee shall on behalf of the President direct the President's Committee and its functions.

(d) The Chairman may from time to time prescribe such necessary rules, procedures, and policies relating to the President's Committee, the Executive Committee, and the Advisory Council, and to their affairs, as are not inconsistent with law or with the provisions of this Order.

(e) The Vice Chairmen shall advise and counsel the Committee and shall represent the Committee on appropriate occasions.

(f) All members (including the Chairman and Vice Chairmen) of the President's Committee, the Executive Committee, and the Advisory Council shall serve without compensation. The Chairman and the Vice Chairmen of the President's Committee may receive transportation and per diem allowances as authorized by law for persons serving without compensation. Persons with disabilities serving as Chairman or Vice Chairmen may be compensated for attendant expenses, consistent with government procedures and practices.

(g) Employees of the President's Committee shall be appointed, subject to law, and shall be directed by the Chairman of the Committee. To such extent as may be mutually arranged by the Chairman of the Committee and the Secretary of Labor, employees of the Committee shall be subject to the administrative rules, regulations, and procedures of the Department of Labor.

(h) The Department of Labor is requested to make available to the President's Committee necessary office space and to furnish the Committee, under such arrangements respecting financing as may be appropriate, necessary equipment, supplies, and services. The estimates of appropriations for the operations of the Committee shall be included within the framework of the appropriations structure of the Department of Labor, in such manner as the Director of the Office of Management and Budget may prescribe. The Chairman of the Committee, in cooperation with the Assistant Secretary for Administration and Management of the Department of Labor, shall be responsible for the preparation and justification of the estimates of appropriations for the Committee.

Sec. 6. Reporting. The President's Committee shall report annually to the President, who may apprise the Congress, and other interested organizations and individuals on the progress and problems of maximizing employment opportunities for people with disabilities.

Sec. 7. Prior Orders; Transition. (a) To the extent that this Order is inconsistent with any provision of any prior order, or with any provisions of any regulation or other measure or disposition, heretofore issued, made, or taken by the President or by any other officer of the Executive branch of the Government, this Order shall control. Executive Order No. 11480 of September 9, 1969, as amended, is hereby superseded.

(b) Without further action by the President or the Chairman of the Committee, all members, employees, records, property, funds, and pending business of the President's Committee on Employment of the Handicapped provided for in Executive Order No. 11480 of September 9, 1969, as amended, shall on the date of this Order become members, employees, records, property, funds, and pending business of the Committee established by this Order.

(c) The tenure of persons as members of the Committee in pursuance of the provisions of section 7(b) of this Order, (i), in the case of persons appointed to the predecessor Committee by the President, shall be at the pleasure of the President, and (ii), in the case of other members, shall be for periods equal to their respective unexpired terms under Executive Order No. 11480, as amended, but shall also be subject to the provisions of the last sentence of Section 1(b) of this Order.

RONALD REAGAN

The White House,
May 10, 1988.

[*Filed with the Office of the Federal Register, 10:49 a.m., May 11, 1988*]

Message to the Congress Transmitting the Annual Report of the Corporation for Public Broadcasting
May 10, 1988

To the Congress of the United States:

In accordance with the Communications Act of 1934, as amended (47 U.S.C. 396(i)), I transmit herewith the Annual Report of the Corporation for Public Broadcasting for Fiscal Year 1987. The report implies that funding to the Corporation should be expanded. This does not reflect my views. My budget requests that the Congress freeze funding to the Corporation at its 1988 level of $214 million. I request that the Congress appropriate no more than the level I have proposed.

RONALD REAGAN

The White House,
May 10, 1988.

Proclamation 5818—Just Say No Week, 1988
May 10, 1988

By the President of the United States of America

A Proclamation

This year again we observe a period of time to reflect on our efforts as individuals and as a Nation to create a drug-free society. We do so in the knowledge that we have both cause for hope and cause to redouble our efforts.

Dedicated law enforcement officers and government personnel continue to fight the drug traffickers here and abroad who make war on all of us. Families, churches, schools, and communities are fostering wholesome and healthy attitudes and behavior that are guiding young and old alike. Public opinion polls and other measures show an increasing awareness of the seriousness of illegal drug use and alcohol abuse. And more and more of us see in our American heritage of faith, freedom, spiritual values, and personal achievement a true, rewarding way of life that far outstrips the false, harmful, and joyless path of drug addiction.

America's young people are responding to education and prevention efforts, but continued and intensified work is needed—and at earlier ages. Positive peer pressure can significantly affect children and can create environments in which illegal drug use and alcohol abuse are unacceptable. The "Just Say No" movement, which grew out of great public concern and strong and effective encouragement by the First Lady, is now a rallying cry for youth who want to say "Yes" to life and to the future.

During Just Say No Week this year, on May 11, children across our land will take part in a national "Just Say No" walk against drugs. This week of observance is an excellent time for each of us to commend—and to assist—the young people of our country and all of the parents, educators, and so many other Americans who continue to develop and carry out efforts against illegal drug use and alcohol abuse.

The Congress, by House Joint Resolution 545, has designated the week of May 8 through May 14, 1988, as "Just Say No Week" and has authorized and requested the President to issue a proclamation in observance of this event.

Now, Therefore, I, Ronald Reagan, President of the United States of America, do hereby proclaim the week of May 8 through May 14, 1988, as Just Say No Week. I call upon the American people and officials at every level of government, the clergy, the private sector, civic groups, educators, and the communications media to observe this week with appropriate programs, ceremonies, and activities.

In Witness Whereof, I have hereunto set my hand this 10th day of May, in the year of our Lord nineteen hundred and eighty-eight, and of the Independence of the United States of America the two hundred and twelfth.

RONALD REAGAN

[*Filed with the Office of the Federal Register, 12:08 p.m., May 11, 1988*]

Proclamation 5819—National Osteoporosis Prevention Week, 1988
May 10, 1988

By the President of the United States of America

A Proclamation

This year we again set aside a week to mark our concern over osteoporosis. This bone-weakening disease is the most common cause of bone fractures in the elderly and is a major health problem that afflicts millions of Americans. Osteoporosis can occur in men, but women are the majority of its victims. In fact, it affects half of American women over age 45 and 90 percent of women over age 75.

A fall, blow, or lifting action that would not injure the average person can easily cause one or more bones to break in a person with severe osteoporosis. Any bones may be affected, although fractures of the spine, wrists, and hips are the most common. Osteoporosis is the underlying reason for 1.3 million bone fractures a year, and its incidence will increase as our population ages.

Fortunately, scientific knowledge about this disease has grown, and there is reason for hope. Research is revealing that prevention may be achieved through estrogen replacement therapy for older women and through adequate calcium intake and regular weight-bearing exercise for people of all ages. New approaches to diagnosis and treatment are also under active investigation. For this work to continue and for us to take advantage of the knowledge we have already gained, public awareness of osteoporosis and of the importance of further scientific research is essential.

The Congress, by Senate Joint Resolution 250, has designated the week of May 8 through May 14, 1988, as "National Osteoporosis Prevention Week" and has authorized and requested the President to issue a proclamation in observance of this event.

Now, Therefore, I, Ronald Reagan, President of the United States of America, do hereby proclaim the week of May 8 through May 14, 1988, as National Osteoporosis Prevention Week. I urge the people of the United States and educational, philanthropic, scientific, medical, and health care organizations to observe this week with appropriate programs, ceremonies, and activities.

In Witness Whereof, I have hereunto set my hand this tenth day of May, in the year of our Lord nineteen hundred and eighty-eight, and of the Independence of the United States of America the two hundred and twelfth.

RONALD REAGAN

[*Filed with the Office of the Federal Register, 12:09 p.m., May 11, 1988*]

Proclamation 5820—National Foster Care Month, 1988
May 10, 1988

By the President of the United States of America

A Proclamation

The family is the indispensable foundation of society; at its best, it performs tasks that no other entity can hope to duplicate. The family has the primary responsibility for nurturing children, transmitting our culture, and building the character traits that make for healthy adults and good citizens. Upon the strength of the family rests the future of our Nation.

For a variety of reasons, however, some parents are unable to provide a minimally acceptable level of care for their children, and temporary or permanent alternative placement is necessary. National Foster Care Month presents an appropriate opportunity for all of us—public officials, business, religious, and community leaders, and parents alike—to reflect on the pressures facing families today and on the need for increased efforts to ensure that abandoned or abused children have the opportunity to live in healthy, loving homes.

The emphasis in foster care must be on the well-being of the child, and public policy must serve to promote alternative placement that represents actual care and not mere custody. Because the tasks facing foster parents often include special challenges, such as care of a child who is physically or mentally handicapped or who has been emotionally or physically abused, the mothers and fathers whom society qualifies to accept this added responsibility must be held to a high standard. To accomplish this goal, many more happy and successful families must be willing to step forward and to offer to share heart and home with children desperately longing for both. The aim of all foster care must be the establishment for the child of a sense of permanence and belonging.

National Foster Care Month also provides an opportunity to offer public thanks for the sacrifices and dedication of the many foster parents and concerned professionals working in the field of foster care. Their jobs require extraordinary patience and love, and their rewards are often reaped only years after their primary labor is done—when the child is grown and fully appreciates what has been done for him or her, or when society pauses from its hectic rush forward to recognize the good they have accomplished.

Finally, this month-long observance calls us to deeper thought on the role of values and ideas in the very formation of families. For if the goal of child care is the creation of a warm, stable environment, it is self-evident that the best place to start is in the pursuit of strong and stable marriages. If the need for foster care is not to outstrip our society's capacity for remedial action, it is critical to focus more efforts on policies that promote and protect the triad of mother, father, and child as the harmonious chord God intended for them to be.

To demonstrate our esteem and appreciation for those who devotedly and selflessly share their lives with foster children, the Congress, by Senate Joint Resolution 59, has designated the month of May 1988 as "National Foster Care Month" and has requested the President to issue a proclamation in its observance.

Now, Therefore, I, Ronald Reagan, President of the United States of America, do hereby proclaim the month of May 1988 as National Foster Care Month. I call upon all educators, churches, health care providers, the media, public and private organizations, and the people of the United States to observe this month with appropriate ceremonies and activities.

In Witness Whereof, I have hereunto set my hand this tenth day of May, in the year of our Lord nineteen hundred and eighty-eight, and of the Independence of the United States of America the two hundred and twelfth.

RONALD REAGAN

[*Filed with the Office of the Federal Register, 12:10 p.m., May 11, 1988*]

Proclamation 5821—Older Americans Month, 1988
May 10, 1988

By the President of the United States of America

A Proclamation

Celebration of Older Americans Month summons us as individuals and as a Nation to careful reflection on our attitudes toward and treatment of those of us who are elderly.

If we answer this summons, the need for commensurate action will be apparent to us. Senior citizens merit our express appreciation for their countless, invaluable contributions, past and present, to our Nation. They deserve as well our best efforts to avoid and to dispel false ideas about aging. This requires all of us to become more willing to familiarize ourselves with the many ways older people continue to achieve in every area of endeavor as they begin second careers, further their educations, and voluntarily serve their neighbors both at home and abroad. We can also resolve to lend our support as the private sector and public agencies help senior citizens maintain independence and as State and Area Agencies on Aging work with community leaders and groups to create responsive service systems for older Americans.

By every indication, those systems are working well, as is the overall economy whose growth and vitality are necessary for these systems to function as they are designed. The Social Security system, which began the decade in desperate straits, has been rescued and is on solid ground as we near the end of the '80s. Reform of the tax code has brought relief to many elderly taxpayers, and up to a quarter of all of these citizens will pay no Federal income tax whatsoever. The poverty rate among the elderly has been reduced to the lowest level in our history.

The true wealth of our older Americans—some 30 million men and women over the age of 65 whose life expectancy continues to grow—lies in the wisdom and experience they have to offer succeeding generations. We are wise ourselves to tap that accumulation of knowledge and good judgment and to pay the tribute of close attention to our venerable fellow citizens, the prime architects of the peace, freedom, and prosperity that are our present blessing and future hope.

The Congress, by House Joint Resolution 508, has recognized the month of May 1988 as "Older Americans Month" and has requested the President to issue a proclamation in observance of this event.

Now, Therefore, I, Ronald Reagan, President of the United States of America, do hereby proclaim May 1988 as Older Americans Month. I call upon the American people to observe this month with appropriate programs, ceremonies, and activities.

In Witness Whereof, I have hereunto set my hand this tenth day of May, in the year of our Lord nineteen hundred and eighty-eight, and of the Independence of the United States of America the two hundred and twelfth.

RONALD REAGAN

[*Filed with the Office of the Federal Register, 12:11 p.m., May 11, 1988*]

Nomination of Richard Llewellyn Williams To Be United States Ambassador to Mongolia

May 10, 1988

The President today announced his intention to nominate Richard Llewellyn Williams, of the District of Columbia, a career member of the Senior Foreign Service, Class of Minister-Counselor, as Ambassador to the Mongolian People's Republic. Diplomatic relations were established at the ambassadorial level with the Mongolian People's Republic in January 1987.

Mr. Williams is currently Country Director of the Office of Chinese and Mongolian Affairs at the Department of State in Washington, DC. Previously, he served as deputy consul general in Hong Kong from 1981 to 1985, and as consul general in Guangzhou (Canton). He was Deputy Director of the Office of Micronesian Status Negotiations, 1978–1979, and a student at the National War College, 1977–1978. Mr. Williams was a country officer for Fiji and Papua New Guinea at the Department of State, 1975–1977; an international relations officer for the Bureau of Intelligence and Research, 1972–1975; and a political officer for the U.S. consulate general in Hong Kong, 1968–1972. He attended the Foreign Institute for Chinese language training, 1967–1968. From 1965 to 1967, he was detailed to the White House correspondence staff. He served in the United States Army, 1953–1955, and joined the Foreign Service in 1956.

Mr. Williams graduated from the University of Chicago (A.B., 1948), Purdue University (B.S., 1951), and Harvard University (M.B.A., 1953). He was born December 28, 1929, in Chicago, IL. He is married, has two children, and resides in Washington, DC.

Nomination of Philip D. Winn To Be United States Ambassador to Switzerland
May 10, 1988

The President today announced his intention to nominate Philip D. Winn to be Ambassador to Switzerland. He would succeed Faith Ryan Whittlesey.

Since 1987 Mr. Winn has served as chairman of the board of the Philips Development Corp., in Englewood, CO. Prior to this he served as chairman of the board for Philip D. Winn & Associates, Inc., 1976–1987. From 1981 to 1982, he was Assistant Secretary at the Department of Housing and Urban Development and Federal Housing Commissioner. Mr. Winn also served as senior vice president of Witkin Homes/U.S. Homes, 1964–1976.

Mr. Winn graduated from the University of Michigan (B.A., 1948). He was born February 1, 1925, in New Britain, CT. He served in the United States Army, 1943–1945. Mr. Winn is married, has two children, and resides in Englewood, CO.

Nomination of W. Allen Wallis To Be Alternate United States Governor of the International Bank for Reconstruction and Development and the Inter-American Development Bank
May 10, 1988

The President today announced his intention to nominate W. Allen Wallis to be United States Alternate Governor of the International Bank for Reconstruction and Development for a term of 5 years, and to be United States Alternate Governor of the Inter-American Development Bank for a term of 5 years. This is a reappointment.

Since 1982 Mr. Wallis has been Under Secretary of State for Economic Affairs at the Department of State in Washington, DC. Prior to this he served at the University of Rochester as chancellor, 1970–1982, and president, 1962–1970. Mr. Wallis was also with the University of Chicago, serving as dean of the graduate school of business, 1956–1962, and as chairman of the department of statistics, 1949–1957. He has also worked at the National Bureau of Economic Research, the Ford Foundation, and the Center for Advanced Study in the Behavioral Sciences.

Mr. Wallis graduated from the University of Minnesota (A.B., 1932). He was born November 5, 1912, in Philadelphia, PA. He is married, has two children, and resides in Washington, DC.

Appointment of Louis F. Laun as a Commissioner-Observer on the Commission on Security and Cooperation in Europe
May 11, 1988

The President today announced his intention to appoint Louis F. Laun to be an executive branch Commissioner-Observer on the Commission on Security and Cooperation in Europe. He would succeed Alfred Hugh Kingon.

Since 1986 Mr. Laun has been an Assistant Secretary for International Economic Policy at the Department of Commerce in Washington, DC. Previously he was Deputy

Assistant Secretary of Operations for the U.S. Foreign and Commercial Service at the Department of Commerce in 1986. From 1977 to 1986, he was president of the American Paper Institute. Mr. Laun was also Deputy Administrator of the Small Business Administration, 1973–1977, and Associate Administrator in 1973.

Mr. Laun graduated from Yale University (A.B., 1942). He was born May 19, 1920, in Battle Creek, MI. He served in the United States Marine Corps, 1942–1946. He is married, has three children, and resides in Washington, DC.

Nomination of John Thomas McCarthy To Be United States Ambassador to Lebanon

May 11, 1988

The President today announced his intention to nominate John Thomas McCarthy, of New York, a career member of the Senior Foreign Service, Class of Minister-Counselor, to be Ambassador to the Republic of Lebanon. He would succeed John Hubert Kelly.

Since 1985 Mr. McCarthy has been deputy chief of mission at the American Embassy in Islamabad, Pakistan. Prior to this, he was Deputy Assistant Secretary of State for Public Affairs, 1983–1985, and Director of the Office of Investment in the Economic Bureau, 1980–1983. In 1976 he was assigned to Brussels, Belgium, as trade officer at the U.S. Mission to the European Communities, followed by an assignment as economic counselor at the U.S. Embassy in Brussels from 1978 to 1980. He was the European Community desk officer, 1973–1976, and attended Harvard University for Atlantic affairs training, 1972–1973. Mr. McCarthy was a political officer in the Bureau of International Organization Affairs at the Department of State, 1971–1972. In 1968 he attended the Foreign Service Institute for Thai language training, followed by a position as vice consul at the American consulate in Chiang Mai, Thailand, 1969–1971. Mr. McCarthy entered the Foreign Service in 1962.

Mr. McCarthy graduated from Manhattan College (B.A., 1961) and Harvard University (M.P.A., 1973). He was born December 27, 1939, in New York City. He is married, has three children, and resides in Brentwood, NY.

Appointment of George James Benston as a Member of the Interim Board of Directors of the Federal Agricultural Mortgage Corporation

May 11, 1988

The President today announced his intention to appoint George James Benston to be a member of the Interim Board of Directors of the Federal Agricultural Mortgage Corporation. This is a new position.

Since 1987 Dr. Benston has been the John H. Harland Professor of Finance, Accounting, and Economics at the School of Business Administration at Emory University, in Atlanta, GA. Prior to this he was a professor of accounting, economics, and finance at the University of Rochester, 1969–1987. He has also been an honorary visiting professor for City University, London School of Economics, in London, England, since 1985.

Dr. Benston graduated from Queens College (B.A., 1952), New York University

(M.B.A., 1953), and the University of Chicago (Ph.D., 1963). He was born March 18, 1932, in New York City. He served in the United States Navy, 1953–1956, and the Reserves, 1956–1961. Dr. Benston is married, has two children, and resides in Atlanta, GA.

Appointment of Erwin P. Bettinghaus as a Member of the National Cancer Advisory Board
May 11, 1988

The President today announced his intention to appoint Erwin P. Bettinghaus to be a member of the National Cancer Advisory Board for a term expiring March 9, 1994. He will succeed Barbara Gregg Ingalls Shook.

Since 1976 Mr. Bettinghaus has been the dean of the college of communication arts and sciences at Michigan State University in East Lansing, MI. Prior to this he was the chairperson and professor in the department of communication at Michigan State, 1972–1976.

Mr. Bettinghaus graduated from the University of Illinois (B.A., 1952), Bradley University (M.A., 1953), and the University of Illinois (Ph.D., 1959). He was born October 28, 1930, in Peoria, IL. He is married, has three children, and resides in East Lansing, MI.

Statement on the Death of Tabatha Foster
May 11, 1988

Nancy and I are saddened to hear about the death of Tabatha Foster. Many Americans were drawn to her because of her courageous battle against birth defects. We extend our deepest sympathies to her family.

Remarks at the Annual Republican Congressional Fundraising Dinner
May 11, 1988

Thank you, and thank you, Lee Greenwood. Lee, your music is an inspiration to America. Now it's my turn to sing for my supper. [*Laughter*] Ladies and gentlemen, thank you all very much for being here tonight. I want to thank all those who worked so hard to make tonight's dinner a success, especially the waiters: Al Gore, Bruce Babbitt, Dick Gephardt, and Paul Simon. [*Laughter*] But really, David Murdock, our dinner chairman, has done such a terrific job I may not let him go back to California until I do. And Rabbi Balkany, thank you for your outstanding efforts toward tonight's dinner.

By the way, in a few weeks a new film opens: "Rambo III." You remember, in the first movie Rambo took over a town. In the second, he singlehandedly defeated several Communist armies. And now in the third Rambo film, they say he really gets tough. [*Laughter*] Almost makes me wish I could serve a third term. [*Laughter*]

But what I really want is for the next

Republican President to have a Congress that will work with him, not against him. And that is exactly what Congressman Guy Vander Jagt and Senator Rudy Boschwitz are working to achieve and what tonight is all about. In the Senate we can win back control just by picking up five seats. And with our excellent candidates, I know we can do it.

I remember when George Bush and I took office, January 1981—or as another Republican President might have put it: 4 months and 7 years ago. You know, I've waited 125 years to say that. [*Laughter*] When we took office, the American economy was sinking rapidly in quicksand. Government spending was soaring out of control. Business was being crushed by massive regulation and taxation. Two consecutive years of double-digit inflation had raised consumer prices by a whopping 27.2 percent. And with inflation driving people into higher and higher tax brackets, take-home pay didn't go very far. The prime rate was at a record 21½ percent. Business failures and unemployment were climbing. Economists called it stagflation; the Democrats called it malaise; the liberal pundits said it was part of America's inevitable decline.

But we came in and said the only thing that was inevitable was that bad policies produced bad results. We said there may be no easy solutions, but there's a simple solution: Get government out of the way, and let free people in a free economy work their magic. When we proposed cutting tax rates and letting working people keep more of their own money, our critics warned that it would lead to runaway inflation. Instead, inflation was slashed to a fraction of what it had been, and interest rates were cut by more than half. The top tax bracket has now been lowered from 70 percent to 28 percent, and tax revenues are at an all-time high. Our critics warned that if we slowed the growth in government spending the economy would suffer. When I spoke to you last year, I reported that the U.S. economy had had 53 consecutive months of growth. Well, tonight I have to take that back because it's now 65 months. It is the longest peacetime expansion in our history. And jobs—at the 1984 convention, I said the expansion had created 6½ million new jobs. Now it's over 16 million new jobs.

Now, does all this good news mean, as our critics argue, that America's prosperity has run its course? Hardly. The Democrats were wrong before, and they're wrong again. Our prosperity is based on sound fundamentals: increased production by individuals in the world's most dynamic and freest economy. And now new advances in the physical sciences, information systems, biology, and applied mathematics are producing new industries, new jobs, and increased productivity that will power our economy well into the next century. So, the best is yet to come. If the American people vote in November to continue the progrowth economic policies of the last 7 years, believe me, the next decade will be known as the Roaring Nineties.

But the opposition that controls Congress has made perfectly clear where they stand. When I send them budgets that limit spending, they call them dead on arrival. And when they talk about reducing the Federal deficit, it's just a code word for raising taxes. That's why the 1988 elections are so important. We need a new Congress willing to hold the line on taxes and spending. And I promise you this, even after I leave office, I will never stop campaigning for the tools needed to limit the insatiable fiscal appetite of government. To protect our prosperity, the President needs the line-item veto, and America needs a constitutionally mandated balanced budget.

There are only two things that the liberals don't understand: the things that change and the things that don't. [*Laughter*] The economy, technology, industry—these things change. But America's basic moral, spiritual, and family values—they don't change. And I think you agree with me that those values are the source of our strength and the root of our liberty. America's moral and economic strength at home helped power the cause of freedom around the world. And today, with America proud and respected, it's easy to forget how different things were in the late 1970's. Our military had been allowed to decline. We had planes that didn't fly and ships that didn't sail. Our foreign policy had lost its direction. Instead of being a world leader, America was bend-ing over backward to avoid offending its enemies, and our nation's influence and respect in the world declined. As Jeane Kirkpatrick put it: "It was as if the United States was wearing a sign saying, 'Kick me.' "

With the leader of the free world sitting on the sidelines, the consequences were tragic for world freedom and our own security. Just think of the year 1979. In that one year, Iran, Nicaragua, and Grenada were all lost. Iran fell to the Ayatollah. Nicaragua and Grenada were taken by the Communists. In that one year, our Embassy in Iran was seized not once, but twice. Our Ambassador to Afghanistan was assassinated by gunmen, and that country invaded by Soviet troops—add to that the economic decay at home. That was 1979. Don't we have a right to ask the American people tonight, if the Democrats return to the White House, what happens in 1989? [*Applause*]

Well, there is a choice. Over the last 7 years, we've rebuilt our armed forces and reversed America's slide. We have spoken openly and directly about the fundamental moral differences between the United States and the Soviet Union. We have rejected containment and made our policy the expansion of freedom around the world. We sent a new message of strength by restoring democracy in Grenada. And by supporting courageous freedom fighters around the world, we're shining a light on the path out from communism. And this Sunday, the Soviet Army is scheduled to begin its long-awaited withdrawal from Afghanistan. And isn't it time we apply the lessons of Afghanistan in Nicaragua and show the same commitment to freedom fighters in our own hemisphere as we do to others in distant lands? [*Applause*]

Just as we have rejected the permanence of totalitarianism, so too have we worked to put an end to nuclear terror. While our opponents were shouting for a nuclear freeze, we stood firm and demanded the total elimination of an entire class of U.S. and Soviet nuclear missiles, to be verified by on-site inspection. That's what we demanded, and I can tell you, that's what we got. The INF treaty has swept away the failed ideas of arms control or nuclear freeze. The new vision is nuclear arms reduction. Add to that our plan for a Strategic Defense Initiative, and we can give our children a world free from nuclear terror and the brighter, safer future they deserve.

It was not too many years ago that some people were saying the Republican Party was finished. They said our philosophy of opportunity at home and firmness abroad was out of touch. Well, in 1980 and 1984 we proved them wrong. And I have more bad news for them: Not only are we not finished, we're just beginning. Last week a New York Times editorial asked why New York primary voters showed such little concern about the economy and national security. The Times concluded: "What this seems to add up to, bluntly, is peace and prosperity." Well, carrying a record of peace and prosperity into a national election is a good beginning. But we're also going to keep talking about excellence in education, cracking down on crime, and continuing to press the war against drugs on every front. And that means passing new, tough laws, including the death penalty for drug kingpins and those who kill police officers. It means appointing no-nonsense judges, blocking drugs at our borders, confiscating it in our cities, and eradicating it in the fields where it is grown. And it also means—and Nancy has led the way here—teaching our children to just say no.

Eight years ago, George Bush and I said to the American people, "The time is now." And it still is. The story of America is one of people who've made their dreams come true by realizing that the time for action is always now. It began with 13 Colonies in their battle for independence; and then westward expansion, an Industrial Revolution, the building of a great nation, and finally America's ascendance on the world stage. At every point, the time was now. It is history's greater story, and its greater chapters have not yet been written.

If I may, I'd like to take a moment to say just a word about my future plans. In doing so, I'll break a silence I've maintained for some time with regard to the Presidential candidates. I intend to campaign as hard as I can. My candidate is a former Member of Congress, Ambassador to China, Ambassador to the United Nations, Director of the

CIA, and National Chairman of the Republican Party. I'm going to work as hard as I can to make Vice President George Bush the next President of the United States. Thank you, and God bless you.

Now it's on to New Orleans and on to the White House!

Note: The President spoke at 9:52 p.m. in Hall A at the District of Columbia Convention Center. The dinner was sponsored by the National Republican Senatorial Committee and the National Republican Congressional Committee.

Statement Endorsing George Bush's Candidacy for President

May 12, 1988

I was surprised by the news reports that have said my endorsement last evening of the Vice President was "lukewarm." I am enthusiastic, fully committed and, as I have said, will go all out to make Vice President Bush the next President of the United States. George has been a partner in all we have accomplished, and he should be elected. He has my full confidence and my total support. I will campaign actively on his behalf.

Proclamation 5822—National Tuberous Sclerosis Awareness Week, 1988

May 12, 1988

By the President of the United States of America

A Proclamation

Tuberous sclerosis is an inherited disease whose neurological symptoms can run the gamut from speech disorders, mental retardation, and behavioral problems to motor difficulties and seizures. Small benign tumors may grow on the face and eyes, as well as in the brain, kidneys, and other organs. In its most devastating form, tuberous sclerosis leaves patients completely helpless and dependent.

Approximately one in every 10,000 Americans has tuberous sclerosis, placing this malady among the more common genetic disorders. Yet it often goes unrecognized. White spots that generally appear on the skin early in life are one characteristic sign, but symptoms often take considerable time to develop and are easily misdiagnosed.

There is currently no cure for tuberous sclerosis, but some of its symptoms are treatable. Seizures may be controlled by new anticonvulsant drugs. Children with learning, speech, and language disabilities may benefit from sophisticated educational techniques. People with motor handicaps can learn skills to increase their mobility and enhance daily living.

The best hope for alleviating the suffering brought on by this disease lies in biomedical research. The National Institute of Neurological and Communicative Disorders and Stroke (NINCDS), the focal point within the Federal government for research on neurogenetic disorders, encourages studies on tuberous sclerosis. Some investigators are striving to develop improved methods of treatment; others search for the location of the responsible gene so that the defect that leads to tuberous sclerosis can one day be identified, analyzed, and corrected.

Two private, voluntary health agencies, the American Tuberous Sclerosis Association and the National Tuberous Sclerosis Association, share with the NINCDS the task of informing Americans about this disorder and stimulating more scientific research. All Americans can take heart in the success of this cooperative effort, which is fundamental to the conquest of this disorder.

To further enhance public awareness of tuberous sclerosis, the Congress, by Senate Joint Resolution 212, has designated the week of May 8 through May 14, 1988, as "National Tuberous Sclerosis Awareness Week" and has authorized and requested the President to issue a proclamation in observance of the week.

Now, Therefore, I, Ronald Reagan, President of the United States of America, do hereby proclaim the week of May 8 through May 14, 1988, as National Tuberous Sclerosis Awareness Week, and I call upon the people of the United States to observe this week with appropriate ceremonies and activities.

In Witness Whereof, I have hereunto set my hand this twelfth day of May, in the year of our Lord nineteen hundred and eighty-eight, and of the Independence of the United States of America the two hundred and twelfth.

RONALD REAGAN

[*Filed with the Office of the Federal Register, 10:18 a.m., May 13, 1988*]

Appointment of Peter M. Robinson as Special Assistant to the President and Speechwriter
May 13, 1988

The President today announced the appointment of Peter M. Robinson to be Special Assistant to the President and Speechwriter.

Since October 1983 Mr. Robinson has served as Speechwriter to the President. Previously he was Chief Speechwriter to Vice President Bush.

Mr. Robinson received his bachelor of arts degree from Dartmouth College in 1979. He received his M.A. in 1981 from Christ Church, Oxford University. Mr. Robinson was born on April 18, 1957, and resides in Alexandria, VA.

Remarks on Signing the National Safe Kids Week Proclamation
May 13, 1988

The President. I'm sorry for the delay. We were waiting for one very special person, who apparently is not going to be able to get here. But I want to thank you all very much, and I'd like to welcome everyone gathered here at the White House for the National Safe Kids Campaign.

Being here in the Rose Garden reminds me of the story of another President, Teddy Roosevelt, and his son Quentin when they were living here. Quentin was on stilts, walking through one of the flower gardens. And President Teddy Roosevelt said, "Quentin, get out of there." And Quentin, from up on his stilts, looked down at his father and said, "I don't see what good it does me for you to be President." [*Laughter*]

But seriously, I'm grateful for the contributions that the Children's Hospital National Medical Center, the National Safety Council, and Johnson & Johnson have made to save our most precious resource: our children. And seeing all of you young people here today reminds me of a story of my youth. Well, it was even more than youth. It was back to when I was 3 years old in a little town of Tampico, Illinois, where I'd been born.

We were living in a house, and in front of

the house across the street was a park. And on the far side of the park was a railroad track, and the depot. And my brother, who was 2 years older than I—we were out there one day. And you children—would be hard to realize that there was a time when you didn't have ice cream wagons and things like that coming around. And so, the morning tour of the ice wagon—we didn't have refrigerators either, so the ice wagon would come and deliver to each house some ice. And we who were young thought the greatest thing in the world was to be able to intercept that ice wagon and get a chunk of the ice that chipped off when they were getting the ice ready for the ice boxes and to suck on those pieces of ice. Well, my brother, the 5-year-old, saw the ice wagon pull up over there on the other side of the park and the railroad tracks, and he called to me. And the two of us started across the park. And before we got there, a train pulled in and stopped between us and the ice wagon. Well, upon my brother's cue, I followed him, and we crawled under the train, came out the other side, and barely gotten out and on our way to the ice wagon when the train pulled out. My mother had come out on the porch and seen all of this. We got our ice—[*laughter*]—but about halfway through the park we met our mother—[*laughter*]—on the way through, and we got something else beyond the ice that let us know we were never to crawl under trains again.

Luckily my pride was really the only injury suffered that day, but for many others physical harm is altogether too personal and too real. With me are—or with all of us here are several families whose stories I'd like to share with you.

On a hot August afternoon—now, this is the individual we've been waiting for and is apparently not yet here—Nancy Dunning was on the phone with her husband when she heard a loud thud. And as Mrs. Dunning ran into the backyard, she saw her neighbor rushing toward the street, where her 4-year-old son, Chris, lay bleeding. He'd been hit by a car. As the neighbor comforted Chris, Nancy ran and called the telephone number 911. Suffering serious neck and leg injuries, Christopher could easily have been paralyzed had any of the people who treated him made the slightest mistake. But fortunately his paramedics had completed a pediatric trauma course. And today he is fully healed. His mother Nancy Dunning describes herself as a much more cautious mother now. "I know that the worst can happen, and I'm doing everything I can to make sure it doesn't happen again," are her words.

Joan and Jerry Langdon consider themselves conscientious parents who've taken much care to make their home safe for their baby daughter, Heather. Yet one evening Heather's natural curiosity led her to grab a hot, bright light bulb. At such a tender age this little girl's reflexes didn't tell her to pull away from the scorching heat. Her scream attracted Jerry's attention, and he pulled her hand off the light, but only after she'd been badly burned. Heather has received several skin grafts and, thank goodness, will heal completely.

Kristin Godown is a 12-year-old student who's being honored by the National American Automobile Association for saving the life of a kindergartner. On March 18th, 1987, Kristin was the lead school safety patrol member riding with kindergartners on their way home from Hybla Valley Elementary School in Alexandria, Virginia. At one of the stops, Kristin got off the bus to make sure the children exited safely. And just as the bus was about to pull away, a schoolchild ran under the vehicle to retrieve a piece of paper. Kristin shouted for the bus driver to stop, and because of her quick action, Anita Murphy is alive today. Next week Kristin will be honored, along with other children who've made similar heroic efforts, with the Triple A School Safety Patrol Lifesaving Medal at an awards luncheon here in Washington.

As these experiences show, many childhood accidents and, yes, sometimes death, resulted from situations which should be and are avoidable. Tragically, preventable accidents are the leading causes of death among our children every year. This means 8,000 children die in one year from accidental drowning, poisoning, and auto accidents in which kids were not wearing seat belts. As Surgeon General Koop has recently said, "If a disease were killing our children in the proportions that accidents are, people would demand that that killer disease be halted."

Well, today we're taking action to stop this needless waste. By proclamation, I am designating the week of May 16th through May 22d, 1988, National Safe Kids Week. As the President of the United States and a concerned parent and grandparent myself, I urge everyone in America to please protect our children. And once again I thank you all for coming here today, and I'd like to leave you with one last thought. It's an old proverb that says simply, "There is only one pretty child in the world, and every parent has it."

Well, I thank you, and God bless you. And now I'm going to ask if a few people would come up here with me. I guess Chris Dunning hasn't yet arrived. No, he's not here. So, now would Heather come up and Kristin.

Well, now I'm going to sign the proclamation and the joint resolution that have been passed by the Congress.

And now it's official; we're all going to be careful.

Mrs. Langdon. President Reagan, the Safe Kids would like to present you this T-shirt.

The President. Well, thank you very much. And I promise you, I'll be a safe kid. [*Laughter*]

Note: The President spoke at 11:56 a.m. in the Rose Garden at the White House.

Proclamation 5823—National Safe Kids Week, 1988
May 13, 1988

By the President of the United States of America

A Proclamation

During National Safe Kids Week parents, relatives, teachers, and everyone responsible for the care and safety of children should take notice of the many ways in which we can help youngsters avoid accidents and grow up safely. Children themselves should also become increasingly aware of ways to protect themselves and other young people. Each year accidents take a tragic toll of perhaps 8,000 young lives lost and 50,000 children disabled. We need to recall that we can prevent the majority of these incidents—and we need to do as much as we can about it, in homes, schools, places of work and recreation, on the highways, and throughout our communities.

Much has been done already. Americans continue to take responsibility by exercising extra care around the house, as well as by using items such as infant and toddler car seats and seat belts, smoke detectors, flame-retardant clothing, and child-proof packaging; and emergency medical services are developing still greater capacities in the prevention of death and of serious aftereffects of injury.

As more and more of us understand that accidental injuries are avoidable, and as we act accordingly, we will substantially reduce this major source of death, disability, and injury to our hope for the future—our "safe kids." That is a goal to which we can all look forward.

The Congress, by Senate Joint Resolution 240, has designated the period of May 16 through May 22, 1988, as "National Safe Kids Week" and authorized and requested the President to issue a proclamation in observance of this event.

Now, Therefore, I, Ronald Reagan, President of the United States of America, do hereby proclaim the period of May 16 through May 22, 1988, as National Safe Kids Week. I call upon the people of the United States to observe this week with appropriate ceremonies and activities.

In Witness Whereof, I have hereunto set my hand this thirteenth day of May, in the year of our Lord nineteen hundred and eighty-eight, and of the Independence of the United States of America the two hundred and twelfth.

RONALD REAGAN

[*Filed with the Office of the Federal Register, 4:11 p.m., May 13, 1988*]

Nomination of David S.C. Chu To Be an Assistant Secretary of Defense
May 13, 1988

The President today announced his intention to nominate David S.C. Chu to be an Assistant Secretary of Defense (Program Analysis and Evaluation). This is a new position.

Since 1981 Mr. Chu has been Director of Program Analysis and Evaluation at the Department of Defense in Washington, DC. Prior to this he was Assistant Director for the National Security and International Affairs Division of the Congressional Budget Office, 1978–1981. He was also an associate head of the economics department for the Rand Corp., 1975–1978, and senior economist, 1970–1978.

Mr. Chu graduated from Yale University (B.A., 1964; M.A., 1965; M. Phil., 1967; Ph.D., 1972). He was born May 28, 1944, in New York, NY. He served in the United States Army, 1968–1970. He is married, has one child, and resides in Washington, DC.

Nomination of Kenneth P. Bergquist To Be an Assistant Secretary of the Navy
May 13, 1988

The President today announced his intention to nominate Kenneth P. Bergquist to be an Assistant Secretary of the Navy (Manpower and Reserve Affairs) at the Department of Defense. He would succeed Charles G. Untermeyer.

Since 1986 Mr. Bergquist has been Deputy Assistant Attorney General for Legislative Affairs at the Department of Justice. Prior to this, he was Deputy Assistant Secretary of the Army (Readiness, Force Management, and Training) at the Department of Defense, 1983–1986, and Deputy Assistant Secretary of the Army (Reserve Affairs and Mobilization), 1982–1983. He was chief counsel and staff director for the Committee on Veterans' Affairs of the United States Senate, 1981–1982, and minority counsel and staff director for the Committee on Veterans' Affairs, 1980–1981. Mr. Bergquist was also legislative counsel for the office of Senator Alan K. Simpson, 1979–1980, and an operational intelligence officer for the Central Intelligence Agency, 1977–1979.

Mr. Bergquist graduated from Stanford University (B.A., 1967) and the University of Texas School of Law (J.D., 1977). He was born April 12, 1944, in Washington, DC. He served in the United States Army from 1967 to 1974, receiving a Silver Star, 6 Bronze Stars, and 2 Purple Hearts. He is married, has two children, and resides in McLean, VA.

Nomination of Edward Peter Djerejian To Be United States Ambassador to Syria

May 13, 1988

The President today announced his intention to nominate Edward Peter Djerejian, of Maryland, a career member of the Senior Foreign Service, Class of Minister-Counselor, as Ambassador to the Syrian Arab Republic. He would succeed William L. Eagleton, Jr.

Mr. Djerejian is currently the Principal Deputy Assistant Secretary of State for Near Eastern and South Asian Affairs. From 1985 to 1986, he was assigned on detail to the White House as Special Assistant to the President and Deputy Press Secretary for Foreign Affairs. Mr. Djerejian was heavily involved in the President's November 1985 summit meeting in Geneva with General Secretary Gorbachev and in the Tokyo economic summit in May 1986. He was assigned in January 1985 as Deputy Spokesman of the Department of State and Deputy Assistant Secretary of State for Public Affairs. Mr. Djerejian's last overseas assignment was in Amman, Jordan, where he was the deputy chief of mission at the American Embassy, 1981–1984. His previous Middle East assignments in both the field and in Washington included positions in the Near Eastern Bureau of the Department of State as Deputy Director of Northern Arabian Affairs, 1972–1974; political/labor officer in Casablanca, Morocco, 1969–1972; and political officer in Beirut, Lebanon, 1966–1969. He also served as staff assistant to the Under Secretary of State, 1963–1965, and special assistant to the Under Secretary of State for Political Affairs, 1974–1975. From 1975 to 1977, Mr. Djerejian served as principal officer at the consulate general in Bordeaux, France. After training assignments in the Russian language and Eastern European and Soviet affairs, Mr. Djerejian served at the American Embassy in Moscow from 1979 to 1981, first as chief of external affairs in the political section and then as acting political counselor. Mr. Djerejian served in the United States Army from 1960 until joining the Foreign Service in 1962.

Mr. Djerejian received a B.S.F.S. from the School of Foreign Service, Georgetown University, in 1960. He was born March 6, 1939, in New York City. He is married, has two children, and resides in Bethesda, MD.

Designation of Becky Norton Dunlop as Special Representative to the Northern Mariana Islands-United States Negotiations

May 13, 1988

The President has designated Becky Norton Dunlop, Deputy Under Secretary of the Interior, as Special Representative to meet and to consider in good faith such issues affecting the relationship between the Northern Mariana Islands and the United States. She would succeed Richard Thomas Montoya.

Since 1987 Mrs. Dunlop has been Deputy Under Secretary at the Department of the Interior in Washington, DC. Prior to this she was Special Assistant to the Attorney General for Cabinet Affairs at the Department of Justice, 1985–1987. She was Deputy Assistant to the President and Deputy Director of Presidential Personnel at the White House, 1983–1985; Special Assistant to the President and Director of the Office of Cabinet Affairs, 1982–1983; and Deputy Director of the Office of Presidential Personnel, 1981–1982.

Mrs. Dunlop graduated from Miami University, Ohio (B.A., 1973). She was born October 2, 1951, in Minneapolis, MN. She is married and currently resides in Arlington, VA.

Radio Address to the Nation on Free and Fair Trade
May 14, 1988

My fellow Americans:

Yesterday Congress decided to send me a trade bill that threatens to destroy jobs and that would begin to reverse the policies of the last 7 years. After 3 years of hard work by the Congress and the Executive, it is unfortunate that I have no choice but to send this back to Congress. While there are many positive aspects of this legislation, some of its provisions would move us a step further toward protectionism. Others would create new bureaucracies. But my main objection to the trade bill involves the mandatory requirements it sets down for business to give advance notice of layoffs or plant closings.

Now, let me state very clearly that I believe businesses should give workers and communities just as much warning as they can when it looks as though layoffs or plant closings are going to become unavoidable. Advance notice gives the community and the workers themselves some time to begin adjusting. It's the humane thing to do. But when big government gets in the middle of something like this—dictating all its rules and regulations—well, the humane has a way of becoming inhumane. And what's intended to help everyday working men and women can actually end up hurting them.

When you study the plant-closing provisions of the trade bill, you see that there are circumstances in which they would actually force a business to shut down. Once a struggling business issued a notice that it is likely to close or substantially reduce its work force, then creditors, suppliers, and customers would disappear, eliminating any chance of survival the business might have had. Under these conditions, temporary layoffs are sometimes necessary to manage costs and production. And while the bill does contain a so-called struggling company exemption, this exemption is too vague and unclear to be workable. Then, too, businesses will be very reluctant to add workers when it would put them over the arbitrary thresholds in this bill and subject them to yet another regime of Federal regulation. Make no mistake, these concerns are very real. One independent study shows that if these provisions had been in effect between 1982 and 1986 America today would have almost half a million fewer jobs.

Yes, as I've said, our country should support advance notification of layoffs and plant closings. But this should be decided by bargaining between labor and management, not by some arbitrary rules laid down by politicians and enforced by Washington bureaucrats. And if I feel especially strong about this, I guess it's because I was a union president for years myself. There were times when the union, the Screen Actors Guild, took a hard line in negotiating with management. But, yes, there were also times when the motion picture industry was having its ups and downs, times when the union decided not to press quite so hard because we wanted to make sure the whole industry remained healthy and profitable. The point is, it was up to us, the unions and management, to run the motion picture industry together. We didn't need Washington in on this act.

I guess what it all really comes down to is this: Just what kind of a government do we want? For these past 7 years, the administration has limited government, cutting taxes and regulations alike. The result: the longest peacetime expansion in American history, unemployment at the lowest level in almost 14 years, the creation of 16 million new jobs. And I might add, in the last 3 years, four times as many businesses have opened as have closed. We could go back to big government, and indeed many of those in favor of these plant-closing provisions argue that they're already in effect in many European countries. Well, to tell you the truth, I'm sort of proud of being an American, proud that since 1983 the United States has created six times as many jobs as has Western Europe.

I don't want to leave the impression that the trade bill is completely bad. On the contrary, it contains a number of good and important measures, including new authority for American negotiators seeking to open markets abroad. It also included my proposal for helping workers affected by business failings by providing them with training, education, and job placement services—the truly humane approach. That's why I want a trade bill and why I so regret the addition of counterproductive measures that outweigh the positive features of this legislation. So, I urge Congress to schedule prompt action on a second trade bill immediately after it sustains my veto on this one.

And now one final message. At noon tomorrow in Washington, hundreds will gather to pay tribute to police officers and other law enforcement officials who've died in the line of duty. So, wherever you are at noon, I hope you'll join me in bowing your head and in resolving to let our law enforcement officials know that we understand what our mothers and fathers taught us: The policeman is our friend.

Until next week, thanks for listening, and God bless you.

Note: The President spoke at 12:06 p.m. from Camp David, MD.

Proclamation 5824—Flag Day and National Flag Week, 1988
May 16, 1988

By the President of the United States of America

A Proclamation

Two hundred and eleven years have now gone by since that June day in 1777 when the Continental Congress adopted a flag for the United States of America, then a brand-new Nation fighting for its independence and for the novel notion that individual liberty was everyone's God-given birthright. The banner adopted then, the beautiful Stars and Stripes, was soon raised by a rebel hand for all the world to see. Our task and our glory as Americans is to keep the flag flying high, because freedom waves in its broad stripes and bright stars.

The preservation of freedom is ours to fulfill for our children and for the hope of mankind, just as our forebears fulfilled it for us in years of peace or peril. We will succeed as our countrymen did before us, but only if we make their spirit our own; we must always revere, just as deeply as did they, the Red, White, and Blue—our battle-scarred flag. The heroism, service, and sacrifice of those who have followed Old Glory on many a hard-fought field and at many a guardpost of peace make this our solemn trust. We will keep faith with them and with generations yet unborn just as long as we can sing of flag and freedom as wholeheartedly as did Francis Scott Key in the last stanza of our National Anthem, "The Star-Spangled Banner":

> Oh! thus be it ever, when freemen shall stand Between their loved home and the war's desolation!
> Blest with victory and peace, may the heav'n rescued land Praise the Power that hath made and preserved us a nation.
> Then conquer we must, when our cause it is just, And this be our motto: "In God is our trust."
> And the star-spangled banner in triumph shall wave O'er the land of the free and the home of the brave.

To commemorate the adoption of our flag, the Congress, by joint resolution approved August 3, 1949 (63 Stat. 492), designated June 14 of each year as Flag Day and requested the President to issue an annual proclamation calling for its observance and for the display of the flag of the United States on all government buildings. The Congress also requested the President, by joint resolution approved June 9, 1966 (80 Stat. 194), to issue annually a proclamation designating the week in which June 14 occurs as National Flag Week and calling upon all citizens of the United States to display the flag during that week.

Now, Therefore, I, Ronald Reagan, Presi-

dent of the United States of America, do hereby designate June 14, 1988, as Flag Day and the week beginning June 12 as National Flag Week, and I direct the appropriate officials of the government to display the flag of the United States on all government buildings during that week. I urge all Americans to observe Flag Day, June 14, and Flag Week by flying the Stars and Stripes from their homes and other suitable places.

I also urge the American people to celebrate those days from Flag Day through Independence Day, set aside by the Congress as a time to honor America (89 Stat. 211), by having public gatherings and activities in which they can honor their country in an appropriate manner, especially by ceremonies in which all renew their dedication by publicly reciting the Pledge of Allegiance to the Flag of the United States of America and to the Republic for which it stands, one Nation under God, indivisible, with liberty and justice for all.

In Witness Whereof, I have hereunto set my hand this sixteenth day of May, in the year of our Lord nineteen hundred and eighty-eight, and of the Independence of the United States of America the two hundred and twelfth.

RONALD REAGAN

[*Filed with the Office of the Federal Register, 10:18 a.m., May 17, 1988*]

Remarks to Direct Connection Program Participants
May 16, 1988

The President. You know, we can take credit for the fact that the Sun is shining out there, because this morning it was supposed to rain this afternoon, and as sure as we canceled it or moved it in here, why, the Sun is out, and it's not going to rain.

But a month ago in the Oval Office, I met with eight of you and wished you good luck and Godspeed. You were off to Helsinki to meet with a group of young Soviets to discuss issues of importance to all of you and to your countrymen. And I've heard you were even more successful than you had anticipated. You agreed to a set of resolutions on ways to develop better communication and understanding, to protect the environment, and to press for increased cooperation between our two countries. I know you've already presented your proposal to General Secretary Gorbachev and that you've come here today to present it to me. In a few days from now, I understand you'll also hand it to Secretary-General Perez de Cuellar at the United Nations. First, let me say: "You all do get around."

In all seriousness, I know how satisfied you must be with your efforts. I can see that in your faces—they're bright, expectant, and determined. I don't need to tell you that Mr. Gorbachev and I are both older than you—a little bit. [*Laughter*] We've both lived through the horrors of World War II and its aftermath and the division of Europe and the cold war. I've always tried to be candid about our fundamental differences and will continue to be. I believe this helps, not hinders, the peace process. But so, too, our attitudes and those of our contemporaries have been deeply affected by a history we cannot ignore. And I hope we've all learned enough from that history not to repeat its mistakes. I hope you share with me the conviction that by acknowledging real differences we can, working together, reach across the great divide that has gripped us. I assure you that Nancy and I give you all the encouragement we can in this endeavor. And we trust that some of the aura of enthusiasm and renewal that surrounds you will be contagious as we negotiate with Soviet leaders in the days and months ahead.

Now, I hope to expand our cooperative exchanges with the Soviet Union to increase the cultural, educational, and people-to-people contacts, like yours, that are indispensable. And I want you to know that I'll read your proposal carefully and take it to heart as I leave for Moscow for my next meeting with the General Secretary. We older folks must temper our enthusiasms with the wisdom and experience of age and by the reality of today's world. But that doesn't mean that we still cannot learn much from you young people. You know, I've often said, and I deeply believe, that if all the young people of the world could get together and get to know each other there would never be another war.

You know, as I look at your faces—and I'll bet this is true for you, what I am going to say right now, too—I can't tell which of you are from America and which are from the Soviet Union or if there are some of you from Finland. I see only freshness and beauty and intelligence and determination. Youth united can be a mighty force.

Almost 2,000 years ago, standing on a hilltop near Galilee, the greatest man who ever lived expressed in mighty and inspired words the hopes of your generation for a peaceful future. And if you don't mind, I find his words especially fitting today: "Blessed are the peacemakers," He said, "for they shall be called the sons of God. Blessed are the gentle, for they shall inherit the earth."

Well, thank you all for coming here today, and God bless all of you. And now we're going to come down and shake hands.

Audience member. Mr. President, we, the youth representatives of the United States and the Union of Soviet Socialist Republics and Finland, gathered to create a vision for the 21st century. We believe that we have to help lay groundwork of a new and positive relationship of our two nations in the future.

The President. Thank you very much.

Audience member. We are eager to present our generation's ideas and preparations for our future. Thus, we have carefully recorded some of the beliefs, visions, and tactical ideas which were produced at the conference. We would like now to present to you the fruits of our joint work: our agenda for the 21st century. Thank you for your time considering our ideas, and we ask for your support with our proposals by discussing them at the Moscow summit.

The President. Thank you very much, and I look forward to reading it.

Note: The President spoke at 2:05 p.m. in the East Room at the White House. Direct Connection was a student organization dedicated to promoting communication between the United States and the Soviet Union.

Nomination of Margaret Chase Hager To Be a Member of the National Council on the Handicapped

May 16, 1988

The President today announced his intention to nominate Margaret Chase Hager to be a member of the National Council on the Handicapped for a term expiring September 17, 1990. She would succeed John S. Erthein.

Mrs. Hager has been involved in numerous civic and political activities throughout her career. She has also been director of training administration for the International Banking Group in New York City, 1969–1970. Prior to this she was with First National City Bank (CitiCorp), 1967–1969. From 1966 to 1967, she was an administrative assistant to the director of the International Monetary Fund. Mrs. Hager served as an assistant to the director of loan exhibitions at the Wildenstein Gallery, 1964–1965, and was an assistant registrar and assistant to the editor at the Virginia Museum, 1963–1964.

Mrs. Hager graduated from Wheaton College (B.A., 1963). She was born November 16, 1940, in Richmond, VA. She is married, has two children, and currently resides in Richmond, VA.

Appointment of William Evans as United States Commissioner of the International Whaling Commission
May 16, 1988

The President today announced his intention to appoint William Evans to be United States Commissioner of the International Whaling Commission. He would succeed Anthony J. Calio.

Dr. Evans is currently Under Secretary of Commerce for Oceans and Atmosphere in Washington, DC. Prior to this he was an Assistant Administrator of the National Oceanic and Atmospheric Administration for Fisheries. He has also been executive director and senior scientist at Hubbs-Sea World Research Institute, 1977–1986, head of the bioanalysis group at the Naval Undersea Center, 1974–1976, and an advanced study fellow and visiting scientist for the National Marine Fisheries Service, 1972–1974.

Dr. Evans graduated from Bowling Green State University (B.S., 1953), Ohio State University (M.A., 1954), and the University of California at Los Angeles (Ph.D., 1975). He served in the United States Army, 1954–1956. He was born October 11, 1930, in Elkhart, IN. Dr. Evans is married, has two children, and currently resides in Silver Spring, MD.

Statement on Bipartisan Congressional Efforts To Improve United States Intelligence Capabilities
May 17, 1988

I strongly support bipartisan efforts by the Senate Committees on Intelligence and Armed Services to work with the administration to modernize and upgrade our intelligence capabilities.

It is important as we work toward future arms reduction agreements that our country have all of the means necessary to assure compliance with these agreements. With or without future arms control agreements, it is important for our national security interests that we keep pace with changes in technologies in other nations.

For that reason, I welcome bipartisan support to start this year on a multiyear program to improve these systems. I will also include funding for the second year of this program in the final budget which I submit to the Congress, and I will urge the next administration to assure continuity of this vital effort. After 1989 the funding for the program should be additive to the 2-percent real growth objective for national security spending.

Statement by Assistant to the President for Press Relations Fitzwater on the President's Meeting With Foreign Minister Shimon Peres of Israel
May 17, 1988

Today President Reagan met with Israeli Foreign Minister Shimon Peres. The President and the Foreign Minister discussed bilateral issues, the upcoming U.S.-Soviet summit, and the urgent need to make progress toward peace in the Middle East. The President emphasized the value of deepening U.S.-Israeli bilateral relations and the emergence of meaningful strategic cooperation between our two countries. He remarked that the progress we've made together, embodied in the recently signed MOA [memorandum of agreement, April 21, 1988], owed much to Shimon Peres' efforts, both as Foreign Minister and as Prime Minister.

In discussing the summit, the President spoke of our four-part agenda—bilateral relations, human rights, arms reduction, regional conflicts—and emphasized that we will, as always, press for the unimpeded right of Soviet Jewry to emigrate. The President also spoke of our determination to make progress toward Middle East peace. He thanked Foreign Minister Peres for his efforts in behalf of peace and his continuing commitment to negotiate it.

While being steadfast in his commitment to Israeli strength and security, the Foreign Minister has a vision for the future, recognizes the increasing danger of the status quo, and understands the negative consequences of passivity and delay in the search for a settlement. The Foreign Minister is creative and has the courage and wisdom to say yes when real opportunities arise.

Such a positive attitude toward peace is essential for both Israeli and Arab leaders if there is to be a comprehensive settlement in the region. A settlement must be grounded on the realistic basis of UNSC [United Nations Security Council] Resolution 242 and its call for an exchange of territory for peace. Those leaders who are negative, consistently reject new ideas, and fail to exploit realistic opportunities to bring about negotiations make progress impossible. In the end, they will have to answer to their own people for the suffering that will inevitably result.

The President also told the Foreign Minister that Secretary of State Shultz would be going to the Middle East after the summit to pursue our initiative, an initiative that we continue to believe offers the only realistic basis on which to make progress toward peace. The alternative is a drift toward a much graver future in the region. Extremist forces will gain strength at the expense of moderates at the very moment that proliferating ballistic missiles and chemical weapons are creating a far more ominous military environment.

Foreign Minister Peres agreed that regional trends should add to our collective sense of urgency in pursuing Middle East peace. He also thanked the President for his efforts on behalf of Soviet Jewry and world peace.

Message on the Observance of Police Week and Police Officers' Memorial Day, May 1988

May 17, 1988

There can be no more noble vocation than the protection of one's fellow citizens. Police Week, and in particular Police Officers' Memorial Day, affords each one of us the yearly opportunity to reflect upon the countless contributions made by our Nation's police officers.

No single group is more fully committed to the well-being of their fellow Americans and to the faithful discharge of duty than our law enforcement personnel. Danger is a routine part of their job, and all too often we lose one of these valiant men and women to the sickness that is crime.

I invite all Americans to honor the memories of these courageous heroes on Police Officers' Memorial Day. Our Nation is blessed with the most able, professional, and caring peace officers in the world. What better time to show our deep appreciation for their selfless devotion than during Police Week.

RONALD REAGAN

Remarks and a Question-and-Answer Session With Reporters
May 17, 1988

INF Treaty and the Trade Bill

The President. I have a statement here, a brief statement. First, I am pleased that Senate Majority Leader Bob Byrd and Republican Leader Bob Dole have agreed to take up consideration of the treaty to eliminate an entire class of U.S. and Soviet intermediate-range nuclear missiles. This treaty, which was signed last December, has placed U.S.-Soviet arms discussions on a path that goes beyond arms control and toward real nuclear arms reduction. I am both hopeful and confident that after careful consideration the Senate will agree that this treaty is a diplomatic milestone and will give its consent to United States participation.

Second, the March trade figures were good news—the best news on this front since March of 1985. With the trade deficit dropping $4.1 billion and with exports up $5.4 billion, this is clear evidence that the trade balance is improving as our economy continues to grow. Now, several days ago I received a trade bill from Congress, and my message to Congress on this matter is currently under review, and I expect to issue it within a couple of days. But today's news emphasizes what we've been saying all along: that this is not the time to be imposing restrictions on trade or reducing incentives for free, open markets or closing job opportunities. We want more jobs, not less, and we want a job market open to all working men and women in this country. I'm ready to roll up my sleeves and go to work with the Congress once again in crafting a trade bill that will continue this trend of more job creation and greater economic growth.

General Noriega of Panama

Q. Mr. President, why have you authorized the dropping of the drug indictment against General Noriega, and doesn't that give the Democrats ammunition for the Presidential campaign?

The President. Not if they'll wait until there's something to be announced. We're negotiating right now, and therefore I can't comment on negotiations that are underway. It would be foolish to do so. Some things you have to keep to yourself when you're arguing with someone else. But we're not—as I say, negotiations are underway. There has been no decision made on some of the things that are being discussed, and I have to say that I think that much of what many of you've been dealing with as a story is based on some kind of leaks or misinformation because there are no facts to sustain it.

Q. If I could clear up that one point, though, sir, haven't you authorized the dropping of the indictment in return for something on Mr. Noriega's part?

The President. As I have to say, when you're negotiating—and I did that for 25 years as a union officer in labor-management relations—you don't go out and talk about what you're negotiating.

Attorney General Edwin Meese III

Q. Mr. President, now that the conservatives, personified by the Washington Times, have jumped ship on Attorney General Edwin Meese. And the loss of morale in the Department and loss of respect for the Justice Department in the country and its integrity—are you still backing Meese and have total confidence in him, or are you going to ease him out?

The President. No, I have complete confidence in him, and I know——

Q. Why?

The President. Because there have been a great many allegations made, but nothing has been proven. And I've seen no evidence of any wrongdoing on his part of the kind that is inferred in the allegations that they kicked around. And right now, on this particular thing, I think you'd have to talk to him about that. I think there's more than meets the eye with regard to this latest departure.

Q. What do you mean?

The President. What?

Q. What are you referring to? Do you

mean that Eastland [former Director of the Office of Public Affairs at the Justice Department] did something to undermine the Attorney General?

The President. No, he made a statement himself that there was no animus of anything that had happened. But I think that you should talk to the Attorney General about that and what happened.

Q. Well, is that the role of the press officer—to be a defense attorney?

The President. Well, once again, somebody speculated that that's what was the reason there. And I think that you should talk to the Attorney General.

Democracy in Panama

Q. Mr. President, if you can't discuss the negotiations with Noriega, I'd like to ask you, however, about your policy goal. You have said in the past the goal was to see that Noriega step down from power. And at various times you've talked about leaving the country and various times you haven't. Is your goal to see that not only Noriega leaves power but that none of his cronies continue to exercise power in his name?

The President. I've said I wouldn't comment, but I'll make one comment on that. What we're interested in seeing is a restoration of democracy in Panama. It didn't start with this particular man. But some time back, under another one, the commanding officer of the National Guard in Panama suddenly began to take precedence over the President of Panama and dictate to the Government. We feel that it's time that democracy return to Panama, and this is what we're negotiating toward.

Q. Well, sir, if someone controls the Government—if Noriega pulls strings behind the scenes, is that acceptable to you?

The President. Not if we have reinstituted democracy there in Panama. But, again, I can't comment further on this. We are in the midst of real negotiations.

Q. But sir, the fear is that you're selling out. The fear is that you are going to agree to a deal which has a fig leaf of some restoration of democracy but, in fact, leaves Noriega in power.

The President. Oh, I know. I've been reading that and hearing it in the newscasts——

Q. Well, when you won't comment, sir——

The President.——and no, I'm not going to back away from what we're trying to do.

Q. Well, sir——

Drug Trafficking and Aid to the Contras

Q. Mr. President, there have been charges also that this government was aware of drug running involved with the possibly illegal *contra* supply operation. Can you tell us and the congressional committees that have been investigating that there was no involvement by this government, the CIA, or any other agencies of this government in running drugs on the same airplanes that were bringing weapons to the *contras*? And are you investigating, if you didn't know about it, to see whether there is any truth——

The President. All that I knew about any of this, until the indictment came down with evidently evidence enough to get to an indictment—that previously there had been some rumors he was providing information on—situation in Central America, I think, to our intelligence people at the CIA. Some rumors came up about possible drug and—but no one ever received or could get any evidence to substantiate those rumors. And then this latest thing happened, and I don't know whether he just had started or whether there was anything really going on.

Q. But, sir, there are other charges that there was other involvement by this government in drugs on the same airplanes that were delivering weapons to the *contras* beyond Noriega. Did you know anything about that? Is there any truth to that?

The President. No. No, the only thing I knew was when we operated a sting operation and found that the Sandinistas were shipping out drugs.

Q. Well——

The President. And unfortunately, the pilot of that plane in that particular sting operation was shot down in the streets of an American city shortly after the——

Q. But are you checking into these latest allegations?

The President. Yes, we are.

Q. Mr. President, how can you, given the

hard line that you took at the very beginning in the situation in Panama—saying that Noriega had to leave the country, saying once that the Dominican Republic wasn't far enough—and our recognition of Mr. Delvalle as the President, how can you do anything in the way of a compromise without appearing to back down from your original policy goals?

The President. Again, you're asking me—that would lead into what's being talked about, and I can only tell you that we're not going to just whitewash anyone.

Q. Mr. President——

The President. I suggested two more. So, three, and then——

Astrology

Q. Mr. President, you have repeatedly denied that astrology played any role in the setting of policy, but you have ducked the question as to whether or not it played a role in the setting of schedule. A number of aides, besides Mr. Regan, have indicated that astrology did play a role in the setting of schedule, including the timing of the signing of the INF treaty. Why did you allow that to go on, sir?

The President. It didn't go on. And this whole thing is built around an incident in which it was printed that this had to do with the scheduling of one of my operations. Well, it didn't happen that way at all. And you know something else: It didn't have anything to do with me being sworn in as Governor, taking the oath of office at midnight—or 1 minute after midnight. Back when I first was elected Governor—what I was doing that time was because once I became Governor-elect the incumbent Governor whom I defeated started filling up the ranks of term appointments and judges, to the place where I would have had a government all set up long before I got in. Well, I couldn't do much about it. He was still in office till I was signed in. I asked the people who'd been in charge of my campaign, Bill Roberts, when was the earliest that I could become Governor. And he said, well, the minute after midnight, the night before the inaugural ceremonies. And I said, I'm going to get sworn in a minute after midnight. And I got sworn in and at least had headed off a half a day's appointments that he wouldn't have time, because the next afternoon I was inaugurated.

Q. You're talking about a couple of specific incidents. Are you denying that either you or Mrs. Reagan, though, used astrology on any occasion during your time here at the White House to help set the schedule for trips or the signing of the INF treaty? I must say this goes against what a lot of aides are telling us, sir.

The President. Well, no, I'm only going to tell you that one thing, and that is that after I'd been shot, which was quite a traumatic experience for my wife——

Q. And you?

The President. ——and it was not a—no, I was confident I was going to be all right. [*Laughter*] Other people can't know that. But she was getting a great many calls from friends, and a friend called and said that—or wished that he'd known what I was going to do that day and so forth because of—he mentioned someone, that all the signs were bad and everything else. And Nancy was—it was a trauma that didn't go away easily. And when suddenly things of the same kind just for a short period there—when I was booked for something of the same kind where the accident occurred, why, she would ask, what does it look like now? And no changes were ever made on the basis of whether I did nor did not conduct this——

Q. But why something like the signing of an INF treaty, sir?

The President. What?

Q. Why something like the signing——

The President. No, it wasn't. Nothing of that kind was going on. This was all, once again, smoke and mirrors, and we made no decisions on it, and we're not binding our lives to this. And I don't mean to offend anyone who does believe in it or who engages in it seriously——

Q. Do you believe in it?

The President. What?

Q. Do you believe in it?

The President. I don't guide my life by it, but I won't answer the question the other way because I don't know enough about it to say is there something to it or not.

Q. Do you think the attempt on your life

could have been prevented?

The President. No, this friend thought that had I been told that that was supposed to be a horrendous time for me, that I might have done something—well, we didn't.

Attorney General Edwin Meese III

Q. Mr. President, you have often spoke of your belief in the integrity and honesty of your Attorney General. I'd like to ask you another question, which is: Don't you think that all of these resignations and the difficulty of filling the job and the attacks from so many directions are—even if he is a man of integrity and ability—don't you think this is getting in the way of the Justice Department doing its job? And isn't that a reason for him to step aside on those grounds?

The President. No, because I think that there's been a wave—and for quite a long time, and not just with him, but with others—in which accusation or allegation is taken to mean conviction. And there's been too much of that. In this land of ours, you are innocent until you are proven guilty beyond a reasonable doubt. And nothing has been proven. These allegations continue to be made. This has been true of others. This was true of Ray Donovan [former Secretary of Labor]. And his poignant line, I think, fit the situation. When he was declared totally innocent of any wrongdoing at all, he said, "Where do I go to get back my reputation?" This also applies to Beggs, who finally stood up and resigned from NASA because of things he was supposed to have done before he came into government and was found innocent of every—there wasn't an iota of any kind of support for any of the accusations.

Q. Are you saying then, sir, that unless Mr. Meese would be indicted that he should remain in office? Or can there be lesser allegations that don't require an indictment that would be grounds for him stepping aside?

The President. I think that for him to step aside would be what he himself once said: that he would then live for the rest of his life under this cloud, with nothing that had ever been proven.

Q. Sir, what about the——

The President. But you had recognized her all right. So, you're the last one.

General Noriega of Panama

Q. Thank you, sir. One more about Noriega. The combination of sanctions and negotiations have been going on for an awfully long time, and it seems as if the United States looks progressively weaker. Aren't you a little angry that Noriega has managed to humiliate and embarrass the United States?

The President. Well, we had hoped that we could maybe make it possible for the people of Panama themselves to exert some pressure and do something, and I guess having run into their own armed troops willing to shoot, and shooting, kind of cooled that down. So, we're continuing to negotiate. And our goal remains the same.

Q. But, sir, are you not angry about the fact that the United States has been looking so weak when it's gone up against this man?

The President. Whether I'm angry or not doesn't count. On the situation in Panama, I will not comment on the negotiations that are going on in Panama. And at the appropriate time, I expect to have a full statement and make it to the American people.

Q. Will that be soon?

The President. I wish I knew.

Q. Mr. President, how badly have you been hurt by——

Q. Do you have a message for Don Regan [former Chief of Staff to the President]?

Free and Fair Trade

Q. Some people are saying, Mr. President, that if the trade bill were to be overridden by Congress the effect of the trade bill would be similar to Smoot-Hawley. Why is it that the administration now is basically saying that it's only the plant closings provision that's wrong with this trade bill, that otherwise you would support it?

The President. Well, that is the main thing. There are other things in there that I don't think are helpful or belong there. There's been a habit of adding pork items to almost everything that's up on the Hill, and that's true there. But this is the main one.

And when all of my colleagues at the economic summit from the other countries, the heads of state of the countries with which we trade—when they call what we have seen here in the last 5½ years—called the American miracle—and when I have talked to them, they've asked me for questions about what are some of the things that we had done. I found out in answering their questions that they themselves deplore the fact that in their countries the rules and regulations imposed on government—including things like this and rules about hiring and firing—are part of what they say is holding them back and keeping them from having the kind of economic recovery we have.

Q. Ready for Gorbachev?

Q. Has Regan hurt your reputation? Has Regan hurt your reputation? Has Regan damaged your reputation, Mr. President?

The President. Well, I was worried about his.

Note: The exchange began at 3:49 p.m. in the Briefing Room at the White House.

Remarks at the United States Coast Guard Academy Commencement Ceremony in New London, Connecticut

May 18, 1988

The President. Thank you, Admiral Cueroni, and thank you, Secretary Burnley, Admiral Yost, Senator Weicker, Senator Dodd. I thank you all. And it's an honor to be able to participate in the commencement exercises of the United States Coast Guard Academy. I'm especially delighted to be here with the class of 1988. You see, in certain ways I envy you. For one thing, all of you know what you'll be doing next year. [*Laughter*]

The fact is many young people have trouble choosing their life's work. I was an exception. After college, I knew exactly where my future lay. I became a radio sports announcer. It was just a lucky guess. But I know what I would say to any young people who told me that they were torn between different careers. If they said they wanted to help people in distress, guard our borders, conserve fisheries, battle drug smugglers, enforce maritime law, test their courage against stormy seas, and defend America in times of war, and wear proudly each day the uniform of this great country, then I would tell them just one thing—I'd tell them: Join the Coast Guard.

I know a lot has happened since you started here as swabs, were presented with a copy of "Running Light," and first rode the wind on America's mighty square-rigger, the *Eagle.* Soon, it'll be time for you to receive your commissions and bid farewell to the Academy. It's been said that graduation is a time of sentimental goodbyes coupled with extreme relief. One student departing his alma mater wrote inside the cover of his yearbook: "All things must pass—though I almost didn't." [*Laughter*] Now, I don't imagine that any of you wrote anything like that inside of your copy of "Tide Rips."

You know, as President, I have a military aide from each of the five services. My Coast Guard aides have been excellent. One of them taught me that "The Coast Guard is that hard nucleus about which the Navy forms in time of war." But there's one thing I haven't been able to get a straight answer on. What I want to know is, how's the awning?

Cadets. Aye, aye, sir!

The President. Well—[*laughter*]—I hope that means it's all right. [*Laughter*] Well, graduation day belongs to the graduates, but I want to take just a moment to speak to some special people here today: your mothers and fathers. You know, I've often said that there's nothing that makes me prouder than America's young men and women in uniform. I want to ask the parents: Are you as proud of these soon-to-be officers as I am? [*Applause*] During World War II, one general said that America's secret weapon was "just the best darn kids in the world." Now, that may not have been the exact word he used—[*laughter*]—but when I look at your sons and daughters today, I know exactly what he meant. And cadets, let me ask you something: For your parents, or that special teacher or friend who helped you to be here today, can we give them a very loud salute? [*Applause*]

Well, since your service was founded by the first Congress nearly 200 years ago, it has served with courage and honor in every war our nation has fought. The first Coast Guard casualty of World War II came the day after Pearl Harbor, when a transport evacuating American families out of Singapore came under attack. On D-day, when our soldiers hit the beaches at Normandy, there were Coast Guardsmen piloting the landing craft. And some 1,500 soldiers whose craft were sunk by enemy fire were rescued by the Coast Guard on that fateful day. Back when Washington bureaucrats were not as sophisticated or numerous as they are today, we named things more nearly for what they were. One of my favorite examples is that one of the predecessors of today's Coast Guard was known simply as the Life Saving Service. And though the Coast Guard does many jobs, I suspect seafarers in distress will always think of you that way.

In March of last year, some 200 miles off our New Jersey coast, in stormy Atlantic waters, a Soviet freighter sent out a desperate SOS. The ship was listing 26 degrees to port in seas that were running 20 feet. Gale force winds were gusting up to 55 knots, and the skies were dark with rain and sleet. The Soviet ship was sinking. Well, three Coast Guard helicopters came to the rescue. Their fuel was low; there was little time. And despite screaming winds and pitching seas, each helicopter in turn managed to hover above the ship's heaving deck. And the helicopter crews, with infinite care, lowered a wire basket and lifted up to safety, one by one, each of the 37 people on board. It was one of the most dramatic rescues in Coast Guard history and a heroic demonstration of what we mean when we say the Coast Guard is "an armed service and more."

Today, one of the Coast Guard's most important missions is to fight the importation of illegal drugs. In the last 10 years you have arrested more than 8,500 drug smugglers, and for that, America salutes you. It's time to make illegal drugs public enemy number one. It's time to make—well, it's time to say America's tolerance for illegal drugs is zero. The Congress made a serious mistake when our fiscal year '88 budget request for the Coast Guard was reduced by $72 million and forced a curtailment in the drug interdiction effort. I hope the Congress will restore the funds necessary for you to accomplish your vital mission.

While that is one thing, it's not the only thing that all of us as a nation must do. But before I talk about what remains to be done, let's take stock of what has already occurred. Yes, it's true that across the breadth of the Federal Government we have assembled a strong antidrug team and enacted tough antidrug policies. In 1982 we set up the South Florida Task Force, which was headed by Vice President Bush. Hundreds of additional drug agents were sent to Florida, along with extra judges and prosecutors. More Coast Guard cutters were deployed, and the other military services provided surveillance assistance for the first time. We made record drug seizures, and major crime in South Florida decreased nearly 20 percent.

Because of that success, the next year we formed the National Narcotics Border Interdiction System, also led by the Vice President, to coordinate Federal, State, and local law enforcement efforts against drug smuggling nationwide. Since the formation of the Border Interdiction System in 1983, annual cocaine seizures involving the Coast Guard are up more than 20 times what they had been. In 1987 I established the National Drug Policy Board in order to coordinate all of the administration's efforts in this crusade. This board, chaired by Attorney General Meese, has developed a series of comprehensive strategies to reduce both the supply and demand for illicit drugs.

And let me stress, the Coast Guard and the other armed services have played a major role in this unprecedented campaign. In addition to the Coast Guard's tremendous efforts, last year the Pentagon provided over 2,500 ship days of maritime support and more than 16,000 hours of air surveillance. The Coast Guard and the Department of Defense gained important new resources for their drug-fighting efforts from the Antidrug Abuse Act of 1986. And last year the Coast Guard and agencies with which it works seized nearly 26,000 pounds of cocaine—26,000 pounds of a drug that has a street value of $1,000 an ounce. Don't try to figure that out in your head; it's $416 million. And by keeping deadly drugs from reaching our communities, I think the Coast Guard earned yet another good reason to be known as the Life Saving Service.

Another key part of the war on drugs has been the appointment of no-nonsense Federal judges. Not only have drug convictions doubled since 1979 but prison sentences are 40 percent longer. And last year, new, tougher sentencing guidelines were issued. The Comprehensive Crime Control Act, passed in 1984, helps put drug dealers out of business. Last year alone over $500 million in drug-related assets were seized. Drug eradication programs are now underway in 23 countries, up from just 2 in 1981. More funds than ever before are being spent on drug education and public awareness, and more funds still have been requested. Since 1981 we've tripled the antidrug law enforcement budget, and I'm asking for another 13-percent increase. That would give the Federal Government a total of $3.9 billion next fiscal year to fight this menace.

All told, it's an extraordinary demonstration of our commitment and a remarkable record of achievement. And that having been said, you know what else—extraordinary as it is, remarkable as it is, as much a testimony as it is to those in law enforcement and the Coast Guard—more has to be done. There's an additional step we must take, and without it, I don't know if we can succeed. I want to use this opportunity today to call for a special initiative. One of America's greatest strengths is our unique capacity for coming together during times of national emergency. We set aside those differences that divide us and unite as one people, one government, one nation. We've done this before. We must do it now.

Illegal drug use is the foremost concern in our country. And frankly, as I finish my final year in office and look ahead, I worry that excessive drug politics might undermine effective drug policy. If America's antidrug effort gets tripped up in partisanship, if we permit politics to determine policy, it will mean a disaster for our future and that of our children. That's why today, I'm calling on both Houses of the Congress, both sides of the aisle, to join with my representatives in a special executive-legislative task force to advance America's unified response to the problem of illegal drug use. Because if we cannot remove the politics from drugs, how can we hope to remove the drugs from our communities, workplaces, and schools?

Our task force should agree on solutions for every area of the drug problem, from blocking supplies to curtailing demand, from treatment to education to prosecution, from interdiction and confiscation to eradication—nothing should be overlooked or left out. Our policy is one of zero tolerance for illegal drugs, and we're looking for solutions, not just a restatement of the problem. And no later than 45 days from now there should be a report to me and to the bipartisan leadership of Congress laying out our proposals.

Let me take a minute to spell out some specific items that need to be considered. First, to deter violent crime and narcotics trafficking, we have to deal with the drug syndicates on our terms. That means when a death results from narcotics trafficking or when a law enforcement officer is killed in the battle the law must provide for swift, certain, and just punishment—including capital punishment. We've got to send a loud, clear message to drug kingpins and cop-killers. We also need to appoint more tough Federal judges who take drug crime seriously and to pass mandatory penalties for those who sell drugs to children.

Our military assets can be used for greater command and control functions in surveillance and drug detection. And we should consider allowing our Governors greater use of the National Guard in this effort. But one thing must be clear: When it comes to the military, let's give them a clear mission for specific situations. To assist in this effort I have also today directed Secretary of Defense Carlucci to tap the best minds both inside and outside of government to come up with creative solutions on how we can better use military resources and technologies to detect drugs and support civil law enforcement agencies in interdiction.

We need stepped-up international eradication programs to reduce the supply of drugs, and additional education and prevention programs to reduce demand, including the use of civil sanctions, such as fines and loss of Federal privileges. Our encouragement, our goal, should be for those who have never tried drugs to remain drug free.

I'm especially proud of the antidrug work that Nancy has done, which has changed the way we talk and think about drugs. You see, at the root of the drug crisis is a crisis of values and a spiritual hunger. I believe that as a society we're still paying for the permissiveness of the 1960's and 1970's, when restrictions on personal behavior came under attack by a cultural establishment whose slogan was "just say yes." There were numerous calls for repealing our prohibitions on drugs. And those who favored tougher drug laws, or even just keeping the ones we had, were labeled conservative, moralistic, reactionary, and old-fashioned—and that was back before those words were meant as compliments. [*Laughter*] The none-too-subtle message to young people was that they had to use drugs if they wanted to be cool. What greater shame can there be than that many of our young people began to use drugs not to rebel but to fit in? So, in the crusade for a drug free America, the next step is to enforce a policy of zero tolerance of illegal drug use. So, when we say no to drugs, it'll be clear that we mean absolutely none, no exceptions.

This concern with values goes beyond just the issue of drugs, of course. We worked hard in the early eighties on our national recovery so that we might be able to recognize, indeed, deal with social problems that had been too long ignored and sometimes obscured in the past. Well, today America is facing head-on social problems like drugs and crime. And this, as I say, stems from the renewal of our fundamental beliefs and values as a nation. And this renewal goes beyond just our own borders.

In one week I will depart for the Moscow summit. It'll be my first visit to the Soviet Union and my fourth meeting with General Secretary Gorbachev. Our goals there are something that I've been discussing for the last several months in detail, but let me summarize. There are four main agenda items in the U.S.-Soviet relationship: human rights, regional conflicts, arms reduction, and bilateral exchanges. With regard to human rights, though we note some improvements, we'll continue to press for full respect for the freedom of expression, travel, religion, and other rights contained in the Helsinki accords, and for institutional reforms that would guarantee such rights and the rule of law. We'll discuss a number of regional conflicts in which the United States supports the forces of freedom against brutal Communist dictatorships. In particular, we will note the progress of the Soviet withdrawal from Afghanistan. We will reaffirm America's support for the brave Mujahidin freedom fighters and the goal of an independent, nonaligned, and undivided Afghanistan, free to determine its own future. In the area of arms control, General Secretary Gorbachev and I will continue our dialog on the reduction of nuclear weapons, focusing in particular on strategic offensive systems. And with respect to bilateral exchanges, I especially want to encourage more student exchanges between our two countries. I hope that more Soviet young people can view firsthand America's democratic system and way of life.

Just the other day I met with 70-some students, 38 Americans and 38 Soviet students, who've held a conference in Helsinki, in Moscow, and are now here in the United States holding one. And I looked out at them, as I'm looking at you, and you couldn't tell which were Russian and which were American. And I had to say to them: If all the young people of the world could get to know each other, there'd never be another war.

Well, I should also mention that part of our meetings will focus on the U.S.-Soviet Maritime Search and Rescue Agreement that has just been concluded. Other maritime issues we're currently discussing include the issue of fisheries and plans for dealing with emergency pollution spills. So, yes, the Coast Guard's concerns are the Moscow agenda.

It's been a great honor to be here with all of you. And you can be sure that when I'm in Moscow I'll think of all of you here today. You represent the best of America and carry in your hearts the values that are the source of our liberty and our spiritual strength. This is reflected in the path of the service that you've chosen. We're a nation of free men and women, who use our God-given liberty to serve our country because we love her and all that she represents. It's our earnest prayer to serve America in peace. It is our solemn commitment to defend her in time of war.

I believe that America is standing before the brightest future the world has ever known, and that future is yours. And properly so, because you've chosen to wear the uniform of your country and risk all that you have and all that you are in her defense. I wish not only to congratulate you on your graduation, but as your Commander in Chief, I salute you! Thank you, and God bless you all.

Note: The President spoke at 1:11 p.m. at Nitchem Field. In his opening remarks, he referred to Rear Adm. Richard Cueroni, Superintendent; James H. Burnley IV, Secretary of Transportation; Adm. Paul A. Yost, Commandant; and Senators Christopher J. Dodd and Lowell P. Weicker, Jr., of Connecticut. Prior to his remarks, the President visited the USCG "Vigorous" for briefings and demonstrations of procedures used for the interdiction of vessels. Following his remarks, the President returned to Washington, DC.

Interview With Foreign Television Journalists
May 19, 1988

Helsinki Accords

Q. This is the Oval Office in the White House. First, Mr. President, let me thank you for this opportunity to give us an interview before the Moscow summit. And my name is Mikko Valtasaari. I'm from the YLE, Finland. And I'm here with Edward Stourton, ITN, Britain; Antonello Marescalchi, RAI, Italy; Kenichi Iida, NHK, Japan; Wolf von Lojewski, ARD, West Germany, and Jacques Abouchar, Antenne-2, France.

And, Mr. President, you are soon in Helsinki, and next Friday you will speak from the very same stage where the Helsinki document was signed in 1975. And at that time, President Gerald Ford was criticized by going there and signing on to something that was cause of détente, which only served the Soviet interest, as it was said. How do you evaluate the document now?

The President. Well, I value it very much because it specified the agreement of a number of governments to recognize those basic rules of freedom for people. And since our country, this country here, is the first one that ever declared that government is the servant of the people, not the other way around, we heartily endorsed it.

Right now our concern, as I'm sure the concern of a great many other people is that there has not been a complete keeping of those pledges in that agreement by some of the participants—by the Soviet Union, particularly—in recognizing the fundamental rights of people to leave a country, return to a country, worship as they will, and so forth.

Q. Do you think that the Soviet Union has moved that way?

The President. That what?

Q. ——has moved that direction after this document——

The President. I am, I think, reasonably optimistic in view of the summit meetings that we've had, and the meeting we're going to have, that we have made progress with the Soviet Union on a number of those things under the present leader.

Strategic Arms Control

Q. Mr. President, you hoped, I think, to have an agreement on strategic nuclear weapons ready to sign in Moscow. You haven't got one. Is it still realistic to expect a START agreement in the lifetime of this administration, or is Mr. Gorbachev simply going to sit on his hands and wait for the next President?

The President. Well, I don't know whether he necessarily wants to do that and gamble that much. But we're working as hard as we can, and it's a far more complex treaty than the INF treaty, which we did sign here at the summit in Washington. But we're working as hard as we can. We'll continue to work there at the summit if it is not completed, and none of us really think that it will be because of the complexity. But I think that it is possible that we could have that, yes, while this administration is still here.

Allegations of Former Staff Members

Q. Since the last time you saw Mr. Gorbachev, your former press spokesman has said that he manufactured quotations on your behalf, including one at a summit. Your former Chief of Staff has said that astrology played a part in your scheduling, indeed, in summit planning. How do you think that may change the way Mr. Gorbachev views the President and the administration he's dealing with?

The President. Well, I hope Mr. Gorbachev has heard some of the things that I have been saying about those charges, because no decision was ever made by me on the basis of astrology. And some of these other things—the quotations by a former Press Secretary—actually, I have to say he was not too far wrong with some of the things that were being said in our earlier summit meetings.

I remember that the General Secretary and I, together in a room, one on one, remarked about the uniqueness of our situation and that very possibly, between us, war and peace for the world could be decided, depending on what we did. And I remember also saying to him that I didn't think that we distrusted each other because of our armaments. We were armed because we distrusted each other. And therefore, while we were going to talk about weapons and reducing the number of weapons and so forth, at the same time we should recognize that we ought to try and eliminate those things that cause the mistrust between us.

Middle East Peace Efforts

Q. Among the many discussions you will have in Moscow, probably you will talk with Mr. Gorbachev about the Middle East. What is your opinion for the future of the occupied territories? And do you know there is a projected program of a possibility of sending some European troops under the United Nations flag? What is your opinion about that in the Arab-occupied territories?

The President. Well, I don't know about the sending of troops or anything of that kind. I'd like to be a little more optimistic and say that I believe there is a desire in the Middle East to settle once and for all what is still technically a state of war between the Arab nations and Israel. We have made a proposal, and this proposal could involve putting together an international conference of nations. But we've made it plain: not an international conference to dictate a settlement but to be helpful if we can, to give advice and to make proposals that might help them arrive at a fair and just peace. And if the Soviet Union is to be a member of that conference, I think there they have a step they have to take, and that is to resume diplomatic relations with the State of Israel.

Q. With the State of Israel. But who will represent the Palestinians—the PLO?

The President. There, I think, is an issue. And actually I think that a lot of that has to do with the feeling that some of the Arab States—because I know that there is a great difference in many of the nations about who could be a proper representative for the Palestinian people and a great feeling that that could hardly be Arafat's element, since here again you have a group that refuses to recognize the right of Israel to exist as a nation.

Soviet Domestic Reforms

Q. Mr. President, do you honestly support

a statement made by British Prime Minister Thatcher that the West should support Mr. Gorbachev's domestic reform because it is not only to the benefit of the Soviet people but also to the West?

The President. Well, yes, I think that if there's any way that outside nations could be helpful in this they should because many of the reforms that he is undertaking are aimed at the things that we have always criticized in the Soviet Union. And if there is a way to be helpful in that, and certainly to at least acknowledge our approval of what he is doing, that we should do that.

Q. Could you tell me what's your personal opinion of Mr. Gorbachev's ability to reform his country and chance of success?

The President. Well, I think it is evident that he is running into opposition, that there are those who want to cling to what are more the Stalinist policies, and yet he is apparently going forward with the recommendations. Just recently it became public information that he had met with the heads of the Russian Orthodox Church and discussed some loosening of their opposition to worship.

Arms Control

Q. Mr. President, with Mr. Gorbachev running into some kind of opposition and your term of office expiring, have you ever discussed what is solid and will definitely remain of the arms control process, for example, whoever is in the White House, whoever is in the Kremlin, or do you see the chance that this thing might falter, for example, like détente did?

The President. Well, I have to be more optimistic than that, because I would hope that whoever is there in that office, and whoever is here in this office, would recognize the truth of a statement I made once in addressing the British Parliament and the legislature in Japan and elsewhere: We have to recognize, I think, that a nuclear war cannot be won and should never be fought. Once you engage in that kind of conflict, how do you declare a victor if their country is so poisoned by radiation that there's no place for the people to live? And that's what would result if we began exchanging the weapons that we have today. I think that's what has led us to some success in the reduction of nuclear weapons, is that recognition. Possibly in the Soviet Union it was their tragic experience with Chernobyl and to see that how an area would be made unlivable for the people who had lived all their lives there. And when you stop to think that that explosion was less than the power of one single warhead, and we're talking about exchanges of thousands of warheads.

I was interested one day not too long ago, back around the time of our summit meeting here, to hear in this room my own words coming back to me, not with any acknowledgement that they were mine—maybe he didn't know it—but from a Soviet official who word for word said, "a nuclear war cannot be won and should never be fought."

Q. Mr. President, on the future strategy of the arms control talks, especially among the western NATO nations, sometimes there still is a bit of confusion. The Germans, for example—there are a few people across a political aisle who after INF believe—or are very nervous about modernizing short-range nuclear missiles. They say the shorter the range of the nuclear missiles in central Europe the more dead are the Germans. How can you reconcile these people?

The President. Well, I know, and I have talked with the Chancellor [Helmut Kohl] many times about this. And they see the possibility of—if such a war would occur—they would be the battlefield, largely. And I think that has to be recognized. But at the same time, as I say, those weapons—I have to repeat myself—those weapons are the thing that right at the moment are kind of wiping out the imbalance in conventional weapons. And when you look at that imbalance, you have to say that the Soviet Union's military does not really represent a defensive force; it is far beyond the bounds of what is needed for defense. And so, you look at that as an offensive force. And since the nuclear weapons have been hailed as a deterrent to prevent war, I think that it is only logical that if we negotiate those battlefield tactical weapons and their reduction or elimination, that must be accompanied by the same kind of negotiations with regard to conventional weapons so that we come down to a parity and do not suddenly eliminate a form of weapon that leaves the other side with a great superiority. That might be too much of a temptation to some future leader.

American Hostages in Lebanon

Q. In the last 2 years, France has obtained the release of 10 French hostages while 9 U.S. hostages are still held in Beirut. So, what's your idea about it? Do you think the French are more efficient than you are, or do you suspect the French to have made a deal with the terrorists?

The President. I can't say, and I can't hazard a comment because I know none of the elements that were involved in that transaction. And until I do, I just won't comment.

I still think that all of us want our hostages free. I believe it's the duty of government when the citizens of a country are—their human rights are being unjustly denied by a means of that kind of kidnaping—that the government should take advantage of everything it can to get those people free. At the same time, we must recognize we can't do something in the form of ransom that creates an advantage for those other countries in taking hostages.

I've labored under a misapprehension here—well, worldwide, I guess—about the so-called Iran-*contra* affair. We were not dealing with the Khomeini or with the Iranian Government. Some individuals had sought a meeting with us on the basis of better relations in the event of the passing of the Khomeini and that it would be a new government. And they had an idea of a different kind of government and a relationship with us. And at one time, asking us to prove our credentials, they made the proposal of us violating our policy and selling, really, a token force of weapons to them, and also that they could use those to build some prestige for themselves with the military, which they would need if they were to become important in the next government.

Well, I said back to them that, yes, we could do that, even though it was against our policy of providing weapons for nations that supported terrorism. But they had made it plain that they did not support terrorism. And I said we have kidnaped now some Americans held hostage by an organization, the Hizballah, that we understand has a relationship with the Government of Iran, and said maybe you would have some influence, that if we did this, you could be helpful to us to try to get some of our hostages free.

Now, we argued right in this room about it, and some people said that would appear to be trading arms for hostages. Well, no, because we weren't giving them to the Government, and we weren't—or we weren't giving them, I should say, to the kidnapers. We were doing nothing to make an advantage for them. And I likened it to if I had a child who was kidnaped. I don't think that you should pay ransom, but if I found there was another individual that could get that child back for me in return for my doing something for him, that would be all right. And that this was much the same point.

And the truth was we got two hostages back and had two more that were scheduled to be released in the next 48 hours. And that was when the story was leaked, of what was going on, in that Lebanese paper. And all of a sudden the world media was full of this and translating it as trading arms for hostages. And I went on the air and tried to convince all of them that we weren't trading arms for hostages and tell them what the truth was, but that's what it's been made to appear.

Persian Gulf Conflict

Q. Speaking of Iran, France is reestablishing diplomatic ties with Tehran while the U.S. is still in a situation of undeclared war in the Gulf against Iran. How do you explain such a difference between close allies?

The President. Well, I don't know. We've been doing everything we can behind the scenes to try and bring about peace between Iraq and Iran. The U.N. proposal that was made about them coming to a peace was accepted by Iraq, but not by Iran. And our position in the Gulf—yes, it's brought us into combat with Iranian forces, but we've had naval forces there since 1949 to ensure that that international waterway comes under the international rules of freedom of the seas. And it is Iran that has been trying to close that off and shut down an international waterway, and we don't think that that should be allowed. And that's what we're intending to do, is to try and keep it open.

Afghanistan

Q. Mr. President, you're going to certainly talk about Afghanistan while in Moscow. Is it United States policy now to support the rebels or give the Soviet Union a hand by trying to calm down the situation?

The President. We feel that as long as the Soviet Union has provided support and arms and so forth and advisers to the Afghan force of their puppet government, that even though they go, we must continue to support the Mujahidin so that the people of Afghanistan can now, without the absence of the Soviet Union—I mean without the presence of the Soviet Union, that they can bring about a government that is a government chosen by the people of Afghanistan. And we do not recognize that the government there in Kabul is anything but a puppet government established by the Soviet Union. And so, yes, as long as weapons are being supplied to that other side, we're going to do whatever is necessary to support the Mujahidin.

General Noriega of Panama

Q. Mr. President, the Vice President yesterday broke publicly with you over the negotiations with Panama's General Noriega. He said he wouldn't negotiate with a drug dealer. Isn't his stand rather more consistent with the administration's hard line on drugs than your own?

The President. Well, I think that I have not changed my mind about the hard line on drugs. But you have me now in a situation in which I can't comment on what has been going on because there has been no resolution as yet. And I've never believed that when, say, negotiations are going on that you go public and tell what's being debated and negotiated. So, I can't comment there.

I can see why the Vice President said what he said because the impression has been given, based not on information from us but based on rumors and news leaks and so forth, that we are in negotiation somehow over—or with a participant in the drug trade and all. And I think he was making himself plain that you don't negotiate with people of that kind with regard to their activity in drugs.

Our goal, what we're trying to achieve, is the restoration of democracy in Panama. Right now we have a situation where, not legally but just through custom and tradition and started by a previous general, that you have a military dictatorship, in effect, in which even if the people elect a President, the dictator, using force, maintains control. And our goal is a democratic Panama with a government chosen by the people.

Strategic Defense Initiative

Q. When you speak about—I know you hate the word, the name, but they are Star Wars in Moscow—but at what stage are we? Could you elaborate a little bit about the Star Wars?

The President. On?

Q. The American——

The President. Well, yes, our SDI. Well, this started a number of years ago when I first came here and I met with the military of our own country and asked, is it possible, can you foresee that our science and technology is such that we could create a defensive weapon against nuclear missiles, ballistic missiles, that could literally make them obsolete because there would be so much doubt as to whether, if they were once employed, they could ever get through that defense? And a few days later, they came back and told me that, yes, they believed such a weapon could be designed. And I said, go to it! And so the Strategic Defense Initiative was adopted. It has made such great progress—some scientific breakthroughs—that the people involved believe that not only can we have such a system but that it will come much earlier than we had believed was possible. There have been a number of breakthroughs that have advanced the timing on this.

And then, once you have such a weapon, I believe that that is when we could then really move worldwide, even if it meant sharing that weapon. And I would be amenable to that, that if we had such a weapon, a defensive weapon, that we could eliminate the offensive missiles. Now, the question arises naturally, well, then, why would you need that system if you'd eliminated the weapons? Well, you can't wipe out of people's minds the knowledge of how to build a nuclear missile. And someday there could be a madman loose in the world, as we've seen in our own lifetime a number of times, who, with that knowledge, could then secretly build the only one. I've likened it to when, after World War I, the nations all met in Geneva and decided to eliminate poison gas. But everybody kept their gasmasks.

Korean Peninsula

Q. Mr. President, you deserve credit for including a Far East Asian region for elimination of INF at the Washington summit. What is your next logical step to ease the tensions in the Asian region, for example, Korean Peninsula, where, as you know, the Olympic games will be hurt?

The President. Well, now, I'm not quite sure I understand your question there.

Q. How do you plan to propose to Mr. Gorbachev in order to ease the tensions in the Asian region?

The President. Oh, well, I think that will be a subject for us to talk about and discuss. I think that all of us have an obligation to see that in the world tensions that nothing—if I'm answering you correctly—in the area of terrorism or something could be employed to upset the Olympic games. And I think what that would require are those nations that probably have a more friendly relationship with North Korea than we do, by virtue of the war that was fought there, that if some of those other nations would make it plain that North Korea should not take advantage of their proximity to the games and do anything of a terrorist nature to upset those games.

Vice President Bush

Q. Mr. President, how would you like to be remembered in history? I'm asking about the Reagan legacy, something like that—just a remark. The two frontrunners struggling for your succession—both of them seem to be of quite a different brand of politician, more the managerial type of candidate as compared to a Reagan revolution and inspiration and these kinds of things. Has the mood changed in America?

The President. Well, now, wait a minute. I have to say something about the Republican candidate for President. Now I can safely say that since everyone else has dropped out of the race. I have to say that the Vice President has been an important part of everything that we've achieved in this so-called revolution in these last 7 years or so. I could just give you a figure here of one thing from the very beginning. I had always believed that Vice Presidents in our system of government were relegated to a kind of just standing and waiting position. And I think that's a waste of talent. I have always believed that your Vice President should be like a vice president in a private corporation. He should be an executive with duties and functions.

So, one of the first jobs that I put on the Vice President was to set up a task force and find out how many government regulations imposed on the private sector, on people and on local communities and State governments and business and industry—how many could be removed. And that task force, under his direction, was so successful that we estimate that we have eliminated 600 million man-hours a year of filling out government paperwork on the part of the citizens and businesses and the local and State governments. The book that registers—or contains all those regulations—is only half as thick as it used to be.

And then I put—in the next time, in the task force when the State of Florida—it became disgraceful, the extent to which drugs were being flooded through there into the United States—and put him in charge of a task force there. And for the first time, he put together the law enforcement agencies from the Federal, the State, and the local level, and including cooperation from the military. And that was so successful there that then moved him to a task force for the whole southern border, across the 2,000 miles, the border between our country and Mexico. And again success, and the figures sound so great, except that with the boundaries such as we have and the two great seacoasts, that isn't really the answer to the problem because of all of the thousands of tons of drugs and the planes and ships and trucks and so forth that we have confiscated, and the hundreds of millions of dollars that we've confiscated. As long as there is a demand, the drug dealers can get the drugs through—with these task forces. I don't think it would be helpful to eliminate them and just let them come in free with no interference, because we're doing that. At the same time, we're trying to win the battle where it must be won, and that is in taking the user away from the drugs, not the other way around—to convince the people that they should not.

One last little thing here. I know I'm taking a great deal of time. My wife has been very active in that area, and all on her own. She's not a government employee. But she answered a little girl's question in a schoolroom one day when she was talking to them about drugs and why they, as children, should not engage in this. And the little girl stood up and said to her, "Well, what do we do when someone offers us drugs?" And Nancy said, "Just say no." One answer in a schoolroom to one little girl—today there are over 12,000 Just Say No Clubs in the schools across the United States. And that's why we're going to try to win that battle.

But that all started from what you were saying about differences with the Vice President. And, no, I think that, as I say, he's been a part of all that we've done here with regard to the economy. We've had the longest period of economic expansion in the history of our country. In the last 5 years, we have created 16 million new jobs for the workers in our work force. We have the lowest unemployment rate in many years. And we have the highest rate of employment among what is considered the potential employment pool—all of the people that could be considered as potential for jobs—the highest percentage of them today are employed than has ever been true in our history. And as I say, the Vice President's been a part of all of the things that helped bring this about.

Soviet General Secretary Gorbachev

Q. Mr. President, do you consider Mikhail Gorbachev as a friend—I mean, a real friend?

The President. Well, I can't help but say yes to that because the difference that I've found between him and other previous leaders that I have met with is that, yes, we can debate, and we disagree, and it is true he's made it apparent that he believes much of the Communist propaganda that he's grown up hearing about our country that—the big corporations and whether they dictate to government or not and things of that kind. I try to disabuse him of those beliefs. But there is never a sense of personal animus when the arguments are over, and I'm reasonably optimistic, although at the same time I'm realistic. The only Russian I know is a little Russian proverb. And I've used it so many times on him that he's going to hit me over the head one day if I use it again. And that is, *Dovorey no provorey*—trust but verify.

Q. Thank you, Mr. President. I'm pleased, as a Finn, to welcome you and Mrs. Reagan to our country on your way to Moscow, and we all wish you a very happy journey.

The President. Well, thank you very much. We're looking forward to it because we're celebrating, as you perhaps know, mutually the 350th anniversary of the Finnish-United States relationship and the Finnish community here in our country at that time that was established.

Note: The interview began at 11:35 a.m. in the Oval Office at the White House.

Proclamation 5825—National Rural Health Awareness Week, 1988
May 19, 1988

By the President of the United States of America

A Proclamation

During National Rural Health Awareness Week, we can be grateful for the significant progress made over the years by countless devoted Americans in providing rural health care. We should remember as well, however, the continuing need for citizens to redouble their efforts in this regard.

A quarter of all Americans live in the towns, villages, and farms of rural America. Their location in remote areas with frequently limited transportation, together with their employment on the land and in forests, mines, and factories, presents continuing and sometimes formidable obstacles to the delivery of health services. For instance, rural areas are finding it hard to attract enough health care providers; just 12 percent of our physicians and a declining number of professional nurses and providers of long-term care currently serve our more than 50 million rural citizens.

Fortunately, dedicated Americans are striving to overcome challenges and make good health care, including the benefits of our ever-increasing knowledge about health, nutrition, and disease and the advantages of rapidly evolving medical technology, accessible to rural citizens. Further such efforts, and further enhancement of public awareness of rural health care needs, will reaffirm our commitment to the well-being of rural citizens.

The Congress, by Senate Joint Resolution 254, has designated the week of May 15 through May 21, 1988, as "National Rural Health Awareness Week" and authorized and requested the President to issue a proclamation in observance of this week.

Now, Therefore, I, Ronald Reagan, President of the United States of America, do hereby proclaim the week of May 15 through May 21, 1988, as National Rural Health Awareness Week, and I call upon the people of the United States to observe this week with appropriate programs, ceremonies, and activities.

In Witness Whereof, I have hereunto set my hand this nineteenth day of May, in the year of our Lord nineteen hundred and eighty-eight, and of the Independence of the United States of America the two hundred and twelfth.

RONALD REAGAN

[*Filed with the Office of the Federal Register, 10:55 a.m., May 20, 1988*]

Statement on Signing the Appalachian States Low-Level Radioactive Waste Compact Consent Act
May 19, 1988

Today, I am signing into law H.R. 3025, legislation granting congressional consent to the Appalachian States Low-Level Radioactive Waste Compact.

In granting its consent to the creation of this Compact, the Congress has given its approval to yet another effort at the State level to resolve concerns regarding radioactive waste. More than three-quarters of the States have now entered such compacts, demonstrating the major progress that has been achieved in addressing the problem of radioactive waste. Our continued success in this effort, along with the passage of last year's amendments to the Nuclear Waste Policy Act, underscore this Nation's commitment to take those actions needed to ensure the future availability of nuclear power as an energy supply option for this country. Continued growth in the availability of nuclear power promises significant benefits to our energy security, decreasing this Nation's reliance on insecure sources of foreign oil.

In signing this bill, I note that one of the many provisions of the Compact suffers from a constitutional defect in that it assigns Federal law enforcement responsibilities to the Appalachian States Low-Level Radioactive Waste Commission, but does not require that the Commission be appointed in a manner consistent with the Appointments Clause of the Constitution. Any effort by the Commission to enforce Federal regulations would contravene the Constitution. While I hope that no such effort would occur, I expect the Nuclear Regulatory Commission to take note of and report to the Attorney General on any such actions of the Commission in this area.

RONALD REAGAN

The White House,
May 19, 1988.

Note: H.R. 3025, approved May 19, was assigned Public Law No. 100–319.

Remarks at the White House News Photographers Association Annual Dinner
May 19, 1988

Well, thank you, Ken, and thank all of you. And my congratulations again to the award winners. I'm delighted to be at this 1988 White House News Photographers Dinner, the last one that Nancy and I will be attending.

I've always considered photographers, the cameramen, and the crew, my favorites among the press. [*Laughter*] So, I knew that, being friends, you wouldn't mind if I got a few things off my chest tonight. [*Laughter*] There's been a lot in the papers in recent weeks about insiders' views of the White House. Well, I've had it with all that. So, tonight I'm going to give you the view from the ultimate insider—me. [*Laughter*] I'm going to tell the real story of this administration. It's been a wonderful two terms, with lots of accomplishments. And I've even brought the slides to prove it. So, Marlin, hit the lights. [*Laughter*]

Now, one of the most interesting episodes was General Secretary Gorbachev's visit to the United States. I tried to help him understand our culture. In this photo, I'm saying: "This is the way it works, Mikhail. If Domino's doesn't get the pizza here in 35 seconds—[*laughter*]—we get it free." [*Laughter*] I like Mikhail personally, but you have to watch the Soviets every minute. Someone accidentally noticed that several weeks after they left—noticed they planted bugs all over the place. [*Laughter*] And by the way, on the matter of the INF treaty, I told the Senate not to worry about verification. I told them I'd take care of it. [*Laughter*] And while Gorbachev was here, I even made him write 100 times, "I will not cheat. I will not cheat." [*Laughter*]

[*Showing a slide of Mrs. Reagan and Don Regan*]——Oops! Oops! [*Laughter*]

Well, now, during my Presidency I've always emphasized diplomacy. But sometimes it comes to the point you have to use force in foreign affairs. [*Laughter*] And here I am, arm wrestling General Noriega for Panama. [*Laughter*]

We really enjoyed our trip to China and were amazed that the population was over a billion people. And as you can see here, the lines are terrible. [*Laughter*]

On another trip, the Government of Indonesia gave us these gifts—and they're our friends. [*Laughter*] Actually, I love this shirt. I finally found something louder than Sam Donaldson. [*Laughter*]

And speaking of the press, remember during the *contra* aid vote when the networks wouldn't let me on the air? I bet you wondered how I finally got my message out. [*Laughter*] It's no secret that the press and I sometimes don't get along. In addition to my standard ploy of using helicopter noise to avoid reporters' questions, I've now added a new method to avoid questions—tear gas. [*Laughter*]

I've loved almost every minute I've been in office, although there were a couple of trips to the hospital. In case you're wondering what happened here, I had just said: "So, Don, you say you're going to write a book." [*Laughter*] But while I was recuperating the congressional leadership came to see me. And here I am asking for a colon donor. [*Laughter*]

One of my greatest enjoyments is talking to the young men and women who defend us from attack. Here I am on top of the White House—[*laughter*]—and the soldier is explaining where he thinks the next book will come from. [*Laughter*] It's fortunate that not everything has been spilled in these books, however. [*Laughter*] I mean, I hope the environmentalists never find out about this one. [*Laughter*] We used to fly Air Force One over Wyoming low and shoot buffalo from the window. [*Laughter*]

But I'll tell you someone I trust totally—George Bush. He's been a wonderful Vice President, and he'll make an excellent President. And that's why I endorsed him and why I'll work hard for him this fall. Here we are listening to one of his speeches. [*Laughter*]

You do get to meet lots of wonderful people as President, and they're always bringing me things to try on. [*Laughter*] What struck me about this photo is that this hat fit Don Regan fine. [*Laughter*]

Now, this is an interesting photo. This young man down front there in the picture later told me he had a vision of Michael Dukakis in the Oval Office. [*Laughter*]

And I like this one of Lucky sitting on my lap. Unfortunately, my raincoat was on the seat just behind me. [*Laughter*]

Now, this is a sight I've seen many times. And you do sometimes get in the way, and you do sometimes cause a commotion. But your work has produced a permanent historical record of my two terms as President. You've been there with me. You've captured me in moments of hope and excitement during the campaign; moments of disappointment, like when General Secretary Gorbachev and I parted there in Iceland; moments of grief, such as when we were with the families of the *Challenger* crew; many, many moments of joy and optimism, and of course, moments of love whenever I look in Nancy's direction. You've captured what life has meant for Nancy and me over these past 8 years. And for that, I genuinely thank you.

And you know, there's one picture you've taken time and time again: that of me saluting the troops. I do that out of respect. You here tonight do good, hard, creative work; and I respect that, too. So, as we say our farewells here tonight, this salute's for you. And now, tonight, good night, and God bless you.

Note: The President spoke at 9:28 p.m. in the main ballroom at the Sheraton Washington Hotel. He was introduced by Kenneth L. Blaylock, president of the White House News Photographers Association. Marlin Fitzwater was Assistant to the President for Press Relations.

Remarks at a Cuban Independence Day Ceremony
May 20, 1988

Speaking for myself, and I think speaking for the Vice President also, it gives us great pleasure to join with the Cuban-American community in commemorating the anniversary of a great day in the cause of a free Cuba: the establishment of the Cuban Republic 86 years ago. On that day, May 20th, 1902, the bonds of friendship between the peoples of Cuba and of the United States were reaffirmed. The birth of the Cuban Republic was the culmination of a long and arduous struggle, of revolts, political imprisonment, executions, and exile. Today that passion for a free Cuba remains alive in the hearts of thousands of Cubans everywhere. Cuban-Americans have demonstrated what a free people can accomplish unencumbered by tyranny, and I am confident that the time will come when the spirit of freedom will reign in Cuba itself.

And let me just say, throughout this administration, in good times and bad, I've always known that I could look to the Cuban-American community for support. Your support, your friendship has meant more to me than I can say. Having suffered personally the evils of communism, you have an acute understanding of the danger that Communist expansion poses to this hemisphere. You have stood in support of people everywhere who seek freedom, such as the people of Nicaragua. And let me assure you, as far as this administration is concerned, the freedom of Cuba is a nonnegotiable demand. We will never, ever, negotiate away the dream of every Cuban-American—a dream that I, too, hold in my heart—that Cuba will again join the family of free and democratic nations.

Only 90 miles of ocean separate the island of Cuba from the United States, but between our governments is an unbridgeable gulf—the gulf between freedom and tyranny, between respect for human rights and the rejection of individual freedom. "Within the revolution, everything," Castro has proclaimed, "against the revolution, nothing." Well, "nothing" has meant no freedom of speech, assembly, religion, or economic activity. "Nothing" has increasingly meant a Cuba dependent on subsidies from the Soviet Union to keep its unworkable Communist economy from complete ruin. "Everything" has meant every conceivable cruelty, abuse, and torture—to the point that Cuba, today, has the worst human rights record in the entire Western Hemisphere. "Everything" means the Cuban political prisons where, writes that brave freedom fighter, Armando Valladares, Castro's prisoners "have been held longer than any other political prisoners in Latin America, perhaps in the world. The violence, repression, and beatings are facts of life for them. And today, at this very moment, hundreds of political prisoners are naked, sleeping on the floors of cells whose windows and doors have been sealed. They never see the light of day or, for that matter, artificial light." Denied medical care, even visits, their spirit remains unbroken. If they who suffer so greatly will not negotiate away their freedom with Castro, neither will the United States of America.

José Marti said: "One revolution is still necessary: the one that will not end with the rule of its leader. It will be the revolution against revolutions, the uprising of all peaceable men who will become soldiers for once so that neither they nor anyone else will ever have to be a soldier again." Well, at a time when young Cubans are shipped abroad to advance foreign designs, the rulers in Havana are necessarily worried about the new generation's interest in Marti's message.

In this anniversary of the Cuban Republic, I join a million free Cuban-Americans in reaffirming our solidarity with the long-suffering Cuban people. In the heart of the Americas, the long night of totalitarian rule cannot endure forever. Long live the dawn of freedom! *Viva Cuba Libre!*

Note: The President spoke at 1:03 p.m. in the Roosevelt Room at the White House.

Proclamation 5826—Prayer for Peace, Memorial Day, 1988

May 20, 1988

By the President of the United States of America

A Proclamation

Once each May, amid the quiet hills and rolling lanes and breeze-brushed trees of Arlington National Cemetery, far above the majestic Potomac and the monuments and memorials of our Nation's Capital just beyond, the graves of America's military dead are decorated with the beautiful flag that in life these brave souls followed and loved. This scene is repeated across our land and around the world, wherever our defenders rest. Let us hold it our sacred duty and our inestimable privilege on this day to decorate these graves ourselves—with a fervent prayer and a pledge of true allegiance to the cause of liberty, peace, and country for which America's own have ever served and sacrificed.

During our observance of Memorial Day this year we have fresh reason to call to mind the service and sacrifices of the members of our merchant marine during World War II—these gallant seafarers have now deservedly received veteran status. More than 6,000 of them gave their lives in the dangerous and vital duty of transporting materiel to our forces around the globe. We will never forget them as we honor our war dead.

Our pledge and our prayer this day are those of free men and free women who know that all we hold dear must constantly be built up, fostered, revered, and guarded vigilantly from those in every age who seek its destruction. We know, as have our Nation's defenders down through the years, that there can never be peace without its essential elements of liberty, justice, and independence.

Those true and only building blocks of peace were the lone and lasting cause and hope and prayer that lighted the way of those whom we honor and remember this Memorial Day. To keep faith with our hallowed dead, let us be sure, and very sure, today and every day of our lives, that we keep their cause, their hope, their prayer, forever our country's own.

In recognition of those brave Americans to whom we pay tribute today, the Congress, by joint resolution approved May 11, 1950 (64 Stat. 158), has requested the President to issue a proclamation calling upon the people of the United States to observe each Memorial Day as a day of prayer for permanent peace and designating a period when the people of the United States might unite in prayer.

Now, Therefore, I, Ronald Reagan, President of the United States of America, do hereby designate Memorial Day, Monday, May 30, 1988, as a day of prayer for permanent peace, and I designate the hour beginning in each locality at eleven o'clock in the morning of that day as a time to unite in prayer. I urge the press, radio, television, and all other information media to cooperate in this observance.

I also direct all appropriate Federal officials and request the Governors of the several States and the Commonwealth of Puerto Rico, and the appropriate officials of all units of government, to direct that the flag be flown at half-staff until noon during this Memorial Day on all buildings, grounds, and naval vessels throughout the United States and in all areas under its jurisdiction and control, and I request the people of the United States to display the flag at half-staff from their homes on this day for the customary forenoon period.

In Witness Whereof, I have hereunto set my hand this twentieth day of May, in the year of our Lord nineteen hundred and eighty-eight, and of the Independence of the United States of America the two hundred and twelfth.

RONALD REAGAN

[*Filed with the Office of the Federal Register, 11:04 a.m., May 23, 1988*]

Appointment of Roger Bolton as Special Assistant to the President for Public Liaison
May 20, 1988

The President today announced the appointment of Roger Bolton to be Special Assistant to the President for Public Liaison. He will serve as liaison with business and professional organizations.

Since July of 1985 Mr. Bolton has been

Assistant United States Trade Representative for Public Affairs and Private Sector Liaison. Previously, he served as Deputy Assistant Secretary of the Treasury for Public Affairs, 1984–1985; director of speechwriting for the Reagan-Bush campaign, 1984; press secretary for the Joint Economic Committee, 1983; administrative assistant and press secretary for Representative Clarence J. Brown, 1975–1982; and a reporter for the Marion (Ohio) Star, 1972–1974.

Mr. Bolton graduated from Ohio State University (B.A., 1972). He was born June 12, 1950, in St. Louis, MO. He is married and resides in Reston, VA.

Statement on Signing the Radiation-Exposed Veterans Compensation Act of 1988
May 20, 1988

I have today approved H.R. 1811, the "Radiation-Exposed Veterans Compensation Act of 1988." The Act adjusts the law governing eligibility for disability benefits for certain veterans due to the unique circumstances of their military service in the early days of the atomic age.

The adjustment applies in limited circumstances to three specific categories of American veterans:

—veterans who served with U.S. forces occupying Hiroshima or Nagasaki, Japan during the period beginning on August 6, 1945, and ending on July 1, 1946;

—veterans interned as prisoners of war in Japan during World War II (or who served on active duty in Japan immediately following such internment), if their internment resulted in an opportunity for exposure to ionizing radiation comparable to that of veterans who served in the forces occupying Hiroshima and Nagasaki; and

—veterans who participated on-site in a test involving the atmospheric detonation of a nuclear device.

The adjustment applies only with respect to specified diseases—primarily cancer of various organs—that manifest themselves within 40 years after the veteran last participated in the military radiation-related activity or, in the case of leukemia, 30 years after such participation. Thus, for veterans who served in Hiroshima and Nagasaki or were prisoners of war in Japan, the period for manifestation of the disease already has passed.

The existing fair and equitable system for adjudication of veterans' claims for disability benefits requires demonstration of a connection between a veteran's disability and the veteran's military service. While this legislation bypasses the requirement for demonstration of such a connection, it does so only in specific, narrow circumstances for a truly unique group of veterans.

Enactment of this legislation does not represent a judgment that service-related radiation exposure of veterans covered by the Act in fact caused any disease, nor does it represent endorsement of a principle of permitting veterans to receive benefits funded through veterans programs which bear no relationship to their former military service.

Instead, the Act gives due recognition for the unusual service rendered by Americans who participated in military activities involving exposure to radiation generated by the detonation of atomic explosives. The Nation is grateful for their special service, and enactment of H.R. 1811 makes clear the Nation's continuing concern for their welfare.

RONALD REAGAN

The White House,
May 20, 1988.

Note: H.R. 1811, approved May 20, was assigned Public Law No. 100–321.

Nomination of William Andreas Brown To Be United States Ambassador to Israel
May 20, 1988

The President today announced his intention to nominate William Andreas Brown, of New Hampshire, a career member of the Senior Foreign Service, Class of Career Minister, as Ambassador to Israel. He would succeed Thomas R. Pickering.

In 1956 Mr. Brown entered the Foreign Service in the Department of State. He served as consular and commercial officer in Hong Kong, 1957–1959. From 1959 to 1961, he served as political officer in Singapore, followed by a tour in Kuching, Sarawak, as principal officer until 1965. He then studied the Russian language at the Foreign Service Institute, 1965–1966. He served as political officer in Moscow, 1966–1968, and New Delhi, 1968–1970. In 1970 he became Deputy Director in the Office of Asian Communist Affairs. He attended the National War College, 1972, and studied Mongolian at Leeds, England. Mr. Brown was detailed to the Environmental Protection Agency, where he served as Special Assistant to the Administrator, 1974–1976. In 1977 he went to Moscow as political counselor, where he served until 1978, when he departed for Taipei as deputy chief of mission, Chargé d'Affaires, and, then, first acting director. He served as deputy chief of mission in Tel Aviv, Israel, in 1979–1982. From 1982 to 1983, he was visiting professor at the University of New Hampshire, and from 1983 to 1985, he served as the Principal Deputy Assistant Secretary of State for East Asian and Pacific Affairs. Mr. Brown currently serves as U.S. Ambassador to the Kingdom of Thailand.

Mr. Brown graduated from Harvard College (B.A., 1952) and Harvard University Graduate School (M.A., 1955; Ph.D., 1963). He was born September 7, 1930, in Winchester, MA. He served in the U.S. Marine Corps, 1952–1954, and the U.S. Marine Corps Reserve, 1954–1960. Mr. Brown is married, has four children, and resides in Hillsboro, NH.

Message to the Senate Transmitting the Convention Against Torture and Inhuman Treatment or Punishment
May 20, 1988

To the Senate of the United States:

With a view to receiving the advice and consent of the Senate to ratification, subject to certain reservations, understandings, and declarations, I transmit herewith the Convention against Torture and Other Cruel, Inhuman or Degrading Treatment or Punishment. The Convention was adopted by unanimous agreement of the United Nations General Assembly on December 10, 1984, and entered into force on June 26, 1987. The United States signed it on April 18, 1988. I also transmit, for the information of the Senate, the report of the Department of State on the Convention.

The United States participated actively and effectively in the negotiation of the Convention. It marks a significant step in the development during this century of international measures against torture and other inhuman treatment or punishment. Ratification of the Convention by the United States will clearly express United States opposition to torture, an abhorrent practice unfortunately still prevalent in the world today.

The core provisions of the Convention establish a regime for international cooperation in the criminal prosecution of torturers relying on so-called "universal jurisdiction." Each State Party is required either to prosecute torturers who are found in its territory or to extradite them to other countries for prosecution.

In view of the large number of States concerned, it was not possible to negotiate a treaty that was acceptable to the United States in all respects. Accordingly, certain reservations, understandings, and declarations have been drafted, which are discussed in the report of the Department of State. With the inclusion of these reservations, understandings, and declarations, I believe there are no constitutional or other legal obstacles to United States ratification. The recommended legislation necessary to implement the Convention will be submitted to the Congress separately.

Should the Senate give its advice and consent to ratification of the Convention, I intend at the time of deposit of United States ratification to make a declaration pursuant to Article 28 that the United States does not recognize the competence of the Committee against Torture under Article 20 to make confidential investigations of charges that torture is being systematically practiced in the United States. In addition, I intend not to make declarations, pursuant to Articles 21 and 22 of the Convention, recognizing the competence of the Committee against Torture to receive and consider communications from States and individuals alleging that the United States is violating the Convention. I believe that a final United States decision as to whether to accept such competence of the Committee should be withheld until we have had an opportunity to assess the Committee's work. It would be possible for the United States in the future to accept the competence of the Committee pursuant to Articles 20, 21, and 22, should experience with the Committee prove satisfactory and should the United States consider this step desirable.

By giving its advice and consent to ratification of this Convention, the Senate of the United States will demonstrate unequivocally our desire to bring an end to the abhorrent practice of torture.

RONALD REAGAN

The White House,
May 20, 1988.

Appointment of Ronald P. Andrade as a Member of the National Advisory Council on Indian Education
May 20, 1988

The President today announced his intention to appoint Ronald P. Andrade to be a member of the National Advisory Council on Indian Education for a term expiring September 29, 1990. He would succeed Fred L. Nicol, Jr.

Mr. Andrade is currently a management consultant in Valley Center, CA. Prior to this he was senior planner for La Jolla Indian Tribe, 1986–1987. From 1986 to 1987, he was an American Indian Affairs Specialist of the Equal Opportunity Office at the Department of Agriculture. From 1983 to 1984, he was Staff Assistant to the Assistant Secretary for Indian Affairs of the California Indian Task Force at the Department of the Interior, and executive director of the National Congress of American Indians, 1980–1983. He was executive director of the Native American Student Alliance, 1978–1979, and executive director for San Francisco Indian Center, 1977–1978.

Mr. Andrade was born May 14, 1947, in Los Angeles, CA. He served in the United States Marine Corps Reserve, 1966–1970. He is married, has one child, and resides in Valley Center, CA.

Message to the Senate Transmitting the Protocol on Acts of Violence at International Airports

May 20, 1988

To the Senate of the United States:

I transmit herewith, for the advice and consent of the Senate to ratification, the Protocol for the Suppression of Unlawful Acts of Violence at Airports Serving International Civil Aviation, done at Montreal on February 24, 1988. The report of the Department of State is also enclosed for the information of the Senate.

The Protocol will extend and supplement the legal framework of the Convention for the Suppression of Unlawful Acts against the Safety of Civil Aviation, done at Montreal on September 23, 1971, to which the United States is already a party. It provides for enhanced international cooperation in the fight against terrorism at airports serving international civil aviation. The Protocol was negotiated under the auspices of the International Civil Aviation Organization.

The United States played a leading role in the negotiation of the Protocol. Early ratification by the United States will encourage similar action by other nations.

I recommend that the Senate give early and favorable consideration to the Protocol and give its advice and consent to ratification.

RONALD REAGAN

The White House,
May 20, 1988.

Executive Order 12641—John C. Stennis Space Center

May 20, 1988

Designating Certain Facilities of the National Aeronautics and Space Administration in the State of Mississippi as the John C. Stennis Space Center

Senator John C. Stennis has served his country as a United States Senator for over 40 years and has steadfastly supported the Nation's space program since its inception. He has demonstrated visionary leadership and has consistently worked to assure United States world leadership and preeminence in space.

The installation now to be renamed has played and will continue to play a major role in the United States space program and has been the recipient of the Senator's unwavering support from the moment the decision was made to establish that installation.

Now, Therefore, I, Ronald Reagan, President of the United States of America, by virtue of the authority vested in me by the Constitution and laws of the United States, do hereby direct the Administrator of General Services to designate the facilities of the National Space Technology Laboratories of the National Aeronautics and Space Administration in the State of Mississippi as the John C. Stennis Space Center; and such facilities shall be thereafter known and referred to by that name.

RONALD REAGAN

The White House,
May 20, 1988.

[*Filed with the Office of the Federal Register, 11:06 a.m., May 23, 1988*]

Radio Address to the Nation on Armed Forces Day
May 21, 1988

My fellow Americans:

You may have heard me say before that one of the things I like most about my job as President is visiting and talking with our young men and women in uniform. I've met them all over the world—at our Army outposts along the demilitarized zone in South Korea, on board the U.S.S. *Constellation*, in the hangars of Tempelhof Air Base in West Berlin, at Parris Island in South Carolina, and at the Coast Guard Academy a few days ago. And everywhere, I've seen that their commanders are right: They're the best we've ever had. I mention this because today is Armed Forces Day. Yes, this is the day for all of us to salute the soldiers, sailors, marines, and aviators who stand sentry on the frontiers of freedom all over the world. We say thanks to the patriots who, whether under the midnight star or the noonday Sun, are always alert so that America's peace and liberty will always be safe.

Seven years ago, when we came to Washington, we found that our armed forces had been badly neglected. We found airplanes that could not fly and ships that could not sail for lack of trained people and spare parts. The military couldn't recruit enough good people or hold on to those they had. Today that's changed. The men and women in the services are well-trained and well-equipped. Almost all new recruits have a high school diploma. Never before in peacetime have we had a military that is as well-prepared.

Just last month, the world saw what those who serve America on freedom's front—what they can do when the chips are down. I'm speaking of the story of the U.S.S. *Samuel B. Roberts*, a guided-missile frigate and part of our task force to help protect passage through international waters in the Persian Gulf. The *Roberts* was on patrol when it hit a submerged mine. The mine blew a huge hole in the ship's hull, sent a fireball shooting up the exhaust stack and 150 feet in the air, and almost tore the *Roberts* in half. Luckily, no one was killed. Some might have said that she was doomed—head for the life rafts. Well, that's not what the men of the *Roberts* said. They were determined to show what they could do. Acting fast, they held the *Roberts* together with bolts and wire, took care of their injured, escaped the mine field, and with the help of other Navy ships got safely to harbor. The captain [Comdr. Paul X. Rinn] summed up the spirit and determination of the entire crew when he closed his report saying of the *Roberts*: "We saved her, we'll fix her, and we'll fight again." And he signed off with their motto, "No higher honor." That's the spirit, skill, and dedication that has been rebuilt in all our armed services today. "No higher honor" could be the motto of every American in uniform.

Yesterday, to show the Nation's gratitude again, I signed into law three bills expanding veterans' benefits in education, job training, health care, and other areas. The men and women on duty today should know that we'll still be behind them when their service is done. They also deserve to know that, like them, we're all doing our part to keep the peace. This week I was pleased that the Senate began floor debate on the Intermediate-Range Nuclear Forces, or INF, treaty. This treaty has had a thorough and useful examination in committee. Now the Senate can join with me and show both our allies and adversaries that it, too, wants to help build a brighter peace and better world. I hope the Senate will provide its consent to ratification of the INF treaty in time to bring it into force during my meetings with the General Secretary in Moscow.

On this Armed Forces Day, let's also remember the important role the armed services have been playing in supporting law enforcement agencies in the fight against drugs. I asked the Secretary of Defense this week to find even more ways to use military resources against drug smugglers. I also called for a joint task force—executive branch and Congress—to draw up a unified plan to fight drugs. I hope the leaders of Congress agree with me that the campaign against illegal drugs must not be hostage to headline seeking and partisan politics.

This week we had another sign of America's strength, its economic strength, which undergirds all of our national security efforts. Trade figures came out for March. America exported in March more than ever before. Against this background of good news on trade, I am going to veto the ill-advised trade bill Congress has sent me. Once my veto is sustained, we'll work hard to get a responsible trade bill, one that will strengthen, not weaken, our economy.

One last thought for Armed Forces Day and every day: If you see someone in uniform, would you go up, shake their hand, and thank them.

Until next week, thanks for listening, and God bless you.

Note: The President spoke at 12:06 p.m. from the Oval Office at the White House.

Remarks at the American Film Institute's Preservation Ball Honoring Fred Astaire
May 21, 1988

Talk about a surprise! [*Laughter*] I usually know when I'm going to be on "The Late, Late Show." [*Laughter*] Incidentally, I just have to say—and about show business—that the movie of that great Irving Berlin production, which was his second—because the first was "Yip, Yip, Yaphank" for World War I—[*laughter*]—and then this one—Warners made it. And the total $10 million that came in in profits on the picture was donated to the Army Emergency Relief. And those of us that were back and in the picture—we were already in uniform for real. It's the first time I ever made a movie for a second lieutenant's salary. [*Laughter*]

But again, as I say, thank you. And before saying anything else, I want to salute Bonita Granville Wrather. Bunny, you've guided the American Film Institute through its 20th anniversary, leading the Institute with dedication and inspiration into its third decade of service to this country. And I know that everyone here wants to join Nancy and me—they've already done it, but can do it again, in applauding you. [*Applause*]

"Dancing is a sweat job," Fred Astaire once said. "It takes time to get a dance right, to create something memorable." Fred took the time, and he created some of the most memorable films ever made, as we've seen tonight. He danced with Rita Hayworth atop a wedding cake—"You'll Never Get Rich," 1941. He danced on roller skates—"Shall We Dance?," 1937. He danced while hitting golf balls off a tee—"Carefree," 1938. He danced up the walls and across the ceiling—"Royal Wedding," 1951. And by the way, there's still nobody who's quite sure how he did that. [*Laughter*] He danced in an airplane, aboard ship, and in ballrooms—countless ballrooms, huge, magnificent rooms, with chandeliers and vast expanses of polished floors. And you know, it was a funny thing about those ballrooms. They may have been jammed with people, but they always looked sort of empty until the floor cleared and Fred and Ginger began to dance.

He was a marvel, a distinctly American marvel. Europe had never produced anything like him, neither had anyplace else on Earth. And in devoting his talents to another distinctly American marvel, the movies, Fred Astaire added immeasurably to our heritage, to our sense of ourselves.

It's important work the American Film Institute is doing, in preserving our nation's film heritage. Just think of it: A century from now, young people will still be able to see that thin, lovable, sandy-haired man, 5 feet 9 inches tall—see the way he tilts his hat to one side and smiles, starts to dance the way nobody ever danced before. And they'll be able to say: Yes! That's part of us. That's part of America.

You know, in Hollywood, if you don't sing or dance, you become an after-dinner speaker. [*Laughter*] And look where I wound up. [*Laughter*] But I have to tell you, I was an official of the Screen Actors Guild, president of the union and—so, I'd be out there making my personal appearances on the mashed-potato circuit, and I started out—what would I talk about? You didn't have speechwriters, you did it yourself. And I decided that I would try to correct some of the misapprehensions about show people and about Hollywood.

And I remember one example, and somehow it just does come back to my mind today and in the present circumstances. There had been a movement started because of some of the shenanigans of some of the people in show business that society looked down on. A movement had started in the Congress to pass a law that actors would have to be licensed by the Government in order to perform and be actors. And that gave me a line for my speech. I called that to the people's attention when I was speaking, and I said, "I think it's kind of funny: There are no actors in prison or jail. There are two United States Senators in prison right now." [*Laughter*] The line went over well. [*Laughter*] But I think that's enough from me.

And again, what a happy surprise that was. And thank you all and for all that you're doing in what I think is a very wonderful undertaking. And God bless you all.

Note: The President spoke at 10:40 p.m. in the Independence Ballroom at the Grand Hyatt Hotel. Bonita Granville Wrather was chairman of the board of trustees of the American Film Institute. In his opening remarks, the President referred to the film "This is the Army."

Remarks at the Presentation Ceremony for the "E" and "E Star" Awards

May 23, 1988

The President. Secretary Verity, Secretary McLaughlin, Secretary Lyng, and ladies and gentlemen: I'd like to welcome all of you to the White House. We have quite an array of experts here today, including Members of Congress; representatives from the President's Export Council, the Export Now Advisory Committee, the Departments of Commerce, Labor, and Agriculture; and of course, members of trade and professional groups.

And now, for these garden events, I've always followed Lyndon Johnson's guidelines. He said there are two basic kinds of speeches. The first is the Mother Hubbard speech, which covers everything but touches nothing. The second is the bikini speech, which covers only the essentials. And today I'll try to stick to the second and cover only the essential points. That's obviously the 12 winners here today, who are the recipients of the 1988 "E" and "E Star" Awards for their sustained contributions to our nation's export expansion efforts. Your work is the vital machine that produces prosperity for America. Exports mean jobs for our people and you—the growth and—well, that's why it's always a pleasure, I was going to say—the profits for our businesses and the jobs for our people that you mean and the growth of our economy. And I think thats why it's a pleasure to present the well-deserved "E" and "E Star" Awards.

And this year's ceremony couldn't have come at a better time. Last week the Commerce Department announced a remarkable reduction in the Nation's trade deficit. The trade deficit declined to $9¾ billion for March from the February figure of $13.83 billion. This was overwhelmingly due to the 23-percent jump in exports that the award winners here today helped fuel. Yet even with all this profoundly optimistic news, the pessimists just won't give up. You've got to hand it to them, they see the dark cloud behind every silver lining. Sometimes economic reporting resembles nothing so much as a hall of mirrors where good news becomes bad. Dropping unemployment means "rising fears of inflation." The fact that we're in the longest peacetime expansion in history can only mean calamity is just around the corner. And just the other night, one network managed to turn the American export boom into economic gloom. "An export boom," they said, and I'm quoting, "may also mean a bust in the same region."

Well, it reminds me of the story about Harry Truman and his use of colorful language. It seems that Eleanor Roosevelt called Bess one day and in the course of the conversation asked where Harry was and what he was doing, and Bess said, "He's out putting manure on the flower garden." And Eleanor said, "Oh, Bess, can't you get him to use some other term like fertilizer instead of manure?" And Bess said, "It's taken me 20 years to get him to call it manure." [*Laughter*]

Well, I won't keep you here all day, but before handing out the awards, there's one other point I want to bring up. As many of you know, I launched the Export Now campaign on February 24, and I'm glad to say it's in full swing. Our aim is to make sure that all American businesses—small, medium, and large—are aware of the great opportunities that exist in exporting. Of course, the recent trade figures, with a genuine boom in exports, show that plenty of businesses have already received the message. But there are thousands more that are still hesitant and uncertain, and it is these we want to reach. More than 40 States are on board the Export Now campaign, and they've appointed their trade experts to work with Commerce Department offices around the country. The Export Now staff has handled over 1,000 requests for information and arranged for speakers and other participation in over 300 events nationwide. And soon we'll have solid figures on new companies that have entered exporting or present exporters and have found new markets. That will be the test of how well we're doing, but it's still too early to rack up the results.

For myself, I have no doubts that the Yankee trading spirit is alive and well. Our products are of world-class quality. Our costs are now among the lowest in the world. And we're shipping overseas everything from doughnut makers to locomotives. It's people like you who will catapult America into the Roaring Nineties. So, keep up the good work. And thank you, and God bless you. And now, with Secretary Verity's help, we'll present the awards.

Reporter. Are you going to make a deal with Noriega, Mr. President? How about Noriega? Are you going to make a deal before Wednesday?

The President. We're not going by time; we're going by quality.

Q. Have you agreed to drop the drug charges, Mr. President?

The President. Nothing has been settled; it's still in the works.

Note: The President spoke at 11:34 a.m. in the Rose Garden at the White House. In his opening remarks, the President referred to Secretary of Commerce C. William Verity, Jr., Secretary of Labor Ann D. McLaughlin, and Secretary of Agriculture Richard Lyng. Recipients of the "E" Awards were Rod Canion, of Compaq Computer Corp., Houston, TX; G. Gregory Smith, of Electrical South, Inc., Greensboro, NC; Karsten Solheim, of Karsten Manufacturing Co., Phoenix, AZ; Walter LeCroy, of LeCroy Corp., Chestnut Ridge, NY; Gary Parker, of Lindsay International Sales Corp., Lindsay, NE; J. Walter Kisling, of Multiplex Co., Ballwin, MO; Raymond Gawronski, of Dresser Industries, Salisbury, MD; and Ralph Nolte, of Port Longview, Longview, WA. Recipients of the "E Star" Awards were G. William Hunter, of the Port of Oakland, Oakland, CA; Pauline Chambers Yost, of Technical Rubber Co., Johnstown, OH; R.E. Cartledge, of Union Camp Corp., Savannah, GA; and Dorothy Weaver, of the Greater Miami Chamber of Commerce, Miami, FL.

Nomination of John P. LaWare To Be a Member of the Board of Governors of the Federal Reserve System

May 23, 1988

The President today announced his intention to nominate John P. LaWare, of Massachusetts, District 1, to be a member of the Board of Governors of the Federal Reserve System for a term of 14 years from February 1, 1988. He would succeed Henry C. Wallich.

Since 1978 Mr. LaWare has been chairman and director of Shawmut National Corp. and Shawmut Bank in Boston, MA. He was named chairman and chief executive officer of both the corporation and the bank in 1980. Mr. LaWare joined Chemical Bank & Trust Co. in 1953, serving in various capacities: senior vice president, vice president, assistant vice president and assistant secretary.

Mr. LaWare graduated from Harvard University (B.A., 1950) and the University of Pennsylvania (M.A., 1951). He was born February 20, 1928, in Columbus, WI. He served in the United States Air Force, 1951–1953, and the New York Air National Guard, 1954–1959. He is married, has two children, and resides in Brookline, MA.

Address to the Citizens of Western Europe

May 23, 1988

Good afternoon. As you know, some 24 hours from now, I'll be leaving Washington to fly to Helsinki, Finland, on my way to Moscow to meet with General Secretary Gorbachev. I thought that on this, the eve of my fourth summit meeting with the new Soviet leader, it would be appropriate to address a few words to our fellow democracies with whom we share the dream of freedom and peace. I'd like first to discuss with you the policy that has brought this summit meeting about and that I believe has done much to advance the interests of freedom and peace throughout the world.

From the beginning, our administration has sought to pursue a policy toward the Soviet Union based on realism, on reasoned interchange with the Soviets and, yes, on strength, especially Western unity. The Soviet leaders talk, to use their phrase, of a common European home. Well, I believe that the true homeland of Europe is one defined by transcendent beliefs—a belief in the sacred liberty of the individual, in the importance of the family, in a just and loving God, and in democracy. The Atlantic community is not limited to a military alliance. It is composed instead of nations committed to democracy and free enterprise. Nor is it limited any longer to the West, for the community of democratic nations has spread beyond the Atlantic to encompass Japan, Australia, the Philippines, India, many countries in Latin America, and others around the world.

In dealing with the Soviet Union, the United States has remained in constant consultation with this community of free nations—with our North Atlantic allies and other friends. NATO itself remained steadfast and united in the face of severe challenges in the early 1980's. Already we've witnessed one historic result: the signing during the Washington summit last December of the historic INF treaty. That treaty, which for the first time in history will eliminate a whole class of U.S. and Soviet nuclear missiles, was made possible by the solidarity and, yes, courage of NATO. It offers an essential lesson for Western policy toward the Soviet Union and the Warsaw Pact: that free nations will gain their objectives when they stand firm. The alliance did not waver or fail to carry out its decision of 1979, a decision to go forward with the deployment of INF missiles. Similarly, an agreement was reached to eliminate the threat posed by the newly deployed Soviet SS–20 missiles, and the alliance did not waver in this. The result is the SS–20 threat is about to end because the Soviets had reason to withdraw those SS–20's and the other missiles which they're required to eliminate under this treaty.

Now we're applying these lessons of the INF treaty to negotiations on a strategic arms reduction treaty. We hope to reach a START agreement this year, though it is the requirements of a good treaty and not some arbitrary deadline that will determine the timetable. As we negotiate from strength, we're guided by realism—realism about just what can be achieved in our relations with the Soviet Union and about what the Soviets themselves seek to achieve. We do not expect a quick, radical transformation of the Soviet system. We do not expect to turn a corner one day to find that all our problems have gone away because our adversary has been transformed. We must continue to fulfill our own responsibility to stand firm and vigilant, to provide the incentive for a new Soviet policy in contrast to the old; for there still remain profound political and moral differences between the Soviet system and our own.

As the birthplace of the Conference on Security and Cooperation in Europe, or CSCE, the city I'll be visiting on my way to Moscow, Helsinki, has given its name to a process that lies at the heart of the East-West relationship. The Helsinki Final Act of 1975 codified international standards of behavior in human rights and defined a new standard of openness in social, economic, and security affairs as a benchmark of East-West relations. It's not too much to say that the 1975 Final Act redefined East-West exchanges, enshrining human rights as an issue of permanent importance. The process is now continuing in the CSCE followup meeting—a meeting that has been underway in Vienna since 1986.

The United States is committed to working with the other CSCE states to achieve a balanced result in Vienna, a result that must include significant improvement in Soviet and Eastern European practices in human rights to balance new cooperation in security and economic affairs. Balance here is the essence of the Helsinki process. As signatories of the Helsinki Final Act, the Governments of the Soviet Union, Europe, Canada, and the United States have formally and publicly committed themselves to the recognition of fundamental freedoms: freedom of religion, freedom of thought and expression, freedom of the press, and freedom of movement. Only when these freedoms are observed can the greatest resource of any nation—the creativity, ideas, and initiative of its individual citizens—prosper and grow.

In Moscow, I will welcome the progress we've seen in the Soviet human rights record, especially since the end of 1986. More than 300 political and religious prisoners have been released from labor camps. Emigration, still too low, has improved. Many cases of divided families and separated spouses have been satisfactorily resolved. And censorship of films, books, and other creative works has eased. Yet despite this progress, the human rights situation in the Soviet Union and Eastern Europe is far from good—repressive policies persist. Peaceful demonstrations by national minorities, refuseniks, and others are still being broken up by police. Freedom of religion is still being denied, and members of unregistered religious groups are still being persecuted. Unofficial publications are banned. Dozens of political prisoners and religious dissenters remain imprisoned, and many prisoners of conscience are still being held in psychiatric hospitals. Freedom of movement is still restricted.

All of us who are united by our belief in democracy will continue to press the Soviet Union to improve its practices in these vital areas, in short, to grant full recognition of fundamental human rights. To raise these issues is not only our inclination by tradition and principle but, under the Helsinki Final Act, our responsibility. For our part, the United States is prepared for useful exchanges. We will listen when the Soviets criticize us, and we will discuss their concerns as openly and constructively as possible. And yet I would stress that our interchange with the Soviets has a basis; it is not neutral or value-free. This basis is not just a matter of American standards; they are moral standards, the standards of Western civilization itself that we Americans inherited from Europe. We have fought in Europe twice in this century to help defend them. These shared standards and beliefs tie us to Europe today. They are the essence of the community of free nations to which we belong.

I've mentioned arms reduction, and I've mentioned human rights. My agenda with Mr. Gorbachev, like the agenda which most of your governments discuss with the Soviets, has two other elements. One is Soviet policy in the regional conflicts. We're pleased to see the Soviet Army departing Afghanistan. Once that withdrawal is complete and Afghan self-determination has returned to this country, this will be an historic triumph. I will also raise other issues with him, seeking to engage Soviet cooperation in getting political solutions to other conflicts, such as southern Africa, the Iran-Iraq War, Cambodia, Central America, Ethiopia, and the Arab-Israeli conflict.

In addition, our discussions will cover the need for greater openness and a freer exchange of people. Information and ideas—government barriers to peoples' understanding of the outside world and to contact with that outside world must be eliminated. All of us believe that people must be free to communicate with one another, whether they're journalists, scientists, academics, tourists, or high school students. And so, I'll urge General Secretary Gorbachev to join us in greatly expanding people-to-people exchanges between East and West. One matter in this regard is especially close to my heart: that of seeing more young people travel between East and West. I will discuss youth exchanges with General Secretary Gorbachev because they hold such promise for better understanding in the years to come. Young people should be free—free to come and go as they will, free to travel to and live in each other's country, free to make friends the world over.

When I was in Berlin nearly a year ago, I called upon General Secretary Gorbachev to tear down the wall dividing that city. In so many senses, dividing Europe itself, East from West, the wall is still there, a scar, a grim reminder of the division of Europe. That division is cruel. It is unnecessary. It has gone on too long. We'll work on, unrelentingly, until that division gives way to peace and freedom. The day may still be long in coming, but the United States will always remain utterly committed to bringing that full liberty into being. In the meantime, we'll stand by you in defending our common heritage and beliefs, our common homeland of freedom.

Thank you, and God bless you all.

Note: The President spoke at 10 a.m. from the Oval Office at the White House. It was broadcast live by the U.S. Information Agency's Voice of America and WORLDNET television. The address was released by the Office of the Press Secretary on May 24.

Nomination of Harold G. Christensen To Be Deputy Attorney General

May 24, 1988

The President today nominated Harold G. Christensen to be Deputy Attorney General at the Department of Justice. He would succeed Arnold I. Burns.

Mr. Christensen is currently chairman of the board of directors of Snow, Christensen & Martineau in Salt Lake City, UT. He has also been involved in numerous associations and committees, including: fellow of the American College of Trial Lawyers, and State chairman, 1986 and 1987; member of the ad hoc committee of the Judicial Conference of the United States on American Inns of Court, 1984–1986; charter president of the American Inns of Court I, 1980; and president of the Utah State Bar, 1975–1976.

Mr. Christensen graduated from the University of Utah (A.B., 1949) and the University of Michigan (J.D., 1951). He was born June 25, 1926, in Springville, UT.

Nomination of Edward S.G. Dennis, Jr., To Be an Assistant Attorney General
May 24, 1988

The President today announced his intention to nominate Edward S.G. Dennis, Jr., to be an Assistant Attorney General (Criminal Division) at the Department of Justice. He would succeed William F. Weld.

Since 1983 Mr. Dennis has been United States Attorney for the Eastern District of Pennsylvania in Philadelphia. Prior to this he was chief of the narcotic and dangerous drug section at the Department of Justice in Washington, DC, 1980–1983. Mr. Dennis was Deputy Chief of the Criminal Division of the United States Attorney's Office in Philadelphia, 1978–1980, and Assistant U.S. Attorney in the U.S. Attorney's Office, 1975–1980. He was a law clerk for the Honorable A. Leon Higginbotham, Jr., at the U.S. District Court in Philadelphia, 1973–1975.

Mr. Dennis graduated from the U.S. Merchant Marine Academy (B.S., 1967) and the University of Pennsylvania (LL.D., 1973). He was born January 24, 1945, in Salisbury, MD. He is married, has one child, and resides in Pennsylvania.

Nomination of Warren Zimmermann To Be United States Ambassador to Yugoslavia
May 24, 1988

The President today announced his intention to nominate Warren Zimmermann, of Virginia, a career member of the Senior Foreign Service, Class of Career Minister, to be Ambassador to the Socialist Federal Republic of Yugoslavia. He would succeed John Douglas Scanlon.

Mr. Zimmermann was a staff reporter for the Munroe News Bureau before entering the Foreign Service in 1961. From 1962 to 1964, he was consular and political officer in Caracas, Venezuela. In 1964, he was assigned to the Foreign Service Institute to study Serbo-Croatian and served as political officer in Belgrade, Yugoslavia, 1965–1968. He returned in 1968 to the Bureau of Intelligence and Research as a Soviet policy analyst and served as a special assistant to the Secretary of State in the Office of the Counselor, 1970–1973. In 1973, he studied Russian at the Foreign Service Institute and from there became deputy counselor of embassy for politico-military affairs in Moscow. From 1975 to 1977, he was special assistant for policy planning at the Bureau of European and Canadian Affairs at the Department of State. He was counselor for political affairs in Paris, France, 1977–1980; Deputy Chairman of the U.S. delegation to the Conference on Security and Cooperation in Europe (CSCE) in Madrid, Spain; and deputy chief of mission at the U.S. Embassy in Moscow, 1981. He was a visiting fellow on the Council on Foreign Relations, 1984–1985; and deputy to the head of the U.S. delegation to the arms reduction negotiations in Geneva with the personal rank of Ambassador, 1985. He currently is Chairman of the U.S. delegation to the Vienna followup meeting of the Conference on Security and Cooperation in Europe.

Mr. Zimmermann graduated from Yale University (B.A., 1956) and Cambridge University (M.A., 1958). He was born November 16, 1934, in Philadelphia, PA. He served in the U.S. Army in 1959. He is married, has three children, and resides in Virginia.

Nomination of John Alderson To Be Administrator of General Services

May 24, 1988

The President today announced his intention to nominate John Alderson to be Administrator of General Services. He would succeed Terence C. Golden.

Mr. Alderson has been serving as Acting Administrator since April 1, 1988. Prior to this, he served as Associate Administrator in the Office of Congressional and Industry Relations at the General Services Administration in Washington, DC, from February 1988 until April; Deputy Associate Administrator in the Office of Operations, 1987–1988; and Deputy Commissioner of the Public Buildings Service, 1982–1983. Since 1965 he has been owner of John Alderson Agency, Inc., in Daleville, VA. He was also a vice president of Basic Development and Investment Corp., 1971–1975.

Mr. Alderson was born September 3, 1933, in Botetourt County, VA. He is married, has three children, and resides in Arlington, VA.

Letter to the Speaker of the House of Representatives and the Chairman of the Senate Foreign Relations Committee Reporting on the Cyprus Conflict

May 24, 1988

Dear Mr. Speaker: (Dear Mr. Chairman:)

In accordance with Public Law 95–384, I am submitting to you a bimonthly report on progress toward a negotiated settlement of the Cyprus question.

Major meetings were held by U.S. officials with Cypriot leaders during the past two months. Secretary of State Shultz visited Cyprus on April 8, 1988, during the course of travel to a number of Middle Eastern countries. The Secretary met with Cypriot Foreign Minister Iacovou and stressed to him our desire to be helpful in the effort to achieve a Cyprus solution. The Secretary also underlined our continuing support for the United Nations Secretary General's good offices mission.

Special Cyprus Coordinator M. James Wilkinson visited Cyprus, Greece, and Turkey in late March and early April, meeting in Cyprus with President Vassiliou, Foreign Minister Iacovou, Turkish Cypriot community leader Denktash, and other political and government leaders. Mr. Wilkinson strongly emphasized our belief that negotiations should be started as soon as possible under the aegis of the U.N. Secretary General and his representative in Cyprus, Oscar Camilion. Mr. Wilkinson also stated that the United States wishes to be helpful in the effort to start negotiations, but that the parties themselves must elect to begin the process.

The new U.S. Ambassador to the Republic of Cyprus, Bill K. Perrin, arrived in Cyprus on April 28 and presented his credentials to President Vassiliou on May 3, 1988. Ambassador Perrin begins his tour of duty at a time when we enjoy excellent bilateral relations with Cyprus and stands ready to lend all possible support to efforts to solve the Cyprus dispute.

During the period under review both Greek and Turkish Cypriot leaders expressed their continued interest in working with the U.N. Secretary General in pursuit of a settlement. At the same time, both parties pointed to statements and actions by the other side that they argue call into question the sincerity of such expressions.

Also, during the reporting period, the Turkish Cypriot authorities began stamping the passports of certain travelers entering the Turkish Cypriot sector across the U.N.-controlled buffer zone. The Turkish Cypriots have asserted that the new measures were established in response to long-standing Greek Cypriot restrictions on travel between the two sectors. We and others have questioned the initiative and urged maximum effort by all parties to restart serious negotiations.

Financial problems for the United Nations Force in Cyprus [UNFICYP] remain severe. In mid-April, UNFICYP troop contributors vigorously renewed their appeal for a switch in UNFICYP's funding base to assessed contributions in place of the present voluntary contributions. The United Nations Force in Cyprus's cumulative deficit is over $160 million, borne entirely by the troop-contributing countries. We continue to consult with U.N. officials and the troop contributors on this problem.

Regarding congressional interest in Cyprus, I applaud House Concurrent Resolution 274 that commends the Prime Ministers of Greece and Turkey "on their statesmanship in initiating their current dialogue." I agree with the positive thoughts expressed in that Resolution and, like its authors, hope that the high-level meetings between Greece and Turkey "may result in the creation of an atmosphere that is conducive to . . . a resolution of the Cyprus problem."

The United States continues to believe that the time is ripe for resuming negotiations without preconditions. An early meeting, facilitated as appropriate by the U.N. Secretary General, between the leaders of the two communities also appears desirable. At the same time, we continue to favor expanded contacts at all levels to reduce tensions and to complement, not substitute for, substantive negotiations.

Sincerely,

RONALD REAGAN

Note: Identical letters were sent to Jim Wright, Speaker of the House of Representatives, and Claiborne Pell, chairman of the Senate Foreign Relations Committee.

Message to the House of Representatives Returning Without Approval the Omnibus Trade and Competitiveness Act of 1988
May 24, 1988

To the House of Representatives:

It is with sincere regret that today I must disapprove and return H.R. 3, the Omnibus Trade and Competitiveness Act of 1988. We worked long and hard to produce legislation that would enhance our country's ability to meet foreign competition head-on—to strengthen our trade laws and remove restrictions on America's great economic engine. And we came very close to developing such a bill. Unfortunately, as the process came to a close, provisions were included that simply make this bill, on balance, bad for America—particularly working men and women. The criteria I used in reaching this decision were whether this legislation will create jobs and help sustain our economic growth. I am convinced this bill will cost jobs and damage our economic growth.

During this Administration the American economy has created 16 million new jobs. Our unemployment rate is the lowest in 14 years with more Americans working than ever before in our history. And we are experiencing the longest peacetime expansion this country has ever seen.

While this has been going on at home, many of our trading partners have had a different economic situation. Perhaps the most compelling and important comparison is that over the past decade, the United

States has created more than twice as many jobs as Europe and Japan combined.

The United States economy, which foreign leaders have dubbed the "American Miracle," is not a freak accident or a statistical curiosity. It is the result of 7 years of consistent policies: lower tax rates, reduced regulation, control returned to State and local governments. The Washington tendency to have government be all things to all people has been reversed, and we have gotten government off the backs of the American people. In contrast, many foreign countries remain hamstrung by archaic policies and are now trying to remove these impediments, to reform tax systems, to make labor markets more flexible, and to encourage entrepreneurs.

That is not to say that we cannot do more here at home—we can. That is why I forwarded proposals to improve our competitive strength and why we worked hard with the Congress to try to achieve a positive, forward-looking bill. Unfortunately, that is not the bill the Congress passed and sent to my desk.

The issue receiving the most attention in this bill is the mandatory requirement for businesses to give advance notice of closings or layoffs. I support voluntarily giving workers and communities as much advance warning as possible when a layoff or closing becomes necessary. It allows the workers, the employer, the community, time to adjust to the dislocation. It is the humane thing to do.

But I object to the idea that the Federal Government would arbitrarily mandate, for all conditions and under all circumstances, exactly when and in what form that notification should take place. There are many circumstances under which such mandatory notification would actually force a faltering business to close—by driving away creditors, suppliers, customers, and—in the process destroying jobs. While the legislation attempts to mitigate this outcome, its "faltering business" exemption is too ambiguous to be workable and invites untold litigation.

These concerns are real, not simply philosophical or theoretical. The experience of the Caterpillar Company in the early 1980's, for example, is indicative of the need to be flexible to meet foreign competition and indeed to survive. They had to utilize layoffs and temporary plant closings to respond to competitive developments. And, as one executive of that company stated, they did not have the luxury then, nor do they now, of knowing with certainty what business conditions would be like 60 days in the future. Without the ability to be agile and responsive, they might have closed their doors permanently.

Caterpillar's experience is repeated many times over throughout our economy. One independent analysis shows that if this law had been in place between 1982 and 1986, the United States would have produced almost one-half million fewer jobs. And that is what this debate is about—creating jobs and keeping them—not losing jobs by the straightjacket of regulations.

Over a year ago, I submitted legislation that would provide assistance to workers, employers, and communities in the event of a layoff or closing. The program would serve virtually every dislocated worker who needs it with training, education, and assistance in securing a new job and provide an incentive for giving advance notice of layoffs and closings. Ironically, the one piece of that package that the Congress rejected was a direct incentive for business to give advance notices of closing and layoffs. We need labor laws that fit the flexible, fast-paced economy of the 1990's, not restrictive leftovers from the 1930's agenda. And I encourage the Congress in any subsequent trade bill to include a program that provides incentives for such notice.

There are other provisions in the legislation that provide disincentives to our sustained economic growth or serve some narrow special interests:

—New restrictions on the export, transportation, and even utilization of Alaskan oil further complicate the overbearing regulatory scheme that already impedes the development of Alaskan oil fields. It is the wrong policy. We need to provide incentives, not restrictions, for the production of oil in the United States so that we can reduce our dependence on foreign suppliers. Further, as the Congress has now recognized, it amounts to an unconstitutional discrimination against a single State.

—A mistaken effort to revive discredited industrial policy planning through a so-called Council on Competitiveness that will open even more venues for special pleaders.

—A requirement to negotiate a new centralized international institution to arrange the forgiveness of billions of dollars of debt around the world—all supposedly without increasing U.S. taxes or adding to *our* debt.

—Expanded ethanol imports that could harm U.S. grain producers.

—An amendment to the Trading with the Enemy Act that prevents the President from moving swiftly to block blatant enemy propaganda material from entering the United States, *even during wartime*.

While the Congress did a remarkable job in watering down or eliminating the most protectionist provisions, there remain sections of the bill that push us in the direction of protectionism. Closing our borders is not the solution to opening foreign markets. We need to demand to be treated fairly and take a strong stand against barriers abroad. In short, we need to open markets, not close them.

While there are objectionable portions of the bill, there are also desirable provisions. There is negotiating authority so that the next President will have congressional support to continue to seek agreements that open markets abroad. That, coupled with new trade law tools to strengthen the hand of America in international trade negotiations, will mean that this country can enter the next decade with new agreements that reduce barriers and encourage trade. There are strengthened protections for intellectual property, such as copyrights, and a reduction in various handicaps to U.S. exporters. Finally, the bill would remove a major impediment to U.S. oil production by repealing the windfall profits tax.

That is why I want a trade bill, and why I like much of this bill. But I regret that the addition of a few counterproductive and costly measures outweigh the positive features of this particular legislation. I will continue to work vigorously to secure sound legislation this year.

Let me reiterate what I have said on a number of occasions. I am committed to enactment of a responsible trade bill this year. I have heard some say that there is not time to send me a second bill after my veto is sustained; my response is that there are many months left in 1988—time enough to set aside partisanship and finish the job. I want to sign a trade bill this year. I urge prompt action on a second bill immediately after the Congress sustains my veto.

RONALD REAGAN

The White House,
May 24, 1988.

Nomination of Timothy L. Coyle To Be an Assistant Secretary of Housing and Urban Development
May 24, 1988

The President today announced his intention to nominate Timothy L. Coyle to be an Assistant Secretary of Housing and Urban Development (Legislation and Congressional Relations). He will succeed Stephen May.

Since 1986 Mr. Coyle has been Deputy Under Secretary for Field Operations for the Department of Housing and Urban Development in Washington, DC. Prior to this he served as Deputy Assistant Secretary for Legislation for the Department of Housing and Urban Development from 1984 to 1986. From 1983 to 1984, he was Assistant to the Chairman for the Federal Home Loan Bank Board. From 1981 to 1983, Mr. Coyle was Executive Assistant for Field Operations at the Department of Housing and Urban Development. He was a consultant for the Presidential inaugural committee, 1980–1981.

Mr. Coyle graduated from San Diego State University (B.A., 1976). Mr. Coyle was born October 29, 1953, in Los Angeles, CA. He is married, has two children, and resides in Alexandria, VA.

Nomination of Sheldon Jack Krys To Be an Assistant Secretary of State

May 24, 1988

The President today announced his intention to nominate Sheldon Jack Krys to be Assistant Secretary of State (Administration). He would succeed Donald J. Bouchard.

Since 1985 Mr. Krys has been the United States Ambassador to the Republic of Trinidad and Tobago. Prior to this he was Executive Assistant to the Under Secretary of State for Management, 1984–1985. He was also Deputy Director of Management Operations, 1983–1984, and Executive Director of the Bureau of Near Eastern and South Asian Affairs, 1979–1983.

Mr. Krys attended the University of Maryland. He was born on June 15, 1934, in New York, NY. He is married, has three children, and resides in Potomac, MD.

Statement on Aid to the Nicaraguan Democratic Resistance

May 24, 1988

Two months have passed since the Congress limited U.S. assistance to the Nicaraguan democratic resistance to food, shelter, clothing, and medicine. The Congress stopped U.S. military assistance to the resistance while the Soviet bloc continued its military assistance to the Communist Sandinista regime in Nicaragua. Some thought that U.S. forbearance would bring democracy and peace to Nicaragua through negotiations between the resistance and the Sandinista regime, but it has not.

Tomorrow, as I leave on the first leg of my trip to Moscow, the resistance and the Sandinistas are scheduled to meet again. The Sandinistas will again have the opportunity to carry out the promises they have made—beginning a decade ago with promises to the Organization of American States—of establishment of freedom and democracy in Nicaragua. We do not need more pieces of paper bearing empty Sandinista promises and Sandinista signatures. We need deeds, not more words.

During the 60-day truce established under the Sapoa agreement signed March 23, the Sandinistas have continued, and indeed intensified, their repression of the Nicaraguan people. They have not carried out their commitments under the Guatemala accord of August 7, 1987, or under the Sapoa agreement. The Sandinistas have gone so far as to make it impossible to arrange through neutral parties to deliver food and medicine to resistance members inside Nicaragua.

The men and women of the Agency for International Development who have worked long and hard to ensure that the members of the resistance have the basic necessities of life deserve the thanks of our nation. The work of AID keeps the chance for democracy alive in Nicaragua.

The United States continues to support those fighting for freedom and democracy in Nicaragua. The freedom fighters of the Nicaraguan democratic resistance deserve the continued support of the United States.

If the current stalemate in the peace process persists and the Sandinistas continue their policies of repression, then we will call upon the Congress to reconsider its February 3 decision to curtail assistance to the Nicaraguan freedom fighters.

White House Statement on the 1989 Federal Education Budget Amendments
May 24, 1988

The President today sent to the Congress fiscal year 1989 budget amendments totaling $5,969 million for the Department of Education. The regular fiscal year 1989 budget already included this amount as items proposed for later transmittal pending enactment of necessary authorizing legislation. The legislation, the Augustus F. Hawkins-Robert T. Stafford Elementary and Secondary School Improvement Amendments of 1988, was signed into law by the President on April 18, 1988, as Public Law 100–297. At the signing ceremony and again in his transmittal of these amendments, the President has urged Congress to concentrate funding on the ongoing, successful programs of compensatory education and school improvement. He urged funding only these programs, plus a few new initiatives, rather than dissipating the effects of scarce Federal resources by scattering funding among the many other lower priority, narrow-purpose programs.

The President's 1989 budget recognizes the high priority of these education programs by proposing increases in budget authority in excess of the average of 2 percent that applies to the total for domestic discretionary programs in the bipartisan budget agreement. In addition, the transmittal includes a request for $3.4 million for the Education Department's statistics programs to finance activities as required by Public Law 100–297. These proposals also include $1 million in fiscal year 1989 for the National Commission on Migrant Education. This temporary commission would study education problems of the children of migrant workers. The total package of amendments provides no significant increase to the fiscal year 1989 budget and is consistent with the bipartisan budget agreement.

Written Responses to Questions Submitted by Southeast Asian News Organizations
May 23, 1988

Cambodia

Q. Will you raise the Cambodia question when you meet with General Secretary Gorbachev? Will you be pushing for a solution to this problem at the Moscow summit, as you did for Afghanistan at the recent Washington summit? Do you believe China has a role to play, especially in regards to the Khmer Rouge?

The President. We have been actively discussing Cambodia with the Soviet Union at various levels for a number of years now, and I raised the issue with General Secretary Gorbachev at the last summit. We believe that the Soviet Union can play a positive role in encouraging Vietnam to be responsive to efforts to resolve the Cambodian conflict. We will continue urging the Soviet Union to play such a role. Vietnam should meet directly with Prince Sihanouk and should commit itself to a firm timetable for rapid withdrawal from Cambodia. China supports Prince Sihanouk and the ASEAN [Association of South East Asian Nations] nations in their efforts to end the Vietnamese occupation of Cambodia and restore that country's sovereignty and independence. I am sure that China's policy will make a constructive contribution to settling the Cambodian conflict.

Southeast Asia Nuclear Free Zone

Q. The Soviet Union agreed to a nuclear free zone in Southeast Asia, a proposal raised by members of ASEAN. Do you see a possibility of the U.S. agreeing to such a proposal?

The President. Nuclear arms reduction is a vital goal, and one that we will continue to pursue energetically. But there are no shortcuts. Nuclear free zone treaties are at their best when they prevent nuclear proliferation and promote regional stability and global security, as might be the case in Latin America. In general, however, we must look with caution at the proposition that walling off a portion of the world from nuclear weapons will contribute to world peace. It could instead weaken nuclear deterrence and, in so doing, could heighten rather than reduce the risk of war. For this reason, we cannot support the proposal for a nuclear free zone in Southeast Asia.

U.S. Role in the Pacific Region

Q. In the Pentagon's 1988 Review of Soviet Military Power, it is said that Cam Ranh Bay in Vietnam is the largest Soviet naval base outside the Soviet Union. What kind of role do you think the United States should play in the Pacific, especially Southeast Asia, in light of the Soviet expansion in the area?

The President. Russian interest in the East Asian and Pacific region has waxed and waned through history. Until recently, Soviet efforts to improve their status in the Pacific area were based almost entirely on military power. After a period of military buildup in Asia, General Secretary Gorbachev has made overtures to become more involved in the region in a nonmilitary way. Unlike our own extensive and longstanding commercial, economic, cultural, political, and military links with the region, however, the Soviet Union lacks a firm basis for greater peaceful involvement in Asia. Though Soviet rhetoric has changed under Mr. Gorbachev, Moscow's military posture in the region remains a major concern to us and our friends in Asia.

The United States and most Asian nations agree about what needs to be done on a large number of real issues, such as ceasing Soviet support for the Vietnamese occupation of Cambodia; dealing with the Soviet military buildup, including Cam Ranh Bay; encouraging North Korea to open a dialog with the South Koreans to reduce tensions on the Peninsula; and resolving the Northern Territories dispute with Japan. The Soviet Union already knows it can do a great deal for peace and stability in Asia by resolving these important, tangible problems. We take every opportunity to remind them of that. We are also working closely with our friends and allies in Asia and the Pacific on real-world issues, like economic development, security, the movement for greater democracy, and growth of trade in free-market conditions. We think that real contributions to human welfare beat lofty phrases. We will continue pursuing such contributions.

Soviet-U.S. Summit Meeting in Moscow

Q. Are you optimistic that a START accord can still be signed in Moscow? Do you think that a Moscow summit without a START agreement could maintain the momentum?

The President. Our goal is a good agreement, not a quick agreement. Our negotiators have been working long and hard in Geneva toward an equitable and effectively verifiable agreement to reduce United States and Soviet strategic nuclear arms by 50 percent. Our goal is to reduce the risk of war and strengthen strategic stability through deep cuts in strategic nuclear arsenals and reduced reliance on those weapons systems that are most destabilizing: ballistic missiles, especially heavy intercontinental ballistic missiles with multiple warheads.

Despite the considerable progress that we have made, important differences remain, and it looks increasingly unlikely that a START treaty will be ready before my meeting with General Secretary Gorbachev later this month. Nevertheless, I believe that a START treaty can be concluded this year, but only with hard work and constructive negotiating by both sides. We want a treaty that makes the world a safer place for all of us. We will continue to do our part to achieve an equitable and effectively verifiable START treaty.

I am proud of the achievements we have registered in U.S.-Soviet relations in recent months, including the signing of the INF treaty and reaching an agreement that gets Soviet troops out of Afghanistan. My approach to U.S.-Soviet relations has been based on the principles of strength, realism, and dialog. This approach has served us well through three previous summits, and I remain confident it will produce a good, substantive meeting with Mr. Gorbachev later this month. In Moscow, I intend to seek further progress in all four parts of the U.S.-Soviet agenda, covering human rights, regional issues, bilateral relations, and arms control. My goal is to bequeath to my successor next January the firm basis for a stable, sustainable relationship with the Soviet Union.

Regional Conflicts

Q. How useful have your summits been with General Secretary Gorbachev in the search for peace in the Third World?

The President. We have pursued a vigorous dialog with the Soviet Union on regional conflicts in recent years. In addition to my own discussions with General Secretary Gorbachev, Secretary Shultz and our regional experts have recently had intensive exchanges with their Soviet counterparts on such topics as Afghanistan, southern Africa, the Middle East peace process, Cambodia, and the Korean Peninsula. Our goal, as laid out in my 1985 United Nations General Assembly speech, is the achievement of political settlements based on an end to the fighting, prompt withdrawal of outside forces, and facilitation of a process of genuine national reconciliation.

I had serious discussions with Mr. Gorbachev on regional issues last December and expect to follow up on them in Moscow. The Soviet Union leadership has indicated they see the Afghanistan settlement as opening the way to progress on other conflicts. I am all in favor of this and intend to press Mr. Gorbachev for details later this month. For not only do these conflicts, many of them involving Soviet client states or proxies, pose a serious threat to regional security balances, they also hold the danger of triggering superpower confrontations with negative consequences for regional states.

East Asia-U.S. Trade

Q. The United States has yet to resolve its trade problems with Japan and the newly industrialized countries of Asia. What measures would you advocate that the United States and these countries take to narrow the trade imbalances with minimum disruption to the economies of the Asian nations?

The President. We have urged Japan to boost domestic economic growth and to improve access to the Japanese market for foreign products. Japan has made progress in these areas. In 1987 the Japanese Government enacted spending measures to assure good economic growth, which marked over 4 percent last year. Firm growth has continued this year and has benefited all of Japan's trading partners as Japanese imports have increased. We also have worked with Japan to resolve some difficult bilateral economic issues, most recently in construction and science and technology cooperation, by working out agreements that provide valuable benefits for both nations. However, more remains to be done, particularly in market liberalization of the agricultural sector.

The newly industrialized economies—Hong Kong, Korea, Singapore, and Taiwan—of Asia have for the most part pursued an export-oriented strategy of development. The economic success they have achieved is to a large degree dependent on the relatively free access their wide range of export products have had to the U.S. market. While Hong Kong and Singapore have virtually open markets, Korea and Taiwan have in place laws and regulations which restrict or even ban U.S. exports of goods and services. Both Korea and Taiwan have taken significant steps to reduce their trade barriers, but much more remains to be done. We also have urged these four trading partners to allow their currencies to reflect the underlying strength of their economies.

If the liberal international trading system that has so benefited the United States and all the economies of East Asia is to survive, it is important that all our major trading partners take immediate action to further reduce tariff and nontariff barriers. They also should join us in making every effort to ensure the success of the Uruguay round of the ongoing multilateral trade negotiations.

Thai Intellectual Property Laws

Q. Will the United States further pressure Thailand to include protection of U.S. intellectual property and computer software in Thai copyright laws? To what extent does the United States want its intellectual property protected in Thailand?

The President. The United States looks forward to continuing to work with the Royal Thai Government in a cooperative effort to improve the protection afforded all intellectual property in Thailand. I am convinced that it is in the best economic, cultural, and social interest of any nation to enhance the intellectual property conditions of its own authors and creators and to offer that enhanced protection to creators from other nations as well.

Vietnamese Refugees in Malaysia

Q. Malaysia has announced that it would be closing Pulau Bidong, a Vietnamese refugee transit camp, and new arrivals would be turned away. Does the United States think that Malaysia is serious or merely making a threat? What action is being taken by the United States to speed up resettlement of these refugees?

The President. The Government of Malaysia has indicated its concern and is reviewing its policy as a result of the increasing flow of refugees to its shores in recent months. We have no information that Malaysia has decided to turn away refugees, however. The Malaysians have confirmed to us that they have plans to close Pulau Bidong refugee camp over the course of the coming years, but not in a precipitous way. Residents of the camp and all new arrivals will be transferred to a camp near Kuala Lumpur. We have been assured that every effort will be made to carry out this decision in a humanitarian way.

I want to remind you that we have repeatedly urged the Vietnamese Government to honor its commitment to the orderly departure program so that people do not have to resort to clandestine flight out of Vietnam. We are currently considering admission of up to 1,000 additional refugees from Malaysia who are harder to resettle because they lack family ties in the United States or elsewhere. This decision demonstrates our continuing commitment to first asylum and was made in response to the dramatic increase in Malaysia's boat arrivals in recent months.

Economic Assistance for the Philippines

Q. Do you support the proposed mini-Marshall plan for the Philippines? Do you see burden-sharing in foreign aid as an answer to the foreign assistance needs of the Philippines?

The President. The United States Government is strongly committed to helping democracy and prosperity flourish in the Philippines. We have also been talking with our friends and allies in Asia and Europe about the possibility of increasing assistance and stimulating trade and investment to sustain economic growth in the Philippines. These discussions are continuing. President Aquino enjoys enormous international support, and I am confident the donor community will continue to respond generously to her government.

Note: The questions were submitted by the Singapore Straits Times; the Nation, of Thailand; Business World, of the Philippines; Kompas, of Indonesia; and the Bernama News Agency, of Malaysia. The questions and answers were released by the Office of the Press Secretary on May 25.

Remarks on Departure for the Soviet-United States Summit in Moscow
May 25, 1988

My fellow Americans and all our Ambassadors of our friends and allies who are here: On the eve of my first meeting with General Secretary Gorbachev in 1985, I told you that my mission, simply stated, was a mission for freedom and peace. I wanted to sit down across the table from Mr. Gorbachev and try to set out with him a basis for peaceful discourse and cooperation between our two countries, at the same time working to advance the cause and frontiers of human freedom. As I approached that first meeting in Geneva, I wanted to establish a better working relationship with the Soviet Union—one no longer subject to the dangerous highs and lows of the past; a working relationship that would be based on realities, not merely on a seeming relaxation of tensions between our two countries that could quickly disappear. To accomplish that, the United States needed to see solid and steady progress in four major areas: human rights, regional conflicts, arms reductions, and bilateral exchanges. Well, we've come a long way since then.

Now, as I depart on this trip to Moscow, fulfilling the agreement I made with General Secretary Gorbachev back in 1985 that we would visit each other's country, I can point to achievements we can all be proud of in each of the areas of our four-part agenda. The United States and the Soviet Union have signed the Geneva accords providing for the withdrawal of all Soviet troops from Afghanistan, and the first withdrawals have begun. We have signed an arms reduction treaty that will reduce the level of nuclear arms for the first time in history, eliminating an entire class of U.S. and Soviet nuclear missiles. We've made progress on the main points of a treaty that will cut in half our arsenals of strategic offensive nuclear weapons. Our new nuclear risk reduction centers are already transmitting messages that reduce the risk of conflict.

Our representatives have held broad-ranging discussions on human rights, and we've seen concrete steps taken. The levels of emigration have risen. Some political and religious prisoners have been released, and a number of divided families have been reunited. Somewhat more diversity of expression is permitted. There has been a recognition of religious persecution in the past and a pledge that some restrictions on the right to worship will be eased. We have greatly expanded our bilateral exchanges. The number of travelers between our two countries is rising sharply, with unprecedented totals expected this year. There's more, of course, but I'd miss my plane if I went through the entire list. [*Laughter*] And yet impressive as these achievements may be, they represent only a beginning.

In my talks with General Secretary Gorbachev next week, we will be looking to the future, for there remains much to be done. Permit me to outline the substance of our four-part agenda for those talks:

On human rights, I will press to see that the positive trends I've mentioned continue and the reforms are made permanent. We certainly welcome the recent signs of Soviet progress toward greater freedom of religion, greater freedom of speech, greater freedom of movement. There have been indications that this progress may be written into Soviet law and regulations so that it can be a more permanent part of Soviet life. We will be doing all we can to encourage just that.

Concerning regional conflicts, we'll be looking for Soviet actions to help advance negotiations on the Angola and Namibia problems and to support U.N. efforts to end the Iran-Iraq war. We will ask the Soviets to use their influence with the Ethiopian Government to prevent a manmade crisis of starvation there. We'll urge the Soviets to help move the Middle East peace process closer to a just and lasting solution. And we'll look for ways to help the parties resolve other regional conflicts in Africa, Asia, and, yes, Central America.

Regarding arms reductions, we'll strive to

resolve the issues that still stand in the way of our agreement to cut U.S. and Soviet strategic offensive nuclear arms in half. As we make progress, our negotiators will be able to move forward in their work on the draft START treaty. We'll continue to seek ways to improve the verification procedures of two existing treaties on nuclear testing—the Peaceful Nuclear Explosions treaty and the Threshold Test Ban treaty—so that those treaties can be ratified. And I will urge the Soviets to move ahead at the Vienna followup meeting of the Conference on Security and Cooperation in Europe. At these discussions, negotiators from 35 nations are working on ways to advance human rights and strengthen the confidence- and security-building measures they negotiated at Stockholm in 1986. Separately, the 23 members of the Atlantic alliance and Warsaw Pact are negotiating a mandate for new talks on conventional forces. Success here means the Soviets must make continued progress on human rights, for the security in Europe involves much more than military arrangements. It must be based on a solid foundation of respect for the rights of individuals.

Concerning the final portion of our four-part agenda, our bilateral relations, we will address both new agreements and renewals of existing agreements to extend the areas in which we cooperate. This will include everything from practical matters of nuclear safety to radio navigation and the protection of our global environment. We'll seek to broaden still further our people-to-people contacts and, especially, to give more of our young people the opportunity to participate in such exchanges.

So, as you see from the outline of that agenda, there will be plenty of work for Mr. Gorbachev and me in Moscow next week. I don't expect it to be easy. We may have many differences, deep differences, moral differences, but we're still fellow human beings. We can still work together to keep the peace. And in working with the Soviet Union, the United States can still remain true to its mission of expanding liberty throughout the world.

Since my first meeting with Mr. Gorbachev, we have, as I've said, come a long way. My task next week will be to go still farther—farther in the interests of peace, farther toward a universal respect for fundamental human rights, farther toward world freedom, and farther toward a safer world for all people. And now, as I embark upon this great task, I ask for your prayers. Thank you, and God bless you all.

Note: The President spoke to supporters and members of the White House staff at 9:51 a.m. at the South Portico of the White House.

Written Responses to Questions Submitted by the Finnish Newspaper Helsingin Sanomat
May 19, 1988

President's Visit to Helsinki

Q. Why did you choose Helsinki as your stopover on your flight to Moscow?

The President. For starters, 1988 is an official U.S. Year of Finnish-American Friendship. I was most pleased to have welcomed Prime Minister Holkeri in Washington and to have this chance to stop in your capital. Moreover, Secretary of State Shultz, who as you know has visited Finland on several occasions during the past year, made two persuasive points. First, he told me that Finnish hospitality is too good to be missed. He has found Helsinki an excellent place to rest and prepare for the work ahead and thought that I would, too. Second, he pointed out to me that Finland is a country that has learned to live in close proximity to the Soviet Union. Finnish leaders have a unique perspective on that country, which Secretary Shultz has found informative on his previous trips. I hope to benefit in the same way from my conversation with President Koivisto and other Finnish leaders.

Naval and Air Forces in Europe

Q. The President of Finland, Mauno Koivisto, has proposed talks on confidence- and security-building measures in the Northern Sea areas. Do you think such talks could be linked to other negotiations on conventional force reductions or with proposals for a Nordic nuclear free zone?

The President. We consider freedom of navigation in international air and sea spaces vitally important to the maintenance of peace and security. Western naval and air activities, including those in the Northern Sea areas, form an essential element in current NATO defensive strategy. Unconstrained access to air and sea lines of communication constitute the lifeline between North America and all of our European friends. The strength of Warsaw Pact ground forces on the European land mass makes it all the more important that Western naval and air forces remain free from restriction on the periphery of the continent. Constraints would, in our view, weaken Western deterrence against those who might contemplate military aggression or political intimidation, thereby diminishing stability and security in Europe.

As naval and air forces tend to have global, not region-specific, commitments and responsibilities, it would seem inappropriate to regulate their activities in the context of a regional security regime. Moreover, compliance with restrictions on naval/air maneuvers over the high seas would be extremely difficult—indeed, impossible for most countries—to verify.

For these and other reasons, East and West have traditionally agreed to omit naval forces from conventional arms control negotiations in Europe. This is true for the Mutual and Balanced Force Reduction (MBFR) talks taking place in Vienna, for the upcoming Conventional Stability Talks (CST), and for the Conference on Security and Cooperation in Europe (CSCE). In the concluding document of the Madrid CSCE followup meeting, for example, the 35 participating states acknowledge that independent naval and air force activities fall outside the scope of CSCE security-related negotiations. We continue to believe this is the best course.

Helsinki Final Act

Q. The final document of the Conference on Security and Cooperation in Europe was signed in Helsinki in 1975. How do you assess the implementation, or lack of implementation, of the document? How do U.S. friends and allies around the world measure up to the human rights aspects of the document?

The President. In the strictest sense, the Helsinki Final Act applies only to the 35 signatory states. Among those states, implementation has varied widely between East and West.

For the Western countries, the United States and our NATO allies as well as the neutral and nonaligned states in CSCE, the Final Act, in many respects, merely codified existing practice with regard to human rights and fundamental freedoms. The West has fully met its commitments in all three dimensions of the Helsinki process—humanitarian, military security, and economic/scientific cooperation.

Sadly, the Eastern record has been poor. During the period 1975–85, Soviet performance with regard to the human rights provisions of the Final Act actually deteriorated. The Soviets continued to arrest and jail their citizens for expressing their political and religious beliefs. Prohibitions continued on religious teaching. Emigration rates decreased dramatically by the early 1980's, particularly following the Soviet invasion of Afghanistan. The invasion itself was a clear violation of the basic principles of the Final Act. Similar repression, in varying degrees, occurred in Eastern Europe, such as the declaration of martial law in Poland in 1981 and the suppression of the free trade union Solidarity. In all Eastern states, citizens who had joined together to monitor their governments' implementation of the Final Act were imprisoned, harassed, or forced into exile. Even in the security area, which the Soviets have tried to emphasize over humanitarian issues, the East did only the minimum necessary to comply with the Final Act's provisions and in some instances failed to comply at all.

However, there has been some improvement in the Soviet Union's human rights practices in the past 2 years. A number of political and religious prisoners have been released, and some limited voices of dissent have been allowed to be heard under the policy of *glasnost*. Emigration rates have increased, although they remain well below those of the late 1970's. There have been promises of institutional reform, although concrete steps have been slow to materialize.

Even with these improvements, the East still has far to go to meet the standards set down in the Final Act. Accordingly, at the current CSCE followup meeting in Vienna, we and our NATO allies continue to press the East to improve further its human rights performance. We have made improved performance one of our requirements for a successful conclusion to the meeting. I should note that Eastern implementation of the military confidence- and security-building measures adopted in Stockholm has been generally good. We are pressing the East to show the same spirit with regard to all of its CSCE commitments.

Now, you asked about other countries around the world. As I pointed out earlier, the Helsinki Final Act applies only to the 35 signatory states. Of course, the human rights standards embodied in the Final Act are universal principles also set forth in documents such as the Universal Declaration of Human Rights, to which all United Nations members subscribe. If we take this document as a literal checklist of what ought to be, the world has a very long way to go to meet the standards which its member nations have set for themselves.

Some progress is being made. This year we will see an investigation by the United Nations Human Rights Commission of human rights practices in Cuba, and we are seeing some improvements in other countries in the world. We and our friends and allies continue to work as hard as we can to encourage improved human rights practices throughout the world.

Foreign Criticism of U.S. Policy

Q. The United States has on occasion shown considerable irritation when Sweden, for example, has criticized American policies in Central America and elsewhere. Is it then the U.S. view that neutral countries, such as Sweden and Finland, should as a rule avoid taking stands on international issues? How should neutral countries behave?

The President. The United States is a leading proponent of free speech and firmly believes neutral countries have the same full right as any other country to express their views publicly and privately on any issue that they wish. Every country is of course individually responsible for its own foreign policies and pronouncements. We have questioned the appropriateness of foreign leaders offering public advice to U.S. legislators on issues under heated domestic partisan debate, but this is a consideration that would apply to any country, neutral or otherwise.

U.S. and World Economies

Q. How does the United States plan to assure the world's unstable financial markets of the strength of its own economic policies? What kinds of agreements does the United States want with Japan and Western Europe on the revitalization of the global economy?

The President. The strength of United States economic policies is clear when one examines U.S. economic performance. The United States is in the sixth year of the current expansion. Productivity is rising. Over 16 million new jobs have been created, while inflation, previously in double digits, has come down to about 4 percent per year. Real GNP grew 4 percent in 1987 (fourth quarter to fourth quarter). Real exports increased nearly 17 percent in 1987 and made a significant contribution to real growth for the first time in 7 years. We have also made considerable progress in reducing the Federal deficit; the recent agreement between the administration and Congress produced a 2-year $76 billion deficit reduction package. In addition, the United States continues to eliminate structural rigidities in its own economy through various policy measures. The deregulation of the airline industry, for example, has increased competition, expanded the market, improved consumer choice, and lowered prices. We encourage our European partners to adopt fiscal, labor, social, welfare, and industrial policies which free up resources and make them more responsive to market signals.

There are many ways in which the United States, Europe, and Japan are cooperating to sustain world growth. The major industrial nations are supporting the economic policy coordinating process adopted at the Tokyo and Venice summits. This will be reaffirmed at the Toronto summit as well. Another step involves redressing the current external imbalances. As I pointed out earlier, the United States has taken bold steps to reduce its fiscal deficit. We are also determined to continue reducing the trade deficit and have begun to see results in this area as well. The surplus countries must also do their part in this readjustment process. Economic growth remains strong in the industrial economies, while domestic demand in Europe and especially in Japan has begun to rebound. This is a welcome and positive contribution.

All countries must also make a concerted effort to reduce trade barriers in all areas through negotiations in the Uruguay Round [multilateral trade negotiations], particularly in agriculture. Costly and inefficient agricultural subsidies distort comparative advantages, drain national treasuries, and ultimately cost consumers dearly. We must all do our share. I am determined to fight protectionist pressure in the United States in the belief that open markets benefit everyone and closed markets harm everyone. As the European Community moves toward a single market, both Finland and the United States have an interest in encouraging not only the European Community but all nations to resist the temptation to erect barriers which keep out the rest of the world.

Soviet-U.S. Relations

Q. This will be your fourth face-to-face meeting with the Soviet leader, Mr. Gorbachev, whose country you once called the evil empire. Have you seen him develop or change as a leader? Has the Soviet Union changed? How can U.S.-Soviet relations develop?

The President. General Secretary Gorbachev has spoken clearly about the need for a broad range of political and economic reforms in the Soviet Union. At this point, it is not clear, and it may not be for years, whether significant change has occurred. We would like to see a Soviet Union that deals with its own people and with its neighbors through dialog rather than intimidation.

I think there has been a change in the nature of the U.S.-Soviet dialog in recent years. It used to be that we met only infrequently, and the subject was almost exclusively arms control. Now we have a regular dialog embracing a four-part agenda that includes human rights, regional affairs and bilateral matters, as well as arms reduction. This maturing relationship has already borne some fruit, including the INF agreement, the Afghanistan withdrawal accords, progress in human rights, and a great expansion of opportunities for U.S. and Soviet citizens to have contacts. We have a great many other subjects under discussion, including a treaty on 50-percent reductions in strategic nuclear arms and agreements on expanded cultural exchanges, as well as scientific and technical cooperation.

The United States and Soviet Union will always have differences because our political systems and views of the role of the individual in society are so different. We must be frank with each other about that. But we can also—and this has been at the root of our policy since I have been President—have a constructive relationship which is sustainable over the long term. We have made progress with this four-part agenda, and I think it provides us a good blueprint for future progress.

Arms Control

Q. How would a 50-percent reduction of long-range strategic arms affect the power realities and the political atmosphere in the world? What would be the next step?

The President. One of my highest priorities as President has been the achievement of deep reductions in strategic nuclear arms. As you know, we've made important progress toward that goal and have agreed on the basic outline of a treaty calling for 50-percent reductions in U.S. and Soviet strategic offensive nuclear arms. These reductions would make an historic contribution to international stability and security and would reduce the risk of war by establishing a framework of mutual restraint and responsibility.

The challenges of concluding such an agreement are extraordinary, and several difficult issues remain unsolved. Nonetheless, we will continue our efforts to reach agreement on a treaty that is both equitable and effectively verifiable. As we look ahead, we must also seek constructive solutions to other priority areas of security and arms reduction, including chemical weapons and conventional forces, where the Soviets have a marked advantage. The United States and its NATO allies are committed to making concrete progress in these areas: We seek greater stability at lower levels of conventional forces in Europe and a truly global and effectively verifiable ban on chemical weapons.

Of course, arms reduction alone is not a solution to the problems of East-West relations. We must address the root causes of mistrust and tension between the superpowers, such as our differing political systems and values, our contrasting views of the role of the individual within society, and the need to protect basic rights and freedoms. Our dialog over the coming years must include all issues—human rights, regional conflicts, bilateral matters, as well as arms reduction—as we continue our efforts to build a safer world.

Q. Are you today as committed to space defense and rendering ballistic missiles obsolete as you were when you gave your celebrated speech in 1983? In Reykjavik you seemed to come close to accepting the idea of a world completely free of nuclear weapons as a viable goal. Do you do so now? Under what conditions?

The President. I remain committed today to reducing our reliance for deterrence on ballistic missiles and ultimately to rendering them obsolete. I also support, as a long-term goal, the ultimate elimination of nuclear weapons. However, a world free of nuclear weapons is still far from becoming a reality. In the interim, I believe strongly that we should establish a stable peace which relies more on defense than on the threat of nuclear retaliation to deter war.

There are also many other factors that must be addressed before we can realistically hope to achieve the eventual elimination of nuclear weapons. For example, we must bring about a stable balance of conventional forces, a verifiable global ban on chemical weapons, greatly expanded confidence-building measures, and an overall improvement in East-West relations. Until we achieve these objectives, we must ensure that our security is protected through a safe and stable deterrent capability.

Administration Accomplishments

Q. Are you planning to write your memoirs? What would you most want your Presidency to be remembered for, and what is your greatest regret?

The President. I haven't given much thought to writing my memoirs. I am still too busy with my agenda for my remaining time in office. In terms of what I will list as my successes, on the domestic side, I think all Americans can take pride in the great economic success we have witnessed over the past few years. Inflation is well in the single-digit numbers, and economic growth is in its 66th consecutive month. We have restructured our tax policy, which has assisted in this economic growth. On the foreign policy side, we have taken real steps toward the actual elimination of nuclear weapons by the signing of the INF treaty. We have witnessed a growth of democracy worldwide, particularly in the Western Hemisphere. In Central America now, for example, of the five states we have four democracies, where when I came into office there was only one. These are just limited examples of what I would consider successes not just of my administration but of the American people. But I will leave it to historians to judge the record.

Note: The questions and answers were released by the Office of the Press Secretary on May 26.

Interview With European Journalists
May 24, 1988

Q. Let me first thank you, Mr. President, for giving us this interview on the eve of this historic and first trip to Moscow.

The President. Well, I thank you for doing it.

Soviet General Secretary Gorbachev

Q. I'm asked to ask you the first questions. My name is Fritz Wirth of the journal Die Welt, and everybody else will introduce himself when he asks his first question.

In another interview a few days ago in Moscow, Mr. Gorbachev gave a remarkable characterization of your qualities as a politician, and he praised your realism. After three meetings and many talks one-to-one, how would you characterize Mr. Gorbachev, and what do you regard as his main qualities?

The President. Well, I think he's very forthright. We can get into discussions where perhaps we're disagreeing quite firmly, and yet there is no personal animus in that with him. I think he solidly represents his country. I have suspected sometimes that he, having been raised in that particular country from childhood, believes some of their propaganda about us. But as I say, we can debate and discuss, and I think he's very sincere about the progressive ideas that he is introducing there and the changes that he thinks should be made. But as I say, even if the discussion gets, well, pretty meaningful, there is no animus. When it's over, I think that there's actually a degree of friendship between us.

Human Rights in the Soviet Union

Q. Mr. President, I am Francis Unwin of Le Soir, Brussels. According to the State Department, we are moving toward an agreement that would allow American psychiatrists to visit Soviet mental hospitals to determine if dissidents are being imprisoned there. The Assistant Secretary of State for Human Rights was quoted as saying that there seems to be a genuine interest in the idea of such a visit and in bringing the problem of abuse of psychiatry to an end. Do you think that a formal agreement could be ironed out during your visit to Moscow?

The President. I'm hopeful that it can. I think that some of these things with regard to human rights is not just trying to interfere with their internal affairs at all. But in view of the fact that our country is made up of people from all over the world—and I have used the term myself previously in discussing with them that when a man takes a wife, he doesn't stop loving his mother—and you perhaps are aware that Americans all retain a feeling of their heritage, even those whose grandparents or great-grandparents first came to this country. I think when Americans get acquainted with each other the first thing they inquire is, you know, what is your background. And Americans are accustomed to saying well, I'm this or that. And as time has gone on, most of us have to name three or four countries in our heritage if our ancestors came a few generations back. And the result of that is that in becoming closer and developing a relationship between the two countries we are affected by public opinion and by people in our country who resent if they think that in the land of their heritage people are being treated unfairly.

So, this is one of the reasons why I'm trying to impress upon the General Secretary that if we are to develop relationships, and better relationships in trade and so forth, that can be done better if there aren't elements in our country that believe that somehow the country of their heritage is—the government is being unfair to the people, because they still consider they have a relationship there. And so, it isn't a case of just wanting to impose our rules on them. It is to try and impress them with the need to eliminate some of the things that have grown with their system and that are unfair treatment, that are denying human rights to their own people.

Strategic Nuclear Arms Agreement

Q. Mr. President, I'm Christopher Thomas of the London Times. Could you please assess the prospects for a strategic arms treaty with the Soviet Union before you leave office on January the 20th. And do you see any possibility of another summit with Mr. Gorbachev later this year to sign such an agreement?

The President. Well, I won't rule it out. I won't say it's impossible because it does look as if a START agreement—I don't think there's any way now that the START agreement could come to a signing point in this summit. It is a far more complex treaty than the INF treaty that we did agree upon. Now, with ratification of that, I think that this summit will advance us further in the START discussions, and those people of ours and theirs that have been negotiating in Geneva on this will continue. And I hope that it can come about while I'm still here, and I think they feel the same way just because they believe that there would be perhaps unnecessary delay then if you had to wait while a newcomer in this office settled in and got around to working with them. And so, I would hope that we can iron out the still-undecided points before I leave. And then I could see where we might decide that it should be signed in a meeting rather than several thousand miles apart in the—when the signatures take place. And I've wondered, then, if perhaps the—since we will have each been to each other's country, rather than try to choose which country to do it in, maybe we'd pick a neutral locale.

President's Political Philosophy

Q. My name is Alberto Pasolini Zanelli, Il Giornale, Milan, Italy. And I want to remind you for some of your prophecies. You said very interesting things just at the beginning your first term not just about America but about the Eastern bloc. You said they are bound to be in very difficult times if they don't change the—will be going downstairs in the dustbin of history—or something like that. I think you are a very good prophet—[*laughter*]—but they've changed lots of things—*perestroika*, Hungary, Chinese. How do you feel like a prophet?

The President. Well, I didn't set out to be a prophet, but I just believe strongly that government can become too domineering and when—well, I thought in our own country that we had drifted to a point where government was, in a sense, at an adversarial relationship with its own business and private sector. And so, we set out to reduce regulations that we thought were unnecessary, to return authority to our States. We are unique in the world in that we were created as a federation of sovereign States. And much of our law and so forth was left with the States and the local communities nearest to the people, and then certain things that had to be done by the Federal Government.

But this was not new with me in feeling that the central government had gone too far in imposing itself on these other elements. Franklin Delano Roosevelt, when he ran for election in 1932—one of his platform planks was that he would restore authority and autonomy to the States and local communities that he said had been unjustly seized by the Federal Government. So, this wasn't—and he was of the opposite party. But this we have done. And I think it has been responsible for the longest economic expansion in our nation's history, which we're in right now.

And so, I could obviously see that, well, I disagreed with the whole theory of socialism and its advanced partner, communism, because that was a total imposition on the people. We set out, Vice President Bush was put in—I put him in charge of a task force to investigate how many regulations we could eliminate that had been imposed on the people and on local governments and so forth. And that commission was so successful that we estimate that we have eliminated 600 million man-hours a year of complying with government paperwork throughout the country. So, I'm still critical of that system, but again I think that's not too far away from what the General Secretary is trying to do. He has found and is advocating changes. He's getting resistance from some of the bureaucracy, but he is suggesting changes that are obviously based on improving the economic situation in his country.

NATO Defense Spending

Q. Mr. President, I am Boudouin Ballaert

from the French paper, Le Figaro. And the question of whether the NATO allies of the United States are bearing their fair share of the Western defense burden has triggered an important foreign policy debate here in Washington and was raised recently in Brussels by Mr. William Taft. Mr. President, what's your view about the burden-sharing problem?

The President. Well, there is no question but that if we take it on a percentage of our gross national income we are perhaps having a higher figure in our defense spending than our trading partners are in NATO. And we have believed that since our Congress is making it more difficult for us to continue our rate of spending in defense that maybe our allies could increase their share somewhat. I don't think it is a problem that should cause any ill will between us, but we have in our meetings with our NATO partners suggested that it could be most helpful if they would assume a little bit more of the burden.

Changes in Eastern Europe

Q. May I come back, Mr. President, to Eastern Europe? We had these developments in Hungary last weekend, and we had a peaceful change of power in Czechoslovakia last year. How do you see these developments? Could this be the beginning of a process which could reach the Communist hierarchy in Romania, in Bulgaria, in East Germany as well?

The President. Well, I think that is possible that the—the most recent one—I think we can't rule out the fact that there was an age problem, that one man had been there quite a long time. And this is a younger man. I don't know exactly what his beliefs and policies are, but they seem to be somewhat, well, let's say, in the same mold as the General Secretary of the Soviet Union. And I think we have to expect that, and it probably is a good thing to see happening with those countries, that *glasnost* is practiced in them also.

Advice to the President's Successor

Q. Mr. President, if, as it is currently expected, the dialog continues between Mr. Gorbachev and the next President of the United States, what piece of advice will you give to your successor, depending on his name—Mr. Bush or Mr. Dukakis, presumably?

The President. The advice that I would give to my successor with regard to relationship with——

Q. Yes, in regard to his name—I mean——

The President. Well, I would certainly try to inform him fully of all that had been accomplished in these last few years, now with this relatively new head of state. And I think I would try to convince him that this progress should continue. As I said in the first meeting, one-on-one with the General Secretary, I pointed out to him that it was rather unique that there we were in a room in Geneva, Switzerland, probably the two men in the world that had within our power to maintain the peace or to start a third world war, and neither one of us seemed to want a third world war. And there can be no denying that there is something of the "superstate" about our two nations, and we can have a bearing on the peace and prosperity of the world, depending on how we get along. And so, I suggested to him that we didn't mistrust each other because of our weapons, we had our weapons because we mistrusted each other, and that maybe what we should do is not just deal with arms and numbers of weapons but see if we could not get at the things that made us mistrust each other. And I think we've been doing quite a bit of that. And so, I would try to pass that on as a chore that the next President should continue.

General Manuel Noriega of Panama

Q. Mr. President, your Panama policy seems to be in deep trouble. You rejected a military solution to overthrow General Noriega, and your economic sanctions have so far failed to force him out, despite inflicting grievous harm on the Panamanian economy. And now Vice President Bush is saying that he opposes the dropping of drug charges against General Noriega. Where does your Panama policy go now?

The President. Well, he and I disagree on that. I recognize how it looks to some people with regard to that as a part of our effort. And I think he's aligned with this—that the goal must be the removal of Noriega from power. He is a military dictator. Here is a man who is able to actually drive the President of Panama into hiding for, literally, fear of his life. And he is an absolute dictator. Now that is the goal, and we tried to do that with economic measures. They didn't succeed. We are still in a position of negotiating. Our representatives are down there right now. I have to say the process is still going on. There had been no decision reached.

The disagreement, however, over whether we were doing business with a drug dealer or not was based on a rather unusual thing. And that is when lawyers in this country got an indictment against Noriega on the basis of dealing with the drug dealers, they overlooked—you know, when I say it's unusual, it's unusual that you indict literally the head of another state—but they overlooked the fact that the Panamanian Constitution makes it impossible to extradite this man in response to the indictment. Well, then you have to say the alternative is that he stays there in power and able to continue his drug trafficking. And if it means quashing an indictment that cannot be enforced, I would suggest that that's not too high a price to pay for getting rid of him.

U.S. Economic Recovery

Q. Mr. President, will you explain some secret of the American mind that is about economy. It is flourishing. It is booming—this 65 or 66th month [of] uninterrupted expansion, full employment, low inflation, everything looks fine. Why are still so many people talking gloom in the middle of a boom?

The President. I made some remarks about that to an audience just a few days ago in a speech of mine. It's amazing how even much of our media can—well, I described it like being in a hall of mirrors and coming up with a false image. We announce a figure that we had the highest amount of exports in our history just last week. And how do they get at that? They somehow say, well that, oh, we think inflation is coming back. They'll find some—I described it as their ability to see the dark cloud behind the silver lining. And I think the silver lining is very definitely real.

We took some practical steps in addition to those regulations that I mentioned. We had a complete overhaul of our tax system. Now, I'm not a genius that thought of this all at once by myself, but I know that if you look back through our history invariably tax reductions have resulted in an increase of revenue for the Government. As a matter of fact, centuries ago there was a man named ibn-Khaldun who said in the beginning of the empire, the rates were low, and the revenue was high. At the end of the empire, the rates were high, and the revenue was low.

Well, it happened. When we got our tax reform, that brought the top bracket in our income tax, for example, down from 70 percent on the people who could earn in that bracket. When we brought that down to—well, now it's 28 percent. But first, our first move was to bring it down to 50 percent. Well, even that resulted in a great increase in the revenues from that same segment of people. Well, now, this has to mean that those people were so busy at that 70-percent rate in tax shelters that they were seeking, or in just simply not earning any more beyond a certain point because how much was taken away from them, once you made an incentive that they could keep almost three-quarters of every dollar they earned, they started earning more dollars and stopped looking for tax shelters. And the same has been through all of the brackets. That was one of the great features, I think, of our recovery. And then the other was getting government out of the way of the private sector.

Our country, I think, probably leads the world in entrepreneurship. We have created in the last 5 years 16 million new jobs. Now, most of those jobs have been created by new or small businesses—not the great corporations with their thousands and thousands of employees, but the individual with an idea that goes into business for himself or the individual that's got a few employees and then suddenly he's got 200. Let us say that the bulk of the new jobs were in those industries that employed less than 500 people.

Well, all of this is what has resulted in what the leaders of your countries in our meetings have called the American miracle. And as a matter of fact, many of those leaders have been very frank in saying to me that they would like to be able to remove some of the restrictions and restraints on the private sector, private enterprise in your countries. And we talk about that a great deal, and maybe we're going to see some results elsewhere.

Q. The last one?

The President. Sorry.

Administration Accomplishments

Q. Mr. President, I know you are still very much in charge, of course, but next January you will leave the White House. And how would you like to be remembered, and what about the Reagan legacy?

The President. Well, I would like to feel that what I had left will be continued—the economic policies and the restraints on government. And one other thing, when we came into office, our defense capacity had been so reduced that on any given day 50 percent of our military aircraft could not fly for lack of spare parts, 50 percent of our naval vessels couldn't leave harbor for the same reason or for lack of crew. So, at the same time that I was trying to reduce the spending of government and the share that it was taking in the private sector, I had promised in the campaign I was going to restore our military.

Well, we not only did that, but at that time, there was a great wave of feeling across our country that, well, that things weren't the way they used to be, and there was a lack of patriotism. I likened it to the fact that I said I thought the people were ready for a spiritual revival. And I'm pleased to tell you that that has happened, and I get more mail and more people stopping me, if I'm out on a public appearance or something, to tell me that the thing they're grateful for is the renewal of patriotism and feeling about our country.

So, I don't know. Maybe I ought to just be happy to be remembered at all, but I'd kind of like it if those were the things they remembered. [*Laughter*]

Q. Thank you very much.

The President. That's it? Well——

President's Future Plans

Q. May I just give you a suggestion?

The President. Yes.

Q. When you leave office, please go on doing your Saturday message. [*Laughter*]

The President. Well, whether I do that or not, I can assure you, I am—I've always described it this way: that you know the business that I used to be in, and I've always described that in Hollywood, if you didn't sing or dance, you wound up as an after-dinner speaker. And so, I didn't sing or dance, and I was out on what I—all my personal appearances were out making public speeches. And I did my own speeches and talked on what I wanted to talk about. And basically, it was—even then, with no thought of ever being in public life—it was against the growth of government and the imposition.

When I was making those speeches in those days in Hollywood, the top bracket of the income tax was 90 percent. And I knew what it was like to refuse a good script and not make a picture because I wasn't going to work for 10 cents on the dollar after I'd reached that bracket. So, I can assure you, I'm going to—there are a lot of things I want to campaign for that still haven't been done. So, I will be out there addressing the people. In America—I don't know whether it's true in your countries—we have a great many private organizations, and there's always a demand for speakers. So, I'll be doing that.

And as a matter of fact, I've already picked out one topic I'm going to speak on. You know that an amendment to the Constitution came about a few years ago that limited the President of the United States to two terms; there cannot be a third. Well, now, I can't object to that while I'm in this job. It would sound like I'm doing it for myself. But as soon as I'm out of here, I'm going to try to arouse the American people to get that constitutional amendment changed, canceled, because I think it's an interference with their democratic rights. They should have the right to vote for whoever they want to vote for, for as long as they want to vote for them. And I'm going to see if I can't arouse the people to get that changed.

Q. Mr. President, may I, on behalf of my colleagues, thank you very much for this interview. We wish you a pleasant trip to Moscow and a most successful summit.

The President. Well, thank you very much.

Note: The interview began at 11:35 a.m. in the Oval Office at the White House. It was released by the Office of the Press Secretary on May 26.

Proclamation 5827—Take Pride in America Month, 1988
May 25, 1988

By the President of the United States of America

A Proclamation

Our beautiful land is blessed from sea to shining sea with bountiful natural and cultural resources on Federal, State, and local lands. We are also blessed that the American people possess a unique volunteer spirit rooted in our frontier tradition.

It is truly fitting that we take a special period of time to recognize our Nation's recreational and cultural resources and how they contribute to the economic and social well-being of our communities and our country. Through our stewardship of these natural wonders and great monuments to history, we can express our love for our country, our pride in America, and our desire to preserve our resources and our heritage for the future.

The Take Pride in America campaign, with its theme, "Take Pride in America: You Can Make a Difference," encourages all of us to do just this. The campaign is a partnership of public and private groups, Federal agencies, and State and local governments that fosters public awareness of the need for wise stewardship of our natural resources and for retention of our countless cultural resources as well. Let us remind ourselves often, this month and always, to do our share and "Take Pride in America."

The Congress, by House Joint Resolution 530, has designated May 1988 as "Take Pride in America Month" and authorized and requested the President to issue a proclamation in observance of this event.

Now, Therefore, I, Ronald Reagan, President of the United States of America, do hereby proclaim May 1988 as Take Pride in America Month. I call upon the people of the United States and government officials at every level to observe this month with appropriate programs, ceremonies, and activities.

In Witness Whereof, I have hereunto set my hand this twenty-fifth day of May, in the year of our Lord nineteen hundred and eighty-eight, and of the Independence of the United States of America the two hundred and twelfth.

RONALD REAGAN

[*Filed with the Office of the Federal Register, 11:09 a.m., May 26, 1988*]

Note: The proclamation was released by the Office of the Press Secretary on May 26.

Proclamation 5828—National NHS-NeighborWorks Week, 1988
May 25, 1988

By the President of the United States of America

A Proclamation

Socially, culturally, economically, spiritually, and in so many ways, our neighborhoods tell the American story of family, faith, and freedom. The motto *E pluribus unum,* or "Out of many, one," is an appropriate description of our myriad neighborhoods and their residents. We all love and cherish this blessed land of liberty; therefore, let us join together as partners and neighbors to enrich it, each other, and every one of our neighborhoods with all of the strengths our many heritages provide us. That is something for us to reflect upon, and observance of National NHS-NeighborWorks Week presents a fine opportunity for reflection and action in our communities.

Both reflection and action are already taking place around our land in neighborhoods where residents, business owners, concerned citizens, community groups, and government agencies are turning decay and despair into promise and prosperity. They are using some of the most powerful sources of America's greatness—our volunteer spirit, our spiritual strength, the love and caring of our families, our hard work and determination, our civic energy—to create opportunities and bring renewed inspiration and hope.

Among them are the groups from which this week of observance takes its name. NeighborWorks is a national organization composed of Neighborhood Housing Services (NHS), Apartment Improvement Programs, and Mutual Housing Associations, cooperative ventures that are resident-business-government partnerships relying primarily on volunteer effort and private and local resources. They are revitalizing more than 200 neighborhoods and have generated more than $4 billion in reinvestment funds. These efforts are clearly a major contribution to our Nation and deserve our gratitude, encouragement, cooperation, and emulation during National NHS-NeighborWorks Week and in the future as well.

The Congress, by Public Law 100–261, has designated the week of June 5 through June 11, 1988, as "National NHS-NeighborWorks Week" and authorized and requested the President to issue a proclamation in observance of this week.

Now, Therefore, I, Ronald Reagan, President of the United States of America, do hereby proclaim the week of June 5 through June 11, 1988, as National NHS-NeighborWorks Week. I call upon the people of the United States to observe this week with appropriate ceremonies and activities.

In Witness Whereof, I have hereunto set my hand this twenty-fifth day of May, in the year of our Lord nineteen hundred and eighty-eight, and of the Independence of the United States of America the two hundred and twelfth.

RONALD REAGAN

[*Filed with the Office of the Federal Register, 11:10 a.m., May 26, 1988*]

Note: The proclamation was released by the Office of the Press Secretary on May 26.

Remarks to the Paasikivi Society and the League of Finnish-American Societies in Helsinki, Finland
May 27, 1988

Mr. President, Mr. Speaker, Mr. Prime Minister, and ladies and gentlemen, let me begin by saying thank you to our hosts, the Finnish Government, the Paasikivi Society, and the League of Finnish-American Societies. It's a particular honor for me to come here today. This year—the Year of Friendship, as Congress has proclaimed it, between the United States and Finland—this year marks the 350th anniversary of the arrival of the first Finns in America and the establishment of a small Scandinavian colony near what is today Wilmington, Delaware—an ancient people in a new world. And that is the story not only of those Finns but of all the peoples who braved the seas to settle in and build my country, a land of freedom for a nation of immigrants.

Yes, they founded a new world, but as they crossed the oceans, the mountains, and the prairies, those who made America carried the old world in their hearts—the old customs, the family ties, and most of all the belief in God, a belief that gave them the moral compass and ethical foundation by which they explored an uncharted frontier and constructed a government and nation of, by, and for the people.

And so, although we Americans became a new people, we also remain an ancient one, for we're guided by ancient and universal values, values that Prime Minister Holkeri spoke of in Los Angeles this February when, after recalling Finland's internationally recognized position of neutrality, he added that Finland is "tied to Western values of freedom, democracy, and human rights." And let me add here, that for America those ties are also the bonds of our friendship. America respects Finland's neutrality. We support Finland's independence. We honor Finland's courageous history. We value the creative statesmanship that has been Finland's gift to world peace. And in this soaring hall, which is the great architect Alvar Aalto's statement of hope for Finland's future, we reaffirm our hope and faith that the friendship between our nations will be unending.

We're gathered here today in this hall because it was here, almost 13 years ago, that the 35 nations of the Conference on Security and Cooperation in Europe signed the Helsinki Final Act, a document that embodies the same ethical and moral principles and the same hope for a future of peace that Finns and so many other European immigrants gave America. The Final Act is a singular statement of hope. Its "three baskets" touch on almost every aspect of East-West relations, and taken together form a kind of map through the wilderness of mutual hostility to open fields of peace and to a common home of trust among all of our sovereign nations—neutrals, nonaligned, and alliance members alike. The Final Act sets new standards of conduct for our nations and provided the mechanisms by which to apply those standards.

Yes, the Final Act goes beyond arms control, once the focus of international dialog. It reflects a truth that I have so often noted: Nations do not distrust each other because they are armed; they are armed because they distrust each other. The Final Act grapples with the full range of our underlying differences and deals with East-West relations as an interrelated whole. It reflects the belief of all our countries that human rights are less likely to be abused when a nation's security is less in doubt; that economic relations can contribute to security, but depend on the trust and confidence that come from increasing ties between our peoples, increasing openness, and increasing freedom; and that there is no true international security without respect for human rights. I can hardly improve on the words President Koivisto used in this hall 2 years ago when he recalled that "security is more than the protection of borders and social structures. It is emphasized in the Final Act that individual persons who live in the participating states have to feel in their own lives security which is based on respect for fundamental human rights and basic freedoms."

And beyond establishing these integrated standards, the Final Act establishes a process for progress. It sets up a review procedure to measure performance against standards. And despite the doubts of the critics—for the past 13 years, the signatory states have mustered the political will to keep on working and making progress.

Let me say that it seems particularly appropriate to me that the Final Act is associated so closely with this city and this country. More than any other diplomatic document, the Final Act speaks to the yearning that Finland's longtime President, Urho Kekkonen, spoke of more than a quarter century ago when he said, in his words: "It's the fervent hope of the Finnish people that barriers be lowered all over Europe and that progress be made along the road of European unity." And he added that this was, as he put it, "for the good of Europe, and thus of humanity as a whole." Well, those were visionary words. That vision inspired and shaped the drafting of the Final Act and continues to guide us today.

Has the Final Act and what we call the Helsinki process worked or not? Many say it hasn't, but I believe it has. In the security field, I would point to the most recent fruit of the process: the Stockholm document of confidence- and security-building measures in Europe. This agreement lays down the rules by which our 35 states notify each other of upcoming military activities in Europe; provides detailed information on these activities in advance; and lets the others know their plans for very large military activities 1 or 2 years in advance and agrees not to hold such maneuvers unless this notice is given; invites observers to their larger military activities; and permits on-site inspections to make sure the agreement is honored.

I am happy to note that since our representatives shook hands to seal this agreement a year and a half ago, all 35 states have, by and large, honored both the letter and the spirit of the Stockholm document. The Western and neutral and nonaligned states have set a strong example in providing full information about their military activities. In April, Finland held its first military activity subject to the Stockholm notification requirements and voluntarily invited observers to it. The Soviet Union and its allies also have a generally good record of implementation, though less forthcoming than the West. Ten on-site inspections have been conducted so far, and more and more states are exercising their right to make such inspections. I can't help but believe that making inspections a matter of routine business will improve openness and enhance confidence.

Nor was Stockholm the end of the process. In Vienna all 35 signatory states are considering how to strengthen the confidence- and security-building measures in the context of a balanced outcome at the CSCE followup meeting that includes significant progress on human rights. In the economic field, as in the security field, I believe there has been progress, but of a different kind. Issues and negotiations regarding security are not simple, but military technology makes arms and armies resemble each other enough so that common measures can be confidently applied. Economic relations, by contrast, are bedeviled by differences in our systems. Perhaps increases in nonstrategic trade can contribute to better relations between East and West, but it's difficult to relate the state-run economies of the East to the essentially free-market economies of the West. Perhaps some of the changes underway in the state-run economies will equip them better to deal with our businessmen and open new arenas for cooperation. But our work on these issues over the years has already made us understand that differences in systems are serious obstacles to expansion of economic ties, and since understanding of unpleasant realities is part of wisdom, that, too, is progress.

The changes taking place in the Eastern countries of the continent go beyond changes in their economic systems and greater openness in their military activities. Changes have also begun to occur in the field of human rights, as was called for in the Final Act. The rest of us would like to see the changes that are being announced actually registered in the law and practice of our Eastern partners and in the documents under negotiation in the Vienna followup to the Helsinki conference.

Much has been said about the human rights and humanitarian provisions in the Final Act and the failure of the Eastern bloc to honor them. Yet for all the bleak winds that have swept the plains of justice since that signing day in 1975, the accords have taken root in the conscience of humanity and grown in moral and, increasingly, in diplomatic authority. I believe that this is no accident. It reflects an increasing realization that the agenda of East-West relations must be comprehensive, that security and human rights must be advanced together or cannot truly be secured at all. But it also shows that the provisions in the Final Act reflect standards that are truly universal in their scope. The accords embody a fundamental truth, a truth that gathers strength with each passing season and that will not be denied—the truth that, like the first Finnish settlers in America, all our ancient peoples find themselves today in a new world and that, as those early settlers discovered, the greatest creative and moral force in this new world, the greatest hope for survival and success, for peace and happiness, is human freedom.

Yes, freedom—the right to speak, to print; the right to worship, to travel, to assemble; the right to be different, the right, as the American philosopher Henry David Thoreau wrote, "to step to the music of a different drummer"—this is freedom as most Europeans and Americans understand it and freedom as it is embodied in the Universal Declaration of Human Rights and, yes, in the Helsinki accords. And far more than the locomotive or the automobile, the airplane or the rocket, more than radio, television, or the computer, this concept of liberty is the most distinct, peculiar, and powerful invention of the civilization we all share.

Indeed, without this freedom there would have been no mechanical inventions, for inventions are eccentricities. The men and women who create them are visionaries, just like artists and writers. They see what others fail to see and trust their insights when others don't. The same freedom that permits literature and the arts to flourish; the same freedom that allows one to attend church, synagogue, or mosque without apprehension; that same freedom from oppression and supervision is the freedom that has given us, the peoples of Western Europe and North America, our dynamism, our economic growth, and our inventiveness. Together with Japan and Australia and many others, we have lived in this state of freedom, this house of democracy, since the end of the Second World War.

The house of democracy is a house whose doors are open to all. Because of it, because of the liberty and popular rule we've shared, today we also share a prosperity more widely distributed and extensive, a political order more tolerant and humane than has ever before been known on Earth. To see not simply the immediate but the historic importance of this, we should remember how far many of our nations have traveled and how desolate the future of freedom and democracy once seemed. For much of this century, the totalitarian temptation, in one form or another, has beckoned to mankind, also promising freedom, but of a different kind than the one we celebrate today. This concept of liberty is, as the Czechoslovak writer Milan Kundera has put it, "the age-old dream of a world where everybody would live in harmony, united by a single common will and faith, without secrets from one another"—the freedom of imposed perfection.

Fifty, forty, even as recently as thirty years ago, the contest between this utopian concept of freedom on one hand and the democratic concept of freedom on the other seemed a close one. Promises of a perfect world lured many Western thinkers and millions of others besides. And many believed in the confident prediction of history's inevitable triumph. Well, few do today. Just as democratic freedom has proven itself incredibly fertile—fertile not merely in a material sense but also in the abundance it has brought forth in the human spirit—so, too, utopianism has proven brutal and barren.

Albert Camus once predicted that, in his words, "when revolution in the name of power and of history becomes a murderous and immoderate mechanism, a new rebellion is consecrated in the name of moderation of life." Isn't this exactly what we see happening across the mountains and plains of Europe and even beyond the Urals today? In Western Europe, support for utopian ideologies, including support among intellectuals, has all but collapsed, while in the nondemocratic countries, leaders grapple with the internal contradictions of their system and some ask how they can make that system better and more productive. In a sense, the front line in the competition of ideas that has played in Europe and America for more than 70 years has shifted East. Once it was the democracies that doubted their own view of freedom and wondered whether utopian systems might not be better. Today the doubt is on the other side.

In just 2 days, I will meet in Moscow with General Secretary Gorbachev. It will be our fourth set of face-to-face talks since 1985. The General Secretary and I have developed a broad agenda for U.S.-Soviet relations, an agenda that is linked directly to the agenda of the Final Act. Yes, as does the Final Act, we will discuss security issues. We will pursue progress in arms reduction negotiations across the board and continue our exchanges on regional issues. Yes, we will also discuss economic issues, although, as in the Helsinki process, we have seen in recent years how much the differences in our systems inhibit expanded ties and how difficult it is to divorce economic relations from human rights and other elements of that relationship. And, yes, as our countries did at Helsinki, we will take up other bilateral areas as well, including scientific, cultural, and people-to-people exchanges, where we've been hard at work identifying new ways to cooperate. In this area, in particular, I believe we'll see some good results before the week is over.

And like the Final Act, our agenda now includes human rights as an integral component. We have developed our dialog and put in place new mechanisms for discussion. The General Secretary has spoken often and forthrightly on the problems confronting the Soviet Union. In his campaign to address these shortcomings, he talks of *glasnost* and *perestroika,* openness and restructuring, words that to our ears have a particularly welcome sound. And since he began his campaign, things have happened that all of us applaud. The list includes the release from labor camps or exile of people like Andrei Sakharov, Irina Ratushinskaya, Anatoly Koryagin, Josef Begun, and many other prisoners of conscience; the publication of books like "Dr. Zhivago" and "Children of the Arbat"; the distribution of movies like "Repentance" that are critical of aspects of the Soviet past and present; allowing higher levels of emigration; greater toleration of dissent; General Secretary Gorbachev's recent statements on religious toleration; the beginning of Soviet withdrawal from Afghanistan.

All this is new and good. But at the same time, there is another list, defined not by us but by the standards of the Helsinki Final Act and the sovereign choice of all participants, including the Soviet Union, to subscribe to it. We need look no further through the Final Act to see where Soviet practice does not—or does not yet—measure up to Soviet commitment. Thirteen years after the Final Act was signed, it's difficult to understand why cases of divided families and blocked marriages should remain on the East-West agenda or why Soviet citizens who wish to exercise their right to emigrate should be subject to artificial quotas and arbitrary rulings. And what are we to think of the continued suppression of those who wish to practice their religious beliefs? Over 300 men and women whom the world sees as political prisoners have been released. There remains no reason why the Soviet Union cannot release all people still in jail for expression of political or religious belief, or for organizing to monitor the Helsinki Act.

The Soviets talk about a "common European home" and define it largely in terms of geography. But what is it that cements the structure of clear purpose that all our nations pledged themselves to build by their signature of the Final Act? What is it but the belief in the inalienable rights and dignity of every single human being? What is it but a commitment to true pluralist democracy? What is it but a dedication to the universally understood democratic concept of liberty that evolved from the genius of

European civilization? This body of values—this is what marks, or should mark, the common European home.

Mr. Gorbachev has spoken of, in his words, "the artificiality and temporariness of the bloc-to-bloc confrontation and the archaic nature of the 'iron curtain.'" Well, I join him in this belief and welcome every sign that the Soviets and their allies are ready not only to embrace but to put into practice the values that unify and, indeed, define contemporary Western European civilization and its grateful American offspring.

Some 30 years ago—another period of relative openness—the Italian socialist Pietro Nenni, long a friend of the Soviet Union, warned that it was wrong to think that the relaxation could be permanent in, as he said, "the absence of any system of judicial guarantees." And he added that only democracy and liberty could prevent reversal of the progress underway.

There are a number of steps, which, if taken, would help ensure the deepening and institutionalization of promising reforms. First, the Soviet leaders could agree to tear down the Berlin Wall and all barriers between Eastern and Western Europe. They could join us in making Berlin itself an all-European center of communications, meetings, and travel. They could also give legal and practical protection to free expression and worship. Let me interject here that at one time Moscow was known as the City of the Forty Forties because there were 1,600 belfries in the churches of the city. The world welcomes the return of some churches to worship after many years, but there are still relatively few functioning churches and almost no bells. Mr. Gorbachev recently said, as he put it, "Believers are Soviet people, workers, patriots, and they have the full right to express their conviction with dignity." Well, I applaud Mr. Gorbachev's statement. What a magnificent demonstration of good will it would be for the Soviet leadership for church bells to ring out again not only in Moscow but throughout the Soviet Union.

But beyond these particular steps, there's a deeper question. How can the countries of the East not only grant but guarantee the protection of rights? The thought and practice of centuries has pointed the way. As the French constitutional philosopher Montesquieu wrote more than 200 years ago, "There is no liberty if the judiciary power be not separated" from the other powers of government. And like the complete independence of the judiciary, popular control over those who make the laws provides a vital, practical guarantee of human rights. So does the secret ballot. So does the freedom of citizens to associate and act for political purposes or for free collective bargaining.

I know that for the Eastern countries such steps are difficult, and some may say it's unrealistic to call for them. Some said in 1975 that the standards set forth in the Final Act were unrealistic, that the comprehensive agenda it embodied was unrealistic. Some said, earlier in this decade, that calling for global elimination of an entire class of U.S. and Soviet intermediate-range nuclear missiles was unrealistic, that calling for 50-percent reductions in U.S. and Soviet strategic offensive arms was unrealistic, that the Soviets would never withdraw from Afghanistan. Well, is it realistic to pretend that rights are truly protected when there are no effective safeguards against arbitrary rule? Is it realistic, when the Soviet leadership itself is calling for *glasnost* and democratization, to say that judicial guarantees or the independence of the judiciary or popular control over those who draft the laws or freedom to associate for political purposes are unrealistic? And finally, is it realistic to say that peace is truly secure when political systems are less than open?

We believe that realism is on our side when we say that peace and freedom can only be achieved together, but that they can indeed be achieved together if we're prepared to drive toward that goal. So did the leaders who met in this room to sign the Final Act. They were visionaries of the most practical kind. In shaping our policy toward the Soviet Union, in preparing for my meetings with the General Secretary, I have taken their vision—a shared vision, subscribed to by East, West, and the proud neutral and nonaligned countries of this continent—as my guide. I believe the standard that the framers of the Final Act set, including the concept of liberty it embodies, is a standard for all of us. We can do no less than uphold it and try to see it turn, as the Soviets say, into "life itself."

We in the West will remain firm in our values, strong and vigilant in defense of our interests, ready to negotiate honestly for results of mutual and universal benefit. One lesson we drew again from the events leading up to the Intermediate-range Nuclear Forces treaty was that, in the world as it is today, peace truly does depend on Western strength and resolve. It is a lesson we will continue to heed.

But we're also prepared to work with the Soviets and their allies whenever they're ready to work with us. By strength we do not mean *diktat,* that is, an imposed settlement; we mean confident negotiation. The road ahead may be long, but not as long as our countries had before them 44 years ago when Finland's great President J.K. Paasikivi, told a nation that had shown the world uncommon courage in a harrowing time: "A path rises up to the slope from the floor of the valley. At times the ascent is gradual, at other times steeper. But all the time one comes closer and closer to free, open spaces, above which God's ever brighter sky can be seen. The way up will be difficult, but every step will take us closer to open vistas."

I believe that in Moscow Mr. Gorbachev and I can take another step toward a brighter future and a safer world. And I believe that, for the sake of all our ancient peoples, this new world must be a place both of democratic freedom and of peace. It must be a world in which the spirit of the Helsinki Final Act guides all our countries like a great beacon of hope to all mankind for ages to come.

Thank you, and God bless you. And bear with me now—*Onnea ja menestystä koko Suomen kansalle* [Good luck and success to the entire Finnish people].

Note: The President spoke at 3:05 p.m. in Finlandia Hall. In his opening remarks, he referred to President Mauno Koivisto, Speaker of the Parliament Matti Ahde, and Prime Minister Harri Holkeri.

Statement on Senate Ratification of the Intermediate-Range Nuclear Forces Treaty
May 27, 1988

I am very pleased with the action of the United States Senate in consenting to ratification of the INF treaty. In 2 days, I will arrive in the Soviet Union to meet with General Secretary Gorbachev to discuss our four-part agenda. Today's action by the Senate clearly shows support for our arms reduction objectives.

I want to express my appreciation for the leadership demonstrated by Majority Leader Bob Byrd and Republican leader Bob Dole in securing the timely approval of this treaty. I have invited them to join me for the exchange of ratification documents in Moscow.

I continue to have concerns about the constitutionality of some provisions of the resolution of ratification, particularly those dealing with interpretation, and I will communicate with the Senate on these matters in due course.

Statement on the Retirement of Representative John Duncan of Tennessee
May 27, 1988

Today I learned that my good friend John Duncan has announced that he will not run for reelection to the House of Representatives from the Second District of Tennessee. John was first elected to the House in 1964 to the seat held by Howard Baker's father and then his mother. John's service in the succeeding decades has demonstrated the highest dedication and commitment to the well-being of the Nation and his beloved State of Tennessee. In recent years, his leadership as ranking Republican on the House Ways and Means Committee has proved critical to ensuring fiscal responsibility in the Federal Government.

Nancy and I wish John and Lois the very best of everything always.

Written Responses to Questions Submitted by the Soviet Magazine Ogonek
May 19, 1988

President's Accomplishments

Q. A few words about yourself, your own personal and political experiences, your career? Has your life thus far been a success? How do you evaluate the path you have traveled?

The President. Historians will make the final judgment about my years as Governor of California and as President of the United States, but personally, I feel good about what I have been able to accomplish, both in and out of government. My professional career has been varied. I have worked as a sportscaster, an actor, a labor leader, a lecturer, and a public official. This is something that is characteristic of the American way of life. The opportunity to advance oneself based on one's desires and abilities is a valued part of our existence and one to which I owe my success.

Soviet-U.S. Relations

Q. You are an experienced politician. The years of your Presidency have made you even more experienced, and nevertheless, you have preserved the wonderful ability to change your mind. In my country, many people remember your words, expressed in December of last year, about the changed image of the "evil empire" in your statement—to the effect that your attitude toward the U.S.S.R. had improved. What has changed in your perception of the U.S.S.R.?

The President. I have always believed that people and nations must be judged by their actions and not their words. I have tried to speak out about the positive developments I see as much as I try to draw attention to the negative ones. My guiding principles have been candor, realism, dialog, and strength. In that regard it is fair to say I have noted some progress, such as the Soviet Government's commitment to withdrawal from Afghanistan. We are also seeing resolution of individual human rights cases and more open discussion of these issues. On the other hand, I do not understand, nor do other Americans understand, why the Soviet Government restricts, for example, the practice of religion and freedom of movement. We do not accept limitations on free speech.

I think what has changed is that both the U.S. and the Soviet people are being more candid about areas in which we agree and disagree. We must discuss not only restraint of the arms competition, but also basic issues of human rights and international behavior. Disagreements over these issues have fueled the mistrust that lies between our countries. Nations do not mistrust each other because they are armed; they arm themselves because they mistrust each other.

That is why in Moscow, as we have in our three previous meetings, General Secretary Gorbachev and I will discuss human rights and regional conflicts as vigorously and as seriously as we will discuss arms reductions. We live in an interconnected world with instant communication and a global conscience. How you treat your own citizens is of concern to the whole world. And the world watches and judges each country based not on what it wants the world to hear, but on the actions and policies that it sees. At the same time, the Soviet Union is a country of influence in many regions of the world. With that influence comes a responsibility to work towards peace and to help solve the many regional disputes which plague mankind.

President's Visit to Moscow

Q. You are coming to the U.S.S.R. for the first time. What do you expect from your meeting with our country—not only from the negotiations but personally from your meeting with the U.S.S.R.?

The President. I am looking forward with great anticipation to visiting Moscow and in particular to talking with the people in the Soviet Union. As your question implies, the negotiations are important, but so is the opportunity to understand the other fellow's point of view. I think General Secretary Gorbachev left Washington with a deeper understanding of the American people, and I anticipate the same benefit from my meetings with the people of Moscow.

Political and Economic Freedom

Q. The irreversibility of our chosen path, *perestroika*, is very important to us. Do you feel that there is a link between the process underway here and what is happening in the United States? If so, what is it?

The President. No country can compete successfully in the global market today unless it unleashes the human spirit and lets individuals drive toward their own goals. Society, as a whole, benefits from the progress made by individuals. America is built on the principle of what we call free enterprise, a system which permits each individual to seek his own happiness based on his or her needs and desires. Americans make all sorts of choices within that system, often balancing economic prosperity with job satisfaction, family, recreation, artistic achievement, and other goals. The interaction of all those personal choices makes for a strong and dynamic system.

Perestroika also can play an important role in information exchange. Your government is known for its high regard for secrecy, and you pay a price for that policy. Much of the progress made in the West comes about from information sharing. Free access to the body of knowledge possessed by the society enables our citizens to build on the advances made by others. As long as Soviet society remains off limits to the rest of the world, inhibiting the free flow of information and restricting travel in and out of the U.S.S.R., your economy will be limited in its ability to be part of the world economy.

Regional Conflicts

Q. Your second term as President is coming to an end. You have achieved a great deal. What have you not succeeded in achieving in your relations with the U.S.S.R., but would like to achieve?

The President. I agree that we have made significant progress. The treaty on the elimination of an entire class of U.S. and Soviet intermediate-range nuclear missiles has been a milestone not only for what it accomplishes in its own right but as a precedent for future agreements which will actually reduce nuclear weapons and not just restrain them.

I would like to see progress toward resolving conflicts around the world. For example, the war between Iran and Iraq has been going on for 7 years with hundreds of thousands of casualties. A generation of young lives is being bled away in this tragic conflict. Chemical weapons have been used with consequences that horrify the world. Much of the world has united in an effort to bring an end to this war by supporting U.N. Security Council Resolution 598, which calls for an immediate cease-fire across the board and withdrawal to the internationally recognized boundaries. The Security Council members, including your government, agreed that if either belligerent refused to honor this call by the U.N. Security Council there should be a second resolution mandating an arms embargo against that party. Both the United States and the Soviet Union supported Resolution 598. Iraq has now accepted the resolution and agreed to abide by its terms. Iran is resisting and insists on continuing the war. The Soviet Union is a key actor in this situation. You sell arms to both sides. If the Soviet Union strongly endorsed a second resolution and a strong effort by the United Nations to prevent arms from reaching Iran, I firmly believe we could bring this tragedy to a halt.

In Ethiopia a great tragedy is imminent, as the effects of a terrible drought are being compounded by that government's policies blocking international relief efforts. The Soviet Union is that Marxist government's principal supplier of weapons and has influence there. It would be good if the Soviet Union cooperated with efforts to help prevent a manmade catastrophe.

These are urgent issues I will be discussing with General Secretary Gorbachev. We will also look at ways we can bring about settlements to conflicts in southern Africa, Cambodia, Central America, and the Middle East.

U.S. Political System

Q. What is the mechanism for succession of power in the United States? Are you certain that your successor will continue what you have started?

The President. Our mechanism for succession is a free and open election in which candidates from different parties compete vigorously against each other, arguing their positions in public debates, speeches, and media interviews for some months. Members of our press vigorously question the candidates. We have an election campaign underway right now. In November the American people will go into polling booths across the country and vote in complete secrecy for the candidate of their choice. In addition to electing a new President and Vice President in November, Americans will elect Senators, Members of Congress, State Governors, and local representatives. All of this is provided for under our Constitution.

I have read the constitutions of many countries, including your own. Many nations of the world have written into their constitution provisions for freedom of speech and freedom of assembly. If this is true, some ask, then why is the Constitution of the United States so exceptional? Our Constitution begins with three simple words: "We the People. . . ." This short phrase tells the full story. In other constitutions, the Government tells the people of those countries what they are allowed to do. In our Constitution, we the people tell the Government what it can do. And it can do only those things listed in that document and nothing else. In America, the people are in charge.

Soviet-U.S. Relations

Q. How do you imagine, or envisage, the future of mankind? How can we reach a future without war? Is such a future realistic?

The President. My vision is of a world free of war. A nuclear war cannot be won and should never be fought. General Secretary Gorbachev joined me in affirming that basic truth when we first met in Geneva. We have kept the peace by having enough nuclear weapons to retaliate if the other started a war. Well, that is not much of a defense. There would be no victors in that kind of war. That is why I want to start reducing nuclear weapons. Our INF treaty is an excellent beginning, and we are making progress on a strategic arms reduction treaty, which will cut in half U.S. and Soviet strategic arsenals. At the same time we need to think about getting parity in conventional forces in Europe to make sure one country won't have an advantage over the other. There is today a serious imbalance in your favor.

This is why I am seeking to move our strategy of deterrence toward defensive systems, which threaten no one, and away from offensive systems. That is the purpose behind my Strategic Defense Initiative: to make obsolete the most threatening weapon ever invented—the ballistic missile. I call upon the Soviet leadership to join me in these efforts toward strategic defenses and to move to a world based on defense rather than offense. The reasonableness of this proposal is demonstrated by the fact that your government has been engaged in its own strategic defense programs long before we started SDI.

But we must also keep in mind that arms agreements alone will not make the world safer. We must also deal with the core source of mistrust between our nations. This is why our dialog must cover a broad agenda of human rights, regional and bilateral issues, as well as arms reductions.

Q. Recently, speaking at Moscow University, I told my audience about this interview and asked them to think up a question for you. One of the questions submitted was the following: "Mr. President, do you feel that future generations of Soviet and American citizens will relate to each other better? If so, what have you done to make that possible—to ensure that progress in our relations and a relaxation of tensions begins today?"

The President. I hope that future generations of American and Soviet citizens will have closer relations and better understanding. But much depends on the way your government deals with the basic issue of human rights.

Cultural exchanges and individual travel are the underpinnings for establishing closer relations. I look forward to expanding these and thus broadening the scope of our mutual contacts. Americans hope for a world in which all people can enjoy the freedom they cherish. We will continue to work to fulfill our dreams for peace through understanding.

Note: The questions and answers were released by the Office of the Press Secretary on May 28.

Interview With Soviet Television Journalists Valentin Zorin and Boris Kalyagin
May 20, 1988

Q. Good evening, comrades. We are in the White House in Washington, DC, the residence of the head of the American Government. This is the place where the Presidents of the United States do their work. President Reagan is receiving us in order to give an interview for Soviet television. And since our time is very limited, I think that we will get down to questions right away.

Soviet-U.S. Summit Meeting in Moscow

Mr. President, there's an upcoming visit to Moscow for you. This will be your first trip to our country. What feelings are you traveling to the Soviet Union with, and what do you anticipate from this upcoming summit meeting?

The President. Well, this will be the fourth meeting between the General Secretary and myself. I'm obviously looking forward to the trip for one reason, because I have never been there. And I'm looking forward to seeing your country—well, as much as possible with the meetings that will be going on. And we have discussed in the previous meetings with your General Secretary such matters as arms reductions, and we've been successful on the one treaty. We're both working on the present treaty that we call START—the 50-percent reduction of intercontinental ballistic missiles—but also some differences that we've had on our interpretation of human rights, on regional affairs—and we're greatly heartened by the fact that your forces are withdrawing from Afghanistan—and on bilateral issues: such things as rescue-at-sea agreements, fisheries agreements, things of that kind in which we've made great progress.

Soviet-U.S. Relations

Q. At Geneva, in Reykjavik, in Washington, you and Mr. Gorbachev took steps which have great significance. Thanks to that, the threat of war has been reduced and cooperation has increased between our countries, despite the different social systems we have. What kind of opinion do you have about future prospects for movement in this same direction?

The President. Well, I have to be optimistic about it. I have read "Perestroika" cover to cover, and the goals that were outlined there for your own country and by your present leader were such that I think it would reduce some of the differences between us further and make it possible for future leaders of our countries to eliminate—well, what I called for in our first meeting in Geneva, when just the General Secretary and I were talking to each other, I pointed out that we didn't mistrust each other because we were armed, we're armed because we mistrust each other, and that we had a unique opportunity, the two of us, to go to work not just to try and reduce arms but to reduce the causes of the mistrust. And I think we've carried on in that manner in the succeeding meetings.

Q. I'd like to ask you, Mr. President, what do you think—how do you think—in today's world, what is most important: the power—muscle power, so to speak, or the power of reason? What's more important in today's world?

The President. Well, the power of reason. But I think that can be achieved more quickly if we show our mutual desire for a peaceful world by eliminating some of the most horrendous of the weapons, such as the nuclear weapons. I made a statement to the parliaments of one or two other countries several years ago and have been repeating it since and have heard some of your officials say the same thing: A nuclear war cannot be won and must never be fought.

Q. Starting out from the premise that there shouldn't ever be a nuclear war, is there any sense then in continuing having arms?

The President. Well, I would think that once—I think the weapons that are the most destabilizing are the nuclear weapons, the idea in the minds of people that once those weapons are fired devastation is going to follow and there's no way to halt them. They're more destabilizing than the people's concern about weapons that we're familiar with—airplanes, battleships, things of this kind, artillery. And so, I think that this is the immediate problem. But then if we continue to work out our differences and a better understanding, then I think we engage in the reduction of conventional weapons.

Strategic Arms Control

Q. Mr. President, since we've already touched on the question of nuclear weapons, I wouldn't like to seem pessimistic, but I get the impression that in Moscow there will hardly be an opportunity to sign a treaty about 50-percent reductions of strategic nuclear weapons while observing the ABM treaty. Still, despite that, what are your attitudes about the prospects of concluding such a very, very important treaty for the world?

The President. Well, I still think it can be concluded, but it would be, I think, overly optimistic, with the time limitations, to believe that it could be ready for signature as the INF treaty was here in the previous meeting. But we're going to continue negotiating. It would be nice if we could have achieved a signing ceremony there on this visit, but this treaty is far more technical and complicated than the treaty we did sign. And so, the experts on both sides who have been working on this in Geneva have not been able to make the progress that was made in the earlier treaty. But they're going to continue, I'm sure. And I think that perhaps we can advance it in our conversations, discussion, in Moscow on this. But we must—the idea is to continue until we have the treaty that is correct, and not simply try to meet a date and sign a treaty that might not be all that we would desire.

Q. But you think that the treaty will be signed—such a treaty will be signed?

The President. Yes, I do. I don't think either of us have gone this far with the idea that it wasn't a good idea.

Soviet-U.S. Relations

Q. Mr. President, I'd like to ask you a sort of personal question. Could you, in the beginning of your Presidency, when you just came into the Oval Office, could you have imagined the possibility of your upcoming visit to Moscow?

The President. Probably not, because very frankly, I have to say I think there is a difference between this General Secretary and other leaders of your country that I had met with in the past. I don't think they had any dreams of *perestroika.* And yet, I felt that we had to exist in the world together. Our systems are different, we're going to be competitive in a number of ways, and that'll continue, but we can be competitive without being hostile to the point of conflict with each other. And I think this is what we're aiming at. And no, I could not have foreseen your present leader.

Q. Well, new times bear new leaders, bring about new leaders.

The President. Yes.

Q. So, we can conclude that you think that your successor will continue stabilizing Soviet-American relations, that there won't be a pause in the dialog between our countries?

The President. Well, if the next President is the President I would like to see there, the present Vice President, I know he would continue on this track. But I think that our people want this. I have had a visit, just the other day, here in the White House with 78 young teenagers, and half of them were from the Soviet Union and half were students of ours. They had been holding a conference in Finland, then in Moscow, and now here in the United States. And you looked out at those young people and you couldn't say, well, those are Russians and those are Americans. You just saw young people who had learned to know each other, exchange ideas, get acquainted. And I found myself saying to them, if all the young people of the world could get to know each other, there'd never be another war.

Soviet Expansionism

Q. Mr. President, I can't help but ask you a question which is very interesting to Soviet people, many ordinary people in our country. You, in your speeches, many times have quoted the works of Lenin; you've made reference to his works; you quoted him about expansionistic aims of Soviet Communists. Soviet specialists, insofar as I know, in the U.S. press and people who work in the Library of Congress have studied all of the compositions of Lenin's, and they haven't found one similar quotation or anything that's even close to some of those quotations. So, I would like to ask you what works of Lenin did you read, and where were those quotations that you used taken from?

The President. Oh, my. I don't think I could recall and specify here and there. But I'm old enough to have had a great interest in the Soviet Union, and I know that in the things I studied in college, when I was getting my own degree in economics and sociology, that the declarations of Karl Marx, for example, that Karl Marx said your system, communism, could only succeed when the whole world had become Communist. And so, the goal had to be the one-world Communist state.

Now, as I say, I can't recall all of the sources from which I gleaned this, and maybe some things have been interpreted differently as in modern versions, but I know that Lenin expounded on that and said that that must be the goal. But I also know—and this didn't require reading Lenin—that every leader, every General Secretary but the present one had, in appearances before the Soviet Congress, reiterated their allegiance to that Marxian theory that the goal was a one-world Communist state. This man has not said that. So, I wasn't making anything up; these were the things we were told. For example, here in our government, we knew that Lenin had expressed a part of the plan that involved Latin America and so forth. And the one line that sounded very ominous to us was when he said that the last bastion of capitalism, the United States, would not have to be taken; it would fall into their outstretched hand like overripe fruit.

Q. I'd like to say that, as it says in the Bible, everybody wants to go to paradise, but nobody is proposing to do that—anything for us or to hurry up the process. Everything has to go by in its own time; that's our point of view.

The President. Well, wouldn't you think, though, that these two systems obviously were competitive in the world with each other in the economic situation—industry and so forth, the difference between private ownership and government ownership of the sources of material, industry and so forth, agriculture—well, wouldn't you think that it would make the most sense to compete legitimately, as business firms compete with each other, and see which does the better job?

Q. Without question, when we talk about the fact that we think that sooner or later that the world is going to come to socialism, we're just talking about a historic process. Every country has to decide for itself. And we think that capitalist countries and socialist countries have to coexist peacefully on our very small planet and to cooperate with each other.

The President. Well, yes, we believe that also. But there was a time when, as I say, we were faced with declarations of the need to take over and expand. And on the part of, in this instance, of the communist philosophy, I think, as I've said earlier here, just this normal competition and find out which system is best. And then we have this one thing in which possibly we differ. And that is that we believe the people of a country have the right to determine what form of government they'll have. You have a constitution; we have a constitution. The difference between our two constitutions is very simple; it's contained in three words. Both of the constitutions announce things for the people's benefit and so forth. Your constitution says, these are the privileges, rights that the government provides for the people. Our constitution says, we the people will allow the government to do the following things. And the government can do nothing that is not prescribed by the people in that constitution. And so, where we run into conflicts sometimes in countries where there's a stirring and a division in trying to determine a government, our view is, the people must have the right to say this is the government we want. It must not be imposed on them.

Nicaragua

Q. Mr. President, in that connection I'd like to say that democracy is, of course, a great goal for all peoples. But if you take a specific situation now—social opinion in the United States, the polls and Congress and so forth—Congress is against actions that are being taken in Nicaragua. And despite that, the administration is acting in a somewhat different fashion, despite some of the opinions expressed in Congress.

The President. Yes. Of course, you must remember that each Congressman is elected only by a district—his congressional district. This is the only job in our country that is elected by all of the people. And the responsibility that the people have laid on this office in the Constitution is that the President is responsible for our national security, and that is a duty he cannot shirk. And so, he is the final word as to what is essential to that national security. You were going to say something.

U.S. Human Rights

Q. Yes, I wanted to say, going back to our conversation about coexistence—the coexistence of capitalist and socialist governments—I wanted to remind you that Lenin, our first leader—it was his idea to have peaceful coexistence. That was his idea.

But I'd like to talk about another question. In your statements, in your speeches, you frequently touch a very important question: the human rights question. As a rule, you talk about the human rights situations in other countries. I'd like today to ask you—you, as the President of the United States, as a citizen of the United States—are you satisfied with the situation concerning human rights in your own country?

The President. Well, I don't think—you'll never be completely satisfied. Individuals are going to have prejudice and so forth. But we have laws in our country that make it law-breaking to implement those prejudices and to try to do things unjustly to other people.

You have to remember one great difference about our country. A man put it to me in a letter once. And that is that you could leave here and go to France to live, but you could not become a Frenchman; or you could go to live in Germany or Turkey or—name any country—you could not become one of them; this is the only country in the world in which anyone from any corner of the world can come here and become an American, because that's our history. We came from every corner of the world. If you meet with a group of Americans—if we went around this room for the Americans present and asked them their background, their ancestry and so forth, you'd have quite a collection. As a matter of fact, my own background, going back to grandparents and great-grandparents, covers four different countries—but here in this melting pot. So, the result is that the people that came here came not only with the desire for freedom, but they also brought with them many of the prejudices that existed because of national differences between various countries. And this is something we've had to guard against.

So, the human rights here are protected. People may have and do have—there are people who have a prejudice against someone of another faith, someone of another background or race. But if they do anything to hurt that person because of that prejudice, the law takes care of them.

Q. I think that in terms of human rights, lately, a lot has been said. Therefore, I'd like to ask you a question and return to your upcoming visit to Moscow. Mr. President, I don't want to try and pry any secrets out of you, but could we find out what you're taking to Moscow in your diplomatic briefcase, so to speak, and what you hope to bring back from there? [*Laughter*]

The President. Well, as I said earlier, the same things that we've talked about before and tried to come together in a meeting of the minds—basically, those four major areas. Yes, that's what we'll talk about.

Now, I recognize that one country can't dictate to another as to how they must run their own affairs, and maybe some of the things that we'll talk about are things that I believe maybe we could be—based on our own experience—be helpful; for example, among human rights. I was quite interested recently when the General Secretary, meeting with the leaders of your Orthodox Church, lessened some of the restrictions that government had imposed on the practice of that religion. Well, I've wondered if a further expansion of that—you see, our country came into being because people were being denied, in other countries, the right to worship God as they saw fit. And so, they left those countries and came to this new land as pioneers in order to worship. Well, I've just wondered if there isn't a field there in your own country for more openness and the allowing of people to practice religion in the ways they chose. And here we call it separation of church and state. The government cannot deny people the right to worship, but by the same token, the churches cannot impose on government their beliefs.

Q. I think that really the question of human rights deserves lots of discussion. In that connection, I'd like to ask you, recently in Washington—I read about this in the U.S. press—General Stroessner was here in the United States. He's a dictator from Paraguay. When you meet with the Soviet leaders—or met with them in Geneva and Reykjavik and Washington, you always touched on the question of human rights. That's probably the right thing. Do you talk about that question with General Stroessner, with the leaders of Chile, South Korea, South Africa? In your conversations, do you discuss with them the question of human rights?

The President. Oh, yes, there's no question but that we believe in our getting along with these other countries, that this is an issue, for one reason, because of the background of all of our people. Government is influenced by public opinion. We are supposed—as you mentioned earlier, we are supposed to do in the Congress and here in this office basically what—meet the needs of the people, what the people want. And so, when we are seeking to be neighbors and friends of another country and that country is jailing people for just their expression of political difference or wanting to practice religion and things of that kind—we have a great many people whose heritage is in those countries. And you have to remember that even though we're all Americans—a man doesn't give up love for his mother because he's taken a wife. And so, the people in our country all still feel a kind of heritage and relationship with the countries of their ancestry, or maybe their own if they're new immigrants who are here in the country.

One out of eight of our people have our background in your area. And those people can rise up and oppose us in some agreement that we may want to make of friendship if they feel that the country of their ancestry is being unfair in denying what they consider a human right. Now, maybe your country, you don't place that much importance on public opinion, but here in our system, it is the very basis of our system. And so, we can get along and make treaties much better with each other as governments if our people are not rebellious about something that your government is doing to what they consider their ancestry.

President's Memoirs

Q. Soon you'll be in Moscow, and I think that you'll have the opportunity to get acquainted with the influence of public opinion in the U.S.S.R. and about freedom of religion in the U.S.S.R. Excuse me, I'd like—our time is sort of running out, and in conclusion, I'd like to ask you a personal question, Mr. President. The majority of Presidents in this country, when they left office, write memoirs. Are you getting ready to write your memoirs when you leave office, and if so, when are we going to get a chance to read your memoirs?

The President. Well, I've been thinking very seriously about writing a book. In view of the fact that several people who have left government have written some books, I think maybe I better straighten out the record and tell things as they really are. And so, it's possible that I will. But remember, there's another thing in our country that has become a tradition: People, not government, voluntarily provide money and funds and build what is called a Presidential library and museum, and this is happening with me. This is going forward. There is a group in the country; they've raised the millions of dollars. In California will be built this structure. Now, in that building will be the millions of papers from this administration. They will be open; scholars can come and study them and research and so forth. And there will be also many things that will be of interest to the people—memorabilia that we've accumulated here. And this has happened with all the Presidents in the recent years. So there, too, will be a record that is open for public view. But I'll probably get around to writing a book. I don't look forward to it. I wrote a book once and found it was quite a chore.

Q. Since time is up, more or less, I'd like to thank you for this interview, and I'd like to wish you huge success in your upcoming mission. Thank you, Mr. President.

Soviet Women

The President. Well, thank you very much. May I just say one thing also—in going to your country, and I would relish the opportunity, if I could, to say a few words here—that is never discussed very much. I have a great admiration for the women of the Soviet Union, particularly in the Russian area. From the outside looking in, they seem to be a great bulwark of strength and solidity in the maintaining of the home and the things that they stand for—the standing in lines to bring home what is necessary for the family and all of that. And I just wonder if they're getting the credit within your country that I think they deserve.

Q. They deserve it. They don't just stand in lines, but the majority of them work together with men. They teach, they take care of children, they work in administrative posts, and so forth. And I hope that with your own eyes you will be able to see all of that when you come to our country.

The President. Well, you've said it better than I did, but, yes, I recognize all of those things and just wondered if they get the recognition they deserve within their country.

Q. Once again, thank you very much, Mr. President, for this very interesting interview.

The President. Well, I'm pleased, and I welcome you and enjoyed it very much. And I appreciate greatly the opportunity to speak to your people.

Q. Thank you. It is not our fault; the people here are guilty. They were telling us all the time that we should finish up, but I guess we ran over our schedule.

The President. Yes.

Q. Tell the President there's an interpretation coming through, so I guess you understood what I said.

The President. Yes.

Q. But I want to say to you that this interview will be broadcast on the eve of your arrival—I think the 27th of May. I have the impression that you'll be able to see it, because the 27th, I think, you're going to be in Helsinki, and you can see Soviet television in Finland very well. And it's going to be on one of our channels. There are going to be about 200 million Soviets that will see this interview, and it will be broadcast all over Eastern Europe, as well. So, everything that you said will reach all the Soviet people, and I think it will be a good beginning for your visit to the Soviet Union.

The President. Well, thank you. I appreciate this very much. And we'll look forward to it. If they don't have me scheduled for something in Helsinki, I'll see it.

Q. In conclusion, I would like one personal memory to share with you. Please don't think this is some sort of compliment, but in my office in Moscow there are a number of photographs hanging on the wall, and among them is a photograph where I was photographed with the Governor of California, Mr. Ronald Reagan, in Sacramento. It is a very precious souvenir to me. I treasure it very much. A lot of time has gone by since then, but I don't see that you've changed much. I think that you have some kind of recipe against the course of time somehow.

The President. Well, for heaven sakes! Well, thank you very much. But that was the meeting then with a group of you—a group of press came to Sacramento and met in the Cabinet Room with me, and then later we were all at our home.

Q. Yes, yes, that's right.

The President. Yes, I remember that.

Q. Yes, that was the meeting. And at that time, I asked you the same thing that I am going to ask you now, that the group should go over to the side and that you and I be photographed together. And then I will have this picture hanging on this wall, too.

The President. Alright. Okay.

Q. Thank you.

Note: The interview began at 11:36 a.m. in the Oval Office at the White House and was released by the Office of the Press Secretary on May 28.

Radio Address to the Nation on the Soviet-United States Summit Meeting in Moscow
May 28, 1988

My fellow Americans:

As this pretaped broadcast reaches you, I'm in Helsinki, Finland, on my way to the Soviet Union, where I arrive on Sunday. When I meet in the coming days with Soviet General Secretary Gorbachev, it will be our fourth set of face-to-face talks in 3 years. Through our conversations, U.S.-Soviet relations have moved forward on the basis of frankness and realism. This relationship has not rested on any single issue, but has been built on a sturdy four-part agenda that includes human rights, regional conflicts, arms reduction, and bilateral exchanges. What has been achieved in this brief span of time offers great hope for a brighter future and a safer world.

Through Western firmness and resolve, we concluded the historic INF treaty that provides for the global elimination of an entire class of U.S. and Soviet intermediate-range nuclear missiles. Soviet armed forces are now withdrawing from Afghanistan, an historic event that should lead finally to peace, self-determination, and healing for that long-suffering people and to an independent and undivided Afghan nation.

It is also encouraging to hear General Secretary Gorbachev speak forthrightly about *glasnost* and *perestroika*—openness and restructuring in the Soviet Union—words that to Western ears have a particularly welcome sound. And since he began his campaign, we can list developments that the free world heartily applauds. We've seen many well-known prisoners of conscience released from harsh labor camps or strict internal exile, courageous people like Josif Begun and Andrei Sakharov. Soviet authorities have permitted the publication of books like "Dr. Zhivago" and the distribution of movies such as "Repentance" that are critical of aspects of the Soviet past and present. Greater emigration has been allowed. Greater dissent is being tolerated. And recently, General Secretary Gorbachev has promised to grant a measure of religious freedom to the peoples of the Soviet Union.

All this is new and good, but at the same time, there's another list that the West cannot ignore. While there are improvements, the basic structure of the system has not changed in the Soviet Union or in Eastern Europe, and there remain significant violations of human rights and freedoms. In Asia, Africa, and Central America, unpopular regimes use Soviet arms to oppress their own people and commit aggression against neighboring states. These regional conflicts extract a terrible toll of suffering and threaten to draw the United States and the Soviet Union into direct confrontation.

These and related concerns will be at the top of my agenda in the days ahead. I shall say, among other things, that the Soviet Union should fully honor the Helsinki accords. In view of that document, signed in Helsinki in 1975, it is difficult to understand why almost 13 years later cases of divided families and blocked marriages should remain on the East-West agenda or why Soviet citizens who wish by right to emigrate should not be able to do so. And there are other issues: the recognition of those who wish to practice their religious beliefs and the release of all prisoners of conscience.

In working for a safer world and a brighter future for all people, we know arms agreements alone will not make the world safer; we must also reduce the reasons for having arms. As I said to General Secretary Gorbachev when we first met in 1985, we do not mistrust each other because we're armed; we're armed because we mistrust each other. History has taught us that it is not weapons that cause war but the nature and conduct of the Governments that wield the weapons. So, when we encourage Soviet reforms, it is with the knowledge that democracy not only guarantees human rights but also helps prevent war and, in truth, is a form of arms control. So, really, our whole agenda has one purpose: to protect peace, freedom, and life itself.

We would like to see positive changes in the U.S.S.R. institutionalized so that they'll become lasting features of Soviet society. And I would like to see more Soviet young people come here to experience and learn from our society. And that's why we're ready to work with the Soviets, to praise and criticize and work for greater contact and for change because that is the path to lasting peace, greater freedom, and a safer world.

I'm grateful for your prayers and support as I embark on this journey. Until next week, thanks for listening, and God bless you.

Note: The President's address was recorded on May 23 in the Library at the White House for broadcast on May 28.

Remarks at the Opening Ceremony of the Soviet-United States Summit Meeting in Moscow
May 29, 1988

The General Secretary. Esteemed Mr. Ronald Reagan, President of the United States of America; esteemed Mrs. Nancy Reagan: On behalf of the people and Government of the Soviet Union, I extend to you my sincere greetings on the occasion of your visit. Welcome!

It is now almost 6 months since our meeting in Washington, which went down in history as a major milestone in Soviet-American and in international relations. Now, on this return trip, you, Mr. President, have traversed the great distance that lies between our two capitals to continue our political dialog. This is a fact we duly appreciate. As this is our fourth meeting, we can already make some meaningful assessments. As we see it, long-held dislikes have been weakened; habitual stereotypes stemming from enemy images have been shaken loose. The human features of the other nation are now more clearly visible. This in itself is important, for at the turn of the two millenniums, history has objectively bound our two countries by a common responsibility for the destinies of mankind. The peoples of the world and, in the first place, the Soviet and the American people welcome the emerging positive changes in our relationship and hope that your visit and talks here will be productive, providing a fresh impetus in all areas of dialog and interaction between our two great nations.

You and I are conscious of our two peoples' longing for mutual understanding, cooperation, and a safe and stable world. This makes it incumbent upon us to discuss constructively the main aspects of disarmament: the set of issues related to 50-percent cuts in strategic offensive arms, while preserving the 1972 ABM treaty; problems of eliminating chemical weapons; reductions in armed forces and conventional armaments in Europe; cessation of nuclear testing. The world is also looking to us, Mr. President, for responsible judgments on other complex issues of today, such as the settlement of regional conflicts; improving international economic relations; promoting development; overcoming backwardness, poverty, and mass diseases; and humanitarian problems.

And of course, we shall discuss bilateral relations. Our previous meetings have shown that constructive Soviet-U.S. relations are possible. The treaty on intermediate and shorter range missiles is the most impressive symbol of that. But even more complex and important tasks lie ahead. And so, Mr. President, you and I still have a lot of work to do. And it is good when there is a lot of work to be done and people need that work. We are ready to do our utmost in these coming days in Moscow.

Mr. President, you and Mrs. Reagan are here on your first visit to the Soviet Union, a country which you have so often mentioned in your public statements. Aware of your interest in Russian proverbs, let me add another one to your collection: "It is better to see once than to hear a hundred times." Let me assure you that you can look forward to hospitality, warmth, and good will. You will have many meetings with Soviet people. They have a centuries-old history behind them. They love their land and take pride in their accomplishments. They resent things that are presently standing in their way, and they are heatedly discussing how their country can best progress. They are full of plans for the future.

Being ardent patriots, Soviet people are open to friendship and cooperation with all nations. They harbor sincere respect for the American people and want good relations with your country. Here, within the walls of the ancient Kremlin, where one feels the touch of history, people are moved to reflect over the diversity and greatness of human civilization. So, may this give greater historical depth to the Soviet-American talks to be held here, infusing them with a sense of mankind's shared destinies. Once again, I bid you welcome.

The President. Mr. General Secretary, Mrs. Gorbachev: Mr. General Secretary, thank you for those kind words of welcome. We've traveled a long road together to reach this moment—from our first meeting in Geneva in November, 1985, when I invited you to visit me in Washington and you invited me to Moscow. It was cold that day in Geneva, and even colder in Reykjavik when we met the following year to work on the preparations for our exchange of visits. We've faced great obstacles; but by the time of your visit to Washington last December, although we still had to grapple with difficult issues, we had achieved impressive progress in all the areas of our common agenda—human rights, regional issues, arms reduction, and our bilateral relations.

We signed a treaty that will reduce the level of nuclear arms for the first time in history by eliminating an entire class of U.S. and Soviet independent [intermediate-] range missiles. We agreed on the main points of a treaty that will cut in half our arsenals of strategic offensive nuclear arms. We agreed to conduct a joint experiment that would allow us to develop effective ways to verify limits on nuclear testing. We held full and frank discussions that planted the seeds for future progress.

It is almost summer; and some of those seeds are beginning to bear fruit, thanks to the hard work we have both done since our last meeting, including monthly meetings by our Foreign Ministers and the first meeting of our Defense Ministers. We have signed the Geneva accords, providing for the withdrawal of all Soviet troops from Afghanistan, and the first withdrawals have begun. We and our allies have completed technical arrangements necessary to begin implementing the INF treaty as soon as it enters into force. For the next major step in arms control, reductions in U.S. and Soviet strategic offensive arsenals, our negotiators in Geneva have produced hundreds of pages of joint, draft treaty text recording our areas of agreement, as well as those issues yet to be resolved. Our new nuclear risk reduction centers have begun their transmissions of routine notifications to reduce the risk of conflict. Our scientists are installing the equipment for our joint experiment to verify limits on nuclear testing. Our experts have held broad-ranging discussions on human rights, and important steps have been taken in that area. We have greatly expanded our bilateral exchanges since we signed our agreement in 1985. I hope you'll agree with me that more of our young people need to participate in these exchanges, which can do so much to lay the basis for greater mutual understanding in the next generation.

I could go on; the list of accomplishments goes far beyond what many anticipated. But I think the message is clear: Despite clear and fundamental differences, and despite the inevitable frustrations that we have encountered, our work has begun to produce results. In the past, Mr. General Secretary, you've taken note of my liking for Russian proverbs. And in order not to disappoint anyone on this visit, I thought I would mention a literary saying from your past, another example of your people's succinct wisdom: *Rodilsiya ne toropilsiya*—It was born, it wasn't rushed.

Mr. General Secretary, we did not rush. We have taken our work step by step. And I have come here to continue that work. We both know it will not be easy. We both know that there are tremendous hurdles yet to be overcome. But we also know that it can be done because we share a common goal: strengthening the framework we have already begun to build for a relationship that we can sustain over the long term, a relationship that will bring genuine benefits to our own peoples and to the world.

Thank you, and God bless you.

Note: The General Secretary spoke at 2:55 p.m. in St. George's Hall at the Grand Kremlin Palace. The President spoke in English, and the General Secretary spoke in Russian. Their remarks were translated by interpreters.

Remarks to Religious Leaders at the Danilov Monastery in Moscow
May 30, 1988

It's a very great pleasure to visit this beautiful monastery and to have a chance to meet some of the people who have helped make its return to the Russian Orthodox Church a reality. I am also addressing in spirit the 35 million believers whose personal contributions made this magnificent restoration possible.

It's been said that an icon is a window between heaven and Earth through which the believing eye can peer into the beyond. One cannot look at the magnificent icons created, and recreated here under the direction of Father Zinon, without experiencing the deep faith that lives in the hearts of the people of this land. Like the saints and martyrs depicted in these icons, the faith of your people has been tested and tempered in the crucible of hardship. But in that suffering, it has grown strong, ready now to embrace with new hope the beginnings of a second Christian millennium.

We in our country share this hope for a new age of religious freedom in the Soviet Union. We share the hope that this monastery is not an end in itself but the symbol of a new policy of religious tolerance that will extend to all peoples of all faiths. We pray that the return of this monastery signals a willingness to return to believers the thousands of other houses of worship which are now closed, boarded up, or used for secular purposes.

There are many ties of faith that bind your country and mine. We have in America many churches, many creeds, that feel a special kinship with their fellow believers here—Protestant, Catholic, Jewish, Orthodox, and Islamic. They are united with believers in this country in many ways, especially in prayer. Our people feel it keenly when religious freedom is denied to anyone anywhere and hope with you that soon all the many Soviet religious communities that are now prevented from registering, or are banned altogether, including the Ukrainian Catholic and Orthodox Churches, will soon be able to practice their religion freely and openly and instruct their children in and outside the home in the fundamentals of their faith. We don't know if this first thaw will be followed by a resurgent spring of religious liberty—we don't know, but we may hope. We may hope that *perestroika* will be accompanied by a deeper restructuring, a deeper conversion, a *mentanoya*, a change in heart, and that *glasnost*, which means giving voice, will also let loose a new chorus of belief, singing praise to the God that gave us life.

There is a beautiful passage that I'd just like to read, if I may. It's from one of this country's great writers and believers, Aleksandr Solzhenitsyn, about the faith that is as elemental to this land as the dark and fertile soil. He wrote: "When you travel the byroads of central Russia, you begin to understand the secret of the pacifying Russian countryside. It is in the churches. They lift their belltowers—graceful, shapely, all different—high over mundane timber and thatch. From villages that are cut off and invisible to each other, they soar to the same heaven. People who are always selfish and often unkind—but the evening chimes used to ring out, floating over the villages, fields, and woods, reminding men that they must abandon trivial concerns of this world and give time and thought to eternity."

In our prayers we may keep that image in mind: the thought that the bells may ring again, sounding throughout Moscow and across the countryside, clamoring for joy in their new-found freedom. Well, I've talked long enough. I'm sure you have many questions and many things on your minds, and I'm anxious to hear what you have to say.

Note: The President spoke at 2:35 p.m. in the reception room at the Father Superior's residence. Prior to his remarks, the President viewed restored icons at the monastery and discussed restoration techniques.

Remarks to Soviet Dissidents at Spaso House in Moscow
May 30, 1988

Well, thank you all, and welcome to Spaso House. After the discussions we've just had I thought it might be appropriate for me to begin by letting you know why I so wanted this meeting to take place. You see, I wanted to convey to you that you have the prayers and support of the American people, indeed of people throughout the world. I wanted to convey this support to you that you might in turn convey it to others so that all those working for human rights throughout this vast land, from the Urals to Kamchatka, from the Laptev Sea to the Caspian, might be encouraged and take heart.

In one capacity, of course, I speak as a

head of government. The United States views human rights as fundamental, absolutely fundamental to our relationship with the Soviet Union and all nations. From the outset of our administration, we've stressed that an essential element in improving relations between the United States and the Soviet Union is human rights and Soviet compliance with international covenants on human rights. There have been hopeful signs; indeed, I believe this a hopeful time for your nation.

Over the past 3 years more than 300 political and religious prisoners have been released from labor camps. Fewer dissidents and believers have been put in prisons and mental hospitals. And in recent months, more people have been permitted to emigrate or reunite with their families. The United States applauds these changes, yet the basic standards that the Soviet Union agreed to almost 13 years ago in the Helsinki accords, or a generation ago in the Universal Declaration of Human Rights, still need to be met. If I may, I'd like to share with you the main aims of our human rights agenda during this summit meeting here in Moscow.

Freedom of religion—in the words of the Universal Declaration of Human Rights, "Everyone has the right to freedom of thought, conscience, and religion." I'm hopeful the Soviet Government will permit all the peoples of the Soviet Union to worship their creator as they themselves see fit, in liberty.

Freedom of speech—again in the words of the Universal Declaration of Human Rights, "Everyone has the right to freedom of opinion and expression." It is my fervent hope for you and your country that there will soon come a day when no one need fear prison for offenses that involve nothing more than the spoken or written word.

Freedom of travel—I've told the General Secretary how heartened we are that during the past year the number of those permitted to emigrate has risen. We're encouraged as well that the number of those permitted to leave for short trips, often family visits, has gone up. And yet the words of the Universal Declaration go beyond these steps: "Everyone has the right to leave any country, including his own, and to return to his own country." It is our hope that soon there will be complete freedom of travel.

In particular, I've noted in my talks here the many who have been denied the right to emigrate on the grounds that they held secret knowledge, even though their secret work had ended years before and their so-called secrets had long since become either public knowledge or obsolete. Such cases must be rationally reviewed.

And finally, institutional changes to make progress permanent. I've come to Moscow with this human rights agenda because, as I suggested, it is our belief that this is a moment of hope. The new Soviet leaders appear to grasp the connection between certain freedoms and economic growth. The freedom to keep the fruits of one's own labor, for example, is a freedom that the present reforms seem to be enlarging. We hope that one freedom will lead to another and another; that the Soviet Government will understand that it is the individual who is always the source of economic creativity, the inquiring mind that produces a technical breakthrough, the imagination that conceives of new products and markets; and that in order for the individual to create, he must have a sense of just that—his own individuality, his own self-worth. He must sense that others respect him and, yes, that his nation respects him—respects him enough to grant him all his human rights. This, as I said, is our hope; yet whatever the future may bring, the commitment of the United States will nevertheless remain unshakable on human rights. On the fundamental dignity of the human person, there can be no relenting, for now we must work for more, always more.

And here I would like to speak to you not as a head of government but as a man, a fellow human being. I came here hoping to do what I could to give you strength. Yet I already know it is you who have strengthened me, you who have given me a message to carry back. While we press for human rights through diplomatic channels, you press with your very lives, day in, day out, year after year, risking your jobs, your homes, your all.

If I may, I want to give you one thought

from my heart. Coming here, being with you, looking into your faces, I have to believe that the history of this troubled century will indeed be redeemed in the eyes of God and man, and that freedom will truly come to all. For what injustice can withstand your strength, and what can conquer your prayers? And so, I say with Pushkin: "It's time my friend, it's time. The heart begs for peace, the days fly past, it's time, my friend, it's time."

Could I play a little trick on you and say something that isn't written here? Sometimes when I'm faced with an unbeliever, an atheist, I am tempted to invite him to the greatest gourmet dinner that one could ever serve and, when we finished eating that magnificent dinner, to ask him if he believes there's a cook. Thank you all, and God bless you.

Note: The President spoke at 4:29 p.m. in the ballroom at the U.S. Ambassador's residence.

Toasts of the President and General Secretary Gorbachev of the Soviet Union at the State Dinner in Moscow
May 30, 1988

The General Secretary. Esteemed Mr. President, esteemed Mrs. Reagan, ladies and gentlemen, comrades, I welcome you in the Moscow Kremlin. For five centuries, it has been the site of events that constituted milestones in the life of our state. Decisions crucial to the fate of our nation were made here. The very environment around us is a call for responsibility to our times and contemporaries, to the present and to the future.

It is here that we wish to emphasize the importance of the newly discovered truth that it is no longer possible to settle international disputes by force of arms. Our awareness of the realities of the present-day world has led us to that conclusion. I like the notion of realism, and I also like the fact that you, Mr. President, have lately been uttering it more and more often.

Normal and, indeed, durable Soviet-American relations, which so powerfully affect the world's political climate, are only conceivable within the framework of realism. Thanks to realism, for all our differences, we have succeeded in arriving at a joint conclusion which, though very simple, is of historic importance: A nuclear war cannot be won and must never be fought. Other conclusions follow with inexorable logic. One of them is whether there is any need for weaponry which cannot be used without destroying ourselves and, indeed, all of mankind. I believe the realization of this became Reykjavik's pivotal idea.

Our Warsaw treaty allies firmly adhere to this position. This is our powerful support in all matters related to nuclear disarmament. They have given the Soviet leadership a clear mandate to negotiate radical nuclear arms limitations and reductions with the United States. My talks with leaders of Socialist countries and with authoritative representatives of other nations make it clear to me that there is a common desire to overcome military confrontation and to end the race in both nuclear and conventional arms.

To this, it should be added that a realistic approach is making a way for itself in all directions and on all continents. And the idea of resolving today's problems solely by political means is gaining increasing authority. There is an ever-broadening desire of the most diverse political and social forces for dialog, for exchanges, for better knowledge of each other, and for mutual understanding. If this is indeed so, if this is the will of the peoples, an effort is needed to ensure that the stocks of the ferment of realistic policies keep growing and never run out. For that, it is essential to understand each other better, to take into account the specific features of life in various countries, the historical conditions that shape them, and the choice made by their peoples.

I recall the words you once spoke, Mr. President, and I quote: "The only way to resolve differences is to understand them." How very true. Let me just add that seeking to resolve differences should not mean an end to being different. The diversity of the world is a powerful wellspring of mutual enrichment, both spiritual and material.

Ladies and gentlemen, comrades, the word *perestroika* does not sound anachronistic, even within these ancient walls, for renewal of society, humanization of life, and elevated ideals are—at all times and everywhere—in the interests of the people and of each individual. And when this happens, especially in a great country, it is important to understand the meaning of what it is going through. It is this desire to understand the Soviet Union that we are now seeing abroad. And we regard this as a good sign because we do want to be understood correctly. This is also important for civilized international relations. Everyone who wants to do business with us will find it useful to know how Soviet people see themselves.

We see ourselves even more convinced that our Socialist choice was correct, and we cannot conceive of our country developing without socialism—based on any other fundamental values. Our program is more democracy, more *glasnost,* more social justice with full prosperity and high moral standards. Our goal is maximum freedom for man, for the individual, and for society. Internationally, we see ourselves as part of an integral civilization, where each has the right to a social and political choice, to a worthy and equal place within the community of nations.

On issues of peace and progress, we believe in the primacy of universal human values and regard the preservation of peace as the top priority. And that is why we advocate the establishment of a comprehensive system of international security as a condition for the survival of mankind. Linked with this is also our desire to revive and enhance the role of the United Nations on the basis of the original goals, which the Soviet Union and the United States, together with their allies, enshrined in the charter of that organization. Its very name is symbolic: the United Nations—united in their determination to prevent new tragedies of war, to banish war from international relations, and to affirm just principles securing a worthy life for any nation, whether large or small, strong or weak, rich or poor.

We want to build contacts among people in all forums, to expand and improve the quality of information, and to develop ties in the spheres of science, culture, education, sports, and any other human endeavor. But this should be done without interfering in domestic affairs, without sermonizing or imposing one's views and ways, without turning family or personal problems into a pretext for confrontation between states. In short, our time offers great scope for action in the humanitarian field. Nations should understand each other better, know the truth about each other, and free themselves from bias and prejudice.

As far as we know, most Americans, just like us, want to get rid of the demon of nuclear war; but they, just like us, just like all people on Earth, are becoming increasingly concerned over the risk of environmental disaster. Such a risk can only be averted if we act together. Increasingly urgent is the truly global problem of the economic state of the world—in the North and South, in the West and East of this planet. The economic foundation of civilization will be destroyed unless a way is found to put an end to the squandering of funds and resources for war and destruction, unless the problem of debt is settled and world finances are stabilized, unless the world market becomes truly worldwide by incorporating all states and nations on an equal footing.

It is across this spectrum of issues that we approach international affairs and, of course, our relations with the United States of America. We are motivated by an awareness of the realities and imperatives of the nuclear and space age, the age of sweeping technological revolution when the human race has turned out to be both omnipotent and mortal. It was this awareness that engendered the new thinking, which has made possible a conceptual and practical breakthrough in relations between us as well.

Mr. President, this meeting, while taking stock of a fundamentally important period in Soviet-American relations, has to consolidate our achievements and give new impetus for the future. Never before have nuclear missiles been destroyed. Now we have an unprecedented treaty, and our two countries will be performing for the first time ever this overture of nuclear disarmament. The performance has to be flawless.

The Soviet Union and the United States are acting as guarantors of the Afghan political settlement. This, too, is a precedent of tremendous importance. As guarantors, our two countries face a very responsible period, and we hope they both will go through it in a befitting manner. The whole world is watching to see how we are going to act in this situation.

Our main task continues to be the working out of an agreement on 50-percent reductions in strategic offensive arms while observing the ABM treaty. In our talks today, you and I devoted a lot of attention, and with good cause, to discussing the entire range of these problems. Mr. President, we are expected to ensure that the Moscow summit open up new horizons in the Soviet-American dialog, in relations between the U.S.S.R. and the U.S., for the benefit of our two nations and the entire world. This is worth any effort and any amount of good will.

To cooperation between the Soviet Union and the United States of America, to their better mutual knowledge and mutual understanding. I wish good health and happiness to you, Mr. President, to Mrs. Nancy Reagan, and to all our distinguished guests.

The President. Mr. General Secretary, I want to thank you again for the hospitality that we've encountered this evening and at every turn since our arrival in Moscow. We appreciate deeply the personal effort that you, Mrs. Gorbachev, and all of your associates have expended on our behalf.

Today has been a busy day. I want to thank you for the opportunity to meet with so many divergent members of Soviet society. As you know, I traveled to Danilov and met there with the clergy at that ancient monastery, and later in the day had most interesting exchanges with other members of Soviet society at Spaso House. These meetings only confirmed, Mr. General Secretary, the feelings of admiration and warmth that Americans harbor toward the peoples of the Soviet Union. As wartime allies, we came to know you in a special way. But in a broader sense, the American people, like the rest of the world, admire the saga of the peoples of the Soviet Union. The clearing of the forest, the struggle to build a society, the evolution into a modern state, and the struggle against Hitler's armies. There are other ways, too, that we know you: "Happy or sad, my beloved, you are beautiful," says one of your folk songs, "as beautiful as a Russian song, as beautiful as a Russian soul."

As expressed in the great music, architecture, art—we need only look about us this evening—and literature that over many centuries you've given the world, we have beheld the beauty and majesty of your peoples' national experience. And without belittling the serious business before us, all of the fundamental issues that separate our governments, I hope you'll permit me tonight to say that in the eyes of the American people, your people truly are, as the folk song suggests, a people of heart and mind, a people—to use our vernacular—with soul. And that's why we believe there's common ground between our two peoples and why it is our duty to find common ground for our two governments.

Over the next 3 days, General Secretary Gorbachev and I will review what has been accomplished over the past 3 years and what our two nations might accomplish together in the months to come. We have a great deal to discuss on both accounts. What we have achieved is a good beginning. We have taken the first step toward deep reductions of our nuclear arsenals. We have taken the first step toward dealing with the reality that much of the tension and mistrust between our two countries arises from very different concepts of the fundamental rights and role of the individual in society. We have taken the first step to build that network of personal relationships and understanding between societies, between people, that are crucial to dispelling dangerous misconceptions and stereotypes.

These are good first steps, Mr. General

Secretary, and we can both take pride in them, but as I said, they are just a start. Nuclear arsenals remain too large. The fighting continues needlessly, tragically, in too many regions of the globe. The vision of freedom and cooperation enshrined in the Helsinki Final Act remains unrealized. The American and Soviet peoples are getting to know each other better, but not well enough. Mr. General Secretary, you and I are meeting now for the fourth time in 3 years—a good deal more often than our predecessors. And this has allowed our relationship to differ from theirs in more than a quantitative state or sense.

We have established the kind of working relationship I think we both had in mind when we first met in Geneva. We've been candid about our differences, but sincere in sharing a common objective and working hard together to draw closer to it. It's easy to disagree and much harder to find areas where we can agree. We and our two governments have both gotten into the habit of looking for those areas. We found more than we expected. I intend to pursue the search for common ground during the months left to me as President. When I pass the job on to my successor, I intend to tell him it is a search that must be continued. Based on the achievements of the last few years, I will also tell him it is a search that can succeed.

Once again, Mr. General Secretary, I want to extend my thanks for your hospitality. I also hope you'll permit me to mention that, as you have been a gracious host, we've tried to be gracious guests by bringing along some small expressions of our gratitude. There's one gift in particular that I wanted to mention not only in view of my own former profession but because it has, I think, something important to say to us about what is underway this week in Moscow. It is a film, not as well-known as some but an American classic. It is a powerfully acted and directed story of family and romantic love, of devotion to the land and dedication to higher principle. It is also fun, it has humor. There's a renegade goose, a mischievous young boy, a noisy neighbor, a love-struck teenager in love with a gallant soldier, an adolescent struggling for manhood, a loving, highly principled wife, and a gentle but strong father. It's about the good and sometimes difficult things that happen between man and wife, and parent and child. The film also has sweep and majesty and power and pathos. For you see, it takes place against the backdrop of our American epic, the Civil War. And because the family is of the Quaker religion and renounces violence, each of its characters must, in his or her own way, face this war and the moral dilemma it poses. The film shows not just the tragedy of war, but the problems of pacifism, the nobility of patriotism, as well as the love of peace.

I promise not to spoil its outcome for you, but I hope you'll permit me to describe one scene. Just as the invading armies come into southern Indiana, one of our States, the Quaker farmer is approached by two of his neighbors. One is also a Quaker who earlier in the story, when times are peaceful, denounces violence and vows never to lift his hand in anger. But now that the enemy has burned his barn, he's on his way to battle and criticizes his fellow Quaker for not joining him in renouncing his religious beliefs. The other visitor, also on his way to battle, is the intruding but friendly neighbor. Yet it is this neighbor, although a nonbeliever, who says he's proud of the Quaker farmer's decision not to fight. In the face of the tragedy of war, he's grateful, as he says, that somebody's holding out for a better way of settling things.

It seems to me, Mr. General Secretary, that in pursuing these summit meetings we, too, have been holding out for a better way of settling things. And by the way, the film's title is more than a little appropriate. It's called "Friendly Persuasion." So, Mr. General Secretary, allow me to raise a glass to the work that has been done, to the work that remains to be done, and let us also toast the art of friendly persuasion, the hope of peace with freedom, the hope of holding out for a better way of settling things. Thank you, and God bless you.

Note: The General Secretary spoke at 7:37 p.m. in St. Vladimir's Hall at the Grand Kremlin Palace. The President spoke in English, and the General Secretary spoke in Russian. Their remarks were translated by interpreters.

Remarks at a Luncheon Hosted by Artists and Cultural Leaders in Moscow
May 31, 1988

As Henry VIII said to each of his six wives, I won't keep you long. [*Laughter*] But thank you, Vladimir Vasilievich. It's with some humility that I come here today. You here—writers, artists, dramatists, musicians of this vast country—are heirs to the seminal figures in many of the arts as they have developed in the 20th century, Europe and America. I'm thinking of such giants as Kandinski, Stravinsky, Stanislavsky, Dostoyevski, to name a few—men whose vision transformed all of ours.

I've been very impressed with what I've heard just now. For my contribution to this dialog I thought I would deal here briefly with the question whose answer might open up some new insights for all of us. You see, I've been told that many of you were puzzled that a former actor could become the leader of a great nation, particularly the United States. What does acting have to do with politics and statecraft? Whatever possessed the American people to entrust this high office to me? You might feel reassured to know you aren't the first to ask that question. Back in Washington, just about every member of the political opposition has been asking it for the last 8 years, and they're not the first. It's been happening ever since. Almost a quarter of a century ago, I announced that I was going to run for what turned out to be the first public office I ever held, Governor of California. Yes, I had served as president of my union, the Screen Actors Guild. Yes, in that role I'd led a successful strike by the union against the studios. And, yes, I'd campaigned actively for a number of candidates for office, including candidates for President. But I was still known primarily as an actor.

In the movie business, actors often get what we call typecast; that is, the studios come to think of you as playing certain kinds of roles, so those are the kinds of roles they give you. And no matter how hard you try, you just can't get them to think of you in any other way. Well, politics is a little like that, too. So, I've had a lot of time and reason to think about my role not just as a citizen turned politician but as an actor turned politician.

In looking back, I believe that acting did help prepare me for the work I do now. There are two things, two indispensable lessons, that I've taken from my craft into public life. And I hope you won't think it excessively opportune if I use the words of a Soviet filmmaker to explain one of them. He was, after all, one of the world's greatest filmmakers, and so, like so many of your artists, indeed, like so many of you, belongs in a broader sense to all of humanity.

It was during the production of "Ivan the Terrible" when Eisenstein noted that in making a film, or in thinking through any detail of it—which to my mind would include the acting of a part—in his words, "The most important thing is to have the vision. The next is to grasp and hold it. You must see and feel what you are thinking. You must see and grasp it. You must hold and fix it in your memory and senses. And you must do it at once." To grasp and hold a vision, to fix it in your senses—that is the very essence, I believe, of successful leadership not only on the movie set, where I learned about it, but everywhere. And by the way, in my many dealings with him since he became General Secretary, I've found that Mr. Gorbachev has the ability to grasp and hold a vision, and I respect him for that.

The second lesson I carried from acting into public life was more subtle. And let me again refer to a Soviet artist, a poet—again, one of the world's greatest. At the beginning of "Requiem," Anna Akhmatova writes of standing in a line outside a prison when someone in the crowd recognizes her as a well-known poet. She continues, "Then a woman standing behind me, whose lips were blue with cold and who, naturally enough, had never even heard of my name, emerged from that state of torpor common to us all and, putting her lips close to my ear—there everyone spoke in whispers—

asked me, 'And could you describe this?' And I answered her, 'I can.' Then something vaguely like a smile flashed across what once had been her face."

That exchange—"Can you describe this?" "I can"—is at the heart of acting as it is of poetry and of so many of the arts. You get inside a character, a place, and a moment. You come to know the character in that instant not as an abstraction, one of the people, one of the masses, but as a particular person—yearning, hoping, fearing, loving—a face, even what had once been a face, apart from all others; and you convey that knowledge. You describe it, you describe the face. Pretty soon, at least for me, it becomes harder and harder to force any member of humanity into a straitjacket, into some rigid form in which you all expect to fit. In acting, even as you develop an appreciation for what we call the dramatic, you become in a more intimate way less taken with superficial pomp and circumstance, more attentive to the core of the soul—that part of each of us that God holds in the hollow of his hand and into which he breathes the breath of life. And you come to appreciate what another of your poets, Nikolai Gumilev, meant when he wrote that "The eternal entrance to God's paradise is not closed with seven diamond seals. It is a doorway in a wall abandoned long ago—stones, moss, and nothing more."

As I see it, political leadership in a democracy requires seeing past the abstractions and embracing the vast diversity of humanity and doing it with humility, listening as best you can not just to those with high positions but to the cacophonous voices of ordinary people and trusting those millions of people, keeping out of their way, not trying to act the all-wise and all-powerful, not letting government act that way. And the word we have for this is freedom.

In the last few years, freedom for the arts has been expanded in the Soviet Union. Some poems, books, music, and works in other fields that were once banned have been made available to the public; and some of those artists who produced them have been recognized. Two weeks ago, because of the work of the Writers Union, the first step was taken to make the Pasternak home at Peredelkino into a museum. In the meantime, some artists in exile—the stage director Yuri Lubimov, for example—have been permitted to return and to work, and artists who are here have been allowed a greater range.

We in the United States applaud the new thaw in the arts. We hope to see it go further. We hope to see Mikhail Baryshnikov and Slava Rostropovich, artists Mrs. Reagan and I have seen perform in Washington, perform again in Moscow. We hope to see the works of Aleksandr Solzhenitsyn published in the land he loves. And we hope to see a permanent end to restrictions on the creativity of all artists and writers. We want this not just for your sake but for our own. We believe that the greater the freedoms in other countries the more secure both our own freedoms and peace. And we believe that when the arts in any country are free to blossom the lives of all people are richer.

William Faulkner said of poets—although he could have been speaking of any of the arts—it is the poet's privilege to help man endure by lifting his heart, by reminding him of the courage and honor and hope and pride and compassion and pity and sacrifice which have been the glory of our past. The poet's voice need not merely be the record of man. It can be one of the props, the pillars, to help him endure and prevail. Thank you for having me here today and for sharing your thoughts with me, and God bless you all.

Note: The President spoke at 1:44 p.m. in the dining room at the A. Fadeyev Central House of Men of Letters. He was introduced by Vladimir Vasilievich Karpov, first secretary of the board of the Soviet Writers' Union.

Remarks and a Question-and-Answer Session With the Students and Faculty at Moscow State University
May 31, 1988

The President. Thank you, Rector Logunov, and I want to thank all of you very much for a very warm welcome. It's a great pleasure to be here at Moscow State University, and I want to thank you all for turning out. I know you must be very busy this week, studying and taking your final examinations. So, let me just say *zhelayu vam uspekha* [I wish you success]. Nancy couldn't make it today because she's visiting Leningrad, which she tells me is a very beautiful city, but she, too, says hello and wishes you all good luck.

Let me say it's also a great pleasure to once again have this opportunity to speak directly to the people of the Soviet Union. Before I left Washington, I received many heartfelt letters and telegrams asking me to carry here a simple message, perhaps, but also some of the most important business of this summit: It is a message of peace and good will and hope for a growing friendship and closeness between our two peoples.

As you know, I've come to Moscow to meet with one of your most distinguished graduates. In this, our fourth summit, General Secretary Gorbachev and I have spent many hours together, and I feel that we're getting to know each other well. Our discussions, of course, have been focused primarily on many of the important issues of the day, issues I want to touch on with you in a few moments. But first I want to take a little time to talk to you much as I would to any group of university students in the United States. I want to talk not just of the realities of today but of the possibilities of tomorrow.

Standing here before a mural of your revolution, I want to talk about a very different revolution that is taking place right now, quietly sweeping the globe without bloodshed or conflict. Its effects are peaceful, but they will fundamentally alter our world, shatter old assumptions, and reshape our lives. It's easy to underestimate because it's not accompanied by banners or fanfare. It's been called the technological or information revolution, and as its emblem, one might take the tiny silicon chip, no bigger than a fingerprint. One of these chips has more computing power than a roomful of old-style computers.

As part of an exchange program, we now have an exhibition touring your country that shows how information technology is transforming our lives—replacing manual labor with robots, forecasting weather for farmers, or mapping the genetic code of DNA for medical researchers. These microcomputers today aid the design of everything from houses to cars to spacecraft; they even design better and faster computers. They can translate English into Russian or enable the blind to read or help Michael Jackson produce on one synthesizer the sounds of a whole orchestra. Linked by a network of satellites and fiber-optic cables, one individual with a desktop computer and a telephone commands resources unavailable to the largest governments just a few years ago.

Like a chrysalis, we're emerging from the economy of the Industrial Revolution—an economy confined to and limited by the Earth's physical resources—into, as one economist titled his book, "The Economy in Mind," in which there are no bounds on human imagination and the freedom to create is the most precious natural resource. Think of that little computer chip. Its value isn't in the sand from which it is made but in the microscopic architecture designed into it by ingenious human minds. Or take the example of the satellite relaying this broadcast around the world, which replaces thousands of tons of copper mined from the Earth and molded into wire. In the new economy, human invention increasingly makes physical resources obsolete. We're breaking through the material conditions of existence to a world where man creates his own destiny. Even as we explore the most advanced reaches of science, we're returning to the age-old wisdom of our culture, a wisdom contained in the book of Genesis in the Bible: In the beginning was the spirit, and it was from this spirit that the material abundance of creation issued forth.

But progress is not foreordained. The key is freedom—freedom of thought, freedom of information, freedom of communication. The renowned scientist, scholar, and founding father of this university, Mikhail Lomonosov, knew that. "It is common knowledge," he said, "that the achievements of science are considerable and rapid, particularly once the yoke of slavery is cast off and replaced by the freedom of philosophy." You know, one of the first contacts between your country and mine took place between Russian and American explorers. The Americans were members of Cook's last voyage on an expedition searching for an Arctic passage; on the island of Unalaska, they came upon the Russians, who took them in, and together with the native inhabitants, held a prayer service on the ice.

The explorers of the modern era are the entrepreneurs, men with vision, with the courage to take risks and faith enough to brave the unknown. These entrepreneurs and their small enterprises are responsible for almost all the economic growth in the United States. They are the prime movers of the technological revolution. In fact, one of the largest personal computer firms in the United States was started by two college students, no older than you, in the garage behind their home. Some people, even in my own country, look at the riot of experiment that is the free market and see only waste. What of all the entrepreneurs that fail? Well, many do, particularly the successful ones; often several times. And if you ask them the secret of their success, they'll tell you it's all that they learned in their struggles along the way; yes, it's what they learned from failing. Like an athlete in competition or a scholar in pursuit of the truth, experience is the greatest teacher.

And that's why it's so hard for government planners, no matter how sophisticated, to ever substitute for millions of individuals working night and day to make their dreams come true. The fact is, bureaucracies are a problem around the world. There's an old story about a town—it could be anywhere—with a bureaucrat who is known to be a good-for-nothing, but he somehow had always hung on to power. So one day, in a town meeting, an old woman got up and said to him: "There is a folk legend here where I come from that when a baby is born, an angel comes down from heaven and kisses it on one part of its body. If the angel kisses him on his hand, he becomes a handyman. If he kisses him on his forehead, he becomes bright and clever. And I've been trying to figure out where the angel kissed you so that you should sit there for so long and do nothing." [*Laughter*]

We are seeing the power of economic freedom spreading around the world. Places such as the Republic of Korea, Singapore, Taiwan have vaulted into the technological era, barely pausing in the industrial age along the way. Low-tax agricultural policies in the subcontinent mean that in some years India is now a net exporter of food. Perhaps most exciting are the winds of change that are blowing over the People's Republic of China, where one-quarter of the world's population is now getting its first taste of economic freedom. At the same time, the growth of democracy has become one of the most powerful political movements of our age. In Latin America in the 1970's, only a third of the population lived under democratic government; today over 90 percent does. In the Philippines, in the Republic of Korea, free, contested, democratic elections are the order of the day. Throughout the world, free markets are the model for growth. Democracy is the standard by which governments are measured.

We Americans make no secret of our belief in freedom. In fact, it's something of a national pastime. Every 4 years the American people choose a new President, and 1988 is one of those years. At one point there were 13 major candidates running in the two major parties, not to mention all the others, including the Socialist and Libertarian candidates—all trying to get my job. About 1,000 local television stations, 8,500 radio stations, and 1,700 daily newspapers—each one an independent, private enterprise, fiercely independent of the Government—report on the candidates, grill them in interviews, and bring them together for debates. In the end, the people vote; they decide who will be the next President.But freedom doesn't begin or end with elections.

Go to any American town, to take just an example, and you'll see dozens of churches, representing many different beliefs—in many places, synagogues and mosques—and you'll see families of every conceivable nationality worshiping together. Go into any schoolroom, and there you will see children being taught the Declaration of Independence, that they are endowed by their Creator with certain unalienable rights—among them life, liberty, and the pursuit of happiness—that no government can justly deny; the guarantees in their Constitution for freedom of speech, freedom of assembly, and freedom of religion. Go into any courtroom, and there will preside an independent judge, beholden to no government power. There every defendant has the right to a trial by a jury of his peers, usually 12 men and women—common citizens; they are the ones, the only ones, who weigh the evidence and decide on guilt or innocence. In that court, the accused is innocent until proven guilty, and the word of a policeman or any official has no greater legal standing than the word of the accused. Go to any university campus, and there you'll find an open, sometimes heated discussion of the problems in American society and what can be done to correct them. Turn on the television, and you'll see the legislature conducting the business of government right there before the camera, debating and voting on the legislation that will become the law of the land. March in any demonstration, and there are many of them; the people's right of assembly is guaranteed in the Constitution and protected by the police. Go into any union hall, where the members know their right to strike is protected by law. As a matter of fact, one of the many jobs I had before this one was being president of a union, the Screen Actors Guild. I led my union out on strike, and I'm proud to say we won.

But freedom is more even than this. Freedom is the right to question and change the established way of doing things. It is the continuing revolution of the marketplace. It is the understanding that allows us to recognize shortcomings and seek solutions. It is the right to put forth an idea, scoffed at by the experts, and watch it catch fire among the people. It is the right to dream—to follow your dream or stick to your conscience, even if you're the only one in a sea of doubters. Freedom is the recognition that no single person, no single authority or government has a monopoly on the truth, but that every individual life is infinitely precious, that every one of us put on this world has been put there for a reason and has something to offer.

America is a nation made up of hundreds of nationalities. Our ties to you are more than ones of good feeling; they're ties of kinship. In America, you'll find Russians, Armenians, Ukrainians, peoples from Eastern Europe and Central Asia. They come from every part of this vast continent, from every continent, to live in harmony, seeking a place where each cultural heritage is respected, each is valued for its diverse strengths and beauties and the richness it brings to our lives. Recently, a few individuals and families have been allowed to visit relatives in the West. We can only hope that it won't be long before all are allowed to do so and Ukrainian-Americans, Baltic-Americans, Armenian-Americans can freely visit their homelands, just as this Irish-American visits his.

Freedom, it has been said, makes people selfish and materialistic, but Americans are one of the most religious peoples on Earth. Because they know that liberty, just as life itself, is not earned but a gift from God, they seek to share that gift with the world. "Reason and experience," said George Washington in his Farewell Address, "both forbid us to expect that national morality can prevail in exclusion of religious principle. And it is substantially true, that virtue or morality is a necessary spring of popular government." Democracy is less a system of government than it is a system to keep government limited, unintrusive; a system of constraints on power to keep politics and government secondary to the important things in life, the true sources of value found only in family and faith.

But I hope you know I go on about these things not simply to extol the virtues of my own country but to speak to the true greatness of the heart and soul of your land. Who, after all, needs to tell the land of Dostoyevski about the quest for truth, the home of Kandinski and Scriabin about imagination, the rich and noble culture of the Uzbek man of letters Alisher Navoi about beauty and heart? The great culture of your diverse land speaks with a glowing passion to all humanity. Let me cite one of the most eloquent contemporary passages on human freedom. It comes, not from the literature of America, but from this country, from one of the greatest writers of the 20th century, Boris Pasternak, in the novel "Dr. Zhivago." He writes: "I think that if the beast who sleeps in man could be held down by threats—any kind of threat, whether of jail or of retribution after death—then the highest emblem of humanity would be the lion tamer in the circus with his whip, not the prophet who sacrificed himself. But this is just the point—what has for centuries raised man above the beast is not the cudgel, but an inward music—the irresistible power of unarmed truth."

The irresistible power of unarmed truth. Today the world looks expectantly to signs of change, steps toward greater freedom in the Soviet Union. We watch and we hope as we see positive changes taking place. There are some, I know, in your society who fear that change will bring only disruption and discontinuity, who fear to embrace the hope of the future—sometimes it takes faith. It's like that scene in the cowboy movie "Butch Cassidy and the Sundance Kid," which some here in Moscow recently had a chance to see. The posse is closing in on the two outlaws, Butch and Sundance, who find themselves trapped on the edge of a cliff, with a sheer drop of hundreds of feet to the raging rapids below. Butch turns to Sundance and says their only hope is to jump into the river below, but Sundance refuses. He says he'd rather fight it out with the posse, even though they're hopelessly outnumbered. Butch says that's suicide and urges him to jump, but Sundance still refuses and finally admits, "I can't swim." Butch breaks up laughing and says, "You crazy fool, the fall will probably kill you." And, by the way, both Butch and Sundance made it, in case you didn't see the movie. I think what I've just been talking about is *perestroika* and what its goals are.

But change would not mean rejection of the past. Like a tree growing strong through the seasons, rooted in the Earth and drawing life from the Sun, so, too, positive change must be rooted in traditional values—in the land, in culture, in family and community—and it must take its life from the eternal things, from the source of all life, which is faith. Such change will lead to new understandings, new opportunities, to a broader future in which the tradition is not supplanted but finds its full flowering. That is the future beckoning to your generation.

At the same time, we should remember that reform that is not institutionalized will always be insecure. Such freedom will always be looking over its shoulder. A bird on a tether, no matter how long the rope, can always be pulled back. And that is why, in my conversation with General Secretary Gorbachev, I have spoken of how important it is to institutionalize change—to put guarantees on reform. And we've been talking together about one sad reminder of a divided world: the Berlin Wall. It's time to remove the barriers that keep people apart.

I'm proposing an increased exchange program of high school students between our countries. General Secretary Gorbachev mentioned on Sunday a wonderful phrase you have in Russian for this: "Better to see something once than to hear about it a hundred times." Mr. Gorbachev and I first began working on this in 1985. In our discussion today, we agreed on working up to several thousand exchanges a year from each country in the near future. But not everyone can travel across the continents and oceans. Words travel lighter, and that's why we'd like to make available to this country more of our 11,000 magazines and periodicals and our television and radio shows that can be beamed off a satellite in seconds. Nothing would please us more than for the Soviet people to get to know us better and to understand our way of life.

Just a few years ago, few would have imagined the progress our two nations have made together. The INF treaty, which General Secretary Gorbachev and I signed last December in Washington and whose instruments of ratification we will exchange tomorrow—the first true nuclear arms reduction treaty in history, calling for the elimination of an entire class of U.S. and Soviet nuclear missiles. And just 16 days ago, we saw the beginning of your withdrawal from Afghanistan, which gives us hope that soon the fighting may end and the healing may begin and that that suffering country may find self-determination, unity, and peace at long last.

It's my fervent hope that our constructive cooperation on these issues will be carried on to address the continuing destruction and conflicts in many regions of the globe and that the serious discussions that led to the Geneva accords on Afghanistan will help lead to solutions in southern Africa, Ethiopia, Cambodia, the Persian Gulf, and Central America. I have often said: Nations do not distrust each other because they are armed; they are armed because they distrust each other. If this globe is to live in peace and prosper, if it is to embrace all the possibilities of the technological revolution, then nations must renounce, once and for all, the right to an expansionist foreign policy. Peace between nations must be an enduring goal, not a tactical stage in a continuing conflict.

I've been told that there's a popular song in your country—perhaps you know it—whose evocative refrain asks the question, "Do the Russians want a war?" In answer it says: "Go ask that silence lingering in the air, above the birch and poplar there; beneath those trees the soldiers lie. Go ask my mother, ask my wife; then you will have to ask no more, 'Do the Russians want a war?' " But what of your one-time allies? What of those who embraced you on the Elbe? What if we were to ask the watery graves of the Pacific or the European battlefields where America's fallen were buried far from home? What if we were to ask their mothers, sisters, and sons, do Americans want war? Ask us, too, and you'll find the same answer, the same longing in every heart. People do not make wars; governments do. And no mother would ever willingly sacrifice her sons for territorial gain, for economic advantage, for ideology. A people free to choose will always choose peace.

Americans seek always to make friends of old antagonists. After a colonial revolution with Britain, we have cemented for all ages the ties of kinship between our nations. After a terrible Civil War between North and South, we healed our wounds and found true unity as a nation. We fought two world wars in my lifetime against Germany and one with Japan, but now the Federal Republic of Germany and Japan are two of our closest allies and friends.

Some people point to the trade disputes between us as a sign of strain, but they're the frictions of all families, and the family of free nations is a big and vital and sometimes boisterous one. I can tell you that nothing would please my heart more than in my lifetime to see American and Soviet diplomats grappling with the problem of trade disputes between America and a growing, exuberant, exporting Soviet Union that had opened up to economic freedom and growth.

And as important as these official people-to-people exchanges are, nothing would please me more than for them to become unnecessary, to see travel between East and West become so routine that university students in the Soviet Union could take a month off in the summer and, just like students in the West do now, put packs on their backs and travel from country to country in Europe with barely a passport check in between. Nothing would please me more than to see the day that a concert promoter in, say, England could call up a Soviet rock group, without going through any government agency, and have them playing in Liverpool the next night. Is this just a dream? Perhaps, but it is a dream that is our responsibility to have come true.

Your generation is living in one of the most exciting, hopeful times in Soviet history. It is a time when the first breath of freedom stirs the air and the heart beats to the accelerated rhythm of hope, when the accumulated spiritual energies of a long silence yearn to break free. I am reminded of the famous passage near the end of Gogol's "Dead Souls." Comparing his nation to a speeding troika, Gogol asks what will be its destination. But he writes, "There was no answer save the bell pouring forth marvelous sound."

We do not know what the conclusion will be of this journey, but we're hopeful that the promise of reform will be fulfilled. In this Moscow spring, this May 1988, we may be allowed that hope: that freedom, like the fresh green sapling planted over Tolstoy's grave, will blossom forth at last in the rich fertile soil of your people and culture. We may be allowed to hope that the marvelous sound of a new openness will keep rising through, ringing through, leading to a new world of reconciliation, friendship, and peace.

Thank you all very much, and *da blagoslovit vas gospod*—God bless you.

Mr. Logunov. Dear friends, Mr. President has kindly agreed to answer your questions. But since he doesn't have too much time, only 15 minutes—so, those who have questions, please ask them.

Strategic Arms Reductions

Q. And this is a student from the history faculty, and he says that he's happy to welcome you on behalf of the students of the university. And the first question is that the improvement in the relations between the two countries has come about during your tenure as President, and in this regard he would like to ask the following question. It is very important to get a handle on the question of arms control and, specifically, the limitation of strategic arms. Do you think that it will be possible for you and the General Secretary to get a treaty on the limitation of strategic arms during the time that you are still President?

The President. Well, the arms treaty that is being negotiated now is the so-called START treaty, and it is based on taking the intercontinental ballistic missiles and reducing them by half, down to parity between our two countries. Now, this is a much more complicated treaty than the INF treaty, the intermediate-range treaty, which we have signed and which our two governments have ratified and is now in effect. So, there are many things still to be settled. You and we have had negotiators in Geneva for months working on various points of this treaty. Once we had hoped that maybe, like the INF treaty, we would have been able to sign it here at this summit meeting. It is not completed; there are still some points that are being debated. We are both hopeful that it can be finished before I leave office, which is in the coming January, but I assure you that if it isn't—I assure you that I will have impressed on my successor that we must carry on until it is signed. My dream has always been that once we've started down this road, we can look forward to a day—you can look forward to a day—when there will be no more nuclear weapons in the world at all.

Young People

Q. The question is: The universities influence public opinion, and the student wonders how the youths have changed since the days when you were a student up until now?

The President. Well, wait a minute. How you have changed since the era of my own youth?

Q. How just students have changed, the youth have changed. You were a student. [*Laughter*] At your time there were one type. How they have changed?

The President. Well, I know there was a period in our country when there was a very great change for the worse. When I was Governor of California, I could start a riot just by going to a campus. But that has all changed, and I could be looking out at an American student body as well as I'm looking out here and would not be able to tell the difference between you.

I think that back in our day—I did happen to go to school, get my college education in a unique time; it was the time of the Great Depression, when, in a country like our own, there was 25-percent unemployment and the bottom seemed to have fallen out of everything. But we had—I think what maybe I should be telling you from my point here, because I graduated in 1932, that I should tell you that when you get to be my age, you're going to be surprised how much you recall the feelings you had in these days here and that—how easy it is to understand the young people because of your own having been young once. You know an awful lot more about being young than you do about being old. [*Laughter*]

And I think there is a seriousness, I think there is a sense of responsibility that young people have, and I think that there is an awareness on the part of most of you about what you want your adulthood to be and what the country you live in—you want it to be. And I have a great deal of faith. I said the other day to 76 students—they were half American and half Russian. They had held a conference here and in Finland and then in the United States, and I faced them just the other day, and I had to say—I couldn't tell the difference looking at them, which were which, but I said one line to them. I said I believe that if all the young people of the world today could get to know each other, there would never be another war. And I think that of you. I think that of the other students that I've addressed in other places.

And of course, I know also that you're young and, therefore, there are certain things that at times take precedence. I'll illustrate one myself. Twenty-five years after I graduated, my alma mater brought me back to the school and gave me an honorary degree. And I had to tell them they compounded a sense of guilt I had nursed for 25 years because I always felt the first degree they gave me was honorary. [*Laughter*] You're great! Carry on.

Regional Conflicts

Q. Mr. President, you have just mentioned that you welcome the efforts—settlement of the Afghanistan question and the difference of other regional conflicts. What conflicts do you mean? Central America conflicts, Southeast Asian, or South African?

The President. Well, for example, in South Africa, where Namibia has been promised its independence as a nation—another new African nation. But it is impossible because of a civil war going on in another country there, and that civil war is being fought on one side by some 30,000 to 40,000 Cuban troops who have gone from the Americas over there and are fighting on one side with one kind of authoritative government. When that country was freed from being a colony and given its independence, one faction seized power and made itself the government of that nation. And leaders of another—seeming the majority of the people had wanted, simply, the people to have the right to choose the government that they wanted, and that is the civil war that is going on. But what we believe is that those foreign soldiers should get out and let them settle it, let the citizens of that nation settle their problems.

And the same is true in Nicaragua. Nicaragua has been—Nicaragua made a promise. They had a dictator. There was a revolution, there was an organization that—and was aided by others in the revolution, and they appealed to the Organization of American States for help in getting the dictator to step down and stop the killing. And he did. But the Organization of American States had asked, what are the goals of the revolution? And they were given in writing, and they were the goals of pluralistic society, of the right of unions and freedom of speech and press and so forth and free elections—a pluralistic society. And then the one group that was the best organized among the revolutionaries seized power, exiled many of the other leaders, and has its own government, which violated every one of the promises that had been made. And here again, we want—we're trying to encourage the getting back those—or making those promises come true and letting the people of that particular country decide their fate.

Soviet MIA's in Afghanistan

Q. Esteemed Mr. President, I'm very much anxious and concerned about the destiny of 310 Soviet soldiers being missing in Afghanistan. Are you willing to help in their search and their return to the motherland?

The President. Very much so. We would like nothing better than that.

U.S. Constitution

Q. The reservation of the inalienable rights of citizens guaranteed by the Constitution faces certain problems; for example, the right of people to have arms, or for example, the problem appears, an evil appears whether spread of pornography or narcotics is compatible with these rights. Do you believe that these problems are just unavoidable problems connected with democracy, or they could be avoided?

The President. Well, if I understand you correctly, this is a question about the inalienable rights of the people—does that include the right to do criminal acts—for example, in the use of drugs and so forth? No. No, we have a set of laws. I think what is significant and different about our system is that every country has a constitution, and most constitutions or practically all of the constitutions in the world are documents in which the government tells the people what the people can do. Our Constitution is different, and the difference is in three words; it almost escapes everyone. The three words are, "We the people." Our Constitution is a document in which we the people tell the Government what its powers are. And it can have no powers other than those listed in that document. But very carefully, at the same time, the people give the government the power with regard to those things which they think would be destructive to society, to the family, to the individual and so forth—infringements on their rights. And thus, the government can enforce the laws. But that has all been dictated by the people.

President's Retirement Plans

Q. Mr. President, from history I know that people who have been connected with great power, with big posts, say goodbye, leave these posts with great difficulty. Since your term of office is coming to an end, what sentiments do you experience and whether you feel like, if, hypothetically, you can just stay for another term? [*Laughter*]

The President. Well, I'll tell you something. I think it was a kind of revenge against Franklin Delano Roosevelt, who was elected four times—the only President. There had kind of grown a tradition in our country about two terms. That tradition was started by Washington, our first President, only because there was great talk at the formation of our country that we might become a monarchy, and we had just freed ourselves from a monarchy. So, when the second term was over, George Washington stepped down and said he would do it—stepping down—so that there would not get to be the kind of idea of an inherited aristocracy. Well, succeeding Presidents—many of them didn't get a chance at a second term; they did one term and were gone. But that tradition kind of remained, but it was just a tradition. And then Roosevelt ran the four times—died very early in his fourth term. And suddenly, in the atmosphere at that time, they added an amendment to the Constitution that Presidents could only serve two terms.

When I get out of office—I can't do this while I'm in office, because it will look as I'm selfishly doing it for myself—when I get out of office, I'm going to travel around what I call the mashed-potato circuit—that is the after-dinner speaking and the speaking to luncheon groups and so forth—I'm going to travel around and try to convince the people of our country that they should wipe out that amendment to the Constitution because it was an interference with the democratic rights of the people. The people should be allowed to vote for who they wanted to vote for, for as many times as they want to vote for him; and that it is they who are being denied a right. But you see, I will no longer be President then, so I can do that and talk for that.

There are a few other things I'm going to try to convince the people to impress upon our Congress, the things that should be done. I've always described it that if—in Hollywood, when I was there, if you didn't sing or dance, you wound up as an after-dinner speaker. And I didn't sing or dance. [*Laughter*] So, I have a hunch that I will be out on the speaking circuit, telling about a few things that I didn't get done in government, but urging the people to tell the Congress they wanted them done.

American Indians

Q. Mr. President, I've heard that a group of American Indians have come here because they couldn't meet you in the United States of America. If you fail to meet them here, will you be able to correct it and to meet them back in the United States?

The President. I didn't know that they had asked to see me. If they've come here or whether to see them there—[*laughter*]—I'd be very happy to see them.

Let me tell you just a little something

about the American Indian in our land. We have provided millions of acres of land for what are called preservations—or reservations, I should say. They, from the beginning, announced that they wanted to maintain their way of life, as they had always lived there in the desert and the plains and so forth. And we set up these reservations so they could, and have a Bureau of Indian Affairs to help take care of them. At the same time, we provide education for them—schools on the reservations. And they're free also to leave the reservations and be American citizens among the rest of us, and many do. Some still prefer, however, that way—that early way of life. And we've done everything we can to meet their demands as to how they want to live. Maybe we made a mistake. Maybe we should not have humored them in that wanting to stay in that kind of primitive lifestyle. Maybe we should have said, no, come join us; be citizens along with the rest of us. As I say, many have; many have been very successful.

And I'm very pleased to meet with them, talk with them at any time and see what their grievances are or what they feel they might be. And you'd be surprised: Some of them became very wealthy because some of those reservations were overlaying great pools of oil, and you can get very rich pumping oil. And so, I don't know what their complaint might be.

Soviet Dissidents

Q. Mr. President, I'm very much tantalized since yesterday evening by the question, why did you receive yesterday—did you receive and when you invite yesterday—refuseniks or dissidents? And for the second part of the question is, just what are your impressions from Soviet people? And among these dissidents, you have invited a former collaborator with a Fascist, who was a policeman serving for Fascist.

The President. Well, that's one I don't know about, or maybe the information hasn't been all given out on that. But you have to understand that Americans come from every corner of the world. I received a letter from a man that called something to my attention recently. He said, you can go to live in France, but you cannot become a Frenchman; you can go to live in Germany, you cannot become a German—or a Turk, or a Greek, or whatever. But he said anyone, from any corner of the world, can come to live in America and become an American.

You have to realize that we are a people that are made up of every strain, nationality, and race of the world. And the result is that when people in our country think someone is being mistreated or treated unjustly in another country, these are people who still feel that kinship to that country because that is their heritage. In America, whenever you meet someone new and become friends, one of the first things you tell each other is what your bloodline is. For example, when I'm asked, I have to say Irish, English, and Scotch—English and Scotch on my mother's side, Irish on my father's side. But all of them have that.

Well, when you take on to yourself a wife, you do not stop loving your mother. So, Americans all feel a kind of a kinship to that country that their parents or their grandparents or even some great-grandparents came from; you don't lose that contact. So, what I have come and what I have brought to the General Secretary—and I must say he has been very cooperative about it—I have brought lists of names that have been brought to me from people that are relatives or friends that know that—or that believe that this individual is being mistreated here in this country, and they want him to be allowed to emigrate to our country—some are separated families.

One that I met in this, the other day, was born the same time I was. He was born of Russian parents who had moved to America, oh, way back in the early 1900's, and he was born in 1911. And then sometime later, the family moved back to Russia. Now he's grown, has a son. He's an American citizen. But they wanted to go back to America and being denied on the grounds that, well, they can go back to America, but his son married a Russian young lady, and they want to keep her from going back. Well, the whole family said, no, we're not going to leave her alone here. She's a member of the family now. Well, that kind of a case is brought to me personally, so I bring it to the General Secretary. And as I say, I must say, he has been most helpful and most agreeable about correcting these things.

Now, I'm not blaming you; I'm blaming bureaucracy. We have the same type of thing happen in our own country. And every once in a while, somebody has to get the bureaucracy by the neck and shake it loose and say, Stop doing what you're doing! And this is the type of thing and the names that we have brought. And it is a list of names, all of which have been brought to me personally by either relatives or close friends and associates. [*Applause*]

Thank you very much. You're all very kind. I thank you very much. And I hope I answered the questions correctly. Nobody asked me what it was going to feel like to not be President anymore. I have some understanding, because after I'd been Governor for 8 years and then stepped down, I want to tell you what it's like. We'd only been home a few days, and someone invited us out to dinner. Nancy and I both went out, got in the back seat of the car, and waited for somebody to get in front and drive us. [*Laughter*]

[*At this point, Rector Logunov gave the President a gift.*]

That is beautiful. Thank you very much.

Note: The President spoke at 4:10 p.m. in the Lecture Hall at Moscow State University. Anatoliy A. Logunov was rector of the university.

Toasts at a State Dinner Hosted by the President at Spaso House in Moscow

May 31, 1988

The President. Mr. General Secretary, Mrs. Gorbachev, distinguished guests and friends, it's a pleasure to host all of you tonight and to reciprocate, in a small way, the hospitality you lavished upon us yesterday evening. While the General Secretary and I had already held three meetings before this one began here in Moscow, each of those earlier encounters took place in the autumn. The days were growing short, the weather ever grayer and colder. It makes for a bracing, delightful change to have this meeting take place at the high point of spring, a time of long, light-filled days.

I know that Nancy found her springtime visit to Leningrad earlier today both magnificent and moving. The play of light upon the rivers and canals added the special splendor of the season to a city splendid in any season. And everywhere, Nancy has told me, there was a sense of history, especially of Leningrad's immense courage and sacrifice during the Second World War, surely one of the most stirring epics in the whole human story.

Here in Moscow, I've been reminded a number of times during this springtime visit of a passage in a book about your country by Laurens Van der Post. Especially struck by the city's churches, Van der Post wrote that when he caught his first sight of the Moscow skyline he saw "the light of an unusually pure evening upon it. That light was alchemical, and it transformed Moscow into a city of gold. The tops of the spires and pinnacles drawing the rigid forms of the skyscrapers after them into arrows of gold aimed at the arched and timeless blue." So, we, too, have found Moscow a city of beauties. A city, especially, whose pinnacles and spires reminded one at virtually every turn of man's ancient capacity for aspiration, for reaching out toward the light.

It's a particular pleasure to be able to welcome you to Spaso House—a house of considerable beauty in its own right—the residence of our Ambassadors to the Soviet Union. During the 55 years of diplomatic relations between our two nations, Spaso House has served as one of the principal settings for exchanges between us—exchanges formal and informal alike. There have been some splendid moments within these walls. Prokofiev once conducted his marvelous "The Love for Three Oranges" in this very room. As wartime allies, our representatives met often under this roof. And Ambassador and Mrs. Matlock have continued the tradition of making Spaso House a centerpiece of American culture, a place to receive and talk with Soviet officials and with people from all walks of life and from all parts of the Soviet Union. But there have also been quiet times in this house—unnaturally quiet times. Times when difficult relations between us meant that this house, this huge, magnificent house, stood virtually empty of visitors. I'm told that it was even possible to hear the Moscow Metro rumbling past, ever so faintly, deep in the Earth below.

Mr. General Secretary, we know that on matters of great importance we will continue to differ profoundly, and yet you and I have met four times now, more often than any previous President and General Secretary. While our discussions have sometimes been pointed or contentious, we possess an enlarged understanding of each other and of each other's country. On specific matters of policy, we have made progress, often historic progress. And perhaps most important, we have committed our nations to continuing to work together, agreeing that silence must never again be permitted to fall between us. We have agreed always to continue the interchanges between our nations because, I believe, we both hear the same voice, the same overwhelming imperative. What that voice says can be expressed in many ways. But I have found it in vivid form in Pasternak's poem "The Garden of Gethsemane." Listen, if you will, to Pasternak's account of that famous arrest:

> "There appeared—no one knew from where—a crowd of slaves and a rabble of knaves, with lights and swords and, leading them, Judas with a traitor's kiss on his lips.
>
> "Peter repulsed the ruffians with his sword and cut off the ear of one of them. But he heard: 'You cannot decide a dispute with weapons; put your sword in its place, O man.' "

That's the voice. "Put your sword in its place, O man." That is the imperative, the command. And so, we will work together that we might forever keep our swords at our sides.

Mr. General Secretary, ladies and gentlemen, Spaso House has, as I said, seen quiet times, yet the animated conversation of this evening has already done much to make up for them. And so, I would like to raise a glass to the continued interchange between our two nations and, if I may, to Spaso House itself, as a symbol of our relations. May this lovely home never lack for visitors and shared meals and the sounds of spirited conversation and even the peal of hearty laughter. Thank you, and God bless you. And to the General Secretary, to Mrs. Gorbachev, to the relationship that I believe must continue.

The General Secretary. Esteemed Mr. President, esteemed Mrs. Reagan, ladies and gentlemen, comrades: I thank you, Mr. President for the words of greeting you just addressed to us.

Two great nations have given the two of us a mandate to determine what Soviet-American relations should be like. Since our first meeting in Geneva, relations between our two countries have overcome a long, drawn out period of confrontation to reach an acceptable level from which it is now easier to move forward. In Reykjavik, in Washington, and during this present visit of yours, our dialog has been intense. Its most important result has been the now-ratified first treaty to reduce nuclear weapons. A search is continuing to find a solution for problems relating to 50-percent cuts in strategic offensive arms. The Geneva accord in Afghanistan has come into force. We now have as many as 47 bilateral agreements on cooperation.

The visit by a President of the United States to the Soviet Union is an occasion for a glance at the past and a look into the future. The history of relations between our two countries has known all kinds of things, good and bad. Of the good things, we remember particularly well the Soviet-American comradeship-in-arms in World War II. Those grim years saw the emergence of the first shoots of Soviet-American friendship. And there was not one single Soviet citizen who did not feel bitter when that glorious page in the history of our relations gave way to cold war. That was a hard test for our peoples. The world found itself in a dangerous situation. We all felt the breath of impending catastrophe. Even today, we're sometimes chilled by cold winds.

But world developments in their main tendency are turning toward a search for political solutions, toward cooperation and peace. We are, all of us, witnesses to momentous changes, though a lot still has to be done to achieve irreversible change. Although everything urges cooperation and trust, prejudices and stereotypes are still with us, as is rivalry, above all in the military sphere. A great deal has been said at this meeting, too, about how pointless and catastrophic it is. More importantly, we can register some headway toward better mutual understanding in this area as well.

Today, I would like to address another major world problem: the situation in the developing world, which cannot but affect our countries, too. The problems which the developing countries face have turned out to be difficult [to] the point of tragedy. Glaring backwardness, hunger, poverty, and mass diseases continue to beset entire nations. An incredibly high debt has become an excruciating and universal problem. It would seem that everybody can see its complexity, involving as it does extremely diverse and truly vital interests, and understand that a way out must be solved.

We believe that if the international community and, above all, the great powers are to be of any help the starting point and the essential thing is to recognize unconditionally the freedom of choice. We are insisting on fairness. We have seriously studied the economic system in developing nations, and I am convinced that a way out is possible along the lines of a radical restructuring of the entire system of world economic relations, without any discrimination for political reasons. This would promote a political settlement of regional conflicts which not only impede progress in that part of the world but also cause turmoil in the entire world situation. With such an approach, our differences as to what kind of a future awaits the Third World would not take on confrontational forms. So, in this matter, too, our relationship is doomed to have an international dimension.

Turning now to our bilateral relations, we envision there opportunities and prospects primarily in light of internal evolution in both countries, but also in the context of world developments. Many Americans who are studying us and who have visited the U.S.S.R., and now, I hope, those present here as well, have been able to see for themselves the sweeping scope of change in our country. It is based on comprehensive democratization and radical economic reform. I'm gratified to note that today the President and I have had an in-depth exchange of views on this subject. We have also discussed our *perestroika* a number of times with other Americans. This is all to the good. It, too, is a sign of change in our relationship.

We, for our part, are trying to closely follow the profound trends in the United States. We see how little similarity there is between what is happening in our country and in yours, in two very different societies based on different values. But we do not regard this as an obstacle to identifying promising areas for mutually beneficial ties or for cooperation in the interests of the two peoples. We're in favor of competition and comparison.

And another thing, whatever the ups and downs of our dialog with America, Soviet representatives have been upholding the interests of the Soviet state. In their contacts with us, American officials have been acting in exactly the same way, vis-a-vis their own interests. The truth is that in building their relationship the Soviet Union and the United States can effectively serve their own interests only if they have a realistic view and take account of each other's interests and intentions. We must learn the difficult art of not just existing side by side but of building bridges of mutually beneficial cooperation.

Soviet and American people want to live in peace and communicate in all areas in which they have a mutual interest. The interest is there, and it is growing. We feel no fear. We are not prejudiced. We believe in the value of communication. I see a future in which the Soviet Union and the United States base their relations on disarmament, a balance of interest, and comprehensive cooperation rather than on deterring each other or upgrading their military capabilities. I see a future in which solutions to real problems are not impeded by problems historically outdated or artificially kept alive, inherited from the times of the cold war, and in which the policies of confrontation give way to a joint quest based on reason, mutual benefit, and readiness to compromise. I see a future in which our two countries, without claiming any special rights in the world, are always mindful of their special responsibility in a community of equal nations. It'll be a world that is safer and more secure, which is so badly needed by all people on Earth, by their children and grandchildren, so that they could gain and preserve the basic human rights: the right to life, work, freedom, and the pursuit of happiness. The path towards this future can be neither easy nor short. We may be standing at the threshold of a uniquely interesting period in the history of our two nations. This new meeting between the two of us, Mr. President, confirms that 3 years ago in Geneva we took the right decision.

May the years to come bring a healthier international environment. May life be triumphant. To the very good health of the President, to the very good health of Mrs. Nancy Reagan, to cooperation between our two peoples.

Note: The President spoke at 10 p.m. in the Chandelier Room at the Ambassador's residence. The President spoke in English, and the General Secretary spoke in Russian. Their remarks were translated by interpreters.

Statement by Assistant to the President for Press Relations Fitzwater on the Soviet-United States Strategic Ballistic Missile Launch Notification Agreement

May 31, 1988

The agreement between the United States and the Soviet Union on notification of launches of strategic ballistic missiles is a practical new step designed to reduce the risk of misinterpretation, miscalculation, or accident.

In the START negotiations, both sides have proposed that there be notification of launches of ICBM's and SLBM's. Both sides launch such missiles from time to time for purposes of testing, training, and maintaining their reliability. The sides have very similar language to implement such notifications in the joint draft text of the START agreement in Geneva. Given this common approach to launch notification, the United States proposed at the meeting of Foreign Ministers in mid-May in Geneva that we separate this provision from the START treaty and reach an agreement on this subject now. Our START negotiator subsequently gave his counterpart in Geneva a draft text of an agreement. On Sunday the Soviets agreed to this concept and gave us a draft very similar to ours. Our START negotiators have completed the text, and it was signed today by Secretary Shultz and Foreign Minister Shevardnadze.

The agreement requires notification of all ICBM and SLBM launches at least 24 hours in advance. The notification would include the planned date of launch, the launch area, and the impact area. The notifications will be made through the Nuclear Risk Reduction Centers.

Remarks at the Exchange of Documents Ratifying the Intermediate-Range Nuclear Forces Treaty
June 1, 1988

The General Secretary. Esteemed Mr. President, esteemed Mrs. Reagan, distinguished ladies and gentlemen, comrades, we are approaching the end of the meeting between the leaders of the Soviet Union and the United States of America, the fourth such meeting in 3 years. The visit of the United States President to our country is drawing to a close.

The President and I have summed up the results of a dialog between our two countries at the highest level. We have discussed both the immediate and longer term prospects for Soviet-U.S. relations. We have signed documents which record what has been achieved and provide guidelines for the future. Among them, an historic place will belong to the ratification documents which give effect to the treaty on intermediate and shorter range missiles. The exchange a few minutes ago of the instruments of ratification means that the era of nuclear disarmament has begun.

Assessing the work done over these past few days, we can say our satisfaction, say that what has been happening these days in Moscow is big politics, politics that affect the interests of millions and millions of people. Each such meeting dealt a blow at the foundations of the cold war. Each of them made huge breaches in the cold war fortress and opened up passages to modern, civilized world politics worthy of the truly new times.

But big politics means difficult politics in which every step is not easy to take. Weighing carefully each one of our new steps, we measure it against the security interests of our two nations and of the world as a whole, for that is the only way to achieve truly substantial results with the necessary margin of viability. Big politics also means big responsibility, and so it cannot be built on pursuing only one's own interest, which is always inherently one-sided. Such politics also needs a great idea. Humankind has conceived that idea in the pangs of wars and disasters, tragedies and calamities, strivings and discoveries of the 20th century. This, in our view, is the idea of a nuclear-free and nonviolent world. It is that idea that is inscribed in the mandate which the Soviet people give to their representatives at the start of any negotiations. This particularly applies to our negotiations with the United States of America.

Addressing the Soviet people and the Americans, addressing all nations from these hallowed steps of the Moscow Kremlin, I hereby declare we have been working honestly and with perseverance, and we shall continue to do so to fulfill that historic mandate.

The first lines have already been written into the book of a world without wars, violence, or nuclear weapons. I believe that no one can now close that book and put it aside. President Ronald Reagan and I have agreed that the immediate task before us, which is to conclude a treaty on a 50-percent reduction in strategic offensive arms, can and must be accomplished. In our joint endeavors and discussions, we have learned to understand each other better, to take into account each other's concerns, and to search for solutions. The atmosphere in our relations is improving. We're working to make it a constant not only in our official contacts but also in the day-to-day management of Soviet-U.S. relations. In this, too, we are guided by a mandate from our peoples.

Thanks to the atmosphere of the meetings in Washington and in Moscow, and as a result of the agreements reached, Americans and Soviet people now have more opportunities for communication and for getting to know each other. I'm convinced that scientists, students, schoolchildren, cultural personalities, ordinary tourists, athletes, and of course businessmen will continue to enlarge and add new colors to the fabric of cooperative and even friendly relations. Sometimes, they can do that better than politicians.

Historians who will one day describe and

evaluate what is now being done have probably not yet been born. But every day, babies are being born who will live in the 21st century and to whom we must bequeath a safe and humane world. On behalf of the Soviet leadership and the Soviet people, I wish to tell all those who are concerned, and yet hopeful about the future, we shall work to achieve that goal, and we can only do it by working together. Thank you.

The President. Mr. General Secretary, these are historic moments. As we exchange these documents, the instruments of ratification, this treaty, the terms of which we formally agreed to last December in Washington, enters into force.

Mr. General Secretary, you know that our way here has not been easy. At crucial moments your personal intervention was needed and proved decisive, and for this we are grateful. So, too, Mr. General Secretary, you are aware of how important the objective not just of arms control but of arms reduction has been to my own thinking and to the policy of my administration since its outset. Seven years ago, when I first suggested the concept of a double-zero treaty, there were those who said that this was so unrealistic an idea that it was irresponsible to even propose it. Others simply dismissed the concept as a propaganda ploy or a geopolitical gambit. But skepticism and doubt bring a barren harvest. And today, on this table before us, we see the fruits of hope, evidence of what candor and realism can accomplish. We have dared to hope, Mr. General Secretary, and we have been rewarded.

For the first time in history, an entire class of U.S.-Soviet nuclear missiles is eliminated. In addition, this treaty provides for the most stringent verification in history. And for the first time, inspection teams are actually in residence in our respective countries. And while this treaty makes possible a new dimension of cooperation between us, much remains on our agenda. We must not stop here, Mr. General Secretary; there is much more to be done. As will be seen in our joint statement later today, more progress has been made toward a strategic arms treaty during our meetings. We must try to move forward in the months ahead to complete this START treaty as soon as possible. So, let us continue to expand the frontiers of trust, even as we verify, Mr. General Secretary—even as we verify.

Mr. General Secretary, we've agreed many times that there remain differences, important fundamental differences, between us. Yet as we work over the long run to narrow these differences, as we work for what I hope will be a new era of peace and expanded human freedom, we must also acknowledge our solemn responsibility to take steps now to reduce the chances of conflict and to prevent war. This we have done today, a first step toward a brighter future, a safer world. America's allies and friends welcome this treaty, too. We consulted them fully during its negotiation. We made clear that we would never put their security or their interests at risk, that on the contrary we would sign a treaty only if it enhanced their security, as this one does.

And finally, if I may, I would like to take a moment to thank the United States Senate for their work on this treaty. The way of democracy is sometimes a complicated way and sometimes trying, but it is a good way, and we believe the best way.

And once again, Mr. General Secretary, I want to extend to you and to all those who labored so hard for this moment, my warmest personal thanks.

Note: The General Secretary spoke at 12:15 p.m. in St. Vladimir's Hall at the Grand Kremlin Palace. The President spoke in English, and the General Secretary spoke in Russian. Their remarks were translated by interpreters.

Joint Statement Following the Soviet-United States Summit Meeting in Moscow
June 1, 1988

In accordance with the understanding reached during the U.S.-Soviet summit meeting in Geneva in November 1985, and confirmed at the Washington summit in December 1987, Ronald W. Reagan, President of the United States of America, and Mikhail S. Gorbachev, General Secretary of the Central Committee of the Communist Party of the Soviet Union, met in Moscow May 29–June 2, 1988.

Attending on the U.S. side were Secretary of State George P. Shultz; Secretary of Defense Frank C. Carlucci; Presidential Chief of Staff Howard H. Baker, Jr.; Assistant to the President for National Security Colin L. Powell; Ambassador at Large and Special Adviser to the President and the Secretary of State on Arms Control Matters, Paul H. Nitze; Special Adviser to the President and the Secretary of State on Arms Control Matters, Ambassador Edward L. Rowny; Ambassador of the U.S. to the USSR Jack F. Matlock; and Assistant Secretary of State for European and Canadian Affairs Rozanne L. Ridgway.

Attending on the Soviet side were Members of the Politburo of the CPSU Central Committee, Chairman of the Presidium of the USSR Supreme Soviet, Andrei A. Gromyko; Member of the Politburo of the CPSU Central Committee, Minister of Foreign Affairs of the USSR Eduard A. Shevardnadze; Member of the Politburo of the CPSU Central Committee, Secretary of the CPSU Central Committee Alexander N. Yakovlev; Alternate Member of the Politburo of the CPSU Central Committee, Minister of Defense of the USSR, Dimitri T. Yazov; Secretary of the CPSU Central Committee Anatoly F. Dobrynin; Assistant of the General Secretary of the CPSU Central Committee, Anatoly S. Chernyaev; Deputy Minister of Foreign Affairs of the USSR, Alexander A. Bessmertnykh; and Ambassador of the USSR to the United States of America Yuri V. Dubinin.

The President and the General Secretary view the Moscow summit as an important step in the process of putting U.S.-Soviet relations on a more productive and sustainable basis. Their comprehensive and detailed discussions covered the full agenda of issues to which the two leaders agreed during their initial meeting in Geneva in November, 1985—an agenda encompassing arms control, human rights and humanitarian matters, settlement of regional conflicts, and bilateral relations. Serious differences remain on important issues; the frank dialogue which has developed between the two countries remains critical to surmounting these differences.

The talks took place in a constructive atmosphere which provided ample opportunity for candid exchange. As a result, the sides achieved a better understanding of each other's positions. The two leaders welcomed the progress achieved in various areas of U.S.-Soviet relations since their last meeting in Washington, notwithstanding the difficulty and complexity of the issues. They noted with satisfaction numerous concrete agreements which have been achieved, and expressed their determination to redouble efforts in the months ahead in areas where work remains to be done. They praised the creative and intensive efforts made by representatives of both sides in recent months to resolve outstanding differences.

Assessing the state of U.S.-Soviet relations, the President and the General Secretary underscored the historic importance of their meetings in Geneva, Reykjavik, Washington, and Moscow in laying the foundation for a realistic approach to the problems of strengthening stability and reducing the risk of conflict. They reaffirmed their solemn conviction that a nuclear war cannot be won and must never be fought, their determination to prevent any war between the United States and Soviet Union, whether nuclear or conventional, and their disavowal of any intention to achieve military superiority.

The two leaders are convinced that the

expanding political dialogue they have established represents an increasingly effective means of resolving issues of mutual interest and concern. They do not minimize the real differences of history, tradition and ideology which will continue to characterize the US-Soviet relationship. But they believe that the dialogue will endure, because it is based on realism and focused on the achievement of concrete results. It can serve as a constructive basis for addressing not only the problems of the present, but of tomorrow and the next century. It is a process which the President and the General Secretary believe serves the best interests of the peoples of the United States and the Soviet Union, and can contribute to a more stable, more peaceful and safer world.

I. Arms Control

The President and the General Secretary, having expressed the commitment of their two countries to build on progress to date in arms control, determined objectives and next steps on a wide range of issues in this area. These will guide the efforts of the two governments in the months ahead as they work with each other and with other states toward equitable, verifiable agreements that strengthen international stability and security.

INF

The President and the General Secretary signed the protocol on the exchange of instruments of ratification of the Treaty between the United States of America and the Union of Soviet Socialist Republics on the Elimination of Their Intermediate-Range and Shorter-Range Missiles. The two leaders welcomed the entry into force of this historic agreement, which for the first time will eliminate an entire class of U.S. and Soviet nuclear arms, and which sets new standards for arms control. The leaders are determined to achieve the full implementation of all the provisions and understandings of the Treaty, viewing joint and successful work in this respect as an important precedent for future arms control efforts.

Nuclear and Space Talks

The two leaders noted that a Joint Draft Text of a Treaty on Reduction and Limitation of Strategic Offensive Arms has been elaborated. Through this process, the sides have been able to record in the Joint Draft Text extensive and significant areas of agreement and also to detail positions on remaining areas of disagreement. While important additional work is required before this Treaty is ready for signature, many key provisions are recorded in the Joint Draft Text and are considered to be agreed, subject to the completion and ratification of the Treaty.

Taking into account a Treaty on Strategic Offensive Arms, the sides have continued negotiations to achieve a separate agreement concerning the ABM Treaty building on the language of the Washington Summit Joint Statement dated December 10, 1987. Progress was noted in preparing the Joint Draft Text of an associated Protocol. In connection with their obligations under the Protocol, the sides have agreed in particular to use the Nuclear Risk Reduction Centers for transmission of relevant information. The leaders directed their negotiators to prepare the Joint Draft Text of a separate agreement and to continue work on its associated Protocol.

The Joint Draft Treaty on Reduction and Limitation of Strategic Offensive Arms reflects the earlier understanding on establishing ceilings of no more than 1600 strategic offensive delivery systems and 6000 warheads as well as agreement on subceilings of 4900 on the aggregate of ICBM and SLBM warheads and 1540 warheads on 154 heavy missiles.

The draft Treaty also records the sides' agreement that as a result of the reductions the aggregate throw-weight of the Soviet Union's ICBMs and SLBMs will be reduced to a level approximately 50 percent below the existing level and this level will not be exceeded.

During the negotiations the two sides have also achieved understanding that in future work on the Treaty they will act on the understanding that on deployed ICBMs and SLBMs of existing types the counting rule will include the number of warheads referred to in the Joint Statement of December 10, 1987, and the number of warheads which will be attributed to each new type of ballistic missile will be subject to negotiation.

In addition, the sides agreed on a counting rule for heavy bomber armaments according to which heavy bombers equipped only for nuclear gravity bombs and SRAMs will count as one delivery vehicle against the 1600 limit and one warhead against the 6000 limit.

The delegations have also prepared Joint Draft Texts of an Inspection Protocol, a Conversion or Elimination Protocol, and a Memorandum of Understanding on data, which are integral parts of the Treaty. These documents build on the verification provisions of the INF Treaty, extending and elaborating them as necessary to meet the more demanding requirements of START. The START verification measures will, at a minimum, include:

A. Data exchanges, to include declarations and appropriate notifications on the number and location of weapons systems limited by START, including locations and facilities for production, final assembly, storage, testing, repair, training, deployment, conversion, and elimination of such systems. Such declarations will be exchanged between the sides before the Treaty is signed and updated periodically.

B. Baseline inspections to verify the accuracy of these declarations.

C. On-site observation of elimination of strategic systems necessary to meet the agreed limits.

D. Continuous on-site monitoring of the perimeter and portals of critical production facilities to confirm the output of weapons to be limited.

E. Short-notice on-site inspection of:
- (i) declared locations during the process of reducing to agreed limits;
- (ii) locations where systems covered by this Treaty remain after achieving the agreed limits; and
- (iii) locations where such systems have been located (formerly declared facilities).

F. Short-notice inspection, in accordance with agreed upon procedures, of locations where either side considers covert deployment, production, storage or repair of strategic offensive arms could be occurring.

G. Prohibition of the use of concealment or other activities which impede verification by National Technical Means. Such provisions would include a ban on telemetry encryption and would allow for full access to all telemetric information broadcast during missile flight.

H. Procedures that enable verification of the number of warheads on deployed ballistic missiles of each specific type, including on-site inspection.

I. Enhanced observation of activities related to reduction and limitation of strategic offensive arms by National Technical Means. These would include open displays of treaty-limited items at missile bases, bomber bases, and submarine ports at locations and times chosen by the inspecting party.

The two sides have also begun to exchange data on their strategic forces.

During the course of this meeting in Moscow, the exchanges on START resulted in the achievement of substantial additional common ground, particularly in the areas of ALCMs and the attempts to develop and agree, if possible, on a solution to the problem of verification of mobile ICBMs. The details of this additional common ground have been recorded in documents exchanged between the sides. The Delegations in Geneva will record these gains in the Joint Draft Text of the START Treaty.

The sides also discussed the question of limiting long-range, nuclear-armed SLCMs.

Ronald Reagan and M.S. Gorbachev expressed their joint confidence that the extensive work done provides the basis for concluding the Treaty on Reduction and Limitation of Strategic Offensive Arms which will promote strategic stability and strengthen security not only of the peoples of the USSR and the USA, but of all mankind.

Guided by this fundamental agreement, the U.S. President and the General Secretary of the Central Committee of the CPSU agreed to continue their efforts in this area energetically and purposefully. The Delegations of the two countries have been instructed to return to Geneva on July 12, 1988. It has been agreed as a matter of principle that, once the remaining problems are solved and the Treaty and its associated documents are agreed, they will be signed without delay.

Ballistic Missile Launch Notifications

The agreement between the U.S. and the USSR on notifications of launches of Intercontinental Ballistic Missiles and Submarine-Launched Ballistic Missiles, signed during the Moscow summit, is a practical new step, reflecting the desire of the sides to reduce the risk of outbreak of nuclear war, in particular as a result of misinterpretation, miscalculation or accident.

Nuclear Testing

The leaders reaffirmed the commitment of the two sides to conduct in a single forum full-scale, stage-by-stage negotiations on the issues relating to nuclear testing. In these negotiations the sides as the first step will agree upon effective verification measures which will make it possible to ratify the U.S.-USSR Threshold Test Ban Treaty of 1974 and Peaceful Nuclear Explosions Treaty of 1976, and proceed to negotiating further intermediate limitations on nuclear testing leading to the ultimate objective of the complete cessation of nuclear testing as part of an effective disarmament process. This process, among other things, would pursue, as the first priority, the goal of the reduction of nuclear weapons and, ultimately, their elimination. In implementing the first objective of these negotiations, agreement upon effective verification measures for the U.S.-USSR Threshold Test Ban Treaty of 1974, the sides agreed to design and conduct a Joint Verification Experiment at each other's test sites.

The leaders therefore noted with satisfaction the signing of the Joint Verification Experiment Agreement, the considerable preparation underway for the Experiment, and the positive cooperation being exhibited in particular by the substantial numbers of personnel now engaged in work at each other's test sites. They also noted the substantial progress on a new Protocol to the Peaceful Nuclear Explosions Treaty and urged continuing constructive negotiations on effective verification measures for the Threshold Test Ban Treaty.

Expressing their conviction that the progress achieved so far forms a solid basis for continuing progress on issues relating to nuclear testing, the leaders instructed their negotiators to complete expeditiously the preparation of a Protocol to the Peaceful Nuclear Explosions Treaty and to complete the preparation of a Protocol to the Threshold Test Ban Treaty as soon as possible after the Joint Verification Experiment has been conducted and analyzed. They confirmed their understanding that verification measures for the TTBT will, to the extent appropriate, be used in further nuclear test limitation agreements which may subsequently be reached. They also declared their mutual intention to seek ratification of both the 1974 and 1976 Treaties when the corresponding protocols to the Threshold Test Ban Treaty and the Peaceful Nuclear Explosions Treaty are completed, and to continue negotiations as agreed in the Washington joint summit statement.

Nuclear Non-Proliferation

The two leaders noted that this year marks the 20th Anniversary of the Nuclear Non-Proliferation Treaty, one of the most important international arms control agreements with over 130 adherents. They reaffirmed their conviction that universal adherence to the NPT is important to international peace and security. They expressed the hope that each state not a party to the Treaty will join it, or make an equally binding commitment under international law to forego acquisition of nuclear weapons and prevent nuclear weapons proliferation. This will enhance the possibility of progress toward reducing nuclear armaments and reduce the threat of nuclear war.

The two leaders also confirmed their support of the International Atomic Energy Agency, and agreed that they would continue efforts to further strengthen it. They reaffirmed the value of their regular consultations on non-proliferation and agreed that they should continue.

Nuclear Risk Reduction Centers

The leaders expressed satisfaction over the activation of the new communications link between the Nuclear Risk Reduction Centers in Moscow and Washington, established in accordance with the U.S.-Soviet agreement of September 15, 1987. It was agreed that the Centers can play an important role in the context of a future Treaty on reducing U.S. and Soviet strategic nuclear arms.

Chemical Weapons

The leaders reviewed the status of ongoing multilateral negotiations and bilateral U.S.-Soviet consultations toward a comprehensive, effectively verifiable, and truly global ban on chemical weapons, encompassing all chemical weapons-capable states. They also expressed concern over the growing problem of chemical weapons proliferation and use.

The leaders reaffirmed the importance of efforts to address, as a matter of continuing urgency, the unique challenges of a chemical weapons ban and to achieve an effective convention. While noting the progress already achieved in the talks and the difficult problems with regard to effective monitoring of the global prohibition of chemical weapons and the non-use of dual-capable chemicals for chemical weapons purposes, the leaders underlined the need for concrete solutions to the problems of ensuring effective verification and undiminished security for all convention participants. They gave instructions to their respective delegations to this effect.

Both sides agreed on the vital importance of greater openness by all states as a way to build confidence and strengthen the foundation for an effective convention. The leaders also emphasized the necessity of close coordination on a multilateral basis in order to ensure the participation of all CW-possessing and CW-capable states in the convention.

Both sides strongly condemned the dangerous spread and illegal use of chemical weapons in violation of the 1925 Geneva Protocol. They stressed the importance of both technical and political solutions to this problem and confirmed their support for international investigations of suspected violations. Noting the initial efforts being made to control the export of chemicals used in manufacturing chemical weapons, the leaders called on all nations with the capability of producing such chemicals to institute stringent export controls to inhibit the proliferation of chemical weapons.

Conventional Arms Control

The leaders emphasized the importance of strengthening stability and security in the whole of Europe. They welcomed progress to date on development of a mandate for new negotiations on armed forces and conventional armaments. They expressed their hope for an early and balanced conclusion to the Vienna CSCE Follow-Up Meeting. The President and the General Secretary also noted that full implementation of the provisions of the document of the Stockholm Conference on Confidence- and Security-Building Measures and Disarmament in Europe can significantly increase openness and mutual confidence.

They also discussed the situation in the Mutual and Balanced Force Reduction (MBFR) negotiations in Vienna.

Conference on Security and Cooperation in Europe

They expressed their commitment to further development of the CSCE process. The U.S. and USSR will continue to work with the other 33 participants to bring the Vienna CSCE follow-up meeting to a successful conclusion, through significant results in all the principal areas of the Helsinki Final Act and Madrid Concluding Document.

Ballistic Missile Technology Proliferation

The leaders agreed to bilateral discussions at the level of experts on the problem of proliferation of ballistic missile technology.

Third Special Session of the UN General Assembly

The President and the General Secretary noted the importance of the ongoing Third Special Session on Disarmament.

II. HUMAN RIGHTS AND HUMANITARIAN CONCERNS

The President and the General Secretary engaged in a detailed discussion of human rights and humanitarian concerns. The leaders reviewed the increasingly broad and detailed U.S.-Soviet dialogue in this area and agreed that it should be conducted at all levels in order to achieve sustained, concrete progress. They noted that this dialogue should seek to maximize assurance of the rights, freedoms and human dignity of individuals; promotion of people-to-people communications and contacts; active sharing of spiritual, cultural, historical and other values; and greater mutual understanding and respect between the two countries. Toward this end, they discussed the possible establishment of a forum which, meeting regularly, would bring together participants from across the range of their two societies. They noted steps already taken to establish the exchange of information and contacts between legislative bodies of both countries, as well as discussions between legal experts, physicians and representatives of other professions directly involved in matters pertaining to human rights, and between representatives of non-governmental organizations.

III. Regional Issues

The President and the General Secretary thoroughly discussed a wide range of regional questions, including the Middle East, the Iran-Iraq war, southern Africa, the Horn of Africa, Central America, Cambodia, the Korean Peninsula, and other issues. They expressed satisfaction with the April, 1988, conclusion in Geneva of accords on an Afghanistan settlement. Although the discussions revealed serious differences both in the assessment of the causes of regional tensions and in the means to overcome them, the leaders agreed that these differences need not be an obstacle to constructive interaction between the U.S. and USSR.

They reaffirmed their intention to continue U.S.-Soviet discussions at all levels aimed at helping parties to regional conflicts find peaceful solutions which advance their independence, freedom and security. They emphasized the importance of enhancing the capacity of the United Nations and other international institutions to contribute to the resolution of regional conflicts.

IV. Bilateral Affairs

The President and the General Secretary reviewed progress in further expanding bilateral contacts, exchanges and cooperation since their meeting in Washington, D.C. in December 1987. They noted the increasingly important role that mutually beneficial interchange between the two countries can play in improving mutual understanding and providing stability in the U.S.-Soviet relationship. They stated their intention to intensify such ties.

They noted with particular satisfaction that concrete agreements had been reached in most of the areas identified at their meetings in Geneva, Reykjavik and Washington.

Bilateral Agreements and Cooperative Activities

The President and the General Secretary welcomed the conclusion of a number of bilateral agreements which open new opportunities for fruitful cooperation in the following fields: cooperation in transportation science and technology; maritime search and rescue; operational coordination between U.S. and Soviet radionavigation systems in the Northern Pacific and Bering Sea; and mutual fisheries relations.

The two leaders welcomed the recent signing of a new Memorandum on Civilian Nuclear Reactor Safety under the bilateral agreement on Peaceful Uses of Atomic Energy. There was an exchange of notes to extend that Agreement.

They expressed satisfaction with the recent signing of a new protocol under the bilateral Housing Agreement for cooperation in construction research relating to extreme geological and unusual climatic conditions.

They reviewed the status of negotiations between the two countries concerning maritime shipping, the U.S.-USSR maritime boundary, basic scientific research, and emergency pollution clean-up in the Bering and Chukchi Seas. They instructed their negotiators to accelerate efforts to achieve mutually acceptable agreements in these areas at the earliest opportunity.

The two leaders welcomed the start of bilateral discussions on combatting narcotics trafficking. They noted with satisfaction ongoing consultations between the two sides concerning law of the sea, air and sea transportation safety, and areas of mutual interest in the field of law.

Cultural and People-to-People Exchanges

Noting the expansion of exchanges in the areas of education, science, culture and sports under the General Exchanges Agreement, the two leaders welcomed the signing of a new implementing program for 1989–91 under the Agreement and expressed their intention to continue expansion of such exchanges. During the time in which this program is in force, the two sides, taking into consideration their mutual interest as well as financial and technical conditions, will conduct negotiations on the opening of culture/information centers in the U.S. and the USSR with the aim of signing an appropriate agreement on behalf of the governments of both countries.

They expressed satisfaction that, over the course of their dialogue, people-to-people contacts and exchanges between non-governmental organizations have significantly increased and become one of the most dynamic elements in the bilateral relationship. They reaffirmed their commitment to further growth of such exchanges, which contribute to mutual understanding, and welcomed plans for increased exchanges of young people in the future. In this context, they expressed their readiness to consider in practical terms the idea of further developing exchanges of high school students. They cited recent joint U.S.-Soviet initiatives on culture, theater and the cinema as examples of new opportunities to engage those involved in the creative arts.

Noting the rapidly growing sports ties between the two countries, including their national Olympic committees, the two leaders expressed their support for the International Olympic movement, which promotes international cooperation and understanding through athletic competition.

Other Cooperative Activities

The President and the General Secretary noted the successful expansion of scientific cooperation within the framework of bilateral agreements in Environmental Protection, Medical Science and Public Health, Artificial Heart Research and Development, Agriculture, and Studies of the World Ocean, and expressed their intention to continue to expand activities under these Agreements in areas of mutual benefit to the two sides.

The President and the General Secretary noted with pleasure the commencement of work on a conceptual design of an International Thermonuclear Experimental Reactor (ITER), under the auspices of the International Atomic Energy Agency, between scientists and experts from the United States, Soviet Union, European Atomic Energy Community, and Japan. The two leaders noted the significance of this next step toward the development of fusion power as a cheap, environmentally sound, and essentially inexhaustible energy source for the benefit of all mankind.

The President and the General Secretary welcomed agreement by representatives of the United States, Soviet Union, Canada and France, to institutionalize in the near future the COSPAS/SARSAT space-based, life-saving global search and rescue system.

Both leaders reaffirmed their support for the WHO/UNICEF goal of reducing the scale of preventable childhood death through the most effective methods of saving children. They urged other countries and the international community to intensify efforts to achieve this goal.

Global Climate and Environmental Change Initiative

The two leaders expressed their satisfaction with activities since the Washington summit in expanding cooperation with respect to global climate and environmental change, including in areas of mutual concern relating to environmental protection, such as protection and conservation of stratospheric ozone and a possible global warming trend. They emphasized their desire to make more active use of the unique opportunities afforded by the space programs of the two countries to conduct global monitoring of the environment and the ecology of the Earth's land, oceans and atmosphere. They underscored the need to continue to promote both bilateral and multilateral cooperation in this important area in the future.

Initiative for Expanded Civil Space Cooperation

Recognizing the long-standing commitment of both countries to space science and exploration, and noting the progress made under the 1987 U.S.-USSR Cooperative Agreement in the Exploration and Use of Outer Space for Peaceful Purposes, the two leaders agreed to a new initiative to expand civil space cooperation by exchanging flight opportunities for scientific instruments to fly on each other's spacecraft, and by exchanging results of independent national studies of future unmanned solar system exploration missions as a means of assessing prospects for further U.S.-Soviet cooperation on such missions. They also agreed to expand exchanges of space science data and of scientists, to enhance the scientific benefit that can be derived from the two countries' space research missions. They noted scientific missions to the Moon and Mars as areas of possible bilateral and international cooperation.

Arctic Contacts and Cooperation

Taking into account the unique environmental, demographic and other characteristics of the Arctic, the two leaders reaffirmed their support for expanded bilateral and regional contacts and cooperation in this area. They noted plans and opportunities for increased scientific and environmental cooperation under a number of bilateral agreements as well as within an International Arctic Science Committee of states with interests in the region. They expressed their support for increased people-to-people contacts between the native peoples of Alaska and the Soviet North.

The President and the General Secretary noted the positive role played by the multilateral Antarctic Treaty and emphasized the importance of U.S.-Soviet scientific and environmental cooperation in that region.

Trade and Economic Affairs

The two sides reconfirmed their strong support for the expansion of mutually beneficial trade and economic relations and noted recent activity in this area. They reiterated their belief that commercially viable joint ventures complying with the laws and regulations of both countries could play a role in the further development of commercial relations. They welcomed the results of the meeting of the Joint U.S.-USSR Commercial Commission in April and noted with satisfaction that working groups had been created under the Commission to further the establishment of better conditions under which mutually advantageous trade can develop. Taking note of the 1974 Joint Statement and Protocol amending the Long-Term Agreement between the United States of America and the Union of Soviet Socialist Republics to Facilitate Economic, Industrial and Technical Cooperation issued at the conclusion of the Joint Commercial Commission, they agreed that the Commission should continue to meet to build upon the forward momentum which has been generated.

The two leaders cited expanding relations between Aeroflot and Pan American Airlines under the government-to-government Civil Air Transportation Agreement as a positive example of mutually beneficial cooperation.

Consulates Exchange/Diplomatic and Consular Missions

The President and the General Secretary reaffirmed their agreement to open Consulates General in Kiev and New York as soon as practicable.

The two leaders discussed questions relating to ensuring adequate and secure conditions for U.S. and Soviet diplomatic and consular establishments and their personnel in each other's territory. They agreed on the need to approach problems relating to such matters constructively and on the basis of reciprocity.

V. FUTURE MEETINGS

The President and the General Secretary, recognizing the importance of their personal involvement in the development of relations in the months ahead, instructed Secretary of State Shultz and Foreign Minister Shevardnadze to meet as necessary and to report to them on ways to ensure continued practical progress across the full range of issues. Expert-level contacts will also continue on an intensified basis.

Note: The joint statement was not issued as a White House press release.

The President's News Conference Following the Soviet-United States Summit Meeting in Moscow
June 1, 1988

The President. I have a statement. First, if just this one time I might speak for all of you as well as myself, I would like to extend my thanks to General Secretary Gorbachev, all of his associates in the Soviet Government, and the people of Moscow for all they've done to make our stay here a pleasant one and this summit conference the success it has been.

This is my fourth summit. For some in our governments and some of you in the media, the number is higher. But a good deal of important work has been accomplished here in Moscow. And the relationship between Mr. Gorbachev and me, and the various members of our respective delegations, has continued to deepen and improve. But personal relationships and hopes for peace are not by themselves enough. I think history will note that in our approach to the summit process the United States has sought a consistency of expression as well as purpose. While at every turn I've tried to state our overwhelming desire for peace, I have also tried to note the existence of fundamental differences. And that's why it's a source of great satisfaction that those differences, in part as a result of these meetings, continue to recede.

In addition, spokesmen for the Soviet Government have noted the change of policy, indeed, the profound change of policy that has occurred in their own government. The United States is fully cognizant of this change and aware of its implications. In noting the differences that still stand between us, therefore, my desire has not been to sound a note of discouragement but one of realism, not to conduct a tutorial but to give the kind of emphatic testimony to the truth that, over the long run, removes illusion and moves the process of negotiation forward.

From our standpoint, this approach has borne fruit at previous meetings and at this summit conference. And here, permit me to go back for just a moment to our first summit meeting at Geneva. There we agreed on certain fundamental realities that would govern our relations: that a nuclear war cannot be won and must never be fought, that the United States and the Soviet Union bear special responsibilities for avoiding the risk of war, that neither side should seek military superiority over the other. We affirmed our determination to prevent war, whether nuclear or conventional, and our resolve to contribute in every way possible, along with other nations, to a safer world.

We also set out a broad agenda and initiated a new process of dialog to address the sources of tension in U.S.-Soviet relations. Since Geneva, we have achieved, through a sustained effort, progress across this broad agenda. Our first discussions here in Moscow focused on the important matter of human rights, individual freedoms. The United States views human rights as fundamental to our relationship with the Soviet Union and all nations. From the beginning, we've stressed this point and are encouraged by recent signs of progress in the Soviet Union. I believe that where people have the right to speak, write, travel, and worship freely, creative energies are released. On several occasions I've said that nations do not distrust each other because they're armed; they are armed because they distrust each other.

For the past 3 years, General Secretary Gorbachev and I have worked to build a relationship of greater trust. And we both recognize that one way to do that is to improve understanding between our two countries through broader people-to-people contacts. A series of agreements to expand U.S.-Soviet bilateral cooperation, including cultural exchanges, have been concluded. We agreed to expand our student exchange programs, with a goal of allowing hundreds, and eventually thousands, of Soviet and American high school students to study in each other's classrooms. For our future relations, academic, cultural, and other exchanges are of greater importance.

Turning to regional issues, Mr. Gorbachev and I agree that there must be peaceful solutions to these conflicts. Our goal is to advance independence, security, and freedom. The Soviet decision to withdraw from Afghanistan is significant, and we agree that building on the Afghan settlement leads to an approach to other regional problems. Our discussions also dealt with Cambodia, Angola, Ethiopia, the Middle East and the Persian Gulf, and Central America.

Each of our summit meetings moved us farther toward an INF treaty, capped by today's exchange of ratification instruments, which now makes it a reality. Each meeting has also moved us farther toward meeting the even greater challenge of crafting a treaty to reduce our strategic nuclear arsenals. In Geneva, the General Secretary and I agreed on the concept of 50-percent reductions; and in Reykjavik, on numerical limits for warheads and delivery vehicles; in Washington, on intensive work to complete a START treaty, including comprehensive verification provisions building upon those in INF.

Here in Moscow, we've made important additional strides toward that objective. Verification is one of the most important and most difficult issues for us, and I'm pleased to report progress in this area, too. We've moved forward in other areas as well, including agreements on an experiment to improve the verification of existing nuclear testing treaties and on notification of strategic ballistic missile launches.

Finally, let me say how deeply moving I have found my discussions with various citizens of the Soviet Union. The monks of Danilov, the dissidents and refuseniks, the writers and artists, the students and young people have shown once again that spiritual values are cherished in this nation. It's my fervent hope that those values will attain even fuller expression.

And now I will be happy to take your questions. And, Helen [Helen Thomas, United Press International], we begin with you.

Soviet-U.S. Relations

Q. Mr. President, I know you've touched on this, but at your first news conference in 1981, you said that the Soviets lie and cheat and pursue their ends of world domination. What has really changed your mind? Can the American people really trust the Russians now? And I'd like to follow up.

The President. Well, Helen, that was the first press conference that I'd held since being elected President. And the question that came to me was: Could we believe the Russians, or would they lie to us? And my answer at that time was not expressing my opinion. I said, I will answer that with their own words. And then I cited some of the leaders of the Communist movement in the Soviet Union that said that the only immorality was anything that slowed the growth of socialism and that there was no immorality in lying or cheating or doing anything of that kind, as long as it advanced the cause of socialism. Now, that was my answer. So, it wasn't an opinion. I was quoting what their leaders themselves—the beginners of that particular system—had said.

Q. Well, that's what you thought then. Do you still think that, and can you now declare the cold war over?

The President. I think right now, of course, as I've said, *dovorey no provorey*—trust but verify.

Q. Well, is that the atmosphere now?

The President. But I think that there is quite a difference today in the leadership and in the relationship between our two countries. And we have held very productive meetings that I think were productive for both sides.

Arms Control

Q. Mr. President, on the START treaty, what are the areas of progress, and what's the specific progress that you achieved here? And why do you think that you can conclude a treaty this year, when Senate leaders are urging you to go slow, and this summit, with all its momentum, wasn't able to break the impasse?

The President. Well, the Senate leaders themselves brought the verification—or the ratification papers here that we just received today on the INF treaty. It meant changing their own schedules a great deal and speeding up the ratification process. I think that we could count on them to feel the same if we are coming to final agreement on a START treaty.

But I want to remind you of one thing that we've said over and over again. The START treaty is infinitely more complex than the INF treaty, and therefore, there is going to be continued negotiation on a number of points. And then it will depend on the Senate once—if we have agreed upon a treaty, it is their responsibility to thoroughly study that treaty and then issue ratification of it if they find it satisfactory.

We can hope. I would hope that before the year is out that we could eliminate the differences that still exist. But if not, I would hope that my successor would continue because here we are getting at, I think, the most important reduction that should take place in nuclear weapons. The most destabilizing are the intercontinental ballistic missiles in which someone pushes a button and minutes later a part of the Earth blows up. And the thing that I express my hope about is that not only have we said 50 percent, but in that first meeting in Geneva the General Secretary proposed the idea also of reducing by half our nuclear missiles.

Q. To follow up, sir: Could you go over the areas of progress on START that you achieved here?

The President. No, I don't think that I should go on. The conversations are still going on, and there are things still being discussed. And as I say, progress has been made, or we wouldn't still be talking the way we are. But—

There's a young lady in the back that I think is native to the scene.

Soviet-U.S. Relations

Q. Mr. President, is there something in Soviet-American relations that you would advise your successor to leave behind? And is there something that you would especially advise to take to the future?

The President. Wait a minute. If I heard the entire question—special advice on what?

Q. Is there something in Soviet-American relations that you would advise your successor to leave behind, and is there something specific that you would advise him to take to the future? To follow up, yes.

The President. Yes. If these negotiations and so forth are still going on, I will do everything I can to persuade my successor to follow up and to continue. And as a matter of fact, I think I'll tell him that he will find the Russian people most warm and hospitable and friendly.

Human Rights

Q. Mr. President, Soviet officials have told us they have dossiers on all of the dissidents and that some of those people—in fact, they've said that all those people are not the best people representing Soviet society. How do you feel about the fact that they have kept dossiers on these dissidents with whom you met, and doesn't that contradict your view that there have been improvements here and that this is a more open society under Mr. Gorbachev?

The President. Well, no, the figures themselves reveal that improvements have been made. Some 300 people have been freed from imprisonment. The lists that we bring are names that have been brought to our attention by relatives or friends—their own relatives, for example, living in our country now—and I have brought those names to the General Secretary and explained the personal interest that we have in them. And a great many of them have since been allowed to come to our country or to other countries that they preferred, such as Israel. And so, I think there has been a sizable improvement, and we still are going to continue doing that.

Q. But, sir, what about the fact that the very people with whom you met have now been investigated by Soviet authorities and might be subject to some form of retaliation? Mr. Gorbachev said today that you no longer feel that this is the "evil empire," that you told him that within the Kremlin walls. Doesn't this contradict your new feeling of optimism about the Soviet Union?

The President. No, because as I say, he

has received the latest list that I brought here, and previous experiences with this—a great many of those people have been allowed to come to our country.

Soviet-U.S. Relations

Q. Sir, yesterday you did say you no longer believed the Soviet Union is an "evil empire." You said that was another time, another era. What's changed? Is it just Mr. Gorbachev's succession to the General Secretaryship, or have you yourself changed or expanded your view of the Soviet Union?

The President. No, I think that a great deal of it is due to the General Secretary, who I have found different than previous Soviet leaders have been; but that also as we have pursued this, we have found them willing to enter into negotiations with us. And I think that enough progress has been made that we can look with optimism on future negotiations.

Q. Sir, I suppose I'm asking if you think that there's anything that you have learned, that you personally have expanded or changed your views because you've had an opportunity to learn more about this country over the years and about their system so that you think you are part of the process; or is it just Gorbachev?

The President. Well, a large part of it is Mr. Gorbachev as a leader. And I think there have been changes here as they have sought to make—well, I read *"Perestroika,"* and I found much in it that I could agree with.

Bill [Bill Plante, CBS News]?

Strategic Defense Initiative

Q. Mr. President, Mr. Gorbachev said in his news conference that he thought you could have achieved more in this summit. Specifically, he went on to say that on the issue of the ABM interpretation of the treaty—said that you had gone back on your word, that in Geneva you had agreed that you would no longer seek military superiority, and that by holding to the development of SDI you were seeking superiority in outer space, and that, therefore, you had gone back on your word. Are you seeking superiority in outer space? Can you reach a START agreement without some accommodation on SDI and the ABM question?

The President. SDI, in my mind—maybe some of my people wouldn't agree with me—but the whole thing was my idea to see if there could not be developed a defensive weapon that would make it virtually impossible for nuclear missiles to get through to their targets in another country. And from the very beginning, I have said that if and when such a system can be developed I would support the idea of making it available worldwide, because since we all know how to make nuclear missiles, sometime there could be a madman come along, as a Hitler came along, who could then make those missiles—but that my idea would be the sharing of the knowledge of SDI as a defensive weapon—would be accompanied by the total elimination of nuclear weapons. And I happen to believe that this will be a lot better world if we get rid of all the nuclear weapons. And that is what my dream of SDI is: that it can be the tool by which we eliminate.

Q. Well, sir, if I may follow up, Mr. Gorbachev said today that he did not believe that it's for defensive purposes.

The President. I know you said that before, and I——

Q. Well, you failed to convince him, despite the fact that you're on such good terms with him.

The President. Well, maybe he just doesn't know me well enough. But from the very first, I have said that that is my goal for that defensive weapon. There is nothing offensive about it. It cannot hurt or kill anyone. It can just make it impossible for missiles to get through the screen.

Now, you, and then I'm going to start spreading around here.

Arms Control

Q. Mr. President, I want to ask you about this effort you again stated today to try to get a START treaty before you leave office. You have less than 8 months left in office. Mikhail Gorbachev could have 20 years. By setting up any kind of deadline, no matter how unofficial, aren't you putting all the pressure on the U.S. side?

The President. Oh, no, no. We set no deadline. I said we're going to continue working toward that. And I could hope that maybe in that period of time—but, no, I am dead set against deadlines. You don't make a treaty just to simply have it be achieved at a certain point in time. The treaty is ready when it is a good treaty and good for all sides involved. And that's what we'll do instead of setting a deadline and then saying, well, let's sign it because we've reached the deadline. It has to be good.

Future Soviet-U.S. Summit Meeting

Q. If I might follow up, sir: There is also talk about a fifth summit sometime this year to sign a treaty, which might come sometime in the fall. To prevent U.S.-Soviet relations from being mixed up in politics, are you willing to rule out a summit until the Presidential campaign is over in November?

The President. I'd make any decision of that kind based on how I thought it could affect the situation. And if it gave a promise of success, then go for it.

Terms for National Leaders

Q. Mr. President, you were asked by one of the students at Moscow University yesterday about the practice in the United States of limiting Presidential terms. I believe you said you were going to go out on the mashed-potato circuit next year and campaign for repeal of that constitutional amendment. Were you aware that Mr. Gorbachev, as part of his reforms, is promoting the idea of limited terms for the leader of the Soviet Union? And do you think it's a good idea for the Soviet Union?

The President. Well, I would hesitate to comment on that. I mean, this system of government here—you do not have a national election in which all of the people vote to see who would be the leader. My objection to the constitutional amendment that was passed in our country limiting a President to two terms was the fact that that is the only office in the United States in which all the people vote for the candidates for that office. And it seems to me that it is an infringement on the rights of our people in a democracy to tell them that they can't vote for someone because of a time limit. I think it impinges on their right to vote for whoever they want to vote for as many times as they want to vote for them. That is the principle of democracy.

Soviet-U.S. Relations

Q. Mr. President, if I may just ask one more question on the students, you talked a lot about how it is a positive thing for students from both countries to mix and mingle, to get to know each other, to understand each other. Do you think part of your positive feeling about the Soviet Union these days comes as a result of greater tolerance that you've developed as a result of your meetings with Mr. Gorbachev over the past few years?

The President. Well, I have found that Mr. Gorbachev and I have, I think, a very satisfactory relationship. But at the same time, I am never going to relax my belief in the need for verification of agreements that we might make, and I'm quite sure he feels the same way.

Now, where is the gentleman?

Troop Reductions in Europe

Q. I'm here, Mr. President. I understand that in your first meeting with Mr. Gorbachev he suggested the reduction of half-a-million military personnel as certain condition, but there was no followup, as it were. Was this subject raised again, and what was your response?

The President. No, this proposal—that was just—been a suggestion made of the removal of a half-a-million men on the NATO line in the European front. This has to be considered. We think that we are coming to a point—and that he himself is willing to—of reductions in conventional weapons along that front, and conventional forces as well as the nuclear forces. But the simple removing of a half-a-million men would not be exactly equal because his military would be moved a short distance back away from the front. Well, there's a 3,000-mile ocean between where our men would have to be moved, and in the event of an emergency, we'd have an ocean to cross to get our men back there and equal. So, that has to be considered.

Human Rights in the Soviet Union

Q. Mr. President, General Secretary Gorbachev, in his remarks earlier this afternoon, was talking about your comments here on human rights, and he said, "I did not have a lot of admiration for that part of the trip." When you met with the General Secretary privately, we know, of course, that you discussed human rights. Did he say anything to you specifically about the meeting with dissidents or your remarks at Danilov Monastery or the remarks yesterday at the Writers Union?

The President. No, but I do know that he and others have had a feeling that in some way our concern with this is interfering with your internal government policies. I have explained to him, and I think maybe he has seen the point. Our country is very unique. All of us, either by ourselves or through our ancestors or our grandparents or parents, came from someplace else—about the only nation in the world that can say that. As a matter of fact, the estimate is that one out of eight Americans trace their parentage and their heritage, if not their own immigration, to the Eastern bloc.

And so, I have put it this way: that you don't stop loving your mother because you've taken unto yourself a wife. So, the people in America do have a feeling for the countries of their heritage. In my case, it was a great-grandfather on one side and a grandmother and grandfather on my mother's side. Well, Americans retain that feeling of friendship and loyalty to the countries that, as I say, are their heritage. And so, when we feel that people are being unjustly treated—imprisoned for something that in our country would not be a crime, calling for such a sentence—our people get aroused, and they come to us, and they want help. They want something done.

A wife, who's been waiting for 8 years for her husband to be allowed to leave this country to join her—things of this kind we don't think are really interfering with someone else's business. We think it's very much our business to bring it to the attention where we feel that there is an injustice to the Government. And I have explained this to the General Secretary, and I think he has seen the justice of what I've said because many of the individuals that we've brought to his attention have now been released from confinement here and have been allowed to emigrate—come to other countries, to our country.

"Peaceful Coexistence" Pledge

Q. Mr. President, Mr. Gorbachev says that he proposed a draft statement that would use the words "peaceful coexistence." And he said that your first response to that was, "I like it." But that when you came back from meeting with your aides, you seem to have changed your mind. Did you, and why?

The President. Well, I liked the whole tone, the general tone of it, and what it was seeking to achieve was what we're both seeking to achieve. But I said at the same time, I would take it to our people. And I took it there, and they studied it and saw where there could have been certain ambiguities in there that would not achieve the general thought of what was being proposed. We were in agreement with the general thought. So, some rewriting was done by our own people. And when the total statement is released to you, I think you will find that we have achieved what it was he had with the paragraph that he proposed. And it's been achieved and improved to the point that it is clear and unmistakable, that it achieves the purpose that he had in mind.

Q. Well, if I could follow up, sir: You've sort of teased us now. If you could give us some sense of what you've proposed to substitute for peaceful coexistence? What's the better term that your aides had advised you to use?

The President. No, peaceful coexistence—both pieces achieve the same end, but the other one had ambiguities in it. And I don't think they were intentional, but they could have been used to justify doing something else that was not in keeping with the entire goal of the statement here.

Government Bureaucracy

Q. Mr. President, if I could follow up on your comments on emigration: Yesterday when you were talking about a family denied the right to emigrate, you called it a bureaucratic problem; you said you blamed the bureaucracy. Do you believe that essentially it is just bureaucratic lethargy that has caused that problem in the Soviet Union?

The President. Well, now, somebody distracted me back there. I think someone else thought I had pointed at them instead of you.

Q. Yesterday, when you spoke to the students about—you were talking about emigration and a family in particular that had been denied the right to emigrate, and you said you blamed the bureaucracy. Do you view the emigration problem from the Soviet Union as essentially a problem of just a lethargic bureaucracy?

The President. I'm afraid that I have to confess to you that I think one of the sins of government, and one with which we must deal and never have been able to be completely successful with, and this includes our own government, is that the bureaucracy once created has one fundamental rule above all others: Preserve the bureaucracy. And I think that governments will always find that they are having to check on bureaucracy and make sure that it is not abiding by its own rules and taking the easiest course. And so, I wouldn't—picking on one government other than another.

Human Rights in the United States

Q. If I could follow up: You said that you believed you persuaded Mr. Gorbachev on some of these emigration questions. But he said on human rights in the United States that you—he did not find your arguments convincing. Do you consider that a failure in this summit?

The President. I think that there is a mistaken view, and, oh, how I yearn to have him come to our country for long enough to see some of our country. I think there is a mistaken view about the things that occasionally dominate the press about prejudice, racial or religious, in our country, about the so-called street people that apparently have no place to live. And I think these are socioeconomic problems in our land; we have them, of course. We also try to deal with them. But I don't think he quite could understand a recent situation. A young lady living on the sidewalks of New York, living out there on the sidewalk, winter and summer. And so, for her own sake, the police picked her up to bring her to where she could be placed in a shelter. And she took her case to court and won her case in court that she should be allowed to go back and sleep on the sidewalk where she had been because that's what she preferred to do. Well, when you have a free country, how far can we go in impinging on the freedom of someone who says this is the way I want to live. And I think we can straighten him out if he saw what we did in our country.

Soviet Emigration

Q. Mr. President, in this room on Monday, you heard moving stories of people who had been—[*inaudible*]—and you wrote it off to bureaucracy. Is that really your view that it is only the bureaucracy? It is not a willful policy of the Government here to keep these people from emigrating?

The President. No, I can't say that it's one. I don't know that much about the system, but it was a question that was presented to me on the basis that it possibly was a bureaucratic bungle. Maybe I should illustrate to you why I feel the way I do about bureaucracies. Once during the war, I happened to be involved in a situation in which one level of the military wanted a warehouse full of filing cabinets—wanted permission to destroy the files so they could use those filing cases. And they were able to prove that the documents had no historic value. They had no bearing on present-day government at all. They were just useless. And so, the message went up through the ranks, requesting permission to destroy these obsolete files. And then, back down through the ranks, from the top command, endorsed by each level of command, came the reply: Permission granted, providing copies were made of each file destroyed.

Q. Can I follow that up? Don't you think you're letting Mr. Gorbachev off a little easy on just saying it's a bureaucracy?

The President. No, as I said, I don't. The way the question was framed, I thought that there was a possibility of that. No, but I just have to believe that in any government some of us do find ourselves bound in by bureaucracy, and then sometimes you have to stomp your foot and say, unmistakably, I want it done. And then maybe you get through with it. But I have great confidence in his ability to do that. Lou [Lou Cannon, Washington Post]?

Strategic Arms Control

Q. Thank you, sir. You said starting at the beginning of this year and going into this summit that if there was this progress toward a START treaty you would be willing to come together a fifth time and sign it, but only if it was a good treaty. You've referred to that today again several times. What is your judgment, your best judgment, on the basis of this summit: Have you made enough progress that you now think that a START treaty is likely within your term?

The President. Lou [Lou Cannon, Washington Post]—and I honestly cannot answer that. I don't know. Let me just give you what the mechanics are: that our people have been steadily in Geneva—both sides, Soviet people and our people—working on this treaty, knowing what we hope to achieve, and they're working there. And as I say, they've made progress. There is no way to judge, and there is no way that I would give them a date and say, please, you have to get this by such and such a time because that's not the way to get a good treaty. I want a good treaty.

Future Soviet-U.S. Summit Meeting

Q. Sir, if I could follow up: Is the only condition under which you would have a fifth summit with Mr. Gorbachev is if there was, in fact, what you thought was a good START treaty ready to be signed?

The President. Well, you can't rule out. Something else might come up that necessitates our getting together and settling something other than that particular treaty. So, no one can say, no, there will be no need for a summit.

Q. Thank you, Mr. President.

The President. When Helen [Helen Thomas, United Press International] says that, I'm sorry, I have to leave.

Soviet Women

Q. Mr. President, what have you learned about the Soviet Union? What have you learned in your first trip to Moscow?

The President. I'm going to do one answer because I've wanted to say this, and I say it anytime I get a chance. I think that one of the most wonderful forces for stability and good that I have seen in the Soviet Union are the Russian women.

Note: The President's news conference began at 4 p.m. in the ballroom at Spaso House.

Announcement of the Appointment of Admiral Frank B. Kelso II as Supreme Allied Commander, Atlantic
June 1, 1988

The President has nominated and the NATO Defense Planning Committee today has appointed Adm. Frank B. Kelso II, U.S. Navy, to succeed Admiral Baggett as Supreme Allied Commander, Atlantic.

The Committee has been informed of the contents of a letter from the President of the United States of America to the Secretary General of the North Atlantic Treaty Organization and Chairman of the Committee, in which the President asked the member governments to agree to release Admiral Baggett. The Committee agreed with great regret to release Admiral Baggett from his assignment as Supreme Allied Commander, Atlantic. They expressed to Admiral Baggett, in the name of the governments represented on the Committee, lasting gratitude for his distinguished service.

The Committee requested that the President of the United States of America nominate an officer of the United States Navy for appointment by the Committee as Supreme Allied Commander, Atlantic, to succeed Admiral Baggett. In response to this request, the President of the United States informed the Committee of his nomination of Admiral Kelso for consideration by the Committee as successor to Admiral Baggett. Admiral Kelso is now serving as Commander in Chief, U.S. Atlantic Fleet/Deputy Commander in Chief, U.S. Atlantic Command. At its meeting today, the Committee adopted a resolution appointing Admiral Kelso Supreme Allied Commander, Atlantic, as successor to Admiral Baggett with the same powers and functions.

In addition to the NATO position, Admiral Kelso will be assigned as the Commander in Chief, U.S. Atlantic Command. The transfer of commands will take place in the fall of 1988.

Remarks Following the Soviet-United States Summit Meeting in Moscow
June 2, 1988

The General Secretary. Esteemed Mr. President and Mrs. Reagan, 1 hour from now you will be leaving Moscow. In the first place, I want to thank you and your colleagues for cooperation, openness, and a businesslike approach to the talks that we've had here. I believe that both of us have every reason to regard this meeting and your visit as a useful contribution to the development of dialog between the Soviet Union and the United States.

Mr. President, you and I have been dealing with each other for 3 years now. From the first exchange of letters to the conclusion of this meeting, we've come a long way. Our dialog has not been easy, but we mustered enough realism and political will to overcome obstacles and divert the train of Soviet-U.S. relations from a dangerous track to a safer one. It has, however, so far been moving much more slowly than is required by the real situation, both in our two countries and in the whole world. But as I have understood, Mr. President, you're willing to continue our joint endeavors. For my part, I can assure you that we will do everything in our power to go on moving forward. Now, with the vast experience of Geneva, Reykjavik, Washington, and Moscow and backed up by their achievements, we are, in duty, bound to display still greater determination and consistency. That is what the Soviet and American peoples, international public opinion, and the entire world community are expecting of us.

I hope you will have pleasant memories of your stay in this country. Mr. President, Mrs. Reagan, when you return to America, please convey to the American people best wishes from the peoples of the Soviet Union. Over the past 3 years, our two nations have come to know each other better. They have now taken a really good look in each other's eyes and have a keener sense of the need to learn to live together on this beautiful planet Earth. I wish you good journey back home, Mr. President and Mrs. Reagan. To you and to all members of the U.S. delegation, I wish good health. Goodbye.

The President. Mr. General Secretary, Mrs. Gorbachev, this is an emotional moment for Mrs. Reagan and me. We have been truly moved by the warmth and the generous hospitality that we've received from all of our Soviet hosts during this brief visit—but most especially from the two of you.

During this meeting, as in all of our previous meetings, I appreciated and valued our exchanges and the long hours of hard work that we and our experts put in to make progress on the difficult issues we face. But this meeting has added something else for Mrs. Reagan and me. Our time here has allowed us to know, if only briefly, your art treasures and your people: artists, writers, individuals from all walks of life—people who were willing to share with us their experiences, their fears, their hopes.

Mr. General Secretary, it is fitting that we are ending our visit as we began it, in this hall, named for the Order of St. George. I would like to think that our efforts during these past few days have slayed a few dragons and advanced the struggle against the evils that threaten mankind—threats to peace and to liberty. And I would like to hope that, like St. George, with God's help, peace and freedom can prevail. And, Mr. General Secretary, if you will permit me just one more proverb, I think a very old and popular saying you have here about last Sunday, the day of our arrival, spoke to the promise that we've seen fulfilled at this summit in this Moscow spring. Truly, then, *Troitsa: ves' les raskroitsya* [At the Feast of the Trinity, the whole forest blossoms].

And now, if I might just conclude on a personal note, earlier this week at Moscow State University I mentioned to the young people there that they appeared to my eyes exactly as would any group of students in my own country or anywhere else in the world; so, too, did Nancy. And I find the faces, young and old, here on the streets of Moscow. At first, more than anything else, they were curious faces, but as the time went on, the smiles began and then the waves. And I don't have to tell you, Nancy and I smiled back and waved just as hard.

Mr. General Secretary, I think you understand we're not just grateful to both you and Mrs. Gorbachev but want you to know we think of you as friends. And in that spirit, we would ask one further favor of you. Tell the people of the Soviet Union of the deep feelings of friendship felt by us and by the people of our country toward them. Tell them, too, Nancy and I are grateful for their coming out to see us, grateful for their waves and smiles, and tell them we will remember all of our days their faces: the faces of hope—hope for a new era in human history, an era of peace between our nations and our peoples.

Thank you and God bless you.

Note: The General Secretary spoke at 10:07 a.m. in St. George's Hall at the Grand Kremlin Palace. The President spoke in English, and the General Secretary spoke in Russian. Their remarks were translated by interpreters.

Remarks to Members of the Royal Institute of International Affairs in London
June 3, 1988

My Lord Mayor, Prime Minister, Your Excellencies, my Lords, aldermen, sheriffs, ladies and gentlemen, I wonder if you can imagine what it is for an American to stand in this place. Back in the States, we're terribly proud of anything more than a few hundred years old; some even see my election to the Presidency as America's attempt to show our European cousins that we, too, have a regard for antiquity. [*Laughter*]

Guildhall has been here since the 15th century, and while it is comforting at my age to be near anything that much older than myself—[*laughter*]—the venerable age of this institution is hardly all that impresses. Who can come here and not think upon the moments these walls have seen, the many times that people of this city and nation have gathered here in national crisis or national triumph? In the darkest hours of the last World War, when the tense drama of Edward R. Murrow's opening, "This is London," was enough to impress on millions of Americans the mettle of the British people, how many times in those days did proceedings continue here, a testimony to the cause of civilization for which you stood? From the Marne to El Alamein, to Arnhem, to the Falklands, you have in this century so often remained steadfast for what is right—and against what is wrong. You are a brave people, and this land truly is, as your majestic, moving hymn proclaims, a "land of hope and glory." And it's why Nancy and I, in the closing days of this historic trip, are glad to be in England once again. After a long journey, we feel among friends, and with all our hearts we thank you for having us here.

Such feelings are, of course, especially appropriate to this occasion; I have come from Moscow to report to you, for truly the relationship between the United States and Great Britain has been critical to NATO's success and the cause of freedom. This hardly means that we've always had a perfect understanding. When I first visited Mrs. Thatcher at the British Embassy in 1981, she mischievously reminded me that the huge portrait dominating the grand staircase was none other than that of George III, though she did graciously concede that today most of her countrymen would agree with Jefferson that a little rebellion now and then is a good thing. [*Laughter*] So, there has always been, as there should be among friends, an element of fun about our differences. But let me assure you, it is how much we have in common and the depth of our friendship that truly matters.

I have often mentioned this in the States, but I have never had an opportunity to tell a British audience how, during my first visit here 40 years ago, I was, like most Americans, anxious to see some of the sights and those 400-year-old inns I had been told abound in this country. Well, a driver took me and a couple of other people to an old inn, a pub really—and what in America we would call a "mom and pop" place. This quite elderly lady was waiting on us, and finally, hearing us talk to one another, she said, "You're Americans, aren't you?" And we said we were. "Oh," she said, "there were a lot of your chaps stationed down the road during the war." And she added, "They used to come in here of an evening, and they'd have a songfest. They called me mom, and they called the old man pop." And then her mood changed, and she said, "It was Christmas Eve, and you know, we were all alone and feeling a bit down. And suddenly they burst through the door, and they had presents for me and Pop." And by this time she wasn't looking at us anymore; she was looking off into the distance, into memory, and there were tears in her eyes. And then she said, "Big strapping lads they was, from a place called Ioway." [*Laughter*]

From a place called Ioway—and Oregon, California, Texas, New Jersey, Georgia; here with other young men from Lancaster, Hampshire, Glasgow, and Dorset—all of them caught up in the terrible paradoxes of that time: that young men must wage war to end war, and die for freedom so that freedom itself might live. And it is those same two causes for which they fought and died—the cause of peace, the cause of freedom for all humanity—that still brings us, British and American, together.

For these causes, the people of Great Britain, the United States, and other allied nations have for 44 years made enormous sacrifices to keep our alliance strong and our military ready. For them we embarked in this decade on a new postwar strategy, a forward strategy of freedom, a strategy of public candor about the moral and fundamental differences between statism and democracy, but also a strategy of vigorous diplomatic engagement; a policy that rejects both the inevitability of war or the permanence of totalitarian rule, a policy based on realism that seeks not just treaties for treaties' sake but the recognition and resolution of fundamental differences with our adversaries.

The pursuit of this policy has just now taken me to Moscow, and, let me say, I believe this policy is bearing fruit. Quite possibly, we're beginning to take down the barriers of the postwar era; quite possibly, we are entering a new era in history, a time of lasting change in the Soviet Union. We will have to see. But if so, it's because of the steadfastness of the allies—the democracies—for more than 40 years, and especially in this decade.

The history of our time will undoubtedly include a footnote about how, during this decade and the last, the voice of retreat and hopelessness reached a crescendo in the West—insisting the only way to peace was unilateral disarmament, proposing nuclear freezes, opposing deployment of counterbalancing weapons such as intermediate-range missiles or the more recent concept of strategic defense systems. These same voices ridiculed the notion of going beyond arms control, the hope of doing something more than merely establishing artificial limits within which arms buildups could continue all but unabated. Arms reduction would never work, they said, and when the Soviets left the negotiating table in Geneva for 15 months, they proclaimed disaster.

And yet it was our double-zero option, much maligned when first proposed, that provided the basis for the INF treaty, the first treaty ever that did not just control offensive weapons but reduced them and, yes, actually eliminated an entire class of U.S. and Soviet nuclear missiles. This treaty, last month's development in Afghanistan, the changes we see in the Soviet Union—these are momentous events; not conclusive, but momentous. And that's why, although history will duly note that we, too, heard voices of denial and doubt, it is those who spoke with hope and strength who will be best remembered.

And here I want to say that through all the troubles of the last decade, one such firm, eloquent voice, a voice that proclaimed proudly the cause of the Western alliance and human freedom, has been heard. A voice that never sacrificed its anticommunist credentials or its realistic appraisal of change in the Soviet Union, but because it came from the longest-serving leader in the alliance, it did become one of the first to suggest that we could "do business" with Mr. Gorbachev. So, let me discharge my first official duty here today. Prime Minister, the achievements of the Moscow summit as well as the Geneva and Washington summits say much about your valor and strength and, by virtue of the office you hold, that of the British people. So let me say, simply: At this hour in history, Prime Minister, the entire world salutes you and your gallant people and gallant nation.

And while your leadership and the vision of the British people have been an inspiration, not just to my own people but to all of those who love freedom and yearn for peace, I know you join me in a deep sense of gratitude toward the leaders and peoples of all the democratic allies. Whether deploying crucial weapons of deterrence, standing fast in the Persian Gulf, combating terrorism and aggression by outlaw regimes, or helping freedom fighters around the globe, rarely in history has any alliance of free nations acted with such firmness and dispatch, and on so many fronts. In a process reaching back as far as the founding of NATO and the Common Market, the House of Western Europe, together with the United States, Canada, Japan, and others—this House of Democracy—engaged in an active diplomacy while sparking a startling growth of democratic institutions and free markets all across the globe; in short, an expansion of the frontiers of freedom and a lessening of the chances of war.

So, it is within this context that I report now on events in Moscow. On Wednesday, at 08:20 Greenwich time, Mr. Gorbachev and I exchanged the instruments of ratification of the INF treaty. So, too, we made tangible progress toward the START treaty on strategic weapons. Such a treaty, with all its implications, is, I believe, now within our grasp. But part of the realism and candor we were determined to bring to negotiations with the Soviets meant refusing to put all the weight of these negotiations and our bilateral relationship on the single issue of arms control. As I never tire of saying, nations do not distrust each other because they are armed; they are armed because they distrust each other.

So, equally important items on the agenda dealt with critical issues, like regional conflicts, human rights, and bilateral exchanges. With regard to regional conflicts, here, too, we are now in the third week of the pullout of Soviet troops from Afghanistan. The importance of this step should not be underestimated. Our third area of discussion was bilateral contacts between our peoples, an expanding program of student exchanges and the opening of cultural centers—progress toward a broader understanding of each other. And finally, on the issue of human rights—granting people the right to speak, write, travel, and worship freely—there are signs of greater individual freedom.

Now, originally I was going to give you just an accounting on these items. But, you know, on my first day in Moscow Mr. Gorbachev used a Russian saying: "Better to see something once than to hear about it a hundred times." So, if I might go beyond our four-part agenda today and offer just a moment or two of personal reflection on the country I saw for the first time.

In all aspects of Soviet life, the talk is of progress toward democratic reform—in the economy, in political institutions, in religious, social, and artistic life. It is called *glasnost*—openness; it is *perestroika*—restructuring. Mr. Gorbachev and I discussed his upcoming party conference, where many of these reforms will be debated and perhaps adopted—such things as official accountability, limitations on length of service in office, an independent judiciary, revisions of the criminal law, and lowering taxes on cooperatives. In short, giving individuals more freedom to run their own affairs, to control their own destinies.

To those of us familiar with the postwar era, all of this is cause for shaking the head in wonder. Imagine, the President of the United States and the General Secretary of the Soviet Union walking together in Red Square, talking about a growing personal friendship, and meeting together average citizens, realizing how much our people have in common. It was a special moment in a week of special moments. My personal impression of Mr. Gorbachev is that he is a serious man seeking serious reform. I pray that the hand of the Lord will be on the Soviet people—the people whose faces Nancy and I saw everywhere we went. Believe me, there was one thing about those faces that we will never forget: They were the faces of hope—the hope of a new era in human history and, hopefully, an era of peace and freedom for all.

And yet, while the Moscow summit showed great promise and the response of the Soviet people was heartening, let me interject here a note of caution and, I hope, prudence. It has never been disputes between the free peoples and the peoples of the Soviet Union that have been at the heart of postwar tensions and conflicts. No, disputes among governments over the pursuit of statism and expansionism have been the central point in our difficulties. Now that the allies are strong and expansionism is receding around the world and in the Soviet Union, there is hope. And we look for this trend to continue. We must do all we can to assist it. And this means openly acknowledging positive change and crediting it. But let us also remember the strategy that we have adopted is one that provides for setbacks along the way as well as progress. Let us embrace honest change when it occurs. But let us also be wary; let us stay strong; and let us be confident, too.

Prime Minister, perhaps you remember that upon accepting your gracious invitation to address the members of the Parliament in 1982, I suggested then that the world could well be at a turning point when the two great threats to life in this century—nuclear war and totalitarian rule—might now be overcome. In an accounting of what might lie ahead for the Western alliance, I suggested that the hard evidence of the totalitarian experiment was now in and that this evidence had led to an uprising of the intellect and will, one that reaffirmed the dignity of the individual in the face of the modern state. I suggested, too, that in a way Marx was right when he said the political order would come into conflict with the economic order; only he was wrong in predicting which part of the world this would occur in, for the crisis came not in the Capitalist West but in the Communist East. Noting the economic difficulties reaching the critical stage in the Soviet Union and Eastern Europe, I said that at other times in history the ruling elites had faced such situations and, when they encountered resolve and determination from free nations, decided to loosen their grip.

It was then I suggested that the tides of history were running in the cause of liberty, but only if we, as free men and women, joined together in a worldwide movement toward democracy, a crusade for freedom, a crusade that would be not so much a struggle of armed might, not so much a test of bombs and rockets, as a test of faith and will. Well, that crusade for freedom, that crusade for peace is well underway. We have found the will. We have held fast to the faith. And, whatever happens, whatever triumphs or disappointments ahead, we must keep to this strategy of strength and candor, this strategy of hope—hope in the eventual triumph of freedom.

But as we move forward, let us not fail to note the lessons we've learned along the way in developing our strategy. We have learned the first objective of the adversaries of freedom is to make free nations question their own faith in freedom, to make us think that adhering to our principles and speaking out against human rights abuses or foreign aggression is somehow an act of belligerence. Well, over the long run, such inhibitions make free peoples silent and, ultimately, half-hearted about their cause. This is the first and most important defeat free nations can ever suffer, for when free peoples cease telling the truth about and to their adversaries, they cease telling the truth to themselves. In matters of state, unless the truth be spoken, it ceases to exist.

It is in this sense that the best indicator of how much we care about freedom is what we say about freedom; it is in this sense that words truly are actions. And there is one added and quite extraordinary benefit to this sort of realism and public candor: This is also the best way to avoid war or conflict. Too often in the past, the adversaries of freedom forgot the reserves of strength and resolve among free peoples; too often they interpreted conciliatory words as weakness; and too often they miscalculated and underestimated the willingness of free men and women to resist to the end. Words of freedom remind them otherwise.

This is the lesson we've learned and the lesson of the last war and, yes, the lesson of Munich. But it is also the lesson taught us by Sir Winston [Churchill], by London in the Blitz, by the enduring pride and faith of the British people. Just a few years ago, Her Majesty Queen Elizabeth and I stood at the Normandy beaches to commemorate the selflessness that comes from such pride and faith. It is well we recall the lessons of our alliance. And I wonder if you might permit me to recall one other this morning: Operation Market Garden. It was called 3 months after Overlord and the rescue of Europe began—a plan to suddenly drop British and American airborne divisions on The Netherlands and open up a drive into the heart of Germany. A battalion of British paratroopers was given the great task of seizing the bridge deep in enemy territory at Arnhem. For a terrible 10 days they held out.

Some years ago, a reunion of those magnificent veterans—British, Americans, and others of our allies—was held in New York City. From the dispatch by the New York Times reporter Maurice Carroll, there was this paragraph: " 'Look at him,' said Henri Knap, an Amsterdam newspaperman who headed a Dutch underground's intelligence operation in Arnhem. He gestured toward General John Frost, a bluff Briton who had committed the battalion that held the bridge. 'Look at him—still with that black mustache. If you put him at the end of a bridge even today and said "keep it," he'd keep it.' "

The story mentioned the wife of Cornelius Ryan, the American writer who immortalized Market Garden in his book, "A Bridge Too Far," who told the reporter that just as Mr. Ryan was finishing his book—writing the final paragraphs about General Frost's valiant stand at Arnhem and about how in his eyes his men would always be undefeated—her husband burst into tears. That was quite unlike him; and Mrs. Ryan, alarmed, rushed to him. The writer could only look up and say of General Frost: "Honestly, what that man went through." A few days ago, seated there in Spaso House with Soviet dissidents, I had that same thought and asked myself: What won't men suffer for freedom? The dispatch about the Arnhem veteran concluded with this quote from General Frost about his visits to that bridge. " 'We've been going back ever since. Every year we have a—what's the word?—reunion. Now, there's a word.' He turned to his wife, 'Dear, what's the word for going to Arnhem?' 'Reunion,' she said. 'No,' he said, 'there's a special word.' She pondered. 'Pilgrimage,' she said. 'Yes, pilgrimage,' " General Frost said.

As those veterans of Arnhem view their time, so, too, we must view ours; ours is also a pilgrimage, a pilgrimage toward those things we honor and love: human dignity, the hope of freedom for all peoples and for all nations. And I've always cherished the belief that all of history is such a pilgrimage and that our Maker, while never denying us free will, does over time guide us with a wise and provident hand, giving direction to history and slowly bringing good from evil—leading us ever so slowly but ever so relentlessly and lovingly to a moment when the will of man and God are as one again.

I cherish, too, the hope that what we

have done together throughout this decade and in Moscow this week has helped bring mankind along the road of that pilgrimage. If this be so, prayerful recognition of what we are about as a civilization and a people has played its part. I mean, of course, the great civilized ideas that comprise so much of your heritage: the development of law embodied by your constitutional tradition, the idea of restraint on centralized power and individual rights as established in your Magna Carta, the idea of representative government as embodied by the mother of all parliaments. But we go beyond even this. Your own Evelyn Waugh, who reminded us that "civilization—and by this I do not mean talking cinemas and tinned food nor even surgery and hygienic houses but the whole moral and artistic organization of Europe—has not in itself the power of survival." It came into being, he said, through the Judeo-Christian tradition and "without it has no significance or power to command allegiance. It is no longer possible," he wrote, "to accept the benefits of civilization and at the same time deny the supernatural basis on which it rests."

And so, it is first things we must consider. And here it is, a story, one last story, that can remind us best of what we're about. It's a story that a few years ago came in the guise of that art form for which I have an understandable affection—the cinema. It's a story about the 1920 Olympics and two British athletes: Harold Abrahams, a young Jew, whose victory—as his immigrant Arab-Italian coach put it—was a triumph for all those who have come from distant lands and found freedom and refuge here in England; and Eric Liddell, a young Scotsman, who would not sacrifice religious conviction for fame. In one unforgettable scene, Eric Liddell reads the words of Isaiah. "He giveth power to the faint, and to them that have no might, he increased their strength, but they that wait upon the Lord shall renew their strength. They shall mount up with wings as eagles. They shall run and not be weary."

Here, then, is our formula for completing our crusade for freedom. Here is the strength of our civilization and our belief in the rights of humanity. Our faith is in a higher law. Yes, we believe in prayer and its power. And like the Founding Fathers of both our lands, we hold that humanity was meant not to be dishonored by the all-powerful state, but to live in the image and likeness of Him who made us.

More than five decades ago, an American President told his generation that they had a rendezvous with destiny; at almost the same moment, a Prime Minister asked the British people for their finest hour. This rendezvous, this finest hour, is still upon us. Let us seek to do His will in all things, to stand for freedom, to speak for humanity. "Come, my friends," as it was said of old by Tennyson, "it is not too late to seek a newer world." Thank you.

Note: The President spoke at 12:10 p.m. in the Great Hall at Guildhall. In his opening remarks, he referred to Sir Greville Spratt, the mayor of London, and Prime Minister Margaret Thatcher.

Remarks to United States Embassy Personnel in London
June 3, 1988

Well, now I'm a little embarrassed to come up here after all those wonderful things were said about me, because I happen to think that we have a very wonderful Ambassador and his wife here representing the United States in this nation. And I also happen to have had the chance to observe and know what a wonderful staff there is in this Embassy, also. But the reason it makes it a little difficult is because I know how much we upset the routine when we drop in. [*Laughter*]

Nancy and I want to thank Ambassador Price, his lovely lady, and all the members of the Embassy staff for your extraordinary efforts to assure the success of this visit, as you have done so before. This, as you've been told, is my third visit to London and probably my last as President, and I know how much time and hard work must be devoted to a Presidential visit. I also know that a visit like this is an exceptional one, one that takes you away from your day-to-day business.

And let me express my deep appreciation for the work you do to represent United States interests in the United Kingdom. I know you spend long hours working to secure our foreign policy objectives, to strengthen our economy, to enhance our national security, and to protect United States citizens overseas. And I know the many times when you have been called upon for some individual citizen to overcome something that is upsetting them at the time when they're far away from home and here in this land. Your work here in London has proven invaluable in ensuring that the special relationship we enjoy with Great Britain continues to bear fruit.

Nancy and I wish to thank you, all the men and women of the Embassy, not just the American employees, but also the Foreign Service nationals without whose hard work and support this visit and the execution of our foreign policy would not be possible. And, Charlie, I just—there are no words to express the appreciation that we have. You have a great staff, and now it's coming time for me to say so long.

I have to tell you, though, I want to tell you one little incident that occurred recently in my meeting with the General Secretary over there. And knowing, of course, that officially their nation is atheist, and we know that ours is based on the Judeo-Christian religion, and I couldn't resist one day—I told him that I was looking forward to having prepared the greatest gourmet dinner that anyone could ever think of, the most wonderful and delicious foods, and having him to that dinner. And then when the dinner was over, I was going to ask him if he believed there was a cook. [*Laughter*]

Well, God bless all of you. And on behalf of Nancy and myself now, we've got to take the walk down to the helicopter, and we'll be on our way home. But we'll be on our way home with the warmest of memories and feeling of gratitude to all of you. Thank you. God bless you all.

Note: The President spoke at 1:45 p.m. from the terrace at Winfield House. Charles H. Price II was the U.S. Ambassador to the United Kingdom.

Remarks Upon Returning From the Soviet-United States Summit Meeting in Moscow
June 3, 1988

The Vice President. Mr. President and Mrs. Reagan, I'm delighted to say on behalf of the people of the United States of America, welcome home, and well done! Everyone in America watched your historic trip and hoped for the best and pulled for you. And now it's over, and we can all say that you've made a historic contribution to peace in the world.

On arms control, Mrs. Thatcher probably put it best when she said that you have bravely gone forward in spite of the voices of denial and doubt. You showed the only way to succeed is by retaining your resolve and speaking with conviction. As for the latter, I suspect you know, Mr. President, that you caught a little flack for bringing up the issue of human rights so forcefully right there in the heart of the Soviet system. But most Americans felt as I did: We have a tradition of freedom and a history of free speech, and what's wrong with telling the other guy how you feel?

The fact is you made us proud. This week an American President strode the hard ground of Red Square and reminded the world through the sureness of his step and the lilt of his words what a bracing thing freedom is—what a moving and bracing thing. So, welcome back, Mr. President. It's good to see you. God bless you and Nancy.

The President. Well, thank you all very much. As some of you may have heard, Mr. Gorbachev and I've been trading Russian proverbs this week. [*Laughter*] But you know, flying back across the Atlantic today, it was an American saying that kept running through my mind. Believe me, as far as Nancy and I are concerned, there's no place like home.

We want to thank all of you for coming out today. We're grateful for your enthusiasm and for the warmth of your welcome. And take it from me, all this red, white, and blue scenery hits these two weary travelers right where we live. If I might paraphrase George M. Cohan: Some may call it a flag-waving, but right now I can't think of a better flag to wave.

We're a little tired, but we're exhilarated at what has happened—exhilarated, too, at the thought of the future and what may lie ahead for the young people of America and all of the world. The events of this week in Moscow were momentous—not conclusive perhaps, but momentous. And believe me, right now momentous will do just fine.

You know, it's occurred to me that time does have a way of sorting things out. For many years now, Americans have seen the danger of war and pleaded the cause of peace. And other Americans have seen the danger of totalitarianism and pleaded the cause of freedom. So, I was just thinking, why don't we just agree today on something that maybe we should have been saying to each other all along: that we're all Americans and that we all have one and the same burning cause in our hearts—the cause of world peace and the cause of world freedom.

Peace and freedom are what this trip was about, and we saw some real progress in several areas in Moscow—on human rights, on regional conflicts, on greater contacts between the people of the Soviet Union and the United States. We exchanged the documents that put into force an historic treaty that eliminates for the first time an entire class of U.S. and Soviet nuclear weapons and establishes real breakthroughs in verification procedures. And we made tangible progress toward an even more historic treaty on strategic weapons—yes, a 50-percent reduction in nuclear weapons. All of this was good and promising for the future.

But there's something else I want to tell you about. I wish you could've seen the faces we saw in the Soviet Union. As I said to the young people at Moscow State University, it was hard, really, to tell them apart from any other group of students—in our country or anywhere else in the world. And as I told Mr. Gorbachev, there were also the faces, young and old, we saw on the streets of Moscow. At first, more than anything else, they were curious faces, but as time went on, the smiles began and then the waves. And I don't have to tell you Nancy and I smiled back and waved just as hard. The truth came home to us once again. It isn't people, but governments that make war. And it isn't people, but governments that erect barriers that keep us apart.

Much is happening in the Soviet Union. We hope and pray that the signs of change continue there. Our pledge—Mr. Gorbachev and I—is to work to continue building a better understanding between our two countries. But let's remember, too, that just as our forward strategy of peace and freedom anticipated positive changes, it remains ready to take us over any bumps in the road. And that's because our strategy is based on faith in the eventual triumph of human freedom.

That faith in freedom, that abiding belief in what the unfettered human spirit can accomplish, defines us as a people and a nation. And you know, I've been told that even a few veteran journalists said a chill went through them this week at a sight they never thought they would see in their lifetime: an American President there in the heart of Moscow talking about economic, political, and individual freedoms to the future leaders of the Soviet Union; explaining that freedom makes a difference, and explaining how freedom works; talking, too, about the possibility of a new age of prosperity and peace, where old antagonisms between nations can someday be put behind us, a new age that can be ours if only we'll reach out to it.

Ladies and gentlemen, all across our country during these weeks of spring it's graduation time. And I hope our young graduates know what a sudden, startling future may now be before them, a future brought about by a technological and information revolution based on a growing understanding of the nexus between economic growth and creative freedom. But I hope, too, that young Americans—and all Americans—will always remember that this revolution is only the continuation of a revolution begun two centuries ago, a revolution of hope, a hope that someday a new land might become a place where freedom's light would beacon forth. That faith in freedom, that belief in the unalienable rights of man begun in Carpenters Hall in Philadelphia, traveled last week to the Lenin Hills in Moscow.

It was the selflessness of so many Americans that brought it there, selflessness by Americans for over two centuries, but especially by those Americans who fought what has truly been called the twilight struggle of the postwar years, a struggle where national interest was not always clearly defined or adversaries easily identified or sacrifice fully appreciated. Now, more than ever, we must continue. The judgment of future generations will be harsh upon us if, after so much sacrifice and now at the hour of hope, we falter or fail. Let us resolve to continue, one nation, one people, united in our love of peace and freedom, determined to keep our defenses strong, to stand with those who struggle for freedom across the world, to keep America a shining city, a light unto the nations.

And let us remember, too, that there's work remaining here at home, that whatever the accomplishments of America, we must never be prideful toward others. We have much to learn from peoples of foreign lands and other cultures, nor should we ever grow content. Let us never rest until every American of every race or background knows the full blessing of liberty, until justice for all is truly justice for all. And most of all, let us remember that being an American means remembering another loyalty, a loyalty as, the hymn puts it, "to another country I have heard of, a place whose King is never seen and whose armies cannot be counted."

And yet if patriotism is not the only thing, it is one of the best things. And we can be grateful to God that we have seen such a rebirth of it here in this country. And you know, it's true, frequently when such moments happen in a nation's history, there's a popular saying or song that speaks for that time. And just maybe this verse sounds familiar to you: "If tomorrow, all things were gone I'd worked for all my life, and I had to start again with just my children and my wife, I'd thank my lucky stars to be living here today 'cause the flag still stands for freedom and they can't take that away."

Nancy and I have full hearts today. We're grateful to all of you and to the American people, grateful for the chance to serve, grateful for all the support and warmth that you've given us over the years. And you know what else? We think our friend Lee Greenwood has it just right, "All our days, and especially today, there ain't no doubt we love this land. God bless the U.S.A.!"

Note: The President spoke at 4:46 p.m. in Hangar 3 at Andrews Air Force Base, MD.

Letter to the Speaker of the House of Representatives and the President of the Senate on Trade With Hungary and China
June 3, 1988

Dear Mr. Speaker: (Dear Mr. President:)

I hereby transmit the documents referred to in subsection 402(d)(5) of the Trade Act of 1974 with respect to a further 12-month extension of the authority to waive subsections (a) and (b) of section 402 of the Act. These documents constitute my decision to continue in effect this waiver authority for a further 12-month period.

I include as part of these documents my

determination that further extension of the waiver authority will substantially promote the objectives of section 402. I also include my determination that continuation of the waivers applicable to the Hungarian People's Republic and the People's Republic of China will substantially promote the objectives of section 402. The attached documents also include my reasons for extension of the waiver authority, and for my determination that continuation of the waivers currently in effect for the Hungarian People's Republic and the People's Republic of China will substantially promote the objectives of section 402.

Sincerely,

RONALD REAGAN

Report to Congress Concerning Extension of Waiver Authority

Pursuant to subsection 402(d)(5) of the Trade Act of 1974 (hereinafter "the Act"), I have today determined that further extension of the waiver authority granted by subsection 402(c) of the Act for 12 months will substantially promote the objectives of section 402 and that continuation of the waivers currently applicable to the Hungarian People's Republic and the People's Republic of China will also substantially promote the objectives of section 402 of the Act. My determination is attached and is incorporated herein.

The general waiver authority conferred by section 402 of the Act is an important means for the strengthening of mutually beneficial relations between the United States and certain countries of Eastern Europe and the People's Republic of China. The waiver authority has permitted us to conclude and maintain in force bilateral trade agreements with Hungary, Romania, and the People's Republic of China. These agreements continue to be fundamental elements in our political and economic relations with those countries, including important exchanges on emigration and human rights matters. Granting of Most Favored Nation (MFN) status pursuant to these agreements gives U.S. companies the ability to compete in those markets. Moreover, continuation of the waiver authority would permit future expansion of our bilateral relations with other countries now subject to subsections 402 (a) and (b) of the Act, should circumstances permit. I believe that these considerations clearly warrant this renewal of the general waiver authority.

I continue to believe that extending the current waivers applicable to Hungary and the People's Republic of China will substantially promote the objectives of section 402 of the Act.

Hungary. Hungary has continued to take a relatively positive and constructive approach to emigration matters. Nearly all Hungarians who are eligible to apply to emigrate for purposes of family reunification receive permission to depart. During the past year there have been, in fact, no instances of refusal of emigration permission in family reunification cases. The American Embassy in Budapest issued 139 immigrant visas in 1987, considerably more than the number issued for 1986 (102). There have been no divided family cases since the spring of 1987, when the three cases brought to the Foreign Ministry's attention in January 1987 were resolved. Although there are some restrictions on emigration, there are no systematic official sanctions imposed on persons seeking to emigrate.

People's Republic of China. Although China's population will shortly exceed 1.1 billion persons, only 10 percent of the country's land area is suitable for farming. China's standard of living is low—per capita GNP was under $300 in 1987; urban overcrowding is endemic; and unemployment is a growing problem. In consequence, China faces exceptional challenges to adequately feed and house even its present population. Furthermore, birth rates have recently picked up again and are adding another 12–13 million people each year to the population. If present trends continue, China's population will exceed 1.25 billion by the year 2000. These circumstances contribute to the maintenance of a relatively open emigration policy. In addition, the Chinese Government, as part of its policies of economic reform and opening to the outside world, continues to encourage students, scientists, and industrial managers to travel to Western countries for training and orientation. The principal limitation on increased emigration appears not to be Chinese policy, but the ability and willingness of other nations to absorb Chinese immigrants.

China's relatively liberal policy on emigration is reflected in the steadily rising number of immigrant visas issued by our embassy and consulates in China since the normalization of relations in 1979. In Fiscal Year 1987, our China posts issued 16,263 immigrant visas (versus 14,051 in FY 1986) and 50,519 non-immigrant visas (versus 44,254 in FY 1986). This represents a rise of 16 percent for immigrants and 14 percent for non-immigrants. Non-immigrant visas were issued to Chinese who wished to study, conduct business, and visit relatives in the United States. Other Western countries continue to experience increases in Chinese travel and emigration.

For the above reasons, I have determined that continuation of the waivers for Hungary and the People's Republic of China will substantially promote the objectives of the Act.

Romania. Since Romania has renounced extension of Most-Favored-Nation tariff treatment by the United States conditioned on the requirements of section 402 of the Act, I am permitting the waiver for Romania to expire on July 3, 1988.

Note: The letter was released by the Office of the Press Secretary on June 4.

Presidential Determination No. 88–18—Trade With Hungary and China

June 3, 1988

Memorandum for the Secretary of State

Subject: Determination Under Subsection 402(d)(5) of the Trade Act of 1974—Continuation of Waiver Authority

Pursuant to the authority vested in me under the Trade Act of 1974 (Public Law 93–618), January 3, 1975 (88 Stat. 1978) (hereinafter "the Act"), I determine, pursuant to subsection 402(d)(5) of the Act, that the further extension of the waiver authority granted by subsection 402(c) of the Act will substantially promote the objectives of section 402 of the Act. I further determine that the continuation of the waivers applicable to the Hungarian People's Republic and the People's Republic of China will substantially promote the objectives of section 402 of the Act.

This determination shall be published in the *Federal Register.*

RONALD REAGAN

[*Filed with the Office of the Federal Register, 3:17 p.m., June 6, 1988*]

Note: The memorandum was released by the Office of the Press Secretary on June 4.

Radio Address to the Nation on the Soviet-United States Summit Meeting in Moscow and the Toronto Economic Summit

June 4, 1988

My fellow Americans:

It was just yesterday that I returned from my historic Moscow summit meeting with General Secretary Gorbachev. And it so happens that later this month I'll be visiting Canada for an economic summit with the leaders of the world's industrialized nations. I thought I'd take a few moments to tell you about both.

First, my meeting with General Secretary

Gorbachev in Moscow—the event that held perhaps the most immediate historic importance took place on Wednesday. It was then that General Secretary Gorbachev and I exchanged the instruments of ratification, bringing into effect the INF treaty. The effect of this treaty will be, very simply, to eliminate an entire class of U.S. and Soviet intermediate-range nuclear missiles. The significance of the INF treaty can hardly be overstated. For the first time ever, the levels of nuclear arms will actually be reduced rather than having caps placed on their growth. These missiles will not simply have been shuffled around on the map or placed in storage; they will have been destroyed.

The exchange of these instruments of ratification alone would have made the Moscow summit a success, but the General Secretary and I made important progress in other areas as well. We moved ahead on START negotiations, negotiations that would lead to a dramatic reduction in both sides' arsenals of strategic nuclear arms.

On bilateral issues, I'm especially pleased by our agreement to hold increased exchanges involving high school students. The number of students will at first be in the hundreds, but could grow into the thousands. Imagine it—hundreds and then thousands of young people who have firsthand knowledge of each other's country and, yes, who have made friends. Turning to regional conflicts, Mr. Gorbachev and I discussed ways to reduce tension in areas around the globe—Southeast Asia, Africa, Central America, the Persian Gulf, and the Middle East. The withdrawal of Soviet troops from Afghanistan, of course, represents an historic step in itself, one that the General Secretary and I agreed could serve as a model for settling other regional conflicts.

A key part of my agenda for this Moscow summit, as for my previous meetings with the General Secretary, involved human rights. Recently, the Soviets have begun to show somewhat more respect for human rights. In the past year, for example, they have released some 300 political detainees from detention. It's my hope that what took place on my Moscow visit will lead to still greater individual freedom for the peoples of the Soviet Union.

You see, in addition to my meetings with Mr. Gorbachev, I held other meetings—with monks at a monastery in Moscow; with nearly 100 dissidents and refuseniks, men and women who have worked for years for the freedom to speak, to worship, to assemble, and to travel; and at Moscow University with students, indeed, with the very students likely to become the Soviet Union's next generation of leaders. To the dissidents and refuseniks, I was able to say: The people of the United States and elsewhere support you. To the students, I suggested: There is another way to live and govern your country, a way of democracy and economic growth, a way in which creative human energies are released. If anyone had suggested, even as recently as 10 years ago, that an American President would one day be able to meet with Soviet dissidents inside Moscow itself or be able to speak to Soviet students in their own university about human freedom, well, I think you'll agree that a prediction like that would have been dismissed. But this past week, it happened. Seeds of freedom and greater trust were sown. And I just have to believe that, in ways we may not even be able to guess, those seeds will take root and grow.

Accompanying these new political freedoms are a series of economic reforms that may begin to inject elements of free enterprise into the Soviet economy. In 2 weeks, I'll be attending my final economic summit in Toronto, where the Western countries will celebrate the success of free markets. It's my belief that liberty should be as important a concern in Toronto as it was in Moscow. Liberty in the economic sphere means low taxes. It means paring away needless regulations and reducing counterproductive government planning and interference. And it means keeping down barriers to international trade, here and around the world.

Until next week, thanks for listening, and God bless you.

Note: The President spoke at 12:06 p.m. from the Oval Office at the White House.

Remarks to World Gas Conference Participants
June 6, 1988

Well, thank you, John, thank you all. And to all of you of the International Gas Union and George Lawrence and all of you of the American Gas Association, my warmest greetings. And as you've just been told, I've just returned from an historic meeting in the Soviet Union, and I thought it would be fitting to report on that summit meeting before this, an international audience. And by the way, I'd like to extend a particular word of greeting to the members of the Soviet delegation who are here today. I guess it shows just how much things have changed that Ronald Reagan can say to a group of visiting Soviet citizens: My friends, if you're wondering about the weather back in Moscow, well, lately most of the days have been sunny and mild. [*Laughter*]

But before I report in any detail on the events that took place in Moscow, I want to recognize Secretary of Energy John Herrington. The Department of Energy recently completed an important study that greatly adds to our knowledge of natural gas. As John himself has described it: "This study is a useful national inventory of a vital strategic asset." He went on to say that the study "confirms that there are adequate supplies in the United States to help stem the predicted rise in oil imports over the next decade."

It goes without saying that our own supply of natural gas is vital to a strong and growing American economy. You might remember that when our administration took office the Federal Government seemed more intent on hampering the natural gas industry than helping it. Since then we've presided over the—as you've been told—the 1985 expiration of new gas wellhead price controls and over the enactment of legislation to remove Fuel Use Act gas restrictions. Those two steps have brightened America's energy future. I want to thank so many of you in America's gas industry for your support, your crucial support, in bringing these changes about. And I want to urge all of you in the natural gas industry to build on your industry's natural strengths. Natural gas is a clean-burning, abundant, competitively priced fuel found within our borders, a fuel that is poised to play a major role in containing the rise of imported oil from insecure sources while keeping America energy-secure. And there's a whole universe of new applications, including the natural gas bus that will soon be tested in New York City. And you know what the song says: "If you can make it there, you'll make it anywhere." [*Laughter*]

Progress has been made, but much still remains to be done. Congress must act now to decontrol the wellhead price of natural gas and to provide more efficient pipeline transportation. These measures, coupled with the access to Canadian natural gas supplies that is ensured by the U.S.-Canada free trade agreement, will do a great deal to reduce the demand for imported oil.

But to turn now to the events that took place last week in Moscow, permit me to begin with perhaps my strongest impression: an impression of change in the Soviet Union; an impression of new possibilities, of new hope. Indeed, Soviet officials have themselves spoken of the profound change of policy that has taken place in their own government. Differences remain, and it is still much too early to tell just where the changes in the Soviet Union itself will lead. But when a President of the United States is able to meet on Soviet soil with dissidents and refuseniks, able to exchange thoughts with cultural and intellectual leaders, able to discuss with Soviet young people the importance of individual freedoms, well, there is, as I said, a sense of new hope—a powerful hope.

The event in Moscow of the most immediate impact on East-West relations took place last Wednesday. It was then that General Secretary Gorbachev and I met in the Kremlin to exchange the instruments of ratification of the INF treaty. And the moment we exchanged those instruments, that historic treaty entered into force. For the first time ever, an entire class of U.S. and Soviet nuclear missiles is being eliminated. And with the treaty's stringent verification measures, a new dimension of cooperation and trust will open between us.

The world can also take satisfaction at the continued progress we made on 50-percent reductions in strategic ballistic missiles—a treaty we call START. And on this issue, permit me to review for just a moment the four summit meetings between myself and Mr. Gorbachev. For in assessing their impact, it's important to see them as a whole.

In Geneva the General Secretary and I agreed on the concept of 50-percent reductions; in Reykjavik, on numerical limits for warheads and delivery vehicles; in Washington, on intensive work to complete a START treaty, including comprehensive verification provisions building upon those in the INF treaty. And in Moscow, we made important additional strides toward that objective. Verification in particular represents one of the most important and difficult issues. In Moscow we moved forward in reaching an agreement on a joint experiment in each other's country to improve the verification of existing nuclear testing treaties, and another agreement on notification of strategic ballistic missile test launches. When will the START treaty be completed? We still do not know. But I can say that we are moving forward on the treaty and its associated documents with renewed vigor and cooperation. I won't set deadlines. I've said that many times.

I am also gratified that this summit has borne out again the wisdom of our approach, which has been to expand the agenda of Soviet-American relations beyond just arms control or, more to the point, arms reduction. Too often in the past, the full weight of our relations hinged on this one issue while other fundamental issues were not raised. As I never tire of saying, nations distrust each other not because they are armed; they are armed because they distrust each other.

So, building for a better understanding between our two countries is important. Getting at those fundamental problems is essential. And that's why I am pleased to report to you that in the areas of human rights, regional conflicts, and bilateral and people-to-people exchanges, the Moscow summit has moved our full agenda forward.

Beginning with bilateral exchanges, I am deeply pleased that the Soviets agreed to take an important step toward expanding people-to-people exchanges, not just making occasional, symbolic gestures that involve a few carefully selected groups. Our goal is to have an ongoing series of widespread exchanges involving a cross section of citizens from both of our societies. In this connection, we agreed on an exchange each year of hundreds of students of high school age. This is a far larger number than in the past, and this is an inaugural step, not a final one. So, too, there is a new dimension to our cultural exchanges. In the spirit of *glasnost* and *perestroika,* the [Secretary] General and I expanded and updated an earlier cultural agreement and agreed to a plan that will establish culture and information centers in each other's capital.

Turning to regional issues, Mr. Gorbachev and I had a full and frank exchange. We agreed that the Soviet decision to withdraw from Afghanistan set a positive precedent for the resolution of other conflicts, and I expressed my expectation that the Soviet withdrawal would proceed on schedule, bringing peace to the region and self-determination to Afghanistan. We discussed Southeast Asia, both of us welcoming Vietnam's recent commitment to remove some of its troops from Cambodia. I noted, however, that a solution there required the withdrawal of all troops and a dialog between Prince Sihanouk and Vietnam. We also discussed the new prospects for a solution in southern Africa. This will restore an early target date for the removal of Cuban troops and all foreign troops from Angola and national reconciliation within Angola.

Other regional tensions were not neglected. I once again pressed the Soviets to support a second U.N. Security Council resolution, to enforce Resolution 598, calling for a negotiated end to the Iran-Iraq war. I pressed Mr. Gorbachev to help avert a manmade famine in Ethiopia. I stated my interest in moving forward our initiative in the Middle East peace process, again pressing the Soviets to play a more helpful role. And I emphasized our concerns about Central America, calling on Moscow to stop its vast supply of weaponry to the Communist Sandinistas in Nicaragua and the Communist guerrillas in El Salvador.

And finally, in the area of human rights, I am encouraged. Our discussions here focused on the recognition of the right to speak, write, travel, and worship freely. Our joint statement reaffirms the need to assure the rights, freedoms, and human dignity of individuals; the promotion of people-to-people communications; and an active sharing of cultural, historical, and spiritual values. Here I want to stress that those increased bilateral contacts I noted earlier include steps to establish wider exchanges among the leaders of human rights organizations, as well as lawyers, physicians, and representatives of other professions involved in this work. I think the growth of such contacts, under the aegis of the summit process, could over the long run become one of the most fruitful products of these discussions.

But beyond the official agenda I've just described, there was something else taking place in Moscow last week, something that had to do with the power of words. I said earlier that there were unmistakable signs that things are changing in the Soviet Union. Consider, if you will, what I was able to say to Soviet refuseniks and dissidents. I said, "Coming here, being with you, looking into your faces, I have to believe that the history of this troubled century will indeed be redeemed in the eyes of God and man and that freedom will truly come to all, for what injustice can withstand your strength, and what can conquer your prayers." Or consider these words that I was able to speak to a group of Russian Orthodox monks when I visited the Danilov Monastery: "We hope that *perestroika* will be accompanied by a deeper restructuring, a deeper conversion, a *metanoia,* a change in heart; and that *glasnost,* which means giving voice, will also let loose a new chorus of belief, singing praise to the God that gave us life." Or picture the scene last Tuesday at Moscow State University, where the next generation of Soviet leaders is being trained. To several hundred students I said: "Freedom is the recognition that no single person, no single authority or government has a monopoly on the truth, but that every individual life is infinitely precious." "Democracy," I added, "is less a system of government than it is a system to keep government limited and unintrusive." Later in that same address, I quoted Boris Pasternak's novel "Doctor Zhivago," just published in the Soviet Union for the first time, which speaks of the "irresistible power of unarmed truth," even the power of a simple phrase.

Yes, these are signs of change that are encouraging. They're promising. And I hope that General Secretary Gorbachev continues to press for additional reforms. You might remember that Nancy and I took an unscheduled stroll last Sunday on the Arbat—that's a lively pedestrian street. We greeted as many people as we could. There were ordinary, everyday people, of course; and through an interpreter, I said a few words. After Nancy and I left, reporters stayed behind to interview some of the people we'd met. Now, I didn't read this particular report, this report of the effect a simple phrase had had, until after Nancy and I had left Moscow. But when I did, well, it made me feel humble. That's the only way you could feel. And it made me think that visiting Moscow on behalf of the American people was one of the highest privileges of my life. The Wall Street Journal reported that after Nancy and I left the Arbat on Sunday "one elderly lady was clearly elated. 'It is very good. I'm glad he comes.' she said. And then, tears welling up in her eyes, she confided: 'I am a Christian myself, and I like it that he says God bless you.' "

And there, perhaps, lies the greatest significance of what took place in Moscow last week, not that Ronald Reagan spoke there. I was only giving voice to the abiding beliefs of the American people, indeed, of free people everywhere. No, it was that the words that were spoken were words of faith, words of freedom, words of truth, words, well—and in power that unarmed truth is irresistible. So, thank you all, and, yes, God bless you all.

Note: The President spoke at 11:12 a.m. in the Sheraton Washington Ballroom at the Sheraton Washington Hotel. In his opening remarks, he referred to John Kean, president of the International Gas Union, and George H. Lawrence, president of the American Gas Association. The World Gas Conference was a triennial event sponsored by the International Gas Union, which had members from 45 countries.

Statement on the Death of Clarence Pendleton
June 6, 1988

Yesterday, with the sudden death of Clarence Pendleton, America lost a leading apostle of a just and colorblind society. Clarence Pendleton early in life took up the banner of equal rights for all Americans and boldly carried that banner forward. It was my good fortune to have known Penny, to have shared his good will and good humor, to have traversed time and Earth with him on the path to a more just society for all Americans. With Penny's passing, I have lost a loyal friend and a compatriot deeply committed to my administration and its commitment to fight against discrimination wherever it exists. And the loss to our nation is no less.

In his uncompromising articulation of the ideal of a colorblind society open to all without regard to race, giving no quarter to either prejudice or preference, Penny insisted that the full brunt of the law should be brought to bear on discrimination. At the same time, he understood that the law must itself not deviate from the Constitution's mandate of nondiscrimination for any reason lest it become a double-edged sword, harming the innocent and poorly serving those most in need of protection. And it was in part through his participation in the public discussion of civil rights that the racial quota has been vanquished from our society.

Penny has been taken from us—and my heart goes out to his family and friends—but what Penny leaves us are fond memories of a man who loved life and made us love it more for his time among us, and a fuller confidence, because of his work, that one day all Americans will be judged not by stereotypes and prejudices but on their own merits, qualifications, performance—as Penny often quoted Martin Luther King, Jr., "not . . . by the color of their skin but by the content of their character."

Nomination of John F. Kordek To Be United States Ambassador to Botswana
June 6, 1988

The President today announced his intention to nominate John F. Kordek, of Illinois, a career member of the Senior Foreign Service, Class of Career Minister, as Ambassador to the Republic of Botswana. He would succeed Natale H. Bellocchi.

Mr. Kordek joined the Foreign Service in 1964. He began his diplomatic career as vice consul at the U.S. consulate general in Zagreb, Yugoslavia. Since then he has been posted in Belgrade, Brussels, Warsaw, Caracas, and Washington, holding positions such as counselor and Chargé d'Affaires. Upon his return to Washington in 1983, Mr. Kordek was assigned as Director of USIA operations in Latin America and the Caribbean. In February 1985, Mr. Kordek was appointed as Director of USIA's European operations. Mr. Kordek currently holds the position as Counselor of the USIA, the third ranking job in the USIA and the most senior career position.

Mr. Kordek graduated from Johns Hopkins University (M.A., 1967) and DePaul

University (Ph.B., 1964). Mr. Kordek was born June 9, 1938, in Chicago, IL. He is married, has two children, and resides in Annandale, VA.

Nomination of Thomas Edmund McNamara To Be United States Ambassador to Colombia
June 6, 1988

The President today announced his intention to nominate Thomas Edmund McNamara, of Connecticut, a career member of the Senior Foreign Service, Class of Minister-Counselor, as Ambassador to the Republic of Colombia. He would succeed Charles A. Gillespie, Jr.

Mr. McNamara joined the Department of State in 1965. He has served overseas in Paris, Lubumbashi, Bukavu, Moscow, and most recently as deputy chief of mission in Kinshasa, Zaire, 1980–1983. In Washington, he has worked in the Bureau of European Affairs, the Arms Control and Disarmament Agency, and the Bureau of Politico-Military Affairs. Until September 1986, he served for 3 years as Deputy Assistant Secretary of State for Politico-Military Affairs. Since January 1987 he has been the Director of Counterterrorism and Narcotics on the staff of the National Security Council.

Mr. McNamara graduated from Manhattan College (B.A., 1962) and the University of Notre Dame (M.A., 1964). He was born September 16, 1940, in New Haven, CT. He is married, has two children, and currently resides in Washington, DC.

Nomination of John J. Maresca for the Rank of Ambassador While Serving as Chief of the U.S. Delegation to the Conference on Confidence and Security Building Measures and Disarmament in Europe
June 6, 1988

The President today announced his intention to nominate John J. Maresca, of Connecticut, a career member of the Senior Foreign Service, Class of Minister-Counselor, for the rank of Ambassador in his capacity as chief of the United States delegation to the Conference on Confidence and Security Building Measures (CSBM).

Mr. Maresca joined the Foreign Service in 1966 and was vice consul in Amsterdam, Netherlands. In 1967–1968, he was the political officer at the U.S. Embassy in The Hague, Netherlands. In 1968–1970, he served as the assistant French desk officer in the Department of State, and in 1970 he went to Brussels, Belgium, as the Deputy Director of the Office of the Secretary General of NATO. From 1973 to 1975, he served as the Deputy Chief of the U.S. delegation to the Conference on Security and Cooperation in Europe (CSCE) in Helsinki, Finland, and Geneva, Switzerland. He returned to the Department in 1975 and was the officer in charge of NATO political affairs. From 1977 to 1980, Mr. Maresca served as the deputy political counselor in Paris, France, and in 1977 was the Deputy Chief of the U.S. delegation to the CSCE in Belgrade, Yugoslavia. From 1980 to 1982, he was the Director, Office of Western European Affairs in the Department of State, before returning to Paris in 1982 to serve as the deputy chief of mission. Mr. Maresca was a visiting fellow at Georgetown University's School of Foreign Service from 1985 to 1986. Since 1986 he has been serving as the Deputy Assistant Secretary for European and NATO Policy at the Department of Defense.

Mr. Maresca received a B.A. in 1959 from Yale University. He served in the United States Navy from 1959 to 1965. He was born December 9, 1937, in Stresa, Italy. Mr. Maresca is married, has one child, and resides in Chevy Chase, MD.

Nomination of Timothy Lathrop Towell To Be United States Ambassador to Paraguay

June 6, 1988

The President today announced his intention to nominate Timothy Lathrop Towell, of Ohio, a career member of the Senior Foreign Service, Class One, as Ambassador to the Republic of Paraguay. He would succeed Clyde D. Taylor.

Mr. Towell joined the Foreign Service in 1963. He has served as vice consul in Valencia, Spain, 1963–1965; second secretary at the U.S. Embassy in Madrid, Spain, 1965–1966; and consul for the U.S. consulate in Cochabamba, Bolivia, 1967–1968. In 1968 he was detailed to the Agency for International Development at the U.S. Embassy in La Paz, Bolivia. He returned to Washington and served as Bolivian desk officer at the Department of State, 1968–1970, and Spanish desk officer, 1970–1972. He has also served as U.S. consul in Porto Alegre, Brazil, 1972–1974; first secretary at the U.S. Embassy in Brussels, Belgium, 1975–1979; political-economic officer for the U.S. Interests Section in Havana, Cuba, 1979–1980; and legislative management officer for Europe in the Office of Congressional Relations at the Department of State, 1980–1983. Since 1983, he has been Deputy Chief of Protocol at the Department of State.

Mr. Towell graduated from Yale University (B.A., 1957) and Case Western Reserve University (M.A., 1962). He was born January 31, 1934, in Cleveland, OH. He served in the United States Army Reserve, 1959. Mr. Towell is married, has two children, and resides in Washington, DC.

Nomination of Harry E. Bergold To Be United States Ambassador to Morocco

June 6, 1988

The President today announced his intention to nominate Harry E. Bergold, of Florida, a career member of the Senior Foreign Service, Class of Career Minister, as Ambassador to the Kingdom of Morocco. He would succeed Thomas Anthony Nassif.

Mr. Bergold entered the Foreign Service as an international economist in the Department of State in 1957. He was third secretary in Tegucigalpa, Honduras, 1959–1961, and second secretary in Mexico City, 1961–1963. He then returned to the Department of State, where he served as the desk officer for Mexico, 1964–1966. From 1967 to 1972, Mr. Bergold was politico-military officer in Madrid, Spain, and political counselor in Panama, 1972. In 1973, he was detailed to the Department of Defense, first as Deputy Assistant Secretary for European and NATO Affairs, 1973; then as Principal Deputy Assistant Secretary for Legislative Affairs, 1976. He served as Director for International Affairs of the White House energy staff, 1977, and was then detailed to the Department of Energy as Assistant Secretary for International Affairs, 1978–1979. From 1980 to 1983, he was Ambassador to Hungary. He was Ambassador to the Republic of

Nicaragua, 1984–1987. Since 1987 Mr. Bergold has been diplomat-in-residence at the Center for Strategic and International Studies in Washington, DC.

Mr. Bergold graduated from Yale University (B.A., 1953; M.A., 1957). He was born November 11, 1931, in Olean, NY. He served in the United States Army, 1954–1956. He is married and resides in Washington, DC.

Appointment of Abe Pollin as a Member of the International Cultural and Trade Center Commission

June 6, 1988

The President today announced his intention to appoint Abe Pollin to be a Member of the International Cultural and Trade Center Commission for a term expiring August 20, 1989. This is a new position.

Since 1973 Mr. Pollin has been chairman of the board of the Capital Centre in Landover, MD. He is also the owner of the Washington Bullets professional basketball team.

Mr. Pollin graduated from George Washington University (B.A., 1945). He was born on December 3, 1923, in Philadelphia, PA. He is married, has two children, and resides in Bethesda, MD.

Nomination of Joseph Francis Glennon To Be a Member of the Advisory Board for Radio Broadcasting to Cuba

June 7, 1988

The President today announced his intention to nominate Joseph Francis Glennon to be a member of the Advisory Board for Radio Broadcasting to Cuba for a term expiring October 27, 1991. This is a reappointment.

From 1956 to 1980, Mr. Glennon was a Foreign Service officer for the Department of State. He served as a counselor for host country relations at the U.S. Mission to the United Nations in New York City, 1960–1980. Prior to this he was the attaché for the U.S. Embassy in Ankara, Turkey, 1956–1960. He was also an assistant director of personnel for Radio Free Europe, 1950–1956, and an FBI agent, 1947–1950.

Mr. Glennon graduated from Seton Hall University (B.S., 1947). He was born February 12, 1919, in Newark, NJ. He served in the U.S. Air Force during World War II. He is married, has six children, and resides in Boynton Beach, FL.

Statement on Signing the South Pacific Tuna Act of 1988

June 7, 1988

I am pleased to sign into law S. 1989, the South Pacific Tuna Act of 1988. This bill implements the South Pacific Regional Fisheries Treaty by making U.S. domestic legislation consistent with our treaty obligations. The treaty is historic in both its complexity and scope and culminates over 2 years of difficult negotiations. Its successful implementation will set a tone of cooperation rather than confrontation in our fisheries relations with 15 island nations of the South Pacific.

Under the terms of the treaty, U.S. tuna fishermen may purchase regional licenses to fish in some 10 million square miles of tuna-rich waters in the South Pacific Ocean, including waters under the jurisdiction of the Pacific Island signatories. It will set to rest the fisheries-related problems we have experienced stemming from our differing juridical positions concerning highly migratory species of tuna. In addition, the license fees and the economic assistance agreement associated with the treaty will further the economic development and strengthen the democratic traditions of the Pacific Island states participating in the treaty.

The peoples of the United States and the South Pacific have a long history of contact and cooperation. Beginning in the early 19th century when American seamen first ventured into the region, through the dark days of World War II when we fought side by side in defense of our homes and freedom, to today when we sit together at the negotiating table to work out mutually beneficial solutions to complex problems, our peoples have together faced and overcome adversity and challenge. I am proud of that history and of the fact that through the peoples of Hawaii, American Samoa, Guam, and the Northern Mariana Islands the United States has contributed to the rich cultural and spiritual traditions of the Pacific Islands. I am pleased that my signature on this legislation will reinforce the bonds of friendship and affection that unite our peoples.

RONALD REAGAN

The White House,
June 7, 1988.

Note: S. 1989, approved June 7, was assigned Public Law No. 100–330.

Appointment of Walter Gellhorn as a Member of the Council of the Administrative Conference of the United States
June 7, 1988

The President today announced his intention to appoint Walter Gellhorn to be a member of the Council of the Administrative Conference of the United States for a term of 3 years. This is a reappointment.

Since 1974 Mr. Gellhorn has been a professor emeritus at the Columbia University Law School. From 1972 to 1974, he was a professor at the Columbia University Law School.

Mr. Gellhorn graduated from Amherst College (A.B., 1927), Columbia University (LL.B., 1931), and the University of Pennsylvania (LL.D., 1963). He was born September 18, 1906, in St. Louis, MO. Mr. Gellhorn is married, has two children, and resides in New York, NY.

Appointment of Rebecca Gernhardt Range as a Member of the Interagency Committee on Women's Business Enterprise
June 7, 1988

The President today announced his intention to appoint Rebecca Gernhardt Range to be a member of the Interagency Committee on Women's Business Enterprise. She would succeed Gwendolyn S. King.

Ms. Range is currently Deputy Assistant to the President and Director of the Office of Public Liaison at the White House. Prior to this, she was Assistant Secretary for Governmental Affairs at the Department of

Transportation, 1985–1987; Counselor to the Secretary of Transportation, 1984–1985; and Deputy Assistant Secretary for Governmental Affairs at the Department of Transportation, 1983–1984. Ms. Range served as chief of staff, legislative assistant, and staff assistant for Senator Ted Stevens, 1977–1983.

Ms. Range graduated from DePauw University (B.A., 1976) and Catholic University, Columbus School of Law (J.D., 1981). She was born October 23, 1954, in Mansfield, OH. Ms. Range is married, has two children, and resides in Washington, DC.

Appointment of Douglas A. Riggs as a Member of the Panel of Conciliators of the International Centre for the Settlement of Investment Disputes

June 7, 1988

The President today announced his intention to appoint Douglas A. Riggs to be a member of the Panel of Conciliators, International Centre for the Settlement of Investment Disputes, for a term of 6 years. He would succeed James Coffin Greene.

Mr. Riggs is currently vice president for corporate communication for Pitney Bowes World Headquarters in Stamford, CT. Prior to this he was General Counsel at the Department of Commerce, 1985–1988. Mr. Riggs has served as Special Assistant to the President for Public Liaison at the White House, 1983–1985, and Associate Director, 1983. He was a partner with the law firm Bogle & Gates, 1980–1983.

Mr. Riggs graduated from Brigham Young University (B.S., 1966), the University of West Virginia (M.S., 1967), and Cornell University (J.D., 1973). He served in the United States Army, 1967–1970. He was born August 20, 1944, in Rigby, ID. He is married, has one child, and resides in Bethesda, MD.

Nomination of Charles S. Warner To Be Alternate United States Executive Director of the International Monetary Fund

June 7, 1988

The President today announced his intention to nominate Charles S. Warner to be United States Alternate Executive Director of the International Monetary Fund for a term of 2 years. He would succeed Mary Kate Bush.

Since 1986 Mr. Warner has been Deputy Director-General for the United Nations Industrial Development Organization in Vienna, Austria. Prior to this he was director for international trade services for Coopers & Lybrand, 1984–1986. He worked at the Department of Commerce from 1981 to 1984 as Deputy Assistant Secretary of the Economic Development Administration and Director of the Office of Export Trading Company Affairs at the International Trade Administration. He was president and chief executive officer of the Piedmont Land Co., 1976–1981; director of finance for the William P. Lipscomb Co., 1972–1976; and chairman and chief executive officer for Taconic Group, Inc., 1968–1972.

Mr. Warner graduated from the University of Virginia (B.A., 1954). He served in the United States Marine Corps, 1951–1957. Mr. Warner was born September 10, 1931, in Washington, DC. He is married and currently resides in Vienna, Austria.

Nomination of James B. Coles To Be a Member of the Board of Directors of the National Corporation for Housing Partnerships
June 7, 1988

The President today announced his intention to nominate James B. Coles to be a member of the Board of Directors of the National Corporation for Housing Partnerships for the term expiring October 27, 1990. He would succeed Barbara W. Schlicher.

Since 1972 Mr. Coles has been president of Coles Communities in San Diego, CA. He has also been involved in several civic and community organizations.

Mr. Coles graduated from San Diego State University (B.A., 1967). He served in the United States Army, 1960–1963. He was born September 29, 1941, in Camden, NJ. He is married, has two children, and resides in La Jolla, CA.

Nomination of Charles L. Hosler, Jr., To Be a Member of the National Science Board
June 7, 1988

The President today announced his intention to nominate Charles L. Hosler, Jr., to be a member of the National Science Board, National Science Foundation, for a term expiring May 10, 1994. This is a reappointment.

Since 1985 Dr. Hosler has been vice president for research and dean of the graduate school at Pennsylvania State University. Prior to this he was dean of the College of Earth and Mineral Sciences at Pennsylvania State University, 1966–1985.

Dr. Hosler graduated from Pennsylvania State University (B.S., 1947; M.S., 1948; Ph.D., 1951). He was born June 3, 1924, in Honey Brook, PA. He is married, has four children, and resides in State College, PA.

Nomination of William H. Fite To Be an Assistant Director of the United States Arms Control and Disarmament Agency
June 7, 1988

The President today announced his intention to nominate William H. Fite to be an Assistant Director of the United States Arms Control and Disarmament Agency (Bureau of Strategic Programs). He would succeed Michael A. Mobbs.

Since 1977 Mr. Fite has been minority director for national security affairs on the Subcommittee on Arms Control, International Security, and Science for the House Committee on Foreign Affairs in Washington, DC. Prior to this he was legislative assistant to Representative William F. Goodling, 1975–1977.

Mr. Fite graduated from Messiah College (B.A., 1970) and Pennsylvania State University (M.A., 1972). He was born April 11, 1948, in Mechanicsburg, PA. He is married and currently resides in Alexandria, VA.

Appointment of Mark Greenberg as a Special Assistant to the President for Legislative Affairs
June 7, 1988

The President today announced the appointment of Mark Greenberg to be Special Assistant to the President for Legislative Affairs (Senate) at the White House.

Prior to joining the White House staff, Mr. Greenberg served as administrative assistant and legislative director for Senator Paul Trible of Virginia. He was also chief of minority staff of the ways and means committee in the Massachusetts State Legislature.

Mr. Greenberg graduated from Kenyon College and received a master of arts degree from Claremont Graduate School and completed course work on his Ph.D. at Boston College. Mr. Greenberg is married, has one child, and resides in Alexandria, VA.

Message to the Congress Reporting on the National Emergency With Respect to Iran
June 7, 1988

To the Congress of the United States:

This report with respect to Iran is made pursuant to section 204(c) of the International Emergency Economic Powers Act, 50 U.S.C. 1703(c), and section 505(c) of the International Security and Development Cooperation Act of 1985, 22 U.S.C. 2349aa–9. This report discusses only matters concerning the national emergency with respect to Iran that was declared in Executive Order No. 12170 of November 14, 1979, and matters relating to Executive Order No. 12613 of October 29, 1987. This report covers events through April 30, 1988, including those that occurred since my last report under Executive Order No. 12170 dated November 20, 1987. That report covered events through October 15, 1987.

1. On October 29, 1987, after prior consultation with the Congress, I issued Executive Order No. 12613 invoking, *inter alia*, the authority of the International Security and Development Cooperation Act of 1985 to prohibit the importation of goods and services from Iran. As reported to the Congress on that date, this action was taken in response to the actions and policies of the Government of Iran in support of terrorism and acts of aggression against U.S. forces, U.S.-flag vessels, and other merchant vessels of nonbelligerent nations engaged in lawful and peaceful commerce in international waters of the Persian Gulf and territorial waters of nonbelligerent nations of that region. The Executive Order and my report noted that the import prohibition was in response to actions of the Government of Iran taken after the conclusion of the Claims Settlement Agreement of January 19, 1981 (the "Algiers Accords").

Pursuant to Executive Order No. 12613 (the "Embargo Order"), the Secretary of the Treasury, in consultation with the Secretary of State, issued the Iranian Transactions Regulations, 31 C.F.R. Part 560 (the "ITRs"), administered by the Office of Foreign Assets Control ("FAC"). A copy of these regulations is attached.

The ITRs provide, by general license, an exception to the import embargo for goods in transit at the October 29, 1987, effective date of the Embargo Order. Additionally, the ITRs provide for importation pursuant to specific FAC license for several categories of goods of Iranian origin, including those (a) imported prior to January 1, 1988, pursuant to a contract predating the Embargo Order, (b) located outside Iran as of the effective date of the Embargo Order and for which no benefit or payment would accrue to Iran after the effective date relating to the sale or importation, or (c) received by U.S. claimants pursuant to an award of, or in settlement of claims brought before, the Iran-United States Claims Tribunal (see paragraph 2 of this report).

In the period ended April 30, 1988, FAC issued 74 specific licenses for imports of goods under preexisting contracts and 94 specific licenses for goods located outside Iran on the effective date of the Embargo Order. We believe that nearly all goods eligible for importation pursuant to the "in transit" exception were admitted within this reporting period.

Numerous Customs Service detentions and seizures of Iranian-origin goods (including carpets, caviar, dates, pistachios, and gold) have taken place, and a number of FAC and Customs investigations into potential violations of the ITRs are pending. Several of the seizures have led to forfeiture actions and imposition of civil monetary penalties. An indictment relating to the importation of 1.7 tons of Iranian caviar was returned on April 21, 1988, in Miami, Florida.

2. The Iran-United States Claims Tribunal (the "Tribunal"), established at The Hague pursuant to the Algiers Accords, continues to make progress in arbitrating the claims before it. Since my last report, the Tribunal has rendered 42 awards, for a total of 360 awards. Of that total, 259 have been awards in favor of American claimants: 154 of these were awards on agreed terms, authorizing and approving payment of settlements negotiated by the parties, and 105 were decisions adjudicated on the merits. The Tribunal has dismissed a total of 25 other claims on the merits and 52 for jurisdictional reasons. Of the 24 remaining awards, two represent withdrawals and 22 were in favor of Iranian claimants. As of April 30, 1988, total payments to successful American claimants from the Security Account held by the NV Settlement Bank stood at approximately $1.051 billion.

To date, the Security Account has fallen below the required balance of $500 million 11 times. Each time, Iran has replenished the account, as required by the Algiers Accords, by transferring funds from the separate account held by the NV Settlement Bank in which interest on the Security Account is deposited. Iran has also replenished the account once when it was not required by the Accords, for a total of 12 replenishments. The most recent replenishment occurred on April 20, 1988, in the amount of $500,000, bringing the total in the Security Account to $500,367,792. The aggregate amount that has been transferred from the interest account to the Security Account is approximately $549.5 million.

In July 1987, the Government of Iran appointed Mr. Seyed Khalil Khalilian to replace Dr. Hamid Bahrami-Ahmadi as the Iranian arbitrator to Chamber Two.

3. As stated in my last report, the Tribunal continues to make progress in the arbitration of claims of U.S. nationals for $250,000 or more. Over 64 percent of the nonbank claims have now been disposed of through adjudication, settlement, or voluntary withdrawal, leaving 184 such claims on the docket. The largest of the large claims, the progress of which has been slowed by their complexity, are finally being decided, sometimes with sizable damage awards to the U.S. claimant. Since the last report, 21 large claims have been decided. One U.S. company received an award for $54.4 million.

4. The Tribunal continues to process claims of U.S. nationals against Iran of less than $250,000 each. As of April 30, 1988, a total of 210 small claims have been resolved, 71 of them since my last report, as a result of decisions on the merits, awards on agreed terms, or Tribunal orders. Eight contested claims have been decided since my previous report, raising the total number of contested claims decided to 21, 12 of which favored the American claimant. These decisions will help in establishing guidelines for the adjudication or settlement of similar claims. To date, American claimants have also received 25 awards on agreed terms reflecting settlements of claims under $250,000.

Since my last report, the three Tribunal Chambers have selected 53 small claims for active arbitration, bringing the total number of small claims currently under active Tribunal consideration to 185. The Tribunal has held hearings in six of these claims since my last report. The Tribunal has recently decided three significant "wrongful expulsion" test cases. The general thrust of the holdings in this area is that claimants may recover for losses associated with expulsion from Iran only when officials of the Islamic Revolutionary Government perpetrated specific acts directed at the claimant and the claimant clearly left Iran as a result of those acts.

5. In coordination with concerned government agencies, the Department of State continues to present U.S. Government claims against Iran, as well as responses by the United States Government to claims brought against it by Iran. Since my last report, the Department has filed pleadings in 12 government-to-government claims based on contracts for the provision of goods and services.

In five related government-to-government claims, the Tribunal awarded damages to Iran Air for aircraft services and supplies it found to be owed by U.S. agencies. With these decisions, the Tribunal to date has made five awards in favor of the United States and nine in favor of Iran. The Tribunal has dismissed 12 claims that had been filed by the United States and three claims that had been filed by Iran. In addition, Iran has withdrawn 13 of its government-to-government claims, while the United States has withdrawn five. No government-to-government claims have been finally settled since my last report, so 26 remain pending.

The Tribunal has not issued any opinions in claims concerning the interpretation or performance of various provisions of the Algiers Accords since my last report. One interpretive dispute brought by Iran was withdrawn by Iran and terminated. Iran recently filed an interpretive dispute in which it challenges a claimant's right to attach Iranian assets abroad in advance of an award by the Tribunal. The Department of State has filed two pleadings in interpretive disputes since my last report.

6. Since my last report, three bank syndicates have completed negotiations with Bank Markazi Jomhouri Islami Iran ("Bank Markazi," Iran's central bank) and have been paid a total of $691,912.40 for interest accruing for the period January 1–18, 1981 ("January Interest"). These payments were made from Dollar Account No. 2 at the Bank of England.

As indicated in my report of June 16, 1987, on May 4, 1987, the Tribunal directed that about $454 million in Iranian funds held at the Federal Reserve Bank of New York ("FRBNY") be transferred to the Bank of England for credit to the account of Bank Markazi. These funds were transferred on May 13, 1987, with my approval. The Tribunal's May 4, 1987, order also directed that the United States and Iran pursue the settlement of remaining claims pending against the FRBNY account from which the money was transferred, and an amount was reserved for those claims. On April 13, 1988, FRBNY, acting on behalf of the United States Government, and Bank Markazi, acting on behalf of the Government of Iran, agreed on the disposition of the remaining Iranian funds held at FRBNY. As a result, on April 15, 1988, $37.9 million not needed to cover any of the claims pending against the account at FRBNY were returned, as required under the Tribunal's order. Further, a procedure was established for the disposition of the remaining claims—which are claims of bank syndicates of which a U.S. bank is a member—against the remainder of these funds (approximately $31.6 million).

7. Since my last report, there has been one amendment to the Iranian Assets Control Regulations, 31 C.F.R. Part 535 (the "Regulations"), administered by the Office of Foreign Assets Control. On January 26, 1988, FAC established administrative procedures for the imposition of civil monetary penalties for violation of the Regulations, as provided in section 206 of the International Emergency Economic Powers Act, 50 U.S.C. 1705. 53 *Fed. Reg.* 7355 (March 8, 1988). A copy of these amendments to the Regulations is attached. The new prepenalty and penalty procedures do not alter substantive obligations imposed by the Regulations.

There have been no amendments to the Iranian Transactions Regulations since their publication on November 17, 1987.

8. The situation reviewed above continues to implicate important diplomatic, financial, and legal interests of the United

States and its nationals and presents an unusual challenge to the national security and foreign policy of the United States. The Iranian Assets Control Regulations issued pursuant to Executive Order No. 12170 continue to play an important role in structuring our relationship with Iran and in enabling the United States properly to implement the Algiers Accords. Similarly, the Iranian Transactions Regulations issued pursuant to Executive Order No. 12613 continue to advance important objectives in combatting international terrorism. I shall continue to exercise the powers at my disposal to deal with these problems and will continue to report periodically to the Congress on significant developments.

RONALD REAGAN

The White House,
June 7, 1988.

Appointment of the 1988–1989 White House Fellows
June 7, 1988

The President today announced the appointments of the 1988–1989 White House fellows. This is the 24th class of fellows since the program began in 1964. The 14 fellows were chosen from among 825 applicants and screened by 11 regional panels. The President's Commission on White House Fellowships, chaired by Vice Admiral James B. Stockdale, USN, Ret., interviewed the 33 national finalists before recommending the 14 persons to the President. Their year of government service will begin September 1, 1988.

Fellows serve for 1 year as Special Assistants to the Vice President, members of the Cabinet, and the President's principal staff. In addition to the work assignments, the fellowship includes an education program that parallels and broadens the unique experience of working at the highest levels of the Federal Government. The program is open to U.S. citizens in the early stages of their careers and from all occupations and professions. Federal Government employees are not eligible, with the exception of career Armed Forces personnel. Leadership, character, intellectual and professional ability, and commitment to community and nation are the principal criteria employed in the selection of fellows.

Applications for the 1989–1990 program are available from the President's Commission on White House Fellowships, 712 Jackson Place, NW, Washington, DC. 20503.

The 1988–89 White House fellows are:

Bradford B. Baker, 28, of Florida. Mr. Baker, an entrepreneur, is currently president of Advanced Printer Technologies, Inc. He is very active in his community, where he has served as president of the Venice, Florida, Chamber of Commerce; a director of the United Way; and as vice president of the Triangle Economic Development Association.

Jeffrey W. Colyer, 28, of Kansas. Dr. Colyer is currently a surgical resident at the Washington Hospital Center. He has worked with the International Medical Corps, designing surgical medic training programs and setting up surgical clinics for the Afghan freedom fighters. In addition to his medical background, he received his master's degree in international relations from Cambridge University.

Charles P. Garcia, 27, of the Republic of Panama. Captain Garcia serves in the U.S. Air Force. He was born in Washington, DC, and raised in Panama, where he is currently stationed. A graduate of the U.S. Air Force Academy, he was chairman of the cadet honor committee. He is the editor-in-chief of the USSOUTHCOM Intelligence Quarterly.

Jonathan D. George, 31, of California. Captain George is currently serving as a U–2 instructor pilot for the U.S. Air Force. He is the recipient of the coveted Koren Kolligian Jr. Trophy, the Distinguished Flying Cross for heroism in flight, and the Humanitarian Service Medal. He is a member of the Comanche Nation of Oklahoma.

David E. Greenberg, 38, of Colorado. Mr. Greenberg is a communications consultant and newspaper columnist in Denver, CO. Active in his community, he is president of the board of directors of the Denver Children's Museum, a trustee of the American Center for International Leadership, an adviser to Governor Roemer's Task Force on AIDS, and a member of the Chancellor's Advisory Board at the University of Colorado at Denver.

Nancy J. Kelley, 32, of Connecticut. Mrs. Kelley is a recent graduate of the Harvard Law School and the Kennedy School of Government at Harvard University. While at Harvard, she was director of the Community Revitalization Project. A magna cum laude graduate of Yale University, she was a Harry Truman scholar and banner bearer for Saybrook College.

Michael T. Lempres, 28, of California. Mr. Lempres is an attorney with the law firm of McCutchen, Doyle, Brown & Enersen in San Francisco. A graduate of Dartmouth University and the Boalt Hall School of Law at the University of California, he has served as a law clerk for the Honorable Robert P. Aguilar, U.S. District Judge for the Northern District of California.

Alan W. Marty, 31, of Texas. Mr. Marty is currently a regional sales manager for Applied Materials, Inc., where he has generated record sales. After receiving his bachelor's degree in materials science engineering from Iowa State University, he earned master's of business administration and education degrees at Stanford University.

Mark E. Readinger, 35, of Texas. Mr. Readinger is currently the senior strategic planner for Texas Instruments, Inc. He is a graduate of the U.S. Military Academy and served in the armor branch of the U.S. Army from 1975 through 1980. He serves on the board of directors of his local Boys and Girls Club and is active in other civic organizations.

Mitchell B. Reiss, 30, of New York. Mr. Reiss is an attorney with the firm of Fried, Frank, Harris, Schriver & Jacobson in New York City. He has received a bachelor's degree from Williams College, a master's degree from the Fletcher School of Law and Diplomacy, a doctorate from Oxford University, and a law degree from Columbia Law School. His dissertation was published and nominated for four national book awards.

John E. Shephard, Jr., 32, of New York. Major Shephard is a U.S. Army officer currently teaching at the U.S. Military Academy. A graduate of the U.S. Military Academy, he earned a master's degree from the Massachusetts Institute of Technology. His articles on civil-military relations have appeared in professional journals and on the editorial pages of the Wall Street Journal and the Washington Post.

David L. Simms, 31, of Massachusetts. Mr. Simms is currently a manager with Bain and Company in Boston. He is a summa cum laude graduate of the University of Pennsylvania, where he earned degrees in economics and applied science. He is a graduate of the Harvard University joint J.D./M.B.A. program. He has served as a trustee of the University of Pennsylvania and on the management board for Christians for Urban Justice/Habitat for Humanity.

Clifford L. Stanley, 41, of Virginia. Lt. Col. Stanley is a U.S. Marine Corps officer currently attending the National War College. He earned a master's degree with honors from Johns Hopkins University. He has been awarded the Meritorious Service Medal, Navy Commendation Medal, and the Navy Achievement Medal.

Patrick M. Walsh, 33, of Texas. Lt. Comdr. Walsh is a U.S. naval officer currently attending the Armed Forces Staff College. A graduate of the U.S. Naval Academy, he is an accomplished naval aviator. He has served aboard five aircraft carriers, as an operational test director for the Chief of Naval Operations and as a member of the Blue Angels. He has been active in the Big Brothers and the Make-a-Wish Foundation.

Appointment of Michael J. Astrue as Associate Counsel to the President

June 8, 1988

The President today announced the appointment of Michael J. Astrue to be Associate Counsel to the President. He will succeed Peter D. Keisler.

From 1985 to 1988, Mr. Astrue served in the Department of Health and Human Services as counselor to the Commissioner of Social Security; legal counsel to the Deputy Commissioner for Programs, Social Security Administration; and Acting Deputy Assistant Secretary for Human Services Legislation. In addition, he was an associate with the law firm of Ropes and Gray in Boston (1984–1985) and a law clerk to the Honorable Walter J. Skinner, U.S. District Court Judge for the District of Massachusetts (1983–1984).

Mr. Astrue graduated from Yale University (B.A., 1978) and Harvard Law School (J.D., 1983). He was born October 1, 1956, in Fort Dix, NJ. Mr. Astrue is married, has one child, and is a resident of Belmont, MA.

Appointment of Kevin H. Kruke as Special Assistant to the President and Deputy Director of the Office of Public Liaison
June 8, 1988

The President today announced the appointment of Kevin H. Kruke to be Special Assistant to the President and Deputy Director of the Office of Public Liaison. He will succeed Donald A. Danner.

Since 1986 Mr. Kruke has served as the executive vice president of the American Trucking Association's Foundation and the Trucking Research Institute. From 1985 to 1986, Mr. Kruke worked at the U.S. Department of Transportation, where he served as a congressional relations officer in the Office of Intergovernmental Affairs. From 1976 to 1984, Mr. Kruke served in a variety of positions at the Highway Users Federation for Safety and Mobility.

A 1975 graduate of the University of Wisconsin at Milwaukee, Mr. Kruke received his B.A. in economics. He received his master of philosophy degree from George Washington University, specializing in environmental economics and industrial organization, in 1985. He was born April 22, 1954, in Wauwatosa, WI, and resides in Washington, DC.

Nomination of William G. Goetz To Be a Member of the National Advisory Council on Educational Research and Improvement
June 8, 1988

The President today announced his intention to nominate William G. Goetz to be a member of the National Advisory Council on Educational Research and Improvement for a term expiring September 30, 1990. He would succeed Onalee McGraw.

Since 1967 Mr. Goetz has been dean of the school of business and administration, and the executive vice president of the Dickinson State University Foundation at Dickinson State University. He has also served since 1987 as assistant minority leader in the North Dakota House of Representatives.

Mr. Goetz graduated from Minot State University (B.A., 1966) and the University of North Dakota (M.A., 1967). He was born January 6, 1944, in Hazen, ND. He is married, has three children, and resides in Dickinson, ND.

Nomination of Keith Lapham Brown To Be United States Ambassador to Denmark
June 8, 1988

The President today announced his intention to nominate Keith Lapham Brown to be Ambassador to Denmark. He would succeed Terence A. Todman, who has served with distinction in Denmark for more than 4½ years.

Mr. Brown is an attorney at law and a member of the Texas, Oklahoma, and Colorado Bar Associations. He was a founder and original partner of Vail Associates and served as a director for many years. Mr. Brown has served as a director of the Public Service Co. of Colorado; Griffith Realty, Inc.; Caulkins Oil Co.; National Western Stock Show Association; Boys Club of Denver, Inc.; Boys Club of America, Inc.; and the Colorado State Bank. He is an honorary trustee and past president of the board of Colorado Academy. He serves on the Advisory Board for the Center for Strategic and International Studies, Washington, DC. He is chairman of the International Institute of Education/Denver World Affairs Council and is a past executive board member for Downtown Denver, Inc. Mr. Brown served as the United States Ambassador to Lesotho from 1982 to 1983 and is a member of the Council of American Ambassadors. He was most recently the chairman of the Republican National Finance Committee in Washington, DC.

Mr. Brown attended the University of Illinois, the University of Texas, Northwestern University Law School, and graduated from the University of Texas Law School (LL.B., 1949). He served in the United States Navy from 1943 to 1946. He was born June 18, 1925, in Sterling, IL. Mr. Brown is married, has three children, and resides in Denver, CO.

Nomination of Michael H. Newlin To Be United States Representative to the Vienna Office of the United Nations and Deputy Representative to the International Atomic Energy Agency
June 8, 1988

The President today announced his intention to nominate Michael H. Newlin, of Maryland, a career member of the Senior Foreign Service, Class of Minister-Counselor, as the Representative of the United States of America to the Vienna Office of the United Nations and Deputy Representative of the United States of America to the International Atomic Energy Agency, with the rank of Ambassador. He would succeed Bruce Chapman.

Mr. Newlin is a career diplomat who joined the Foreign Service in 1952. He has held posts in Europe, the Middle East and Africa, as well as in the Department of State and the U.S. Mission to the United Nations. Mr. Newlin was Ambassador to Algeria from 1981 to 1985. He is currently Principal Deputy Assistant Secretary of State for Consular Affairs.

Mr. Newlin graduated from Harvard University (B.A., 1949; M.B.A., 1951). He was born May 16, 1926, in Greensboro, NC. Mr. Newlin is married, has one child, and resides in Bethesda, MD.

Appointment of Helen M. Scheirbeck as a Member of the National Advisory Council on Indian Education

June 8, 1988

The President today announced his intention to appoint Helen M. Scheirbeck to be a member of the National Advisory Council on Indian Education for a term expiring September 29, 1990. She would succeed Thomas E. Sawyer.

Since 1987 Ms. Scheirbeck has been development director of the Indian Cultural Center in Pembroke, NC. Prior to this, she was director of the American Indian Nations Region, Save the Children Federation, in Westport, CT, 1982–1987, and director of Indian information programs, Lumbee Regional Development Association, 1981–1982. Ms. Scheirbeck also served with the White House Conference on Children and Youth, 1980–1981.

Ms. Scheirbeck graduated from Berea College (B.S., 1958) and Virginia Polytechnic Institute and State University (Ed.D., 1980). She was born August 21, 1935, in Lumberton, NC. She has one child and resides in Fairfax, VA.

Nomination of Roland W. Schmitt To Be a Member of the National Science Board

June 8, 1988

The President today announced his intention to nominate Roland W. Schmitt to be a member of the National Science Board, National Science Foundation, for a term expiring May 10, 1994. This is a reappointment.

Dr. Schmitt is currently president of Rensselaer Polytechnic Institute in Troy, NY. Prior to this, Dr. Schmitt was with General Electric from 1951 to 1986, serving most recently as senior vice president for science and technology, 1986–1988; and senior vice president for corporate research and development, 1980–1986.

Dr. Schmitt graduated from the University of Texas (B.A., 1947; B.S., 1947; M.A., 1948) and Rice University (Ph.D., 1951). He was born July 24, 1923, in Seguin, TX. Dr. Schmitt is married, has four children, and resides in Rexford, NY.

Message to the Congress Transmitting the Pro-Life Act of 1988

June 8, 1988

To the Congress of the United States:

I am pleased to transmit for your immediate and favorable consideration the "President's Pro-Life Act of 1988." This important legislation carries out my commitment to protect the rights of unborn children by prohibiting any Federal dollars from being used to fund abortion unless a mother's life would be physically endangered by carrying the fetus to term.

Since the legalization of abortion on demand in 1973, there have been an estimated 21 million abortions in this country. The bill I am sending you has been named the "President's Pro-Life Act of 1988" to emphasize the urgent need to reduce the number of abortions in this country and to reaffirm life's sacred position in our Nation.

The findings that would underlie the mandate of the statute point out that abortion takes the life of a living human being, that there is no right to abortion secured by the Constitution, and that the Supreme Court erred in its decision in *Roe* v. *Wade* in failing to recognize the humanity of the unborn child.

The key provision of the bill would enact, on a permanent and government-wide basis, the anti-abortion provision—commonly known as the Hyde Amendment—that is included annually in the appropriation act for the Department of Health and Human Services. Enacting this prohibition on the funding of abortion in general legislation will extend its application to all agencies and to all Federal funds.

None are more powerless than the unborn. I urge you to pass this measure promptly and thereby join me in helping to protect their rights to life, liberty, and the pursuit of happiness.

RONALD REAGAN

The White House,
June 8, 1988.

Nomination of James B. Werson To Be a Member of the Board of Directors of the National Corporation for Housing Partnerships
June 8, 1988

The President today announced his intention to nominate James B. Werson to be a member of the Board of Directors of the National Corporation for Housing Partnerships for the term expiring October 27, 1991. He would succeed Alfred J. Fleischer, Sr.

Since 1947 Mr. Werson has been with the law firm of Severson, Werson, Berke and Malchior in San Francisco, CA, and currently serves as president. Mr. Werson was with the Federal Bureau of Investigation from 1942 to 1946.

Mr. Werson graduated from the University of California at Berkeley (A.B., 1938) and Boalt Hall School of Law, University of California at Berkeley (J.D., 1942). He was born December 29, 1916, in Butte, MT. He is married, has three children, and resides in El Cerrito, CA.

Remarks and a Question-and-Answer Session at a Luncheon With Radio and Television Journalists
June 8, 1988

The President. Well, if you don't feel welcome already, welcome to the White House. There's a story we had in Hollywood about Cecil B. deMille, the producer of all those great historical spectacles. It was after the big earthquake in March 1933. And a famous actress of that time, Janet Gaynor, had been in one of the studio buildings when the quake began and all the shaking took place. And when it was over and the ground had stopped moving, she turned to a friend and said, "I thought for a moment we'd dropped into one of those deMille pictures." That's just how I felt last week, during the Moscow summit—dropped into a grand historical moment. I know that you have questions to ask about the summit, and I don't want to take too much time at the start, but I thought I'd quickly review what we set out to do and what we did.

As you know, our relationship with the Soviets is like a table. It's built on four legs: arms reduction, resolving of regional conflicts, improvement of human rights within the Soviet Union, and expansion of bilateral exchanges. The Soviets have indicated many times that they'd prefer the discussions be confined to the arms issues alone, but we believe that sustained improvement in relations can't rest stably on one leg. We saw what happened in the détente period of the early seventies. There were arms and trade agreements and what was billed as a general thaw, but because of Soviet behavior in so many areas, these could not be sustained. Weapons are a sign of tensions, not a cause of them. I know all of you have heard me say this time and again, but let me repeat it here: Nations do not distrust each other because they're armed; they are armed because they distrust each other.

And we began building our new relationship with the Soviets 7½ years ago. Strengthening America's defenses was and is part of it. Our zero-option proposal for intermediate-range nuclear missiles was part of it, coupled with NATO's deployment of Pershing II and ground-launched cruise missiles. It was a carrot-and-stick response to the highly destabilizing deployment of the Soviet INF missiles. Our policies regarding emigration from the Soviet Union, human rights problems, and the Soviet presence in a variety of Third World conflicts were also aspects of it.

Progress was stalled for a long time. The Soviets tested our resolve, and that of our allies, at the bargaining table and in the deployment of INF weapons. They also went through a series of leaders, none of whom lived long enough to change the longstanding Brezhnev-era policies. That was one of my problems, my delay in getting started in dealings with the Soviet Union—they kept dying on me. And now, under Mr. Gorbachev, the Soviets have a leader who appears to want to change things and who may actually be able to change things. Internally, his promotion of *perestroika* and *glasnost* gives us hope, although we remember that old American political adage: "Trust everybody, but cut the cards." In foreign affairs, he's begun the withdrawal from Afghanistan and agreed to our zero option for INF, something the Soviets spent a number of years denouncing.

I hope you'll forgive me for saying this, but too often in the past, it's appeared to me that coverage of summits has been geared more to the hunt for headlines than to the realities of business. If there wasn't the blockbuster agreement, a summit was dismissed. In fact, each of my four meetings with Mr. Gorbachev has produced significant steps forward. Take just one area: reduction in the level of strategic arms. In Geneva the General Secretary and I agreed to the concept of 50-percent reductions; and in Reykjavik, on numerical limits for warheads and delivery vehicles; in Washington, on intensive work to complete a START treaty, including comprehensive verification provisions building on those in the INF treaty. And in Moscow, we moved forward in reaching an agreement on an experiment to improve the verification of existing nuclear testing treaties, and another agreement on notification of strategic ballistic missile launches.

I've heard repeated many times the old rule that you should never go to a summit unless everything has been fully scripted in advance. Well, as you might have guessed, I don't fully accept that. I can't tell you the shock the first time when they said that we should put out the statement in advance that we were going to finish the summit with. I believe that if relations between the United States and the Soviet Union are genuinely to improve, from time to time the top leaders must step in and exercise leadership. They must agree on a common set of broad goals so that those under them have a clear and common green light to move forward. That's been the purpose and the accomplishment of these four summits.

Today we can say, with caution, that we may be entering a new era of U.S. and Soviet relations. It's been a long time coming, but unlike past improvements that saw only a brief day, I think this one will have a broad and stable footing. If the Soviets want it to grow, it can, and it will.

And now, rather than going on, I know that you have questions that you want to ask and that I want to answer. Think of what a refreshing change this will be for me—to hear someone shout a question and realize it's not Sam Donaldson. [*Laughter*] Yes?

Administration Transition

Q. I'm not close to Sam, I'm afraid—background, at least. I'd like to ask you: With the administration coming to a close, and in your own mind and the mind of many others, so much accomplished at the summit, how are you going to prepare for the transition—whether it's a Republican or Democratic administration—so that you can continue what you've started? And I have a followup I'd like to ask.

The President. Well, I'll be pretty handicapped if it goes one way. But if it goes the way I'd like it to go—George Bush, who has been a part of everything that we've accomplished in these several years—why, I would want to point out to my successor the things that we didn't get accomplished that are still needed: the improvement in the whole budgeting process, the line-item veto and what it means. As a Governor for 8 years, I did 943 line-item vetoes without ever being overridden once, and we left the State with a surplus, not a deficit. But, no, I'll want to be of help if I can, but there are a number of things that in these succeeding months we're still going to try to get forward.

Q. My followup is: Nothing is going to be accomplished in terms of an arms agreement without your support, even after you're out of office. Do you think there should be some kind of formalized relationship between yourself and the next President and next administration so that you could be privy to what's being prepared along the way?

The President. Well, let me say, there is such a situation or arrangement now. Regularly we keep each of the former Presidents informed in writing with the policies and where we are and things like the summit and all of that. That goes on regularly, and they're all kept completely informed. And I think that's all that an ex-President should ask for.

Strategic Arms Control

Q. Mr. President, Paul Linnman, from KATV in Portland, Oregon. Acknowledging that you are pleased with the progress made in Moscow and your administration—there is the possibility of agreement before your term ends. Will you press for that if it becomes realistic to include going so far as to invoking your powers to recall Congress for ratification?

The President. Oh, I wouldn't mind recalling them for anything. [*Laughter*] No, the thing is—let me make clear that we have refrained from setting deadlines. I think the idea to set down some line and then you find yourself tempted to agree to something less good than it could be, but because of the deadline—so, if it isn't, I'd think it would be great if the START agreement could be finished, the negotiations go on between our representatives. If that could be done before I left office and it could be signed, that would be fine, because then we could move on to some other things that need dealing with—conventional weapons and so forth. But if it isn't, why, we'll just keep on negotiating and then try to impress on whoever comes in next where we are.

I've got to come over to this side here sometime.

Presidential Candidates

Q. My name is Ted Trulock. I'm with WCTV in Tallahassee, Florida. We both went to Dixon High School——

The President. Well!

Q. ——in Dixon, Illinois. Anyway, sir, what I was going to ask you about was the Democratic side on Presidential politics. How do you see the Reverend Jackson's campaign? Do you think that he is a viable Vice Presidential candidate? Can you give us some advice? I'd like to follow up, if I could.

The President. Well, I hate to give any suggestions that might be of help to the other side. But there's no question that he has impressed a great number of followers. And I want to say—and without any inference to any racial difference or anything—I would have to say that I find myself in great disagreement with policies that he has proposed, as well as those of the other candidate, Dukakis. But I think that goes with the game. They obviously have different goals in mind than we have. But I think he's certainly been a viable candidate all the way.

Q. Your friend George Bush seems to be having some problems in California. What can you do to help him there?

The President. Everything I can. I've had to be neutral for a long time—until there was a definite candidate—because in this job you are titular head of the party, so you have to remain neutral. But as I say, he's been a part of everything that we've accomplished in this administration.

Soviet People

Q. I'm Sharon Crockett, from LAC Radio in Nashville. What is your impression of the people of the Soviet Union—just the regular people?

The President. My opinion of the——

Q. The people—just the plain old everyday working people in the Soviet Union.

The President. In the Soviet Union?

Q. Yes.

The President. There are several people at my table here that are going to have to listen again. One of the most exciting things—I couldn't believe it, after all the years of propaganda that we're all villains on this side of the ocean and everything. The Soviet people were the warmest, friendliest, nicest people you could ever meet. Every place we went, whether it was night or day, the streets would be lined with thousands of them, as if there was going to be a parade—and their friendly waves. And then in the opportunities when we did have a chance to get out in the street and come in contact with them, and they all wanted to shake hands and visit. They were really wonderful. And I'm going to add something in there that you didn't ask, but that I had said once before up here. I voiced this a few times when I had a chance publicly in the Soviet Union: that not only were they all so wonderful and friendly, but I think the women of the Soviet Union are the biggest and most powerful stabilizing force in that society. They're just wonderful.

Soviet-U.S. Relations

Q. Mr. President, my name is Cameron Harper. I'm from KTVK Television in Phoenix. And I heard you say in speeches that the summit was a turning point in East-West affairs, and you've said that it planted the seeds of freedom and liberty. Vice President George Bush, as recently as yesterday, was saying that he's not so sure, that he's not sure it represents a fundamental change in direction in the Soviet Union and its relations with this country. Is he reading a different set of briefing papers, perhaps?

The President. No, and I think he's being as careful as we all must be. It's all right to be optimistic and all of that, but I—I'm not a linguist, but I learned a Russian proverb, and Gorbachev wishes to hell I hadn't. [*Laughter*] It is: *Dovorey no provorey.* It means trust, but verify. And we have the greatest verification worked out in the INF treaty that's ever taken place. There will be, I think, sixty-some Americans permanently stationed in the Soviet Union, and they will have as many of theirs permanently stationed here. And that's never been attempted in any treaties before.

There's a young lady there. Yes?

General Secretary Gorbachev

Q. Mr. President, you know Mikhail Gorbachev probably better than any American, have had four summits with him, spent many hours one-on-one with him. If he has the good fortune to have your good health and stamina, he could conceivably be the Secretary General for 20 to 25 years. I'd like first your impressions of the man and any advice you might offer to the next President on going toe-to-toe with Mikhail Gorbachev.

The President. Well, I have known a number of their leaders and met with a number of their leaders before, and I must say this: He is different. And this doesn't mean I mean that you lower your guard precipitantly at all, but he definitely—his *perestroika*—and I read his book—and *glasnost*—he definitely wants changes in the social structure there. And he's faced with a great economic problem, literally a basket case. And he has plans, and these other things I've just mentioned are part of his plan for trying to build up the economy and make it more viable than it presently is. And I have to say that I think the Russian people have taken to both of these, *glasnost* and *perestroika,* and have a far better feeling about their system. I didn't run into the kind of cynicism that I've seen so often in the past among them. And I think that Margaret Thatcher was right when she said, "He's someone you can do business with."

Meetings With the Press

Q. Mr. President, Howard Caldwell, from

Indianapolis, Indiana. In light of the heavy coverage of the summit, I'm curious why you invited us out here today. Were you dissatisfied about coverage? [*Laughter*]

The President. No, let me tell you. We've gone too long without people like you being here. I started in the beginning having, several times a year, people like yourselves from all over the country here in this same room and doing what we're doing right now, because I recognize that your only sources of information were coming from certain elements of the press within the beltway and in the East here. And I sometimes have found some of those sources biased. And I thought that you had a right to be able to ask, and you ask good questions, too.

This young lady here, and then I'll get you.

Presidential Candidates

Q. This is to play off the question that was asked to you earlier. I'm Nancy Chandler, from WITI–TV in Milwaukee. I'm wondering, with the approaching election, you knowing Gorbachev, if you had talked at all—certainly we know your preference in the Presidential race—if he had expressed one way or another which candidate he might appreciate negotiating with in the future.

The President. No, I think he's been very careful to not ever get into that subject, and he's never brought that up or not. But I've made it plain to him that I'm going to do everything I can to impress upon my successor where we are and what the goals should continue to be.

Now, that young man.

American Indians

Q. Mr. President, some remarks you made in Moscow caused great consternation among Indian leaders. One of the kinder assessments was by Navajo Tribal Chairman Peter McDonald, who happens to be a Republican and suggested it might behoove you to visit the Navajo reservation this fall. I'm wondering whether you have any regrets about the remarks you made about American Indians in Moscow and what the chances are of you visiting the Navajo reservation this fall.

The President. Well, I don't know whether I can, whether the schedule will permit—I'm still trying to find the fellow that tells me where—I'm going to be doing every 15 minutes every day. But, no, I don't regret that, and I do think that there were mistakes made back in the very beginning of our country with regard to the Indians and the manner of handling them. But the question that I was answering was in effect—was that somehow I had refused to meet with them. I've never refused to meet with any Americans and certainly haven't refused to meet with them and have on a number of occasions. And I don't know just what the specific complaint is, but I know that we've been doing for a long time our utmost to provide education for those who wanted to maintain Indian life as it was on the reservation, in contrast to those who leave and come out and join the rest of us and become more like us.

I've got to turn back this way again. May I go back here once, and then I'll come to you.

Soviet-U.S. Cooperation in Space

Q. Mr. Reagan, Steve Rondinaro, WESH Television, Orlando. Thank you for having us for lunch. I enjoyed the fingerbowl. [*Laughter*] Let me ask you, sir—our area covers the Kennedy Space Center. We follow space very closely and paid a lot of attention to Mr. Gorbachev's first motions about a joint mission to Mars. Did you weigh that prospect at all? Do you see that happening? And how do you view our space program, as opposed to where their's is? They just put three cosmonauts up yesterday.

The President. Yes, there's no question but that the *Challenger* tragedy has put us behind, and we are back of where our schedule called for—because we wanted to be underway on a space station by this time. With regard to the Mars trip—incidentally, we've already sent a craft to Mars, as you know, in the past—taken some pictures that make you wonder why anyone would want to go there. [*Laughter*] But they've specified theirs would be unmanned, also. I have turned that over to our people in that field because I don't know just exactly what the scheduling problems are for getting us back into operation again and whether that would set us back. But I'm going to wait for their reporting before making a decision on whether we do something jointly.

Q. They have a space station up already. I know you wanted to have ours up there by 1990, originally.

The President. Yes.

Q. Do you have a money battle to make that happen? Will that become reality?

The President. Well, as I say, we were set back by that tragedy and then the extensive research and all that went on so that we wouldn't have a repeat. And so, we're behind. There's no question, we're behind schedule in all of our space activity other than the things that we put aloft, such as the satellites that can give us the weather and that can photograph the Earth as if they were—[*laughter*]—just on the second floor and so forth, that type of thing. But generally we are behind schedule, and right now, as I understand, we're having a little problem—since the explosion in one of our rocket fuel plants—we're having trouble.

Cuba

Q. Mr. President, Bill Bayer, from Miami. You're coming to Miami later this month, I understand, but some of the Cuban-American community and many of the people down there say that the Reagan administration has betrayed us. You've heard this, of course.

The President. Yes.

Q. Okay. What is your answer to this? Of course, betrayal is a very provocative word, but nonetheless it's bounced around the headlines all over the country. What would you answer them? And then I have a followup.

The President. I would answer that they're misinformed. We certainly haven't betrayed them, nor is there anything to this idea that we've softened up our relationship with Castro. As you know, we were instrumental—in fact I would think that we were the ones that got the United Nations to authorize a team to go to Castro—or to Cuba and look into the charges of violation of human rights there. So, no, we're not doing anything of that kind. Since Cardinal O'Connor went down there, if it is true that he is going to release several hundred of their political prisoners, I have firsthand knowledge of what those prisoners have been going through, and some of them for more than 20 years, and the torture that they've gone through. But before I would take Castro's word as to the number and that he's releasing the bulk of them—only a few—no, I'd want somebody else to be there counting.

Regional Conflicts

Q. Mr. President, did the subject of the backyard, the Caribbean and South America, come up during the Moscow summit at all, and the cancer of communism seeping through?

The President. We always bring that up in connection with that one thing about regional activities and regional developments. You don't get definite and specific yes and no answers to things. We think that there is a big improvement—the Afghanistan thing that has happened. We think that there is a probability—maybe I should say possibility, but I believe even a probability—of, now, relief in Angola from this same kind of a situation. But, yes, they know our feelings, and we have laid out the places where we believe that something must be done.

Ms. Board. We have time for one more question.

Q. Mr. President, Ray Briem, of ABC, Los Angeles. And first of all, as a member of the Rotary Club of Pacific Palisades, we know you're an honorary member, and after January, we invite you back. [*Laughter*]

The President. Thank you.

Strategic Defense Initiative

Q. Regarding SDI, a few months ago you said that the Soviets may be preparing to break out of the ABM treaty and deploy a nationwide ABM system. Did you talk that over with Mr. Gorbachev? And what was his answer?

The President. Oh, we have told him that we believe that they're in violation. We know they're in violation of the ABM treaty, particularly with Krasnoyarsk. And we've made it plain that we know that and that that is going to be factored in in any of our dealings, and particularly with SDI.

We know that they have been spending far more on defensive programs than we have with SDI. But evidently their technology must not have kept pace with ours, because our system is one that I think, in spite of some of the pessimists who claim otherwise, that it is a research program aimed at a target. And the research has—there have been a number of breakthroughs that has made most of our scientists optimistic that it is a system that can work. And if it can, I have often said—and have said to General Secretary Gorbachev—that this could be the answer to the dream of no more nuclear weapons if we could make them obsolete with this kind of defensive system. And I have said that I would be pleased to share it with the world if we had such a thing because someday—you know, we know how to make those nuclear missiles, and someday there could be a madman come along, another Hitler or something, and try to blackmail the Earth. But not if we all had a protective system against them that was almost invulnerable. And we're very optimistic about it.

There's—did you mean that one or that—there was one that I was going to take right back there with his hand up.

Vice President Bush

Q. Mr. President, Wayne Weinberg, with WDVO Radio in Orlando. If I could play a game of "what if " with you: If I were Vice President, if I were George Bush, and we were in the Oval Office, and it was just you and I, and I said, "Gee, Mr. President, all the polls show that I'm behind Michael Dukakis." What would you tell him to give encouragement and perhaps to advise some strategy to reverse that?

The President. I'd say, George, wait till you and I get out there on the trail and start pinning him down on the things he claims which we know are not true. And then we would say such things as some of our own accomplishments. You know, if I listened to him long enough, I would be convinced that we're in an economic downturn and that people are homeless and people are going without food and medical attention and that we've got to do something about the unemployed. Do you know what the potential pool of employment is in the United States? I didn't till I got here. It is everyone, male and female, 16 years of age and up. That is the potential employment pool—all of those students, all of those retired people, everything. Today the highest percentage of that pool is employed than ever in our history.

There were other things we wanted to do. We wanted to get the Government to act a little bit more like business and do things more effectively and efficiently than it can. I put George Bush in charge of a task force to see how many Federal regulations could be eliminated. The book containing those regulations now is only half as big as it was when we came. And our estimate is that the people, the communities, the States, and businesses have now been able to reduce the amount of time spent on government-required paperwork by 600 million man-hours a year.

And there are other little items, like just the other day some figures came in: that it used to take 43 days to get a passport; it only takes 10 now. And there's one that used to take 100 days to get an urban renewal loan set in motion. And it doesn't take 100 days anymore; it takes about 16. I may be getting some of these figures inaccurate, but that's how much the improvement has come in businesslike ways and things that we've done to imitate business instead of attack business.

Now, I know that I'm way past my schedule, and Elizabeth isn't—she could hit me over the head if I don't say—there's one thing that's typical of this, as well as the regular press conferences. And that is that, darn it, I always have to walk away with about 30 hands that have been waving that I haven't been able to get to. I just try to point in directions here and not play any favorites. And since you're all new to me, I couldn't play any favorites, but I'm grateful for your being here. And maybe if you feel like writing some questions and handing them to our people, we can send you back some answers if we didn't get to them at all. But I have to get back to the office now. Thank you all very much.

Note: The President spoke at 1:08 p.m. in

the State Dining Room at the White House. Elizabeth Board, Special Assistant to the President and Director of Media and Broadcast Relations, also attended the luncheon.

Executive Order 12642—Designation of the Secretary of Defense as the Presidential Designee Under Title I of the Uniformed and Overseas Citizens Absentee Voting Act
June 8, 1988

By virtue of the authority vested in me as President by the Constitution and laws of the United States of America, including section 101(a) of the Uniformed and Overseas Citizens Absentee Voting Act (Public Law 99–410) ("the Act"), it is hereby ordered as follows:

Section 1. The Secretary of Defense is hereby designated as the "Presidential designee" under Title I of the Act.

Sec. 2. In order to effectuate the purposes of the Act, the Secretary of Defense is hereby authorized to delegate any or all of the functions, responsibilities, powers, authority, or discretion devolving upon him in consequence of this Order to any person or persons within the Department of Defense.

RONALD REAGAN

The White House,
June 8, 1988.

[*Filed with the Office of the Federal Register, 12:29 p.m., June 9, 1988*]

Statement on Senate Action Sustaining the President's Veto of the Omnibus Trade Bill
June 8, 1988

I am pleased the Senate voted to sustain my veto of H.R. 3, the Omnibus Trade bill. As I said in my veto message on the bill, I am committed to enactment of a responsible trade bill this year. I am directing my senior advisers to stand ready to assist the congressional leadership on a new trade bill—one that will strengthen America's international competitiveness and create even more new jobs for Americans.

Appointment of Jerry J. Naylor as a Member of the National Commission for Employment Policy
June 9, 1988

The President today announced his intention to appoint Jerry J. Naylor to be a member of the National Commission for Employment Policy for a term expiring September 30, 1991. This is a reappointment.

Since 1985 Mr. Naylor has been president of International Syndications, Inc., and senior vice president for corporate development of Newslink, Inc., in Agoura, CA. Prior to this he was president of the Jerry Naylor Co., 1982–1985. Mr. Naylor is a veteran of the entertainment industry. He was a member of the rock group Buddy Holly and the Crickets and became lead singer after the death of Buddy Holly in 1959.

Mr. Naylor attended the University of Maryland. He served in the United States Army, 1957–1958. He was born March 6, 1939, in Erath County, TX. Mr. Naylor is married, has three children, and resides in Agoura, CA.

Remarks at the National Conference on Corporate Initiatives for a Drug Free Workplace
June 9, 1988

Well, thank you, Irwin Lerner. Thank you all very much. And I join you in recognizing Congressman Ben Gilman for all that he has been doing up on the Hill in regard to this problem. It's a pleasure to be here with you, this National Conference on Corporate Initiatives for a Drug Free Workplace, and I am delighted by the strong leadership that the business community is showing in this vital effort.

You know, I've been speaking out about the problem of illegal drugs for a very long time now. When I began doing so as Governor of California, the times were very different. In fact, a conference of this type would have been unlikely, and had it been held, there probably would have been pickets out in front. Well, when I arrived here today there were no pickets and no petitions, no demonstrators, no protests. I circled the block a couple times while we checked to make sure it was the right hotel. [*Laughter*] The truth is that attitudes toward illegal drugs really have changed. We can see it in the media. We can see it among our youth. And we can see it on the floor of Congress.

Though the struggle for a drug free America has not yet been won, the moral and cultural battle to define the threat of illegal drugs is clear. And it's all of us who are on the winning side, part of the overwhelming consensus against illegal drugs in America. An important symbol of that consensus and of the distance that we've traveled as a society is that our drug policy today is one of zero tolerance. That means absolutely, positively none—no exceptions.

I have to tell you that I am especially proud of the antidrug work that Nancy, who you so generously mentioned, has done that's changed the way we talk and think about illegal drugs. It was not that long ago that the message to our young people was that experimenting with illegal drugs was not only harmless but was kind of a good thing, an instant path to popularity and sophistication. The social stigma all too often was not on the drug user but on the young person who refused to try drugs. As I've said before, the tragic fact is that many young people began using drugs not to rebel or escape but just to fit in.

In many ways our country is still paying for the erosion of our values and the decline in self-responsibility that occurred in the 1960's and the 1970's. The students of that period who used illegal drugs in high school or college have, in many cases, taken their destructive drug habits with them into their places of employment. What we've found is that drug users at work pose a threat to their coworkers and represent a corporate crisis and a national catastrophe.

What was once defended as a so-called victimless crime we now find is costing America billions of dollars a year in lost productivity. We're finding that drug users are two or three times more likely to skip work as nonusers and three or four times as likely to be involved in accidents when they do show up. They're more likely to steal from their employers, and their health care costs are substantially higher. It's no surprise that 92 percent of all Americans say they don't want to work around someone who gets high during the day, and who can blame them? Having seen the damage caused by illegal drugs in the workplace, our message is simple: Let's get those blasted drugs out now!

The good news is that there has been a major change of attitude in America, and the work that you're doing now is an important part of it. The momentum has shifted from those who celebrated the drug subculture to the people who just say no and help others to do the same. Illegal drugs and drug use are not being tolerated anymore. Yes, the enemy, illegal drug use, is still out there and still a threat. But today illegal drug use is an enemy that has no defenders. Not only is an ever-increasing number of Americans personally rejecting the use of illegal drugs, but the country as a whole is moving to deglamorize and depopularize their use.

Law enforcement authorities, such as the police, the Coast Guard, the Drug Enforcement Administration, and the Customs Service, are critical players in the war on drugs—but there are limits on what can be accomplished on the supply side. There must also be stern social sanctions on the user of illegal drugs and broad societal support for individuals being drug free. It is this change in attitudes that, I believe, makes total victory in the war on drugs not just possible but ultimately certain.

The glamorizing of drugs in film and music that was so much a part of the "progressive" culture has declined, and instead the most popular entertainment stars and sports celebrities are warning our young people that using drugs is dangerous for their health and bad for their image. Now, it just seems the other day, a quite popular motion picture, a comedy starring several feminine stars, one of the big comedy scenes was all of them sitting around and passing the joint around, and then the hilarity and so forth, and that was considered just fine to get laughs in the theater and all. Well, thank heaven we don't see that anymore. The entertainment world has joined your club.

We're also becoming increasingly intolerant of illegal drugs on our college and university campuses. And employers are stating right up front that illegal drug use will be hazardous to their workers' careers. Some very encouraging news about the prospects for a drug free work force came in last year's annual survey of high school seniors. The survey showed that the Just Say No message is getting through to the new generation of workers. Almost all students said it was wrong to even try a drug like cocaine. And the percentage of students who indicated that they were currently using illegal drugs was lower, much lower, than in previous years.

You in the business community are playing a critical role in America's transition to a drug free society. You're providing drug education to your employees. You're offering counseling and treatment to help men and women escape from drug dependency. You're providing drug testing to help deter and detect illegal drug use. And you send a strong message to your work force and community that your company has zero tolerance for illegal drugs and that users must be held responsible for their illicit drug use. You make it clear that not only are drug users not part of the "in crowd," but unless they quit taking illegal drugs they'll be part of the out-of-work crowd.

Most importantly, in everything you do, you keep the focus on the user, and this is vital. We're confiscating more drugs at the border than ever before in history. We're convicting more drug dealers and giving them longer sentences. We're eradicating more drug fields around the world, devoting more resources to drug enforcement than ever before, and bringing the military into an unprecedented level of support in the battle against illegal drugs. But in the final analysis, the focus must be on the user, because so long as there's a demand for illegal drugs, there will be a powerful financial incentive for drug traffickers to satisfy that demand. Ultimately, the solution requires transforming illegal drug users into nonusers. And the antidrug programs you're conducting in the workplace are an essential part in this effort.

As you work to get drugs out of your offices and plants, it's important to remember the problem of illegal drug use is a global problem. You may know, for example, that Nancy, in addition to all that she's done at home, has organized two international conferences of first ladies to discuss the drug problem, one held at the White House, the other held at the United Nations. And just this afternoon, Nancy will be addressing 1,300 women from countries around the world who are attending the World Gas Conference. So, in many nations and in many languages, there are young people learning the words "just say no."

I've got to interject something here about that. You know where that came from? Nancy was speaking to a school, to a classroom out in Oakland, California. And a little girl stood up and said, "But what do we do when someone offers us drugs?" And Nancy said, "Well, just say no." Today there are over 12,000 Just Say No clubs in schools across the United States—all from just one single remark in one single classroom.

I hope that the leading role taken by American business to get illegal drugs out of the workplace will be expanded here at home and duplicated abroad. Some people may look at the drug problem and throw up their hands, not knowing where to begin. Then there are people like you who look at the drug problem and roll up their sleeves and get to work. What you're doing is making a real difference. Drug education, counseling, treatment, and testing—these are powerful tools. I'm proud that American business has willingly taken on this vital effort. By doing this, you're helping your coworkers, you're helping your companies, you're helping the American economy, and you're helping to bring us closer to fulfilling our goal of a drug free America.

And with regard to the private initiative, early in my first term, at a dinner party at the White House, the wife of an Ambassador of a European country sitting beside me heard some talk at our table about one or two of the programs going on here, not just for drugs but I mean of a private nature. And very quietly she said to me, "Yes, but you're unique." And I said, "What? What do you mean unique?" She said, "Yes, in America, you'll do that that way—private people." She said, "The rest of us in the rest of the world, we wait for government to do it."

Well, I'm sure that many of you know already that in the last couple of years meetings have been held in Paris and in London at the invitation of our neighboring and friendly trading partners in the world, and they have invited people like you to come over there and tell them how to establish private sector initiatives and private sector work in getting problems solved. And here in our own country, just last year the private giving of money, alone, to worthy causes totaled $84 billion. You know how much the Government would have to raise to be able to spend $84 billion? [*Laughter*] About three times that amount for the administrative overhead. [*Laughter*] Well, again, I just want to thank you all. And I feel greatly honored to be a part of this, even for these few minutes.

Note: The President spoke at 11:22 a.m. in the Constitution Ballroom at the Grand Hyatt Hotel. He was introduced by Irwin Lerner, president and chief executive officer of Hoffmann-La Roche, which sponsored the conference.

Remarks at the Presentation Ceremony for the President's Volunteer Action Awards

June 10, 1988

The President. Good afternoon, and welcome to the White House. It's my honor to be here today to award the 1988 President's Volunteer Action Awards. When we came to Washington 7 years ago, one of our goals was to restore the promise of hope upon which our great nation was founded, to once again have communities where neighbor helps neighbor and the spirit of caring is put into action by ordinary citizens.

In 1982 we presented the first Volunteer Action Awards to recognize and honor those citizens who had dedicated themselves to these ideals. Since then, thousands and thousands of applications have been received telling of Americans who give generously of themselves to aid their fellow man. Each is worthy of recognition, but you, the winners of the Volunteer Action Awards, are unique. Through your lives and the principles that you uphold, you set an example, not just for your communities but the Nation and the world. You've made the words "I can't" obsolete and have brought hope that doesn't disappoint to those in need. To many of you, service to your fellow man is not just part of your life but has become your life's work.

As the wife of an Army colonel stationed in Korea, Harriet Hodges was just trying to help one family in 1972, when she arranged for their child to be flown to the United States for lifesaving heart surgery. But when other mothers with their little ones gathered at her door for help, she responded, and one by one, Harriet Hodges has arranged, without cost to their families, for 2,000 Korean children to have the surgery they need in the United States.

In Dallas, Texas, Margaret Gallimore seeks out those in need—the worst need—those dying with nowhere to go. Last spring, Margaret opened her home to victims of AIDS. With only the help of her children, Pamela, Phillip, Willie, and a friend, Margaret, a registered nurse, bathes and cooks and takes care of 20 people.

At 91 most of us would be content to retire, but Arnolta Williams, or "Mama" Williams, as she is known in Jacksonville, Florida, just keeps going. Following a routine she established almost 70 years ago, she's up every day volunteering. During her life she's raised the funds and gathered the support to build a nursery for the children of low-income mothers, acted as a community leader to bring harmony during the racial turmoil of the 1960's, and served on the board of countless nonprofit organizations. In fact, "Mama" Williams has done so much during her lifetime to help others it would be impossible to mention every project now, but I think it's sufficient to say that, if you think about it, you know that she isn't called "Mama" without reason. And I like another thing about her, too. She did a little personal job on me. [*Laughter*] She's made me—she talked me into feeling young again. [*Laughter*]

And it makes me proud as I look around the room to see the familiar faces of my friends from the entertainment industry like Martha Lyles, who works with SHARE, another of today's award recipients.

President Eisenhower said: "There is nothing wrong with America that the faith, love of freedom, intelligence, and energy of her citizens cannot cure." It's this optimism put into action through our private sector initiatives that differentiates America from much of the world. The 18 Americans that we honor today demonstrate that spirit. I think that each of you would be interested to know that the banner of hope that you wave is being recognized around the world. Recently, his Royal Highness, the Prince of Wales, and Prime Minister Thatcher addressed a conference of American and British business leaders gathered to discuss what they could do to increase private sector initiatives internationally.

Today's the last time that I will bestow these prestigious awards, so before I close, I'd like to recognize two gentlemen who have dedicated themselves to promoting voluntarism in our country, Governor George Romney and W. Clement Stone. W. Clement Stone, born into poverty in Chicago at the turn of the century, rose from his humble beginnings to become one of our country's greatest businessmen and philanthropists. In addition to giving away hundreds of millions of dollars to needy causes, Clem has demonstrated through his personal service and leadership the formula for success in America. He's done a magnificent job as chairman of the ACTION Advisory Board. Governor Romney, the founder of American Motors Company and former Governor of Michigan, has spent a lifetime in service to his fellow man—stopping not even at retirement. In 1973 he helped form what we now know as VOLUNTEER: The National Center [for Citizen Involvement]. Through his efforts, volunteer centers across the country have helped assist those who wish to volunteer their time.

Governor, and Clem, thank you.

And now if Donna Alvarado, our Director of ACTION, and Governor Romney will step forward, we'll present the Volunteer Action Awards.

Ms. Alvarado. Mr. President, Mrs. Reagan, in response to the call you issued to the American people from the beginning of your administration to reach out and assist their neighbors and according to the inspiring example of volunteer service to the Nation that has been set by that extraordinary lady who is ever at your side, I am pleased to introduce to you the 18 outstanding volunteers you have selected to receive the 1988 President's Volunteer Action Awards.

First, the Red River Revel Arts Festival involves over 3,000 volunteers in the 8-day festival, which provides a variety of arts experiences for more than 300,000 people who attend annually. Accepting for Red River Revel is James Montgomery, president.

Zachary Fisher has been the leading force in the development of the Intrepid Sea-Air-Space Museum located on the U.S.S. *Intrepid*, and of the Veterans Bedside Network. He formed the Elizabeth and Zachary Fisher Armed Forces Charitable Foundation to provide scholarship assistance to members of the armed services and their families. Zachary Fisher.

Verlyn and Martha Roskam founded Educational Assistance Unlimited, a unique barter program which matches goods contributed by corporations with colleges which need the items with the cash value of the contributions given as scholarships by the colleges in the name of the companies. Accepting for Verlyn and Martha Roskam is their son, Peter Roskam.

Thomas W. Evans founded the Mentor Program, which matches high school students with law firms to teach them the workings of the law and has led in the development of the National Symposium on Partnerships in Education. Thomas W. Evans.

Kaye Kiker was instrumental in the formation of Alabamians for a Clean Environment and has been the leader in educating local residents about the impact of the Nation's largest toxic-waste landfill located in their county. Kaye Kiker.

Mission Air Ministries, founded in 1981, provides no-cost air transportation to hospitals and medical centers for over 200 patients each year. Mission Air pilots and medical personnel are among the more than 400 volunteers involved in this program. Accepting for Mission Air is Donald Simpson, founder.

Margaret Gallimore, who has worked in nursing for 24 years, has housed over 20 people with AIDS in the house adjacent to her own home, providing meals, care, and support and serving as their adopted family. The home is the only facility for nonambulatory people with AIDS in the Dallas area. Margaret Gallimore.

Mrs. Arnolta "Mama" Williams has been a volunteer leader in her community of Jacksonville, Florida since 1920. She was a founder and president of Gateway Nursery and Kindergarten for underprivileged children and is the chairperson of the Jacksonville Foster Grandparent Program. At age 91, "Mama" Williams shows the dynamic role of seniors in community service. "Mama" Williams.

SHARE Incorporated, an organization of 100 women from the entertainment industry, annually raises over $1 million through special events to provide grants to 28 organizations that serve mentally disabled and abused children. Accepting the award is Miriam Nelson Meyers, one of SHARE's founders.

Robert Mosbacher, Jr., was instrumental in the development of the InfoNet Task Force, which provides referral and information services to the unemployed in the Houston, Texas, area, and the After School Partnership, which assists latchkey children at 14 sites. Rob Mosbacher.

Harriet Hodges, who resides with her husband in Seoul, Korea, has developed a network of 15 hospitals across the United States that has provided lifesaving heart surgery for over 2,000 needy Korean youngsters in the past 15 years. Mrs. Hodges is known as the Korean heart lady. Harriet Hodges.

Dr. Luis Gomez has been providing no-cost medical care to more than 50 people with leprosy in Juarez, Mexico, since 1980 and founded the Father Damien Fund to help purchase medicine and equipment for the work. Dr. Luis Gomez.

The 1987 International Summer Special Olympics Committee involved over 23,000 volunteers in the games held in South Bend, Indiana, during which 5,000 mentally disabled athletes from all 50 States and 50 foreign countries participated in 14 Olympic style sports. Accepting the award is the

Special Olympics Committee president and chairman, Ervin Derda.

Roberta R. Roper founded the Stephanie Roper Committee and Foundation in memory of her daughter, in order to develop and guarantee victims' rights in the court system and to provide assistance to crime victims and their families. Roberta Roper.

Operation Comeback is sponsored by Valencia Community College to involve college students as counselors for court-referred young people who participate in community service projects as a way of providing positive experiences and building self-esteem. Accepting is Dr. William Prentiss, founder of Operation Comeback.

First Bank System, Community First Program of Minneapolis involves over 2,000 employee volunteers in 23 community service programs which have provided nearly 600,000 hours of volunteer service in 1987. Accepting for the Community First Program is D.H. Ankeny, chairman and CEO of First Bank System.

Time, Incorporated, Time to Read Program involves over 500 employee volunteers who tutored more than 600 functionally illiterate adults and young people in reading at 20 sites in 1987, using specially designed curriculum and popular reading material published by Time, Incorporated. Accepting for Time to Read is Donald M. Wilson, corporate vice president.

And finally, the Barberton Free Clinic was developed by the Council of Labor to provide free medical assistance to unemployed residents of the Ohio community, which has a 33-percent unemployment rate. Accepting the award is Charles Lemmon, president of the Barberton Council of Labor.

And now, Mr. President, we have a special addition to the program, which may come as a bit of a surprise to you. For the past 6 years, Presidential Volunteer Action Awards have been conferred at ceremonies here in the East Room of the White House. This program was created by you to recognize and reward the best in America—our volunteer spirit. And as a result of the executive order which you signed, this will become a permanent Presidential program. For years to come, outstanding volunteers from across this country will receive the personal thanks from future Presidents of the United States.

Well, Mr. President, the volunteer community of this country would like to do some thanking of its own. To represent the millions of volunteers across this country, we have asked Mr. Bobby Trimble to join us today. Bobby was recognized at the very first President's Volunteer Action Awards Luncheon for a program he created called Christmas in April. It did not have much national recognition back then in 1982, but through your assistance, it has spread all across America. Through Christmas in April programs across the Nation, thousands of volunteers work each year to rebuild homes and indeed lives of those who are in need. Now, may I ask Bobby Trimble to please come forward.

Mr. Trimble. As you can tell, I'm a little bit nervous. [*Laughter*] What an honor. It feels good. I'm president of the Christmas in April program in Midland, Texas, which has been going on for 16 years, and from this humble beginning 16 years ago, has spread out to a number of other cities in the United States. We did not grow very much until after the 1982 awards, which I was very fortunate to receive this from Mrs. Reagan. She was volunteering also that day for her husband because he was out of town. [*Laughter*] And so I appreciated that very much.

Let me give you just a little bit—so many people say, well, what is Christmas in April? So, I always like to explain just a little bit in a short, short way. We take volunteers from all walks of life, buy the materials for them, and let them overhaul an old, beat-up house. And it's amazing what volunteers who've had no experience of being a carpenter or a roofer or a plumber or a painter—to see what they can do to an old house. But then you get the question: "I have no skills." So, the first thing you do—put them on the trash details. [*Laughter*] The next year, I guarantee you, that person will have a skill when they came back to work. [*Laughter*] So, if that—try that in your community when somebody tells you they have no skills.

So—but Mr. President, so like so many

successful volunteer programs in this country, Christmas in April began as an idea of what one town could do for its neighbors in need. Today it has spread across the country; new programs are beginning each year. I believe Christmas in April has spread because of the recognition Mrs. Reagan gave me 6 years ago when I received their Volunteer Action Award. As a result, a lot more people heard about our program and wanted to find out how to get it started in their community. But Mr. President, what you have done goes far beyond simply presenting awards to volunteer programs. Your leadership has helped to renew an old American tradition of neighbor helping neighbor. You have inspired the Nation to reach for the best in itself, and to devote its energies to making our communities, our nation, and the world a better place. Under your Presidency, voluntarism and charitable giving in our country have reached an all-time high. And it hasn't stopped here. In the past few years, we have seen a tremendous interest by other countries who have observed what has happened in America, then duplicated it beyond our shores. Over the past 5, 6, 7 years, I have had requests of how to get a Christmas neighbor program started from all over the United States, Canada, and as far away as Israel. So, you can see what good publicity does.

Mr. President, today I've a special honor. On behalf of millions of volunteers in America, I want to say thank you for what you have done, to recognize your leadership and to inspire future generations of Americans to meet the standards you have established. We, the volunteers of America, have created a new award. This award will be presented each year, by all future Presidents of the United States, to the individual that symbolizes the very best of voluntarism in our country. And Mr. President, this new medal will be called "The Ronald Reagan Award for Volunteer Excellence."

And now, I would like to present you with the first strike of the Ronald Reagan Award for Volunteer Excellence. And in future years, the recipient of this award will be selected personally by the President of the United States. But this year, to keep this a surprise, you were not able to make the personal decision. [*Laughter*] However, the leaders of VOLUNTEER, the National Center, the ACTION Advisory Commission, and your Private Sector Initiatives Board of Advisors have picked the person they feel represents the type of volunteer spirit you have encouraged.

Mr. President, I would ask you to announce the first recipient of the Ronald Reagan Award for Volunteer Excellence. [*Laughter*]

The President. Well, I couldn't be more proud. The winner of the Ronald Reagan Award for Volunteer Excellence goes to "Mama" Williams. Well, I—yes, I was surprised. I am very much surprised. But also——

Ms. Williams. Great-great-grandmother's surprised too. [*Laughter*]

The President. And very proud. And proud of all of you and grateful to all of you. I'd like to just stay here and talk to you all afternoon, but Nancy tells me that I've got to help her with the dishes. [*Laughter*]

Ms. Williams. Don't you make another joke like that. [*Laughter*]

Mrs. Reagan. That's right! [*Laughter*]

Mrs. Reagan. Did you hear what she said?

The President. No. What?

Ms. Williams. Don't make another joke like that. [*Laughter*]

The President. "Mama"—well, "Mama" Williams, that may not be as much of a joke as you think. Because—[*laughter*]—one of the better jobs I had in my entire life, working my way through Eureka College, was washing dishes in the girls dormitory. [*Laughter*]

Ms. Williams. That was before you were married. [*Laughter*]

The President. Yes. [*Laughter*] Well, again, God bless you all. Thank you all for what you've done. And this is—and as you've heard here today and those that have spoken already—all of this is going around the world, too, because there have been meetings abroad. And as a matter of fact, at the economic summit a year ago in Venice, Italy, between meetings, I was invited to a house and found myself looking at some Americans who were there, and who were helping Italy with their implementation of a private enterprise program of their own, so that they could do things as you do, without waiting to see if government's going to do them first. And this is spreading all over the world, and it all started right here under that grand old flag.

So, God bless all of you, and thank you.

Note: The President spoke at 1:15 p.m. in the East Room at the White House.

Message to the Senate on the Soviet-United States Intermediate-Range Nuclear Forces Treaty
June 10, 1988

To the Senate of the United States:

I was gratified the United States Senate gave its advice and consent to the ratification of the Treaty Between the United States of America and the Union of Soviet Socialist Republics on the Elimination of Their Intermediate- and Shorter-Range Missiles (INF Treaty). It was my honor to exchange instruments of ratification on June 1 in Moscow, and the Treaty has now entered into force.

During the past 4 months, the Senate has performed its constitutional duties with respect to the advice and consent to this Treaty in an exceptionally serious and diligent manner. On the Administration's part, we spared no effort to respond to the Senate's needs, and to do our best to ensure that the Senate had all the information it needed to carry out its constitutional responsibilities. Administration witnesses appeared in more than 70 formal hearings and many more informal briefings; we provided detailed written answers to over 1,300 questions for the record from the Committees and individual Senators; and we provided access to the negotiating record of the Treaty, comprising 31 bound volumes.

In short, I believe the Executive branch and the Senate took their responsibilities very seriously and made every effort to work together to fulfill them in the common interest of advancing the national security of the United States and our Allies and friends. The Treaty will bear witness to the sincerity and diligence of those in the Executive branch and the Senate who have taken part in this effort.

As noted in my statement issued on May 27, the date of final Senate action, one provision of the Resolution to Ratification adopted by the Senate causes me serious concern.

The Senate condition relating to the Treaty Clauses of the Constitution apparently seeks to alter the law of treaty interpretation. The accompanying report of the Committee on Foreign Relations accords primacy, second only to the Treaty text, to all Executive branch statements to the Senate above all other sources which international forums or even U.S. courts would consider in interpreting treaties. It subordinates fundamental and essential treaty interpretative sources such as the treaty parties' intent, the treaty negotiating record and the parties' subsequent practices.

Treaties are agreements between sovereign states and must be interpreted in accordance with accepted principles of international law and United States Supreme Court jurisprudence. As a practical matter, the Senate condition only can work against the interests of the United States by creating situations in which a treaty has one meaning under international law and another under domestic law. Unilateral restrictions on the United States should be avoided, especially in a treaty affecting vital national security interests. With respect to U.S. law, the President must respect the mutual understandings reached with the Senate during the advice and consent process. But Executive statements should be given binding weight only when they were authoritatively communicated to the Senate by the Executive and were part of the basis on which the Senate granted its advice and consent to ratification. This is in accordance with the legal standards applied by our courts in determining legislative intent. I commend the thoughtful statements made during the Senate debate by Senators Specter, Roth, Wilson, and others which amplify these concerns.

This Administration does not take the position that the Executive branch can disregard authoritative Executive statements to the Senate, and we have no intention of changing the interpretation of the INF Treaty which was presented to the Senate. On the contrary, this Administration has made it clear that it will consider all such authoritative statements as having been made in good faith. Nonetheless the principles of treaty interpretation recognized and repeatedly invoked by the courts may not be limited or changed by the Senate alone, and those principles will govern any future disputes over interpretation of this Treaty. As Senator Lugar pointed out during the debate, the Supreme Court may well have the final judgment, which would be binding on the President and Senate alike. Accordingly, I am compelled to state that I cannot accept the proposition that a condition in a resolution to ratification can alter the allocation of rights and duties under the Constitution; nor could I, consistent with my oath of office, accept any diminution claimed to be effected by such a condition in the constitutional powers and responsibilities of the Presidency.

I do not believe that any difference of views about the Senate condition will have any practical effect on the implementation of the Treaty. I believe the Executive branch and the Senate have a very good common understanding of the terms of the Treaty, and I believe that we will handle any question of interpretation that may arise in a spirit of mutual accommodation and respect. In this spirit I welcome the entry into force of the Treaty and express my hope that it will lead to even more important advances in arms reduction and the preservation of world peace and security.

RONALD REAGAN

The White House,
June 10, 1988.

Proclamation 5829—Entry Into the United States of Certain Panamanians

June 10, 1988

Suspension of Entry as Immigrants and Nonimmigrants of Persons Who Formulate or Implement the Policies of the Noriega/Solis Palma Regime

By the President of the United States of America

A Proclamation

In light of the current political and economic crisis in Panama and the actions of Manuel Antonio Noriega and Manuel Solis Palma and their forces that engendered this crisis and are preventing the legitimate government of President Eric Arturo Delvalle from restoring order and democracy to that country, I have determined that it is in the interests of the United States to restrict the entrance into the United States as immigrants and nonimmigrants of certain persons who formulate or implement the policies of Manuel Antonio Noriega and Manuel Solis Palma.

Now, Therefore, I, Ronald Reagan, by the power vested in me as President by the Constitution and laws of the United States of America, including section 212(f) of the Immigration and Nationality Act of 1952, as amended (8 U.S.C. 1182(f)), having found that the unrestricted immigrant and nonimmigrant entry of officers and employees who formulate or implement the policies of Manuel Antonio Noriega and Manuel Solis Palma would, except as provided for in Section 2 of this Proclamation, be detrimental to the interests of the United States, do proclaim that:

Section 1. The entry into the United States as immigrants and nonimmigrants of

Panamanian nationals (and their immediate families), who formulate or implement the policies of Manuel Antonio Noriega and Manuel Solis Palma and who are designated by the Secretary of State or his designee, is hereby suspended.

Sec. 2. Nothing in this Proclamation shall be construed (1) to derogate from United States Government obligations under applicable international agreements or (2) to prohibit the entry into the United States of individuals for the purpose of submitting to legal proceedings initiated by the United States Government.

Sec. 3. This Proclamation is effective immediately and shall remain in effect until such time as the Secretary of State determines that democracy has been restored in Panama.

In Witness Whereof, I have hereunto set my hand this tenth day of June, in the year of our Lord nineteen hundred and eighty-eight, and of the Independence of the United States of America the two hundred and twelfth.

RONALD REAGAN

[*Filed with the Office of the Federal Register, 10:32 a.m., June 13, 1988*]

Nomination of Richard Clark Barkley To Be United States Ambassador to the German Democratic Republic

June 10, 1988

The President today announced his intention to nominate Richard Clark Barkley, of Michigan, a career member of the Senior Foreign Service, Class of Minister-Counselor, as Ambassador to the German Democratic Republic. He would succeed Francis J. Meehan.

Mr. Barkley served in the United States Army from 1955 to 1957. From 1959 to 1961, he was a part-time instructor at the University of Maryland abroad. In 1962 he entered the Foreign Service. Mr. Barkley was a junior officer trainee until 1965, when he became vice consul, Santiago de los Caballeros, Dominican Republic, 1965–1967. From 1967 to 1968, he was in university training at Columbia University. He then returned to the Department of State, where he served as international relations officer, NATO desk, 1968–1969, and in the same capacity for the German desk, 1969–1971. Mr. Barkley continued as international relations officer abroad and served at the U.S. Embassy in Bonn, Federal Republic of Germany, 1971–1972, and the U.S. Embassy in Berlin, German Democratic Republic, 1972–1974. He served as executive assistant to Ambassador Ellsworth Bunker at the Department of State, 1974–1977, and Deputy Country Director of the Office of Central European Affairs, 1977–1979. From 1979 to 1982, he was deputy chief of mission in Oslo, Norway, and political counselor for the U.S. Embassy in Bonn, Federal Republic of Germany, 1982–1985. Since 1985 Mr. Barkley has been deputy chief of mission in Pretoria, Republic of South Africa.

Mr. Barkley graduated from Michigan State University (B.A., 1954) and Wayne State University (M.A., 1955). He was born December 23, 1932, in Chicago, IL. He is married and currently resides in Washington, DC.

Nomination of Ken Kramer To Be an Assistant Secretary of the Army
June 10, 1988

The President today announced his intention to nominate Ken Kramer to be an Assistant Secretary of the Army (Financial Management). He would succeed Michael P.W. Stone.

Since 1986 Mr. Kramer has been an attorney in Colorado Springs, CO. Prior to this, he was a Member of the United States House of Representatives from the 5th District of Colorado, 1979–1986. He was a State representative for the State of Colorado, 1973–1978.

Mr. Kramer graduated from the University of Illinois (B.A., 1963) and Harvard Law School (J.D., 1966). He served in the U.S. Army, 1967–1970. He was born February 19, 1942, in Chicago, IL. He has two children and resides in Colorado Springs, CO.

Statement by Assistant to the President for Press Relations Fitzwater on the Nicaraguan Peace Negotiations
June 10, 1988

The President is disappointed at the Sandinista rejection of the Nicaraguan resistance proposal to achieve democracy and an end to the war in Nicaragua. Sandinista promises of democracy date back to 1979 in commitments made to the Organization of American States and repeated in the Guatemala accord of August 7, 1987, the San José declaration of January 16, 1988, and the Sapoa agreement of March 23, 1988. If the dialog between the resistance and the Sandinistas is to resume, the Sandinistas must show a willingness to carry out the promises to establish democracy that they have made, and broken repeatedly, over the past decade.

In the June 7–9 round of talks, the resistance proposed specific steps to implement a calendar of previous Sandinista commitments for establishing democracy in Nicaragua in conjunction with the cease-fire process. However, it became clear that the Sandinistas were not interested in democratization and national reconciliation. Their sole goal was the disarmament of the resistance. Deeds, not more words, are needed. Those who insisted that the best way to achieve peace and democracy in Nicaragua was to withdraw military pressure on the Sandinistas now bear a special responsibility to press for democracy in Nicaragua.

Ambassador Max Kampelman, the Counselor of the Department of State, had scheduled visits to the Central American democracies to brief their leaders on events at the recent summit in Moscow, including the summit discussions on regional issues. The President now has directed that the Ambassador seek the views of the leaders of the democracies on the current situation in Nicaragua as well.

Radio Address to the Nation on Economic Growth and Free and Fair Trade
June 11, 1988

My fellow Americans:

In one week, I go to Toronto for the annual economic summit with the leaders of the major industrial democracies. The United States along with our strong allies—Canada, France, Germany, Great Britain, Italy, Japan, and the European Community—form the industrial and technological backbone of the free world.

This will be my eighth and final economic summit, and there'll be much to celebrate. Perhaps foremost will be the worldwide economic revolution that has unleashed ever greater levels of prosperity with lower tax rates. America led the way with major tax cuts and tax reform, and the other major industrial democracies have either cut their tax rates or are now in the process of doing so. I'm proud to say that we now lead the world with the lowest top personal tax rate of any of the major economic powers. We are also leading the way in creating jobs, providing employment for a greater percentage of our labor force than any of the other major industrial democracies. In fact, U.S. employment is at its highest level ever, and we've also brought down inflation and interest rates.

It's not surprising that country after country has followed us on the path to greater economic freedom and begun to replace their statist policies with deregulation, privatization, and freer trade. One of the great lessons of the last 7 years is that when people in free economies are allowed to trade with one another around the world the result is greater prosperity for us all. Certainly, the United States has been one of the biggest gainers in the global economy. You've probably heard that we're now in the longest peacetime economic expansion in U.S. history. But this is also the first economic expansion in the postwar period in which the U.S. economy has grown faster than most of its major trading partners. So, yes, we're doing particularly well, but when free countries trade and invest with one another, there are no losers, only winners.

Today we have a global economy in which the United States is at the very center. Of total foreign direct investment in the world, nearly 40 percent, by far the largest share, consists of Americans investing overseas. But it's not a one-way street. At the same time, the United States also receives more foreign investment from abroad than any other country. So, we truly are the investment capital of the world. The same thing is true regarding trade. We import more and export more than any other country on Earth.

With that in mind, I want to reaffirm my commitment to enactment this year of responsible trade legislation. To help achieve positive trade legislation, I've directed my senior advisers to stand ready to assist the congressional leadership on a new trade bill—one that will strengthen America's international competitiveness and create even more new jobs for Americans. And make no mistake, the global economy is the basis of our prosperity and the foundation of our economic future. I can think of no surer way of derailing our economy than to try through protectionist measures to seal America off from trade and investment with the other countries of the world.

I'm reminded of the story of the Sunday school teacher who asks her class, "Who wants to go to heaven?" Well, all of the children raise their hands except for one little boy in the back of the room. The teacher, astounded, says, "Charlie, don't you want to go to heaven?" "Sure I do," he says, "just not with this bunch." Well, fortunately, we and our trading partners are going to deal with economic matters together because that's the only way to move ahead. I'm glad to say we're moving away from protectionism and toward greater economic growth and job creation.

One of the historic events of our time is the U.S.-Canada free trade agreement that I entered into this year with Prime Minister Brian Mulroney. This agreement between the world's two greatest trading partners will eliminate tariff barriers between the United States and Canada by the year 1999 and establish the largest free trade area on Earth. The advantages to both our countries will be enormous in terms of jobs and prosperity. But as much as this pathbreaking agreement does for the people of the United States and Canada, this agreement, looked at in the sweep of history, is truly a gift to the world. It creates a model that can be imitated and expanded and ultimately made universal among free nations. And that's something we can truly be proud of.

And finally, Tuesday is Flag Day, the anniversary of the first official American flag. Nancy and I hope that you'll join us and millions of other Americans Tuesday evening at 7 p.m. eastern daylight time in the annual "Pause for the Pledge."

Until next week, thanks for listening, and God bless you.

Note: The President spoke at 12:06 p.m. from Camp David, MD.

Message to the Congress Transmitting the Portugal-United States Social Security Agreement
June 13, 1988

To the Congress of the United States:

Pursuant to Section 233(e)(1) of the Social Security Act, as amended by the Social Security Amendments of 1977 (P.L. 95–216, 42 U.S.C. 433(e)(1)), I transmit herewith the Agreement between the United States of America and the Portuguese Republic on Social Security that consists of two separate instruments: a principal agreement and an administrative arrangement. The Agreement was signed at Lisbon on March 30, 1988.

The U.S.-Portugal Agreement is similar in objective to the social security agreements already in force with Belgium, Canada, the Federal Republic of Germany, Italy, Norway, Spain, Sweden, Switzerland, and the United Kingdom. Such bilateral agreements provide for limited coordination between the United States and foreign social security systems to overcome the problems of gaps in protection and of dual coverage and taxation for workers who move from one country to the other.

I also transmit for the information of the Congress a comprehensive report prepared by the Department of Health and Human Services, which explains the provisions of the Agreement and provides data on the number of persons affected by the Agreement and the effect on social security financing as required by the same provision of the Social Security Act.

The Department of State and the Department of Health and Human Services join with me in commending the U.S.-Portugal Social Security Agreement and related documents.

RONALD REAGAN

The White House,
June 13, 1988.

Remarks at the Annual Meeting of the Atlantic Council
June 13, 1988

Well, thank you very much. And thank you, General Goodpaster, Secretary Shultz, John Gray, General Seignious, Gene Bradley, James Shinn, and ladies and gentlemen. Just a week and a half ago, I had the honor to address the British people, the Atlantic community, and the world from the ancient and historic podium of Guildhall in London.

After my report on the Moscow summit, Mrs. Thatcher graciously said that she believed that "There is now more hope between East and West than ever before in the lifetime of most of those" there. And she spoke of the new confidence and optimism in the West, and she recalled the words of Sir Winston Churchill when he wrote: "Where we are able to stand together and work together for righteous causes, we shall always be thankful, and the world will always be free." Well, this message of unity and optimism and hope and strength is the message that I bring to you today.

You've been talking here today about "rebuilding the consensus on East-West relations." And I would admit that at times in recent years a free world consensus in this area seemed particularly elusive, rather like the story that Franklin Roosevelt liked to tell about the marine who was ordered home from Guadalcanal. The marine was very unhappy because he hadn't shot a single enemy soldier, so his sergeant just told him, "Just go up on that hill over there and shout, 'To the devil with Tojo.' " Well, the marine did as he was told, and sure enough, out of the jungle ran a Japanese soldier shouting, "To the devil with Roosevelt." "And of course," said the marine afterward, "how could I shoot a fellow Republican?" [*Laughter*]

But our consensus is built not only on what we're against but on what we're for. And we are against totalitarianism. We're for freedom and democracy—for them without hesitation or apology, and virtually, I would venture, without division. This is the first great truth to keep in mind. There may be divisions within our countries as to methods, but there are none as to fundamental goals.

In the last decade and a half, we in the democracies have, in true democratic fashion, tested the various propositions about the methods for best approaching East-West affairs. Now that we have an INF treaty, the first agreement ever to eliminate an entire class of U.S. and Soviet nuclear missiles and with the most stringent verification procedures in arms control history; now that the Soviets have begun withdrawing from Afghanistan; now that we've begun to see internal changes within the Soviet Union—can there be any doubt that we were right about a forward strategy for freedom, right about the importance of candor regarding the differences between our systems, and right to say that the road to peace is not through weakness, division, or preemptive concession, but through unity, confidence, and strength?

In just a few days I will attend another summit, the economic summit in Toronto, as the General has told you. And this is an excellent forum before which to talk about our hopes for that summit. I know that the Atlantic Council is examining how to best integrate economics and security. The International Management and Development Institute is meeting to discuss economic challenges facing us.

Over the years, the economic summits have been a cornerstone of cooperation among the major democratic economies. They're part of the superstructure of Western strength and East-West affairs. And here again, our democracies have, as democracies do, tested among ourselves various propositions about economic growth and vitality since the first of the summits that I attended in 1981.

Everywhere in the democratic world we're seeing the emergence of a new consensus: that growth and opportunity must go hand in hand. Consider taxes. In the past 3 years, Britain, Canada, Japan, and France, among others, have all let their top tax rates tumble. Why? Well, here's what Nigel Lawson, Britain's Chancellor of the Exchequer, said not long ago, in his words: "The reason for the worldwide trend toward lower top rates of tax is clear. Excessive rates of income tax destroy enterprise, encourage avoidance, and drive talent to more hospitable shores overseas. Far from raising additional revenue, over time they actually raise less." And he concluded, "By contrast, a reduction in the top rates of income tax can, over time, result in a higher, not lower, yield to the Exchequer." Well, it seems I've heard somebody else say that before, somewhere.

But this new consensus doesn't stop with taxation. Country after country has begun to sell off state-owned industries. Restrictive regulations have begun to fall. Paying for the excesses of government spending with high inflation has all but stopped. And at least in the United States, deficit spending by government is falling. The idea that connects all this is the market. The industrial world, the entire world, is turning away from state control of economies and returning to the marketplace. From India to Argentina, from Africa to China, and even in the Soviet Union, the shackles of state economic domination are beginning to loosen. And you know something's happening when there's talk of lower taxes in the Soviet Union.

Now, I don't need to tell you that the United States has led the way or that the remarkable performance of our economy since our expansion began has been the driving force behind this new consensus. I don't need to recite all we've done—the longest peacetime expansion on record; more than twice as many jobs created as the other six summit countries combined—and they have 50 percent more employment-age population than we do; the family income is up sharply after riding a falling roller coaster through the previous decade; a larger percentage of the work force employed than ever before; exports the highest in our history. I don't need to tell you all this, but you might guess that I'm a little proud of it. And I have to watch myself when I talk about it. I don't want people to get the impression that I think of politics the way Will Rogers thought of the movies. He said, "The only business where you can sit out front and applaud yourself." [*Laughter*]

This new consensus has not only brought the economies of America, Britain, Canada, and so many other countries roaring back, it has also opened the way for a coordination of economic policy among the summit countries that would have been unthinkable just a few years ago. Whether it's through what's known as the G–7 [the economic summit participants] or in managing the debt crisis in so many Third World countries or responding to the tremors in the world financial markets last October, we work together. Today we use a common set of books to tell how our policies are doing, and we're working in common for balance in trade and capital flows and government budgets and for surefootedness in the world's financial markets. Starting with the United States, the summit countries have had nearly 6 years of uninterrupted growth. I'd like to make it 60 and more.

But it can't happen if we try to live as if we're the only economy on Earth. The summit nations are working together as never before because our economies are tied together as never before. To give an example of this, someone pointed out to me recently, while the New York Stock Exchange does $8 billion of business on a good day, the foreign exchange markets do over 25 times as much business every day. In this global marketplace, industries around the world rise and fall together. The decline in the worldwide demand for steel was felt in the Rhine Basin of Europe in just the same way it was felt in our Lehigh Valley. Thousands of jobs disappeared in both places, and not just to foreign competition. Here in America, high-tech minimills melted down the business of many old, integrated producers.

But there's one difference in the way we in America dealt with the decline. We lost the same kind of jobs other countries lost, but unlike those European nations that lag behind in cutting taxes, regulations, and government ownership, we created new jobs in place of the old ones. Allentown in Lehigh Valley was once a home of heavy industry. Then the steel mill and the truck factory shut down. Many people wrote off Allentown—too soon. In place of a few big, old companies, dozens of new companies started up. Small companies that were already open grew. Entrepreneurs created what David Birch, MIT's authority on job creation, calls a hidden economy. He adds that all across America "the small companies, not the big ones that get so much attention, are building a new economy that is providing jobs and making the country competitive again." And that's why today Allentown has an unemployment rate of only 5.4 percent.

Throughout what used to be called the Rust Belt, the story is the same. One midwesterner recently told the New York Times, as he said, "I go through the newspapers from county-seat-size towns, and I'm finding dozens of announcements of new plants and plans for new plants and expansion projects." And new or expanding entrepreneurial companies and bigger, older, but now streamlined manufacturers are leading an export boom that some say has stretched our production capacity to the limit. Not long ago, for example, Business Week reported that America's steelmakers had become among the world's most productive and announced in its headline: "Cancel the Funeral, Steel is on the Mend."

Yes, America is leading the world, both as consumer and producer, into the global marketplace of the next century. For all of us, what's happening in Japan or Germany, Britain, France, Italy, or Canada is as momentous as what's happening in California, Florida, New York, or Illinois. There's a lesson in all this—in the story of Allentown and one of the so-called Rust Belt, as well as the globalization of trade and finance—and the lesson is that the future belongs to the flexible. It belongs to those who look at the problem and see an opportunity, to those who look at the unknown and see an adventure, to those who look at the untried and see a challenge, to those who have shed the weight of structural rigidities and protective subsidies and face the future with energy and excitement.

In no field do we all have more weeding to do than agriculture, where subsidies cost the consumers and taxpayers of Europe, North America, and Japan $200 billion a year. Agriculture is "planted" on the agenda of the Uruguay round of trade talks—as are the issues of establishing rules for trade in intellectual property, investment, services, and the lowering of tariff and nontariff trade barriers. Those talks were scheduled to go for 4 years. They are now nearing the halfway point. It's time to narrow down and lay out specific goals, a roadmap, and a timetable to the finish line. In Toronto, we, the heads of the major industrial states, can push our ministers to have that job completed by the end of the year—no excuses. You know, sometimes when I hear people say why we can't do this or that in the trade talks, it reminds me of how Chico Marx, one of the Marx Brothers, used to try to walk off the Hollywood sets in the middle of the afternoon. As he explained, "But it's after quitting time in New York." [*Laughter*]

Well, it's time that we in the summit nations forget about quitting time and join in a great venture to progress—a joint venture that opens the international marketplace and that also strengthens the weak links in the international economy. Let's join together to help restore the economies of two countries: one, the Philippines, an heroic democracy ravaged by Communist-led insurrection; the other, Afghanistan, a victim of brutal aggression. Let's join together to bring the newly industrialized countries into the full and mature place in the world trading system that they have earned. Let's join together in helping the countries of sub-Saharan Africa work out their debt problems. We'll take up their problems, as we have those of other debtor nations, on a case-by-case basis, working to help develop economic policies that promote growth and opportunity. The United States has already indicated its willingness to consider new ways of rescheduling the debt of the poorest countries, ways that can produce substantial new relief. And let us join together to attack the lifeblood of one trade that should never be part of international trade: the international narcotics trade. At this summit, we should join in a common offensive against money laundering and the flow of drug profits through the world's financial institutions.

Pushing forward the trade negotiations, a joint venture for progress, strengthening the system of policy coordination—this is the agenda of the Toronto summit. We'll be building on a decade of progress, on the new economic consensus in our countries. We'll be looking to continue the building of the global marketplace. I know there are some who want to turn back, who want to return to the more insular and isolationist days of old. I vetoed the trade bill last week because I don't believe we can or should turn back. Critics of our policies complain that, on one hand, America is, as they say, "exporting jobs," which is to say our companies invest overseas, and on the other hand, that America is "selling itself to foreigners," which is to say that foreign companies are investing here. Put it together, and what they're really saying is "turn back." The isolationism of their foreign policy walks hand in hand with the isolationism of their economic policy, and both will lead us to disaster.

We're in a new age of invention and exploration, a time when the vast capacity of the human imagination is opening new universes for exploration. "To see the universe in a grain of sand" is no longer a poetic metaphor, but the daily reality of the silicon chip. F. Scott Fitzgerald wrote that when the early explorers just looked on this land, they must have held their breath. They had, for the last time in history, come face to face with something commensurate to man's infinite capacity for wonder. Yet it was not for the last time. We, too, stand on the shores of something as vast: of an economic and technological future immense with promise.

If we seize it, if we don't turn away from it, that future will transform the democratic world and, I am confident after my visit to Moscow, the countries of the Soviet bloc as well. I believe that the house of democracy's current consensus for strength and growth will usher in a new age of which we can only dream. But if we have the courage and the resolve, I believe that age will give us a world of peace and freedom, of opportunity and hope for generations to come. And I believe that even more after the summit that we've just been to and what I saw on the faces of the rank and file, the people of the Soviet Union.

And I can't resist now—I brought back a story that was being told there—I didn't bring it back, one of our Secret Service agents did and told it to me. The story has it—this is what they tell among themselves—that General Secretary Gorbachev and I were in the limousine with the head of our Secret Service unit, Ray, and he had a security man with him. And we were sightseeing. And they pulled up before a magnificent big fall, a waterfall, and we got out to look at it. And Gorbachev said to Ray, "Go ahead, jump over." And Ray said, "I've got a wife and three kids." And Gorbachev turned to his man and said to jump over, and he did. And Ray, with great humanity, went down around the waterfall, scrambling over the rocks to the bottom, and found the man wringing out his clothes. And he said, "When he told you to jump, why did you jump?" The man says, "I've got a wife and three kids." [*Laughter*]

Note: The President spoke at 2:06 p.m. in Loy Henderson Auditorium at the Department of State. In his opening remarks, he referred to Gen. Andrew J. Goodpaster, USA, Ret., council chairman; Secretary of State George P. Shultz; Lt. Gen. George M. Seignious, USA, Ret., council president; John E. Gray and Gene E. Bradley, council directors; and James W. Shinn, director of the council's NATO information office.

Statement by Assistant to the President for Press Relations Fitzwater on the Resignation of Howard H. Baker, Jr., as Chief of Staff to the President

June 14, 1988

President Reagan today announces with deep regret the resignation of Chief of Staff Senator Howard H. Baker, who has asked the President's permission to return to private life at this juncture in the administration. The President has enjoyed a close, personal working relationship with Senator Baker since his appointment as Chief of Staff on February 27, 1987. The President has known Senator Baker for many years, having worked with him as Senate majority leader to implement so many of the Reagan initiatives of the first term.

"Senator Baker has been a close friend and adviser, who has guided my staff deftly and effectively for the last 16 months," the President said. "He held a steady hand in the operation of the White House while the

Iran-*contra* investigations were being conducted, and his wise counsel fostered the spirit of cooperation in which those issues were presented to the American people. Similarly, he was a steady force for peace in helping to move our negotiators toward an INF agreement and in ensuring two successful summits with the leader of the Soviet Union. He has served America long and well. I wish he and his wife, Joy, all the best in the years ahead."

Senator Baker's resignation will be effective July 1, 1988. He intends to return to private law practice. A copy of Senator Baker's letter of resignation will be available today, and a response by the President will be available soon.

Statement on the Appointment of Kenneth M. Duberstein as Chief of Staff to the President

June 14, 1988

I am today announcing the appointment of Kenneth M. Duberstein to be Chief of Staff at the White House. Ken will assume his new duties on Friday, July 1, 1988.

Ken has been Deputy Chief of Staff since March 23, 1987, and has been a close confidant and adviser since that time. In addition, Senator Baker recommended him for this new position. I have known Ken since the earliest days of my administration, when he served in our Office of Legislative Affairs. I welcome his leadership in the next several months, as we attend the eighth economic summit of industrialized nations and conduct the affairs of government for the next 7 months.

Ken will be my principal aide and will lead the White House staff as we head into the homestretch. He is an outstanding manager and skilled strategist, who has been fundamental to the significant accomplishments, foreign and domestic, we have achieved since Ken returned as Deputy Chief of Staff in March 1987. Ken has given me firm and effective counsel, and I look forward to his tenure as Chief of Staff.

Informal Exchange With Reporters Prior to a Meeting With Prime Minister Ciriaco De Mita of Italy

June 14, 1988

Resignation of Howard H. Baker, Jr.

Q. Mr. President, do you think that your administration is going to be considered lameduck in view of the departure of Howard Baker?

The President. Well, I don't think it should be. We're going to miss him, of course. He has served very well. But he had his reasons for what he's had to do.

Q. Mr. President, Senator Baker said he'd be the one to turn out the lights here at the White House. Does that mean the lights are out on your administration?

The President. No, that means, I think, a little change has occurred.

Trade Deficit

Q. Did you see the trade figures this morning, Mr. President? It's one of the best trade reports in some time—something like under $10 billion for the monthly reported. Do you have a comment on that?

The President. Yes. It would be a happy comment because it shows that we have continued to bring down the trade deficit. It has been on a pretty continual decline, and it's been brought about this time by not only an increase in exports but a decrease in imports.

Plant Closings

Q. Could you clarify your position, Mr. President, on the business of plant closing? Would you support a move in Congress toward a voluntary provision of plant closing that would not be mandatory?

The President. We already have that, and we have a number of plants that have relations with their unions, that in their union labor contract have provisions for that. It is just that I believe that excessive controls and regulations by government—well, we've seen a comparison with some of our trading partners that have too much of that, and they've not been able to match our economic expansion.

Aid to the Contras

Q. Will you seek more military aid for the *contras,* Mr. President, or is that a lost cause?

The President. Well, this is something that's under discussion right now.

Resignation of Howard H. Baker, Jr.

Q. Are you going to miss Howard Baker?

The President. What?

Q. Are you going to miss Howard Baker?

The President. I said that, Helen [Helen Thomas, United Press International]. Yes, I will miss him.

Q. What kind of job has he done, Mr. President?

The President. He's done a fine job, both as leader of the Senate and now, as he came over here, in this position.

Q. Are you going to miss his picture-taking?

The President. What?

Q. Will you miss his picture-taking?

The President. [*Laughter*] He's quite a photographer.

Note: The exchange began at 11:34 a.m. in the Oval Office at the White House. Following their meeting, the President and the Prime Minister had lunch in the Residence.

Letter of Resignation of Howard H. Baker, Jr., as Chief of Staff to the President

June 14, 1988

Dear Mr. President:

As we discussed previously, I would like to leave your Administration before the end of the term. I think this is a particularly good time to do that and, therefore, I ask that I be relieved of my responsibilities as Chief of Staff as of the close of business on June 30th.

When you asked me to undertake this job in February of 1987 we discussed a number of objectives. First and foremost was to navigate the troubled waters of the Iran-contra affair. I believe that task is now behind us, and I think your representations have been fully supported by the record. I especially pay tribute to Arthur B. Culvahouse, Jr., White House Counsel, and his staff for their excellent work in these matters. The second item was to see that, notwithstanding the hearings and inquiries related to Iran-contra, we were able to carry forward your agenda. I believe that has been done; indeed, I think that far from being immobilized, the past 16 months have been among the most energetic and successful of your Administration. I particularly wish to single out Tom Griscom, your Assistant for Communications and Planning, for his excellent assistance in planning the schedule and events that made this possible. And finally, we discussed the foreign policy opportunities that lay before you, particularly in the field of arms control. I think the completion of the INF treaty and its ratification by the Senate followed by a successful Moscow Summit ranks among the most historic of your achievements during your Presidency. I believe that we owe a special debt of gratitude, first, to Frank Carlucci as your National Security Adviser and later, Colin Powell, as well, of course, as Secretary Shultz for these accomplishments.

There is still much to be done, particularly a full legislative schedule as well as continuing negotiations in the arms control field. However, you have a good staff in place, and I am confident that they can continue to receive your guidance and carry out your wishes for the remaining months of the Administration. I recommend Ken Duberstein, my able and experienced Deputy, to take my place as Chief of Staff. Therefore, Mr. President, for these reasons and for personal reasons, I make this request effective June 30th.

It has been my pleasure to work with you as fellow politicians dating from 1966, when you were elected Governor and I was elected U.S. Senator, as Majority Leader in the U.S. Senate during your first term, and now as your Chief of Staff. I will always treasure that experience and be grateful to you and the First Lady for your historic contribution to this country.

Sincerely,

HOWARD

Remarks Following Discussions With Prime Minister Ciriaco De Mita of Italy
June 14, 1988

The President. Ladies and gentlemen, it's been my great pleasure to meet today with Prime Minister De Mita of Italy, who is no stranger to the White House. But this is the first time that he comes as Prime Minister, and I want to begin by offering our warmest congratulations.

I regard this visit as extremely important. As members of the Atlantic alliance and as major industrial states, the United States and the Republic of Italy have much to discuss and much to do. Accordingly, our discussions today were wide-ranging and extremely useful. Although our agenda was far too long for me to discuss in detail, let me just give you some of the highlights. First, I gave the Prime Minister my views on where our relationship stands with the Soviet Union and where it is going. I told him that we're very pleased with the progress that we've made on the broad agenda and, of course, with the entry into force of the INF treaty. I also told him of my firm belief that without Italy's courage, determination, and support throughout INF deployment and negotiations there would have been no treaty. In arms reductions and the other areas on our agenda, much work remains to be done. We will continue to depend, and gratefully so, upon Italy's support as an ally and advice as a friend.

One of the important issues before our alliance is where we will redeploy the 401st Tactical Fighter Wing, the F–16's. Italy's willingness, at NATO invitation, to consider accepting the planes on its soil is typical of Italy's serious approach toward its alliance commitments. Its willingness to do its part, to share the risks and responsibilities as well as the benefits of NATO membership, is exemplary.

The Prime Minister and I will meet again shortly in Toronto, where we'll participate in our economic summit. We reviewed some of the issues that we expect to discuss there, including Italy's welcome initiative to strengthen international environmental protection activities. Prime Minister De Mita and I also talked about our mutual desire for a peaceful end to the conflict between Iran and Iraq and for a comprehensive peace in the Middle East. I know there's deep interest and concern among the Italian people on these issues, and we appreciate the positive role that the Government of Italy has played in that troubled region.

Another issue of great concern to all of us is international terrorism. In the last 6 months, Italy has been the victim of two shocking incidents: the death of one of your close friends, Mr. Prime Minister, in which I want to extend again my deepest condolences, and an attack on a USO club in Naples, in which an American servicewoman was killed. These incidents, terrible as they are, only serve to strengthen our resolve. And they remind us of the importance of our cooperative efforts against the human scourge of terrorism.

Mr. Prime Minister, in closing, I must confess that 6 months ago I said that U.S.-Italian relations could hardly be better, but remarkably, they are. In fact, I believe that we've made significant progress in a number of areas, and I'm confident that we'll continue this trend for the foreseeable future. Mr. Prime Minister, we're indeed pleased and honored to have had you as our guest.

The Prime Minister. I should like to thank President Reagan for the welcome extended to me today, which bears witness to the longstanding bonds of friendship that exist between Italy and the United States.

I have once again expressed to the President the admiration and esteem of the Italian Government for the courage and determination with which he has pursued his farsighted plan to effectively ease the tensions between East and West during his recent discussions with the General Secretary of the Soviet Communist Party, Gorbachev. Italy warmly welcomes the outcome of the Moscow summit and believes that it is a prelude to further and more wide-ranging agreements along the paths of peace.

I reaffirm the fact that Italy will continue with conviction to share in the commitments and undertakings of the alliance which binds us, safeguards our freedoms, and underpins the development of the West. The prospects for a lasting peace which are now emerging in the world require us to prevent any weakening of Atlantic solidarity, to refrain from any actions of unilateral disarmament, and to ensure that differential security zones are not created in Europe. I also stressed to President Reagan the importance we attribute to strengthening the relationship between the United States and Europe—that Europe which represents the other major goal of the Italian Government and the major contribution which a strong, united, and prosperous Europe—coupled with a solid Euro-American partnership—can make towards the peace and development of the whole world.

With President Reagan, I reviewed the main aspects of the international situation. We expressed a shared concern at the protracted states of crisis in the Middle East, Southeast Asia, southern Africa, and Latin America. We also expressed the hope that the improved climate of trust which now characterizes the dialog between East and West may exercise a favorable effect on these crises and help lead to peaceful and fair settlements.

Particular attention was devoted to the preparations for the summit of the seven most industrialized nations in Toronto in relation to economic growth, trade issues, and problems of international indebtedness. In Toronto, the seven will have to demonstrate their political farsightedness in order to withstand any backward protectionist tendencies and any selfish inward-looking attitudes. I also reminded President Reagan of the particular importance which Italy attaches to the risks connected with the deterioration of the environment and the fight against the worldwide scourge of drugs.

Lastly, we reviewed bilateral relations between the United States and Italy and expressed our satisfaction at how well they are faring, along with the hope that cooperation and exchanges in every sector will continue to increase and intensify. There is a fundamental bond which unites Italy and the United States in this respect, and that is represented by Americans of Italian origin. They continue to make a growing contribution to strengthening the ties between our two countries.

Today's conversations have enhanced my personal conviction that there exists a special relationship between Italy and the United States, a permanent political solidarity from which our two countries will greatly benefit in their commitment to the pursuit of a future characterized by peace, justice, and progress.

Note: The President spoke at 1:29 p.m. at the South Portico of the White House. The Prime Minister spoke in Italian, and his remarks were translated by an interpreter.

Nomination of C. Paul Robinson for the Rank of Ambassador While Serving as United States Negotiator for the Nuclear Testing Talks

June 14, 1988

The President today accorded the personal rank of Ambassador to C. Paul Robinson, of New Jersey, in his capacity as the United States Negotiator for the Nuclear Testing Talks, and nominated him for the rank of Ambassador while so serving. The accordance of the personal rank of Ambassador is an interim measure pending his confirmation by the Senate.

Since 1988 Mr. Robinson has been U.S. Negotiator for Nuclear Testing Talks for the Department of State in Geneva. Prior to this he was senior vice president and principal scientist with Ebasco Services, Inc., 1985–1988. From 1967 to 1985, he was associated with Los Alamos National Laboratory, serving in several capacities: Principal Associate Director, 1981–1985; division leader of the applied photochemistry division, 1976–1980; associate division leader of the laser research division, 1974–1976; alternate group leader for chemical lasers in the laser research division, 1972–1974; staff member in the advanced concepts group in the nuclear propulsion division, 1970–1972; and staff member and chief test operator in the field test division, 1967–1970.

Mr. Robinson graduated from Christian Brothers College (B.S., 1963) and Florida State University (Ph.D., 1967). He was born October 9, 1941, in Detroit, MI. He is married, has two children, and resides in Chatham, NJ.

Nomination of Donna R. Fitzpatrick To Be Under Secretary of Energy

June 14, 1988

The President today announced his intention to nominate Donna R. Fitzpatrick to be Under Secretary of Energy at the Department of Energy. She would succeed Joseph F. Salgado.

Since 1985 Miss Fitzpatrick has been Assistant Secretary for Conservation and Renewable Energy at the Department of Energy in Washington, DC. Prior to this, she was Principal Deputy Assistant Secretary for Conservation and Renewable Energy, 1984–1985. She was a sole practitioner in the general practice of law, 1983–1984, and an associate attorney with the law firm of O'Connor & Hannan, 1980–1983. In 1980 Miss Fitzpatrick was a member of the transition team for the National Science Foundation for the office of the President-elect. She has also been a legal assistant with O'Connor & Hannan, 1976–1980; faculty member at the Academy of the Sacred Heart, 1974–1976; and a faculty member at Georgetown Visitation Preparatory School, 1972–1974.

Miss Fitzpatrick graduated from American University (B.A., 1972) and George Washington University (J.D., 1980). She was born May 9, 1948, in Washington, DC, where she currently resides.

Nomination of Joseph F. Salgado To Be Deputy Secretary of Energy
June 14, 1988

The President today announced his intention to nominate Joseph F. Salgado to be Deputy Secretary of Energy. He would succeed William F. Martin.

Since 1985 Mr. Salgado has been Under Secretary of Energy in Washington, DC. Prior to this he was Associate Director for Presidential Personnel at the White House, 1983–1985. From 1982 to 1983, he served as the Associate Commissioner for Enforcement at the Immigration and Naturalization Service, Department of Justice. Mr. Salgado has also served as deputy district attorney and senior trial attorney for the Alameda County district attorney's office in California, 1973–1981, and as a sergeant with the Oakland Police Department, 1966–1973.

Mr. Salgado graduated from the University of San Francisco (B.S., 1968) and San Francisco Law School (J.D., 1972). He was born January 10, 1943, in San Diego, CA, and currently resides in Alexandria, VA.

Nomination of Danford L. Sawyer, Jr., To Be a Member of the Advisory Board for Radio Broadcasting to Cuba
June 14, 1988

The President today announced his intention to nominate Danford L. Sawyer, Jr., to be a member of the Advisory Board for Radio Broadcasting to Cuba for a term expiring October 27, 1991. This is a reappointment.

Since 1987 Mr. Sawyer has been president, chairman, and treasurer of Omni Investments International, Inc., in Sarasota, FL. Prior to this he was vice president for international development at R.R. Donnelley and Sons Co., 1984–1987. He has also served as president of Sawyer & Associates Advertising, Inc., and president of Area Guides, Inc.

Mr. Sawyer attended the University of the South, 1957–1959. He was born November 11, 1939, in New York, NY. Mr. Sawyer is married, has three children, and resides in Sarasota, FL.

Proclamation 5830—National Recycling Month, 1988
June 14, 1988

By the President of the United States of America

A Proclamation

Americans have become increasingly aware of health and environmental problems associated with the careless or improper management of municipal solid waste. In many densely populated regions, increasing waste volumes, shrinking landfill capacity, and rising costs of disposal have added to our concerns about the need for proper waste management.

Recycling is becoming increasingly important in municipal solid waste management. Many communities have recognized the value of recycling in waste management for some time. Volunteer programs exist in many towns and counties, and some States have recently enacted mandatory recycling laws. In addition, the recycling of scrap metals, paper, and glass has become a well-developed industry. Despite these efforts, however, only 10 percent of our Nation's municipal solid waste is recycled; nearly 80 percent of municipal solid waste is disposed of in landfills and the remaining 10 percent is incinerated.

The benefits of recycling waste materials are substantial. Recycling saves energy and thus preserves important fuel resources. It also avoids the pollution created in extracting resources from their natural environment. Through recycling, wastes are diverted from landfills and our limited landfill space is preserved. Communities can use recycling to generate revenues from the materials recovered from the waste stream. Finally, recycling can save us money by avoiding the high costs of landfills or incineration.

These benefits can only be realized through more recycling. The Environmental Protection Agency considers feasible a recycling level of 25 percent nationally by the early 1990's through the efforts of States and municipalities and the cooperation of individual households and businesses in separating recyclable materials from their waste and in not generating unnecessary waste.

The Congress, by House Joint Resolution 469, has designated June 1988 as "National Recycling Month" and has authorized and requested the President to issue a proclamation in observance of this event.

Now, Therefore, I, Ronald Reagan, President of the United States of America, do hereby proclaim June 1988 as National Recycling Month. I urge the people of the United States to observe this month with appropriate programs, ceremonies, and activities.

In Witness Whereof, I have hereunto set my hand this fourteenth day of June, in the year of our Lord nineteen hundred and eighty-eight, and of the Independence of the United States of America the two hundred and twelfth.

RONALD REAGAN

[*Filed with the Office of the Federal Register, 10:51 a.m., June 15, 1988*]

Proclamation 5831—Baltic Freedom Day, 1988
June 14, 1988

By the President of the United States of America

A Proclamation

In June 1940, acting under the color of a secret protocol to the infamous Ribbentrop-Molotov Non-Aggression Pact signed the previous year, Soviet forces occupied the independent Baltic States of Estonia, Latvia, and Lithuania. These small, democratic republics were crushed by the armies of their expansionist neighbor and illegally incorporated into the Soviet empire. In the aftermath of the Soviet takeover, tens of thousands of Balts were imprisoned, deported, or killed. Their religious and cultural heritage was denigrated and repressed. An alien political system, inimical to the ideals of individual liberty and self-determination, was imposed upon them.

The end of World War II saw the defeat of ambitious empire-builders in Germany and Japan, but foreign domination of the Baltic States that resulted from the collusion of Hitler and Stalin remained in place. For nearly five decades, the Soviet Union has tried in vain to convince the Baltic peoples to accept its hegemony, but its efforts are doomed to failure.

The situation has improved for some Soviet human rights activists in recent months, but Baltic men and women still suffer imprisonment, banishment, and persecution for daring to protest the continuing suppression of their national independence and cultures. Yet, despite the risks, they continue to speak out, to plead, and to claim their rights to religious, cultural, and political freedom.

Our government has never recognized the forcible incorporation of the Baltic States into the Soviet Union, and we never will. The American people, citizens of a land conceived in liberty and dedicated to equality under God for all, support the aspirations of the Baltic people to regain the freedom that was theirs and to chart their own course. To this goal we pledge anew our unswerving commitment.

By Senate Joint Resolution 249, the Congress of the United States has authorized and requested the President to designate June 14, 1988, as "Baltic Freedom Day."

Now, Therefore, I, Ronald Reagan, President of the United States of America, do hereby designate June 14, 1988, as Baltic Freedom Day. I call upon the people of the United States to observe this day with appropriate remembrances and ceremonies and to reaffirm their commitment to principles of liberty and freedom for all oppressed people.

In Witness Whereof, I have hereunto set my hand this fourteenth day of June, in the year of our Lord nineteen hundred and eighty-eight, and of the Independence of the United States of America the two hundred and twelfth.

RONALD REAGAN

[*Filed with the Office of the Federal Register, 10:52 a.m., June 15, 1988*]

Statement by Assistant to the President for Press Relations Fitzwater on the Defense Department Procurement Practices Investigation

June 15, 1988

President Reagan has urged the Justice Department to make a thorough and exhaustive investigation of allegations concerning fraud and bribery associated with defense contracts. The President received a briefing from Secretary of Defense Carlucci on Tuesday afternoon concerning the investigation. The FBI confirmed Tuesday that an investigation has been underway for some time regarding fraudulent activity within the Department of Defense contracting process.

At the President's direction, Senator Baker called the Attorney General this morning to discuss the President's conviction that the investigation by the Department of Justice and the FBI must be pursued thoroughly and conclusively. Fraud and abuse will not be tolerated. We trust the Bureau to leave no stone unturned in pursuing this investigation.

Message to the Congress Transmitting the Annual Report of the National Science Foundation

June 15, 1988

To the Congress of the United States:

I am pleased to send you the annual report of the National Science Foundation for Fiscal Year 1987. This report describes research supported by the Foundation in the mathematical, physical, biological, social, behavioral, and computer sciences; engineering; and education in those fields.

Achievements such as those described in this report are the basis for much of our Nation's strength—its economic growth, national security, and the overall well-being of our people.

The National Science Foundation has been and will remain a key part of the national effort to expand our research achievements and productivity and to remain competitive in world markets through innovation and new discoveries.

I commend the Foundation's work to you.

RONALD REAGAN

The White House,
June 15, 1988.

Appointment of Robert S. Pastorino as Special Assistant to the President for National Security Affairs
June 15, 1988

The President today announced the appointment of Robert S. Pastorino as Special Assistant to the President for National Security Affairs at the White House. Mr. Pastorino will succeed Jose S. Sorzano as Senior Director of Latin American Affairs on the National Security Council staff.

Mr. Pastorino is a career Foreign Service Officer who joined the Department of State in 1966. His early overseas assignments included political, economic, and commercial positions in Embassies in Caracas, Bogota, and Lisbon and in the U.S. consulate general in Hermosillo, Mexico. He was assigned to Mexico City as economic counselor in 1984, and as political counselor in 1985. He served as Chargé d'Affaires in Tegucigalpa, Honduras between July and November 1986 and as deputy chief of mission until May 1987. Mr. Pastorino was then appointed Deputy Assistant Secretary of Defense for Inter-American Affairs. He has also served as a commodities negotiator and financial analyst at the Department of State.

Mr. Pastorino graduated from San Francisco State University. He was born in San Francisco, CA, in 1940, is married, and has three children.

Excerpts From an Interview With International Newspaper Journalists
June 15, 1988

Speaker of the House of Representatives

Q. Mr. President, Jim Gerstenzang, Los Angeles Times. I'd like to shift to the domestic arena and ask if you think that Speaker Wright's book deal might mute the political impact of the ethics questions in the Presidential campaign, and also, just generally what your thoughts are on these reports now?

The President. You mean with regard to the Speaker?

Q. Yes.

The President. Well, this is—once again, I'm going to fall back on the same thing I've done when it's been with other people. I think it is proper that there is an investigation going forward with regard to these charges, but I don't think that anyone should give an opinion until we know whether they are just accusations or whether they have really happened.

Q. Can I just ask if you think there should be an independent counsel involved in this or if the House is the proper investigatory——

The President. I have to wonder if it should not be an independent counsel from the standpoint of the relationship of the Speaker to the majority of the committee. And I think everyone would feel that it was more proper if it was done by an appointed investigator.

Aid to the Contras

Q. Mr. President, on the issue of the assistance for the Nicaraguan resistance, you're coming under renewed pressure to provide that assistance on the one hand from the State Department. There are those who are saying that you won't be able to get it through Congress. Have you reached any decision? What's your thinking at this point on what's needed? Is it time for more military assistance to push the negotiations back on track?

The President. I think it is so apparent that that is what is necessary it would be ridiculous for anyone to oppose it. We went along with the peace plan that was agreed to among all the Central American states and to give it a chance. It is apparent that the Sandinistas are not going to democratize. They're resisting at the same time that they demand the *contras* set a date for laying down their arms. But they won't set a date for when they will meet the other terms of that peace plan, which were a pluralistic, democratic society in Nicaragua, a government in which the people had a decision to make in elections and so forth. And it seems to me that the efforts that have been made in the Congress and succeeded in reducing and eliminating our ability to help the freedom fighters—that that has literally given a signal to the Sandinistas that they can continue to hold out.

Now, if we want them to continue meeting and arriving at the settlement that the peace plan was supposed to bring about, which had as one of its aims democracy in Nicaragua, well, I think then that we've got to restore the threat to the Sandinistas, that they must see that the people of Nicaragua do have a force there that can be used to bring about an equitable settlement.

Q. So, you will ask for renewed military aid?

The President. We're discussing—I'm not going to give any answer to anything right now. We're discussing where we go from here and what we're going to do. And some of their leaders, as you know, are here in Washington right now. But I think it is evident that the Sandinistas were encouraged into thinking that maybe they could continue to hold out.

Remember that when the revolution was going on against Somoza the revolutionaries went to the Organization of American States and asked them to ask Somoza, the dictator, to step down in order to end the killing. And the Organization of American States asked the revolutionaries what were the goals of the revolution, and they were provided in writing. And they were democracy and freedom for the people and all the things that the rest of us have and believe in. And this is what was promised, and Somoza stepped down. And then the only really centrally organized group in the revolution, the Sandinista organization, a Communist organization, began getting rid of the other revolutionaries, either by exile or execution or whatever. And they established their Communist government, not a democracy.

And what this whole fight is about is to bring them back to the promises that were made to all the rest of us here in America about what kind of a democratic government they would have. But as I say, when the help was denied to the freedom fighters and it looked like if the Sandinistas just held out longer the freedom fighters would have to give up—this isn't good enough.

Note: The interview began at 1:35 p.m. in the Oval Office at the White House. Participants in the interview included Robert Hepburn, Toronto Star, of Canada; Renzo Gianfanelli, Corriere Della Sera, of Italy; François Sergent, Liberation, of France; Ian Brodie, Daily Telegraph, of the United Kingdom; Carlos Widmann, Sueddeutsche Zeitung, of the Federal Republic of Germany; Yoshio Murakami, Asahi Shimbun, of Japan; and James Gerstenzang, Los Angeles Times.

Appointment of Walter F. Beran as a Member of the President's Export Council
June 15, 1988

The President today announced his intention to appoint Walter F. Beran to be a member of the President's Export Council. He would succeed David C. Scott.

Since 1972 Mr. Beran has been vice chairman of Ernst & Whinney in Los Angeles, CA. Prior to this he was partner in charge of client relations for Ernst & Whinney in Cleveland, OH, 1965–1972.

Mr. Beran graduated from Baylor University (B.B.A., 1948). He was born April 20, 1926, in Grove, TX, and served in the U.S. infantry during World War II. He is married, has two children, and resides in Venice, CA.

Appointment of Earl H. Cunerd as a Member of the Committee for Purchase From the Blind and Other Severely Handicapped
June 15, 1988

The President today announced his intention to appoint Earl H. Cunerd to be a member of the Committee for Purchase from the Blind and Other Severely Handicapped for a term expiring April 24, 1993. This is a reappointment.

From 1967 to 1984, Mr. Cunerd was executive director of the United Cerebral Palsy Association, Inc., in New York. Prior to this, Mr. Cunerd was an assistant vice president and divisional vice president for Girard Trust Bank, 1956–1967, and assistant vice president for the First Pennsylvania Company, 1955–1956. Mr. Cunerd has served as president, vice president, and a member of the board of the National Health Council.

Mr. Cunerd graduated from the University of Pennsylvania (B.A., 1940) and Rutgers University (M.B.A., 1956). He was born January 26, 1918, in Philadelphia, PA. He is married, has one child, and resides in Moorestown, NJ.

Appointment of Alfred Gottschalk as a Member of the United States Holocaust Memorial Council
June 15, 1988

The President today announced his intention to appoint Alfred Gottschalk to be a member of the United States Holocaust Memorial Council for a term expiring January 15, 1993. This is a reappointment.

Since 1971 Dr. Gottschalk has been president of Hebrew Union College in Cincinnati, OH. Prior to this he was a dean at Hebrew Union College, 1959–1971.

Dr. Gottschalk graduated from Brooklyn College (A.B., 1952); Hebrew Union College (M.A., 1956); and the University of Southern California (Ph.D., 1965). He was born March 7, 1930, in Oberwesel, Germany. He is married, has two children, and resides in Cincinnati, OH.

Appointment of Keith B. Geiger as a Member of the Commission on Presidential Scholars
June 15, 1988

The President today announced his intention to appoint Keith B. Geiger to be a member of the Commission on Presidential Scholars. This is an initial appointment.

Since 1983 Mr. Geiger has been vice president of the National Education Association in Washington, DC. Previously he was president of the Michigan Education Association, 1977–1983.

Mr. Geiger graduated from Asbury College (B.A., 1962) and Peabody College (M.A., 1967). He was born October 9, 1940, in Pigeon, MI. Mr. Geiger is married, has two children, and resides in Fairfax, VA.

Letter of Resignation of Thomas C. Griscom as Assistant to the President for Communications and Planning
June 16, 1988

Dear Mr. President:

It is with deep regret that today I ask to be relieved of my duties as Assistant to the President for Communications and Planning effective June 30. There is never a good time to make such a request. But after careful consideration of both personal and professional obligations, I have reached this decision.

Over the past seven years, I have had the opportunity to be involved—either directly or indirectly—in implementing many of the policies that you have advanced. As an aide to then-Senate Majority Leader Howard Baker, I was able to observe the early steps that you took to chart a new spirit in America and to begin the longest peacetime economic expansion in history. In February 1987, I was privileged to be asked to become part of the White House team that was put together by your new chief-of-staff, Senator Baker. This was a period of great challenge, but also of great promise. With your direction, the past 16 months have been a time to finish the work of today, and to look ahead to tomorrow.

To have been part of the team that worked on the Washington and Moscow summits will remain as the high points of my tenure at the White House, because not only did you achieve the first agreement to reduce U.S. and Soviet nuclear missiles, but you also laid the foundation for a continued, broad relationship between our two countries.

So when I think back to these last several months, it will be with fond memories and a sense of pride to have been on this team. I feel the White House staff under Senator Baker's leadership has performed extremely well. I am confident that same performance will continue under the leadership of Ken Duberstein, because much remains to be done over the next seven months.

My best wishes are with you and Mrs. Reagan in the months and years ahead.

Sincerely,

THOMAS C. GRISCOM

Note: The original was not available for verification of the content of the letter.

Remarks at the Presentation Ceremony for the Presidential Scholars Awards
June 16, 1988

How do you do? Thank you all. I'm delighted to have all of you here today. And I want to thank Ronna Romney and the commissioners and the program sponsors for their generous contributions that make all this possible.

I want you to know the Presidential Scholars program has been a personal favorite; it always gives me a chance to reveal my own uneasiness in greeting such accomplished young scholars as yourselves. I like to remind people that some years ago my alma mater, Eureka College, gave me a degree in economics and sociology. But then 25 years later, they invited me back and gave me an honorary degree, and that just compounded a sense of guilt I'd been nursing for 25 years because I thought the first one was honorary. [*Laughter*]

We do have something in common though this morning: All of you are seniors, and I'm a sort of senior myself. [*Laughter*] Believe me, when you get to be my kind of senior status there's no greater fun than a chance to meet your kind of senior. All those cliches you've been hearing from your commencement speakers about how much you mean to us and how you represent the future and hope and the best in our lives—well, they're more than just cliches. So, having all of you here today is a morale boost, and I thank you for coming by.

I know I'm also supposed to remind you about something your commencement speakers have been talking to you about: gratitude. And by the way, that reminds me of a story. Maybe you've been warned about me and stories. [*Laughter*] Just think of this as part of the historical experience of the Reagan White House. Anyway, this involves a missionary. He was being chased by a hungry lion. And the lion was getting very close and just about within reach and ready to pounce. And the missionary dropped to his knees in prayer and said, "Oh, Lord, transform this beast into a believer." And the lion dropped to his knees and brought his paws together and said, "Oh, Lord, let us be grateful for what we're about to receive." [*Laughter*]

But then I've been reading some of the comments you wrote about being a Presidential scholar, and I realize you're way ahead of me on the matter of gratitude. For example, James Grove from Missouri wrote, "Thanks to mom and dad for letting me stay up so late." And Tom Tsao from New York thanks his parents for "waking me up in the morning." And then there's Wil Shapton in Michigan who thanks "my grandmother for reading to me out of the encyclopedia when I was little and my father for teaching me how to perform a kinematic structural analysis of my matchbox cars." [*Laughter*] But more seriously, Brian Curtis says he's grateful "to my parents for supporting all my academic endeavors always with unconditional love, not dependent on success or failure." And Deeling Liu Teng of Illinois, "I would like to thank my family. Their strength has enabled me to strive for goals above my own expectations."

So, you can see that I don't have to do much reminding. You're wise to remember your parents and teachers and counselors and principals who worked so hard with you for this moment. And I hope you know that gratitude isn't mentioned by us old folks just because we want to get in on the action and take a little credit for your success. Really it's another way of trying to pass along to you something valuable we've learned, something that will help in the future.

Secretary of Education Bennett has quoted a scholar who said that he sometimes worried about young people because while many of them know "where they are in space, they don't know where they are in time." Well, he meant simply that many young people have a sense of the dynamics of the modern world, but may not be quite as aware of the older values and deeper wisdom that made the creativity of this modern world possible.

Gratitude is a way of reminding ourselves where we are in time, a way of reminding ourselves that becoming a truly sophisticated and learned person begins with understanding the great teachings of our civilization about God and humanity, teachings that make ideas like human dignity, democracy, the rule of law and representative institutions possible. And it's why all of us can be grateful to Bill Bennett for what he's done to remind us of the importance of the values implicit in civilization and the need to teach and transmit from generation to generation a moral education. Loyalty, faithfulness, commitment, courage, patriotism, the ability to distinguish between right and wrong—I hope that these values are as much a part of your life as any calculus course or social science study. And so, do remember: Gratitude is a way to a deeper wisdom. Look for that deeper wisdom; believe me, there's a great hunger for it. And here you're in luck. As Americans, you have a special claim on it.

I got a sense of that hunger, by the way, 2 weeks ago, when I was in Moscow talking to the young people there at Moscow State University. And you know, I told them about a gathering much like this one that had occurred just before I left for the summit meeting. We had here in the East Room a group of students about your age, half of them Russian and half of them American. They had been in a joint conference together. And I made the point then that really it was very difficult to tell any of them apart, that young people are much the same all across the world, as are people of every age. It's just our governments that are based on different principles.

And that's the job before you and those students in Moscow for the remainder of this century and into the next one: to bring peoples of other cultures together in that common bond of humanity and to understand that the best way to do this is to stand forthrightly for the values of our whole way of life and what it is based upon, to speak for freedom, to argue the cause for democracy, and always to bear in mind those fundamental, moral distinctions between systems of government that believe in the dignity of the individual and other systems that simply see the individual as a cog in the great machine of the state.

Now, I know all of this strikes a very serious note on what is and should be a tremendously joyful moment for all of you. So, that's why I want to tell each of you that we're grateful to you, too. We're grateful for all the hard work you've done, but also for believing in yourselves, for reminding us that there are such things as the future and hope and capable young hands to take up the great tasks that we must leave unfinished.

So, congratulations to all of you. From one senior to another, I wish you all the best as we both set out to begin yet another chapter in our lives. I'm nearing the epilog, and you're barely through the introduction. But I'm grateful for this moment in which we could come together. Now, I'm going to go back inside and do what a little girl told me to do in a letter she wrote to me the first week I held this job. She wrote all the tasks that confronted me, and believe me, she had the problems down just about in proper order, too. And she urged me to get ahead with the business and solve them. Then she wound up with the last line in the letter that said, "Now get back to the Oval Office, and go to work." [*Laughter*] And she was right all the way.

So, I think I'll do that and let you get in the shade. We maybe should have had this particular function indoors, but we hadn't counted on exactly this weather. So, again, thanks to all of you, and congratulations to all of you, and God bless you. [*Applause*]

Thank you, and God bless you all. Thank you all. Keep clapping. The press are yelling questions at me. [*Laughter*]

Note: The President spoke at 11:31 a.m. in the Rose Garden at the White House. In his opening remarks, he referred to Ronna Romney, Chairman of the Commission on Presidential Scholars.

Appointment of Mari Maseng as Assistant to the President for Communications
June 16, 1988

The President today announced the appointment of Mari Maseng to be Assistant to the President for Communications, effective July 1, 1988.

Ms. Maseng has served President Reagan in the White House on two separate occasions during this administration. She was Director of the Office of Public Liaison from May 1986 to July 1987 and was a member of the President's speechwriting staff from January 1981 to November 1983. Most recently Ms. Maseng served as press secretary for the Dole for President campaign. She was Assistant Secretary of Transportation for Public Affairs from November 1983 to April 1985 and was also vice president of the Beatrice Companies in Chicago, IL. Mari Maseng has served the President and the administration with distinction in three important capacities in the past 7 years. Her close relationship with the President during this period and her previous service in the White House should ensure a smooth transition in the Office of Communications.

Ms. Maseng graduated from the University of South Carolina (B.A., 1975). She was born March 15, 1954, in Chicago, IL, and resides in Washington, DC.

Proclamation 5832—To Amend the Quantitative Limitations on Imports of Certain Cheese
June 16, 1988

By the President of the United States of America

A Proclamation

1. Quantitative limitations previously have been imposed on the importation of certain cheeses pursuant to the provisions of Section 22 of the Agricultural Adjustment Act of 1933, as amended (7 U.S.C. 624). Section 701 of the Trade Agreements Act of 1979, Public Law 96–39, provides that the President shall by proclamation limit the quantity of quota cheeses specified therein which may enter the United States in any calendar year after 1979 to not more than 111,000 metric tons.

2. By Proclamation No. 5618 of March 16, 1987, the quantitative limitations in part 3 of the Appendix to the Tariff Schedules of the United States (TSUS) were modified to reflect the Government of Portugal's accessions to the European Economic Community (EEC). The quota allocations previously made to Portugal were transferred to the European Economic Community. Proclamation No. 5618 also implemented certain undertakings to the EEC.

3. Due to a technical error, Proclamation No. 5618 failed to delete the quota for Portugal for certain cheeses under TSUS Item 950.10D, while transferring that quota to the EEC. Accordingly, I have determined that a technical correction is appropriate.

Now, Therefore, I, Ronald Reagan, President of the United States of America, acting under the authority vested in me by the Constitution and the statutes of the United States of America, including Section 701 of the Trade Agreements Act of 1979 and Section 22 of the Agricultural Adjustment Act of 1933, as amended, do hereby proclaim that, effective upon signature of this Proclamation, part 3 of the Appendix for the Tariff Schedules of the United States (TSUS) is modified as follows:

TSUS Item 950.10D is modified by deleting the line beginning with "Portugal".

In Witness Whereof, I have hereunto set my hand this sixteenth day of June, in the year of our Lord nineteen hundred and eighty-eight, and of the Independence of the United States of America the two hundred and twelfth.

RONALD REAGAN

[*Filed with the Office of the Federal Register, 11:19 a.m., June 17, 1988*]

Proclamation 5833—National Scleroderma Awareness Week, 1988
June 16, 1988

By the President of the United States of America

A Proclamation

Scleroderma, which literally means "hard skin," is a painful and debilitating connective tissue disease characterized by excessive deposits of collagen in the skin. The hallmark of this disease is skin thickening, but scleroderma can also involve other organs such as the gastrointestinal tract, lungs, heart, or kidneys. The disease can begin at any age, but it usually affects people in their most productive years, and women more frequently than men.

New research findings and new approaches to diagnosis and treatment are being developed to combat scleroderma. Research studies on scleroderma include investigations of various causes of the disease, research on vascular alterations, research on regulation of collagen synthesis, and development of diagnostic probes. Such fundamental research may lead to new and improved treatment strategies that will effectively attack the disease itself.

If this work is to continue and we are to take advantage of knowledge already gained, public awareness about scleroderma and about continuing scientific research is crucial. Private voluntary organizations and the Federal government are working together to achieve this goal.

The Congress, by Senate Joint Resolution 266, has designated the week beginning June 12, 1988, as "National Scleroderma Awareness Week" and has authorized and requested the President to issue a proclamation in observance of this event.

Now, Therefore, I, Ronald Reagan, President of the United States of America, do hereby proclaim the week beginning June 12, 1988, as National Scleroderma Awareness Week, and I call upon the people of the United States and educational, philanthropic, scientific, medical, and health care organizations and professionals to observe this week with appropriate ceremonies and activities.

In Witness Whereof, I have hereunto set my hand this sixteenth day of June, in the year of our Lord nineteen hundred and eighty-eight, and of the Independence of the United States of America the two hundred and twelfth.

RONALD REAGAN

[*Filed with the Office of the Federal Register, 11:20 a.m., June 17, 1988*]

Letter to Members of Congress on Funding for Science, Space, and Technology Programs
June 16, 1988

Dear ________:

As the Congress prepares to consider the HUD-Independent Agencies Appropriations Act for fiscal year 1989, I want to emphasize the importance to the Nation's future of full funding and support for science, space and technology programs. These programs are essential if the United States is to maintain its leadership in space exploration and development and its preeminence in science and technology.

The Space Shuttle, the Space Station, the Commercially Developed Space Facility (CDSF), and the National Science Foundation programs are essential to maintain national security, economic growth and international competitiveness.

Timely restoration of the Nation's Space Shuttle capability is critical to national security. Establishment of the Space Station will advance the frontiers of scientific knowledge and strengthen cooperation in space among the United States and its Allies. Deployment of the CDSF will begin to tap the commercial potential of space to serve the Nation's economic needs. The program initiatives of the National Science Foundation to increase the number of research awards, to improve undergraduate science and engineering programs, and to establish new Science and Technology Centers all are essential ingredients for improvement of the Nation's science infrastructure.

Last November, we reached a Bipartisan Budget Agreement to put the Federal Government firmly on the path toward elimination of the budget deficit. Achievement of that critically important objective requires those in office to make difficult choices among competing priorities.

We have considered the full range of Federal programs and their competing demands on scarce taxpayers' dollars and have concluded that full funding of science, space and technology programs must remain a top priority. I urge the Congress to provide full funding and support for these programs.

Sincerely,

RONALD REAGAN

Note: Identical letters were sent to Senators William Proxmire of Wisconsin and Jake Garn of Utah and Representatives Edward P. Boland of Massachusetts and Bill Green of New York. The original was not available for verification of the content of the letter.

Nomination of Carl Copeland Cundiff To Be United States Ambassador to Niger
June 16, 1988

The President today announced his intention to nominate Carl Copeland Cundiff, of Nevada, a career member of the Senior Foreign Service, Class of Minister-Counselor, as Ambassador to the Republic of Niger. He would succeed Richard Wayne Bogosian.

Mr. Cundiff entered the Foreign Service in 1965. From 1966 to 1968, he was assigned to the U.S. Embassy in Singapore. He was then an economist for the Agency for International Development in Saigon, Vietnam, 1968–1969; the U.S. Mission to the Organization for Economic Cooperation and Development in Paris, 1970–1973; and the Department of State in the Office of Monetary Affairs of the Economic Bureau, 1974–1977. He was an office director of the economic policy staff of the Economic Bureau, 1977–1980; an economic counselor for the U.S. Embassy in Lagos, Nigeria, 1980–1982; and deputy chief of mission for the U.S. Embassy in Abidjan, Cote d'Ivoire, 1982–1986. Since 1986 he has been office director in the office of food and policy programs for the Economic Bureau of the Department of State.

Mr. Cundiff graduated from the University of the South (B.A., 1963); Fletcher School of Law and Diplomacy (M.A., 1964; M.A.L.D., 1965; Ph.D., 1968); and Harvard University, Kennedy School of Government (M.P.A., 1974). He was born March 29, 1941, in New Orleans, LA. He is married, has two children, and resides in Washington, DC.

Remarks to the American Coalition for Trade Expansion With Canada

June 16, 1988

Thank you all very much, and welcome to the White House. I know that sounds strange, but they consider all this part of the White House complex.

But I want to thank each one of you for being a part of the American Coalition for Canada Free Trade, and in particular, let me thank Jim Robinson for taking the lead in this effort. I know you've already heard from Jim Baker and Clayton Yeutter. I think you know the key role that they've played in achieving this historic agreement, which will mean greater jobs and prosperity for generations to come.

If there was ever a case of being on the right side of history, it's certainly true of the Americans and the Canadians who have helped achieve our free trade agreement. I think people on both sides of the border realize that this mutually beneficial agreement is part of a shared destiny, but it's the hard work of people like you, in both countries, who made it happen and who are now helping to finish the job.

And that's reminding me of a story—things usually do remind me of a story. [*Laughter*] It can be illustrated. It has to do with an old farmer who had a piece of creek-bottom land and decided one day to make something out of it. It was covered with rocks and brush, and he set to work hauling the rocks away and then grubbing out the brush and all. And then he cultivated, and he fertilized, and he planted. And finally he had the most beautiful garden down there that you've ever seen. And one Sunday morning after church service, he said to the minister—he was so proud of this—he asked him if he wouldn't like to come out and see what he'd been doing out there along the creek. And so, the minister came out, and they went down. And the Reverend looked, and he said, "I've never seen anything like it." He said, "These melons—how the Lord has blessed this land. And look at that corn." He said, "God has really been good to this place." And he went on like that about the beans and everything else that was there, and the old boy was getting pretty fidgety. And finally the minister came to him and said, "Oh," he said, "what has happened here with the help of the Lord." And the old boy said, "Reverend, I wish you could have seen this place when the Lord was doing it by himself." [*Laughter*]

Well, the truth is that a lot of people have come together behind the free trade agreement. And I'm very pleased by the bipartisan cooperation that we've received in Congress. Actually, even the protectionists could help in their own way. You see, if protectionists in the United States say that the agreement favors Canada, and I could write that down and send it to Prime Minister Mulroney, and he could show that to the Canadian Parliament. And if the protectionists in Canada say it benefits the United States more, then the Prime Minister could copy that and send that to me, and I could show that to our Congress. And I figure with that kind of support coming from both sides of the border we just couldn't lose. [*Laughter*]

The truth is that the biggest winners in this agreement are the citizens of both the United States and Canada: Both will get more jobs, faster growth, lower prices, and come out miles ahead of the protectionist countries of the world. Under this trade pact, Americans and Canadians, the world's two greatest trading partners, will, by doing business with each other, have an alternative to the tariffs and trade barriers that we both face in doing business with other countries. So, in creating the largest free trade area on Earth, both of our countries can become more competitive.

What the U.S.-Canada agreement accomplishes on a bilateral basis is a tremendous example of what we can, and ultimately must, achieve multilaterally. In that sense, this agreement is a gift to the world. It creates a model that can be imitated and expanded and, ultimately, made universal among free nations.

And America has been performing strongly in world markets. In a report released this week, the Nation's April trade deficit fell by 15.5 percent, bringing it down to $9.9 billion, which is the lowest monthly figure in more than 2½ years. These results continue the progress that's been underway for several quarters. In fact, in the first quarter of this year, U.S. exports in goods and services rose at an annual rate of over 20 percent. Now, this is the kind of good news that I'm delighted to carry to the Toronto summit.

When I meet in a few days with the heads of the major industrial democracies, I will urge that we continue to work together to open our markets. We need to give the Uruguay round of GATT [General Agreement on Tariffs and Trade] negotiations another push forward.

One of the most difficult trade problems facing the United States and Canada is in agriculture. Trade-distorting subsidies are so pervasive around the world that no single nation—or two nations—can afford to give up these practices unilaterally or bilaterally. We must seek a multilateral solution.

In the important new areas of trade in services and trade-related investment, the agreement with Canada breaks new ground and shows the way to a multilateral accord. The multilateral trade talks are scheduled to go for 4 years. But we can't afford to let those talks languish now, as we near the halfway point. In Toronto, we, the heads of the major industrial states, should push our ministers to lay down specific goals and a timetable to the finish line by the end of this year—no excuses. Our goal must be universal free trade among free people and free countries, and that's the shape of the future.

Protectionism has no future; it's a dead and discredited idea. In a global economy, there can be no surer way of impoverishing ourselves than to try to make America go it alone, by cutting us off from trade and investment with the other countries of the world. The protectionists make me think of the story of that Sunday school teacher who asks her class, "Who wants to go to heaven?" And all of the children raise their hands except for one little boy in the back of the room. The teacher, astounded, says, "Charlie, don't you want to go to heaven?" And he says, "Yep, but not with this bunch." [*Laughter*]

Well, today, we have a global economy in which the United States is at the very center. We import and export more than any other country on Earth. Of total foreign investment in the world, nearly 40 percent, by far the largest share, consists of Americans investing overseas. But it's not a one-way street. At the same time, the United States also receives more foreign investment from abroad than any other country. So, we truly are the investment capital of the world.

One of the reasons world capital has been drawn to the United States is that we have led the world in reducing tax rates. Back in the 1970's, the top personal income tax rate in the United States was 70 percent. That was even higher than the average of the other leading democracies—industrial democracies. Well, today, instead of taxing our citizens more heavily than those other countries, our top Federal rate of 28 percent is the lowest, most progrowth, most competitive top personal rate of any of the leading industrial democracies in the world. And when the people around the world see the American economy booming, it's not surprising that they want to join in.

I had that experience. My first time was in Canada at the first summit. My freshman year here was held in Ottawa. And I was kind of a new kid in school. And they didn't listen much if I did talk, and I didn't talk too much and all. But it was a great thrill a couple of years later when our—economic plan had started working. When I appeared at the table for the next summit meeting, and my six colleagues across the table were looking, and all they wanted to hear was how did we explain the American miracle that was taking place. And I took great delight in telling them about—well, to follow our lead by cutting taxes and excess regulation and opening things up to freer trade.

America has produced nearly 17 million jobs over the last 5½ years, putting employment at an all-time high. And we're providing jobs for a larger percentage of our population than any of the other major industrial democracies. Since 1982 we've created jobs in the United States at twice the rate of Japan and Britain, 8 times the rate in Italy, and 14 times the rate of West Germany. So, anyone who thinks that we've somehow lost jobs through trade not only has it wrong, they've got it upside down and backward.

You know, I don't know whether you've known this. I had to get this job to learn that the statisticians have as our potential employment pool everyone in the United States 16 years of age and up, both sexes. Now, that includes all the youngsters still getting education; that includes all of the people retired and everything else. But that's our potential employment pool. And today, when I said the largest rate of employment—62.6 percent of that entire pool is employed in America today. I used to get upset not too many weeks ago at some of the Presidential candidates and things that they were saying about how we must do something to get jobs for people.

Well, we're now in the longest peacetime expansion on record, the first in the postwar period in which we've grown faster than most of our major trading partners. And after 65 consecutive months of growth not only have we kept inflation under control but the inflation rate is a good deal lower than it was before the expansion began. And with the American economy booming, not only is the end not in sight but I believe that the best is yet to come. If the progrowth economic policies of the last 7 years are continued, the next decade will be known as the Roaring Nineties.

The U.S.-Canada free trade agreement will help assure that this type of growth and prosperity continues and expands to embrace everyone in our society. Our protectionist opponents do not know how to create real prosperity, so they try to freeze the status quo. It's like a flim-flam version of the $1 million lottery: The winner gets $1 a year for a million years. [*Laughter*]

Well, what we're offering is the real thing—real jobs, real growth, real prosperity for America and for Canada. And again, I want to thank you for all that you're doing to support the U.S.-Canada free trade agreement and for taking the time this year to be a part of history. I can't thank you enough, and without you, I don't think we'd be where we are today. I told a few of you just a little earlier today, a few of you, that really what we did that I think made all of this happen was we just got out of your way. As long as I'm around, we're going to keep on staying out of your way as much as we possibly can.

Thank you all, and God bless you.

Note: The President spoke at 2:33 p.m. at a briefing in Room 450 of the Old Executive Office Building. In his opening remarks, he referred to James D. Robinson III, Chairman of the President's Advisory Committee on Trade Negotiations; Secretary of the Treasury James A. Baker III; and U.S. Trade Representative Clayton Yeutter.

Remarks on Free and Fair Trade to Members of the United States Information Agency Volunteer International Council
June 17, 1988

Thank you all very much, and welcome back to the White House. I would like to begin by thanking Charlie Wick for bringing you all together today. As many of you know, Charlie has served as Director of the USIA longer than any other Director in our history. And Charlie's been not only a trusted adviser but a good personal friend. Thank you, Charlie.

Well, it's my job just now to say a few words. But whenever I'm asked to speak after lunch, there's a certain story that comes to mind. It dates back to ancient Rome. And on Sunday afternoon, there was going to be a feeding of the hungry lions. And a little cluster of Christians were going to be brought out into the Colosseum, and the lions turned loose. And there they were, huddled there, and in came the lions roaring toward them. And one man stepped out of the little group and said a few quiet words, and the lions just laid down. Well, the crowd was furious. And Caesar sent for the man, and they brought the man before him. And he said, "What did you say that made the lions act like that?" He said, "I just told them that after they ate there would be speeches." [*Laughter*] So, with your permission, I'll keep these remarks brief.

As you know, I'll be leaving on Sunday for Toronto to attend the 14th annual economic summit. These annual meetings of the leaders of the major industrial democracies have proven invaluable in setting broad policy guidelines. And I can't resist pointing out that when I attended my first economic summit in 1981 my views on the need to strengthen free markets were not exactly popular. Today things have changed. Statism and socialism are now on the defensive, even in the Communist world. There's global understanding that, yes, the free market is the engine of economic growth.

World trade will, of course, represent a topic of central concern at the Toronto summit, and so I thought I'd share with you some of my thoughts about the international economy. First, underlying principles—listen, if you will, to these words written by Thomas Jefferson: "Our interest will be to throw open the door of commerce and to knock off all its shackles, giving perfect freedom to all persons for the vent of whatever they may choose to bring into our ports, and asking the same in theirs." In short, protectionism in any country does damage to all. And so, the goal of the administration has been to open the markets of other countries, not to close America's markets.

Yes, the news this week of continued improvement in the American trade deficit is encouraging and welcome. But consider what the trade deficit arose from: the unparalleled American economic expansion, now in its sixth year; and the openness of the American market to foreign exports. These two factors have generated export-led economic growth in Europe, Japan, and in the Third World. To cite but one example, in the past year the United States absorbed roughly two-thirds of Mexico's total exports. Other developing nations are likewise dependent on exports to America for their economic growth. But to be able to import, Americans must be able to export. So, it damages the entire world economy when foreign countries fail to offer the same opportunities to American exports that America offers to their products. It's this basic sense of fairness that has helped generate protectionist pressures in America. And let me repeat: Protectionism, the closing of America's markets, is the wrong response. Opening markets—that, I firmly believe—is the answer.

So, our administration, working with Congress, eliminated many, but not all, of the protectionist measures from the recent omnibus trade bill. And I'm looking forward to signing an improved version of this bill as soon as Congress sends me a bill that will strengthen America's international competitiveness and create even more new jobs for Americans. One of the central components of this bill, and this is crucial, is negotiating authority that will allow us to forcefully pursue open markets everywhere. After all, that was the original intent of the framers of the General Agreement on Tariffs and Trade 40 years ago.

The United States has played a leading role in opening this new round of international trade negotiations—the Uruguay round, agreed upon at Punta del Este, Uruguay, in September 1986. These negotiations will build on the achievements of previous trade rounds and provide a much-needed framework for expanding trade in services, investment, and intellectual property. And they will also focus on the crisis in world agricultural trade.

Now, I don't want to say a great deal about this matter of the world agricultural trade crisis. You'll be hearing a great deal about it as the negotiations progress this year. But there's a simple rule that's as true in agriculture as in any other endeavor: When you tax something, you get less of it, and when you subsidize something, you get more of it. It so happens that this year the world's industrialized nations are subsidizing agriculture to the tune of $200 billion a year. Is it any wonder there are world surpluses of so many crops or that so many markets for agricultural goods have become so distorted? Our position on this is simple: By the year 2000, all subsidies and market barriers that distort trade in agriculture should be eliminated—all of them. Is that a tall order? You bet. But we've filled tall orders before. In fact, the European press has given our position on agricultural subsidies a nickname that sort of appeals to me. They've started calling it the zero option. [*Laughter*]

I've enjoyed economics ever since I started studying it during my college days. And, no, it's not true that I was able to tell you the story of the prisoners and the lions because I was an eyewitness. [*Laughter*] But there's one quotation about world trade that I especially cherish. It comes from the 18th century French economist Frederic Bastiat, who wrote that protectionism "is the sacrifice of the consumer to the producer, of the end to the means." And I guess that's what a belief in free trade comes down to: keeping the ends in view. The ends of continued world growth, that the lives of individuals—of men and women and children—might become even better. Those are the ends that brought me to this high office, and those are the ends I'll continue to fight for until the very day I leave this grand old house.

I appreciate the personal commitment that each of you has made to be a part of the USIA International Council. Through you, the business and opinion leaders of the world, we are better able to understand international perceptions of our country and directly communicate our message. And again, I thank you all, and thank you for being here, and God bless you all. You'll forgive us, but we've got to get back to work.

Note: The President spoke at 2:01 p.m. following a luncheon in the East Room at the White House. The Council examined overseas perceptions of U.S. leadership in world affairs and ways the United States could improve its image abroad.

Proclamation 5834—National Dairy Goat Awareness Week, 1988
June 17, 1988

By the President of the United States of America

A Proclamation

For many centuries, dating perhaps to prehistoric times, dairy goats have provided mankind with a reliable and abundant source of milk and milk products, meat, and clothing. Here in the United States, goats have been valued throughout our history primarily as dairy animals. Because of their ability to thrive in either lush or arid country, efficiently converting a wide variety of vegetation into nutritious milk and meat, these animals often accompanied American pioneer families in the days of westward expansion. Goats have long been a part of the typical mix of animals on farms in every region of the United States.

Today, among the contributions of dairy goat farming to our Nation's economy is an impressive array of dairy products. The interest of both domestic and foreign consumers in U.S. domestic goat cheeses, or Chevre, continues to increase, as does awareness of all dairy goat products. These trends deserve every encouragement.

The Congress, by House Joint Resolution 423, has designated the period beginning the second Saturday and ending the third Saturday of June 1988 as "National Dairy Goat Awareness Week" and has authorized and requested the President to issue a proclamation in its observance.

Now, Therefore, I, Ronald Reagan, President of the United States of America, do hereby proclaim the period beginning the second Saturday and ending the third Saturday of June 1988 as National Dairy Goat Awareness Week. I call upon the people of the United States to observe this week with appropriate programs, ceremonies, and activities.

In Witness Whereof, I have hereunto set

my hand this seventeenth day of June, in the year of our Lord nineteen hundred and eighty-eight, and of the Independence of the United States of America the two hundred and twelfth.

RONALD REAGAN

[Filed with the Office of the Federal Register, 10:16 a.m., June 20, 1988]

Statement by Assistant to the President for Press Relations Fitzwater on the Drought Emergency

June 17, 1988

The President met for 30 minutes this afternoon at 3:30 p.m. to discuss the drought situation with Vice President Bush, Secretary of Agriculture Lyng, OMB Director Miller, Deputy Chief of Staff Duberstein, and John Tuck [Deputy Assistant to the President and Executive Assistant to the Chief of Staff].

Secretary Lyng summarized the severity of the drought, using a chart of the United States, color-coded to indicate the areas of greatest severity. Secretary Lyng indicated the largest area of severe drought is in the North Central States. He indicated the drought severity of that region stretched well into Canada, including the provinces of Saskatchewan and Alberta, and that Prime Minister Mulroney will undoubtedly share our concern for the drought at the Toronto summit. The Secretary also summarized actions already taken to relieve the shortages of grazing land for livestock.

President Reagan asked to be kept informed on a regular basis. Secretary Lyng will provide daily reports on drought conditions to the White House. In addition, the first meeting of the Interagency Drought Policy Committee will be held Monday at the Department of Agriculture.

Secretary Lyng will accompany Vice President Bush on a tour of the drought area near Springfield, IL, this weekend. He will report to the President and the Cabinet next week.

Secretary Lyng summarized actions taken to date, including:

—Opening conservation reserve acreage to haying in 297 drought-designated counties in 13 States. The move will help provide feed for livestock in hard-hit drought areas.

—To date, USDA has approved haying and grazing on acreage conservation and conserving use land (acreage normally idle under these farm programs) in 1,937 counties in 22 States.

—Emergency feed programs have been approved for 95 counties in 9 States. Other provisions allowing farmers to receive 92 percent of their normal farm program payments if they are prevented from planting due to disaster have been approved for 20 counties in 7 States.

Radio Address to the Nation on Economic Growth and the Situation in Nicaragua

June 18, 1988

My fellow Americans:

Seven years ago, as a newly elected President, I traveled to Canada for my first economic summit with the leaders of the other major industrial democracies. Tomorrow I will attend my eighth and final economic summit, and it's remarkable to think how much things have changed.

When I took office, unemployment was climbing, inflation was soaring, Federal spending was out of control, and interest rates had topped 20 percent. The economic mess we faced was clear. And it was also clear that without a recovery in the United States there was little chance for the world economy to get back on its feet. The world stood, as one foreign leader put it, in the "trough of the recession," faced with the "twin evils of inflation and unemployment." It was, as another head of government said at the time, "one of the most difficult periods of the Western industrial countries." The question was what to do.

And that was when we presented a bold new program of cutting tax rates and excessive regulation, opening world markets, and letting the private sector lead the way to economic recovery. Today we're in the longest peacetime economic expansion on record. We have created nearly 17 million jobs in the last 5½ years. That's twice as many new jobs as the other six summit countries combined, and those countries have a working-age population that's over 60 percent larger than the United States.

But our own prosperity is only part of our achievement. We have also led the world toward a remarkable consensus: that economic freedom, not state planning and intervention, holds the key to growth and development. Yes, the other industrial democracies have joined us on this path. But it goes further than that. From India to Argentina, from Africa to China and even in the Soviet Union, the shackles of state economic domination are beginning to loosen. So, in winning this battle of ideas, we're helping to enrich and liberate the working people and entrepreneurs of the entire world.

And at the Toronto summit, we're going to work together to make sure that this great "venture to progress" continues. That means further opening the international marketplace and increasing the coordination of our policies. That means bringing the newly industrialized countries into the full and mature place in the world trading system that they have earned. And it also means working together, however, to put an end to one type of trade: illegal drug trafficking. So, these topics and others, such as the rebuilding of Afghanistan and the Philippines, international debt, and agricultural subsidies—these will be on the Toronto agenda.

But before I travel across our northern border to Canada, I'd like to talk for a minute about a situation south of our border, in Central America. This is a problem that's close to home and that demands our strong attention.

Back on February 3d this year, the Congress, by just an 8-vote margin, took a dangerous gamble with our national security and the prospects for democracy in Central America. You see, on that day the House of Representatives voted down my request to continue effective support for the Nicaraguan freedom fighters. The opponents of aid argued that they were giving peace a chance by unilaterally disarming the freedom fighters. But today the Nicaraguan talks are at an impasse, the victim of the Sandinistas' bad faith and Congress' bad judgment. The leaders of the resistance who courageously went to Managua to seek concrete democratic freedoms were instead subjected to lies, abuse, harassment, and threats of physical harm by the Communist government. Costa Rican President Arias said that the democratization that was required of Nicaragua "has not happened," citing Sandinista "intransigence." The Sandinistas have proved repeatedly that they will not democratize without pressure. As they've shown at Contadora, Manzanillo, San José, Esquipulas, and Sapoa: Peace talks for them are just political theater, a way to weaken the democratic resistance while consolidating their militant Communist regime.

I've warned that if we fail in Nicaragua we could one day face a Communist Central America spreading subversion northward and southward. As I said in 1984, this would pose "the threat that 100 million people from Panama to the open border of our South could come under the control of pro-Soviet regimes." That is why we must work for a free Nicaragua. Even the Washington Post, in an editorial last Sunday, urged one key faction of House Democrats to "stop chasing ghosts and playing political games." We can still secure peace and freedom in Central America, but time is growing short, and the stakes ever larger. If we fail to act in time, the American people will demand to know why.

Until next week, thanks for listening, and God bless you.

Note: The President spoke at 12:06 p.m. from the Oval Office at the White House.

Remarks on Signing the Japan-United States Science and Technology Cooperation Agreement
June 20, 1988

The President. Prime Minister Takeshita and I have just signed a new agreement on cooperation in research and development in science and technology. This agreement provides for joint initiatives to strengthen our bilateral science and technology relationship. It's based on the principles of mutual and equitable contributions and benefits. In it, we set forth the policy framework for this overall relationship. Our hope is to strengthen the relationship for peaceful purposes.

The United States and Japan have a long history of scientific and technological cooperation. This cooperation has benefited both our nations. It has included joint government-to-government research projects, exchanges of students and scholars, and private industry research. When we look to the future, it is clear that science and technology will grow even more important to our mutual well-being. With this in mind, and recognizing the great contributions both of our scientific establishments have to offer to world prosperity, we seek to enhance cooperation in a number of research areas of national importance. Under this agreement we will establish a joint high-level committee to meet at least annually for the purpose of reviewing matters of importance in the field of science and technology. This joint committee will also review and discuss policy issues related to the overall science and technology relationship between our two countries and the cooperative activities under this agreement. I might add that this new agreement is already bearing fruit, and I thank the Prime Minister for his efforts in this regard.

Thank you, and God bless you.

The Prime Minister. It is my deep pleasure to join you, Mr. President, in signing this Japan-U.S. Science and Technology Cooperation Agreement. This agreement lifts our sights to the 1990's and beyond, establishing a practical framework for cooperation between Japan and the United States, two leading nations on the cutting edge of the pursuit of new knowledge. I wish to stress that our collaboration under this agreement is not exclusive. It is open to be shared by all the world. Indeed, I cherish the hope that our joint endeavors, particularly on the frontiers of advanced science and technology, will bear rich fruit and will contribute significantly, not only to the well-being of our two peoples, but also to peaceful progress and prosperity throughout the world. I offer my sincere appreciation to you, Mr. President, and I extend my warm thanks to all those in both our nations whose vision and efforts have shaped this important understanding.

Thank you.

Note: The President spoke at 4:43 p.m. in the ballroom at the Royal York Hotel in Toronto, Canada. The Prime Minister spoke in Japanese, and his remarks were translated by an interpreter.

Statement on Japanese Import Quotas on Beef and Citrus
June 20, 1988

The news from Tokyo of an agreement on beef and citrus products was most welcome. Ambassador Yeutter, our Trade Representative, advises that agreement was reached to eliminate Japanese import quotas on beef and citrus products. I am pleased that Prime Minister Takeshita's government has joined us in liberalizing agricultural trade. We made tough choices in order to open these markets. This important achievement strengthens the U.S.-Japan relationship and demonstrates our mutual commitment to an open trading system.

Toronto Economic Summit Conference Political Declaration
June 20, 1988

East-West

1. We the leaders of our seven countries, and the representatives of the European Community, uphold common principles of freedom, respect for individual rights, and the desire of all men to live in peace under the rule of law. Our peoples stand in solidarity within the framework of our existing alliances for the cause of freedom, to safeguard democracy and the prosperity which it has produced. In our discussions we considered how these goals and values could be pursued in the field of foreign affairs, particularly with regard to East-West relations.

2. We discussed a wide range of regional questions and these discussions are continuing throughout the Summit.

3. We confirmed our belief in constructive and realistic dialogue and cooperation, including arms control, human rights and regional issues, as the way to build stability between East and West and enhance security at lower levels of arms. We also reaffirmed that for the foreseeable future nuclear deterrence and adequate conventional strength are the guarantees of peace in freedom.

4. In several important respects changes have taken place in relations between Western countries and the Soviet Union since we last met. For our part this evolution has come about because the industrialized democracies have been strong and united. In the Soviet Union greater freedom and openness will offer opportunities to reduce mistrust and build confidence. Each of us will respond positively to any such developments.

5. We welcome the beginning of the Soviet withdrawal of its occupation troops from Afghanistan. It must be total and apply to the entire country. The Afghan people must be able to choose their government freely. Each of us confirms our willingness to make our full contribution to the efforts of the international community to ensure the return of the refugees to their homeland, their resettlement, and the reconstruction of their country. We now look to the Soviet Union to make a constructive contribution to resolving other regional conflicts as well.

6. Since our last meeting, progress has been made between the United States and the Soviet Union in agreeing to reduce nuclear weapons in a manner which accords fully with the security interests of each of our countries. The INF Treaty, the direct result of Western firmness and unity, is the first treaty ever actually to reduce nuclear arms. It sets vitally important precedents for future arms control agreements: asymmetrical reductions and intrusive verification arrangements. We now look for deep cuts in U.S. and Soviet strategic offensive arms. We congratulate President Reagan on what he has already accomplished, along with General Secretary Gorbachev, toward this goal.

7. Nonetheless, the massive presence of

Soviet conventional forces in Eastern Europe, the ensuing conventional superiority of the Warsaw Pact, and its capacity to launch surprise attacks and large scale offensive operations, lie at the core of the security problem in Europe. The Soviet military buildup in the Far East is equally a major source of instability in Asia. These threats must be reduced. Our goal is enhanced security and stability at lower levels of forces, after having eliminated the present imbalances. We seek the early establishment of a comprehensive, effectively verifiable and truly global ban on chemical weapons.

8. Genuine peace cannot be established solely by arms control. It must be firmly based on respect for fundamental human rights. We urge the Soviet Union to move forward in ensuring human dignity and freedoms and to implement fully and strengthen substantially its commitments under the Helsinki process. Recent progress must be enshrined in law and practice, the painful barriers that divide people must come down, and the obstacles to emigration must be removed.

9. We pay special attention to the countries in Eastern Europe. We encourage them to open up their economies and societies, and to improve respect for human rights. In this context we support the continuation and strengthening of the Helsinki process.

10. We take positive note of Eastern countries' growing interest in ending their economic isolation, for example in the establishment and development of relations with the European Community. East-West economic relations can be expanded and serve our common interests so long as the commercial basis is sound, they are conducted within the framework of the basic principles and the rules of the international trade and payments system, and are consistent with the security interests of each of our countries.

Terrorism

11. We strongly reaffirm our condemnation of terrorism in all its forms, including the taking of hostages. We renew our commitment to policies and measures agreed at previous Summits, in particular those against state-sponsored terrorism.

12. We strongly condemn recent threats to air security, in particular the destruction of a Korean airliner and the hijacking of a Kuwaiti airliner. We recall the principle affirmed in previous declarations that terrorists must not go unpunished. We appeal to all countries who are not party to the international conventions on civil aviation security, in particular the Hague Convention, to accede to those conventions.

13. We express support for work currently under way in the International Civil Aviation Organization aimed at strengthening international protection against hijackings. We welcome the most recent declaration adopted by the ICAO Council which endorses the principle that hijacked aircraft should not be allowed to take off once they have landed, except in circumstances as specified in the ICAO declaration.

14. We welcome the adoption this year in Montreal and Rome of two international agreements on aviation and maritime security to enhance the safety of travellers.

15. We reaffirm our determination to continue the fight against terrorism through the application of rule of law, the policy of no concessions to terrorists and their sponsors, and international cooperation.

Narcotics

16. The illegal use of drugs and the illicit trafficking in them poses grave risks to the peoples of Summit countries as well as the peoples of source and transit countries. There is an urgent need for improved international cooperation in all appropriate fora on programs to counter all facets of the illicit drug problem, in particular production, trafficking, and financing of the drug trade. The complexity of the problem requires additional international cooperation, in particular to trace, freeze and confiscate the proceeds of drug traffickers, and to curb money laundering.

17. We look forward to the successful negotiation in Vienna in November of a United Nations Convention on illicit trafficking.

18. We supported the initiative of the Government of the United States for a special task force to be convened to propose

methods of improving cooperation in all areas including national, bilateral and multilateral efforts in the fight against narcotics.

Note: The declaration was not issued as a White House press release.

Toronto Economic Summit Conference Chairman's Summary of Political Issues
June 20, 1988

The following represents an agreed summary of the discussions on the Middle East, South Africa and Cambodia.

Middle East

We express our deep concern at the increasing instability in the Near East. The current violence in the Occupied Territories is a clear sign that the status quo is not sustainable. An early negotiated settlement to the underlying Arab/Israeli dispute is essential. We declare our support for the convening of a properly structured international conference as the appropriate framework for the necessary negotiations between the parties directly concerned. In this perspective we salute current efforts aimed at achieving a settlement, particularly the initiative pursued by Mr. Shultz since February. We urge the parties to cooperate fully in the search for a solution.

We have pursued our consultations about the continuing war between Iran and Iraq, which remains a source of profound concern to us. We reaffirm our support for Security Council Resolution 598, which was adopted unanimously. We express our warm appreciation for the efforts of the Secretary General to work for a settlement on this basis and reiterate our firm determination to ensure implementation of this mandatory resolution by a follow-up resolution. We condemn the use of chemical weapons by either party, deplore proliferation of ballistic missiles in the region, and renew our commitment to uphold the principle of freedom of navigation in the Gulf.

South Africa

We declare our abhorrence of apartheid, which must be replaced through a process of genuine national negotiations by a non-racial democracy.

We expressed our urgent opinion on three particular matters:

(1) all legal options available in South Africa should be used to secure clemency for the Sharpeville Six;

(2) the enactment of legislation designed to deprive anti-apartheid organizations of overseas aid would place severe strain on the relations each of us has with South Africa;

(3) we strongly support the current negotiations seeking national reconciliation within Angola, an end to the Angola/Namibia conflict, and early implementation of UN Security Council Resolution 435.

Cambodia

As the recent message from Prince Sihanouk has reminded us, the continuing Cambodian conflict and the suffering of the Cambodian people is of deep concern. We join the vast majority of the nations of the world in calling for the prompt withdrawal of all Vietnamese troops. We support a political settlement in Cambodia which will provide for Cambodian self-determination and lead to the re-emergence of a free and independent Cambodia.

Note: The summary was not issued as a White House press release.

Toronto Economic Summit Conference Economic Declaration
June 21, 1988

1. We, the Heads of State or Government of seven major industrial nations and the President of the Commission of the European Communities, have met in Toronto for the fourteenth annual Economic Summit. We have drawn lessons from the past and looked ahead to the future.

2. Over the past fourteen years, the world economy and economic policy have undergone profound changes. In particular, the information-technology revolution and the globalization of markets have increased economic interdependence, making it essential that governments consider fully the international dimensions of their deliberations.

3. We observed a sharp contrast between the 1970s and 1980s. The former was a decade of high and rising inflation, declining productivity growth, policies dominated by short-term considerations, and frequently inadequate international policy cooperation. In the 1980s inflation has been brought under control, laying the basis for sustained strong growth and improved productivity. The result has been the longest period of economic growth in post-war history. However, the 1980s have seen the emergence of large external imbalances in the major industrial economies, greater exchange rate volatility, and debt-servicing difficulties in a number of developing countries. Our response to these developments has been an increased commitment to international cooperation, resulting in the intensified process of policy coordination adopted at the 1986 Tokyo Summit and further strengthened at the Venice Summit and in the Group of Seven.

4. Summits have proven an effective forum to address the issues facing the world economy, promote new ideas and develop a common sense of purpose. Especially in the 1980s they have helped bring about an increasing recognition that the eradication of inflation and of inflationary expectations is fundamental to sustained growth and job creation. That recognition has been underpinned by a shift from short-term considerations to a medium-term framework for the development and implementation of economic policies, and a commitment to improve efficiency and adaptability through greater reliance on competitive forces and structural reform. Over this period we have also singled out for concerted attention a number of other issues of decisive importance: the overriding need to resist protectionism and strengthen the open, multilateral trading system; to maintain and strengthen an effective strategy to address the challenge of development and alleviate the burden of debt; and to deal with the serious nature of the world agricultural problem.

5. Since we last met, our economies have kept up the momentum of growth. Employment has continued to expand generally, inflation has been restrained, and progress has been made toward the correction of major external imbalances. These encouraging developments are cause for optimism, but not for complacency. To sustain non-inflationary growth will require a commitment to enhanced cooperation. This is the key to credibility and confidence.

International Economic Policy Cooperation

Macroeconomic Policies and Exchange Rates

6. The Tokyo and Venice Summits have developed and strengthened the process of coordination of our economic policies. Developments in the wake of the financial strains last October demonstrate the effectiveness and resilience of the arrangements that have emerged. The policies, the short-term prospects, and the medium-term objectives and projections of our economies are being discussed regularly in the Group of Seven. The policies and performance are assessed on the basis of economic indicators. We welcome the progress made in refining the analytical use of indicators, as well as the addition to the existing indicators of a commodity-price indicator. The progress in coordination is contributing to the process

of further improving the functioning of the international monetary system.

7. Fiscal, monetary and structural policies have been undertaken to foster the adjustment to more sustainable economic and financial positions in the context of non-inflationary growth. Efforts in those directions, including continued reduction of budgetary deficits, will continue. We need to maintain vigilance against any resurgence of inflation. We reaffirm our determination to follow and, wherever feasible, strengthen our agreed strategy of coordinated efforts to reduce the growth of spending in countries with large external deficits and to sustain the momentum of domestic demand in those with large external surpluses. The reduction of large external imbalances, however, will require not only our cooperative efforts, but also those of smaller economies, including newly industrializing economies, with large external surpluses.

8. The exchange rate changes in the past three years, especially the depreciation of the U.S. dollar against the Japanese yen and the major European currencies, have played a major role in the adjustment of real trade balances. We endorse the Group of Seven's conclusion that either excessive fluctuation of exchange rates, a further decline of the dollar, or a rise in the dollar to an extent that becomes destabilizing to the adjustment process, could be counterproductive by damaging growth prospects in the world economy.

Structural Reforms

9. International cooperation involves more than coordination of macroeconomic policies. Structural reforms complement macroeconomic policies, enhance their effectiveness, and provide the basis for more robust growth. We shall collectively review our progress on structural reforms and shall strive to integrate structural policies into our economic coordination process.

10. We will continue to pursue structural reforms by removing barriers, unnecessary controls and regulations; increasing competition, while mitigating adverse effects on social groups or regions; removing disincentives to work, save, and invest, such as through tax reform; and by improving education and training. The specific priorities that each of us has identified are outlined in the attached Annex on Structural Reforms.

11. We welcome the further development of the OECD's surveillance of structural reforms. Such surveillance would be particularly useful in improving public understanding of the reforms by revealing their impact on government budgets, consumer prices, and international trade.

12. One of the major structural problems in both developed and developing countries is in the field of agricultural policies. It is essential that recent significant policy reform efforts undertaken by a number of parties be continued through further positive action by all Summit participants. More market-oriented agricultural policies should assist in the achievement of important objectives such as preserving rural areas and family farming, raising quality standards and protecting the environment. We welcome the OECD's increased emphasis on structural adjustment and development in the rural economy.

13. Financial and technological innovations are rapidly integrating financial markets internationally, contributing to a better allocation of capital but also increasing the speed and extent to which disturbances in one country may be transmitted to other countries. We will continue to cooperate with other countries in the examination of the functioning of the global financial system, including securities markets.

MULTILATERAL TRADING SYSTEM/URUGUAY ROUND

14. A successful Uruguay Round will assure the integrity of an open, predictable multilateral trading system based on clear rules and will lead to trade expansion and enhanced economic growth. At Punta del Este, Ministers committed themselves to further trade liberalization across the wide range of goods and services, including such new areas as trade-related intellectual property and trade-related investment measures, to strengthen the multilateral trading system, and to allow for early agreements where appropriate. Countries must continue to resist protectionism and the temptation to adopt unilateral measures outside the framework of GATT rules. In order to

preserve a favourable negotiating climate, the participants should conscientiously implement the commitments to standstill and rollback that they have taken at Punta del Este and subsequent international meetings.

15. We strongly welcome the Free Trade Agreement between Canada and the USA, and the steady progress towards the target of the European Community to complete the internal market by 1992. It is our policy that these developments, together with other moves towards regional cooperation in which our countries are involved, should support the open, multilateral trading system and catalyze the liberalizing impact of the Uruguay Round.

16. We attach major importance to strengthening the GATT itself. It is vital that the GATT become a more dynamic and effective organization, particularly in regard to the surveillance of trade policies and dispute settlement procedures, with greater Ministerial involvement, and strengthened linkages with other international organizations. GATT disciplines must be improved so that members accept their obligations and ensure that disputes are resolved speedily, effectively and equitably.

17. Trade plays a key role in development. We encourage the developing countries, especially the newly industrializing economies, to undertake increased commitments and obligations and a greater role in the GATT, commensurate with their importance in international trade and in the international adjustment process, as well as with their respective stages of development. Equally, developed countries should continue to strive to ensure more open markets for the exports of developing countries.

18. In agriculture, continued political impetus is essential to underpin the politically difficult efforts at domestic policy reform and to advance the equally difficult and related process of agricultural trade reform. Although significant progress was made in 1987 in the Uruguay Round negotiations, with the tabling of major proposals, it is necessary to ensure that the Mid-Term Review in Montreal in December, 1988 adds impetus to the negotiations in this as in other fields. We support efforts to adopt a framework approach, including short as well as long-term elements which will promote the reform process as launched last year and relieve current strains in agricultural markets. This would be facilitated by a device for the measurement of support and protection. Also, ways should be developed to take account of food security and social concerns. To move the issue forward, and noting among other things the diversity of our agricultural situations, our negotiators in Geneva must develop a framework approach which includes short-term options in line with long-term goals concerning the reduction of all direct and indirect subsidies and other measures affecting directly or indirectly agricultural trade. The objective of the framework approach would be to make the agricultural sector more responsive to market signals.

19. As the Uruguay Round enters a more difficult phase, it is vital to ensure the momentum of these ambitious negotiations. The Mid-Term Review will provide a unique opportunity to send a credible political signal to the trading world. The greatest possible advance must be made in all areas of the negotiations, including, where appropriate, decisions, so as to reach before the end of the year the stage where tangible progress can be registered. To this end, we support efforts to adopt a framework approach on all issues in the negotiations, i.e. reform of the GATT system and rules, market access, agriculture and new issues (such as trade in services, trade-related intellectual property rights, and trade-related investment measures). For our part, we are committed to ensure that the Mid-Term Review establishes a solid base for the full and complete success of the negotiations, in accordance with the Punta del Este Declaration.

20. We all recognize the critical and expanding role of international investment in the world economy and share a deep concern that increased protectionism would undermine the benefits of open investment policies. We resolve to progressively liberalize international investment policies and urge other countries to do likewise.

Newly Industrializing Economies

21. Certain newly-industrializing econo-

mies (NIEs) in the Asia-Pacific region have become increasingly important in world trade. Although these economies differ in many important respects, they are all characterized by dynamic, export-led growth which has allowed them to treble their share of world trade since 1960. Other outward-oriented Asian countries are also beginning to emerge as rapidly-growing exporters of manufactures. With increased economic importance come greater international responsibilities and a strong mutual interest in improved constructive dialogue and cooperative efforts in the near term between the industrialized countries and the Asian NIEs, as well as the other outward-oriented countries in the region. The dialogue and cooperative efforts could centre on such policy areas as macroeconomic, currency, structural and trade to achieve the international adjustment necessary for sustained, balanced growth of the world economy. We encourage the development of informal processes which would facilitate multilateral discussions of issues of mutual concern and foster the necessary cooperation.

Developing Countries and Debt

22. The performance of developing countries is increasingly important to the world economy. Central to the prospects of the developing countries are a healthy global economic environment and an open trading system, adequate financial flows and, most important, their commitment to appropriate economic reform. The problems of many heavily-indebted developing countries are a cause of economic and political concern and can be a threat to political stability in developing countries. Several countries find themselves in that situation in various regions of the world: Latin America, Africa and the Pacific, particularly the Philippines, and that merits our special attention.

Middle-Income Countries

23. A number of highly-indebted middle-income countries continue to have difficulties servicing their external debt and generating the investment necessary for sustainable growth. The market-oriented, growth-led strategy based on the case-by-case approach remains the only viable approach for overcoming their external debt problems.

24. We are encouraged that many indebted countries have begun the difficult process of macroeconomic adjustment and structural reform necessary for sustained progress, encouraging the return of flight capital and new investment flows. The success of these efforts is essential for improving the economic performance and strengthening the creditworthiness of these countries.

25. Official financing has played a central role in the debt strategy through the Paris Club (US $73 billion of principal and interest have been consolidated since 1983) and the flexible policies of export credit agencies. The international financial institutions will continue to have a pivotal role. We endorse the recent initiatives taken by the International Monetary Fund to strengthen its capacity to support medium-term programs of macroeconomic adjustment and structural reform and to provide greater protection for adjustment programs from unforeseen external developments. We strongly support the full implementation of the World Bank's US $75 billion General Capital Increase to strengthen its capacity to promote adjustment in middle-income countries. We also support greater awareness by international financial institutions of the environmental impact of their development programs.

26. Commercial banks have played an important role in supporting debtor countries' reform efforts through an expanded menu of financing options which has facilitated the channelling of commercial bank lending into productive uses. Their continued involvement is indispensable to the debt strategy. In this regard, the World Bank and IMF can play an important catalytic role in mobilizing additional financing from private (and official) sources in support of debtor countries' adjustment programs.

27. We note that in recent years there has been increasing recourse to innovative financing techniques. The important characteristics of these techniques are that they are voluntary, market-oriented, and applied on a case-by-case basis. The "menu ap-

proach" has engendered new financial flows and, in some cases, reduced the existing stock of debt. The flexibility of the present strategy would be enhanced by the further broadening of the menu approach and the encouragement of innovative financing techniques to improve the quality of new lending, but particular initiatives would have to be carefully considered.

28. International direct investment plays an important role in spurring economic growth and structural adjustment in developing countries. Thus it contributes to alleviating debt problems. Developing countries should welcome and encourage such investment by creating a favourable investment climate.

Debt of the Poorest

29. An increase in concessional resource flows is necessary to help the poorest developing countries resume sustained growth, especially in cases where it is extremely difficult for them to service their debts. Since Venice, progress in dealing with the debt burden of these countries has been encouraging. Paris Club creditors are rescheduling debt at extended grace and repayment periods. In addition, the recent enhancement of the IMF's Structural Adjustment Facility; the World Bank and Official Development Assistance (ODA) agencies' enhanced program of co-financing; and the fifth replenishment of the African Development Fund will mobilize a total of more than US $18 billion in favour of the poorest and most indebted countries undertaking adjustment efforts over the period 1988/90. Out of this total, US $15 billion will be channelled to sub-Saharan African countries.

30. We welcome proposals made by several of us to ease further the debt service burdens of the poorest countries that are undertaking internationally-approved adjustment programs. We have achieved consensus on rescheduling official debt of these countries within a framework of comparability that allows official creditors to choose among concessional interest rates usually on shorter maturities, longer repayment periods at commercial rates, partial write-offs of debt service obligations during the consolidation period, or a combination of these options. This approach allows official creditors to choose options consistent with their legal or budgetary constraints. The Paris Club has been urged to work out necessary technicalities to ensure comparability by the end of this year at the very latest. This approach will provide benefits over and above the impressive multilateral agreements to help the poorest countries over the past year. We also welcome the action taken by a number of creditor governments to write-off or otherwise remove the burden of ODA loans, and also urge countries to maintain a high grant element in their future assistance to the poorest.

Environment

31. We agree that the protection and enhancement of the environment is essential. The report of the World Commission on Environment and Development has stressed that environmental considerations must be integrated into all areas of economic policy-making if the globe is to continue to support humankind. We endorse the concept of sustainable development.

32. Threats to the environment recognize no boundaries. Their urgent nature requires strengthened international cooperation among all countries. Significant progress has been achieved in a number of environmental areas. The Montreal Protocol on Substances that Deplete the Ozone Layer is a milestone. All countries are encouraged to sign and ratify it.

33. Further action is needed. Global climate change, air, sea and fresh water pollution, acid rain, hazardous substances, deforestation, and endangered species require priority attention. It is, therefore, timely that negotiations on a protocol on emissions of nitrogen oxides within the framework of the Geneva Convention on Long-range Transboundary Air Pollution be pursued energetically. The efforts of the United Nations Environment Program (UNEP) for an agreement on the transfrontier shipment of hazardous wastes should also be encouraged as well as the establishment of an intergovernmental panel on global climate change under the auspices of UNEP and the World Meteorological Organization (WMO). We also recognize the potential impact of agriculture on the environment,

whether negative through over-intensive use of resources or positive in preventing desertification. We welcome the Conference on the Changing Atmosphere to be held in Toronto next week.

FUTURE SUMMITS

34. We, the Heads of State or Government, and the representatives of the European Community, believe that the Economic Summits have strengthened the ties of solidarity, both political and economic, that exist between our countries and that thereby they have helped to sustain the values of democracy that underlie our economic and political systems. Our annual meetings have provided the principal opportunity each year for the governments of the major industrialized countries to reflect, in an informal and flexible manner, upon their common responsibility for the progress of the world economy and to resolve how that responsibility should have practical manifestation in the years ahead. We believe that the mutual understanding engendered in our meetings has benefitted both our own countries and the wider world community. We believe, too, that the opportunities afforded by our meetings are becoming even more valuable in today's world of increasing interdependence and increasing technological change. We have therefore agreed to institute a further cycle of Summits by accepting the invitation of the President of the French Republic to meet in France, July 14-16, 1989.

OTHER ISSUES

Human Frontier Science Program

1. We note the successful conclusion of Japan's feasibility study on the Human Frontier Science Program and are grateful for the opportunities our scientists were given to contribute to the study. We look forward to the Japanese Government's proposal for the implementation of the program in the near future.

Bioethics

2. We note that, as part of the continuing review of the ethical implications of developments in the life sciences, the Italian Government hosted the fifth conference on bioethics in April 1988, and we welcome the intention of the European Communities to host the sixth conference in the spring of 1989.

ANNEX ON STRUCTURAL REFORMS

—Europe is pursuing structural reforms to complement macroeconomic policies in order to spur job creation, enhance growth potential, and achieve a sustainable pattern of external balances. Structural reform measures are being put into place in the framework of the Communities' program for a unified internal market by 1992; including full liberalization of capital movements; removal of physical, administrative and technical barriers to allow the full mobility of persons, goods and services and an improvement of competition policy. However, full achievement will depend on complete and timely implementation of the measures and on complementary policies including those in the fields of regional, social and environmental policies and of technological co-operation.

—The main elements of Germany's structural reforms are tax reform and reduction, deregulation and privatization, reform of the postal and telecommunication system, increased flexibility in the labour market, and reform of the social security system.

—In France, the main structural reforms will deal with improving the level of education and professional training and development for workers, and with major improvements in the functioning of financial markets in order to facilitate the financing of the economy at the lowest possible cost.

—Italy will seek to promote training and education, increase the flexibility of the labour market to spur employment, improve the functioning of financial markets, revise the tax system to promote efficiency and eliminate distortions, and enhance public sector efficiency.

—In the United Kingdom, there has already been a substantial program of tax reform, trade union law reform, deregulation, opening up of markets and privatization of state industries. This will continue. Further measures are being introduced to improve both the quality of education and the flexibility of the housing market.

—Japan will pursue further structural reforms to support and sustain the greater reliance on domestic demand-led growth which has quickened remarkably. Japan will promote reform of government regulations in key sectors including land use policies and the distribution system, and reform of the tax system.

—For the United States, where recent indications that the declining trend in private savings may have bottomed out are encouraging, it is nonetheless a priority to increase incentives to save. Also the United States will strengthen the international competitiveness of its industrial sector.

—The most promising areas of structural reform in Canada are implementation of the second stage of tax reform, the proposed liberalization of the financial services sector, and, most important, the implementation of the Free Trade Agreement with the United States.

Note: The declaration was not issued as a White House press release.

The President's News Conference in Toronto, Canada
June 21, 1988

The President. I have a little statement here first I'd like to impose on you. This will be before taking questions.

Today's ceremonies, as you know, mark the end of my eighth economic summit. And over the years, I've come to regard the summit process as extremely important in forging a coordinated economic approach for the United States and the other industrialized democracies. It's helped return the nations represented here to steady growth and helped to establish a consensus among us that only free and open markets and only free and open societies foster economic progress and opportunity.

Maybe one of the best ways to view these economic summits is to compare discussions at them, whether heralded in our communiques or not, with later results. For example, our 1981 communique from Ottawa said the primary challenge we addressed at this meeting was the need to revitalize the economies of the industrial democracies. Revitalization, of course, has been achieved in part because the common commitment at Ottawa inaugurated a search for consensus on how to work together to release the productive energies of our peoples. And today gross national products are growing, as are employment numbers and real personal incomes. Our economic expansion in the United States got the ball rolling and helped crystallize the new consensus. And now everyone is part of the act.

To take another example, in our 1986 Tokyo economic communique, we said there should be close and continuous coordination of economic policy among the seven summit countries. Today policy coordination is a major pillar of the economic policies of all our countries. It's a significant reason why the world market instable—instabilities, I should say, of last October had so little impact on our underlying economies. The summit in Tokyo gave the political push that ensured that the fledgling process of coordination grew strong and robust.

So, here we are celebrating this summit with a measure of pride. Some significant items are still in need of attention, but all in all, how things have changed over the years! The economies of the summit countries have come roaring back, driven by a common commitment to replace government control with market-oriented policies. These summits are building blocks for tomorrow. Goals we set in earlier years have borne fruit. I believe that the goals we're setting now will become the landmarks for the future.

Looking back at how much has been achieved since the last time the summit was in Canada, is it any wonder that our seven free democratic industrialized nations are turning with confidence to the future, to the challenges and opportunities that new technology, more closely knit global markets, and a free world will bring in working together.

During our meetings here, we discussed the international economic and political situation. We reviewed the economic policy coordination process; the world debt situation, particularly that of the poorer countries; the state of the Uruguay round of trade negotiations, particularly in agriculture; and international cooperation to stop the production and flow of illegal drugs. We also had a fruitful exchange of views on East-West relations, terrorism, and regional political issues.

Yesterday afternoon Prime Minister Mulroney organized an informal session, where leaders shared their thoughts on the economic future of the summit countries. In that session, I said that I believe that the expansion of global markets and the enormous technological advances that are coming in the years ahead will demand even closer coordination of economic policies. All of our economies must be flexible and open, not burdened by excessive regulations, high taxes, and all the other rigidities that too many economies have known too well.

Last night my colleagues and I spoke of the future; of the education of our children; of assisting those displaced by the rapid pace of economic change, most notably our farmers; of removing structural impediments in our economies so that we're all flexible enough to meet the challenges of the rapid technological changes and economic integration that is the hallmark of the future.

The summit nations can be partners in a great "venture to progress." Yes, we can seize our opportunities, or we can watch the world go by. I'm confident which path our nations will choose. As I said before leaving Washington, the future belongs to the flexible. Eight years ago, you'd have heard arguments about that; today it defines the consensus among the seven nations that meet at these economic summits.

And finally in closing, let me say thank you to the people of Toronto and to Prime Minister Mulroney for hosting us with such courtesy and enthusiasm. They made all of us in the American delegation, and I'm confident those in the other delegations as well, feel right at home. After just 3 days here, we share one common sentiment: We love Canada!

So, thank you, and Terry [Terence Hunt, Associated Press], tee off.

Defense Department Investigation

Q. Mr. President, I want to ask you about the investigation of corruption at the Pentagon. Caspar Weinberger, your former Defense Secretary, says that perhaps the Defense Department wasn't as vigilant as it should have been. Do you share any responsibility for that, sir, or feel any sense of failure or disappointment?

The President. Well, I think all of us are disappointed and upset that such things could happen. I think that Cap Weinberger was just being—or trying to join in here. I think he was one of the finest Secretaries of Defense this country has had, and I think he was doing all that he could to bring a national security out of chaos—the kind that we inherited. For him to take some responsibility—of course, he was heading up there, and I suppose I could do the same thing. Except that you have to look at what is being unveiled here. That one tip came from one individual, and immediately the Naval intelligence—or investigative unit began an investigation based on that single tip and then called for help from the Federal Bureau of Investigation. They joined in, and for 2 years they've been tracking this down to, finally, the place where they have come to the point in which they feel they can serve indictments.

And I have to say that I think it should be understandable how such things can happen in something as big as our government is. But I think we also ought to recognize that within our government—and the minute there was one tip of something of that nature was going on, the units to which we entrust such things, this Naval unit and the FBI, set to work and now is ready to act.

Q. How much ammunition do you think that this gives Michael Dukakis on the so-called sleaze factor?

The President. I don't think it really gives him any at all. I don't think this is a case apparently at high levels. I think the very fact that it was investigated—let me just point something out: that there's almost an accusation in the fact of why didn't some of us know. I think the tip that came and the investigation that was started reflected that there wasn't anyone, up to and including me, that the investigators could feel free to inform of this. They had no idea where this leveled off or how far it went or how high it went. So, they set out keeping their own decisions to themselves and investigated. And now they have come forth with this, and some of us have been notified now about what was going on. But I think they were proper—the danger of leaks and everything else and not knowing where this investigation might take them—to do just as they did.

Helen [Helen Thomas, United Press International]?

Q. Mr. President, you didn't know about the divergence of funds, you say, in the Iran-*contra* scandal. Weinberger doesn't know about all of this alleged rampant bribery, fraud. Who's in charge? I mean, where does the buck stop? Why aren't you accountable to the public trust? And I'd like to follow up.

The President. We are accountable. On the other hand, I think there are some things you can see. And something as complex as that whole process and the number of corporations and all—corporate heads probably are surprised at what they're learning also—because you can't be down there watching several million people and the total of all of the companies and of the Defense Department every day, and what they're doing, or what phone calls they're making. And I'm quite sure that no one would think that we should be tapping all of those phones and listening in on conversations of everybody just on the suspicion that someone might be out of line.

Admiral Poindexter and Colonel North

Q. Mr. President, in terms of the scandals, Senator Mitchell has asked that you specifically—that you not pardon Colonel North [former National Security Council staff member] and Admiral Poindexter [former Assistant to the President for National Security Affairs] before they are tried, because he said that otherwise there might be a perception of purchasing silence. Are you willing to give that commitment?

The President. Well, I have said already that while I don't think that those men were guilty of any lawbreaking of any kind—but of course, the new case has to go forward, or they would live the rest of their lives under a shadow of guilt. So, I have no intention of—now, wait a minute! Let me move back for some of our visitors.

The gentleman right——

Drought

Q. Mr. President, do you plan a visit to the areas of the country that have been afflicted by the drought and recognized just by the drought? Do you plan a visit to the drought areas of the country, sir? And recognizing that your Interagency Committee on the Drought has not made its report, could you give us an idea what specific steps you are considering to help the farmers in view of the drought?

The President. Oh, well, here the Secretary of Agriculture has taken his place, and we have a task force out there, taking a firsthand look at the situation. And we're going to have to see what we can do. We don't underestimate the seriousness of this at all. And I'm here in this summit; they're out there finding out. And outside of praying for rain, there isn't anything I can do until we hear from them.

Q. If I may follow up sir: Are you planning to visit the drought area yourself and take a firsthand look yourself?

The President. That's going to depend on whether the task force sees that there might be any value in doing that.

Defense Department Investigation

Q. Thank you, Mr. President. You suggested the other day, and you seem to be suggesting today, that the Pentagon scandal is just the case of a few people gone wrong. But in fact there are 200 subpoenas out in this case. A number of the top procurement officers of the Pentagon are under investigation, and so are almost all of the top defense contractors. Isn't the greater likelihood that this is a very widespread scandal?

The President. Oh, listen, I'm aware of the numbers, and if I gave that impression that this is minor in some way—not at all. I don't feel that way at all. As a matter of fact, I'm very upset. The only thing I'm calling attention to is that that same Department, the Department of Defense, is the one that uncovered and then proceeded to investigate and pin down where there was guilt. But we now have to wait and find out under the due process of law that it definitely is guilt on individuals' part. There may be some people that are falsely suspected, and we should know that, too. But, no, I'm not taking this lightly at all. But I do think that you all ought to pay attention to the fact that it wasn't an outside investigation.

Q. If I may follow up, sir: It's been suggested that contracts with some of these defense contractors may have to be suspended until the investigation proves out. Are you concerned about the impact on the national security, either in terms of slowing down the defense buildup or the further erosion of support for your defense buildup?

The President. Well, I'm concerned about anything that affects our national security. At the same time, however, I recognize that we have established a national security system that we didn't have a few years ago and that we have produced enough strength that resulted in things like the INF treaty with a potential adversary, the Soviet Union. And that has to be taken into account, too. But I haven't seen any—we can't judge yet whether there's something specific in all of these things that might have in some way lessened the recovery of our defensive strength.

I'm looking for somebody from the local press, and then I'll come back down front.

Savings and Loan Industry

Q. Mr. President, I'd like to ask about the savings and loan industry. This year there were record losses in the industry. Close to $4 billion has been spent bailing out savings and loans. It's estimated that it will take $75 billion to get it on its feet. Is there a crisis in the savings and loan industry, and will the American taxpayer have to bail it out?

The President. Well, I certainly hope not, and I don't think so. And I don't believe there's a crisis. The market today went up 25 points, and our growth is still continuing, and there's no sign of inflation and things of that kind—or panic. But, yes, there is a problem there, and we're trying to deal with the problem.

Sam [Sam Donaldson, ABC News]?

Gun Control

Q. Mr. President, recently, Washington columnist Carl Rowan believed he was threatened by people in his backyard. He took a gun which was unregistered, and he shot—he said as a warning shot. A young man was nicked in the wrist. Do you think it's a good idea for citizens to have guns in their home and to go out and to use them if they feel threatened?

The President. Well, Sam, as I understand it, what Carl was saying was that his son, who was entitled to have a gun, left that gun there and it was a registered gun with regard to his son. On the other hand, I try to keep thinking this was 2 o'clock in the morning. Someone is coming toward him. He had that—but you asked the question in general, not just about him. You asked whether people should have—Sam, I'm going to answer by way of a letter, a very interesting letter that I received when I was Governor of California.

It came from a burglar who was serving time in San Quentin prison. And there was a big movement on in California at that time, as there continually is everyplace, to eliminate the citizens having weapons. And this burglar, prisoner, wrote to me and said, "I just want to tell you that if that goes through, that law, there will be hundreds of very happy people here in San Quentin." He said, "We case a place that we've planned for robbery or burglary. We get to know the habits of the people and their comings and goings and so forth." But he said, "The one thing we never can know in advance is in that household, in a drawer by the bed, does the householder have a gun." And he says, "If you can ever tell us that none of them do, that they don't have them, then I can assure you that all us burglars are going to be very happy." I think we ought to pay heed to that.

Q. Well, sir, is it worth it? Statistics show that when homeowners or citizens use handguns, normally they shoot themselves, their loved ones, or strangers who are not engaged in a criminal act by mistake. Is it worth all these lives in order to attempt to try to shoot one burglar?

The President. Well, Sam, I'll tell you, there's some certain things I would go for. For example, in California, for a citizen to buy a gun, that citizen has to come in and lay down the money, of course, name, address, and so forth, and then doesn't get the gun. And this goes to an agency in the State Government that looks into that person's entire background as to who and what they are, and then they come back after that investigation, and if they don't have a record of any crimes or mental problems or anything of that kind, they are allowed to take their gun home. Now, I would like to see that generally, and I think that all States ought to take a look at that system. But in addition, I think that maybe we could tie to that making sure that they aren't just totally absent of any knowledge of weapons. I taught my entire family out at the Ranch how to shoot a gun in case they ever had to. And I think maybe there could be some restrictions, that there had to be a certain amount of training taken.

Now let me—here, and then back to you. No, no, Lou [Lou Cannon, Washington Post]. Now, don't you sit. You get up, yes. [*Laughter*] No, and then I'll take him.

Q. My name is Jerry O'Leary [Washington Times], and I'm——

The President. I know, Jerry.

Situation in Panama

Q. Mr. President, have you given up on doing anything forceful about the continuing chaos in Panama and Nicaragua and now, once again, in Haiti since you have not used up all of your options, including the option of military force? And is there any prospect at all in the rest of your administration for resuming military assistance to the resistance fighters?

The President. Well, Jerry, on the first thing of Panama, I have to say to you that there are many things I can't comment, that we still have some of our economic measures in place. We still feel, as we always did, that a military dictatorship in Panama under General Noriega is not what we want to see continue, but I can't speculate or even hint at what might be options that are being considered or anything of that kind because I just don't think it would be suitable and I don't think it would be helpful. But we have not changed our minds about the fact that Panama should return to a civilian democracy.

Michael S. Dukakis

Q. What did you mean when you said today when you were asked if Mr. Dukakis would win, and you said, "over my live body."

The President. Well, because the old expression is "my dead body," and I wouldn't want somebody to take me up on that. [*Laughter*]

The gentleman back there.

Canada-U.S. Relations

Q. If I could ask briefly about the economic summit—[*laughter*]—the communique——

The President. I was all set for that, too.

Q. The communique praises the Canadian-American free trade deal. If for whatever reason the deal doesn't go through, what would that do to Canadian-American relations?

The President. Well, I certainly don't think it would change the relationship that the Prime Minister and I have. And I also don't think that it would do away with the friendship that exists between Americans and Canadians. We're pretty unique in the world. There's no place quite like—well, there isn't any place like this—5,000 miles of border, as your Prime Minister has said, without a loaded gun along that border. I think we're very proud of that.

And I've had an idea here. I know that in your Parliament there are critics; there are in our Congress. And I've had it figured out that if I could get what the critics in the Parliament are saying about maybe this bill favoring the United States and take it down and show it to our Congress, and in turn send what our Congress are saying about this favoring Canada up here to the Parliament, I think it would be passed in a minute and a half. And I'm not going to do that, but I'm optimistic that we can get it. And I think it will have an effect on the entire trade of the world. We are the two biggest trading partners in the world. And for us to establish the biggest free trading area in the world is right in keeping with all the things that we've been doing.

Iran Arms and Contra Aid Controversy

Q. Mr. President, during the Iran-*contra* scandal, America learned that there were people in the White House making foreign policy, in effect, without your knowledge and that of some of your other senior officials. Now we have the situation in the Pentagon, sir, where there is apparently a burgeoning scandal which happened without the knowledge of you or your Secretary of Defense. Reflecting on this, sir, have you thought that you might have changed your style of management? Would you wish to have had a more hands-on approach now that you're at the end of your term? Would that have changed things? Would it have helped?

The President. I don't think it would have changed anything in this present situation at all. I don't think there's any way that anyone at higher levels could have had access to this information on what was going on. With regard to the Iran-*contra* affair, I would just like—I haven't had a chance to do this for a long time—I'd like to remind you all that I'm the one who told all of you of what had just been discovered. And it was discovered after the leak came out of a newspaper in Lebanon, charging the trading of hostages for arms and that I was dealing with the Ayatollah. Let me say with great emphasis and to all the rest of you who aren't as close to Washington as some of the people here: There's no scandal.

We were not doing business with the Ayatollah. We were keeping the operation covert because—by way of a third country—some individuals from Iran who were heeding the warnings that we were being given at about that time that the Ayatollah might not live out the week and there was factionalism rising as to who was going to have to do with the new government. These individuals, we were assured, were pretty responsible by that third country, which—much closer to the situation. And they wanted to meet to discuss with us what might be the future relations between our two countries when the Ayatollah was gone, and I sent a team. Now, you couldn't send the Secretary of State or people of that kind there because it wouldn't be covert any longer—they're recognizable. I don't mean that he'd tell. [*Laughter*] He's just—you know, he can't be anonymous anymore, or people like him.

But anyway, we sent them there to make contact, and now back came this request from them that what it would do for them in the event of forming new government and so forth—more or less—token shipment of a type of weapon. I sent word back that we didn't do business with countries that supported terrorism. Well, they sent back reminding us that they weren't representing the country; they weren't that government. And they wouldn't, if they were—be a government—they wouldn't do these things. And so, then was when I sent word back and said, well, all right, but I know that there are connections in Iran with the Hizballah [radical terrorist group in Lebanon] who are holding American hostages. We'll do this if you will use your influence, if you have any, to see if you can get our hostages back. And they said yes.

Well, they got two of them back, and we were supposed to get two more within 48 hours. Now, all of this I told to you when, after it broke and the news had broken that we were doing this, our own investigation began and we found one memorandum that indicated that there was more money than we had received for our weapons. We got the money that we had coming to us, but suddenly we had—and I told you that, and that we were trying to find out, and that I was appointing a commission under Senator Tower to find out how could there be additional money there. And after all the months of investigation by the Congress, I still haven't found out how there was extra money.

Q. Well, sir, if you had kept a tighter rein on what was going on and inquired more closely into what was happening in this and in other situations, might it not have happened?

The President. I don't see how I could have without endangering the people we were doing business with. If they were identified, they could be executed. They weren't representing the Government, and to tell you the truth, I don't know whether they're alive today. And as a matter of fact, when this all broke, one of our hostages had just been released, Jacobsen, and he pled with you one day out in the Rose Garden at that time to please not talk about this because we could get some people killed.

Defense Management and Spending

Q. Mr. President, but in this case, you have said that Cap Weinberger helped take the national security out of chaos. Can you really disagree with both Republicans and Democrats who are saying that your administration threw so much money at the Pentagon and hired people to manage it who were hired for their conservative values rather than their management skills, and that in this administration there was a different structural approach to controlling the spending of these billions of dollars?

The President. No, I don't believe that or agree with it. And they were appointed because of their business skill. I had made statements many times during the campaign that I didn't want people that were out looking for a job in government. I wanted people that would make a sacrifice to work for government, then take them for as long as they could stay there. And this we did. But with regard to throwing this money at the Pentagon, I'd like to call your attention to something.

When I took office, on any given day, 50 percent of our military planes couldn't take off for lack of spare parts and fuel. Half of our naval vessels couldn't leave port for the same reason, or in addition, and lack of crew. I had promised during the campaign in answer to questions from just people in audiences over and over again that with regard to deficit spending and all—where did this figure, the military thing—and I said, if it comes to a choice, the prime responsibility of government is the defense of the Nation. I have to do that. But I would like to call attention to this fact. President Carter evidently realized the situation before he left office. And as you know, a President leaving office gives you a 5-year projection of his plan—what his budget—the first budget when I came in was passed by the previous President, but then, where it goes. We have not yet spent as much money on defense as he had advocated should be spent for the next 5 years.

Q. But, sir, how do you feel about the fact that, even though you pride yourself on cutting government spending and regulations, that the legacy you may well leave is a counterreaction, where there is an erosion of public support for defense spending and a public reaction that actually hurts rather than helps national security?

The President. Well, you're just saying some things that—I don't know how I would answer that. But I think if people will listen and get the explanation and exactly what the situation was and wait until the facts are in, for example, on this particular investigation, that I don't think that they will find that we were derelict in our duty.

Now, there's a young lady just there.

Value of the U.S. Dollar

Q. Thank you, Mr. President. Was there any concern when you met with summit leaders this week that higher interest rates in the United States would push the dollar too high?

The President. I don't recall any conversation of that kind. All of us have been feeling pretty confident of what we're doing and the stability we have and——

Q. So, the dollar is on the right track?

The President. I think we have stability right now, and I'm afraid to look at Jim Baker—[*laughter*]—because I might find myself asking him to answer the question for you.

Drug Trafficking and Interdiction

Q. Mr. President, what do you really think you've really achieved in terms of drug interdiction here? How many drug traffickers are going to be apprehended as a result of these deliberations?

The President. Well, more have been apprehended in this past year or so than ever before. And more thousands of, literally, tons of illegal drugs seized, more airplanes, more ships, more trucks and automobiles, and more money has been seized than ever before. But we have come to the conclusion, with boundaries like ours and coastlines like ours, the only answer that is ever going to win this war for us—we keep this up; we keep doing that, of course—but the real answer is going to be a bigger effort at taking the customer away from the drugs. That's why we're going to implement all the programs we can about appealing to the people and getting former drug addicts who are—many of them in the entertainment world and the athletic world are doing more than their duty to speak to young people about their ex—they're exaddicts and about this. But that is going to be the only way we can really succeed. But we have stepped up this interception thing, and I think more than has ever been intercepted before.

Q. Is the course of it by national arrangements rather than multinational, do you think?

The President. Oh, well, you're talking about the summit and our—oh, well, listen, we were all in agreement here. And I think we've discussed this today, and we thought of a number of things. And we're going to be working on this and putting a team together that will represent more than us. We're going to do such things, and we're agreed. And we're going to do such things as tracking money, and interfering with the laundering of illegal drug money and so forth. So, we are united on this; there's no question about that.

Well, wait a minute—for all the hands. Helen's in charge, and she tells me I've used up all my time. I can't do it. So, I'm sorry. I'm always sorry I have to leave hands that——

Situation in Haiti

Q. ——talk to you about Haiti after this week. Have you found out anything more about the situation there?

The President. I thought you already all knew everything about it because you didn't ask me any questions about it.

Note: The President's news conference began at 5:30 p.m. in the ballroom at the Royal York Hotel.

Remarks to Members of the Empire and Canadian Clubs in Toronto, Canada

June 21, 1988

Thank you all very much, and, Brian, I thank you from the bottom of my heart. Tony van Strawbenzee, Gordon Riel, and ladies and gentlemen, it's a pleasure to be here today. I should tell you that, for me, this is a season for antiquity. Two weeks ago I spoke in one of the most venerable chambers in the democratic world, London's Guildhall. And today, here with two of the oldest regularly assembling groups of their kind in our young continent—how I love to find anything that's older than I am. [*Laughter*] But it's a pleasure to join you. And for 3 days now, I've enjoyed the beauty and vibrancy of your magnificent city. Your mayor recently said that Toronto has excitement, but hasn't lost civility, and I can vouch for that.

But I tell you, I have to interrupt my remarks here with Brian's farewell and the fact of what's going to happen to me. I don't know why it should have reminded me of a little something. But Nancy and I were in Ireland at Cashel Rock, and a young guide was taking us through the cemetery at the ruins of the old cathedral where Saint Patrick first erected a cross. And he brought us to a great tombstone, and inscribed on it was, "Remember me as you pass by, for as you are, so once was I. But as I am, you too will be. So, be content to follow me." [*Laughter*] And that had proven too much for some later Irishman, who had scratched underneath, "To follow you, I am content. I wish I knew which way you went." [*Laughter*]

Well, Brian has told me about Toronto's extraordinary dynamism and spirit of enterprise, its low crime and high quality of life. But as an old sportscaster, what says the most to me is the way this hometown cheers its Blue Jays. Toronto, like Canada itself, is brimming with strength, vitality, and self-assurance.

Those qualities, together with our similar heritages and common values, have made the relationship between the United States and Canada unique in world history. We have been best friends, important trading partners, and allies for more than a century and a half. In many ways, America's relationship with Canada has been the vanguard of our relations with other nations. Our first environmental treaty, over boundary waters, involved Canada. Our first permanent mutual defense relationship was with Canada. And the agreement to remove ships of war from the Great Lakes was our first arms reduction pact. You may have heard me say that nations don't distrust each other because they are armed, they are armed because they distrust each other. With the longest undefended border in the world, Canada and the United States are proof of the flip-side of that: When nations live in trust and friendship, they live in peace.

Today our relations are better than ever. Over the last 4 years, the Canadian-U.S. partnership has grown and strengthened. That's all for the good. In a world that's changing before our eyes, we need each other's friendship as never before. And in many ways, that is what, for Brian and me, the last 3 days here in Toronto have been about: the changing world and the role of North America in it.

As you know, we've just finished meeting with the leaders of the five other major industrial democracies. These annual economic summits have played an important role in the revival of growth in the industrial world. Each year, of course, a different country serves as host. Over the past 8 years, I've noticed that the leader of the host nation sets the tone and, to a large extent, determines the success of the meetings. Well, this year's summit was informal yet highly focused. It was a get-down-to-basics, open-for-business summit. And the progress achieved may not become fully evident for months, but it was essential—I should say, substantial. Much of the credit for this success belongs to one of the democratic world's strongest and best leaders and someone whose friendship I cherish. It is rare that a personal friendship between two leaders can change the course of history, rarer still that it changes for the better. But I believe that's the case here. I believe that future generations will regard our work together as one of the great legacies of North America to the world in this half century. No, we don't always see eye-to-eye, but then what two Irishmen ever did? [*Laughter*] So, let me just pause here to say thank you for his vision, leadership, and friendship to my colleague and your Prime Minister, Brian Mulroney.

You know, as I said, economic summits are not intended to produce blockbuster announcements. They are regular business meetings. They give those of us around the table a feel for what the others are thinking. They're a forum for us to raise issues or to advance the many ways in which our governments work together.

In economics at this summit, we advanced the process of coordinating policy. From now on, our seven governments will examine structural reform issues in their talks and will include a commodity price indicator in coordinating policy. We also reviewed our commitment to achieving progress in the Uruguay round of trade negotiations. Finally, we agreed to work together to ease the debt situation in the poorest countries of Africa.

Turning from economics, in East-West relations we reaffirmed a common position on human rights, on the need to reduce the massive conventional forces imbalance in favor of the Soviet Union and its allies, and the conditions by which we're ready to expand economic ties with Eastern countries. In other areas, we underscored the need for a common fight against terrorism and the international narcotics trade. And I'll have more to say about the drug trade in a moment. And finally, we said once again that we would work to resolve regional conflicts in the Middle East, the Persian Gulf, Cambodia, and South Africa.

You'll see a great deal about our discussions in tomorrow's headlines. But sometimes, maybe most of the time, history is not made in headlines, and we don't recognize great turning points until they're long past. This was an economic summit, and in economics I believe that today history is made at summits, yes, but in broader and more profound ways as well. This summit was held against the backdrop of a transformation as dramatic as the one you find at the place on the prairie where the Rockies meet the Plains. Less than a decade ago, inflation, as Brian told us, stagnation, decline, and despair characterized, in one measure or another, the economies of nearly all the summit nations. And today we live in a time of hope.

I know that I don't need to tell you this because, as it was in the summit, Canada is a leader. In the last 4 years, among industrial nations, only Japan matched Canada's economic growth, while Canada created more than a million jobs and, confounding the experts of just a few years ago, did it while keeping inflation in check. How? One answer, of course, is that you've been deregulating industry, moving government out of the ownership and management of industry, and reducing marginal tax rates.

But another, and I believe truer, answer is that you have reaffirmed an old faith—faith in the abiding, universal truth that economic growth does not spring from the numbers and graphs in government bureaus but from the hopes and aspirations of ordinary people. You have said, in effect, that the key to the future is in a simple human face. It's not the face of someone famous, someone whose name is likely to appear in the history books, but of someone, a man or a woman, who carries in his or her heart a dream, an excitement, a drive. And despite others calling that person impractical, he or she goes out and builds a dream into a business. Sometimes the dream is technologically sophisticated. Sometimes it's as simple as the store on the corner. Either way, this person, this dreamer, this entrepreneur, whether on his or her own or as a determined leader within a firm, is the driving force behind all growth. And because he or she can come from any part of society with ideas that will often seem eccentric, at least until they are tested, we in government cannot help this individual. We can't effectively target money or other assistance. We can only keep out of his or her way. We can, as you have, reduce taxes and regulations and open markets. We can give freedom.

Like you, we in the United States have always rediscovered that human face, that enduring truth. And as it has been for you, the spark from this faith in freedom has rekindled our fires of opportunity, invention, and growth. It's transforming life on this great, splendid continent we share, and more and more it's transforming life throughout the world.

Yes, as I looked around that summit table these last 3 days, it seemed to me we've come to a moment in which, as it must have when John Cabot landed on the shores of Newfoundland nearly 500 years ago, humanity stands on the shores of a new world and for a moment holds its breath in awe and wonder. Each of the summit nations has turned away from statism and toward the market. This movement toward freer enterprise is worldwide, stretching from India to Argentina and beginning to reach even into China and, now, the Soviet Union. And everywhere there are those who say we must dim this light of opportunity and turn back from this frontier of the future. And the question is, will we?

Already on this continent that light has ignited a bonfire of entrepreneurship and technological innovation unlike anything mankind has ever seen. As one physicist noted not long ago: "The entire Industrial Revolution enhanced productivity by a factor of one hundred. The microelectronic revolution has already enhanced productivity in information-based technology by a factor of more than a million." And he added, "the end isn't in sight yet." Today a phone call, a television report, or a currency transaction bounces from Toronto to Tokyo by way of satellite, often starting from a dish antenna that fits on the top of a truck. Satellite and dish replace tons of wire and miles of cable that once carried those signals. And they do the job better.

The heart of the technological revolution that produced them, that has, at the same time, put desktop computers in homes across our continent while making North American industry vastly more productive—the heart of this revolution is a tiny silicon chip that you can hold on the tip of your finger and still see most of the finger. Today a single chip has the incredible power of a million transistors, that is, of the biggest computer of the 1960's. Yet one of North America's most prominent research directors predicts that in less than 15 years, the power of a billion transistors will be packed on a chip. That's the power of 20 of today's most advanced supercomputers, all in a laptop computer, available to every entrepreneur and executive.

Already this new technology is transforming our offices and factories, creating many jobs, eliminating others. And for that reason, some people fear it. I understand that. I remember returning to Hollywood from the service. Before the War, I'd achieved the status symbol of all contract players in movie studios. I could get away with saying, "I quit at 6 o'clock." Well, when I got back, I decided I'd better reestablish this right from the start, having been gone 4 years. The first day of shooting, I sought out the first assistant director, and I said, "I think we should get one thing straight. I quit at 6 o'clock." He shot back, "Well, you're going to be pretty lonesome for that last hour. We quit at 5." [*Laughter*]

It seemed that with wartime excess-profits tax, everyone started to think of production costs as mostly government money, so why not share the wealth. They started leaving early and loosening standards. Pretty soon, though, Hollywood had to shape up. It faced a new challenge from a new technology called television. Within a few years, studio employment dropped by thousands and many predicted Hollywood would die—but Hollywood adapted. Many Hollywood people found work in TV, and that included a certain actor. The studios themselves discovered new markets, and among them the television market. And today almost as many people have jobs in the movies as at the peak, and even more work in broadcasting, which now faces the new technologies of video and cable.

This story of challenge and growth is not just the story of movies and television but of all humanity in its long climb from the swamp to the stars. Do we dare stop climbing? Would we want to stop, especially we North Americans, we who, as Winston Churchill said when he addressed your Parliament during the bleakest days of the Second World War, have not journeyed all this way across the mountains, across the prairies, across the centuries because we're made of sugar candy? Nothing could turn us back faster from the new technological horizon and the morning of its promise than to do what some would have us do and hide from the growing global marketplace.

Your Prime Minister and I want to keep the world on the path of hope. And that's why we've joined together in pressing for a new round of international trade talks, in working for reform of the agricultural policies of the summit nations, and of course in negotiating a Canada-U.S. free trade agreement. That historic agreement, once approved by your Parliament and our Congress, will throw open the doors to the world's largest free trade area. It will benefit not only our two countries but all nations now wrestling against the siren temptation of protection. Already Canada and the United States produce the world's largest volume of trade. The U.S. has a larger volume of trade with Ontario alone than with most other countries. Who better than Canada and America to show those who hear the call of protection that there is a better way? As I told the Parliament last year: "We will overcome the impulse of economic isolationism with a brotherly embrace, an embrace that may someday extend throughout the Americas and ultimately to the free world."

Well, with the European Community scheduled to remove internal barriers by 1992, we can hope that the two great continents of Europe and North America will become the dynamic engines of an even faster, expanding, open, world economy. Our free trade agreement will create in North America the world's most powerful market, a market that includes many of the most exciting centers of commerce and invention on Earth, a market that brings together two of the freest peoples on Earth. In the past, whenever we North Americans have lowered trading restrictions, we have seen our economies bloom like mountain meadows after a spring rain. Well, hasn't the moment come for another flowering?

Some say that open trade and easier access will lead to an erosion of cultural distinctions. But I believe that to find North America's true future under this agreement we need to look no farther than Canada itself, where distinct cultures have lived, worked, and traded together while respecting each other's differences for generations.

With protectionist storms brewing everywhere, the choice in both our nations and among all the summit countries is between moving forward toward freer trade or backward toward the protection and isolation that are relics of another age. We cannot, for example, expect the limited free trade of today to remain secure if trade in other products becomes more and more restricted. We cannot stand still, but then we North Americans never have. We've always risen to meet a challenge. Our hearts quicken to the call; our eyes brighten; our pace picks up.

Let's remind those who call for sweeping separation that we have long worked in common for common goals—to protect our common security and peace, for example. Of course, some have criticized this security partnership, often saying that if we build weapons we're bound to use them, which makes me wonder where they've been for the last 40 years.

In my country's Air Force museum there is an entire B–36 bomber, one of the first planes used for mutual security in an early part of NATO's nuclear umbrella. It has wings two-thirds the length of a football field, six rear-mounted propeller engines, four jet booster engines, and lots of vacuum tubes. At one time it could carry a 10,000 pound bomb load and fly 10,000 miles. Three hundred and eighty-five were built. Most have been junked. None was ever flown in combat.

These last 40 years, whole generations of missiles and nuclear weapons have been built and dismantled. Their only job was to keep the peace. It was kept. And now, because of NATO's strength and steadfastness, the Soviets have agreed for the first time to join us and eliminate an entire class of nuclear weapons. Is there any better answer to those who, in the name of peace, oppose a strong defense partnership?

Canada and America have been partners for peace not just in maintaining a strong Western defense but all over the world. From Cyprus to the Sinai, from pressuring the Soviets to get out of Afghanistan to supporting democracy in the Philippines, we have worked together. I saw one of the fruits of our partnership during my recent visit to Moscow. I had some contact—not enough—with the Soviet people. They lined the streets by the thousands. I was amazed by their sincere warmth. Their faces were filled with hope—the hope, I believe, that they might be entering a new era in human history, an era of peace and, yes, of freedom.

As I said at Guildhall, I found Mr. Gorbachev to be a serious man seeking serious reform. And he and I talked about those reforms, as well as about regional conflicts, human rights, and arms reduction. Our discussions focused on freedom of choice and other individual freedoms and on the fact that recognition of these basic rights must never be taken for granted. I know I speak for all of us in saying our prayers go with the Soviet peoples. But as I also said at Guildhall of the security partnership between North America and Europe in NATO, let us stay strong. Without our strength, the tide of oppression and expansion would never have been halted. Our partnership and that of our allies is the hope of all peoples who yearn for freedom. So, as the Prime Minister said so well in his speech to Congress in April: "We wish Mr. Gorbachev well, but history obliges us to retain a strong measure of skepticism about the Soviet system. We can all be," as the Prime Minister said, "in some ways from Missouri."

Over the last 3 days, the summit partners here in Toronto discussed East-West relations. And we took up another threat to the security of our nations, a comparatively new but frightening one: illegal drugs. Drugs have only once before been on our agenda. A North American dialog between Prime Minister Mulroney and Vice President Bush put them there this time. Over breakfast in Washington in April, the Prime Minister and the Vice President exchanged thoughts on how our countries could work together to fight the drug kingpins. One area they discussed was appropriate for the talks at this summit: how to prevent the laundering of money across international borders. Handling of money is proving the drug trade's weakest point. The drug trade is conducted primarily in cash and needs international banking to move and launder its money. Canada's strong support for the Bush initiative is reflected in the historic commitment endorsed by all the summit leaders in the Toronto communique. It's time to shut the teller's window to drug lords and close the money laundries for good.

So, yes, in ensuring the security not only of our nations but our ideals, in fighting the drug scourge, in leading the world economy to a future of opportunity and growth, the partnership between our countries is at the center. It is the example to our allies and the world. It is the hope of peoples and nations.

And so, today, mankind—standing on the shore of a new continent, a new age of invention, adventure, and growth—holds its breath and for one lingering moment wonders: Go forward or go back? And what we North Americans decide together will, to a large measure, answer that question for the entire world. Let us choose life. And let us choose hope. And let us turn to the horizon and greet the morning and continue the adventure that our forefathers started so many years ago when, with faith and freedom, they landed on this great, strange continent and began to build a new world.

Before I leave completely, with regard to what I have said about drugs and all the things that is going forward, I couldn't help but think very proudly today at the table—with all of that being accomplished between our seven nations—I couldn't help but think that one tiny young lady a few years ago, moving to Washington, set out on her own on a crusade against drugs. And today she's got a lot of company.

And now, I thank you. And since this is my last official visit to Canada, let me add here publicly to Brian Mulroney, a colleague for 4 years and a friend for life, a particular thank you. Brian and Mila, God bless you, and God bless you all. And I have to tell you—you've probably guessed from what he said and what I said—that in this summit business, the head man in the country where you're meeting is the chairman of all the meetings. And I have to tell you that on a performance rating of, say, from 1 to 10, your Prime Minister, in my book, gets an "11".

Thank you.

Note: The President spoke at 7:25 p.m. in the Canadian Room at the Royal York Hotel. In his opening remarks, he referred to Canadian Prime Minister Brian Mulroney. He also referred to Tony van Strawbenzee and Gordon Riel, presidents of the Empire and Canadian Clubs, respectively.

Statement by Assistant to the President for Press Relations Fitzwater on the Fair Housing Amendments Act of 1988

June 21, 1988

The President is encouraged that the Fish-Michel-Sensenbrenner amendment will be adopted by the House during the consideration of H.R. 1158, the bill to amend the Fair Housing Act. This legislation, as amended, will go a long way to strengthen laws against discrimination in housing, a goal we all share. Among other things, the bill achieves a longstanding legislative objective of the President: to prohibit invidious discrimination in housing against those with handicaps.

The Fish-Michel-Sensenbrenner amendment preserves the constitutional right of

Americans to jury trials in civil lawsuits. This amendment is a major step forward on the road to timely enactment of fair housing legislation. We are also encouraged by the amendment Congressman Clay Shaw plans to offer to protect the rights of older Americans and Americans without children.

Among our remaining concerns are two particular problems for which we would support corrective amendments: (1) preserving executive branch discretion in instituting civil lawsuits, thereby avoiding constitutional separation-of-powers litigation that could delay effective enforcement, and (2) maintaining litigation authority in the Department of Justice. The action anticipated by the House will advance major civil rights legislation which is long overdue.

White House Statement on the President's Meeting With the First United States On-Site Inspection Team for the Intermediate-Range Nuclear Forces Treaty

June 22, 1988

The President met this morning with Brig. Gen. Roland LaJoie, Director of the On-Site Inspection Agency, and members of the first team of U.S. inspectors who will be monitoring Soviet compliance with the INF treaty. The team is departing today for its staging area in Japan so that it will be in position to begin the on-site inspections by July 1. These will be the first of the extensive on-site inspections called for in the INF treaty, which entered into effect on June 1, 1988.

The first inspections—the baseline inspections—are to take place during July 1–September 1 and will cover 133 Soviet facilities. The Soviets will simultaneously conduct inspections of 26 U.S. INF facilities in the U.S. and in our allied basing countries. On July 1, we will also begin resident on-site monitoring of the Soviet missile facility at Votkinsk. U.S. inspectors will also be watching the elimination of Soviet INF missiles and associated equipment.

These inspection activities are an essential element of our verification regime for the INF treaty. In addition, the experience gained will be useful as we develop verification provisions for a strategic arms reduction agreement. Full and faithful implementation of the INF treaty will contribute to the confidence necessary to make further progress in arms reductions.

Statement on the Death of Representative John Duncan of Tennessee

June 22, 1988

With great sadness, I learned that John Duncan passed away. Nancy and I will miss our good friend, and our prayers are with Lois and the Duncan family.

John was first elected to the House in 1964 to the seat held by Howard Baker's father and then his mother. He set the highest standards of excellence and integrity in public service. The Nation and the people of the State of Tennessee have benefited beyond measure from his statesmanship and commitment to the national well-being.

Nomination of Jack R. Stokvis To Be an Assistant Secretary of Housing and Urban Development
June 22, 1988

The President today announced his intention to nominate Jack R. Stokvis to be an Assistant Secretary of Housing and Urban Development (Community Planning and Development). He would succeed Alfred Clinton Moran.

Since 1981 Mr. Stokvis has been General Deputy Assistant Secretary for Community Planning and Development for the Department of Housing and Urban Development in Washington, DC. Prior to this he was director of the department of planning and grants for the city of East Orange, NJ, 1980–1981. He has also been special project manager for the Great Falls National Historic District in New Jersey, 1976–1980; principal planner for the city of Paterson, 1975–1976; and a senior planner for Jersey City, 1973–1975.

Mr. Stokvis graduated from Union College (A.B., 1967) and received a master of urban planning degree from New York University in 1973. He was born December 10, 1944, in Hartford, CT. He is married, has two children, and resides in Arlington, VA.

Nomination of Maynard Wayne Glitman To Be United States Ambassador to Belgium
June 22, 1988

The President today announced his intention to nominate Maynard Wayne Glitman, of Vermont, a career member of the Senior Foreign Service, Class of Career Minister, as Ambassador to the Kingdom of Belgium. He would succeed Geoffrey Swaebe.

Mr. Glitman entered the Foreign Service in 1956. From 1956 to 1957, he was an economic officer in the Department of State and then was a fiscal and financial officer, 1957–1959. He was a consular and economic officer in Nassau, 1956–1961, and also in Ottawa, 1961–1965. He attended Atlantic affairs studies at the University of California (Berkeley) from 1965 to 1966. From 1967 to 1968, he was an international relations officer in the Department of State, following which he was detailed to the United Nations General Assembly in 1967 and to the National Security Council in 1968. From 1968 to 1973, he was a political officer in Paris. He returned to the Department of State to be Director of the Office of International Trade Policy and subsequently was a Deputy Assistant Secretary of State for International Trade Policy. He was then detailed to the Department of Defense, where he was Deputy Assistant Secretary of Defense for International Security Affairs, 1976–1977. From 1977 to 1981, he was deputy chief of mission at the United States Mission to NATO in Brussels. He was then appointed Department of State representative and deputy negotiator to the Intermediate-Range Nuclear Forces Negotiations, with the rank of Ambassador, in Geneva from 1981 to 1984. In 1984 Mr. Glitman was chief U.S. representative at the Mutual and Balanced Force Reduction (MBFR) Talks in Vienna. Since 1985 he has been the chief U.S. negotiator for Intermediate-Range Nuclear Forces in Geneva.

Mr. Glitman graduated from the University of Illinois (B.A., 1955) and Fletcher School of Law and Diplomacy (M.A., 1956). He was born December 8, 1933, in Chicago, IL. Mr. Glitman is married, has five children, and resides in Geneva, Switzerland.

Nomination of John Andrew Burroughs, Jr., To Be United States Ambassador to Uganda
June 22, 1988

The President today announced his intention to nominate John Andrew Burroughs, Jr., of Maryland, a career member of the Senior Foreign Service, Class of Counselor, as Ambassador to the Republic of Uganda. He would succeed Robert G. Houdek.

From 1960 to 1963, Mr. Burroughs was a passport examiner with the Department of State, and from 1963 to 1964, he was assistant chief of the special services branch of the Passport Office. From 1964 to 1966, he was administrative assistant in the Bureau of Economic and Business Affairs at the Department of State. He was an employee relations specialist in the Office of Civilian Manpower Management at the Department of the Navy, 1966–1970, and Special Assistant (Equal Opportunity) to the Assistant Secretary of the Navy, 1970–1977. He was Deputy Assistant Secretary for Equal Employment Opportunity at the Department of State, 1977–1981; U.S. Ambassador to the Republic of Malawi, 1981–1984; and a foreign affairs fellow at the Joint Center for Political Studies, 1984–1985. Since 1985 Mr. Burroughs has been American Consul General in Cape Town, Republic of South Africa.

Mr. Burroughs graduated from the University of Iowa (B.A., 1959). He was born July 31, 1936, in Washington, DC. He is married and currently resides in Temple Hills, MD.

Nomination of Antonio Navarro To Be a Member of the Advisory Board for Radio Broadcasting to Cuba
June 22, 1988

The President today announced his intention to nominate Antonio Navarro to be a member of the Advisory Board for Radio Broadcasting to Cuba for a term expiring October 27, 1991. This is a reappointment.

Since 1987 Mr. Navarro has been vice chairman of Jack Hilton, Inc., in New York City. Prior to this he was senior vice president and group executive at W.R. Grace & Co., 1982–1987.

Mr. Navarro graduated from Georgia Institute of Technology (B.S., 1944). He was born September 26, 1922, in Havana, Cuba. He is married, has three children, and resides in New York City.

Nomination of Clair W. Burgener To Be a Member of the Board for International Broadcasting
June 22, 1988

The President today announced his intention to nominate Clair W. Burgener to be a member of the Board for International Broadcasting for a term expiring April 28, 1991. This is a reappointment.

Since 1983 Mr. Burgener has been president of Burgener Properties in Rancho Santa Fe, CA. Prior to this he served as a Member of Congress in the House of Representatives from 1973 to 1983.

Mr. Burgener graduated from California State University (A.B., 1950). He was born

December 5, 1921, in Vernal, UT. Mr. Burgener is married, has three children, and resides in Rancho Santa Fe, CA.

Appointment of Lucille Clarke Dumbrill as a Member of the Advisory Council on Historic Preservation
June 22, 1988

The President today announced his intention to appoint Lucille Clarke Dumbrill to be a member of the Advisory Council on Historic Preservation for a term expiring June 10, 1992. She would succeed Mimi Rodden.

Mrs. Dumbrill has been involved with numerous community, historical, and political organizations in the State of Wyoming. Mrs. Dumbrill graduated from the University of Wyoming (M.A., 1951). She was born May 16, 1928, in Laketown, UT. She is married, has three children, and resides in Newcastle, WY.

Nomination of MacDonald G. Becket To Be a Member of the Board of Directors of the National Institute of Building Sciences
June 22, 1988

The President today announced his intention to nominate MacDonald G. Becket to be a member of the Board of Directors of the National Institute of Building Sciences for a term expiring September 7, 1990. This is a reappointment.

Since 1969 Mr. Becket has been chairman of the board of the Becket Group in Santa Monica, CA. Mr. Becket has also been active in community and professional organizations in California.

Mr. Becket graduated from the University of Southern California (B.A., 1952). He was born November 2, 1928, in Seattle, WA. He is married, has four children, and resides in Los Angeles, CA.

Letter to the Chairman and Ranking Minority Member of the Senate Appropriations Committee on the Space Station Program
June 22, 1988

Dear Mr. Chairman: (Dear Senator Hatfield:)

In anticipation of the Senate Appropriations Committee meetings this week, I am writing to urge your support for the Space Station program while preserving the integrity of the budget agreement we reached with the bipartisan congressional leadership last November.

The Senate is now at a critical decision point. The FY 1989 appropriation bill as marked by the HUD-Independent Agencies Subcommittee would provide only $200 million for the Space Station and effectively force termination of the Space Station program. This would be totally unacceptable.

Equally unacceptable, however, would be any plan that takes critical funds away from another national priority, our country's defense budget. I understand that the Defense Appropriations Subcommittee has proposed to do just that by transferring more than $600 million from Defense research and development into an account to pay for the Space Station. Not only is this counterproductive to our goals for both Defense and the Space Station, but funding the Space Station at the expense of national security violates the budget agreement.

In my FY 1989 budget, within the terms of our agreements on overall spending levels, I put the Space Station among the top priorities and included the necessary funding of about $1 billion in FY 1989. In addition, because of the importance of a stable, long-term commitment to this program, I proposed that appropriations be made for FY 1990 and 1991 as well.

We all know that the space program has been the source of innovation and technological growth here on Earth. The Space Station is an important vehicle of international cooperation—the largest cooperative science and technology project ever undertaken. We need the Space Station for all these reasons and for an even more important, but less tangible, reason: our Nation's leadership role in the peaceful exploration and use of space.

The Soviet Union already has an active space station program and is using it increasingly to support civilian space goals and to advance foreign policy objectives. Meanwhile, our closest friends and allies in Europe, Japan, and Canada have agreed to join with us in a cooperative relationship that will substantially increase the capabilities of the U.S. station; indeed, we are about to sign intergovernmental agreements with these partners, who collectively will contribute over $7 billion to the Space Station. The Congress's failure now to fund adequately this vital project will significantly undermine our national space effort and raise serious questions about our reliability as a leader and partner in an area where our leadership has been so vital for three decades.

I am fully aware of the difficult decisions that must be made in setting priorities among the competing demands for funding this year, but this is not the time to turn our backs on the future or on needed defense spending. By making these difficult but necessary decisions, we can achieve the priorities our Nation needs. If we are to insure our future, funding of science, space, and technology programs must remain a top priority.

I am asking you to help assure that future by supporting appropriation of the funds necessary for the space program our Nation needs without sacrificing national security and other vital programs our Nation requires.

Sincerely,

RONALD REAGAN

Note: Identical letters were sent to John C. Stennis of Mississippi and Mark O. Hatfield of Oregon, chairman and ranking minority member of the Senate Appropriations Committee, respectively.

Message to the Congress Transmitting the Soviet-United States Fishery Agreement
June 22, 1988

To the Congress of the United States:

In accordance with the Magnuson Fishery Conservation and Management Act of 1976 (MFCMA) (Public Law 94–265; 16 U.S.C. 1801 *et seq.*), I transmit herewith an Agreement Between the Government of the United States of America and the Government of the Union of Soviet Socialist Republics on Mutual Fisheries Relations, signed at Moscow on May 31, 1988 (the "Agreement"). This Agreement conforms with U.S. law and will replace both the Agreement Between the Government of the United States and the Government of the Union of Soviet Socialist Republics Concerning Fisheries Off the Coasts of the United States of November 26, 1976, as amended, and the Agreement Between the

Government of the United States and the Government of the Union of Soviet Socialist Republics Concerning Fisheries Off the Coasts of the Union of Soviet Socialist Republics of February 21, 1988.

The Agreement provides opportunities for fishermen from each country to conduct fisheries activities on a reciprocal basis in the other country's waters. The Agreement also establishes a framework for cooperation between the two countries on other fisheries issues of mutual concern. Several U.S. industry interests have urged prompt consideration of this Agreement because of their desire to conclude joint fisheries ventures with the Soviet fishing industry.

In light of the importance of our fisheries relationship with the U.S.S.R., I recommend that the Congress give favorable consideration to this Agreement at an early date.

RONALD REAGAN

The White House,
June 22, 1988.

Message to the Congress Transmitting the Report on the Administration of the Refugee Admissions Program
June 22, 1988

To the Congress of the United States:

In accordance with Public Law 100–204, section 904(d), I am pleased to transmit a report on the roles and responsibilities of the Immigration and Naturalization Service and the Department of State in administering the United States refugee admissions program. Recommendations for improving the program's effectiveness and efficiency over the next few years are also included.

I am proud of the roles both the Immigration and Naturalization Service and the Department of State have played in the implementation of the Refugee Act of 1980. While improvements can still be made in the operations of both the Immigration and Naturalization Service and the Department of State as well as in other aspects of the admissions program, the programs, procedures, and processes established since 1980 represent a positive legacy for the next administration.

RONALD REAGAN

The White House,
June 22, 1988.

Appointment of Terry Weeks as a Member of the Commission on Presidential Scholars
June 22, 1988

The President today announced his intention to appoint Terry Weeks to be a member of the Commission on Presidential Scholars during his tenure as National Teacher of the Year (1988). He would succeed Donna Hill Oliver.

Mr. Weeks is currently a teacher of social studies for Central Middle School in Murfreesboro, TN. Mr. Weeks was also named Teacher of the Year for 1988.

Mr. Weeks graduated from Middle Tennessee State (B.S., 1972; M.S., 1974). He was born February 17, 1951, in Murfreesboro, TN. He is married and currently resides in Murfreesboro.

Appointment of Ruth Govorchin as a Member of the President's Committee on Mental Retardation

June 22, 1988

The President today announced his intention to appoint Ruth Govorchin to be a member of the President's Committee on Mental Retardation for a term expiring May 11, 1991. She would succeed Madeline B. Harwood.

Since 1983 Mrs. Govorchin has served as a special education teacher for Melbourne Trainable Mentally Retarded School in Lakewood, CA. Prior to this she served as a temporary teacher for the Los Angeles County schools in 1983. She has also been a guest lecturer on mental retardation for California State University.

Mrs. Govorchin graduated from California State University (B.A., 1980) and received her master's degree from the University of San Francisco in 1985. She was born November 25, 1940, in Denver, CO. She is married, has three children, and resides in Yorba Linda, CA.

Nomination of Hillel Fradkin To Be a Member of the National Council on the Humanities

June 22, 1988

The President today announced his intention to nominate Hillel Fradkin to be a member of the National Council on the Humanities, National Foundation on the Arts and the Humanities, for a term expiring January 26, 1991. He would succeed A. Lawrence Chickering.

Since 1986 Mr. Fradkin has been senior program officer for the Lynde and Harry Bradley Foundation in Milwaukee, WI. Prior to this he was program officer for the grant program in research and education for the John M. Olin Foundation, 1983–1986. He has also been a visiting lecturer of Jewish thought at the University of Chicago since 1987; adjunct professor of Jewish thought for the department of religion at Barnard College, 1979–1984; and visiting instructor for the department of political science at Yale University, 1977–1979.

Mr. Fradkin graduated from Cornell University (B.A., 1967) and the University of Chicago (Ph.D., 1978). He served in the United States Army, 1969–1972. Mr. Fradkin was born March 30, 1947, in New York, NY. He is married, has one child, and resides in Whitefish Bay, WI.

Appointment of Thomas Allen Sands as a United States Commissioner of the Red River Compact Commission, and Designation as Chairman

June 22, 1988

The President today announced his intention to appoint Maj. Gen. Thomas Allen Sands, United States Army, to be United States Commissioner to the Red River Compact Commission. This is a new position. General Sands will also serve as Chairman of the Commission.

Since 1984 General Sands has been Commanding General of the U.S. Army Engineering Division for the Lower Mississippi

Valley in Vicksburg, MS. Prior to this he was Commanding General of the U.S. Army Engineering Division in New York City, 1981–1984. He was also district engineer for the U.S. Army Engineering District in New Orleans, 1978–1981; personnel management officer, then chief, of the programs branch of the U.S. Army Military Personnel Center in Alexandria, VA, 1975–1978; and Assistant Director of Civil Works in the Office of Chief of Engineers for the United States Army in Washington, DC, 1974–1975.

General Sands attended the U.S. Army War College and received a B.A. degree from the U.S. Military Academy and an M.S. from Texas A&M University. He has been in the United States Army since 1958. He was born June 7, 1935, in Columbia, TN. He is married, has two children, and resides in Vicksburg, MS.

Remarks at the Business Roundtable Annual Dinner

June 22, 1988

Well, thank you, Roger, and thank you all. By the way, Roger, the Presidential limousine is running just fine. [*Laughter*] But I have to tell you, I think you fellows went a little overboard when I said I wanted the car to be absolutely worry-free. The other day my Secret Service driver pulled into a gas station, and I leaned forward and said, "But the gas gauge still shows 'full.' " And the agent said, "Yes, that doesn't matter. Mr. Smith painted it that way." [*Laughter*] And one other thing, Roger. Does everybody who buys that kind of a car get a warranty that reads, "Good until whichever comes first: 60,000 miles or 2 terms"? [*Laughter*]

Roger, ladies and gentlemen, it's an honor to be able to speak to you this evening. I've come here at a time when the creative energies of the American people have carried our economy into the midst of the longest peacetime expansion—as Roger told you—in our nation's history, at a time when world trade is strong and growing, when we see all around us technological breakthroughs that promise to carry us forward into a dazzling new era. Yet even today there is still work to do, a great deal of work, to make the economy of our nation and the world all that we would like them to be.

Some of that work our administration can do in the coming months. And let me interject here that one item of unfinished business that I know you're particularly concerned about is product liability law reform. Outlandish court awards have placed tremendous burdens on U.S. companies as they try to compete in an international marketplace. If Congress is serious about enhancing the competitiveness of American firms, it should pass meaningful product liability law reform this year—reform that protects legitimate claims by consumers, but limits the level of awards to reasonable losses. But as I was saying, we must leave whatever part of our agenda is unfinished to those who will follow us, trusting that they'll benefit from the lessons that we've learned. And so, this evening I'd like to speak to you about both practical policy—reporting to you in particular on the economic summit that just took place in Toronto—and about the enduring lessons that have emerged from the experience of these 8 years.

First, if I may, I'd like to establish the scope of the topic under discussion. For when we speak about the economy, we're dealing with more than mere numbers, more than statistics about productivity and employment. We're dealing instead with one of the most basic aspects of human existence: We're dealing with the way the great majority of men and women spend most of their hours, most days, throughout the most productive years of their lives.

The historian William McNeill described the rise of social organization in the ancient Middle East this way: "Only on irrigated land could rich crops be harvested year after year from the same fields, and only where irrigation was needed did large numbers of men find it necessary to cooperate in digging and diking. An agricultural surplus that could support specialists, together with habits of social organization embracing large numbers of men, this could and did emerge in the flood plains of the principal Middle Eastern rivers, and, until much later, not elsewhere." In other words, there was a surplus of goods to be traded, and that is economy. There, and only there, did civilization arise.

Now, it's not my intention to give a history lesson. But I believe it's important to remind ourselves that in dealing with the economy we're dealing with human creativity. This insight has represented the underpinning of our economic expansion. We cut tax rates, reduced government regulation, and restrained Federal spending; and we unleashed the creativity of individuals and businesses. We gave them freedom to create; to keep the rewards of their own risktaking and hard work; and to reach for new, bold ideas.

As I noted a moment ago, today we're in the midst of our nation's longest peacetime expansion. Real family income is up. Twice as many new jobs have been created here in the United States as in the other six industrialized nations combined. Unemployment has fallen to its lowest level in 14 years. And during this economic expansion, the number of Americans living below the poverty line has fallen, reversing its upward trend.

The lesson that we've learned about releasing the creative energies of private firms and individuals is one that's being taken up around the world. From the early days in 1981 of skepticism to today, nation after nation has moved toward a free enterprise economy. Using high inflation to pay for expanding government spending has halted. And most of the industrialized democracies have either cut their top tax rates or are now in the process of doing so. And why has this happened? Well, I quote: "The reason for the worldwide trend toward lower top rates of tax is clear. Excessive rates of income tax destroy enterprise. By contrast, a reduction in the top rates of income tax can, over time, result in a higher, not lower, revenue yield." Those were the words of Britain's Chancellor to the Exchequer, Nigel Lawson. I've been making that argument for 8 years now, but it's not really authoritative until you hear it in a British accent. [*Laughter*]

But in India and Argentina, in Botswana, in China, and, yes, even in the Soviet Union, state control of the economy is loosening in favor of freer markets. And the lesson is clear: If you want economic growth, work for economic and individual freedom. Another way of putting this is what I said before and during the Toronto summit. The future belongs to the flexible. It belongs to those countries that don't straitjacket the initiative of their people; to those who give reign to the creative, enterprising spirit that is in all people; to those who see the limit of government's understanding and its ability to respond to a world that is changing before our eyes.

The greatest historymakers in our time are not politicians and statesmen, but inventors, entrepreneurs, and others who are transforming the technological base of civilization and whose search for new markets is leading us into a more global economy. These people are making the world anew and knitting all of our nations together in ways more diverse and wonderful than we can fully comprehend. So, by flexibility, I mean, in a greater sense, humility—humility of governments before the vastly diverse creativity of their peoples. At the Toronto summit our goal was to apply that lesson of flexibility to discussions on world finance and trade, including, of course, the troublesome question of agriculture.

On world trade, there are some substantial inequities, but the answer is not to close American markets: The answer is to open foreign ones. And that's why we leaders used this summit to encourage the international trade negotiations, what is called the Uruguay round, now going on in Geneva. Those negotiations are approaching their midway point. We hope by year's end to see agreement on specific goals for the final 2 years in such major areas as agriculture, services, intellectual property, and investment, along with a roadmap and timetable to the finish line.

Opening, not closing, markets is why a new trade bill at home must encourage free and fair trade and not establish barriers that will lead to retaliation. Our goal, the goal of both the executive and legislative branches, should be sound, coherent, consistent trade policy, a trade bill that does not seek short-term political gains but long-term economic prosperity for all Americans in a market-driven world economy. What Thomas Jefferson said long ago still applies: "Our interest will be to throw open the door of commerce and to knock off all its shackles, giving perfect freedom to all persons for the vent of whatever they may choose to bring into our ports, and asking the same of theirs." Clear back then—Thomas Jefferson. And by the way, that a 20th century President can quote Jefferson on trade says a great deal about America's abiding interest in free markets, even from our earliest days. I told Tom that when he said it. [*Laughter*]

In Toronto, the other leaders and I confirmed once more that free markets must be our goal. Now, that doesn't mean that areas of disagreement don't remain. Take agriculture, for example: We agreed to keep looking for an agreement. There's a simple rule that's as true of agriculture as it is of any other endeavor: When you subsidize something, you get more of it. This year the world's industrialized nations are subsidizing agriculture to the tune of $200 billion a year. There are world surpluses of agricultural products, and the result is that many markets for agricultural goods have become distorted. We in the United States want to eliminate all agricultural subsidies that distort trade. A tall order, perhaps, but we've filled tall orders before. In fact, the European press has given our position on agricultural subsidies a nickname that sort of appeals to me. They're calling it a second zero-option.

In Toronto we talked about many issues. We agreed to direct our agriculture negotiators in Geneva to reach decisions that will reduce subsidies that directly or indirectly affect trade. We stated our belief that we should make agriculture more responsive to market signals. We further agreed on a general framework for dealing with Third World debt, particularly the debt of the poorest nations. And we discussed how to help debt-ridden countries that are making the transition to democracy—for example, the Philippines.

We also talked about how we coordinate our economic policies. I know many people question the summit process. What do the summits do? Are they just so much sound and fury? Well, not on your life! Today, all year round, the summit countries are working more closely together than ever before, and the summits are a key reason why. One payoff is that last October, when the world markets began to shake, the international economy stayed steady. Working together, we guided the world ship through the storm.

Finally, we talked about East-West relations, terrorism, regional political issues, and something I know every American family will cheer, the Bush initiative to stop drug-money laundering. Thanks to Vice President Bush, the major industrial democracies have committed themselves to hanging up "Gone Out of Business" signs in drug-money laundries all over the world.

Now, I've spoken of economic freedom and of the practical way to put that lesson into effect. Permit me to close now with one other practical matter, one that will put the great lesson of free markets into effect in an especially dramatic and historic way: the U.S.-Canada free trade agreement. Prime Minister Mulroney and I entered into this agreement in January of this year. It presently awaits enactment of implementing legislation by our Congress and the Canadian Parliament.

Today, as we await this final approval, the United States and Canada already generate the world's highest volume of trade. We are the two greatest trading partners in the world. The United States has a larger volume of trade with the Province of Ontario than with most other nations. United States citizens are by far the principal foreign investors in Canada, and on a per capita basis, Canadians are even greater investors in our country. This two-way traffic in trade and investment has created countless thousands of jobs and added immeasurably to the prosperity of both our nations.

And now, with the free trade agreement, our two nations can do still more.

Upon enactment of the implementing legislation, the agreement will make Canada and the United States the largest free trade area in the world. For the United States, this agreement will remove all Canadian tariffs; secure improved access to the Canadian market for our manufacturing, agriculture, high technology, and financial sectors; and give us important additional access to Canadian energy supplies. For Canada, this agreement will make available the enormous United States market. Canadian producers of every kind of good and service will be able to benefit from enormous economies of scale. But beyond the benefits this free trade agreement will bestow upon our two nations, there is the immeasurable importance of the example it will present to all the world. To those who would engage in all the bitterness, all the destructiveness, of round upon round of trade battles, Canada and the United States will show the better way.

I'm confident that final approval of this free trade agreement will be completed during my own term in office. But I'd hope that those who'd follow me will not view it as an item of finished business, but rather as only a beginning. In Toronto, when we gave a push to the Uruguay round, we moved the world a step closer to free and fair trade for all nations. I would hope that in the years to come, America's leaders will fix upon the vision of a day when the free flow of trade, from the southern tip of South America to the northern outposts of the Arctic Circle, unites the people of the Western Hemisphere in a bond of mutually beneficial exchange. I would hope that America's leaders will fix upon the vision of a day when all borders become what the U.S.-Canadian border so long has been: a meeting place, rather than a dividing line. I would hope that America's leaders will fix upon that vision and work tirelessly to make it come true.

That's the thought that I would most like to leave you with: that even in economics—the subject we're so often tempted to think of merely in terms of numbers and techniques—even there, men and women are moved by the power of vision, by the power of dreams. Just a few decades ago, who would have thought that sand, mere sand, possessed the power to change the world? And yet today silicon, the stuff of sand, goes into the microchips that are ushering in the profoundest economic changes since the Industrial Revolution. Vision at the high technology firms like those so many of you represent—vision has made it so.

We've done much during these 8 years to act upon the vision of economic freedom. Well, I'm convinced that today we stand on the verge of an economic and technological future of vast promise. We've embarked on an economic course that has led to new jobs, lower taxes, steady growth. And the challenge now is to recognize those voices that would construct barriers on this road to economic prosperity. These are the decisions that will be made over the next several months: individual opportunity and incentive or renewed government restriction and burden.

Already, we've seen new prosperity throughout the democratic world. And after my visit to Moscow, it's my belief that human creativity, expressed in economic freedom, can transform even the nations of the Soviet bloc. If we have the resolve, the patience, the willingness to work, and, yes, the vision, we can lead the world into a new age of prosperity and freedom.

And I can't leave you and resist exposing my latest hobby, which has become discovering stories that are told between the citizens of the Soviet Union, among themselves, which show a great sense of humor and also a little cynicism about certain things that are going on. This one happens to be with the life of someone that's no longer with us. This was when Chernenko died as General Secretary, and he met St. Peter. And St. Peter said, "Well, I can't let you in here—an atheist like you." Well, he said, "You'll have to go down to hell." But he said, "You have two choices: There is a Communist hell and a Capitalist hell." And Chernenko said, "Well, I choose the Communist hell, of course." St. Peter said, "I think I ought to tell you, the Capitalist hell is a little more comfortable." And Chernenko said, "Yes, but the Communist hell is the only one where I can be sure that the heating system will fail." [*Laughter*]

Thank you, God bless you.

Note: The President spoke at 6:30 p.m. in the Capitol Ballroom at the J.W. Marriott Hotel. He was introduced by Roger B. Smith, chairman of the Business Roundtable and General Motors Corp.

Remarks Following Discussions With Prime Minister Robert Hawke of Australia
June 23, 1988

The President. I was pleased to welcome Prime Minister Bob Hawke to Washington again, especially because this year Australia is commemorating its bicentennial. The United States and Australia have been steadfast partners through times of war and times of peace, and I'm sure the Prime Minister's visit to Washington and other cities in the United States will deepen the already close ties between our two countries.

During the Prime Minister's last visit in 1986, I promised to reciprocate Australia's contribution to our own bicentennial celebration. Last year Congress appropriated $5 million for a U.S. national gift to Australia that will be used for a permanent U.S. gallery in the Australian National Maritime Museum, with an exhibition commemorating 200 years of bilateral maritime relations. I expect this exhibit, along with other public and private efforts too numerous to list, will serve as a lasting testament of our two peoples' enduring friendship.

Our discussions have covered a range of topics, including security and progress in arms control. I shared with the Prime Minister my detailed assessment of my meetings a few weeks ago in Moscow with General Secretary Gorbachev. Australia is an important ally in our efforts to reach meaningful arms reduction agreements with the U.S.S.R. The joint facilities that Australia hosts are essential to deterrence and to the West's ability to monitor Soviet compliance with arms accords. The U.S. greatly appreciates Australia's contributions to the vital task of preserving peace in both the South Pacific and throughout the world.

Prime Minister Hawke and I also talked a good deal about bilateral trade issues. The U.S. and Australia have closely parallel interests in the current round of multilateral trade negotiations. We're in full agreement on the need to open up international trade in agricultural products, a keystone of both our economies. We also agree on the need to redouble our efforts toward the elimination of trade-distorting government subsidies of agricultural products. The Toronto summit resulted in a strong, unified position on the pressing need to invigorate the multilateral trading system. I noted that the United States will continue to work closely with Australia and other like-minded countries to carry us through to a positive conclusion of the ongoing trade negotiations. Until we achieve that goal, we will ensure that any measures that the United States may take to counter unfair subsidization of agriculture take fully into account the interests of countries like Australia.

We also exchanged views on refugees and regional issues, particularly on the importance of cooperation among Pacific States to maintain a secure, peaceful, and prosperous environment in which democratic government can flourish. The stabilizing role the United States-Australia alliance plays in supporting our common efforts has helped foster the phenomenal growth the Pacific region has enjoyed.

In summing up, I cannot overstate the importance we attach to our relationship with Australia. Australia has made major contributions to our mutual security over the past 40 years as a responsible ally, a staunch defender of democratic freedoms, and as a major trading partner.

Bob, you've been a good friend, and I

value your counsel. This is our fourth meeting, and I'm delighted that we've been able to have regular, personal exchanges of views and ideas. I know the American people will extend to you a warm welcome, in the tradition of hospitality that both Aussies and Yanks are famous for, as you continue your visit in the United States.

The Prime Minister. Thank you, Mr. President. Ladies and gentlemen, I confirm that the President and I have been able to engage in a very useful discussion covering the range of topics to which the President has alluded. We have confirmed the strengths and the enduring nature of the relationship between our two great countries, a relationship which, as I was able to say in Congress and confirm with the President, is based upon a shared commitment to principles which we regard as fundamental to the operation of a free and open society.

I took the opportunity of thanking the President for the fact that during my Prime Ministership, as he has said, he has welcomed me here on a number of occasions; and I observed that this would almost certainly be the last occasion on which I would have the opportunity of meeting with him as President of the United States. And I expressed to him personally and on behalf of the Government and people of Australia our gratitude for the contribution of his Presidency to the improvement not merely of his own people but globally.

The fact that today, as I said to the Congress, we have more than at any other stage in the postwar period reason to look with optimism to a future where the world can live more constructively at peace is in very large measure, as I told the President, due to his ideas, to his persistence, to his strength, to his determination to shape the agenda and the context of the discussions between the two superpowers. He has ensured properly that when he has come to speak he has spoken both from a position of strength and from a position where he knows that he has consulted and has the support of his allies and friends.

He has insisted that, in those discussions, that the vital question of human rights shall be a central part of the agenda. And the results have shown not merely in the negotiation for the first time of an agreement which has eliminated a particular class of nuclear weapons but also in the area of human rights, the significant advances that have been made in the attitudes and practices of the Soviet Union, that his determination in the shaping of the agenda has been right and that it has borne fruit. And I repeat that we are this day able to look with a greater degree of confidence to a world in which the resources of mankind may be able, with a greater degree of confidence, to be channeled into constructive uses is significantly a result, Mr. President, as I told you, of the time of your Presidency. And we are indebted to you for that.

We are also indebted to you for the fact that in your own country, you have presided over a period of record growth and uninterrupted prosperity. Our relationship, as I've said to you, is so good and so mature that where we do have any differences we are able to discuss those.

I expressed to the President, in particular, the appreciation of the Government and the people of Australia for the way in which he has reflected the fact that the correspondence that takes place between us is no mere formality, but that the President reads, takes account of, and carries with him in his presentations the consideration of the Australian position. And in particular, of course, I refer to the fact that I—for some time now and particularly just before the recent Toronto summit, wrote to the President—stressed the importance that we attach to the attainment of a liberalized international trading system in general, and in particular, in regard to agricultural commodities. And as you know, ladies and gentlemen, the President took those matters seriously into account and pressed them at the Toronto summit. So, I expressed our appreciation to the President.

And so, I conclude, Ron, as I began in our private talks, in saying in front of the media, thank you for a contribution to the relations between our two countries, which I believe has been unique on your part. And thank you for the contributions that you have made, which means that at the end of your Presidency the world is going to be a better and safer place than it was when you took office.

Note: The President spoke at 1:44 p.m. in the East Room at the White House. Earlier, the President and the Prime Minister met in the Oval Office and then attended a luncheon in the Residence.

Nomination of Frederick K. Goodwin To Be Administrator of the Alcohol, Drug Abuse, and Mental Health Administration
June 23, 1988

The President today announced his intention to nominate Frederick K. Goodwin to be Administrator of the Alcohol, Drug Abuse, and Mental Health Administration at the Department of Health and Human Services. He would succeed Donald Ian Macdonald.

Since 1982 Dr. Goodwin has been Scientific Director of the National Institute of Mental Health for the Department of Health and Human Services. Prior to this he was Chief of Clinical Psychobiology for the National Institute of Mental Health, 1977–1982. He has also served as chief of the section on psychiatry in the laboratory of clinical science. Dr. Goodwin's clinical research interests have been focused on biological and psychological factors in major depressive illness and in manic-depressive illness.

Dr. Goodwin graduated from Georgetown University (B.S., 1958) and St. Louis University School of Medicine (M.D., 1963). He was born April 21, 1936, in Cincinnati, OH. He is married, has three children, and resides in Chevy Chase, MD.

Appointment of Allan C. Carlson as a Member of the National Commission on Children
June 23, 1988

The President today announced his intention to appoint Allan C. Carlson to be a member of the National Commission on Children for a term expiring March 31, 1989. This is a new position.

Since 1986 Mr. Carlson has been president and director of the Center on the Family in America for the Rockford Institute in Rockford, IL. Prior to this he was executive president of the Rockford Institute, 1981–1986. He has also been an assistant to the president and lecturer in history at Gettysburg College, 1979–1981; NEH fellow of the American Enterprise Institute for Public Policy Research in 1979; and assistant director in the office for governmental affairs at the Lutheran Council in the U.S.A.

Mr. Carlson graduated from Augustana College (A.B., 1971) and Ohio University (Ph.D., 1978). He was born May 7, 1949, in Des Moines, IA. He served in the Iowa National Guard, 1971–1979. He is married, has three children, and resides in Rockford.

Message on the Observance of Independence Day, 1988
June 23, 1988

The Fourth of July is much more than a date on the calendar—it is celebrated here in the United States, and recognized around the world, as a turning point in history. No matter how many Fourths we Americans have seen, every new one revives in our hearts the pure patriotism of childhood. With each flag, with each parade and picnic and burst of fireworks, we can't help but recall the first stirrings of our deep love for America.

This year, on our Nation's 212th birthday, we recall another special anniversary, the Bicentennial of our first Independence Day under our newly ratified Constitution. In his diary entry for that date, John Quincy Adams recorded how the news of the latest State ratification was received in Boston: "(I)mmediately the bells were set to ringing, and the guns to firing again, without any mercy, and continued all the remainder of the afternoon." For two centuries now, the Constitution whose birth these patriots so exuberantly hailed has endured, ensuring our liberty and preserving this great Republic.

The passage of time has only brought us even more reason to celebrate. Our Founders marked the Fourth of July, uncertain that the Union would be formed; our ancestors at the time of the Civil War marked it as well, uncertain that the Union would survive; and our parents and grandparents marked it, uncertain that it would withstand the ravages of global conflict. We can rejoice—and be grateful to God—that peace and prosperity, the hope of every generation, reign for us on this July 4, 1988.

To all my fellow Americans, Happy Fourth of July!

RONALD REAGAN

Statement by Deputy Press Secretary Popadiuk on the President's Meeting on the Drought With Secretary of Agriculture Richard Lyng
June 23, 1988

The President and the Vice President were briefed this afternoon by Agriculture Secretary Richard Lyng on the drought situation. The Vice President and the Secretary also reported to the President on their recent trip to view the farm situation in Illinois.

Secretary Lyng showed the President a map that demonstrated the worsening condition of the drought in many areas of the United States. Despite the serious potential effects of the drought, the Secretary said rainfall in the next 2 weeks would alleviate much of the potential damage. The Secretary said that in discussions he has had with Congressmen and Senators, farm groups and Governors, there was agreement that it is too early for emergency relief measures. He also said that the Agriculture Department and other agencies have taken some steps to help, including haying and grazing on acreage conservation reserve and conserving use land and haying on conservation reserve program land.

The Secretary reported on his meeting this morning with Governors on the National Governors' Association Agriculture Committee, who told him they are pleased with the administration's reaction to the drought. Secretary Lyng also told the President and Vice President that the Presidential Interagency Drought Policy Committee is establishing a toll-free hotline to answer questions about Federal services available to citizens in drought-stricken areas. (The hotline begins operation Friday, June 24, from 8 a.m. to 6 p.m. eastern daylight time on weekdays, and from 9 a.m. to 1 p.m. on

Saturdays. The toll-free number is 1–800–541–3375. In the Washington metropolitan area, the number is 202–447–8455).

Chief of Staff Howard Baker, Deputy Chief of Staff Ken Duberstein, OMB Director James Miller, and Cabinet Secretary Nancy Risque also attended the meeting. Following that session Secretary Lyng briefed the Cabinet on the drought situation.

The President expressed serious concern about the drought and after the meeting said: "Our number one worry right now is the effects of the drought on the farmers and their families and making certain they receive any help we can provide."

Remarks at a Dinner Honoring Senator John C. Stennis of Mississippi

June 23, 1988

Thank you, Sam, and thank you all. And I want to thank you especially for extending your gracious southern hospitality to this fellow who happened to be raised up north in Illinois. In fact, being here with all you southerners—would you be surprised if it reminded me of a story? [*Laughter*]

It has to do with a Yankee who was driving through the deep South, in Mississippi, and there was a car on the road with a native son driving. And there was an accident—they collided. The cars were pretty much wrecked. But both got out, and fortunately neither one was seriously injured. And the hometowner, the constituent of our guest of honor, said, "Wait a minute." He said, "you look a little shaken up. Just a second." He went back to his wrecked car and came back with a bottle of bourbon and said, "Here, take this. It'll settle your nerves." So, he took a shot and tried to give it back, and he says, "No, no, no. Go on. No. Take another one. Go ahead." [*Laughter*] And about two or three drinks later, the Yankee said, "Hey, look, wait a minute! Southern hospitality is all right, but here, you haven't had a drop. You take one." He says, "No, I'm just going to stand here and wait until the police come." [*Laughter*]

Well, while we're all sorry to see Senator Stennis leave Washington, I want you to know that I have a special reason. You see, Senator, you're one of the few fellows left in this town who calls me kid. [*Laughter*]

But, Senator Stennis, honored guests, and ladies and gentlemen, this gathering tonight truly is a celebration. And the man we honor is no ordinary individual. The life and career of John Stennis are legendary in his home State of Mississippi and here in Washington, where he has served, as you've been told several times tonight, with quiet dignity for 41 years. Forty-one years—consider that if you will. Senator Stennis has served in the Senate for one-fifth of the life of this nation.

Probably half of the people in this room tonight had not even been born when John Stennis came to Washington, and I suppose there are plenty in the other half who would hardly care to admit it—[*laughter*]—over four decades of service in the United States Senate, a period during which this great country has undergone tremendous challenge and change. The humble man who came to Washington from a small town in Mississippi has made an impression on American government that is difficult to measure and hard to fully describe. He has demonstrated for all of us that one man, committed to God and country, willing to work hard and sacrifice personal gain and comfort, can make a difference. Mississippi can take pride in the accomplishments of John Stennis, but he is a United States Senator, and so we celebrate his contribution to all of America.

Tangible evidence of the difference Senator Stennis has made abounds. Our strong and able military, represented so splendidly here tonight, owes much of its strength to this man who has always been an unwavering advocate of peace through strength. As chairman of the Senate Armed Services

Committee in the seventies, Senator Stennis led some of the most crucial legislative battles in history on behalf of our national defense.

Back home in Mississippi, the economic opportunities that Senator Stennis has helped to bring about are beyond counting. Today there's room for even more economic growth in Mississippi, as there is in all the 50 States. But now Mississippi fully shares in the economic life of the Nation.

And yet perhaps John Stennis' greatest contribution to American Government has been his abiding example of integrity in public service. From the time he was elected to represent the people of Kemper County in the Mississippi House of Representatives in 1928 until this moment six decades later, Senator Stennis has been under the oath of public office. And for these six decades, he has done that oath constant honor. Here in Washington, John Stennis established his reputation early in his Senate career, always recognizing that the effectiveness of the Senate is harmed when Members fail to uphold the highest standards. It's no wonder the Senate looked to John Stennis as a leader when the Select Committee on Standards and Conduct was formed in 1965.

And now, if I might, I'd like to add a personal note. Life has not always been easy for Senator Stennis. We all recall his remarkable recovery from gunshot wounds in 1973. His sense of purpose, his commitment to duty, would not allow him to stop or even to slow down. Then there was heart surgery in 1983. And then in 1984 there was more surgery, radical surgery. I remember visiting Senator Stennis at Walter Reed Army Medical Center just days after the removal of his left leg. I admit I felt great pain for him, this fiercely independent man forced to undergo such a life-altering operation.

I went to Walter Reed to encourage Senator Stennis, but when I left, it was I who had been strengthened. For even then, from his hospital bed, John Stennis talked of the future of this nation. Determination to return to his post was evident in everything he said. It was December 4th when I made that visit to Walter Reed. And just over a month later, I stood inside the Capitol to take the oath of office for the second term as President, and, yes, there was John Stennis in the front row.

Senator, when I consider your career, there's a certain comparison that comes to my mind. In troubled places, you've brought calm resolve, like one of the many great fighting ships you've done so much to obtain for the Navy. Serene, self-possessed, but like a ship of the line possessed of a high sense of purpose—that is John Stennis.

And, Senator, if you think I'm leading up to something, I am. Senator Stennis, and ladies and gentlemen, it's my honor to announce tonight that, as an expression of the Nation's gratitude for the public service of the man we honor tonight, the Navy's next nuclear-powered aircraft carrier, CVN–74, will be christened the U.S.S. *John C. Stennis.*

Senator, you have devoted your life to the service of our nation. I can do no more tonight than say, on behalf of the American people: Thank you for your dedicated service. Godspeed in your further endeavors, and God bless you.

Note: The President spoke at 9:25 p.m. in the Sheraton Ballroom at the Sheraton-Washington Hotel. He was introduced by Senator Sam Nunn of Georgia.

Executive Order 12643—International Committee of the Red Cross
June 23, 1988

By virtue of the authority vested in me as President by the Constitution and laws of the United States of America, including the International Organizations Immunities Act (P.L. 79–291, as amended by Section 743 of P.L. 100–204), I hereby extend to the International Committee of the Red Cross the privileges, exemptions, and immunities provided by the International Organizations Immunities Act.

This Order is not intended to abridge in any respect privileges, exemptions, or immunities that the International Committee of the Red Cross may have acquired or may acquire by international agreements or by statute.

RONALD REAGAN

The White House,
June 23, 1988.

[*Filed with the Office of the Federal Register, 3:12 p.m., June 23, 1988*]

Note: The Executive order was released by the Office of the Press Secretary on June 24.

White House Statement on the President's Meeting with Patriarch Nasrallah Sfeir of Lebanon

June 24, 1988

The President was pleased to meet today with Maronite Catholic Patriarch Nasrallah Sfeir of Lebanon. The Vice President also met separately with Patriarch Sfeir. The President and the Vice President reaffirmed U.S. support for the restoration of Lebanon's unity, sovereignty, and territorial integrity, and the withdrawal of all foreign forces from Lebanon. Both emphasized that the suffering of the Lebanese people must end and that a process of national reconciliation is urgently needed, including agreement on political and security reform. They also recognized that durable peace and security for Lebanon can best be assured by a comprehensive peace settlement for the Middle East and pledged the continued efforts by this administration on the peace process.

The United States considers the upcoming Lebanese Presidential election to be very important for Lebanon's unity and stability. The election should proceed constitutionally, with a new President taking office as scheduled on September 23. It should also be orderly so that a smooth, legitimate transition can occur. The election provides an excellent opportunity for national reconciliation and should be seen in that light. In this context, the United States has responded to the request of Lebanese leaders to help Lebanese Moslems and Christians devise and agree upon a new arrangement for sharing political power. We are convinced by our conversations with these leaders that responsible Lebanese want to find fair guidelines for a process to establish a central government that exercises full authority over a unified, sovereign state. In that state, all Lebanese would enjoy comparable opportunities for advancement. The United States believes an agreement on such guidelines is possible and ought to be achieved as soon as possible.

The United States is particularly concerned about the plight of innocent civilians in Lebanon. The tragic casualties from the recent fighting between rival militias in Beirut's southern suburbs and from terrorist bombings and the continued taking and detention of hostages, both Lebanese and foreign, demonstrate the urgent need to restore the authority of the central government throughout the country. Only the central government has the clear, unencumbered right and responsibility to maintain law and order. The continued existence of armed militias and terrorist groups frustrates the desire of the vast majority of the Lebanese people to have the legal order and authority reestablished.

The Lebanese and American peoples have had a long and close relationship. Out of that friendship emerges both our deep concern about Lebanon's future and our enduring commitment to help the Lebanese ease their suffering and achieve national reconciliation. To those ends, the United States pledges both continuing humanitarian assistance and political support.

Nomination of Robert L. Pugh To Be United States Ambassador to Chad

June 24, 1988

The President today announced his intention to nominate Robert L. Pugh, of Virginia, a career member of the Senior Foreign Service, Class of Minister-Counselor, as Ambassador to the Republic of Chad. He would succeed John Blane.

Mr. Pugh entered the Foreign Service in 1961. He studied at the Foreign Service Institute and then served as an international economist for the Department of State, 1961–1963. In 1963 he returned to the Institute for further study. He served as political-military officer in Ankara, Turkey, 1964–1967, and as principal officer of the American consulate in Isfahan, 1967–1969. From 1969 to 1972, he was political officer in the Office of Turkish Affairs for the Bureau of Near Eastern and South Asian Affairs in the Department of State. He served as political-military officer in Athens, Greece, 1972–1976; congressional relations officer at the Department of State, 1976–1977; political adviser to CINCUSNAVEUR in London, 1977–1979; and Deputy Director of the Office of Southern European Affairs in the Bureau of European Affairs, 1979–1981. Mr. Pugh was a personnel placement officer in the Bureau of Personnel, 1981–1982, and deputy chief of mission at the U.S. Embassy in Beirut, 1982–1984. From 1984 to 1985, he attended the Executive Seminar in National and International Affairs at the Foreign Service Institute. Since 1985 he has been U.S. Ambassador to the Islamic Republic of Mauritania.

Mr. Pugh graduated from the University of Washington (B.A., 1954). He served in the United States Marine Corps, 1954–1961. He was born October 27, 1931, in Clinton, PA. He is married and has two children.

Remarks at the Presentation Ceremony for the Prisoners of War Medal

June 24, 1988

Well, thank you all very much. Secretary [of Defense] Carlucci, and members of the Congress who are here, and honored guests, thank you all. I've often noted that, in my lifetime, America has fought four wars: the First World War, World War II, Korea, and Vietnam. You, the men here today, are the Americans who fought those wars. You survived the battles, you survived captivity, and you came home. I salute your valor, and I thank you for being here today as we present a new medal that honors those who served honorably as prisoners of war.

You symbolize the sacrifice that our nation has made, and you can be proud of what you helped achieve—a Western Europe that is strong and free, a democratic and prosperous Japan that is our critical ally in the Pacific, a South Korea whose remarkable economic and political achievements have become a model for building freedom in the developing world. And in Vietnam, you fought a noble battle for freedom. On the battlefield you knew only victory, only to have your victory lost by a failure of political will.

Nonetheless, you did honor to America. Your resistance to the evil of communism foreshadowed the growing movement toward democracy that we see today around the world. With your blood and valor, you won time for the rest of Southeast Asia and for the rest of humanity. You sustained the dream of freedom and leave as your legacy the free and vibrant nations of that region and the recognition that only free nations can prosper for their peoples. You, all of our former POW's, embody America's indomitable will to be free. Through your heroism, you have woven your lives into the fabric of American history and bound your flesh and spirit into our 200-year unbroken chain of freedom. Through your courage, you have demonstrated to the world that the American people shall always do that which is necessary to remain free. And for this the people of our nation and free people everywhere are in your debt.

In 10 days, it will be the Fourth of July, Independence Day. There'll be parades and fireworks. Americans will display the flag. And some children may ask, "Well, what are we celebrating? What does independence mean?" And all of you, better than most, know what independence means. You know the price at which it was won. As former prisoners of war, you know what it is to lose your freedom and to recover it. You know that freedom has its enemies, you've stared them in the eye, and you've suffered at their hands. You've seen that those who hate America hate us not for our flaws but for our strengths. You know what it means to be Americans, and in fact to be punished for it by those who despise what our country stands for. A former Vietnam POW, Captain Larry Chesley, tells of one instance when a fellow prisoner was taken from his cell—this was after the systematic torture had ceased—and he was savagely beaten as an example to the others. His crime was that there in the prison camp, he had made an American flag. The same flag too many of us will take for granted this Fourth of July.

I recall that returning prisoners of war said there were three things that helped them survive captivity and return with honor: faith in God, faith in their fellow prisoners, and faith in their country. As prisoners, many of you were subjected to terrible hardship and pain, which you resisted to the limits of your endurance, showing extraordinary courage time after time. You gained strength from each other and found it deep within yourselves.

Admiral James Stockdale, a long-term guest at the Hanoi Hilton, told of the time that he was left exposed outdoors for 3 days and nights in leg irons and handcuffs. He was periodically beaten and prevented from sleeping. As he grew weak, two fellow prisoners, despite the close watch of guards, spoke short words of encouragement that helped to sustain him. And another POW sent him a message in code by snapping a towel. The message was "God bless you." Yes, when things seemed most hopeless, you spoke words of prayer. In your time of greatest suffering, your faith did not falter but instead grew stronger. And in the face of evil, you put your trust in God and praised His name.

You also kept faith with America. And who can love this country more than the men and women who've been prisoners of a foreign power? When survivors of the Bataan Death March—World War II—being held in a POW camp, learned of the end of the war and their impending liberation, instead of taking vengeance on the prison guards there in their place of pain and torment, they said a prayer of thanksgiving and then sang "God Bless America." In the words of the song, America's soldiers "stood beside her," and we must stand beside them. Our country has not forgotten your former comrades who are still missing, those who fought in Korea and Vietnam and who have not returned home or been accounted for. We must keep faith with them and their families and demand the fullest possible accounting of the fate of the Americans who are missing in action. I know that the "River Rats" have a scholarship fund for the MIA children, and many of you've supported our efforts to learn the fate of their fathers. And let me say, we write no final chapter here. If there are living Americans being held against their will, we must bring them home.

America must also remain strong and vigilant, so that we can prevent war. A strong defense is one of our most basic human needs because it's the price of maintaining peace. And the same is true of supporting our allies and friends. Those resisting tyranny and aggression today in Nicaragua, in Afghanistan, in Cambodia, in Angola, and elsewhere, these fighters for freedom are part of the age-old tradition of human courage in the face of oppression. All of our efforts in Central America, particularly our support for the Nicaraguan freedom fighters, are designed to help those people secure their own freedom, so that we will never have to go to war to defend that critical region. And who can know better than you, how much better it is to deter a war than to fight one.

I know I've spoken before and told of when the Vietnam POW's returned home. I was Governor of California then, and Nancy and I were fortunate enough to have several hundred of them, in a number of groups, in our home. And we heard such stories and saw such courage. And one night afterward, when they'd gone, I said to Nancy, "Where did we find such men?" And the answer came almost as quickly as I'd asked it. We found them where we've always found them—on the farms, in the shops, in the offices and stores, on the streets, in the towns and cities of America. They're just the product of the greatest, freest system man has ever known.

Speaking for Nancy and myself, you and all those others will forever be in our prayers. I thank you, and God bless you. And God bless America!

And now, it's my honor to present the POW Medal to Americans representing World War II, the Korean conflict, and the Vietnam war.

Note: The President spoke at 2:01 p.m. at the South Portico at the White House. Recipients of the Prisoners of War Medal included: Sgt. Albert J. Bland, USAF, Pacific Theater, World War II; Lt. Gen. Charles M. Williams, USAF, European Theater, World War II; Cpl. Charles A. Burton, USA, Korean war; Col. Jesse "Davy" Booker, USMC, Korean war; Col. Floyd James "Jim" Thompson, USA, Vietnam war; and Comdr. Everett Alvarez, USN, Vietnam war.

Proclamation 5835—50th Anniversary of the Javits-Wagner-O'Day Act, 1988

June 24, 1988

By the President of the United States of America

A Proclamation

We can all be grateful that during the past 50 years a special effort has made more employment opportunities available to blind and other severely disabled Americans. The Wagner-O'Day Act, which became law on June 25, 1938, directed Federal agencies to purchase products from sheltered workshops staffed by blind Americans. In 1971, amendments proposed by Senator Javits extended this program by including workshops employing those with severe disabilities and by expanding the role of the Committee for Purchase from the Blind and Other Severely Handicapped in the administration of the program.

Today, more than 16,000 blind and other severely disabled people work in nearly 350 facilities under this program. From a modest beginning, when traditional products such as mops and brooms were produced, the program has grown to include a broad range of sophisticated goods and services.

Under this law, now known as the Javits-Wagner-O'Day Act, countless blind and other severely disabled Americans have received training and employment and have developed and displayed the skills and abilities to take competitive jobs outside sheltered settings and to reach their full potential and independence. Our Nation benefits from such contributions, and the Federal government benefits from the program because fine products and services are provided at fair market prices. Achievements under the program have been many, but we must continue our efforts to hire and train the majority of disabled people of working age who have not yet become employed.

We should all appreciate the wisdom and dedication of Senators Jacob Javits and Robert Wagner and of Congresswoman Caroline O'Day, by whose names this Act is known. We should also commend the efforts of the Committee for Purchase from the Blind and Other Severely Handicapped, the National Industries for the Blind, and the National Industries for the Severely Handicapped, whose goals are making the wisdom of the Act a reality.

The Congress, by Senate Concurrent Resolution 121, has requested the President to issue a proclamation commemorating June 25, 1988, as the 50th Anniversary of the Javits-Wagner-O'Day Act.

Now, Therefore, I, Ronald Reagan, President of the United States of America, do hereby commemorate the 50th Anniversary of the Javits-Wagner-O'Day Act on June 25, 1988. I call upon the people of the United States to observe this day with appropriate ceremonies and activities designed to reaffirm the Act's historical objectives of providing employment opportunities to blind and other severely handicapped Americans.

In Witness Whereof, I have hereunto set my hand this twenty-fourth day of June, in the year of our Lord nineteen hundred and eighty-eight, and of the Independence of the United States of America the two hundred and twelfth.

RONALD REAGAN

[*Filed with the Office of the Federal Register, 10:41 a.m., June 27, 1988*]

Remarks at the Ford's Theatre Gala
June 24, 1988

Thank you, and thank you all. And special thanks to Jimmy Stewart, who was so gracious in introducing my roommate, Nancy. [*Laughter*] There's no denying it; the Stewarts and the Reagans go back a long way. In fact, when my old boss, Jack Warner, first heard that I was running for Governor of California, he thought for a moment and then said, "No, Jimmy Stewart for Governor. Reagan for best friend." [*Laughter*] But even that was an improvement over what Jack Warner's brother, Harry, said way back in the very old days. Somebody told him about that new technique that would make it possible to add soundtracks to motion pictures—up until then, of course, there had been nothing but silent movies—and Harry answered, "Who the . . . wants to hear actors talk?" [*Laughter*]

But we're here tonight not to celebrate the movies but the theater—Ford's Theatre. This has been quite an evening, and on behalf of everyone here tonight, I want to express my gratitude to all those who've made it possible. Thanks go to the general chairmen, Betty Wright and Carol Laxalt; to the chairman of this evening's gala, Mary Jane Wick; and to the executive producer of this evening's performance, Frankie Hewitt; to our hosts, Jane Seymour and Harry Hamlin; and, yes, to this entire cast.

It was 125 years ago this year that Ford's Theatre first opened, as we've been told. And Washington in those days was, for the most part, a village—modest frame houses, dirt roads, chickens and livestock everywhere. The theatrical manager, John T. Ford, came here from Baltimore because he realized that Washington had a large natural audience—the thousands of Union troops quartered here with little to do. But Ford's Theatre did much more than give the troops a way to fight off their boredom; it brought pleasure and refreshment into the heart of a city struggling with the Civil War. Think how uplifting it must have been to the people who crowded this theater in those dark days to be able to laugh, to be able to participate in an evening that lifted them out of themselves. His biographers tell us that Mr. Lincoln loved the theater and nothing could have pleased him more than the performances that he saw here.

Today the village of Washington has become a great international city, even a center of culture and the arts. But the work of this splendid little theater remains unchanged: to refresh, to uplift, and to give joy. And so, in supporting Ford's Theatre, we're both helping to preserve a piece of our own history and to provide theater of the highest standards for the audiences today. May Ford's first 125 years be followed by 125 to come.

I can't resist, seeing all these splendid people up here entertaining us, as they have tonight, giving away the only thing they have to sell. Some years back, some entertainer in show business did something that affronted the public morals; and the press took off on that individual and then on all of show business and said that show people were just childish in their ways, in their thinking, in the things that they did, and complete children in their attitude. And it remained for a columnist named Irvin S. Cobb to respond. And he said: "If this be true, and if it be true when the final curtain falls all must approach the gates bearing in their arms that which they have given in life, the people of show business will march in the procession carrying in their arms the pure pearl of tears, the gold of laughter, and the diamonds of stardust they spread on what might otherwise have been a rather dreary world. And when at last, all reach the final stage door, the keeper will say, 'Open, let my children in.' "

Thank you, and God bless you.

Note: The President spoke at 10:50 p.m. at Ford's Theatre.

Radio Address to the Nation on the Fight Against Illegal Drugs
June 25, 1988

My fellow Americans:

This past week I traveled to Canada for my eighth economic summit with leaders of the industrialized democracies. The summit produced important results. We agreed on a plan to provide debt relief for some of the poorest countries of the world. We moved important agricultural reform negotiations forward. And we rededicated our nations to combating the modern day evils of airplane hijackings, terrorism, and illegal drugs.

It's this last matter, the fight against illegal drugs, that I'd like to take a moment to discuss with you this afternoon. This past week's meeting in Canada wasn't the first time the drug problem had been discussed among my summit colleagues. At the 1985 summit in Bonn, we established an expert group to identify areas for enhancing effectiveness and cooperation in fighting the scourge of illegal drugs. The expert group presented its report at our 1986 summit in Tokyo, and the report proved useful in setting our countries on a path of cooperation in combating drug abuse and illicit drug trafficking. Now the summit leaders have supported an initiative for a special group, launched by Vice President Bush and Canadian Prime Minister Mulroney, that would extend and promote the work done by the Bonn summit. This group will propose methods to improve international cooperation in combating production, trafficking, and financing of the drug trade. I'm hopeful this group can identify measures for a major coordinated assault on drugs.

But today the battle against drugs extends far beyond the seven industrialized democracies represented in Toronto. Just 1 year ago, 138 nations, members of the United Nations, met in Vienna to participate in the historic International Conference on Drug Abuse and Illicit Trafficking. This conference proved a resounding success in bringing together representatives from around the globe. Each of the participating governments declared its commitment to vigorous action against drug abuse and illicit drug trafficking. Perhaps even more important, the 138 nations adopted a comprehensive outline of activities all nations can undertake to fight illegal drugs. These activities include the reduction of demand for illegal drugs, the suppression of illicit drug production and trafficking, and the treatment and rehabilitation of drug-dependent people.

One suggestion coming out of the U.N. Conference was the recommendation for a commemorative day: an International Day Against Drug Abuse and Illicit Trafficking. The U.N. General Assembly then set aside June 26th to serve as this day of observance. Around the world, nations will join the United Nations commemorating the international fight against drugs, and I'm pleased that the United States will be among them. Attorney General Meese, who headed our delegation to the conference in Vienna, will host a ceremony to draw attention to the international day and to reaffirm the commitment of the United States to a drug free America and, yes, a drug free world.

Here at home this past week, the White House Conference for a Drug Free America released its report. This document included more than 100 recommendations for combating drug abuse and illicit drug trafficking. We'll be giving these recommendations careful consideration in the days ahead.

And there's another important antidrug effort underway here at home. It was on May 18th that I called on—to use my own words—"both Houses of the Congress, both sides of the aisle, to join with my representatives in a special executive-legislative task force to advance America's unified response to the problem of illegal drug use." My goal is to combine the expertise of the executive and legislative branches to identify the next steps we should take to stop the illegal use, distribution, and production of drugs and to begin taking these steps on a bipartisan basis. I'm sure you'll agree the drug problem is a national problem that demands national solutions and is too important for us to permit partisan bickering. I was pleased that the House and Senate minority leaders, Bob Dole and Bob Michel, appointed their representatives to the task force, and I urge the Speaker of the House and the majority leader of the Senate to appoint their own representatives quickly so we can get to work. Next week my National Drug Policy Board will recommend specific proposals that would be important to any new drug legislation. Today illegal drug use is down in our high schools. Cocaine and heroin seizures are up. And perhaps most important, attitudes about illegal drugs have changed. But we're working to make our beloved land what we know it ought to be and can be: a truly drug free America.

Until next week, thanks for listening, and God bless you.

Note: The President spoke at 12:06 p.m. from the Oval Office at the White House.

Written Responses to Questions Submitted by the Turkish Newspaper Hurriyet
June 22, 1988

Turkey-U.S. Relations

Q. Turkish President Mr. Kenan Evren will pay an official visit to Washington, DC, this June upon your invitation. What are your expectations in respect to this visit?

The President. I look forward to meeting President Evren, a man who holds a special place in the modern history of Turkey. He and I have the opportunity to reinforce the ties of mutual interest, friendship, and cooperation that have historically linked our nations and peoples. As a major ally of the United States, Turkey is a country of great importance to the American people. President Evren's visit will mark another vital step in the development of this relationship.

Q. How would you assess the course of the Turkish-American relationship during your Presidency? What were your priorities? What has given you the most personal satisfaction in regard to the Turkish-American relationship during this period? What have been your disappointments?

The President. Hosting the Turkish President gives me great satisfaction because the visit symbolizes the importance of the Turkish-American partnership to both our peoples. The interests and the democratic values of our nations and peoples coincide. In the past 7½ years, we have strengthened our friendship. Like all friends and allies, we have had occasional areas of disagreement, but when the overall relationship is as strong as it is between our two countries, disagreements do not prejudice the fundamental relationship. Today, following Turkey's successful resolution of the problems of anarchy and violence which it confronted during the 1970's, Turkey and the United States once again deal with each other and with the world as strong, self-confident democracies. This is a powerful bond between our two peoples. In addition, I think it very important that over the past 8 years there has been significant growth in the support for the Turkish-American relationship in our Congress.

President's View of Turkey

Q. How would you describe your perception of Turkey in the economic, political, and security fields?

The President. Turkey is of great importance. Its democratic values, its secular orientation, and the political commitment it has made to full involvement in the Western community of nations are very significant. A glance at a map explains the unique geographic and strategic situation of your country. I have admired the way Turkey overcame the forces of terrorism and anarchy which threatened your freedoms in the late 1970's. The commitment of the Turkish people to democracy is obviously very strong. Turkey's economic potential has always been very great. I have been impressed by Turkey's economic advances in the 1980's through a market-oriented approach to economic growth and progress.

Turkey's Role in the Middle East

Q. Although participating fully in such Western institutions as NATO, Turkey is an Islamic country and also a part of the Middle East. How does this fact affect the U.S. policy considerations towards Turkey? In your view, what is Turkey's role in the region?

The President. Turkey clearly can and does play a special role in the Middle East. In part, this role is a product of its traditions and its achievements, which gives it a special relationship to the area. We value the insights of your leaders into developments and trends throughout the region. More broadly, Turkey's success as a Western, modern, and secular state has a significant impact as a potential model for the region.

Turkey-U.S. Relations

Q. Several developments in Washington are contributing to a growing uneasiness towards the United States in the Turkish public and official circles. Among these developments, declining assistance levels, conditions added on assistance programs in Congress, and restrictions imposed on Turkish exports could be named. How do you plan to address those problems? What would you recommend to the next administration in this respect?

The President. None of the issues which you have raised are new, and all are more than outweighed by newer, positive elements in our relationship. As I noted earlier, I think the relationship between Turkey and the United States is stronger, in part, because of the greater appreciation in this country of its importance to both Turkey and the United States. While budget austerity in this country limits assistance levels, we have found ways to make the assistance itself more effective through the extension of forms of assistance which do not require repayment and through the development of such programs as the Southern Region Amendment, under which we were able to provide 40 F–4E aircraft to Turkey last year. The United States and Turkey have enjoyed excellent bilateral relations during the past 7½ years. And as President, I have worked to expand the ties between Turkey and the United States beyond our security relationship. Today our two countries are increasingly linked by a growing variety of economic and cultural ties, and this gives me great satisfaction.

Q. There is a persistent feeling in the Turkish public that Turkey is taken for granted by the United States. How would you respond to this concern?

The President. First, I would say it would be very sad if either partner should take the relationship for granted. It is too important to us both for that attitude to prevail. But secondly, I must disagree with your statement. Such an approach assumes that Turkey does more for the United States than the United States does for Turkey. I believe that both nations are making great contributions to our common objectives. Our relationship with Turkey, like our relationships with our other allies, rests on the principle of collective defense. There is no doubt that both the United States and Turkey are more secure because of their alliance. The money the United States spends on strategic defense and conventional forces is money spent on the defense of Turkey as well. Our many years of sustained assistance to Turkey demonstrate that our commitment to the relationship is strongly rooted in American policy and belies the allegation that we take Turkey for granted. Finally, I think that President Evren's visit to the United States clearly indicates the importance which we give to our Turkish ally.

Turkey's Role in NATO

Q. What are the implications for Turkey of the ongoing dialog between you and Soviet leader Mr. Mikhail Gorbachev? In your opinion, what role would Turkey play in the post-INF period?

The President. Turkey, like all members of NATO, will benefit from the dialog between the United States and the Soviet Union, since this dialog is carried out within the context of, and with full recognition for, our NATO commitments. In the post-INF period, Turkey will remain, as it has always been, NATO's bulwark on the southern flank against Soviet aggression.

Cyprus Conflict

Q. How do you view the recent trends in Turkish-Greek relations? Are you hopeful that the "spirit of Davos" could lead to the solution of the Cyprus problem?

The President. As a friend and ally of both Greece and Turkey, we can only welcome the reduction in tensions that has followed the meeting of Prime Ministers Özal and Papandreou at Davos. As I suggested earlier, we believe strongly in the utility of dialog to solve international problems. Certainly the efforts of the U.N. Secretary-General through his good offices mission, which we strongly support, provide a vehicle for getting such a dialog underway. The issues are difficult and complex and will take time to resolve.

Note: The questions and answers were released by the Office of the Press Secretary on June 27.

Remarks at the Welcoming Ceremony for President Kenan Evren of Turkey
June 27, 1988

President Reagan. The founder of the Turkish Republic, Mustafa Kemal Atatürk, once said, "Happy is he who can call himself a Turk." Well, I can say that I understand that sentiment. And I can also say that, "Happy is the American President who can welcome the Turkish President." So, let me welcome you to the United States on behalf of myself and the American people.

We are proud to have the Turkish President here. Turkey and the United States have the strongest of bonds: friendship and alliance. Our relations have been characterized by success. Together with their NATO allies, Turkey and the United States have been partners in the most successful alliance the world has ever known, an alliance that has maintained the peace for nearly 40 years.

The modern Turkish-American partnership began in 1947. The Turkish people demonstrated the will and the courage that were required to meet the threat of aggression. The American people, with similar will and courage, were able to support them. In the 40 years that have followed, the strength and durability of our partnership, and of the NATO alliance, have discouraged aggression. In Korea, Turks and Americans shed blood together on the battlefield in defense of freedom. Today the solidarity of our mutual commitment to collective security keeps us safe and enables us to seek improved relations with our adversaries from a position of strength.

The ties between Turkey and the United States are broader than our common security interests. We are brought together by the strong bonds that derive from shared values as well. And I might say, Americans have admired the way that Turkey pulled itself back to democracy when challenged by the violent forces of terrorism and anarchy a decade ago. We are well aware of your own distinguished role, Mr. President, in maintaining Turkey's devotion to the ideals of Atatürk. Your country's pride in that accomplishment is understandable. For our part, the American people are proud of the decades of support they have given to Turkey. Friendships must never be taken for granted. We want our ties with the Turkish Nation to grow and to deepen. Happily, that process is well underway. As vigorous democracies, our peoples should get to know each other better.

Last year the "Süleyman the Magnificent" exhibit, magnificent in itself, opened the eyes of Americans to the richness of the Turkish heritage. Visits between American Congressmen and women and Turkish parliamentarians have increased in recent years, and with that increase has come better understanding. Our trade relations are growing, and Turkey is strongly attracting American investors. And I firmly believe that trade and investment are the surest ways that Turkey can find to ensure the prosperity its people seek.

Mr. President, Turkey and the United States are allies and friends; as such, we have a record of success together. In our coming meetings, I know that we will enhance that friendship and add to the record of success. I am confident, too, that your full schedule, with its intense program of contacts with American political, economic, and cultural leaders, will further strengthen mutual understanding and our sense of common purpose. I look forward to discussing with you the ways in which we can strengthen our established ties and create new forms of cooperation in defense of these purposes and values. As Turkey and the United States look ahead to the next century, our continuing friendship and alliance will continue to serve us well. It cannot be otherwise, for at the root of our relationship are common goals: democracy, peace, and security for our peoples.

And now, Mr. President, I have the honor of presenting to you the Legion of Merit, Chief Commander, one of the highest military honors our country awards, for the service of Turkish forces in the Korean conflict. I present this not only as a tribute to the valor of the Turkish military and the people of your nation but as a symbol of our alliance on so many fronts over so many years in the cause of peace and freedom.

President Evren. Mr. President, Mrs. Reagan, I thank you for the kind invitation to visit the United States of America and for your generous hospitality. Your warm words of welcome have moved us. This ceremony, which marks the beginning of my visit, brings together the national flags of Turkey and the United States, allies whose ties have stood the test of time.

Thousands of Turks like myself still recall the memories of fighting shoulder-to-shoulder with American soldiers in Korea for the defense of freedom. We have been allies at war and in peace. This Legion of Merit award is a reflection of the fact that the outstanding services of the Turkish brigade in Korea are still fresh in the minds of our American friends, and I accept it with deep appreciation on behalf of the entire Turkish Nation. In so doing, I express not only my own personal thanks but also those of my 54 million fellow Turks who share with me the pride of their nation on this occasion. Recalling our comrades in arms who made the ultimate sacrifice in Korea, I assure you that the dedication of the Turkish people to the principle of freedom and democracy remains as undiminished today as it did 40 years ago.

Mr. President, my visit to your country is also the natural consequence of the interest and support which your administration from the outset has extended to Turkey and to the development of Turkish-American friendship. This interest, which we much appreciate, is rooted in Turkey's dedication to Western ideals of democracy, peace, and stability. As in the past, the core of Turkish-American relations continues to consist of commonly held political views and values. Those elements constitute the most valid guarantee of the durability and closeness of our friendship, as well as the fruitfulness of our cooperation. The stable development of Turkish-American relations, based on equality and mutual interests, is to the benefit of our countries, the free world, and international peace and security.

Mr. President, I am confident that my visit will provide the opportunity for a productive dialog on how we can further expand and deepen our bonds. At the same time, I hope that my visit will also contribute to a better recognition of Turkey and the United States by our respective peoples, and particularly of Turkey as a reliable partner.

Mr. President, the people of Turkey follow with admiration your determined efforts for the defense of freedom, strengthening of peace, and development and reduction of international tensions. Strengthening of peace, freedom, and independence remain high on the global agenda. Situated in a region where these issues are paramount, Turkey is determined to continue her contribution to peace and stability. Turkey serves as an anchor of democracy, freedom, and stability in a region in turmoil. Your own Thomas Paine once wrote: "Those who expect to reap the blessings of freedom must undergo the fatigue of supporting it." Mr. President, let me say that in Turkey we do not feel fatigued by our support of the Western allies because we know that by supporting the allies we may all continue to reap the blessings of freedom.

Mr. President, I am delighted to meet you, the distinguished members of your administration, and be among the great people of this country. As a final word, let me say that I look with hope and confidence to the future of the relations between our two countries sharing the ideals of peace, stability, freedom, and prosperity. I thank you once again for your kind invitation.

Note: President Reagan spoke at 10:12 a.m. at the South Portico of the White House, where President Evren was accorded a formal welcome with full military honors. Following the ceremony, the two Presidents met in the Oval Office.

Statement on the Report of the Presidential Commission on the Human Immunodeficiency Virus Epidemic
June 27, 1988

I have just been briefed on the unanimous report of the Commission on the Human Immunodeficiency Virus Epidemic by Adm. James D. Watkins, the Commission's Chairman. The report represents an impressive effort and significantly increases our level of understanding to deal with AIDS. To begin implementing this report, I am today directing Dr. Ian Macdonald, a distinguished physician and my Special Assistant for Drug Policy, to present to me within 30 days a course of action that takes us forward. At Admiral Watkins' suggestion, I have also directed Dr. Macdonald to include among his priorities consideration of specific measures to strengthen implementation of the policy guidance from "AIDS in the Workplace," recently issued by the Office of Personnel Management.

The report embraces the major concepts

my administration laid out over a year ago: to be compassionate towards victims of the disease; to care for them with dignity and kindness; and at the same time, to inform and educate our citizens so that we can prevent the further spread of the disease.

There is a direct relationship between drug abuse and the spread of the HIV virus that becomes AIDS. It is critical that particular attention be focused on this relationship now, while developing a national consensus on additional anti-drug abuse measures.

I want to express my sincere appreciation to Admiral Watkins and all of the Commission participants for their perseverance and diligence in completing their work. It is my hope that we can continue to approach this problem, which is more than a medical crisis or a public health threat, in a thoughtful and bipartisan manner.

Designation of Anne E. Brunsdale as Vice Chairman of the United States International Trade Commission
June 27, 1988

The President today announced his intention to designate Anne E. Brunsdale as Vice Chairman of the United States International Trade Commission for the term expiring June 16, 1990.

Since 1985 Miss Brunsdale has been a member of the International Trade Commission in Washington, DC. Prior to this, she was a resident fellow for the American Enterprise Institute for Public Policy Research (AEI), 1983–1985, and managing editor of Regulation, 1977–1985. From 1970 to 1977, she was director of publications for AEI, and a research associate, 1967–1970.

Miss Brunsdale graduated from the University of Minnesota (B.A., 1945; M.A., 1946) and Yale University (M.A., 1949). She was born October 1, 1923, in Minneapolis, MN, and she currently resides in Washington, DC.

Toasts at the State Dinner for President Kenan Evren of Turkey
June 27, 1988

President Reagan. Ladies and gentlemen, I've been told of a Turkish proverb that states: "A cup of coffee will bear the fruit of 40 years of friendship." Well, my sense of this expression is that in the give and take of conversation over coffee people establish the sense of caring and loyalty, and of shared hopes and expectations, that define friendship.

Now, Americans and Turks sitting here will soon be sharing a cup of coffee. And earlier today, you and I shared our ideas and our hopes for the United States, for Turkey, and for the partnership between our peoples. And that's why I've long hoped that you would come to the United States, and that's why I'm glad you're here.

But you and I are building on a solid structure. The United States and Turkey have, for more than 40 years, shared much more than a cup of coffee. We've worked together to preserve the integrity of Turkey when it was threatened by aggression in 1947. We've been partners in the world's most successful partnership: the NATO alliance of democracies. Together with our allies, we have withstood aggression and made progress toward peace. Turks and Americans shed blood together in Korea. Americans have been proud to help Turkey in securing its democracy and seeking prosperity.

Our aspirations for our partnership remain large: peace, security, and freedom for our peoples; close cooperation in securing these objectives; and success in defending them. I am confident that 40 years from now Turks and Americans will look back and say that through their friendship Turks and Americans secured for themselves the kind of world we have envisioned together.

And now please join me in a toast to President Evren, to the Turkish-American relationship, and to the friendship between our two peoples. And as you say in Turkish: *Serefinize* [To your honor].

President Evren. Mr. President, Mrs. Reagan, distinguished guests: Mr. President, I thank you for your kind remarks. I am indeed moved by them. Our talks today with you and with the distinguished members of your administration have reaffirmed the strength and depth of the bond of friendship which we have continuously developed over the years between our countries. I am most pleased to observe this.

During your administration, Turkish-American relations have gained additional momentum, and the scope of our cooperation has vastly expanded. I am confident that I speak for the Turkish people in stating that we see you not only as a distinguished statesman of our era but also as a good friend of Turkey. We hope that future administrations will carry and further build on the revitalization process in our relations.

The strategic interdependence between our two countries, which we mutually identified almost 40 years ago, retains its validity today. But Turkish-American cooperation rests not only on strategic interests but also on common values embedded in the principles of respect for human rights, freedom, and democracy. We in Turkey are proud that, like other NATO countries with whom we share a common destiny, we have succeeded in establishing a democracy with all its institutions based on respect for human rights. Though this characteristic may not be all that well-known, it is the basis for Turkey's position as an island of peace and stability in a region in turmoil.

Mr. President, we followed with satisfaction and great interest the positive developments at the Moscow summit. It is the hope of Turkish and other peoples that the historical step taken by concluding the INF agreement will be followed by more comprehensive ones in the direction of disarmament. I would like to express my appreciation for this constructive initiative on the part of the United States and the Soviet Union and congratulate you for your tremendous success. We support the efforts of your administration to seek better relations with the Soviet Union without neglecting our defense requirements. It would be a tremendous achievement if, through these efforts, we could leave to future generations a more secure world.

Mr. President, with its present capabilities and future potential, Turkey can become an important economic partner. Internal stability and peace have fostered and sustained high rates of economic growth. This encourages us as we look to the future with confidence for a prosperous Turkey. We consider the economic dimension of our relations with the United States as integral to our traditional friendship and security partnership. Expanded economic cooperation will be an additional source of strength for our political and security relations. That is why we seek more dynamic and comprehensive economic collaboration as part of a multifaceted and therefore more robust relationship. We want our American friends to know of our desire for wide-ranging cooperation in this regard.

Mr. President, I thank you once again for your kind invitation, for the generous hospitality that the American people have extended to us, and for this beautiful evening. And I propose a toast to you; to your charming wife, Mrs. Reagan; and to the continuation of the excellent relations between Turkey and the United States.

Note: President Reagan spoke at 9:54 p.m. in the Rose Garden at the White House.

Letter Accepting the Resignation of Howard H. Baker, Jr., as Chief of Staff to the President
June 28, 1988

Dear Howard:

It is with especially deep regret that I accept your resignation as Chief of Staff, effective June 30.

You and I have known each other for many years as public servants, partisan allies, and good friends. You came to the United States Senate the same year I went to the Statehouse in California; and, as I'm sure you would agree, things haven't been the same for either of us since. Our paths often brought us together in those early years and helped determine the future direction of our Party and our country. And let me add: Our Nation has rarely seen a more dedicated and capable leader in its capital than Howard Baker.

Your dedication to public service was renowned during your 18 years in the Senate, but it became even more so when you set aside your personal and political interests to answer my call to service in the Executive branch. For that, I am particularly appreciative. You accepted the position of Chief of Staff and quickly assembled a top-flight team of senior aides to move my agenda forward. A tone of cooperation and conciliation in those difficult early months of 1987 was communicated to the public and to those in the Congress. At the same time, the White House functioned efficiently and effectively in setting out and pursuing my policy goals.

I clearly appreciate the challenges you faced. Your tireless efforts on my behalf with your former colleagues to forge a sense of cooperation last October to reach a budget agreement; your counsel on many issues that enabled me to make the best decisions on behalf of all the people; your significant contributions to bring about the first reduction in United States and Soviet nuclear arms; and also your gentle Tennessee wit that can relax a tense moment—these are attributes that come from the heart and that have made our relationship not a job but a friendship that will last forever.

No one understands better than Nancy and I the personal reasons that lead you to relinquish your responsibilities at this time. That, too, is a tribute to your character and your integrity. With all the years you and I have been associated, this truly is no farewell, but rather a note of enduring and heartfelt thanks for a job well done.

Our best wishes for happiness and good health to you, Joy, and your entire family now and for the future. God bless you.

Sincerely,

RON

Note: Mr. Baker's letter of resignation appears on p. 771 of this volume.

Appointment of M.B. Oglesby, Jr., as Assistant to the President and Deputy Chief of Staff
June 28, 1988

The President today announced the appointment of M.B. Oglesby, Jr., to be Assistant to the President and Deputy Chief of Staff, effective July 5, 1988. He would succeed Kenneth M. Duberstein.

Mr. Oglesby is currently vice chairman of the board of Hecht, Spencer & Oglesby, Inc., government relations representatives in Washington, DC. He joined the firm in March 1986, having come from the White House, where he served as Assistant to the President for Legislative Affairs. Previously, he served as minority staff associate for the House Energy and Commerce Committee, dealing principally with railroad, environmental, and commerce-related legislation. Mr. Oglesby also served as deputy director and acting director of the State of Illinois Washington office and as executive assistant to Congressman Edward Madigan (R–IL). Prior to coming to Washington, he served in Illinois State Government as an assistant to Governor Richard Ogilvie and as executive assistant to the speaker of the house. Mr. Oglesby also spent 3½ years in management positions with the Illinois Bell Telephone Co.

He attended the University of Illinois in Champaign. He is married, resides in Bethesda, MD, and was born October 1, 1942, in Flora, IL.

Appointment of John C. Tuck as Assistant to the President and Director of the Office of the Chief of Staff
June 28, 1988

The President today appointed John C. Tuck as Assistant to the President and Director of the Office of the Chief of Staff.

Since April 1987 Mr. Tuck has been serving as Deputy Assistant to the President and Executive Assistant to the Chief of Staff. Prior to this, he served as Deputy Assistant to the President for Legislative Affairs from October 1986 to April 1987 and Special Assistant to the President for Legislative Affairs from March 1986 to October 1986. He was assistant secretary for the majority, United States Senate, 1981–1986. He also serves as a member of the President's Commission on White House Fellowships.

Mr. Tuck graduated from Georgetown University, School of Foreign Service (B.S., 1967). He served in the U.S. Navy, 1968–1973, and was detailed to the White House as a social aide from September 1971 to December 1972. He is a commander in the Naval reserve. He was born May 28, 1945, in Dayton, OH. Mr. Tuck is married to the former Jane L. McDonough. They have three children, and they currently reside in Arlington, VA.

Statement by Assistant to the President for Press Relations Fitzwater on the Soviet-United States Nuclear Testing Negotiations
June 28, 1988

The United States and the Soviet Union concluded round two of the nuclear testing talks on June 28 in Geneva. The round, which began on February 15, is part of U.S.-Soviet step-by-step negotiations on nuclear testing. The first priority of these talks is agreement on effective verification measures for two existing, but unratified treaties: the Threshold Test Ban Treaty and the Peaceful Nuclear Explosions Treaty.

During the round, we made considerable progress toward our goal of effective verification of these treaties. The two sides are now close to agreement on the verification protocol for the Peaceful Nuclear Explosions Treaty. Agreement on this protocol will facilitate further progress on the verification protocol for the Threshold Test Ban Treaty. However, in the case of this treaty, the Soviets have insisted that the joint verification experiment is necessary before the protocol is finalized.

Preparations for the joint verification experiment are well advanced. Based on procedures detailed in an agreement signed in Moscow during the summit, personnel from each side are now on the other's test site, making arrangements for the experiment. We expect the joint verification experiment to be conducted this summer. We believe that the experiment will provide the Soviets the information they need to accept routine U.S. use of CORRTEX—the most accurate method we have identified for verifying compliance with these treaties—for treaty verification.

We hope that with the continued cooperation of the Soviet Union we will be able to reach early agreement on effective verification measures so that these two treaties can be ratified.

Statement by Assistant to the President for Press Relations Fitzwater on the Assassination of the United States Naval Attaché in Athens, Greece
June 28, 1988

We condemn this senseless act of brutality. As of this time, no group has claimed responsibility for the act. Our deepest sympathies are extended to Captain Nordeen's family. We will work with Greek authorities to bring the murderers to justice.

Note: William Nordeen's automobile was blown up as it passed a parked vehicle loaded with dynamite. The Greek terrorist group "November 17" claimed responsibility.

White House Statement on the President's Discussions with Israeli Defense Minister Yitzhak Rabin
June 28, 1988

The President, the Vice President, and other top officials have met with Israeli Defense Minister Yitzhak Rabin over the past 2 days. The President noted that Israel and the United States will soon sign a memorandum of understanding (MOU) for the joint development of an antitactical ballistic missile (ATBM) which will be able to deal with ballistic missile threats. The U.S. contribution will be approximately 80 percent and that of Israel 20 percent. This joint development is an outgrowth of research on SDI.

The President expressed his concern about ominous new military developments in the region. In particular, he called attention to the proliferation of ballistic missiles and chemical capabilities. He observed that such capabilities could change the military situation, making any future war far more costly, difficult to control, and dangerous. Both the President and Vice President emphasized in their meetings with Defense Minister Rabin the need for international efforts to stop this proliferation. They also stressed that these trends put a premium both on continuing U.S.-Israeli defense cooperation and energetically working for peace in the area.

The President paid tribute to what Defense Minister Rabin has done to strengthen Israeli capability for self-defense. Defense Minister Rabin has also done much to develop our strategic partnership and give it substance. He has recognized realistically what Israel can develop on its own and in partnership with the United States.

The President and Vice President reaffirmed America's commitment to Israel's security, noting that Israel could never be fully secure without peace. Realism and a willingness to nurture, rather than reject, possible opportunities for peace are essential, as is a climate that makes negotiations possible. While Israel should not be expected to make concessions under the threat of violence, the preservation of order in the territories must neither provide a justification for civilian lawlessness nor act as an excuse for avoiding political discourse with the Palestinians of the West Bank and Gaza. Neither should violence nor controls on violence become ends in themselves, making a political solution more difficult.

Nomination of Charles A. Gillespie, Jr., To Be United States Ambassador to Chile

June 28, 1988

The President today announced his intention to nominate Charles A. Gillespie, Jr., of California, a career member of the Senior Foreign Service, Class of Minister-Counselor, as Ambassador to the Republic of Chile. He would succeed Harry George Barnes, Jr.

Since joining the Foreign Service in 1965, Ambassador Gillespie has served at American Embassies in Manila, Brussels, Mexico City, and Managua, and at the U.S. mission to the North Atlantic Treaty Organization in Belgium. In 1981 he joined the staff of the State Department's Assistant Secretary for Inter-American Affairs as a special assistant. Ambassador Gillespie was named Deputy Assistant Secretary for Inter-American Affairs in 1983. In October 1983 he was selected to establish the first American Embassy on the island of Grenada. He assumed his current duties as Ambassador to the Republic of Colombia in August 1985.

Ambassador Gillespie graduated from the University of California at Los Angeles (B.A., 1958). He served in the United States Army, 1958–1962. He was born March 22, 1935, in Long Beach, CA. He is married, has two children, and resides in Bogotá, Colombia.

Nomination of William H. Twaddell To Be United States Ambassador to Mauritania

June 28, 1988

The President today announced his intention to nominate William H. Twaddell, of Rhode Island, a career member of the Senior Foreign Service, Class of Counselor, as Ambassador to the Islamic Republic of Mauritania. He would succeed Robert L. Pugh.

Mr. Twaddell was a member of the United States Peace Corps from 1963 to 1965. From 1968 to 1969, he was a reporter for the New York Daily News in Washington, DC. He entered the Foreign Service in 1969, and was a consular officer for the American consulate general in Dhahran, Saudi Arabia, 1970–1972. He was an economic-commercial officer for the American Embassy in Caracas, Venezuela, 1973–1975, and an economic analyst in the Bureau of Intelligence and Research, 1975–1976. He was an operations officer in the Operations Center at the Department of State, 1976–1977, and then Special Assistant to the Secretary of State, 1977–1980. Mr. Twaddell has served as deputy chief of mission and Chargé d'Affaires at the American Embassy in Maputo, Mozambique, 1980–1983; instructor in the department of humanities at the U.S. Coast Guard Academy, 1983–1985; and deputy chief of mission for the American Embassy in Bamako, Mali, 1985–1987. Since 1987 he has been attending the senior seminar at the Foreign Service Institute.

Mr. Twaddell attended Brown University (B.A., 1963). He was born January 25, 1941, in Madison, WI. He served in the United States Army, 1965–1967. Mr. Twaddell has two children and currently resides in Washington, DC.

Nomination of Noreen C. Thomas To Be a Member of the National Advisory Council on Educational Research and Improvement
June 28, 1988

The President today announced his intention to nominate Noreen C. Thomas to be a member of the National Advisory Council on Educational Research and Improvement for a term expiring September 30, 1991. This is a reappointment.

Since 1987 Mrs. Thomas has been a second and third grade teacher at the Chase Lake Elementary School in Edmonds, WA. She was previously a first and second grade teacher at the Evergreen Elementary School, 1979–1987.

Mrs. Thomas graduated from Washington State University (B.A., 1957). She was born August 13, 1935, in Port Angeles, WA. She is married, has one child, and resides in Edmonds, WA.

Appointment of David Zwiebel To Be a Member of the National Commission on Children
June 28, 1988

The President today announced his intention to appoint David Zwiebel to be a member of the National Commission on Children for a term expiring March 31, 1989. This is a new position.

Since 1984 Mr. Zwiebel has been general counsel and director of governmental affairs for Agudath Israel of America in New York City. Prior to this he was with the law firm of Paul, Weiss, Rifkin, Wharton & Garrison, 1979–1984.

Mr. Zwiebel graduated from Brooklyn College, CUNY (B.S., 1975) and Yeshiva University (J.D., 1979). He was born December 29, 1952, in the Bronx, NY. He is married, has six children, and resides in Brooklyn, NY.

Nomination of James G. Stearns To Be a Director of the Securities Investor Protection Corporation, and Designation as Chairman
June 28, 1988

The President today announced his intention to nominate James G. Stearns to be a Director of the Securities Investor Protection Corporation for a term expiring December 31, 1991. This is a reappointment. Upon appointment, he will be redesignated Chairman.

Since 1975 Mr. Stearns has been a self-employed rancher and farmer in Nevada and Oregon. He was also director of the Office of Alcohol Fuels at the Department of Energy in Washington, DC, in 1981.

Mr. Stearns was born January 29, 1922, in Lapine, OR. He served in the United States Army Air Corps, 1942–1945. He is married, has three children, and resides in Reno, NV.

Appointment of Theodore N. Lerner To Be a Member of the United States Holocaust Memorial Council
June 28, 1988

The President today announced his intention to appoint Theodore N. Lerner to be a member of the United States Holocaust Memorial Council for the remainder of the term expiring January 15, 1991. He would succeed Seymour Siegel.

Since 1951 Mr. Lerner has been a real estate developer in Washington, DC. He is also president of Lerner Corp. in North Bethesda, MD. Mr. Lerner is a member of the building committee for the U.S. Holocaust Museum and a trustee of the George Washington University.

Mr. Lerner graduated from George Washington University (B.A., 1948; LL.B., 1950). He was born October 15, 1925, in Washington, DC. He served in the United States Army, 1944–1946. He is married, has three children, and currently resides in Chevy Chase, MD.

Proclamation 5836—Withdrawal of Nondiscriminatory Treatment for Products of Romania
June 28, 1988

By the President of the United States of America

A Proclamation

1. Pursuant to section 402(c) of the Trade Act of 1974, as amended ("the Act") (19 U.S.C. 2432(c)), I previously waived the requirements of sections 402(a) and (b) of the Act (19 U.S.C. 2432(a) and (b) with respect to the Socialist Republic of Romania ("Romania"). As a result, articles the product of Romania imported into the United States were eligible for nondiscriminatory treatment (most-favored-nation status). Romania also was eligible to participate in programs of the U.S. Government that extend credits, credit guarantees, or investment guarantees. Pursuant to section 404(a) of the Act (19 U.S.C. 2434(a)), I extended most-favored-nation status to Romania under the terms of a commercial agreement that entered into force on August 3, 1975, and was entered into under the authority of section 405 of the Act (19 U.S.C. 2435), with such status contingent upon the annual renewal of a waiver pursuant to section 402(c) of the Act (19 U.S.C. 2432(c)).

2. The Government of Romania has announced that it has decided to renounce the renewal of nondiscriminatory treatment accorded to the products of Romania by the United States subject to the terms of section 402 of the Act (19 U.S.C. 2432).

3. Accordingly, I have decided to allow the waiver for Romania under section 402 of the Act (19 U.S.C. 2432) to expire as scheduled at the close of July 2, 1988, without renewal at that time, and I have so reported to the Congress. Therefore, effective July 3, 1988, all articles the product of Romania that are entered, or withdrawn from warehouse for consumption, into the customs territory of the United States shall be subject to the customs duties set forth in the Rates of Duty column 2 of the Tariff Schedules of the United States (TSUS) (19 U.S.C. 1202). Furthermore, effective as of that date, Romania shall no longer be eligible to receive credits or guarantees under any program of the U.S. Government that extends credits, credit guarantees, or investment guarantees, including the Commodity Credit Corporation and the Export-Import Bank of the United States.

4. Section 404(c) of the Act (19 U.S.C. 2434(c)) authorizes the President to suspend or withdraw any extension of nondiscriminatory treatment to any country pursuant to section 404(a) of the Act (19 U.S.C.

2434(a)).

5. Section 604 of the Act (19 U.S.C. 2483) authorizes the President to embody in the TSUS the substance of the relevant provisions of that Act, of other acts affecting import treatment, and of actions taken thereunder.

Now, Therefore, I, Ronald Reagan, President of the United States of America, acting under the authority vested in me by the Constitution and statutes of the United States of America, including but not limited to sections 402, 404, and 604 of the Act, do proclaim that:

(1) Effective with respect to all articles the product of Romania that are entered, or withdrawn from warehouse for consumption, into the customs territory of the United States on or after July 3, 1988, such articles, whether imported directly or indirectly, shall be subject to duty at the rates set forth in the Rates of Duty column 2 of the TSUS.

(2) General Headnote 3(d) to the TSUS, setting forth those countries whose products, whether imported directly or indirectly, shall be dutied at the rates of duty shown in the column numbered 2 of such schedules, is modified by inserting in alphabetical sequence "Socialist Republic of Romania".

(3) Romania will no longer be eligible to receive credits or guarantees under any program of the U.S. Government that extends credits, credit guarantees, or investment guarantees.

(4) The action taken in this Proclamation shall be effective July 3, 1988.

In Witness Whereof, I have hereunto set my hand this twenty-eighth day of June, in the year of our Lord nineteen hundred and eighty-eight, and of the Independence of the United States of America the two hundred and twelfth.

RONALD REAGAN

[*Filed with the Office of the Federal Register, 12:23 p.m., June 29, 1988*]

Statement by Assistant to the President for Press Relations Fitzwater on the Supreme Court's Decision Upholding the Constitutionality of the Independent Counsel Act

June 29, 1988

The United States Supreme Court today upheld the constitutionality of the Independent Counsel Act. In so doing, the Court reversed a decision by the United States Court of Appeals for the DC Circuit. Justice Kennedy did not participate in the decision of the case.

The President signed an extension of the Independent Counsel Act in December 1987. At that time, he expressed his full support for the goal of ensuring public confidence in the impartiality and integrity of criminal law investigations of high-level executive branch officials. At the same time, the President expressed concern that the act's procedures were inconsistent with the text of the Constitution and the principle of separation of powers. Despite these doubts about the constitutionality of the Independent Counsel Act, the administration has faithfully and consistently complied with all of the act's requirements, even offering the ongoing Independent Counsels parallel appointments within the Department of Justice to protect them against constitutional challenge. Thus, today's decision by the Court will have no practical effect on the administration's implementation of the Independent Counsel Act or on the ongoing investigations. We cannot comment on the consequences of this decision for any existing cases.

Remarks at a Campaign Fundraising Luncheon for Representative Connie Mack in Miami, Florida
June 29, 1988

Thank you. Connie, I could have listened all day. [*Laughter*] Thank you all very much. Connie and Priscilla, Governor Bob Martinez and Mary Jane, Jeannie Austin, Alec Courtelis, Tommy Thomas, Jeb Bush, and Paula Hawkins, ladies and gentlemen, I thank you all. The Florida Republican Party fills my heart with sunshine. You know, it's always great to be in Florida, but it's not true that I keep returning just because Ponce de Leon thought that this was the place to find the Fountain of Youth. [*Laughter*] The fact is Ponce de Leon never did find the Fountain of Youth. I know, I was with him on that trip. [*Laughter*]

Well, actually, the truth is, you know what keeps me young—it's cutting taxes. [*Laughter*] The other thing that keeps me young is helping elect outstanding Republicans, and that's why I'm here today. I came to campaign for the next United States Senator from Florida: Congressman Connie Mack.

Now of course, Connie Mack's grandfather and namesake was the grand old man of baseball. Back then, if Connie had told his grandfather that he wanted to go to Washington to be a Senator, Mr. Mack probably would have figured that Connie meant the baseball team, the old Washington Senators. [*Laughter*] In those days, we used to jokingly say, "Washington, first in war, first in peace, and the last in the American League." [*Laughter*] But next year, thanks to you, Washington will have a new winning team, and I mean real major leaguers: Senator Connie Mack and President George Bush. And Connie, you'll have to pitch because he was a catcher. [*Laughter*]

Well, since his election to Congress in 1982, Connie has stood with us for reducing taxes, spending, and government; strengthening our defense, expanding world freedom; and restoring a strong, proud, and free America that puts its faith in God and trust in the people themselves. What the 1988 elections are all about is whether we continue to build on that progress and move ahead to an even brighter future or whether we hesitate and return to those worn-out policies that Connie mentioned that bring high taxes, low growth, and a loss of direction and purpose.

When George Bush and I took office, the other party, which had long controlled Washington, had left America with its economic and foreign policy in disarray. Government spending was soaring out of control. Business was being crushed under massive regulation and taxation. Unemployment and business failures were climbing. The prime rate was at a record 21½ percent. And working people had suffered under 2 consecutive years of double-digit inflation that had raised consumer prices an incredible 27.3 percent. Yes, soaring prices and a sinking economy—that's what the other fellows, with all their lip service about compassion, inflicted on the American people. The economists called it stagflation. The Democrats termed it malaise. The liberal pundits said it was part of America's inevitable decline. But we came in and said the only thing that was inevitable was that bad policies produce bad results. We said there may be no easy solutions, but there's a simple solution: Get government out of the way and let free people and a free economy work their magic.

We refused to believe the so-called experts who announced that fuel shortages and gas lines were here to stay, that we had entered an age of scarcity and Americans would have to learn to get by with less. Instead we deregulated oil prices, said goodbye to Federal price fixing and fuel rationing, and helped put America back to work. When we proposed cutting tax rates and letting working people keep more of their own money, the Washington establishment immediately launched a counterattack, rolling out liberal economists to warn that lowering tax rates would cause runaway inflation.

Well, we pushed ahead and cut the tax

rates, as you know. And the result was that inflation was slashed to a fraction of what it had been; interest rates were more than cut in half; the economy boomed; employment soared; and Federal revenues actually increased. The top tax bracket has now been lowered from 70 percent to 28 percent, and in the Senate, Connie Mack will help keep the rates down and work with George Bush and his fellow Republicans in Congress to cut the capital gains rate and open our economy for more jobs and growth.

But what about the Democrats? The $64 billion question is this: Should we expect that if the Democrats' all but certain Presidential candidate is elected that he would raise taxes? Yep. In fact, he just did. Not only has he hiked taxes as Governor of Massachusetts, but in the last 5 years he has increased Massachusetts' State spending at double the rate of Federal spending. He has spent every dime and more of the revenue generated in his State by the Reagan-Bush recovery. And since 1986, while the Federal budget deficit has been cut sharply, his deficit in Massachusetts has ballooned. So, yes, the man expected to head up the Democratic ticket that Connie faces is a true liberal who, instead of controlling government spending, raises taxes. The sad truth is that whenever liberals talk about reducing the deficit it's just a code word for boosting taxes. And once they raise taxes, they raise spending even more.

This November, if the people of Florida don't want an increase in Federal taxes or a big-spending Congress, all they need to do is to go to the polls and vote Republican. See, I know what I'm talking about, because for most of my life, I was a Democrat. [*Laughter*] But then, you know, as the Scripture says, "When I was a child, I spake as a child; I thought as a child"—[*laughter*]—"and then I put aside childish things." [*Laughter*]

Well, Connie Mack knows that to fight the deficit you must control spending. He supports the balanced budget amendment and the line-item veto, which your Governor has and which I had as a Governor, but which—for some reason they just don't want to give it to a President. He helped lead the fight to pass Gramm-Rudman, and that law is already helping to put a lid on Federal spending. Connie knows that the American people are not undertaxed; the Federal Government overspends. Isn't that the kind of man Florida needs in the Senate? [*Applause*]

You see, the new liberals—or the liberals, not new—the liberals in Congress have opened a new front in their assault on limited government and fiscal responsibility with a tactic designed to circumvent the budget process and slip past Gramm-Rudman. Their new strategy is to try to enact their multimillion-dollar social agenda by requiring private businesses, primarily small businesses, to carry out and directly pay for expensive social programs.

Now, here's an example: Senator Kennedy has tried for years to pass an exorbitantly expensive program of socialized medicine, and it hasn't happened. So, now he's proposing—and the expected Democratic nominee has endorsed this plan—that the Government pass a law requiring private companies to directly pay for a federally mandated health insurance program, a program not targeted to the needy and which would not provide for the retired or unemployed.

According to the Congress' own budget office, this law would cost the American people a whopping $27.1 billion a year. But the political angle of this scheme is that the tremendous expense of this mandatory program will not be called what it obviously is, a gigantic tax, a $27 billion tax, mostly falling on small businesses, that would reduce jobs, growth, wages, and economic opportunity across every segment of American society. The fact that the liberals try to disguise their big government ideology inside a legislative Trojan horse is proof that they haven't given up. It's up to conservatives like Connie Mack to just say no to big government and to lead the fight for greater opportunity and prosperity for America.

In 1988 the American people face a choice, really the same choice we've faced before, and much the same choice most of the world has recently had to make. And each time the people have made the same decision to continue in the direction of economic freedom, entrepreneurship, and individual opportunity, and to move away from the heavy hand of government which seeks to control the people and the economy.

Now, I have to tell you, this reminds me of a story. Actually, it's an old baseball story. You see, one day, old Lucifer down there from his headquarters called St. Peter in Heaven, said they wanted to challenge him to a baseball game. And St. Peter said, "Sure, let's play. But to be fair, I have to tell you all the great ones are up here. We've got Babe Ruth, Lou Gehrig, Satchel Paige, Roberto Clemente. We've got all the best players, and our manager is the legendary Connie Mack. You won't have a chance." Well, old Lucifer says, "That doesn't matter, we'll win anyway." And St. Peter says, "How do you expect to do that?" "Well," he says, "simple, we've got all the umpires." [*Laughter*]

You see, we can either have an economy that puts the private citizen at the center—the consumer, the worker, the entrepreneur—and lets each individual be the judge of what to buy or sell, where to work, where to invest, and what to create; or we can put the Government at the center of the economy and let bureaucrats and politicians call the balls and strikes and decide who's out, and who's out of work, who's out of business, or who will get the big contract and be home free.

What is euphemistically called government-corporate partnership is just government coercion, political favoritism, collectivist industrial policy, and old-fashioned Federal boondoggles nicely wrapped up in a bright-colored ribbon. And it doesn't work. This kind of approach was tried in Europe, and it's being abandoned because it only resulted in economic stagnation and industrial decay. The fact is that in the last 5 years, while American businesses, mostly small companies, were creating nearly 17 million new jobs, Western Europe created none, not one. Back in 1981, we passed a true jobs bill. We cut taxes, spending, and regulation, and got government out of the way and let free people create new jobs and businesses. Well, our jobs bill, what was once dismissed as Reaganomics—funny, they don't call it that anymore—has produced over 250,000 jobs a month over 66 straight months; and that is a record that no spending program or political gimmick can ever match. And do you know that most of those new jobs, those almost 17 million, were created by small, independent businesses in these 66 months?

Connie Mack and the Republican Party stand for opportunity and jobs. We represent working people and entrepreneurs. The liberal leadership of the Democratic Party represents big government at the expense of the American worker and taxpayer. But the fact is that the Democrats have controlled both Houses of Congress for 27 of the last 33 years, and now more than ever it's time for a change.

Let me add to those figures I just gave you with regard to the other party. When we took office in January 1981, the Democrats had controlled both Houses of the Congress for 44 of the preceding 48 years. But in the 1980 election, we won control of one House: the Senate. And for 6 years, we had that. Now, we're back to the Democrats having both Houses. We couldn't have achieved the economic recovery we have if both Houses had remained in Democratic hands as they are now. We must get the Senate back if we're to continue our economic growth.

And let's talk for a moment about foreign policy. Let me offer here a simple, straightforward message: No more Vietnams, no more Nicaraguas, no more Bay of Pigs. Never again! Connie Mack and I stand with the Nicaraguan resistance. We will not rest until we've won for them the full support they need and until they've won for themselves the genuine democracy and freedom for which they've so bravely struggled. By supporting courageous freedom fighters around the world, we're shining a light on the path out from Communism, and nowhere has that light shone brighter than in Afghanistan. And isn't it time we apply the lessons of Afghanistan in Nicaragua and show the same commitment to freedom fighters in our own hemisphere as we do to others in distant lands?

I just came from a meeting with Cuban-American leaders, and I want to tell you what I told them. In Communist Cuba, a man like Armando Valladares is considered a criminal. In the United States, we're honored to have him represent our nation before the world. In Communist Cuba, a man like Ramon Puig is labeled an enemy of the Government. In the United States, he's a respected citizen and a hero. And while Havana spreads communism, terror, and death in Central America, many Cuban-Americans like Dr. Manuel Alzugaray are providing food, medicine, and humanitarian assistance to the victims of Communist aggression.

So, yes, there is an unbridgeable gulf between the Governments of the United States and Cuba; it is the gulf between freedom and tyranny. And as far as this administration is concerned, freedom for Cuba, liberty for her people, is a nonnegotiable demand. And so long as Cuba remains an inhuman Communist dungeon, so long as it exports terrorism and revolution in the Western Hemisphere; has some 60,000 military, secret police, and other personnel propping up brutal Communist dictatorships around the world; and, yes, so long as Cuba is used as the personal instrument of Fidel Castro's violent anti-Americanism—there cannot and must not be any normalization of relations with Cuba.

You can count on Connie Mack to defend freedom, to defend America, to defend the taxpayer, and to defend the family. He supports the Strategic Defense Initiative that would protect us from nuclear attack. And he supports tough Federal judges who would put violent criminals behind bars. And to protect our children from the menace of illegal drugs, he favors the toughest, most comprehensive drug enforcement policies, including the death penalty when narcotics traffickers commit murder. And when it comes to looking out for the rights and concerns of retired people, you can count on Connie Mack to be there. He has staunchly defended the Social Security system to ensure that it will be fiscally sound and available for Americans who worked so many years to earn its benefits.

Yes, Connie Mack cares about people. Ask Anatoly Michelson, who immigrated to America 30 years ago, only to have the Soviet Union keep his family from joining him. As a Member of Congress, Connie took up their cause, and last year—after three decades apart—a reunion took place. And Anatoly, who is here today, was reunited in America with his wife, daughter, and grandson.

And when I look at this tremendous group here today, all of you, I just wish I could take you all back to Washington with me, but I have to leave you here so you can get out the vote in November. I want to thank each one of you for everything that you're doing to help put Congressman Connie Mack in the Senate and to help build the Republican Party throughout the State of Florida.

So, thank you all. God bless you all.

Note: The President spoke at 2 p.m. in the International Ballroom at the Omni International Hotel. In his opening remarks, he referred to Connie and Priscilla Mack; Robert and Mary Jane Martinez; Jeannie Austin, Florida State Republican chairman; Alex Courtelis, chairman of the luncheon; L.E. (Tommy) Thomas, former Republican State chairman; John E. Bush, Dade County Republican Party Chairman; and Senator Paula Hawkins. Following his remarks, the President returned to Washington, DC.

White House Statement on the President's Meeting With Jonas Savimbi of Angola

June 30, 1988

The President met at the White House this morning with Dr. Jonas Savimbi, leader of the opposition National Union for the Total Independence of Angola (UNITA), who is in the United States on a private visit. Dr. Savimbi enjoys significant support among the Angolan population. He seeks the withdrawal of all foreign forces and a process of internal political reconciliation in Angola. The United States believes that true peace in Angola can only result from national reconciliation and that UNITA has the right to participate in such a process.

The President and Dr. Savimbi discussed a range of issues concerning the situation in southern Africa. The President supports UNITA's struggle against the presence of Soviet and Cuban forces in Angola. Dr. Savimbi supports the ongoing U.S.-brokered negotiations with South Africa, Angola, and Cuba aimed at achieving Cuban troop withdrawal from Angola and independence for neighboring Namibia. During the recent Toronto summit, participating nations expressed strong support for the negotiations and the goal of national reconciliation within Angola.

Informal Exchange With Reporters on Allegations of Illegal Drug Use by Members of the White House Staff
June 30, 1988

Q. Mr. President, were you surprised by allegations of drug use in the White House?

The President. No, we've known this for a while, and the investigation goes on. And I think it's just evidence of what we've been saying, and particularly what Nancy has been saying, and that is that this problem— no one is exempt. This problem crosses all kinds of lines.

Q. What should happen to those who have been—if they are proven to have used drugs?

The President. Well, if it's just a case of using them, I would like to see us do our best to get them in a drug treatment organization—and that they will agree to accepting a cure.

Q. So, the policy is going to be, give them a second chance?

The President. I have always said that I think that—this is another indication of why compulsory drug testing is not bad. It is, I think, one of the principal answers. But let the people know that we'll do our best to salvage anyone who has been addicted.

Q. Isn't it true, Mr. President, that it wasn't drug testing that caught these people; it was actually a tip?

The President. I'm not commenting on the investigation, but it certainly wasn't drug testing, no, because we haven't been doing that.

Q. Well, wouldn't that mean that you should encourage whistle-blowers instead of drug testing?

The President. No, I think drug testing is the best way.

Q. Are you——

The President. What's that?

Q. Are you upset that it was here in the White House?

The President. Well, yes, of course, I'm upset when it's found anywhere. Incidentally, I've taken my test. [*Laughter*]

Q. Was Mrs. Reagan upset? Mrs. Reagan upset about this? Have you discussed it?

The President. Of course you're upset about something of this kind. Any evidence of it——

Q. But you and your wife were never in any personal danger due to the nature of their duties?

The President. No, I wouldn't think so.

Note: The exchange began at 11:56 a.m. in the Cabinet Room at the White House.

Proclamation 5837—National Safety Belt Use Week, 1988
June 30, 1988

By the President of the United States of America

A Proclamation

Today, 32 States and the District of Columbia have laws requiring the use of safety belts, and all 50 States and the District of Columbia have child safety seat laws requiring the use of safety seats and belt systems. These laws were enacted because of the widespread recognition of the tremendous benefits provided by the use of these essential protective devices.

Studies of motor vehicle crashes show that front-seat occupants who do not wear safety belts are twice as likely to be killed or seriously injured as occupants who wear their belts. In 1987 alone, safety belts saved the lives of 2,450 front-seat passengers and prevented thousands of serious injuries. "Buckling up" is clearly one of the most valuable acts we can perform for ourselves and our loved ones.

With the increase in publicity about safety belts and the enactment of safety belt use laws, belt use has been steadily increasing. But there is still a long way to go: Less than half of our citizens are using safety belts regularly. A higher percentage of children are restrained by child seats, but many of these seats are incorrectly installed. Each of us can help improve safety by wearing safety belts at all times, by encouraging others to do so, and by making sure that our children ride in safety seats that are properly installed.

In order to encourage the people of the United States to wear safety belts, to have their children use child safety seats, and to encourage safety and law enforcement agencies and other concerned organizations, individuals, and officials to promote greater use of these essential safety devices, the Congress, by H.J. Res. 485, has designated June 26 through July 2, 1988, as "National Safety Belt Use Week" and authorized and requested the President to issue a proclamation in observance of this week.

Now, Therefore, I, Ronald Reagan, President of the United States of America, do hereby proclaim June 26 through July 2, 1988, as National Safety Belt Use Week. I call upon the Governors of the States, Puerto Rico, the Northern Mariana Islands, the Virgin Islands, Guam, and American Samoa, the Mayor of the District of Columbia, and the people of the United States to observe this week with appropriate ceremonies and activities and to reaffirm our commitment to encouraging universal seat belt use.

In Witness Whereof, I have hereunto set my hand this thirtieth day of June, in the year of our Lord nineteen hundred and eighty-eight, and of the Independence of the United States of America the two hundred and twelfth.

RONALD REAGAN

[*Filed with the Office of the Federal Register, 11:19 a.m., July 1, 1988*]

Statement on the Recommendations of the National Drug Policy Board
June 30, 1988

Today Attorney General Edwin Meese, Chairman of the National Drug Policy Board, presented me with the Board's report in response to my request for additional recommendations to strengthen our national drug policy. Next week I plan to approve an administration package that will be presented to the bipartisan executive-legislative drug task force.

The Board's excellent work builds upon

the solid foundation already laid by this administration's strategy to reduce the supply and demand for illegal drugs. These recommendations send a strong message to drug-law offenders, including users and traffickers. I join the Chairman in emphasizing that we cannot tolerate criminals who violate our borders, terrorize our communities, or poison our citizens. Likewise, we cannot tolerate drug users who provide the illegal market for the drugs or who benefit from the taxpayers' generosity through Federal grants, contracts, or loans. We must hold people responsible for their drug use through accountable treatment programs and through our parole and probations systems. This problem touches all of us at home, at school, at work, whether in government or in the private sector.

The recommendations of the Drug Policy Board are intended to strengthen America's drug enforcement policies to implement six essential goals:

- first, a drug free work force, both in the Government and in the private sector, through measures such as random drug testing and effective treatment programs;
- second, drug free schools through Nancy's Just Say No program and by requiring effective antidrug policies on campuses as a condition to Federal aid;
- third, expanded drug treatment accountability to ensure through testing that those programs eliminate drug use and move toward drug free environments;
- fourth, expanded international cooperation through interdiction, joint detection, apprehension, and eradication programs, including a coordinated role for the U.S. military and drug enforcement agencies;
- fifth, strengthened law enforcement with essential tools, such as the Federal death penalty for drug-related murders;
- sixth, expanded public awareness of the dangers of drug use by working together at all levels.

On May 18, 1988, I called for a joint executive-legislative task force, a summit meeting of leaders in the Congress and the administration, to develop a comprehensive legislative package to address every aspect of the drug problem. I urge the task force to begin its deliberations with an initial meeting soon after the Fourth of July weekend so we can enact the necessary legislation quickly.

In addition, it is imperative for the Congress to restore hundreds of millions in cuts in our law enforcement budget requests and expeditiously pass legislation needed to successfully implement our drug strategy. The Drug Policy Board recommendations are a good starting point to pull together so that we can stop the sale and use of illegal drugs.

Nomination of Robert S. Muller To Be a Member of the National Council on the Handicapped
June 30, 1988

The President today announced his intention to nominate Robert S. Muller to be a member of the National Council on the Handicapped for a term expiring September 17, 1991. This is a reappointment.

Since 1966 Mr. Muller has been with Steelcase, Inc., in Grand Rapids, MI, and currently serves as administrator of human services. Since 1978 Mr. Muller has also been an adjunct assistant professor at Aquinas College.

Mr. Muller graduated from Aquinas College (B.A., 1974). He was born June 22, 1941, in Grand Rapids, MI. He is married, has three children, and resides in Grandview, MI.

Nomination of Elizabeth Anne Moler To Be a Member of the Federal Energy Regulatory Commission

June 30, 1988

The President today announced his intention to nominate Elizabeth Anne Moler to be a member of the Federal Energy Regulatory Commission, Department of Energy, for a term expiring October 20, 1991. She would succeed Charles G. Stalon.

Since 1977 Ms. Moler has been with the Committee on Energy and Natural Resources for the United States Senate in Washington, DC, serving as senior counsel, 1987–present; minority counsel, 1981–1987; counsel, 1977–1981; and professional staff member, 1976–1977.

Ms. Moler graduated from American University (B.A., 1971) and George Washington University (J.D., 1977). She was born January 24, 1949, in Salt Lake City, UT. She is married, has one child, and resides in McLean, VA.

Appointment of Kathleen Day Koch as Associate Counsel to the President

June 30, 1988

The President today announced the appointment of Kathleen Day Koch to be Associate Counsel to the President at the White House.

Since 1987 Ms. Koch has served as an Assistant Counsel in the Office of the Counsel to the President. Prior to this, she was a senior attorney in the Office of the General Counsel at the Department of Commerce, 1984–1987; an attorney and deputy ethics official for the Merit Systems Protection Board, 1979–1984; and an attorney with the Department of Housing and Urban Development, 1977–1979.

Ms. Koch received a B.S. degree in 1971 from the University of Missouri, St. Louis, and a J.D. degree in 1977 from the University of Chicago School of Law. She was born November 27, 1948, in St. Louis, MO, and resides with her three children in Annandale, VA.

Appointment of Valdas V. Adamkus To Be a United States Commissioner on the Ohio River Valley Water Sanitation Commission

June 30, 1988

The President today announced his intention to appoint Valdas V. Adamkus to be a Commissioner representing the United States Government on the Ohio River Valley Water Sanitation Commission. He would succeed Jack E. Ravan.

Since 1981 Mr. Adamkus has been an Administrator of the United States Environmental Protection Agency (EPA) for Region V in Chicago, IL. Prior to this he served as a Deputy Regional Administrator for the EPA, 1970–1981. Mr. Adamkus has also served as Deputy Director and then Director of the Ohio River Basin Regional Office in Cincinnati.

Mr. Adamkus attended the University of Munich and graduated from the Illinois Institute of Technology (B.S., 1960). He was born November 3, 1926, in Kaunas, Lithuania. He served in the United States Army Reserve, 1950–1959. He is married and resides in Hinsdale, IL.

Appointment of Robert Boone Hawkins, Jr., as a Member of the Advisory Commission on Intergovernmental Relations, and Designation as Chairman

June 30, 1988

The President today announced his intention to appoint Robert Boone Hawkins, Jr., to be a member of the Advisory Commission on Intergovernmental Relations for a term of 2 years. This is a reappointment. Upon appointment, he will be redesignated Chairman.

Since 1986 Dr. Hawkins has been president and cofounder for the Institute for Contemporary Studies in San Francisco, CA. Prior to this he was president of the Sequoia Institute, 1978–present.

Dr. Hawkins graduated from San Francisco State College (B.S., 1965) and the University of Washington (Ph.D., 1969). He was born September 6, 1941, in Berkeley, CA. He served in the United States Army in 1970. Dr. Hawkins is married, has two children, and resides in Loomis, CA.

Appointment of John M. Engler as a Member of the Intergovernmental Advisory Council on Education

June 30, 1988

The President today announced his intention to appoint John M. Engler to be a member of the Intergovernmental Advisory Council on Education for the remainder of the term expiring July 27, 1989. He would succeed Betty Easley.

Since 1979 Mr. Engler has been a member of the Michigan State Senate. Since 1984 he has been senate majority leader. Prior to this he was a representative for the Michigan State Assembly, 1971–1978.

Mr. Engler graduated from Michigan State University (B.S., 1971) and Thomas M. Cooley Law School (J.D., 1982). He was born October 12, 1948, in Mount Pleasant, MI, where he currently resides.

Statement on the 20th Anniversary of the Treaty on the Non-Proliferation of Nuclear Weapons

July 1, 1988

The Non-Proliferation Treaty is one of the international community's most vital instruments for preventing the spread of nuclear weapons and strengthening international peace and stability. I firmly believe that nuclear war can never be won and must never be fought. If we are to succeed in halting the spread of nuclear weapons, the nations of the world must continue to work together.

I call on all countries that have not yet adhered to the Non-Proliferation Treaty to do so to demonstrate their commitment to preventing the spread of nuclear weapons and to strengthening the foundations of peace. I also urge all parties to the treaty to rededicate themselves to achieving its objective.

Statement by Assistant to the President for Press Relations Fitzwater on the Treaty on the Non-Proliferation of Nuclear Weapons

July 1, 1988

Twenty years ago today, 61 nations, including the United States, signed the Treaty on the Non-Proliferation of Nuclear Weapons. This treaty serves as a cornerstone of international efforts to prevent the further spread of nuclear weapons, which is one of the most direct and serious threats to regional and global stability. Nations from around the globe have committed themselves to the treaty and its objectives. Indeed, with 136 parties, the Non-Proliferation Treaty has the widest adherence of any arms control treaty in history. The important role of the treaty has been repeatedly reaffirmed.

The participants at the third Non-Proliferation Treaty Review Conference in 1985 concluded that universal adherence to the treaty is the best way to strengthen the barriers against proliferation. They urged all states not party to the treaty to accede to it. The nuclear-weapon states which are parties to the treaty have agreed not to assist non-nuclear-weapon states to acquire nuclear explosives. The non-nuclear-weapon states, in turn, pledge not to acquire nuclear explosives. These mutual pledges acknowledge that the technology of nuclear weapons and nuclear explosives cannot be distinguished and that their further spread threatens the security of all nations.

The Non-Proliferation Treaty also calls for parties to cooperate in the development of the peaceful uses of nuclear energy, especially in non-nuclear-weapon states which are parties to the treaty. The peaceful uses of nuclear energy are important to the social and economic well-being of many peoples, and the United States has long been in the forefront of countries providing technical assistance and other cooperation in the nuclear field. We are committed to continuing such cooperation under effective international safeguards. The comprehensive safeguards applied by the International Atomic Energy Agency under the treaty provide essential assurance of the peaceful intent of the nuclear activities of the states involved, thus benefiting all mankind.

The United States has taken the initiative in negotiations to substantially reduce nuclear arsenals as called for in article VI of the Non-Proliferation Treaty. The conclusion by the U.S. and the U.S.S.R. of the treaty on the elimination of intermediate-range and shorter range missiles (INF), which entered into force on June 1, is clear evidence of our deep commitment to nuclear arms reductions. This treaty, which contains the most stringent verification measures of any arms control agreement, will eliminate an entire class of U.S. and Soviet nuclear missiles.

The United States also continues its negotiations with the U.S.S.R. to complete a treaty to reduce U.S. and Soviet strategic offensive arms by 50 percent. We are, in addition, committed to seeking effective and verifiable agreements with the Soviet Union on nuclear testing limitations that could strengthen security for all nations. When discussions of two existing treaties are completed and they are ratified, we are prepared to pursue negotiations on a step-by-step parallel program to limit and ultimately end nuclear testing, in association with a program to reduce and ultimately eliminate all nuclear weapons.

In 1981 the President outlined U.S. policy to prevent the proliferation of nuclear explosives and declared that this issue was critical to international peace as well as regional and global stability. If we are to succeed in halting the spread of nuclear weapons, however, the nations of the world must work together. Each state has a responsibility to refrain from seeking nuclear weapons and to take all steps necessary to avoid contributing to the spread of nuclear weapons through the export of nuclear equipment and technology.

As the President has stated on a number of occasions, he believes that a nuclear war can never be won and must never be fought. In order to eliminate the threat of nuclear war, we have sought to achieve deep reductions in the level of nuclear weapons worldwide. The INF agreement is a concrete example of our success. However, in order to completely rid the world of the risk of nuclear war, particularly at the time when the United States and the U.S.S.R. have agreed to reduce their nuclear arsenals, it is equally vital to prevent any further spread of nuclear weapons. The Non-Proliferation Treaty is clearly the most important means we have for accomplishing this goal.

The United States played a major role in the negotiation of the Non-Proliferation Treaty, and over its lifetime, all U.S. Presidents have strongly supported it. On this, the 20th anniversary of the opening for a signature of the treaty, the President calls upon all countries that have not yet adhered to it to do so in order to demonstrate their commitment to preventing the spread of nuclear weapons and to reducing the risk of nuclear war. Further, he urges all parties to the treaty to rededicate themselves to achieving its objectives and to ensuring its continued vitality. This is both our shared responsibility and our contribution to peace for this and future generations.

Proclamation 5838—National Literacy Day, 1988
July 1, 1988

By the President of the United States of America

A Proclamation

We know that America offers freedom and opportunity to every citizen; yet we know too that the burden of illiteracy keeps some of us from taking full advantage of all our country has to offer and from contributing all we can. Fortunately, dedicated citizens have been working hard to help their neighbors learn to read and write; and in recent years the Adult Literacy Initiative has encouraged many people to volunteer in this effort.

We can be proud of the volunteers and the public-private partners who are carrying America's promise to their fellow citizens. National Literacy Day gives us a special chance to let more people know of the help and hope that are available—that they can truly learn to read and write. On this day and throughout the year, let us extend a helping hand to our fellow citizens and offer them the priceless opportunity of literacy and the world of potential it creates.

The Congress, by Senate Joint Resolution 304, has designated July 2, 1988, as "National Literacy Day" and authorized and requested the President to issue a proclamation in observance of this occasion.

Now, Therefore, I, Ronald Reagan, President of the United States of America, do hereby proclaim July 2, 1988, as National Literacy Day. I invite the Governors of the several States, local officials, and all Americans to observe this day with appropriate programs, ceremonies, and activities to increase awareness about illiteracy and to encourage participation in the fight for literacy and learning in our land.

In Witness Whereof, I have hereunto set my hand this first day of July, in the year of our Lord nineteen hundred and eighty-eight, and of the Independence of the

United States of America the two hundred and twelfth.

RONALD REAGAN

[*Filed with the Office of the Federal Register, 4:53 p.m., July 1, 1988*]

Remarks on Signing the Medicare Catastrophic Coverage Act of 1988

July 1, 1988

It was in my 1987 State of the Union Address—and by the way, one of the best parts of this job is that from time to time you get to quote yourself—[*laughter*]—but it was in my State of the Union Address that I said, "Let us remove a financial specter facing our older Americans: the fear of an illness so expensive that it can result in having to make an intolerable choice between bankruptcy and death." Well, our administration, I went on to say, would soon submit legislation "to help free the elderly from the fear of catastrophic illness."

Well, that initiative has produced an historic piece of legislation, and in a moment, I will sign the Medicare Catastrophic Coverage Act of 1988. This legislation will help remove a terrible threat from the lives of elderly and disabled Americans, the threat of an illness requiring acute care, one so devastating that it could wipe out the savings of an entire lifetime. The scene is only too easy to picture. An elderly couple, perhaps one has a very long stay in the hospital; the other forced to empty the savings account, to skimp on groceries. And even for those never actually forced into this situation, there's the gnawing worry, the fear, that someday it might just happen. This legislation will change that, replacing worry and fear with peace of mind.

I'm proud to be able to note that the legislation follows the same premise as all sound insurance programs. It will be paid for by those who are covered by its services. Even so, I must add a word of caution. Every administration since the Medicare program was passed has worried about the seemingly uncontrollable cost increases in our government health care programs. Whoever the President in office, program costs have exceeded the best congressional budget estimates. Unless we're careful, it's possible that aspects of this legislation will do the same.

In particular, the legislation provides many new benefits, benefits like respite care and prescription drugs. Since these have never been covered by Medicare, we have no real way of knowing how much these services will cost. So, if future administrations and Congresses aren't diligent, these new benefits could contribute to a program we can't afford. This could be more than a budget problem; it could be a tragedy. The program, after all, is to be paid for by the elderly themselves. So, we must control the costs of these new benefits, or we'll harm the very people we're trying to help. And yet, if administered with prudence, this program can, as I said, provide countless Americans with peace of mind.

Many people share the credit for this achievement. In fact, I feel a little like an Academy Award winner back in my old profession: No matter how many I thank, I'm afraid I'll leave somebody out. There were the hundreds who testified at the regional meetings. There was the public-private working group consisting of many of the Nation's leading health experts. There were the Senators and Representatives of both parties, like Dan Rostenkowski, chairman of the House Ways and Means Committee; Lloyd Bentsen, chairman of the Senate Finance Committee; John Dingell, chairman of the House Energy and Commerce Committee; Bill Gradison; Pete Stark; and many others, some of whom are on the dais with me today, who toiled, compromised, and sacrificed. There were the elderly and their organizations who agreed to pay for this new benefit rather than have it placed on the backs of their children. And there was our Secretary of Health and Human Services, Dr. Otis Bowen, working tirelessly to bring this achievement about.

On behalf of a grateful nation, I thank you all. And now let me sign this historic legislation, the Medicare Catastrophic Coverage Act of 1988.

Note: The President spoke at 10:31 a.m. in the Rose Garden at the White House. H.R. 2470, approved July 1, was assigned Public Law No. 100–360.

Nomination of Charles G. Stalon To Be a Member of the Federal Energy Regulatory Commission
July 1, 1988

The President today announced his intention to nominate Charles G. Stalon to be a member of the Federal Energy Regulatory Commission, Department of Energy, for the remainder of the term expiring October 20, 1989. He would succeed C.M. Naeve.

Since 1984 Mr. Stalon has been a Commissioner of the Federal Energy Regulatory Commission in Washington, DC. Prior to this he was a commissioner with the Illinois Commerce Commission in Springfield, 1977–1984. He was an associate professor at Southern Illinois University, Carbondale, 1963–1977.

Mr. Stalon graduated from Butler University (B.A., 1959) and Purdue University (M.S., 1963; Ph.D., 1966). He was born October 29, 1929, in Cape Girardeau, MO. He served in the United States Navy, 1948–1949 and 1952–1954. He is married, has two children, and resides in Bethesda, MD.

Proclamation 5839—United States-Canada Days of Peace and Friendship, 1988
July 1, 1988

By the President of the United States of America

A Proclamation

The enduring friendship between the American and Canadian peoples is based on our similar aspirations for liberty, justice, individual rights, and democratic values. Our governments differ in form but embody these same principles. Bound by a common vision of the future, the United States and Canada are working together to fulfill international responsibilities in the defense of freedom and lasting peace throughout the world.

Our friendship is reflected as well in our extensive trade with each other. Canada and the United States are each other's most important trading partners. We also have the world's largest bilateral trading relationship, and the recently signed Free Trade Agreement, when implemented, will increase prosperity in both our countries and further strengthen the close ties we enjoy.

July 2 and 3 are an especially good time to commemorate the unique relationship between Americans and Canadians, because these two days fall between beloved holidays—Canada Day on July 1 and America's Independence Day on the Fourth of July. May our celebration of U.S.-Canada Days of Peace and Friendship ever remind us of the history of mutual goodwill that unites us and of the sacrifices so many have made in each country for the freedom, justice, and peace we cherish.

The Congress of the United States, by House Joint Resolution 587, has designated

July 2 and 3, 1988, as "United States-Canada Days of Peace and Friendship" and authorized and requested the President to issue a proclamation in observance of this event.

Now, Therefore, I, Ronald Reagan, President of the United States of America, do hereby proclaim July 2 and 3, 1988, as United States-Canada Days of Peace and Friendship. I call upon the people of the United States to observe these days with appropriate programs, ceremonies, and activities.

In Witness Whereof, I have hereunto set my hand this 1st day of July, in the year of our Lord nineteen hundred and eighty-eight, and of the Independence of the United States of America the two hundred and twelfth.

RONALD REAGAN

[*Filed with the Office of the Federal Register, 11:25 a.m., July 6, 1988*]

White House Statement on the Report of Presidential Emergency Board No. 213 Concerning the Investigation of a Railroad Labor Dispute

July 1, 1988

Presidential Emergency Board No. 213 today submitted its report to the President concerning a dispute between the Chicago and North Western Transportation Company and certain of its employees represented by the United Transportation Union.

The President, in his discretion, under the Railway Labor Act, and on the recommendation of the National Mediation Board, established the three-member Board by Executive Order 12636, effective April 22, 1988. It was established because of a threatened strike by approximately 2,200 members of the United Transportation Union. The strike would have affected the carrier's freight train operations in the 10 States of Illinois, Iowa, Kansas, Michigan, Minnesota, Missouri, Nebraska, South Dakota, Wisconsin, and Wyoming. It would also have affected suburban commuter passenger service operated under contract by the North Western for the Regional Transportation Authority ("METRA") in Chicago, IL.

The Board was chaired by Robert O. Harris, Arbitrator, of Washington, DC. Richard R. Kasher, Arbitrator, of Bryn Mawr, PA, and Robert E. Peterson, Arbitrator, of Briarcliff Manor, NY, served as members of the Board.

The central issue in dispute concerned the number of train service-employees that shall be used on each crew employed in road, freight, and yard service operations. The North Western had sought to revise agreements to permit it the unrestricted right to determine when and if any train-service employees shall be used on a train. The union rejected such a demand. It proposed that the *standard* crew consist of not less than one conductor and one foreman and two helpers in yard service. Further, the union contended that in no event should a *minimum* crew consist of less than one conductor/foreman and one brakeman/helper.

The North Western offered employees adversely affected by implementation of its rules changes a one-time severance allowance of $25,000 or, in the alternative, a supplemental unemployment allowance for 1 year.

Appendix A—Digest of Other White House Announcements

The following list includes the President's public schedule and other items of general interest announced by the Office of the Press Secretary and not included elsewhere in this book.

January 3

The President returned to the White House following his stay in Palm Springs, CA.

January 4

The President met at the White House with:
—the Vice President; Howard H. Baker, Jr., Chief of Staff to the President; and Colin L. Powell, Assistant to the President for National Security Affairs;
—the 1987 Sports Illustrated Sportsmen and Sportswomen of the Year.

January 5

The President met at the White House with:
—the Vice President; Howard H. Baker, Jr., Chief of Staff to the President; and Colin L. Powell, Assistant to the President for National Security Affairs;
—the Vice President; James C. Miller III, Director of the Office of Management and Budget; and members of the White House staff, to discuss the 1989 fiscal year Federal budget;
—the 1988 White House fellows.

The White House announced that President Reagan has invited President Mohammed Hosni Mubarak of Egypt to make a state visit to the United States. President Mubarak has accepted the invitation and will meet with President Reagan at the White House on January 28.

The President announced his intention to appoint the following individuals to be United States Commissioners on the United States section of the Pacific Salmon Commission for terms expiring January 5, 1992. These are reappointments.

Sherman Timothy Wapato, of Oregon. Since 1982 Mr. Wapato has been executive director of Columbia River Intertribal Fish Commission in Portland, OR.

William R. Wilkerson, of Washington. Since 1986 Mr. Wilkerson has been director of the Washington Department of Revenue in Olympia, WA.

The President announced his intention to appoint the following individuals to be members of the White House Conference for a Drug Free America. These are initial appointments.

Mark S. Gold, M.D., of New Jersey. Since 1978 Dr. Gold has been director of research at Fair Oaks Hospital in Summit, NJ.

Edward O. Fritts, of Virginia. Since 1982 Mr. Fritts has been president and chief executive officer of the National Association of Broadcasters in Washington, DC.

Luke V. McCarthy, of California. Since 1978 Mr. McCarthy has been president of August Financial Corp. in Long Beach, CA.

William J. Rudolph, of Georgia. From 1977 to 1987, Mr. Rudolph has been principal of Northside High School in Atlanta, GA.

Gale E. Sayers, of Illinois. Mr. Sayers, formerly with the Chicago Bears, has been president of Crest Computer Supply in Skokie, IL, since 1984.

Frank R. Tully, of Ohio. Since 1986 Mr. Tully has been vice president of human resources at Goodyear Tire & Rubber Co. in Akron, OH.

Robert O. Voy, M.D., of Colorado. Since 1985 Dr. Voy has been chief medical officer and director of sports medicine and science for the U.S. Olympic Committee in Colorado Springs, CO.

January 6

The President met at the White House with:
—the Vice President; Howard H. Baker, Jr., Chief of Staff to the President; and Colin L. Powell, Assistant to the President for National Security Affairs;
—Secretary of State George P. Shultz.

January 7

The President met at the White House with:
—the Vice President; Howard H. Baker, Jr., Chief of Staff to the President; and Colin L. Powell, Assistant to the President for National Security Affairs;
—members of the U.S. delegation to the intermediate-range nuclear force reduction negotiations, to express his appreciation for their work.

January 8

The President met at the White House with:
—the Vice President; Howard H. Baker, Jr., Chief of Staff to the President; and Colin L. Powell, Assistant to the President for National Security Affairs;
—Secretary of State George P. Shultz.

The President declared that a major disaster existed in Hawaii as a result of heavy rains that began on December 11, which caused widespread flooding and mudslides. He directed the Federal Emergency Management Agency to provide assistance to supplement State and local recovery efforts.

In the afternoon, the President left the White House for a weekend stay at Camp David, MD.

January 10

The President returned to the White House from a weekend stay at Camp David, MD.

January 11

The President met at the White House with the Vice President; Howard H. Baker, Jr., Chief of Staff to the President; and Colin L. Powell, Assistant to the President for National Security Affairs.

January 12

The President met at the White House with:

—the Vice President; Howard H. Baker, Jr., Chief of Staff to the President; and Colin L. Powell, Assistant to the President for National Security Affairs;

—the Commission on Integrated Long-Term Strategy, to receive its report on the implications of advanced technologies for U.S. defense policies and military strategy over the next 20 years;

—the board of directors of the Hoover Institution;

—the Economic Policy Council and the National Security Council, to discuss Japan-U.S. relations;

—U.S. Ambassadors Henry A. Grunwald (Austria), Warren Zimmermann (Conference on Security and Cooperation in Europe), Ronald D. Palmer (Mauritius), and Stephen Ledogar (European conventional arms negotiations), prior to their departure for their overseas posts.

The President announced his intention to appoint/designate the following individuals to be members of the White House Conference for a Drug Free America. These are initial appointments.

Wilford S. Bailey, of Alabama. Since 1987 Mr. Bailey has been president of the National Collegiate Athletic Association at Auburn University.

Joseph R. Barbera, of California. Since 1957 Mr. Barbera has been president of Hanna-Barbera Productions, Inc., in Hollywood, CA.

R.V. Durham, of North Carolina. Since 1973 Mr. Durham has been director of safety and health for the International Brotherhood of Teamsters in Washington, DC.

Mary George, of Hawaii. Since 1974 Mrs. George has been a Republican State senator in the Hawaii State Senate and minority leader since 1987.

Daniel M. O'Hare, of New York. Since 1973 Mr. O'Hare has been founder, executive director, and chairman of the Board of Americans Mobilized to End Narcotics Abuse (A.M.E.N.) in Newburgh, NY.

Jesse Philips, of Ohio. Since 1957 Mr. Philips has been founder and chairman of Philips Industries in Dayton, OH.

Tim Reid, of California. Since 1987 Mr. Reid has been the coexecutive producer and an actor on "Frank's Place," for the CBS Television Network in Culver City, CA.

Carol Sager, of Massachusetts. Mrs. Sager is currently superintendent for the Highwood-Highland Park School District in Highland Park, IL.

E. Clay Shaw, Jr., of Florida (to be designated). Since 1981 Mr. Shaw has been the U.S. Representative from Florida (15th District) in Washington, DC.

January 13

The President met at the White House with the Vice President; Howard H. Baker, Jr., Chief of Staff to the President; and Colin L. Powell, Assistant to the President for National Security Affairs.

January 14

The President met at the White House with:

—the Vice President; Howard H. Baker, Jr., Chief of Staff to the President; and Colin L. Powell, Assistant to the President for National Security Affairs;

—Secretary of Labor Ann D. McLaughlin;

—Secretary of Defense Frank C. Carlucci;

—Brian Stevenson, president of Lions Clubs International.

January 15

The President met at the White House with:

—the Vice President; Howard H. Baker, Jr., Chief of Staff to the President; and Colin L. Powell, Assistant to the President for National Security Affairs;

—Secretary of State George P. Shultz.

In the afternoon, the President went to Bethesda Naval Hospital for his biannual physical examination as a followup to his surgery in 1985 and 1987. Following the examination, he went to Camp David, MD, for a weekend stay.

January 16

The President directed the Federal Emergency Management Agency to provide assistance to Kwajalein Atoll in the Marshall Islands to supplement local efforts to recover from damage caused by Typhoon Roy, which struck the area on January 9.

January 18

The President returned to the White House from a weekend stay at Camp David, MD.

January 19

The President met at the White House with:

—Howard H. Baker, Jr., Chief of Staff to the President, and Colin L. Powell, Assistant to the President for National Security Affairs;
—Ashley Hovey, the 1988 March of Dimes Poster Child.

The President recess-appointed Ronald A. Cass as a member of the U.S. International Trade Commission for a term expiring June 16, 1996. He would succeed Paula Stern.

The President announced his intention to appoint the following individuals to be members of the Advisory Committee for Trade Negotiations for terms of 2 years:

Linda Lugenia Arey, of Virginia. She would succeed Bob J. Murphy. Ms. Arey was Special Assistant to the President and Deputy Director of the Office of Public Liaison at the White House, 1985–1987.

Philip E. Lippincott, of New Jersey. He would succeed Barbara McConnell Barrett. Since 1983 Mr. Lippincott has been chairman and chief executive officer of Scott Paper Co., in Philadelphia, PA.

William G. Moore, Jr., of Texas. He would succeed Murray H. Finley. Since 1982 Mr. Moore has been chairman and chief executive officer of Recognition Equipment, Inc., in Dallas, TX.

Earl Wantland, of Oregon. He would succeed Benjamin Frank. Since 1974 Mr. Wantland has been president and chief executive officer of Tektronix, Inc., in Beaverton, OR.

January 20

The President met at the White House with:
—the Vice President; Howard H. Baker, Jr., Chief of Staff to the President; and Colin L. Powell, Assistant to the President for National Security Affairs;
—the Vice President, for lunch;
—Secretary of State George P. Shultz.

The President directed the Federal Emergency Management Agency to provide assistance to the Territory of Guam and the island of Rota in the Northern Mariana Islands to supplement local efforts to recover from damage caused by Typhoon Roy.

January 21

The President met at the White House with:
—Howard H. Baker, Jr., Chief of Staff to the President, and Colin L. Powell, Assistant to the President for National Security Affairs;
—West German Foreign Minister Hans-Dietrich Genscher;
—Senator John G. Tower, to discuss current arms control negotiations and efforts to secure Senate ratification of the Soviet-U.S. Intermediate-Range Nuclear Forces treaty;
—representatives of the International Confederation of Free Trade Unions;
—William F. Buckley, for lunch;
—Richard Berkley, president of the U.S. Conference of Mayors;
—representatives of the National Fish and Wildlife Foundation.

The White House announced that the test results from the President's physical examination of January 15 indicated that the President was in good health.

January 22

The President met at the White House with:
—Howard H. Baker, Jr., Chief of Staff to the President, and Colin L. Powell, Assistant to the President for National Security Affairs;
—Jim McCrery, Republican candidate for the U.S. House of Representatives from Louisiana;
—Secretary of State George P. Shultz.

In the afternoon, the President left the White House for a weekend stay at Camp David, MD.

The White House announced that President Reagan has invited President Vigdis Finnbógadottir of Iceland to meet with him during her private visit to the United States. President Finnbógadottir has accepted the invitation and will meet with President Reagan at the White House on January 26.

January 24

The President returned to the White House from a weekend stay at Camp David, MD.

January 25

The President met at the White House with:
—Howard H. Baker, Jr., Chief of Staff to the President, and Colin L. Powell, Assistant to the President for National Security Affairs;
—the Cabinet.

January 26

The President met at the White House with:
—Howard H. Baker, Jr., Chief of Staff to the President, and Colin L. Powell, Assistant to the President for National Security Affairs;
—the Republican congressional leadership;
—the bipartisan congressional leadership;
—William H. Webster, Director of Central Intelligence;
—President Vigdis Finnbógadottir of Iceland.

The President transmitted the following reports to the Congress:
—the 17th annual report of the Department of Transportation for fiscal year 1983;
—the sixth annual report of the Tourism Policy Council for fiscal year 1987;
—the 11th annual report of the National Institute for Building Sciences for 1987;
—the sixth annual report on Alaska's mineral resources.

The President announced his intention to appoint or designate the following individuals to be members of the White House Conference for a Drug Free America:

Walton E. Burdick, of New York. Since 1980 Mr. Burdick has been vice president of personnel for IBM Corp. in Armonk, NY.

Morris E. Chafetz, of the District of Columbia. Since 1976 Dr. Chafetz has been president of the Health Education Foundation in Washington, DC.

Daniel J. Devine, of Arizona. Since 1987 Mr. Devine has been director of community education/substance abuse at Arizona State University.

Glenn English, Jr., of Oklahoma. Since 1974 Mr. English has been a United States Representative from Oklahoma.

John R. Hall, of Texas. Since 1962 Mr. Hall has been owner of John Hall Gold & Porcelain Lab, Inc., in Fort Worth, TX.

Ed Koch, of New York. Since 1978 Mr. Koch has been mayor of New York City.

January 27

The President met at the White House with:
—Howard H. Baker, Jr., Chief of Staff to the President, and Colin L. Powell, Assistant to the President for National Security Affairs;
—Vladislav Naumov, a Soviet soldier who defected while serving in Afghanistan; and Ludmila Thorne, of Freedom House, a New York-based organization concerned with human rights in the Soviet Union;
—Democratic Members of Congress, to discuss aid for the Nicaraguan democratic resistance;
—Secretary of State George P. Shultz;
—Republican Members of the House of Representatives, to discuss aid for the Nicaraguan democratic resistance.

The President announced his intention to appoint Frank C. Carlucci as a Governor of the Board of Governors of the American National Red Cross for a term of 3 years. He would succeed Caspar W. Weinberger.

January 28

The President met at the White House with:
—Howard H. Baker, Jr., Chief of Staff to the President, and Colin L. Powell, Assistant to the President for National Security Affairs;
—Republican Members of the House of Representatives, to discuss aid for the Nicaraguan democratic resistance.

January 29

The President met at the White House with:
—Howard H. Baker, Jr., Chief of Staff to the President, and Colin L. Powell, Assistant to the President for National Security Affairs;
—Secretary of State George P. Shultz.

The President designated the following individuals to be members of the White House Conference for a Drug Free America:

Benjamin A. Gilman, of New York. Since 1972 Mr. Gilman has been the United States Representative from New York for the 22d District.

Charles B. Rangel, of New York. Since 1970 Mr. Rangel has been the United States Representative from New York for the 16th District.

Pete Wilson, of California. Since 1983 Mr. Wilson has been a United States Senator from California.

January 30

In the evening, the President attended the Alfalfa Club dinner at the Capital Hilton Hotel.

February 1

The President met at the White House with:
—the Vice President; Howard H. Baker, Jr., Chief of Staff to the President; and Colin L. Powell, Assistant to the President for National Security Affairs;
—members of the White House staff, for an issues briefing luncheon;
—Secretary of Defense Frank C. Carlucci.

The President announced his intention to appoint the following individuals to be members of the National Advisory Council on Indian Education:

For a term expiring September 29, 1989:

Omar J. Lane, of Wyoming. He would succeed Evalu Ware Russell. Since 1986 Mr. Lane has been president of Prime Industries International in Lander, WY.

For a term expiring September 29, 1990:

W.L. (Buck) Martin, of Wisconsin. This is a reappointment. Since 1986 Mr. Martin has been intergovernmental affairs adviser for the office of the Governor in Madison, WI.

February 2

The President met at the White House with:
—Howard H. Baker, Jr., Chief of Staff to the President, and Colin L. Powell, Assistant to the President for National Security Affairs;
—Members of Congress;
—Charles S. Robb, former Governor of Virginia;
—Members of Congress.

In the evening, the President attended the Republican Eagles dinner at the Capital Hilton Hotel.

February 3

The President met at the White House with:
—Howard H. Baker, Jr., Chief of Staff to the President, and Colin L. Powell, Assistant to the President for National Security Affairs;
—Secretary of State George P. Shultz.

February 4

The President met at the White House with:

—Howard H. Baker, Jr., Chief of Staff to the President, and Colin L. Powell, Assistant to the President for National Security Affairs;

—Members of Congress;

—representatives of the Women's Sports Foundation.

February 5

The President met at the White House with:

—Howard H. Baker, Jr., Chief of Staff to the President, and Colin L. Powell, Assistant to the President for National Security Affairs;

—the 1988 class of the U.S. Senate Youth Program;

—Warren E. Burger, former Chief Justice of the U.S. Supreme Court, to receive a bust of Benjamin Franklin.

The President declared that a major disaster existed in areas of California as a result of severe storms and flooding that began on January 17. He directed the Federal Emergency Management Agency to provide funds to supplement State and local recovery efforts.

The President announced his intention to designate the following individuals to be members of the Supplemental Health Insurance Panel:

Lewis R. Crist, of Missouri. Since 1986 he has been director of insurance for the State of Missouri in Jefferson City.

John S. Greeno, of Alabama. Since 1987 he has been commissioner of insurance for the department of insurance in Montgomery, AL.

In the afternoon, the President left the White House for a weekend stay at Camp David, MD.

February 7

The President returned to the White House from a weekend stay at Camp David, MD.

February 8

The President met at the White House with Howard H. Baker, Jr., Chief of Staff to the President, and Colin L. Powell, Assistant to the President for National Security Affairs.

February 9

The President met at the White House with:

—Howard H. Baker, Jr., Chief of Staff to the President, and Colin L. Powell, Assistant to the President for National Security Affairs;

—Saudi Foreign Minister Sa'ud al-Faysal, to receive letters from King Fahd regarding the U.N. arms embargo resolution against Iran and the situation in the Israeli-occupied territories;

—representatives of the Boy Scouts of America, to receive their annual report to the Nation.

The President announced his intention to appoint the following individuals to be members of the United States Holocaust Memorial Council for terms expiring January 15, 1993:

Harry H. Levitch, of Tennessee. He would succeed Dorothy Height. Since 1950 Mr. Levitch has been president of Harry Levitch Jewelers in Memphis, TN.

Miles Lerman, of New Jersey. This is a reappointment. Since 1955 Mr. Lerman has been president of Miles Lerman Enterprises in Vineland, NJ.

Edward M. Rosenfeld, of California. He would succeed Raul Hilberg. Since 1986 Mr. Rosenfeld has been a partner with Patterson, Belknap, Webb & Tyler in Los Angeles, CA.

Murray Pantirer, of New Jersey. He would succeed Theodore Hesburgh. Since 1952 Mr. Pantirer has been a partner with Bertram Associates in Union, NJ.

Arnold Thaler, of Illinois. He would succeed Norman Lamm. Since 1981 Mr. Thaler has been chairman and chief executive officer for the View-Master International Group in New York, NY.

In the evening, the President hosted a reception for the diplomatic corps in the Residence.

February 10

The President met at the White House with:

—the Vice President; Howard H. Baker, Jr., Chief of Staff to the President; and Colin L. Powell, Assistant to the President for National Security Affairs;

—Jean-Pascal Delamuraz, Vice President and Public Economy Minister of Switzerland, to discuss trade issues;

—the Vice President, for lunch;

—William H. Webster, Director of Central Intelligence;

—Secretary of State George P. Shultz.

February 11

The President met at the White House with:

—Howard H. Baker, Jr., Chief of Staff to the President, and Colin L. Powell, Assistant to the President for National Security Affairs;

—the Cabinet, to discuss the Federal budget;

—leaders of the Masons.

February 12

In the morning, the President traveled to Los Angeles, CA, to attend a State Republican fundraising reception.

February 17

The President returned to the White House following a 4-day stay at his ranch in Santa Barbara County, CA.

February 18

The President met at the White House with Howard H. Baker, Jr., Chief of Staff to the President, and Colin L. Powell, Assistant to the President for National Security Affairs.

The President designated Francis C. Coleman as Chairman of the Board of Regents of the Uniformed Services University of the Health Sciences, Department of Defense. He would succeed David Olch. Mr. Coleman has served as a member of the Board since 1982.

The President announced that C. Paul Robinson would serve as a negotiator and head of the delegation to the Soviet-United States nuclear testing talks.

February 19

The President met at the White House with:

—Howard H. Baker, Jr., Chief of Staff to the President, and Colin L. Powell, Assistant to the President for National Security Affairs;

—Secretary of State George P. Shultz.

The President transmitted the following reports to Congress:

—the 17th annual report on hazardous materials transportation for calender year 1986;

—the second biennial report of the Interagency Arctic Research Policy Committee;

—the fiscal year 1986 annual report on mine safety and health activities as submitted by the Secretary of Labor.

The President announced his intention to appoint the following individuals to be members of the National Commission on Agricultural Policy:

Marjorie A. Albin, of Illinois. Since 1978 Mrs. Albin has been vice president and chief executive officer of the Longview State Bank in Illinois.

Glen E. Brown, of Utah. Since 1987 Mr. Brown has been speaker of the house of representatives at the State capitol in Salt Lake City, UT.

E.C. Downes, Jr., of Virginia. Mr. Downes has been a self-employed farmer of vegetables and grain for over 40 years.

Don Heinz, of Hawaii. Mr. Heinz is currently president of Hawaii Sugar Planters' Association in Aiea, HI.

Charles Knigge, of Wisconsin. Mr. Knigge is currently a dairy farmer in Omro, WI.

The President announced his intention to appoint the following individuals to be members of the National Council on Vocational Education:

For a term expiring January 17, 1989:

Robert Case II, of Washington. He would succeed Ray Shamie. Since 1984 Mr. Case has been owner-broker at Coldwell Banker Thayer-Case in Ellensburg, WA.

For terms expiring January 17, 1991:

Dee Brown, of Texas. He would succeed Marva Nettles Collins. Since 1955 Mr. Brown has been president and chairman of the board for Dee Brown, Inc., in Dallas, TX.

Gertrude McDonald, of California. This is a reappointment. Mrs. McDonald is a retired educator from Fremont, CA.

Patricia Glaser Silversmith, of Colorado. This is a reappointment. Mrs. Silversmith is a retired volunteer teacher.

Jhoon Goo Rhee, of Virginia. He would succeed Mary B. Liu. Since 1962 Mr. Jhoon Rhee is the founder and president of the Jhoon Rhee Institute of Tae Kwon Do, Inc., and World Martial Congress for Arts Education.

The President appointed the following individuals to be Commissioners of the United States section of the Great Lakes Fishery Commission:

For a term of 2 years:

James M. Ridenour, of Indiana. Mr. Ridenour has been director of the Indiana Department of Natural Resources. This is a reappointment.

For a term of 4 years:

Charles C. Krueger, of New York. He would succeed Claude Ver Duin. Since 1984 Mr. Krueger has been assistant professor of the department of natural resources at Cornell University.

For terms of 6 years:

Jim Cady, of Minnesota. He would succeed W. Mason Lawrence. Since 1960 Mr. Cady has been owner and operator of the Peterson Trout Farm in Peterson, MN.

William P. Horn. Mr. Horn has been Assistant Secretary for Fish and Wildlife at the Department of Interior. He will continue to serve as the United States Government Representative at the pleasure of the President.

In the afternoon, the President left the White House for a weekend stay at Camp David, MD.

February 21

The President returned to the White House from a weekend stay at Camp David, MD.

February 22

The President met at the White House with:

—Howard H. Baker, Jr., Chief of Staff to the President, and Colin L. Powell, Assistant to the President for National Security Affairs;

—members of the White House staff, for an issues briefing luncheon;

—staff members of the Office of Management and Budget, to thank them for their work on the 1989 fiscal year Federal budget;

—the Cabinet, to discuss the Economic Report and trade legislation.

In the morning, the President attended the swearing-in ceremony for Wendy Lee Gramm as Commissioner and Chairman of the Commodity Futures Trading Commission in the Roosevelt Room at the White House.

The President designated Edward J. Philbin as Acting Chairman of the Federal Maritime Commission. Mr. Philbin has served as a member of the Commission since November 1984.

The President announced his intention to appoint Caspar W. Weinberger as a member of the

President's Foreign Intelligence Advisory Board for a term of 2 years. This is a new position. Mr. Weinberger is currently a designated member of the National Economic Commission.

The President announced his intention to nominate the following individuals to be members of the Architectural and Transportation Barriers Compliance Board for terms expiring December 3, 1990:

William H. McCabe, of Connecticut. He would succeed Charles R. Hauser. Since 1986 Mr. McCabe has been a partner with the international accounting firm of Deloitte Haskins & Sells in Hartford, CT.

Glen R. Stotler, of West Virginia. He would succeed Truman H. Cline. Since 1985 Mr. Stotler has been a commissioner for Morgan County in Berkeley Springs, WV.

The President announced his intention to appoint the following individuals to be members of the National Commission on Agricultural Policy. These are new positions.

Arthur R. Brown, Jr., of New Jersey. Since 1982 Mr. Brown has been the secretary of agriculture for the State of New Jersey.

Fred Bruning, of Nebraska. Since 1975 Mr. Bruning has been owner and operator of Bruning Farms Partnership, a grain and livestock farm in Thayer County, NE.

Henry J. Voss, of California. Since 1981 Mr. Voss has been president of the California Farm Bureau Federation in Sacramento, CA.

February 23

The President met at the White House with:

—Howard H. Baker, Jr., Chief of Staff to the President, and Colin L. Powell, Assistant to the President for National Security Affairs;

—Lady Olga Maitland, who was a British supporter of strong Western defense policies.

The President transmitted to the Congress a report on the activities of the U.S. Government in the United Nations and its affiliated agencies during the 1986 calendar year.

February 24

The President met at the White House with:

—Howard H. Baker, Jr., Chief of Staff to the President;

—Secretary of State George P. Shultz, to discuss the Secretary's recent meetings with Soviet leaders in Moscow;

—congressional leaders.

February 25

The President met at the White House with:

—Howard H. Baker, Jr., Chief of Staff to the President, and Colin L. Powell, Assistant to the President for National Security Affairs;

—business community leaders, to discuss the Federal budget and the Intermediate-Range Nuclear Forces treaty;

—William H. Webster, Director of Central Intelligence;

—entertainer Wayne Newton;

—Members of the Senate, to discuss their recent meetings with NATO representatives on the Intermediate-Range Nuclear Forces treaty;

—members of the President's Cancer Panel, to receive their report.

In an Oval Office ceremony, the President met with 8-year-old Shawn Dennsteadt, of Mount Laurel, NJ. Shawn presented the President with the 54th edition Easter Seals.

The President announced his intention to appoint the following individuals to be members of the National Commission on Agriculture Policy. These are new positions.

Povy Bigbee, of New Mexico. Since 1986 Mr. Bigbee has been a broker with Western Equities Real Estate in McKenzie, NM.

Terry L. Murphy, of Montana. Since 1979 Mr. Murphy has been president of Montana Farmers Union in Great Falls, MT.

The President announced his intention to appoint the following individuals to be members of the White House Conference for a Drug Free America:

John Ashcroft, of Missouri. Since 1985 Mr. Ashcroft has been Governor of Missouri.

Betty Parker Blackmon, of Missouri. Since 1981 Ms. Blackmon has been executive director of the Johnson County Substance Abuse Center, Inc., in Shawnee, KS.

James E. Burke, of New Jersey. Since 1976 Mr. Burke has been chairman of the board and chief executive officer of Johnson & Johnson in New Brunswick.

John S. Chamberlin, of New Jersey. Since 1985 Mr. Chamberlin has been president and chief operating officer of Avon Products, Inc., in New York City.

William F. Dohr, of California. Since 1987 Mr. Dohr has been vice president of Sterling Homes Corp. in Irvine.

Apolonio Flores, of Texas. Since 1979 Mr. Flores has been executive director of the San Antonio Housing Authority.

Charles Grantham, of New York. Since 1984 Mr. Grantham has been executive vice president of the National Basketball Players Association in New York City.

Robert D. Kight, of Texas. Since 1983 Mr. Kight has been business manager and president of the International Union of Operating Engineers in Houston.

Jeane J. Kirkpatrick, of Maryland. Since 1985 Ms. Kirkpatrick has been senior fellow for the American Enterprise Institute for Public Policy in Washington, DC.

M. David Lewis, of California. Since 1982 Mr. Lewis has been founder, president, and medical director of the ASAP Family Treatment program in Van Nuys.

William H. Lindsey, of Florida. Since 1974 Mr. Lindsey has been executive director of the Fort Lauderdale Housing Authority.

Carol Mann, of Texas. Since 1985 Ms. Mann has been president of the Women's Sports Foundation in New York City.

J. Willard Marriott, Jr., of Maryland. Mr. Marriott has been with the Marriott Corporation since 1964, serving as president, chief executive officer, and he currently serves as chairman of the board in Washington, DC.

G.W. (Hank) McCullough, of California. Presently, Mr. McCullough is self-employed in Woodside.

Adm. Daniel J. Murphy, USN, Ret., of Maryland. Since 1986 Mr. Murphy has been vice chairman of public affairs worldwide at Hill & Knowlton Public Affairs Worldwide Co. in Washington, DC.

Robert P. Neuschel, of Illinois. Since 1979 Mr. Neuschel has been managing director of the transportation center at Northwestern University in Evanston.

Edward James Olmos, of California. Since 1984 Mr. Olmos has been an actor on NBC's "Miami Vice" in Miami, FL.

Camilo A. Padreda, of Florida. Since 1979 Mr. Padreda has been a general contractor for Cipicorp Construction, Inc., in Miami.

R. Dale Patchett, of Florida. Since 1984 Mr. Patchett has been house minority leader of the Florida House of Representatives.

Jessie M. Rattley, of Virginia. Since 1986 Mr. Rattley has been mayor of the city of Newport News.

Bruce Ritter, of New York. Since 1969 Mr. Ritter has been president of Covenant House in New York City.

Mitchell S. Rosenthal, of New York. Since 1970 Mr. Rosenthal has been president and chief executive officer of Phoenix House in New York City.

Sue Rusche, of Georgia. Since 1977 Ms. Rusche has been executive director of Families in Action in Atlanta.

George H. Ryan, of Illinois. Since 1983 Mr. Ryan has been Lieutenant Governor of Illinois.

Carol L. Schwartz, of the District of Columbia. Since 1985 Ms. Schwartz has been a member-at-large of the city council of the District of Columbia.

John W. Snow, of Florida. Since 1987 Mr. Snow has been president and chief executive officer of CSX Transportation Group in Jacksonville.

Joseph (Bo) Sullivan, of New Jersey. Since 1964 Mr. Sullivan has been president and chief executive officer of Bormont Industries in Totowa.

Reggie Williams, of Ohio. Since 1976 Mr. Williams has been a professional football player with the Cincinnati Bengals.

February 26

The President met at the White House with:
—Howard H. Baker, Jr., Chief of Staff to the President, and Colin L. Powell, Assistant to the President for National Security Affairs;
—Southern Republican State chairmen, for lunch;
—leaders of service organizations, to discuss the national campaign against drug abuse.

The President transmitted the following reports to the Congress:
—the 16th annual report on the administration of the Federal Railroad Safety Act of 1970;
—the fourth annual report of the National Endowment for Democracy, which covered fiscal year 1987.

The President today announced his intention to appoint the following individuals to be members of the National Commission on Agricultural Policy. These are new positions.

George Betton, of Delaware. From 1961 to 1987 Mr. Betton was vice president of operations for Delaware Farm Credit in Dover.

Donald G. Butcher, of New York. Since 1957 Mr. Butcher has been commissioner of the New York State Department of Agriculture and Markets in Albany.

D.M. (Pete) Gossett, of Tennessee. Since 1987 Mr. Gossett has been vice president for agriculture at the University of Tennessee in Knoxville.

February 28

The President and Mrs. Reagan hosted "In Performance," one of a series of concerts televised by the Public Broadcasting Service, in the Residence.

February 29

The President met at the White House with:
—Howard H. Baker, Jr., Chief of Staff to the President, and Colin L. Powell, Assistant to the President for National Security Affairs;
—James C. Miller III, Director of the Office of Management and Budget, and agency representatives, to receive the report on management in the U.S. Government for fiscal year 1989;
—the Vice President, for lunch;
—Ambassador Mike Mansfield;
—Secretary of Defense Frank C. Carlucci.

March 1

The President arrived at Zaventem Airport in Brussels, where he was met by Belgian Prime Minister Wilfried Martens. The President then went to Chateau Stuyvenberg, his residence during his stay in Belgium.

March 2

In the morning, the President met with Secretary of State George P. Shultz at Chateau Stuyvenberg to discuss the Secretary's recent trip to the Middle East.

In the afternoon, the President attended the opening ceremonies of the NATO summit and participated in a working session at NATO Headquarters. After attending a reception and luncheon for heads of state, the President participated in a second working session with allied leaders.

In the evening, the President attended a reception and working dinner for NATO leaders at Val Duchesse. He then returned to Chateau Stuyvenberg.

March 3

In the morning, the President attended a working session with allied leaders at NATO Headquarters and met with American NATO personnel.

In the afternoon, he met with King Baudouin I of Belgium at Laeken Palace. After a working luncheon with his advisers, the President met with Belgian Prime Minister Wilfried Martens and Foreign Minister Leo Tindemans at Chateau Stuyvenberg.

In the evening, the President returned to Washington, DC.

March 4

The President met at the White House with the Mexican delegation to the Mexico-U.S. Interparliamentary Conference.

The White House announced that Caspar W. Weinberger will visit Australia on March 16–22 as the U.S. representative to Australia's bicentennial celebration.

The President today announced his intention to nominate the following individuals to be members of the Board of Trustees of the Institute of American Indian and Alaska Native Culture and Arts Development for a term of years prescribed by Public Law 99–498 of October 17, 1986:

William Stewart Johnson, of the District of Columbia. Upon confirmation, he will be designated Chairman. Since 1978 Mr. Johnson has been director of government programs for the IBM Corp. in Washington, DC.

Alfred H. Qöyawayma, of Arizona. Upon confirmation, he will be designated Vice Chairman. Since 1971 Mr. Qöyawayma has been manager of the environmental services department of the Salt River Project in Tempe, AZ.

Gail Bird, of New Mexico. Since 1976 Miss Bird has been a jewelry designer in Ojo Caliente, NM.

Edith Colvard Crutcher, of Kansas. Ms. Crutcher is currently a part-time Commissioner for Indian Arts & Crafts and an adviser to the Museum for Women in the Arts. She resides in Washington, DC.

Roy M. Huhndorf, of Alaska. Since 1975 Mr. Huhndorf has been president and chief executive officer of Cook Inlet Region, Inc., in Anchorage, AK.

Jim Jennings, of Virginia. Since 1981 Mr. Jennings has been executive vice president of Hill & Knowlton, Inc., in Washington, DC.

Duane H. King, of Oklahoma. Since 1982 Mr. King has been executive director of Cherokee National Historical Society in Tahlequah, OK.

Beatrice Rivas Sanchez, of Michigan. Since 1982 Miss Sanchez has been dean of Cranbrook Academy of Art in Bloomfield Hills, MI.

James D. Santini, of Nevada. Since 1984 Mr. Santini has been a partner with Bible, Santini, Hoy & Miller in Washington, DC.

Irving James Toddy, of Arizona. Since 1987 Mr. Toddy has been executive director for the division of youth development and services of the Navajo Nation in Window Rock, AZ.

March 7

The President met at the White House with:
—Howard H. Baker, Jr., Chief of Staff to the President, and Colin L. Powell, Assistant to the President for National Security Affairs;
—members of the White House staff, for an issues briefing luncheon;
—Secretary of State George P. Shultz, to discuss his recent trip to the Middle East.

The White House announced that the President has invited Prime Minister Brian Mulroney of Canada to make an official visit to the United States. Prime Minister Mulroney has accepted the invitation and will meet with the President at the White House on April 27.

In the afternoon, the President hosted a reception for media executives in the Residence.

March 8

The President met at the White House with:
—Howard H. Baker, Jr., Chief of Staff to the President, and Colin L. Powell, Assistant to the President for National Security Affairs;
—Chinese Foreign Minister Wu Xueqian;
—former Senator Paul Laxalt of Nevada, for lunch;
—the Cabinet, to discuss the NATO summit meeting in Brussels, Belgium;
—officers of the U.S. League of Savings Institutions;
—the leadership of the National Jewish Coalition.

The President transmitted a report to the Speaker of the House of Representatives and the chairman of the Senate Foreign Relations Committee concerning the late transmittals of certain international agreements.

The President announced his intention to appoint the following individuals to be members of the Architectural and Transportation Barriers Compliance Board for terms expiring December 3, 1990:

Stephen B. Bull, of the District of Columbia. He would succeed Steven A. Diaz. Since 1978 Mr. Bull has been director of Washington relations for Philip Morris, Inc., in Washington, DC.

Eugene C. Johnson, of Maryland. He would succeed Norman Hughes. Since 1985 Mr. Johnson has been executive vice president and chief operating officer for TCOM Systems, Inc., in Washington, DC.

March 9

The President met at the White House with Howard H. Baker, Jr., Chief of Staff to the President, and Colin L. Powell, Assistant to the President for National Security Affairs.

March 10

The President met at the White House with Howard H. Baker, Jr., Chief of Staff to the President, and Colin L. Powell, Assistant to the President for National Security Affairs.

The President today announced his intention to appoint the following individuals to be members of the President's Foreign Intelligence Advisory Board for terms of 2 years:

Zbigniew Brzezinski of Virginia. This is a new position. Since 1981 Mr. Brzezinski has been a counselor for the Center for Strategic and International Studies, in Washington, DC. Prior to this he was the Assistant to the President for National Security Affairs at the White House, 1977–1981.

Gordon C. Luce of California. He would succeed Clare Boothe Luce. Since 1979 Mr. Luce has been chairman of the board and chief executive officer of Great American First Savings Bank in San Diego, CA. He was president of the Great American First Savings Bank, 1969–1979.

The President today announced his intention to nominate the following individuals to be members of the National Museum Service Board:

For a term expiring December 6, 1991:

Arthur C. Beale, of Massachusetts. He would succeed Ann Duncan Haffner. Mr. Beale has been director of research for the Museum of Fine Arts in Boston, MA, 1986-present.

For a term expiring December 6, 1992:

Willard L. Boyd, of Illinois. He would succeed Peter H. Raven. Upon confirmation, he will be designated Chairperson. Since 1981 Mr. Boyd has been president of the Field Museum of Natural History in Chicago, IL.

In the evening, the President hosted a dinner for members of the Ronald Reagan Presidential Foundation in the Residence.

March 11

The President met at the White House with:
—Howard H. Baker, Jr., Chief of Staff to the President, and Colin L. Powell, Assistant to the President for National Security Affairs;
—Secretary of State George P. Shultz.

The White House announced that the President approved Federal aid to assist the North Slope Borough in Alaska to recover from damages to an elementary school complex that was struck by fire on February 10.

In the afternoon, the President left the White House for a weekend stay at Camp David, MD.

March 13

The President returned to the White House from a weekend stay at Camp David, MD.

March 14

The President met at the White House with:
—Howard H. Baker, Jr., Chief of Staff to the President, and Colin L. Powell, Assistant to the President for National Security Affairs;
—West German Defense Minister Manfred Woerner, to discuss the Minister's upcoming term as Secretary General of NATO;
—members of the White House staff, for the issues briefing luncheon;
—Secretary of Defense Frank C. Carlucci.

The President transmitted to the Congress the annual report of ACTION for fiscal year 1987.

March 15

The President met at the White House with:
—Howard H. Baker, Jr., Chief of Staff to the President, and Colin L. Powell, Assistant to the President for National Security Affairs;
—congressional leaders, to discuss foreign policy issues;
—chief executive officers of the Swedish-American Chamber of Commerce.

In the evening, the President attended the Inner Circle dinner for major National Republican Senatorial Committee fundraisers.

March 16

The President met at the White House with Howard H. Baker, Jr., Chief of Staff to the President, and Colin L. Powell, Assistant to the President for National Security Affairs.

The President announced his intention to nominate the following individuals to be members of the Federal Retirement Thrift Investment Board:

For a term of 4 years:

Roger W. Mehle, of New York. This is a reappointment. Upon confirmation, he will be designated Chairman. Since 1985 Mr. Mehle has been a partner with Royer, Shacknai & Mehle in Washington, DC.

For a term of 2 years:

Richard H. Headlee, of Michigan. This is a reappointment. Since 1972 Mr. Headlee has been chief executive officer and president of Alexander Hamilton Life Insurance Companies in Farmington Hills, MI.

In the afternoon, the President hosted a reception for Members of Congress in the Residence.

In the evening, the President was briefed in the Residence by Howard H. Baker, Jr., Chief of Staff to the President, and Colin L. Powell, Assistant to the President for National Security Affairs, on the incursion by Sandinista armed forces into Honduras. The President then ordered U.S. combat troops sent to Palmerola Air Force Base in Honduras.

March 17

The President met at the White House with:

—the Vice President; Howard H. Baker, Jr., Chief of Staff to the President; and Colin L. Powell, Assistant to the President for National Security Affairs;
—Irish Ambassador Padraic N. MacKernan, to receive shamrocks from Ireland in observance of St. Patrick's Day.

Throughout the day, the President telephoned Members of Congress to discuss his veto of the Civil Rights Restoration Act of 1987.

The President designated Dennis M. Devaney as Acting General Counsel of the Federal Labor Relations Authority.

March 18

The President met at the White House with:
—the Vice President; Howard H. Baker, Jr., Chief of Staff to the President; and Colin L. Powell, Assistant to the President for National Security Affairs;
—the Vice President, for lunch;
—Secretary of State George P. Shultz.

March 21

The President met at the White House with:
—the Vice President; Howard H. Baker, Jr., Chief of Staff to the President; and Colin L. Powell, Assistant to the President for National Security Affairs;
—members of the White House staff, for an issues briefing luncheon;
—members of the U.S. delegation of observers for the Salvadoran legislative and municipal elections.

The White House announced that the President has invited Prime Minister Eddie Fenech Adami of Malta to meet with him at the White House on July 13. Prime Minister Adami has accepted the President's invitation.

March 22

The President met at the White House with:
—the Vice President; Howard H. Baker, Jr., Chief of Staff to the President; and Colin L. Powell, Assistant to the President for National Security Affairs;
—José Antonio Ardanza, President of the Basque region of Spain.

In an Oval Office ceremony, the President received diplomatic credentials from Ambassadors Jan Kinast of Poland, Ataul Karim of Bangladesh, Roble Olhaye Oudine of Djibouti, Denis Daudi Afande of Kenya, Harold Huyton Francis of New Zealand, Carlos Delius Evers of Bolivia, and Paul Desire Kabore of Burkina Faso.

March 23

The President met at the White House with:
—the Vice President; Howard H. Baker, Jr., Chief of Staff to the President; and Colin L. Powell, Assistant to the President for National Security Affairs;
—former President Chun Doo Hwan of the Republic of Korea, to discuss the transition of newly elected President Roh Tae Woo and its effect on South Korean democracy;
—Secretary of State George P. Shultz.

March 24

The President met at the White House with:
—the Vice President; Howard H. Baker, Jr., Chief of Staff to the President; and Colin L. Powell, Assistant to the President for National Security Affairs;
—Hans-Jochen Vogel, chairman of the West German Social Democratic Party, to discuss West German-U.S. relations;
—the winners of the White House News Photographers Association contest.

The President announced his intention to appoint the following individuals to be members of the Board of Directors of the Federal National Mortgage Association for terms ending on the date of the annual meeting of the stockholders in 1989:

Samuel W. Bartholomew, of Tennessee. This is a reappointment. Since 1976 Mr. Bartholomew has been founder and principal with the law firm of Donelson, Stakes, and Bartholomew in Nashville, TN.

Henry C. Cashen II, of the District of Columbia. This is a reappointment. Since 1973 Mr. Cashen has been a partner in the law firm of Dickstein, Shapiro and Morin in Washington, DC.

Vance C. Miller, of Texas. This is a reappointment. Mr. Miller is currently chairman of the board for Vance C. Miller Interests in Dallas, TX.

The President announced his intention to nominate the following individuals to be members of the Board of Directors of the Overseas Private Investment Corporation:

For a term expiring December 17, 1990:

Allie C. Felder, Jr., of the District of Columbia. This is a reappointment. Since 1987 Dr. Felder has been the senior vice president emeritus of the National Cooperative Business Association in Washington, DC.

For the remainder of the term expiring December 17, 1988:

Richard F. Hohlt, of Indiana. He will succeed Thomas A. Bolan. Since 1984 Mr. Hohlt has been senior vice president for government affairs at the U.S. League of Savings Institutions in Washington, DC.

March 25

The President met at the White House with:
—the Vice President; Howard H. Baker, Jr., Chief of Staff to the President; and Colin L.

Powell, Assistant to the President for National Security Affairs;
—Archbishop Iakovos of the Greek Orthodox Archdiocese of North and South America, for the observance of Greek Independence Day;
—Secretary of State George P. Shultz.

The President announced his intention to designate the following individuals to be members of the International Centre for Settlement of Investment Disputes for terms of 6 years:

To be members of the Panel of Conciliators:

Richard A. Hauser, of the District of Columbia. He would succeed Peter Heinz Kaminer. Since 1986 Mr. Hauser has been a partner in the law firm of Baker & Hostetler in Washington, DC.

Cecil Jay Olmstead, of Connecticut. He would succeed Bayless Andrew Manning. Since 1980 Mr. Olmstead has been a counsel for Steptoe & Johnson in Washington, DC.

Michael Stephan Shaw, of Illinois. He would succeed Seymour Jeffrey Rubin. Since 1980 Mr. Shaw has been a principal with the law firm of Shaw & Miller in Chicago, IL.

To be members of the Panel of Arbitrators:

Robert Michael Kimmitt, of Virginia. He would succeed Myres Smith McDougal. Since 1987 Mr. Kimmitt has been a partner in the law firm of Sidley & Austin in Washington, DC.

Robert F. Pietrowski, Jr., of Maryland. He would succeed Detlev Frederick Vagts. Since 1984 Mr. Pietrowski has been a partner in the law firm of Bracewell & Patterson in Washington, DC.

The President today selected the following individuals to be members of the Board of Directors of the National Railroad Passenger Corporation for terms of 2 years:

Samuel H. Hellenbrand, of New York. This is a reappointment. Since 1983 Mr. Hellenbrand has been the director of the Security Capital Corp. in New York City.

Frank W. Jenkins, of Pennsylvania. This is a reappointment. Since 1964 Mr. Jenkins has been a partner with the law firm of Jenkins, Tarquini, and Jenkins in Ambler, PA.

March 26

In the evening, the President attended the Gridiron dinner at the Capital Hilton Hotel.

March 28

The President met at the White House with:
—Howard H. Baker, Jr., Chief of Staff to the President, and Colin L. Powell, Assistant to the President for National Security Affairs;
—William H. Webster, Director of Central Intelligence.

The President announced his intention to appoint the following individuals to be members of the International Cultural and Trade Center Commission. These are new positions.

For terms of 6 years expiring August 20, 1993:

Charles H. Percy. Upon appointment, he will be designated Chairman. Since 1985 Mr. Percy has been with Charles H. Percy and Associates in Washington, DC. Prior to this he was a United States Senator for Illinois from 1967 to 1985.

Harry McPherson. Upon appointment, he will be designated Vice Chairman. Since 1969 Mr. McPherson has been a partner with the law firm of Verner, Lipfert, Bernhard, McPherson and Hand. From 1965 to 1969, Mr. McPherson was Counsel, then Special Counsel to the President at the White House.

For terms of 4 years expiring August 20, 1991:

Donald A. Brown. Since 1960 Mr. Brown has been a founding partner with JBG Associates in Washington, DC, and since 1955 Mr. Brown has been founder and partner with the firm of Brown, Gildenhorn and Jacobs.

Michael R. Gardner. Since 1982 Mr. Gardner has been a partner and head of the communications law section of Akin, Gump, Strauss, Hauer and Feld in Washington, DC. From 1977 to 1982, Mr. Gardner was a partner with Bracewell and Patterson.

For a term of 2 years expiring August 20, 1989:

Judah C. Sommer. Since 1984 Mr. Sommer has been vice president and manager of Goldman and Sachs in Washington, DC. From 1977 to 1984, Mr. Sommer was a partner with Stroock, Stroock & Lavan.

March 29

The President met at the White House with:
—Howard H. Baker, Jr., Chief of Staff to the President, and Colin L. Powell, Assistant to the President for National Security Affairs;
—the Republican congressional leadership;
—George F. Will, for lunch;
—Members of Congress, to discuss space, science, and technology.

The White House announced the resignations of Deputy Attorney General Arnold I. Burns and Assistant Attorney General William F. Weld.

The President transmitted to the Congress the 21st annual report of the U.S.-Japan Cooperative Medical Science program.

March 30

The President met at the White House with:
—Howard H. Baker, Jr., Chief of Staff to the President, and Colin L. Powell, Assistant to the President for National Security Affairs;
—Senator Robert Dole of Kansas, to discuss issues currently under consideration by the Congress;
—Secretary of State George P. Shultz.

President Reagan discussed the Afghan peace negotiations in a telephone conversation with President Mohammed Zia-ul-Haq of Pakistan.

March 31

The President met at the White House with:

—the Vice President; Howard H. Baker, Jr., Chief of Staff to the President; and Colin L. Powell, Assistant to the President for National Security Affairs;
—the Vice President, for lunch;
—the Cabinet, to discuss trade, aid to the Nicaraguan democratic resistance, and the situation in Panama.

In the afternoon, the President attended the kickoff of the Malcolm Baldrige National Quality Awards program in the Roosevelt Room at the White House.

April 1

In the morning, the President left the White House to visit his ranch in Santa Barbara County, CA, and Las Vegas, NV.

April 4

In the afternoon, the President attended a luncheon for members of the Ronald Reagan Presidential Foundation at the home of Gen. William Lyon, USAF, Ret., in Cota de Caza, CA. Following the luncheon, the President returned to his ranch in Santa Barbara County, CA.

April 7

The President discussed the situation in Panama, Afghanistan, and the Middle East in by telephone with Howard H. Baker, Jr., Chief of Staff to the President, and Colin L. Powell, Assistant to the President for National Security Affairs.

The White House announced that:
—at the invitation of the President, the University of Kansas Jayhawks, the 1988 men's NCAA basketball champions, and the Louisiana Tech Lady Techsters, the 1988 women's NCAA basketball champions, will visit the White House on April 11;
—the President has accepted an invitation to address a luncheon hosted by the World Affairs Council of Western Massachusetts in Springfield on April 21.

April 10

The President returned to the White House after his visit to California and Nevada.

April 11

The President met at the White House with:
—the Vice President; Howard H. Baker, Jr., Chief of Staff to the President; and Colin L. Powell, Assistant to the President for National Security Affairs;
—members of the White House staff, for an issues briefing luncheon;
—Secretary of State George P. Schultz and Secretary of Defense Frank C. Carlucci, to discuss the Afghanistan accords.

In the evening, the President hosted a dinner for King Carl XVI Gustaf and Queen Sylvia of Sweden in the Residence at the White House.

April 12

The President met at the White House with:
—Howard H. Baker, Jr., Chief of Staff to the President, and Colin L. Powell, Assistant to the President for National Security Affairs;
—conservative leaders, to discuss foreign policy;
—Secretary of Defense Frank C. Carlucci.

The President appointed the following individuals to be members of the Board of Directors of the Federal Financing Bank:

M. Peter McPherson, Deputy Secretary of the Treasury. He would succeed Richard G. Darman.

Mark Sullivan III, General Counsel for the Department of the Treasury. He would succeed Robert Michael Kimmitt.

The President announced his intention to appoint Secretary of Labor Ann Dore McLaughlin to be a member of the Advisory Commission on Intergovernmental Relations for a term of 2 years. She would succeed William Emerson Brock III.

In the afternoon, the President hosted a reception for employees of the Public Broadcasting Service in the Residence.

April 13

The President met at the White House with:
—Howard H. Baker, Jr., Chief of Staff to the President, and Colin L. Powell, Assistant to the President for National Security Affairs;
—Prime Minister Lee Kuan Yew of Singapore.

The President transmitted to the Congress the 16th annual report on Federal advisory committees covering fiscal year 1987.

April 14

The President met at the White House with:
—Howard H. Baker, Jr., Chief of Staff to the President, and Colin L. Powell, Assistant to the President for National Security Affairs;
—the State chairmen of the President's Dinner, an annual fundraiser for Republican congressional election campaigns;
—the leaders of Childhelp U.S.A.;
—Terry M. Weeks, the 1988 Teacher of the Year;
—the executive committee of the Republican National Hispanic Assembly.

The President announced his intention to appoint the following individuals to be members of the Cultural Property Advisory Committee:

For terms of 1 year:

James G. Crowley III, of South Carolina. This is a reappointment. Since 1976 Mr. Crowley has been a private art dealer in Spartanburg, SC.

Denver Fred Wendorf, Jr., of Texas. This is a reappointment. Since 1968 Dr. Wendorf has been chairman of the department of anthropology at Southern Methodist University in Dallas, TX.

For terms of 2 years:

Patricia Rieff Anawalt, of California. This is a reappointment. Since 1975 Dr. Anawalt has been a consulting curator for the Museum of Cultural History at the University of California at Los Angeles.

Leslie Elizabeth Wildesen, of Colorado. This is a reappointment. Since 1984 Dr. Wildesen has been the Colorado State Archaeologist in Denver, CO.

For terms of 3 years:

James William Alsdorf, of Illinois. This is a reappointment. Since 1983 Mr. Alsdorf has been chairman of the board, director, and chief executive officer of Alsdorf International in Winnetka, IL.

Clemency Chase Coggins, of Massachusetts. This is a reappointment. Since 1979 Dr. Coggins has been an associate professor of Pre-Columbian art of the Peabody Museum of Archaeology and Ethnology at Harvard University.

Thomas K. Seligman, of California. He would succeed Arthur A. Houghton III. Since 1972 Mr. Seligman has been deputy director for education and exhibitions at the Fine Arts Museum of San Francisco.

April 15

The President met at the White House with:
- —Howard H. Baker, Jr., Chief of Staff to the President, and Colin L. Powell, Assistant to the President for National Security Affairs;
- —members of the National Conference of Lieutenant Governors;
- —Secretary of State George P. Shultz.

The President transmitted the following reports to the Congress:
- —the 1987 annual report of the Federal Council on Aging;
- —the 22d annual report of the National Endowment for the Humanities covering 1987.

In the afternoon, the President left the White House for a weekend stay at Camp David, MD.

April 17

In the afternoon, the President returned to the White House from a weekend stay at Camp David, MD.

In the evening, the President met in the Residence with administration officials; Adm. William J. Crowe, Jr., Chairman of the Joint Chiefs of Staff; and congressional leaders to consider options for taking action against Iran for the attack on the U.S.S. *Samuel B. Roberts* in the Persian Gulf. Subsequently, the President ordered a military strike against the Sassan and Sirri oil platforms.

April 18

The President met at the White House with:
- —Howard H. Baker, Jr., Chief of Staff to the President, and Colin L. Powell, Assistant to the President for National Security Affairs;
- —the Cabinet.

The President hosted a luncheon for the Western Republican State party chairmen in the Cabinet Room at the White House.

The President announced his intention to nominate the following individuals to be members of the National Council on the Humanities for terms expiring January 26, 1994:

Gary L. McDowell, of Louisiana. He would succeed Rita Ricardo-Campbell. Since 1987 Mr. McDowell has been a fellow with the Woodrow Wilson International Center for Scholars at the Smithsonian Institution in Washington, DC.

William P. Wright, Jr., of Texas. He would succeed Peter J. Stanlis. Since 1957 Mr. Wright has been owner and chairman of the board for Westner Marketing, Inc., in Abilene, TX.

In the evening, the President attended the eighth annual Basque Lamb Fry dinner, hosted by former Senator Paul Laxalt of Nevada at the Georgetown Club.

April 19

The President met at the White House with:
- —Howard H. Baker, Jr., Chief of Staff to the President, and Colin L. Powell, Assistant to the President for National Security Affairs;
- —the Republican congressional leadership;
- —the Heisman Trophy winners;
- —a delegation from the California Agricultural Leadership program, a nonprofit educational program to benefit California farming.

The President transmitted to the Congress the annual report of the National Endowment for the Arts and the National Council on the Arts for fiscal year 1987.

The White House announced that the President has invited Prime Minister Thorsteinn Palsson of Iceland to make an official working visit to the United States. The Prime Minister has accepted the invitation and will meet with the President at the White House on May 16.

The White House also announced that the President has invited Prime Minister Robert Hawke of Australia to make an official working visit to the United States. The Prime Minister has accepted the invitation and will meet with the President at the White House on June 23.

April 20

The President met at the White House with:
- —the Vice President; Howard H. Baker, Jr., Chief of Staff to the President; and Colin L.

Powell, Assistant to the President for National Security Affairs;
—the Vice President, for lunch.

April 21

The President met at the White House with:
—the Vice President; Howard H. Baker, Jr., Chief of Staff to the President; and Colin L. Powell, Assistant to the President for National Security Affairs;
—members of the Soviet-U.S. delegation to the bilateral information talks.

April 22

The President met at the White House with:
—Howard H. Baker, Jr., Chief of Staff to the President, and Colin L. Powell, Assistant to the President for National Security Affairs;
—Foreign Minister Sitthi Sawetsila of Thailand.

The President announced his intention to appoint the following individuals to be members of the United States Holocaust Memorial Council for terms expiring January 15, 1993:

David T. Chase, of Connecticut. He would succeed Norman Braman. Since 1953 Mr. Chase has been president of Chase Enterprises in Hartford, CT.

Ronald S. Lauder, of New York. He would succeed Irving Greenberg. Since 1987 Mr. Lauder has been with Estee Lauder Co. in New York City. Previously he was the United States Ambassador to Austria, 1985–1987.

Franklin Littell, of Pennsylvania. This is a reappointment. Since 1975 Mr. Littell has been founder and honorary chairman of the Anne Frank Institute of Philadelphia.

The White House announced that the President has invited Premier John W.D. Swan of Bermuda for a private meeting at the White House. The Premier has accepted the invitation and will meet with the President on May 3.

The White House announced that the President will meet with Eberhard Diepgen, Governing Mayor of Berlin, on April 28.

The White House announced that the President has invited Prime Minister Harri Holkeri of Finland to visit the White House. The Prime Minister has accepted the invitation and will meet with the President on May 2.

In the afternoon, the President left the White House for a weekend stay at Camp David, MD. Enroute, he stopped briefly at Bethesda Naval Hospital for routine dental x rays.

April 24

In the afternoon, the President returned to the White House from a weekend stay at Camp David, MD.

In the evening, the President and Mrs. Reagan hosted "In Performance," one of a series of concerts televised by the Public Broadcasting Service, in the Residence.

April 25

The President met at the White House with:
—Howard H. Baker, Jr., Chief of Staff to the President, and Colin L. Powell, Assistant to the President for National Security Affairs;
—members of the White House staff, for an issues briefing luncheon;
—religious and human rights leaders, to receive a petition for religious freedom in the Soviet Union;
—William H. Webster, Director of Central Intelligence.

In the evening, the President attended a reception at Blair House honoring those involved in its restoration.

April 26

The President met at the White House with:
—Howard H. Baker, Jr., Chief of Staff to the President, and Colin L. Powell, Assistant to the President for National Security Affairs;
—Secretary of State George P. Shultz;
—William H. Webster, Director of Central Intelligence.

The President hosted a luncheon for America's outstanding teachers in the Roosevelt Room at the White House.

The White House announced that the President has asked former Governor Richard L. Thornburgh of Pennsylvania to be his representative at the Australia-American Friendship Week celebrations, April 29–May 8. Australia-American Friendship Week commemorates the Battle of the Coral Sea and the ANZUS alliance.

The President appointed the following individuals to be members of the President's Emergency Board No. 213, created by Executive Order No. 12636 on April 20, 1988:

Robert O. Harris, of Washington, DC, who will serve as Chairman, is an attorney and arbitrator. He is currently ombudsman for the International Monetary Fund. Previously he was a member of the National Mediation Board. He was born November 11, 1929.

Richard R. Kasher, of Pennsylvania, is an attorney and arbitrator in Bryn Mawr. Previously he was director of labor relations for the Consolidated Rail Corp. in Philadelphia. He was born May 30, 1939.

Robert E. Peterson, of New York, is an independent arbitrator in Briarcliff Manor. Previously he was chief personnel officer for the Long Island Rail Road. He was born December 2, 1929.

April 27

The President met at the White House with:
—the Vice President; Howard H. Baker, Jr., Chief of Staff to the President; and Colin L.

Powell, Assistant to the President for National Security Affairs;
—Senator James A. McClure of Idaho;
—the Vice President, for lunch.

April 28

The President met at the White House with:
—the Vice President; Howard H. Baker, Jr., Chief of Staff to the President; and Colin L. Powell, Assistant to the President for National Security Affairs;
—Eberhard Diepgen, Governing Mayor of Berlin;
—Michael Neufeldt, the 1987 Muscular Dystrophy Poster Child;
—members of the National Drug Policy Board to receive a report.

The President hosted a private luncheon in the Residence for Prime Minister and Mrs. Mulroney of Canada.

April 29

The President met at the White House with:
—Howard H. Baker, Jr., Chief of Staff to the President, and Colin L. Powell, Assistant to the President for National Security Affairs;
—Secretary of State George P. Shultz.

May 2

The President met at the White House with:
—the Vice President; Howard H. Baker, Jr., Chief of Staff to the President; and Colin L. Powell, Assistant to the President for National Security Affairs;
—members of the White House staff, for an issues briefing luncheon;
—William H. Webster, Director of Central Intelligence;
—Representative Robert H. Michel and members of the Illinois Chamber of Commerce.

The White House announced that the President has invited Prime Minister and Crown Prince Sa'd al-'Abdallah al-Salim Al Sabah of Kuwait to make an official working visit to the United States. The Prime Minister has accepted the invitation and will meet with the President at the White House on July 12.

The President announced his intention to appoint the following individuals to be members of the President's National Security Telecommunications Advisory Committee:

Carl F. Bailey, of Alabama. He would succeed Bennet R. Miller. Since 1983 Mr. Bailey has been president and chief executive officer for South Central Bell Telephone Co. in Birmingham, AL.

R.A. Fuhrman, of California. He would succeed Harry Jack Gray. Since 1986 Mr. Fuhrman has been president and chief executive officer for Lockheed Corp. in Calabasas, CA.

John T. Hartley, of Florida. He would succeed Joseph A. Boyd. Since 1986 Mr. Hartley has been chairman, president, and chief executive officer for the Harris Corp. in Melbourne, FL.

To be designated Chairman:

Paul H. Henson, of Kansas. He would succeed Rocco John Marano. Since 1985 Mr. Henson has been chairman of the board for United Telecommunications, Inc., in Kansas City, MO.

The President announced his intention to appoint the following individuals to be members of the Arctic Research Commission for the terms indicated:

For the remainder of the term expiring February 26, 1989:

Ben C. Gerwick, Jr., of California. He would succeed James Herbert Zumberge. Since 1971 Mr. Gerwick has been a professor of civil engineering at the University of California at Berkeley and president of Ben C. Garrick, Inc.

For a term expiring February 26, 1992:

Elmer E. Rasmuson, of Alaska. This is a reappointment. Since 1982 Mr. Rasmuson has been chairman of the budget and planning committee for the National Bank of Alaska in Anchorage.

May 3

The President met at the White House with:
—the Vice President; Howard H. Baker, Jr., Chief of Staff to the President; and Colin L. Powell, Assistant to the President for National Security Affairs;
—Premier John W.D. Swan of Bermuda;
—Myroslav Cardinal Lubachivsky of the Ukrainian Catholic Church;
—Gov. James Martin of North Carolina.

May 4

The President met at the White House with the Vice President; Howard H. Baker, Jr., Chief of Staff to the President; and Colin L. Powell, Assistant to the President for National Security Affairs.

May 5

The President met at the White House with:
—the Vice President; Howard H. Baker, Jr., Chief of Staff to the President; and Colin L. Powell, Assistant to the President for National Security Affairs;
—William F. Burns, Director of the U.S. Arms Control and Disarmament Agency;
—the Kilgore College women's basketball team;
—the National Collegiate Athletic Association hockey champions from Lake Superior State University;
—members of the National Day of Prayer organizing committee.

The White House announced that the President directed Assistant Secretary of the Treasury Francis Anthony Keating II to perform the duties of the office of the Associate Attorney General at the Department of Justice.

The President announced his intention to appoint the following individuals to be members of the National Cancer Advisory Board for terms expiring March 9, 1994:

David G. Bragg, of Utah. He would succeed Victor Braren. Since 1970 Dr. Bragg has been a professor and chairman of the department of radiology at the University of Utah School of Medicine in Salt Lake City, UT.

Louis V. Gerstner, Jr., of Connecticut. He would succeed Richard A. Bloch. Since 1985 Mr. Gerstner has been president of the American Express Co. in New York City.

Walter Lawrence, Jr., of Virginia. He would succeed Geza J. Jako. Since 1980 Dr. Lawrence has been a professor and chairman of the division of surgical oncology at the Medical College of Virginia in Richmond, VA.

Howard M. Temin, of Wisconsin. This is a reappointment. Since 1974 Dr. Temin has been a professor of viral oncology and cell biology for the American Cancer Society at the University of Wisconsin in Madison, WI.

Samuel A. Wells, Jr., of Missouri. He would succeed Ed L. Calhoon. Since 1981 Dr. Wells has been Bixby Professor of Surgery and chairman of the department of surgery at Washington University in St. Louis, MO.

May 6

The President met at the White House with:
—the Vice President; Howard H. Baker, Jr., Chief of Staff to the President; and Colin L. Powell, Assistant to the President for National Security Affairs;
—Alfred Dregger, member of the West German Bundestag;
—Josip Vrhovec, member of the Yugoslav Presidency, to discuss U.S. and International Monetary Fund financial assistance for Yugoslavia;
—the Cabinet;
—Secretary of State George P. Shultz.

In the afternoon, the President left the White House for a weekend stay at Camp David, MD.

May 8

In the afternoon, the President returned to the White House from a weekend stay at Camp David, MD.

May 9

The President met at the White House with:
—the Vice President; Howard H. Baker, Jr., Chief of Staff to the President; and Colin L. Powell, Assistant to the President for National Security Affairs;
—former Japanese Prime Minister Yasuhiro Nakasone;
—Carl T. Rowan, political commentator, for lunch;
—Secretary of Defense Frank C. Carlucci;
—members of the Council of the Americas.

May 10

The President met at the White House with:
—the Vice President; Howard H. Baker, Jr., Chief of Staff to the President; and Colin L. Powell, Assistant to the President for National Security Affairs;
—Republican Senators;
—Chinese Premier Jiyun Tian, to discuss China-U.S. trade expansion;
—Secretary of State George P. Shultz.

The President announced his intention to appoint the following to be members of the President's Commission on Executive Exchange for terms of 2 years:

Frank C. Carlucci, Secretary of Defense. He would succeed Caspar Willard Weinberger. Mr. Carlucci has served as Secretary of Defense since 1987. Previously he was Assistant to the President for National Security Affairs.

C. William Verity, Jr., Secretary of Commerce. He would succeed Malcolm Baldrige. Mr. Verity has served as Secretary of Commerce since 1987. Previously he was chairman of the board of Armco.

The President announced his intention to appoint the following to be members of the Interim Board of Directors of the Federal Agricultural Mortgage Corporation. The following are new positions:

John R. Dahl, of North Dakota. Upon appointment, he will be designated chairperson. Currently, Mr. Dahl is a rancher with Dahl Land & Cattle Co. in Gackle, ND.

B. Dale Harrison, of Ohio. Since January 1988 Mr. Harrison has been chairman of the Fourth Farm Credit District Board in Eaton, OH. He is also a farmer.

Leslie G. Horsager, of New Jersey. Since 1985 Mr. Horsager has been vice president of the Prudential Investment Corp. and head of Prudential Agricultural Investments Group in Sea Bright, NJ.

Randall A. Killebrew, of Illinois. Since 1974 Mr. Killebrew has been president of the First National Bank of Petersburg in Petersburg, IL.

Thomas H. Olson, of Nebraska. Since 1973 Mr. Olson has been president of Lisco State Bank in Lisco, NE.

James A. Pierson, of Massachusetts. Since 1987 Mr. Pierson has been president and chief executive officer of Farm Credit Banks of Springfield in Agawam, MA.

Donald R. Rogge, of Texas. Since 1986 Mr. Rogge has been president of Federal Land Bank of Texas in Austin, TX.

Edward Charles Williamson, Jr., of Georgia. Since 1978 Mr. Williamson has been manager, director, and vice president of J.L. Adams Farms in Camilla, GA.

May 11

The President met at the White House with:
- —the Vice President; Howard H. Baker, Jr., Chief of Staff to the President; and Colin L. Powell, Assistant to the President for National Security Affairs;
- —the Republican congressional leadership;
- —major contributors to the President's Dinner, a Republican congressional fundraiser.

The President transmitted to the Committee on Foreign Relations and the Select Committee on Intelligence of the Senate and to the Committee on Foreign Affairs and the Permanent Select Committee on Intelligence of the House of Representatives a classified report required by section 601 of the Intelligence Authorization Act for Fiscal Year 1985 (P.L. 98–618) on reciprocity and equivalence of foreign governments that engage in intelligence activities within the United States that are harmful to our national security.

The President announced the appointment of Robert Holmes Tuttle to be Assistant to the President and Director of Presidential Personnel. Since February of 1985 Mr. Tuttle has served as Deputy Assistant to the President and Director of Presidential Personnel.

In the afternoon, the President hosted a luncheon for Soviet experts in the Roosevelt Room at the White House.

In the evening, the President hosted a reception for major contributors to the President's Dinner, a Republican congressional fundraiser.

May 12

The President met at the White House with:
- —Howard H. Baker, Jr., Chief of Staff to the President, and Colin L. Powell, Assistant to the President for National Security Affairs;
- —the executive committee of the International Council of the World Conference on Soviet Jewry.

The President received the report "America's Waiting Children" from the Interagency Task Force on Adoption.

The President transmitted to the Congress the eighth and ninth annual reports describing Federal actions with respect to the conservation and use of petroleum and natural gas in Federal facilities.

May 13

The President met at the White House with:
- —Howard H. Baker, Jr., Chief of Staff to the President, and Colin L. Powell, Assistant to the President for National Security Affairs;
- —the Cabinet.

In the afternoon, the President left the White House for a weekend stay at Camp David, MD.

May 15

In the afternoon, the President returned to the White House from a weekend stay at Camp David, MD.

May 16

The President met at the White House with:
- —Howard H. Baker, Jr., Chief of Staff to the President, and Colin L. Powell, Assistant to the President for National Security Affairs;
- —Secretary of State George P. Shultz;
- —the Capitol Regents of the National Federation of Republican Women;
- —the Working Group on Financial Markets, to receive the group's interim report.

The President announced his intention to appoint the following individuals to be members of the National Commission for Employment Policy:

For a term expiring March 20, 1991:

Donald W. Jones, of Missouri. He would succeed Walton E. Burdick. Since 1984 Mr. Jones has been a partner with Hulston, Jones, and Sullivan in Springfield, MO.

For a term expiring September 30, 1991:

James W. Winchester, of Mississippi. This is a reappointment. Since 1986 Dr. Winchester has been president of Winchester and Associates in Washington, DC.

May 17

The President met at the White House with:
- —Howard H. Baker, Jr., Chief of Staff to the President, and Colin L. Powell, Assistant to the President for National Security Affairs;
- —Senator David K. Karnes of Nebraska;
- —a group of human rights activists.

May 19

The President met at the White House with Howard H. Baker, Jr., Chief of Staff to the President, and Colin L. Powell, Assistant to the President for National Security Affairs.

May 20

The President met at the White House with:
- —the Vice President; Howard H. Baker, Jr., Chief of Staff to the President; and Colin L. Powell, Assistant to the President for National Security Affairs;
- —the Vice President, for lunch;
- —Secretary of State George P. Shultz;
- —the Joint Chiefs of Staff.

The President designated William W. Fox, Jr., as Chairman of the Marine Mammal Commission. He would succeed Robert Elsner. Mr. Fox has served as a member since November of 1987.

May 23

The President met at the White House with the Vice President; Howard H. Baker, Jr., Chief of Staff to the President; and Colin L. Powell,

Assistant to the President for National Security Affairs.

The President transmitted to the Congress fiscal year 1989 budget amendments totaling $1.4 million for the legislative branch and fiscal year 1988 and 1989 appropriations language for the judiciary.

May 24

The President met at the White House with:

—the Vice President; Howard H. Baker, Jr., Chief of Staff to the President; and Colin L. Powell, Assistant to the President for National Security Affairs;

—congressional leaders, to discuss the trade bill veto, the Intermediate-Range Nuclear Forces treaty, and the legislative-executive branch drug task force;

—the Vice President, for lunch;

—the Foreign Intelligence Advisory Board, to discuss the START negotiations;

—the Cabinet.

The White House announced that the President has invited Prime Minister Ciriaco De Mita of Italy for an official working visit to the United States. The Prime Minister has accepted the invitation and will meet with the President at the White House on June 14.

The White House also announced that President Reagan has invited President Kenan Evren of Turkey to make a state visit to the United States. President Evren has accepted the invitation and will meet with President Reagan at the White House on June 27.

May 25

In the evening, President Reagan arrived at Helsinki-Vantaa Airport, where he was greeted by Finnish President Mauno Koivisto. President Reagan then went to a government guest house, his residence during his stay in Finland.

May 27

In the afternoon, President Reagan went to the Presidential Palace for a formal welcoming ceremony. President Reagan met with President Koivisto, and the two Presidents had lunch in the Hall of Mirrors. President Reagan then returned to his residence.

May 28

In the afternoon, the President met with administration officials at his residence.

May 29

In the morning, President Reagan said goodbye to President Koivisto and U.S. Embassy personnel at Helsinki-Vantaa Airport.

In the afternoon, the President arrived at Vnukovo II Airport in Moscow. He was welcomed by Andrei Gromyko, Chairman of the Presidium of the Supreme Soviet, in a formal arrival ceremony.

After participating in the opening ceremonies of the Soviet-U.S. summit, the President met privately with Soviet General Secretary Gorbachev in St. Catherine's Hall at the Grand Kremlin Palace. Following the meeting, the President went to Spaso House, his residence during his stay in the Soviet Union. He then met with administration officials.

May 30

In the morning, the President met with administration officials at Spaso House. Later in the morning, he met with the General Secretary in a plenary session in St. Catherine's Hall at the Grand Kremlin Palace. Following the meeting, the President returned to Spaso House and met with administration officials.

May 31

In the morning, the President met with administration officials at Spaso House. Later in the morning, he met privately with the General Secretary in the General Secretary's office in the Soviet Government Building at the Kremlin. The President and the General Secretary toured the grounds of the Kremlin before participating in a plenary session in St. Catherine's Hall at the Grand Kremlin Palace. The two leaders then witnessed the signing of two Soviet-U.S. arms control agreements by Secretary of State George P. Shultz and Foreign Minister Eduard Shevardnadze in the Palace's Red Room. After the signing ceremony, the President returned to Spaso House.

June 1

In the morning, the President met with administration officials at Spaso House. Later in the morning, he met with the General Secretary in a plenary session in St. Catherine's Hall at the Grand Kremlin Palace. Following the meeting, the President returned to Spaso House, where he had lunch with senior advisers.

In the evening, the President and Mrs. Reagan, accompanied by General Secretary and Mrs. Gorbachev, attended a performance of the Bolshoi ballet. Afterward, they had dinner with General Secretary and Mrs. Gorbachev at the General Secretary's dacha outside Moscow. Following dinner, the President and Mrs. Reagan returned to Spaso House.

June 2

In the morning, the President met with U.S. Embassy personnel. He left Spaso House and attended a farewell ceremony at the Grand Kremlin Palace with the General Secretary. After a departure ceremony with Chairman Gromyko at Vnukovo II Airport, the President traveled to London.

In the afternoon, after a private lunch with the U.S. Ambassador, the President went to Buckingham Palace, where he had tea with Queen Elizabeth II and reviewed the honor guard.

In the evening, the President met with Prime Minister Margaret Thatcher at 10 Downing Street. The two leaders attended a dinner after their meeting. Following the dinner, the President went to Winfield House, his residence during his stay in the United Kingdom.

June 3

In the morning, the President met with Japanese Prime Minister Noboru Takeshita at Winfield House.

In the afternoon, the President returned to Washington, DC.

June 6

The President met at the White House with:

—Howard H. Baker, Jr., Chief of Staff to the President, and Colin L. Powell, Assistant to the President for National Security Affairs;

—members of the White House staff, for an issues briefing luncheon.

The President designated Eugene J. McAllister, an Assistant Secretary of State (Economic and Business Affairs), to serve as a member of the Board of Directors of the Overseas Private Investment Corporation. He would succeed Douglas W. McMinn.

The President announced the appointment of the following individuals to be members of the National Commission for Employment Policy:

For the remainder of the term expiring September 30, 1989:

William M. Taylor, of Florida. He would succeed Barbara Collins McQuown. Since 1973 Mr. Taylor has been president of Bill Taylor and Associates, Inc., in Jacksonville, FL.

For a term expiring March 20, 1991:

J. Michael Levesque, of Rhode Island. He would succeed Juan Rangel. Since 1987 Mr. Levesque has been chairman of the Republican Party for the State of Rhode Island.

The President announced the appointment of the following individuals to be members of the Administrative Conference of the United States for terms of 3 years:

James C. Miller III, of the District of Columbia. This is a reappointment. Since 1985 Mr. Miller has been Director of the Office of Management and Budget at the White House. Upon appointment, he will be redesignated Vice Chairman.

Curtis H. Barnette, of Pennsylvania. He would succeed Edith Dinneen Hakola. Mr. Barnette is a senior vice president and general counsel for Bethlehem Steel Corp. in Bethlehem, PA.

Phillip D. Brady, of Virginia. He would succeed Arnold I. Burns. Since 1988 Mr. Brady has been Deputy Counsel to the President at the White House.

Trudi Morrison, of Colorado. She would succeed Otis M. Smith. Since 1987 Ms. Morrison has been president of the Morrimunt Corp. in Great Falls, VA.

R. Carter Sanders, Jr., of Virginia. He would succeed William R. Jackson. Since 1985 Mr. Sanders has been a senior partner with Sanders & Associates, P.C., in Washington, DC.

Edward L. Weidenfeld, of the District of Columbia. This is a reappointment. Since 1982 Mr. Weidenfeld has been in practice with the law office of Edward L. Weidenfeld, Esq., in Washington, DC.

June 7

The President met at the White House with:

—Howard H. Baker, Jr., Chief of Staff to the President, and Colin L. Powell, Assistant to the President for National Security Affairs;

—the Economic Policy Council, to discuss the Toronto economic summit.

The President announced his intention to appoint the following individuals to be members of the Board of Governors of the United Service Organizations, Inc., for terms of 3 years:

John S. Autry, of Virginia. He would succeed Mary Carol Rudin. Since 1980 Mr. Autry has been vice president for government relations of Unisys Corp. in Washington, DC.

Lois Haight Herrington, of California. She would succeed Carole Curb. Since 1987 Mrs. Herrington has been Chairman and Executive Director of the White House Conference for a Drug Free America in Washington, DC.

The President announced his intention to appoint the following individuals to be members of the Committee for Purchase From the Blind and Other Severely Handicapped:

Nancy Marie Flynn, of Virginia, to be the Department of Labor member of the Committee for Purchase From the Blind and Other Severely Handicapped. She would succeed Herbert J. Cohen. Miss Flynn is currently Deputy Administrator of the Wage and Hour Division of the Employment Standard Administration at the Department of Labor in Washington, DC. Prior to this she was Assistant Administrator in the Office of Program Operations for the Employment Standards Administration, 1987–1988.

Susan S. Suter, of Illinois, to be the Department of Education member of the Committee for Purchase From the Blind and Other Severely Handicapped. She would succeed George A. Conn. Mrs. Suter is currently Commissioner of the Rehabilitation Services Administration at the Department of Education in Washington, DC. Prior to this she was executive director of the Illinois Department of Rehabilitative Services.

The President announced his intention to nominate the following individuals to be members of the National Council on the Handicapped:

For the remainder of the term expiring September 17, 1989:

George H. Oberle, Jr., of Oklahoma. He would succeed Carolyn L. Vash. Since 1974 Dr. Oberle has been a professor and director of the school of health, physical education & leisure at Oklahoma State University.

For the term expiring September 17, 1990:

Justin W. Dart, Jr., of Texas. He would succeed Roxanne S. Vierra. From 1986 to 1987, Mr. Dart was a Commissioner of the Rehabilitative Services Administration at the Department of Education in Washington, DC.

For terms expiring September 17, 1991:

Joni Tada, of California. This is a reappointment. Since 1979 Mrs. Tada has been founder of Joni and Friends in Agoura, CA.

Phyllis D. Zlotnick, of Connecticut. This is a reappointment. Since 1983 Ms. Zlotnick has been a legislative consultant in the office of protection and advocacy for the State of Connecticut.

In the evening, the President attended a fundraiser for Congressman Trent Lott of Mississippi at the Grand Hotel.

June 8

The President met at the White House with:

—the Vice President; Howard H. Baker, Jr., Chief of Staff to the President; and Colin L. Powell, Assistant to the President for National Security Affairs;

—Lauren Dutton, the National Arthritis Poster Child;

—members of the Polish American Congress.

The President announced his intention to nominate the following individuals to be members of the National Commission on Libraries and Information Science for terms expiring July 19, 1993:

Wanda L. Forbes, of South Carolina. This is a reappointment. From 1975 to 1978, Mrs. Forbes was with the South Carolina Commission on Higher Education.

Margaret Phelan, of Kansas. This is a reappointment. Since 1977 Miss Phelan has been owner of Phelan Business Research in Shawnee Mission, KS.

Charles E. Reid, of New Jersey. He would succeed Bessie Boehm Moore. Since 1980 Mr. Reid has been senior vice president of Prodevco Group in Fort Lee, NJ.

The President announced his intention to appoint the following individuals to be members of the National Commission on Children for terms expiring March 31, 1989. These are new positions.

Daniel R. Coats, Member, U.S. House of Representatives. Since 1981 Mr. Coats has been a Member of the U.S. House of Representatives for the 4th District of Indiana.

Theresa Harlow Esposito, of North Carolina. Since 1984 Mrs. Esposito has been State representative in the North Carolina House of Representatives.

A. Louise Oliver, of the District of Columbia. Mrs. Oliver is currently a consultant for the Department of Education in Washington, DC.

Nancy J. Risque, of Maryland. Since 1987 Ms. Risque has been Assistant to the President and Cabinet Secretary at the White House in Washington, DC.

The President announced his intention to appoint the following individuals to be members of the Cultural Property Advisory Committee:

For a term of 1 year expiring April 25, 1989:

John J. Slocum, of Rhode Island. This is a reappointment. Since 1971 Mr. Slocum has been a trustee and member of the executive committee of the Archaeological Institute of America in Rhode Island.

For a term of 2 years expiring April 25, 1990:

Michael Kelly, of Illinois. This is a reappointment. Upon appointment, he will be redesignated Chairman. Since 1963 Mr. Kelly has been chairman of the board and chief executive officer for Kelco Industries, Inc.

June 9

The President met at the White House with:

—the Vice President; Howard H. Baker, Jr., Chief of Staff to the President; and Colin L. Powell, Assistant to the President for National Security Affairs;

—President Mobutu Sese Seko of Zaire.

The President announced his intention to appoint the following individuals to be members of the Cultural Property Advisory Committee:

For a term of 2 years expiring April 25, 1990:

Alfred E. Stendahl, of California. This is a reappointment. Since 1966 Mr. Stendahl has been director of Stendahl Art Galleries in Los Angeles, CA.

For a term of 3 years expiring April 25, 1991:

Glenn C. Randall, of the District of Columbia. He would succeed James Berry Hill. Since 1974 Mr. Randall has been owner and chairman of the board of G. Randall, Inc., in Washington, DC.

June 10

The President met at the White House with:

—Howard H. Baker, Jr., Chief of Staff to the President, and Colin L. Powell, Assistant to the President for National Security Affairs;

—community leaders participating in a 2-day workshop on self-help and welfare reform efforts;

—the Economic Policy Council, to discuss the Toronto economic summit.

In the afternoon, the President left the White House for a weekend stay at Camp David, MD.

June 12

In the afternoon, the President returned to the White House from a weekend stay at Camp David, MD. Later in the afternoon, the President and Mrs. Reagan hosted the annual White House tennis tournament.

June 13

The President met at the White House with:
- —the Vice President; Howard H. Baker, Jr., Chief of Staff to the President; and Colin L. Powell, Assistant to the President for National Security Affairs;
- —Prince Sadruddin Aga Khan, Coordinator for U.N. Humanitarian and Economic Assistance, to discuss the international relief effort for Afghanistan;
- —members of the White House staff, for an issues briefing luncheon;
- —Secretary of State George P. Shultz;
- —members of the North Atlantic Assembly;
- —Republican candidates for the upcoming congressional elections.

The President and Mrs. Reagan sent a telegram to the widow of novelist Louis L'Amour to express their sympathy on the loss of her husband.

June 14

The President met at the White House with:
- —the Vice President; Howard H. Baker, Jr., Chief of Staff to the President; and Colin L. Powell, Assistant to the President for National Security Affairs;
- —members of the Republican congressional leadership;
- —William H. Webster, Director of Central Intelligence.

June 15

The President met at the White House with:
- —the Vice President; Howard H. Baker, Jr., Chief of Staff to the President; and Colin L. Powell, Assistant to the President for National Security Affairs;
- —Members of Congress, to discuss the Nicaraguan peace negotiations;
- —Republican State chairmen from the Northeastern States, for lunch;
- —representatives of the Ronald Reagan Home Preservation Foundation.

The President announced his intention to appoint the following individuals to be members of the National Commission on Children for terms expiring March 31, 1989. These are new positions.

Mai Bell Hurley, of Tennessee. Since 1986 Mrs. Hurley has been president in a volunteer capacity for the Child Welfare League of America in Washington, DC.

Kay C. James, of Virginia. Since 1985 Mrs. James has been director of public affairs for the National Right to Life Committee in Washington, DC.

Gerald P. Regier, of Virginia. Mr. Regier has been president and chief executive officer for the Family Research Council of America, Inc., in Washington, DC.

June 16

The President met at the White House with:
- —the Vice President; Howard H. Baker, Jr., Chief of Staff to the President; and Colin L. Powell, Assistant to the President for National Security Affairs;
- —the Economic Policy Council, to discuss the Toronto economic summit.

The President announced his intention to appoint Andrew H. Card, Jr., Deputy Assistant to the President and Director of the Office of Intergovernmental Affairs at the White House, to be a member of the Advisory Commission on Intergovernmental Relations for a term of 2 years. He would succeed Gwendolyn S. King.

June 17

The President met at the White House with:
- —the Vice President; Howard H. Baker, Jr., Chief of Staff to the President; and Colin L. Powell, Assistant to the President for National Security Affairs;
- —Secretary of State George P. Shultz.

June 19

In the morning, the President arrived at Lester B. Pearson International Airport in Toronto, Canada. He then went to the Royal York Hotel, his residence during the economic summit.

Early in the afternoon, the President attended the official welcoming ceremony at Nathan Phillips Square. Following the ceremony, he met privately with Canadian Prime Minister Brian Mulroney at the city hall. Upon returning to the Royal York Hotel, President Reagan met with administration officials and then with President François Mitterrand of France.

Later in the afternoon, the President attended the opening session of the economic summit at the Metro Toronto Convention Center.

In the evening, the President attended a reception and dinner for summit leaders at the Toronto Hunt Club. He then returned to the Royal York Hotel.

June 20

In the morning, the President began the first full day of the economic summit by meeting privately with summit leaders and participating in a plenary session at the Metro Toronto Convention Center.

In the afternoon, after attending a working luncheon with summit leaders and Foreign Ministers at L'Hotel, the President participated in a plenary session at the Metro Toronto Convention Center.

In the evening, the President attended an informal working session and dinner for summit leaders at Hart House at the University of Toronto. He then returned to the Royal York Hotel.

June 21

In the morning, the President attended a plenary session at the Metro Toronto Convention Center.

In the afternoon, the President attended a final luncheon for summit participants hosted by Canadian Governor General Jeanne Sauvé at the Art Gallery of Ontario.

In the evening, the President returned to Washington, DC.

June 22

The President met at the White House with:
—the Vice President; Howard H. Baker, Jr., Chief of Staff to the President; and Colin L. Powell, Assistant to the President for National Security Affairs;
—Secretary of State George P. Shultz.

The President announced his intention to appoint the following individuals to be members of the Board of Trustees of the John F. Kennedy Center for the Performing Arts for terms expiring September 1, 1998. These are reappointments.

Lois M. Ribicoff, of Connecticut. Mrs. Ribicoff is actively involved in the music and art community in New York City.

Dennis Stanfill, of California. Since 1981 Mr. Stanfill has been president of Stanfill, Doig & Co., in Los Angeles, CA. Prior to this he was chairman of the board and chief executive officer of Twentieth Century Fox.

June 23

The President met at the White House with:
—the Vice President; Howard H. Baker, Jr., Chief of Staff to the President; and Colin L. Powell, Assistant to the President for National Security Affairs;
—recipients of the Life Achievement Award from Puerto Rico;
—the Cabinet.

In an Oval Office ceremony, the President presented Frances Gershwin Godowsky, sister of George and Ira Gershwin, with the Congressional Gold Medal, in recognition of her brothers' achievements.

The President announced his intention to nominate the following individuals to be members of the Board of Directors of the Federal Agricultural Mortgage Corporation. These are new positions.

John R. Dahl, of North Dakota. Upon confirmation, he will be designated Chairperson. Mr. Dahl has been a rancher with Dahl Land & Cattle Co., in Gackle, ND.

George James Benston, of New York. Since 1987 Dr. Benston has been the John H. Harland Professor of Finance, Accounting, and Economics for the Emory University School of Business Administration in Atlanta, GA.

Derryl McLaren, of Iowa. Since 1972 Mr. McLaren has been a farmer of grain and livestock in Farragut, IA.

Gordon Clyde Southern, of Missouri. Since 1954 Mr. Southern has been a farmer and president of Southern Farm Co., Inc., in Steele, MO.

Edward Charles Williamson, Jr., of Georgia. Since 1978 Mr. Williamson has been manager, director, and vice president for J.L. Adams Farms in Camilla, GA.

June 24

The President met at the White House with:
—the Vice President; Howard H. Baker, Jr., Chief of Staff to the President; and Colin L. Powell, Assistant to the President for National Security Affairs;
—Secretary of State George P. Shultz.

In the afternoon, the President hosted a reception for the Ford's Theatre Gala in the Residence.

The President designated Senator Ted Stevens of Alaska as his representative to the Farnborough Air Show to be held in September.

The President directed Salvatore R. Martoche, Assistant Secretary of Labor (Enforcement), to perform the duties of the office of Assistant Secretary of the Treasury (Enforcement).

The President appointed the following individuals as members of the National Commission on Migrant Education. These are new positions.

Linda Chavez, of Maryland. Upon appointment she will be designated Chairman. Since 1987 Ms. Chavez has been president of U.S. English in Washington, DC.

Donna Garner, of Texas. Since 1986 Mrs. Garner has been a teacher at Temple High School in Temple, TX.

Michael J. Lavelle, of New York. Since 1984 Mr. Lavelle has been president of Diversified Research, Inc., in New York, NY.

Robert G. Simmons, Jr., of Nebraska. Since 1949 Mr. Simmons has been a practicing attorney and a county attorney in Scottsbluff, NE.

June 27

The President met at the White House with the Vice President; Howard H. Baker, Jr., Chief of Staff to the President; and Colin L. Powell, Assistant to the President for National Security Affairs.

June 28

The President met at the White House with:
—Howard H. Baker, Jr., Chief of Staff to the President, and Colin L. Powell, Assistant to the President for National Security Affairs;
—congressional leaders, to discuss plant-closing notification, aid to the Nicaraguan democratic resistance, and defense appropriations;
—Secretary of Defense Frank C. Carlucci; Attorney General Edwin Meese III; Arthur B. Culvahouse, Jr., Counsel to the President;

and Assistant Attorney General-designate Edward S.G. Dennis, Jr., to discuss the investigation of Defense Department procurement practices;
—Republican congressional candidates.

In the afternoon, the President received the report of the White House Conference for a Drug Free America.

The President announced his intention to appoint the following individuals to be members of the President's Committee on Mental Retardation for terms expiring May 11, 1991:

Dorothy Corbin Clark, of Utah. This is a reappointment. Mrs. Clark is currently a secretary and nurse for Stanley N. Clark, M.D., in Provo, UT.

Matthew J. Guglielmo, of California. This is a reappointment. Since 1974 Mr. Guglielmo has been president of Fairview Families and Friends, Inc., for Fairview State Hospital in California.

William Kerby Hummer, of California. This is a reappointment. Since 1969 Dr. Hummer has been a physician in Santa Monica, CA.

Dagne B. Olsen, of North Dakota. She would succeed Martha Lois Eargle. Since 1980 Mrs. Olsen has been a State legislator in the North Dakota House of Representatives in Bismarck, ND.

B. Dean Owens, of Washington. He would succeed Roger Stanley Johnson. Since 1976 Mr. Owens has been director of career planning and placement for Central Washington University in Ellensburg, WA.

The President designated the following individuals to be members of the U.S. delegation to the Kingdom of Tonga to commemorate the 100th anniversary of the signing of the Treaty of Amity, Commerce, and Navigation between the United States of America and the Kingdom of Tonga and to celebrate the 70th birthday of His Majesty, King Taufa' ahau Tupou IV of Tonga, July 4, 1988. The U.S. delegation will be led by Representative Patricia Saiki of Hawaii.

Leonard Rochwarger, U.S. Ambassador to Fiji, the Kingdom of Tonga, Tuvalu, and the Republic of Kiribati.

Peter Coleman, former Governor of American Samoa.

Maureen Zatarga, Associate Director, Office of Presidential Personnel, the White House.

June 30

The President met at the White House with:
—Howard H. Baker, Jr., Chief of Staff to the President, and Colin L. Powell, Assistant to the President for National Security Affairs;
—Senator Strom Thurmond of South Carolina, to discuss a production nuclear reactor;
—Members of Congress, to discuss drug abuse and trafficking;
—Pat Riley, coach of the 1988 world champion Los Angeles Lakers basketball team;
—the 1988 Ronald Reagan Scholars;
—Shelli Breed and Donald L. Towslee, Multiple Sclerosis Mother and Father of the Year.

The President announced his intention to appoint the following individuals to be members of the Board for International Food and Agricultural Development:

For terms expiring July 28, 1992:

Gwendolyn S. King, of Maryland. She would succeed Paul Findley. Since 1988 Ms. King has been executive vice president of Gogol and Associates in Washington, DC.

Leo M. Walsh, of Wisconsin. This is a reappointment. Since 1979 Mr. Walsh has been dean and director of the College of Agricultural and Life Sciences at the University of Wisconsin at Madison.

For the remainder of the term expiring July 28, 1989:

Wendell G. Rayburn, of Missouri. He would succeed Leonard H.O. Spearman. Since 1988 Mr. Rayburn has been president of Lincoln University in Jefferson City, MO.

The President announced his intention to appoint the following individuals to be members of the President's Committee on Mental Retardation:

For the remainder of the term expiring May 11, 1990:

Kate Semerad, of Maryland. She would succeed Robert V. Bush. Since 1985 Mrs. Semerad has been president of Semerad International, Ltd., in Kensington, MD.

For a term expiring May 11, 1991:

George M. Wilson, of Minnesota. He would succeed U. Yun Ryo. Mr. Wilson has been president of Worldwide Publications in Minneapolis, MN, for 15 years.

July 1

The President met at the White House with:
—Kenneth M. Duberstein, Chief of Staff to the President, and Colin L. Powell, Assistant to the President for National Security Affairs;
—Secretary of Agriculture Richard Lyng, to discuss the drought situation.

In the afternoon, the President left the White House for a weekend stay at Camp David, MD.

Appendix B—Nominations Submitted to the Senate

The following list does not include promotions of members of the Uniformed Services, nominations to the Service Academies, or nominations of Foreign Service officers.

Submitted January 26

Eugene J. McAllister,
of Virginia, to be an Assistant Secretary of State, vice Douglas W. McMinn, resigned.

Chester E. Norris, Jr.,
of Maine, a career member of the Senior Foreign Service, Class of Minister-Counselor, to be Ambassador Extraordinary and Plenipotentiary of the United States of America to the Republic of Equatorial Guinea.

Edward Morgan Rowell,
of California, a career member of the Senior Foreign Service, Class of Minister-Counselor, to be Ambassador Extraordinary and Plenipotentiary of the United States of America to the Republic of Portugal, to which position he was appointed during the last recess of the Senate.

L. Francis Bouchey,
of Virginia, to be a member of the Board of Directors of the Inter-American Foundation for a term of 6 years (new position).

Jack Katzen,
of Connecticut, to be an Assistant Secretary of Defense, vice Robert B. Costello.

Roger J. Marzulla,
of California, to be an Assistant Attorney General, vice Frank Henry Habicht II, resigned.

Carol Pendas Whitten,
of Maryland, to be a member of the National Advisory Council on Educational Research and Improvement for a term expiring September 30, 1990, vice Penny Pullen, term expired.

Don E. Newquist,
of Texas, to be a member of the United States International Trade Commission for the remainder of the term expiring December 16, 1988, vice Susan Wittenberg Liebeler.

Ronald A. Cass,
of Massachusetts, to be a member of the United States International Trade Commission for the term expiring June 16, 1996, vice Paula Stern, resigned, to which position he was appointed during the last recess of the Senate.

Submitted January 27

Charles Franklin Dunbar,
of Maine, a career member of the Senior Foreign Service, Class of Minister-Counselor, to be Ambassador Extraordinary and Plenipotentiary of the United States of America to the Yemen Arab Republic.

Milton Frank,
of California, to be Ambassador Extraordinary and Plenipotentiary of the United States of America to the Kingdom of Nepal.

April Catherine Glaspie,
of California, a career member of the Senior Foreign Service, Class of Counselor, to be Ambassador Extraordinary and Plenipotentiary of the United States of America to the Republic of Iraq.

Bill K. Perrin,
of Texas, to be Ambassador Extraordinary and Plenipotentiary of the United States of America to the Republic of Cyprus.

Ronald F. Lehman II,
of Virginia, to be an Assistant Secretary of Defense, vice Richard N. Perle, resigned.

Submitted January 28

William F. Burns,
of Pennsylvania, to be Director of the United States Arms Control and Disarmament Agency, vice Kenneth L. Adelman, resigned.

Submitted February 2

George M. Marovich,
of Illinois, to be United States District Judge for the Northern District of Illinois, vice Susan C. Getzendanner, resigned.

Bernard A. Friedman,
of Michigan, to be United States District Judge for the Eastern District of Michigan, vice Robert E. DeMascio, retired.

Emilio M. Garza,
of Texas, to be United States District Judge for the Western District of Texas, vice William S. Sessions, resigned.

Nanette Fabray MacDougall,
of California, to be a member of the National Council on the Handicapped for a term expiring September 17, 1990 (reappointment).

Thomas J. Simon,
of Virginia, to be a member of the Railroad Retirement Board for the term of 5 years from August 29, 1987, vice Robert A. Gielow, term expired.

Withdrawn February 2

Robert N. Miller,
of Colorado, to be United States District Judge for the District of Colorado, vice a new position created by P.L. 98–353, approved July 10, 1984, which was sent to the Senate on February 5, 1987.

Submitted February 5

Deborah J. Daniels,
of Indiana, to be United States Attorney for the Southern District of Indiana for the term of 4 years, vice John D. Tinder, resigned.

Grover W. Garrison,
of Louisiana, to be United States Marshal for the Middle District of Louisiana for the term of 4 years, vice James L. Meyers, retired.

Frances Mathews,
of Colorado, to be a member of the National Advisory Council on Educational Research and Improvement for a term expiring September 30, 1990, vice Elaine Y. Schadler, term expired.

Howard W. Cannon,
of Nevada, to be a member of the Board of Trustees of the Barry Goldwater Scholarship and Excellence in Education Foundation for a term of 4 years (new position).

Submitted February 16

Thomas S. Zilly,
of Washington, to be United States District Judge for the Western District of Washington, vice Walter T. McGovern, retired.

Paul Freedenberg,
of Maryland, to be Under Secretary of Commerce for Export Administration (new position).

Marc G. Stanley,
of Maryland, to be an Assistant Secretary of Commerce, vice Gerald J. McKiernan, resigned.

Mark E. Buchman,
of California, to be President, Government National Mortgage Association, vice Glenn R. Wilson, Jr., resigned.

Ernest C. Baynard III,
of Virginia, to be an Assistant Secretary of Energy (Environment, Safety and Health), vice Mary L. Walker, resigned.

Leslee Kathryn Alexander,
of Tennessee, to be a member of the Board of Directors of the Corporation for Public Broadcasting for a term expiring March 26, 1991, vice Harry O'Connor, term expired.

Richard C. Crawford,
of Oklahoma, to be a member of the Board of Trustees of the Harry S. Truman Scholarship Foundation for a term expiring December 10, 1993, vice Robert Michael Isaac, term expired.

John E. Higgins, Jr.,
of Maryland, to be a member of the National Labor Relations Board for the term of 5 years expiring December 16, 1992, vice Donald L. Dotson, term expired.

Tirso del Junco,
of California, to be a Governor of the United States Postal Service for the remainder of the term expiring December 8, 1991, vice John R. McKean, resigned.

Submitted February 18

Daniel G. Amstutz,
of New York, for the rank of Ambassador during his tenure of service as chief agricultural negotiator in the Uruguay round of multilateral trade negotiations.

William Evans,
of California, to be Under Secretary of Commerce for Oceans and Atmosphere (new position).

Submitted February 19

Donald E. Abrams,
of Colorado, to be United States District Judge for the District of Colorado, a new position created by P.L. 98–353, approved July 10, 1984.

Alan Marshall Elkins,
of Maine, to be a member of the Board of Regents of the Uniformed Services University of the Health Sciences for a term expiring May 1, 1993, vice David I. Olch, deceased.

Robert Earl Farris,
of Tennessee, to be Administrator of the Federal Highway Administration, vice Ray A. Barnhart, resigned.

David L. Chatfield,
of Alaska, to be a member of the National Credit Union Administration Board for the remainder of the term expiring August 2, 1989, vice P.A. Mack, Jr., resigned.

Submitted February 22

Shannon T. Mason, Jr.,
of Virginia, to be United States District Judge for the Eastern District of Virginia, vice D. Dortch Warriner, deceased.

Submitted February 25

Alex R. Munson,
of the Northern Mariana Islands, to be Judge for the District Court for the Northern Mariana Islands for a term of 10 years, vice Alfred Laureta, term expiring.

Kenneth J. Beirne,
of Virginia, to be an Assistant Secretary of Housing and Urban Development, vice June Q. Koch, resigned.

Hugh Hewitt,
of Michigan, to be Deputy Director of the Office of Personnel Management, vice James E. Colvard, resigned.

Submitted February 29

John C. Lifland,
of New Jersey, to be United States District Judge for the District of New Jersey, vice Clarkson S. Fisher, retired.

Jill E. Kent,
of the District of Columbia, to be an Assistant Secretary of the Treasury, vice John F.W. Rogers, resigned.

Robert H. Brumley II,
of Virginia, to be General Counsel of the Department of Commerce, vice Douglas A. Riggs, resigned.

Frank DeGeorge,
of Maryland, to be Inspector General, Department of Commerce, vice Sherman Maxwell Funk.

Robert L. Pettit,
of the District of Columbia, to be Associate Deputy Secretary of Transportation, vice Jennifer Lynn Dorn, resigned.

Karen Borlaug Phillips,
of Virginia, to be a member of the Interstate Commerce Commission for a term expiring December 31, 1991, vice Malcolm M.B. Sterrett, term expired.

Jesse D. Winzenried,
of Wyoming, to be a Director of the Securities Investor Protection Corporation for a term expiring December 31, 1990, vice Roger A. Yurchuck, term expired.

Submitted March 14

George Arthur Trail III,
of Pennsylvania, a career member of the Senior Foreign Service, Class of Minister-Counselor, to be Ambassador Extraordinary and Plenipotentiary of the United States of America to the Republic of Malawi.

M. Alan Woods,
of the District of Columbia, to be a member of the Board of Directors of the Inter-American Foundation for a term expiring September 20, 1992, vice M. Peter McPherson.

Gordon A. Smith,
of Maryland, to be an Assistant Secretary of Defense, vice Donald C. Latham, resigned.

William Lockhart Ball III,
of South Carolina, to be Secretary of the Navy, vice James H. Webb, Jr., resigned.

James R. McGregor,
of Pennsylvania, to be United States District Judge for the Western District of Pennsylvania, vice Hubert I. Teitelbaum, retired.

Stanley J. Glod,
of Virginia, to be Chairman of the Foreign Claims Settlement Commission of the United States for the remainder of the term expiring September 30, 1988, vice Bohdan J. Futey, resigned.

Edward R. Hamberger,
of Maryland, to be an Assistant Secretary of Transportation, vice Rebecca Gernhardt Range.

Barry M. Goldwater, Jr.,
of California, to be a member of the Board of Trustees of the Barry Goldwater Scholarship and Excellence in Education Foundation for a term of 6 years (new position).

Richard V. Backley,
of Virginia, to be a member of the Federal Mine Safety and Health Review Commission for a term

of 6 years expiring August 30, 1994 (reappointment).

The following-named persons to be members of the Board of Trustees of the Harry S. Truman Scholarship Foundation for terms expiring December 10, 1993:

Margaret Truman Daniel, of New York (reappointment).

Gary Eugene Wood, of Texas, vice Gloria Ann Hay, term expired.

Walter C. Wallace,
of New York, to be a member of the National Mediation Board for the term expiring July 1, 1990 (reappointment).

The following-named persons to be members of the Board of Trustees of the Institute of American Indian and Alaska Native Culture and Arts Development for terms prescribed by Public Law 99–498 of October 17, 1986 (new positions):

Gail Bird, of New Mexico.
Edith Colvard Crutcher, of Kansas.
Roy M. Huhndorf, of Alaska.
James Courtney Jennings, of Virginia.
William Stewart Johnson, of the District of Columbia.
Duane H. King, of Oklahoma.
Alfred H. Qöyawayma, of Arizona.
Beatrice Rivas Sanchez, of Michigan.
James D. Santini, of Nevada.
Irving James Toddy, of Arizona.

The following-named persons to be members of the National Museum Services Board for the terms indicated:

For a term expiring December 6, 1991:

Arthur C. Beale, of Massachusetts, vice Ann Duncan Haffner, term expired.

For a term expiring December 6, 1992:

Willard L. Boyd, of Illinois, vice Peter H. Raven, term expired.

David E. Baldelli,
of Texas, to be United States Marshal for the Northern District of Texas for a term of 4 years, vice Clinton T. Peoples, term expired.

Submitted March 16

Michael E. Zacharia,
of California, to be an Assistant Secretary of Commerce (new position).

Submitted March 18

Barbara McConnell Barrett,
of Arizona, to be Deputy Administrator of the Federal Aviation Administration, vice Richard H. Jones, resigned.

Susan S. Suter,
of Illinois, to be Commissioner of the Rehabilitation Services Administration, vice Justin W. Dart, Jr., resigned.

Submitted March 23

Frederick M. Bernthal,
of Tennessee, to be Assistant Secretary of State for Oceans and International Environmental and Scientific Affairs, vice John Dimitri Negroponte.

Robert S. Gelbard,
of Washington, a career member of the Senior Foreign Service, Class of Minister-Counselor, to be Ambassador Extraordinary and Plenipotentiary of the United States of America to the Republic of Bolivia.

E. Allan Wendt,
of California, a career member of the Senior Foreign Service, Class of Minister-Counselor, for the rank of Ambassador during his tenure of service as Senior Representative for Strategic Technology Policy in the Office of the Under Secretary of State for Coordinating Security Assistance Programs.

George F. Murphy, Jr.,
of Maryland, to be Deputy Director of the United States Arms Control and Disarmament Agency, vice David F. Emery, resigned.

William H. Erickson,
of Colorado, to be United States District Judge for the District of Colorado, vice John P. Moore, elevated.

G. Philip Hughes,
of Virginia, to be an Assistant Secretary of Commerce (new position).

The following-named persons to be members of the Federal Retirement Thrift Investment Board for the terms indicated:

For a term of 2 years:

Richard H. Headlee, of Michigan (reappointment).

For a term of 4 years:

Roger W. Mehle, of New York (reappointment).

Submitted March 24

Michael J. Norton,
of Colorado, to be United States Attorney for the District of Colorado for the term of 4 years, vice Robert N. Miller, resigned.

Joy Cherian,
of Maryland, to be a member of the Equal Employment Opportunity Commission for a term expiring July 1, 1993 (reappointment).

L. Clair Nelson,
of Virginia, to be a member of the Federal Mine Safety and Health Review Commission for a term of 6 years expiring August 30, 1994 (reappointment).

Submitted March 28

David Courtland O'Neal,
of Illinois, to be Assistant Secretary of Labor for Mine Safety and Health, vice David A. Zegeer, resigned.

Elaine L. Chao,
of California, to be a Federal Maritime Commissioner for the remainder of the term expiring June 30, 1991, vice Edward V. Hickey, Jr., deceased.

The following-named persons to be members of the Board of Directors of the Overseas Private Investment Corporation for the terms indicated:

For the remainder of the term expiring December 17, 1988:

Richard F. Hohlt, of Indiana, vice Thomas A. Bolan.

For a term expiring December 17, 1990:

Allie C. Felder, Jr., of the District of Columbia (reappointment).

Susan E. Alvarado,
of Virginia, to be a Governor of the United States Postal Service for the term expiring December 8, 1996, vice Ruth O. Peters, term expired.

Withdrawn March 28

Alfred C. Schmutzer, Jr.,
of Tennessee, to be United States District Judge for the Eastern District of Tennessee, vice Robert L. Taylor, retired, which was sent to the Senate on December 18, 1987.

Submitted March 29

Randall R. Rader,
of Virginia, to be a Judge of the United States Claims Court for the term of 15 years, vice Robert M.M. Seto, term expired.

Submitted March 30

Karl S. Forester,
of Kentucky, to be United States District Judge for the Eastern District of Kentucky to fill an additional position created November 30, 1987, pursuant to the provisions of section 372(b) of title 28 of the United States Code.

Simeon Timothy Lake III,
of Texas, to be United States District Judge for the Southern District of Texas, vice Ross N. Sterling, Jr., deceased.

Dennis M. Devaney,
of Maryland, to be General Counsel of the Federal Labor Relations Authority for a term of 5 years, vice John Carl Miller, term expired.

Submitted March 31

Michael P.W. Stone,
of California, to be Under Secretary of the Army, vice James R. Ambrose, resigned.

Margaret P. Currin,
of North Carolina, to be United States Attorney for the Eastern District of North Carolina for the term of 4 years, vice Samuel T. Currin, resigned.

F. Clifton White,
of Virginia, to be a member of the Advisory Board for Radio Broadcasting to Cuba for a term of 2 years (new position).

Submitted April 13

Paul D. Taylor,
of New York, a career member of the Senior Foreign Service, Class of Minister-Counselor, to be Ambassador Extraordinary and Plenipotentiary of the United States of America to the Dominican Republic.

Richard Newton Holwill,
of the District of Columbia, to be Ambassador Extraordinary and Plenipotentiary of the United States of America to the Republic of Ecuador.

Walter Leon Cutler,
of Maryland, a career member of the Senior Foreign Service, Class of Career Minister, to be Ambassador Extraordinary and Plenipotentiary of the United States of America to the Kingdom of Saudi Arabia.

George Edward Moose,
of Maryland, a career member of the Senior Foreign Service, Class of Counselor, to be Ambassador Extraordinary and Plenipotentiary of the United States of America to the Republic of Senegal.

Rush Walker Taylor, Jr.,
of Texas, a career member of the Senior Foreign Service, Class of Counselor, to be Ambassador Extraordinary and Plenipotentiary of the United States of America to the Republic of Togo.

Henry F. Cooper,
of Virginia, for the rank of Ambassador during his tenure of service as United States Negotiator for Defense and Space Arms.

Stephen R. Hanmer, Jr.,
of Virginia, for the rank of Ambassador during his tenure of service as United States Negotiator for Strategic Nuclear Arms.

Mark T. Cox IV,
of Florida, to be United States Alternate Executive Director of the International Bank for Reconstruction and Development for a term of 2 years, vice Hugh W. Foster, resigned.

William G. Cambridge,
of Nebraska, to be United States District Judge for the District of Nebraska, vice Clarence A. Beam, elevated.

Richard A. Schell,
of Texas, to be United States District Judge for the Eastern District of Texas, vice William M. Steger, retired.

Patrick Butler,
of Maryland, to be a member of the National Council on the Humanities for a term expiring January 26, 1994, vice Walter Berns, term expired.

Lemoine V. Dickinson, Jr.,
of Virginia, to be a member of the National Transportation Safety Board for the remainder of the term expiring December 31, 1988, vice Patricia A. Goldman, resigned.

Joseph Wentling Brown,
of Nevada, to be a member of the Board of Directors of the State Justice Institute for a term expiring September 17, 1989 (new position).

Withdrawn April 13

George D. Hardy,
of Maryland, to be a member of the Board of Trustees of the Barry Goldwater Scholarship and Excellence in Education Foundation for a term of 6 years (new position), which was sent to the Senate on July 15, 1987.

Submitted April 14

Donna F. Tuttle,
of California, to be Deputy Secretary of Commerce, vice Clarence J. Brown, resigned.

Judith Richards Hope,
of the District of Columbia, to be United States Circuit Judge for the District of Columbia Circuit, vice Robert H. Bork, resigned.

Submitted April 15

Jay B. Stephens,
of Virginia, to be United States Attorney for the District of Columbia for the term of 4 years, vice Joseph E. diGenova, resigned.

Submitted April 19

Robert South Barrett IV,
of Virginia, a career member of the Senior Foreign Service, Class of Minister-Counselor, to be Ambassador Extraordinary and Plenipotentiary of the United States of America to the Republic of Djibouti.

William Graham Walker,
of California, a career member of the Senior Foreign Service, Class of Minister-Counselor, to be Ambassador Extraordinary and Plenipotentiary of the United States of America to the Republic of El Salvador.

W. Allen Moore,
of Virginia, to be Under Secretary of Commerce for International Trade, vice S. Bruce Smart, Jr., resigned.

S. Jay Plager,
of Indiana, to be Administrator of the Office of Information and Regulatory Affairs (new position).

The following-named persons to be members of the National Council on the Humanities for terms expiring January 26, 1994:

Gary L. McDowell, of Louisiana, vice Rita Ricardo-Campbell, term expired.
William P. Wright, Jr., of Texas, vice Peter J. Stanlis, term expired.

James Eugene Burnett, Jr.,
of Arkansas, to be Chairman of the National Transportation Safety Board for a term of 2 years (reappointment).

Submitted April 20

Daniel Anthony O'Donohue,
of Virginia, a career member of the Senior Foreign Service, Class of Minister-Counselor, to be Ambassador Extraordinary and Plenipotentiary of the United States of America to the Kingdom of Thailand.

John K. Stewart,
of California, to be a member of the Board of Directors of the National Consumer Cooperative Bank for a term of 3 years (new position).

Salvatore R. Martoche,
of New York, to be a member of the National Mediation Board for the term expiring July 1, 1991, vice Helen M. Witt, term expiring.

Submitted April 21

Fowler C. West,
of Texas, to be a Commissioner of the Commodity Futures Trading Commission for the term expiring April 13, 1992 (reappointment).

William H. LeBlanc III,
of Louisiana, to be a Commissioner of the Postal Rate Commission for the term expiring November 22, 1994 (reappointment).

Submitted April 22

Arch Madsen,
of Utah, to be a member of the Board for International Broadcasting for the remainder of the term expiring May 20, 1989, vice Lilla Burt Cummings Tower.

Francis Anthony Keating II,
of Oklahoma, to be Associate Attorney General, vice Stephen S. Trott.

Submitted April 26

Mary A. Ryan,
of Texas, a career member of the Senior Foreign Service, Class of Minister-Counselor, to be Ambassador Extraordinary and Plenipotentiary of the United States of America to the Kingdom of Swaziland.

Pamela Ann Rymer,
of California, to be United States Circuit Judge for the Ninth Circuit, vice Anthony M. Kennedy, elevated.

Norwood Carlton Tilley, Jr.,
of North Carolina, to be United States District Judge for the Middle District of North Carolina, vice Hiram H. Ward, retired.

Charles Ray Ritcheson,
of California, to be a member of the National Council on the Humanities for the remainder of the term expiring January 26, 1990, vice William Allen, resigned.

Warren J. Baker,
of California, to be a member of the National Science Board, National Science Foundation, for a term expiring May 10, 1994 (reappointment).

Submitted April 27

Jan W. Mares,
of Connecticut, to be an Assistant Secretary of Commerce, vice Paul Freedenberg.

Wendy Monson DeMocker,
of Virginia, to be an Assistant Secretary of Transportation, vice Dale A. Petroskey, resigned.

Jane A. Kenny,
of Virginia, to be Deputy Director of ACTION, vice Henry M. Ventura, resigned.

Marian North Koonce,
of California, to be a member of the National Council on the Handicapped for a term expiring September 23, 1990 (reappointment).

Submitted April 28

Charles R. Butler, Jr.,
of Alabama, to be United States District Judge for the Southern District of Alabama, vice Emmett Ripley Cox, elevated.

Eric H. Holder, Jr.,
of the District of Columbia, to be an Associate Judge of the Superior Court of the District of Columbia for the term of 15 years, vice Virginia L. Riley, deceased.

Withdrawn April 28

Thomas W. Pauken,
of Texas, to be a member of the Board of Directors of the Inter-American Foundation for the term expiring October 6, 1992, vice Luis Guerrero Nogales, term expired, which was sent to the Senate on April 24, 1987.

Submitted May 9

Charles A. Gargano,
of New York, to be Ambassador Extraordinary and Plenipotentiary of the United States of America to the Republic of Trinidad and Tobago.

Jeffrey Davidow,
of Virginia, a career member of the Senior Foreign Service, Class of Counselor, to be Ambassa-

dor Extraordinary and Plenipotentiary of the United States of America to the Republic of Zambia.

Charles S. Whitehouse,
of Virginia, to be an Assistant Secretary of Defense, vice Chapman B. Cox, resigned.

Fern M. Smith,
of California, to be United States District Judge for the Northern District of California, vice Samuel Conti, retired.

Charles E. Cobb, Jr.,
of Florida, to be Under Secretary of Commerce for Travel and Tourism, vice Donna F. Tuttle.

James P. Moore, Jr.,
of Pennsylvania, to be an Assistant Secretary of Commerce, vice Charles E. Cobb, Jr.

William W. Erwin,
of Indiana, to be a member of the Board of Directors of the Farm Credit System Assistance Board, subject to the provisions prescribed by P.L. 100–233 (new position).

Edwin J. Delattre,
of Maryland, to be a member of the National Council on the Humanities for a term expiring January 26, 1994, vice George Carey, term expired.

The following-named persons to be members of the National Museum Services Board for terms expiring December 6, 1992:

Helmuth J. Naumer, of New Mexico, vice Donald Moncrief Muchmore, term expired.
Richard J. Schwartz, of New York, vice Louis Roman DiSabato, term expired.

Henry R. Folsom,
of Virginia, to be a Commissioner of the Postal Rate Commission for the term expiring October 14, 1994 (reappointment).

Submitted May 10

Jan E. DuBois,
of Pennsylvania, to be United States District Judge for the Eastern District of Pennsylvania, vice Clifford Scott Green, retired.

Richard W. Cameron,
of California, to be United States Marshal for the Southern District of California for the term of 4 years, vice James R. Laffoon, deceased.

Withdrawn May 10

David C. Treen,
of Louisiana, to be United States Circuit Judge for the Fifth Circuit, vice Albert Tate, Jr., deceased, which was sent to the Senate on July 22, 1987.

Submitted May 11

Christopher W.S. Ross,
of California, a career member of the Senior Foreign Service, Class of Minister-Counselor, to be Ambassador Extraordinary and Plenipotentiary of the United States of America to the Democratic and Popular Republic of Algeria.

Richard Llewellyn Williams,
of the District of Columbia, a career member of the Senior Foreign Service, Class of Minister-Counselor, to be Ambassador Extraordinary and Plenipotentiary of the United States of America to the Mongolian People's Republic.

Philip D. Winn,
of Colorado, to be Ambassador Extraordinary and Plenipotentiary of the United States of America to Switzerland.

Edward Noonan Ney,
of New York, to be a member of the Board for International Broadcasting for a term expiring April 28, 1991 (reappointment).

Charles C. Cox,
of Texas, to be a member of the Securities and Exchange Commission for the term expiring June 5, 1993 (reappointment).

Submitted May 16

John Thomas McCarthy,
of New York, a career member of the Senior Foreign Service, Class of Minister-Counselor, to be Ambassador Extraordinary and Plenipotentiary of the United States of America to the Republic of Lebanon.

Edward Peter Djerejian,
of Maryland, a career member of the Senior Foreign Service, Class of Minister-Counselor, to be Ambassador Extraordinary and Plenipotentiary of the United States of America to the Syrian Arab Republic.

W. Allan Wallis,
of New York, to be United States Alternate Governor of the International Bank for Reconstruction and Development for a term of 5 years and United States Alternate Governor of the Inter-

American Bank for a term of 5 years (reappointments).

David S.C. Chu,
of the District of Columbia, to be an Assistant Secretary of Defense (new position—P.L. 100–180).

Kenneth P. Bergquist,
of Virginia, to be an Assistant Secretary of the Navy, vice Charles G. Untermeyer, resigned.

Submitted May 17

Herbert J. Hutton,
of Pennsylvania, to be United States District Judge for the Eastern District of Pennsylvania, vice Clarence C. Newcomer, retired.

Submitted May 20

Margaret Chase Hager,
of Virginia, to be a member of the National Council on the Handicapped for a term expiring September 17, 1990, vice John S. Erthein, term expired.

Submitted May 24

William Andreas Brown,
of New Hampshire, a career member of the Senior Foreign Service, Class of Career Minister, to be Ambassador Extraordinary and Plenipotentiary of the United States of America to Israel.

Withdrawn May 24

John R. Wall,
of Ohio, to be a member of the Occupational Safety and Health Review Commission for the term expiring April 27, 1993 (reappointment), which was sent to the Senate on May 5, 1987.

Submitted May 25

Sheldon J. Krys,
of Maryland, to be an Assistant Secretary of State, vice Donald J. Bouchard, resigned.

Warren Zimmermann,
of Virginia, a career member of the Senior Foreign Service, Class of Career Minister, to be Ambassador Extraordinary and Plenipotentiary of the United States of America to the Socialist Federal Republic of Yugoslavia.

Harold G. Christensen,
of Utah, to be Deputy Attorney General, vice Arnold I. Burns, resigned.

Edward S.G. Dennis, Jr.,
of Pennsylvania, to be an Assistant Attorney General, vice William F. Weld, resigned.

Richard L. Nygaard,
of Pennsylvania, to be United States Circuit Judge for the Third Circuit, vice Joseph F. Weis, Jr., retired.

Timothy L. Coyle,
of California, to be an Assistant Secretary of Housing and Urban Development, vice Stephen May, resigned.

Robert O. Hunter, Jr.,
of California, to be Director of the Office of Energy Research, vice Alvin W. Trivelpiece, resigned.

John Alderson,
of Virginia, to be Administrator of General Services, vice Terence C. Golden, resigned.

Submitted June 7

John Florian Kordek,
of Illinois, a career member of the Senior Foreign Service, Class of Career Minister, to be Ambassador Extraordinary and Plenipotentiary of the United States of America to the Republic of Botswana.

Thomas Edmund McNamara,
of Connecticut, a career member of the Senior Foreign Service, Class of Minister-Counselor, to be Ambassador Extraordinary and Plenipotentiary of the United States of America to the Republic of Colombia.

Harry E. Bergold,
of Florida, a career member of the Senior Foreign Service, Class of Career Minister, to be Ambassador Extraordinary and Plenipotentiary of the United States of America to the Kingdom of Morocco.

Timothy Lathrop Towell,
of Ohio, a career member of the Senior Foreign Service, Class One, to be Ambassador Extraordinary and Plenipotentiary of the United States of America to the Republic of Paraguay.

John J. Maresca,
of Connecticut, a career member of the Senior Foreign Service, Class of Minister-Counselor, for the rank of Ambassador in his capacity as Chief of the United States Delegation to the Conference on Confidence and Security Building Measures.

Submitted June 8

William H. Fite,
of Pennsylvania, to be an Assistant Director of the United States Arms Control and Disarmament Agency, vice Michael A. Mobbs, resigned.

Charles S. Warner,
of Virginia, to be United States Alternate Executive Director of the International Monetary Fund for a term of 2 years, vice Mary Kate Bush, resigned.

Joseph Francis Glennon,
of Florida, to be a member of the Advisory Board for Radio Broadcasting to Cuba for a term expiring October 27, 1991 (reappointment).

James B. Coles,
of California, to be a member of the Board of Directors of the National Corporation for Housing Partnerships for the term expiring October 27, 1990, vice Barbara W. Schlicher, term expired.

The following-named persons to be members of the National Council on the Handicapped for the terms indicated:

For the remainder of the term expiring September 17, 1989:

George H. Oberle, Jr., of Oklahoma, vice Carolyn L. Vash, resigned.

For a term expiring September 17, 1990:

Justin W. Dart, Jr., of Texas, vice Roxanne S. Vierra, term expired.

For terms expiring September 17, 1991:

Joni Tada, of California (reappointment).

Phyllis D. Zlotnick, of Connecticut (reappointment).

Charles L. Hosler, Jr.,
of Pennsylvania, to be a member of the National Science Board, National Science Foundation, for a term expiring May 10, 1994 (reappointment).

Submitted June 10

Keith Lapham Brown,
of Colorado, to be Ambassador Extraordinary and Plenipotentiary of the United States of America to Denmark.

Michael H. Newlin,
of Maryland, to be the Representative of the United States of America to the Vienna Office of the United Nations and Deputy Representative of the United States of America to the International Atomic Energy Agency, with the rank of Ambassador.

Roland W. Schmitt,
of New York, to be a member of the National Science Board, National Science Foundation, for a term expiring May 10, 1994 (reappointment).

William G. Goetz,
of North Dakota, to be a member of the National Advisory Council on Educational Research and Improvement for a term expiring September 30, 1990, vice Onalee McGraw, term expired.

James B. Werson,
of California, to be a member of the Board of Directors of the National Corporation for Housing Partnerships for the term expiring October 27, 1991, vice Alfred J. Fleischer, Sr., term expiring.

The following-named persons to be members of the National Commission on Libraries and Information Science for terms expiring July 19, 1993:

Wanda L. Forbes, of South Carolina (reappointment).

Margaret Phelan, of Kansas (reappointment).

Charles E. Reid, of New Jersey, vice Bessie Boehm Moore, term expiring.

Submitted June 14

Richard Clark Barkley,
of Michigan, a career member of the Senior Foreign Service, Class of Minister-Counselor, to be Ambassador Extraordinary and Plenipotentiary of the United States of America to the German Democratic Republic.

C. Paul Robinson,
of New Jersey, for the rank of Ambassador while serving as the U.S. negotiator for the nuclear testing talks.

Robert P. Patterson, Jr.,
of New York, to be United States District Judge for the Southern District of New York, vice Whitman Knapp, retired.

Ken Kramer,
of Colorado, to be an Assistant Secretary of the Army, Vice Michael P.W. Stone.

Dennis C. Vacco,
of New York, to be United States Attorney for the Western District of New York for the term of 4 years, vice Salvatore R. Martoche, resigned.

Submitted June 17

Carl Copeland Cundiff,
of Nevada, a career member of the Senior Foreign Service, Class of Minister-Counselor, to be

Ambassador Extraordinary and Plenipotentiary of the United States of America to the Republic of Niger.

John P. LaWare,
of Massachusetts, to be a member of the Board of Governors of the Federal Reserve System for a term of 14 years from February 1, 1988, vice Henry C. Wallich, resigned.

Submitted June 20

Adriane J. Dudley,
of the Virgin Islands, to be a Judge of the District Court of the Virgin Islands for a term of 10 years, vice Almeric L. Christian, retired.

Submitted June 23

Maynard Wayne Glitman,
of Vermont, a career member of the Senior Foreign Service, Class of Career Minister, to be Ambassador Extraordinary and Plenipotentiary of the United States of America to the Kingdom of Belgium.

John Andrew Burroughs, Jr.,
of Maryland, a career member of the Senior Foreign Service, Class of Counselor, to be Ambassador Extraordinary and Plenipotentiary of the United States of America to the Republic of Uganda.

Lewis T. Babcock,
of Colorado, to be United States District Judge for the District of Colorado, vice John L. Kane, Jr., retired.

Melinda Harmon,
of Texas, to be United States District Judge for the Southern District of Texas, vice John V. Singleton, Jr., retired.

Jack R. Stokvis,
of New York, to be an Assistant Secretary of Housing and Urban Development, vice Alfred Clinton Moran, resigned.

Frederick K. Goodwin,
of Maryland, to be Administrator of the Alcohol, Drug Abuse, and Mental Health Administration, vice Donald Ian Macdonald, resigned.

Antonio Navarro,
of New York, to be a member of the Advisory Board for Radio Broadcasting to Cuba for a term expiring October 27, 1991 (reappointment).

Hillel Fradkin,
of Wisconsin, to be a member of the National Council on the Humanities for a term expiring January 26, 1994, vice A. Lawrence Chickering, term expired.

MacDonald G. Becket,
of California, to be a member of the Board of Directors of the National Institute of Building Sciences for a term expiring September 7, 1990 (reappointment).

Submitted June 24

The following-named persons to be members of the Board of Directors of the Federal Agricultural Mortgage Corporation:

John R. Dahl, of North Dakota (new position).
George James Benston, of New York (new position).
Derryl McLaren, of Iowa (new position).
Gordon Clyde Southern, of Missouri (new position).
Edward Charles Williamson, Jr., of Georgia (new position).

Submitted June 27

Robert L. Pugh,
of Virginia, a career member of the Senior Foreign Service, Class of Minister-Counselor, to be Ambassador Extraordinary and Plenipotentiary of the United States of America to the Republic of Chad.

John M. Duhe, Jr.,
of Louisiana, to be United States Circuit Judge for the Fifth Circuit, vice Albert Tate, Jr., deceased.

Jacques L. Wiener, Jr.,
of Louisiana, to be United States Circuit Judge for the Fifth Circuit, vice Robert M. Hill, deceased.

Appendix C—Checklist of White House Press Releases

The following list contains releases of the Office of the Press Secretary which are not included in this book.

Released January 2

Fact sheet:
Canada-U.S. free trade agreement

Released January 8

Transcript:
Press briefing on the report of the Presidential Task Force on Market Mechanisms—by Nicholas Brady, Chairman of the task force

Released January 11

Advance text:
Remarks to the City Club of Cleveland in Cleveland, OH

Released January 13

Statement:
President's health and public schedule changes—by Marlin Fitzwater, Assistant to the President for Press Relations

Announcement:
Presentation of the Presidential Medal of Freedom to Roger L. Stevens, departing Chairman of the Board of Trustees of the John F. Kennedy Center for the Performing Arts

Released January 15

Statement:
President's biannual physical examination at Bethesda Naval Hospital—by Col. John E. Hutton, Jr., Physician to the President

Released January 19

Fact sheet:
National security strategy report

Fact sheet:
Prince George's County Public Schools/Suitland High School

Fact sheet:
Magnet schools

Announcement:
Presentation of the Presidential Citizens Medal to Brooke Astor

Released January 22

Fact sheet:
Participants in the President's meeting with Right to Life volunteers

Released January 25

Fact sheet:
Reserve Officers Association

Advance text:
State of the Union Address

Excerpts:
State of the Union Address

Fact sheet:
State of the Union Address

Fact sheet:
1988 legislative and administrative message to the Congress

Fact sheet:
Crusade for a drug free nation

Fact sheet:
Federal budget reform

Fact sheet:
Freedom and peace

Fact sheet:
Education reform

Announcement:
Proposal to establish a Thomas A. Edison Prize

Released January 29

Fact sheet:
Generalized System of Preferences

Released February 2

Statement:
On the refusal of the television networks to broadcast the President's address requesting additional aid for the Nicaraguan democratic resist-

ance—by Marlin Fitzwater, Assistant to the President for Press Relations

Statement:
On the refusal of the television networks to broadcast the President's address requesting additional aid for the Nicaraguan democratic resistance—by Howard H. Baker, Jr., Chief of Staff to the President

Announcement:
Nomination of Bernard A. Friedman to be United States District Judge for the Eastern District of Michigan

Announcement:
Nomination of Emilio M. Garza to be United States District Judge for the Western District of Texas

Announcement:
Nomination of George M. Marovich to be United States District Judge for the Northern District of Illinois

Released February 4

Announcement:
Nomination of Grover W. Garrison to be United States Marshal for the Middle District of Louisiana

Announcement:
Nomination of Deborah J. Daniels to be United States Attorney for the Southern District of Indiana

Released February 8

Advance text:
Remarks at a seminar on substance abuse in the workplace: Strategies for the 1990's, in Durham, NC

Fact sheet:
Toward a drug free workplace

Released February 11

Transcript:
Press briefing on national space policy—by James C. Fletcher, Administrator of the National Aeronautics and Space Administration, Secretary of Commerce C. William Verity, and Secretary of Transportation James H. Burnley IV

Fact sheet:
Presidential directive on national space policy

Fact sheet:
President's space policy and commercial space initiative to begin the next century

Announcement:
Nomination of Thomas S. Zilly to be United States District Judge for the Western District of Washington

Advance text:
Remarks at the annual Conservative Political Action Conference dinner

Released February 13

Transcript:
Press briefing on President Reagan's meeting with President De la Madrid of Mexico in Mazatlán—by Secretary of State George P. Shultz, Secretary of the Treasury James A. Baker III, Attorney General Edwin Meese III, and U.S. Trade Representative Clayton Yeutter

Released February 18

Fact sheet:
President's 1989 fiscal year budget

Transcript:
Press briefing on the President's 1989 fiscal year budget—by Secretary of the Treasury James A. Baker III; Beryl W. Sprinkel, Chairman of the Council of Economic Advisers; and James C. Miller III, Director of the Office of Management and Budget

Released February 19

Fact sheet:
U.S.-German Youth Exchange Council

Announcement:
Nomination of Donald E. Abram to be United States District Judge for the District of Colorado

Released February 22

Announcement:
Nomination of Shannon T. Mason, Jr., to be United States District Judge for the Eastern District of Virginia

Released February 23

Advance text:
President's address to the citizens of Western Europe

Fact sheet:
Superconductivity Competitiveness Act of 1988

Released February 24

Fact sheet:
Truth in Federal Spending Act of 1988

Released February 25

Announcement:
Nomination of Alex R. Munson to be Judge for the District Court for the Northern Mariana Islands

Released February 29

Announcement:
Nomination of John C. Lifland to be United States District Judge for the District of New Jersey

Transcript:
Press briefing on the U.S. management report for fiscal year 1989—by James C. Miller III, Director of the Office of Management and Budget; Joseph R. Wright, Deputy Director of the Office of Management and Budget; and Gerald Riso, Chief Financial Officer of the Office of Management and Budget

Released March 1

Advance text:
Remarks on departure for the North Atlantic Treaty Organization summit in Brussels, Belgium

Released March 3

Transcript:
Interview of Howard H. Baker, Jr., Chief of Staff to the President, by Bill Plante, CBS News

Transcript:
Interview of Colin L. Powell, Assistant to the President for National Security Affairs, by Chris Wallace, NBC News

Transcript:
Interview of Colin L. Powell, Assistant to the President for National Security Affairs, by Sam Donaldson, ABC News

Transcript:
Interview of Howard H. Baker, Jr., Chief of Staff to the President, by Andrea Mitchell, NBC News

Transcript:
Interview of Colin L. Powell, Assistant to the President for National Security Affairs, by Frank Sesno, Cable News Network

Transcript:
Interview of Secretary of State George P. Shultz by Wyatt Andrews, CBS News

Transcript:
Press briefing on the North Atlantic Treaty Organization summit—by Secretary of State George P. Shultz

Transcript:
Interview of Secretary of State George P. Shultz by John McWethy, ABC News

Transcript:
Interview of Secretary of State George P. Shultz by Ralph Begleiter, Cable News Network

Released March 4

Statement:
Unemployment rate for February—by Marlin Fitzwater, Assistant to the President for Press Relations

Announcement:
Designation of Caspar W. Weinberger as the U.S. representative to Australia's bicentennial celebration

Released March 8

Announcement:
Nomination of James R. McGregor to be United States District Judge for the Western District of Pennsylvania

Released March 9

Advance text:
Remarks at the dedication ceremony for the Knute Rockne Commemorative Stamp at the University of Notre Dame in West Lafayette, IN

Released March 10

Transcript:
Press briefing on the President's request for revisions in the fiscal year 1988 appropriations—by James C. Miller III, Director of the Office of Management and Budget

Fact sheet:
President's request for revisions to the fiscal year 1988 appropriations

Released March 11

Statement:
U.S. economic sanctions against Panama—by Leslye A. Arsht, Special Assistant to the President and Deputy Press Secretary

Transcript:
Press briefing on U.S. economic sanctions against Panama—by Secretary of State George P. Shultz

Released March 14

Announcement:
Nomination of David Eric Baldelli to be United States Marshal for the Northern District of Texas

Released March 16

Fact sheet:
Civil Rights Protection Act of 1988

Released March 18

Transcript:
Press briefing on the final report of the President's Commission on Privatization—by David F. Linowes, Commission Chairman

Released March 23

Announcement:
Nomination of William H. Erickson to be United States District Judge for the District of Colorado

Released March 24

Announcement:
Nomination of Michael J. Norton to be United States Attorney for the District of Colorado

Advance text:
Remarks to students and faculty of Oakton High School in Vienna, VA

Released March 28

Advance text:
Remarks to employees of Reynolds Metals Co., in Richmond, VA

Released March 29

Announcement:
Nomination of Randall R. Rader to be a Judge of the United States Claims Court

Released March 30

Announcement:
Nomination of Simeon Timothy Lake III to be United States District Judge for the Southern District of Texas

Announcement:
Nomination of Karl S. Forester to be United States District Judge for the Eastern District of Kentucky

Announcement:
Nomination of Margaret P. Currin to be United States Attorney for the Eastern District of North Carolina

Released April 5

Transcript:
Press briefing on international issues—by Colin L. Powell, Assistant to the President for National Security Affairs

Released April 6

Statement:
President and Mrs. Reagan's lease of a home in Bel Air, CA—by Marlin Fitzwater, Assistant to the President for Press Relations

Released April 7

Transcript:
Press briefing on domestic and foreign issues—by Howard H. Baker, Jr., Chief of Staff to the President, and Colin L. Powell, Assistant to the President for National Security Affairs

Released April 8

Statement:
President and Mrs. Reagan's 1987 Federal income tax return

Released April 11

Transcript:
Press briefing on the Afghanistan accords—by Secretary of State George P. Shultz

Released April 12

Announcement:
Nomination of William G. Cambridge to be United States District Judge for the District of Nebraska

Announcement:
Nomination of Richard A. Schell to be United States District Judge for the Eastern District of Texas

Released April 14

Announcement:
Nomination of Judith Richards Hope to be United States Circuit Judge for the District of Columbia Circuit

Released April 15

Announcement:
Nomination of Jay B. Stephens to be United States Attorney for the District of Columbia

Released April 19

Advance text:
Remarks at a campaign fundraising reception for Pete Dawkins

Advance text:
Remarks at the Electronic Industries Association's annual government-industry dinner

Released April 21

Advance text:
Remarks to the World Affairs Council of Western Massachusetts in Springfield, MA

Released April 22

Announcement:
President's attendance at a reception following the restoration of Blair House

Announcement:
President's address to the National Strategy Forum and his attendance at an Illinois State Republican Party fundraiser in Chicago, IL

Released April 26

Announcement:
Nomination of Pamela Ann Rymer to be United States Circuit Judge for the Ninth Circuit

Announcement:
Nomination of Charles R. Butler, Jr., to be United States District Judge for the Southern District of Alabama

Announcement:
Nomination of Norwood Carlton Tilley, Jr., to be United States District Judge for the Middle District of North Carolina

Fact sheet:
American Education: Making it Work

Transcript:
Press briefing on the economy—by Beryl W. Sprinkel, Chairman of the Council of Economic Advisers

Transcript:
Press briefing on the report "American Education: Making it Work"—by Secretary of Education William J. Bennett

Released April 28

Announcement:
Nomination of Eric H. Holder, Jr., to be an Associate Judge of the Superior Court of the District of Columbia

Released May 3

Announcement:
Nomination of Fern M. Smith to be United States District Judge for the Northern District of California

Released May 4

Advance text:
Remarks to members of the National Strategy Forum in Chicago, IL

Released May 6

Fact sheet:
Public Service Recognition Week

Released May 10

Announcement:
Nomination of Jan E. DuBois to be United States District Judge for the Eastern District of Pennsylvania

Transcript:
Presidential Medal of Freedom citation for Lord Peter Carrington of NATO

Released May 11

Transcript:
Remarks to reporters on a campaign announcement to be made at the President's Dinner, a Republican congressional fundraiser

Released May 12

Fact sheet:
America's Waiting Children: summary of the report of the Interagency Task Force on Adoption

Transcript:
Press briefing on the report of the Interagency Task Force on Adoption—by Mary Gall, task force Chairwoman

Released May 17

Announcement:
Nomination of Herbert J. Hutton to be United States District Judge for the Eastern District of Pennsylvania

Transcript:
Press briefing on the Moscow summit—by Rozanne L. Ridgway, Assistant Secretary of State for European and Canadian Affairs

Released May 18

Fact sheet:
Remarks at the U.S. Coast Guard Academy commencement ceremony in New London, CT

Advance text:
Remarks at the U.S. Coast Guard Academy commencement ceremony in New London, CT

Released May 19

Announcement:
President's attendance at the American Film Institute's 1988 Preservation Ball on May 21

Released May 20

Transcript:
Press briefing on security and arms control issues at the Moscow summit meeting—by Ambassadors Max M. Kampelman, Paul H. Nitze, and Edward L. Rowny

Released May 23

Fact sheet:
Recipients of the "E" and "E Star" Awards

Transcript:
Press briefing on the Soviet-U.S. summit meeting in Moscow—by Michael H. Armacost, Under Secretary of State for Political Affairs

Released May 24

Transcript:
Press briefing on the President's visit to Helsinki, Finland—by Rozanne L. Ridgway, Assistant Secretary of State for European and Canadian Affairs

Announcement:
Nomination of Richard L. Nygaard to be United States Circuit Judge for the Third Circuit

Released May 25

Advance text:
Remarks upon departure for the Soviet-U.S. summit meeting in Moscow

Released May 27

Advance text:
Remarks to the Paasikivi Society and the League of Finnish-American Societies in Helsinki, Finland

Released May 28

Transcript:
Press briefing on the Soviet-U.S. summit meeting in Moscow—by Marlin Fitzwater, Assistant to the President for Press Relations; Thomas C. Griscom, Assistant to the President for Communications and Planning; Colin L. Powell, Assistant to the President for National Security Affairs; and Rozanne L. Ridgway, Assistant Secretary of State for European and Canadian Affairs

Released May 30

Announcement:
Soviet citizens attending the President's reception at Spaso House on May 30

Released May 31

Fact sheet:
Soviet-U.S. high school exchange proposal

Fact sheet:
Soviet-U.S. general exchanges agreement: 1989–1991 program on cooperation and exchanges

Fact sheet:
Agreement between the U.S. and the Soviet Union on cooperation in transportation science and technology

Fact sheet:
Agreement between the U.S. and the Soviet Union on cooperation in outer space

Fact sheet:
Agreement between the U.S. and the Soviet Union on cooperation in peaceful uses of atomic energy

Fact sheet:
Soviet-U.S. comprehensive fishing agreement

Fact sheet:
Agreement between the U.S. and the Soviet Union on cooperation in radio navigation

Fact sheet:
Soviet-U.S. joint arms control verification experiment agreements

Fact sheet:
Agreement between the U.S. and the Soviet Union on cooperation in maritime search and rescue

Released June 1

Transcript:
Press briefing on Soviet-U.S. relations—by Senate Majority Leader Robert C. Byrd and Senate Minority Leader Robert Dole

Transcript:
Interview of Colin L. Powell, Assistant to the President for National Security Affairs, by Bernard Shaw, of Cable Network News

Transcript:
Interview of Secretary of State George P. Shultz by Tom Brokaw, of NBC News

Transcript:
Interview of Secretary of State George P. Shultz by Robin MacNeil, of the MacNeil/Lehrer Newshour

Transcript:
Interview of Howard H. Baker, Jr., Chief of Staff to the President, by Peter Jennings, of ABC News

Transcript:
Interview of Secretary of Defense Frank C. Carlucci by Bill Plante, of CBS News

Released June 2

Advance text:
Remarks to members of the Royal Institute of International Affairs in London

Released June 10

Transcript:
Press briefing on self-help and welfare reform efforts—by community leaders

Released June 13

Advance text:
Remarks to the Atlantic Council

Transcript:
Press briefing on international agricultural trade reform—by Ambassador Daniel Amstutz

Released June 14

Fact sheet:
Biographical information on Kenneth M. Duberstein

Announcement:
Nomination of Dennis C. Vacco to be United States Attorney for the Western District of New York

Announcement:
Nomination of Robert P. Patterson, Jr., to be United States District Judge for the Southern District of New York

Transcript:
Press briefing on the Toronto economic summit—by W. Allen Wallis, Under Secretary of State for Economic Affairs, and David C. Mulford, Assistant Secretary of the Treasury for International Affairs

Transcript:
Press briefing on the President's meeting with Italian Prime Minister De Mita—by Rozanne L. Ridgway, Assistant Secretary of State for European and Canadian Affairs

Released June 15

Announcement:
Nomination of Robert C. Bonner to be United States District Judge for the Central District of California

Transcript:
Press briefing on general topics—by Secretary of State George P. Shultz and Secretary of the Treasury James A. Baker III

Released June 16

Fact sheet:
Biographical information on Mari Maseng

Fact sheet:
Presidential Scholars program

Transcript:
Press briefing on the Toronto economic summit—by U.S. Trade Representative Clayton Yeutter

Released June 17

Announcement:
Nomination of Adriane J. Dudley to be a Judge of the District Court of the Virgin Islands

Released June 19

Transcript:
Interview of Secretary of the Treasury James A. Baker III by David Brinkley, of ABC News

Released June 20

Fact sheet:
Japan-U.S. agreement on cooperation in science and technology

Transcript:
Press briefing on the Toronto economic summit—by Rozanne L. Ridgway, Assistant Secretary of State for European and Canadian Affairs

Transcript:
Press briefing on the Toronto economic summit—by Secretary of the Treasury James A. Baker III

Released June 21

Advance text:
Remarks to the members of the Empire and Canadian Clubs in Toronto, Canada

Released June 22

Advance text:
Remarks at the annual Business Roundtable dinner

Released June 23

Transcript:
Press briefing on the Nation's economy—by Beryl W. Sprinkel, Chairman of the Council of Economic Advisers

Announcement:
Nomination of Lewis T. Babcock to be United States District Judge for the District of Colorado

Announcement:
Nomination of Melinda Harmon to be United States District Judge for the Southern District of Texas

Transcript:
Press briefing on the President's discussions with Prime Minister Robert Hawke of Australia—by Gaston J. Sigur, Assistant Secretary of State for East Asian and Pacific Affairs

Released June 27

Announcement:
Nomination of John M. Duhe, Jr., to be United States Circuit Judge for the Fifth Circuit

Announcement:
Nomination of Jacques L. Wiener, Jr., to be United States Circuit Judge for the Fifth Circuit

Announcement:
President's attendance at a fundraising reception for Senator David Karnes of Nebraska on July 11

Released June 29

Advance text:
Remarks at a fundraising luncheon for Congressman Connie Mack of Florida in Miami, FL

Released June 30

Fact sheet:
Recommendations of the National Drug Policy Board for 1988 anti-drug abuse legislation

Released July 1

Fact sheet:
Medicare Catastrophic Coverage Act of 1988

Transcript:
Press briefing on the drought situation and Federal emergency relief plans—by Secretary of Agriculture Richard Lyng

Appendix D—Acts Approved by the President

Approved January 2

H.J. Res. 436 / Public Law 100–229
Providing for the convening of the second session of the One Hundredth Congress

Approved January 5

H.R. 1454 / Public Law 100–230
To permit certain private contributions for construction of the Korean War Veterans Memorial to be invested temporarily in Government securities until such contributed amounts are required for disbursement for the memorial

H.R. 2401 / Public Law 100–231
Renewable Resources Extension Act Amendments of 1987

H.R. 3435 / Public Law 100–232
Charitable Assistance and Food Bank Act of 1987

Approved January 6

H.R. 3030 / Public Law 100–233
Agricultural Credit Act of 1987

H.R. 3479 / Public Law 100–234
Notice to Lessees Numbered 5 Gas Royalty Act of 1987

Approved January 8

H.R. 145 / Public Law 100–235
Computer Security Act of 1987

H.R. 1162 / Public Law 100–236
To amend title 28, United States Code, to provide for the selection of the court of appeals to decide multiple appeals filed with respect to the same agency order

H.R. 1340 / Public Law 100–237
Commodity Distribution Reform Act and WIC Amendments of 1987

H.R. 3395 / Public Law 100–238
Making technical corrections relating to the Federal Employees' Retirement System, and for other purposes

Approved January 11

H.R. 2598 / Public Law 100–239
Commercial Fishing Industry Vessel Anti-Reflagging Act of 1987

S. 1389 / Public Law 100–240
To amend the National Fish and Wildlife Foundation Establishment Act with respect to management requisition, and disposition of real property, reauthorization, and participation of foreign governments

Approved February 3

H.R. 278 / Public Law 100–241
Alaska Native Claims Settlement Act Amendments of 1987

Approved February 5

S. 825 / Public Law 100–242
Housing and Community Development Act of 1987

Approved February 9

S.J. Res. 196 / Public Law 100–243
To designate February 4, 1988, as "National Women in Sports Day"

S.J. Res. 201 / Public Law 100–244
To designate January 28, 1988, as "National Challenger Center Day" to honor the crew of the space shuttle Challenger

Approved February 10

H.J. Res. 402 / Public Law 100–245
To designate the week of February 7–13, 1988, as "National Child Passenger Safety Awareness Week"

Approved February 11

S.J. Res. 172 / Public Law 100–246
To designate the period commencing February 21, 1988, and ending February 27, 1988, as "National Visiting Nurse Associations Week"

S.J. Res. 39 / Public Law 100–247
To provide for the designation of the 70th anniversary of the renewal of Lithuanian independence, February 16, 1988, as "Lithuanian Independence Day"

S.J. Res. 143 / Public Law 100–248
To designate April 1988, as "Fair Housing Month"

Approved February 16

H.R. 1983 / Public Law 100–249
Authorizing the Secretary of the Interior to preserve certain wetlands and historic and prehistoric sites in the St. Johns River Valley, Florida, and for other purposes

H.R. 2566 / Public Law 100–250
To amend the National Parks and Recreation Act of 1978, as amended, to extend the term of the Delta Region Preservation Commission, and for other purposes

H.R. 3884 / Public Law 100–251
To rescind certain budget authority recommended in Public Law 100–202

Approved February 29

H.R. 1612 / Public Law 100–252
To authorize appropriations under the Earthquake Hazards Reduction Act of 1977 for fiscal years 1988, 1989, and 1990

S. 2022 / Public Law 100–253
Veterans' Home Loan Program Emergency Amendments of 1988

S.J. Res. 122 / Public Law 100–254
To designate the week beginning October 16, 1988, as "Gaucher's Disease Awareness Week"

H.R. 3923 / Public Law 100–255
To make a technical correction to section 8103 of title 46, United States Code

Approved March 8

S.J. Res. 251 / Public Law 100–256
Designating March 4, 1988, as "Department of Commerce Day"

S.J. Res. 262 / Public Law 100–257
To designate the month of March 1988, as "Women's History Month"

Approved March 14

S. 1447 / Public Law 100–258
To designate Morgan and Lawrence Counties in Alabama as a single metropolitan statistical area

Passed March 22, over the President's veto

S. 557 / Public Law 100–259
Civil Rights Restoration Act of 1987

Approved March 23

S.J. Res. 126 / Public Law 100–260
To designate March 16, 1988, as "Freedom of Information Day"

S.J. Res. 252 / Public Law 100–261
Designating June 5–11, 1988, as "National NHS-Neighbor Works Week"

S.J. Res. 265 / Public Law 100–262
To designate March 20, 1988 as "National Agriculture Day"

Approved March 24

S.J. Res. 125 / Public Law 100–263
To designate the period commencing on May 9, 1988, and ending on May 15, 1988, as "National Stuttering Awareness Week"

Approved March 25

H.R. 3689 / Public Law 100–264
To designate the United States Post Office Building located at 300 Sycamore Street in Waterloo, Iowa, as the "H.R. Gross Post Office Building"

S.J. Res. 216 / Public Law 100–265
Approving the location of the Black Revolutionary War Patriots Memorial

S.J. Res. 218 / Public Law 100–266
To designate March 25, 1988, as "Greek Independence Day: A National Day of Celebration of Greek and American Democracy"

Approved March 28

S.J. Res. 225 / Public Law 100–267
Approving the location of the Korean War Memorial

S.J. Res. 229 / Public Law 100–268
To designate the day of April 1, 1988, as "Run to Daylight Day"

S.J. Res. 253 / Public Law 100–269
Designating April 9, 1988, as "National Former Prisoners of War Recognition Day"

Approved March 29

S.J. Res. 244 / Public Law 100–270
To designate the month of April 1988, as "National Know Your Cholesterol Month"

H.R. 3967 / Public Law 100–271
To amend the Department of Defense Authorization Act, 1985, to extend medical benefits for certain former spouses

Approved March 30

S.J. Res. 185 / Public Law 100–272
To designate the period commencing on May 2, 1988, and ending on May 8, 1988, as "National Drinking Water Week"

S.J. Res. 255 / Public Law 100–273
To authorize and request the President to issue a proclamation designating April 24 through April 30, 1988, as "National Organ and Tissue Donor Awareness Week"

Approved March 31

H.R. 2631 / Public Law 100–274
To authorize appropriations for the Bureau of the Mint for fiscal year 1988, and for other purposes

S. 854 / Public Law 100–275
Nevada-Florida Land Exchange Authorization Act of 1988

H.J. Res. 523 / Public Law 100–276
To provide assistance and support for peace, democracy, and reconciliation in Central America

Approved April 4

S. 2151 / Public Law 100–277
To amend section 416 of the Agricultural Act of 1949, and for other purposes

Approved April 6

H.R. 4263 / Public Law 100–278
To designate interstate route I–195 in the State of New Jersey as the "James J. Howard Interstate Highway"

H.J. Res. 470 / Public Law 100–279
To designate March 29, 1988, as "Education Day, U.S.A."

H.J. Res. 519 / Public Law 100–280
To continue the withdrawal of certain public lands in Nevada

S. 1397 / Public Law 100–281
To recognize the organization known as the Non Commissioned Officers Association of the United States of America

S.J. Res. 206 / Public Law 100–282
To designate April 8, 1988, as "Dennis Chavez Day"

Approved April 7

S. 2117 / Public Law 100–283
Age Discrimination Claims Assistance Act of 1988

H.R. 3981 / Public Law 100–284
To make section 7351 of title 5, United States Code, inapplicable to leave transfers under certain experimental programs covering Federal employees, except as the Office of Personnel Management may otherwise prescribe

H.J. Res. 480 / Public Law 100–285
Granting the consent of the Congress to amendments made by Maryland, Virginia, and the District of Columbia to the Washington Metropolitan Area Transit Regulation Compact

S.J. Res. 223 / Public Law 100–286
To designate the period commencing from April 10, 1988, and ending on April 16, 1988, as "National Productivity Improvement Week"

S.J. Res. 245 / Public Law 100–287
To designate April 21, 1988, as "John Muir Day"

S.J. Res. 260 / Public Law 100–288
To designate the week beginning April 10, 1988, as "National Child Care Awareness Week"

Approved April 12

H.J. Res. 513 / Public Law 100–289
To designate April 6, 1988, as "National Student-Athlete Day"

H.R. 2819 / Private Law 100–8
For the relief of Tracy McFarlane

Approved April 18

H.R. 3459 / Public Law 100–290
Orphan Drug Amendments of 1988

S.J. Res. 234 / Public Law 100–291
Designating the week of April 17, 1988, as "Crime Victims Week"

Approved April 20

H.J. Res. 527 / Public Law 100–292
To designate the week of April 17, 1988, through April 24, 1988, as "Jewish Heritage Week"

Approved April 22

H.R. 1207 / Public Law 100–293
Prescription Drug Marketing Act of 1987

Approved April 25

H.R. 1900 / Public Law 100–294
Child Abuse Prevention, Adoption, and Family Services Act of 1988

H.J. Res. 347 / Public Law 100–295
Recognizing the identical plaques initiated by Sami Bandak, created by Margareta Hennix and Ginvanni Bizzini, and depicting the Calmare Nyckel, the ship that brought the first Swedish settlers to North America, as significant symbols of the "Year of New Sweden"; and providing for the placement of one of such plaques at Fort Christina in the State of Delaware

Approved April 26

H.J. Res. 373 / Public Law 100–296
To designate May 1988 as "National Trauma Awareness Month"

Approved April 27

S. 1609 / Private Law 100–9
For the relief of James P. Purvis

Approved April 28

H.R. 5 / Public Law 100–297
Augustus F. Hawkins-Robert T. Stafford Elementary and Secondary School Improvement Amendments of 1988

S. 858 / Public Law 100–298
Abandoned Shipwreck Act of 1987

S.J. Res. 246 / Public Law 100–299
To designate the month of April 1988, as "National Child Abuse Prevention Month"

Approved April 29

H.R. 3971 / Public Law 100–300
International Child Abduction Remedies Act

S. 90 / Public Law 100–301
Big Cypress National Preserve Addition Act

S.J. Res. 227 / Public Law 100–302
To express gratitude for law enforcement personnel

S.J. Res. 247 / Public Law 100–303
To authorize the President to proclaim the last Friday of April 1988 as "National Arbor Day"

H.J. Res. 552 / Public Law 100–304
Making emergency mandatory veterans supplemental appropriations for the fiscal year ending September 30, 1988

Approved May 2

S.J. Res. 235 / Public Law 100–305
Deploring the Soviet Government's active persecution of religious believers in Ukraine

Approved May 3

H.J. Res. 421 / Public Law 100–306
Designating May 1988 as "National Digestive Disease Awareness Month"

Approved May 5

S. 1378 / Public Law 100–307
To provide for setting aside the first Thursday in May as the date on which the National Day of Prayer is celebrated

S.J. Res. 222 / Public Law 100–308
To designate the period commencing on May 1, 1988, and ending on May 7, 1988, as "National Older Americans Abuse Prevention Week"

S.J. Res. 242 / Public Law 100–309
Designating the period commencing May 2, 1988, and ending on May 8, 1988, as "Public Service Recognition Week"

H.R. 2139 / Private Law 100–10
For the relief of John H. Teele

H.R. 3439 / Private Law 100–11
For the relief of Marisela, Felix, and William Marrero

Approved May 6

H.J. Res. 508 / Public Law 100–310
Designating May 1988 as "Older Americans Month"

H.J. Res. 541 / Public Law 100–311
Commending the State of Israel and its people on the occasion of the fortieth anniversary of the reestablishment of the independent State of Israel

S.J. Res. 190 / Public Law 100–312
To authorize and request the President to issue a proclamation designating June 6–12, 1988, as "National Fishing Week"

Approved May 10

H.J. Res. 545 / Public Law 100–313
Designating May 8–14, 1988, as "Just Say No Week"

S.J. Res. 59 / Public Law 100–314
To designate the month of May, 1988 as "National Foster Care Month"

S.J. Res. 250 / Public Law 100–315
Designating the week of May 8, 1988, through May 14, 1988, as "National Osteoporosis Prevention Week of 1988"

Approved May 12

S.J. Res. 212 / Public Law 100–316
To designate the period commencing May 8, 1988, and ending on May 14, 1988, as "National Tuberous Sclerosis Awareness Week"

Approved May 13

S.J. Res. 240 / Public Law 100–317
To designate the period commencing on May 16, 1988 and ending on May 22, 1988, as "National Safe Kids Week"

S. 2273 / Public Law 100–318
To provide for the transfer of certain funds to the Secretary of the Interior for the benefit of certain members of the Crow Tribe

Approved May 19

H.R. 3025 / Public Law 100–319
Appalachian States Low-Level Radioactive Waste Compact Consent Act

S.J. Res. 254 / Public Law 100–320
To designate the period commencing on May 15, 1988, and ending on May 21, 1988, as "National Rural Health Awareness Week"

Approved May 20

H.R. 1811 / Public Law 100–321
Radiation-Exposed Veterans Compensation Act of 1988

H.R. 2616 / Public Law 100–322
Veterans' Benefits and Services Act of 1988

S. 999 / Public Law 100–323
Veterans' Employment, Training, and Counseling Amendments of 1988

H.R. 2889 / Private Law 100–12
For the relief of Frances Silver

H.R. 3606 / Private Law 100–13
For the relief of Brenda W. Gay

S. 393 / Private Law 100–14
For the relief of Emilie Santos

Approved May 30

H.R. 1430 / Public Law 100–324
Merchant Marine Decorations and Medals Act

H.R. 4083 / Public Law 100–325
To amend title 5, United States Code, to authorize the establishment of the Federal Bureau of Investigation and Drug Enforcement Administration Senior Executive Service, and for other purposes

Approved June 7

H.R. 2878 / Public Law 100–326
To designate certain national forest system lands in the States of Virginia and West Virginia as wilderness areas

H.R. 3987 / Public Law 100–327
To designate the United States Post Office Building located at 500 West Chestnut Expressway in Springfield, Missouri, as the "Gene Taylor Post Office Building"

H.J. Res. 530 / Public Law 100–328
Designating May 1988 as "Take Pride in America Month"

S. 1988 / Public Law 100–329
To amend the Merchant Marine Act, 1920, and for other purposes

S. 1989 / Public Law 100–330
South Pacific Tuna Act of 1988

Approved June 14

H.R. 4556 / Public Law 100–331
To amend the provisions of the Agricultural Act of 1949 relating to certain cross compliance requirements under the extra long staple cotton program

H.J. Res. 469 / Public Law 100–332
To designate June 1988 as "National Recycling Month"

Approved June 16

H.R. 2210 / Public Law 100–333
Organotin Antifouling Paint Control Act of 1988

H.R. 2969 / Public Law 100–334
Retiree Benefits Bankruptcy Protection Act of 1988

S.J. Res. 266 / Public Law 100–335
To designate the week beginning June 12, 1988, as "National Scleroderma Awareness Week"

Approved June 17

H.R. 1100 / Public Law 100–336
To authorize the Secretary of the Interior to provide assistance to Wildlife Prairie Park, in the State of Illinois, and for other purposes

H.R. 3869 / Public Law 100–337
To amend the Act providing for the establishment of the Tuskegee Institute National Historic Site, Alabama, to authorize an exchange of properties between the United States and Tuskegee University, and for other purposes

H.R. 4799 / Public Law 100–338
To extend the withdrawal of certain public lands in Lincoln County, Nevada

S. 1652 / Public Law 100–339
To authorize the establishment by the Secretary of Agriculture of a plant stress and water conservation research laboratory and program at Lubbock, Texas

S. 2304 / Public Law 100–340
To amend the Departments of Commerce, Justice, and State, the Judiciary, and Related Agencies Appropriation Act, 1986, to extend the life of the Commission on the Ukraine Famine

Approved June 22

H.J. Res. 423 / Public Law 100–341
To designate the third week in June 1988 as "National Dairy Goat Awareness Week"

S. 1539 / Public Law 100–342
Rail Safety Improvement Act of 1988

S.J. Res. 249 / Public Law 100–343
Designating June 14, 1988, as "Baltic Freedom Day"

Approved June 23

S.J. Res. 147 / Public Law 100–344
Designating the week beginning on the third Sunday of September in 1988 as "National Adult Day Care Center Week"

Approved June 24

H.R. 4448 / Public Law 100–345
To designate the Cleveland Ohio General Mail Facility and Main Office in Cleveland, Ohio, as the "John O. Holly Building of the United States Postal Service"

S. 794 / Public Law 100–346
To amend chapter 13 of title 18, United States Code, to impose criminal penalties for damage to religious property and for obstruction of persons in the free exercise of religious beliefs

Approved June 27

H.R. 1212 / Public Law 100–347
Employee Polygraph Protection Act of 1988

H.R. 1044 / Public Law 100–348
San Francisco Maritime National Historical Park Act of 1988

H.R. 2652 / Public Law 100–349
To revise the boundaries of Salem Maritime National Historic Site in the Commonwealth of Massachusetts, and for other purposes

H.R. 4621 / Public Law 100–350
To provide Congressional approval of the Governing International Fishery Agreement between the United States and the Government of the German Democratic Republic

H.R. 4638 / Public Law 100–351
To amend the effective date provision of the Augustus F. Hawkins-Robert T. Stafford Elementary and Secondary School Improvement Amendments of 1988

S. 952 / Public Law 100–352
To improve the administration of justice by providing greater discretion to the Supreme Court in selecting the cases it will review, and for other purposes

S. 1901 / Public Law 100–353
To designate the Federal Building located at 600 Las Vegas Boulevard in Las Vegas, Nevada, as the "Alan Bible Federal Building"

S. 1960 / Public Law 100–354
To designate the Federal Building located at 215 North 17th Street in Omaha, Nebraska, as the "Edward Zorinsky Federal Building"

Approved June 28

H.R. 2203 / Public Law 100–355
To increase the amount authorized to be appropriated with respect to the Sewall-Belmont House National Historic Site

S. 2156 / Public Law 100–356
To amend the National School Lunch Act to require eligibility for free lunches to be based on the nonfarm income poverty guidelines prescribed by the Office of Management and Budget

S. 2167 / Public Law 100–357
National Appliance Energy Conservation Amendments of 1988

Approved June 29

H.R. 3927 / Public Law 100–358
Indian Housing Act of 1988

Approved June 30

H.J. Res. 485 / Public Law 100–359
Designating June 26 through July 2, 1988, as "National Safety Belt Use Week"

Approved July 1

H.R. 2470 / Public Law 100–360
Medicare Catastrophic Coverage Act of 1988

H.J. Res. 587 / Public Law 100–361
Designating July 2 and 3, 1988, as "United States-Canada Days of Peace and Friendship"

Subject Index

Name Index

Document Categories List